Table 2. New Privately Owned Housing Units Started: 1959–Present*

Period	Total	In Structures With				MSAs		Regions			
		1 Unit	2 Units	3 and 4 Units	5 Units or More	Inside	Outside	North-east	Mid-west	South	West
Annual Data											
1959	1,517.0	1,234.0	55.9	227.0	NA	1,054.9	462.1	268.7	367.4	511.4	369.5
1960	1,252.2	994.7	44.0	213.5	NA	864.5	387.7	221.4	292.0	429.4	309.4
1961	1,313.0	974.3	43.9	294.8	NA	913.6	399.4	246.3	277.7	472.7	316.3
1962	1,462.9	991.4	49.2	422.3	NA	1,034.1	428.8	263.8	289.6	531.2	378.3
1963	1,603.2	1,012.4	52.9	537.8	NA	1,125.4	477.8	261.0	329.2	586.2	426.8
1964	1,528.8	970.5	53.9	54.5	450.0	1,079.8	449.0	254.5	339.7	577.8	356.9
1965	1,472.8	963.7	50.8	35.8	422.5	1,011.9	460.9	270.2	361.5	574.7	266.3
1966	1,164.9	778.6	34.6	26.5	325.1	787.7	377.1	206.5	288.3	472.5	197.6
1967	1,291.6	843.9	41.4	30.2	376.1	902.9	388.7	214.9	337.1	519.5	220.1
1968	1,507.6	899.4	46.0	34.9	527.3	1,096.4	411.2	226.8	368.6	618.5	293.7
1969	1,466.8	810.6	43.0	42.0	571.2	1,078.7	388.0	206.1	348.7	588.4	323.5
1970	1,433.6	812.9	42.4	42.4	535.9	1,017.9	415.7	217.9	293.5	611.6	310.5
1971	2,052.2	1,151.0	55.1	65.2	780.9	1,501.8	550.4	263.8	434.1	868.7	485.6
1972	2,356.6	1,309.2	67.1	74.2	906.2	1,720.4	636.2	329.5	442.8	1,057.0	527.4
1973	2,045.3	1,132.0	54.2	64.1	795.0	1,495.4	549.9	277.3	439.7	899.4	428.8
1974	1,337.7	888.1	33.2	34.9	381.6	922.5	415.3	183.2	317.3	552.8	284.5
1975	1,160.4	892.2	34.5	29.5	204.3	760.3	400.1	149.2	294.0	442.1	275.1
1976	1,537.5	1,162.4	44.0	41.9	289.2	1,043.5	494.1	169.2	400.1	568.5	399.6
1977	1,987.1	1,450.9	60.7	61.0	414.4	1,377.3	609.8	201.6	464.6	783.1	537.9
1978	2,020.3	1,433.3	62.2	62.8	462.0	1,432.1	588.2	200.3	451.2	823.7	545.2
1979	1,745.1	1,194.1	56.1	65.9	429.0	1,240.6	504.6	177.9	349.2	747.5	470.5
1980	1,292.2	852.2	48.8	60.7	330.5	913.6	378.7	125.4	218.1	642.7	306.0
1981	1,084.2	705.4	38.2	52.9	287.7	759.8	324.3	117.3	165.2	561.6	240.0
1982	1,062.2	662.6	31.9	48.1	319.6	784.8	277.4	116.7	149.1	591.0	205.4
1983	1,703.0	1,067.6	41.8	71.7	522.0	1,351.1	351.9	167.6	217.9	935.2	382.3
1984	1,749.5	1,084.2	38.6	82.8	544.0	1,414.6	334.9	204.1	243.4	866.0	436.0
1985	1,741.8	1,072.4	37.0	56.4	576.1	1,493.9	247.9	251.7	239.7	782.3	468.2
1986	1,805.4	1,179.4	36.1	47.9	542.0	1,546.3	259.1	293.5	295.8	733.1	483.0
1987	1,620.5	1,146.4	27.8	37.5	408.7	1,372.2	248.2	269.0	297.9	633.9	419.8
1988	1,488.1	1,081.3	23.4	35.4	348.0	1,243.0	245.1	235.3	274.0	574.9	403.9
1989	1,376.1	1,003.3	19.9	35.3	317.6	1,128.1	248.0	178.5	265.8	536.2	395.7
1990	1,192.7	894.8	16.1	21.4	260.4	946.9	245.7	131.3	253.2	479.3	328.9
1991	1,013.9	840.4	15.5	20.1	137.9	789.2	224.7	112.9	233.0	414.1	254.0
1992	1,199.7	1,029.9	12.4	18.3	139.0	931.5	268.2	126.7	287.8	496.9	288.3
1993	1,287.6	1,125.7	11.1	18.3	132.6	1,031.9	255.8	126.5	297.7	561.8	301.7
1994	1,457.0	1,198.4	14.8	20.2	223.5	1,183.1	273.9	138.2	328.9	639.1	350.8
Monthly Data (Seasonally Adjusted Annual Rates)											
1994											
January	1,266	1,122	23		121	NA		89	251	554	372
February	1,318	1,112	32		174	NA		131	260	592	335
March	1,499	1,259	30		210	NA		137	349	641	372
April	1,463	1,209	31		223	NA		150	355	615	343
May	1,489	1,197	36		256	NA		135	323	684	347
June	1,370	1,174	18		178	NA		137	306	602	325
July	1,440	1,219	32		189	NA		131	340	600	369
August	1,463	1,174	40		249	NA		148	319	681	315
September	1,511	1,235	42		234	NA		136	337	659	379
October	1,451	1,164	39		248	NA		130	313	648	360
November	1,536	1,186	62		288	NA		159	380	661	336
December	1,545	1,250	33		262	NA		139	341	714	351
1995											
January	1,366	1,055	38		273	NA		117	288	621	340
February	1,315	1,041	44		230	NA		132	284	552	347
March	1,211	979	29		203	NA		137	268	531	275

* Components may not add to totals because of rounding. Units in thousands.

Source: Bureau of the Census, Department of Commerce

REAL ESTATE FINANCE

REAL ESTATE FINANCE

Theory and Practice

Third Edition

TERRENCE M. CLAURETIE
University of Nevada, Las Vegas

G. STACY SIRMANS
Florida State University

Prentice Hall
Upper Saddle River, New Jersey 07458

Library of Congress Cataloging-in-Publication Data

Clauretie, Terrence M.
    Real estate finance : theory and practice / Terrence M. Clauretie,
  G. Stacy Sirmans.
        p.   cm.
    Includes bibliographical references and index.
    ISBN 0-13-974916-0
    1. Mortgage loans--United States.   2. Real property--United
States--Finance.   3. Housing--United States--Finance.   I. Sirmans,
G. Stacy.   II. Title.
HG2040.5.U5C6   1999
332.7'2--dc21   99-19265
                                                                  CIP

Acquisitions Editor: *Elizabeth Sugg*
Editorial Assistant: *Maria Kirk*
Production Editor: *Lori Harvey, Carlisle Publishers Services*
Production Liaison: *Eileen M. O'Sullivan*
Director of Manufacturing & Production: *Bruce Johnson*
Managing Editor: *Mary Carnis*
Marketing Manager: *Danny Hoyt*
Production Manager: *Marc Bove*
Compositor: *Carlisle Communications, Ltd.*
Cover Design: *Miguel Ortiz*
Printer/Binder: *Courier Westford*

 © 1999, 1996 by Prentice-Hall, Inc
Simon & Schuster/A Viacom Company
Upper Saddle River, New Jersey 07458

This text was published by The Dryden Press, a division
of Harcourt Brace & Company, in its first edition as
The Theory and Practice of Real Estate Finance by
Terrence M. Clauretie and James Webb (copyright ©
1993 by The Dryden Press).

Printed in the United States of America

10 9 8 7 6 5 4 3 2 1

ISBN 0-13-974916-0

Prentice-Hall International (UK) Limited, *London*
Prentice-Hall of Australia Pty. Limited, *Sydney*
Prentice-Hall Canada Inc., *Toronto*
Prentice-Hall Hispanoamericana, S.A., *Mexico*
Prentice-Hall of India Private Limited, *New Delhi*
Prentice-Hall of Japan, Inc., *Tokyo*
Simon & Schuster Asia Pte. Ltd., *Singapore*
Editora Prentice-Hall do Brasil, Ltda., *Rio de Janeiro*

To Patty, Sean, and Kevin

TMC

To Elaine, Stace, Candace, and Berkeley

GSS

CONTENTS

PREFACE   xv

Goals and Foundation of the Text   xv
Topic Coverage   xv
Background of the Student   xvi
Acknowledgments   xvi

PART ONE
Finance and Real Estate   1

CHAPTER 1   *Real Estate Finance: An Overview   2*

The Nature of Real Estate Finance   2
What Is Finance?   2
What Is Real Estate Finance?   3
What Is the Environment of Real Estate Finance?   4
A Closer Look at Financial Intermediaries and Financial Markets   6
Commercial Banks   6
Thrift Institutions   6
Investment Companies   7
Insurance Companies   7
Pension Funds   7
Direct Financing   7
Secondary Mortgage Market   7
Primary and Secondary Markets   7
Money and Capital Markets   8
Organization of the Book   8

CHAPTER 2   *Money, Credit, and the Determination of Interest Rates   15*

The General Level of Interest Rates   15
Money, the Economy, and Inflation   16
The Equation of Exchange   17
The Fisher Equation   17
The Gibson Paradox   19
Liquidity, Income, and Price-anticipation Effects   19
The Determination of Interest Rates on Specific Credit Market Instruments   20
Default Risk   20
Callability Risk   21
Maturity Risk   22
Marketability Risk or Liquidity Risk   22
The Yield Curve and Future Interest Rates   22
Liquidity Premium Theory   24

Market Segmentation Theory   24
Expectations Theory   24

CHAPTER   3   *Finance Theory and Real Estate   28*

Asset Valuation   28
Amount of After-tax Cash Flows   29
Timing of Cash Flows   29
Risk of Cash Flows   29
Role of Risk in Valuation   32
The Theory of Financial Leverage and Optimal Capital Structure   32
Leverage and Value   32
Irrelevance of Capital Structure   33
Options and Real Estate Finance   33
Definition of Options   33
Examples of Options in Real Estate Finance   34
The Theory of Financial Intermediation   36
Portfolio Theory   37
Efficient Market Theory   38
Agency Theory   39

PART TWO
Residential Real Estate Finance   43

CHAPTER   4   *The Early History of Residential Finance and Creation
of the Fixed Rate Mortgage   44*

Pre-American Developments   44
Roman Law   44
German Influence   45
American Residential Finance: Early American History Through the Depression Years   46
Mechanics of the Fixed-rate Mortgage (FRM)   48
The Mortgage Payment   48
Amortization of the Mortgage   49
The Outstanding Balance of the Mortgage   50
The Effective Cost of the Mortgage   50
Calculating the APR   51
Effective Cost and Early Repayment   51
The Effect Cost of Prepayment Penalties   52
Fixed-rate Mortgages and Interest Rate Risk   53
APPENDIX A   Elements of the Discounted Cash Flow Model of Valuation   57
APPENDIX B   Maturity, Duration, and the Interest Rate Risk of Mortgages   58

CHAPTER   5   *Postwar Residential Finance   61*

Background   61
The 1950s: A Decade of Stability   62
The 1960s: Creeping Inflation, Disintermediation, and the Rise of the Secondary Mortgage Market   64
The 1970s: Problems of the Fixed-rate Mortgage in an Inflationary Environment   66
Demand Problems   66
Supply Problems   68
Introduction of Alternative Mortgage Instruments   68
Continued Growth of the Secondary Market   70
The 1980s: Deregulation, the Growth of Alternative Mortgage Instruments, and the Thrift Crises   70
Interest Rate Risk Increases: Value of Assumption Option Becomes an Issue   70
The Era of Creative Financing   73
Widespread Savings and Loan Failures   77
Post-FIRREA Regulatory Structure of the Mortgage Market   84

Categories of Capitalization   86

The 1990s: Dominance of the Secondary Mortgage Market   88
    Risk-based Guidelines Expanded to Cover Interest Rate Risk   89

C H A P T E R   6   *Alternative Mortgage Instruments   93*

Problems of Supply: Interest-rate Risk and the Adjustable Rate Mortgage   93
    Description of ARMs   94
    Comparison of ARM Performance   98
    Pricing Adjustable Rate Mortgages   100
    Problems in ARM Calculations   105
Problems of Demand: The Tilt Effect and the Graduated Payment Mortgage   106
Simultaneously Solving the Problems of Supply and Demand: The Price Level Adjusted
    Mortgage   109
Other Alternative Mortgage Instruments   112
    Shared Appreciation Mortgage (SAM)   112
    Reverse Annuity Mortgage (RAM)   113
    Pledged-account Mortgage   114
Alternative Mortgage Instruments and the Tax Deductibility of Interest Payments   116
Mortgage Refinancing   116
Refinancing Owner-occupied Residential Property   117
APPENDIX A   Computing Initial Payment on a GPM Loan   123

C H A P T E R   7   *Financing and Property Values   125*

Creative Financing   126
    FHA/VA Discount Points   126
    Assumable Loans   128
    Other Creative Financing: Buy-downs, Wraparound Loans, and Land Contracts   132
    Implications for Appraisal Practices and Market Studies   135
Mortgage Revenue Bonds   135
    Role of State Housing Finance Authorities (HFA)   135
    MRBs, House Prices, and Wealth Distribution   137

C H A P T E R   8   *Federal Housing Policies: Part I   144*

Housing Affordability   144
    Economic Support of Financial Institutions   144
    Mortgage Insurance, Direct Grants, and Subsidies   146
    Income Tax Provisions   149
Efficiency and Stability   150
    Efficient Markets   150
    Deregulation   151
Competition in the Real Estate Finance Market   152
    Interstate Land Sales Full Disclosure Act (ILSFDA, 1968)   152
    Consumer Credit Protection Act (Truth-in-Lending Law, 1968)   152
    Real Estate Settlement Procedures Act (RESPA, 1974)   156
APPENDIX A   Major Federal Legislation and Executive Orders Authorizing HUD
    Programs   164
APPENDIX B   ARM Examples   168
    Variable-rate Mortgage Sample   168
    Rescission Model Form (General)   170

C H A P T E R   9   *Federal Housing Policies: Part II   172*

Equity in Housing   172
    Fair Housing Act (1968)   172
    Equal Credit Opportunity Act (ECOA, 1974)   173

Home Mortgage Disclosure Act (HMDA, 1975) and Community Reinvestment Act (CRA, 1978)   177

Fair Housing Amendments Act of 1988   181

APPENDIX A   Summary of Major Federal Legislation Affecting Real Estate   184

C H A P T E R   1 0   *The Secondary Mortgage Market   188*

Nature of Secondary Market   188
    What Is a Secondary Mortgage Market?   188
    Why Does the Secondary Mortgage Market Exist?   189
Mortgage-related Securities (MRSs)   190
    Characteristics of Mortgage-related Securities   190
    Types of Mortgage-related Securities   191
    Swaps   195
    Tax and Accounting Issues of Mortgage-related Securities   196
Secondary Mortgage Market Agencies and Firms   197
    Federal National Mortgage Association (FNMA)   198
    Government National Mortgage Association (GNMA)   198
    Federal Home Loan Mortgage Corporation (FHLMC)   201
    Federal Credit Agencies   202
    State and Local Credit Agencies   204
    Private Firms   205
Developing a Secondary Mortgage Market: a Year-by-year Summary   205
The Flow of Funds Through the Primary and Secondary Mortgage Markets   209
Regulation of Government Sponsored Enterprises (GSEs)   214

C H A P T E R   1 1   *Valuation of Mortgage Securities   217*

Valuation of Traditional Debt Securities   218
Mortgage-related Securities   220
    Pass-throughs   221
    Senior/Subordinated Pass-throughs   232
    Mortgage-backed Bonds   233
    Collateralized Mortgage Obligations   236
    Interest-only and Principal-only Strips   241
    Floaters and Inverse Floaters   245
    Servicing Rights   246
    Data on Mortgage Pools   248
Value Creation in Mortgage-related Securities   249

C H A P T E R   1 2   *Controlling Default Risk Through Borrower Qualification,
                           Loan Underwriting, and Contractual Relationships   254*

Borrower Qualification and Loan Underwriting   254
    Theories of Default   255
    Characteristics of the Property   257
    Characteristics of the Borrower   257
    HUD/FHA Guidelines   257
    VA Borrower Qualification   259
    Conforming Conventional Loan Qualification   260
    Borrower Qualification Comparison   260
Contractual Relationships in Residential Loans   262
    Promissory Notes   263
    Deed-of-trust or Trust Deeds   266

C H A P T E R   1 3   *Loan Origination, Processing, and Closing   270*

Loan Processing   270
    Property Appraisal   270
    Analysis of Application   273

Submission for Insurance 274
Loan Closing 276
Mortgage Banking 277
Sources of Funds 278
Revenues 278

CHAPTER 14   *Mortgage Default Insurance, Foreclosure,*
                           and Title Insurance 280

Mortgage Default Insurance 280
Government Insurance 281
The Rural Housing Service 285
Private Mortgage Insurance 286
Comparison of Government and Private Mortgage Insurance Programs 289
State Foreclosure Laws 289
Foreclosure 289
Default Risk, Mortgage Insurance, and State Foreclosure Laws 291
Title Insurance 294
APPENDIX A   FHA GPM Program 298

PART THREE
Commercial Real Estate Finance 301

CHAPTER 15   *Value, Leverage, and Capital Structure 302*

Valuation of Real Estate Investments 303
General Principles 303
Financial Leverage 304
Debt and Returns to Equity: A Real Estate Example 306
Basic Assumptions 308
Annual Operating Cash Flows 309
Sale of Property 309
Value of the Cash Flows 311
Arguments Against an Optimal Capital Structure 313
Resolution of the Modigliani–Miller Proposition with the Use of Debt Financing
for Real Estate Properties 315
Some Practical Considerations in the Use of Debt to Finance
Real Estate Properties 316
Real Estate Investing in the Real World 318

CHAPTER 16   *Federal Taxation and Real Estate Finance 322*

Classification of Real Property 324
Tax Shelters 325
Taxes, Cash Flows, and Discount Rates: Some Examples 325
Real Estate Tax Regulations 329
Definition of Income 329
Determination of Taxes 337
Effect of Tax Reform Act of 1986 on Real Estate Investment 343
Tax-deferred Exchanges of Real Estate Properties 345
Basic Requirements 345
Three-party Exchanges 345
Delayed Exchanges 345
Boot 346
Technical Requirements 346
Installment Sale Financing 347
APPENDIX A   Tax Preference Items for Alternative Minimum Tax 354

C H A P T E R 1 7   *Sources of Funds for Commercial Real Estate Properties* *355*

Debt Financing of Real Estate Properties 355
    Estimates of the Stock of Debt 355
    Flow of Debt Funds 357
    A Closer Look at Commercial Collateralized Mortgage Obligations (CMOs) 360
    Recent Trends in Debt Financing 362
Equity Financing of Real Estate Properties 363
    Equity Financing Through Securities 363
    Institutional Investors 364
    Public/Private Partnerships 368
    Finding Sources of Financing 369

C H A P T E R 1 8   *Acquisition, Development, and Construction Financing* *373*

Acquisition 374
    The Land Loan 374
    Institutional Lenders 375
    Seller Accommodation 375
Development 377
Construction 379
    Underwriting Construction Loans 379
    The Construction Loan Commitment 380
    Construction Loan Provisions 380
    Construction Loan Administration 382
    Determination of Loan Amount and Disbursements 382

C H A P T E R 1 9   *Permanent Financing of Commercial Real Estate Properties* *398*

Long-term, Fixed-rate Loans 398
Alternatives to Standard Long-term Fixed-rate Loans 399
    Equity Participation Loans 399
    Lease Versus Own Analysis 405
    Leases and Sale-leaseback Agreements 406
Ground Lease Mortgages 415
Credit-based Financing 416
APPENDIX A Supporting Schedules for Example 2 420

C H A P T E R 2 0   *Ownership Structures for Financing and Holding Real Estate* *421*

Forms of Real Estate Ownership 422
    Sole Ownership 422
    Corporate Form of Ownership 423
    Partnerships 424
    Real Estate Investment Trusts 424
A Closer Look at Real Estate Limited Partnerships and Real Estate Investment Trusts 425
    Real Estate Limited Partnerships 425
    Real Estate Investment Trusts 427
A Closer Look at Corporate Versus Partnership Form of Ownership 433

PART FOUR
Special Topics in Real Estate Finance 439

CHAPTER 21 *Real Estate in a Portfolio Context 440*

The Nature of Diversification 440
    Benefits of Diversification 445
    Theories of Asset Pricing 447
Real Estate in a Mixed Asset Portfolio 450
    The Problem with Appraised Values 450
    Sources of Real Estate Data 451
    The Diversification Benefits of Real Estate 452
Within-real-estate Diversification 454
    Diversification by Property Type 455
    Geographic Diversification 456
    Other Methods of Diversification 457
APPENDIX A The Capital Asset Pricing Model Derived from Combining an Asset with the Existing Market Portfolio 460

CHAPTER 22 *Liability, Agency Problems, Fraud, and Ethics in Real Estate Finance 461*

Lenders' Legal Liability 461
    Hazardous Waste Disposal 462
April 1992 EPA Regulation 467
    Recent Court Decision 467
    Risk Management for Lender Liability 468
    Lenders and the Drug War 468
    Liability from Lender/Borrower Relationship 469
    Other Theories of Lender Liability 473
    Liability to Third Parties: Bankruptcy and Agency Law 475
Bankruptcy and Agency Costs 476
    Bankruptcy Law and the "Cramdown" Process 477
    Practical Considerations 478
Ethics, Fraud, and Agency Costs 479
    Agency Relationships and Mortgage Insurance 480
    Agency Relationships and Recent Thrift Failures 480

APPENDIX 1 *A Refresher Course on the Time Value of Money and Related Concepts 485*

Discounting and Compounding (Coming and Going) 485
Discounting and Compounding Annuities 488
Discounting and Compounding at Intervals Other than One Year 490
Concluding Remarks 492

APPENDIX 2 *Acronym List 541*

APPENDIX 3 *Software to Accompany Real Estate Finance 543*

GLOSSARY 549
NAME INDEX 569
SUBJECT INDEX 571

PREFACE

Goals and Foundation of the Text

The title of this textbook, Real Estate Finance: Theory and Practice, suggests that the material covered here reflects a blend of theory and practice. In fact, our goal is to apply the theoretical aspects of financial economics to explain how real estate financial institutions and markets have developed and evolved to their present state, and why they take the form they do. We are not content with providing only descriptions of institutions and definitions of terms. Our goal is to promote a greater understanding of how real estate financial markets work. To do this we present the material based on a foundation of economic and finance theories.

We want to provide a real estate finance textbook that is comparable to those in the area of managerial finance by basing it on sound economic and finance principles. A foundation of theory will allow you to understand the structure of the real estate finance market as it changes throughout your lifetime. Although the institutions, regulations, and structure of the real estate finance market will continue to change, the theoretical underpinnings on which economic behavior takes place will not. We feel strongly that "education is what remains after you have forgotten the facts".

We not only provide you with a solid foundation for which to examine and understand the real estate financial market, we also introduce some of the more important results of empirical research done by experts in that market. In addition to presenting the questions, so to speak, we also attempt to provide some answers.

Even with this emphasis on economic and financial theory, we do not neglect the descriptive approach that is necessary to understand the structure of real estate finance markets. You will gain an understanding of major institutions and the roles they play in the real estate finance market. You will learn about the major federal legislation that impacts real estate finance, particularly the residential area. And you will understand how law shapes and affects the form of the real estate finance market.

Topic Coverage

The textbook is divided into four parts. The first part (Chapters 1 through 3 deals with financial markets in general, finance theory, and the application of finance theory to real estate. Here, we lay down the foundation for understanding how financial markets operate. We discuss the primary tools of financial analysis and show, in general, how they apply to real estate. Part one of the text is designed to give the student a basic understanding of finance theory as it applies to real estate and mortgage markets.

Part two of the book deals with issues related to residential real estate finance. After developing the history of real estate finance in chapters four and five, we investigate alternative mortgage instruments and the effect of terms of financing on property values in chapters six and seven. Next, we look at federal housing policies and their impact on the residential real estate market. Chapter eight focuses on the support that the federal government has given to depository institutions as well as reporting requirements by mortgage lenders. Chapter nine centers on the issues of discrimination and the federal laws passed to ensure equal opportunity for housing and financing for all citizens. The next two chapters are devoted to the secondary mortgage market, one to a description of this market and one to issues related to the valuation of securities created in the secondary mortgage market. We complete the second part of the textbook with three chapters on residential loan underwriting, loan processing and origination, and mortgage insurance. In the third edition we have added material on prepayment protection mortgages, risk based capital guidelines for interest rate risk for financial institutions regulated by the government, and on floaters and inverse floaters (types of mortgage derivative securities).

The third part of the textbook deals with commercial real estate finance. We present issues concerning the use of debt (leverage) in financing properties, the impact of tax laws on financing commercial properties, and sources of commercial real estate financing. In this section we also discuss various methods of financing commercial properties, including equity participation loans and sale lease-back agreements.

The final chapter in this section deals with the different ownership structures that are available for holding commercial real estate. For the third edition we have included more material on optimal capital structure, tax deferred exchanges, and lease versus own analysis.

The fourth and final part deals with special topics. In one chapter we discuss real estate in a portfolio context, and, in the last two chapters, we present material related to lender legal liability, ethics and fraud in real estate finance, and agency problems in real estate finance.

Throughout the third edition we provide updated tables and exhibits. We also have updated the references of empirical work by authors who have made valuable contributions to the understanding of the topics discussed in the textbook. Also, we have provided software with each text so that you may be able to explore many of the complicated models of real estate finance. The software is user-friendly and will help you understand many of the financial relationships of the models, and facilitate solving some of the homework problems at the end of the chapters. The software utilizes EXCEL© worksheets and is located on the enclosed CD. We have also removed many of the exhibits from the text and placed additional material on federal laws, tables and other interesting real estate topics on the CD, also in microsoft WORD© format.

Background of the Student

The textbook has been written under the assumption that you, the reader, have some foundation in economics and finance. However, we present the material in a manner that those without such a background can follow along at a moderate pace. If you do not have a background in finance, we suggest that you first consult the appendix on the time value of money at the end of the book. Unlike many other textbooks on real estate finance, we do not introduce this material in the body of the text. Nevertheless, an understanding of the discounting and compounding process is necessary before you begin reading. If you have a background in finance, you can begin with Chapter 1. If not, read the appendix and ask your instructor for some review material that may strengthen your understanding of the discounting and compounding process.

Finally, we would like to continually develop this textbook and make it better with each edition. If you have any comments or would like to make suggestions that would improve it for future editions, please write us at:

Terrence M. Clauretie
G. Stacy Sirmans
c/o Real Estate Editor
Prentice Hall
One Lake Street Drive
Upper Saddle River, New Jersey 07458
Also feel free to e-mail Terrence M. Clauretie at mikec@ccmail.nevada.edu

Acknowledgments

We would like to acknowledge with grateful appreciation the contributions of several colleagues to the development of this textbook. From inception through completion, their suggestions were invaluable in improving the presentation of the material. We, of course, are responsible for the final version, so if there are any errors or omissions, they are our responsibility only. Those who helped develop this textbook and to whom we owe our gratitude include: Robert J. Aalberts, University of Nevada, Las Vegas; Wayne Archer, University of Florida; J'Noel Ball, Northeastern University; Jerome Dasso, University of Oregon-Emeritus; Patrick Egger, PriMerit Bank, Las Vegas; Donald Johnson, College for Financial Planning; Will McIntosh, Prudential Realty Group; Theron Nelson, University of North Dakota; Philip Rushing, University of Illinois; Jay Sa-Aadu, University of Iowa; James Shilling, University of Wisconsin; Rock Tarantello, Tarantello and Associates.

REAL ESTATE FINANCE

Finance and Real Estate

The three chapters in Part One of the text set the stage for applying financial economics to real estate. Here, the text discusses the nature of finance and economics and describes financial markets with reference to those institutions that play a role in real estate finance. It also looks at money, credit, and interest rates. Interest rates, as you may expect, play an integral role in real estate finance. The determination of both the general level of interest rates and those on particular debt securities is presented. Finally, in this section we present the major finance concepts and principles and show how they apply to real estate markets.

CHAPTER **1**

Real Estate Finance: An Overview

LEARNING OBJECTIVES

After reading this chapter, you should understand the relationship between finance and real estate. You also should understand how financial markets work in terms of the flow of funds from those with credit to lend to those with a demand for borrowed funds. You also will learn which major financial institutions direct the flow of funds.

INTRODUCTION

Each chapter in this textbook tackles a different subject in real estate finance. The text is by no means exhaustive. In fact, it is quite modest in its coverage. Be aware that when you have completed this course, your knowledge of real estate finance will be greater than it is now but still lacking in many respects. You can gain additional knowledge of real estate finance from more in-depth study of the various subjects in this textbook, as well as from real-world experiences. If your professional goals direct you to the world of real estate finance, expect to gain much knowledge through your day-to-day experiences. With this in mind, you will nonetheless need to get as much from this text as possible. To accomplish this, you need to begin in this chapter by understanding the framework of real estate finance—what real estate finance is and the environment within which it takes place. Chapter by chapter, you will learn about individual real estate finance topics. As each topic is introduced, we will attempt to place it in the framework of general finance models. You should understand that real estate finance subjects are applications of more general finance principles. We tend to focus as much on finance principles and concepts as on descriptions of real estate finance institutions. The application of general finance principles to real estate is discussed in detail in Chapter 3. For now, we discuss what real estate finance is all about.

THE NATURE OF REAL ESTATE FINANCE

The nature of real estate finance can be framed by three questions:

- What is finance?
- What is real estate finance?
- What is the environment of real estate finance?

What Is Finance?

Finance is the study of the process, institutions, markets, and instruments used to transfer money and credit between individuals, businesses, and governments. Finance is applied economics. Economics is the study of the allocation of resources for the purpose of producing goods and services for various members of society. Finance is the study of how the flow of money and credit facilitates that production and allocation. Although finance can be seen as a segment of the more general field of economics, there are differences in the focus of the two fields of study. This is not to say that finance is different or unrelated to economics; it is not. It does have a different focus, however, and utilizes certain concepts more than the traditional study of economics does. The focus of finance differs from that of economics in several ways.

If you have had a course in economics and one in finance, you can appreciate how the two subjects differ in their approach. First, in the theory of the firm, for example, microeconomics focuses on the profit maximizing assumption. Policies of the firm are geared toward maximizing profits within the constraints of the structure of the industry. In finance, at least managerial finance, the focus is on maximizing the value of equity interest of owners. This involves a lot more than maximizing the profits of the firm. In fact, a myopic view of maximizing profits could lead to less than a maximization of the value of the firm's equity position. Thus, finance is concerned with issues such as the character of securities (debt or equity) issued by the firm in order to finance assets. Seldom, if ever, in a microeconomics course does one consider the character of the securities issued by firms.

Second, the focus of finance is more on the intertemporal transfer of funds between individuals. This is another way of saying that finance considers the time value of money and the implications for interest rates on the time value of money and financing decisions. Finance is concerned with the valuation of assets, and the valuation process explicitly considers the timing of the cash flows associated with the ownership of an asset.

Third—and this is also related to the valuation of an asset—finance focuses on cash flows, not profits. Cash flows are important because they can be either reinvested in other income-earning assets, or they can reduce expense-costing liabilities. Again, microeconomics focuses on profits.

Finally, the study of finance makes extensive use of the concept of risk. **Risk** is the possibility (and associated probabilities) that the actual result (return on investment, for example) will differ from the expected outcome. Finance considers the effect of risk on the valuation (the cash flows) of an asset. It also analyzes the risk-return tradeoff, the general principle that states that investors require additional expected returns for taking on additional risk.

These are just several ways in which the focus of the study of finance differs from that of economics. Again, finance can be considered a subfield of economics. Yet, most agree, the focus of finance is different from that of economics.

What Is Real Estate Finance?

There are several subdisciplines within finance including

- Managerial or corporate finance
- Investment and securities (including real estate) analysis and portfolio theory
- Financial institutions and financial services
- Personal finance
- Insurance and risk management
- Real estate finance

Each of the subdisciplines deals with a different area of finance. Real estate finance is a very broad category and includes the study of the institutions, markets, and instruments used to transfer money and credit for the purpose of developing or acquiring real property. Real property, in turn, is the rights, powers, and privileges associated with the use of real estate. Real estate is land and all fixed and immovable improvements on it. Real estate finance would include, but not be limited to, a study of

Owner-occupied residential property
Rental residential property
Terms of residential property leases

Appraisal of residential properties

Loans (mortgages) on residential properties

Sales and exchange of residential properties

Economics of brokerage of residential properties

Markets for exchange of residential mortgages

Valuation of residential mortgages

Commercial properties, including urban office buildings, suburban office buildings, hotels/motels, retirement communities, recreation facilities, mini-warehouses, warehouses, apartment complexes, industrial facilities, and retail trade facilities

Loans on commercial properties

Markets for the exchange of commercial property loans

Valuation of loans on commercial properties

Appraisal of commercial properties

Investment in commercial properties

Portfolios of real estate investments

Real estate taxation issues

Law and real estate lending

Since real property includes not only real estate, but all of the rights and privileges of the use of real estate that can be transferred, the study of real estate finance does not have a narrow focus.

What Is the Environment of Real Estate Finance?

Financial instruments are used to transfer money and credit for the purpose of developing and acquiring real property. The institutions that create and purchase those instruments and the markets within which they are transferred constitute the environment of real estate finance. In essence, the environment is the financial system of the United States. This portion of the financial system is not insignificant. Hartzell, Pittman, and Downs estimate the value of commercial real estate in the United States in 1989 to be $2.43 trillion. This constitutes 23.7 percent of the total value of the traditional institutional investment asset classes. This is less than corporate equity and government securities, but more than corporate debt. They estimate the value of residential property to be $8.7 trillion. [1]

In considering the economy as a whole, there is an identity called the **savings—investment cycle.** The identity indicates that, by definition, the amount of savings equals the total amount invested. Table 1–1 shows the gross savings and investment in the United States for 1996. Savings are identified by three groups: individuals, businesses, and government. Not surprisingly, the federal government's savings in 1996 was negative. Twenty-two percent of the total

TABLE 1–1
U.S. Gross Saving and Investment; 1996
(Billions of Dollars)

Personal Saving	292.2	
Total personal savings		292.2
Gross Business Savings:		
Undistributed profits	176.5	
Depreciation allowance	723.4	
Total business savings		899.9
Total savings		1,192.1
Government Surplus or Deficit (−)	135.0	
Gross savings		1,327.1
Gross Private Domestic Investment	1,381.9	
Net Foreign Investment	−149.4	
Statistical Discrepancy	194.6	
Gross Investment		1,327.1

Source: *Survey of Current Business,* 1997, Washington, D.C.: U.S. Government Printing Office.

FIGURE 1–1

Flow of Funds in the Savings–Investment Cycle

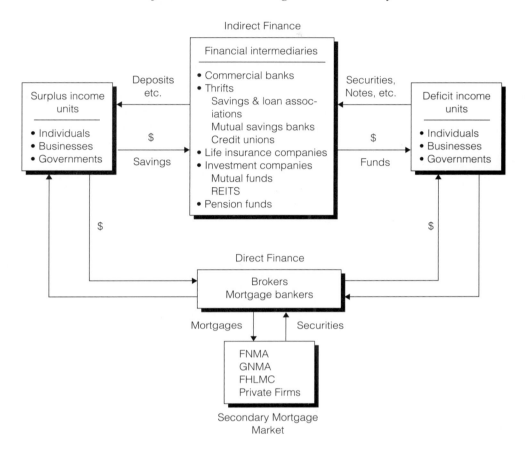

savings came from individuals. Businesses saved $176.5 billion in undistributed profits (retained earnings) and another $723.4 billion of savings resulted from corporate and noncorporate depreciation allowance. The total savings of $1,327.1 billion resulted in an equal amount of "investment." This does not mean investment by purchasing stocks and bonds but rather investment in the sense of new plant construction, equipment, and real property.

The financial marketplace is the system whereby savings are transferred from what are termed *surplus income units* to what are termed *deficit income units*. The best way to understand the process is to consider a simple example. If an individual has more income than consumption, he or she is a surplus income unit and adds to the amount of savings. On the other hand, a corporation that needs to construct a manufacturing facility and does not have sufficient revenue above expenses to meet the cost will have to borrow funds. This deficit income firm may issue a bond. If the bond is purchased by the income surplus unit, a small portion of the national savings-investment cycle is completed. Of course, this is a very simple example. The actual process involves sophisticated markets and institutions that facilitate the closing of the cycle.

Figure 1–1 illustrates a simple **flow of funds** in the savings-investment cycle. This is the environment of real estate finance. On the left side of the figure are the surplus income units with funds to lend. On the right side are the deficit income units with a need to borrow credit. Surplus and deficit income units are broken down into three categories: individuals (households), businesses, and governments. Both surplus and deficit income units exist within each category, but some categories will be dominated by one type. Recently, for example, the federal government has been a deficit income unit (but some state governments are surplus income units).

Excess funds flow from the surplus income to the deficit income units either directly or through intermediaries. Direct financing takes place when the surplus income unit advances funds directly to the deficit income unit. The transaction usually involves a surplus unit purchasing the security (a bond, for example) issued by the deficit unit. Brokers may facilitate the transaction but are not necessary in many cases. **Financial intermediaries** are financial institutions that channel funds from the surplus income units to the deficit income units. Intermediaries provide special services that will be discussed later in the text under the theory of financial intermediation. Of special interest to real estate finance are the activities of the secondary mortgage market. Here, intermediaries purchase residential and commercial mortgages from other intermediaries or from brokers that deal with surplus income units. They purchase the mortgages with funds raised through the sale of securities that they create. As an example, a secondary mortgage market agency will sell a security to a surplus income unit through a broker and use the proceeds of the sale to purchase a mortgage from a deficit income unit, again through a broker.

A CLOSER LOOK AT FINANCIAL INTERMEDIARIES AND FINANCIAL MARKETS

The intermediaries shown in Figure 1–1 vary in purpose and form but fulfill the same function—facilitating the flow of funds in the financial system. Intermediaries perform several functions discussed in detail in Chapter 3. In short, because of their special position in the financial market, they take on (for a fee) several risks or offer services associated with lending. First, they provide liquidity to savers (for example, checking accounts). Second, they borrow short and lend long, exposing themselves to adverse (upward) movements in interest rates. Third, they can evaluate the credit risks of borrowers. Because of this ability to evaluate credit risk, they are in a good position to take on the risk that a borrower may default on a loan.

Government regulation and supervision of some of the financial intermediaries are outlined in Exhibit 1–1. As you can see, a rather large and complex system has developed to regulate and supervise financial intermediaries, both at the federal and state level. Let's consider briefly the principal financial intermediaries.

Commercial Banks

Commercial banks accept demand deposits (checking accounts) and time deposits (savings accounts and certificates of deposit). They also may borrow funds from other sources. Together these funds are advanced to individuals, businesses, and the government. Commercial banks are supervised by the Federal Reserve System. Their deposits are insured by the Federal Deposit Insurance Corporation (FDIC). They are an important source of commercial real estate loans, especially loans for the acquisition, development, and construction (ADC loans) of real estate projects. They are also a source of residential loans.

Thrift Institutions

Thrift institutions include savings and loan associations, mutual savings banks, and credit unions. They are called thrifts because they are a major depository of individuals' savings. Prior to the early 1980s, they were prohibited from accepting demand deposits. They could only accept time deposits. Now, they can compete with commercial banks for demand deposits. The distinction between savings and loan associations and mutual savings banks is in the form of ownership. The mutual savings bank form of ownership (a cooperative as opposed to a stock company) must be approved by state law. There are a dozen or so states that allow this form of ownership. There is little practical distinction between them, however. They share the same trade association, the U.S. Savings and Loan League, and are supervised by the same government agency, the Office of Thrift Supervision (formally the Federal Home Loan Bank Board). Their deposits are insured by the FDIC. (Prior to 1990 their deposits were insured by the Federal Savings and Loan Insurance Corporation [FSLIC]). Credit unions are restricted by their charters to serving members of a designated affiliation, such as employees of a corporation, government unit, or other entity. They are supervised by the **National Credit Union Association**

Board (NCUAB), and their deposits are insured by the federally insured National Credit Union Share Insurance Fund. Thrifts are the largest single source of residential mortgage credit. Prior to 1982, thrifts were restricted in their investment activities. Savings and loans, in particular, were directed to invest in residential mortgages. Deregulation of thrifts beginning in 1982 allowed them to broaden their investments to include more commercial real estate investments.

Investment Companies

Investment companies pool the funds of many savers and invest the funds in a portfolio of assets. Many companies invest only in stocks, and some of these specialize only in growth stocks, income stocks, or stock of companies in certain industries. Some investment companies, called real estate investment trusts (REITs), specialize in real estate properties or mortgages on real estate properties. Others invest in mortgage-type securities such as Government National Mortgage Association (GNMA) bonds.

Insurance Companies

Insurance companies, especially life insurance companies, receive periodic or lump-sum payments from individuals or organizations in return for a promise to make future payments if certain events occur. They have a need to invest these funds to build a reserve until the event occurs, at which time there will be a claim. Since they have a long investment horizon, life insurance companies invest in many commercial real estate properties.

Pension Funds

Private **pension funds** pool the contributions of employees and invest the funds just as insurance companies do. They need to build a reserve to meet the retirement needs of the contributors. Currently, they invest modestly in commercial real estate properties. It is expected, however, that their investment in real estate will increase in the future.

Direct Financing

Much of the flow of funds in the savings-investment cycle takes place without the use of intermediaries. Surplus income units advance funds directly to deficit income units with the aid of brokers that facilitate the transaction. Thus, when an individual purchases a bond directly from the federal government or when a home seller grants a note to the home buyer, **direct financing** takes place. Often a broker may be involved, as is the case with the purchase of most corporate securities.

Secondary Mortgage Market

Of particular interest to those involved in real estate finance is the role of the **secondary mortgage market** agencies and firms. These agencies and firms include the Federal National Mortgage Association (FNMA), the Government National Mortgage Association (GNMA), the Federal Home Loan Mortgage Corporation (FHLMC), and many private firms. They obtain funds by issuing securities (often through brokers) called mortgage-related securities (MRS). They then use the funds to purchase mortgages. The cash flow stream from the mortgages is used to service the interest payments on the mortgage-related securities. Let's distinguish between secondary and primary markets and look at the importance of secondary markets to the efficient flow of funds in the financial system.

Primary and Secondary Markets

You are undoubtedly aware of the exchanges, such as the New York Bond Exchange and the New York Stock Exchange. Existing securities are bought and sold on these exchanges. On these exchanges, the owners of the securities did not originate or create them. When a security is created and sold for the first time by a deficit income unit, that transaction takes place in the **primary market.** Secondary mortgage market agencies and firms are classified as such because they purchase (and sell) mortgages that have been previously originated by other lenders. That is, they themselves do not originate the mortgage to the borrowing household. When a mortgage is originated by a lender to a household, this takes place in the primary market. New securities are created in the primary market, and any subsequent sale of the security takes place in the **secondary market.**

Secondary markets are helpful, if not necessary, to the success of primary markets. A large and active secondary market makes securities more liquid. A buyer of a security in the primary market will be concerned if it is difficult to resell the security. Investors do not like securities that are not easily sold (not liquid). The reduction in marketability (or liquidity) risk due to a large and efficient secondary market leads to a reduction in the yield required by investors in the primary market. But a reduction in the investors' required yield also translates into a lower interest cost for borrowers. In this way, secondary markets lower the costs of completing the savings-investment, or flow-of-funds, cycle.

Money and Capital Markets

Financial markets can be broken into two categories: money markets and capital markets. Both involve the flow of funds between users and suppliers of credit. **Money markets** deal in short-term securities (maturities of 1 year or less), and capital markets deal in long-term securities (over 1 year in maturity). Many organizations deal in both markets. The federal government, for example, issues both short-term Treasury bills and long-term Treasury bonds to finance its deficits. Corporations finance their assets with long-term bonds and equity but have an occasional need for short-term financing. When they do, they borrow for the short term from commercial banks or issue commercial paper. Most real estate financing takes place in the **capital markets**. Mortgages are long-term securities. The exception would be the need for short-term acquisition, development, and construction loans that are refinanced with long-term permanent loans when the real estate project is complete.

ORGANIZATION OF THE BOOK

The remainder of this text is organized as follows. Chapters 2 and 3 complete Part One. Chapter 2 deals with the determination of interest rates. The interest rate is the "price" of credit, and an understanding of how interest rates are determined is essential to understanding the real estate finance market. Chapter 3 outlines some of the fundamental principles of finance and indicates how these can be applied to real estate. They include asset valuation, leverage and capital structure, option valuation, the theory of financial intermediation, portfolio theory, efficient market theory, and agency theory. These basic finance principles are applied wherever possible throughout the remainder of the text.

The eleven chapters in Part Two of the text deal with residential real estate finance. Chapter 4 outlines the history of residential finance until World War II, including the development of the fixed rate amortizing mortgage. Chapter 5 breaks the postwar era into decades and shows how the residential real estate market has evolved to arrive at the current market structure. Chapter 6 examines alternative mortgage instruments—mortgages other than the standard fixed-rate 30-year loan. Chapter 7 is devoted entirely to the relationship between the method of financing property acquisition and transaction prices. Chapters 8 and 9 discuss federal policies on residential housing. Federal laws related to four issues are considered: housing affordability, market efficiency, competition in the housing finance market, and equity (fairness).

The next two chapters are designed to acquaint you with the secondary mortgage market. Chapter 10 presents the structure of the secondary mortgage market and includes a description of the major secondary mortgage market agencies and the mortgage-related securities that they create. Chapter 11 follows with a discussion on the cash flows and valuation of those mortgage-related securities. Chapter 12 focuses on risk management by lenders. It discusses standard borrower qualification and loan underwriting procedures. Chapter 13 describes the steps in the loan origination and processing procedures. It also presents a summary of the activities of mortgage bankers. Finally, Chapter 14 closes the section on residential finance with a discussion of government and private mortgage insurance programs.

Part Three is concerned with commercial real estate finance. Chapter 15 looks at the theoretical aspects of leverage and capital structure. The federal tax environment of commercial real estate is presented in Chapter 16. Chapter 17 briefly describes the sources of funds for commercial real estate acquisition and development. The next three chapters discuss several different finance arrangements. Chapter 18 outlines acquisition, development, and construction financing. Chapter 19 looks at various permanent loan arrangements, including equity participation loans and sale-leaseback arrangements. The last chapter of this section, Chapter 20, discusses the various forms of ownership of commercial real estate. Such investment vehicles as real estate investment trusts and real estate limited partnerships are discussed here.

Part Four completes the text with a presentation of related finance topics. Chapter 21 examines portfolio considerations for large investors (sometimes referred to as institutional investors) in commercial real estate. Chapter 22 discusses issues such as lender liability, agency problems, fraud, and ethics in real estate finance. As mentioned, throughout the text we focus on the application of finance principles to real estate.

KEY TERMS

Capital market

Commercial banks

Direct financing

Finance

Financial intermediaries

Flow of funds

Insurance companies

Investment companies

Money market

National Credit Union Association Board

Pension funds

Primary market

Risk

Savings-investment cycle

Secondary market

Secondary mortgage market

Thrift institutions

SUGGESTED READINGS

Brick, J.R., ed. 1981. *Financial Markets: Instruments and Concepts.* Richmond, VA: Robert F. Dame.

Dasso, J., J.D. Shilling, and A.A. Ring. 1995. *Real Estate,* 12th ed. Englewood Cliffs, NJ: Prentice-Hall.

Hancock, Diana and James A. Wilcox, 1997. Bank Capital, Nonbank Finance, and Real Estate Activity. *Journal of Housing Research.* 8:1, 75–105.

Jaffe, A.J. and C.F. Sirmans. 1995. *Fundamentals of Real Estate Investment,* 3d ed. Englewood Cliffs, NJ: Prentice-Hall.

Miles, M. et al. 1991. *Real Estate Development Principles and Process.* Washington, DC: Urban Land Institute, ch. 3.

Moyer, R.C. et al. 1990. *Contemporary Financial Management.* St. Paul: West Publishing Company, ch. 2.

Smith, C. 1990. The theory of corporate finance: An historic overview. In C. Smith, ed., *The Modern Theory of Corporate Finance.* New York: McGraw-Hill.

REVIEW QUESTIONS

1–1   a. Define the study of finance.

       b. How is the focus of finance different from the field of traditional economics?

1–2   a. Define real estate finance.

       b. What real estate-related topics are of concern to real estate finance?

1–3   What does the flow-of-funds cycle show?

1–4   List five types of financial intermediaries and give a brief description of each.

1–5   a. Distinguish between primary and secondary markets.

       b. Give an example of each.

1–6   a. Distinguish between money and capital markets.

       b. In which of these markets does most real estate financing take place? Why?

ENDNOTE

1.   David J. Hartzell, Robert H. Pittman, and David H. Downs, "An Updated Look at the Size of the U.S. Real Estate Market Portfolio." *Journal of Real Estate Research* 9 (Spring 1994), 197–212.

WEB SITES

www.fdic.gov/databank   FDIC data on commercial banks and savings and loans
www.financenet.gov   federal government financial management information
www.real-jobs.com   career interests in real estate and potential employers

EXHIBIT 1–1

Regulatory Environment of Financial Institutions

Depository Institutions and Their Regulators

	Chartering & Licensing	Branching
	1.	2. Intra-state
A. National Banks	Comptroller	Comptroller
B. State Member Banks	State authority	Federal Reserve & state authority
C. State Nonmember Banks Insured	State authority	FDIC & state authority
D. Noninsured State Banks	State authority	State authority
E. Insured Savings Associations Federal (1)	OTS	OTS
Insured Savings Associations State (2)	State authority	OTS & state authority
F. Uninsured Savings Associations State	State authority	State authority
G. Credit Unions Federal	NCUAB	(5)
Credit Unions State	State authority	State authority
H. Bank Holding Companies	Federal Reserve & state authority	Federal Reserve & state authority
I. Savings Association Holding Companies	OTS & state authority (3)	OTS & state authority
J. Foreign Branches of U.S. Banks National & State Members	Federal Reserve & state authority	N/A
Foreign Branches of U.S. Banks Insured State Nonmembers	State authority	N/A
K. Edge Act Corporations	Federal Reserve	Federal Reserve
Agreement Corporations	State authority (4)	Federal Reserve
L. U.S. Branches & Agencies of Foreign Banks—Federal	Comptroller	Comptroller & FDIC (6)
U.S. Branches & Agencies of Foreign Banks—State	State authority	State authority & FDIC (6)

The Matrix provides an overview of primary regulators of depository institutions as of April 1992. It is not intended to cover each area of regulatory responsibility in detail. Further, the Matrix and accompanying footnotes should not be considered either a substitute for or an interpretation of the regulations. Regulatory agencies should be consulted for answers to specific questions.

April 1992

Federal Reserve Bank of New York

(1) Federal savings associations include any thrift institution such as federal savings banks, federally chartered under Section 5 of the Home Owners' Act.

(2) State savings associations include any state chartered savings bank, savings and loan association, building and loan association, homestead association, or cooperative bank.

(3) Savings association holding companies are required to register with the OTS.

(4) Agreement Corporations are subject to the restrictions on powers established by the Federal Reserve for Edge Act Corporations.

(5) Federal credit unions are not required to receive NCUA approval before opening a branch.

(6) The establishment of federal branches and agencies is subject to the within-state branching restrictions of the McFadden Act. The establishment of state branches or agencies is regulated by state banking law. A foreign bank may not relocate any insured branch within the state without the prior written consent of the FDIC.

(7) While the McFadden Act prevents interstate branching by national and state member banks, banks can provide certain services on an interstate basis.

(8) While the McFadden Act's interstate branching restrictions are not applicable to insured state non-member and non-insured state banks, state laws generally prohibit branching by out-of-state banks.

(continued)

EXHIBIT 1–1 (*Continued*)

Regulatory Environment of Financial Institutions

	Mergers, Acquisitions & Consolidations		Reserve Requirements
3. Inter-state	4. Intra-state	5. Inter-state	6.
(7)	Comptroller (11)	(19)	Federal Reserve (21)
(7)	Federal Reserve & state authority (12)	(19)	Federal Reserve (21)
(8)	FDIC & state authority (13)	FDIC & state authority	Federal Reserve (21)
(8)	State authority (14)	State authority (14)	Federal Reserve (21)
OTS (9)	OTS	OTS (9,15)	Federal Reserve (21)
OTS & state authority	OTS & state authority (15)	OTS & state authority	Federal Reserve (21)
State authority	State authority	State authority	Federal Reserve (21)
(5)	NCUA	NCUA	Federal Reserve (21)
State authority	NCUA & state authority (16)	NCUA & state authority (16)	Federal Reserve (21)
Federal Reserve & state authority	Federal Reserve & state authority	Federal Reserve & state authority (20)	N/A
OTS & state authority	OTS & state authority	OTS & state authority	N/A
N/A	N/A	N/A	(22)
N/A	N/A	N/A	(22)
Federal Reserve	Federal Reserve (17)	Federal Reserve (17)	Federal Reserve (21)
Federal Reserve	Federal Reserve (17)	Federal Reserve (17)	Federal Reserve (21)
Comptroller & Federal Reserve (10)	Comptroller & Federal Reserve (18)	(18)	Federal Reserve (21)
State authority & Federal Reserve (10)	FDIC or Federal Reserve and state authority (18)	(18)	Federal Reserve (21)

(9) Federal savings associations are prohibited from out-of-state branching unless they qualify as domestic building and loan associations under the tax laws or meet certain other requirements.

(10) Foreign banks with state or federal branches or agencies (or commercial lending companies or bank subsidiaries) are not permitted to establish a federal or state branch or agency outside their home state unless: (a) it is permitted by law in the state in which it will operate and (b) in the case of a branch, an agreement with the Federal Reserve has been entered that will limit deposits at the non-home state branch to those permitted to Edge Act Corporations.

(11) The Comptroller must approve the merger or acquisition if the resulting bank is a national bank. However, if a non-insured bank merges into a national bank, the FDIC must approve the merger.

(12) The Federal Reserve must approve the merger or acquisition if the resulting bank is a state member bank. However, if a non-insured bank merges into a state member bank, the FDIC must approve the merger.

(13) The FDIC must approve the merger or acquisition if the resulting bank is an insured state non-member bank or if a non-insured bank merges into an insured state non-member bank.

(14) In addition to state authority, the FDIC must approve mergers or acquisitions between insured depository institutions and non-insured institutions.

(15) The OTS must approve the merger or acquisition if the resulting institution is an insured savings association. However, if a non-insured institution merges into an insured savings association, the FDIC must approve the merger.

(16) The NCUA must approve the merger or acquisition if the resulting credit union is federally insured.

(17) The Federal Reserve supervises acquisitions made by Edge Act Corporations and Agreement Corporations. Agreement Corporations may merge as permitted by state authority.

EXHIBIT 1 – 1 *(Continued)*

Regulatory Environment of Financial Institutions

LEGEND

FDIC	Federal Deposit Insurance Corporation
FTC	Federal Trade Commission
Federal Reserve	Board of Governors of the Federal Reserve System/Federal Reserve Banks
IBF	International Banking Facility

Access to the Discount Window	Deposit Insurance	Supervision & Examination
7.	8.	9.
Federal Reserve (23)	FDIC	Comptroller (27)
Federal Reserve (23)	FDIC	Federal Reserve & state authority (27)
Federal Reserve (23)	FDIC	FDIC & state authority
Federal Reserve (23)	None or state insurance fund (24)	State authority
Federal Home Loan Bank & Federal Reserve (23)	FDIC	OTS (27,28)
Federal Home Loan Bank & Federal Reserve (23)	FDIC	OTS & state authority (27,28)
Federal Home Loan Bank & Federal Reserve (23)	None or state insurance fund (24)	State authority (28)
Central Liquidity Facility & Federal Reserve (23)	Credit Union Share (25)	NCUA
Central Liquidity Facility & Federal Reserve (23)	Credit Union Share or state insurance fund (25)	State authority
N/A	N/A	Federal Reserve
N/A	N/A	OTS
N/A	N/A	Comptroller or Federal Reserve (29)
N/A	N/A	FDIC or state authority (29)
N/A	N/A	Federal Reserve
N/A	N/A	Federal Reserve & state authority
Federal Reserve (23)	FDIC (26)	Comptroller & Federal Reserve (27,30)
Federal Reserve (23)	FDIC (26)	FDIC, state authority & Federal Reserve (27,30)

(18) The International Banking Act of 1978 makes foreign banks that have branches or agencies in the U.S. subject to the provisions of the Bank Holding Company Act of 1956 with respect to non-bank acquisitions. Acquisitions of banks are subject to the Bank Holding Company Act and the home state limitations imposed by the International Banking Act.

(19) The McFadden Act prevents interstate branching by national and state member banks.

(20) The Douglas Amendment to the Bank Holding Company Act allows bank holding companies to acquire banks in other states if the state of the acquired bank specifically allows out-of-state holding companies to acquire in-state banks.

(21) Under the Depository Institutions Deregulation and Monetary Control Act of 1980, the Federal Reserve is required to set a uniform system of reserve requirements (Regulation D) for virtually all depository institutions. Non-insured state banks eligible for deposit insurance may be subject to reserve requirements. Regulation D provides that IBF deposits satisfying the requirements of that Regulation are exempt from reserve requirements.

(22) Deposits at foreign branches of U.S. banks payable only outside the U.S. are generally not subject to reserve requirements.

(23) Nearly all depository institutions in the U.S., including branches and agencies of foreign banks, have

access to the discount window. These depository institutions are expected to make reasonable use of their usual sources of funds before requesting loans from Federal Reserve Banks. For example, savings associations and credit unions should first go to the Federal Home Loan Banks and the Central Liquidity Facility, respectively, for loans.

(24) Deposits which are not insured by the FDIC may be insured by states or state authorized insurance funds.

(25) Shares in all federal credit unions and many state credit unions are insured by the National Credit Union Share Insurance Fund, which is administered by the NCUA. Shares in some state credit unions

(continued)

EXHIBIT 1 – 1 *(Continued)*

Regulatory Environment of Financial Institutions

NCUA	National Credit Union Administration
Member	Member of the Federal Reserve System
N/A	Not Applicable
OCC	Office of the Comptroller of Currency
OTS	Office of Thrift Supervision

Prudential Limits, Safety & Soundness	Consumer Protection	
10.	**11. Rulemaking**	**12. Enforcement**
Comptroller	Federal Reserve	Comptroller
Federal Reserve & state authority	Federal Reserve & state authority	Federal Reserve & state authority
FDIC & state authority	Federal Reserve & state authority	FDIC & state authority
State authority	Federal Reserve & state authority	State authority & FTC (31)
OTS & FDIC	Federal Reserve & OTS	OTS
OTS, FDIC & state authority	Federal Reserve, OTS & state authority	OTS & State authority
State authority	Federal Reserve & state authority	State authority & FTC (31)
NCUA	Federal Reserve & state authority	NCUA
State authority	Federal Reserve & state authority	State authority & FTC (31)
Federal Reserve	Federal Reserve & state authority	FTC (31)
OTS	Federal Reserve & state authority	FTC (31)
Comptroller & Federal Reserve	N/A	N/A
FDIC & state authority	N/A	N/A
Federal Reserve	N/A	N/A
Federal Reserve	N/A	N/A
Comptroller	Federal Reserve & state authority	OCC or FTC
Federal Reserve or FDIC & state authority	Federal Reserve & state authority	OCC or FTC & state authority

may be insured by state or state-authorized insurance funds.

(26) Federal branches of foreign banks which accept retail deposits generally must obtain FDIC insurance. State branches of foreign banks which accept retail deposits generally must also obtain FDIC insurance if they are located in a state in which a state bank is required to have deposit insurance.

(27) The FDIC has some residual examination authority over all FDIC-insured depository institutions.

(28) Federally insured Savings Associations are supervised and examined by the OTS; non-federally insured state Savings Associations by state authority.

(29) Foreign branches of national banks are supervised and examined by the OCC; foreign branches of state member banks by the Federal Reserve; foreign branches of insured state non-member banks by the FDIC; and foreign branches of non-insured state non-member banks by state authority.

(30) Federal branches and agencies are examined by the OCC; state branches insured by the FDIC are examined by the FDIC and state authority; and state non-insured branches and agencies are examined by state authority. The Federal Reserve has residual examining authority over all banking activities of foreign banks.

(31) Enforcement of federal consumer regulations is generally left to the FTC where the institution is not otherwise a federally insured depository institution.

Public Information Department
Federal Reserve Bank
of New York
33 Liberty Street
New York, NY 10045

CHAPTER 2

Money, Credit, and the Determination of Interest Rates

LEARNING OBJECTIVES

When you have finished this chapter, you should understand how the supply and demand for money and credit affect (and are affected by) the economy and, in turn, affect the general level of interest rates. The level and volatility of interest rates have a great effect on real estate activity, as you will see in later chapters. Interest rates affect the demand for mortgages and housing; an increase in rates reduces the affordability of housing. Rate increases also affect the timing and value of the cash flows associated with mortgages and other real estate securities. As an example, if interest rates fall, many homeowners will refinance their existing mortgage, shortening its maturity. You also should understand how yields on individual debt instruments are determined. Finally, you should understand why, at any point in time, securities of different maturities may have different yields and what this difference may imply about how financial markets view changes in interest rates in the future.

INTRODUCTION

In this chapter we explore the determination of interest rates. We begin with a discussion of the relationship between the economy and interest rates. We are interested in the manner in which the general level of interest rates is determined. We often hear about the periodic changes in interest rates in the financial markets. It is this "general" level of rates that is the focus of the first part of this chapter. Next, we explore the determination of interest rates on specific, individual debt securities. We discover those security-specific characteristics that determine interest rate or yield (the terms *interest rate* and *yield* are used interchangeably in this chapter). Finally, we expose what current interest rates may indicate about the future direction of interest rate changes.

THE GENERAL LEVEL OF INTEREST RATES

To understand how various forces interplay to determine the level of interest rates in the economy, it is helpful to begin by assuming that there exists only one type of credit instrument. In actuality there are hundreds of different credit instruments. Each has its own interest rate (yield) that reflects not only the general economy but the various elements of risk particular to the issuer. In this section we will focus on the general level of interest rates and not individual rates that are affected by the peculiar risk characteristics of different credit instruments. To do this, it is useful to assume that there is only one type of credit market instrument in the economy. For the purpose of this simplified model we will consider a bond.[1]

Assume that the bond is riskless in all respects. The issuer will meet all interest and principal payments with certainty, and the instruments can be sold instantly for cash at a stated price. Finally, assume there is no expectation of inflation (or deflation) at any time in the future.

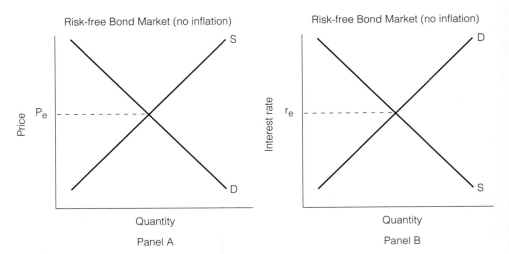

FIGURE 2–1

Supply and Demand for Bonds

The price of the bond is inversely related to, and determined by, the market-required yield. If the bond promises to pay $1 per year into perpetuity (no repayment of principal ever) and the market yield is 10 percent, then its price will be $10. The $1 annual payment will yield 10 percent on the $10 investment ($1/$10 = 0.1). If the required market yield is 12.5 percent, then the bond will sell for $8, the $1 payment being 12.5 percent of the investment ($1/0.125 = $8). Note that the market value of the bonds can be defined in terms of either their price or their yield.

Figure 2–1 shows the supply and demand for the bonds in terms of either concept. Panel A represents the market in terms of the price and Panel B in terms of the yield. Panel A is the conventional graph with an upward-sloping supply curve and a downward-sloping demand curve. As the price increases, suppliers (those demanding credit) will desire to place more bonds in the market. This makes sense since higher bond prices reflect a lower yield or interest cost to the issuer. Lower prices (higher yields) lead to an increase in the quantity demanded. The intersection of the curves establishes the equilibrium price. The curves are reversed in Panel B because the yield, measured on the vertical axis, is the inverse of the price.

What might be the value of the equilibrium rate of interest in this simple model? It is difficult to say because the assumptions employed to demonstrate this market are never fully met in the real world. No such rate has ever been observed. The closest approximation is the market for Treasury securities in a no- or low-inflation time period, such as during the 1930s or the early 1950s. At those times, Treasuries sold to yield approximately 2 to 3 percent annually. Investors in Treasuries during these periods could expect a 3 percent yield with no deterioration in return due to inflation. For that reason the yield is referred to as the real rate of interest. The real rate of interest is the equilibrium rate on riskless bonds in a noninflationary environment.

Once consideration is made for risk, the possibility of inflation, or other factors, the supply and demand curves in Figure 2–1 will shift. While the figure implies a rather simplistic determination of interest rates, a large number of real-world factors determine the position of the curves and, thus, the rate of interest on specific securities. Those factors are considered next, beginning with a discussion of inflation.

MONEY, THE ECONOMY, AND INFLATION

In this section we outline a transition mechanism of money and interest rates that operates somewhat as follows:

money supply → economy → inflation → inflationary expectations →
credit markets → interest rates

This money–inflation–interest rate mechanism has been studied and outlined for decades. One of the economists who explored these relationships was Irving Fisher, an early twentieth-century American economist.

The Equation of Exchange

Fisher is known for developing the **Equation of Exchange:**[2]

$$MV = PT \qquad \text{(Equation 2–1)}$$

where, for a given period of time, for example, 1 year, M represents the money supply, V its **velocity of circulation,** P the general price level, and T the volume of trade. The velocity of circulation is the average number of times \$1 turns over in 1 year. It is the total annual dollar transactions divided by the supply of money.

The equation holds by a definition of the terms. The left side is the product of a stock (M) and a flow (V) and represents the total amount spent on goods and services. The right side is also the product of a stock (P) and a flow (T) and represents the total amount received from the sale of goods and services. It is true by definition since what is spent in the economy during a year equals what is received. The value of the equation lies in the assumptions that are made about the behavior of, and the relationships between, the variables. Fisher's statistical studies indicated that the velocity of money was fairly stable and only changed gradually over long periods of time. Also, for a fully employed economy, the volume of trade can expand only at a modest rate, constrained by the amount and growth of real resources. This view leaves the money supply and the price level positively related (by the equation) and free to take on values of an unlimited range. Furthermore, the price level becomes the passive variable in the model, determined by changes in the money supply.

Consider some possible values for the variables in the equation on a year-to-year basis. If the volume of trade can increase only with the growth in real resources (historically about 2 to 3 percent annually), then growth in the supply of money in excess of this rate will cause the price level to rise. Given the stability of the velocity of money and the constraint on the growth rate of the volume of trade, the rate of the growth in prices (inflation) should be 2 or 3 percent below the rate of growth of the money supply. The greater the rate of growth in money, the greater the rate of inflation. This **monetary theory of inflation** is well known and generally accepted by many economists, Milton Friedman[3] among the foremost. It is evident that, for a fully employed economy, the limit on growth in the real volume of trade is determined by growth in real resources. The velocity of money is stable, Friedman says, because it depends upon the demand for real money (the demand to hold real money balances by the public), which is determined primarily by only slowly changing institutional factors. This leaves money supply and prices to be linked, he says. Evidence also suggests that the direction of causation runs from money to prices. That is, increases in the supply of money lead to subsequent changes in the level of prices. There is no evidence to suggest that an increase in prices is followed by a subsequent change in the supply of money. In summary, theory and evidence give strong support to the proposition that inflation is a monetary phenomenon, resulting from an increase in the money supply in excess of the increase in goods and services.

The Fisher Equation

The rate of inflation plays an important role in the determination of market interest rates. In another work, Fisher developed a well-known equation bearing his name.[4] This is not to be confused with the Equation of Exchange he developed earlier. The **Fisher Equation** completes the final portion of the money–inflation–interest rate mechanism. Generally, economists agree that inflation, especially if it is consistent year after year, creates expectations of future inflation. The **adaptations model of inflationary expectations** postulates that credit market participants adapt their expectations of near-term future inflation on the basis of the most recent experience.

Fisher begins with the **real rate of interest,** observing that it is a rate that would exist on default-free bonds, which are at no risk that the principal will not be repaid, in a noninflationary environment. Investors expect to be better off in a real sense as a result of their saving and investing. By investing $100 at the real rate, they would receive, for example, $103 at the end of one year. In the absence of inflation they are 3 percent wealthier in real terms. However, if during the year unexpected inflation of 5 percent occurred, then the real purchasing power of the $103 end-of-year wealth would be only about $98 ($103/1.05). Investors who expect 5 percent annual inflation in the future would require approximately an 8 percent yield to offset the rise in general prices ($108/1.05 = $103). Moreover, borrowers who anticipate the same inflation rate expect to repay the principal with depreciated dollars. They are willing to pay the higher nominal rate. In this fashion, inflationary expectations become incorporated in nominal interest rates. The Fisher Equation expresses this relationship as

$$i + r = p \qquad \text{(Equation 2–2)}$$

where i is the equilibrium nominal rate of interest observed in the credit market, r is the real rate of interest, and p is the expected inflation over the maturity of the bond. For our example, 8% = 3% + 5%. You now can see why it is difficult to observe the real rate of interest. Although the nominal rate is observed in the market, a precise measure of inflationary expectations cannot be observed, only estimated. If one views the money–inflation–interest rate mechanism from beginning to end, the line of causation runs from money to the economy to inflation to inflationary expectations to credit markets to interest rates. Furthermore, consistent and substantial increases in the money supply at one end create higher market rates of interest at the other. The experience of the 1960s and 1970s, when rapid increases in the money supply were associated with very high market interest rates (peaking in 1981 after several years of very loose monetary policy), is an excellent example of the mechanism in action. Figure 2–2 shows the relationship between the 1-year Treasury bill (T-bill) rate and the rate of inflation in the previous year for each year from 1959 through 1996. For example, in 1980 the rate on 1-year T-bills was approx-

FIGURE 2–2

Inflation/T-bill Yield

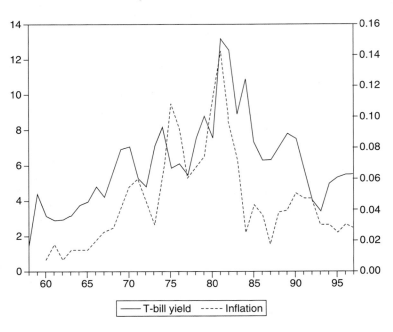

imately 13 percent. The figures show that the inflation rate the year before was also about 13 percent. The nearly coincident lines indicate a very close correlation between interest rates and the year-earlier level of inflation. It is dramatic evidence of the link between inflation and interest rates.

The Gibson Paradox

Despite the evidence in support of the money–inflation–interest rate mechanism, not all economists agree that increases in the growth rate of money will necessarily result in higher nominal interest rates. They argue that an increase in the money supply will lead to an increase in the demand for bonds as well as for goods and services. This results in upward pressure on bond prices, forcing interest rates down. This is called the liquidity effect and was well accepted by Keynesian economists of the postwar era (1940s–1960s). Curiously, Keynes himself noted a series of articles written in *Bankers Magazine* by A. H. Gibson.[5] The articles noted and emphasized the close positive correlation over more than a century between the interest yield on bonds and the wholesale price index in England. Gibson noted the same relationship as in Figure 2–2. Keynes thought the relationship to be more than coincidence and believed that a general model could be developed to explain it. In other words, Keynes himself did not accept the liquidity effect without reservations. It turns out the Fisher Equation is a model that explains the relationship.

Those who were convinced that increases in the supply of money should depress interest rates concentrated only on one element of the entire mechanism. They explained the impact of money on the demand for goods and services (inflation) and on the demand for bonds but ignored the further effects of inflation and inflationary expectations on credit markets. These effects are discussed next.

Liquidity, Income, and Price-Anticipation Effects

An increase in the supply of money can have three effects on credit markets: liquidity, income, and price-anticipation effects. The **liquidity effect,** recognized by Keynesian economists, refers to the initial short-run effect of an increase in the money supply on interest rates. An increase in the supply of money will cause individuals to possess excess cash, which will lead them to readjust their portfolios by purchasing more bonds. The increase in the demand for bonds will depress interest rates. This is only a short-term effect. Eventually, the increase in money also will spill over into a greater demand for goods and services, creating an increase in national income.

The **income effect** comes into play when the higher level of income causes an increase in the demand for credit (supply of bonds). Businesses will demand more credit (issue bonds) to expand their plant and equipment to meet the increased demand for their products. Households will increase their demand for credit in order to purchase durable goods such as houses, autos, and appliances. The increase in the demand for credit by both sectors will place upward pressure on the level of interest rates. Finally, the **price-anticipation effect,** captured in the Fisher Equation, reflects the decrease in the supply of credit (at current rates) as a result of future expected inflation.

The three effects are summarized and demonstrated in Figure 2–3. The supply and demand curves, S and D, duplicate those from Panel A in Figure 2–1, the initial curves for a riskless bond in a noninflationary environment. They establish the real rate of interest in terms of price at P_1. The vertical axis measures the price of the bond. Recall that an increase in the price represents a fall in interest rates and vice versa. The liquidity effect is demonstrated by an increase in the demand for bonds from D to D′. Bond prices (interest rates) rise (fall) initially to P_2. As the increase in the supply of money causes an increase in income, businesses and households demand more credit—that is, they supply additional bonds. The shift of the supply curve to the right from S to S′ lowers the price of bonds to P_3; interest rates are now rising. Finally, market participants who expect inflation to occur in the future reduce their supply of credit (demand for bonds) from D′ to D″. The final equilibrium price P_4 is lower than the initial price, indicating that market rates have risen from their initial level.

FIGURE 2–3

Supply and Demand for Bonds

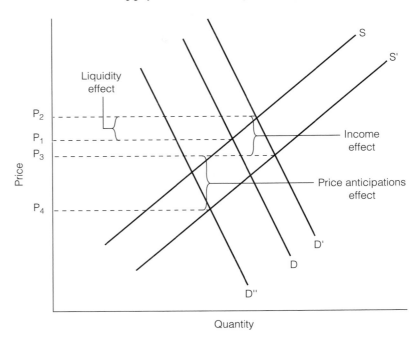

THE DETERMINATION OF INTEREST RATES ON SPECIFIC CREDIT MARKET INSTRUMENTS

In 1996 the inflation rate in the U.S. economy was about 2.75 percent. If the Fisher Equation is used to explain the nominal rate on risk-free bonds (given a real rate of 2 percent), then short-term Treasury bills should have yielded about 4.75 percent in 1997. For 1997 the average treasury bill yield was, indeed, about 5.00 percent, very close to 4.75 percent. In July 1997, 1-year T-bills had an average yield of 5.54 percent. This indicates a perception of future inflation somewhat greater than the 1996 experience. Also, an inspection of other securities at that time reveals an array of yields.

Table 2–1 shows a selection of such yields. The difference in the yields reflects different risk characteristics of the securities. Risk characteristics include default, callability, maturity, and marketability.

Default Risk

Default risk is the risk that the bond issuer will be unable to pay the interest and principal on the obligation. Rating agencies such as Standard and Poor's and Moody's investigate the financial strength of corporations and municipalities that issue bonds. A description of the ratings of these agencies is presented in Table 2–2. Since a lower rating reflects a greater possibility of default, the yield on lower-rated bonds will be greater than that on higher-rated bonds. The difference between the 9.1 percent yield on the bonds of Showboat (rated B−) and the 7.9 percent yield of IBM (rated AAA) at least partially reflects the additional default risk. Note that the Showboat bonds have a shorter maturity. Thus, the difference in yields would not be attributed to term structure (maturity). Although the default risk on IBM bonds is minimal, it is nonetheless positive. IBM bonds yield slightly more than the 10-year Treasury bonds, which have no default risk.

TABLE 2–1

Yields on Selected Bonds, July 1997

Bond	Yield
One-year T-bills	5.70
Ten-year T-bills	6.52
GNMA 8s	7.56
GNMA 12s	7.80
Bell of PA, 2013	8.30
IBM, 2013	7.80
Showboat, 2008	9.10

TABLE 2–2

Description of Agency Ratings

Moody's	Standard and Poor's	Quality Indication
Aaa	AAA	Highest quality
Aa	AA	High quality
A	A	Upper medium grade
Baa	BBB	Medium grade
Ba	BB	Contains speculative elements
B	B	Outright speculative
Caa	CCC & CC	Default definitely possible
Ca	C	Default, only partial recovery likely
C	DDD-D	Default, little recovery likely

Callability Risk

Callability risk refers to the possibility that an issuer of a bond may call it (demand to buy it back) prior to maturity for an amount equal to or near its face (principal amount) value. Noncallable bonds cannot be called prior to maturity. The investor in a noncallable bond benefits if market interest rates fall below the rate offered on these bonds. The bondholder will be entitled to receive the higher coupon rates until maturity. The market value of a noncallable bond with a coupon rate in excess of the market rate will be above its face value. If market rates for bonds of equivalent risk are 10 percent, the market value of a noncallable bond with a coupon rate of 14 percent ($140 annual coupon payment on a $1000 face-value bond) will be about $1200. When issued an equivalent bond that is callable will have a lower value, or higher yield, because of the likelihood that the issuer will take advantage of its right to call the bond at near its face value ($1000). The issuer will likely finance the call by issuing new bonds at a lower interest rate.

The premium for callability risk can be seen in the yields of the Government National Mortgage Association (GNMA) securities. These bonds are described in greater detail in Chapters 10 and 11. Essentially, they are securities backed by a pool of mortgages. The mortgages have a coupon rate 0.5 percent greater than the rate on the bonds. If a homeowner decides to prepay his mortgage prior to maturity, the entire principal is passed through to the GNMA bondholder and no further interest payments on this amount will be forthcoming. The homeowner has issued a callable bond (mortgage) and is likely to exercise the call option if market rates fall below that on the mortgage. Homeowners will refinance their mortgage at the lower interest rate. Since GNMA bondholders do not benefit from an increase in value should rates fall, they are exposed to callability risk. The GNMA 8s in Table 2–1 had a current coupon yield (8 percent) above that of the 10-year Treasury bonds (6.52 percent). (GNMA 8 means the investor obtains an 8 percent annual yield on the security.) Since they have callability risk, they are priced lower in the market and have a slightly higher (7.56 percent) yield to maturity. The higher yield is not due to default risk since the mortgages backing GNMA bonds are all FHA-

or VA-insured. In addition, GNMA, an agency within the Department of Housing and Urban Development, guarantees the timely payment of interest and principal to the bondholders. Therefore, the higher yield must be due to callability risk.

Maturity Risk

Maturity risk refers to the risk associated with bonds with longer maturities. There are actually two related risks here. First, the values of bonds with longer maturities change more than those with shorter maturities when interest rates change. This is called interest rate risk. Appendix A to Chapter 4 shows how changes in interest rates affect the value of bonds with various maturities. Longer-term bonds have more interest rate risk because they have longer lives over which it is possible for market rates to change. Also, purchasing power risk increases with maturity. Purchasing power risk is the risk that inflation will erode the value of the principal amount of the bond. Other things being equal, longer-term bonds will be priced lower to yield more than shorter-term bonds. This yield difference is exemplified, in part, by the difference in the yield on the 10-year Treasury and the 1-year Treasury.

Marketability Risk or Liquidity Risk

Marketability risk refers to the risk that the bond may not trade in a large, organized (liquid) market. The inability to sell the security quickly for cash for its intrinsic value will cause investors to require a yield premium. Although not represented in Table 2–1, such securities exist. Examples would include the bonds issued by very small municipalities or small companies. If all of these risks are combined into the notion of a risk premium *k*, the following equation will describe the return on a particular security:

$$i = r + p + k \qquad \text{(Equation 2–3)}$$

where *i* is the nominal rate, *r* the real rate, *p* the expected inflation rate, and *k* represents other risk factors specific to the security.

For example, the yield on GNMA 12s can be decomposed into the following approximation:

$$7.80\% = 3\% + 3\% + 1.80\%$$

THE YIELD CURVE AND FUTURE INTEREST RATES

The yield spread between the 10- and 1-year Treasuries in Table 2–1 is approximately 0.75 percent. Why does this difference exist? There is no difference in either default, callability, or marketability risk between the instruments. In fact, Table 2–3 shows that different maturity Treasuries in July 1997 had different yields, generally increasing as maturity lengthened.

TABLE 2–3

Yields on Treasuries
July 1997

Maturity	Yield
3 month	5.30
1 year	5.70
2 year	5.96
3 year	6.08
5 year	6.18
7 year	6.29
10 year	6.52
20 year	6.67
30 year	6.62

FIGURE 2–4

Yield Curve; July, 1997

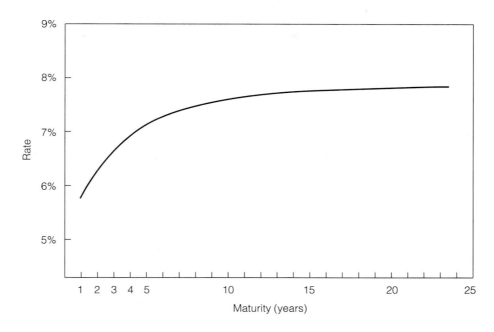

FIGURE 2–5

Examples of Yield Curves

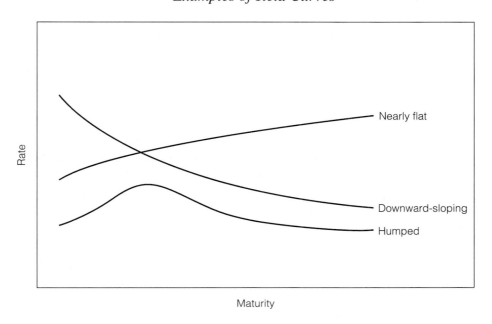

However, the difference in yield among securities may be more than justified by maturity risk alone. Figure 2–4 demonstrates visually the relationship between the maturity of the various Treasury obligations and their yields from Table 2–3. It is called a **yield curve.** A yield curve is a line that relates maturity and yield on bonds of the same grade at a point in time. The yield curve on a given date does not always appear as it does in Figure 2–4. Examples of other yield curves are shown in Figure 2–5. You may wonder why the yield curve is not flat or why there is such a variety of curves at different times. There are three principal theories of the shape of the yield curve, and this is where we see that the shape of the yield curve may be different from what one would expect from maturity risk alone.

Liquidity Premium Theory

According to the **liquidity premium theory,** long-term rates tend to be higher than short-term rates because a premium must be paid to investors who are reluctant to tie up their funds for long periods of time.

   If there is a liquidity premium, it is likely to be small and certainly does not explain the situations in which long-term rates occasionally fall below the shorter-term rates. A more general explanation is required.

Market Segmentation Theory

The **market segmentation theory** suggests that there are two (or more) markets for securities of different maturities. Just as there are two markets for apples and oranges, each with their own equilibrium price, so it is with security markets, according to this theory. Different markets may exist because some institutional investors may have different needs for short- versus long-term bonds.

   Pension funds, for example, may demand long-term investments only, while commercial banks may prefer shorter-term securities. Populated by different participants, the markets will have different equilibrium interest rates. This theory makes the heroic assumption that investors will not change their preference for securities as a result of yield discrepancies. This is unlikely. If an investor who prefers a short-term investment notices a higher yield on a long-term security, she will have an incentive to shift to the longer-term security. As long as it can be sold in a liquid market (Treasuries, for example), she can sell it at any time, effectively causing its maturity to meet her particular needs. Note that this investor may not shift to the longer-term security if she expects interest rates to rise by the time she intended to sell it in the market. An increase in interest rates would result in a decline in its value, possibly resulting in a loss. In the absence of any expectation of a change in interest rates, there is no reason to expect that investors would segment themselves in one end of the maturity spectrum and ignore superior returns in the other end. Segmentation may occur if there are expectations of changing interest rates, however. Higher yields will be necessary to attract investors to a maturity segment of the market if they have certain expectations of interest rate changes. This is a third explanation of the yield curve.

Expectations Theory

To understand the expectations theory, consider the yields in Table 2–3. Let us begin by analyzing two yields, a 1-year and a 2-year Treasury, 5.70 and 5.96, respectively. These two rates were the observed equilibrium yields in July 1997. Since they were equilibrium rates, the supply and demand for these two securities were equal. There was no desire for investors to shift from one to the other and cause the equilibrium rates to shift.

   Consider an investor with a 2-year investment horizon and $1 to invest. In July 1997 he has (at least) two choices. One is to purchase a 2-year Treasury priced to yield 5.96 percent compounded annually. The other is to purchase a 1-year Treasury priced to yield 5.70 percent and to roll it over in July 1997 into another 1-year Treasury at a rate to be determined in the market at that time. With an initial investment of $1, his wealth in July 1999 under each alternative will be

$$\text{Choice 1} \qquad \$1(1.0596)^2$$

$$\text{Choice 2} \qquad \$1(1.057) \times (1 + r_1)$$

where r_1 equals the 1-year rate of interest established in the market in July 1998.

   Since both the 1-year and 2-year security markets are in equilibrium in July 1997, investors must view the choices as identical. They are indifferent to them because they expect the same wealth position in July 1999, regardless of which choice is pursued. Therefore, investors must feel that

$$\$1(1.0596)^2 = \$1(1.057)(1 + r_1)$$

or

$$(1 + r_1) = (1.0596)^2/(1.057) = 1.0622$$

To be indifferent between the two choices, investors in July 1997 expect that the 1-year rate to be established in the market in July 1998 will be 6.22 percent. They expect interest rates to rise. Investors will receive the same 2-year return if they invest in a 2-year bond at a rate of 5.96 percent annually or a 1-year bond at 5.70 percent followed by rolling the investment over to another year at 6.22 percent.

This same logic can be used to compute r_2, the 1-year yield investors expect 2 years in the future (July 1999 through July 2000, in this example). Since the 3-year yield in Table 2–3 is 6.08, the following equation is used:

$$\$1(1.0596)^2 (1 + r_2) = \$1 (1.0608)^3$$

$$(1 + r_2) = (1.0608)^3 /(1.0596)^2 = 1.0632$$

$$r_2 = 6.32\%$$

Investors believe in July 1997 that rates will rise slightly in the third year over the second.

At times, the longer-term yields have been below the short-term yields. It is not unusual to observe a 1-year rate above those of a 2-year rate, for example. In such cases it can be shown that investors expect that rates will fall in the future.

The expectations hypothesis explains a wide range of yield curves with varying slopes. Generally, upward-sloping curves indicate that market participants expect rates to rise in the future, and downward-sloping curves indicate expectations of falling rates.

SUMMARY

Economic conditions, including actual inflation and inflationary expectations, establish the general level of interest rates. In the absence of inflationary expectation the risk-free rate would equal the real rate. For a risk-free bond the nominal rate can be described with the Fisher Equation, by which inflationary expectations are added to the real rate to provide the nominal rate. Risk characteristics of individual issues cause the nominal rate on their securities to be larger by those risk factors. Specific and different risk factors of individual securities include default, maturity, callability, and marketability (liquidity).

The yield curve shows the yield on securities of varying maturity. It incorporates the market expectation of future interest rates. An upward-sloping curve signals expectations of rising rates, and a downward-sloping curve indicates falling rates.

KEY TERMS

Adaptation model of inflationary expectations	Liquidity premium theory
Callability risk	Market segmentation theory
Default risk	Marketability (liquidity) risk
Equation of Exchange	Maturity risk
Expectations theory	Monetary theory of inflation
Fisher Equation	Price-anticipation effect
Gibson Paradox	Purchasing power risk
Income effect	Real rate of interest
Interest rate risk	Velocity of circulation
Liquidity effect	Yield curve

SUGGESTED READINGS

Evans, M.D., and K.K. Lewis. 1995. Do expected shifts in inflation affect estimates of the long-run Fisher relation? *Journal of Finance,* L(1):225–253.

Laidler, D.E. 1985. *The Demand of Money,* 3rd ed. New York: Harper & Row, chs. 5 and 7.

Poole, W. 1978. *Money and the Economy: A Monetarist View.* Reading, MA: Addison-Wesley Publishing, chs. 2, 3, 5.

Price, K., and J. Brick. 1985. The term structure: Forecasting implication. In J. Brick, ed., *Financial Markets Instruments and Concepts.* Richmond, VA.: Robert F. Dame.

Reilly, F., and R. Sidhu. 1981. The many uses of bond duration. In J. Brick, ed., *Financial Markets Instruments and Concepts.* Richmond, VA.: Robert F. Dame, Inc.

REVIEW QUESTIONS

2–1   a. What is the real rate of interest?

      b. Give two reasons why the actual yield on a corporate bond would be greater than the real rate of interest.

2–2   a. What is the Equation of Exchange?

      b. How can the Equation of Exchange be used to explain the monetary theory of inflation?

2–3   a. What is the Gibson Paradox?

      b. What is the Fisher Equation?

      c. What is the relationship between these two concepts?

2–4   List and explain the types of risk associated with specific securities.

2–5   a. What is the yield curve?

      b. Give three explanations why long-term and short-term Treasuries would have different yields on the same date.

2–6   a. Presently, a 1-year Treasury yields 7.8 percent and a 2-year Treasury yields 9 percent. What does this say about market expectations of the 1-year Treasury rate that will be observed one year from now?

      b. Will it be higher or lower than the present 1-year rate?

      c. Give an estimate of its value.

2–7   What does it mean when we say that mortgages (or pass-through securities backed by mortgages) are callable?

PROBLEMS

2–1   Provide the missing data, assuming that the Fisher Equation is accurate.

Case	Real Interest Rate	Nominal Interest Rate	Expected Inflation
A	3%	8%	
B	3		3%
C	3	6	

2–2   Provide the missing data, assuming the Equation of Exchange is accurate.

Case	Money Supply	Velocity	Index of Price Level	Real Transactions	GNP
A	$1,000B	4	8	500B	
B	1,000B		10		5,000B
C		5	10	900B	
D		5		800B	4,000B

2–3   Assume the current money supply is $1,000 B and that the velocity of circulation is 5. Real transactions are $500 billion and the price level index is 10. Next year, the Federal

Reserve is expected to increase the money supply to $1,200 B and real transactions are expected to increase by $50 billion. If the velocity of money remains constant, what will be the rate of inflation if the Equation of Exchange holds each year?

2–4   Determine the price of a bond that promises to pay $10 annually in perpetuity for the following interest rates.

Interest Rate	Price
8%	_____
9	_____
12	_____
14	_____

2–5   Provide the missing data in the following table.

Case	Risk Free Rate	Nominal Rate	Maturity Risk Premium	Callability Risk Premium	Default Risk Premium
A	3.0%	9.0%	2.0%	1.0%	
B	3.0		2.0	2.0	2.5%
C	2.5	8.5	1.0	2.0	
D		10.0	2.0	1.5	4.0

2–6   a. Given the following yields on risk-free Treasury securities, determine the one-year expected rate for the period January 1, 1998, to December 31, 1998 (current date January 1, 1996).

Maturity Date	Rate
December 31, 1996	8%
December 31, 1997	10
December 31, 1998	11

b. What is the expected 1-year rate for the period January 1, 1997 to December 31, 1997?

ENDNOTES

1.   In the most general sense a mortgage is a bond.
2.   Irving Fisher, *The Purchasing Power of Money* (New York: The MacMillan Company, 1922).
3.   Milton Friedman, *Studies in the Quantity Theory of Money* (Chicago: University of Chicago Press, 1956).
4.   Irving Fisher, *The Theory of Interest* (New York: The MacMillan Company, 1930).
5.   John Maynard Keynes, *A Treatise on Money,* vol. 2 (New York: MacMillan and Company, 1930), 198.

WEB SITES

www.interest.com   information on mortgage rates
www.cnnfn.com/markets/rates   market interest rates
http://woodrow.mplsfrb.fed.us/economy/charts   interest rate graphs
www.hsh.com/   graphs of historical interest rates
www.msa2000.com/r.htm   history of interest rates, relative rates by loan type, comparative loan costs
www.mkts.com.spsindex.htm   U.S. Bond market overview
www. Nmnews.fgray.com   national mortgage news
www.mortgagemag.com   latest mortgage news
www.newspage.com   latest national mortgage news

CHAPTER 3

Finance Theory and Real Estate

LEARNING OBJECTIVES

After reading this chapter, you should understand how basic finance principles can be applied to real estate. An overview of several finance principles is presented, including asset valuation, the theory of leverage and optimal capital structure, option valuation, the theory of financial intermediation, portfolio theory, efficient market theory, and agency theory. In-depth analysis of the applications of these principles to real estate are presented later in the text. After reading this chapter, you should see how finance principles can be applied to a wide variety of real estate topics.

INTRODUCTION

Many principles of financial analysis have been developed within the framework of corporate managerial finance and corporate securities markets. But these same principles can be and are applied in practice to real-estate-related subjects. Therefore, in addition to describing the institutions, laws, and markets for real property and real property securities, we will show how finance principles also can be applied to these areas. That is, we seek to integrate finance theory with a description of real estate institutions and markets. We begin with one of the more fundamental finance concepts: asset valuation.

ASSET VALUATION

Asset valuation is concerned with those principles that maximize the wealth of the investor. An asset provides cash flows over time to its owner. The valuation of the asset depends on the expected amount, timing, and risk associated with the cash flows. These elements are all included in the **discounted cash flow (DCF) model** of valuation in this equation:

$$\text{PRESENT VALUE} = \sum_{i=1}^{n} \frac{CF_i}{(1 + r)^i} \qquad \text{(Equation 3–1)}$$

In this equation, *CF* stands for periodic cash flows, *r* is the appropriate discount rate, and *n* is the number of cash flows.

The formula applies to any asset capable of providing cash flows to its owner. In real estate, those assets include equity positions, such as land and buildings; mortgages collateralized by real estate; securities backed by pools of mortgages (pass-through, mortgage-backed bonds); options to purchase real estate; stock in corporations that invest in real estate equity and mortgages (Real Estate Investments Trusts); rights to the servicing income from a portfolio of mortgages; and many others.

Since each asset can be valued in terms of the amount, timing, and risk of the cash flows, there are four elements in the equation: (1) the (present) value, (2) the amount of the cash flows, (3) the time period in which or over which the cash flows occur, and (4) the discount rate. Given any three of the four elements in this basic valuation equation, the fourth can be computed. Furthermore, different situations in real estate finance call for determining each of the four elements.

Amount of After-tax Cash Flows

Each asset provides its owner with an expected cash flow. For valuation purposes, the relevant amount is the after-tax cash flows. Because of the tax shelter characteristics of real estate, actual cash flows are often different from the (accounting) income generated by the asset. Net operating income (NOI) is determined by subtracting the actual "out-of-pocket" expenses of operating the real estate asset from the revenues. Operating expenses will include maintenance, utilities, and property taxes. Federal and state income taxes will be based on the NOI, less depreciation, and represent a cash outflow. Depreciation, however, is a noncash expense and, although it is a deduction for the purpose of determining taxable income, it is not a cash outflow. Why do we focus on after-tax cash flows as opposed to NOI (or accounting profits) in determining value? Because cash flows not only recognize profits, they go further to indicate the amount of cash, on a periodic basis, that is available to the owner of the asset to increase his wealth. While the taxable income on an investment may be negative, indicating a loss, the cash flow available to the owner may be positive. The owner has the opportunity to reinvest this cash flow and obtain a market rate-of-return. In fact, if this income and after-tax cash flow relationship were to prevail in each year of the life of the investment, the reinvested cash flows would continue to accumulate. While the original investment would show annual accounting losses, the investor's wealth would be substantial. It is the asset's cash flows that determine the rate at which the investor's wealth accumulates and thus the value of the asset. The difference between NOI and cash flows is reflected in the practice of many industrial firms that use two alternative accounting practices for income reporting and for tax purposes. In accounting for ending inventory, for example, one method called *first-in-first-out* (FIFO) may maximize reported earnings whereas an alternative method called *last-in-first-out* (LIFO) will reduce earnings, thus, taxes. This practice recognizes that the added cash flows from minimizing taxes allows for a greater accumulation of wealth, since the cash flows can be reinvested in other corporate investments.

Timing of Cash Flows

The timing of the cash flows simply refers to the idea that, other things being equal, the sooner a cash flow is received, the greater its present value. This is so because the sooner it is received, the sooner it can be employed to increase interest-earning assets or reduce interest-costing liabilities, both of which will increase owner's wealth. This principle is recognized in the DCF model by the fact that the later in the life of the asset that a cash flow is received, the larger is the discount factor $[(1 + r)^t]$ that is applied. Also, as seen in the appendix to Chapter 4, values of assets with early cash flows change less when market interest rates change than do other assets.

Risk of Cash Flows

The concept of risk involves the recognition that probabilities can be assigned to alternative (possible) future cash flows. If a probability of 100 percent can be assigned to a future cash flow, there is no risk. The common example of a risk-free investment is that of a Treasury bill for which there is no possibility of default. Most other investments pose at least some possibility that the actual cash flow will differ from the expected cash flow. When probabilities cannot be assigned to these possibilities, uncertainty is said to exist. When probabilities can be assigned, risk is said to exist. Thus, risk exists when there is the possibility that the actual cash flows will differ from those expected (for any reason), and probabilities can be assigned to those possibilities. All assets involve risk, especially real-estate-related assets. Consider the risk of the following real estate assets.

Commercial Project

The cash flows of a commercial project, such as a hotel, apartment complex, or office building, will depend upon a large number of elements, all subject to risk. These include the actual revenues and a multitude of expenses. The revenues, in turn, will depend upon many other risk factors, such as the state of the local and national economy, amount of competition, expertise of the property management, and so forth. The terminal cash flow, the amount received by the investor when the asset is sold or otherwise disposed of, is also subject to risk. It will depend upon the projected cash flows at that time, which are all subject to risk. The value of the real estate asset will be more sensitive to some of these variables than to others. Nonetheless, all represent elements of risk in the sense that their actual amounts may differ from the expected amounts.

Real Estate Limited Partnerships

Many people invest in real estate through limited partnerships (RELPs). These are discussed more fully in Chapter 20. Limited partnerships are partnerships that provide limited liability to the partner-investors, just as corporate stock does. This form of investment involves no management of or decision making about the underlying real estate asset, but gives the investor a right to receive some of the cash flows associated with the real estate, such as tax benefits and appreciation in value. As an example, a partnership may be formed with many investor-partners pooling their funds to purchase a hotel. The partners would receive cash flows from the investment after the expenses of forming and operating the partnership. Thus, in addition to the risk of the cash flows of the real estate, the RELP investor incurs other risks. There may be risk associated with the actual cash flow taken by the general partner for operating the partnership. There is also the risk of the value of the partnership interest upon resale. Since there is no organized, liquid marketplace for RELPs, there may exist substantial liquidity or marketability risk for these investments.

Real Estate Investment Trusts

Some investors invest in real estate through **real estate investment trusts** (REITs). These are also discussed in Chapter 20. This form of investment consists of purchasing stock in a corporation that in turn purchases real estate properties (equity REIT), mortgages on real estate properties (mortgage REIT), or a combination (hybrid REIT). As long as the corporation meets certain Internal Revenue Service (IRS) regulations, it can pass the cash flows of the real estate along to the stockholders without incurring a tax liability at the corporate level. The stockholder in the REIT incurs the same risk as the underlying real estate asset, in addition to the operating risk of the REIT and liquidity risks associated with the resale of the REIT stock. (The stock of large REITs is exchanged on the major stock exchanges, however).

Residential Mortgage

Consider a lender of a residential mortgage. The amount and timing of the payments are spelled out in the note as part of the contract between the lender and the mortgagor. Yet, the possibility remains that the amount and timing of the cash flows may differ from that outlined in the note or even that expected by the lender. The mortgagor could be delinquent in some payments or, worse, default on the mortgage. If the latter occurs, the lender will be forced to foreclose on the property and will have to liquidate the REO (real estate owned). The precise value at liquidation is unknown and also subject to risk. In the case where the property has positive equity and there is no delinquency, the mortgagor may prepay the loan because she desires to sell the property or refinance the loan at a lower interest rate. Thus, the timing and amount of the cash flows are subject to risk, despite the terms of the note indicating the amount and dates of the payment.

Mortgage-backed Securities

The same risk associated with individual mortgages applies to securities backed by pools of mortgages, especially if those securities are of the pass-through type (see Chapter 10). An investor who purchases $100,000 in a mortgage-backed security (MBS) will "own" a small (prorated) portion of several hundred mortgages. She will receive a prorated share of all monthly principal and interest payments, as if she were the original lender. The investor also will receive a prorated share of any mortgages that are prepaid in a given month. The investor faces the same prepayment risk as the originator of a loan who would hold it in a portfolio. Because MBSs represent large pools of mortgages, the portfolio effect may reduce the risk, such as a default, associated with individual mortgages. However, systematic risks, such as a substantial decline in market rates that would lead to accelerated prepayments, would not be diversified away. In fact, prepayment assumptions are such an important element in the valuation of MBSs that the research staffs of large institutional investors expend great effort to identify those variables that affect prepayments and the manner in which they do so—that is, their functional relationship. Investors also wish to identify MBSs that may have greater or lesser prepayment rates than average. If they can be successful in doing so and still purchase the security at the average value for all such securities, they may reap excess returns. A lot of research has been devoted to establishing the prepayment risk associated with MBSs.

Collateralized Mortgage Obligations

Collateralized mortgage obligations (CMOs), discussed in Chapter 10, are similar to MBSs, except the timing of the cash flows associated with the underlying mortgages (that serve as collateral) have been "rearranged" to serve the needs of various types of investors. Precisely because many investors do not like the risk associated with MBSs, financial institutions have created CMOs. As with an MBS, the underlying collateral is a pool of residential mortgages. An investor can purchase various "tranches" in the CMO. A tranche promises bond-like payments on certain dates. The originator of the CMO estimates the payment and prepayment behavior of the underlying mortgages and constructs the tranches accordingly. All payments and prepayments from the entire pool of mortgages may go to the first tranche until it is paid off with known payments on known dates. (Any excess prepayments are invested for payment to later tranches, and any shortfalls are made up from the originator's funds.) While this arrangement makes the payments of the first tranches more certain, it increases the risk associated with the later, or "residual," tranches.

Interest-only and Principal-only Securities (IOs and POs)

From a pool of mortgages, it is possible to sell rights to receive principal payments only or rights to receive interest payments only (see Chapter 11). These two cash flows will behave differently when, for example, market interest rates change. If market rates rise, mortgagors will tend to prepay less often. The owner of the **PO** will receive the same total payments as she otherwise would, but they now will be stretched over a longer period of time. This factor, and the fact that (discount) rates have risen, will lower the value of the PO. On the other hand, because interest is paid on any outstanding principal, the owner of the **IO** now will receive a larger stream of payments than she otherwise would have. The value of the IO will, therefore, rise. Thus, the size or the timing of the cash flows associated with IOs and POs are subject to risk and will behave differently from each other in response to a change in market rates.

Servicing Rights

Continuing with the residential loan example, the value of the **servicing rights** (Chapter 11) to mortgages depends upon expected cash flows, which are subject to risk. Servicing rights arise when an originator of a portfolio of mortgages sells that portfolio to an investor, perhaps on the secondary mortgage market, but continues to service the loans for a fee. The originator will collect the monthly payment, send out delinquency notices, collect delinquent penalty payments, and so forth. He will forward the payments to the new owner in return for a portion of the payment. For example, 0.25 percent of the loan balance would be a reasonable fee. The originator's after-tax cash flow is composed of this fee, less any operating expenses and taxes associated with servicing the loans. These cash flows have value and can be sold. That is, many originators will, subsequent to the sale of the mortgages, also sell the servicing rights. The value is determined with reference to the size and timing of the flows in relation to the risk. The major risk comes through prepayments that, should they accelerate, would eliminate the remaining servicing fees associated with the prepaid loans. A decline in market rates will cause the value of servicing rights to decline.

Role of Risk in Valuation

The importance of considering risk in a real estate investment lies in the determination of the discount rate to employ in the discounted cash flow model. A basic principle of finance requires that the greater the perceived risk, the greater will be the required rate of return (discount rate) of an investment. Unfortunately, there are no formulae by which one can translate a given level of risk of a real estate investment into a proper discount rate. The returns on an individual real estate project cannot easily be related to the marketplace (as can be done with common stock) in order to determine systematic risk, for example. In the stock market the capital asset pricing model (CAPM) can be utilized to suggest a discount rate for equity. With the CAPM the risk-free rate, the return on the market, and the stock's systematic risk are employed to suggest a proper equity discount rate.

Such convenient formulae are not available to real estate analysts, but general guidelines can be followed. One example is that the discount rate associated with the equity portion of a real estate investment should be higher than the rate associated with the debt on the project. The risk of the debt is less since the debtor stands first to receive any cash flows after operating expenses and usually will have a lien on the property should there be a default. Since debt holders presumably estimate their risk in calculating their required rate on debt, an upward adjustment is justified for the risk of equity cash flows. There are some well-known problems associated with using risk-adjusted discount rates.[1] Even if subjective in nature, however, the principle remains that the greater the perceived risk, the greater should be the appropriate discount rate.

THE THEORY OF FINANCIAL LEVERAGE AND OPTIMAL CAPITAL STRUCTURE

Financial leverage is the concept of using debt in financing an investment project. The two primary sources of capital for financing any project are debt and equity. Real estate projects are most often financed with a mix of these two. Financial leverage can best be illustrated by examining the relationship between the overall return on the project and the return on the equity. For example, say that a particular real estate asset provides a 12 percent return. That is, the annual after-tax cash flow is 12 percent of the cost of the asset. If the asset is financed with all equity, the return to the equity investor is equal to the overall return on the asset, 12 percent. If, however, debt can be obtained at a favorable rate (less than 12 percent) it can be used to enhance the return to the equity. A portion of an asset that yields 12 percent is financed by lower cost debt, the difference flowing through to the equity holder. This means that favorable financial leverage will result in an equity yield greater than 12 percent. The amount of debt used and the cost of the debt will determine the extent to which the equity yield is increased.

The process of incurring debt at a cost less than the return on the investment is positive (favorable) financial leverage. Negative (unfavorable) financial leverage occurs when the cost of borrowing exceeds the return on the investment. This would result in a decline in the return on the equity. Thus, financial leverage creates financial risk if there is some chance that the cost of the debt may exceed the return to the investment. This risk usually is created by variability in either the return on the investment or the cost of the debt or both. The effect of financial leverage on equity yield is illustrated in later chapters.

Leverage and Value

The value of the equity position of the investor increases, to a point, with the use of **leverage.** As seen, the basic principle that drives the process is that the investor can borrow at a rate less than the return on the asset. One reason why debt financing may carry a smaller cost for reasonable levels of loan-to-value ratios is the perceived degree of risk associated with debt payments. Lenders are given preference before equity holders to receive cash flows in the form of interest payments because of their legal position. Additionally, with the exception of default, the amount of the payments is not subject to risk, as is the case with equity that represents a claim on the residual cash flows.

Irrelevance of Capital Structure

The proposition offered by Modigliani and Miller is that, in a world without taxes, rearranging the cash flows of a corporation due to different proportions of debt and equity cannot create value.[2] They offer as proof the ability of an equity holder to use homemade leverage (borrow personally) to purchase the stock in an all-equity firm. After paying interest on the personal indebtedness, the residual cash flows are identical to those that would occur had the firm issued the debt. Since the replication of the cash flows does not depend upon the firm issuing the debt, the capital structure of the firm itself does not create or enhance value. That is, while there may be value created by sorting the cash flows of a firm into debt and equity returns (because, for instance, of different risk preferences of investors), there is no need for the division to be done at the firm level. It can be done at the personal level. The question becomes, if Modigliani and Miller are correct about the valuation of the firm, can value be created through the use of leverage in real estate projects? The answer is yes, as we will demonstrate with an example.

Assume that an investor owned a 100 percent equity position in an office building and desired to use leverage to increase value. Following Modigliani and Miller, the division of the cash flows into debt and equity components can be done either by leveraging the property or borrowing personally. Assume that a lender advances funds to the property owner personally. The owner pledges to make loan payments from the cash flows of the property. It would appear that the lender stands to receive the same cash flow, regardless of whether the loan was collateralized by the real estate or advanced to the property owner personally. In such a case, however, the property owner would now be in a position to borrow additional funds from a second lender by pledging the property as a loan, leaving the first lender in a subordinated and, much more risky position. To prevent just such an occurrence, the first lender would demand that the loan be collateralized by the property. In this fashion, the leverage is forced to be applied at the property, and not the personal, level. Because leverage cannot be created as cheaply anywhere else, leverage can add value.

OPTIONS AND REAL ESTATE FINANCE

Definition of Options

Options are rights. The owner of an option has a right, but not an obligation, to purchase (**call** option) or sell (**put** option) an asset at a predetermined price (strike price) from or to another individual on or before a given date (exercise date). The student may be most familiar with stock options, the right to buy or sell common stock at a given price. Options have intrinsic value and market value, the latter generally being greater than the former. The intrinsic value is the excess of the current price of the asset over the strike price for a call or the excess of the strike price over the current market price for a put.

An option that gives the holder the right to buy a share of stock at a strike price of $50 has an intrinsic value of $6, if the current market price is $56 and transaction costs are ignored. This is so because the holder can exercise his right and immediately resell the stock in the market. However, this action is unlikely. The value of all call options (without dividends) and some put options is greater unexercised at any time prior to the expiration date. This is another way of saying that the value of the option will be greater than its intrinsic value. Additionally, options with no intrinsic value will nonetheless have some positive market value because of their nature as a right and not an obligation.

Consider the above call option where the market price of the stock is $45. The option has no intrinsic value. The value on the expiration date will be positive only if the market price rises above $50 and will be equal to the differential. Figure 3–1 shows a probability distribution of the market value of the stock on two dates: three months in the future and six months in the future. The shaded areas of the two curves represent the portions where the market value will exceed the

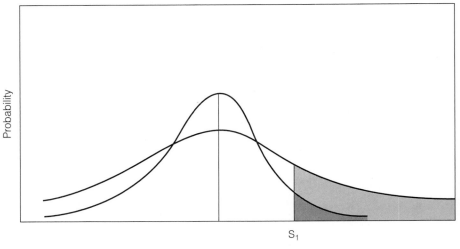

FIGURE 3–1

Probability Distribution of Stock Prices

strike price on each date. The probability distribution which represents the market values for a date six months in the future is more dispersed than that for three months in the future. The reason lies in the behavior of market values that change over time. Through time, stock prices follow a pattern that has a large random component, due to the unpredictable manner in which information arrives to the marketplace. The longer the time period over which prices can move, the greater the cumulative effect of the random components. Put another way, the distribution of possible market values tomorrow is more constrained than the distribution a year from now. Furthermore, the greater the volatility of price movements, the wider will be the probability distribution of prices on any given date. In other words, you also can view the two distributions in Figure 3–1 as that of the prices of two different stocks on the same date, the wider distribution representing the more volatile stock. Figure 3–1 shows that the greater portion of the six-month probability distribution lies above the strike price S_1. Thus, there is a greater chance that the market value will exceed the strike price by a larger amount in six months versus three months. If the exercise date of the option is in six months, as opposed to three months, the current value of the option will be greater. Thus, two important determinants of the value of an option are the time to expiration of the option and the volatility in the value of the underlying security.

In addition to options on common stock, there are also traded options on debt instruments such as Treasury securities or mortgage-backed securities. The value of debt securities fluctuates as a result of several factors, the most important being the change in market interest rates. The values of debt securities move inversely to changes in interest rates. Furthermore, for a given change in the market rate, the magnitude of a change in the value of a debt security is dependent upon its duration (similar to maturity). Translating from our discussion of options on equities, this means that an option on a debt security will have a greater value the longer the duration of the security and the more volatile interest rates are expected to be (during the term of exercise). As the volatility in interest rates increases and is extrapolated into the future, the value of options pertaining to real-estate-related debt increases.

Examples of Options in Real Estate Finance

With the exception of options on mortgage-backed securities, there are no standardized option contracts that are traded on an organized exchange. This does not mean that options in real estate are limited to those on MBSs. Various real estate contracts grant valuable options to one or both parties to the transaction. Consider the following real-estate-related transactions.

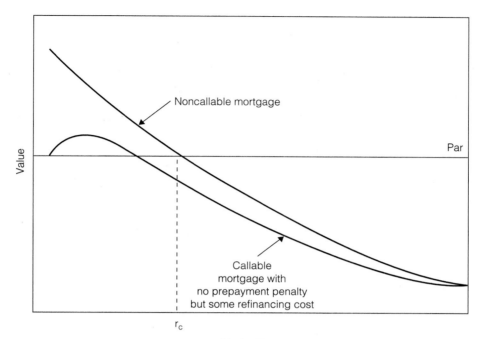

FIGURE 3–2

Value of Mortgages

Residential Mortgage

When a homeowner obtains a mortgage with a lien on a residence, she also has contracted for some options. A call option gives the homeowner the right to prepay the current balance on the mortgage at any time prior to its maturity. Since prepayment penalties (payments required in order to prepay prior to maturity) are rare in residential mortgages, being prohibited by law in some states and by the FHA or VA on insured loans, they are viewed by lenders as a provision that would place them at a competitive disadvantage. The mortgagor has essentially issued a callable bond. That is, she has issued a note (in return for current cash to purchase the residence) that allows her to call the mortgage at any time prior to maturity. The strike price is the balance of the mortgage at the time it is called (prepaid). The value of the remaining payments at the time of call is a function of the market rate of interest on mortgages of like risk at the time of the call. If the market rate of interest falls so that the value of the remaining payments increase, the mortgagor is likely to call the note since its strike price (balance) is less than its value (to the lender).

Figure 3–2 shows the value of two securities with identical contract rates—one a noncallable bond, the other a callable mortgage—as a function of the market rate of interest. At very high market rates both obligations are valued below their face value and identically. As interest rates decrease, the values of both obligations rise. As the interest rate approaches the coupon rate, the value of the mortgage increases less than the value of the noncallable bond, reflecting the increased probability of prepayment. In the case where the market rate is slightly below the contract (coupon) rate, both obligations will have a value slightly above the face value. Mortgagors are unlikely to prepay their mortgage on the basis of very small differences in rates. As the market rate falls further, the likelihood of prepayment increases and, at some point, becomes so great that the value of the mortgage is equal to its balance. The value of the noncallable bond continues to increase as the market rate continues to fall below the contract rate. The difference between the two curves is the value of the call option on the mortgagor. This difference will widen if the market anticipates an increased volatility of interest rate. That is, if expected volatility increases, the two curves will be redrawn with a larger gap between them.

The mortgagor has another option as well—the put option. The mortgage is secured by a lien on the residence. In the event of default (nonpayment of any contractual obligation, primarily, but not restricted to, the principal and interest), the lender can foreclose on the property and liquidate it to satisfy the obligation. If the situation is such that the lender has no recourse to the personal assets of the mortgagor (as would be the case in a state that has enacted such a prohibition or if the mortgagor has little or no other assets), then the only remedy is to access the market value of the property. In the case where the market value of the property falls below the balance of the loan (negative equity), the mortgagor has a put option that has intrinsic worth. That is, the mortgagor in putting (selling) the property to the lender in satisfaction of the loan obligation exercises a put option at a strike price (value of the property) less than the value of the obligation (loan balance). Now, the mortgagor may not choose to exercise the option in this situation. A person may believe that the property could have a greater value in the future and continue to make the monthly payments. Of course, if an unavoidable event such as involuntary unemployment, a divorce, or a move to another residence occurs, this would precipitate the exercise of the default put option. In essence, the unavoidable event moves the exercise date to the present.

Options on Commercial Properties

The same default option pertains to commercial properties financed in part by debt. In the event the development does not work out as planned and the market value of the property falls below the indebtedness, the owner will put (sell) the property to the lender. In contrast to residential debt, there may be some slight differences in the exercise of the option. If the property is suffering a net operating loss, the owner will be quicker to put the property to the lender rather than hold the put option. The lender also may require contractual provisions that reduce the value of such a put option, such as a personal note that allows the lender to attach assets other than the property used to secure the debt. The lender also may require a larger down payment than is typically required for residential properties. This reduces the probability that the value of the property will fall below the loan balance and, thus, reduces the value of the put option.

Explicit Options

Finally, there are explicit option contracts that are entered into routinely, often in relation to the purchase of raw (undeveloped) land. A developer may wish to secure the right to purchase land while completing the development package, including arranging the financing of the project. Purchasing an option to buy the land at a given price in the future allows the developer to do this. The price of the option generally will be small relative to the purchase price. A developer may pay $40,000 for the right to purchase a parcel of land for $2 million anytime within the next nine months. The value of the option to the developer may well be worth its price. Should land values escalate over the period of exercise, the option will be valuable. If the value of the land in question rises to $2.2 million by the last day of the exercise period, the option will be worth $200,000. If prices fall significantly, the option holder can buy the property in the market at a lower price, losing the option premium. Of course, in an efficient market the option should be priced at an amount that reflects, among other factors, the volatility of land values in the area.

THE THEORY OF FINANCIAL INTERMEDIATION

As the word *intermediary* suggests, financial institutions "stand between" the suppliers and users of credit. The most common **financial intermediaries** are commercial banks, savings and loan associations, mutual savings banks, and life insurance companies. The common understanding is that an intermediary, such as a depository institution, receives credit from suppliers when it issues a liability (deposit). It lends the credit, creating an asset for itself, at a higher rate of interest than it provides on the deposit. The margin between the two rates is expected to cover the costs of operations and provide a normal return to the capital invested in the institution by stockholders. As we will see below, this scenario is often difficult for financial intermediaries to achieve. For now, let us focus on this simple notion of an intermediary.

Given that this is a simplified version of what intermediaries do, you may ask why they exist. It appears that suppliers and users of credit could deal with each other directly and eliminate (share) the margin charged by the intermediary. In fact, this is done quite often when investors purchase corporate, municipal, Treasury, and other securities directly from the issuer. Money-market funds have been established to aid the small investor in this process of direct lending. Yet, intermediaries continue to exist. If this is so, they must provide an economic service. In a competitive economy consumers will not pay for a service they can provide for themselves without cost.

In fact, intermediaries perform several valuable economic functions. In order to understand them, consider a direct loan from you to your neighbor so that she may purchase a house. Here you are the mortgagee, and you and your neighbor have bypassed the intermediary. An alternative is to deposit your funds in an intermediary institution, which would then advance a loan to your neighbor. From your perspective, are there reasons for which the latter arrangement would be superior to the former? Several reasons are evident.

Liquidity Risk.   When a deposit is made in a financial intermediary, the depositor receives a liquid asset. The deposit can be made in the most liquid of all assets, a transaction or demand deposit upon which the depositor can write checks. It can also be made in the form of very short-term deposits with maturities generally less than one year. Contrast this liquidity to a direct loan in the form of a mortgage to your neighbor.

Credit Evaluation and Risk Management.   Intermediaries may have a superior knowledge of the credit risks associated with either the mortgagor or the property being mortgaged. They are also aware of various measures for reducing risk. The intermediary will place various covenants in a mortgage to reduce risk. Examples are the escrow requirements for property taxes and hazard insurance, provisions for penalties for delinquent payments, and so forth. Intermediaries also reduce risk through diversification—that is, through holding many mortgages. In short, financial intermediaries often have better credit-evaluation and risk-reduction procedures than do most individuals.

Interest Rate Risk.   Mortgages generally have long maturities. Fixed-rate mortgages specify a contract rate of interest that will remain unchanged over their life. Accordingly, they are subject to **interest rate risk.** This risk is increased by the prepayment option held by the mortgagor. By issuing short-term deposits and investing in long-term fixed-rate mortgages, intermediaries transfer interest rate risk to their stockholders, noteholders, or deposit insurer. To the extent that intermediaries do not properly judge interest rate risk, they will fail to obtain a sufficient margin between the rate they pay on deposits and the rate they charge on long-term fixed-rate mortgages. As we will see in another chapter, it is apparent that this has caused some intermediaries great difficulties in recent years.

Many savings and loan associations have reduced their exposure to interest rate risk by either issuing adjustable-rate mortgages (ARMs) or selling off their fixed-rate mortgages while retaining the servicing fees. The former approach has narrowed the spread between the rate they pay on deposits and the rate they receive on their assets, the yield on adjustable-rate mortgages being less than that on fixed-rate loans. The narrowing reflects the reduced risk. The latter approach allows an institution to focus on the first two functions: providing liquidity and credit evaluation and risk reduction. Notice that where the need for liquidity or credit evaluation is unnecessary, as with investment in short-term Treasury securities, the role of intermediaries is nonexistent. The function is taken over by nonintermediaries, such as money market funds. Because lack of liquidity and credit evaluation is a problem with investment in real estate securities such as mortgages, financial intermediaries will continue to be involved in real estate finance.

PORTFOLIO THEORY

As with an individual asset, a portfolio of several assets has an expected return and expected risk (as measured by the variance in returns). When assets are combined to form a portfolio, the expected return on the portfolio will be equal to an average of the expected returns on the individual assets, weighted by the relative amount of each asset included in the portfolio. This should be no surprise. The same cannot be said about the risk, however. The risk of the portfolio is not equal to a weighted average of the risk of the individual assets because risk is a measure of the extent to which the actual returns of an asset can differ from the expected returns, as measured by their probabilities. Risk refers to the random component of returns over time. Portfolio construction exploits the random element in the returns of individual assets by combining several assets whose returns are less than perfectly positively correlated (move in exact synchronization, up and down) with each other. In fact, if the returns of two assets are random yet perfectly negatively correlated (move in the opposite direction), it is possible that the return on a portfolio can be constructed with no risk at all—that is, the returns will be certain.

In short, portfolio construction allows a reduction in the risk of the portfolio over that present in individual assets, without a sacrifice in expected returns. Furthermore, if the transaction costs required to establish a portfolio of a given size are identical to the total transaction costs on the individual assets (which is likely), then the risk reduction available through portfolio construction can be achieved without additional cost.

Several studies have demonstrated the benefits of diversification through portfolio construction of real estate assets. The benefits occur when properties of different types (hotels, warehouses, office buildings, farmland) and/or different geographical regions are combined. The greatest reduction in risk is through geographical diversification, where regions are defined in terms of their economy (manufacturing, mineral extraction, and so on). Today, large institutional investors such as life insurance companies and pension funds employ staffs of analysts to select real estate investments that meet portfolio requirements of risk reduction and return retention.

EFFICIENT MARKET THEORY

The term **efficient market** refers to the notion that an asset trades in a market where its value reflects all available information about that asset. The asset is priced "efficiently" in the sense that no one individual is able to trade on the basis of information available to all other market participants and, in the process, make excess returns. The term *excess returns* is important. The concept of an efficient market does not preclude an individual from making normal returns (a return for effort) in seeking out and effectively analyzing information available to the market. An investor cannot make returns in excess of normal returns by employing information that is available to everyone. The two concepts—that the price of an asset includes all available information and that no one can make returns in excess of normal by trading in an efficient market—are essentially identical. To make excess returns, a trader would have to have information that the asset is misprized. But if the trader has that information, and it is available to all market participants, then the asset would not be misprized.

Market efficiency can be discussed in terms of the type of information that is available about assets. **Weak-form** market efficiency exists where the price of the asset completely reflects its historical prices (including the present price), so that knowledge of only those historical prices provides a trader no advantage over other market participants in earning an excess return. **Semi-strong** market efficiency exists when the price of the asset reflects not only past price behavior but any other publicly available information. **Strong** market efficiency exists when the current price reflects all information, whether public or private (inside information).

The conditions that lead to market efficiency in any form include the existence of many investors (market participants), uniform and widespread information, no market restrictions, no transaction costs, and investor preferences that value greater returns and less risk. The large organized stock markets come closest to meeting the requirements of an efficient market. It is no surprise then that numerous studies have shown stock markets to be efficient. Virtually no study has demonstrated a scheme whereby past price behavior alone can be used to make excess returns above transaction costs in the stock market. Any such scheme, upon discovery, would be so quickly exploited by market participants as to obviate its usefulness for this purpose. That is, the scheme would represent new information that would be made available quickly to all market participants, and market prices would quickly reflect this new information.

Many studies also have shown that market prices of stocks quickly react to new information that affects their value. Unless action is taken within minutes of new information, excess returns cannot be made. It is not surprising that some studies have demonstrated that markets are not efficient with regard to nonpublic (inside) information. Inside knowledge can be used to make excess returns, although, even here, the time frame within which an investor must act is very limited.

As markets for assets lose the qualities of an efficient market, the ability to make excess returns by acquiring and trading on information, especially nonpublic information, increases. Markets tend to be less efficient when they are dominated by a few large investors, involve assets that are traded infrequently, and have large transaction and information costs. This latter description may apply to some real estate markets. Although some studies have demonstrated that real estate markets are efficient in terms of past price information (weak efficiency), there is less evidence that this is so for other types of information. Information that may affect the value of real estate may not be widely disseminated, including knowledge about proposed changes in zoning laws and regulations, road improvements, the availability of public utilities, other nearby developments, and so forth. Most analysts agree that real estate markets do not enjoy the efficiency of more liquid markets dominated by many participants.

AGENCY THEORY

Agency theory and agency problems deal with the relationship between principals and agents. An agent is someone who is retained by another (principal) to conduct activities for the latter's benefit. Agency problems are situations where the agent has an incentive to act in his own behalf to the detriment of the principal. These situations give rise to **agency costs.** These are costs born by the principal to minimize or prevent agency problems and include monitoring, bonding, and structuring costs. These costs take various form, but all are intended to prevent the agent from placing his goals ahead of the principal's. **Monitoring costs** are outlays for audits and other control procedures. An out-of-town owner of a property may hire a manager to operate the property. The manager (agent) should have the goal of minimizing expenses, maximizing rental revenues, keeping the property in good condition, and so forth.[3] The owner will incur costs to monitor the operations of the manager, including auditing the books and inspecting the property. The owner should inspect the property to make sure that maintenance costs incurred, per the books of the property, are actually used to keep the property in good condition.

Bonding costs are payments made to third parties to ensure the honest behavior of agents. The bonding company contracts to reimburse the principal for any dishonest behavior of agents. In the above example, if the manager were paying invoices for the maintenance of the property to a repair firm owned by his brother-in-law and the repairs were not actually made, then the dishonest act would be subject to reimbursement by the bonding company.

Structuring costs involve compensation to agents to ensure performance consistent with the interest of the principal. In the above example, the owner of the property may enter into a contract with the manager whereby the latter would receive a portion of any operating profits from the property. This gives the manager an incentive to reduce unnecessary expenses and to keep the property in good operating condition in order to attract tenants.

There are many other examples of agency relationships and agency costs in real estate. The owner of a mall may enter into a lease where revenues received by a tenant over and above a certain amount are shared between the two parties. This gives the mall management an incentive to draw customers to the mall through various promotions. A mortgagee will require that property tax and hazard insurance be escrowed since the property serves as collateral for the loan. The mortgagee of a commercial property will expend effort to make sure that the owner does not encumber the property with other loans. This is done through a recordation of the first mortgage with the county clerk. An agent employed to sell a property will be paid on the basis of a percentage of the sales price. This provides an incentive for the agent to obtain a buyer willing to pay the highest possible price.[4] Or, a lender making a construction loan to a developer will hire a voucher-control agent. The agent will make sure that any loan disbursements are paid to the contractors who build the structure that serves as collateral. Otherwise, if funds are diverted elsewhere, the unpaid contractors will put a lien on the property that will supercede that of the lender. Consider that, in a foreclosure of a residential property, the lender may not have an incentive to expend effort to make repairs on the property because any losses (including those caused by a decline in value) may be insured through a private mortgage insurer. To avoid this possibility, private mortgage insurers provide by contract that repairs to the property must be made before a claim can be submitted, and, furthermore, repair expenses cannot be made part of the claim. This provision ensures that the property is kept in as good condition as possible, maximizing its liquidation value.

In summary, agency problems exist in many real estate activities and transactions. Agency costs are incurred by the principal to minimize activity on the part of the agent that serves the latter's interest at the expense of the former.

SUMMARY

The principles of finance that have commonly been applied to an analysis of corporation finance and corporate debt and equity securities can easily be applied to real estate and securities collateralized by real estate. The principles of asset valuation apply to real estate, mortgages, and other real-estate-related securities such as mortgage-backed securities. Leverage, whereby debt is used to increase the value of equity contributions, is especially relevant to real estate investments. Options—some explicit, others not so obvious—exist in many areas. Real estate finance historically has been intricately tied to our financial institutions. The theory of financial intermediation is important for understanding the role, success, and failures of intermediaries such as thrifts. Real estate assets can be combined by themselves, or with other assets, in portfolios that reduce risk. Large institutional investors, such as pension funds and life insurance companies, explore their risk-reducing opportunities when they invest in real estate. The uniqueness of real estate properties and lack of widespread knowledge of all relevant facts allow for some inefficiencies. There is evidence that this leads to excess returns for some real estate investors. Finally, agency problems and costs to monitor agents are also present in real estate. Contracts and an intricate system of laws address client-agency problems.

KEY TERMS

Agency costs:
   Bonding
   Monitoring
   Structuring
Agency theory
Agent
Asset valuation
Capital structure
Collateralized mortgage obligations
Credit evaluation and Risk management
Discounted cash flow (DCF)
Efficient market theory:
   Semi-strong form
   Strong form
   Weak form
Financial intermediation

Interest rate risk
IOs
Leverage
Limited partnerships
Liquidity risk
Net present value
Options:
   Call
   Put
Portfolio theory
Prepayment (or call) option
POs
Real estate investment trusts (REITs)
Risk
Servicing rights

SUGGESTED READINGS

Black, F. 1988. A simple discounting rule. *Financial Management* 17(2): 7–11.

Brigham, E. F., and L. C. Gapenski. 1990. *Intermediate Financial Management,* 3rd ed. Hinsdale, IL: The Dryden Press, ch. 1.

Cooley, P. L., and J. L. Heck. 1981. Significant contributions to the finance literature. *Financial Management,* tenth anniversary issue, 23–33.

Pogue, G. A., and K. Lall. 1974. Corporate finance: An overview. *Sloan Management Review,* Spring.

Weston, J. F. 1981. Developments in finance theory. *Financial Management,* tenth anniversary issue, 5–22.

REVIEW QUESTIONS

3–1   What are the four terms of the discounted cash flow (DCF) model?

3–2   Differentiate between income and cash flows.

3–3   Why does the DCF model focus on cash flows and not income?

3–4   a. Define risk.

        b. What term in the DCF model reflects risk?

3–5   a. Provide several examples of real estate assets that involve risk.

        b. Explain the source of the risk.

3–6   a. Define leverage.

        b. Explain how leverage can be used to increase the value of equity in a real estate investment.

3–7   Discuss the concept of optimal capital structure as it pertains to real estate investments.

3–8   a. Define options.

        b. Give several examples of options in real estate.

3–9   List three "services" provided by financial intermediaries.

3–10   Explain how financial intermediaries can be exposed to interest rate risk.

3–11   Define an "efficient market."

3–12   Explain why a stock market, such as the New York Stock Exchange, is more efficient than some real estate markets.

3–13   a. Define agency costs.

        b. Give several examples of agency costs in real estate.

ENDNOTES

1. For example, the discounted cash flow model implies that the riskiness of cash flows increases at a compound rate over time since the adjustment to the discount rate for risk is compounded by raising the term $(1 + r)$ to the ith power. This is unlikely to be true in reality.

2. Franco Modigliani and Merton Miller, "The Cost of Capital, Corporation Finance, and the Theory of Investment," *American Economic Review* 48 (1958): 261–297.

3. Sidney Rosenberg and John Corgel, "Agency Costs in Property Management Contracts," *AREUEA Journal* (Summer 1990): 184–201. The authors found expenses of managed properties to be 6 percent greater when the property management was unrelated to the property owner's company.

4. T. S. Zorn and J. E. Larson, "The Incentive Effect of Flat-Fee and Percentage Commission for Real Estate Brokers," *AREUEA Journal* (Spring 1986): 27–41. The authors found that percentage-fee incentives in broker's contracts are superior to a flat-fee structure to obtain higher prices for sellers of real estate.

PART

2

Residential Real Estate Finance

Part Two focuses on residential real estate finance. The main object of study is the one- to four-family (but typically one-family) residential mortgage. Multifamily property (apartments) finance is considered commercial financing and is not discussed in Part Two. Included in this section is a discussion of federal policies and laws related to residential finance, financing terms and their effect on property prices, the structure of the secondary mortgage market, and the pricing of mortgage-related securities. Risk management also is discussed. Here we talk about borrower and property qualification and mortgage insurance—both private and government (FHA/VA).

The Early History of Residential Finance and Creation of the Fixed Rate-Mortgage

LEARNING OBJECTIVES

After reading this chapter, you should have an understanding of how residential lending evolved from the earliest of times through World War II. This early history sets the stage for the modern system of residential finance as we know it. Understanding its development through time will allow you to appreciate the structure of the present system. You also should understand the mechanics of the standard fixed-rate mortgage (FRM) developed in the 1930s.

INTRODUCTION

At its root, real estate finance involves the advancing of funds from a lender to a borrower for the purpose (usually) of buying or improving real property. As with any contract freely entered into by two parties, there are mutual benefits that are derived by virtue of the arrangement. Furthermore, since the transaction involves the movement of funds from one party to another over time, the agreement inherently involves risk to one or both parties. This is unlike a transaction where, for example, goods are exchanged for cash with no future commitment by either party. Various measures have been invented, developed, and employed to minimize the risk of real estate lending. Additionally, legal institutions have promulgated rules and laws that have affected the risks involved by defining the rights and duties of the parties. At times such laws have tended to favor the lender; at other times, they have favored the borrower. When the laws tend to favor one party over the other, markets may be disrupted or altered so as to reintroduce a balance of benefits and risks.

From the standpoint of the lender, risks are minimized when loans are made to credit-worthy individuals for a fraction of the value of the property and when the lender is able to quickly secure possession of the property used as collateral. The timing and the right to possession of the collateral by the lender are very important to minimize risk.

PRE-AMERICAN DEVELOPMENTS

Roman Law

Many aspects of U.S. and Western law can be traced to the Roman Empire. Roman real property law went through several stages. Initially the instrument used in real estate loans was termed the **fiducia,** from the Latin word for trust or confidence. Ironically, it apparently did not mean that the lender had trust or confidence in the borrower since this instrument provided for legal title and possession of the property to be held by the lender. If the obligation of the borrower under the terms of the loan was met, then the fiducia called for a reconveyance of the title and possession to the original owner (borrower). This arrangement apparently became awkward, and the **pigus** was developed. Under this instrument, there was no transfer of the title. The land was "pawned," so to speak, with the title and possession remaining with the borrower. However, the rights of the lender were well protected. Under this arrangement, the lender had the right to take title and possession of the property under a "suspicion of the probability of default" by the borrower. Later, the **hypotheca,** which means pledge, was developed. This instrument was similar to the pigus except that the lender could take possession of the property only in the event of an actual default.

German Influence

As the Roman Empire began to wane, German customs took hold in Europe. German law recognized the concept of a **gage,** a deposit made in promise of the fulfillment of an agreement. Often a borrower would physically deliver portable property as a gage, as would be done today at a pawn shop. In such a case, it was termed a "live" gage. When the collateral for the loan was real property, this arrangement was impossible. The gage in this case stipulated that in the event of default, the lender could take possession of the property but could not look beyond that gage for relief. That is, the borrower had the option of fulfilling the obligation or putting the property to the lender, a put option.

English Developments

The French introduced the Germanic gage system to England after William the Conqueror's invasion in 1066. For loans involving real property where there could be no physical transfer of the pledged property, it was termed a "dead" gage. Since the French word for dead is *mort,* it was appropriately termed a *mort gage,* or mortgage. Lending in England in the Middle Ages was complicated by the prohibition of interest by the church. Charging interest for a loan was termed **usury** and thought to be sinful. The basis of the prohibition, as indicated by the writings of church scholars such as St. Thomas Aquinas, was "natural law." Thomas Aquinas relied heavily on Aristotelian philosophy, which sought guidance in "natural law," or what seemed natural. It was natural in an agrarian economy for land to produce food, for animals to produce offspring, and so forth. But it was not natural that money reproduce, and hence came the judgment that charging interest was unnatural and sinful.

Thomas Aquinas was quick to point out, however, that an interest charge could be justified under some circumstances, such as the case where the lender suffered harm by virtue of the loan. By stretching the definition, harm could be defined as a lost opportunity. In any event, lenders, in order not to run afoul of the church's prohibition, would lend funds not for interest but so that the lender would have the right to possess and reap the benefits of a portion of the land securing the loan. In these early times if there was a default, the lender had the right to take possession of the entire land and had no obligation to give the borrower anything in return. As the common law developed, borrowers were able to invoke the intervention of the Chancery Court during the reign of Queen Elizabeth I (1558–1603) on the basis of unfairness. The Chancery Court ruled that this was unduly harsh, especially where the debt was small and the borrower had only temporary financial difficulties. Borrowers could petition the court, stating how they intended to pay the debt. The court began to allow the borrower to redeem the property (after the default) upon payment of the delinquent amounts. This was termed the **equitable right of redemption.**

This right, in the eyes of the lender, was soon abused. Borrowers could redeem their property long after the actual default. In effect, they had a call option on the real estate with an exercise price equal to the amount of the delinquent payments. Furthermore, the exercise period was unlimited. Lenders sought and received a provision for foreclosure whereby after a certain period of time the borrower was prevented (foreclosed) from redeeming the property in the fashion described. The exercise period of the option was reduced.

Today we experience the remnants of this system. In all states a mortgagor can redeem his property by paying delinquent amounts, including any legal and other expenses, up to the point of actual foreclosure. This is the equitable right of redemption. Additionally, some states, by statute, grant an additional period of time during which the mortgagor can redeem the property. This is called a **statutory right of redemption.**

AMERICAN RESIDENTIAL FINANCE: EARLY AMERICAN HISTORY THROUGH THE DEPRESSION YEARS

During the years following the American Revolution, there was little need for real estate lending. In rural areas, most families lived on small farms that were kept in the family and passed down from generation to generation. The need to finance the sale of these small properties was rare or nonexistent. This remained then, for the most part, until after the Civil War. Occasionally, a "building society" would be formed in an urban area to garner sufficient funds for the organizers to purchase their residences. Once such funds had been accumulated, the society would cease to solicit additional funds. The first such building society was the Oxford Provident Building Association, formed in Philadelphia, in 1831. The "dices" that were collected from the members were not considered deposits or liabilities but rather shares of equity. At first the shareholder was not entitled to a fixed "dividend," or even to redeem the shares on demand. Later, many of the building societies began to provide for liquidation at face value. This change moved the societies away from being stock-ownership corporations toward being thrifts as we know them today. By the time of the Civil War, there were only a handful of such societies.

The post–Civil War westward expansion required that the sale of new farms be financed. The funds required to finance these sales were, for the most part, in the hands of large Eastern institutional investors. It was during this time that the mortgage banker came into prominence. Mortgage bankers were specialists who would originate mortgages in the expanding West for their investor-correspondents in the East. The typical farm mortgage at this time was a short-term loan (usually five years) with only interest paid semiannually. A loan that has interest-only payments is called **nonamortizing,** which means none of the principal is included in any of the payments. The principal balance of these loans is never reduced. For this reason the loans usually covered only 40 to 50 percent of the value of the property. Upon maturity the loan would be refinanced at a new rate of interest for a small origination fee, say 1 percent of the loan's balance.

Mortgage bankers dominated the small-farm mortgage market since there were few savings and loans until the latter part of the 1800s. Neither were commercial banks active in this market. Under the National Banking System (1863–1913), federally chartered banks were prohibited from making real estate loans. This would be changed in 1913 with the establishment of the Federal Reserve System whereby banks were authorized to originate five-year loans with a maximum of 50 percent loan-to-value ratio. State banks that were allowed to issue real estate loans also originated short-term, nonamortizing loans.

It is interesting to note that the type of loan originated in this era was very similar to what today would be considered a five-year adjustable-rate mortgage. By keeping the maturity short, lenders minimized their interest rate risk. If market rates rose subsequent to origination, the lender would be faced with, at most, only a few years of below-market returns. There was some default risk associated with this type of loan, however. Since they were nonamortizing, there was a greater likelihood that the value of the property might slip below the balance of the loan. This was particularly true for properties with second and third mortgages. The default risk associated with such loans became apparent in the late 1920s and early 1930s during America's pre–Depression and Depression years. Huge numbers of borrowers were forced to default on their loans.

During the early 1920s, **building and loan associations** experienced their most rapid growth. Associations grew from 5356 with $571 million in total assets in 1900 to 11,777 with $8.8 billion in assets in 1930. During this time the associations gradually changed the rules on dividends and retirement of shares to compete with commercial banks; this represented essentially a circumvention of the laws that restricted entry into banking. For example, some associations issued "shares" with a definite "interest" (dividend) rate maturing at specific dates. They were analogous to certificates of deposit. Other shares could be redeemed on short notice at par and without a penalty. The growth of associations at this time also was aided by federal income tax regulations that exempted the associations from tax as long as they loaned their funds to members for home building.

During the early 1920s property values rose rapidly as the money supply grew at a historically rapid rate. Lenders were not restrained in advancing funds to purchase high-priced properties. Then, with the collapse of the banking system in the early 1930s, the money supply plummeted. Declining property prices followed, leading to a record number of defaults and further eroding the capital position of lenders.

The default risk of the short-term nonamortizing loan popular at the time can be demonstrated by analyzing the performance of such loans during the 1920s and 1930s. Saulnier discusses the loan histories of the largest 24 insurance companies over this period.[1] From 1920 through 1924, only 24.4 percent of the loans originated by this group of lenders were **fully amortized,** meaning that by the end of the payment stream the debt would be reduced to zero. During this time the foreclosure rate was 5.3 percent of all loans—15 percent on the nonamortizing loans and only 2.8 percent on the amortizing loans. From 1930 through 1934, the worst part of the Great Depression, foreclosure rates rose to 21.1 percent overall—28.1 percent on nonamortizing loans and 17.8 percent on amortizing loans. During the entire decade of the 1920s, the foreclosure rate was 21 percent on loans of four years or less maturity and 13.5 percent on 10- to 14-year maturity loans. Clearly, for this particular set of loans, the shorter nonamortizing mortgages experienced greater foreclosure rates.

This experience led to a change in the type of mortgages originated by all lenders. The changes made by the life insurance companies used in the Saulnier study exemplify those changes. While only 24 percent of the loans originated from 1920 through 1924 were fully amortized and 79 percent had a maturity less than nine years, by 1930 to 1934, 31.5 percent were fully amortized, and the proportion with a maturity less than nine years dropped to 66 percent. During the 1940–1946 period, 94 percent of all loans originated by life insurance companies were fully amortized, and only 3 percent had a maturity less than nine years. The dramatic drop in the proportion of short-term, nonamortizing loans in the latter period also reflects the laws and agencies established by the federal government during the Depression to support the mortgage market.

The collapse of the economy from 1929 through 1933 threw the real estate lending market into disarray. After the 1929 crash, property values fell to about half the 1928 level. The dramatic drop in personal income led to large-scale delinquencies on mortgage loans. As a result, lenders, particularly depository institutions such as thrifts, were caught in the middle. They were not receiving their periodic payments on the loans, and foreclosures offered no remedy due to the drop in property values. Depositors withdrew large sums of cash to meet their living expenses. Between 1931 and 1934, net withdrawals from savings and loan institutions amounted to $1.84 billion, about one-third of their 1930 deposit level. By 1935, one-fifth of all mortgage loans resulted in real estate owned (REO) for the thrifts. Many states passed legislation enacting moratoria on foreclosures. Following Iowa's lead in passing legislation in February 1933, 26 additional states passed such moratoria legislation. Generally intended to last for only two or a few years, some moratoria lasted well into the 1940s.

The chaotic situation led the federal government to enact programs or agencies to aid the real estate lending market. There were six such programs in all.

The **Reconstruction Finance Corporation (RFC),** established in early 1932, used government credit to lend $114 million to savings and loan associations and $290 million to mortgage loan companies from its beginning through October 1937. The loans helped the thrifts survive their liquidity crisis.

The **Federal Home Loan Bank System (FHLBS)** was established by the Federal Home Loan Bank Act in July 1932. The Act established twelve Federal Home Loan Banks, which in turn chartered federal institutions and accepted qualified state institutions as members. Through the sale of bonds and a line of credit to the Treasury, the system lent more than $200 million to thrifts from 1932 through 1937.

The **Home Owners Loan Corporation (HOLC),** established by the Home Owners Loan Act in June 1933, received an initial capitalization of $200 million from the U.S. Treasury. It was authorized to issue up to $4.75 billion in 4 percent notes guaranteed by the government. Through the end of 1936, it loaned more than $3 billion to homeowners with mortgages held by thrifts, commercial banks, and mortgage companies. It also lent money directly to the mortgagor for up to 80 percent of the value of the property. The homeowner could then renegotiate a new mortgage with better terms. It ended its lending in 1936.

The **Federal Savings and Loan Insurance Corporation (FSLIC)** was established by the National Housing Act in 1934. FSLIC, similar to the Federal Deposit Insurance Corporation

(FDIC) for commercial banks, was established to insure the deposits at thrifts. The agency would charge the thrifts a small premium for the insurance and use these funds to pay any claims of depositors of failed institutions. Government backing gave the agency credibility. The duties of the FSLIC were taken over by the FDIC when the agency was abolished in 1989 by a thrift reform act.

The **Federal Housing Administration (FHA),** also established by the National Housing Act, insured mortgages against default. The agency would charge an insurance premium to the mortgagor to cover the cost of expected claims. Again, government backing established credibility for this insurance provider. The FHA would insure loans up to 80 percent of the value of one- to four-family properties as long as they were long-term, amortizing loans. At first the term was for 15 years, but later 20-, 25-, and 30-year loans became common. Lenders, burned by the high default rates on short-term loans during the Depression, were quick to make loans with the new insurance provisions. Conventional loans (nongovernment-insured) also took on the characteristics of the long-term FHA loan. By making the maturity longer, lenders exchanged default risk for interest rate risk. This exchange would not become apparent for a few decades. When it did, it caused thrifts great problems. As one can imagine, in a volatile interest rate environment, the interest rate risk on a long-term mortgage with a prepayment option is very great.

The **Federal National Mortgage Association (FNMA)** was established in 1938. Originally called the National Mortgage Association of Washington, this agency stood ready to purchase and sell FHA-insured mortgages. It raised its funds by borrowing from the Treasury and selling shares in the Association to the financial institutions that it did business with. Its main purpose was to aid the acceptance of FHA-insured loans by establishing a market for these loans. As interest rates rose, the value of some FHA loans fell. The FNMA would purchase them at face value, thus providing lenders with additional funds to originate mortgages. FNMA would sell the loans when interest rates dropped. Temporary losses were covered by its line of credit to the U.S. Treasury. FNMA was eventually given status as a private company in the late 1960s. By the 1990s FNMA was a major secondary mortgage market agency. The current operations of this agency are discussed in Chapter 10.

MECHANICS OF THE FIXED-RATE MORTGAGE (FRM)

One of the most enduring products of the Depression era is the fixed-rate, fixed-payment, long-term, amortizing mortgage. This mortgage has dominated the mortgage market over the last half century. Currently, mortgage lenders also offer a 15-year fixed-rate mortgage. To understand the mechanics of mortgages, we begin with the fixed-rate mortgage by showing how to calculate payments, amortization, outstanding balances, and the effective cost of the loan. The background will be invaluable for understanding much of the remainder of the residential finance section of this text. This section should be reviewed with a calculator at hand. Confirming the values in this section also will provide you with a brief review of the time value of money mechanics.

The Mortgage Payment

Recall from time value of money analysis that the present value of an annuity is

$$\text{Present Value of an annuity} = \text{Payment} \left[\frac{(1 + i)^n - 1}{i(1 + i)^n} \right]$$

From this equation the present value of the annuity can be calculated given that the payment, the interest or discount rate (i), and the number of payments (n) are known. Since the payment on a fixed-rate mortgage is an annuity and given that the present value of the annuity (the initial amount borrowed) is known, the present value of an annuity equation can be rearranged to form the **mortgage constant.** This is written as

$$\text{Mortgage Constant (MC}_{i,n}) = \frac{i(1 + i)^n}{(1 + i)^n - 1} \qquad \text{(Equation 4–1)}$$

The mortgage constant calculates the amount of payment required to amortize one dollar at a certain interest rate and a given number of payments. The mortgage constant multiplied by the amount borrowed yields the payment. Note that mortgage payments are structured as an ordinary annuity which means that the payments fall at the end of each period.

For example, suppose that you borrow $100,000 at 10 percent for 30 years, annual payments. The yearly payment required to repay principal and interest would be

$$\text{Annual Payment} = \$100.000 \ (MC_{i,n}) = \$100,000 \left[\frac{.10(1.10)^{30}}{(1.1)^{30} - 1} \right]$$

$$= \$100,000(0.1060742) = \$10,607.42$$

It is common for mortgages to be repaid monthly; thus the payment must be adjusted to reflect monthly amortization. The mortgage constant would be written as

$$\text{Mortgage Constant} \ (MC_{i,n}) = \left[\frac{i/12(1 + i/12)^{12n}}{(1 + i/12)^{12n} - 1} \right]$$

Using the monthly mortgage constant, the monthly payment to satisfy principal and interest is $877.57. This is calculated as

$$\text{Monthly Payment} = \$100,000 \ (MC_{10,30}) = \$100,000 \left[\frac{0.008333(1.008333)^{360}}{(1.008333)^{360} - 1} \right] = \$877.57$$

Note that even though the mortgage constant is expressed on an annual basis, the interest rate and term are adjusted to reflect monthly amortization. That is, the interest rate is divided by 12 and the term has been multiplied by 12. The interest rate and term must always be measured in the same units (yearly, monthly, etc.).

A financial calculator can be used to solve for the payment. For example, using the HP10B, the keystrokes would be

Enter 100000 as a negative **PV** (-100000)
Enter 10 **I/YR**
Enter 360 **N**
Solve for **PMT**

This solution assumes that the calculator is set on 12 payments per year.

Amortization of the Mortgage

The preceding calculation shows the payment required to fully amortize this mortgage over its specified term. This means that each consecutive payment will reduce the balance of the mortgage such that, when all payments are made, the mortgage balance is zero. In other words, the payback of the mortgage is included in the monthly payment. Thus, each payment is the sum of two components: interest and principal repayment. Although the total payment remains constant, the components do not remain a constant proportion of the payment. The early payments will be comprised primarily of interest with very little going to principal reduction. With each payment, the interest proportion decreases (because the principal balance is decreasing) and the principal repayment proportion increases. Over the total payments, the sum of the individual principal repayments will equal the original amount borrowed.

Table 4–1 shows the allocation between interest and principal repayment for the first six months and the last six months for our example. As seen, the amount of interest paid for a given month is greatest in month one and declines for each consecutive month. The portion of the payment that is principal repayment behaves just the opposite. The smallest proportion of principal repayment is found in the payment for month one. The amortization of the mortgage is a form of forced saving since it requires the borrower to replace debt with equity.

TABLE 4-1
Monthly Amortization Schedule for $100,000 Loan at 10% for 30 Years

		Payment	Beginning Balance	Interest	Principal Repayment	Ending Balance
0	1	$877.57	$100,000	$833.33	$ 44.24	$99,956
0	2	$877.57	$ 99,956	832.96	$ 44.61	99,911
0	3	$877.57	$ 99,911	832.59	$ 44.98	99,866
0	4	$877.57	$ 99,866	832.22	$ 45.35	99,821
0	5	$877.57	$ 99,821	831.84	$ 45.73	99,775
0	6	$877.57	$ 99,775	831.46	$ 46.11	99,729
	—	—	—	—	—	—
	—	—	—	—	—	—
	—	—	—	—	—	—
355		$877.57	$ 5,115	42.63	$834.94	4,280
356		$877.57	$ 4,280	35.67	$841.90	3,438
357		$877.57	$ 3,438	28.65	$848.92	2,589
358		$877.57	$ 2,589	21.58	$855.99	1,733
359		$877.57	$ 1,733	14.44	$863.13	870
360		$877.57	$ 870	7.25	$870.32	0

Balances are rounded to the nearest dollar.

Because only the interest portion of the mortgage payment is tax deductible and since interest is a declining portion of the monthly payment, the after-tax cost of the mortgage is increasing over time. For example, note from Table 4–1 that interest in month one is $833.33 with principal repayment of $44.24. For a borrower in a 28 percent marginal tax bracket, the after-tax cost of the payment is $644.24 (44.24 + (833.33(1 − 0.28))). However the after-tax cost of the 360th payment is much higher at $875.54 (870.32 + (7.25(1 − 0.28))).

The Outstanding Balance of the Mortgage

As the **amortization schedule** shows, the amount owed on the mortgage declines with each payment. Thus, after each payment, the mortgage will have some **outstanding balance.** The balance remaining at any point in time is simply the *present value of the remaining stream of payments discounted at the contract interest rate.* For our example, the outstanding balance at the end of 6 months is

$$\text{Outstanding Balance} = \frac{\$877.57}{MC_{10,29.5}} = \$99,729$$

where the monthly mortgage constant is

$$MC_{10,29.5} = \frac{0.008333(1.008333)^{354}}{(1.008333)^{354} - 1}$$

Recall that the mortgage constant factor is the reciprocal of the present value of an annuity factor. Also, note that the interest rate and number of payments are adjusted to reflect the monthly amortization.

The Effective Cost of the Mortgage

The effective cost of the mortgage is the borrower's actual percentage cost. This is also the effective yield earned by the lender. The effective cost (yield) of the loan is affected by loan fees charged by the lender. In the absence of loan fees, the effective cost (yield) of the loan is equal to the contract interest rate. Any closing costs classified as additional finance charges are loan fees and affect the cost of the loan. Loan fees are charged by the lender to cover expenses incurred in loan processing and preparing the loan documents. It is common for an **origination**

fee to appear on the closing statement. Other items typically classified as finance charges that can affect the cost of the loan include (a) lender inspection fee, (b) assumption fee, (c) underwriting fee, (d) VA funding fee/FHA MIP, (e) tax service fee, (f) document preparation fee, (g) flood certification fee, (h) prepaid interest, and (i) mortgage insurance premium (first year).

The lender may also "discount" the mortgage, i.e., charge the borrower **discount points.** A point is equal to 1 percent of the loan amount and is a cash charge paid by the borrower to the lender at the time of loan origination. In effect, lenders allow borrowers to "buy down" their contract interest rate by paying points. Remember that the contract rate is the rate upon which the mortgage payment is based. Thus a borrower can trade off an initial cash charge for a lower monthly payment. The payment of points has the effect of raising the effective cost (yield) of the loan.

When loan fees and/or points are charged, the lender must disclose to the borrower the effect on the cost of the loan. Along with other items, truth-in-lending laws require the lender to disclose the **annual percentage rate (APR)** of the loan. The APR is the effective cost of the loan assuming that it is held to maturity.

Calculating the APR

The charging of discount points has the effect of increasing the cost of the loan by reducing the amount of funds actually acquired by the borrower. Consider our previous example with a loan amount of $100,000 at 10 percent for 30 years and a monthly payment of $877.57. If no points or loan fees are charged, the APR on the loan will be the contract rate of 10 percent. However, with points or fees, the APR rises above 10 percent. This can be illustrated by considering an equation of which the left side gives the amount of funds effectively received by the borrower (face amount minus the points/fees) and the right side gives the amount that the borrower repays. If the loan is held to maturity, the amount repaid is the series of monthly payments. The following examples help to clarify.

APR With No Points or Fees

$$\$100,000 - 0 = \$877.57 \ (\text{PVAIF}_{i, \ 360})$$

Solving for i (an internal rate of return calculation) yields an interest rate of 0.8333 percent monthly which annualizes to 10 percent (0.8333% $\times$ 12). The left side of the equation is the face amount of the loan minus the points or fees. PVAIF is the present value interest factor for an annuity.

The keystrokes on the HP10B would be

Enter 100000 minus 0 as a negative **PV**
Enter 877.57 as **PMT**
Enter 360 **N**
Solve for **I/YR**

APR With Two Discount Points

$$\$100,000 - 2000 = \$877.57 \ (\text{PVAIF}_{i, \ 360})$$

This equation shows that the amount of funds actually acquired by the borrower is $98,000. However, the payment stream is based on the face value of the loan; thus, the borrower repays 360 payments of $877.57. Solving for i yields an APR of 10.24 percent. A rough rule of thumb is that one point will raise the APR by about one-eighth of 1 percent. The calculator keystrokes to solve this problem are the same as above.

Effective Cost and Early Repayment

Since the typical mortgage is not held for its entire life, an additional consideration for the borrower is the effective cost of the loan (in percentage terms) under a shortened holding period. If a loan doesn't have any financing costs (such as discount points), the effective cost under any holding period is equal to the contract rate. Once financing costs are introduced, however, the holding period becomes critical. As will be illustrated later, when financing costs are present, the effective cost of the loan will be sensitive to the holding period. That is, a loan with two points, for example, will have a different effective cost under two different holding periods.

An understanding of this raises questions about how mortgages are priced, that is, how lenders set the tradeoff between contract rates and discount points. Avery, Beeson, and Sniderman in a 1996 study[2] examine an aspect of this by looking at the relationship between the mortgage rates advertised by lenders and the behavior of borrowers. Specifically, they examine how the quality and number of applicants vary in response to short-run fluctuations in lender rates. They found that lower advertised rates attract more and better quality applicants. They also found that the low-rate lenders tend to be mortgage banks and mortgage subsidiaries of commercial banks and S&Ls that sell off a larger portion of the loans they originate.

Because most mortgages are not held to maturity, it is important to understand how a shortened holding period will affect the interest cost. For now, we also will assume that there is no prepayment penalty on the mortgage. To illustrate with our previous example, suppose that the loan is prepaid at the end of five years. This means that the payment stream for the borrower is the monthly payment for sixty periods plus the outstanding balance at the end of the fifth year. The effective cost would be calculated as

$$\$100,000 - 0 = \$877.57 \, (\text{PVAIF}_{i,60}) + \$96,574 \, (\text{PVIF}_{i,60})$$

where the balance of the mortgage at the end of year five is

$$\text{Bal} = \$877.57/\text{MC}_{10,25} = \$96,574$$

PVIF is the present value interest factor of $1. Note that in deriving the outstanding balance the mortgage constant reflects an interest rate and term adjusted to monthly compounding.

Solving the above equation for the internal rate of return yields an i of 10 percent. This shows that with no discount points or loan fees the holding period does not affect the effective cost (yield) of the loan.

The keystrokes on the HP10B to solve this equation are

Enter 100000 minus 0 as a negative **PV**
Enter 877.57 as **PMT**
Enter 96574 as **FV**
Enter 60 **N**
Solve for **I/YR**

If points and/or loan fees are present, the effective cost over the holding period will be a function of the time the mortgage is held. If we use our example of two points being charged and assume that the mortgage is held for 5 years, the effective cost (yield) is calculated as

$$\$100,000 - \$2000 = \$877.57 \, (\text{PVAIF}_{i,60}) + \$96,574 \, (\text{PVIF}_{i,60})$$

The effective cost is 10.52 percent. Holding other factors constant, the shorter the holding period, the higher the effective cost of the loan.

The Effective Cost of Prepayment Penalties

Some mortgages assess a penalty to the borrower for repaying a mortgage before maturity. The penalty may be stated as a percentage of the outstanding balance at the point of prepayment. The mortgage may have a specified window of time in which the penalty can be assessed. For example, a mortgage may call for a prepayment penalty if the loan is repaid within the first ten years. The prepayment penalty has the effect of increasing the cost (yield) of the loan. Using our previous example, suppose the mortgage has no points or fees, but it does have a prepayment penalty of 5 percent if the loan is repaid within the first ten years. The effect on the cost of the loan if it is repaid at the end of year five would be

$$\$100,000 = \$877.57 \, (\text{PVAIF}_{i,60}) + \$96,574 \, (1.05) \, (\text{PVIF}_{i,60})$$

The prepayment penalty increases the effective cost (yield) from 10 percent to 10.74 percent.

Some lenders offer the **prepayment-protection mortgage (PPM).** This type of mortgage which was prominent in the 1940s faded in the 1970s when high market rates made refinancing unattractive and the mortgage market became more standardized with the emergence of the secondary mortgage market. The use of PPMs continued to fade in the early 1980s. The decreasing rates of the late 1980s and 1990s, however, renewed borrower interest in refinancing and raised concerns by lenders and/or investors in prepayment protection. Primarily, lenders and investors were seeing their returns eroded by borrowers replacing older, higher interest rate loans with new, lower rate mortgages.

The PPM differs from the standard mortgage in that the borrower gives up the right to prepay the mortgage without penalty in exchange for a lower interest rate. This provision does not preclude prepayment, it simply attaches a cost to it. The cost may be assessed in different ways. For example, Freddie Mac has two PPM structures that apply to both fixed-rate and adjustable-rate mortgages. One method restricts prepayment for the first three years of life and charges a penalty of two percent of the outstanding loan balance. The other provision has a five-year restriction and charges a penalty of six months' interest on the remaining balance. The penalty applies only to refinancing and is not triggered by loan repayment resulting from sale of the property.

Countrywide Home Funding Corporation, the largest independent mortgage banker in the United States, offers a program whereby borrowers can reduce their contract rate by accepting a prepayment penalty. The rate is generally reduced by about one-quarter (say from 8 percent to 7.75 percent). The homeowner may sell the property or pay down the mortgage by as much as 20 percent during the first five years without a penalty. Above that, however, the borrower must pay a penalty equal to six months' interest on the outstanding balance after exempting the first 20 percent of principal.

Fixed-Rate Mortgages and Interest Rate Risk

Recall that interest rate risk is the risk of loss due to changes in market interest rates. Fixed-income assets are especially susceptible to interest rate risk due to the fixed nature of their income streams. Fixed-rate, fixed-payment mortgages are fixed-income assets. Thus, their market values will change inversely to market rate changes. That is, as market rates rise, the value of the mortgage will decline. As we discuss later, this is one factor that caused major problems for mortgage lenders in the 1980s.

The effect on the fixed-rate mortgage of a change in market rates can be illustrated using our previous example. A lender originates a mortgage for $100,000 at 10 percent for 30 years in monthly payments. This yields a monthly payment of $877.57. Suppose that five years later the market rate is 12 percent on 25-year, fixed-rate mortgages. The outstanding balance (face value) of this mortgage is $96,574 (as shown above). However, the market value of this loan is

$$\text{Market Value} = \$877.57/\text{MC}_{12,25} = \$83,322$$

The loan would be discounted at the higher market rate to reflect current market conditions and thus the market value of the loan is significantly less than the face value. This loss in value occurs whether the lender holds the loan in portfolio or sells it in the secondary market.

SUMMARY

The government mortgage market programs of the Depression years were established for a twofold purpose. One was to provide liquidity to lenders through direct loans and insuring deposits. Another was the promotion of a long-term, amortizing instrument through default insurance and a secondary market for such loans. The government was successful on both counts. Through these agencies and the establishment of insurance guaranteed by the Veterans Administration in 1947, the postwar residential finance system was in place. America entered this new era with the following:

1. A well-established system of thrifts, insured by the government and able to provide the services of intermediaries;
2. A long-term, fixed-rate, amortizing mortgage as the principal (virtually only) type of loan; and
3. An economy characterized by stable inflation and interest rates.

The mechanics of the fixed-rate, fixed-payment mortgage include calculation of the payment, the outstanding balance, the amortization schedule, and the effective cost. The annual percentage rate (APR) is the effective cost of the loan if it is held to maturity. Calculations show that the holding period is critical in determining the effective cost of the loan if the loan is discounted or has a prepayment penalty. Fixed-rate mortgages are inversely affected by changes in market interest rates.

KEY TERMS

Annual percentage rate (APR)
Amortization schedule
Building and loan associations
Discount points
Duration
Federal Savings and Loan Insurance Corporation (FSLIC)
Equitable right of redemption
Gage
Effective cost
Federal Home Loan Bank System (FHLBS)
Federal Housing Administration (FHA)
Federal National Mortgage Association (FNMA)
Federal Savings and Loan Association
Fiducia

Fully-amortizing
Home Owners Loan Corporation (HOLC)
Hypotheca
Mortgage constant
Mortgage payment
Nonamortizing
Origination fee
Outstanding balance
Pigus
Prepayment penalty
Prepayment protection mortgage (PPM)
Reconstruction finance corporation (RFC)
Statutory right of redemption
Usury

SUGGESTED READINGS

Chandler, L. V. 1970. *America's Great Depression 1929–1941.* New York: Harper and Row.
Colean, M. L. 1950. *The Impact of Government on Real Estate in the United States.* New York: National Bureau of Economic Research.
Goldsmith, R. 1958. *Financial Intermediaries in the American Economy Since 1900.* New York: National Bureau of Economic Research.
Peterson, P. T. History of mortgages. *Secondary Mortgage Markets,* 7(3).
Schwartz, E. 1989. The problems of savings and loans. In E. Schwartz and G. Vasconcellos, eds., *Restructuring the Thrift Industry.* Bethlehem, PA: Lehigh University.
Sirmans, C. F. 1989. *Real Estate Finance.* 2nd ed. New York: McGraw-Hill.

REVIEW QUESTIONS

4–1   Summarize the historical use of property as collateral for a loan to finance its purchase.

4–2   What was the major difference between the fiducia, the pigus, and the hypotheca in Roman law?

4–3   a. Define an equitable right of redemption.
       b. What is the origin of the equitable right of redemption?

4–4   Explain why mortgage bankers were popular in the post–Civil War era.

4–5   a. What were the characteristics of mortgages in the latter half of the nineteenth century?
       b. Explain why they minimized interest rate risk for the lender.

4–6   Outline the causes of the high default rate on mortgages during the 1930s Depression.

4–7   How did federal programs support the mortgage and housing market in the 1930s Depression?

4–8   What was the purpose of the following agencies: (a) FSLIC, (b) FHA, and (c) FNMA?

4–9   Explain how the mortgage market of the 1940s differed from that of the 1920s.

PROBLEMS

4–1   John Corbitt takes a fully amortizing mortgage for $80,000 at 10 percent interest for 30 years, monthly payments. What will be his monthly payment?

4–2   Dave Burns wants to buy a house. To do so, he must incur a mortgage. A local lender has determined that Dave can afford a monthly payment of $600, principal and interest. If the current interest rate on 30-year, fixed-rate mortgages is 9.50 percent, what is the maximum amount of mortgage that Dave could qualify for?

4–3   Mike Long qualifies to borrow $120,000 on a mortgage at 9 percent for 30 years, monthly payments.
    a. What is his monthly payment?
    b. How much interest does Mike pay in the first month of the loan?
    c. How much interest does he pay in the first year of the mortgage?
    d. If he decides to repay the mortgage at the end of year three, what is the outstanding balance at that time?
    e. How much total interest does he pay over this three year period?

4–4   You borrow $75,000 for 30 years with monthly amortization, and your payment is $590.03. What interest rate is being charged?

4–5   You want to purchase a house that has an asking price of $125,000. You can get a loan for 80 percent of the bank's appraised value at 9.50 percent for 30 years, monthly payments. The appraiser values the house at 95 percent of the asking price.
    a. What will be your monthly payment if you take the loan?
    b. What would be the balance of the mortgage after five years?
    c. Set up a five-year amortization schedule showing total annual mortgage payments, total interest and principal paid annually, and the balance at the end of each year. (Do not set up a monthly amortization schedule to answer this problem.)

4–6   Local lenders are offering the following terms for 30-year, fixed-rate mortgages. If your objective is to minimize the cost of borrowing, which alternative do you prefer?

Contract Interest Rate	Discount Points
8.25%	2.75
8.50%	2.00
8.75%	1.00

    a. Assume monthly payments and the mortgage held to its maturity. What is the effective cost (APR) of each alternative?
    b. Assume monthly payments and a holding period of five years. What is the effective cost of each alternative?
    c. Assume that each mortgage has a 3 percent prepayment penalty. What is the effective cost of each alternative?

4–7   Determine the monthly payment for the following mortgages of $90,000 each.

Mortgage	Interest Rate	Maturity (in months)	Payment
A	10%	360	_____
B	11%	300	_____
C	9%	300	_____
D	8%	260	_____

4–8 Determine the yield-to-maturity at origination for the following mortgages.

Mortgage	Monthly Payment	Maturity (in months)	Amount at Origination	Yield-to-Maturity
A	$500	360	$50,000	_____
B	$600	360	$65,000	_____
C	$550	260	$62,000	_____
D	$550	300	$60,000	_____

4–9 How long would it take to pay off the following mortgages? Hint: "Never" is a possible answer.

Mortgage	Payment	Coupon Rate	Initial Loan	Maturity
A	$400	10.0%	$45,000	_____
B	800	10.5%	$75,000	_____
C	600	11.0%	$62,000	_____
D	550	11.0%	$60,000	_____

4–10 Determine the discount points necessary to provide a yield-to-maturity of 10 percent for the following mortgages with 30-year maturities.

Mortgage	Monthly Payment	Coupon Rate	Amount at Origination	Discount Points (in dollars)
A	$800	N/A	$100,000	_____
B	900	N/A	110,000	_____
C	950	N/A	125,000	_____
D	700	N/A	110,000	_____

4–11 Determine the balance of the following 30-year mortgages at the end of the fifth year. Hint: The balance of a standard fixed-rate mortgage at any time is equal to the present value of the remaining payments discounted by the rate on the mortgage.

Mortgage	Original Amount	Contract Rate	Balance
A	$100,000	10%	_____
B	90,000	8%	_____
C	80,000	12%	_____

ENDNOTES

1. R. J. Saulnier, *Urban Mortgage Lending by Life Insurance Companies* (New York: National Bureau of Economic Research, 1950). During this time, insurance companies held about one-sixth of all residential mortgage debt outstanding.
2. R. B. Avery, P. E. Beeson, and M. S. Sniderman, "Posted Rates and Mortgage Lending Activity," *Journal of Real Estate Finance and Economics* 13 (1996): 11–26.

WEB SITES

Time Value of Money Calculator
http://www.Timevalue.com/cgi-bin/tvscalc.exe
Current Mortgage Information, Rates, ARM Indexes, Etc.
http://www.hsh.com
Countrywide Mortgages
http://www.countrywide.com
Coldwell Banker Online
http://www.coldwellbanker.com

APPENDIX A

Elements of the Discounted Cash Flow Model of Valuation

The discounted cash flow model is expressed by the equation:

$$PV = \sum_{i=1}^{n} \frac{CF_i}{(1 + r)^i}$$ (Equation 4A–1)

where PV stands for present value, CF is the amount of the cash flows, r is the discount rate, and n represents the number of periods over which the cash flows are received. Information on three of the terms is sufficient to determine the value of the fourth. Interestingly, different problems in real estate finance may call for solving one of the particular terms in the basic equation. A simple example is the determination of the payment on a standard mortgage, given the amount of the loan PV, the maturity n, and the lender's interest charge r. Although financial tables are available, calculations are easily performed using a standard financial calculator that has at least four keys representing the terms in the equation (PV, PMT, %, n). Let's begin by considering a familiar 30-year, fixed-rate mortgage discussed in this chapter.

Case A.   In this first case, assume that the mortgagor desires to borrow $90,000 (PV). The lender offers a 30-year (360 monthly payments, n) loan with a contract rate of 10 percent (%). This is sufficient information to compute the required monthly payment (PMT) in the following equation:

$$\$90,000 = \frac{PMT}{(1 + .008333)^1} + \frac{PMT}{(1 + .008333)^2} + \cdots + \frac{PMT}{(1 + .008333)^{360}}$$

After inputting 90,000 for PV, 360 for n, and 10/12 for %, the calculator will compute the payment, PMT, and display the solution: $789.81. In this case, we solved for the payment. Now, let's look at a situation where the object is to find a present value.

Case B.   Assume in the above example that the mortgagor decides she cannot afford such a high payment and has only $650 available for the monthly principal and interest payment. She wants to know how much she can borrow. There is sufficient information to determine the amount from the following equation:

$$Amount = \frac{650}{(1 + .008333)^1} + \frac{650}{(1 + .008333)^2} + \cdots + \frac{650}{(1 + .008333)^{360}}$$

Again, we have three of the four necessary elements. After inputting 650 for PMT, 360 for n, and 10/12 for %, the solution would be displayed as: $74,068. Next, let's consider a case where the missing element is the interest rate r.

Case C.   After arranging for the above loan, the mortgagor is informed by the lender that there is a 2 percent discount applicable to this loan (two points charged). In this case the mortgagor will receive only 98 percent of the $74,000 loan, or $72,587. The payment, however, remains $650 per month. This raises the effective interest rate on the loan. The federal truth-in-lending law (see Chapter 8) will require the lender to restate the actual rate as the Annual Percentage Rate (APR). The lender can compute the APR and inform the mortgagor of the rate by solving the following equation for r:

$$\$72,587 = \frac{650}{(1 + r)^1} + \frac{650}{(1 + r)^2} \cdots \frac{650}{(1 + r)^{360}}$$

Inputting 72,587 for the present value, 650 for PMT, and 360 for n, will result in an APR of 0.0853 per month, or 10.25 percent annually. The use of the discount points has raised the effective interest cost on the loan by 0.25 percent annually. Larger discounts will result in higher effective yields. A final example looks at determining the term *n,* of a loan given the other three terms.

Case D.   Here, assume that there are no discount points (Case B). The mortgagor desires to borrow the $74,068 and is willing to pay a 10 percent annual interest cost, but desires to reduce the payment to $640. This can be accomplished by extending the term of the loan beyond 360 months. We can solve for *n* in the following equation:

$$\$74,068 = \frac{640}{(1.008333)^1} + \frac{640}{(1 + .008333)^2} + \ldots + \frac{640}{(1 + .008333)^n}$$

Inputting 74,068 for the present value, 10/12 for %, and 640 for PMT, the solution for *n* appears as: 402. The loan will be amortized in 331/2 years.

To summarize, three of the four terms of the DCF model are required to solve for the fourth. As long as three terms are known, the fourth can be solved. Although financial tables can be used for this purpose, they can be cumbersome. Today most real estate students and professionals become quite adept at solving financial problems with the use of an inexpensive financial calculator. We suggest you acquire one if you have not already done so. It will be quite useful for solving problems in this and the remaining chapters. Also, note that there is a wide variety of situations in real estate finance that will call for solving different terms of the basic valuation model.

APPENDIX B

Maturity, Duration, and the Interest Rate Risk of Mortgages

The discounted cash flow (DCF) model tells us that the value of a mortgage, or any debt instrument, is determined by discounting the expected future payments to the present:

$$\text{Value} = \text{PMT}/(1 + r)^1 + \text{PMT}/(1 + r)^2 + \ldots + \text{PMT}/(1 + r)^n \qquad \text{(Equation 4B–1)}$$

If the payments (PMT) are fixed, then a change in the discount rate will alter the value. Thus, when market rates of interest change, so do the values of debt instruments. As interest (discount) rates rise, the value of the obligations falls.

Consider two mortgages originated today, both for the same balance and at the same rate of interest but with two different maturities.

	Balance	Annual Rate	Maturity	Payment
Mortgage A	$100,000	12%	30 years	$1,028.61
Mortgage B	$100,000	12%	15 years	$1,200.17

Each payment stream when discounted at 1 percent monthly has a value of $100,000. Assume that the day after origination (tomorrow) market rates rise to 14 percent annually. The values of each mortgage will be reduced. According to Equation 4A–1, the two values will be $86,812 and $90,120 for mortgages A and B, respectively. The standard explanation for the difference in the degree of loss is the difference in maturity. When interest rates rise, holders of existing debt have a claim to payments that are lower than would exist on the same size of new debt. The longer those payments are stretched out, the lower their value. Stated differently, the holder of Mortgage B receives larger payments earlier than the holder of Mortgage A. Mortgage B holder has the opportunity to reinvest those payments at the higher market rate. By year 15, Mortgage B is completely paid off and all funds are reinvested at the higher rate. But now consider the following "mortgages."

	Balance ($)	Annual Rate (%)	Maturity (years)	Monthly Payment ($)	Payment at Maturity ($)
Mortgage A	100,000	12	30	1,028.61	0
Mortgage B	100,000	12	30	1,000.00	100,000
Mortgage C	100,000	12	30	0	3,594,964

Mortgage A is a typical amortizing mortgage. Mortgage B is an interest-only mortgage with a repayment of principal at maturity. The payments act as those of a typical corporate bond. Mortgage C has no intermediate payments. Interest is accrued and the total is paid at maturity, the same as a zero-coupon bond. The DCF equations for these mortgages (A, B, C) appear as follows:

A $\$100,000 = \$1,028.61/(1.01)^1 + \$1,028.61/(1.01)^2 + \ldots + \$1,028.61/(1.01)^{360}$

B $\$100,000 = \$1,000/(1.01)^1 + \$1,000/(1.01)^2 + \ldots + \$1,000(1.01)^{360} + \$100,000/(1.01)^{360}$

C $\$100,000 = \$3,594,964/(1.01)^{360}$

Following the above example, if interest rates rise to 14 percent tomorrow, then the values of the three mortgages will be as follows:

A $86,812

B $85,933

C $55,235

Although the mortgages all had the same maturity (30 years), the decline in value as a result of the increase in interest rates was not identical. The explanation lies in the timing and amount of the cash flows. As in the previous example, the mortgages that have large and early intermediate payments decline less in value. The holder of Mortgage C has no intermediate cash flows whatsoever to reinvest at the higher (14 percent) rate. The holder of Mortgage A has the benefit of receiving some principal with each payment. The amortized portion of the payment can be reinvested at the higher rates along with the interest payments.

The difference in the change in values of the mortgages lies in the difference in the extent to which the cash flows of the mortgages are "pushed" back toward their maturities. A measure of the extent to which the cash flows are pushed back is called the duration. Although each of the three mortgages in our example has the same maturity, they have different durations. The duration of a debt instrument is a measure of the average time prior to the receipt of the cash flows. More accurately, it is the weighted average of the lengths of time prior to the receipt of the cash flows using the relative present values of the cash flows as the weights. The formula for duration is as follows:

$$D = \frac{\sum t \times CF_t/(1 + r)^t}{\sum CF/(1 + r)^t} \qquad \text{(Equation 4B–2)}$$

An example is provided in Table 4B–1.

Note that the values in the numerator are weighted by t, the period in which the cash flow occurs. The duration in years of each of the above mortgages is

A = 7.9

B = 8.4

C = 30.0

TABLE 4B–1

Computation of Duration of Bond

coupon, 8%; face value, $1,000; payment, semiannual; maturity, 7 years; market rate, 9%.

1 Period	2 Semiannual Cash Flow (CF)	3 $CF/(1 + r)^t$ (present value of column 2)	4 $txCF/(1 + r)^t$ (column 1 × column 3)
1	40	$ 38.28	$ 38.28
2	40	36.63	73.26
3	40	35.05	105.16
4	40	33.54	134.17
5	40	32.10	160.49
6	40	30.72	184.29
7	40	29.39	205.75
8	40	28.13	225.02
9	40	26.92	242.25
10	40	25.76	257.57
11	40	24.65	271.13
12	40	23.59	283.04
13	40	22.57	293.42
14	1040	$561.57	7,862.00
TOTAL		$948.89	$10,335.83

Duration = 10,335.83/948.89 = 10.89 periods
Comments: Total value of column 3 (denominator of duration formula) is also the value of the bond. Duration is 10.89 periods, or 5.44 years, less than maturity of seven years.

The percent change in the price of debt instrument as a result of a change in interest rates can be determined by

$$\frac{\Delta p}{p} = -D \times \frac{\Delta r}{(1 + r)} \qquad \text{(Equation 4B–3)}$$

For the three mortgages we have

$$A = -14\% = -7.9 \times .02/1.12$$

$$B = -15\% = -8.4 \times .02/1.12$$

$$C = -45\% = -30.0 \times .02/1.12$$

In summary, the change in the price of a debt instrument as a result of a change in market rates of interest is a function of its duration. Duration is closely allied to maturity. Longer-maturity bonds will have longer durations. But, the duration of a bond will be less than its maturity (except for zero-coupon bonds, which have the same duration as maturity). Because duration and maturity are closely related, a common misconception is that a bond's maturity determines the extent to which its value changes as a result of a change in interest rates. To be precise, price changes are determined by duration.

CHAPTER **5**

Postwar Residential Finance

LEARNING OBJECTIVES

After reading this chapter, you should have an understanding of the major forces that changed and shaped the residential mortgage market since the end of World War II. You should understand how changes in the inflationary environment forced changes in the types of institutions that originated mortgages and in the types of mortgages they offered. You will discover why thrifts (savings and loan associations, mutual savings banks, and credit unions) played a less and less important role over the period of transition and why adjustable rate mortgages became popular. This chapter also outlines how federal government policies aided or hindered the transition. An understanding of the developments in residential real estate finance over the last half century is essential to appreciate the current structure of the market.

INTRODUCTION

This chapter provides an overview of the post-World War II residential finance market. From the end of the war through the early 1990s, there have been dramatic changes in the types of mortgages employed to finance residential properties, the types of investors (lenders) in those mortgages, and the methods by which lenders and borrowers are brought together. It is important that you understand the changes that have taken place in this market and the reasons for those changes. In this way you can better appreciate the present structure of the market.

BACKGROUND

The data in Table 5–1 show the amount and holders of mortgage debt outstanding (residential and commercial) at the beginning of each decade since World War II. Included is the share of the total held by each type of lender and the annual growth rate in their holdings for each decade. Some noticeable trends are apparent. During the decade of the '50s, savings and loan associations enjoyed the greatest growth in mortgage lending. They increased their holdings nearly 16 percent annually to raise their share of the total from 19 to 29 percent. The growth came at the expense of a decline in the share held by commercial banks and individuals. Savings and loan associations were granted a favorable tax status for investing in residential mortgages. They continued to increase their share of the market in later decades as well.

After 1950, commercial banks initially lost ground but later recovered their share of mortgage lending. By the 1980s, their share was the same as it was in 1950. Although there was no trend in the share held by individuals, there was some fluctuation due primarily to the interest rate cycle.

When interest rates are relatively high, borrowers tend to hold onto existing mortgages. If they are holding relatively low-cost financing, there is little incentive to repay the debt. Also, it is more difficult for individuals to sell property when interest rates are high. Therefore, they often finance all or part of the sale themselves. The sellers become mortgage holders. These loans,

TABLE 5–1

Mortgage Debt Outstanding by Holder (billions of dollars)

	Savings and Loan Associations	Savings Banks	Commercial Banks	Life Insurance Companies	Federal and Related Agencies	Individuals and Others	Total
1950	13.7(19)	8.3(11)	13.7(19)	16.1(22)	2.8(4)	18.4(25)	73
1960	60.1(29)	29.9(13)	28.8(14)	41.8(20)	11.5(6)	38.4(18)	207.5
Annual % of growth	(15.9)	(12.5)	(7.7)	(10)	(15.1)	(7.6)	(11)
1970	150.3(32)	57.9(12)	73.3(15)	74.4(16)	38.3(8)	79.3(17)	473.5
Annual % of growth	(9.6)	(7.97)	(9.8)	(5.9)	(12.8)	(7.5)	(8.6)
1980	503.2(35)	99.9(7)	262.7(18)	131.1(9)	256.8(18)	203.9(14)	1457.6
Annual % of growth	(12.8)	(5.6)	(13.6)	(5.8)	(21)	(9.9)	(11.9)
1990	801.6(21)[a]		844.8(22)	267.9(7.1)	1361.3(36)	522.1(13.6)	3797.7
Annual % of growth	(4)		(14.3)	(12.0)	(19.8)	(26)	(10.4)
1996	628.7 (12.4)		1136.1 (22)	212.4(4.2)	2363.8(47)	713.4(14.1)	5054.4
Annual % of growth	(-2.8)		(5.9)	(-.5)	(10.1)	(6.7)	(5.1)

( ) = % of market

[a] 1990 and 1996 values are for savings and loan associations and savings banks combined.

termed **purchase money mortgages,** owner-carrybacks, or owner-seconds, are usually short-term loans with balloon payments. The increase in the share held by individuals in the 1980s over the 1970s partially reflects the very high interest rates of the late 1970s.

The most notable trend is that of the share held by federal and related agencies. Several federal agencies were active in the 1970s and 1980s in raising funds for residential finance. They enjoyed the backing (credit) of the federal government and were successful in attracting funds to residential financing via the secondary mortgage market. They were especially successful during periods of high and volatile interest rates. Many lenders that in earlier times held loans in their own portfolios began to avoid interest rate risk by selling off loans that they originated to the federal agencies. In addition, the agencies were given broadened powers by the government to expand the secondary mortgage market. Legislation was passed to eliminate taxation at the entity level. The government believed it was important for the secondary market to provide funds for the housing market during periods of high interest rates. By 1990 the agencies were so successful and such large players in the market that they could virtually dictate the terms, conditions, and underwriting criteria of mortgage instruments offered in the marketplace. If terms of the loans did not conform (conforming loans) with the requirements of the federal agencies, they would not be available for sale or purchase in the secondary market.

The expansion of the secondary mortgage market accelerated in the early 1990s. While the amount of mortgage debt held by savings institutions fell nearly 3 percent annually from 1990 to 1996, the share held by federally related agencies rose by 10 percent annually over this same period. By 1996 federally related agencies held 47 percent of all mortgage debt. A decade-by-decade review of the postwar mortgage market follows.

THE 1950s: A DECADE OF STABILITY

In 1950, one-half of all mortgage debt (residential and commercial) was held by depository institutions. By 1960, the ratio had risen to 56 percent. Because of the widespread acceptance of the 30-year, fixed-rate mortgage, these institutions were particularly vulnerable to interest rate risk. The risk occurs when there is a large difference between the maturity of an institution's assets and liabilities. This is called a **maturity mismatch.** Even if most mortgages are prepaid prior to their 30-year maturity, their expected "life" is still measured in years—several years. Most deposits have maturities of less than 1 year; some are payable on demand.

To appreciate the severe problems associated with the maturity mismatch problem that appeared later in the 1970s and 1980s, consider a typical thrift of the 1950s. It would originate and hold in its portfolio mortgages yielding close to 5 percent. At the time, it would pay 3.5 percent on short-term deposits. The spread would cover operating expenses and provide for a return on

TABLE 5–2
Effect of Changing Interest Rates on Financial Statements of a Savings and Loan

Partial Balance Sheet and Income Statement

Assets		Liabilities	
Long-term mortgages	$50,000,000	Deposits	$50,000,000
Building, furniture, and fixtures	8,000,000	Capital (net worth)	8,000,000
Total	$58,000,000	Total	$58,000,000

Partial Income Statement Prior to Rise in Rates

Interest revenue	$2,500,000	(.05 × 50,000,000)
Interest expense	1,750,000	(.035 × 50,000,000)
Net interest income	750,000	

Partial Income Statement after Rise in Rates

Interest revenue	$2,500,000	
Interest expense	3,000,000	(.06 × 50,000,000)
Net interest income	(500,000)	

Market Value of Assets and Liabilities after Rise in Rates

Assets		Liabilities	
Long-term mortgages	$40,361,297[a]	Deposits	$50,000,000
Building, furniture, and fixtures	8,000,000	Capital (net worth)	(1,638,703)
Total	$48,361,297	Total	$48,361,297

[a]Assumes an annual payment of $3,252,572 amortized over 30 years. In reality, the expected life is shorter because of prepayments. A shorter life assumption would raise the market value somewhat.

the capital invested in the thrift. Consider what would happen if market interest rates rose so that depositors required a higher rate, say 6 percent. Furthermore, assume that there are no regulatory restrictions on the rate the thrift can pay on deposits. As the 3.5 percent deposits matured, they would be rolled over at the 6 percent rate. The yield on new mortgages would also be higher, say 7 percent. This would discourage holders of the old 5 percent mortgages from prepaying them. They would be less likely to accept job transfers or undertake other actions that would result in a sale of their residence and a prepayment of the loan. If the 5 percent loans were assumable—as all FHA, VA, and many conventional loans were during this decade—then they would be passed on to the new buyers of any properties that were sold. In summary, the rise in rates would result in an increase in the thrifts' expenses with little change in their revenues.

The example in Table 5–2 demonstrates this point. A thrift with $50 million in mortgage assets and the same amount of short-term deposits would earn $750,000 before the change in interest rates and lose $500,000 subsequent to the change. The thrift's net worth becomes negative in this example. Neither can the thrift escape the problems caused by the rise in rates by selling its low-rate loans. Their value in the market is significantly less than their balance or the amount of deposit liabilities. The thrift may prefer to retain the loans rather than incur a loss on their sale that would be recorded in their year-end income statement. Once the problem created by the maturity mismatch and the rise in interest rates has occurred, the thrift is "locked in" and must hope for a fall in rates to extricate itself from insolvency.

The maturity mismatch problem is exacerbated by the general lack of prepayment penalties on mortgages. If the profits of a thrift decline when market rates rise, one would expect the reverse when they fall. Recall, however, that borrowers have a valuable prepayment option. With no penalties, they can refinance existing loans at lower rates should rates fall. They incur some refinancing costs, such as appraisal fees and loan origination fees, but the present value of the interest savings derived from the refinance could easily exceed these costs. Thus, when rates fall, the thrifts pay less to retain deposits but also earn less on their long-term assets. Should rates rise, subsequently the maturity mismatch problem reoccurs. The problem is not only one of rising interest rates but one of volatile interest rates. Lenders who originate long-term, fixed-rate mortgages without prepayment penalties grant borrowers valuable options. Recall that such options increase in value when interest rates become more volatile.

Maturity mismatch turned out not to be much of a problem in the 1950s for two reasons. First, the annual inflation rate was low and stable, around 2 percent. This translated into low and stable interest rates. From 1950 through 1958, the 3-month Treasury rate was 3.27 percent at its highest (1957) and was as low as 0.95 percent (1954). There was never any pressure for deposit rates to rise above the yield on mortgages. Second, Regulation Q, issued by the Federal Reserve Board in the 1930s, placed a limit on the rate commercial banks could pay on deposits. Limits on savings and loan deposit rates would not begin until 1966 when the Federal Home Loan Bank Board set the maximum rate that thrifts could pay on savings deposits at 0.25 percent over the commercial bank ceiling. At the time, thrifts were not allowed to issue demand deposits. The Interest Rate Adjustment Act of 1966 authorized the 0.25 percent advantage over banks to compensate for this competitive disadvantage. During the 1950s, the limit on the rates that banks were allowed to offer was intended to preserve their profitability and solvency. Left to compete, they would drive the rate up to whatever the market rate would be, increasing their expenses but not, in the aggregate, attracting more total savings. Of course, if the market rate for deposits was below the Regulation Q ceiling, then it would be nonbinding.

In summary, although the structure of the mortgage market was such as to have potential for serious problems for banks and thrifts, the stable inflation and interest rate environment of the 1950s suppressed any evidence of such problems. It would not remain hidden; hinted at in the 1960s, it emerged as a major concern in the 1970s and led to a restructuring of the mortgage market in the 1980s.

THE 1960s: CREEPING INFLATION, DISINTERMEDIATION, AND THE RISE OF THE SECONDARY MORTGAGE MARKET

The rate of inflation accelerated during the 1960s, partially as a result of the expanded war effort in Vietnam. The 1.5 percent inflation rate in 1960 was quadrupled in 1969 when it reached 6.1 percent. Interest rates reacted accordingly, incorporating inflationary expectations. The 3-year Treasury yield rose gradually from 3.98 percent in 1960 to 7.02 percent in 1969. Short-term rates occasionally rose above the Regulation Q restricted rate offered on bank deposits.

Owners of large deposits began to withdraw their funds and invest in Treasuries. With the development of bond funds, even small savers could take advantage of attractive Treasury yields.[1] The withdrawal of funds from the intermediaries under these circumstances was termed **disintermediation.** Although the regulatory agencies raised the Regulation Q limits when market rates rose enough to cause significant disintermediation, their actions were often delayed. In the meantime, the withdrawal of deposits from banks and thrifts led to a reduction in new funds available for mortgage lending.

Figure 5–1 demonstrates this point. Data on Regulation Q ceiling rates, short-term Treasury yields, the net increase in deposits at savings institutions, and new mortgage lending clearly show the relationship between interest rates, disintermediation, and the mortgage market. As long as market rates were below or only slightly above the Regulation Q limit, disintermediation was not a problem and the regulation served its purpose of preserving the profitability of financial institutions. When market rates rose moderately above the limit, however, depositors withdrew their funds from the thrifts which in turn cut back on mortgage lending. The housing sector at this time was very dependent upon thrifts for funding. Forty-six percent of all mortgage debt outstanding was held by thrifts in 1965. Another 15 percent was held by commercial banks. The housing market suffered during disintermediation because financial institutions were forced to cut back on mortgage lending and homeowners had no financing alternatives.

Unlike the business and government sectors, a prospective homeowner was unable to directly finance his purchase. In simple terms, he was unable to issue a bond (mortgage) in any market in order to obtain the funds necessary to purchase a residence. Intermediation worked best in the mortgage market for the reasons suggested in Chapter 3. The business and government sectors could issue bonds in the market directly to investors, avoiding the intermediation process. Since home buyers were restricted to the intermediaries for loans, they found funds

FIGURE 5–1

Regulation Q Maximum Rates, Market Yields, and Net S&L Deposits

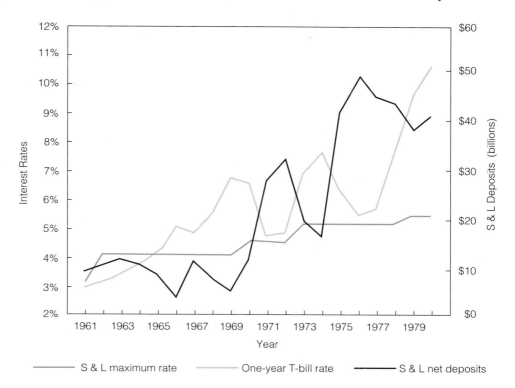

——— S & L maximum rate	········· One-year T-bill rate	——— S & L net deposits

tight whenever the intermediaries experienced an outflow of funds. It was not until the development of the secondary mortgage market that home buyers could finance directly their purchases through the issuance of a bond, so-to-speak (GNMA bonds are discussed in Chapters 10 and 11). It was ironic that the federal government could compete for and divert funds to its own use through direct financing (issuing bonds to the public) at the time it directed financial institutions to limit the rate they could offer on deposits.

The greatest disintermediations of the decade occurred during the 1966 "credit crunch" and again in 1969. In the third quarter of 1966, short-term Treasuries had a yield of 5.38 percent while thrifts paid 4 percent on time deposits. In that quarter there was a $726 million outflow of funds from thrifts. This compares to an average inflow of $2.2 billion per quarter for the previous 4 years. In 1966, one-to four-family housing starts fell to 839,700, a drop of 20 percent from their 1965 level of 1,050,300.

Because of the manner in which it was financed, housing became particularly vulnerable to cyclical movements in interest rates. The bulk of residential loans were made by depository institutions that suffered a maturity mismatch problem in their capital structure and an unreliable supply of funds that resulted from restrictions on deposit rates. Regulation Q limits would continue through the 1970s. The standard fixed-rate mortgage with its tilt (affordability) problem would continue to dominate all forms of residential loans through the early to mid-1970s. But the cyclical nature of the housing market had already evidenced itself in the 1960s and made it clear that residential financing needed help in the form of a well-developed secondary market for mortgages.

A **secondary market** is one in which securities are bought and sold subsequent to their initial origination. It is a market where existing securities are traded. Up until the 1960s, there was limited activity in the secondary market for mortgages. Most lenders were also investors. They held the loans they originated in their own portfolio.

As we discussed in Chapter 1, a secondary market for any security is important for several reasons. First, it increases liquidity. The initial investors in securities (lenders) prefer to originate loans that can be resold quickly and without loss of their intrinsic value. Without a large, organized secondary market, this is unlikely. With no secondary market, lenders will charge for lack of liquidity by requiring a higher rate (offering a lower price) on the loans they originate and must hold in their portfolio.

Second, a secondary market reduces the interest rate risk associated with the maturity mismatch problem. Lenders can continue to exploit their expertise as originators and sell off the loans to other investors. These investors, in turn, avoid the mismatch problem because they need not rely on short-term deposits as a source of funds. They can issue long-term bonds to finance their mortgage purchases. The long-term bonds will not be subject to either fluctuations in short-term rates or Regulation Q restrictions. Alternatively, secondary market investors can finance the purchase of mortgages by issuing bonds which essentially pass through the monthly interest and principal payments of the mortgages to the bondholder. In this manner, the ultimate bondholder becomes the lender. That bondholder may be in a better position to absorb interest rate risk than the thrift.

Third, an organized secondary market can aid the smooth flow of funds from capital-rich areas to capital-deficient areas. Excess funds from the more stable Northeast may be used to satisfy the needs of borrowers in rapidly growing areas of the country such as the Southwest. This would tend to equalize interest rates between the various regions of the country.

At this time two new federal mortgage agencies were created to expand the secondary market. In 1968 the Housing and Urban Development Act established the Government National Mortgage Association (GNMA, often pronounced Ginnie Mae). In the process it also privatized the Federal National Mortgage Association (FNMA, or Fannie Mae) that was created during the 1930s. The second new agency, the Federal Home Loan Mortgage Association (FHLMC, or Freddie Mac), was created in 1970. Both agencies are discussed in detail in Chapter 10. Briefly, GNMA guarantees (but does not actually issue) bonds of the pass-through type as long as the mortgages backing them are government-underwritten (FHA or VA). A pass-through channels each principal and interest payment from the homeowner through to the bondholder. The FHLMC issues various types of bonds, including long-term bonds, in order to raise funds to purchase conventional mortgages.

Because of the activity of GNMA in the 1960s, the share of all mortgage debt held by federal agencies or in pools (which is what GNMAs are) rose to 8 percent from 6 percent in 1960 and 4 percent in 1950. The major expansion of secondary market activity was yet to come, however. As we will see, the share held by agencies and pools would rise to about 47 percent by 1996.

The disintermediation of the late 1960s slowed the growth of thrift participation in the mortgage market. The 16 percent annual growth in the volume of mortgage holdings of savings and loans that characterized the 1950s slowed to 9.6 percent in the 1960s. The disintermediation was also a hint of more severe problems to come in the 1970s, when inflation would accelerate even more. The regulatory authorities felt that they could not eliminate Regulation Q for fear that rapidly rising rates on deposits would result in mass insolvency for thrifts with large portfolios of low-rate mortgages. Yet with Regulation Q in place, the disintermediation problems would accelerate.

THE 1970s: PROBLEMS OF THE FIXED-RATE MORTGAGE IN AN INFLATIONARY ENVIRONMENT

The decade of the 1970s began with a 6 percent rate of inflation and ended in 1979 with prices rising at 13.3 percent annually. Moreover, the volatility in the annual rate of inflation increased significantly. The 1979 rate was the highest inflation rate of the decade, but it had been as low as 3.4 percent in 1972. In addition to the maturity mismatch problem for the thrifts, the high rates of inflation and interest caused housing affordability problems for home buyers. The high-inflation environment caused both supply (thrifts) and demand (affordability) problems for the mortgage market during this decade. It was clear by mid-decade that the standard fixed-rate, 30-year, amortizing loan and the thrift industry were in trouble. Yet up to that point, the housing market had relied almost exclusively on that type of loan and on financial intermediaries to supply it.

Demand Problems

The problems of the fixed-rate mortgage in an inflationary environment may be summarized as follows. First, inflation creates expectations of future inflation and, through the Fisher Equation

(Chapter 2), a rise in long-term interest rates. The home buyer faces a higher rate and a higher payment for a given value of a house. Second, if inflation actually occurs as expected, there is no increase in the real cost of housing over the term of the loan. The real cost is increased in the early part of the loan and decreased in the later part. It is this **"tilt" effect** that causes an afford-ability problem for the home buyer. The lender charges a premium in the interest rate to compensate for future inflation. Home buyers must make their initial payments out of an income that has yet to benefit (rise) from the future inflation.

The examples in Table 5–3 demonstrate this tilt effect on housing affordability. In these examples it is assumed that the borrower's income will rise at an annual rate of 2 percent (for productivity) plus the rate of inflation. In other words, real income grows at 2 percent. It is also assumed that the contract rate on the loan is equal to the real rate (3 percent) plus the rate of inflation. The contract rate establishes the constant dollar payment. For example, annual inflation in Case B is expected to be 2 percent, the borrower's income will grow at 4 percent, and the contract rate on the loan will be 5 percent. The last column for each case is the important column. It shows the real payment divided by the real income of the borrower over the course of the 30-year loan.

In year 5 of Case B, inflation would have reduced the real value of the $429.45 payment to $388.97 ($429.45/(1.02)^5$), while the borrower's monthly income would have risen to $3650, or $3312 in real terms. The real-payment-to-real-income ratio is 11.74 percent ($388.97/$3312). In each case, the tilt effect occurs; the real-payment-to-real-income ratio is greater in the first year of the loan and declines throughout its life. The magnitude of the tilt effect increases as expected inflation rises. The affordability problem caused by inflation and the fixed-rate mortgage is evident. Although the real cost of housing over the 30-year period is identical, in each case a greater portion of that cost is redistributed to the front end of the loan as inflation increases.

By the late 1970s inflation had risen to historically high levels. Interest rates responded and housing affordability plummeted. Mortgage rates, an affordability index, existing single-family home sales, and housing starts during this period are shown in Table 5–4. The **affordability index** is based on the monthly principal and interest payment on a median-priced, existing, single-family home as reported by the National Association of Realtors, and the median family income. The index is calculated as follows. First, the loan amount, equal to 80 percent of the median-priced home, is determined. Existing rates on fixed-rate loans are then used to calculate the interest and principal payment. The median family income is then divided by this payment. As with any index, the base is set at 100. Both rising home values and interest rates reduce the affordability index. The data in Table 5–4 clearly illustrate the relationship between interest rates and affordability during a period when the fixed-rate mortgage was a popular loan instrument.

T A B L E   5 – 3
Effect of Inflation of Real Payment of Fixed-rate Mortgage

$80,000, 30-year mortgage; $3,000/month initial income

	Year	Monthly Payment	Real Payment	Payment/Income
Case A: 0% inflation; 3% interest rate	1	$335.36	$335.36	10.96%
	5	335.36	335.36	10.12
	10	335.36	335.36	9.17
	20	335.36	335.36	7.52
	30	335.36	335.36	6.17
Case B: 2% inflation; 5% interest rate	1	$429.45	$421.03	13.76%
	5	429.45	388.97	11.74
	10	429.45	352.30	9.60
	20	429.45	289.01	6.40
	30	429.45	237.09	4.36
Case C: 8% inflation; 11% interest rate	1	$761.86	$705.42	23.05%
	5	761.86	518.51	15.65
	10	761.86	352.89	9.65
	20	761.86	163.45	3.67
	30	761.86	75.71	1.39

T A B L E   5 – 4

Mortgage Yield, Affordability Index, Home Sales, and Housing Starts: 1977–1985

Year	Mortgage Yields[a]	Housing Affordability Index [b]	Home Sales (thousands of units)	Housing Starts (thousands of units)
1977	9.02	120.6	5651.7	2001.7
1978	9.56	111.4	6022.1	2036.1
1979	10.78	97.2	5587.0	1760.0
1980	12.66	79.9	4285.6	1312.6
1981	14.70	68.9	3519.3	1100.3
1982	15.14	69.5	3062.1	1072.1
1983	12.57	83.2	4431.5	1712.5
1984	12.38	89.1	4619.0	1755.8
1985	11.55	95.5	4958.9	1744.9

[a]Effective rate of conventional mortgages reflecting fees and charges assuming repayment in ten years, Federal Home Loan Bank Board Series.
[b]The housing affordability index measures the percentage of income the median income family has toward qualifying for a median-priced home with a 20 percent down payment. In 1985, the median income family—with an income of $26,300—had 95.5 percent of the income needed to qualify for the $75,500 median-priced home.

The lender includes the expected inflation premium in the contract rate; however, there is no guarantee that the actual rate of inflation over the life of the loan will equal the expected rate. The real cost of housing will be different from the expected cost as well. If inflation turns out to be much greater than expected, the homeowner will face a lower real cost, and the lender will incur a reduction in the real rate-of-return on the loan. The reverse will be true if inflation is lower than expected. Thus, uncertainty about future inflation adds another problem to the workability of the long-term, fixed-rate mortgage. As inflation accelerated in the late 1970s and its variability was magnified, there was increased incentive for the market to develop mortgage loans that eliminated tilt and inflation uncertainty problems.

Supply Problems

The supply problems of the standard, fixed-rate mortgage in an inflationary environment stem from the maturity mismatch structure of financial intermediaries and the use of Regulation Q. During the early part of the 1970s, the yield curve was upward-sloping. Long-term rates were often significantly higher than short-term rates. In 1972, the yield on home mortgages averaged 7.6 percent, whereas 3-month Treasuries yielded 4.07 percent. Intermediaries paid 4.5 percent on savings deposits. The three-point spread was high by historical standards and reflected the steeply upward-sloping yield curve. Lenders who saw profit opportunities in the spread and originated a large volume of fixed-rate mortgages may have failed to consider the implications of the yield curve. Recall from Chapter 2 that an upward-sloping curve is indicative of expectations that market rates will rise. Maturity mismatch and rising rates can combine to produce long-term losses or a savings outflow if deposit rates are restricted, which is exactly what occurred.

By 1979, the rate on 3-month Treasuries had risen to 10.04 percent. Disintermediation became such a problem that the regulatory agencies allowed the deposit rate to rise to 5.5 percent. But even at this rate, the savings outflow continued. Thrifts not only saw the margin between the rate earned on old low-rate mortgages and the rate paid on deposits narrow, they also faced disintermediation.

Introduction of Alternative Mortgage Instruments

The demand and supply problems created by the long-term, fixed-rate mortgage in an inflationary environment led to a rethinking of the type of residential loan that would serve the needs of the housing sector. Many new mortgage designs were suggested. Some solved the tilt problem, others the interest rate risk problem, and still others both. These **alternative mortgage instruments (AMIs)** are discussed at length in the next chapter. The more popular AMIs are briefly described here.

The graduated-payment mortgage (GPM) was introduced to solve the tilt problem. Different versions were employed, but the main concept was to reduce the initial payment below, and raise the later payment above, that which would be required to amortize the standard fixed-rate loan. The contract rate would be fixed just the same as that on a fixed-rate mortgage (FRM). More total dollars would be repaid by the borrower because of the reduction in initial payments.

One problem with the GPM was its provision for negative amortization. The lower initial payments would be less than the interest due so that the difference would be added to the loan balance. **Negative amortization** occurs when the loan balance grows rather than declines over time. Positive amortization would occur only at about the midpoint in the life of the GPM (12 to 15 years). The rising balance could exceed the value of the property at some point, raising the risk of default. The GPM did not gain wide acceptance until the FHA insured these loans. When it did, it required larger down payments than on amortizing loans, partially offsetting their advantage of greater affordability.

Another problem of the GPM is one shared with the FRM: that of unanticipated changes in the inflation rate. The contract rate on a GPM is set at the beginning of the loan, so that increases in the actual rate of inflation over the expected rate would lower the real cost to the borrower and lower the real return for the lender.

The shared appreciation mortgage (SAM) was designed to solve this latter problem. With this loan the lender would offer a low contract rate in return for a share of the appreciation of the property at a later date or when sold. The lower rate would make the loan more affordable. Assuming that the property financed with the loan would appreciate in value at a rate equivalent to general inflation, the share of appreciation received by the lender would be a function of the actual rate, not an expected rate. That is, by tying the yield on the loan, *ex post,* to the actual rate of inflation, the problem of unanticipated changes in the inflation rate was avoided.

The maturity mismatch problem is one of interest rate risk. Recall that with interest rate risk, as the market rate rises, the value of the asset declines. The most popular AMI developed to alleviate this problem was the adjustable-rate mortgage (ARM), at first called the variable-rate mortgage. The ARM allows the lender to shift some or all of the interest rate risk to the borrower. In its most simple terms, the ARM provided for a periodic adjustment of the contract rate to reflect more closely the market rate. The maturity of the loan is effectively the length of time selected between adjustments, for example, 1 year. Initially, adjustment terms ranged from 6 months to 5 years. Eventually, the market settled on the 1-year adjustment period as the most popular term. ARMs are usually amortized over 30 years, just as with FRMs, so that default risk is not as much an issue as with GPMs. Thus, regardless of the periodic interest rate adjustments, the ARM will fully amortize to a zero balance over 30 years.

A thrift with a portfolio of 1-year ARMs and liabilities consisting of 1-year deposits would have no maturity mismatch and no interest rate risk. Most borrowers were not willing to accept a transfer of the total amount of interest rate risk to themselves. Eventually, lenders retained some of the risk by agreeing to limits (caps) on the periodic change in the rate or on the maximum rate over the life of the loan.

Because some of the interest rate risk has been shifted to the borrower and the fact that the periodic adjustments effectively create a series of short-term loans, the initial contract rate on an ARM is less than that on an FRM of the same maturity. One way to compare FRMs and ARMs is to think of the FRM as one 30 year loan whereas a 1-year adjustable ARM is a series of 30 1-year loans. This alleviated the affordability problem in a high-interest-rate era but did not completely eliminate it. There is evidence to suggest that borrowers prefer ARMs when interest rates are high because of the increase in affordability.

One AMI was designed to alleviate both supply and demand problems. The **price level adjusted mortgage (PLAM)** provides for an initial contract rate equal to the real rate. Recall that the nominal rate is the sum of the real rate and the inflation rate. Thus, this contract rate would be less than what is normally observed. The low monthly payment that results helps solve the tilt and affordability problem. Each year thereafter, the balance of the loan and, thus, the payment would be adjusted to reflect changes in inflation. The annual adjustment would be that year's actual rate of inflation multiplied by the ending loan balance. If no inflation occurred, there would be no adjustment, and the lender would receive the real rate of return. The PLAM loan has complicated features that are difficult for the average homeowner to understand. Perhaps for this reason, it never gained popularity. In 1990 the FHA began to explore the possibility of insuring PLAMS but, to date, has not done so.

Continued Growth of the Secondary Market

With the maturity mismatch problem continuing throughout the 1970s, the activities of the federally related agencies (FNMA, GNMA, FHLMC) continued to grow in scope and importance. By 1980 the agencies held (or guaranteed the debt backed by mortgages) slightly more than one-fifth of all mortgage debt outstanding. Lenders were beginning to realize the risk of holding loans in their own portfolios. The prepayment option granted in the typical mortgage magnified this risk. In addition, there was the assumability option. All FHA and VA loans and some conventional loans could be assumed by the buyer of the residence. Under an assumption the buyer "assumes" the liability of, and promises to make the payments on, the existing loan. The assumability option has intrinsic value whenever the current market rate exceeds the contract rate on the mortgage. The seller of the house can pass on the low-rate loan to the buyer, capturing its value in terms of a higher selling price for the property. The seller-mortgagor and buyer benefit at the expense of the lender, who continues to carry a low-rate loan in a period of high market rates. This option, like the prepayment option, has greater value when interest rates are perceived to be more volatile. The two options combined cause interest rate risk to be very burdensome for thrifts when interest rate volatility is high.

The high and volatile interest rates of the late 1970s convinced many lenders to shift the interest rate risk to organizations and investors that were better prepared to handle it. They did so by selling off the mortgages which they originated to the secondary market operators (FNMA, FHLMC, GNMA). In many cases lenders were not even willing to assume the interest rate risk that would exist between the point of origination and point of sale. They were willing to pay the agencies for a commitment to purchase the mortgages at a future date for a given price. The growth of the secondary market participants continued at high levels through the next decade and into the 90's as well.

THE 1980s: DEREGULATION, THE GROWTH OF ALTERNATIVE MORTGAGE INSTRUMENTS, AND THE THRIFT CRISES

From the passage of the Financial Institutions Deregulation and Monetary Control Act (MCA) of 1980 to the passage of the Financial Reform, Recovery, and Enforcement Act (FIRREA) of 1989, this decade witnessed the greatest changes in the residential finance market since the 1930s. The changes were brought about by the recognition of the interest rate risk facing traditional mortgage lenders in the inflationary and volatile interest rate environment of the early part of the decade.

Interest Rate Risk Increases: Value of Assumption Option Becomes an Issue

To appreciate the problems faced by lenders, we will analyze briefly the value of the assumability option discussed above. In 1982 the market rate on mortgages was approximately 15 percent. A 10-year-old loan originated in 1972 would have a contract rate near 7.5 percent. Now, consider the numbers for a typical 30-year loan originated in 1972. With an initial balance of, say, $60,000, the monthly principal and interest payment would be $419. The balance 10 years later in 1982 would be $52,077. If the buyer of a house financed with this loan could assume the loan, she would realize considerable savings. The payment on a new 15 percent loan for $52,077, amortized over 20 years (the remaining life of the old loan), would be $685.74. The assumption results in a monthly savings of $266.75. The seller of the house would be able to obtain a higher price than he would if the loan was nonassumable. That is, the seller is not only selling bricks and mortar, he is selling a monthly payment savings of some magnitude. Later, in

Chapter 7, we will see that economists have been able to verify that houses with assumable mortgages sell for higher prices than their counterparts with nonassumable mortgages when market rates are high.

The value of the assumability option was an issue in the high-interest-rate environment of the early 1980s. Lenders sought to eliminate its value for conventional mortgages through the due-on-sale clause in the mortgage or deed-of-trust.[2] Essentially, the due-on-sale clause stipulated that the entire amount of the remaining balance was due to the lender in the event of a sale of the property. Lenders began to insert the clause more frequently as interest rates rose during the 1970s. By the 1990s, virtually all conventional mortgages had this clause. FHA and VA mortgages continue to be assumable, but recent loans require credit approval of the buyers by these agencies.

The value of the assumability option was so great at times that borrowers fought to recover its value even for loans that had the due-on-sale clause. Borrowers fought in two ways—by attempting to conceal the sale from the lender and by litigating in court. As one can imagine, given the large value of an assumability option in a high-interest-rate period, borrowers would attempt to capture the value by concealing the sale in a variety of ways. Some ways are rather obvious. For example, rather than sell the property, sellers would simply enter into a long-term lease, giving the lessee an option to buy at the end of the lease for a nominal amount. In this way the buyer (who is, in reality, a lessee) makes lease payments that are lower than what the principal and interest payments would be on a new loan, yet greater than the current payments made by the seller (the lessor). The lessor continues to be the owner-of-record and makes the payments on the loan to the lender. At the end of the lease the buyer (lessor) has the right to purchase the property for a nominal amount. The transaction derives value from a continuation of the old, low-rate loan.

Another method employed to retain the value of the low-rate loan in the face of a due-on-sale clause is the land sales contract, or contract for deed. Under this arrangement the seller and the buyer enter into a contract. The seller promises to deliver the deed to the property at some time in the future. The buyer, in consideration for this promise, agrees to make monthly payments for the period of the contract. Title to the property remains in the hands of the seller, who continues to make the payments on the original loan to the lender. This type of arrangement has risk, especially for the buyer. If he should fail to make some of the payments required under the contract, he may be left with no property interest at all. The seller could void the contract, and the buyer may have no recourse. These contracts were very popular in the early 1980s as a way to avoid triggering the due-on-sale clause.

Still another method to circumvent the clause is to transfer the property into a trust for the owner's benefit. Instead of the property being sold, the beneficial use of the property would be transferred.

Sellers and buyers of residential properties also sought to preserve the value of low-rate loans through litigation. Lenders had gradually increased their use of the clause in trust deeds. The trust deed would also indicate the types of actions that would trigger the clause. As borrowers sought additional ways to avoid the exercise of the clause, more conditions were included in the deeds. The three most popular actions that would trigger the clause include a sale, lease, or further encumbrance of the property. These maneuvers led to several test cases, the most famous of which was the Wellenkamp decision in California (1978). To understand the arguments in this case, one should review pre-Wellenkamp litigation in that state.

Wellenkamp Case

At first the courts viewed the due-on-sale clause as a restraint on the free transfer of property rights. Although an early case allowed a "reasonable" enforcement of the clause (*Coast Bank* v. *Minderhout,* 1964, 61 C2d 311), most cases did not allow for its enforcement unless there was a deleterious impact on the security for the loan. In other words, the courts were reluctant to allow the lender to enforce the clause for the purpose of increasing its profits (removing a low-rate loan from its portfolio), but did allow its enforcement where the sale resulted in an impairment of the security for the loan. At the time it was not much of an issue because market rates and contract rates were nearly identical. In the late 1960s the situation changed, and the court held that it was reasonable for the clause to be enforced for the purpose of portfolio restructuring (*Cherry* v. *Home Savings and Loan Association,* 1969, 276 CA2d 574). However, the California State Supreme Court reversed this thinking and ruled that economic considerations other than security impairment could not be used to justify enforcement of the clause (*LaSala* v. *American Savings and Loan Association,* 1971, 5 CA3d 865). The action that triggered the clause in this case was further encumbrance of the property. The lender claimed that the junior mortgage required the borrower to make additional payments and the security of the first loan was impaired. The court rejected this argument. Although the junior financing had additional risk, the original loan was exposed to no greater risk because it stood first to collect any proceeds from the liquidation of the property just as it originally did. Essentially, the court said, trust deeds are to be used to mitigate default risk and not interest rate risk.

In 1974 the California courts once again rejected profit or portfolio considerations as a justification for enforcing the due-on-sale clause (*Tucker* v. *Lassen Savings and Loan Association,* 1974, 12 C3d 629). In this case a land sales contract had triggered the clause.

Up to this time, no case involved a regular sale of the property as a trigger for enforcement of the clause. It was not certain how the courts would rule in such a case. However, in 1978 they followed their previous decisions and rejected the automatic use of the clause in a regular sale where there was no impairment of the lender's security interest (*Wellenkamp* v. *Bank of America,* 1978, 21 C3d 943). The Wellenkamps had contracted to sell their residence to a physician and his wife. They argued that the credit rating of the buyers was so good as to preclude any impairment of the security. Additionally, they argued, the equity in the property was significant. The lenders argued that they had made the original loan on the basis of the credit risk of the Wellenkamps and should not be placed in the position of accepting the credit risk of the buyers. Of course, the lender's motive for the enforcement of the clause was undoubtedly the disparity between the market rate and the contract rate on the loan. This was a period of rising rates, and lenders stood to suffer great losses if they could not enforce the due-on-sale clause for the conventional loans in their portfolio.

Federal Regulators and the Assumability Issue

Federal regulators such as the Federal Home Loan Bank Board (now the Office of Thrift Supervision) were concerned about the profitability of their member associations at this time. They could not keep the interest cost of funds artificially low (through Regulation Q) forever. Money market funds provided small savers with alternatives, and disintermediation was a constant threat. They saw the need for members to be able to raise the yield on their mortgage portfolio when properties with low-rate loans were sold. They directed their members to enforce the clause. As a result, a California case made it to the Supreme Court of the United States in June 1982. The U.S. Supreme Court agreed with the Federal Home Loan Bank Board and allowed the automatic enforcement of the clause for all federally chartered thrifts (*Fidelity Federal Savings and Loan Association* v. *de le Cuesta,* 1982, 458 U.S. 141). Here, the Court indicated that the regulator's requirement to assure the solvency of the nation's thrifts overrode the individual borrower's right to transfer the property with the original financing.

Because of the conflict between the state courts (at least in California) and the FHLBB regulations for federally chartered institutions, there was a period of time during which state-chartered institutions were unable to enforce the due-on-sale clause. In 1982, however, the Garn–St. Germain Act, among other things, allowed state chartered (but federally insured) thrifts to enforce the clause. It thereby established a "window period," during which loans originated or assumed by state-chartered thrifts were exempt from the enforcement of the clause while those originated by federally chartered thrifts were not. That period ran from August 25, 1978, the date of the Wellenkamp decision, to October 15, 1982, the date of the Garn Act. The Act also gave the Federal Home Loan Bank Board the authority to stipulate what actions would trigger the due-on-sale clause. In May and July 1983 the Board issued a set of regulations that spelled out the actions that would trigger the clause. The actions generally relate to a sale, a long-term lease, a lease with an option to buy, a foreclosure on a second deed of trust, a land sale contract (contract for deed), or transfer of the property into a trust.

The stakes involved in the above litigation were not insignificant. With very high interest rates in the late 1970s and early 1980s, thrifts stood to lose (and borrowers gain) large sums through the inability to enforce the due-on-sale clause on conventional mortgages. In California alone, the wealth transfer resulting from the Wellenkamp decision was substantial. By comparing the financial statements and the turnover of conventional mortgages of state and federally chartered savings and loans from 1978 through 1981, Larry Ozanne was able to estimate the magnitude of the wealth transfer.[3] You will recall that during this period the state-chartered associations were not able to enforce the clause, while the federally chartered associations were. Ozanne estimated the net income of the state associations in California was between $58 and $170 million less in 1981 than it would have been had they been able to enforce the due-on-sale clause. In the same year the yield on their loan portfolio was between 0.15 and 0.30 percent less than it otherwise would have been. The market value of their mortgage portfolio was reduced by between $56 and $206 million. The wealth transfer estimated by Ozanne is an indication of the value of the assumability option in residential mortgages that lack a due-on-sale clause. Wealth is transferred from the lender and may be shared by the seller and buyer of the property. A portion of the value of the option is captured by the home seller in the form of higher property prices. The early 1980s was a period in which home prices were affected as much by the terms of financing as by the homes' physical characteristics. It was the era of nonmarket or creative financing.

The Era of Creative Financing

Creative financing refers to sale of real estate with terms of financing that are different from those on new loans with terms established by current market forces. Creative financing has a long history. It was used frequently in the sale of raw or agricultural land shortly after the federal tax law established separate rates for ordinary income and capital gains (1930s and 1940s). A buyer could either finance the purchase with a loan from a third-party lender or a loan from the seller (assuming the seller had no immediate need for cash). In the former case the buyer would pay the market value of the land since he was obtaining market-value financing. Sellers of land realized that they could get a higher-than-market-value price for the property if they were willing to finance the sale themselves at a below-market rate of interest. In this case the buyer would have a larger indebtedness because of the higher price, but because of the lower interest rate, the size of the payment would not be larger than on a conventional loan.[4] In other words, the payment that the buyer would make on the lower rate higher amount loans from the seller would equal that on a higher rate lower amount loan from a third-party lender. If all that mattered to the buyer was the size of the payment, then he would have no preference between the two ways of financing the property.

In the process of arranging the transaction in this manner, the seller would realize a higher capital gains on the sale but would receive lower interest income (ordinary income) in the future. Ordinary income was shifted to capital gains income, and a lower overall tax bill was the result. This was so until the IRS began to impute a (near) market rate on owner-financed loans with rates substantially below market. Later, tax laws eliminated the distinction between ordinary income and capital gains.

The same process developed with regard to residential property transactions in the late 1970s and early 1980s. Because market interest rates were rising rapidly, there were many cases where residential loans had below-market terms. While summarized here, these are discussed in greater detail in Chapter 7.

Government-underwritten Loans

Nonconventional, or creative, financing occurred in several forms. A moderate form was related to government-underwritten loans (FHA, VA). FHA and VA were concerned with default risk and believed that this risk could be lessened by keeping the borrower's payments as low as possible.[5] For this reason the agencies, until the late 1980s, set a maximum, or ceiling, rate of interest on loans that they insured. As long as the market rate on conventional loans was equal to or below that on the ceiling, the terms of each type were identical. If the agencies were slow to respond, rising market rates could exceed the ceiling, sometimes by a substantial margin. Lenders would prefer to originate conventional loans with their higher yield unless they could somehow raise the yield on government-underwritten loans above the ceiling. They did so by discounting.

Consider the following equation for an FHA loan when the market rate *rm* equals the ceiling rate *rc:*

$$BAL = \frac{PMT}{(1 + rc)^1} + \frac{PMT}{(1 + rc)^2} + \cdots + \frac{PMT}{(1 + rc)^{360}} \qquad \text{(Equation 5–1)}$$

The payment, PMT, is set by amortizing the loan over 30 years at the ceiling rate *rc* (which is the same as the market rate *rm*). It is the same payment that would be set on a conventional loan. What happens if the market rate is above the ceiling rate and the lender desires to obtain the market rate on this loan? The lender is unable to raise the payment, PMT, because it must be set with reference to the ceiling rate and the 30-year amortization period. The only term in the equation that can be altered is the amount of the loan. The lender can lower the amount originated, BAL, by charging discount points. A charge of two discount points would reduce the BAL to 0.98 BAL and raise the effective yield (see Chapter 4). The greater the amount of the discount, the greater the impact on the effective yield.

Table 5–5 shows the FHA-VA ceiling rate, the market rate on conventional loans, the spread between those rates, and the discount points charged on government-underwritten loans for selected months from 1978 through 1983. These data are displayed in Figure 5–2 and demonstrate the effect of the spread between the rates on the points charged. Lenders have an opportunity to invest in conventional loans and will charge sufficient points on FHA loans to make risk-adjusted yields on the two types of loans comparable.

When market rates were substantially higher than the ceiling rates, FHA and VA loans were attractive to buyers because the agencies ruled that the buyer of a residence financed by an underwritten loan could not be required to pay the discount points established by the lender. This meant that the seller of the residence had to pay the discount points. A lender making a $50,000 FHA or VA loan with three discount points charges $1500 for the loan. If the buyer is not required to pay the points, he receives the benefit of the below-market-rate financing without incurring the cost established by the lender.

On the other side, the seller of the house would prefer to sell with conventional financing rather than pay the discount points. The seller would agree to government-underwritten financing only if the property sold for $1500 more than if financed with a conventional loan. Since the

TABLE 5–5

Maximum Allowable FHA Rate, Conventional Mortgage Yields, and FHA Discount Points: Selected Months, 1978–1983

Date	Maximum FHA Rate	Conventional Yield[a]	Yield Spread	Points[b]
3/78	8.75	9.40	0.65	2.30
6/78	9.00	9.80	0.80	3.30
5/79	10.00	10.90	0.90	2.50
11/79	11.50	12.50	1.00	3.50
3/80	13.00	15.50	2.55	5.50
6/80	11.50	13.25	1.75	2.00
10/80	13.00	14.70	1.70	5.00
6/81	15.50	16.70	1.20	3.25
12/81	15.50	17.00	1.50	3.25
2/82	16.50	17.20	0.70	2.25
4/82	15.50	16.65	1.15	3.00
9/82	14.00	15.05	1.05	0.25
12/82	12.00	13.62	1.62	3.00
9/83	13.00	13.60	0.60	2.00

[a]Source: Federal Reserve Bulletin, various issues.
[b]Points were computed from data on maximum allowable yield and yield-to-maturity on FHA loans, HUD series, assuming 10-year maturity.

FIGURE 5–2

Discount Points and FHA-Market Yield Spread: 1978–83

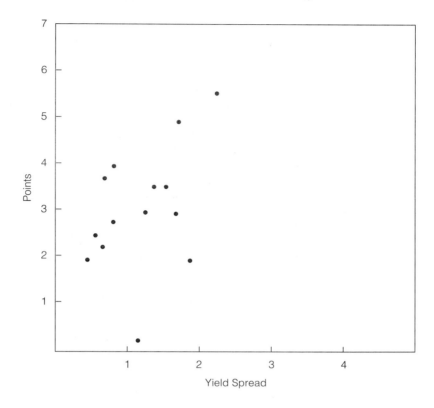

buyer is receiving below-market financing, he may agree to pay more for the property, circumventing the prohibition against the borrower paying the points. In the end, the buyer receiving the low-rate financing pays for the discount points in the form of a higher property price. The transaction price reflects the terms of financing. In Chapter 7, we will review some studies that determined the extent to which FHA-VA points were capitalized into house prices.

Assumable Loans

During this time in which all FHA and VA loans were assumable, some conventional loans lacked a due-on-sale clause, and the clause was found to be unenforceable in others (until 1982). The **assumable loan** is attached to the property, just as a physical characteristic such as a pool, fireplace, or garage. The sale price of a house should reflect the "value" of the assumable loan. It will be shown in Chapter 7 that a buyer of the property could pay more than he or she would for an identical property without an assumable loan and have the same monthly payments. It will also be shown that, for various reasons, the actual "value" of the assumable loan may be less than the present value of the payment savings. Also in Chapter 7, we will discuss the intriguing reasons for this anomaly and review several studies that determined the extent to which the value of assumable loans were included in transaction prices during the early 1980s.

Wraparound Loans

A wraparound loan is a way to obtain additional financing while keeping an existing loan in place. The wrap is a junior mortgage that "wraps" around an existing loan. The amount of the wrap would equal the balance of the existing loan plus whatever additional amount of funds is loaned. The wrap borrower acknowledges (by virtue of the wrapping) the existence of the original loan but accepts no liability for this loan. The original borrower who is now the wrap lender remains liable for making the payments on the original loan. Sometimes the wrap lender may be a third party who has assumed responsibility for the original mortgage. Thus the buyer who is the wrap borrower accepts the property "subject to" the existing mortgage. The process would proceed as thus: the wrap borrower would make the wrap mortgage payment to the wrap lender who in turn would make the payment on the original loan.

Although this process is complex, there are incentives for using this financing structure. Essentially the wrap loan provides additional funds to the borrower above the amount of the existing mortgage. So why not just take a second mortgage for that amount? The answer lies in the advantages to both the borrower and lender. The wrap can allow the borrower to obtain financing at a lower cost than the average cost of her first and second mortgages. For the wrap lender, it is an opportunity to leverage off the existing mortgage and enhance the return to the wrap loan. An example is provided in Chapter 7.

Because the wrap borrower is not responsible for the payments on the original loan, procedures should be put in place to ensure that these payments are made. One way to accomplish this is to require the payments to be made through an escrow arrangement. In fact, all payments could be made through the escrow agent such that all parties are provided some protection.

Wraparound loans may be used in a variety of situations:

- When the interest rate on the existing mortgage is well below the current market rate. This provides an incentive to retain this loan.
- When the property owner wishes to sell a property that has a mortgage with a prepayment lockout. This complicates the sale of the property since the loan cannot be repaid before the lockout period ends. A wrap may provide a means to sell the property.
- When a wrap loan provides the buyer/wrap borrower a way to obtain a higher loan-to-value ratio than what institutional lenders may be willing to grant in either a first or second mortgage.

A seller wishing to do a wrap should seek approval of the arrangement from her original lender. Problems may arise when a wrap is used with an existing mortgage that is not assumable. The sale of the property could trigger the due-on-sale clause in the original mortgage. An assumable mortgage allows a wrap to be done by a third party. This may be an individual or a financial institution. For example, a bank may assume the existing loan from the original lender and become a wrap lender to the buyer of the property.

Buydown Financing

A **buydown mortgage** is a fixed-rate mortgage in which the seller prepays some of the loan interest to "buy down" the interest rate for the buyer/borrower for some period. This type of financing becomes more popular in periods of high interest rates (such as the early 1980s). The seller is usually a builder seeking to promote home sales in a slow market. The buydown allows the borrower to acquire cheaper financing in the early life of the loan. A typical buydown would be: the prepaid interest buys down the borrower's interest rate by 300 basis points, 200 basis points, and 100 basis points over the first 3 years of loan life, respectively. Suppose the contract rate on the loan is 10 percent. This buydown would give the borrower interest rates of 7 percent, 8 percent, and 9 percent, respectively, over the first 3 years. These lower rates would be reflected in a lower payment for the borrower. In the fourth year the payment reverts to normal since the contract rate is now being charged.

The good news with a buydown is that the lower initial payments may allow the buyer/borrower to qualify for the loan when she otherwise might have problems. The bad news is that, as with other types of favorable financing, the seller will likely attempt to capture the value of the buydown into the price of the property.

The secondary mortgage market places certain restrictions on buydowns to make them acceptable for purchase. These restrictions have to do with the amount of contribution the seller can make (10 percent of the lesser of sales price or appraised value for loans of 90 percent or less, for example) and the extent to which the borrower's effective interest rate can move (usually not more than 1 percent per period). Buydowns are permissible on one- to four-unit properties and on a variety of loan types, including fixed-rate, adjustable-rate, and graduated-payment mortgages. An example of a buydown is provided in Chapter 7.

Owner Financing

During periods of high interest rates, sellers often found it difficult to obtain what they believed to be the value of their property. Other sellers with assumable loans, as in the preceding example, had built up substantial equity in their property. They wanted to capture the added value of the assumable loan in the property price. To do so, they had to find a buyer with a sufficient down payment to assume the loan. In some cases the down payment could be sizable. When no buyers with sufficient cash could be located, sellers would often extend owner-financing at below-market rates. Because of this, the owner-financing itself had value. The value of such financing was often limited by the fact that the seller carryback had a short term, say 3 or 5 years, with a balloon payment. The value of owner carrybacks are discussed in Chapter 7 as well. Taken together, assumable loans and owner carrybacks are referred to as seller-supplied financing and are examples of what came to be termed creative financing.[6]

Widespread Savings and Loan Failures

The 1980s witnessed more problems with the solvency of savings and loan associations than did any other period in history. The problems were caused by a combination of the structure of the industry, regulation, legislation, the economy (especially interest rate volatility during this period), and some dishonest and incompetent management. Table 5–6 provides an overview of the problem. Shown are the effective interest rate on new mortgages, the interest cost of savings deposits, the operating expense ratio, and average net earnings spread on new mortgages for FSLIC-insured institutions from 1979 through 1988. Also shown are the number of insolvent FSLIC-insured savings and loan associations (using Generally Accepted Accounting Principles) and the number of insolvencies resolved by the FSLIC.[7]

The data show a clear picture of the financial problems experienced by thrifts as the decade progressed. The spread between the rate received on new mortgages and that paid on deposits narrowed by more than a percentage point from 3.49 in 1979 to 2.39 in 1987. The rate paid to depositors rose to very high levels in the early to mid-1980s as a result of competition and the removal of Regulation Q limits. Although rates on new mortgage loans rose, they did not keep

T A B L E   5 – 6

Interest Revenue, Interest Costs, and Insolvent Savings and Loans: 1975–1988

Year	Effective Interest Rate on Conventional Loans (New homes)	Effective Interest Cost of Savings Deposits (FSLIC-insured)	Operating Expense Ratio (FSLIC-insured)	Average Net Earnings Spread on Mortgages (New homes)	GAAP Insolvent Institutions	FDIC Insolvency Resolutions
	(1)	(2)	(3)	(1)-(2)-(3)		
1975	9.00	6.21	1.20	1.59	17	11
1976	9.00	6.32	1.20	1.49	48	12
1977	9.00	6.39	1.18	1.45	38	10
1978	9.56	6.56	1.20	1.80	38	4
1979	10.78	7.29	1.25	2.24	34	4
1980	12.66	8.78	1.28	2.60	43	32
1981	14.70	10.71	1.38	2.61	85	82
1982	15.14	11.19	1.44	2.51	237	247
1983	12.57	9.71	1.50	1.36	293	70
1984	12.38	9.93	1.57	0.88	445	36
1985	11.55	9.03	1.83	0.69	470	64
1986	10.17	7.84	1.97	0.36	471	80
1987	9.31	6.92	1.94	0.45	515	77
1988	9.02	6.58	1.95	0.49	364	233

pace with those paid on deposits, causing the spread to narrow. Additionally, the yield on the total mortgage portfolio of savings and loans lagged below that on new mortgages, due to the slowing of prepayments on existing loans originated earlier in a period of low rates.

The profit squeeze caused by the narrowing of the rate spread was tightened by an increase in the operating expense ratio. As a result, the average net earnings on new mortgages dropped from 2.61 percent in 1980 to 0.45 percent in 1987, the year in which the number of GAAP-insolvent savings and loans reached its peak at 515. Although this causal evidence suggests that the widespread insolvencies had their origin in the maturity mismatch problem, the actual causes were much more varied and intricate. The scenario of thrift failures in this decade is fascinating and can be outlined as follows.

Pre-1982. Regulatory restriction of competition and risk-taking. Financial Institutions Deregulation and Monetary Control Act of 1980.

1982. Competition and incentives for risk-taking introduced; the Garn–St. Germain Act.

1982–1985. Interest rate risk replaced by credit risk; the put option analogy. FSLIC forbearance. Insolvency is a problem, but liquidity is not.

1985–1988. Insolvency leads to risk-taking, which in turn leads to further insolvency. The **"zombie"** theory of the spread of thrift failure.

1988–1989. Bankruptcy costs emerge, deposit rates rise, and thrifts make greater use of nondeposit borrowed funds.

1989. The Bush Initiative and the Financial Institutions Reform, Recovery, and Enforcement Act of 1989.

Pre-1982.   The problems faced by the thrift industry in the late 1980s can be traced to developments in the late 1970s and early 1980s. Prior to the early 1980s, the regulatory agencies acted to limit competition among, and risk-taking by, thrifts. They limited competition by placing ceilings on the rates thrifts could offer on deposits and limited risk-taking by mandating that thrift assets be held primarily in the form of residential mortgages. Although the Monetary Control Act of 1980 would provide for the gradual elimination of deposit ceilings, by the mid-1980s their effectiveness began to erode prior to their complete elimination. The competition from money market funds forced thrifts to rely on a greater use of borrowed funds (from the Federal Home Loan Bank Board, among others) and less on deposits. Additionally, the Depository Institutions Deregulation Committee (established by the Monetary Control Act of 1980) began to remove rate ceilings on some designated deposits. In 1982 the committee allowed thrifts to offer a money market deposit account with a rate competitive with money market funds. In January of 1983 rate ceilings were removed on Super Now accounts, and in October of the same year, ceilings were removed on small-time deposits (ceilings remained on deposits of 31 days or less and on balances less than $2500).

Gradually during the early 1980s, deposits subject to ceilings became a smaller fraction of the total. But thrift assets remained primarily long-term, residential mortgages or mortgage-backed securities. The maturity mismatch problems surfaced during a period of rising interest rates, with predictable results. Table 5–7 shows the interest income and expense structure for all FSLIC-insured savings and loans for this period. As interest expenses increased dramatically, interest revenue rose modestly, producing losses in 1981 and 1982. Interest revenue rose slowly due to the drop in the prepayment rate of old, low-rate mortgages. The proportion of mortgages

TABLE 5–7
Income and Expense as a Percentage of Average Assets
(FSLIC insured institutions)

	1979	*1980*	*1981*	*1982*	*1983*
Gross operating income	9.03	9.50	10.29	10.69	10.66
Gross interest expense	6.77	8.03	10.00	10.51	9.02
Net interest margin	2.26	1.47	0.29	0.18	1.64
After-tax income	0.67	0.13	−0.73	−0.64	0.26

prepaid annually fell from a range of 12 to 14 percent in the late 1970s to approximately 6 percent in 1981. The maturity mismatch problem caused widespread losses for thrifts. Although there was some recovery with the decline in rates in 1983, a substantial number of savings and loans remained insolvent, as indicated by the data in Table 5–6. Furthermore, the numbers would increase throughout the remainder of the decade.

The losses suffered by savings and loans during this time led regulators to take action to shore up the net worth of their troubled members. In late 1981, the FHLBB and the FSLIC created an instrument called the Income Capital Certificate (ICC). Troubled thrifts were allowed to issue a certificate, which the FSLIC purchased for cash or for a promissory note. The intent was to repurchase the certificates when the weak thrifts became profitable. By 1984, a total of 93 FSLIC-insured institutions had $852 million of these certificates outstanding. Since many of the certificates were issued in exchange for promissory notes, there was little inflow of cash to troubled thrifts. Instead, there was an accounting transaction, whereby the institution would add the amount of the certificate to its net worth and to its assets (the promissory note). In this manner the FSLIC avoided the task of closing institutions with negative net worth.

1982—The Garn–St. Germain Act.

The Garn–St. Germain Act hastened the removal of limits on deposit rates, expanded the types of assets that thrifts could invest in, and instituted measures to alleviate, or "hide," the problem of insolvent thrifts.

With reference to thrift institutions, the Act (1) authorized a savings account to compete with money market funds; (2) authorized a public NOW account; (3) preempted state restrictions on due-on-sale clause enforcement by state-chartered lenders that were insured by the FSLIC (the Supreme Court had, at this time, cleared the way for enforcement of the clause by federally chartered thrifts); (4) called for the savings account interest differential between banks and thrifts to be phased out by 1984; (5) provided FSLIC and FDIC assistance in shoring up the net worth of deficient institutions; (6) facilitated the conversion of thrifts from the mutual to the stock form; (7) allowed thrifts to invest in commercial, agricultural, and consumer loans, as well as other investments, such as real estate development projects; (8) permitted investment in personal property for lease up to 10 percent of assets; and (9) allowed bank holding companies to acquire thrifts across state lines.

Together, these provisions were intended to accomplish at least two broad goals: reduce the maturity mismatch problem, with its attendant interest rate risk, and avoid the cost of resolution of troubled thrifts by reducing or eliminating the negative net worth of many savings and loan associations.

Maturity Mismatch and Interest Rate Risk.

The Garn–St. Germain Act sought to reduce the maturity mismatch problem by giving thrifts the power to diversify their assets beyond long-term, fixed-rate, residential loans. By including short-term real estate development loans, commercial loans, personal loans, and other short-term investments in their asset portfolio, the thrifts would lower the overall maturity of their respective portfolios. Preempting state restrictions on the ability of state-chartered lenders to enforce a due-on-sale clause reduced the number of low-rate mortgages that were assumed on the sale of residences. This provision had the effect of reducing the maturity of the residential-loan portion of thrift portfolios.

Negative Net Worth (Insolvency) of Thrifts.

The resolution of insolvent thrifts proved to be an expensive undertaking for the FSLIC. Basically, the FSLIC had to make good on the amount of the negative net worth. In 1982, at the time of the Garn–St. Germain Act, the FSLIC and federal regulators preferred to address the negative net worth problem in less expensive ways, mainly by keeping the troubled thrifts artificially afloat. The act authorized the issuance of Net Worth Certificates by institutions that had suffered declines in net worth, primarily as a result of interest rate movements and maturity mismatch. The FDIC and FSLIC were permitted to acquire the certificates, which operated similarly to the Income Capital Certificates issued in 1981. They were a temporary solution and represented no real cash infusion into capital. Troubled thrifts that desired to avoid closure issued net worth certificates. By mid-1984, 93 FSLIC-insured savings and loans, with 10 percent of the industry's assets, had issued $852 million in Net Worth Certificates. Only 31 of these institutions were profitable by the second quarter of 1984.

Although the act appeared to accomplish its two main goals, the results were short-lived and created longer-term problems. Thrifts were allowed to invest in shorter-term, but more risky, assets. Many did and, in the process, substituted default risk for interest rate risk. As the following text explains, the system created incentives for risk-taking by thrifts. They responded, and over the next several years, the number of troubled thrifts expanded. Furthermore, the situation was worsened by the FSLIC's failure to close troubled thrifts. They did the exact opposite, shoring them up with accounting transactions that were regulatory additions to net worth and not cash additions.

1982–1985—Incentives for Risk-Taking and FSLIC Forbearance. The equity position in a stock form of savings and loan (or any corporation, for that matter) is similar to holding a put option on the firm's assets. First, consider a nonfinancial corporation. The stockholders that own the equity position also hold an option. If the firm does well, any excess operating cash flows over those paid to the debtholders belong to the stockholders. There is no theoretical limit to the amount of such excess cash flows. If the firm does poorly and has several years of operating losses, the value of the equity position will decline. Given sufficient losses, the value of the equity may go to zero. Stockholders will lose the value of their equity but no more (given limited liability). At the point where the equity (net worth) becomes negative, the value of the debt exceeds the value of the assets. The stockholders will "put" the assets of the firm to the debtholders in satisfaction of the debt.

The same is true for savings and loan associations. In this case, the debtholders are, for the most part, either insured depositors of the institution or the FHLBB. The stockholders desire to maximize the value of their equity. In the case of insolvent thrifts, the value may already be negative. For those thrifts the stockholders have an incentive to take on very risky investments. If the investments perform exceptionally well, the net worth may become positive. If they do not, the stockholders are in no worse position than they were before taking on the risky investments. They will put the (low-valued) assets to the debtholders.

In this case the debtholders are insured against losses by the Treasury-backed FSLIC. In essence, the stockholders have an option to put the assets of insolvent thrifts to the taxpayers. The management of insolvent thrifts also has an incentive to undertake risky investments. If the investments succeed, their employment is secured. If they fail, they also are in no worse position.

The undertaking of risky investments by insolvent thrifts was aided by FSLIC forbearance. Instead of giving equity owners the option of either infusing more cash capital into insolvent thrifts or facing liquidation, the FSLIC allowed many troubled institutions to continue to operate and undertake risky investments. The regulators took actions that gave many troubled thrifts the appearance of accounting solvency even though they were economically insolvent. They did this in two ways: by regulatory additions to net worth and by allowing accounting practices that were at variance with Generally Accepted Accounting Principles.

We already discussed two examples of regulatory, noncash additions to thrift net worth: Income Capital Certificates (1981) and Net Worth Certificates (1982). In addition, the FHLBB authorized FSLIC-insured institutions to add "appraised equity capital" to their net worth in 1982. The appraised equity capital was a one-time adjustment reflecting the difference between the market value and the book value of the thrift's capital assets, which primarily consisted of the thrift's own real estate (building and land). Since they were not required to write down any portfolio assets that may have declined in value, this regulatory addition to net worth led to a biased inflation of the net worth of institutions that elected to add appraised equity to their capital.

Regulatory Accounting Practices Versus Generally Accepted Accounting Principles. Prior to the FIRREA (discussed below), federal regulators allowed thrifts to account for certain income statement and balance sheet items in a manner different from rules imposed on nonfinancial businesses by Generally Accepted Accounting Principles (GAAP). These Regulatory Accounting Practices (RAP) generally allowed thrifts to overstate income or net worth. That is, RAP versus GAAP led to an understatement of the true number of unprofitable and insolvent thrifts during the mid- to late 1980s. The understatement of the number of thrifts that should have been either closed or required to raise more capital from stockholders masked the serious-

FIGURE 5-3

Major Differences in RAP vs GAAP

Income Statement Items

Deferral of gains and losses on assets
Accretion of discounts on securities
Commitment fees
Origination fees

Balance Sheet Items

Definition of net worth and regulatory additions to net worth
Treatment of assets in mergers
Marketable equity securities recorded at cost
Liquid Asset Mutual Funds

ness of the problem. This is how the accounting rules led to an understatement of the insolvency problem. Figure 5–3 shows the accounting statement items most affected by the discrepancy between RAP and GAAP.

RAP allowed thrifts the choice of whether or not to report the gains or losses on the disposition of certain assets. Naturally, given a choice, institutions that had losses on sales of qualifying assets would choose to defer recording the loss, while institutions with gains would choose to record the gain. GAAP requires that all losses and gains be recognized in the income statement. RAP allowed thrifts to record accrued income, using the life of the security or 10 years, whichever is shorter. GAAP requires the accretion to be recorded over the life of the security. When a security is purchased at a discount under its face value, the buyer should record an amount of annual appreciation in income. Assume that a security with a face (maturity) value of $1000 and an expected life of 20 years is purchased for $800. For each of the 20 years, the investor receives a portion of the $200 difference in addition to any coupon payments. If the $200 gain is included in income over a 10-year period, rather than 20 as required by GAAP, reported income will be greater in the early years of the investment. This distorts the income statement by making the thrift appear more profitable in the early years.

Commitment fees are charged by lenders to lock the rate on a mortgage of the borrower. To avoid the risk that rates will rise between the time of application for the loan and the time the loan is made (often several months later), borrowers will pay a commitment fee, which is expressed as a percentage of the loan. Under RAP, thrifts were allowed to include the fee in current income. The maximum amount that could be included was 1 percent for a commitment period less than 1 year, 1.5 percent for a period of 12 to 18 months, and 2 percent for periods in excess of 18 months. GAAP, on the other hand, only allowed commitment fees to be included in current income up to the amount of expenses related to retention of the commitment. The remainder had to be amortized over the combined life of the commitment and the loan term.

Origination fees are charged by the lender to originate a mortgage and, like commitment fees, are expressed as a percentage of the loan, usually 1 or 2 percent. RAP allowed these fees to be included in current income, limited to 2 percent (plus $400) on nonconstruction loans and 2.5 percent (plus $400) on construction loans. GAAP, on the other hand, allows origination fees to be included as income only to the extent of costs incurred by the origination process. The remainder must be amortized.

As previously stated, the FSLIC cooperated with thrifts to artificially buoy the net worth of potentially insolvent institutions. They did so by issuing Income Capital Certificates, Net Worth Certificates, and appraised equity capital. These regulatory additions to net worth were included in the definition of net worth under RAP. There were no reductions in net worth under RAP. With GAAP, none of the regulatory additions could have been included. Furthermore, GAAP required the reduction in net worth by a downward adjustment of assets to market value.

An example would be marketable equity securities (stocks) owned by the thrift. Under RAP, the securities could be recorded at cost, whereas GAAP required that they be recorded at market value (and the loss recorded as a deduction in net worth).

To encourage the acquisition of troubled thrifts, the FSLIC allowed mergers with accounting procedures at variance with GAAP. Thrifts were allowed to extend the period of goodwill amortization (thereby reducing annual expenses) to shorten the lives of loans for the purpose of the accretion of a discount, and they were permitted to include cash infusions by the FSLIC as additions to net worth (as opposed to a debt obligation of the thrift to the FSLIC).

RAP and GAAP diverged in other areas (of minor importance), but it was the differences we have discussed that allowed institutions to consistently overrepresent income and net worth. Many troubled institutions with negative intrinsic net worth continued to operate with the aid of additions of regulatory net worth and lax accounting standards. Rather than swiftly closing insolvent thrifts, the FSLIC exacerbated the problem by artificially increasing their reported income and net worth.

1985–1988—The "Zombie" Theory of the Spread of Thrift Failures. Professor Ed Kane describes the "zombie" theory of the spread of thrift problems as follows: A "zombie" is a growth-obsessed insolvent thrift. The intention of such a thrift is to grow out of its problem by taking on high-risk investments. If the investments work out, the thrift survives and becomes profitable. If they do not, the thrift has nothing to lose since the stockholders presently have no positive net worth. Since its debt (deposits) is insured by the FSLIC, the creditors have no incentive to take control away from the stockholders. Thus, despite its negative net worth, the thrift continues to operate, taking on high-risk investments.[8] The stockholders of such thrifts gain when they take on high-risk investments because gains belong to them, whereas losses are passed along to the FSLIC.

The zombies, as Kane calls them, continued to operate and compete aggressively for deposits and loans. Their competition raised the market rate on deposits and lowered the return on loans. The average net earnings spread (Table 5–6) declined each year in the mid- to late 1980s. The aggressive competitive behavior of the zombies caused the profitability and net worth of more conservative thrifts to fall. As their net worth approached zero, they became zombies as well. By 1987, GAAP counted a record 515 insolvent institutions.

The zombie population of thrifts grew for three reasons. First, the monitoring of troubled thrifts by the FSLIC proved to be inadequate after the fact. It appears that bureaucrats preferred to pass on the problem to their successors. Second, stockholders of troubled thrifts were not required to recapitalize (put up more personal capital). Third, the problem of inadequately capitalized thrifts was masked by accounting rules (RAP) that made zombies appear to be viable institutions.

1989—The Bush Initiative and the Financial Institutions Reform, Recovery, and Enforcement Act. On February 6, 1989, President Bush announced a plan to resolve the growing thrift crisis. The plan was intended, according to the President, to restructure the regulation of the savings and loan industry, improve supervisory controls to prevent abuses, increase the financial strength of the FSLIC, increase penalties for fraud, create a new corporation to handle the closing of insolvent thrifts, and begin placing these institutions under the control of the government in an orderly manner. The initiative was submitted to Congress and, after several revisions, was passed in August as the **Financial Institutions Reform, Recovery, and Enforcement Act (FIRREA).**

FIRREA attempted to solve the problem of insolvent thrifts by, in part, separating them from their former regulatory agency. First, it replaced the FSLIC with the Resolution Trust Corporation (RTC) and placed it under the control of the FDIC. The RTC was given 7 years to dispose of assets acquired when the FSLIC took over failed thrifts. This was done to make the insurance fund more independent of the industry.

Second, the act changed the FHLBB to the Office of Thrift Supervision (OTS) and placed it within the Department of the Treasury. This was done to remove any conflict of interest between the supervisory agency and the insurance fund. Third, the act established a set of capital requirements, including one that is risk-based. A risk-based capital requirement is one that requires the thrift to have more capital (net worth) if its assets are in higher-risk classes. In addition, the act required that overall capital be at least 3 percent of assets and at least 1.5 percent of tangible assets. (Tangible assets are all assets other than goodwill.) Thus, when goodwill is included in the definition of assets, the capital requirement increases. The new capital requirements were to be phased in over a period of 5 years. In addition, investment in certain assets was prohibited.

Fourth, the act reduced the Loan To One Buyer (LTOB) limit from 100 percent of capital to 15 percent of capital as of August 9, 1989. Fifth, the act required that thrifts report financial statements according to GAAP.

The changes in the rules that regulate the investment behavior of thrifts are outlined in Table 5–8. FIRREA changed the definition of what constituted **Qualified Thrift Investments (QTIs).** It created two classes of QTIs: primary QTIs and secondary QTIs. The latter were created under pressure from advocates of low-income families and other concerned groups. Secondary QTIs include loans for low-income homes, hospitals, nursing homes, and education.

FIRREA also raised the minimum proportion of assets that thrifts had to hold in the form of QTIs from 60 to 70 percent. In 1991, banking reform legislation reduced the ratio to 65 percent and allowed thrifts to meet or exceed the ratio on a monthly average basis in 9 out of every 12 months. Furthermore, the definition of assets used for determining this proportion was changed from net tangible assets to portfolio assets. The former is total assets less goodwill. The latter is more narrowly defined, deleting the value of a thrift's property used for business purposes and liquid assets (such as cash). Although thrifts were allowed several years to meet the new requirements gradually, there was no mandate to divest any currently held loans.

Finally, the new rules prohibited investments in some types of assets altogether. Thrifts could not invest in junk bonds—bonds rated below the top four ratings—or in direct-equity investments, either securities or real estate. Thrifts were given until July 1, 1994, to divest themselves of these types of investments. They could, however, invest up to 3 percent of their assets in service companies (subsidiaries) that could hold such investments.

Despite the ambitious intent of the act, many people remained skeptical of its ability to substantially change the behavior of thrifts. Because of several weaknesses, the act failed to alter substantially the situation that led to the crisis in the first place.

For example, the act allowed the continuation of insurance for large deposits ($100,000) and retained the flat premium schedule for institutions. Although institutions with higher-risk

TABLE 5–8
FIRREA Mandated Changes in Thrift Investments

	Old Rules	*New Rules*
QTI's	60% tangible assets[a]	65% of portfolio assets[b]
Assets included in QTIs:	Residential loans, FHLBB stocks, CDs of other S&Ls. Investments in RELPs, others	1. Primary QTIs (55%); residential loans, home equity loans, mortgage backed securities, obligations of FDIC, RTC, and FSLIC resolution fund, stock of FNMA, FHLMC and FHLB.
		2. Secondary QTIs (15%); 50% of residential loans originated and sold within 90 days, 200% of acquisition development and construction loans for low-priced homes, 200% of residential, church and nursing-home loans in low-income neighborhoods; and consumer and education loans (10%)
Commercial real estate loans	40% of tangible assets	400% of capital[c]
Prohibited investments	None	Junk bonds, direct equity investments in securities and real property.[d]

[a]Total assets less Goodwill.
[b]Total assets less Goodwill less value of property used in business less liquid assets. Original requirement of 70% was reduced to 65% by banking reform legislation in 1991.
[c]No divestiture required.
[d]Divestiture required.

assets were required to have greater capital requirements, they nevertheless continued to pay the same flat insurance premium as institutions with lower-risk assets. In fact, the risk-based capital requirements encouraged thrifts to return to low-risk (default) mortgages, which exposed them once again to interest rate risk. Some also argued that the 5-year phase-in for the new requirements was too long and would allow remaining zombies to continue to operate. Additionally, the act failed to establish a mandatory closure level of capital. One weakness of the pre-act regulatory environment was the failure to close (or require recapitalization of) thrifts as their net worth shrank.

Post-FIRREA Regulatory Structure of the Mortgage Market

Figure 5–4 outlines the changes in the regulatory structure of the mortgage market that resulted from FIRREA. The effects of the changes can be summarized as follows.

Federal Asset Disposition Association.   This agency was established prior to FIRREA to dispose of properties owned by thrifts as a result of foreclosures. It was liquidated by the new RTC.

Federal Deposit Insurance Corporation.   The size of the Board of Directors of this agency was increased from three to five members—Comptroller of the Currency, Director of the Office of Thrift Supervision, and three independent members appointed by the President. This agency took over the supervision of state-chartered thrifts from the FHLBB and became the guarantor of the Savings Association Insurance Fund (SAIF). It also manages the Resolution Trust Corporation.

Federal Housing Finance Board.   This agency was established by FIRREA to oversee the twelve federal home loan banks as a result of the dissolution of the Federal Home Loan Bank Board. The five-member board consists of the Secretary of the Department of Housing and Urban Development and four members appointed by the President. This board oversees the advances of the federal home loan banks to member savings and loans.

Federal Home Loan Bank Board.   Abolished by FIRREA, its employees were allocated to the FDIC, RTC, OTS, and the Federal Housing Finance Board.

Federal Savings and Loan Insurance Corporation (FSLIC).   Also abolished by FIRREA, its insurance activities were transferred to FDIC and OTS.

Office of Thrift Supervision.   This agency took over the duties and powers of the FHLBB and its chairman. Under the supervision of the Treasury Department, it establishes capital requirements for savings and loans. By FIRREA mandate, those capital requirements can be no less stringent than those for national banks.

Resolution Trust Corporation.   Its role was to liquidate and dispose of former FSLIC-insured institutions that were placed into conservatorship in the 3 years after January 1, 1989. It also liquidated the Federal Asset Deposition Association (FADA). Its board consists of five members: the Secretary of HUD, Secretary of the Treasury, Chairman of the Board of Governors of the Federal Reserve System, and two members appointed by the President. The RTC established a real estate asset division that identified properties of significant cultural, recreational, or scientific value.

A 1993 study by Forgey, Goebel, and Rutherford provides a look at the disposition of properties by the RTC for the period August 1989 through June 1992.[9] The top five states by number of RTC sales were Texas, Florida, Arizona, Louisiana, and Colorado, respectively, while the top five types of property by number of sales were single-family homes, condominiums, residential developed land, duplexes, and residential unimproved land, respectively. For all property types the mean sale price was $134,326 while the mean appraised value was $168,353. For single-family homes, the mean sale price was $65,112 with a mean appraised value of $74,764.

FIRREA Mandated Changes in Regulation of Mortgage Market

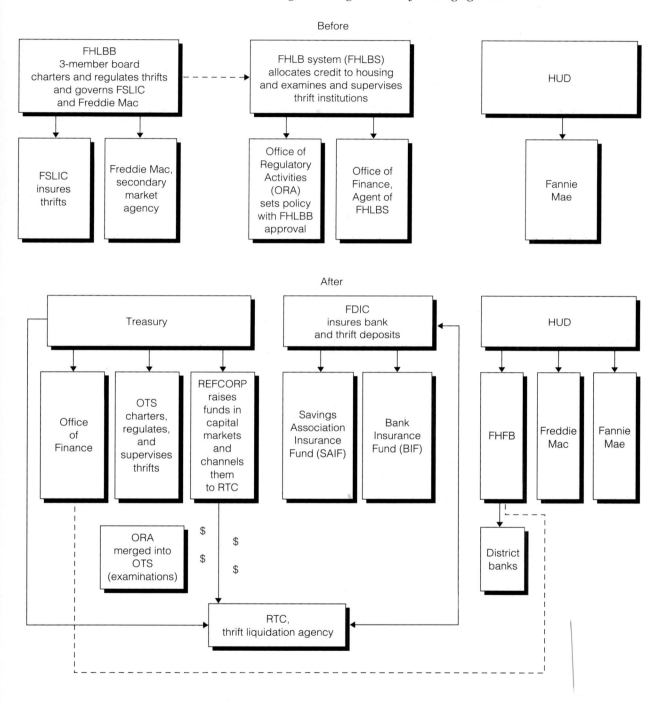

Federal Home Loan Mortgage Corporation (Freddie Mac).   This secondary market agency was given a new, independent board of directors (five appointed by the President and 13 elected by stockholders) and encouraged to expand its purchases of mortgages to include those provided to low- and moderate-income families.

Risk-based Capital Guidelines.   One of the more important provisions of FIRREA was the requirement that thrifts have sufficient capital to absorb risks associated with their assets.

Most nonfinancial corporations will have capital requirements thrust upon them by the rigors of the marketplace. The interest cost on their debt will reflect the risk of their assets and the amount of stockholder equity. Firms with risky assets and little stockholder equity will find the cost of debt (leverage) prohibitive. Regulated financial institutions do not face the same market pressures. Their debt (customer deposits) is insured by the federal government (FDIC and the former FSLIC). Because of federal insurance, depositors will not pressure financial institutions to either invest in less risky assets or obtain sufficient stockholder equity. FIRREA regulations in this area are intended to substitute for market pressures.

The law mandated that thrifts meet three requirements: a risk-based capital standard, a leverage (core) capital standard, and a tangible capital standard. The risk-based capital requirements are established by assigning each asset a risk weight, ranging from 0 to 200 percent. The book value of the asset is multiplied by its risk weight to produce a risk-weighted value. These values are then summed to arrive at a total risk-based asset structure. An institution must have capital equal to a certain ratio of this total. Initially set at 6.4 percent, the ratio rose to 8 percent by the end of 1992. Consider the following simple example of risk-based capital requirement:

Asset	Book Value	Risk Weight	Risk-weighted Assets
Treasuries	$100	0%	$000
Mortgages	100	50	50
Participation certificates	100	20	20
REO	100	200	200
Total	$400		$270

At the end of 1992 the institution would be required to have $21.60 (0.08 × $270) in capital.

The leverage and tangible capital requirements were designed to ensure that all savings and loan associations hold some minimal amount of capital, even if they hold assets with little or no default risk. The core capital requirement was initially set at 3 percent of total assets and the tangible requirement as 1.5 percent of total assets other than goodwill. FIRREA required that by 1995 both requirements be at 3 percent.

Subsequent to FIRREA, capital regulation has been concerned primarily with interest rate risk. Consider the OTS's periodic thrift bulletins (TBs) that further clarify the guidelines for investments. TB-12 requires thrift institutions to show that any derivative securities that they purchase reduce the overall interest rate risk faced by the institution. TB-13 further requires that thrifts evaluate their interest rate risk from a portfolio approach. Together, these two guidelines reflect an interest rate risk approach to capital requirements. Also, a 1990 proposal by the OTS would require thrifts to gauge the effect of a 200-basis point change in interest rates on the value of their assets and liabilities. The required capital would then depend upon the change in the thrift's net worth.

Thrift Versus Bank Capital Requirements.   FIRREA required that the capital standards for thrifts be no less stringent than those for banks. There are some differences, however. First, FIRREA established more severe penalties for a thrift that fails to meet the capital standards. It must file a capital plan with the OTS, describing how it plans to meet the requirement and certifying that its liabilities will not grow while the OTS reviews the plan (except that deposit liabilities can grow by the amount of interest added to deposit accounts). If the thrift fails to present the plan, then OTS can prohibit any further acquisition of assets. OTS also can require that the thrift reduce the interest rate it pays on deposits and eliminate designated-lending programs.

Second, the leverage requirement for thrifts is not applicable to banks. Bank regulators can establish such requirements for banks if they choose, however. Finally, there are some slight differences in the risk weights assigned to certain assets. Table 5–9 shows the present risk-based capital guidelines for thrifts and banks.

Categories of Capitalization

Beginning in 1992 under the Federal Deposit Insurance Corporation Improvement Act thrift capitalization was categorized into five classes. The classes were defined in terms of risk-based cap-

TABLE 5–9
Risk-based Capital Guidelines; December 1992

	National Banks (%)	Savings Association (%)
Minimum ratio of capital to risk-weighted assets	8	8[a]
Risk Weights		
Cash	0	0
U.S. treasuries and securities guaranteed by the U.S. treasury (except mortgage securities)	0	0
FHA-insured, VA-guaranteed mortgage loans	20	20
Qualifying mortgage loans secured by 1- to 4-family homes	50 (if conservatively valued)[b]	50 (if original LTV ≤ 80% or backed by approved MI)[c]
Qualifying multifamily mortgage loans (existing property, 5-36 units, LTV ≤ 80%, 80% occupancy over preceding year)	100	50
Delinquent loans (90 days or more) 1- to 4-family residential	100	100
Other	100	200
Ginnie Mae securities	0	0
Freddie Mac and Fannie Mae mortgage securities	20	20
High-quality nonagency mortgage securities [d] backed by agency securities	20	20
backed by nonagency securities or mortgage loans	50 or 100	20
Other mortgage securities backed by qualifying mortgage loans	50	50
by nonqualifying loans	100	100
Stripped mortgage securities	100	100[a]
Residual mortgage securities	100	100[a]
Retained subordinated class of mortgage securities	Same as underlying collateral, but capital required against transaction	Same as for banks[c]
Goodwill	100[e]	100 for qualifying supervisory goodwill not excluded for assets base[f]
Real estate owned	100	200
Equity investments (equity securities, investments in real property, investments in subsidiaries)	100	100 for amount not excluded from assets; all equity investments except certain subsidiaries must be phased out of asset base over 5 years
Nonresidential construction loans and land loans with LTVs above 80%	100	100, but part above 80% LTV exluded from asset base immediately
Standard risk category for all other assets, including nonqualifying 1- to 4-family mortgage loans, non-qualifying multifamily mortgage loans, customer and commercial loans	100	100

[a] Denotes items that are likely to change once the interest rate component is adopted.
[b] Regulation does not define "conservatively valued."
[c] Denotes items that may have different capital requirements under OTS's forthcoming optional "marginal capital calculation" for mortgage-related assets.
[d] OTS defines these as investment-grade securities (assigned to one of the two highest rating categories by a nationally recognized rating agency) backed by first-lien residential mortgage loans. OTS includes mortgage-backed bonds in this category, but OCC does not.
[e] Most goodwill is excluded from the asset base and deducted from capital.
[f] Nonsupervisory goodwill must be immediately excluded from asset base and thus deducted from capital. Qualifying supervisory goodwill is phased out over 5 years.

ital and what is termed **Tier one risk-based capital.** Without elaboration on the Tier one definitions, the categories of risk as follows: well-capitalized thrifts were defined as those with a total risk-based capital to asset ratio greater than or equal to 10 percent of risk-weighted assets, adequately capitalized thrift have risk-based capital greater than or equal to 8 percent, undercapitalized thrifts have a less than 8 percent ratio, significantly undercapitalized thrifts less than 6 percent, and critically undercapitalized are thrifts with a ratio of tangible to total assets of less than 2 percent. The OTS can take action to require an increase in capitalization for those thrifts that are undercapitalized or worse. Table 5–10 shows that the percentage of well-capitalized thrifts has increased (and less-capitalized thrifts decreased) since 1992 in response to this legislation.

Taken together, the risk-based capital guidelines that required greater capitalization for more risk assets and the capitalization categories that provided for OTS intervention in the case of undercapitalized thrifts, led to a significant reduction in the volume of risky assets held by thrifts. Thrifts over the early 1990s made a concerted effort to purge risky assets from their asset portfolio. Two types of risky assets defined by the risk-based guidelines include real estate owned (REO) and noncurrent loans (loans that are delinquent one or more payments). Table 5–11 shows the decline in the amount and percentage of these low quality assets from 1989 through 1995.

THE 1990S: DOMINANCE OF THE SECONDARY MORTGAGE MARKET

The 1990s saw the government-sponsored enterprises (GNMA, FNMA, FHLMC) and the secondary mortgage begin to dominate the mortgage market. Mortgage bankers gained an increasing share of originations and the percentage of residential loans that become securitized increased rapidly during this period. (Securitized means that entities in the secondary mortgage market issue securities or bonds and use the funds to purchase mortgages.) Table 5–12 shows the originations of residential (one-to-four family and multifamily) loans by thrifts and commercial banks on the one hand and mortgage bankers on the other. Mortgage bankers, of course,

TABLE 5–10

Federal Deposit Insurance Corporation Improvement Act Capital Categories: Year-End 1992–1995 (Number of OTS-Regulated Thrifts Percentage in parentheses—dollars in millions)

Year	Well-Capitalized		Adequately Capitalized		Undercapitalized	Significantly Undercapitalized	Critically Undercapitalized
1992	1,520	(81.2)	273	(14.6)	32 (1.7)	34 (1.8)	13 (1.4)
1993	1,550	(92.9)	109	(6.5)	8 (0.5)	1 (0.06)	1 (0.06)
1994	1,439	(93.3)	95	(6.1)	5 (0.3)	3 (0.19)	1 (0.06)
1995	1,392	(97.0)	38	(2.6)	4 (0.28)	1 (0.07)	0 (0)

TABLE 5–11

Amount and Percentage of Troubled Assets of All Assets, OTS-Regulated Thrifts: 1989–1995 (dollars in billions)

Year	Real Estate Owned		Noncurrent Loans		Total Troubled Assets	
1989	21.8	(1.84)	15.0	(1.26)	36.8	(3.10)
1990	22.6	(2.20)	16.8	(1.63)	39.4	(3.83)
1991	17.3	(1.93)	16.8	(1.87)	34.1	(3.80)
1992	12.6	(1.57)	12.2	(1.51)	24.8	(3.08)
1993	6.9	(.89)	9.9	(1.28)	16.8	(2.17)
1994	3.8	(.49)	7.1	(.91)	10.9	(1.40)
1995	2.5	(.32)	6.8	(.88)	9.3	(1.20)

originate loans exclusively for sale in the seconday market. In 1990 mortgage bankers originated 34 percent of all residential loans compared to 64 percent by depository institutions. By 1995 mortgage bankers originated 54 percent of all loans.

The increased share of originations by mortgage bankers led to a similar increase in loans that were securitized in the secondary mortgage market. Table 5–13 shows the percentage of residential loans securitized in 1990 compared to 1997. Whereas 42 percent of all outstanding residential loans were securitized in 1990 that percentage increased to 53 percent by 1997.

Risk-based Guidelines Expanded to Cover Interest Rate Risk

On June 30, 1995, the Board of Governors of the Federal Reserve System approved two measures related to the supervisory treatment of interest rate risk. The established guidelines to incorporate interest rate risk under Section 305 of the Federal Deposit Insurance Corporation Improvement Act. Section 305 of the Act requires banking regulators to revise risk-based capital standards to include provisions for interest rate risk. In 1995 the Board instituted a two-step approach to implementing the capital standards. The first step revises the capital standards to explicitly account for a bank's exposure to a decline in economic value as a result of a change in interest rates. The rule encourages regulators to utilize a new supervisory measurement process that focuses on a bank's economic value exposure, historical earnings performance, and exposure to interest rate movements. The second step is a rule that establishes an explicit minimum capital charge for interest rate risk that is based on the level of a bank's measured interest rate risk exposure. The supervisory measurement process includes a measure of a bank's underlying economic value and how that value would change in response to changes in interest rates. The bank's economic value is defined as the present value of its assets less the present value of its liabilities plus the net present value of its off balance sheet instruments. The model then estimates a change in the net position as a result of a 200 basis point change in interest rates. In short, the interest rate risk guidelines explicitly accounts for the maturity mismatch problem in assessing adequate capital for banks.

TABLE 5–12
Total Residential Originations (millions)

	Thrifts and Commercial Banks		Mortgage bankers		Total
1990	$313,955	(64)	$166,687	(34)	$490,967
1991	313,206	(53)	265,949	(45)	587,585
1992	471,000	(51)	439,662	(47)	919,412
1993	513,848	(49)	528,502	(50)	1,051,563
1994	381,282	(47)	408,141	(51)	801,433
1995	303,033	(45)	364,813	(54)	678,620

Source: Secondary Mortgage Markets

TABLE 5–13
Securitized Mortgage Debt Outstanding (billions)

	1990				1997I			
	Total	GSE	Private	%	Total	GSE	Private	%
Conventional	2,421	741	56	33%	3,625	1,434	293	48%
FHA/VA	546	460	0	84%	654	562	0	86%
Total	2,967	1,201	56	42%	4,279	1,996	293	53%

Source: Secondary Mortgage Markets, July 1997.

SUMMARY

The residential mortgage and housing market went through some dramatic structural changes from the end of World War II through the early 1990s. The standard, fixed-rate loan that dominated the marketplace at the end of the war was joined by a host of alternative mortgage instruments in the 1980s. The most popular AMI to survive the test of the marketplace was the adjustable-rate mortgage. The FHA-insured GPM made modest gains in acceptability. Other AMIs, such as SAMs and PLAMs, are relegated to a small segment of the market.

The role of the major lenders also shifted. Thrifts lost ground to the mortgage bankers in the share of total originations. Mortgage bankers increased their share when the federal government provided support for the development of the secondary mortgage market. Developed in the late 1960s and early 1970s, the secondary mortgage market exploded in the 1980s until by 1990 it was so large and pervasive that the three government agencies involved could dictate the types and terms of mortgages that would be originated in the primary market. Loans that do not conform to agency requirements are not available for exchange in the secondary market and will not be originated, except for retention in lender's portfolios.

The regulatory structure was also changed, primarily because of the large-scale failure of the savings and loans in the 1980s. The FSLIC was replaced by the RTC and housed within the FDIC. The FHLBB was replaced by the OTS and placed within the Department of the Treasury. This reorganization separated the former supervisory agency from the former insurance fund.

Many of these changes were the result of the introduction of high- and variable-inflation rates in the 1970s. The inflation caused interest rates to rise and become volatile. In turn, the standard, fixed-rate loan became a weak instrument, and previously stable thrifts were exposed to significant interest rate risk. Interest rate risk led to losses, which led to speculation and risky lending behavior. This, in turn, led to widespread failure of thrifts. Although mismanagement and fraud added to the thrift failures, the root cause was the combination of the economic system and a lax regulatory system. The 1990s saw the rapid development of the secondary mortgage market as mortgage bankers became the dominate originators and by 1997 for the first time in history the majority of mortgage loans were securitized.

KEY TERMS

Affordability index
Alternative mortgage instruments (AMIs)
Assumable loan
Creative financing
Depository Institutions Deregulation and
    Monetary Control Act (MCA)
Disintermediation
Due-on-sale clause
Federal Asset Disposition Association (FADA)
Federal Deposit Insurance Corporation (FDIC)
Federal Home Loan Bank Board (FHLBB)
Federal mortgage agencies
Federal Savings and Loan Insurance Corporation
    (FSLIC)
Financial Institutions Reform, Recovery, and
    Enforcement Act (FIRREA)
Forbearance

Garn–St. Germain Act
Generally accepted accounting principles
    (GAAP)
Interest rate risk
Maturity mismatch
Negative amortization
Office of thrift supervision (OTS)
Qualified thrift investments (QTI)
Regulatory accounting principles (RAP)
Resolution trust corporation (RTC)
Risk-based capital guidelines
Secondary mortgage market
Thrift failures
"Tilt" effect
Wellenkamp case
"Zombie" theory of thrift failure

SUGGESTED READINGS

Kane, E. 1989. "The Unending Deposit Insurance Mess," *Science,* October.

Lindsay, R. October 1970. "Regulation Q: The Money Markets and Housing-II." In *Housing and Monetary Policy*. Federal Reserve Bank of Boston Conference Series No. 4, 52–59.

Maisel, S. October 1979. "Risk and Capital Adequacy in Banks." In *The Republication of Financial Institutions*. Conference Series No. 21, Federal Reserve Banks of Boston, 203–224.

Meltzer, A. H. 1970. "Regulation Q: The Money Markets and Housing." In *Housing and Monetary Policy.* Federal Reserve Bank of Boston Conference Series No. 4, October, 41–51.

Ozanne, L. 1984. "The Financial Stakes in Due-on-Sale: The Case of California's State-Chartered Savings and Loans," *AREUEA Journal,* Winter, 473–494.

Parliament, T. J., and J. S. Kaden. 1981. The Shared Appreciation Concept in Residential Financing. In John R. Buck, ed., *Financial Markets.* Richmond, VA: Robert F. Dame, 285–300.

REVIEW QUESTIONS

5–1   Discuss the major changes in the residential finance market from 1950 to the 1990s with regard to

a. the types of mortgage lenders.

b. the types of mortgage loans.

c. the role of the federal government, including legislation.

5–2   Fully explain the concept of interest rate risk as it relates to thrift asset–liability maturity mismatch.

5–3   Explain why increased interest rate volatility increases interest rate risk of the type indicated in Question 2.

5–4   Identify the problems created by Regulation Q during the 1960s and 1970s.

5–5   Define disintermediation and explain why it caused severe disruptions in the housing market.

5–6   Indicate three benefits of a well-organized secondary market for mortgages.

5–7   a. Identify the supply problems of a standard, fixed-rate mortgage in an inflationary environment.

b. Identify the demand problems of a standard, fixed-rate mortgage in an inflationary environment.

5–8   What are the major changes in the regulation of financial institutions that were brought about by the Depository Institutions and Monetary Control Act of 1980 and the Garn–St. Germain Act of 1982?

5–9   Outline the critical issues on each side of the "battle" for enforcement of the due-on-sale clause in the late 1970s and early 1980s.

5–10   Explain how borrowers attempted to circumvent the enforcement of the due-on-sale clause.

5–11   Indicate the major reasons for widespread failure of savings and loans in the 1980s. Include a discussion of (a) FSLIC forbearance, (b) regulatory additions to net worth, and (c) RAP vs. GAAP accounting.

5–12   Explain the "zombie" theory of savings and loan failure as outlined by Professor Kane.

5–13   What provisions of FIRREA addressed the causes of the savings and loan failures?

5–14   What are some of the weaknesses of FIRREA?

5–15   How did FIRREA change the regulatory structure of the mortgage market in terms of (a) the regulators and (b) the rules and regulations.

5–16   a. What are risk-based capital guidelines?

b. Give an example of current risk-based capital guidelines for thrifts.

PROBLEMS

5–1   Determine the Period 1 and Period 2 market net worth of the following savings and loans:

Period 1		Period 2	
Assets		Assets	
30-year mortgages, 9% coupon	$50,000,000	30-year mortgages, 9% coupon	
Building and land	$5,000,000	Building and land	$5,000,000
Liabilities		Liabilities	
1 Year CDs at 1-year market rate	$50,000,000	1 Year CDs at 1-year market rate	$50,000,000
Equity		Equity	
1-year market rate 7%		1-year market rate 8%	
30-year market rate 9%		30-year market rate 10%	

5–2 Determine the required net worth, or capital, of the thrift (based on the following selected assets) under the indicated risk-based capital guidelines (not necessarily real-world guidelines).

Asset	Risk Weight	Book Value
Treasuries	0%	$1,000,000
Residential mortgages	25	3,000,000
Commercial mortgages	50	2,000,000
GNMAs	20	3,500,000
REO	250	800,000

ENDNOTES

1. The first money market fund, the Reserve Fund, was organized in November 1971.
2. A deed-of-trust is an instrument that places title to the property with a trustee (third party) until the loan is fully paid. These concepts are discussed in Chapter 12.
3. Larry Ozanne, "The Financial Stakes in Due-On-Sale: The Case of California's State-Chartered Savings and Loans," *AREUEA Journal* 12(4) (Winter 1984), 473–494.
4. As an example, the payment on a 30-year loan for $100,000 at 10 percent is the same as a $115,307 at 8 percent.
5. In fact, a study by Hendershott and Schultz shows that, after building a substantial capital base in the 1970s, the FHA single-family mortgage insurance fund lost roughly $10 billion in the 1980s. Negative equity, unemployment, and loan size were seen to be significant determinants of default. See Patric H. Hendershott and William R. Schultz, "Equity and Nonequity Determinants of FHA Single-Family Mortgage Foreclosures in the 1980s," *Journal of the American Real Estate and Urban Economics Association* 21 (Winter 1993), 405–430.
6. Creative financing also included such loans as wraparound loans, buydowns, zero interest rate financing, and other nontraditional loans.
7. A savings and loan is defined as a failure when there is a resolution by the FSLIC through (a) liquidation, (b) merger with another financial institution with the aid of the FSLIC, or (c) merger as the result of supervisory action.
8. Edward Kane, "The Unending Deposit Insurance Mess," *Science* (October 1989), 451–456.
9. Fred A. Forgey, Paul R. Goebel, and Ronald C. Rutherford, "Implicit Liquidity Premiums in the Disposition of RTC Assets," *Journal of Real Estate Research* 8 (Summer 1993), 347–364.

WEB SITES

www.fdic.gov/databank FDIC data on commercial banks and savings and loan associations.
www.cob.ohio-state.edu/dept/fin/overview.html Topics of general interest to finance students.
www.ots.treas.gov Information on regulation of thrifts by the Office of Thrift Supervision
www.fhfb.gov Federal Housing Finance Board. Has one of the largest sets of historical mortgage rates by property type and loan type that is available.
www.hamb.org Access to HUD rulings that affect mortgage brokers.
www.clev.frb.org/bsr/dialogue Information on risk based capital guidelines.

CHAPTER **6**

Alternative Mortgage Instruments

LEARNING OBJECTIVES

Alternative mortgage instruments (AMIs) are mortgages other than the standard, fixed-rate, 30-year, amortizing loan (FRM). After reading this chapter, you should understand the basics of several types of AMIs. The basics of AMIs include the determination of standard mortgage terms such as the interest rate, payment, discount points, term of the loan, and so forth. You should understand not only how the terms are determined but how they are interrelated. Finally, you should understand how the characteristics of various AMIs solve the problems of a fixed rate mortgage in an inflationary environment.

INTRODUCTION

In the previous chapter, we saw how an inflationary environment created problems for the standard fixed-rate mortgage. Supply problems are related to the asset-liability maturity mismatch of traditional mortgage lenders. Thrifts hold short-term liabilities (deposits) and originate long-term assets (mortgages). Inflation creates expectations of continued inflation which in turn causes the nominal interest rates on thrift deposits to rise. Mortgage prepayments slow with rising rates, and the thrifts are saddled with relatively low-rate mortgages. This scenario, which exemplifies the interest rate risk of fixed-rate mortgages, turns profits to losses.[1]

Demand problems are related to affordability. Rising interest rates on mortgages cause the payment to increase beyond the affordability range of many potential homeowners. The "tilt" problem causes the "real" payment to be extraordinarily high at the beginning of the FRM and very low at the end.

We will discuss AMIs first from the standpoint of supply problems, then from that of demand problems. Other AMIs are given only cursory treatment.

PROBLEMS OF SUPPLY: INTEREST RATE RISK AND THE ADJUSTABLE-RATE MORTGAGE

The most popular AMI designed to solve the problem of interest rate risk is the adjustable-rate mortgage, originally called the variable-rate mortgage. Another is the price level adjusted mortgage (PLAM). The latter is discussed later in the chapter. We will treat the ARM in detail here.

The basic concept behind the **adjustable rate mortgage (ARM)** is to allow the rate of interest on the loan to move with the market rate. This provision reduces the interest rate risk faced by the lender by shifting it to the borrower. At first, one might conclude that an ARM is no less risky than an FRM because it allows the interest rate on the loan to fall as well as rise. Recall, however, that with an FRM the borrower will prefer to retain the FRM if rates rise, but will refinance with a lower rate if they fall. Thus, the ARM significantly reduces interest rate risk for the lender because it is preferable to an FRM when interest rates rise yet no worse when they fall. Because they face less interest rate risk with ARMs, lenders require a lower return.

Borrowers have proven reluctant to absorb all of the risk associated with rising rates. As a result, nearly all ARMs have provisions that limit the amount by which the rate can increase, either periodically or over the term of the mortgage. All ARMs share a number of characteristics. They have (1) a lower initial interest rate than FRMs, (2) a rate that in some fashion is tied to the market (an index), and (3) provisions for limiting the amount by which the rate or payments can change. We first will describe the characteristics of typical ARMs. Then we will provide an example of how the payments and loan balances of a set of ARMs will behave as a result of changes in the market rate of interest. Finally, we will discuss the pricing of ARMs. Pricing refers to how lenders set the different terms of the ARMs in relation to one another. For example, if the lender agrees to a very strict limit on the periodic change in the interest rate, he may require a higher initial rate than otherwise. Alternatively, he may keep the rate low but raise the amount of discount points. The tradeoff of terms is called the pricing of ARMs.

Description of ARMs

An ARM can be described by a number of different features. These include the frequency of rate change, index, margin, interest rate caps, payment caps, caps on negative amortization, initial period discount (teaser), and convertibility.

One provision of an ARM is the **frequency of rate change**—how frequently the lender can adjust the contract rate on the loan. When ARMs were first developed, rate adjustment periods ranged from 6 months to 5 years. Typical adjustment periods were 6 months, 1 year, 3 years, or 5 years. An ARM that exposed the lender to no interest rate risk whatsoever would adjust nearly instantaneously to changes in the market rate, say, daily. This is impractical, however, so lenders have settled on only a few alternative adjustment periods. The longer the time between adjustments, the greater the interest rate risk assumed by the lender. Between adjustments, ARMs behave as fixed-rate mortgages. Longer adjustment periods increase the probability of prepayment, if market rates decline below that on the ARM, for example.

Over time, as the terms of ARMs became more uniform, the market gravitated to the 1-year adjustable ARM as a standard. Although other adjustment periods can be found, today most ARMs adjust every year. This means that the contract rate is adjusted once a year, and this adjustment is usually reflected in a change in the monthly payment. Having said that, however, in recent years lenders have become more willing to postpone the first payment adjustment until as far as 7 to 10 years into the future. About two-thirds of lenders participating in a Freddie Mac survey reported that they offer a 7/1 ARM. This loan locks in an initial interest rate for 7 years and adjusts annually thereafter. Fifty-two percent of lenders offer a 10/1 ARM.

The **index** is the market rate which provides the basis for adjustment to the interest rate on the ARM. The contract rate on the ARM will not equal the index but rather will equal the value of the index plus a fixed "add-on" or margin. When the index goes up, so will the rate on the ARM and vice versa. In general the index must be (1) beyond manipulation by the lender, (2) not excessively volatile, (3) an established index, and (4) acceptable to the borrower.

The index will be either a rate on a Treasury obligation (bill or bond) or some measure of the cost of funds to the lender. If the index is the yield on a Treasury obligation, the rate will be selected on a Treasury with a maturity corresponding to the frequency with which the rate on the ARM can change. If the ARM adjusts to the market rate every year, then the index will be the yield on a 1-year Treasury bill. If the rate on the ARM changes only every 3 years, then the index will be a 3-year Treasury note yield.

If the index is based on the lender's cost of funds **(Cost of Fund Index, COFI),** then it will be equal to some recent (regional) rate paid on savings deposits as determined by a federal regulatory agency. Thrifts do not change the rate they offer on deposits frequently. They may change the rate only if there is a moderate change in market rates and then only after several weeks or months. As a result, the COFI indices will change more slowly than Treasury rates. They are much less volatile.

The **margin** is the amount, in basis points, added to the index to arrive at the contract rate for the loan. It is expressed in basis points. If the index value is 8 percent and the margin is 150 basis points, then the rate on the loan will be 9.5 percent (until the next adjustment). If a COFI is used as an index, then the margin will represent the amount the lender will have available to cover non-interest costs, such as operating expenses and a return to capital. If a lender decides that, for some reason, he requires a higher yield on a particular ARM, perhaps because its rate adjusts infrequently (5 years), he will increase the margin for new loans so as to obtain the higher yield. The lender has no control over the level of the index. Once stated in the mortgage contract, the margin cannot change for that loan. Thus, changes in the contract rate on the ARM are a result of movements in the index and not changes in the margin. Most margins will range from 150 to 275 basis points.

There are two types of **interest rate caps: adjustment rate caps** (or rate caps) and **life-of-loan rate caps.** The former places a limit on how the contract rate on the loan can change at each date of adjustment (anniversary date). The latter establishes a ceiling that the rate on the loan can never exceed. The life-of-loan cap (life cap) is usually stated as a number of percentage points over the initial rate. If the initial rate on an ARM is 9 percent and the life cap is 6 percentage points, the maximum contract rate over the life of the loan will be 15 percent.

Adjustment caps are usually either 1 or 2 percent. The smaller (tighter) the adjustment cap, the greater the interest rate risk to the lender. A 2 percent adjustment cap on a 1-year ARM means that the rate can rise by, at most, 2 percent (200 basis points) in 1 year. If the market rate has risen by 3 percentage points, the lender will not receive the market return. Adjustment caps also establish a floor of the same size. A 2 percent adjustment cap means that the rate on the loan cannot increase or decrease by more than 2 percent on the adjustment date.

In determining the contract rate for a given period, the lender can never charge a rate greater than the index plus the margin. The adjustment caps mean that the lender cannot charge this amount if he is constrained by the cap. Thus the contract rate for any given period will be either (1) the index plus the margin or (2) the previous period's contract rate plus the adjustment cap.

Some ARMs have **payment caps** which limit the amount by which the borrower's payment may increase on the adjustment date. This cap does not limit the interest rate on the loan. The normal payment cap is 7.5 percent, which means that the payment cannot increase more than that amount for each adjustment period. Payment caps are not very appealing to borrowers since they can produce negative amortization (increasing mortgage balance) by constraining the payment but not the interest. Payment caps also are not especially appealing to mortgage lenders since this type of loan may not be saleable in the secondary market due to investors' concerns of increased delinquency.

Negative amortization is an increase in the loan balance as a result of payments that are less than the full amount of the interest charge. Since negative amortization represents a default risk, lenders may limit the amount of negative amortization on ARMs that have payment caps. (ARMs with rate caps and no optional payment cap generally will not have negative amortization.) The usual limit is 125 percent of the original loan amount. Thus, the balance on a $100,000 loan will not be allowed to exceed $125,000 through negative amortization.

To attract borrowers, lenders sometimes offer an **initial-period discount,** an initial contract rate on the loan that is less than the index plus the margin at that time. If, for example, the index is 8 percent and the margin 150 basis points, the **fully indexed rate** on the loan should be 9.5 percent. The lender may offer a rate, for the initial period only, of 8.5 percent. The initial-period discount is sometimes referred to as a **teaser rate.**

Some ARMs are written to be **convertible.** This means that, within a given window of time, the ARM can be converted to a fixed-rate mortgage. A nominal conversion fee is charged and the mortgage is generally converted at an interest rate slightly above market.

An ARM also may have some other features that are common to other types of loans. They can be assumable or not, have a prepayment penalty (but rarely do), or have up-front discount and origination points.

▉▍ ARM EXAMPLE

The best way to understand the fundamentals of ARM construction and pricing is to consider an example. First, assume that the future indexes (Treasury rates) to which the rate on the example ARMs are tied will behave as indicated in Table 6–1. We have purposely shown them as increasing over a 5-year period. Next, Table 6–2 describes the characteristics of five different ARMs. The terms reflect a tradeoff that is representative of modern ARMs. For example, the first ARM benefits the lender by virtue of an absence on restrictions to rate changes (no rate cap). The borrower benefits by the smaller margin applied to the index. As compared to ARM 2, ARM 3 benefits the borrower by providing a tighter rate cap and compensates the lender by providing for a larger margin. This tradeoff of terms is called the pricing of ARMs and is discussed later.

Because we have chosen a rising-interest-rate scenario for our example, the less restrictive ARMs, in terms of caps, will benefit the lender over the period analyzed. Although ARM 1 has the smallest margin, it has no restrictions on periodic rate changes. It also provides for more frequent rate changes than the other ARMs. Also, ARM 5 has a payment cap. It will display negative amortization with a rising-interest-rate pattern.

For illustration, we will show the initial payment and subsequent adjustment for ARM 1. The initial payment is calculated as

$$\text{PMT}_1 = \text{Loan Amount } [i \, (1 + i)^n / (1 + i)^n - 1]$$

$$\text{PMT}_1 = \$100,000 \, (\text{MC}_{9.5/12, \, 360})$$

$$\text{PMT}_1 = \$100,000 \, (0.0084085)$$

$$\text{PMT}_1 = \$840.85$$

TABLE 6−1
Future Interest Indexes for Adjustable Rate Mortgage Example

Month	6-month ARM	1-year ARM	5-year ARM
1	7.9	8.1	8.7
7	8.1	N/A	N/A
13	8.15	8.6	N/A
19	8.2	N/A	N/A
25	9.0	9.5	N/A
31	9.5	N/A	N/A
37	9.9	10.0	N/A
43	9.8	N/A	N/A
49	9.7	11.0	N/A
55	9.7	N/A	N/A
61	9.7	10.5	12.0

TABLE 6−2
Information for Adjustable Rate Mortgage Example

	ARM 1	ARM 2	ARM 3	ARM 4	ARM 5
Loan amount	$100,000	$100,000	$100,000	$100,000	$100,000
Months amortized	360	360	360	360	360
Rate change interval	6 months	1 year	1 year	5 years	1 year
Margin over index	175.00	200.00	225.00	250.00	250.00
Special initial period rate	9.500	9.000	8.000	9.500	9.000
Discount points	2.000	2.000	3.000	3.000	2.000
Ceiling rate CAP	None	2.000	1.000	2.000	None
Floor rate CAP	None	2.000	1.000	2.000	None
Payment CAP	None	None	None	None	7.500
Lifetime CAP	15.000	15.000	15.000	15.000	15.000
Neg. amort. CAP	None	None	None	None	125.000

Six months later at the first adjustment, the index has a value of 8.10 percent; thus, the fully indexed rate (index plus the margin) is 9.85 percent (8.10 + 1.75). If a ceiling rate cap existed, the lender would have to compare this new rate to the sum of the previous period's rate plus the cap to determine which is smaller.

To determine the payment for period two, one must first know the amount to be financed, i.e., the outstanding balance of the loan at the end of the first 6 months. This is calculated as

$$\text{Outstanding Balance} = \text{Payment} (\text{PVAIF}_{9.5/12,\ 354})$$

$$= \$840.85\ (118.5693)$$

$$= \$99,699$$

The new information needed to determine the new payment is now known: the new contract rate (9.85 percent) and the amount to be financed ($99,699). The new payment is thus

$$\text{PMT}_2 = \$99,699\ (\text{MC}_{9.85/12,\ 354})$$

$$= \$866.32$$

This process is repeated for each adjustment. Note that, regardless of adjustments where the payment may increase in some periods and decrease in others, the loan will fully amortize over the contract period of 30 years.

The payments associated with each of the ARMs in our example are shown in Table 6–3. Several items should be noted. First, the payments on ARM 1 are never restricted by rate caps. They rise over the first 48 months and then decline slightly in the 49th month when the 6-month index falls from 9.8 to 9.7 percent.

Second, although ARM 2 has a 2 percent cap, the payment is never restricted because the index never increases by as much as two percentage points in any 1 year.

Third, because of the 1 percent rate cap on ARM 3, its payments are restricted through the first 4 years. The index in Month 12 (8.6 percent) plus the margin (225 basis points) would result in a rate of 10.85 percent. Yet, the first-year rate was 8 percent, and the ARM has a 1 percent cap. The payment in the second year, $803.39, will be calculated by amortizing the balance of this loan over 29 remaining years at only 9 percent. The payment is also restricted in the third year. In Month 25, the index rises to 9.5 percent, which results in a fully indexed rate of 11.75 percent. Because of the 1 percent cap, the loan rate can rise to only 10 percent, 1 percent over the Year 2 rate. In Month 37, the index rises to 10 percent, which would result in a fully indexed rate of 12.25 percent. The rate on the loan is restricted to 11 percent in the fourth year, however.

TABLE 6–3
Payment Summary for ARM Example

Month	ARM 1	ARM 2	ARM 3	ARM 4	ARM 5
1	$840.85	$804.62	$733.76	$840.85	$804.62
7	866.32	804.62	733.76	840.85	804.62
13	869.95	920.43	803.39[b]	840.85	864.97[a]
19	873.56	920.43	803.39	840.85	864.97
25	931.46	986.61	873.92[b]	840.85	929.84[a]
31	967.92	986.61	873.92	840.85	929.84
37	997.16	1023.40	945.12[b]	840.85	999.58[a]
43	989.88	1023.40	945.12	840.85	999.58
49	982.67	1097.00	1016.83[b]	840.85	1074.55[b]
55	982.67	1097.00	1016.83	840.85	1074.55
61	982.67	1060.54	1070.72	978.26[b]	1154.92

[a]The limit on payment change was hit.
[b]The limit on rate change was hit.

TABLE 6–4

Loan Balance for ARM Example

Month	ARM 1	ARM 2	ARM 3	ARM 4	ARM 5
0	$100,000.00	$100,000.00	$100,000.00	$100,000.00	$100,000.00
12	99,405.26	99,316.88	99,164.60	99,383.38	99,316.88
24	98,782.17	98,773.32	98,418.45	98,705.58	99,995.26
36	98,223.24	98,266.80	97,742.91	97,960.50	100,884.41
48	97,666.08	97,750.23	97,122.47	97,141.48	101,536.56
60	97,023.77	97,265.66	96,544.11	96,241.18	102,401.66

TABLE 6–5

Rate of Return Over 5 Years, ARM Example

Loan	Rate of Return (percent)
ARM 5	11.91
ARM 2	11.53
ARM 1	11.01
ARM 3	10.56
ARM 4	10.28

The contrast in payments between ARM 2 and ARM 3 shows the importance of the size of the rate cap.

Fourth, ARM 4 acts as a fixed-rate loan through the first 5 years and then its payment is restricted by a 2 percent rate cap. Finally, ARM 5 is the loan with the payment cap. The payment on this loan is restricted to a 7.5 percent increase at the end of each of the first 4 years.

The loan balances for each example ARM are shown in Table 6–4. The balances for ARM 5 show negative amortization through Month 60. Maximum negative amortization is reached in Month 60 at 102.4 percent of the original loan, substantially below the 125 percent ceiling.

Next, for additional perspective, let's consider how the payment on ARM 3 is calculated by using the 13th payment as an example. At the end of the 12th month the balance on this loan is $99,164.60. The 1-year Treasury index is 8.6 percent, and the loan's margin is 225 basis points. The fully indexed rate on this loan is 10.85 percent. The rate for the previous (first) year was 8 percent. Since the loan has a 1 percent cap, the maximum rate of interest for the second year is 9 percent. The payment that amortizes a $99,164.60 loan at 9 percent annually over 29 years is $803.39 (see Table 6–3). ■ ■

Comparison of ARM Performance

Lenders are interested in how various ARMs will perform financially over different interest rate scenarios. If lenders trade off the various terms in proper balance, there should be little difference between the performance of each loan. A tight payment cap on a particular loan should be offset by a higher margin, for example.

There are several ways to measure the investment performance of loans. A typical method is to calculate the effective cost (yield for the lender) using an internal rate of return (IRR) calculation. This is the same method as was used for the fixed-rate mortgage, but it is complicated by the fact that only the initial interest rate is known. On an ex ante basis, one may calculate the effective cost on most likely, worst case, and best case scenarios. On an ex post basis, the analysis is easier since the interest rates and payments are known. For our five ARMs, let's assume that each is repaid at the end of Year 5. The effective cost for each is shown in Table 6–5.

In our rising-interest-rate scenario, the effective cost (yield) will be greatest for ARMs that are uncapped, allow for frequent rate changes, have large margins, and do not have large initial-period discounts. For our ARMs, ARM 5 has the highest cost (yield) at 11.91 percent. Even though it had a payment cap, it continued to earn uncapped interest on the unpaid balance. It had a relatively large margin and no deep initial-period discount. ARM 4, which had a fixed interest rate for the 5 years, higher discount points, no low initial-period rate, and normal interest rate caps, had the lowest effective cost at 10.28 percent.

For illustration, let's compute the effective cost (yield) for ARM 2 assuming prepayment at the end of Year 5. The equation is written as

$$\text{Present Value of Loan} = PMT_1/(1+IRR) + PMT_2/(1+IRR)^2$$

$$+ PMT_3/(1+IRR)^3 + PMT_4/(1+IRR)^4 + PMT_5/(1+IRR)^5 + \ldots$$

$$+ PMT_{60}/(1+IRR)^{60} + \text{Balance}_{60}/(1+IRR)^{60} \qquad \text{Equation (6–1)}$$

where PMT is the monthly payment and Balance$_{60}$ is the outstanding balance of the loan at the end of the 60th payment (end of Year 5). For ARM 2, the equation would be

$$\$98,000 = \$804.62 \ (PVAIF_{i\%/12,\ 12})$$

$$+ \$920.43 \ (PVAIF_{i\%/12,\ 12}) \ (PVIF_{i\%/12,\ 12})$$

$$+ \$986.61 \ (PVAIF_{i\%/12,\ 12}) \ (PVIF_{i\%/12,\ 24})$$

$$+ \$1023.4 \ (PVAIF_{i\%/12,\ 12}) \ (PVIF_{i\%/12,\ 36})$$

$$+ \$1097.0 \ (PVAIF_{i\%/12,\ 12}) \ (PVIF_{i\%/12,\ 48})$$

$$+ \$97,265.66 \ (PVIF_{i\%/12,\ 60})$$

This equation can be solved for i either by using a financial calculator or by an interative process of trial and error. Using the financial calculator, the cash flow mode is required to correctly structure the time line since the cash flows change value over time. For the typical financial calculator, the required steps would be

1. Enter 98,000 as a negative cash flow (CF_0).
2. Enter 804.62 as cash flow one (CF_1).
3. Enter the number of payments (in this case 12) by punching shift key N_j.
4. Enter 920.43 as cash flow two (CF_2).
5. Enter the number of payments using step 3.
6. Enter 986.61 as cash flow three (CF_3).
7. Enter the number of payments using step 3.
8. Enter 1023.40 as cash flow four (CF_4).
9. Enter the number of payments using step 3.
10. Enter 1097.00 as cash flow five (CF_5).
11. Enter the first eleven payments by punching shift key N_j.
12. Enter 1097.00 plus 97,265.66 as cash flow six (CF_6).
13. Solve for the interest rate using the IRR function.

Note that, in order to correctly structure the time line, the 60th payment must be added to the outstanding balance since these payments are made simultaneously.

One may also calculate the effective cost by using **terminal wealth.** First, it is assumed that each payment is reinvested as received at the then-prevailing market rate. These reinvested payments accumulate in a fund. At the end of 5 years, the amount in the fund is added to the prepaid loan balance to form the terminal wealth. The rate of return is then computed as follows:

$$R = (TW/BB)^{1/5} - 1$$

where *R* is the rate of return, TW is the terminal wealth, and BB is the beginning balance. If the beginning balance grows at *g* percent annually, then over 5 years the terminal wealth will be

$$TW = BB(1 + g)^5$$

Taking this equation and dividing each side by BB, taking the fifth root of each side, and subtracting 1 results in the above equation. The terminal wealth concept is an alternative to present value as a measure of performance. Terminal wealth has intuitive appeal. Given that two (or more) investments have the same beginning principal, the superior one (from the mortgage lender's standpoint) is that which has the largest value at a future point in time.

Pricing Adjustable-Rate Mortgages

Pricing of ARMs refers to the effect on the value of an ARM of changing one or more of its terms. If the introduction of a term, such as a cap on the rate change, causes the lender more interest rate risk, this will lower the value of the ARM. To compensate, the lender will have to charge discount points or, alternatively, add some basis points to the margin. The tradeoff in terms, an attempt to maintain a certain "value" for the ARM, is referred to as the pricing of the ARM terms.

To understand how ARMs are priced, first consider a "perfect" ARM, one that completely eliminates interest rate risk. Such a theoretical ARM would have an index that changed with the market rate and reflected, at all times, the interest cost of funds to the lender. The lender would set a margin sufficient to cover operating expenses and provide a return to capital invested in the institution. There would be no caps at all on the loan, and its rate would change simultaneously with the index. With this perfect ARM, the lender would be completely hedged against interest rate risk.

The opposite extreme would be a completely bound ARM. Once the rate was established, zero caps on the interest rate would prevent any change at all. Such a bound ARM would be essentially a fixed-rate mortgage, but with an ARM rate of interest—a bad deal for lenders. For the purpose of our discussion, a bound ARM is a hypothetical reference loan. No lender would originate an essentially fixed-rate loan with a lower ARM rate of interest. Between these two extremes lie ARMs that are actually originated by lenders. They have rate caps, life-of-loan caps, payment caps, and initial-period discounts. They do not adjust instantaneously with an index, but only periodically. The longer the period of adjustment, the greater the interest rate risk.

Now, a perfect ARM would always be valued at par, a value equal to 100 percent of its balance. A perfect ARM might look as follows. It would have a rate tied to an index that reflects the lender's cost of funds. (Assume that index is currently 7 percent.) Next, the lender would establish the margin necessary to cover operating costs, say, 200 basis points. The rate on the loan would be 9 percent. At future dates, it would always be valued at the amount of its balance.

The introduction of restrictive terms would lower its value. If the lender adds a 2 percent rate cap, the value may fall to 0.975 percent of par, for example. The 2.5 percent discount is the price of the cap. To restore value, the lender would have to charge 2.5 discount points at origination. Alternatively, the lender could add 25 basis points to the margin. In this case, the present value of the additional basis points over the expected life of the loan would equal the 2.5 discount points. How did we decide that the "price" of a 2 percent cap was 2.5 discount points at origination or 25 basis points added to the margin?

The answer lies in pricing. Pricing methods are the subject of numerous research studies. Although their methodologies have varied, these studies have yielded similar results in terms of establishing the pricing of various ARM terms.

One method uses **historical replication.** By constructing a theoretically perfect ARM and then tracing the movements of an actual index over some historical period, this method can replicate the ARMs cash flows. The present value of the cash flows is then calculated. The process is then repeated with one term changed. For example, a 1 percent rate cap may be added. If the present value of the cash flows of the capped ARM is less than that of the perfect ARM, then a determination is made concerning the discount points or the addition to the margin that would be necessary to equate the present values of the two loans.

Another methodology uses a **simulation** of interest rates rather than actual rates over an historical period (which may not be repeated). With a **simulation model,** the cash flows of a perfect ARM are traced by allowing a random movement in the index. The change in the index from one period to the next may be taken from a normal probability distribution. If the mean of the distribution of rate changes is positive, then rates will drift up over time, and vice versa. If the distribution of rate changes is given a large variance (or standard deviation), then rates will fluctuate more widely around the trend. In this manner the cash flows of the perfect ARM may be generated thousands of times and an average found. The same process is then used for an ARM that is capped or has an initial-period discount. Various discounts are applied to the capped ARM so as to create the same present value as the perfect ARM. Assumptions that are made concerning the trend and volatility of interest rates will have a dramatic effect on pricing relationships.

The results of numerous pricing studies reveal the following approximate prices for various terms.

Adjustment Caps and Periods.   Figure 6–1 shows the relationship between the size of rate caps, the adjustment period, and the value of an ARM. Here, interest volatility is assumed to be about normal (15 percent standard deviation in annual rate). If there were no interest rate volatility, then all the ARMs would be priced at par because there would be no interest rate risk. If the periodic rate cap is zero, the ARM is completely bound, and if it has a contract rate equal to a perfect ARM, it will have a value somewhere below par—0.982, for example. As the size of the cap increases, so will the value of the ARM (interest rate risk is reduced). The longer the adjustment period, the lower the value of the ARM for any given rate cap. None of the ARMs shown has a value of par (100 percent) because none are perfect—that is, they all have some lag in the adjustment to the index.

Initial-period Discount (Teaser Rate).   Figure 6–2 prices initial-period discounts, or teaser rates.[2] Assuming a 7 percent index and 200 basis point margin, the fully indexed rate is 9 percent. Interest rate volatility is again assumed to be normal in this example. The solid line represents the value of a completely bound ARM. It reaches its maximum value when there is no initial-period discount. (For consistency, we place its value with no discount [9 percent]: at the initial value in Figure 6–1.) The dashed line represents the value of an ARM with a 2 percent

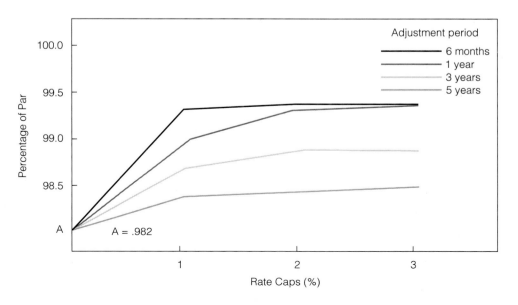

FIGURE 6–1

Periodic Rate Caps, Reset Frequency, and Loan Value

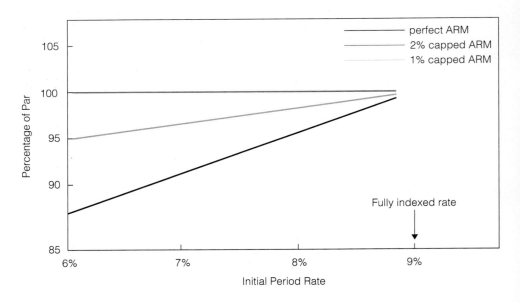

FIGURE 6–2

Teaser Rates and Loan Values

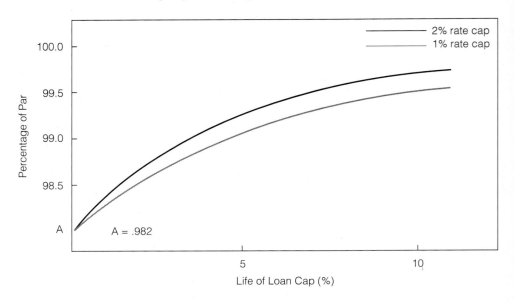

FIGURE 6–3

Life of Loan Caps and Loan Value

cap. For deep initial-period discounts, the cap may prevent the loan from becoming fully indexed on the first or early anniversary dates. For small teaser discounts, the value quickly approaches that of a perfect ARM.

Life-of-loan Caps.   Figure 6–3 shows the value of an ARM with various life caps but with no rate adjustment caps (rates are free to fluctuate). With a zero lifetime cap the ARM is again bound and has the same value as an FRM in the previous figures. As the life of the loan cap increases, the value increases and approaches par for very large caps.

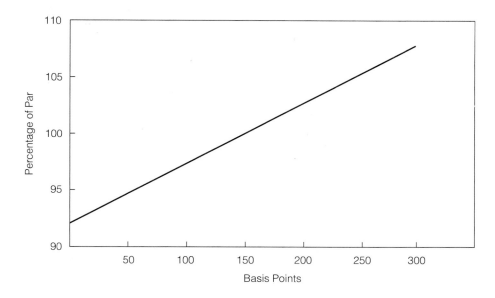

FIGURE 6–4

Margin and Loan Value, Perfect ARM

Margin. An increase in the margin, other things being equal, will raise the value of an ARM. Figure 6–4 shows the value of the perfect ARM in our example reaching 100 percent of par when the margin equals 200 basis points. Research has indicated that the value of an ARM increases about 1 percent for every 25 to 30 basis points added to the margin.

Interest Rate Volatility and Trend. The expectations of borrowers and lenders concerning the direction and volatility of future interest rates also will affect the pricing of ARMs. Interest rate volatility adds value to the borrower's refinance option on a fixed-rate loan, lowering its value to the lender. Also, if interest rates are expected to rise in the future, the value of an ARM will rise relative to a fixed-rate loan.

Figure 6–5 shows the value of a bound ARM (FRM), an ARM with a 2 percent rate cap, and a perfect ARM—all as functions of expected interest rate volatility. Again, if we assume that the normal level of volatility is represented by 15 percent per annum standard deviation, a bound ARM will have a value of approximately 0.982. Point A corresponds with the same points in Figures 6–1 and 6–3. A perfect ARM will be valued at par, regardless of the volatility of interest rates; it adjusts instantaneously to rate changes. The 2 percent capped ARM occupies an intermediary position between the perfect ARM and the bound ARM.

Figure 6–6 shows the values of the same three loans as a function of the average rate of interest subsequent to origination. If rates rise, the value of the bound ARM will fall the greatest, the perfect ARM not at all. For index rates above 7 percent, the difference in the curves represents the value to the lender from originating an ARM over a fixed-rate loan. For levels of the index below 7 percent, the values of the bound ARM and the capped ARM will rise above the perfect ARM. The capped ARM experiences a smaller increase in value, reflecting the fact that the ARM will adjust to the lower rates only within the tolerance of the 2 percent cap. The rate on the bound ARM will not adjust to the lower index. Note, however, that because of the ability to refinance a loan, the bound ARM's value eventually returns to par at sufficiently low interest rates. That is, if the index falls significantly, borrowers will refinance their bound ARM.

In summary, research has predicted what has been illustrated in the preceding figures. Specifically, for normal expectations of interest rate volatility, the following will hold true:

1. In exchange for tighter rate caps and less-frequent rate adjustments, lenders will require either added discount points or a larger margin. For a 2 percent cap and a 1-year adjustment, the discount will lie in the range of 1 discount point.

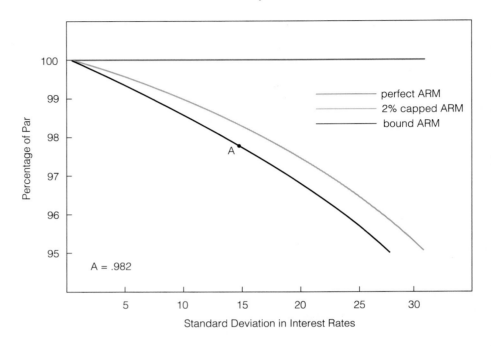

FIGURE 6–5

Interest Rate Volatility and Loan Value

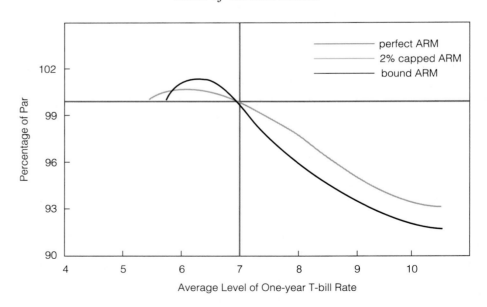

FIGURE 6–6

Value of Various ARMs

2. In exchange for an initial-period discount on the rate, lenders will require an addition to the margin or discount points. For a 2 percent rate-capped ARM, a 1 percent break on the initial rate may require approximately 2 discount points.
3. Lenders require a discount to provide a life-of-loan cap. The discount will depend on whether or not the ARM also has a rate cap. The additional discount is slight if the ARM

has a rate cap. This is so because the rate cap lessens the likelihood that the life cap would become binding in the near future. Without a rate cap, the addition of a 5 percent life cap likely costs between 1 and 1.5 discount points.

4. Other things being equal, an addition of 25 to 30 basis points to the margin adds about 1 percent to the value of the loan. A lender can charge one less point by adding 25 to 30 basis points.

5. Expectations that interest rates will rise or become more volatile will lead lenders to charge greater discounts on fixed-rate loans or strictly bound ARMs.

There is an almost limitless number of combinations of ARM terms. With eight or nine terms to play with, lenders could conceive of virtually endless permutations of ARM loans. Lenders have experimented with many combinations of terms over the years, seeking to find loans that would appeal to borrowers, yet provide interest rate protection. In fact, a 1994 study by Sa-Aadu and Shilling[3] estimated a model of ARM choice over a full set of alternative ARM contracts and found that borrowers perceive a broad array of ARMs as equivalent. They argue that it makes little sense for lenders to offer a wide variety of ARMs that are perceived as the same.

The secondary market agencies have used computer simulation programs to arrange the various terms and construct ARMs that they thought would protect them from interest rate risk. They defined the terms of ARMs they would purchase and to a great degree forced them on lenders who originated loans primarily for sale. As a result of this process, many types of ARMs became almost nonexistent, such as the 5-year adjustable. As more and more combinations of terms became less popular, the market gravitated to only a few different types. Today, the most popular ARM is the 1-year adjustable tied to a 1-year Treasury index. Yet, even for this standardized loan, terms such as the number of discount points will vary, depending on expectations concerning the trend and volatility of interest rates. Such expectations not only have a dramatic effect on the terms of successful ARMs, they also affect the share of total loans represented by ARMs.

Problems in ARM Calculations

Evidence shows that lenders sometimes make errors when ARM adjustments are made. Generally, adjustment errors seem to be unintentional and correctable. Most errors appear to stem from sloppy or faulty procedures, calculation errors, and/or faulty computer software. As Elledge, Fletcher, and Norris[4] point out, errors are most likely to occur during four events: (1) loan origination, (2) the initial entry of the loan data into the system, (3) the loan adjustment date, and (4) the time of changes in the system. Some causes of errors that they cite are: (1) mistakes in the original loan set-up process, (2) lack of agreement of terms disclosed to the borrower and the terms in the note and rider, (3) selection of the wrong index or index value, (4) selection of the index on the wrong date, (5) failure to make any adjustment in some years (or ever), and (6) incorrect allocation of payment between interest and principal. Evidence shows that errors may occur in 20 to 30 percent of ARMs.

Since the loan document is viewed as a contract, lenders must correct any errors that result in overcharges to borrowers and refund any overpayments. On the other hand, undercharges cannot be collected by lenders from borrowers.

FRM–ARM Spread

The rate of interest on an ARM is typically 1 to 3 percentage points below that on a fixed-rate loan. The reason is simple. Lenders accept a lower rate for shifting a portion of the interest rate risk to borrowers. The more risk they can shift to borrowers through loose rate caps and frequent adjustment periods, the lower will be the rate relative to that on a fixed-rate loan. At any particular time the FRM–ARM rate spread will depend on several factors. Two of the most important are the market's expectations of the trend and volatility in interest rates. We saw in Chapter 2 that the yield curve can be used as a simple forecasting tool for future interest rates. When the yield curve is upward-sloping and interest rates have recently been volatile, lenders will offer larger discounts on ARMs and the FRM–ARM spread will widen. When the yield curve is flat, the spread will narrow. On occasion, the yield curve has been downward-sloping, suggesting that interest rates may fall. In this case, lenders have less incentive to offer ARMs and the spread has nearly disappeared. Generally, however, borrowers can expect to get a 1–3 percent break on the ARM rate over the FRM rate.

The demand for ARMs is affected by two primary factors: (a) the level of market interest rates in general and (b) the spread between the prices of FRMs and ARMs. Higher market rates in general reduce the affordability of FRMs and make ARMs more appealing. Likewise, the greater the differential between the rate on FRMs and the rate on ARMs (since it is lower), the greater the demand for ARMs.

PROBLEMS OF DEMAND: THE TILT EFFECT AND THE GRADUATED-PAYMENT MORTGAGE

The tilt effect occurs when expectations of future inflation cause interest rates to rise. Lenders then charge a higher rate on newly originated loans to compensate for expected inflation, preserving a real rate of return. The higher rate, in turn, causes payments on a standard, fixed-rate loan to increase. Since the FRM is an annuity, all payments are raised uniformly. The real (inflation-adjusted) size of the initial payment can be substantially greater than the latter payments. That is, in terms of buying power, a $1000 monthly payment today is much greater than a $1000 payment 10, 20, or 30 years from today.

Although the income of the borrower is expected to increase over the term of the loan, because of the inflationary expectation the borrower must make the initial payments out of current income, not future income. This results in very burdensome payments at the start of the loan and easy payments at the end. Consider that 30 years ago, a $110 payment would have represented about 25 percent of the head of household's income. That sort of payment was common on mortgages at that time.

The principal AMI designed to offset the tilt effect is the **graduated-payment mortgage (GPM).** The concept of the GPM is rather simple. The payments on a fixed-rate loan are rearranged to be lower at the beginning of the loan and higher at the end. The payment pattern is designed to track the income of the borrower as it is affected by inflation. The rate on the loan is not changed, just the pattern of payments. Generally, the payments are constant for a year and then increased in each successive year. For some GPMs the payments are scheduled to increase for only several years before leveling off for the remainder of the mortgage term. Because the interest rate on a GPM is approximately that on a level-payment FRM, the initial smaller payment may be insufficient to meet all of the interest obligation. Any residual is added to the balance of the loan, resulting in negative amortization for about the first half of the term.

GPM EXAMPLE

Let's say that the rate on a level-payment FRM is 12 percent and that, for simplicity, payments are made annually. With no discount points, the equation for a $100,000 loan appears as follows:

$$\$100,000 = \frac{12,414}{(1 + 0.12)^1} + \frac{12,414}{(1 + 0.12)^2} + \cdots + \frac{12,414}{(1 + 0.12)^{30}} \qquad \text{Equation (6–2)}$$

To convert this loan to a GPM with payments rising by 7.5 percent for the first 5 years and fixed thereafter, the payments must be restructured. The initial payment must be chosen such that each of the five succeeding payments are 7.5 percent greater than the preceding, the remaining payments for 24 years are equal to that of the sixth year, and the above equation is maintained. The following payment schedule is the result:

$$\$100,000 = \frac{791.40}{(1.01)^1} + \cdots + \frac{850.72}{(1.01)^{13}} + \cdots + \frac{914.53}{(1.01)^{25}} + \cdots + \frac{983.12}{(1.01)^{37}} + \cdots$$

$$+ \frac{1,056.85}{(1.01)^{49}} + \cdots + \frac{1,136.11}{(1.01)^{61}} + \cdots + \frac{1,136.11}{(1.01)^{360}}$$

The amortization schedule for this loan appears in Table 6–6. Note that negative amortization occurs through the first 5 years. The payment on the GPM is insufficient to meet the interest charges during this period. The payment does not even equal that for a standard level-payment mortgage until approximately the fourth or fifth year of the loan. For example, the interest charge on a $100,000 loan at 12 percent is approximately $12,000 for the first year. Yet the 12 payments of $791.40 add up to only $9496. The difference, $2504, is added to the loan balance. Payments exceed the interest charge only at the end of the fifth year.

A method for solving for the initial monthly payment (the remaining payments are tied to the first payment by the pre-established growth rate) is presented in Appendix A to this chapter. The computations can be somewhat involved, so standard tables have been developed to ease the problem of determining the initial payment. Table 6–7 is an example of such a table. The factors in the table are multiplied by the amount of the loan balance to arrive at the initial payment. Note that the entry for a 12 percent loan with a 7.5 percent growth in payments for 5 years is 0.007914, or $791.40, for a $100,000 loan. ▮ ▮

The most popular GPMs are insured by the FHA. At one time, the FHA had two GPM programs, 245a and 245b. The 245a program set the initial loan-to-value ratio such that the negative amortization would not exceed 97 percent of the initial appraised value of the property. The 245b program was more liberal; under this program negative amortization could bring the loan balance to 113 percent of the property value. The 245b program was terminated in October 1987 because of its default risk. Even though the GPM solves the tilt problem, it has some shortcomings and has not gained widespread acceptance.

TABLE 6–6
Amortization Schedule of GPM Loan
$100,000, 12%, Initial Monthly Payment = $791.37

Year	Beginning Balance	Interest	Payment	Ending Balance[a]
1	$100,000	$12,142[b]	$ 9,496[c]	$102,646
2	102,646	12,439	10,209	104,875
3	104,874	12,677	10,974	106,577
4	106,577	12,845	11,797	107,625
5	107,625	12,928	12,682	107,871
6	107,871	12,905	13,633	107,143
7	107,143	12,813	13,633	106,323
.	.	.	.	.
.	.	.	.	.
.	.	.	.	.
30	13,812	179	13,633	0

[a]Beginning balance = interest + payment − ending balance.
[b]Although the interest rate is 12% per annum, the interest cost is slightly higher than $12,000 because of the negative amortization in the initial months.
[c]12 × $791.37.

TABLE 6–7
Factors to Compute Monthly Payment in First Year of GPM[a]

Growth Rate for First 5 Years	Interest Rate						
	9	9.5	10	10.5	11	11.5	12
0.050	0.006671	0.006986	0.007305	0.007631	0.007961	0.008296	0.008635
0.075	0.006079	0.006372	0.006670	0.006971	0.007283	0.007596	0.007914
0.010	0.005543	0.005816	0.006094	0.006377	0.000666	0.006958	0.007255

[a]First payment = Factor × loan balance

The benefits of the GPM are simple. By partially eliminating the tilt effect (most GPMs have constant payments after the first 6 years, not throughout the life of the loan), borrowers can qualify for a larger loan than with a level payment mortgage. Housing becomes more affordable. Also, the increase in payments each year corresponds with the expected increase in the borrower's income. There are three main problems with the GPM, however: negative amortization, interest rate risk, and inflexible payment schedules.

The most obvious problem of the GPM is the default risk associated with negative amortization. In our example, negative amortization reached 107.8 percent of the loan balance in year five. Assuming no appreciation in housing prices (or a decline, as was the case in some regions of the country during the 1980s), the original loan-to-value ratio would have to be as small as 92.5 percent to avoid negative equity and the likelihood of default. For this reason the FHA 245a program required a larger down payment than for fixed-rate loans, usually about 10 percent. Although the GPM is designed to solve the affordability problem associated with the tilt effect, it creates another affordability problem in terms of the larger down payment required to mitigate default risk.

A second problem of the GPM involves interest rate risk. Although it is common to speak of interest rate risk as related to the maturity of a debt obligation, it is actually related to its effective maturity, or duration. The reader is referred to the appendix to Chapter 4 for a discussion of duration, maturity, and interest rate risk. Recall that duration is related to the maturity of a debt obligation but is not quite the same thing. Generally, the longer the maturity, the longer the duration. The two are related because duration measures the extent to which the payment pattern of a debt obligation is pushed back in time. However, large intermediate payments shorten duration (but not maturity) and lower interest rate risk by allowing the lender to reinvest those payments at current interest rates. A standard mortgage includes some amortization of the principal in its payments and thus has a shorter duration than, say, a corporate bond of equal maturity but with interest-only payments. The latter, in turn, has a shorter duration than a zero-coupon bond. A zero-coupon bond has no intermediate payments at all; its only payment is at maturity. In that case, duration and maturity are the same.

The following examples are intended to clarify the relationship between maturity and duration.

Debt	Maturity	Duration
1-year ARM	1 year	10.8 months
30-year FRM	30 years	7.7 to 8.5 years
GPM	30 years	11 to 12 years
Zero-coupon bond	30 years	30 years

In any event, it is the duration of a debt instrument that determines its interest rate risk. But since duration and maturity are closely related, it is common to speak of interest rate risk as being determined by maturity.

The negative amortization on a GPM lengthens its duration over that of a level-payment loan of equal maturity. This increases its interest rate risk. Simply put, if rates rise subsequent to the origination of a GPM, the lender is placed in the position of having a loan with a growing balance financed at an old, low rate.

Lenders will seek compensation for this risk through a slightly higher rate of interest (the FHA insures against default risk, not interest rate risk) than that on the level-payment loan. This factor partially defeats the affordability advantage of the GPM. Higher down payments (to control for default risk) and higher initial yields (to compensate for interest rate risk) have combined to offset some of the affordability advantage of the GPM.

Another problem with the GPM is the inflexibility of its payment schedule. Although graduated, it is graduated for only several years and for a predetermined set amount. There is no guarantee that the borrower's income will increase in relation to the schedule of payments. One finds it difficult to imagine that a borrower's income will rise by 7.5 percent annually for 6 years and level off for the remaining 24 years. As presently structured, GPMs become standard, fixed-rate loans after the first 6 years. A GPM can be designed such that the payments increase throughout the life of the loan. This would involve an even smaller first year's payment and greater negative amortization until approximately 12 or so years into the life of the loan. It would also increase the loan's duration, further raising interest rate risk for the lender. But there is still no guarantee that borrower's income will increase so as to track the predetermined schedule of payments. Another problem with the GPM involves the treatment of interest expense for tax purposes. The tax ramifications of AMIs are discussed later in this chapter.

SIMULTANEOUSLY SOLVING THE PROBLEMS OF SUPPLY AND DEMAND: THE PRICE LEVEL ADJUSTED MORTGAGE

One AMI, the **price level adjusted mortgage (PLAM),** solves both the tilt and the interest rate risk problems of an FRM.[5] The lender desires to earn a real rate-of-return on a loan and also be compensated for any erosion due to inflation. This is the reason that lenders add an expected inflation premium to the real rate when setting the rate on a standard loan. Unfortunately, this creates a tilt problem. It also does not guarantee that the lender will be protected from erosion due to unexpected inflation. The lender is subject to risk associated with unexpected increases in inflation and market rates of interest.

The PLAM solves these problems by separating the return to the lender into two components: the real return and compensation for inflation. With the PLAM, the inflation component is determined after the inflation has occurred and is equal to the exact amount of the inflation. The contract rate on the PLAM is the real rate, approximately 3 percent. Annually, the balance of the loan is adjusted for the amount of the previous year's rate of inflation. For instance, a lender makes a $100,000 loan, and in the first year the rate of inflation is 6 percent. Under the PLAM, the lender would receive a 9 percent return in the first year—3 percent as the contract rate of interest and a 6 percent increase in the balance of the loan. If there were no inflation at all in the first year, there would be no upward adjustment of the loan balance. The lender would receive only the real rate-of-return, 3 percent, but that would be sufficient in the absence of inflation.

The low contract rate makes the loan more affordable for the borrower. Because inflation need not be anticipated with the PLAM, there is no tilt effect. The borrower only pays the inflation premium through an upward adjustment of the balance after the inflation has occurred. Presumably, the increase in the borrower's income will have approximated the rate of inflation. The only drawback of the PLAM (besides its complexity) is the provision for negative amortization. The negative amortization occurs through the adjustment of the balance for recent inflation.

PLAM EXAMPLE

To understand how a PLAM works, consider Table 6–8. For purposes of illustration, we assume that the inflation rate is 4 percent for the first 3 years, 6 percent for Years 4 through 6, and 5 percent for the remainder of the loan. The initial contract rate is the real rate, 3 percent. Each year the beginning balance is amortized over the remaining life of the loan at the real rate. The PLAM behaves as follows:

Year 1. In the first year, the payment is established by amortizing the $100,000 loan over 30 years at 3 percent. The payment is substantially less than that on a standard loan amortized at 9 percent—$5102 versus $9734. In the absence of inflation, the ending balance would be $97,898. The actual ending balance is adjusted upward by 4 percent ($101,814 = $97,898 × 1.04).

Year 2. This payment is set by amortizing the adjusted balance ($101,814) over 29 years at 3 percent. Since the ending balance from Year 1 was adjusted upward by 4 percent, the payment in Year 2 will be 4 percent greater than in Year 1—$5306 versus $5102. Recall that it is amortized at the same rate, 3 percent. If the borrower's income has kept pace with inflation, there will be no increase in the real payment. The ending balance in the absence of inflation would be $99,562. This is adjusted upward by Year 2 inflation, 4 percent, so that the adjusted ending balance is $103,545.

Year 5. Skipping to Year 5, the beginning balance is $108,750. Amortized at 3 percent the payment rises to $6083. This is a 6 percent increase from the previous year, reflecting the 6 percent inflation in Year 4. Negative amortization continues.

TABLE 6–8
Price Level Adjusted Mortgage Examples[a]

Year	Beginning Balance	Interest (3%)	Payments	Ending Balance Before Adjustment	Ending Balance After Adjustment
1	$100,000	$3,000	$5,102	$97,898	$101,814
2	101,814	3,054	5,306	99,562	103,545
3	103,545	3,106	5,518	101,133	105,178
4	105,178	3,155	5,739	102,595	108,750
5	108,750	3,263	6,083	105,930	112,285
6	112,285	3,369	6,448	109,206	115,758
7	115,758	3,473	6,835	112,395	118,015
.	.	.	.	.	.
.	.	.	.	.	.
.	.	.	.	.	.
14	126,629	3,799	9,618	120,810	126,851
.	.	.	.	.	.
.	.	.	.	.	.
.	.	.	.	.	.
.	.	.	.	.	.
.	.	.	.	.	.
28	53,864	1,616	19,043	36,438	38,259
29	38,259	1,148	19,995	19,412	20,383
30	20,383	611	20,994	0	0

Inflation rate: 4% Years 1–3, 6% Years 4–6, 5% Years 7–30
[a]Loan amount = $100,000; Real rate = 3%.

Remaining Years. Continued inflation causes the loan balance to increase for several years. In this example it reaches a peak in Year 14. The reason the balance does not continue to grow beyond Year 14 is that with each successive year the balance is amortized over a shorter remaining term. For short terms, a large proportion of the payment represents amortization. In Year 14, only $3799 of the $9618 payment is interest; the rest is principal reduction. Eventually, this large amount of amortization exceeds the adjustment of the balance for inflation. The payments in the last few years of the loan appear very high. The last payment, nearly $21,000, is four times greater than the first. This will not be a burden if the borrower's income has kept up with inflation. The last payment is greater than the first by a compounded growth factor of about 5 percent annually over the 30 years. ▮ ▮

The Effective Cost. Calculating the effective cost of the PLAM is an internal rate of return (IRR) process similar to that shown earlier for the ARM. Using our example from Table 6–8, let's calculate the effective cost for a 5-year holding period. The equation would be

$$\$100,000 = \$5,102/(1 + IRR) + \$5,306/(1 + IRR)^2 + \$5,518/(1 + IRR)^3$$

$$+ \$5,739/(1 + IRR)^4 + \$6,083/(1 + IRR)^5 + 112,285/(1 + IRR)^5 \quad \text{(Equation 6–3)}$$

Solving for the IRR shows the effective cost to be 7.62 percent. The steps on the financial calculator would be

1. Enter 100,000 as a negative CF_0.
2. Enter 5,102 as CF_1.
3. Enter 5,306 as CF_2.
4. Enter 5,518 as CF_3.
5. Enter 5,739 as CF_4.
6. Enter the sum of 6,083 plus 112,285 as CF_5.
7. Solve for IRR.

The PLAM is an ideal loan for solving both the demand and supply problems of the fixed-rate mortgage in an inflationary environment. By tying the return to inflation after it has occurred, lenders need not include inflationary expectations in the contract rate. Neither do lenders have to correctly estimate future inflation. The inflation component of the return is determined on an annual basis as the inflation occurs and is exactly equal to the amount of inflation. The PLAM is not a popular AMI for several reasons, however.

The PLAM has several drawbacks that explain its relative obscurity in the mortgage market. First, it is a relatively complex instrument and one that is rather difficult to explain to borrowers. Second, even with moderate inflation, the upward adjustment in the loan balance in the early years creates negative amortization. The PLAM's negative amortization is greater and occurs for a longer time than that of a typical GPM. Even with the moderate inflation in our example, the loan balance reaches 127 percent of the original balance. With such negative amortization, default risk becomes a concern if equity in the property is eroded. Also, payments increase as a result of inflation. If a borrower's income fails to keep up with inflation, payment-to-income ratios above a stress level can result.

There is some difference of opinion on the default risk of PLAMs. Proponents of the PLAM argue that any inflation that drives the negative amortization of the loan also will increase the value of the property. If the two increase in proportion, there should always be positive equity. Also, as indicated above, there should be no payment shock, as the income of the borrower also will increase with inflation. McCulloch argues that since 1920 the experience in the United States has been that nominal incomes and house prices do keep up with inflation.[6] He claims that the payment-to-income ratio over the life of a PLAM will likely be much more stable than that on an ARM. The reason is that when unexpected inflation occurs, the balance of the loan is adjusted after the inflation so as to compensate the lender. With an ARM the lender raises the interest rate on the loan at the anniversary date for all remaining payments. This reintroduces the tilt problem all over again. Manchester tracked the payment-to-income ratios on a hypothetical FRM, ARM, and PLAM originated in 1967.[7] Through 1982 the after-tax payment-to-income ratios on the FRM and ARM fell steadily, from 15.5 and 14.1 percent to 5.8 and 7.6 percent, respectively. The after-tax, payment-to-income ratio on the PLAM remained nearly constant over this time, falling only slightly from 13.6 to 12.6.

In regard to negative amortization, Pesando and Turnbull indicate that the major risk of PLAMs comes from the difference in regional house appreciation rates.[8] Looking at the prices of houses in several Canadian cities, they conclude that there are substantial differences in the rate of home price appreciation by region. Lenders that originate PLAMs for which the negative amortization is tied to a national inflation rate may find that houses in localized areas may not appreciate as rapidly (or may even fall) as the national average. They found, for example, that based on historical differences in regional house appreciation rates, there would be an 11 percent chance that the loan-to-value ratio of a house in Vancouver would exceed 100 percent 5 years after financing with a PLAM. The same probability would be 21 percent in Toronto and 40.5 percent in Mississauga.

Regional variation in the growth in property prices is also characteristic of the U.S. economy. Consider that between 1983 and 1988, home prices rose by 22.9 percent in the South and 81.2 percent in the Northeast, according to figures from the National Association of Realtors. During this time, average home prices rose by only 7.5 percent in Texas, and between 1985 and 1987 they fell by more than 5 percent in that state.

The variance in local house price appreciation around national trends clearly indicates that localized default problems could crop up due to failures in regional economies. This regional risk is likely one of the reasons lenders have not embraced the PLAM, especially in the absence of any provision for default insurance.

Another problem with the PLAM is that it does not quite solve the maturity mismatch problem. At the beginning of the year a lender may offer 8 percent on 1-year deposits. If inflation that year turns out to be only 2 percent, then the rate-of-return on PLAM mortgages will only be 5 percent, less than the interest expense. That is, although the PLAM eliminates the need to accurately predict inflation from the standpoint of the lender's assets, it does not do the same from the standpoint of deposit liabilities. Lenders that originate substantial amounts of PLAMs may have to issue deposits for which the rate is also tied to inflation after the fact. Such price level adjusted deposits (PLADs) would allow the lender to originate mortgages without any risk of predicting future inflation. Whether depositors of thrifts could be persuaded to accept PLADs is another question. Later, we indicate that the PLAM also suffers from an unfavorable income tax treatment of the borrower's interest expense.

OTHER ALTERNATIVE MORTGAGE INSTRUMENTS

Other AMIs include the shared appreciation mortgage (SAM), the reverse annuity mortgage (RAM), and the pledged account mortgage, also called the flexible loan insurance program (FLIP).

Shared Appreciation Mortgage

The high interest rates of the late 1970s and early 1980s provided the motivation for the **shared appreciation mortgage (SAM),** first offered by Advance Mortgage Corporation in 1980. Savings and loans were given permission by the Federal Home Loan Board to offer SAMs in 1982.

The shared appreciation mortgage works similarly to the PLAM, except that it has no annual readjustments of the loan balance and the monthly payment. The lender establishes an initial low rate on the loan and collects for the inflation premium in a lump sum later. The payment consists of a portion of the appreciation in the value of the house. The amount of the appreciation is determined when the property is sold or by appraisal on a predetermined date (say, in 10 years), whichever occurs first. By lowering the initial rate (and payment), the SAM relieves the affordability problem of standard loans. It also provides some diversification benefits for the borrower. Instead of having the majority of wealth tied up in a residence, the borrower can spin off the right to a portion of the property's appreciation in return for reduced payments. The payment savings then can be invested in other nonresidential assets.

One task facing the lender is pricing the SAM. Pricing entails the simultaneous determination of the reduction in the initial interest rate and the share of the appreciation of the property. The lender must decide what share in appreciation will compensate for the reduced interest rate on the loan. The greater the reduction in the rate, the larger the required share of appreciation. The tradeoff must be such that the expected return on the SAM equals that on a standard loan. The required share will depend upon a number of factors, including the lender's tax bracket, the loan-to-value ratio, the reduction in the interest rate, the rate on a standard loan, and expected inflation in housing values. Dougherty, Van Order, Villani developed a pricing model that incorporates the above factors.[9] If the lender is in the 30 percent tax bracket and the nominal rate of interest is 10 percent, for instance, the after-tax nominal rate is 7 percent. If the nominal rate is 10 percent, then inflation expectations could reasonably approximate 7 percent.

Assuming that the after-tax, nominal interest rate equals the expected house price appreciation rate, the model can be stated as

$$\alpha = \frac{\upsilon \cdot \beta}{1-t} \qquad \text{(Equation 6–4)}$$

where α is the share of appreciation, υ is the loan-to-value ratio, β is the reduction in the initial interest rate, and $(1\text{-}t)$ represents one minus the lender's tax bracket.

As an example, if the loan-to-value ratio is 0.9 and there is a one-third reduction in the interest rate on the loan and the lender's tax bracket is 25 percent, then the share of appreciation is

$$0.4 = \frac{0.9 \times 0.333}{0.75}$$

The formula makes intuitive sense. A larger loan-to-value ratio means that the lender is putting up more funds on a given house. The funds are advanced at a reduced rate. With larger loan-to-value ratios, the lender is putting up a greater portion of the funds required to acquire the property and thus will demand a greater portion of the appreciation of the asset. An increase in the loan-to-value ratio from 80 to 90 percent requires a 12.5 percent increase in the share. Also, the greater the reduction in the interest rate, the larger the required share.

There are several considerations not included in the share-determination formula. First, if the expected rate of housing inflation rises above the after-tax nominal rate, then the required share will be reduced. Second, for lenders the SAM is a better hedge against inflation than an FRM. With an FRM the lender loses with increases in inflation but does not gain with a decrease (because of the prepayment option). With the SAM the loss from unanticipated inflation is mitigated by sharing in-house appreciation. For borrowers the SAM is a hedge against the possibility that the price of the house will not rise as rapidly as general house prices. It also has diversification benefits discussed above.

There are some shortcomings of the SAM that have prevented it from becoming a popular AMI. First, the determination of the amount of appreciation can be difficult and will depend on many factors. Second, there is the risk that individual property prices may not appreciate as fast as general housing prices. The Community Reinvestment Act (discussed in Chapter 9) likely will preclude lenders from setting different terms on SAMs to reflect neighborhood risk. Third, there is the risk that the borrower, who has given up a share of the property appreciation, will not have an incentive to maintain the property. Also, the question of improvements may complicate the determination of the appreciation. If the homeowner adds, say, a pool at a cost of $15,000, the property's value may rise by only $9000. Yet the homeowner will want a credit of the full amount when the property's appreciation is determined by appraisal.

Finally, there are problems with the tax treatment of the interest expense, outlined later in the chapter.

Reverse Annuity Mortgage

This type of mortgage was approved by the FHLBB for member thrifts in January 1979. As the name implies, it acts in reverse of a regular mortgage. With a regular mortgage the borrower receives a large cash inflow (loan) in the present and makes monthly payments (cash outflows) over the life of the loan. With a **reverse annuity mortgage (RAM)** the borrower receives a series of monthly payments and, at the end of the loan, makes a large cash repayment. In both types of loans, the house serves as collateral and its value will exceed the amount of the loan. RAMs are designed primarily for retired homeowners with little or no debt on their current residence. Whether or not to remain in a home is a major life decision for most elderly homeowners. Mayer and Simons estimate that 6 million U.S. households could benefit from the use of a RAM.[10] A study by VanderHart shows that this decision is influenced by financial and demographic factors such as income, wealth, home equity, marital status, and health.[11] The terms of RAMs are flexible enough to create several different types.

A fixed payment, fixed term loan provides for a fixed payment for a certain length of time, usually 10 years. If the property is sold or the owner dies prior to the 10-year term, the loan is paid off from the proceeds of the sale of the property. If the owner is still living in the house at the end of 10 years, the loan will have to be paid off. Often, another RAM can be taken out to refinance the existing one, if there has been some appreciation in the property's value.

Table 6–9 shows the payments on a 10-year RAM for $100,000. A graduated-payment, fixed-term loan (not shown) works the same way, except that the initial payments are smaller and the ending payments are larger. Such a RAM is designed to alleviate the fears of retired persons concerning inflation.

A fixed-payment, lifetime RAM is designed to eliminate mortality risk. This is particularly worrisome for some retirees. Many fear that if they outlive the term of the RAM, their payments will cease and they may be forced to sell their property. The lifetime RAM guarantees a monthly payment for as long as the homeowner lives. For example, assume the RAM is for $100,000. The lender will buy a deferred life annuity from a life insurance company with a portion of the loan—in this case, $40,000. The deferred life annuity will begin payments to the homeowner at the end of the loan—in this case, 10 years. The lender will make payments to the homeowner beginning immediately. The payments, with interest, will accumulate to a $60,000 balance in 10 years. At this time payments from the life annuity will begin, and the homeowner can refinance

TABLE 6−9

Reverse Annuity Mortgage[a]

Year	Beginning Balance	Payment	Interest	Ending Balance
1	0	$5,704.13	$570.41[b]	$6,274.54[c]
2	6,275.54	5,704.13	1,197.87	13,176.54
3	13,177.54	5,704.13	1,888.07	20,768.74
4	20,769.74	5,704.13	2,647.29	29,120.15
5	29,120.15	5,704.13	3,482.43	38,306.71
6	38,307.71	5,704.13	4,401.08	48,411.93
7	48,412.93	5,704.13	5,411.61	59,527.66
8	59,528.66	5,704.13	6,523.18	71,754.97
9	71,755.97	5,704.13	7,745.91	85,205.01
10	85,205.01	5,704.13	9,090.91	100,000.06

[a]$100,000, 10%, Ten-Year Loan
[b]10% of Beginning Balance Plus Payment
[c]Beginning Balance Plus Payment Plus Interest

the mortgage balance. If the homeowner dies prior to the life annuity, then the proceeds of the sale of the property pay off the balance of the loan.

This form of transaction takes the mortality risk out of a RAM. The lender does not assume the mortality risk but shifts it to an insurance company that is able to diversify the risk. But, as Boehm and Ehrhardt point out, RAMs have exceptionally high interest rate risk.[12] Also, movements in interest rates contribute to prepayment risk. Klein and Sirmans show that prepayment is most sensitive to marital status, age of the borrower, and term of the loan.[13] In addition, Miceli and Sirmans show that lenders must protect themselves against the risk of undermaintenance by the borrower.[14] This is especially true when the RAM contract calls for the lender to receive either the loan balance or the sale price of the house.

In essence, RAMs are instruments by which retired homeowners can take equity out of their residences. There are alternatives for the homeowner to accomplish the same task. The homeowner can take out a standard mortgage and invest the proceeds in a life annuity. She can then make the standard payments out of the monthly income from the life annuity. Assuming the homeowner's life expectancy is only several years, the payments from the life annuity should cover the mortgage payments and provide additional income for living expenses.

Pledged-account Mortgage

A pledged account mortgage, also referred to as a **flexible loan insurance program (FLIP),** is a loan arrangement that creates graduated payments for the borrower. The arrangement combines a deposit with the lender and a standard, fixed-rate loan to create a graduated-payment structure. Rather than use the funds in the deposit as a down payment (and thereby lower the amount of the standard loan), the borrower uses interest payments and a reduction in the principal of the deposit to supplement payments on the fixed-rate loan. The deposit will be pledged along with the house as collateral for the loan. An example will clarify how this loan arrangement works.

Assume the buyer desires to purchase a $110,000 house and has $30,000 in cash. Instead of financing the acquisition with an $80,000 loan, the buyer makes a down payment of only $10,000, places $20,000 in a pledged account, and borrows $100,000. Assume the interest rate on the loan is 10 percent, while the rate earned on the deposit is 7.5 percent. The monthly payment required to amortize a $100,000 loan over 30 years at 10 percent is $877.57, or $10,531 annually. Also assume the borrower wants payments to increase at 7.5 percent annually for the first 6 years. The arrangement can be structured as indicated in Table 6–10.

In the first year the buyer makes a $4746 payment on the loan. The difference ($10,531 − $4746) is made up of a principal and interest contribution from the pledged account. In the fol-

TABLE 6–10

Pledged Account or FLIP Mortgage[a]

Year	Beginning Deposit Balance	Reduction in Principal	Buyer's Interest	Ending Payment	Total	Balance
1	$20,000	$4,285	$1,500[b]	$4,746	$10,531[c]	$17,215[d]
2	17,215	4,138	1,291	5,102[e]	10,531	14,369
3	14,369	3,969	1,078	5,485	10,531	11,478
4	11,478	3,774	861	5,896	10,531	8,564
5	8,564	3,550	642	6,338	10,531	5,656
6	5,656	3,293	424	6,813	10,531	2,787
7	2,787	2,997	209	7,324	10,531	0
8–30	0	0	0	10,531	10,531	0

[a]$100,000 loan, 10%; $20,000 deposit, 9.5%
payments increase at 7.5% annually
[b]7.5% of beginning balance
[c]12 × 877.57
[d]Beginning balance plus interest less principal reduction
[e]Previous payment × 1.075

lowing year the borrower makes a $5102 payment. This is 7.5 percent larger than the first year's payment and, again, the difference is made up from contributions from the pledged account. Because some principal is being used up, the pledged account is being exhausted. In year seven the borrower's payments are up to $7324, and the deposit is exhausted. After year seven the borrower makes the full payment, $10,531, necessary to amortize the loan.

Had the borrower made a $30,000 down payment and financed $80,000, the monthly payment would have been $702.06, or $8425 annually. The pledged account arrangement, just as a graduated-payment mortgage, causes the initial payments to be below, and the later payments to be above, those on an $80,000 standard FRM.

For the borrower the main advantage of the pledged account arrangement is the lower initial payments and their effect on affordability. The lender may be in a slightly greater default risk position with this arrangement than with an $80,000 loan (down payment of $30,000). Although the account is pledged as collateral, it is quickly exhausted. As with a GPM, the arrangement provides for negative amortization. As the account is exhausted, the loan-to-value ratio increases. As long as the property price does not fall, there will always be positive equity, however.

One disadvantage to the borrower is the larger total finance charges that result. The present value (discounted at the mortgage rate, 10 percent) of the total payments under the pledged account loan is $76,224. Add to this the $10,000 down payment and the $20,000 deposit (which is exhausted), and the total cost in terms of present value is $106,224. The present value of the payments on an $80,000 loan plus a $20,000 down payment is $100,000. The larger finance cost associated with the pledged account loan results from the fact that payments made on the loan financed at 10 percent are made from an account that only earns 7.5 percent. As long as the borrower makes less on the pledged account than is charged on the mortgage, the pledged account arrangement will result in overall higher finance charges. If the borrower could earn a rate on the deposit equal to that charged on the mortgage, the result would be a wash—no higher or lower total finance charges, just a rearrangement of the payment pattern.

In an efficient market one would expect that the loan arrangement will grant neither net benefits nor costs to the borrower or lender. The higher default risk faced by the lender is offset by the larger yield on the loan (resulting from the low-cost, pledged account). If there were no greater default risk, one would expect that lenders would either reduce the rate on the mortgage or offer higher rates on the pledged account, until the total cost on a pledged account loan would equal that on a standard loan with a larger down payment.

ALTERNATIVE MORTGAGE INSTRUMENTS AND THE TAX DEDUCTIBILITY OF INTEREST PAYMENTS

The relative attractiveness to both lenders and borrowers of AMIs is especially affected by the tax treatment of the interest deduction on these loans. The amount and timing of the deduction depends upon the type of mortgage instrument, whether a standard loan or an AMI. With a standard loan all interest payments are taxed as income to the lender and deductions by the borrower. With some AMIs this symmetry may not hold because borrowers, being cash-basis taxpayers, may not fully use interest deductions, while lenders, being accrual-basis taxpayers, must include all interest charges in income.

As an example, consider the GPM. In the initial years the interest expense will be greater than the payment, leading to negative amortization. The borrower cannot deduct the excess of the interest charge over the amount of the payment. The deduction is deferred until positive amortization begins.[15] Thus, although the initial payments are less on a GPM, so are the interest deductions. The lender, on the other hand, must include all of the interest charge in income even though the cash inflow is less.

Negative amortization also characterizes the PLAM. The adjustment for inflation is considered a finance charge, but since it is added to the loan balance and is not a cash payment, the borrower cannot make a deduction for tax purposes. As with the GPM, the lender must include all of the interest charge, including the adjustment for inflation, in interest income.

Under the SAM the lender offers a low rate of interest in exchange for a share of the appreciation in the property. For a very low initial rate, the share of the appreciation will be large. The initial payments on the SAM will provide for few tax benefits. The shared appreciation portion of the interest charge is deductible, but only when paid and for owner-occupied properties.[16] There will be a large deduction when the property is either sold or appraised. If the borrower finances the share of the appreciation (interest) from the same lender, the tax deduction will be disallowed. In this case, it will have to be amortized over the life of the new loan.[17] For SAM loans the interest deduction can be large, late, and in some cases, not fully used. From the standpoint of the lender, the SAM loan is not so onerous. Interest income is reported only to the extent of actual cash payments. As the property appreciates, the lender is obtaining a rate of return but does not have to make any tax payments until the property is sold or appraised. This is similar to the increase in value of a capital asset. The increase in value is not taxed until the asset is sold.

The tax treatment of AMIs might create some sort of clientele effect since some AMIs actually may be advantageous for some types of borrowers. Young borrowers in a low tax bracket may have insufficient itemizations to take advantage of tax deductions. GPMs and PLAMs may be well suited for these types of borrowers. The deferred tax deductions allow these borrowers to "store up" tax benefits until a time when they can be more valuable.

In summary, the tax treatment of AMIs will distort the amount and timing of their after-tax payments. The value of each can be determined by discounting the after-tax cash flows by the after-tax discount rate. Because of the asymmetry of the tax treatment of interest expense for the borrower and interest revenue for the lender, the relative values of AMIs may diverge. It is likely that the tax treatment of negatively amortizing loans has added to their costs and their relative obscurity in the marketplace.

Alternative mortgage instruments emerged partially as a result of interest rate risk faced by lenders. One consequence of interest rate risk was that as rates rose, borrowers had an incentive to retain their loans and not pay them off. However, as rates fell, borrowers, facing no prepayment penalty had an incentive to refinance at the lower rate. We now take up the economics of refinancing from the standpoint of the borrower.

MORTGAGE REFINANCING

The menu of alternative mortgage instruments also must be considered by the mortgage borrower in a mortgage refinancing decision. Although there may be no plans to sell the property to which the mortgage is attached, the borrower may have an incentive to trade an existing mortgage for a new one. For example, in periods of declining mortgage rates, homeowners often will refinance to a lower rate to take advantage of the resulting payment savings. Another borrower may refinance and borrow more than the amount currently owed in order to take out equity (maybe to send their child to college). An owner of an income-producing property may refinance in order to improve cash flow by lowering financing costs. A clear example is the "rush to refinance" that occurred in 1993 when mortgage rates were at their lowest point in two decades. Some borrowers refinanced their mortgages from fixed-rate to fixed-rate, fixed-rate to adjustable-rate or vice versa, adjustable to adjustable, or some other alternative.

The refinancing decision is essentially a net present value decision. If refinancing were a frictionless (i.e., costless) transaction, borrowers would refinance with any decrease in the interest rate. Since it is not costless, however, borrowers will refinance when they are confident that the benefits will outweigh the costs. A paper by Dickinson and Heuson shows that the refinancing decision is quite complicated with a number of factors being considered. These include interest rate movements, transactions costs, changes in borrower income and house value, personal financial opportunities, and the prepayment option embedded in the mortgage.[18] Yang and Maris show that information asymmetry makes it more difficult for the lender to price the refinancing.[19] An example of information asymmetry is the fact that the borrower may have more information about how long she will hold the mortgage than does the lender.

REFINANCING OWNER-OCCUPIED RESIDENTIAL PROPERTY

To make an effective refinancing decision, one must compare the terms on the existing mortgage with those on the new financing. Recall that the general terms of the mortgage will be the amount owed, the contract interest rate, the maturity, discount points, etc. In deciding whether to refinance, one compares the cost of refinancing to the benefits. The costs of refinancing would include the costs of getting out of the existing mortgage (maybe a prepayment penalty) plus the costs of acquiring the new mortgage (origination fee, discount points, etc.) The present value of this total cost is compared to the present value of the payment savings. If the benefit outweighs the cost, the borrower would refinance.

For example, suppose that a borrower took a 30-year, fixed-rate mortgage for $100,000 at a 10 percent contract rate, monthly payments. Five years later the contract rate on 25-year, fixed-rate mortgages is 7.5 percent. The attraction of the lower rate would cause the borrower to consider refinancing. A quick analysis shows the borrower's current position:

current payment = $877.57

outstanding balance = $96,574

prepayment penalty = 3 percent of the outstanding balance if repaid within the first 8 years

Obtaining a new 25-year, fixed-rate mortgage will cost the borrower 4 percent in financing costs. This includes 1 point origination fee, 2 discount points, and 1 percent other costs (such as an appraisal, survey, etc.). Thus, the total cost to get out of the existing mortgage and into the new one is a prepayment penalty on the existing loan of $2897 ($96,574 × 0.03) and financing cost on the new loan of $3863 ($96,574 × 0.04). This is a total of $6760.

Refinancing the outstanding balance for 25 years at the lower 7.50 percent rate results in a payment of $713.67. By refinancing the borrower has a monthly payment savings of $163.90. Since the refinancing decision is essentially an investment decision, all values would be set to present value terms using the borrower's opportunity cost of capital. Suppose this is 8 percent. Assuming that the borrower plans to hold the mortgage for its full term, the present value of the payment savings is $21,236. Comparing this with the cost to refinance of $6760 produces a positive net present value of $14,476. Thus, the borrower would refinance. This calculation can be shown as:

$$\text{NPV} = \$163.90 \ (\text{PVAIF}_{8/12, \ 300}) - \$6{,}760 = \$21{,}236 - \$6{,}760 = \$14{,}476.$$

One important consideration is the length of time the borrower plans to hold the mortgage. The above calculations assumed that the borrower planned either to hold the existing mortgage for its remaining life of 25 years or to hold the new mortgage for its entire 25 years. The analysis would be revised somewhat if the borrower has a planned holding period less than 25 years. Suppose that, when considering refinancing, the borrower knows that the mortgage will be held for eight more years. Thus if no refinancing takes place, the existing loan will be 13 years old (out of its 30-year life) when it is repaid. If refinancing takes place, the new loan will be 8 years old (out of its 25-year life) when it is repaid. Note that at that future point in time, both mortgages will have the same remaining term (17 years).

This becomes an important consideration since the outstanding balances of the two loans will not be equal at that time. Other things constant, the lower the contract rate the faster a loan will amortize.[20] Thus, the refinanced loan will have a lower balance at that time than the existing loan. This is viewed as a savings to the borrower and would be considered a cash inflow. After the additional 8 years, the outstanding balance on the existing mortgage if refinancing did not take place would be $85,934. With refinancing, the balance on the new loan would be $82,153. Note that the prepayment penalty on the existing loan has expired. This produces a savings at that time of $3781. The net present value equation now would be

$$NPV = \$163.90 \, (PVAIF_{8/12, \, 96}) + \$3,781 \, (PVIF_{8/12, \, 96}) - \$6,760$$

$$= \$11,594 + \$1,998 - \$6,760$$

$$= \$13,592 - \$6,760$$

$$= \$6,832.$$

The net present value, although lower than before, is positive, and the borrower would refinance.

SUMMARY

Table 6–11 summarizes the advantages and disadvantages of various AMI loans. Default risk is considered from the standpoint of both the provision for negative amortization and for increases in the payment-to-income ratio. The GPM and the PLAM have the greatest risk of default through negative amortization, while the ARM and FLIP loans join these two in terms of the likelihood that the payment-to-income ratio can increase. The standard, fixed-rate loan and the SAM are the only loans for which the payment cannot increase. In terms of interest rate risk, the ARM is superior to all other loans. While both the GPM and the PLAM have provisions for negative amortization, that on the PLAM compensates for changes in the rate of inflation. Thus, the risk is less with the PLAM than with the GPM, which has a rather long duration.

T A B L E   6 – 1 1
Characteristics of Various Mortgages

	SFR	ARM	GPM	PLAM	SAM	FLIP
Default risk from neg. amortization	Moderate	Moderate	Large	Large	Little	Moderate
Default risk from payment/income ratio	Moderate	Large	Large	Large	Little	Large
Interest and rate risk	Moderate	None	Substantial	Little	Little	Little
Tax savings	Standard	Standard	Poor	Poor	Standard	Standard
Level of complexity	Low	Moderate	Low	High	Moderate	Moderate
Affordability at high interest rates	Poor	Moderate	Good	Excellent	Excellent	Moderate

Loans that do not allow the borrower to deduct all of the interest charges when they occur (GPM, PLAM) are inferior to those that do. ARMs have a moderate level of complexity because of the various cap, margin, and index choices. The GPM is the only AMI for which the payment schedule is predetermined at origination and is, therefore, not complex. When interest rates are high, the GPM, PLAM, and SAM lower the initial payments and solve the tilt problem. The FLIP constructs a graduated-payment schedule through an arrangement that raises the total finance charges to the borrower.

Those loans that rank highest in overall characteristics are the FRM and the ARM. This would explain their dominance in the mortgage market. This is true whether a borrower is seeking funds to purchase a real property or to refinance a property currently owned. Refinancing can be viewed essentially as a present value analysis. If the present value of the future payment savings exceeds the cost of the refinancing, it may make economic sense to refinance the loan.

KEY TERMS

Adjustable rate mortgage (ARM)
Affordability problem
Cost of funds index (COFI)
Flexible loan insurance program (FLIP)
Fully indexed rate
Graduated payment mortgage (GPM)
Index Shared appreciation mortgage (SAM)
Initial-period discount
Life-of-loan rate cap
Margin
Negative amortization

Payment cap
Price level adjusted mortgage (PLAM)
Pricing ARMs
Pledged account mortgage
Rate cap
Reverse annuity mortgage (RAM)
Refinancing
Simulation model
Teaser rate
Terminal wealth
Tilt effect

SUGGESTED READINGS

Gordon, J. D., J. Lugtjes, and J. Feid. 1990. Thrifts' pricing of adjustable rate mortgages. Research Paper No. 90-02. Washington, DC: Office of Thrift Supervision.

Jaffee, D., and J. Kearl. 1975. Macroeconomics simulations of alternative mortgage instruments. *New Mortgage Designs for Stable Housing in an Inflationary Environment,* Conference Series no. 14. Federal Reserve Bank of Boston.

Lessard, D., and F. Modligliani. 1975. Inflation and the housing market: Problems and potential solutions. *New Mortgage Designs for Stable Housing in an Inflationary Environment,* Conference Series no. 14. Federal Reserve Bank of Boston.

Mettling, S. R. 1984. *Modern Residential Financing Methods.* Chicago: Real Estate Education Company, chs. 6, 7, and 8.

Ryding, J. 1990. Housing Finance and the Transmission of Monetary Policy. *Federal Reserve Bank of New York Quarterly Review,* Summer.

REVIEW QUESTIONS

6–1   Name two AMIs that solve the maturity mismatch problem of thrifts and explain how they do so.

6–2   Identify seven common terms that characterize an ARM.

6–3   What is meant by "pricing" ARM terms?

6–4   How would a lender change the margin on an ARM (increase or decrease) in response to (a) imposing a 1 percent rate cap on a previously uncapped ARM (b) granting an initial period discount and (c) removing a life-of-loan cap? Explain each of your answers.

6–5   What factors affect the share of newly originated mortgages that are ARMs?

6–6   What are the major shortcomings of the graduated-payment mortgage?

6–7   Explain how the price level adjusted mortgage compensates the lender for both the real rate of return and the rate of inflation.

6–8   What are the major shortcomings of the price level adjusted mortgage?

6–9   How is the amount of the share of property appreciation given to the lender for a SAM loan determined?

6–10   From the borrower's perspective, what is the major drawback of the pledged account mortgage, or FLIP?

6–11   Why are GPMs and PLAMs poor AMIs from the standpoint of income tax regulations?

PROBLEMS

6–1   Given the following data, determine the first monthly payment for the following types of mortgages listed in a, b, c, and d.

Market rate	10%
Real rate	3%
Mortgage amount	$100,000
Maturity	30 years

a. Standard, fixed-rate mortgage
b. GPM, growth rate first 5 years, 7.5%
c. Price level adjusted mortgage
d. ARM, special first year rate 8%

6–2   Determine the first payment in the second year of the 1-year adjustable ARMs shown in the following table (mortgage amount at origination, $100,000; maturity, 30 years)

ARM	Contract Rate	Teaser Rate	Rate Cap	Margin	Year 1 Index	Year 2 Index
A	9%	8%	1%	100	8%	8%
B	10	8	2	200	8	10
C	11	8	2	300	8	11

6–3   Suppose you are considering an ARM with the following characteristics:

Mortgage amount	$100,000
Index	One-year treasury bill yield
Margin	2.50
Maximum annual adjustment	2%
Lifetime interest cap	6%
Discount points	2.00
Loan maturity	30 years

a. If the TB yield is currently 6 percent, what is the monthly payment for the first year? (Assume the loan is fully indexed at the outset.)
b. If the index moves to 7.5 percent at the end of the first year, what is the monthly payment for year 2?
c. If the loan is paid off at the end of year 2, what is the effective cost (yield)?

6–4   Consider a PLAM with the following features:

Mortgage amount	$90,000
Mortgage term	30 years
Current real rate	5%
Inflation for the next three years respectively	2%, 3%, 5%

Mortgage payments adjusted annually
a. What are the monthly payments for each of the first three years?
b. What is the effective cost if the loan is repaid at the end of year three?
c. What is the effective cost if the loan is repaid at the end of year three and the lender charges two discount points up front?

6–5   Compare the following mortgages and determine which has the lower cost:

	FRM	ARM
Mortgage Amount	$100,000	$100,000
Term	30 years	30 years
Discount Points	2.00	3.25
Initial Contract Interest Rate	9.75%	7.75%
Margin	. . .	2.75
Caps	. . .	2% annual, 6% lifetime
Index Value at Outset	. . .	7.75%
Prepayment	End of year 3	End of year 3

Assume that the ARM rate adjusts from the initial beginning rate and the index has the following values:

Beginning of Year	Index Value
1	7.75%
2	9.00%
3	10.75%

6–6   Determine the share of appreciation the lender should receive on the following SAM loan.

Loan-to-value ratio	90%
Market rate	12%
Rate on loan	10%
Lender's tax bracket	30%

6–7   A widow wishes to take out a reverse annuity mortgage on her house. What annual payment can she get if she decides on a $100,000 debt at the end of 10 years and the current rate is 9 percent?

6–8   Five years ago a borrower incurred a mortgage for $80,000 at 10 percent for 30 years, monthly payments. Currently the market rate is 8 percent on 25-year mortgages. The existing mortgage has a prepayment penalty of 5 percent of the outstanding balance at prepayment for the first ten years of the mortgage and the lender will charge 4 percent financing cost on a new loan. The borrower's opportunity investment rate is 9.5 percent. The borrower is considering refinancing the remaining balance.

   a. If the borrower plans to hold either mortgage (the existing mortgage or the new mortgage) for the next 25 years, should she refinance?

   b. If the borrower plans to hold the mortgage financing for eight more years, should she refinance at the present time?

   c. Assume everything in part A except that, instead of refinancing the outstanding balance, the borrower borrows $100,000. Should she refinance?

ENDNOTES

1. In today's mortgage market, lenders commonly offer the 15-year, fixed-rate mortgage as an alternative to the standard 30-year, fixed-rate loan. The shorter-term loan, by nature, will repay faster, which can be an advantage to the mortgage lender in periods of slow prepayment (such as when interest rates are rising). The borrower would have to weigh the advantages of the shorter-term loan (such as faster equity buildup) with the disadvantages (such as a higher monthly payment). For an analysis of choosing between 15- and 30-year mortgages, see Richard A. Phillips, Eric Rosenblatt, and James H. Vanderhoff, "The Effect of Relative Pricing on the Fixed-Rate Mortgage Term Decision," *Journal of Real Estate Research* 7 (Spring 1992), 187–194.

2. For an example of the research on teaser rates on ARMs, see Joel F. Houston, J. Sa-Aadu, and James D. Shilling, "Teaser Rates in Conventional Adjustable-Rate Mortgage (ARM) Markets," *Journal of Real Estate Finance and Economics* 4 (March 1991), 19–32. See also R. Green and J. Shilling, "Do Teaser Rates on Adjustable-Rate Mortgages Make Owner-Occupied Housing More Affordable?" *Journal of Housing Economics* 3 (December 1994), 263–282.

3. J. Sa-Aadu and J. D. Shilling, "Tests of Borrower Perceptions in the Adjustable-Rate Mortgage Market: Do Borrowers View ARM Contracts as Distinct?" *Journal of Urban Economics* 36 (1994), 8–22.

4. B. Elledge, S. Fletcher, and G. Norris, "Fumbles, Oversights, and Omissions:Bank ARM Calculations," *Real Estate Review* 25 (Fall 1995), 48–54.

5. A paper by Scott, Houston, and Do shows that actually a hybrid PLAM which permits inflation-risk sharing and also accommodates a wide range of amortization-graduation schemes for loan repayment may be the optimal mortgage. See William H. Scott, Jr., Arthur L. Houston, Jr., and A. Quang Do, "Inflation Risk, Payment Tilt, and the Design of Partially Indexed Affordable Mortgages," *Journal of the American Real Estate and Urban Economics Association* 21 (Spring 1993), 1–26

6. J. Huston McCulloch, "Risk Characteristics and Underwriting Standards for Price Level Adjusted Mortgages Versus Other Mortgage Instruments," *Housing Finance Review* 5 (Fall 1986), 65–97.

7. Joyce Manchester, "Evidence of Possible Default Under Three Mortgage Contracts," *Housing Finance Review* 4 (January 1985), 517–536.

8. James Pesando and Stuart Turnbull, "The Timepath of Homeowner's Equity Under Different Mortgage Instruments: A Simulation Study," *House Finance Review* 4 (January 1985), 483–504.

9. Ann Dougherty, Robert Van Order, and Kevin Villani, "Pricing Shared Appreciation Mortgages," *Housing Finance Review* 1 (October 1982), 361–375.

10. Christopher J. Mayer and Katerina Simons, "Reverse Mortgages and the Liquidity of Housing Wealth," *Journal of the American Real Estate and Urban Economics Association* 22 (Summer 1994), 235–255.

11. Peter VanderHart, "An Empirical Analysis of the Housing Decisions of Older Homeowners," *Journal of the American Real Estate and Urban Economics Association* 22 (Summer 1994), 205–233.

12. Thomas P. Boehm and Michael C. Ehrhardt, "Reverse Mortgages and Interest Rate Risk," *Journal of the American Real Estate and Urban Economics Association* 22 (Summer 1994), 387–408.

13. Linda Klein and C. F. Sirmans, "Reverse Mortgages and Prepayment Risk," *Journal of the American Real Estate and Urban Economics Association* 22 (Summer 1994), 409–431.

14. Thomas J. Miceli and C. F. Sirmans, "Reverse Mortgages and Borrower Maintenance Risk," *Journal of the American Real Estate and Urban Economics Association* 22 (Summer 1994), 433–450.

15. Revenue Ruling 77–135.

16. Revenue Ruling 51–83.

17. Revenue Ruling 70–647.

18. Amy Dickinson and Andrea J. Heuson, "Explaining Refinancing Decisions Using Microdata," *Journal of the American Real Estate and Urban Economics Association* 21 (Fall 1993), 293–311.

19. T. L. Tyler Yang and Brian Maris, "Mortgage Refinancing with Asymmetric Information," *Journal of the American Real Estate and Urban Economics Association* 21 (Winter 1993), 491–510.

20. This means that given two loans with everything equal except the contract rates, the loan with the lower contract rate will amortize faster and will have a lower outstanding balance at any point in time between inception and maturity. Only at the beginning and the end (when the balance is zero) will the balances on the loans be equal.

WEB SITES

www.bog.frb.fed.us

Board of Governors of the Federal Reserve System. Provides various interest rate data.

www.coldwellbanker.dom

Provides tips on buying and financing a home. Online mortgage calculations are also available.

www.countrywide.com

Provides online applications for mortgages, loan information and services, and information for real estate professionals.

APPENDIX A

Computing Initial Payment on a GPM Loan

To compute the first payment on a GPM loan, consider that the present value of the loan equals:

$$\text{Year 1} \left[\text{PMT}_1 \sum_{t=1}^{12} \frac{1}{\left(1 + \dfrac{i}{12}\right)^t} \right]$$

$$\text{Year 2} + \left[\text{PMT}_1(1 + g)^1 \sum_{t=1}^{12} \frac{1}{\left(1 + \dfrac{i}{12}\right)} \cdot \frac{1}{\left(1 + \dfrac{i}{12}\right)^{12}} \right]$$

$$\text{Year 3} + \left[\text{PMT}_1(1 + g)^2 \sum_{t=1}^{12} \frac{1}{\left(1 + \dfrac{i}{12}\right)^t} \cdot \frac{1}{\left(1 + \dfrac{i}{12}\right)^{24}} \right]$$

$$\vdots \qquad\qquad\qquad \vdots$$

$$\text{Year 6--30} + \left[\text{PMT}_1(1 + g)^5 \sum_{t=1}^{300} \frac{1}{\left(1 + \dfrac{i}{12}\right)^t} \cdot \frac{1}{\left(1 + \dfrac{i}{12}\right)^{60}} \right]$$

where i is the contract rate, PMT_1, is the monthly payment for Year 1, and g is the growth rate of payment.

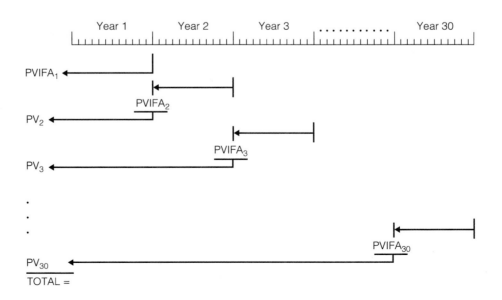

The solution to the equation involves finding the present value of annuities. Each year's series of payments is an annuity for 12 months. They each have a present value as of the first of the year in which they occur. In turn, each of these values has a present value. It works as follows: The $PVIFA_1$ for Year 1 payments is equivalent to their present value. The $PVIFA_2$ for Year 2 payments is equivalent to their present value as of the beginning of Year 2. PV_2 is the present value, as of the loan origination, of $PVIFA_2$, and so forth. As an example, assume a loan for $100,000 at 12 percent with a 7.5 percent graduation in payments through the first 6 years. The following table computes the present value factors.

Year	Payment	Graduated Payment Factor	PVIFA	PVIA	Factors
1	PMT_1	1	11.255[a]	1	11.255
2	$PMT_1(1.075)$	1.0750	11.255	0.8874[b]	10.737
3	$PMT_1(1.075)^2$	1.1556	11.255	0.7876[b]	10.243
4	$PMT_1(1.075)^3$	1.2423	11.255	0.6989	9.772
5	$PMT_1(1.075)^4$	1.3355	11.255	0.6203	9.323
6–30	$PMT_1(1.075)^5$	1.4356	94.946[c]	0.5504	75.031
TOTAL					126.361

[a]Present value interest factor of an annuity for 12 periods at 1 percent (Table 4 Row 12, Column 1).
[b]Present value of future sum discounted at 12 percent.
[c]Present value interest factor of an annuity for 300 periods at 1 percent.

$PMT_1 \times 126.36 = \$100,000$. Therefore, $PMT_1 = \$100,000/126.36 = \$791.39$.

CHAPTER 7

Financing and Property Values

LEARNING OBJECTIVES

After reading the chapter, you should understand how the terms of financing affect the transaction price of real estate, particularly residential real estate. You should understand the theoretical issues related to the interaction of financing and transaction prices and learn that the "true" or "intrinsic" value of real estate may differ from the actual transaction price because of financing terms. You also should learn of the different types of financing alternatives that affect transaction prices.

INTRODUCTION

Terms of financing can affect the transaction price of real estate. They represent items, in addition to the physical characteristics of the property, for which the buyer is willing to pay and the seller is able to charge. **Advantageous financing,** or **creative financing,** indicates that some aspect of the financing, usually the interest rate, is different from the current market terms offered by institutional mortgage lenders and benefits the borrower. In order for advantageous financing to affect the value of the property, it must be "attached" to the property and nontransferable. Advantageous financing that allows the borrower to purchase any property, such as a loan made with funds from a mortgage revenue bond, may not affect the value of a particular property.

There are many examples of financing that carry a lower-than-market rate of interest and are attached to the property. An **assumable loan** may have been originated at a time when market rates were lower than current rates. Such a loan is attractive because of federal regulations (FHA/VA) or because it lacks a due-on-sale clause. With **owner-second** or **carryback financing,** motivated sellers may offer to take back a note at a low rate in order to sell a property quickly or to be able to sell a property with an existing assumable loan and thereby capture its value. Using **buydowns,** home builders often will agree to subsidize a portion of the initial interest payments, thereby lowering the interest cost to the buyer. The previous treatment of discount points in **FHA** loans is another example. At a time when the FHA established a ceiling rate on insured loans, lenders charged discount points to raise the effective yield to a market yield. The rate on the loan, held below the market rate by regulation, represented advantageous financing to the borrower. Now that the FHA allows the contract rate to float with the market, FHA financing is no longer so advantageous. Also, FHA mortgages are no longer nonqualifying assumable loans. **Land contracts** involve a contract to purchase a property. The buyer lives in the property during the contract period and pays a monthly payment. The seller continues to make payments on the low-rate loan to the lender and title to the property is transferred when all the buyer's payments are made.

The volume and importance of advantageous, or creative, financing follows the interest rate cycle. When interest rates are cyclically high, home buyers are priced out of the market, and creative financing takes on greater importance. Also, the volume of loans with rates below the market, some of which are assumable, expands. Conversely, when rates are low, the volume and importance of advantageous financing wanes. If the market rate falls to that on assumable loans, such loans will lose much of their advantage and value. When there is considerable creative financing, the transaction prices of residential properties will be distorted from their "bricks-and-mortar" values. These distortions are of concern for many reasons, one of which is the implication for accurate appraisals. As we will see below, accurate appraisals are essential for informed decisions by lenders.

CREATIVE FINANCING

The issues related to terms of financing and property values are theoretical and empirical. Theoretical issues deal with all the factors that may affect the value that buyers and sellers place on creative financing. For example, perhaps the length of time that a buyer intends to own the property (and thereby take advantage of the assumable loan) will affect the amount she is willing to pay for the right to assume a low-rate loan. Also, the amount of interest payments that buyers are able to deduct from their taxes, as determined by their tax bracket, may affect the value they place on an assumable loan. There are several other factors along these lines that may, in theory, affect the value of creative financing.

The empirical issue is straightforward. How are property prices actually affected by the terms of financing? Do property prices reflect the value of creative financing as determined from a theoretical standpoint? Transaction prices and terms of financing are easily observed, so answers to these empirical questions should be attainable.

We begin our discussion of the theoretical and empirical issues with FHA/VA discount points. One of the first investigations, from an empirical standpoint, concerned FHA/VA discount points. For this reason we begin with a discussion of that research and then consider the other forms of creative financing.

FHA/VA Discount Points

We saw in Chapter 5 that during the late 1970s market rates rose quickly. The FHA and VA established ceilings on the rate of interest on loans they insured, ceilings that changed infrequently. As a result, there were periods of time during which the market rate (on conventional loans) was above, sometimes substantially, the ceiling rate. Lenders would charge discount points to raise the yield on FHA and VA loans to competitive levels. In setting the points, lenders would assume that the loan would be prepaid prior to maturity, say, in 10 or 12 years.

For example, assume that the contract rate on a conventional loan is at c percent but that the maximum rate on an FHA loan is m, and m is less than c. For a conventional loan of amount B dollars and no points, the following equation holds:

$$B = \frac{\text{pmt}c}{(1 + c)^1} + \frac{\text{pmt}c}{(1 + c)^2} + \cdots + \frac{\text{pmt}c}{(1 + c)^{360}} \qquad \text{(Equation 7–1)}$$

PMTc is the payment on a conventional loan necessary to provide a yield of c percent. For an FHA loan of B dollars, the payment must be set with reference to rate m, not rate c. Since the payment PMTm is less than PMTc, the yield on an FHA loan will be equivalent to that on a conventional loan if

$$\alpha B = \frac{\text{pmt}m}{(1 + c)^1} + \frac{\text{pmt}m}{(1 + c)^2} + \cdots + \frac{\text{pmt}m}{(1 + c)^{120}} + \frac{B_{120}}{(1 + c)^{120}} \qquad \text{(Equation 7–2)}$$

where B_{120} is the balance at the end of Year 10, the assumed year of prepayment.

The lender advances only αB dollars, not B, the difference being discount points. If α equals 0.95, then the lender charges 5 discount points for the loan.

A buyer of a property to be financed with an FHA loan makes a lower payment than if it were financed with a conventional loan. He should be willing to pay the points in order to obtain the loan. This is especially true if his expected holding period is longer than that assumed by the lender in determining the points. In that case, the buyer receives the benefits of the lower payments for a longer term than was used to compute the amount of points. However, in an attempt to shift the burden of paying points to the property seller, the FHA prohibited the buyer from paying them.

Now assume that the value of the property with no special financing attached is $100,000—that is, its "bricks and mortar" value. In dollars, 5 points on an FHA loan for 90 percent of value would be $4500 (0.05 × $90,000). The seller would be willing to sell to an FHA-financed buyer and pay $4500 only if he would receive $4500 more for the property than if he sold it with conventional financing and no requirement to pay points. That is, the seller should require a $104,500[1] price if financed with an FHA loan or $100,000 if financed with a conventional loan. In either case he nets $100,000. The buyer should be willing to pay the additional $4500 because of the lower interest rate on the FHA loan. The value of the low rate is ultimately incorporated in the transaction price of the property.

If the theory is sound, FHA-financed properties should sell for an amount greater than comparable conventionally financed properties when the FHA rate is limited and points are charged. Furthermore, the amount of the difference should equal the amount of points charged.

Zerbst and Brueggeman tested this hypothesis.[2] They reasoned that home sellers set an asking price above the eventual sales price. Sellers negotiate downward, but settle on a higher sales price if the property is purchased with an FHA-financed loan. The authors argued that the sales-price-to-asking-price ratio (SP/AP) would be greater for FHA loans by the amount of points. They used price data on a cross sample of 276 housing sales in June 1973, including those financed with FHA, VA, and conventional loans, to statistically test the equation

$$SP/AP = a + b_1 FHA + b_2 VA + b_3 L/V + b_4 Time + e_t \qquad \text{(Equation 7–3)}$$

where FHA and VA were dummy variables (equal to 1, if financed with that type of loan), L/V was the loan-to-value ratio, Time was the time the property was on the market, and e is an error term. They used an ordinary least-squares technique for this purpose.

The coefficient on the FHA variable was 0.0227, indicating that FHA home buyers paid 2.27 percent more, as a percentage of asking price, than conventional buyers in the same sample. Since lenders charged 5.75 discount points at the time, the authors concluded that 43 percent of the discount points (2.27/5.75) was passed on to FHA buyers by sellers. Since the simple theory described above predicts that all of the points should be included in the sales price, their estimates appear low. Either the theory or their estimation procedure was flawed. A more sophisticated theoretical model, developed below, indicates that less than all the points may be included in the price of the house. If this is so, then Zerbst and Brueggeman's results may be reasonable.

Colwell, Guntermann, and Sirmans suggest that Zerbst and Brueggeman's empirical procedure may be flawed.[3] They argue that the asking price AP may be set with reference to the likelihood that the property will be sold with FHA financing. In this case, the dependent variable in Equation 7–3 is misspecified. Colwell et al. propose an equation similar to the one below, called a hedonic price equation. A hedonic price equation is one that explains the price of a residence with reference to its physical characteristics, such as the number of rooms, square feet, presence of a garage, fireplace, neighborhood location, and so forth. An example is

$$price = a + b \,[\text{Rooms}] + c \,[\text{Baths}] + d \,[\text{Square Feet}] + \ldots + \text{etc.}$$

The theoretical value of the terms of financing can be added to this equation. In this case, Colwell et al. added the amount of points charged on each loan. If a property were financed with a conventional loan, then the amount of points included for that observation would be zero. Colwell et al. used price and property description data on 2408 sales in Lubbock, Texas, to test a hedonic equation with the value of FHA points added. The statistical technique they employed was the ordinary least-squares method. The coefficient on the points variable was 0.773, indicating that, for their sample, 77.3 percent of the points was included in the price of properties financed with FHA loans. This value was much closer to 100 percent.

TABLE 7-1

Value of a Low Rate Assumable Loan 1982

Assumable loan	
Originated	1972
Remaining term	20 Years
Payment	$419.00
Rate	7.5%
Original balance	$60,000
1982 balance	$52,077
Alternative new conventional loan	
Term	20 Years
Balance	$52,077
Rate	15%
Payment	$685.74
Payment savings	$266.75
Present value of payment savings	$20,258

Now that the FHA allows the lender to charge a rate reflecting the market, large discount points are seldom charged. However, a lender can offer a very-low-rate FHA loan and charge some points. As a practical matter, the seller of a property should never agree in a sales contract to pay the points associated with an FHA-financed sale before knowing what those points might be. Even if the points on a near-market-rate loan are small, buyers could use the agreement to their advantage by seeking out low-rate loans with large points.

Assumable Loans

Up through the 1960s many conventional loans were assumable. All FHA and VA loans are assumable. For FHA loans originated after December 1, 1986, the FHA has required that persons assuming the loan within 1 year of origination meet certain borrower qualifications. Assumable loans with rates near or below the market rate have value because of their advantageous rate.

Consider the example given in Chapter 5 and repeated here. Table 7–1 shows the terms of an assumable loan and a new conventional loan. A purchaser of the property attached by the assumable loan would be provided with $52,077 in financing but the rate on this amount would be considerably under current rates: 7.5 percent versus 15 percent. By assuming the loan, the buyer saves $266.75 per month over alternative financing at market rates. Since the assumable loan has value, the buyer would be willing to pay more for the house than she would if there were no assumable loan. Stated differently, given two identical houses, one with the assumable loan in this example and one with no assumable loan, the former would demand a higher price in the market. The assumable loan has value, just as any other amenity, and its value will be reflected in the price. The value of such assumable loans has been the subject of much theoretical and empirical discussion.

Cash-equivalent Value

The term *cash equivalent* was coined in the appraisal literature to focus on the issue of the value of assumable loans. Early on, appraisers recognized that the terms of financing would affect the transaction price of residential properties.[4] For example, Lusht and Hanz recently found that row houses selling for cash sold for about 16 percent less than their counterparts that used a mortgage in the sale.[5] An earlier study by Asabere, Huffman, and Mehdian shows that properties in all cash transactions sold for about a 13 percent price discount relative to transactions involving financing terms.[6] **Cash equivalent** refers to the amount for which a residential property would sell if purchased for cash (or if purchased with a combination of cash and current market financing).

The cash equivalent can be found by finding the "value" of the terms of financing. If the residence attached by the assumable loan in our example sold for $72,077, then the terms and their values would be as follows:

Terms	Amount	Value
Cash	$20,000	$20,000
Assumption	$52,077	31,819
Total	$72,077	51,819

Here, the "value" of the assumable loan, $31,819, is the value of the remaining payments discounted at the market rate of interest, 15 percent. That is,

$$\$31,819 = \frac{419}{(1 + 0.15/12)^1} + \frac{419}{(1 + 0.15/12)^2} + \cdots + \frac{419}{(1 + 0.15/12)^{240}}$$

The buyer is paying for the property by giving cash with a value of $20,000 and a promise to make the payments on the assumable loan, the value of those payments being only $31,819. The total value, $51,819, is referred to as the cash equivalent. The cash equivalent is the amount that, presumably, the buyer would pay for the "bricks and mortar" if the property were sold without an assumable loan.

Note that the difference between the transaction price, $72,077, and the cash-equivalent price, $51,819, is $20,258. This amount is also the present value of the payment savings, found by discounting those savings at the current market rate.

When discussing the value of an assumable loan, some prefer to talk in terms of the payment savings and the present value of the payment savings. As a result, the present value of the payment savings occasionally has been referred to as the cash-equivalent value of the assumable loan. We will try to be very explicit in our terminology so as not to be confusing.

Another way of looking at this example is to compare the payments on the property with the assumable loan to the payments on an exactly identical property with no assumable loan. The latter should have a cash-equivalent value of $51,819. The payments would look like this:

	Property with Assumable Loan	*Property without Assumable Loan*
Price	$72,077	$51,819
Down payment	20,000	20,000
Loan	52,077[a]	31,819[b]
Payments	419	419[c]

[a] Amount of assumable loan
[b] New financing
[c] Payment on new financing at 15%

Although the buyer would pay $20,258 more for the property with the assumable loan, his down payment and monthly payments would be the same as those on the property without the assumable loan and purchased at its cash equivalent. The result is identical payments on identical properties, but different transaction prices.

The relationship between assumable loans, market interest rates, and property transaction prices is important to appraisers and others interested in housing prices. Consider an appraiser with an assignment to appraise a house (subject property) identical to the one in this example, but with no assumable loan. The appraiser uses the property sold with assumption financing as a comparable. If the appraiser is unaware of the existence of assumption financing on the comparable, he may overvalue the subject property. The appraiser must be aware of not only the existence of nonmarket financing, but also the impact such financing has on the transaction price of properties used as comparables.

Efficient Markets and Value of Assumption Financing

It was assumed in the above example that the house with an assumable loan was sold for a price that reflected the present value of the payment savings on the loan. The payment savings are said to be **capitalized** into the price of the house. Without an assumable loan, the property's value is $51,819. With the loan, it is $72,077, or $20,258 more. The latter amount includes the capitalized (present) value of the payment savings. Although the numbers work out and appear to be reasonable, there remains the question of whether or not it would work this way in the real market. Early empirical work discovered that properties did not sell for an amount reflective of the full value of the payment savings. In terms of our example, the house with the assumable loan may sell in the market for, say, $65,000. The premium over the cash-equivalent value is only $13,181 ($65,000 − $51,819), or 65 percent of the present value of the payment savings. This peculiar result has implications for the appraisal process and for those concerned with housing values.

It also has implications concerning what can be said about the efficiency of the market for residential properties. If only a portion of the cash-equivalent values of assumable loans are included in the price of the properties, one might conclude that the market is inefficient. Buyers do not pay nor do sellers demand the "full" value of assumable loans. On the other hand, if the full values are included in the prices of the properties, then the market can be said to be efficient, at least from the standpoint of the effect of financing on housing values. Many of the requirements for an efficient market appear to be present in the residential property market. Information concerning the characteristics of properties and the terms of financing is readily available. Reasonably sized markets encompass large numbers of buyers and sellers and no market restrictions. On the other hand, there are transaction costs in this market. But, on balance, there appears to be no overwhelming reason to suspect that the market for residential properties would not be efficient. Why, then, do residential properties not have prices that reflect the value of advantageous financing?

To conclude that the market is not efficient, two things must occur. First, the value of an assumable loan must be determined. It may not be the present value of future payment savings for the term of the loan. Second, empirical research must be done to determine the extent to which the value is included in property prices. In regards to the first issue, there may be reasons why the cash-equivalent value, as determined by finding the present value of the payment savings, may not be the correct value of an assumable loan. After initial empirical studies found that only a portion of the cash-equivalent value was capitalized into property prices, researchers began to rethink the value of an assumable loan. It turns out that there are some good reasons to suggest that the value of an assumable loan is not as great as the present value of the payment savings. We first discuss some empirical results and then show how the exploration of the theoretical issues followed.

Empirical Tests of House Price Capitalization of Creative Financing

One of the first studies in this area was done by Sirmans, Smith, and Sirmans, who looked at the effect of assumption financing on houses in the Atlanta, Georgia, area in 1980.[7] They used ordinary least-squares to test a hedonic equation that included physical characteristics and cash-equivalent value of assumable loans. Their sample included 54 properties for which they collected data on the sales price, physical characteristics, and details of the assumable loans. For each property they computed the present value of the payment savings associated with the assumable loan. They then regressed the transaction price on the characteristics of the property and the cash-equivalent value of the assumable loans. The coefficient on the financing variable was approximately 0.32, leading them to conclude that only about one-third of the cash-equivalent value of assumption financing was capitalized into (included in) the transaction price of the properties. Eleven of the properties studied had additional owner-financing. In a later study the authors added a separate variable to measure the value (present value of payment savings) of owner-financing. This did not change their results.

Although one study did find complete capitalization, most others conducted for the same time period found only partial capitalization.[8] In a large sample of houses sold between 1978 and 1982 in Shreveport, Louisiana, Clauretie found that 64 percent of the value of assumption financing was capitalized.[9] The extent of capitalization varied, however, according to how the sample was partitioned by the year of sale. Using samples of condominiums in Hawaii and Florida, Schwartz found that 30 to 50 percent of the implied cash-equivalent values was capitalized.[10]

Given the less-than-overwhelming empirical support for full capitalization of the cash-equivalency value, researchers next turned to a discussion of the theoretical value of assumable loans. The focus was on factors that would cause the value to be less than the cash-equivalent value. Assume, for example, that the cash-equivalent value of an assumable loan is $10,000, but only $6000 is capitalized into the price of the property. The market appears to be inefficient since only 60 percent of the value is included in the price. But what if the "true" value of the assumable loan was only $6000, even though the cash-equivalent value was $10,000? In this case 100 percent of the value would be included in the price, and the market would be considered efficient.

Several factors with various degrees of validity were considered to explain a reduction in the value of assumable loans. First, it was thought that buyers only valued the payment savings that would accrue during their expected tenure in the house, not their value over the full maturity of the assumable loan. In fact, Sirmans, Smith, and Sirmans stated their results in this fashion, claiming that buyers appear to value only the first 3 years or so of payment savings (the first 3 years of payments savings represent about one-third of the present value of an assumable loan with a 20- to 25-year maturity). Theoretically, however, a buyer could capture the value of the remaining payment savings upon resale and thus should be willing to pay for the entire value at purchase.

Clauretie postulated that the after-tax savings of an assumable loan is less than the before-tax savings.[11] On reflection, this line of inquiry also is flawed. Buyers would discount the after-tax savings by an after-tax discount rate. The applicable after-tax discount rate would be the same as that for the buyer's tax bracket. The result would be a wash, producing the same value as the cash-equivalent value.

Friedman suggested that buyers and sellers could not accurately quantify the present value of good financing.[12] But the actual present value calculations need not be made. All a buyer must do is compare the total payments on properties financed with assumable loans and with conventional financing. In our example the buyer would always prefer the property with the assumable loan over the lower-priced property up to a price of $72,077.

Sunderman, Cannaday, and Colwell show that, when the loan-to-value ratio is not considered, the cash equivalence technique overvalues the assumption financing. They also show that the proportion of financing premium increases as the loan-to-value ratio decreases.[13]

Dale-Johnson Findlay, Schwartz, and Kapplin suggested that most properties sold with assumption financing involve a second and junior loan.[14] If the assumable loan is aged and there has been even moderate house appreciation, the amount of the down payment (cash to loan) may be prohibitive for most buyers. It is claimed that the introduction of a second loan changes the appropriate discount factor. A buyer who assumes the loan must take out a second, or junior, loan to finance the equity. Since second, or junior, loans carry greater risk than conventional firsts, their interest rate will be greater. This increases the amount of payment and reduces the value of the assumable loan. If the additional interest charge is sufficient to reduce the value in our example to $6000, it is fully capitalized. This research supports the view that assumable loans should be valued in this manner; if they are, they appear to be fully capitalized.

It is doubtful, however, that the somewhat higher rate on a second mortgage would cause the value of an assumable loan to fall so much that only one-third to two-thirds of its cash-equivalent value would be included in the price of the property. Not convinced of this argument, Ferreira and Sirmans analyzed the risk of assuming a low-rate mortgage, with the recognition that future interest rates may change.[15] This approach has merit and deserves further explanation.

Assume a home buyer in the above example believes that after the purchase interest rates will either increase or decrease. The buyer is not sure in which direction interest rates will move, but given the historical volatility in interest rates, it is unlikely they will remain at their current level. Recall that the home buyer has the option of buying a house with an assumable loan for $72,077 (House A) or an identical property without an assumable loan for $51,819 (House B). In each case the monthly payment is the same, $419. The house without the assumable loan is purchased with a conventional loan that is smaller than the balance on the assumable loan but carries a higher interest rate.

To keep the analysis simple, assume that interest rates go up or down 1 percent immediately after purchase. If interest rates go up, the value of the assumable loan (House A) increases because the payment savings are now even greater. However, had the buyer purchased the house with the conventional financing (House B), the value of the conventional loan would also increase because its payments are based on a rate that is now lower than the market. Even if the conventional loan is not assumable, the home buyer receives the benefit of relatively lower payments for as long as the residence is occupied.

If interest rates decline, the value of the assumable loan also will decline. The amount of the payment savings is less. One might be quick to note that the value of the conventional loan on House B also would fall. However, if refinancing costs are not substantial, the conventional loan can be refinanced at the lower rate, so there is no loss in value to the borrower. The assumable loan cannot (will not) be financed since it carries a very low rate.

The following figures show the value of the payment "savings" associated with each option.

New Interest Rate	Assumable Loan (House A)	Conventional Loan (House B)
14%	$18,382	$0,000
15	$20,258	$0,000
16	$21,960	$1,702

If interest rates rise immediately to 16 percent, then the value of the payment savings (until maturity) on the assumable loan rises to $21,960. The payment of a balance of $52,077 at 16 percent would be $725, or $306 more than $419. The present value of $306 for 240 months discounted at 16 percent is $21,960. The value increases by $1702 ($21,960 − $20,258). The value of the payment savings on the conventional loan would also increase to $1702 from no value.

Should interest rates fall to 14 percent, the payment savings on the assumable loan will fall as will their present value. The loss in value is $1876. There is no loss for the conventional loan, however, since it can be refinanced at the lower rate. It follows that a rise in rates causes the value of each option to increase by the same amount. A drop in rates causes the value of the assumable loan to fall more than that of the conventional loan. Given this asymmetric payoff, home buyers are likely to value the assumable loan at much less than its cash equivalency ($20,258).

Another way of looking at the issue is to consider what would happen if one looked at the conventional loan alternative without the prepayment option. Assume, for example, that lenders could charge sufficient prepayment penalties so as to eliminate the likelihood of any prepayment. In this case lenders would charge a lower rate on conventional mortgages than they otherwise would, and the difference in payments between such conventional loans and an assumable loan would be smaller. With a smaller payment difference, the cash equivalency also would be smaller. In terms of empirical results, had researchers included in their observations such a smaller amount for the cash equivalent value, they would have obtained larger coefficients on this variable, perhaps much closer to 1.0. That is, there would be 100 percent capitalization of the now smaller cash-equivalent value.

Consideration of transaction costs might increase the value of the assumable loan somewhat because the cost would restrict the ability to refinance the conventional loan alternative when rates fall. However, an increase in expected interest rate volatility would cause the potential loss on the assumable loan relative to the loss of the conventional loan to increase. Increased interest volatility would lower the value of the assumption option.

In summary, the possibility that interest rates may fall subsequent to the purchase of a house with a low-rate assumable loan reduces the value of the loan below its cash-equivalent amount.

Other Creative Financing: Buydowns, Wraparound Loans, and Land Contracts

Other forms of creative financing have been used to aid the sale of houses in periods of high interest rates. Research has indicated that a portion of the value of buydowns and land contracts is also included in the transaction price of houses. Recall from Chapter 5 that a buydown occurs when a seller, often a builder of a "spec" property, pays an amount of money to a lender to "buy down" the interest rate over all or a portion of the loan. The lender receives the funds up front and reduces the interest rate on the loan. The buyer of the property does not receive the benefits of the buydown immediately, but only over the buydown period through reduced interest payments. Again, because interest rates may decline subsequent to the origination of the loan, the value to the buyer may not equal the present value of the payment savings over the entire life of the loan.

To illustrate the buydown process, suppose that a borrower takes a mortgage for $100,000 at 10 percent for 30 years, monthly payments. The seller has agreed to buy down the interest rate for the first 3 years to 7 percent, 8 percent, and 9 percent, respectively. In the fourth year the loan rate reverts to the normal contract rate of 10 percent.

The payment under the normal 10 percent rate is $877.57. The monthly payments for the first 3 years and thereafter would be

$$\text{Year 1: } \$100,000 \ (MC_{7\%,30}) \quad = \$100,000 \ (0.0066530) = \$665.30$$

$$\text{Year 2: } \$100,000 \ (MC_{8\%,30}) \quad = \$100,000 \ (0.0073376) = \$733.76$$

$$\text{Year 3: } \$100,000 \ (MC_{9\%,30}) \quad = \$100,000 \ (0.0080462) = \$804.62$$

$$\text{Years 4–30: } \$100,000 \ (MC_{10\%,30}) = \$100,000 \ (0.0087757) = \$877.57$$

The buydown fee paid by the seller at the outset is the present value of the payment shortage over the buydown period. This would be

$$\text{Buydown fee} = \text{PV of shortage} = \$877.57 - \$665.30 \ (PVIFA_{10\%/12, \ 12})$$

$$+ \ \$877.57 - \$733.76 \ (PVIFA_{10\%/12, \ 12}) \ (PVIF_{10\%/12, \ 12})$$

$$+ \ \$877.57 - \$804.62 \ (PVIFA_{10\%/12, \ 12}) \ (PVIF_{10\%/12, \ 24})$$

$$= \$212.27 \ (11.374508)$$

$$+ \ \$143.81 \ (11.374508) \ (0.905212)$$

$$+ \ \$72.95 \ (11.374508) \ (0.819409)$$

$$= \$2,414.47 + \$1,480.72 + \$679.92$$

$$= \$4,575.11$$

The effective cost of the loan for the borrower can be calculated as:

$$\$100,000 = \$665.30 \ (PVIFA_{i\%/12, \ 12})$$

$$+ \ \$733.76 \ (PVIFA_{i\%/12, \ 12}) \ (PVIF_{i\%/12, \ 12})$$

$$+ \ \$804.62 \ (PVIFA_{\%/12, \ 12}) \ (PVIF_{i\%/12, \ 24})$$

$$+ \ \$877.57 \ (PVIFA_{i\%/12, \ 324}) \ (PVIF_{i\%/12, \ 36})$$

$$i = 9.47\%$$

An important empirical question of the 1980s was the extent to which the buydown fee was capitalized into the selling price of the property. Agarwal and Phillips analyzed the prices of 113 houses sold with full-term buydowns of FHA/VA loans in Virginia Beach, Virginia, in the early 1980s.[16] The average buydown paid by builders was $7959. They found, on average, that 58.3 percent of the buydown was included in the price of the house. This implies that the builder-seller absorbed the remaining proportion.

As pointed out in Chapter 5, another popular creative financing technique when market interest rates are high is the wraparound mortgage. This is especially popular when the desire is to preserve an existing low-rate mortgage. Because of the leverage effect, it may be possible for the lender to write a wrap loan at a rate less than market yet still earn an effective yield greater than the market rate. To illustrate, suppose that you want to purchase a property for $150,000 and you can make a $20,000 down payment. The property has an existing mortgage that can be wrapped. This loan is a fixed-rate loan at 7 percent, monthly payments. The loan had an original balance of $110,000 and has 20 years left on its original 30-year term. The current market rate for a new fixed-rate loan is 10.5 percent for 20 years. The seller will give you a wrap loan for the purchase price at 8.75 percent, monthly payments.

The variable of interest is the effective yield for the wrap lender. This will be affected by the structure of the wrap loan. Let's assume that, to make the payments more affordable for the wrap borrower, the wrap loan is amortized for 30 years with a balloon at the end of 20 years. Thus, this wrap will be simultaneous term, partially amortized since the 20-year term is the same as the remaining term for the existing loan. However, the wrap loan will not be completely amortized over this period.

First, the payments on the respective loans can be calculated:

Existing Loan	*Wrap Loan*
$PMT_{EX} = \$110{,}000\ (MC_{7\%,30}) = \$731.83$	$PMT_W = \$130{,}000\ (MC_{8.75\%,30}) = \$1022.71$
$BAL^{ex}_{10} = \$94{,}394$	$BAL^{w}_{20} = \$81{,}604$

To calculate the effective yield for the wrap lender, we have to determine his equity investment. First, a total of $130,000 is being provided by the wrap lender. However, he has a debt source of funds in the amount of the existing loan balance, $94,393. Thus, the wrap lender is investing only $35,606 of his own equity funds. His return on these funds is the difference in the monthly payments of the two loans, $290.88. Remember what the wrap lender will do is collect the payment on the wrap loan and make the payment on the existing loan. Also, in this structure the wrap lender will collect the balance of the wrap loan at the end of 20 years. The equation to determine his effective yield on these funds is

$$\$35{,}606 = \$290.88\ (PVIFA_{i\%/12,\ 240}) + \$81{,}604\ (PVIF_{i\%/12,\ 240})$$

Solving for the interest rate gives an effective yield of 11.48 percent. Thus, the wrap lender can provide below-market financing to the lender while simultaneously earning a yield greater than the market rate.

There are other ways that a wrap loan can be structured. A **simultaneous term, fully amortized** wrap loan would be written for a term equal to the remaining term on the existing loan, and both would be fully amortized over this period. The wrap loan could be an **extended term** wrap. In this case, the wrap loan would be written for a longer term than the remaining term on the existing loan, and both loans would fully amortized. For the period after which the existing loan is repaid, the wrap lender would lose the leverage effect since he is collecting the wrap payments but there is no payment on the existing loan to provide financial leverage. One could even write a **shorter-term** wrap, in which the wrap loan would be amortized for a shorter term than the remaining term on the existing loan. This presents a problem for the wrap lender since the wrap loan is repaid before the existing loan is fully amortized. Since the wrap borrower would likely demand clear title once the wrap loan is repaid, the wrap lender would be required to repay the existing loan over the period of the wrap loan. This could be accomplished in a number of ways including: (1) the payments on the existing loan could be increased so that it fully amortizes over the shorter wrap loan term or (2) a balloon payment could be made on the existing loan at the end of the wrap term.

Land contracts are another method of financing a property. With a land contract, the buyer makes payments under the terms of a contract to purchase the property at a later time, say, 4 or 5 years. The value of the house is increased if the payments under the contract are lower than those that would exist with a conventionally financed purchase. If the agreement involved a wraparound, the seller would continue to make the low-interest payments under the existing low-rate loan during the period of the land contract. The arrangement benefits both parties because the buyer obtains the use of the property with low payments for several years while the seller obtains a higher price for the property. Both gain at the expense of the lender, who continues to carry the old low-rate loan.

Edgren and Hayworth investigated the use of land contracts for property sales in Ann Arbor, Michigan.[17] They found that the use of land contracts raised the transaction price of the Ann Arbor properties by an average of $4700. This was 6.9 percent of the average price in their sample.

Implications for Appraisal Practices and Market Studies

Appraisers and others interested in house values, such as real estate salespeople and brokers, must be aware of the effect of terms of financing on property values. The use and impact of creative financing flows with the interest rate cycle. When interest rates are high and creative finance is common, then the transaction prices of properties will reflect the terms of financing. This has implications for appraisals and market studies that rely on the use of reported transaction prices. Many appraisers failed to understand the full implications of creative financing in the early to mid-1980s. When appraising a property without assumption financing, an appraiser often would rely on a comparable property that sold with creative financing. If he failed to realize that creative financing was involved in the sale of the comparable, he might have unwittingly appraised the subject property too high. This would subject the lender to greater default risk than expected.

Also, there is greater default risk associated with properties sold with creative financing. If the buyer pays (and finances) a substantial amount above the "bricks-and-mortar" value of a property because of a low-rate, assumable loan and interest rates subsequently fall, the value of the assumption financing will disappear. The property may then have a value less than the existing first and second mortgages. Lenders also must be aware of the effect of creative financing on transaction values and the default risk present if the terms of financing are valued too high.

MORTGAGE REVENUE BONDS

A popular housing-finance tool has been **mortgage revenue bonds.** The bonds, commonly referred to as "municipals" and issued by state and local governments, provide interest that is free from federal income taxes. This means that the municipals can offer a lower rate of interest and still sell at a price that is competitive with fully taxable bonds. A taxpayer in the 30 percent tax bracket would see no difference between a municipal bond that offered $70 in annual interest payments and an otherwise identical corporate bond that offered $100 annually. The after-tax amounts would be identical. The special tax status of municipal bonds allows state and local governments to fund needed programs, such as schools, roads, and public safety programs, at a reduced cost.

In addition to the types of spending programs mentioned here, state and local governments gradually began to fund "nonpublic" activities with municipal bonds. Industrial revenue bonds have long been popular with local governments that desired to attract industry to their locality. They would issue these bonds to construct industrial parks and the like. The low interest payments meant that the local government could offer attractive lease terms to attract industry. The firms leasing the facilities benefited at the expense of the lost revenue to the U.S. Treasury.

Another favorite "nonpublic" activity funded by municipal bonds has been housing. State and local governments saw the need to have affordable housing for the lower-income segments of their population. **Mortgage revenue bonds (MRBs)** were created to stimulate housing activity. MRBs became especially popular when interest rates rose to high levels and housing affordability became an issue, especially with first-time home buyers. Of course, local real estate groups, such as real estate sales firms facing sluggish sales during periods of high rates, put their efforts behind promoting these MRBs. Because interest on the MRBs was tax exempt, the funds raised through such programs could be loaned to borrowers at a low, subsidized rate.

Role of State Housing Finance Authorities

Here is how a typical program might work. A state Housing Finance Agency (HFA) would be given the legislative authority to issue tax-exempt MRBs at, say, 7 percent interest. The funds raised from the sale would be made available to lenders within the state or locality to issue low-rate mortgages, say at 7.5 percent. Payments from the mortgages to the lenders would be returned to the state housing agency so that the interest payments on the bonds could be paid. The rate-differential would be available to pay for loan servicing and other expenses.

Because of the low rate, the demand for mortgages originated with MRB money would increase. Housing activity would be greater than it otherwise would be, home affordability would increase, and real estate sales firms would enjoy enhanced revenue. With MRBs everyone gained, with the exception of the U.S. Treasury.

The first state HFA was created in New York in 1960 to finance and develop rental housing. After the Housing Act of 1968 allowed HFAs to participate in selected federal housing programs for rental housing, the formation of HFAs accelerated. In 1974 the Virginia HFA sold the first tax-exempt MRB to finance the purchase of owner-occupied houses. By 1983 every state but Kansas and Arizona had an HFA capable of issuing mortgage revenue bonds. The Revenue and Expenditure Control Act of 1968 controlled the use of tax-exempt, industrial revenue bonds but permitted them for other purposes including "residential real property for family units." In addition to exemption from federal taxation, interest on MRBs was exempt from state-taxable income in all but five states. By 1984 and 1985, the total amount of MRBs floated by HFAs was $14.5 and $15.5 billion, respectively.

The popularity of the MRBs, especially during periods of high interest rates, can be seen from the experience of an issue by the Shreveport (Louisiana) Mortgage Authority. Funds from a $55.2 million bond issue were made available to Shreveport residents from September 1979 through June 1980 at a rate of 7.5 percent when market rates on conventional loans averaged 12.1 percent. The demand for the funds was very strong. Six days prior to the first day of application (September 13, 1979), potential borrowers began to line up outside the offices of 17 authorized lenders. Because of this interest, the Shreveport Mortgage Authority decided to establish a central processing location at a local athletic stadium. Four days prior to the first day of application, more than 2500 applicants arrived at the stadium. As the number of applicants swelled, the assembly was dubbed "Camp Wannamortgage." Long lines formed, with individuals and families arriving with camping equipment for the four-day wait. Newspaper accounts expressed the concerns of applicants that there might be too few properties to select from as a result of the large increase in demand created by the program. Lenders were quoted as saying that they expected house buyers to run out of houses before they ran out of money to loan.

From experiences such as this, it soon became clear that there was wealth transferred to home buyers from the Treasury as a result of the program. Even though most programs were limited in terms of the income of the borrowers and the value of the property that could be purchased, there was a real concern that the programs were being abused and that the Treasury was losing funds to subsidize an essentially private activity, housing. The Office of Management and Budget had issued a report critical of the MRB programs and their effectiveness for delivering affordable housing to low- and moderate-income families.

As a result, the Treasury Department convinced the legislature to curtail the scope of the MRB programs. Legislation (Mortgage Subsidy Bond Tax Act of 1980) at first limited the total amount of MRBs that could be issued and then called for their complete phase-out by the end of 1988 (Deficit Reduction Act of 1984). The program was given new life and extended until the end of 1989 by the Technical and Miscellaneous Revenue Act of 1988. However, in 1989 MRB funding was limited in each state to $50 per capita or $150 million. Based on the 1990 Census, the total 1991 MRB volume authority for the 50 states was about $14.2 billion. In 1990 the National Council of State Housing Agencies lobbied the House Ways and Means Committee to extend federal authorization for the MRB program.

In November 1990 Congress extended the authorization of MRBs until December 1991. Subsequently, the authority has been renewed annually. It is expected that the renewal of the authorization will become an annual event in the future as well. In 1988 Congress passed a law that, effective January 1, 1991, assessed a recapture tax on homeowners who sold their bond financed property within 9 years of purchase. It allows the government to recapture some of the subsidy enjoyed by the homeowner. The recapture tax applies only to a sale within 9 years, if there is a profit on the sale of the property, and the income of the homeowner exceeds a federal limit. The recapture tax equals 1.25 percent of the loan amount for each year of occupancy until the fifth year at which time the tax is reduced by the same percentage until the end of the ninth year. The recapture tax deters individuals from purchasing properties with below-market loans and then selling the property to make a profit. The tax applies only if there is a gain on the property and is capped at fifty percent of that gain. There is no recapture tax in cases where the original loan was only for home improvements less than $15,000, the house is disposed of due to the death of the owner, or is transferred between spouses as a result of a divorce.

Tables 7–2 and 7–3 summarize MRB activity through 1996. Table 7–2 shows the amount of new issues and debt refunding by state. It shows that some states, given their populations, have been more aggressive than others in funding housing through MRB programs. Table 7–3 gives a picture of the loan amounts, property prices, and borrower characteristics by state in 1996.

Next we turn to the issue of MRBs and their impact on property prices.

MRBs, House Prices, and Wealth Distribution

Since the MRB programs allow for below-market interest rates on home loans, the question of the impact of these programs on house prices and the distribution of wealth is important. Individuals other than the borrower may benefit from the programs if house prices reflect the subsidized interest on the loans.

At first glance, it would appear that all the benefits of the low-interest rates would accrue to the borrower. The special financing does not appear to be attached to any individual property. The borrower, armed with a low-rate loan, is free to purchase any property that meets the price limitations established by the particular program.

There are, however, two ways in which a redistribution of the benefits can occur. First, some MRB programs establish "target" areas. The funds are used to purchase specific properties within a designated area. Often, there may only be one or two developers selling properties in the targeted area. The developers will be aware of the terms of the financing. Second, a large infusion of low-rate funds in a moderately sized market will cause a shift in the demand curve for properties in general, affecting the equilibrium price of housing in the local market. In either case, property sellers will receive a portion or all of the wealth created by the programs.

Two studies have confirmed that property prices in target areas reflect the terms of the low-rate financing. Sa-Aadu, Sirmans, and Benjamin analyzed the prices of 126 newly constructed condominiums in Baton Rouge, Louisiana, over a period of a year and a half, beginning in December 1983.[18] They found that the prices of the properties reflected the full cash-equivalent value of the low-rate financing. Durning and Quigley found that the value of MRB financing was capitalized in the prices of houses in a target area in Little Rock, Arkansas, in late 1981 and early 1982.[19] The implications of these studies is that the ultimate beneficiaries of the MRB programs may not be those intended to benefit, but rather the sellers of the properties financed with the bond funds.

One would expect the story to be different for MRBs that do not target specific properties but allow the borrower to purchase any qualifying property within the market area. Clauretie, Merkle, and Sirmans studied the impact of the Shreveport, Louisiana, MRB discussed earlier.[20] A total of 1291 loans (average amount = $42,786) were originated from September 1979 through June 1980. Approximately half the residences sold during this time were purchased with funds from the bond issue. Funds from the bond issue had an impact on the local market. While individual property prices were not affected by the low-rate loans generated from bond funds, the shift in the demand-curve caused a general increase in property prices. Furthermore, the additional amount paid by home buyers over the period of the bond issue (the average increase in price multiplied by the number of home sales) was approximately equal to the aggregate value of the low-rate financing on the MRB loans. The authors concluded that while the recipients of the low-rate loans benefited, the house-buying public at large paid higher prices for the properties they purchased during the term of the program.

A general conclusion about MRB programs is that there may well be an unintended redistribution of wealth and that parties other than those intended are often the beneficiaries or the victims of the redistribution. These considerations, along with the tax loss to the Treasury during a period of high deficits, have reduced federal support for MRB programs.

TABLE 7–2
1996 Homeownership Survey,
Cumulative Mortgage Bond Activity—New Money Issues

	Total 1996 Issuance			Cumulative Production Through 1996			
	New Money Issues	Refundings	Total 1996 Issuance	New Money	Refundings	Total $ Issuance	Total Loans
Alabama HFA	61,920,000	73,080,000	135,000,000	1,493,195,000	573,025,000	2,066,220,000	35,947
Alaska HFC	159,870,603	0	159,870,603	1,149,750,603	692,000,000	1,841,750,603	17,173
Arkansas DFA	95,333,282	0	95,333,282	1,378,033,282	238,250,000	1,616,283,282	30,965
California HFA	408,800,000	338,240,000	747,040,000	4,963,865,400	2,572,742,920	7,536,608,320	71,865
Colorado HFA	140,584,095	768,013	141,352,108	1,389,312,095	333,562,013	1,722,874,108	27,971
Connecticut HFA	204,420,000	210,580,000	415,000,000	3,263,845,000	2,437,120,000	5,700,965,000	74,819
Delaware SHA	0	0	0	823,693,537	104,880,000	928,573,537	5,484
Dist. of Columbia HFA	0	0	0	438,840,000	91,905,000	530,745,000	9,329
Florida HFA	90,585,000	10,990,000	101,575,000	1,982,188,400	808,278,000	2,790,466,400	23,486
Georgia HFA	25,950,000	49,050,000	75,050,000	1,120,691,788	520,880,000	1,641,571,788	24,252
Hawaii HFDC	0	0	0	939,205,000	285,850,000	1,225,055,000	7,522
Idaho HA	131,850,000	68,150,000	200,000,000	1,437,782,885	311,868,115	1,749,469,000	30,702
Illinois HDA	70,810,000	130,700,000	201,510,000	1,735,089,000	804,862,856	2,539,951,856	34,537
Indiana HFA	34,000,000	87,000,000	121,000,000	1,286,035,000	493,355,000	1,779,390,000	28,703
Iowa FA	0	0	0	753,865,000	172,745,000	926,610,000	17,306
Kentucky HC	51,540,000	38,445,000	89,985,000	1,291,511,000	695,010,000	1,986,521,000	41,211
Louisiana HFA	112,664,015	0	112,664,015	1,080,414,015	75,962,165	1,156,376,180	15,952
Maine SHA	60,000,000	13,385,000	73,385,000	1,110,800,000	636,428,000	1,747,228,000	27,988
Maryland CDA	34,805,000	155,545,000	190,350,000	1,865,395,000	1,486,115,951	3,351,510,951	44,927
Massachusetts HFA	46,975,000	150,920,000	197,895,000	1,660,220,000	1,070,659,355	2,730,879,355	34,237
Michigan SHDA	108,200,000	102,295,000	210,495,000	1,379,722,000	593,030,000	1,972,752,000	42,624
Minnesota HFA	74,335,000	186,850,000	261,185,000	1,990,051,000	1,325,435,000	3,315,486,000	47,401
Mississippi HC	89,460,000	25,701,278	115,161,278	1,171,995,920	303,602,269	1,475,598,189	19,875
Missouri HDC	99,223,567	58,711,305	157,934,872	1,905,523,567	206,380,833	2,111,904	42,560

Montana BoH	65,000,000	0	65,000,000	1,072,015,000	240,185,000	1,312,200,000	21,037
Nebraska IFA	150,171,000	0	150,171,000	2,178,656,000	199,417,516	2,378,073,516	39,941
Nevada HD	106,040,000	62,390,000	168,430,000	1,379,475,000	274,740,000	1,654,215,000	22,390
New Hampshire HFA	27,275,000	32,725,000	60,000,000	1,379,475,000	274,740,000	1,654,215,000	22,390
New Jersey HMFA	200,000,000	0	200,000,000	3,237,285,000	965,554,256	4,202,839,256	42,372
New Mexico MFA	122,460,000	28,245,000	150,705,000	1,531,629,000	372,740,959	1,904,369,959	26,053
New York HDC	16,750,000	0	16,750,000	29,080,000	0	29,080,000	3
New York SONYMA	199,678,000	174,352,000	374,030,000	4,549,417,000	2,661,612,800	7,211,029,800	101,374
North Carolina HFA	132,175,000	42,225,000	175,000,000	1,201,845,000	413,595,000	1,615,440,000	31,331
North Dakota HFA	132,900,000	0	175,000,000	1,201,845,000	413,595,000	1,615,440,000	31,331
Ohio HFA	350,000,000	0	350,000,000	3,647,604,000	635,439,500	4,283,043,500	65,626
Oklahoma HFA	20,000,000	45,475,000	65,475,000	1,242,344,000	344,630,000	1,586,974,000	32,211
Oregon HCSD	78,060,000	99,255,000	177,315,000	804,827,765	595,226,418	1,400,054,183	18,795
Pennsylvania HFA	267,195,000	127,805,000	395,000,000	2,273,484,000	865,370,000	3,138,854,000	67,101
Puerto Rico HFC	0	0	0	468,805,757	0	468,805,757	9,117
Rhode Island HMFC	14,450,000	87,165,000	87,165,000	2,422,191,000	971,119,636	3,393,310,636	45,992
South Carolina SHFDA	100,000,000	10,550,000	25,000,000	1,002,698,540	159,440,825	1,162,139,000	24,350
South Dakota HDA	64,415,000	214,045,000	314,045,000	1,783,467,000	1,185,890,000	2,969,357,000	39,993
Tennessee HDA	85,760,000	95,585,000	160,000,000	2,431,420,000	769,103,000	3,200,523,000	61,084
Texas DHCA	75,560,000	140,870,000	226,630,000	2,156,725,890	692,320,741	2,849,046,631	26,717
Utah HFA	56,708,038	49,440,000	125,000,000	1,678,725,000	919,858,000	2,598,583,000	38,888
Vermont HFA	0	0	56,708,038	975,090,038	55,000,000	1,030,090,038	18,392
Virgin Islands HFA	13,000,000	13,000,000	13,000,000	13,000,000	27,000,000	40,000,000	61
Virginia HDA	58,965,000	274,215,000	333,180,000	3,177,390,132	3,564,362,691	6,741,742,823	97,541
Washington SHFC	46,082,603	48,917,397	95,000,000	1,077,107,603	580,308,882	1,657,416,485	26,456
West Virginia HDF	51,190,000	23,810,000	75,000,000	919,820,000	207,775,000	1,127,595,000	24,598
Wisconsin HEDA	149,655,000	143,785,000	293,440,000	2,258,050,000	954,110,000	3,212,160,000	66,675
Wyoming CDA	99,765,000	65,235,000	165,000,000	1,355,705,000	528,432,975	1,884,137,975	25,521
Totals	4,772,180,203	3,479,499,993	8,251,680,196	84,606,391,124	35,605,728,676	120,212,619,800	1,760,096

Note: Arizona and Kansas agencies are not bond issuers. PR HFC did not issue MRB's in 1996, TN, in addition to the new money issues and refundings, $125,000,000 new money COBs and $40,465,000 refunding COBs were issued.

Source: HFA Homeownership Survey: 1996, National Council of State Housing Agencies, Washington, D.C.

TABLE 7–3

1996 Homeownership Survey Mortgage Characteristics

	Avg MRB Mortgage $ Amount	Avg MRB Purchase Price	Percent Single Parents	Avg Age Head of Household	Average Household Size	Average Borrower Income
Alabama HFA	66,109	67,793	NA	32.4	2.4	31,242
Alaska HFC	90,267	90,634	10.6	34	2.0	38,688
Arkansas DFA	55,750	56,760	18.3	33.1	2.5	28,287
California HFA	106,175	109,614	10.0	NA	3.1	34,078
Colorado HFA	71,172	72,364	13.7	33.0	3.0	30,753
Connecticut HFA	87,830	92,147	16.8	33.8	2.7	42,336
Delaware SHA	90,140	92,797	14.0	33.0	2.0	35,308
Dist. of Columbia HFA	88,919	98,226	85.0	37.0	NA	32,302
Florida HFA	70,585	73,840	50.9	33	2.0	28,318
Georgia HFA	64,096	64,858	NA	32.0	2.0	26,323
Hawaii HFDC	163,583	182,119	NA	33.1	2.6	46,851
Idaho HA	72,098	74,342	8.9	31.0	2.8	29,396
Illinois HDA	66,008	75,801	10.6	32.0	2.0	34,723
Indiana HFA	63,114	65,925	23.0	30.0	2.0	30,584
Iowa FA	45,782	47,872	10.3	30.0	2.0	29,171
Kentucky HC	58,354	58,585	22.5	31.0	2.2	28,562
Louisiana HFA	62,274	64,749	22.6	33.6	2.7	27,749
Maine SHA	59,818	62,053	12.0	32.0	2.0	28,448
Maryland CDA	78,903	103,130	NA	34.0	2.0	36,590
Massachusetts HFA	93,263	103,130	NA	34.0	2.0	36,590
Michigan SHDA	50,320	51,268	25.0	31.0	2.0	24,973
Minnesota HFA	60,268	59,656	16.5	31.2	2.2	25,469
Mississippi HC	53,674	54,254	23.2	31.4	2.4	27,078
Missouri HDC	60,361	61,993	NA	31.0	2.4	32,342
Montana BoH	62,746	63,023	12.2	30.0	2.0	26,782
Nebraska IFA	53,580	54,037	NA	NA	NA	NA
Nevada HD	98,141	99,596	13.0	34.6	2.6	36,219
New Hampshire HFA	73,460	77,157	NA	33.0	2.8	37,404
New Jersey HMFA	92,560	100,673	13.5	33.0	2.0	42,603
New Mexico MFA	72,127	75,770	14.7	32.6	2.4	28,696
New York HDC	NA	NA	NA	NA	NA	NA
New York SONYMA	90,123	104,118	1.2	34.0	2.4	40,268
North Carolina HFA	67,055	68,337	25.0	31.8	2.1	29,863
North Dakota HFA	52,099	53,820	45.8	31.3	2.4	29,894
Ohio HFA	69,277	70,136	NA	32.0	2.0	32,578
Oklahoma HFA	50,782	52,898	NA	NA	4.0	27,189
Oregon HCSD	78,719	83,305	12.3	33.3	2.4	31,447
Pennsylvania HFA	58,034	62,238	25.0	NA	2.6	30,142
Puerto Rico HFC						
Rhode Island HMFC	80,228	86,193	NA	34.0	2.4	32,111
South Carolina SHFDA	55,207	62,949	NA	31.0	2.0	21,822
South Dakota HDA	57,374	58,837	9.3	31.0	2.4	30,527
Tennessee HDA	51,930	51,967	29.6	33.8	2.3	23,525
Texas DHCA	66,119	67,279	NA	NA	2.8	29,595
Utah HFA	85,823	86,919	14.0	29.4	3.1	29,254
Vermont HFA	66,559	71,737	21.8	33.0	2.6	29,540
Virgin Islands HFA	99,000	104,000	NA	NA	NA	NA
Virginia HDA	80,656	82,090	47.4	32.0	2.5	34,187
Washington SHFC	89,190	93,877	22.6	33.6	2.5	34,837
West Virginia HDF	58,418	62,578	NA	32.0	NA	30,585
Wisconsin HEDA	52,940	59,993	15.0	32.0	2.3	29,289
Wyoming CDA	63,474	63,754	NA	32.0	3.0	28,199
National Averages	71,850	75,192	NA	NA	NA	30,915

Source: HFA Homeownership Survey: 1996, National Council of State Housing Agencies, Washington, D.C.

SUMMARY

Terms of financing can affect the transaction prices of residential properties. A favorable term, particularly a below-market rate of interest, has value, just as any physical property characteristic. The value of the low-rate financing is not easily determined, however. The cash-equivalent value, found by discounting the future payment savings over the life of the loan, may overstate the true value of below-rate financing. Uncertainty regarding the future direction of interest rates is a critical factor leading to a constraint on the value of low-rate financing. Simply put, the buyer may not pay the "full" cash-equivalent value because a subsequent drop in rates may reduce or eliminate the value. Empirical studies tend to bear this out. Most studies reveal that less than 100 percent of the cash-equivalent value of assumable loans is included in the price of the property. The same is generally true of other types of advantageous financing.

Mortgage revenue bonds are another form of low-rate financing. The tax-free interest on these bonds allows for mortgage loans with rates below those on conventional loans. The Internal Revenue Service limits the volume of MRBs that states can issue. Empirical evidence suggests that the value of properties in areas targeted by MRB financing is greater than otherwise. Where there is no targeted area, house prices in general may be greater if an MRB program of sufficient size increases the general demand for housing.

KEY TERMS

Advantageous (creative) financing	Fully amortized wrap
Assumable loan	House price capitalization
Buydown	Land contract
Capitalization	Mortgage revenue bonds
Carryback	Owner-second
Cash-equivalent value	Regression analysis
Extended term wrap	Seller-supplied financing
FHA/VA discount points	Simultaneous term, partially amortized wrap

SUGGESTED READINGS

Agarwal, V., and R. Phillips. 1993. The effect of mortgage rate buydowns on housing prices: Recent evidence from FHA-VA transactions. *Journal of the American Real Estate and Urban Economics Association.* Winter.

Benjamin, J. and C. F. Sirmans. 1987. Who benefits from mortgage revenue bonds? *National Tax Journal* 40(1).

Clauretie, T. M. 1984. Capitalization of seller-supplied financing: Implication for assessment. *Property Tax Journal* 3(4).

Durning, D. 1992. Mortgage Revenue Bonds: Housing Markets, Home Buyers and Public Policy. Boston: Kluwer Academic Publishers.

Ferreira, E., and G. S. Sirmans. 1987. Interest rate changes, transaction costs, and assumable loan values. *Journal of Real Estate Research* 29–49, Winter.

Rosen, K. T. 1984. Creative financing and house prices: A study of capitalization effects. *Housing Finance Review* 3(2).

Sa-Aadu, J., C. F. Sirmans, and J. Benjamin. 1989. Financing and house prices. *Journal of Financial Research* 12(1): 83–91.

Sirmans, G. S., S. Smith, and C. F. Sirmans. 1983. Assumption financing and selling prices of single-family homes. *Journal of Financial and Quantitative Analysis* 18: 307–318.

Zerbst, R., and W. Brueggeman. 1977. FHA and VA mortgage discount points and housing prices. *Journal of Finance* 22:1766–1773.

REVIEW QUESTIONS

7–1 List and describe three different types of "advantageous financing."

7–2 Explain what is meant by cash-equivalent value.

7–3 What is meant by capitalizing advantageous financing into the price of the property?

7–4   Why would one expect that the cash-equivalent value of an assumable loan would not be fully capitalized into house prices?

7–5   Summarize the empirical findings on the issue of the capitalization of creative financing into house prices?

7–6   What are the implications of creative financing for appraisal practices?

7–7   Explain how land contracts are used as a form of creative financing.

7–8   In regard to mortgage revenue bonds, (a) what are they? (b) how do they work? (c) what is their purpose?

7–9   Explain the wealth redistribution aspects of mortgage revenue bonds.

7–10   List the various ways to structure a wraparound mortgage.

PROBLEMS

7–1   Determine the cash-equivalent value of the following assumable loan:

Original balance	$67,000
Contract rate	8%
Market rate	12%
Remaining term	18 years
Original term	30 years

7–2   Determine the cash-equivalent value of the above loan one year later if the market rate falls to 10 percent.

7–3   A developer is offering a buydown in order to sell a property. With a market rate of 12 percent, he is willing to buy the rate down for the first two years to 8 percent and 10 percent, respectively. If $80,000 is borrowed on a 30-year term with monthly payments, what is the buydown fee?

7–4   Smith wants to buy a property for $120,000, but he has no money to make a down payment. Jones, the seller, is willing to do a wrap for the purchase price with an existing monthly payment mortgage having a fixed rate of 8 percent. This existing loan had an original balance of $100,000 and has 20 years remaining on its original 30-year term. The current market rate is 12 percent on 20-year mortgages. Jones is willing to write the wrap loan at a 10 percent interest rate.

   a. What is the effective equity yield for Jones if the wrap is written for the remaining term of the existing mortgage and both are held to maturity?

   b. Suppose that, in order to lower the payments on the wrap loan, the amortization period is extended to 30 years. Now what is the effective equity yield for the wrap lender?

   c. Assume the conditions in part B except that a balloon payment is required on the wrap loan at the end maturity of the existing loan. What is the effective equity yield for the wrap lender?

   d. Assume the conditions in part A except that the wrap loan is written for 12 years.

      1. What is the effective equity yield for the wrap lender assuming a balloon payment is required on the original loan?

      2. What is the effective equity yield for the wrap lender assuming increased amortization on the original loan to equalize the maturity of the wrap loan?

ENDNOTES

1. Technically, the price would be $104,712: 100,000 [1 − (0.90 × 0.05)].

2. Robert Zerbst and William Brueggeman, "FHA and VA Mortgage Discount Points and Housing Prices," *Journal of Finance* 22 (December 1977): 1766–1773.

3. Peter F. Colwell, Karl L. Guntermann, and C. F. Sirmans, "Discount Points and Housing Prices: Comment," *Journal of Finance* 34 (September 1979): 1049–1054.

4. See, for example, Ken Garcia, "Sales Prices and Cash Equivalents," *The Appraisal Journal* (January 1972): 7–16.

5. Kenneth M. Lusht and J. Andrew Hanz, "Some Further Evidence on the Price of Mortgage Contingency Clauses," *Journal of Real Estate Research* 9 (Spring 1994): 213–218.

6. Paul K. Asabere, Forrest E. Huffman, and Seyed Mehdian, "The Prime Effects of Cash Versus Mortgage Transactions," *Journal of the American Real Estate and Urban Economics Association* 20 (Spring 1992): 141–153.

7. G. Stacy Sirmans, Stanley D. Smith, and C. F. Sirmans, "Assumption Financing and Selling Prices of Single-Family Homes," *Journal of Financial and Quantitative Analysis* 18 (September 1983): 307–318.

8. Kenneth Rosen, "Creative Financing and House Prices: A Study of Capitalization Effects," Berkeley, CA: University of California Center for Real Estate and Urban Economics, 1982.

9. Terrence M. Clauretie, "Capitalization of Seller Supplied Financing: Implications for Assessors," *Property Tax Journal* 3 (December 1984): 229–238.

10. Arthur L. Schwartz, "Cash Equivalency," *The Real Estate Appraiser and Analyst* (Fall 1983).

11. Terrence M. Clauretie, "How Much Is An Assumable Loan Worth?" *Real Estate Review* 12 (Fall 1982): 52–56.

12. Jack Friedman, "Cash Equivalence: Market Knowledge and Judgments," *The Appraisal Journal* 52 (January 1984): 129–132.

13. Mark A. Sunderman, Roger E. Cannaday, and Peter F. Colwell, "The Value of Mortgage Assumptions: An Empirical Test," *Journal of Real Estate Research* 5 (Summer 1990): 247–257.

14. David Dale-Johnson, M. Chapman Findlay, Arthur L. Schwartz, Jr., and Stephen D. Kapplin, "Valuation and Efficiency in the Market for Creatively Financed Houses," *AREUEA Journal* 13 (Winter 1985): 388–403.

15. Eurico J. Ferreira and G. Stacy Sirmans, "Interest Rate Changes, Transactions Costs, and Assumable Loan Values," *Journal of Real Estate Research* 2 (Winter 1987): 29–49.

16. Vinod B. Agarwal and Richard A. Phillips, "Mortgage Rate Buydowns: Further Evidence," *Housing Finance Review* 3 (April 1984): 191–197.

17. John A. Edgren and Steven C. Hayworth, "The Implications of Land Contracts for Property Tax Assessment Practices," *Housing Finance Review* 3 (April 1984): 177–189.

18. J. Sa-Aadu, C. F. Sirmans, and John D. Benjamin, "Financing and House Prices," *Journal of Financial Research* 12 (Spring 1989): 83–91.

19. Dan Durning and John Quigley, "On the Distributional Implications of Mortgage Revenue Bonds and Creative Finance," *National Tax Journal* 38 (December 1985): 513–523.

20. Terrence M. Clauretie, Paul Merkle, and C. F. Sirmans, "The Effect of Bond Issues on Housing Markets," *Housing Finance Review* 5 (Winter 1986): 207–215.

CHAPTER 8

Federal Housing Policies: Part I

LEARNING OBJECTIVES

The subject of Chapters 8 and 9 is federal housing policies. Federal laws greatly influence the practices of individuals and institutions involved in financing residential property. After reading this chapter, you should understand how federal legislation has affected the mortgage and housing markets in terms of affordability, efficiency, and competition. You should understand how legislation has been passed to increase affordability of housing through subsidies to lenders and borrowers. You also should understand how the federal government has sought to foster efficiency in the housing and mortgage market, and you should know the various laws that have been enacted to promote competition in the real estate services industry. Chapter 9 deals with issues of equity and discrimination in housing.

INTRODUCTION

The United States Congress has determined that housing issues are a concern of the federal government. Through a series of acts, it has set as a priority the availability of adequate and affordable housing for all citizens regardless of race, gender, national origin, or religious affiliation. Federal legislation addresses four housing-market issues: affordability, efficiency and stability, competition, and equity. In this chapter we cover the first three. The important concepts of equity and discrimination are dealt with in Chapter 9.

HOUSING AFFORDABILITY

Federal programs designed to make housing more affordable can be categorized into three areas: economic support of financial institutions that supply mortgage funds; guarantee of mortgage insurance, direct grants, and subsidies; and income tax provisions.

Economic Support of Financial Institutions

The federal government has provided economic support to financial institutions that supply mortgage funds. This financial support has allowed the institutions to deliver mortgage funds at a lower cost than they otherwise could. Economic support has come from two sources: (1) loans at below market rates to savings institutions and commercial banks, and (2) subsidized insurance of deposits. Both programs have reduced the cost of funds, both borrowed funds and deposits, for financial institutions. The following discussion focuses on subsidies to savings institutions.

Federal Home Loan Bank Act (1932).   This act established the Federal Home Loan Bank Board and twelve district banks. The board was terminated in 1989. Its role was to act in a supervisory capacity. The role of the banks is to provide liquidity to member associations, such as

144

thrifts, in periods when deposit growth slows or declines. The liquidity is needed because member associations hold assets in the form of long-term mortgages—loans definitely not payable on demand. Also, prior to the development of a secondary mortgage market, it was difficult for thrifts to meet liquidity needs created by an outflow of deposits by selling off mortgages.

The Federal Home Loan Banks obtain a significant amount of the funds that they lend to thrifts from the sale of Federal Home Loan Bank (FHLB) bonds in the capital market. Member associations are required to purchase stock in the Federal Home Loan Banks. This initial capital serves as a solid equity base to support the bond issues. Although the bonds are not guaranteed by the U.S. government, the banks operate under a federal charter and government supervision. Also, when a district bank advances a loan to a member association, it requires collateral, such as mortgages held in the portfolio of the association. Such a loan is called a secured advance. The bonds that district banks sell in the capital market must be backed in equal amount by these secured advances plus government securities or cash. These factors combine to make the FHLB bonds virtually risk free. The low interest paid by the banks allows them to advance loans to their member associations at a reduced rate.

The borrowing and lending activity of the district banks is portrayed in Table 8–1. The data show how the net deposit gain of savings and loan associations slowed when market interest rates rose. Note the slowdown in 1966, 1969, 1974, and, particularly, 1981. We do not include data subsequent to the Garn-St. Germain Act of 1982 because bank advances to thrifts rose significantly as a result of this act. Net FHLB advances followed deposit flows, rising when deposits slowed and falling (through repayments) when deposit flows increased. Also, the changes in the amount of FHLB bonds outstanding followed closely the advances by the banks to member thrifts.

Figure 8–1 shows what occurs to FHLB bonds and advances to thrifts when interest rates cause deposit inflows to slow. As interest rates fall, the reverse process occurs.

National Housing Act (1934).   This act, in addition to creating the Federal Housing Administration, established the Federal Savings and Loan Insurance Corporation, which was abolished in 1989 and merged with FDIC. The purpose of this agency was to insure consumer

TABLE 8–1

Interest Rates, S&L Deposits, FHLBB Advances,
and FHLBB Bond Activity: 1965–1981
(in millions)

	10-Year Treasury Bond Yield	*Net Deposit Gain[a]*	*Net FHLB Advance[b]*	*Change in Consolidated Bonds and Discount Notes Outstanding*
1965	4.28	8,409	672.3	852.0
1966	4.92	3,589	937.8	1,638.0
1967	5.07	10,574	(2,549.0)	(2,799.0)
1968	5.65	7,381	873.4	641.0
1969	6.67	3,954	4,030.0	3,721.0
1970	7.35	10,809	1,325.6	1,767.1
1971	6.16	27,465	(2,678.4)	(3,349.1)
1972	6.21	32,113	42.5	(169.0)
1973	6.84	19,984	7,168.6	7,778.3
1974	7.56	15,705	6,657.3	4,995.9
1975	7.99	42,118	(3,959.8)	(3,062.3)
1976	7.61	49,991	(1,982.6)	(1,762.9)
1977	7.42	50,453	4,310.9	1,389.0
1978	8.41	44,350	12,497.2	9,100.4
1979	9.44	38,968	9,168.0	5,262.2
1980	11.46	41,211	7,124.7	6,896.8
1981	13.91	13,481	16,231.4	16,862.5

[a]Deposit inflows less withdrawals for all FHLB member associations.
[b]New advances to associations less payments.

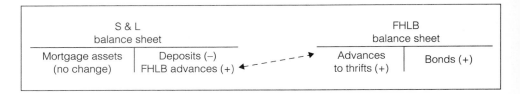

FIGURE 8–1

Flow of Funds through FHLBs When Interest Rates Rise

S & L balance sheet		FHLB balance sheet	
Mortgage assets (no change)	Deposits (–) FHLB advances (+)	Advances to thrifts (+)	Bonds (+)

deposits against loss. It assessed institutions a "flat" rate of one-twelfth of one percent of total deposits as a premium. Deposit insurance allows thrifts to take on excess risk. Without it, depositors would recognize the risk of a thrift's investments and withdraw their funds, effectively closing down the thrift. The rate was flat in the sense that it was based on the amount of an institution's deposits rather than on risk factors. There are several sources of institutional risk.

1. *Interest volatility risk*—changes in market interest rates cause the market value of assets to fall relative to liabilities (because of maturity mismatch).
2. *Credit risk*—borrowers may default on their obligations.
3. *Liquidity risk*—there may be an unpredictable surge in deposit net withdrawals.
4. *Internal fraud risk*—misappropriation of funds by management is one example.
5. *Miscellaneous risk*—risk from foreign exchange, risk of losses from subsidiaries, and risk from unforeseen regulatory actions are included in this category.

Of the sources of risk identified in the preceding list, the first two have been critical for most thrifts. Risk-averting institutions are likely to seek out investments that reduce their maturity mismatch and default exposure. On the other hand, risk- (and return-) seeking institutions are likely to acquire long-term or speculative investments. Equity participations (see Chapter 19) in commercial real estate developments are an excellent example of the latter.

A low, flat-rate insurance premium structure has two faults. First, it misprizes risk and, therefore, encourages thrifts to assume more risk than they could without the insurance. Second, it is distributionally unfair, forcing conservatively managed institutions to subsidize those with risky investments. If regulators are quick to close a thrift as its capital level diminishes and before it has negative net worth, then the risk will be borne by the stockholders—not by the depositors or the government. However, since many thrifts have been undercapitalized to begin with and since bureaucratic regulators are slow to recognize problem thrifts, the deposit insurance ends up as a subsidy to the stockholders of risk-seeking thrifts.

Furthermore, the value of deposit insurance to an institution will vary directly with (1) interest rate volatility, (2) the institution's asset-liability maturity mismatch, and (3) the institution's capital-to-asset ratio. In 1983, McCulloch estimated that FSLIC deposit insurance was worth 2.1 percent of its liabilities per year for an institution with a capital-asset ratio of 100 and an asset-liability maturity mismatch of only 1 year.[1]

In a competitive market the value of the government-provided insurance subsidy will be shifted forward to borrowers and backward to depositors. Low insurance premiums explain why, in some years, the yield on money-market accounts exceeded that of short-term Treasuries and why the majority of mortgage loans have always been of the fixed-rate type.

Mortgage Insurance, Direct Grants, and Subsidies

The National Housing Act, which established the **Federal Housing Administration (FHA),** provides for the bulk of benefits in this category. Insurance, direct grants, and subsidy programs are carried out under the direction of the Department of Housing and Urban Development (HUD), within which the FHA is located. A complete list of HUD-sponsored activities and their legislative authority is provided in Appendix A to this chapter.

Mortgage Insurance

The FHA provides default insurance on a variety of mortgage types for a cost that many believe is less than that justified by the risk. The various government insurance programs are detailed in Chapter 14 and are only briefly mentioned here. The largest FHA insurance program is the One-to-Four-Family Home Mortgage Insurance Program (Section 203 of the National Housing Act). Other FHA insurance programs target loans for high-risk residential properties and include insuring loans for home improvement in declining neighborhoods (Section 223[e]), for home improvement in urban renewal areas (Section 220), and for construction of cooperative housing (Section 213). Still other FHA insurance programs target loans for high-credit-risk borrowers and include insuring loans for special credit risks (those with a less-than-exemplary credit history [Section 237]), for multifamily properties whose tenants are from moderate-income families (Sections 221 [d] [3] and 221 [d] [4]), and for rental housing for the elderly (Section 231). Finally, there are programs that target socially desirable properties such as nursing homes, intermediate-care facilities, board-and-care homes (Section 232), hospitals (Section 242), and group medical practice facilities (Title XI).

Without these insurance programs, it is doubtful that lenders would make many of these high-risk loans, even those for single-family houses. FHA premiums historically have appeared to be less than what would be necessary to compensate for the default risk of residential loans. Because housing prices rose substantially during the 1960s, 1970s, and early 1980s, there were relatively few defaults on FHA-insured, single-family loans during this period. The premiums charged by the FHA did not appear to be low, relative to the risk at that time. This situation changed in the mid-1980s through the early 1990s. Housing price appreciation slowed nationally, and prices declined in locally depressed areas such as the oil-patch states of Texas and Louisiana. Rising numbers of defaults led to large losses for the FHA (see Chapter 14). Since the FHA is backed by the full faith of the U.S. government, lenders are willing to make loans backed by this agency, despite the losses that result from failure to underwrite loans and correctly price insurance. In contrast, when a private mortgage insurer misprizes insurance and suffers large losses, lenders will transfer their business to other insurers. The ability of a private mortgage insurer to pay claims is very important to a lender.[2] Several private mortgage insurers went bankrupt during the late 1980s and early 1990s. In short, the backing of the government has allowed the FHA to subsidize home buyers by charging them a premium that is less than what private insurers would be able to charge, especially for high loan-to-value ratio loans.

It is uncertain how long the government may use the backing of the Treasury to subsidize the insurance premium on FHA loans. There has been a movement to make the FHA actuarially sound. In fact, the Cranston–Gonzalez National Affordability Act of 1990 provided for a restructuring of the premium for FHA insurance in order to accomplish this purpose. The annual charge (premium) has been replaced by a combination of both an up-front and an annual charge. In addition, the Cranston–Gonzalez Act requires that the FHA become actuarially sound in terms of having adequate capital to meet foreseeable future losses. It has established minimum capital ratios that must be met over the next several years.

One must realize that opposing a move to actuarial soundness will be political pressures to make housing affordable, especially for first-time home buyers. If the FHA premium reflects the full risk of high loan-to-value loans, it will obviously reduce housing affordability for those home buyers with little equity to invest in housing.

Direct Grants

In addition to its mortgage insurance program, HUD administers many grant programs. The **Community Development Block Grants** program provides funds to cities and urban counties on a formula basis to entitled communities to carry out a wide range of community development projects. Some of the activities that can be carried out with community development funds include the acquisition of real property; the rehabilitation of residential and nonresidential properties; and the provision of public facilities, such as water and sewerage treatment plants, street maintenance, and neighborhood centers. All projects must benefit low- and moderate-income persons.

Community Development Block Grants for States and Small Cities is a similar program for states and smaller cities. No less than 60 percent of the grant money can be used for projects that benefit low- and moderate-income persons. The Secretary's Discretionary Fund provides Community Block Grants to those communities not eligible for the first two grant types. These grants are available for the insular areas such as Guam, the Virgin Islands, American Samoa, and so forth. Grants in this category are also available for Indian tribes, Alaskan native villages, and work-study programs. The fiscal year 1997 appropriation for this program was $4.6 billion.

Rental Rehabilitation grants are available to cities and states to encourage rehabilitation of rental properties. Rental Rehab funds (generally up to $15,000 per unit) may cover up to half the total eligible rehabilitation costs of a project. After rehabilitation, at least 70 percent of the occupants must be low-income families (less than 80 percent of the median income for the area). Some funds also must be used to aid large families. Rents subsequent to rehabilitation cannot be limited by rent control.

Under the **Urban Homesteading Program,** federally owned properties (primarily foreclosed FHA- or VA-insured properties) are transferred to local governments that have a homestead program approved by HUD. They, in turn, transfer the properties to low-income families for a nominal sum. The homesteaders must occupy the property for at least 5 years and bring the property up to code standards. After these requirements have been met, the homesteaders receive fee-simple title to the property.

The **Emergency Shelter Grants Program** provides grants to states and cities to rehabilitate and convert buildings for shelter for the homeless. The program was established by Section IV of the Stewart B. McKinney Homeless Assistance Act of 1987. Participating local jurisdictions must submit a comprehensive homeless assistance plan (CHAP) outlining the need for assistance, the inventory of facilities available to serve the homeless, and a strategy to meet the long-term needs of the homeless. The act authorized $125 million for fiscal year 1991, $138 million for fiscal year 1992 and $156.8 million for 1995. Funds can be used to pay for maintenance costs, utilities, insurance, and furnishings, but no salaries for staff to operate a shelter may be paid out of grant funds.

Subsidies

HUD also has several subsidy programs, whereby the Department pays a portion of housing costs for low-income families. The most well known of the subsidy programs is the Lower Income Rental Assistance, or Section 8, Program. Under this program, HUD makes up the difference between what low- and very-low-income households can afford and the approved rent for an adequate housing unit. Eligible tenants must pay the highest of either 30 percent of adjusted income, 10 percent of gross income, or a portion of welfare assistance designated to meet housing costs. The subsidized housing must meet certain safety and sanitation standards. The rent cannot exceed the fair market rent for the local area. Funding under this program is no longer available for new construction or for substantially rehabilitated dwellings.

A related program is the Section 8 Existing Housing Voucher Program. It gives assisted families a greater choice of selection by allowing them to rent units with rents above the fair market rent. Monthly housing assistance payments are based on the difference between a payment standard for the area (not the actual rent) and 30 percent of the family's monthly income. Preference is given to those families currently occupying substandard housing or who are involuntarily displaced or are paying more than half their income for rent.

The Section 8 Moderate Rehabilitation Program is a subsidy program that encourages the rehabilitation of dilapidated dwellings. A local Public Housing Agency (PHA) administers the program by selecting landlords to participate on a competitive basis. Landlords agree to rehabilitate properties to meet certain safety and sanitation standards. The PHA sets the rents, based on the costs of maintaining and managing the property. HUD makes the subsidies available for 15 years. Eligible tenants must pay the highest of 30 percent of adjusted income, 10 percent of gross income, or a portion of welfare assistance designated for housing. Preference is given to very-low-income families currently occupying substandard housing or who are involuntarily displaced or paying more than half their income in rent.

HOME and HOPE Programs

The Cranston–Gonzalez National Affordability Housing Act of 1990 had as its primary purpose an increase in the supply of affordable housing for low-income and very-low-income families. It also was designed to improve housing opportunities for disadvantaged minorities (including Native Americans), increase the supply of supportive housing for persons with special needs (such as the disabled), and retain dwellings produced for low-income families with federal assistance (such as low-income housing) so as to prevent their conversion into standard housing. The two main parts of the program are Title II, the HOME Investment Partnership Act, and Title IV, the Homeownership and Opportunity for People Everywhere Program (HOPE).

The HOME program is structured around a loan arrangement whereby the federal government sets up a local home Investment Trust Fund that can be drawn from to increase the supply of low-income housing. Local jurisdictions can use the funds to construct or rehabilitate existing low-income housing. Income from the housing is intended to be returned to the trust for further investment. This portion of the Act emphasizes the need to rehabilitate existing structures, rather than produce new dwellings. The act authorized $1 billion for fiscal year 1991 and approximately $2 billion for fiscal year 1992 for this purpose. These funds may not be used to defray administrative expenses. Also, HUD can place limits on the per-unit cost of the dwellings, according to the cost of construction in the area. Local jurisdictions are required to match the federal funds at no less than 25 percent for rental-assistance programs, 33 percent for rehabilitation of existing structures, and 50 percent for new construction. In general, HUD allocates funds by formula among eligible state and local governments. The fiscal year 1997 appropriation was $1.4 billion subject to some small set-asides for Indian Tribes, insular areas, management information systems, and housing counseling.

The HOPE program is structured as a grant. Grants can be used by local jurisdictions to rehabilitate public housing (and relocate tenants during the rehabilitation), and to acquire public housing for the purpose of transferring ownership to eligible families. Grants also can be used to aid in the formation of rental management corporations for public housing. The goal here is to privatize public housing so as to reduce future deterioration of these properties. The act allocated $68 million in fiscal year 1991 and $380 million in fiscal year 1992 for these purposes. Local jurisdictions are required to match a minimum of 25 percent of the federal grant under the hope program. While still on the books there has been no additional funding requests under this program since 1995. Up to date information for these and all HUD subsidy programs can be obtained by visiting the HUD website referenced at the end of this chapter.

Income Tax Provisions

For simplicity, the annual cost for an owner-occupant of housing under the current tax law can be stated as

$$C = [(1 - t)(i + p) + m + d - f]H \qquad \text{(Equation 8–1)}$$

where C is a dollar cost, H is the value of the house, t is the owner's personal tax rate, i is the interest rate on the mortgage (the amount of the mortgage is assumed to be identical in amount to H), p is the property tax rate, m is maintenance and miscellaneous costs as a percent of H, d is the rate of depreciation, and f is the rate of annual inflation in housing values. Housing inflation reduces the cost of housing and is subtracted from the cost of housing.

Assume, for an individual in the 30 percent tax bracket, a house with a value of $100,000, a mortgage rate of 12 percent, property taxes of 2 percent, miscellaneous expenses and depreciation of 1 percent, and housing inflation of 6 percent. The annual cost of housing for this person is

$$C = [(1 - 0.3)(0.12 + 0.02) + 0.01 - 0.06] \times \$100000$$

$$= (0.098 + 0.01 - 0.06) \times \$100,000 = \$4,800$$

This simple equation can be used to estimate the approximate changes in the total housing cost which result from changes in the components. The components of the equation reflect current tax treatment by the federal government. Both interest charges on mortgages (for primary residences) and property taxes (if itemized) can be deducted for the purpose of determining taxes. Prior to 1997 gains were not taxed as long as the homeowner purchased a new house within 2 years with a higher value than the basis of the old property. Now, the Tax Relief Act of 1997 allows a $250,000 capital gain tax exclusion for single taxpayers and a $500,000 exclusion for married taxpayers as long as they have resided in the house for two of the 5 years prior to sale. This provision effectively eliminates capital gains taxation on housing for the vast majority of U.S. citizens. (If the purchase of the new residence is less than the sales price of the old residence, there will be some tax due. The amount that is sheltered is equal to the difference between the cost of the new residence and the basis of the old residence.) The full amount of housing appreciation f is deducted from the cost.

Many have argued that the current tax treatment favors the production of owner-occupied housing. If interest costs and property taxes were not deductible and owners had to pay tax on the appreciation in house values, the annual housing cost in our example would be expressed as

$$C = [i + p + m + d - f(1 - t)]H$$

$$C = [0.12 + 0.02 + 0.01 - 0.06\,(0.7)] \times \$100,000 \qquad \text{(Equation 8–2)}$$

$$C = 0.108 \times \$100,000 = \$10,800$$

or more than double the tax-subsidized cost.

A complete model of owner-occupied housing is much more complex than the simple equation presented here. A complete model would have to take into account such factors as the tax treatment of rental property (with a deduction for depreciation, for example), the impact of inflation on the cost of rental housing relative to owner-occupied housing, the interaction of inflation and nominal interest rates, and the distribution of households among income classes.

Nonetheless, many have concluded what the simple equation here shows—that current tax laws significantly reduce the cost of owner-occupied housing and encourage its production. James Follain and Robert Dunsky examined the demand for the amount of mortgage debt demanded by U.S. homeowners as a function of the tax rate at which mortgage interest payments can be deducted. They concluded that the elasticity of the demand for mortgage debt with respect to a decrease in the rate at which interest is deductible was −1.5 in 1983 and −3.5 in 1989.[3]

EFFICIENCY AND STABILITY

Legislation designed to foster stability and efficiency in the mortgage and housing market has focused on two areas: (1) creating liquid and efficient markets for loans, and (2) deregulating the market.

Efficient Markets

Capital is used more efficiently and channeled into productive uses when the market for capital is large and liquid. More lenders are willing to invest in debt instruments if they know there is a large, liquid market within which these instruments can be resold. This eliminates marketability risk, which otherwise requires a rate premium. For many years this was not the case for residential mortgages. Many loans were originated and held in the portfolios of lenders until they either prepaid or matured. Consequently, rates on mortgages were relatively high and reflected the default-, interest-rate-, and marketability risks of the lenders' portfolios. Stated differently, the mortgage market was not well integrated into the overall capital market, the latter being large, liquid, and efficient. When not integrated, shifts in the supply and demand for mortgages would cause a divergence between the mortgage rate and capital market rates. The integration of the mortgage market into the larger capital market required the introduction of securitization.

Securitization refers to the process whereby individual, liquid mortgage loans are packaged into securities that are large, riskless (default), and sold on organized exchanges. The process of securitization, by expanding the market for a particular type of debt instrument, lowers the yield required by lenders. While many private financial institutions undertake to securitize mortgages today, the initial task of securitization took place through the activities of the federal government. The structure of the secondary mortgage market is outlined in detail in Chapter 10, so we present only a summary of the legislation here.

The National Mortgage Association of Washington (1938), shortly renamed the Federal National Mortgage Association (FNMA), was authorized to create a secondary market for FHA loans (another purpose was to gain greater acceptance of this new loan insurance by standing ready to buy and sell them). Most of its activities involved buying the loans and holding them in its own portfolio. It raised borrowed money in the capital market in order to finance its purchases. Later, it was allowed to purchase VA loans, and in 1970 the FNMA was given authorization to purchase conventional loans.

The **Housing and Urban Development Act** (1968) privatized the Federal National Mortgage Association (partially to remove its financial activities from the federal budget), while allowing the association to retain a $2.25 billion line of credit with the U.S. Treasury. The act also established the Government National Mortgage Association (GNMA). This agency, housed within HUD, does not buy mortgages. Rather, it guarantees the payment of principal and interest on the securities that are created and backed by mortgages.

The Emergency Home Finance Act (1970) grew out of the success of FNMA and GNMA in creating a liquid market for government-underwritten loans. The industry pressed for more government support of the conventional loan market, and this Act created a new secondary mortgage market agency, the Federal Home Loan Mortgage Corporation, with an objective to create a secondary market for conventional loans. The act also allowed FNMA to purchase conventional loans. The FHLMC issued the first conventional mortgage pass-through security (see Chapter 10) in 1971—the Mortgage Participation Certificate.

Deregulation

During the 1960s and 1970s regulation of mortgage lenders interfered with an efficient flow of capital through the mortgage market. The two most noticeable areas of inefficient regulation were federal Regulation Q limits on institutional deposits and state-imposed ceilings on the rate lenders could charge on mortgages. The Regulation Q limits caused funds to flow out of depository institutions and, therefore, out of the mortgage and housing market. The usury ceilings in various states caused mortgage money to dry up in those states when interest rates rose to cyclical peaks. Well-intentioned laws designed to keep the cost of mortgage funds low for the consumer resulted in unavailable loans, as funds flowed to unrestricted, nonhousing capital markets.

In the early 1980s, the Depository Institutions Deregulation and Monetary Control Act (1980) **deregulated** financial institutions in an attempt to solve these problems. The act eliminated both limits on deposit rates and on mortgage loan rates. It established the Depository Institutions Deregulation Committee to gradually phase out the Regulation Q limits over a few years. In the early 1980s this committee, composed of the heads of the regulatory agencies, eliminated deposit-rate ceilings on first one and then another type of deposit until the rates on all deposits were set by market forces and competition. The act also overrode all state usury ceilings for federally related loans. (Actually, in the year before, the Housing and Community Development Amendments exempted all FHA-insured loans from state and local usury limits.)

The combination of the development of the secondary mortgage market and deregulation has led to a greater integration of the mortgage market into the capital market. In the early 1980s, less than 5 percent of newly issued, fixed-rate conventional mortgages were securitized. By the late 1980s, more than half were securitized by the government agencies.

Hendershott and Van Order conclude that this rise in the securitization of mortgages has led to a substantial increase in the degree of integration.[4] They analyzed the relationship between the rate on GNMA bonds and that on conventional loans from the 1970s through the 1980s. Hendershott and Van Order viewed the GNMA rate as a capital market rate because GNMA bonds sell in a large and liquid market and are guaranteed against default by the U.S. government. They found that, during the early 1970s, the fraction of the change in the GNMA yield that was reflected in the conventional rate within two weeks was only one-sixth. By the early 1980s, the fraction rose to nearly one-half, and by the late 1980s, it had risen to nearly 100 percent. Hendershott and Van Order conclude that, while conventional rates may have been too high or too low relative to GNMA rates in the past, they are currently in line.

COMPETITION IN THE REAL ESTATE FINANCE MARKET

Congress has passed several acts designed to make the real estate finance market more competitive. Economic models have demonstrated the benefits of competition in terms of the efficient allocation of resources. Competitive models assume that market participants have full knowledge of all relevant prices and alternatives. Knowledge of the prices of factors of production and of goods and services is an essential (but not sufficient) condition for a market to be competitive. Accordingly, legislation affecting the competitiveness of the mortgage market has been aimed at making more information available to consumers.

Interstate Land Sales Full Disclosure Act (ILSFDA, 1968)

This act makes it unlawful to offer certain types of land for sale in interstate commerce without disclosing particular information, both to HUD and to prospective purchasers. Motivation for the act came out of hearings by the U.S. Senate Special Committee on Aging, during which testimony was given about land schemes aimed at the elderly. Through manipulative practices (such as land parties) and pressure sales tactics, the elderly often were enticed into purchasing nearly worthless land in swamps, deserts, or remote areas. The ILSFDA is administered by the Office of Interstate Land Sales Registration (OILSR) within HUD. The act applies to all subdivisions within the same promotional scheme (that is, they need not be physically contiguous) that are divided or in the future will be divided into 50 or more lots. A lot is defined as a piece, division, unit, or undivided interest in land. It can include leases, condominiums, and time-sharing arrangements. Subdivisions where the minimum lot is five acres or more are exempt from the provisions of the act. Another exemption is the sale or lease of a subdivision where the purchaser or spouse personally inspects the property, the so-called "on-site" exemption. Also exempt is the sale or lease of lots where a residential or commercial building exists or is required to be built by the buyer within two years of purchase. These exemptions reflect the purpose of the law to restrict the promotion and sale of raw, remote, and nearly worthless land to buyers who have little or no knowledge of the property.

Under this law developers must do two things. First, they have to register a statement-of-record with the OILSR. The statement of record must list, among other things, the developers involved and the characteristics of the land. Second, the developers must provide each prospective buyer or lessee a property report. The property report is similar to the statement-of-record and is designed to provide basic information about the subdivision. The report also advises the prospective buyers that they should seek professional advice, such as from an attorney, before purchasing any lot.

Consumer Credit Protection Act (Truth-in-Lending Law, 1968)

Title I of this act, containing the Truth-in-Lending and Fair-Credit-Billing acts, requires lenders to provide full information about any loan they grant to a customer. The act gives the board of Governors of the Federal Reserve System the authority to set standards and regulate this portion of the act. The regulatory requirements established by the board are referred to as Regulation Z, and they became effective July 1, 1969. They apply to both consumer loans (installment and revolving credit) and to residential mortgages. Loans exempt from Regulation Z include commercial and agricultural loans, loans from a securities dealer to a customer to purchase securities (margin account), student loans, and loans over $25,000 not secured by real property. Residential loans covered by the act include those used to purchase a one- to four-family dwelling, including condominiums, mobile homes, and trailers. Loans for transactions involving dwellings with more than four units are considered commercial and are not covered by the regulations. Also, an owner-seller of a single-family residence who extends credit to a purchaser is not required to conform with the regulations. The regulations do apply to second mortgages. The regulations are not intended to set maximum or minimum loan terms but rather to ensure the consumer is made fully aware of the essential terms of any loan. The motive is to provide consumers with sufficient and early information so that they may shop and compare charges among various loans.

Disclosure must be made in writing and in a form the borrower may keep. Disclosures must be made prior to the consummation of the loan or within three business days after the lender receives an application for the loan. This three-day period coincides with the same period of time that a lender has to provide good-faith estimates of settlement costs under RESPA (discussed later in this chapter). If the lender does not know the precise credit terms, the lender must make the disclosures based on the best information reasonably available and must indicate which items are estimates.

The two most important loan features that must be revealed to the consumer are the total finance charges and the annual percentage rate of interest (APR). These two items must be made more "conspicuous" than any other items of disclosure.

Total Finance Charges

These are the total of all charges over the life of the loan and include interest charges, origination fees (points), discount points, appraisal and credit report fees, premiums for creditor life and accident insurance (should the borrower die, the mortgage balance will be paid), and mortgage-insurance premiums. Not included in finance charges are any fees that would be associated with the sale of the property, even if no mortgage were involved. These typically include application fees, charges for delinquent payments or default, sales taxes, transfer taxes, recording fees, attorney fees, title examination fees, deed preparation fees, and the like. In some cases the lender may charge the seller of the property "points" for extending a mortgage to the buyer. Such charges are not considered finance charges under Regulation Z, even if the seller of the property raises its price to recoup the cost of the points. The same is true for any other seller-paid fees, such as mortgage-insurance premiums.

In addition to the amount of the total finance charges, the lender must disclose the number, amount, and due date of each payment. Disclosure also is required for any prepayment penalties, delinquency and penalty charges, and prepaid finance charges. Prepaid finance charges represent an interest charge for the first partial month payment until regular payments begin.

Annual Percentage Rate

Recall from Chapter 4 the **annual percentage rate** (**APR**) is the effective yield on a loan. The APR on a loan is similar to the yield-to-maturity concept. It will be greater than the contract rate of interest when there are up-front finance charges, such as origination and discount points. To recall how the APR is calculated, first consider a simple mortgage with no finance charges other than the contract rate of interest. The contract rate establishes the payment. When additional finance charges are considered, the monthly payment remains the same and the lender may quote the same contract rate, 10 percent. Origination and discount points will have the effect of reducing the amount of the effective loan amount below the face value. The right side of the equation is the monthly payment annuity. If the left side (loan amount) is reduced, then the equation will no longer be in balance. Balance is restored by raising the discount rate. The discount rate that restores the balance is the annual percentage rate. It is found just as the internal rate-of-return is calculated in traditional capital budgeting problems or commercial real estate investment analysis. As in those cases, lenders have no set formulas that will conveniently yield the APR. Computer programs are available to search for the correct APR.

The regulations require that the APR reported to the borrower be within 0.125 percent of the true APR (0.25 percent for adjustable rate mortgages). Thus, if a fixed-rate mortgage had an APR of 10.57 percent and the lender reported it as 10.5 percent, he would be within the allowed tolerance. A lender may be absolved from any error that is made if the calculation was made through the use of a calculation tool (for example, a computer program) used in good faith. To be absolved, the lender must have taken reasonable steps to verify the accuracy of the calculation tool.

As shown in Chapter 4, the lender calculates the APR of a 30-year loan on the basis of a holding period of the same length. If the borrower repays the loan prior to its maturity, the actual cost increases. The discount and origination points are "spread out" over a fewer number of years. For loans prepaid early in their life, the actual cost can be substantially greater than the contract rate. The actual cost is inversely related to the holding period of the loan. Regulation Z does not require that these other costs be disclosed, only the one based on a 30-year holding period.

Depending upon the borrower's expected holding period for a loan, the APR revealed by the lender can lead to an incorrect choice of loans. To see this, consider two loans, A and B, with different contract rates and up-front points. The actual APRs for each loan as a function of the holding period are shown in Figure 8–2.

Mortgage A has the lower "Reg. Z" APR (based on the term of the loan, N). If the borrower plans to hold the loan less than T* years, Mortgage A will have the higher actual APR. Most borrowers are likely not sophisticated enough to make these subtle distinctions. Yet, there is no current requirement that a loan's APR based on different holding periods be disclosed. Furthermore, there is evidence that home buyers have reasonable knowledge about their expected tenure in a house. Linneman and Voith analyzed data from the Michigan Panel Study on Income Dynamics.[5] They found that many people, including new homeowners, who indicated they expected to move in the near future did, in fact, do so. They argue that since many moves are anticipated by home buyers, APR schedules based on different tenure periods would provide useful information.

Regulation Z and Alternative Mortgage Instruments

Special rules apply to some of the alternative mortgage instruments discussed in the previous chapter, including graduated payment mortgages, adjustable rate mortgages, shared appreciation mortgages, buy-down mortgages, and home equity loans. Examples are included in Appendix B.

FIGURE 8–2

APR as a Function of Holding Period

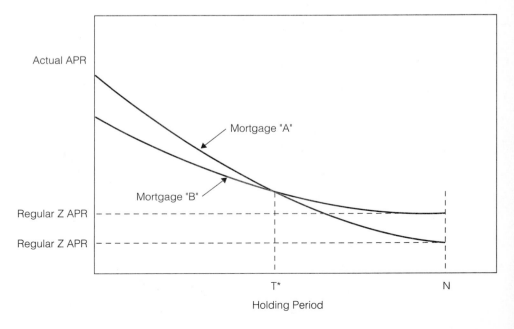

Graduated-Payment Mortgages.   Consider a graduated payment mortgage with a five-year graduation period and a 7.5 percent yearly increase in payments. The loan amount is $44,900 and carries a 14.75 percent rate of interest. Finance charges include two discount points ($898) and an initial mortgage-insurance premium of $225. The following equation can be used to compute the APR:

$$\$43,777 = \frac{446.62}{(1 + r/12)^1} + \cdots + \frac{479.67}{(1 + r/12)^{13}} + \cdots + \frac{515.11}{(1 + r/12)^{25}}$$

$$+ \frac{553.13}{(1 + r/12)^{37}} + \frac{593.91}{(1 + r/12)^{49}} + \cdots + \frac{673.68}{(1 + r/12)^{360}}$$

The resulting APR is 15.37 percent. The lender must advise the borrower that any negative amortization is a finance charge and not part of the amount financed. A sample disclosure appears in Appendix B.

Adjustable Rate Mortgages.   The major problem with estimating the APR on ARMs is that the future payments are not known with certainty. They will go up or down with movements in the index. Disclosure of finance charges is generally based on the initial terms of the loan. Lenders cannot assume that interest rates will change in either direction.

Many ARMs carry a reduced interest rate for the initial period. In such cases the APR is computed as a time-weighted average of the rates over the life of the loan. For example, consider an ARM with a 2 percent margin, originated when the index is 10 percent. The contract rate, if fully indexed, would be 12 percent. The lender may agree to a first-year rate of 9 percent. In this case the APR, assuming no other finance charges, would be 11.90 percent, based on the first year at 9 percent and the remaining years at 12 percent. If the loan were for $100,000, the lender would have to disclose that there would be 12 payments of $804.62, and 348 payments of $1025.31. The lender also must disclose general information about its ARM loans, including the margin; the index used and where information on the index is published (such as the *Wall Street Journal*); the frequency with which the rate can change; any caps on the interest rate change, either periodically or over the life of the loan; any cap on the payment change; and any provision for negative amortization. The lender also is required to provide the borrower with an example showing how payments on its ARM loan would have changed over a recent period of time. Historical indexes are used for this purpose. An example of these disclosures also appears in Appendix B.

Shared Appreciation Mortgages.   With this type of loan, the lender receives a share of the appreciation in the value of the property in return for a reduction in the initial rate of interest. Since the amount of the appreciation is unknown when the loan is originated, all disclosures must be based on the original, fixed interest rate.

Buydown Mortgages.   In certain transactions the seller or another third party may agree to pay an amount to the lender in order to reduce the borrower's payments or to reduce the interest rate for a portion of the loan's term. If the lower rate is reflected in the terms of the contract, then the disclosures must take the buy-down into account. As with ARMs, the APR must be a composite rate that takes into account the lower initial rate and the higher subsequent rate. Payment disclosures also must reflect the two levels. If the lower rate is not reflected in the contract (as might be the case where a side contract is made between the party providing the buy-down and the borrower), then the disclosure provided by the lender cannot reflect the buy-down. The effect of all borrower buy-downs must be included in the disclosure.

Home Equity Loans (HELs).   These loans are usually open-ended; the borrower can "take down" amounts as needed up to a level determined by the value of the equity in the property. There is no amortization schedule, but the loan will generally stipulate minimum monthly payments. The rate on HELs is almost always variable and tied to some money market index, such as short-term Treasury yields. HELs can be best described as open-ended, nonamortizing, adjustable rate mortgages. Disclosure regulations require that the lender inform the borrower that the lender will acquire a security interest in the home. The lender also must inform the borrower that certain conditions may allow the lender to terminate the loan (require full payment of the balance), deny any further extensions of credit, or reduce the credit limit. One such condition would be the failure to meet repayment terms as determined by agreement between the lender and borrower. Payment terms also must be disclosed, including the periodic rate, how the rate is determined, and a statement that paying only the interest charge will not reduce the principal of the loan. The lender also must provide an example of how payments would behave based on a $10,000 extension of credit and the most recent 15-year history of the index value. The example must reflect all significant loan terms, such as negative amortization, rate carryover, rate discounts, and rate and payment limitations that would have been affected by the index movement during that period. The Board of Governors of the Federal Reserve System made several additional minor changes in disclosure requirements as a result of the Home Equity Loan Consumer Protection Act of 1988 (HELCPA). Lenders are no longer required to provide HEL disclosures to a borrower as a result of the latter's inquiry into credit other than a HEL. Also, fees charged to a borrower who voluntarily closes out an HEL account prior to its scheduled maturity need not be disclosed. Since hazard insurance is already carried on the property securing most HELs, the lender need not disclose the amount of insurance premiums but only that property insurance is required.

Other Regulation Z Requirements

Under Regulation Z the borrower has the right to rescind the credit transaction within a short period after it has been consummated. This right allows the cancellation of any agreement which the borrower may have been pressured into accepting. The borrower may cancel the transaction within three business days or the receipt of the Notice of Rescission, whichever occurs later. If a complete and accurate disclosure of the finance charges as required by the regulation has not been made, then the three-day rescission period is extended until such disclosures are made. The borrower may not waive the right of rescission unless a financial emergency arises, and then he may do so only in writing. There can be no preprinted forms for this purpose. The right of rescission does not apply to first mortgages on residential properties where the borrower is not a natural person (if the borrower is a corporation, for example) or if the loan is for a business purpose. Also, the borrower does not have a right to rescind a mortgage transaction for other than a principal dwelling. A borrower cannot rescind a loan made to purchase a second, or a vacation, home. An example of a rescission form is included in Appendix B.

Regulation Z also prescribes certain practices for advertising in the print media (newspaper, billboards, fliers, window displays, and the like). If the advertisement contains any information about a single financing term, such as the down payment, installment payments, number of payments, or length of the loan, then it must also disclose all the other terms, including the cash price; down payment; number, amount, and due dates of payments; and the annual percentage rate of interest. Furthermore, such information cannot be relegated to the "fine print" section of the advertisement.

Finally, Regulation Z provides for both civil remedies and criminal penalties. The civil remedy is an amount equal to twice the finance charge involved (but not less than $100 nor more than $1000), plus attorneys' fees and court costs. Additional damages suffered by the borrower also can be recovered. If, for example, the borrower obtains a loan with an advertised APR of 10 percent and it turns out that the lender miscalculated and the actual APR is 11 percent, the borrower may claim damages. Specifically, the borrower might have been able to obtain another loan with a true APR of 10 percent. The borrower can seek reimbursement for the difference in the finance charges. Criminal penalties for noncompliance (a misdemeanor) include one year in jail or a $5000 fine, or both. Lenders can avoid the civil and criminal penalties if the violation was the result of a miscalculation, but the borrower may still seek damages.

Real Estate Settlement Procedures Act (RESPA, 1974)

This legislation was passed in response to complaints by consumer groups concerning the costs of completing a residential property transaction. Not only were the costs of settlement becoming expensive, but many consumers expressed a frustration over understanding and controlling the various cost elements. The heart of this legislation mandates that reasonable estimates of all **settlement charges** be made known prior to settlement. Just a listing of the possible settlement charges provides an idea of the confusion faced by the typical borrower. Such charges might include an appraisal fee, a credit report fee, inspection fee (termites, for example), mortgage-insurance premium, notary fees, title insurance, title-search fee, document preparation fee, pre-paid interest, attorneys' fees, recording fee, real-estate transfer fee (sometimes called document stamps), sales commissions, and service charges.

Another concern among consumer groups was the manner in which the settlement process lent itself to the practice of kickbacks. Lenders in search of business might be tempted to give kickbacks to real estate salespersons in exchange for directing home buyers to them. Title companies might, in turn, give kickbacks to the lender for directing business to them, and so forth. Since the average home buyer is unaware initially of all of the players in the settlement procedure, it is a ripe area for consumer abuse. Consumer groups felt that some of the settlement services were well overpriced, either in terms of the value to the borrower or the cost of supplying the service. RESPA was designed to make markets more competitive by requiring the dissemination of information to consumers and prohibiting certain practices, particularly kickbacks.

Disclosure Requirements

There are three disclosure requirements mandated by RESPA. First, at the time of the application, the borrower must be given a copy of a booklet that completely details RESPA and the information that must be disclosed. The booklet comes from HUD and provides an explanation of the settlement process and indicates the standard practices and procedures. The booklet also indicates the remedies that are available to the loan applicant in the event the settlement fails to conform with RESPA requirements.

The second disclosure requirement is a "good faith estimate" of the settlement charges that are likely to be assessed against the borrower at settlement. If a range of values is provided for a particular service, then the range must be based on actual experience. The lender also must disclose any special relationship that exists between the lender and another service provider. For example, if the lender uses only one attorney to review the settlement, then the lender must disclose any business relationship that may exist between them. Exhibit 13–5 on the CD shows a typical good faith estimate.

The Uniform Settlement Statement is the third disclosure required by RESPA. It is made on a form provided by HUD. It contains a list of all the charges to be made against the borrower and a complete accounting of all disbursements to be made at settlement. The borrower has the right to review this statement prior to the date of settlement. The Uniform Settlement Statement must be accurate and must contain no estimates of values. Lenders must retain a copy for at least two years and cannot assess a charge for completing the form.

RESPA covers all first mortgages that are secured by one- to four-family residences and made by a federally regulated or insured lender. It does not cover mortgaged property in excess of 25 acres, home-improvement loans, loans to finance the purchase of land where no proceeds are used to construct a dwelling, construction loans to developers, or the execution of a land sales contracts.

Regulation of Abusive Practices

Regulation of practices under RESPA deals with potentially abusive practices, such as kickbacks, required use of certain title services, and unduly large escrow accounts. RESPA requires that the payment of money or something of value be for actual services rendered (that is, not a kickback). If payment exceeds the value of services provided, then it is assumed that a kickback has been provided. Abusive practices are monitored closely, especially in cases where one of the parties can "control" the direction of business to certain service providers. Real estate salespersons often can direct the home buyer to a certain lender. That lender, in turn, can often direct the borrower to a particular attorney, appraiser, or title company. Payments from lenders to realtors are suspect, as are payments from attorneys, appraisers, and title companies to lenders.

RESPA also prohibits a mandatory requirement that the borrower obtain title insurance from a certain title company and limits the amount of funds that can be required in an escrow account. Generally, no more than one-twelfth of the annual taxes and hazard insurance can be included in the monthly payment. Lenders may require an additional amount be placed in escrow to cover any unexpected increases in taxes or insurance. This contingency is limited to one-sixth the current estimate of a reasonable annual charge.

Remedies Under RESPA

Unlike the Land Sales Full Disclosure Act and Regulation Z, RESPA does not provide for either an equitable remedy or a right of rescission. Nothing in the act affects the validity or enforceability of any sale, contract for the sale of real estate, or any loan agreement. Also, unlike the other two acts, the borrower can contract away his rights under RESPA. The act does, however, provide for damages for violations of the abusive practices defined above. In such cases the damaged party can recover attorneys' fees and treble damages. There is also a criminal penalty for abusive practices. Finally, if the laws within a given state provide greater protection than RESPA, those laws will supercede RESPA.

RESPA's Effect on Settlement Services

To assess the need and usefulness of RESPA, we next analyze the market for settlement services. Consider the market for settlement services in the absence of any RESPA regulation. The first thing that the reader should understand about most settlement services is the basis of their value. The purpose of many settlement services is to protect the collateral of the lender. Although paid for by the borrower or the seller of the property, the demand for these services is created by the lender. The borrower, more often than not, will be unaware of either the value of the services or the major suppliers in the local market. Examples of such settlement services are mortgage insurance, title search and insurance, and escrow services. Mortgage insurance protects the lender in the dual event that the borrower defaults and the value of the collateral (residence) is less than the loan balance at the time of default. A title search assures the lender that there are no prior liens on the property that would jeopardize the lender's security. Title insurance hedges the lender against the possibility that the title search was done incorrectly or that fraud or forgery (not detectable by a title search) has occurred within the chain of prior transactions. Escrow accounts ensure that the property taxes and hazard insurance fees are current. The value of settlement services, then, derive from their risk-reduction properties.

The second thing that the reader should be aware of is the inelasticity of demand for settlement services. The demand for settlement services is not responsive to their price for several reasons. One, in aggregate, settlement costs represent a small proportion of either the total transaction or the borrower's total consumption expenditures. Also, they occur infrequently. Consumers are less likely to shop around for services that are purchased so infrequently or represent such a small portion of the overall transaction. Even though the services are demanded by the lender, they are paid for by the borrower.

Third, the suppliers of settlement services (mortgage insurers, title insurers, and so forth) have no incentive to advertise directly to the borrowing public. The borrowing public purchases the services only infrequently, and the public is not the primary beneficiary of services; lenders are. Advertising expenditures for private mortgage insurance companies range from only 2 to 5 percent of total operating costs, for example.

These factors combine to create a system where the cost of services will exceed their value, and referral fees or kickbacks become a common method of soliciting business.

The above discussion indicates the potential for overpricing of settlement services and the accumulation of excess profits by service providers. Evidence of overpricing and excess profits is difficult to obtain, however, because so little is known about the cost curves of providers, either individually or as an industry. Also, while the demand for settlement services as a package is inelastic, the demand-curve faced by each individual service provider may be elastic. That is, while the individual borrower has no incentive to shop around for settlement services, lenders may. They have more time, know the market better, and are knowledgeable about the quality of services provided by suppliers.

There also exists the possibility that, while individual services may be overpriced, the combined package of settlement services and loan charges may be competitively priced so that no excess returns are earned by any single service provider. This may be so even in the absence of regulations, such as those contained in RESPA. While this sounds like a contradiction, Villani and Simonson make such a point.[6] They argue that RESPA may have reduced the prices of individual services while at the same time allowing the price of the entire settlement package to increase.

To understand their argument, consider a situation, again in the absence of RESPA, in which some service providers are competitive. For example, lenders: there are many lenders, entry into the market (especially for mortgage bankers) is not difficult, and borrowers easily can compare and shop around for the best loan terms. Now assume that other service providers are not in a perfectly competitive market. For example, title companies: There may be only a half-dozen or so represented in most regions of the country, they face an inelastic demand-curve, and entry into the market may be regulated by state laws. As a result, they charge rates above those which would be charged had their services been priced competitively. Since each firm charges a rate above its marginal cost, it will seek to expand its sales and capture a larger portion of the market. There is no incentive to advertise to the general public, so solicitation of business will take place through revenue-sharing (kickbacks) with lenders who refer business to the title companies.

The referral fees (kickbacks) become part of the income of lenders and part of the expenses of title companies. Since the lenders are offering a product in a competitive market, they will price their product in a manner that reflects their expenses and revenues (including the referral fees from title insurers). Since each lender perceives that he will receive a referral fee from a title insurer for each loan generated, he has an incentive to compete with other lenders to generate loans. The ultimate beneficiary is the borrower, who may face lower interest rates or discount points and origination fees. Since lenders know the title insurance market and can shop for title companies, they will extract larger and larger referral fees, until the title company's excess profits are eliminated. The pressure of competition at the point of loan origination forces the lender to pass these referral-fee revenues along to the borrower in the form of reduced loan charges. The result of this whole process is a fee structure in which the price paid for title insurance is above the value of the service, the total package of settlement fees and loan charges is competitively priced, and no single service provider makes excess profits.

Curiously, under such a scenario, introducing RESPA-type legislation could actually increase the total cost of settlement. Besides requiring additional paperwork and legal fees, RESPA prohibits referral fees. But, referral fees may make the total settlement process competitive, at least in this hypothetical example. Without referral fees, title companies may keep more of the excess profits generated by their relatively less competitive market position. On the other hand, RESPA-required disclosure may make consumers more aware of the cost of settlement charges, such as title insurance, and more likely to shop for services. This would make that sector of the market more competitive. The causal evidence suggests that the profitability of title companies has declined since RESPA. Pre- and post-RESPA financial data for the title insurance industry are provided in Table 8–2. The table shows that operation revenues have had a somewhat steady increase across pre- and post-RESPA. Likewise, operation expenses have increased steadily. Claims losses have increased over the entire period; however, the increase has been especially dramatic over the last ten years. The operation expense ratio and the combined ratio have increased generally with some dramatic swings in value.

One should interpret the data carefully. For one thing, real estate activity slowed considerably in the late 1970s and early 1980s as interest rates rose to record highs. The title industry is one of high fixed costs and low variable costs (see Chapter 14). Unlike other insurance companies, title insurance companies are unable to reduce expenses when revenues drop. Even with the recovery in real estate in the mid-1980s, title industry profitability did not return to its pre-RESPA levels. On balance, there is no evidence that profits in this industry were abnormally high, relative to other industries, either before or after the act. Plotkin reports that the rate-of-return on invested capital from the underwriting activities of all title insurance companies averaged 4.8 percent from 1970 through 1974.[7] This compares to a rate-of-return on capital of 10.2 percent for a broad spectrum of U.S. industries, as computed by the Securities and Exchange Commission and the Federal Trade Commission.

TABLE 8–2

Financial Performance of Title Companies; Pre- and Post-RESPA

Year	Total Dollar Value of Real Estate Activities	Total Operation Revenue of Title Companies	Total Operation Expenses of Title Ind.	Logs (Claims) (In Dollars)	Operation Expense Rates	Combined Ratio
1968	122.5	367.7	306.0	4.9	83.2	87.2
1969	132.9	383.7	321.0	4.8	83.7	81.3
1970	137.5	375.0	337.1	4.9	89.9	93.5
1971	168.0	525.2	421.5	6.2	80.2	83.5
1972	193.7	644.4	514.1	7.0	79.8	83.4
1973	216.8	720.6	604.0	10.2	83.8	88.5
1974	222.2	674.9	617.3	14.4	91.5	98.0
1975	233.6	684.9	618.6	20.3	90.3	99.0
1976	284.3	899.7	773.9	17.9	86.0	92.3
1977	354.3	1,181.8	996.4	18.8	84.3	89.6
1978	410.0	1,509.2	1,338.7	20.5	88.7	93.7
1979	487.6	1,548.6	1,411.6	24.4	91.2	96.2
1980	454.4	1,403.9	1,380.6	30.0	98.3	104.9
1981	436.1	1,496.5	1,504.2	35.3	100.5	108.6
1982	397.1	1,445.8	1,464.3	33.4	101.3	109.7
1983	494.6	2,181.9	1,954.0	31.4	89.6	95.9
1984	535.8	2,612.8	2,383.7	44.2	91.2	99.1
1985	598.7	2,956.9	2,699.7	48.9	91.3	99.0
1986	675.1	3,770.0	3,279.6	331.7	87.0	95.8
1987	703.7	4,218.3	3,834.4	324.8	90.9	98.6
1988	730.5	4,055.8	3,777.4	389.4	93.1	102.7
1989	734.6	4,107.1	3,871.8	390.2	94.3	103.8
1990	644.4	4,092.9	3,890.4	410.2	95.1	105.1
1991	703.0	4,231.3	4,025.3	424.4	95.1	105.2
1992	767.9	5,231.9	4,725.3	387.7	90.3	97.7
Average 1968–1974					84.6	88.8
Average 1975–1992					92.1	99.9

Source: Title Insurance Industry Statistics, American Land Title Association, 1993, Washington, DC.

RESPA's Effect on Real Estate Sales

After RESPA was passed, technological developments and changing market structure created conflicts of interest within the mortgage-origination sector of the market. Advances in computer technology gave birth to **computer loan origination systems (CLOs).** CLOs allowed borrowers to view, and in some cases apply for, loans from an extensive list provided by lenders. The ability of borrowers to select loans by computer led some large institutional lenders to align themselves with real estate sales firms in order to capture the borrower at the point of first contact. Traditional mortgage lenders, particularly mortgage bankers, saw the new alignments between the large institutional investors and the real estate sales firms as a threat to their market share. They claimed that such arrangements had the potential of violating Title 8 of RESPA.

CLOs, introduced in the early 1980s, are of two types. One type is a loan-information network that allows all lenders the opportunity to display their loans and rates to potential borrowers. Borrowers view the alternative loans and then make separate contact with the lender. The loan listings are updated periodically, either by the lenders or the staff employed by the CLO system. The listings usually are displayed on a computer terminal in a participating realtor's office. Another type of CLO is the integrated origination and processing system. These networks contain loan applications that are filled out on a computer screen and transmitted to a centralized processing and underwriting station for approval. The real estate salesperson takes the application information from the borrower at the point of sale. This type of CLO system also may allow the salesperson to track the loan through its processing stages. This type of CLO generally will have some sort of a prequalification program to make an initial indication of the likelihood that the loan will be approved.

CLOs are either private networks or open networks. Private networks only offer the loans chosen by the sponsor of the network, and only affiliated originators may use the system. Open networks allow any lender who pays a participation fee to list loans on the system and receive processed loans. Private networks have been the object of criticism by those who think they may lead to violations of RESPA.

One example of a controversial private network is Citicorp's Mortgage Power Program. This program began in 1981 on a limited, regional basis and, by 1990, accounted for approximately 5 percent of the national first-mortgage market. The program lined up participating realtors and offered loans at attractive terms to home buyers. In effect, Citicorp used the program to reach the home buyer at the first point of contact, the real estate salesperson.

By marketing its loans in this manner, Citicorp avoided large marketing costs, including those hard costs (bricks-and-mortar) required to open offices throughout the country. Because of these lower marketing costs, Citicorp was able to offer loans with fewer or no origination points or other fees. The participating real estate sales firms were able to charge a fee for their service and still remain competitive.

Critics of the Citicorp program claimed the relationship was a form of disguised referral fees. Instead of charging points for the loans and sending a portion to the referring real estate sales firm, Citicorp simply reduced its origination fees and allowed the real estate firm to substitute its own charges.

Participants claimed that the charges made by the real estate sales firms were compensation for financial advice and loan consultation—charges allowed under RESPA. Citicorp, in fact, sought the opinion of HUD before implementing their program on a nationwide basis. In 1986 the general counsel of HUD issued an opinion that Mortgage Power did not violate RESPA.

Citicorp's position was buttressed by two court cases, *United States* v. *Graham Mortgage Corp.* and *Eisenberg* v. *Comfed Mortgage.*[8] In these cases the courts basically said it was not clear that HUD had intended that the definition of settlement charges include the origination of a loan. One can understand how traditional lenders would be threatened by a mortgage origination system that attracts the consumer at the point of sale and give sales firms the incentive to divert loan business to large institutional investors.

In 1992 HUD issued a rule that allowed companies to pay employees for referrals to affiliated firms as long as customers were informed about the affiliation. In response to pressure from lenders (the Mortgage Bankers Association filed a lawsuit), the Clinton Administration requested HUD revise the rules. The revision, issued in 1994 and proposed as a final rule in 1996, revoked the 1992 rule allowing referrals. It did, however, create several exemptions. The 1996 rule allowed, for example, a managerial employee to be compensated if a certain percentage of her clients do business with affiliated firms. She cannot be paid on a per referral basis. Also, a nonmanagerial employee that does not provide settlement services (stock broker, for example) can be paid for referrals. Finally, a financial services representative who markets services for several companies can be paid on a commission basis but cannot perform settlement services. This 1996 rule also eliminates exemptions for CLO's where the borrower pays the fee but allows all CLO fees (by borrowers, lenders, or others) if the fee reasonably relates to the value of services provided. The revisions incorporated in the 1996 rule brought more complaints from settlement providers and HUD delayed implementation until July 1997. Finally, the 1996 revisions included a policy statement that defined acceptable services of a CLO. The statement indicated that a CLO may:

1. Provide information concerning products or services,
2. Pre-qualify a prospective buyer,
3. Provide consumers with an opportunity to select ancillary services,
4. Provide prospective borrowers with information regarding the rates and terms of loan products,
5. Collect and transmit information on properties for evaluation by lenders,
6. Provide loan origination, processing, and underwriting services, and
7. Make final funding decisions.

Real estate sales firms appear anxious to participate in CLO networks. Some large firms that currently participate include Coldwell Banker Residential Group, Better Homes and Garden Real Estate Service, and Realty World Corporation. The following chart shows the advantages and disadvantages of CLO systems as perceived by advocates and opponents.

Advantages	Disadvantages
Less-costly form of loan origination for lenders	Danger of steering business and paying referral fees (kickbacks)
Access to more geographically dispersed markets	Less professional loan counseling and less quality-control
Incentives for aggressive rate competition	Loss of lender identity
Side-by-side loan comparisons for borrowers	Closing off of a sizeable portion of the market to traditional lenders
Reducing processing and approval time	

SUMMARY

The influence of the federal government in housing issues is pervasive. Legislation is concerned with making housing more affordable, with making borrowers more knowledgeable, and with making the market for housing and mortgages more efficient. The greatest success of the government has occurred in the area of pioneering the secondary mortgage market. The secondary mortgage market has made home financing less expensive by creating a liquid market for mortgages. The government also has made housing more affordable by subsidizing the cost of funds for mortgage lenders, subsidizing costs for mortgage default insurance, and providing direct grants and subsidies for low-income families for the purchase or rental of housing. Rules and regulations designed to make more information available promote competition. Legislation in this area is focused on the cost of credit and the costs associated with residential real estate transactions.

KEY TERMS

Abusive practices
Annual percentage rate (APR)
Community Development Block Grants
Computer loan origination systems
Deregulation
Direct grant
Federal Housing Administration (FHA)
Finance charges
Flood Disaster Protection Act
Home Owner's Loan Act
Housing and Urban Development Act
Interest Rate Readjustment Act

Interstate Land Sales Full Disclosure Act (ILSFDA)
National Housing Act
Real Estate Settlement Procedures Act (RESPA)
Regulation Z (Truth-in-Lending)
Rental Rehabilitation Program
Right of rescission
Securitization
Settlement services
Subsidies
Uniform Settlement Statement
Urban Homesteading Program
Veterans Administration

SUGGESTED READINGS

Ford, D. A. 1982. Title assurance and settlement charges. *Journal of the American Real Estate and Urban Economics Association* 10(3).

Hendershott, Patric H., and Joel Slemrod. 1993 Taxes and the User Cost of Capital for Owner-Occupied Housing, *AREUEA Journal* 11:375–393.

Hendershott, P., and K. Villani. Mortgage and bond yields: Some tests of market efficiency from the GNMA market. National Bureau of Economic Research Working Paper No. 731.

Kent, R. 1981. An analysis of the countercyclical policies of the FHLBB. *Journal of Finance* 36(1).

Merton, R. 1977. An analytic derivation of the cost of deposit insurance and loan guarantees: An application of modern option pricing theory. *Journal of Banking and Finance* 1:3–111.

Tuokey, C. G. 1975. Kickbacks, rebates, and tying arrangements in real estate transactions: The federal real estate settlement act of 1974; antitrust and unfair practices. *Pepperdine Law Review.*

Villani, K. 1981. The tax subsidy to housing in an inflationary environment. Research in Real Estate, vol. 2. Greenwich, CT: JAI Press.

Villani, K., and J. Simonson. 1982. Real estate settlement pricing: A theoretical framework. *Journal of the American Real Estate and Urban Economics Association* 10(7).

Von Furstenberg, G. 1976. Risk structure and the distribution of benefits within the FHA mortgage insurance program. *Journal of Money, Credit and Banking,* August.

REVIEW QUESTIONS

8–1   What are the four housing market issues addressed by federal legislation?

8–2   Describe the federal programs that provide financial support to depository institutions.

8–3   Indicate the main role of the Federal Home Loan Banks and how they finance their operations.

8–4   a. Indicate the source of risk for thrifts.
       b. How did deposit insurance fail to account for such risks?

8–5   How have federal guarantees allowed the FHA to subsidize mortgage insurance?

8–6   Describe at least three HUD grant programs for low-income family housing.

8–7   a. What is the motivation behind the Interstate Land Sales Full Disclosure Act?
       b. What types of properties are covered by the act?

8–8   What are the two main disclosures required by Regulation Z?

8–9   Explain why adding discount points raises the APR on a mortgage.

8–10   What is the effect of prepayment on the actual APR? Explain.

8–11   What are the remedies under Regulation Z for the failure of a lender to adequately disclose financing charges?

8–12   What was the motivation for the Real Estate Settlement Procedures Act?

8–13   What are considered abusive practices under RESPA?

8–14   Discuss the market for settlement services and the arguments for and against the need for regulation.

PROBLEMS

8–1   Determine the annual percentage rate per Regulation Z for the following mortgages.

Mortgage	Coupon Rate	Mortgage Amount	Discount Points	Maturity	APR
A	11%	$100,000	500	30 years	_____
B	10%	100,000	2,500	30 years	_____
C	8%	100,000	3,000	15 years	_____

8–2   For Question 8–1, which mortgage would you choose if you anticipated selling your residence at the end of (a) one year, (b) five years, (c) fifteen years?

8–3   Determine the APR of the following 30-year mortgage for the indicated holding periods (amount, $100,000; coupon, 10 percent, cost of discount points, $4,000).

Mortgage	Holding Period (years)	APR
A	05	_____
B	10	_____
C	25	_____

8–4   What is the APR for the following ARM loan?
       Amount, not applicable; fully indexed rate: 9 percent first year (only); teaser rate: 7 percent; no discount points.

ENDNOTES

1.   J. Huston McCulloch, "Interest-Rate Sensitive Deposit Insurance Premia: Adaptive Conditional Heteroscedastic Estimates," Unpublished manuscript (The Ohio State University, 1983).

2.   *Standard and Poor's* provides ratings for private mortgage insurers, just as it does for corporate bonds. Mortgage lenders consider the ratings to be an important barometer of an insurer's claims-paying ability.

3.   James R. Follain and Robert M. Dunsky, "The Demand for Mortgage Debt and the Income Tax," *Journal of Housing Research,* 8:2 (1997): 155–199.

4.   Patric Hendershott and Robert Van Order, "Integration of Mortgage and Capital Markets," Working Paper No. 89–4 (Tempe, AZ: 1989). Center for Financial Systems Research, Arizona State University.

5. Peter Linneman and Richard Voith, "Would Mortgage Borrowers Benefit from the Provision of APR Schedule?" *Housing Finance Review* 4 (January 1985): 569–576.

6. Kevin Villani and John Simonson, "Real Estate Settlement Pricing: A Theoretical Framework," *AREUEA Journal* 10 (Fall 1982): 249–275.

7. Irving Plotkin, On the Theory and Practice of Rate Review and Profit Measurement in Title Insurance (Cambridge, MA: Arthur D. Little, Inc., 1978).

8. 564 F. Supp. 1239 (E. D. Mich. 1983), rev'd 740 F 2nd 414 (6th Cir. 1984), reh'g den.

WEB SITES

www.hud.gov/hudprog   information on HUD programs for subsidized housing

www.efn.org/~fairhous/eng/afford/programs   information on affordable housing programs

www.ezec.gov/toolbox/guide   information on low income housing programs

www.allregs.com   home lending regulations and compliance for FNMA and GNMA programs.

APPENDIX A

Major Federal Legislation and Executive Orders Authorizing HUD Programs

(in chronological order)

National Housing Act, 1934 (Public Law 73–479)

Title I: Property Improvements
Section 2: Manufactured Housing (Loan Insurance) Property Improvement (Loan Insurance)

Title II:
Section 203: Homes (One- to Four-Family) (Mortgage Insurance)
Section 203(h): Disaster Housing (Mortgage Insurance)
Section 203(i): Suburban and Outlying Areas or Small Communities (Mortgage Insurance)
Section 203(k): Major Home Improvements (Loan Insurance)
Section 207: Multifamily Housing (Mortgage Insurance)
Section 213: Cooperative Housing (Mortgage Insurance)
Section 221(d)(2): Homes for Low- and Moderate-Income Families (Mortgage Insurance)
Section 221(d)(3) and (4): Multifamily Rental Housing (Market Interest Rate) for Low- and Moderate-Income Families (Mortgage Insurance)
Section 221(h): Major Home Improvements (Loan Insurance)
Section 222: Homes for Servicemen (Mortgage Insurance)
Section 223(e): Housing in Declining Neighborhoods (Mortgage Insurance)
Section 223(f): Existing Multifamily Rental Housing (Mortgage Insurance)
Section 231: Senior Citizen Housing (Mortgage Insurance)
Section 232: Nursing Homes and Intermediate Care Facilities (Mortgage Insurance)
Section 233: Experimental Housing (Mortgage Insurance)
Section 234: Condominium Housing (Mortgage Insurance)
Section 235: Interest Supplements on Home Mortgages
Section 236: Interest Supplements on Rental and Cooperative Housing Mortgages
Section 237: Mortgage Credit Assistance for Homeownership Counseling Assistance for Low- and Moderate-Income Families
Section 240: Purchase of Fee Simple Title from Lessors (Mortgage Insurance)
Section 241: Insured Supplement Loans on Multifamily Housing Projects
Section 242: Nonprofit and Public Hospitals (Mortgage Insurance)
Section 245: Graduated Payment and Indexed Mortgages
Section 247: Single Family Mortgage Insurance on Hawaiian Home Lands
Section 248: Single Family Mortgage Insurance on Indian Reservations

Section 249: Reinsurance Contracts
Section 251: Adjustable Rate Single Family Mortgages
Section 252: Shared Appreciation Mortgages for Single Family Housing
Section 253: Shared Appreciation Mortgages for Multifamily Housing
Section 255: Home Equity Conversion Mortgages (Demonstration)

Title III: Governmental National Mortgage Association

Title VIII:
Section 809: Armed Services Housing for Civilian employees (Mortgage Insurance)
Section 810: Armed Services Housing in Impacted Areas (Mortgage Insurance)

Title X: Land Development (Mortgage Insurance)

Title XI: Group Practices Facilities (Mortgage Insurance)

U.S. Housing Act of 1937 (P.L. 93-383 which replaced P.L. 75-412)

Housing Act of 1949 (P.L. 81-171)

Title I: Urban Renewal Projects

Housing Act of 1954 (P.L. 83-560)

Title VII: Section 701: Comprehensive Planning Assistance

Housing Act of 1959 (P.L. 86-372)

Title II: Section 202: Senior Citizen Housing (Direct Loans)

Housing Act of 1964 (P.L. 88-560)

Title III: Section 312: Rehabilitation Loans

Title VIII: Part 1: Federal-State Training Programs

Housing and Urban Development Act of 1965 (P.L. 89-117)

Title I: Rent Supplements

Title VII: Community Facilities
Section 702: Grants for Basic Water and Sewer Facilities
Section 703: Grants for Neighborhood Facilities

Department of Housing and Urban Development Act (P.L. 89-174)

Demonstration Cities and Metropolitan Development Act of 1966 (P.L. 89-754)

Title I: Model Cities

Title X: Sections 1010 and 1011: Urban Research and Technology
Civil Rights Act of 1968 (P.L. 90-284)

Title VIII: Fair Housing

Housing and Urban Development Act of 1968 (P.L. 90-448)

Title I: Homeownership for Lower-Income Families

Title IV: New Communities

Title VIII: Government National Mortgage Association

Title XI: Urban Property Protection and Reinsurance

Title XIV: Interstate Land Sales

Housing and Urban Development Act of 1969 (P.L. 91-152)

Housing and Urban Development Act of 1970 (P.L. 91-609)

Title V: Research and Technology

Title VII: National Urban Policy and New Communities

Housing and Community Development Act of 1974 (P.L. 93-383)

Title I: Community Development Block Grants

Title II: Assisted Housing
Section 8: Lower Income Rental Assistance

Title III: Mortgage Credit Assistance
Section 306: Compensation for Substantial Defects
Section 307: Co-insurance
Section 308: Experimental Financing

Title VI: Mobile Home Construction and Safety Standards

Title VIII: Miscellaneous
Section 802: State Housing Finance Agency Coinsurance
Section 809: National Institute of Building Sciences (NIBS)
Section 810: Urban Homesteading
Section 811: Counseling and Technical Assistance

Emergency Home Purchase Assistance Act of 1974 (P.L. 93-449)

Emergency Housing Act of 1975 (P.L. 94-50)

Title I: Emergency Homeowner's Mortgage Relief

Housing Authorization Act of 1976 (P.L. 94-375)

Housing and Community Development Act of 1977 (P.L. 95-128)

Title I: Community Development

Title II: Housing Assistance and Related Programs

Title III: Federal Housing Administration Mortgage Insurance and Related Programs

Title IV: Lending Powers of Federal Savings and Loan Associations;
Secondary Market Authorities

Title V: Rural Housing

Title VI: National Urban Policy

Title VIII: Community Reinvestment

Title IX: Miscellaneous Provisions

Housing and Community Development Amendments of 1978 (P.L. 95-557)

Title I: Community and Neighborhood Development and Conservation

Title II: Housing Assistance Programs

Title III: Program Amendments and Extensions

Title IV: Congregate Services

Title V: Rural Housing

Title VI: Neighborhood Reinvestment Corporation

Title VII: Neighborhood Self-Help Development

Title VIII: Livable Cities

Title IX: Miscellaneous

Housing and Community Development Amendments of 1979 (P.L. 96-153)

Title I: Community and Neighborhood Development and Conservation

Title II: Housing Assistance Programs

Title III: Program Amendments and Extensions

Title IV: Interstate Land Sales

Title V: Rural Housing

Housing and Community Development Act of 1980 (P.L. 96-399)

Title I: Community and Neighborhood Development and Conservation

Title II: Housing Assistance Programs

Title III: Program Amendment and Extensions

Title IV: Planning Assistance

Title V: Rural Housing

Title VI: Condominium and Cooperative Conversion Protection and Abuse Relief

Housing and Community Development Amendments of 1981; Title III of the Omnibus Budget Reconciliation Act of 1981 (P.L. 97-35)

Subtitle A: Housing and Community Development

Part 1: Community and Economic Development

Part 2: Housing Assistance Programs

Part 3: Program Amendments and Extensions

Part 5: Rural Housing

Part 6: Multifamily Mortgage Foreclosure

Part 7: Effective Date

Housing and Urban-Rural Recovery Act of 1983; Titles I through V of the Domestic Housing and International Recovery and Financial Stability Act (P.L. 98-181)

Title I: Community and Neighborhood Development and Conservation

Title II: Housing Assistance Programs

Title III: Rental Housing Rehabilitation and Production Program

Title IV: Program Amendments and Extensions

Title V: Rural Housing

Housing and Community Development Technical Amendments Act of 1984 (P.L. 98-479)

Housing and Community Development Act of 1987 (P.L. 100-242)

Title I: Housing Assistance

Title II: Preservation of Low-Income Housing

Title III: Rural Housing

Title IV: Mortgage Insurance and Secondary Mortgage Market Programs

Title V: Commun5ity Development and Miscellaneous Programs

Title VI: Nehemiah Housing Opportunity Grants

Title VII: Enterprise Zone Development

Stewart B. McKinney Homeless Assistance Act (P.L. 100-77)

Title IV: Housing Assistance

Subtitle A: Comprehensive Homeless Assistance Plan

Subtitle B: Emergency Shelter Grants

Subtitle C: Supportive and Housing Demonstration

Subtitle D: Supplemental Assistance for Facilities to Assist the Homeless
Section 441: Section 8 Moderate Rehabilitation of Single Room Occupancy Units for Homeless
        Individuals
Title V: Identification and Use of Surplus Federal Property

Indian Housing Act of 1988 (P.L. 100-358)

Title II: Assisted Housing for Indians and Alaska Natives
Section 201: Lower Income Housing on Indian Reservations
Section 202: Mutual Help Homeownership Opportunity

Fair Housing Amendments Act of 1988 (P. L. 100-430, which replaced Title VIII, P.L. 90-284)

Title VIII: Fair Housing and Fair Housing Enforcement

Stewart B. McKinney Homeless Assistance Amendments Act of 1988 (P.L. 100-628)

Title IV: Amendments to Title IV of the Stewart B. McKinney Homeless Assistance Act

Title X: Housing and Community Development Technical Amendments

Anti-Drug Abuse Act of 1988 (P.L. 100-690)

Title V: User Accountability

Subtitle C, Chapter 1: Regulatory and Enforcement Provisions
Subtitle C, Chapter 2: Public Housing Drug Elimination
Subtitle C, Chapter 3: Drug-Free Public Housing
Subtitle D: Drug-Free Workforce
Section 5301, Denial of Federal Benefits to Drug Traffickers and Possessors

APPENDIX B

ARM Examples

Variable-rate Mortgage Sample

This disclosure describes the features of the adjustable-rate mortgage (ARM) program you are considering. Information on other ARM programs is available upon request.

How Your Interest Rate and Payment Are Determined

- Your interest rate will be based on an index rate plus a margin.
- Your payment will be based on the interest rate, loan balance, and loan term.
- —The interest rate will be based on the weekly average yield on United States Treasury securities adjusted to a constant maturity of 1 year (your index), plus our margin. Ask us for our current interest rate and margin.

■ —Information about the index rate is published weekly in the *Wall Street Journal.*

■ Your interest rate will equal the index rate plus our margin unless your interest rate "caps" limit the amount of change in the interest rate.

How Your Interest Rate Can Change

■ Your interest rate can change yearly.

■ Your interest rate cannot increase or decrease more than 2 percent points per year.

■ Your interest rate cannot increase or decrease more than 5 percentage points over the term of the loan.

How Your Monthly Payment Can Change

■ Your monthly payment can change yearly based on changes in the interest rate.

■ For example, on a $10,000, 30-year loan with an initial interest rate of 9.71 percent (the rate shown in the interest rate column below for the year 1987), the maximum amount that the interest rate can rise under this program is 5 percentage points, to 14.71 percent, and the monthly payment can rise from a first-year payment of $85.62 to a maximum of $123.31 in the fourth year.

■ You will be notified in writing 25 days before the annual payment adjustment may be made. This notice will contain information about your interest rates, payment amount, and loan balance.

Example

The example below shows how your payments would have changed under this ARM program based on actual changes in the index from 1977 to 1987. This does not necessarily indicate how your index will change in the future. The example is based on the following assumptions.

```
Amount  . . . . . . . . . . . . . $10,000        Caps  . . . . 2 percent points annual interest rate
Term . . . . . . . . . . . . . . . . 30 years           . . . . . . . .
Payment adjustment  . . . . 1 year             . . . . . . . . 5 percent points lifetime interest rate
Interest adjustment  . . . . . 1 year              . . . . . . . .
Margin . . . . . . . . . . . . . . 3 percentage points   Index  . . . . Weekly average yield on U.S.
                                                   Treasury securities adjusted to a
                                                   constant maturity of one year.
```

Year (as of 1st week ending in July)	Index (%)	Margin* (percentage points)	Interest Rate (%)	Monthly Payment ($)	Remaining Balance ($)
1977	5.72	3	8.72	78.46	9,927.64
1978	8.34	3	10.72**	92.89	9,874.67
1979	9.44	3	12.44	105.67	9,832.70
1980	8.51	3	11.51	98.79	9,776.04
1981	14.94	3	13.51**	113.51	9,731.98
1982	14.41	3	13.72***	115.07	9,683.39
1983	9.78	3	12.78	108.25	9,618.21
1984	12.17	3	13.72***	114.96	9,554.39
1985	7.66	3	11.72**	101.08	9,456.03
1986	6.36	3	9.72**	88.13	9,311.25
1987	6.71	3	9.71	88.07	9,151.55

*This is a margin we have used recently; your margin may be different.
**This interest rate reflects a 2 percentage point annual interest rate cap.
***This interest rate reflects a 5 percentage point lifetime interest rate cap.

To see what your payments would have been during that period, divide your mortgage amount by $10,000; then multiply the monthly payment by that amount. (For example, in 1987 the monthly payment for a mortgage amount of $60,000 taken out in 1977 would be: $60,000/$10,000 = 6; 6 × $88.07 = $528.42.)

Graduated Payment Mortgage Sample

Convenient Savings and Loan   Account number: 4862-88

Michael Jones
500 Walnut Court, Little Creek USA

ANNUAL PERCENTAGE RATE	FINANCE CHARGE	Amount Financed	Total of Payments
The cost of your credit as a yearly rate.	The dollar amount the credit will cost you.	The amount of credit provided to you or on your behalf.	The amount you will have paid after you have made all payments as scheduled.
15.37%	$177,970.44	$43,777	$221,548.44

Your payment schedule will be:

Number of Payments	Amount of Payments	When Payments Are Due
12	$446.62	Monthly beginning 6/1/81
12	$479.67	" " 6/1/82
12	$515.11	" " 6/1/83
12	$553.13	" " 6/1/84
12	$593.91	" " 6/1/85
300	varying from $637.68 to	" " 6/1/86
	$627.37	

Security: You are giving a security interest in the property being purchased.

Late Charge: If a payment is late, you will be charged 5% of the payment.

Prepayment: If you pay off early, you
☒ may   ☐ will not   have to pay a penalty.
☒ may   ☐ will not   be entitled to a refund of part of the finance charge.

Assumption: Someone buying your home cannot assume the remainder of the mortgage on the original terms.

See your contract documents for any additional information about nonpayment, default, any required repayment in full before the scheduled date, and prepayment refunds and penalties

e means an estimate

Rescission Model Form (General)

Notice of Right to Cancel

Your Right to Cancel
You are entering into a transaction that will result in a [mortgage/lien/security interest] [on/in] your home. You have a legal right under federal law to cancel this transaction, without cost, within three business days from whichever of the following events occurs last:

1.   the date of the transaction, which is _____; or
2.   the date you received your Truth in Lending disclosures; or
3.   the date you received this notice of your right to cancel.

If you cancel the transaction, the [mortgage/lien/security interest] is also cancelled. Within 20 calendar days after we receive your notice, we must take the steps necessary to reflect the fact that the [mortgage/lien/security interest] [on/in] your home has been cancelled, and we must return to you any money or property you have given to us or to anyone else in connection with this transaction.

You may keep any money or property we have given you until we have done the things mentioned above, but you must then offer to return the money or property. If it is impractical or unfair for you to return the property, you must offer its reasonable value. You may offer to return the property at your home or at the location of the property. Money must be returned to the address below. If we do not take possession of the money or property within 20 calendar days of your offer, you may keep it without further obligation.

How to Cancel

If you decide to cancel this transaction, you may do so by notifying us in writing at

(creditor's name and business address).

You may use any written statement that is signed and dated by you and states your intention to cancel, or you may use this notice by dating and signing below. Keep one copy of this notice because it contains important information about your rights.

If you cancel by mail or telegram, you must send the notice no later than midnight of

(date)

(or midnight of the third business day following the latest of the three events listed above). If you send or deliver your written notice to cancel some other way, it must be delivered to the above address no later than that time.

I Wish to Cancel

_____   _____

Consumer's Signature   Date

CHAPTER **9**

Federal Housing Policies: Part II

LEARNING OBJECTIVES

After reading this chapter, you should be aware of how federal laws protect the home buyer from discrimination in sales and financing. You should know the major provisions of the Fair Housing Act (and amendments), the Home Mortgage Disclosure Act, and the Community Reinvestment Act. You also should know the theories of discrimination, and what types of discrimination may or may not have occurred in the housing market.

INTRODUCTION

Legislation intended to make the housing market equitable has been aimed at what has been perceived as discriminatory practices in the sale, financing, and rental of houses. Since discrimination on the basis of race, creed, gender, or national origin is decidedly un-American and against the public interest, the federal government has taken an active role in outlawing practices considered to be discriminatory.

EQUITY IN HOUSING

Two principal acts address housing discrimination: the 1968 Fair Housing Act addresses discrimination in the sale of houses and the 1974 Equal Credit Opportunity Act (as amended in 1976) deals with discrimination in the financing of houses. Other legislation includes the 1975 Home Mortgage Disclosure Act and the 1978 Community Reinvestment Act.

Fair Housing Act (1968)

This act was passed as Title VIII of the Civil Rights Act of 1968. It prohibits discrimination in the sale or rental of residential dwellings (or vacant land intended to be used as such) on the basis of race, color, religion, or national origin. Gender was added as a protected class by the Housing and Community Development Act of 1974. Families (those with children under 18) and the handicapped are protected under the Fair Housing Amendment Act of 1988. Under the act, as amended, it is unlawful to

1. refuse to sell or rent, or refuse to negotiate to sell or rent, or to otherwise make unavailable a residential dwelling to those in the protected groups;
2. modify the terms or conditions of a sale or rental on the basis of group membership;
3. advertise that the sale or rental is available to only certain groups;
4. represent to any member of a protected group that a residential dwelling is unavailable for sale or rent when in fact it is;
5. attempt to induce a sale of dwelling units by representing that individuals of any classification are moving into the neighborhood;

6. modify the terms of a mortgage based on the classification of the borrower in a protected group;
7. deny access to a multiple listing service to any individual in a protected group; or
8. deny or make different terms or conditions for home loans by commercial lenders.

The first condition specifically includes brokers in addition to the owner of the property. Condition 5 makes it illegal to engage in what is commonly referred to as blockbusting. In its most unethical form, blockbusting has been used by the unscrupulous to drive prices down so that properties can be purchased cheaply. The "blockbuster" will typically make a statement that certain minority groups are moving into the neighborhood and that property owners should sell quickly at a reduced price to avoid further depreciation. Blockbusters may even pay, or otherwise encourage, a member of a minority group to purchase or show an interest in purchasing neighborhood properties. All this is illegal under the act.

The act does exempt some property owners from its provisions (although no exemptions are made for racial discrimination). An owner-occupant who does not employ a broker or use discriminatory advertising to sell or rent the property is exempt. There are restrictions on who constitutes an owner-occupant, however. For example, the exemption does not apply to anyone owning more than three houses. Also, religious organizations can give preference for their members as long as they do not discriminate on the basis of color, race, gender, national origin, handicap, or families with children. Private clubs also may restrict occupancy of dwellings to their members as long as the facilities are not operated commercially for a profit.

Title VIII also calls for the development and implementation of affirmative, fair-marketing plans in which participants in HUD housing plans must employ an affirmative program to attract buyers and tenants from all minority and majority groups. HUD also has instituted, under Title VIII, voluntary affirmative marketing agreements (VAMAs) with the nation's major housing industry groups, including the National Association of Realtors. The agreements commit the participants to activities designed to make the industry aware of its responsibilities under the law.

The act provides for two legal remedies, which can be pursued simultaneously or in sequence. First, a complaint can be filed with the Department of Housing and Urban Development. HUD will either refer the case to a state agency, if the laws of the state grant essentially the same rights and remedies, or, if not, HUD will investigate the complaint itself. Unable to issue any cease and desist orders, HUD will seek an informal reconciliation of the matter. Its investigation will be conducted at no expense to the complainant, and any evidence it uncovers can be used under the second remedy—a civil suit in federal district court.

A civil suit must be filed within 2 years of the discriminatory act unless the complaint is first filed with HUD. The federal court can order the discriminatory behavior stopped and fine the offender up to $1000. In rare cases of a widespread pattern of abuse by an offender (cases of general public importance), the Attorney General of the United States may file a civil suit. In fiscal year 1988, 4658 complaints were received by HUD; conciliation was attempted in 1539 and was successful in 1122.

Evidence of discrimination is often difficult to accumulate. Government investigators may, therefore, use a system of "checking" or "testing." They may send a black and an equally qualified white buyer into a predominantly white neighborhood to see if the seller of the property or the broker treats the two identically. If the seller or broker tells the black "buyer" that a contract on the house was just signed that day, but tells the white "buyer" (arriving later) that the property is still for sale, then the "checkers" would have gathered sufficient evidence to be used in court.

Equal Credit Opportunity Act (ECOA, 1974)

This act extended the civil rights momentum of the 1960s to credit markets. Though not strictly limited to consumer credit, it concentrates on this area of the capital market. The ECOA grew out of a series of hearings held in 1972 on discrimination against women in the credit market. Witnesses testifying at the hearings of the National Commission on Consumer Finance (NCCF) in May indicated that (especially) married women faced difficulties in obtaining credit. Later in that year the NCCF report was cited by the Senate Committee on Banking, Housing, and Urban

Affairs as justification for federal legislation. The Senate developed a version of a bill that became law in October 1974. This version prohibited discrimination in credit markets based on gender and marital status. Subsequently, the House of Representatives Committee on Banking, Currency, and Housing pushed for an expansion to include discrimination on the basis of age, race, national origin, religion, and color. The Senate amended this bill by adding yet two more protected classes, those receiving income from welfare and those who had, in good faith, exercised their rights under the ECOA. The revised bill became law in March 1976. The act requires lenders to notify applicants of a decision within 30 days of the application for credit and to provide written reasons for any denial of credit.

One difficulty in interpreting and enforcing this legislation has been differentiating between those acts (such as denial of credit) that are discriminatory and those that represent legitimate efforts of lenders to screen applicants for credit. The act assigns that task to the Federal Reserve Board. In Regulation B, the Board states that it is illegal to discriminate by treating one candidate for credit "less favorably" than another. Accurately defining and interpreting discriminatory behavior is more difficult than making this statement, however.

There are at least three ways in which discriminatory lending behavior can be defined or identified. One is the **effects** method. Under this method, discrimination is said to exist if members of minority groups are underrepresented in the class of credit recipients. That is, they represent a smaller proportion of those receiving credit than they do in the general population. Under the **intent** approach, discrimination is held to have existed if a lender intends to treat minority groups less favorably. Finally, the **practices** approach to discrimination holds that discriminatory behavior exists when a lender fails to adhere to a set of guidelines governing the do's and don'ts of the lending procedure. As an example, Board guidelines prohibit the use of "Mr." and "Mrs." on credit application forms and require that a married woman's credit history be considered independently of that of her spouse. Failure to adhere to these "practices" may result in a finding of discriminatory behavior. Lenders are careful to avoid any prohibited practices in taking and evaluating credit applications.

Legitimate credit screening may result in fewer credit approvals for members of minority groups than their proportion in the general population. If, for example, income is a legitimate screening device and blacks have, on average, less income than whites, then the result will be that blacks are underrepresented in the credit-worthy group. This is so, even though race is not a screening factor. This makes the effects approach to discrimination difficult to interpret and enforce. In addition, strict compliance with an effects approach would result in more credit granted to unworthy candidates (based on income) and less to worthy candidates. This would raise the total cost of credit (through a greater number of defaults) to all groups.

It is also difficult to determine a lender's intent. Lenders are not likely to admit discriminatory intent. For these reasons, the federal government has focused on the practices approach to regulate discrimination and enforce the ECOA Act, although Regulation B does mention the effects test in a footnote to Section 202.6(a).

The need for legislation to prevent discrimination in the credit market can be addressed both theoretically and empirically. Theoretically, some markets may be more open to discrimination than others. Whether that is true of the credit market can be partially answered through empirical studies. We look at both approaches.

The Economic Theory of Discrimination

There are two models of discrimination in credit markets. They derive from work done primarily in the economics of labor-market discrimination. One theory states that individuals or firms have a **"taste"** or **preference for discrimination.** This simply means that firms or individuals may derive psychological, but not monetary, satisfaction from discrimination. The other theory states that firms or individuals gain economically from discrimination because there are costs associated with gathering sufficient information to make unbiased decisions.

"Taste" for Discrimination.   One of the first economists to explore the implications of this form of discrimination was Becker.[1] According to this model, an individual or firm has a taste for discrimination if he acts as though he is willing to pay (perhaps in the form of reduced profits) to be associated with some types of people and not others. It is important to note the economic costs associated with discrimination. If, for example, a man and a woman are equally qualified and skilled in all respects for a position, yet the firm hires the man at a higher salary, then it is incurring an additional labor expense for no additional return.

Becker argued that in a perfectly competitive market, firms with a taste for discrimination would, in the long run, be driven out by lower-cost firms without such a preference. That is, the firm with the lowest cost (least discrimination) could undersell all other firms. Although perfect competition in the product market may limit the amount of discrimination, it also may be limited (in long-run equilibrium) in the case where the market is dominated by a monopolist with a taste for discrimination. In this latter case, the owner(s) of the firm would not be maximizing the value (stock) of the company. He could obtain a higher income by selling the firm to new owners who would not discriminate. The new owners would be willing to pay a higher price for the firm because they could manage it more efficiently—that is, without costly discrimination.

One area where discrimination might survive the rigors of the marketplace would be publicly regulated companies. They have a monopoly or near-monopoly in the market for their products. Their profit margin is often regulated. Since excess profits may be regulated away by a mandated price reduction, managers may prefer to take their returns in a nonpecuniary form such as discrimination. This consideration opens up the possibility of discrimination in credit markets when and where financial institutions are heavily regulated. During the 1960s and 1970s, there was a climate of regulation and discouragement of competition. The 1980s brought on deregulation and a spirit of competition. Discrimination in credit markets would have been more likely to survive in the earlier period. Yet, several studies found strong interinstitutional competition during the earlier period.[2]

Economics of Information. A second theory of discrimination derives from a branch of economic theory termed the **economics of information.** Traditional models of perfect competition assumed that all market participants have complete knowledge of product prices and factor productivity (labor, for example). More recent economic models recognize that information is not a free good. Time and money must be used to acquire information. Often the expense of obtaining information may be greater than the benefits. In such a case, discrimination may occur. Here, let us offer a simple working definition of discrimination. Consider discrimination to be "the act of attributing to an individual a characteristic that is known to be true of the group to which he belongs." Without knowledge about the individual, he is tagged with a group characteristic.

A good example relates to automobile insurance. Young males are charged higher rates because as a group they have more frequent and serious accidents than females. Yet, one particular male may have less risk of having an accident than most women. The cost to insurance companies of discovering this information would be prohibitive relative to any benefits. As a result, insurance companies charge all young males higher rates than females. Information about certain driver characteristics that may bear on the severity and frequency of accidents may not be costly to obtain. If married drivers or good students tend to have fewer accidents, then insurance companies might offer discounts to males in these classes because it is not costly to obtain this information.

A similar scenario occurs in credit markets. Prior to ECOA, lenders would compute a "credit score" based on the economic characteristics and group membership of the applicant. Lenders may have operated in the belief that the marital status of an applicant, for example, provided additional useful information concerning the likelihood of default. That is, given two applicants with an identical economic situation, a married applicant may be less likely to default than an unmarried applicant. Being married would increase the probability of obtaining credit. Information on marital status is also costless to obtain.

Now that ECOA is law, lenders cannot obtain or use such information to make a loan decision. The impact of ECOA on the allocation of credit depends upon whether such group membership affects the likelihood of default. If group membership (such as marital status) does not actually affect the probability of default, then the ECOA restrictions would have no effect on credit screening. It would prevent lenders from considering information that was useless anyway. However, if group membership does affect the probability of default, then prohibiting the use of this information will have an effect. It will raise the probability of acceptance of a random applicant from a "risky" group and lower the probability of acceptance of a candidate from a less risky group. This would result in an increase in the proportion of defaulted loans and in the total cost of lending.

Lenders would be expected to attempt to reduce costs by taking other nonprohibited actions. The lender might use a subset of information collected without cost to indirectly screen those who could apply for credit in the first place. If the lender decided to accept an application, then he would seek out additional (costly) information on the applicant. The indirect screening could take the form of refusing applications from certain neighborhoods. An overt refusal to take applications from within a certain area would open the lender to criticism. Indirect screening might take place in more subtle forms, such as failing to open up lending offices in the designated neighborhood. This would be detrimental to a whole class of borrowers that the ECOA was designed to protect. There was some indication that lenders, in fact, responded in this manner to the ECOA. Concerned about this type of lender behavior, the Congress passed the Fair Lending Practices Regulations and the Community Reinvestment Act in 1978, both of which are discussed later in this chapter.

Empirical Evidence of Discrimination

There are several interesting empirical issues raised by the above discussion. One question involves the extent to which membership in any particular demographic group provides information about credit risk. Another concerns the extent to which lenders discriminated against certain groups prior to the enactment of ECOA. Finally, there is the question of whether or not the ECOA has resulted in a reduction in undue discrimination and greater credit opportunities for those in groups protected by the act.

Group Membership and Credit Risk. Tests designed to determine if membership in a particular group affects payment performance are difficult to perform. Data are available on the default experience of actual borrowers and their group membership. But borrowers cannot default until they are given credit. Therefore, any selection bias by lenders automatically would bias the results of a study of default behavior. Some studies have attempted to overcome this "acceptance bias" through statistical techniques. Group characteristics of interest include gender, age, marital status, and race.

Chandler and Ewert analyzed 2000 credit card applicants and account holders at a large bank from 1971 through 1974.[3] They found that, after correcting for economic variables, females had a better payment record than males. Boyes, Hoffman, and Low analyzed the payment history of a large number of credit card holders.[4] They discovered that older borrowers, other things being equal, had better credit histories. Avery analyzed approximately 9900 new accounts opened between 1968 and 1970 at a consumer finance company.[5] He also found that older borrowers had better creditworthiness. Insofar as marital status is concerned, Avery also found this to be important. Married debtors were better credit risks. However, Boyes, Hoffman, and Low found no relationship between marital status and credit risk. Both of these later studies found race to be significant. After controlling for other variables, it appeared that blacks defaulted more often than whites. It must be pointed out, however, that these studies were based on the experience of only two creditors and only for those borrowers accepted for credit. Any selection bias whatsoever tends to bias the results.

Existence of Discrimination. Evidence of lender discrimination on the basis of a group characteristic may show up in a difference in the default rate between members of that group and general debtors. If lenders unwarrantedly discriminated against members of a particular group, they would require of them higher standards of credit-worthiness or higher interest rates on loans. There is no evidence that lenders charged differential loan rates based on membership in a particular group. If discrimination did occur, it would be through the application of tougher qualifying standards. This would, in turn, lead to a lower default rate among members of the group(s) discriminated against. For this reason some research into this issue has focused on default rates among various groups. Peterson and Peterson,[6] and Peterson,[7] looked at the default rates on consumer loans given to 37,000 customers at 30 banks from 1965 through 1971. The data identified the gender of the borrower and the type (purpose) of consumer loan. For most types of loans, the authors found no difference in default rates between male and female borrowers. However, females did default at a disproportionately higher rate for used-car loans and at a disproportionately lower rate for home-improvement loans. This suggests that there may have been some discrimination in favor of females for car loans and against them for home-improvement loans. The authors also found no evidence that females were charged higher interest rates on any type of loan. Marshall analyzed the applications of a large number of borrowers at two finance companies.[8] He found no discrimination on the basis of gender. He did find that older applicants were more likely to be rejected than would be predicted on the basis of their credit scores. In another study Shay and Sexton constructed two scoring models to predict acceptance or rejection for credit.[9] In one model they entered variables for gender, marital status, and age. They found no additional predictive ability for the model that included the group variables. Their results also failed to find evidence of lender discrimination. Altman et al. used much the same methodology and found some evidence of discrimination on the basis of these three group characteristics.[10]

Evidence concerning racial discrimination in credit markets also is mixed but leans toward the view that it was not pervasive either prior or subsequent to ECOA. Responses to surveys that solicit consumer perceptions of discrimination also indicate that loan decisions based on group characteristics are not pervasive. Survey evidence reveals that most consumers did not believe that they had been subject to discriminatory treatment in the credit market.

Effects of ECOA.   Economic theory predicts that discrimination by firms is costly in (long-run) competitive markets. Available evidence suggests that the practice of discrimination in the credit market was not pervasive prior to ECOA. If this is the case, it appears that the legislation should have little or no impact on either the total amount of credit available or on its distribution among potential borrowers. Post-ECOA studies of the credit market suggest that the legislation has not made more credit available to protected classes than would otherwise be the case. In fact, the opposite may have occurred. By preventing lenders from considering group membership, credit available to some protected classes may have been reduced. This is particularly so for females. Chandler and Ewert built several statistical models to predict acceptability for credit.[11] In some they included a variable for gender; in others they did not. The latter would be equivalent to compliance with ECOA. The model that included the variable for gender led to a higher acceptance for female applicants than the model that complied with ECOA. The results suggest that credit risk is affected by gender, and that females, other things being equal, represent less of a risk. If lenders are not able to identify the gender of the applicant, females may lose this advantage. Shinkel found that exclusion of all variables covered by ECOA led to an increase in defaults of up to 2.6 percent, with a reduction in lender profits of 2 to 16 percent.[12]

In summary, four general statements can be made. First, economic theory suggests that discrimination is costly to the individual or the firm with a taste for discrimination. In a competitive market, low-cost producers (nondiscriminators) will attain a competitive edge. Credit markets, especially subsequent to deregulation, are characterized by large numbers of firms and competition. Second, the empirical evidence suggests that lenders engaged in little discrimination. Third, as a result, it is doubtful that ECOA has had any significant impact on making credit available to qualified individuals who would otherwise be cut out of the market because of race, marital status, age, or religion. Fourth, the ECOA does say something about principles of fair-lending practices and, as such, is a valuable statement.

Home Mortgage Disclosure Act (HMDA, 1975) and Community Reinvestment Act (CRA, 1978)

These two acts are closely related to ECOA and reflect the concern of the federal government that all citizens have access to credit markets, regardless of the neighborhood in which they wish to live. The first act discourages lending institutions from avoiding certain neighborhoods, and the second encourages them to evaluate and actively lend in their defined community. The Home Mortgage Disclosure Act requires a lender with assets exceeding $10 million to compile a report on the distribution of its loans, by number and dollar amount, within and outside of any Standard Metropolitan Statistical Area (SMSA) where it has a main or branch office. The report must indicate the distribution of loans by census tract, and the lender must make it available for public inspection. The 1990 census data must be used for all loans made after January 1, 1992.

State-chartered institutions are exempt from the disclosure requirements if they are subject to state laws that are substantially similar to HMDA requirements.

There were some major changes in the HMDA included in the 1989 FIRREA. The changes expanded coverage to include mortgage lenders not affiliated with depository institutions and to include data on home-improvement loans. In addition, the changes required institutions to report the race, sex, and income of mortgage and home-improvement loan applicants and borrowers. Depository institutions with less than $30 million in assets are exempt from these additional provisions, however. In 1991 the Federal Reserve Board issued revised rules that required reporting of data on home-improvement loan refinancing and on rejected loan applications submitted through brokers or correspondents. The revisions also made it clear that civil money penalties could be imposed for violations of the act.

A recent study by Munnell, Browne, McEneaney, and Tootell using the HMDA data shows that the denial rate for whites who apply for mortgages is six percentage points lower than the denial rate for comparable minority applicants. The study concludes that this is due to discrimination since the study controls for applicant characteristics considered by lenders in approving loans.[13] A subsequent editorial in *Forbes* magazine by Brimelow and Spencer[14] challenges this claim of discrimination, citing the Federal Reserve's own finding that the average mortgage default rate for minority neighborhoods is the same as the rate for white neighborhoods. Their rationale is that discriminating lenders would be granting loans to riskier whites while denying them to relatively more qualified minorities. However, a revisiting by Carr and Megbolugbe reinforces the Munnell et al. study by showing that a close examination of the data reveals an even stronger statistical case for discrimination than was originally reported.[15]

As of November 1978, the Community Reinvestment Act requires all federally regulated financial institutions (primarily commercial banks, savings and loan associations, and mutual savings banks) to publicize their lending activities within their community. Under the act an institution must

1. define its "community" by preparing a map, indicating the area from which it accepts deposits and to which it makes loans;
2. list and make available to the public and regulators the types of credit services available;
3. post a notice in its place of business indicating that its lending practices are being evaluated by their federal regulator and that the public can appear and make comments at any hearing for the purpose of authorizing any expansion; and finally,
4. make a periodic report (community support statement) to its regulator concerning its efforts to serve the credit needs of its community.

Based on the community support statement, federal regulators can make written evaluations of an institution's record of meeting the credit needs of the community and can deny a request for expansion to any institution that fails to comply with these provisions.[16]

By amendments made by the FIRREA Act, each evaluation will have a public and confidential section. Under the public portion, the regulatory agency will rate the institution's record of meeting the community's credit needs as either outstanding, satisfactory, in need of improvement, or in substantial noncompliance. The confidential portion is designed to protect the identity of complainants. In 1991 the Federal Housing Finance Board ruled that the Federal Home Loan Bank System could deny access to long-term FHLB advances (loans) by member thrifts that have poor evaluations. If an institution has an outstanding or satisfactory evaluation of its statement, it will be deemed to be in compliance. If it receives a lower evaluation, it must indicate how it expects to cure the deficiencies in an action plan. Access to long-term Federal Home Loan Bank advances will be restricted if an institution has a community-support action plan disapproved or fails to substantially meet the goals of the action plan within one year.

The reason for these acts is that Congress was concerned that discriminatory lending practices could take place other than at the point of loan application. Specifically, citizen groups had long charged that lenders discriminated by refusing to make any loans (or a reduced amount of loans) in certain neighborhoods populated by a greater proportion of individuals in protected groups, especially racial minorities. They claimed that lenders would draw a red line on a map indicating the neighborhoods within which they would not make mortgage loans. The term **redlining** became synonymous with this discriminatory practice.

Those who defended the practice claimed that lenders were simply identifying neighborhoods where the risk of mortgage lending was greater than normal. Default risk is greatest where property values are likely to decline subsequent to originating loans. Borrowers will exercise their put option when the value of the property falls below the amount of the loan. The risk is greater if the borrower lacks sufficient assets that the lender can pursue in satisfaction of any deficiency. The combination of falling property prices and low levels of wealth are typical of neighborhoods that are in transition from predominantly white to a mixture of white and other racial minorities. It is likely that property values stabilize when the transition is complete and a neighborhood is populated predominantly by a racial minority. If lenders are not averse to default risk, then the redlining practice would appear to be racially motivated. Critics of redlining claim that the practice not only discriminates against that segment of the population that needs access to credit the most, but that it also contributes to the decline of neighborhoods. They argue that the inaccessibility of mortgage funds lowers the demand for properties and causes their values to fall. Owners, in turn, have little incentive to maintain their properties. In addition, they are denied access to home-improvement loans. The result is a deterioration of the properties within the redlined area. Whether redlining causes deterioration in neighborhoods or deterioration causes redlining is a difficult cause-and-effect relationship to disentangle. Proponents on each side of the issue have their own point of view.

A related issue is the practice of **FHAing** a neighborhood. Critics of redlining argue that lenders would originate predominantly or only FHA mortgages within a redlined area. If there is a greater risk of default within certain areas, then this would be a reasonable response by a lender. As we will see in Chapter 14, the FHA fully insures the lender against all elements of loss. For conventional loans the lender would either be self-insured, if he held the loan in his own portfolio, or would require private mortgage insurance (PMI). Private mortgage insurance is a coinsurance relationship, however. This means that, under the PMI contract, the lender absorbs a portion of the loss (much like the deductible on your automobile insurance).

Critics of FHAing argue that this practice also contributes to neighborhood decay. They claim that because all elements of loss are covered and the FHA often acts slowly in resolving their claims, many properties in default are left to deteriorate and become the target of vandalism.

Whatever the arguments on each side of the issue, Congress sought a prohibition against the practice of redlining. They saw it as a civil rights issue and not a risk-management issue and passed these two acts.

Empirical Evidence on Redlining

Redlining can occur in several forms. Lenders may make fewer total loans, fewer home-improvement loans, or fewer conventional loans in certain neighborhoods. The motive for redlining can either be risk aversion or discrimination. If redlining occurs because of risk aversion, lenders would be expected to make fewer (conventional) loans in neighborhoods that are undergoing a transition to predominantly black from predominantly white. If redlining occurs because of discrimination, lenders would be expected to make fewer loans in any neighborhood with a significant black population, whether changing or stable. Empirical research is concerned with all of these issues. Hutchinson, Ostas, and Reed studied the lending behavior of four large savings and loan associations in Toledo, Ohio, in 1975.[17] They looked at total loans, home-improvement loans, and the proportion of loans that were conventional in each of Toledo's 123 census tracts. Explanatory variables were taken from the 1970 census and included the percent of the population that was black, the change in the percent that was black (from 1960 to 1970), the average age of structures, unemployment rate, median income, the percent of the population over 55, the average duration of residency, and several other factors. They concluded that the racial composition of a census tract had no effect on the total loans originated within that area. Racial composition did affect the proportion of loans with conventional financing and the number of home-improvement loans, both being reduced in tracts with more blacks. Hutchinson, Ostas, and Reed discovered that the proportion of conventional loans was minimized when the percent of a tract's black population reached approximately 45 percent. Tracts with a homogeneous racial composition (either predominantly white or predominantly black) had higher proportions of conventional loans. The authors concluded that lenders perceive transitional neighborhoods as risky and prefer to originate government-insured loans in those areas.

One could argue that the experience of a sample of four lenders is not representative of the market, that even if those lenders redlined certain neighborhoods (in terms of FHAing or home-improvement loans), those neighborhoods may have had access to other lenders and suffered no lack of borrowing opportunities. Ahlbrandt looked at all mortgage loans made in each of the census tracts in Pittsburgh in 1973 and 1974.[18] Explanatory variables included median family income, percent of units vacant, percent of units that were owner-occupied, percent of the population that was black, the change in the percent black from 1960 to 1970, and the crime rate. Ahlbrandt found that income and neighborhood risk factors (such as crime) were the most important determinants of the number of loans made within a census tract.

The number of loans made was positively related to the change in the percent of black families. This result could be due to the fact that transitional neighborhoods will have more property sales and thus a higher demand for new mortgages. An important finding was that lenders attach more importance to income and neighborhood risk factors in areas with high black populations. Stated differently, a black in such a neighborhood may be required to have more income to qualify for a loan than otherwise would be the case. This conclusion is valid, Ahlbrandt points out, only if one can infer a correspondence between census tract characteristics and mortgage applicant characteristics.

More recent evidence of discrimination surfaced in a report by the Federal Reserve. Based on 1990 Home Mortgage Disclosure Act data, the report was released in late 1991. The data were derived from reports from 9300 lenders covering 6.4 million loan applicants. The Federal Reserve noted the denial rate on loans of families with similar incomes but of different races. Overall, 14.4 percent of all whites applying for conventional loans were denied credit. In contrast, 21.4 percent of Hispanics and 33.9 percent of blacks were denied credit. Interestingly, Asians appeared to be the most favored; only 12.9 percent were denied a loan. In the lowest income group, the rejection rate was 23.1 percent for whites, 17.2 percent for Asians, 31.1 percent for Hispanics, and 40.1 percent for blacks. The pattern remained the same for high-income groups: rejection rates were 8.5 percent for whites, 11.2 percent for Asians, 15.8 percent for Hispanics, and 21.4 percent for blacks.

The pattern also was much the same for government-backed loans (FHA and VA). Here the rejection rates were 12.1 percent for whites, 12.8 percent for Asians, 18.4 percent for Hispanics, and 36.9 percent for blacks. Similar differences in rejection rates were noticed for home-improvement loans.

Interestingly and reflecting previous studies, the report found that the racial mix of the neighborhood was important. The rate of denial to minority families increased as the proportion of minorities in the neighborhood increased. For conventional loans the denial rate was 12 percent for areas with less than 10 percent minority residents, and 24 percent in areas that were 80 percent or more minority. For government-backed loans the pattern was similar.

The Federal Reserve indicated that the results should be interpreted with caution. The HMDA data reveal little about the financial characteristics of the applicants other than their income level. The level of assets, previous credit history, and other factors were not available when the report was prepared. Nonetheless, unless credit histories and asset levels vary systematically with race, the results indicate a possible trend of discrimination.

Recent years have seen a renewed interest in racial discrimination in mortgage lending. It is felt that, in some cases, minorities may be held to a higher standard of loan qualification than nonminorities. If this is the case, then logically, default rates for minorities should be less than the default for nonminorities. Berkovec, Canner, Gabriel, and Hannon test this theory by examining a sample of FHA loans over the period 1987–1989.[19] They find the exact opposite result. Their results indicate a higher likelihood of default by minority households. They do find that the proportion of minorities in a census tract is not strongly correlated with default.

Calem, in a 1996 study, takes a different tack.[20] He examines whether minority loan applicants are denied credit more frequently than nonminority applicants because of information externalities (such as the number of house sales in the area). For predominantly nonminority neighborhoods he found the number of sales in the area for the year previous had a positive effect on the loan approval rate. For minority neighborhoods, however, he found, even in the case of few previous sales, the approval rate exceeded approval rates in nonminority areas.

Fair Housing Amendments Act of 1988

This act, signed in September 1988, became effective in March 1989. It prohibits discrimination in renting on the basis of age, number, and gender of children in the family. It also adds the handicapped to the set of protected groups under the Fair Housing Act of 1968. Its passage was partially the result of complaints by families with children that they had been denied access to rental dwellings or charged higher rental rates. Apparently, the charges were based on practice. A 1980 HUD survey showed that 50 percent of rental units nationwide limited access to families according to the number, age, or gender of their children.[21] Twenty-five percent excluded families with any children. Landlords defended the practice by stating that rental units that accepted families with children incurred higher operating costs.

Familial status under the act includes a parent or other adult having custody of one or more children under the age of 18. It also covers any person who is pregnant or in the process of securing custody of a child under 18. Dwellings covered by the act include apartment complexes, single-family units, condominiums, mobile home parks, and cooperative apartments. The exemptions under the 1968 act remain in effect, however. In addition, housing units for older adults are exempt from the act, provided 80 percent of the dwellings are intended to be occupied by at least one person over the age of 55, if all occupants are over 62 years of age (including spouses), or if such units are operated under a state or federal program designed to assist the elderly. The units must further satisfy a facilities and services test (unless it is not practical to do so) that demonstrates they are specifically designed to meet the physical and social needs of older persons. Relief under the act has been strengthened. It is now the responsibility of the U.S. government to represent the interests of the individual in cases alleging violations. Also, individuals are allowed to pursue civil action on their own and may be awarded punitive damages by the court.

Goebel and Rosenberg looked at the effect on operating expenses of renting to families with children.[22] Prior to the enactment of the federal legislation, sixteen states had enacted some sort of antidiscrimination law based on familial status. Apartment owners in these states would not be able to exclude families with children. Goebel and Rosenberg analyzed the financial statements of a large number of apartment complexes in both states that allowed discrimination and those that did not. In addition to the law in each state, they used demographic and economic variables and the physical characteristics of each apartment complex to explain the level of rents and operating expenses.

They found that rents were higher in states with antidiscrimination laws—that is, in states where families with children could not be excluded. They found no difference in operating expenses, however. The additional rent could not be justified on the basis that admitting families with children raised operating costs. They concluded that antidiscrimination laws in this instance may have hurt those they were intended to protect. One shortcoming of their research was that while they had identified apartment complexes by the laws of the state in which they were located, they did not identify apartment complexes strictly by whether or not they rented to families with children. That is, in those states where discrimination was allowed, some complexes would have discriminated and some would not have. Each type was not identified.

In regards to handicapped individuals the law defines such a person as one having

1. a physical or mental impairment which substantially limits one or more major life activities,
2. a record of having such an impairment, or
3. being regarded as having such an impairment.

Individuals who do not have, or are limited by impairment but are regarded as having an impairment by another person are also protected. The act extends protection to persons who live with or intend to live with a handicapped individual. Congress has extended the original definition of handicapped to include those with Acquired Immunodeficiency Syndrome (AIDS) or Human Acquired Immunodeficiency Virus infection (HIV). In regards to accommodations, housing providers must make reasonable modifications of the structure to allow a handicapped person to use the dwelling. They must also make reasonable accommodations in rules, policies, practices, or services if they are necessary for a disabled person to use the facility. Common areas must be accessible and hallways and doors must be built so as to allow wheelchairs to travel unobstructed. Buildings that have an elevator, four or more units, and are ready for occupancy after March 13, 1991 must conform to these provisions. State laws that are more stringent will supercede this federal law.

SUMMARY

One of the major areas of concern for federal policies toward housing has been discrimination, especially racially based discrimination. Laws have been enacted to discourage discriminatory practices in the sale and financing of houses. The Fair Housing Act of 1968, the Housing and Community Development Act of 1974, and the Fair Housing Amendment Act of 1988 together prohibit discrimination in the sale of properties on the basis of race, color, national origin, gender, familial status, and nature of handicap. The Equal Credit Opportunity Act of 1974 (and amendments in 1976) makes it illegal to discriminate in lending on the basis of age, race, color, national origin, and gender. The Home Mortgage Disclosure Act of 1975 and the Community Reinvestment Act of 1978 prevent lenders from discriminating against minorities by redlining certain areas. All of the acts list practices that are illegal and require brokers and lenders to adhere to a set of guidelines to avoid discrimination.

Economic theory suggests that in a competitive market pure discrimination is costly and should not be pervasive. The empirical evidence suggests that there has been some limited discrimination in the lending area. Discrimination in the sales area, especially on the basis of race, is more likely. Whether or not the legislation outlined in this chapter has had a profound effect in changing the practices of brokers and lenders, the laws may make a difference on the margin and also offer a positive statement concerning the type of behavior that is appropriate for public policy.

KEY TERMS

Blockbusting

Community Reinvestment Act (CRA)

Discrimination, economic theories of discrimination

Discrimination, intent

Discrimination, practices

Equal Credit Opportunity Act (ECOA)

Fair Housing Act and amendments

FHAing

Home Mortgage Disclosure Act (HMDA)

Redlining

SUGGESTED READINGS

Benston, G. J. 1981. Mortgage redlining: A review and critical analysis. *Journal of Bank Research* Vol. 12, Spring.

Board of Governors of the Federal Reserve System. 1977. Equal credit opportunity. *Federal Reserve Bulletin* Vol. 63, February.

Elliehousen, G., and T. Durkin. 1989. Theory and evidence of the impact of equal credit opportunity: An agnostic review of the literature. *Journal of Financial Services Research.*

MacRae, D., M. Turner, and A. Yezer. 1982. Determinants of FHA mortgage insurance in urban neighborhoods. *Housing Finance Review* Vol. 1, January.

Nevin, J. R., and G. A. Churchill, Jr. 1979. The equal credit opportunity act: An evaluation. *Journal of Marketing* Vol. 43, Spring.

Peterson, R. L., and C. M. Peterson. 1978. Testing for sex discrimination in commercial bank consumer lending. Working Paper No. 10. West Lafayette, IN: Purdue University Credit Research Center.

Shear, W., and A. Yezer. 1983. An indirect test for differential treatment of borrowers in mortgage markets. *Journal of the American Real Estate and Urban Economics Association* Vol. 10, Winter.

Squires, G. D. 1997. Insurance Redlining: Disinvestment, Reinvestment, and the Evolving Role of Financial Institutions, Washington, DC. The Urban Institute Press.

REVIEW QUESTIONS

9–1   List the major federal legislation designed to promote equity in the housing market.

9–2   If I own a house and advertise a room for rent, under the Fair Housing Act may I refuse to rent to an individual based on his religion? Race? Explain.

9–3   What is the motivation behind the Equal Credit Opportunity Act?

9–4   Indicate three ways that discriminatory lending practices may be defined. How does Regulation B attempt to define such practices?

9–5   What are the two economic theories of discrimination?

9–6   Do empirical studies support the need for discriminatory lending practices? Explain.

9–7   Has ECOA reduced the amount of discriminatory lending practices?

9–8   What is the motivation behind the Home Mortgage Disclosure Act and the Community Reinvestment Act?

9–9   a. What is redlining?

b. What is FHAing?

ENDNOTES

1. G. S. Becker, *The Economics of Discrimination,* 2d ed. (Chicago: University of Chicago Press, 1971).

2. See, for example, R. P. Shay, "Factors Affecting Price, Volume, and Credit Risk in the Consumer Finance Industry," *Journal of Finance* (May 1970): 503–515; W. L. Sartoris, "The Effects of Regulation, Population Characteristics, and Competition on the Market for Personal Cash Loans," *Journal of Financial and Quantitative Analysis* (September 1972): 1931–1956; and G. E. Boczar, "Competition Between Banks and Finance Companies: A Cross Section Study of Personal Loan Debtors," *Journal of Finance* (March 1978): 245–258.

3. G. G. Chandler and D. C. Ewert, "Discrimination on the Basis of Sex Under the Equal Credit Opportunity Act" (Working Paper No. 8, Credit Research Center, Purdue University, 1976).

4. W. J. Boyes, D. Hoffman, and S. Low, "Lender Reactions to Information Restrictions: The Case of Banks and the ECOA," *Journal of Money, Credit, and Banking* (May 1986): 211–219.

5. R. B. Avery, "Discrimination in Consumer Credit Markets" (Research Papers in Banking and Financing Economics. Washington, DC: Board of Governors of the Federal Reserve System, 1982).

6. R. L. Peterson and C. M. Peterson, "Testing for Sex Discrimination in Commercial Bank Consumer Lending" (Working Paper No. 10, Credit Research Center, Purdue University, 1978).

7. R. L. Peterson, "An Investigation of Sex Discrimination in Commercial Banks' Direct Consumer Lending" *Bell Journal of Economics* 12 (Autumn 1981):547–561.

8. J. Marshall, "Discrimination in Consumer Credit," in A. Heggestad and J. J. Mingo, eds., *The Costs and Benefits of Public Regulation of Consumer Financial Services* (Cambridge, MA: ABT Associates, 1979).

9. R. P. Shay and D. E. Sexton, "Anti-Discrimination Laws in Consumer Credit Markets: Their Impact on Creditors Approval Applications," in A. Heggestad and J. J. Mingo, eds., *The Costs and Benefits of Public Regulation of Consumer Credit Financial Services* (Cambridge, MA: ABT Associates, 1979).

10. E. I. Altman et al. *Application of Classification Techniques in Business, Banking, and Finance* (Greenwich, CT: JAI Press, 1981).

11. G. G. Chandler and D. C. Ewert, "Discrimination on the Basis of Sex Under the Equal Credit Opportunity Act" (Working Paper No. 8, Credit Research Center, Purdue University, 1976).

12. B. A. Shinkel, "The Effects of Equal Credit Opportunity Legislation in Consumer Finance Lending," *Journal of Business Research* (March 1980): 113–134.

13. A. Munnell, L. Browne, J. McEneaney, and G. Tootell, "Mortgage Lending in Boston: Interpreting the HMDA Data" (Working Paper 92–7, Federal Reserve Bank of Boston, 1992).

14. P. Brimelow and L. Spencer, "The Hidden Clue," *Forbes,* 4 Jan. 1993, 48.

15. J. H. Carr and I. F. Megbolugbe, "The Federal Reserve Bank of Boston Study on Mortgage Lending Revisited," *Journal of Housing Research* 4(2) (1993): 277–313.

16. In 1991 the Federal Reserve Board voted against the merger between First Interstate BancSystem of Montana and Commerce BancShares of Wyoming after a group of Northern Cheyenne Indians challenged the lending record of First Interstate Bank of Colstrip, Montana, in regards to loans (or lack of loans) made on the Cheyenne reservation. In the same year, consumer groups challenged the merger between First Interstate Bank and Security Pacific, based on the former's high rejection rate of black and Hispanic loan applicants.

17. P. Hutchinson, J. Ostas, and D. Reed, "A Survey and Comparison of Redlining Influences in Urban Mortgage Lending Markets," *AREUEA Journal* (Winter 1977): 463–472.

18. R. Ahlbrandt, "Exploratory Research on the Redlining Phenomenon," *AREUEA Journal* (Winter 1977): 473–481.

19. J. Berkovec, G. Canner, S. Gabriel, and T. Hannon, "Race, Redlining, and Residential Mortgage Loan Performance," *Journal of Real Estate Finance and Economics* 9 (1994): 263–294.

20. P. Calem, "Mortgage Credit Availability in Low- and Moderate-Income Minority neighborhoods: Are Information Externalities Critical?" *Journal of Real Estate Finance and Economics* 13 (1966): 71–89.

21. R. W. Marans, "Measuring Restrictive Rental Practices Affecting Families with Children" (Office of Policy Planning and Research, Department of Housing and Urban Development, Washington, DC, 1980).

22. P. Goebel and S. Rosenberg, "Economic Analysis of the Impact of Anti-Discrimination Legislation Based on Familial Status" (Working Paper, Texas Tech University, February 1990).

WEB SITES

www.fanniemaefoundation.org   research on federal policies towards housing

www.mtnhomes.com/ffh_act   information on Fair Housing Act

www.nami.org/housing/exec   information from the National Alliance for the Mentally Ill on housing access and problems

www.ffhsj.com/fairlend/fair   a fair lending guide which introduces borrowers to violations of ECOA. Current cases are also profiled.

www.baynet.com/homebuy/discover   foreclosure and fair housing law in California

APPENDIX A

Summary of Major Federal Legislation Affecting Real Estate

1913   Federal Reserve Act. Established the Federal Reserve System and authorized federally chartered commercial banks to make residential real estate loans.

1916   Federal Farm Loan Act. Provided for the formation of Federal Land Bank Associations as units of the Federal Land Bank System. It was given the authority to issue bonds and make loans to farmers.

1932   Reconstruction Finance Act. This act created the Reconstruction Finance Corporation for the purpose of giving liquidity to commercial banks during the Depression.

1932   Federal Home Loan Bank Act. Established the Federal Home Loan Bank System composed of the Federal Home Loan Bank Board and twelve regional banks. One purpose of the banks was to provide liquidity to thrifts.

1932   Home Owners' Loan Act. This act established the Home Owners' Loan Corporation to purchase and refinance defaulted home loans.

1934   National Housing Act. Established the Federal Housing Administration and the Federal Savings and Loan Insurance Corporation. The former insured long-term, fixed-rate loans, and the latter insured the deposits of thrifts against default.

1938   National Mortgage Association of Washington. Established to provide secondary market support for the newly created FHA loans. It was later changed to the Federal National Mortgage Association.

1944   Serviceman's Readjustment Act. Established a mortgage insurance program to be housed within the Veterans Administration.

1949   Housing Act. Proclaimed that the national housing goal was to provide "a decent home and suitable living environment for every American family." It also consolidated the lending programs of the Farmers Home Administration and authorized urban renewal projects.

1959   Housing Act of 1959. Authorized long-term, direct loans through HUD to private, nonprofit sponsors to construct rental and cooperative housing facilities for the elderly and handicapped.

1961   Consolidated Farmers Home Administration Act. Extended the authority of this agency to make residential loans to nonfarmers in rural areas.

1965   Housing and Urban Development Act. Consolidated many housing agencies into the Department of Housing and Urban Development (HUD).

1966   Interest Rate Readjustment Act. Authorized the setting of maximum rates on deposits at thrifts and created the 0.25 percent differential between the maximum rate for thrifts and that for commercial banks.

1968   Fair Housing Act (Title VIII of Civil Rights Act). Prohibited discrimination in real estate sales and mortgage lending on the basis of race, color, national origin, or religion.

1968   Interstate Land Sales Full Disclosure Act. Required the complete disclosure of all relevant facts concerning the interstate sale of certain types of undeveloped land.

1968   Consumer Credit Protection Act. The first title of the act, known as Truth-in-Lending, authorized the Federal Reserve Board to formulate regulations concerning the advance disclosure of certain financial information about consumer loans. The regulations were known as Regulation Z. Title VI of the act is known as the Fair Credit Reporting Act, which established disclosure requirements regarding the information that can be used to grant or deny a loan.

1968   Housing and Urban Development Act. This act privatized the Federal National Mortgage Association (FNMA) and continued its authorization to provide secondary market support for mortgage lending. It also created a new agency, the Government National Mortgage Association (GNMA).

1969   National Environmental Policy Act. This act requires the preparation of an environmental impact statement for real estate developments.

1970   Emergency Home Finance Act. Created a new secondary mortgage market agency, the Federal Home Loan Mortgage Corporation, to support the secondary market in conventional loans originated by thrifts. It also gave FNMA authority to purchase conventional loans in addition to FHA/VA loans.

1974   Flood Disaster Protection Act. Effective in the following year mortgage loans could not be made for the purpose of purchasing dwellings in a flood area unless borrowers obtained flood insurance.

1974   Real Estate Settlement Procedures Act (RESPA) (amended in 1976). This act and the amendments require that mortgage lenders provide borrowers with an advance disclosure of all loan settlement costs and charges. The act also prohibits kickbacks to any person for referring business.

1974   Equal Credit Opportunity Act (ECOA) (amended in 1976). The act prohibits discrimination in lending on the basis of gender, age, marital status, race, religion, or the fact that the applicant receives public assistance (welfare). If rejected, the applicant must be notified within 30 days of the reasons for the rejection.

1975   Home Mortgage Disclosure Act. This act requires the disclosure of an institution's mortgage loans by census tract or zip code. The intention of the act is to prohibit redlining.

1976   RESPA amendments. Requires lenders to provide a good faith estimate of settlement costs and a HUD booklet. Also, a Uniform Settlement Statement (HUD-1) must be provided to the borrower before or at the loan settlement.

1976   ECOA amendments.

1978   Fair Lending Practices Regulations. These FHLB regulations require member thrifts to develop written underwriting standards, keep a loan registry, not deny loans on the basis of the age of the dwelling, and direct advertising to all segments of the community.

1978   Community Reinvestment Act. This act requires federally insured thrifts to adopt a community reinvestment statement. The statement must define the community in which the institution makes loans, maintain a file for public inspection, and post a notice of the CRA requirements.

1979   Housing and Community Development Amendments. This legislation exempts FHA-insured mortgages from then-current state usury laws that established interest rate ceilings.

1980   Depository Institutions Deregulation and Monetary Control Act. Through this act commercial bank and thrift deposit rate ceilings were gradually eliminated (by the Depository Institutions Deregulation Committee, DIDC). The act also overrode all state usury laws for all types of loans. It also simplified the truth-in lending standards and eased lending restrictions for banks and thrifts.

1980   Omnibus Reconciliation Act. Placed limitations on the volume of tax-exempt mortgage revenue bonds that states and municipalities were allowed to issue.

1982   Garn–St. Germain Act. Preempted state due-on-sale restrictions, allowed thrifts to make consumer, commercial, and agricultural loans, and provided FSLIC and FDIC assistance to institutions with deficient net worth.

1984   Deficit Reduction Act. Extended the tax exemption for qualified mortgage subsidy bonds issued by states and local governments.

1984   Secondary Mortgage Market Enhancement Act (SMMEA). Overrode state laws which (a) limited investments in mortgage securities by state-regulated investors such as life insurance companies and pension funds and (b) required tough registration requirements (blue sky laws) for mortgage securities. The legislation allowed states to take back this authority by legislative vote within 7 years. By October 1991, the deadline for this option, about half the states had done so.

1986   Tax Reform Act (TRA). Reduced the corporate tax rate from 46 percent to 34 percent and reduced the bad debt deduction from 40 percent to 8 percent. It also provided for 3-year carrybacks and 15-year carryforwards for the net operating loss (NOL) of savings and loan associations.

1987   Competitive Equity Banking Act. Established to make thrifts competitive with commercial banks, it gave them the flexibility to form different types of holding companies and authorized a $10.8 billion FSLIC recapitalization.

1987   Stewart B. McKinney Homeless Assistance Act. Provided grants through HUD for assisting the homeless. Participating jurisdictions must provide a Comprehensive Homeless Assistance Plan (CHAP) to receive funds that may be used to support the operations of shelters for the homeless.

1988   Home Equity Loan Consumer Protection Act. This act loosened the reporting requirements for home equity loans under Regulation Z.

1989   Financial Institutions Reform, Recovery, and Enforcement Act. This act restructured the regulation of the thrift industry. It replaced the FSLIC with the Resolution Trust Corporation and placed it under the control of the FDIC, changed the FHLBB to the Office of Thrift Supervision and placed it under the U.S. Treasury, established risk-based capital requirements for thrifts, prohibited acquisition of certain investments by thrifts, and required that appraisals on mortgaged properties be done by "certified" appraisers.

1990   Cranston–Gonzalez National Affordable Housing Act. This act contains several programs to increase housing affordability for low-income families. Title II, the HOME Investment Partnerships Act, made available about $3 billion to participating local jurisdictions to construct and preserve housing for low-income families. Title IV, the Homeownership and Opportunity for People Everywhere (HOPE) program made $448 million in grants available for rehabilitations of public housing. Other provisions created incentives for owners of low-income housing not to remove units from this market.

1992   RESPA Amendment (see 1974). The coverage of RESPA is extended to include subordinate financing.

1992   HMDA Amendment (see 1975). Mortgage companies and other nondepository institutions are required to comply with HMDA.

1993   Tax Act. Increased the marginal tax rate on personal income to 39.6 percent but kept the long-term capital gains tax rate at 28 percent. Losses and credits from certain real estate activities are no longer disallowed by the passive loss rules starting in 1994. This relief is designed especially for real estate brokers, salespeople, and other real estate professionals. Increased the write-off period for nonresidential real estate from 31.5 years to 39 years for properties placed in service after May 12, 1993. By relaxing some debt-financed real property exceptions, the tax act made it easier, in limited ways, for pension funds and other exempt organizations to invest in real estate. It also made low-income rental housing tax credits for investors permanent. Among other changes, units occupied by full-time students qualify for these credits, starting in 1993.

1994   Community Development Bank Bill. This new legislation was designed to aid the expansion of the secondary market for commercial and multifamily real estate mortgage loans. The bill helps reduce securitization transaction costs, expand investor markets, and facilitate banks' entry into the secondary market by extending to all highly rated commercial and multifamily real estate securities the same benefits enjoyed by similar residential securities under SMMA (see 1984).

1997   Taxpayer Relief Act. First $500,000 of gain ($25,000 for single persons) on the sale of residence is exempted from taxes if taxpayer resided in house 2 of the 5 years prior to sale. Capital gains rate on commercial properties reintroduced effective May 7, 1997.

CHAPTER **10**

The Secondary Mortgage Market

LEARNING OBJECTIVES

The purpose of this chapter is to introduce you to the workings of the secondary mortgage market. After reading this chapter, you should know why the secondary mortgage market exists, how this market developed, how the market works, why it is important for a more efficient allocation of funds in the real estate market, what the major secondary mortgage market agencies are, and what portion the market commands in real estate lending. Issues such as factors that influence the size and timing of cash flows and the valuation of mortgage-related securities and derivative securities are discussed in the next chapter.

INTRODUCTION

We begin this chapter by answering two important questions: What is a secondary mortgage market? Why does it exist? The answers to these questions will give you a sound understanding of the nature of the secondary mortgage market.

NATURE OF SECONDARY MARKET

What Is a Secondary Mortgage Market?

A **secondary mortgage market** is one in which existing mortgages are bought and sold. This is in contrast to the primary market, where mortgages are originated. Mortgages are originated by the initial lenders, such as thrifts or mortgage bankers. Some thrifts and all mortgage bankers then sell these loans in the secondary market. By definition, the owner of a mortgage that was purchased in the secondary market did not originate the loan. Agencies and firms that purchase mortgages in the secondary market most often raise the funds required for the purchase by issuing bonds or other types of debt instruments. They will pledge the mortgages (now their assets) as collateral for the debt they issue. The debt issue is termed a **mortgage-related security** because it is backed up, or **collateralized,** by mortgages. Mortgage-related securities, sometimes referred to as mortgage-backed securities, also are bought and sold and are considered part of the secondary mortgage market.

A very simple example of how funds might flow in this market is shown in Figure 10–1. The ultimate source of the funds are the investors who purchase the bonds (mortgage-related securities) from the secondary mortgage market agency or firm. The agency or firm then uses the funds to purchase mortgages from, for example, a thrift. The thrift uses the funds to originate mortgages. Although the transactions occur in the reverse order and take some time, it may be useful to think of the entire process as occurring instantaneously as described. The important thing is that investors supply the funds and the homeowners use them to purchase residences. As a result, the amount of funds flowing into mortgages is not restricted by the amount that thrifts and banks can raise through deposits alone.

FIGURE 10–1

Cash Flows in a Simple Secondary Mortgage Market Transaction

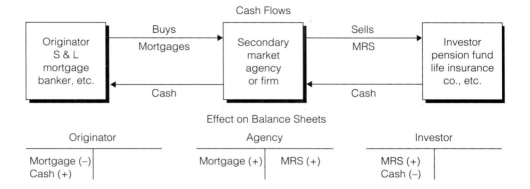

Note that the simple process described here has created a series of assets and liabilities even though there is only one source (investors) and only one use (homeowners) of funds. The homeowner's asset (residence) is partially offset by a liability (mortgage). The mortgage is an asset to the secondary market entity and is offset by a liability (mortgage-related security). The mortgage-related security is, in turn, an asset for the investor. There is no limit to the number of assets and liabilities that can be created in the secondary mortgage market. The investor, for example, might fund the purchase of the mortgage-related securities by issuing its own form of debt and using the mortgage-related securities as collateral. In this case, there would be two mortgage-related securities ultimately backed by the mortgages. We will see an example of just such a secondary mortgage market transaction below.

Why Does the Secondary Mortgage Market Exist?

We all have a picture in our mind of Jimmy Stewart as the beleaguered savings and loan association president in *It's A Wonderful Life,* fending off a mob of depositors anxious to get their money. Either because of rumors of fiscal mismanagement of the institution or just a need for liquidity in times of unemployment, a "run" on the bank was just the sort of dramatic occurrence movie audiences could relate to. In *It's A Wonderful Life,* Jimmy Stewart tried to persuade the anxious depositors that their funds were safe but tied up in the form of residential loans to their neighbors. Such ugly scenes were not far from reality in times when financial institutions faced severe liquidity constraints that resulted from an inability to quickly sell some of their assets in a liquid, efficient market.

Other than stocks and bonds held by commercial banks, much of the assets of lending institutions, particularly thrifts, were illiquid mortgage loans. Up until as recently as the late 1960s, it was very difficult for many thrifts to sell their mortgage assets. There were two reasons for this.

First, their mortgage assets were not homogeneous. The portfolio of a thrift would consist of many different loans with different interest rates, dates of maturity, and loan-to-value ratios. Selling $25 or $50 million of loans with such different characteristics would be very difficult. Second, potential buyers were concerned with the default risk, particularly of conventional loans. Investors nationwide had little or no ability to judge the soundness of loans that were underwritten by a localized thrift.

As a result of the inability to buy and sell mortgages, there was often a persistent mismatch of the supply and demand for capital. The mismatch took two forms. First, there was a regional mismatch. This occurred when there was a greater supply of capital (deposits) in one region and a greater demand (for mortgages) in another. A more stable region with moderate housing growth will have an excess supply of savings, and a rapidly growing area with significant additions to the housing stock will have a deficiency of capital. A secondary market for mortgages alleviated this mismatch, by allowing thrifts in capital-surplus areas to take their excess deposits and purchase mortgages from thrifts in capital-deficit areas. Second, there was an institutional mismatch in the sense that traditional mortgage lenders may have had insufficient funds to meet the mortgage demand and other nonmortgage intermediaries may have had a need to invest funds in long-term assets. This occurred, for example, when individuals began to place more of their savings with pension funds and less with thrifts and banks. The latter have less funds with which to originate mortgages, while the former have a need to invest in long-term assets. The secondary mortgage market offered a solution to this mismatch by facilitating the sale of mortgages from the thrifts and banks to pension funds.

The secondary mortgage market, then, developed because it solved these two mismatch problems. Additionally, the growth of this market in the 1970s and 1980s was stimulated by other developments. During this time, life insurance companies gradually reduced their presence in the mortgage market. There was a need for their correspondent mortgage bankers to find new sources of funds to purchase the loans they originated. Also, pension funds grew in size and needed investments of a long-term nature. We noted in earlier chapters that thrifts were particularly vulnerable to the interest rate risk that resulted from their maturity mismatch and an increase in the volatility of interest rates. Pension funds and long-term investors would be able to handle this risk better. At the same time, some secondary market firms began to purchase mortgages, either because of their risk preference or their ability to issue mortgage-related securities that matched the maturity of the mortgages they purchased. By the 1980s numerous thrifts attempting to avoid interest rate risk sold so many of the loans they originated that they essentially became mortgage bankers. Investors in mortgage-backed securities did not wish to take on default risk, however. So another impetus to the development of a secondary mortgage market was the federal government's willingness to support it through guarantees of timely and full payment.

Finally, the federal government encouraged the development of the secondary mortgage market by overriding state laws that hindered its development. Many states had laws that limited investment in mortgage-backed securities by state-regulated investors, such as life insurance companies and pension funds, and had tough securities registration requirements (blue-sky laws). In 1984 Congress passed the Secondary Mortgage Market Enhancement Act (SMMEA) to overcome these obstacles. The act removed state-imposed limits on the types and quantities of mortgage-backed securities that investors could purchase. At the same time, it exempted mortgage securities from state securities registration requirements. (The charters of Freddie Mac and Fannie Mae exempt them from the registration laws as well.)

At the time the act was passed, Congress gave the states the option of taking back the authority for setting limits on investments by state-regulated investors if the state legislatures voted to override SMMEA within 7 years. By October 1991, the deadline for the override, 21 states had voted to override the preemption from state investment laws and another five opted to override the preemptions on the blue-sky laws. The remaining states, about one-half, are bound by the provisions of SMMEA.

MORTGAGE-RELATED SECURITIES

Characteristics of Mortgage-related Securities

The key to a successful secondary market for mortgages is the creation of mortgage-related securities (MRSs) that are acceptable to investors. There are several characteristics of acceptable securities.

1. MRSs will have some form of **credit enhancement.** This means that the MRS will have less default risk than the underlying mortgages that serve as collateral. There are several methods by which the safety of MRSs can be enhanced. The methods are outlined in a comparison of MRSs in Table 10–1. Just as with corporate bonds, many MRSs are rated by Standard and Poor's and Moody's for their safety. Many investors, such as pension

funds, are prohibited by state law from investing in securities that have less than an investment-grade rating. As a result, a strong rating will broaden the market for the MRS and make it more liquid. This increases the need for credit enhancement.

2. MRSs need to avoid **double taxation.** A secondary market entity that issues MRSs and uses the funds to purchase mortgages will have interest revenue, which it passes through to the investors in the MRSs. MRS issuers must make sure that their revenues and the cash flows to the investors are not both taxed. Otherwise, the double taxation will offset any benefits of the arrangement.

3. MRSs need to **tailor** their cash flows so as to appeal to investors. Many investors do not desire to invest in securities whose cash flows exactly replicate that of a mortgage. If the cash flows from the mortgages can be rearranged in amount and timing and then distributed to the MRS investors, there will be a larger and more liquid market for them.

Types of Mortgage-related Securities

There are four principal types of mortgage-related securities:

1. Mortgage pass-through securities
2. Mortgage-backed bonds
3. Mortgage pay-through bonds
4. Collateralized mortgage obligations

Mortgage Pass-through Securities

Pass-through securities were the first popular MRS. The early successful ones were promoted by the Government National Mortgage Association, a government agency within HUD, in the mid- to late-1960s. With a pass-through, the investor is said to have an undivided interest in the pool of mortgages. The investor has an "ownership" position in the mortgages. What this means is that he will receive the mortgage payments (principal and interest) and any prepayments just as if he were the lender.

Here is a simplified example of how a pass-through works. In Figure 10–1, a thrift (or other originator) groups or packages together, say, 100 fixed-rate loans of $100,000 each, all with the same maturity and contract rate of interest—assume 30 years at 10 percent. It will next issue $10 million in bonds to obtain the cash to finance the mortgages. The bonds may have a minimum denomination of $25,000. There will be 400 such bonds backed by the pool of mortgages. The bonds promise a 9.5 percent yield. Note that the mortgage originator earns 10 percent on the mortgages and pays 9.5 percent to investors in the bonds. The difference, 0.5 percent, will be shared by the originator who services the loan and the agency that provides for credit enhancement. In

TABLE 10–1
Mortgage-related Securities

	Typical Credit Enhancement	Extent to Which Cash Flows Rearranged
Pass-through	FHA/VA loans in pool Agency guarantee	None
Mortgage-backed bonds	Agency equity Pool insurance	Moderate
Mortgage paythrough bonds	Agency equity Pool insurance	Moderate
Collateralized mortgage obligation	Agency equity Pool insurance Letter of credit	Substantial
Debt of agency	FHA/VA loans in pool	Moderate

the case of GNMA bonds, that agency guarantees the timely payment of interest and principal and collects a small fee. Additional enhancement is gained by the provision that the mortgages be held in the hands of a trustee. Investors are satisfied with the 9.5 percent yield because of the credit enhancement and the high yield relative to other "safe" investments.

Assume that an investor buys two bonds ($50,000). At the end of the first month, the mortgagors will remit their payments. If all do so, then the total payments on the $10 million in mortgages will be $87,756.27, of which $83,333.33 will be interest and the remainder, $4422.94, will be principal. The investors will receive this principal (proratedly) and interest at 9.5 percent, or $83,589.61 ($4422.94 + 0.095/12 × $10,000,000). The investor holding two bonds will receive 0.5 percent (2/400) of this amount, or $417.95, of which $22.11 will be principal reduction. The principal balance of his two bonds at the end of the first month will be $49,977.89. The investor will receive the same amount the following month, assuming that no mortgagor in the pool decides to prepay his or her entire loan. If during a given month one or more mortgagors repay their loans, because of a move to a new residence, for instance, the entire amount of the prepayment will be divided proratedly to the investors in the pass-through bonds. In that month the investors' checks will be unexpectedly large and the principal balance of the bond will be reduced more quickly than normal. Essentially, bond investors have a small section of a larger portfolio of loans and receive cash flows that replicate those of a mortgage originator that retains loans in its portfolio.

Investors are attracted to pass-throughs because of their relatively high yield, liquidity, and risk-free quality. However, many investors do not like the uncertainty of the timing of the cash flows, due to unpredictable prepayments of mortgages. Also, mortgages prepay more quickly when interest rates drop, so that the prepayments must be reinvested at lower market rates. Investors in pass-throughs face the same callability risk as mortgage lenders. For these reasons, other MRSs have been developed to avoid the uncertainty surrounding the timing of the cash flows.

Some pass-throughs are rated by the rating agencies (Standard and Poor's and Moody's). Those agencies review the credit risk of the collateral as affected by the types of property, their location, and loan-to-value ratios. They will also rate the capability of the issuer to make cash advances to cover the principal and interest on delinquent and defaulted properties.

Some lenders have pools of mortgages that carry neither FHA/VA nor private mortgage insurance. These pools are difficult to securitize into pass-throughs because of their default risk. Often the lenders do not wish to purchase pool insurance but prefer to self-insure the loans. Pool insurance is private mortgage insurance on the entire pool, not the individual mortgages. Usually only a small percent—for example, 10 percent—of the pool is insured. A pass-through structure that allows for the loans' securitization is the senior/subordinated pass-through. In this arrangement, the lender creates two securities from a pool of mortgages, one having the priority of receiving payments from the pool. From a $100 million pool of mortgages, the lender may create a senior pass-through with a principal balance of $94 million. Since the $94 million pool is secured by $100 million in mortgages, it can be described as overcollateralized.

The lender typically will sell the senior security and retain the rights to the cash flows on the subordinated security—the remaining $6 million, in this example. This overcollateralization enhances the safety of the senior security and gives it investment-grade quality, because cash flows from $100 million in mortgages are available to meet the payments on only $94 million in pass-throughs. There can be a moderate amount of delinquencies and defaults from the pool before the payments on the senior pass-throughs are threatened. Instead of insurance or government guarantees, the overcollateralization provides the credit enhancement.

If properly constructed the senior securities will receive an investment-grade rating from the rating agencies. The agencies will assign an appropriate level of subordination, considering the level of credit risk inherent in the pool. The credit risk is determined by considering the likely amount and timing of defaults, the time required to resolve defaults, and the likely recovery from foreclosures. If an investment grade is assigned, the securities will trade at prices that yield 20 to 40 basis points less than whole loan pass-throughs (those without overcollateralization). If there is a significant number of defaults early in the life of the pool, then some payments on the senior security may be missed. This risk is reduced, however, by increased levels of overcollateralization.

To see how this type of pass-through works, consider a popular arrangement called the interest-shifting mechanism. Under this type of senior/subordinated structure, payments from the mortgage pool are made to both the senior pass-through holders and the holder of the subordinated interest (the lender usually retains the subordinated interest, but on occasion may sell it). However, a disproportionate share of the payments from the pool (including prepayments) are shifted to the senior pass-through holders. This has the effect of lowering the principal balance on the senior security more rapidly than that on the subordinated interest, increasing the level of subordination and safety of the senior security. In addition, the securities can contain a provision that, if losses through delinquency and default are large enough to endanger the promised payments to the senior security, then all future cash flows can be reassigned to that security until a specified level of subordination is achieved.

Since the senior securities are priced higher than whole-loan pass-throughs (they trade at lower yields), the pick-up in value accrues to the lender who retained the subordinated security. In simple terms, the lender may be able to sell the $94 million in pass-throughs for $95 million. Since the lender retains the $6 million in subordinated loans, the total value of the pool to the lender is $101 million. Value has been created by the subordination process. The lender incurs the risk of loss, however, if the default rate on the pool becomes excessive. All defaults are charged to the subordinated position. The lender will benefit from the arrangement as long as defaults are less than the $1 million "profit" picked up from the sale of the senior position. A yield comparison of nonsubordinated pass-throughs with subordinated securities is made in the next chapter.

Mortgage-backed Bonds (MBBs)

Mortgage-backed bonds are mortgage-related securities that promise payments similar to corporate bonds. That is, they promise semiannual payments of interest only until maturity, with the face value due at maturity. The mortgages are owned by the issuer of the bonds; investors have no ownership interest in the mortgages. These bonds are issued primarily by private financial firms. They are usually, but not always, backed by conventional residential and commercial mortgages. The maturity on the bonds will be less than that on the mortgages, and the yield will be slightly below that on the mortgages. Credit enhancement is accomplished through overcollateralization. This means that the face value of the pool of mortgages will be greater than that of the bonds. The issuer makes up the difference with the equity contribution. Figure 10–2 shows an example where an issuer sells $100 million in MBBs, adds an additional $25 million, and purchases $125 million in conventional mortgages. The issuer will attempt to estimate the cash flows coming in from the pool of mortgages, but there will be some uncertainty due to prepayments. Also, the maturity of the MBBs will be less than that of the mortgages, but likely longer than the average life of a mortgage. For example, the maturity on the MBBs may be 15 years and that on the mortgages 30. However, because of prepayments, the average life of the mortgages may be, say, 12 years. A small percentage of mortgages will last the full 30 years, of course. Finally, there is some danger that some of the mortgages may default, and if they are without FHA/VA or private mortgage insurance, the MBB issuer will sustain a loss on such loans.

FIGURE 10–2

Cash Flows for a Mortgage Backed Bond

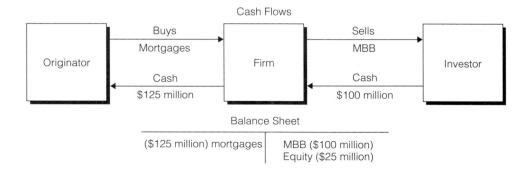

Hopefully, if all goes well, the issuer will take the monthly interest and principal payments from the pool of mortgages and invest them in a fund that earns interest. Then, semiannually, the issuer will remit interest payments to the bondholders from this fund. Any prepayments of mortgages are added to the fund. The fund should continue to grow since interest, principal, and prepayments from the pool of mortgages will be larger than the interest payments on the bonds. At the maturity date, the fund should be large enough to pay the face value of the bonds. Any residual left over will be returned to the issuer as a return on the $25 million equity investment. An example of the cash flows and the pricing of MBBs is provided in the following chapter.

Uncertainty surrounding the achievement of the above scenario is the reason for the overcollateralization. If there is an insufficient fund to pay off the principal on the bonds, then some of the mortgages will have to be sold. This would be true if there were fewer prepayments of mortgages than expected, if there was a large number of defaults, or if the interest rate earned on the reserve fund dropped to a low level. The mortgages are usually placed in the hands of a trustee who will mark-to-market any changes in the value of the mortgages and make sure that the agreed-upon overcollateralization is maintained (125 percent, in this example). **Mark-to-market** refers to valuing the mortgages on a frequent basis as a result of the changes in interest rates. A rise in rates, for example, will cause the market value of mortgages to fall, thus endangering the value of the collateral. If the overcollateralization falls below the agreed upon limit, the trustee will require that the issuer purchase additional mortgages from its own sources and add them to the pool.

Rating agencies such as Standard and Poor's and Moody's rate the MBBs. They consider a number of factors:

1. The quality of the mortgages in the pool. Mortgage quality will be affected by insurance backing (FHA/VA or PMI), loan-to-value ratios, status as residential or commercial, and first or second mortgages, and so forth.
2. The interest rate spread between that on the mortgages and that on the MBBs. The greater the spread, the higher the safety.
3. The likely rate of prepayments of the mortgages. Low-interest mortgages are less likely to prepay if interest rates have risen, for example.
4. The geographic diversification of the mortgages in the pool.
5. The amount of overcollateralization.

All of these considerations affect the rating and, therefore, the amount of overcollateralization chosen by the issuer. The extra $25 million in mortgages is a buffer against the uncertainty of the rate of prepayment and the risk of default. Some issuers will enhance the credit rating of the MBBs further by providing for pool insurance or a letter of credit from a large commercial bank.

Mortgage Pay-through Bonds (MPTBs)

Mortgage pay-through bonds are mortgage-related securities that are a cross between pass-throughs and MBBs. As with MBBs the issuer retains ownership of the pool of mortgages and issues the MPTB as a debt obligation. The issuer also will overcollateralize the debt obligation. Just as with a pass-through, the cash flows to the investor are based on the coupon rate of interest, while principal from amortization and prepayments is passed through as received from the pool of mortgages. Thus, the investor in these bonds faces the same callability risk as those in pass-throughs. Pay-throughs are also rated by the agencies, based on the same factors associated with MBBs. Because the scheduled amortization of the mortgages and prepayments is passed through to reduce the principal of the bonds, the extent of overcollateralization is less than with MBBs.

Collateralized Mortgage Obligations (CMOs)

Collateralized mortgage obligations go the farthest in rearranging the uncertain cash flows from a pool of mortgages into those desired by investors. The restructuring of the cash flows is the most complicated of all mortgage-related securities. The object of CMOs is to rearrange the mortgage cash flows into several different bond-like securities with different maturities. The dif-

TABLE 10-2
Structure of a Collateralized Mortgage Obligation

Assets	Liabilities	Maturity (years)	Coupon (percent)	Amount
Mortgages $106,000,000	Tranche A	5–90	9.25	$ 30,000,000
Yield 10%	Tranche B	9–14	9.50	30,000,000
	Tranche C	12–17	10.00	25,000,000
	Tranche Z	28–30	10.50	15,000,000
	Equity			6,000,000
TOTAL $106,000,000				106,000,000

ferent bond classes are called **tranches.** A typical CMO will have three or four tranches. Because the cash flows from the mortgage pool are uncertain, there will be a tranche into which all residual cash flows accrue. This residual tranche often will be "owned" by the issuer of the CMO. Thus, the issuer will have to have an equity interest in the CMO. The cash flows that accrue to residual are a return-on-equity. A detail of the cash flows of a CMO is outlined in the next chapter, but the basic structure is presented in Table 10–2.

In this example, an issuer sells $100 million in CMOs, adds $6 million of its own equity funds, and purchases $106 million of 10 percent mortgages. The CMO is overcollateralized by $6 million, or 6 percent, of the issue. The CMO has three bond-like tranches and a residual class. The Tranche A bonds earn the lowest rate, 9.25 percent. The other tranches earn somewhat more because of their longer maturity, which results from the order in which cash flows received from the mortgages are distributed to the various tranches. Tranche A bondholders are paid off first. In addition to interest, Tranche A bondholders receive (1) any scheduled amortization of the mortgages; (2) any prepayments of the mortgages, and (3) deferred interest earned by the Tranche Z bondholders but transferred to the Tranche A bondholders. The principal amount of the Tranche A bonds is reduced by these three items. If there are a large amount of prepayments, the maturity of the Tranche A bonds will be shortened. For this reason, the maturity of these bonds is stated as a range of 5 to 9 years. Tranche B bondholders receive interest payments only, but no repayment or prepayment of principal until the Tranche A bondholders are completely paid. After the Tranche A holders are paid, the Tranche B holders receive all repayments and prepayments of principal, as well as interest deferred and transferred from Tranche Z. This pattern is followed for the remaining tranches. In any year, payments not given to any of the tranches is a residual that accrues to the equity interest of the issuer.

A careful inspection of the detailed cash flows of this CMO in the following chapter may clear up any uncertainties as to the flow pattern of funds from the mortgage pool to the various tranches of the CMO.

Some CMOs are backed not by a pool of mortgages but by an MRS issued by another agency. Thus, a private firm might purchase pass-throughs issued by GNMA and rearrange the cash flows to meet the needs of investors. In this situation, the market experiences a "layering" of mortgage-related securities.

A special form of CMO is a stripped mortgage-backed security. Generally, two classes are established. One class of investors has the right to receive all interest payments from a pool of mortgages, while the other has the right to receive all the principal payments—both scheduled amortization and prepayments. The interest-only (IO) and principal-only (PO) securities have some peculiar payment patterns, especially when interest rates are volatile. Some investors purchase them to hedge against the effect of interest rate changes on their other assets. These are also discussed in the following chapter.

Swaps

A **swap** is a secondary mortgage market transaction that occurs when a lender sells mortgages to an agency that in turn issues an MRS, such as a pass-through, back to the lender. Early in the development of the secondary market came the realization that, for various reasons, the investor in the mortgage-related security might very well be the lender that desired to sell the portfolio of mortgages. In such a case, the agency would "swap" the mortgages for the MRS. Why would a lender such as a thrift prefer to hold an MRS backed by its own pool of mortgages rather than the pool itself? The cash flows associated with the underlying pool of mortgages is not altered, yet there are resources expended in converting the pool to a mortgage-related security. Efficient market theory would predict a loss in value due to these expended resources.

One reason for a swap lies in the liquidity advantage of an MRS over individual loans. Thrifts can use them as collateral to borrow funds (this was especially true when Regulation Q set limits on the rate they could offer on deposits but not on borrowed funds). They also can sell them more quickly if there is a need for cash, such as to meet the demands of net withdrawals of deposits. Even if it sells the MRS, the lender will likely retain the servicing and receive a servicing fee. The lender will receive a rate on the MRS from 0.25 to 0.5 percent less than that on the pools of mortgages it originally owned. The spread is the agency's fee for underwriting and guaranteeing the mortgages in the pools and the timely payment of interest and principal. Also, the MRSs are considered an investment in real estate for those regulatory rules that require a certain percentage of assets of thrifts be held in such investments.

Some secondary mortgage market agencies and firms specialize in one or two types of MRSs, while others issue a variety. These agencies and firms are discussed below.

Tax and Accounting Issues of Mortgage-related Securities

Secondary mortgage market agencies and firms that issue MRSs backed by pools of loans have always had to wrestle with the issue of double taxation. Essentially, cash flows from the mortgages to the agency or firm and then to the investors. If the cash flows are taxable when received by the agency, and then again by the investors, the tax burden would be so great as to eliminate the advantages of securitization of mortgages. Avoidance of the double taxation was accomplished in the early years by the creation of a **grantor trust** to own the mortgages. The grantor trust worked especially well for pass-through securities. If the provisions of a qualified grantor trust are met, then the trust is not taxed, only the investor in the pass-through. To qualify, a grantor trust must (1) have a limited life, (2) be self-liquidating (no assets remain after investors are paid off), and (3) require no active management of the assets after they are placed in trust. One can see why a pass-through easily fits these requirements.

When CMOs were developed to meet the cash flow demands of investors, tax and accounting problems developed. Many CMO issuers transferred (sold) the underlying loans to a trust in order to gain the favorable tax treatment and also to remove the loans from their balance sheet (as was the case with pass-throughs). Many thrifts, and certainly mortgage bankers, did not want to carry the loans as assets and MRSs as liabilities on their balance sheets (however, some originators did want to treat CMOs as a financing). Transfer to a trust appeared to solve both problems. The IRS and the accounting profession complicated this arrangement, however. In March 1985, the Financial Accounting Standards Board ruled that an issuer must treat a CMO as a financing (debt), even when the loans are transferred to a trust, if the issuer holds more than a "nominal" residual interest in the collateral. But requirements by the rating agencies for overcollateralization create residual interests that are not nominal. In addition, the size of the residual may increase if prepayments are slower than expected or if reinvestment income exceeds expectations. Some CMO issuers responded by creating a second trust to own the residuals (an owner's trust). Investors could purchase certificates of beneficial interest.

But this did not solve the tax problem. The IRS ruled that CMOs using the trust arrangement were similar to a corporation retaining control and having an equity interest (the residual). The trust arrangement also required active management, as the cash flows not currently distributed to security holders had to be reinvested for later delivery. A few originators who did not mind avoiding the trust arrangement carried the mortgages as assets and the CMOs as debt. For them, the problems were not as severe. However, the residual interest meant that they could not borrow against the full amount of the debt.

Because of these problems, secondary mortgage market participants urged Congress to consider remedial legislation. It came as part of the Tax Reform Act of 1986. The legislation established the **Real Estate Mortgage Investment Conduit (REMIC)** as an entity that could issue CMOs and not be subject to double taxation. A partnership, trust, or other corporation may elect REMIC status and maintain separate records relative to the mortgage pool and management of the funds related to the pool. For tax purposes, income is recorded as received from the pool of mortgages and deductions are allowed for interest paid (on the CMO tranches) to investors and for other pool-related expenses. The net income then can be passed through to the owner of the residual (usually the CMO issuer) as income or loss.

An agency, trust, or firm retains this favorable tax status as long as it does not engage in any prohibited transactions, including (1) receiving income from any asset that is not a "qualified mortgage", (2) receiving fees or compensation for services (other than servicing income from the mortgage portfolio), or (3) buying or selling mortgages out of the pool (except as the pool is liquidated if all proceeds are disbursed within 90 days).

If desired, the user of a REMIC can avoid reporting the mortgages as assets and the CMOs as liabilities; the REMIC is a stand-alone activity. The issuer will report a gain or loss on the "sale" of the mortgages into the REMIC trust, however. If the issuer wants to avoid a loss on the "sale," it will simply report the residual interest owned in the REMIC as an asset. Figure 10–3 shows how REMIC transactions work.

Now that we have considered several types of mortgage-related securities, let's review the agencies and firms that are active in the market.

SECONDARY MORTGAGE MARKET AGENCIES AND FIRMS

There are several agencies that have in the past or presently issue mortgage-related securities:

1. Federal National Mortgage Association (FNMA, Fannie Mae)
2. Government National Mortgage Association (GNMA, Ginnie Mae)
3. Federal Home Loan Mortgage Corporation (FHLMC, Freddie Mac)
4. Federal credit agencies
5. State and local credit agencies
6. Private firms

FIGURE 10–3

Cash Flows for a REMIC

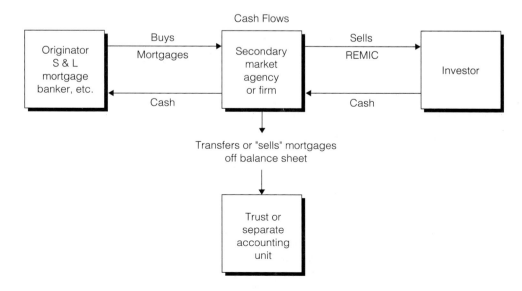

Federal National Mortgage Association

Congress established the Federal National Mortgage Association (FNMA) in 1938 as a subsidiary of the Reconstruction Finance Corporation (RFC). The main purpose was to form secondary market support for FHA and, later, VA loans. Up until the 1980s, the FHA and VA set a limit on the rate interest lenders could charge on these loans so as to keep housing affordable. As interest rates rose, lenders were reluctant to originate FHA and VA loans because of the large amount of points they would have to charge. Additionally, the value of existing loans declined with rising rates. Fannie Mae's purpose was to stand ready to purchase these loans at face value from originators, so as to replenish their funds for new originations. Even though their value was less than face, Fannie Mae hoped to sell them back at face or at a gain when interest rates dropped. In a sense, it was Fannie Mae's purpose to ride the interest rate cycle and take on interest rate risk. Fannie Mae obtained the funds to purchase mortgages by issuing long-term bonds. However, it faced substantial interest rate risk and in the early days relied on the Treasury to cover losses.

In 1950 the agency was transferred to the Housing and Home Finance Agency (an agency that was created in 1942 and later made part of HUD). Its life there was short-lived, as it was rechartered and became a separate agency in 1954. The recharter assigned three tasks to Fannie Mae: (1) continued enhancement of the secondary mortgage market for FHA and VA loans, (2) liquidation of properties and mortgages acquired by default, and (3) management of a subsidized loan program. The recharter also contained a provision that transformed Fannie Mae into an essentially private entity. For this purpose, the 1954 rechartering authorized the issuance of nonvoting preferred and common stock. This would both provide for the restructuring of Fannie Mae as a corporation and provide additional funds with which it could purchase mortgages.

Fannie Mae supports the secondary mortgage market by issuing mortgage-related securities and purchasing mortgages. Credit enhancement comes from the ability of Fannie Mae to borrow from the U.S. Treasury, and its equity results from the sale of common and preferred stock. Originally, Fannie Mae was authorized to purchase FHA and VA loans, but in 1970 Congress, in an act that established the Federal Home Loan Mortgage Corporation (see below), allowed the agency to purchase conventional loans. Fannie Mae holds most of these loans in its own portfolio but occasionally sells some of its inventory to control its interest rate risk exposure. In the 1970s Fannie Mae issued mostly short-term debt, so it faced the same sort of maturity mismatch and interest rate risk problem that thrifts did. It was, essentially, a large thrift. In 1981 its portfolio of $61.4 billion dollars in long-term mortgages was financed partially by $21.2 billion dollars in short-term debt. The amount of liquidating assets within 1 year was $3.6 billion, which produced a 1-year maturity gap of $17.6 billion. This gap represented 29 percent of the agency's assets.

Then, during the mid-1980s FNMA reduced its interest rate risk by issuing pass-throughs and collateralized mortgage obligations as well as purchasing adjustable rate mortgages. By the end of 1988, the liquidating assets and maturing liabilities within 1 year were equal ($36 billion each), so that the 1-year maturity gap was zero. Since that time, the agency has had a more balanced portfolio of assets and liabilities. Table 10–3 shows the recent activity of FNMA.

Fannie Mae held about $366 million in mortgages in its own portfolio in June, 1997. The portfolio was financed with $167.7 million in short-term debt and $177.8 million in long-term debt. Off balance sheet, Fannie Mae had $673.9 million in MBSs outstanding, most of them pass-throughs but some CMOs. In the second quarter of 1997, the corporation earned $970 million in net interest income, the difference between interest income on its mortgage portfolio and interest expense on its liabilities. This represents about 0.3 percent annual return on its assets. It earned an additional $317 million in guarantee fees on its off-balance sheet pass-throughs. After taxes the corporation made $752 million in the second quarter, or $.69 per share.

Government National Mortgage Association

In 1968 Congress passed the Housing and Urban Development Act. Among other things the act established the Government National Mortgage Association (GNMA) and placed it in the newly formed Department of Housing and Urban Development. Ginnie Mae relieved FNMA of two of

T A B L E   1 0 – 3

Federal National Mortgage Association Financial Activity
for Quarter Ending June 1997 (in millions)

Part A: Balance Sheet

Assets	
Mortgage portfolio	296,799
Other assets	69,198
Total assets	365,997
Liabilities	
Debentures, notes, bonds	
Payable in one year	167,682
Payable after one year	177,780
Total	345,462
Other liabilities	7,271
Total liabilities	352,733
Equity	13,264
MBS outstanding	673,900

Part B: Income Statement

Net interest income	970
Guarantee fees	317
Gain on sale of mortgages	—
Miscellaneous income	32
Administrative expense, provision for losses, and foreclosed property expense	(259)
Net income before tax	1,060
Taxes	(308)
Net income	752

its functions: the management and liquidation of previously originated (FHA) mortgages and the loan subsidization program. Under the latter program, termed the special assistance function (SAF), Ginnie Mae subsidized the cost of housing for low-income families. A typical arrangement, called a **Tandem Plan,** authorized Ginnie Mae to make low-interest loans to qualified families. It then would sell the loans at a discount to Fannie Mae. The discount allowed FNMA to earn a market yield. Ginnie Mae absorbed the loss—the difference between the amount of the loan originated and the discounted price received from FNMA. It was Ginnie Mae's only primary market activity. These two functions were never a large part of Ginnie Mae's operations, however. Rather, the agency was given an important third function, support of the secondary mortgage market.

Ginnie Mae's secondary mortgage market operations have been somewhat focused. The agency supports the FHA and VA (and, to a small extent, the Farmers Home Administration) loan market by guaranteeing pass-through securities. Credit enhancement on the pass-throughs comes from two sources. First, the underlying loans are guaranteed against default by the FHA and the VA. Second, Ginnie Mae guarantees the timely payment of interest and principal. So, even if there is a default on some of the loans in the pool, pass-through investors will not have to wait until a claim is made to the FHA or the VA in order to obtain payment. The originator of the mortgages is required to make monthly payments to the investors in the pass-throughs and then seek reimbursement from the FHA, VA, or the Rural Housing Service (RHS). If the originator cannot make the payment, Ginnie Mae will.[1]

It is important to note that Ginnie Mae itself neither purchases mortgages nor issues securities. A balance sheet of Ginnie Mae would show that for its pass-through activity it holds no mortgages nor issues any debt. The agency's activities can be understood by considering its early operations in support of the FHA and VA loan market. Later modifications in operations have been minor. Figure 10–4 shows a typical early Ginnie Mae arrangement. It is useful to view the process in stages.

FIGURE 10–4

Creation of a GNMA Pass-through Security

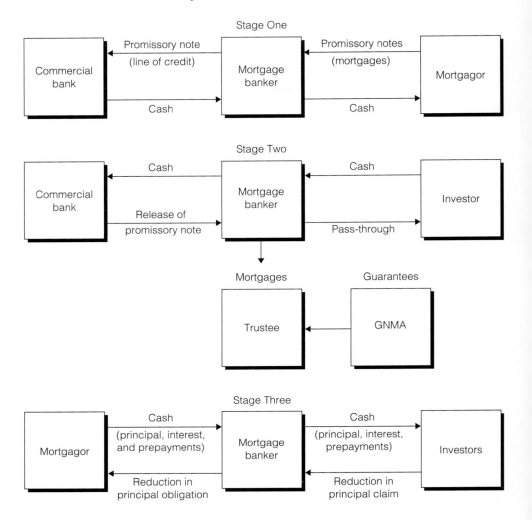

In Stage One a mortgage originator, say a mortgage banker, obtains a line of credit from a commercial bank with which to make mortgage loans. As the loans are made, the line of credit is taken down, and the loans are pledged as collateral for take-down. Recall, this is termed **warehousing.** In this fashion, the originator accumulates a pool of mortgages, say, $100 million in total value. All mortgages must have the same maturity (within a year) and the same rate of interest (within one percentage point), and be guaranteed by the FHA, VA, or RHS (Rural Housing Service) and be within 24 months of origination (except multifamily mature loan program). Next, the originator will request that the pool be qualified for a pass-through security to be issued. Ginnie Mae will qualify the pool if it meets the restrictions mentioned and some other minor conditions. The originator must pay a nonrefundable fee ($500 on the first $1.5 million and $200 for each additional million in the pool) with its request for qualification.

In Stage Two the originator issues the pass-through securities. They will be sold through securities dealers and investment banking firms. They were sold, usually on a forward basis, through an organization called the Ginnie Mae Dealers Association that was merged into the Public Securities Association (PSA) in 1982. Buyers include banks, thrifts, pension funds, life insurance companies, and individual investors. The originator pays off the line of credit with the funds obtained from the sale of the securities. The mortgages then are transferred to a trustee.

The trustee makes sure that the pass-through investors are paid off whenever there is a prepayment of the mortgage.

In Stage Three principal and interest payments are made to the investor. The principal of the investor's security is reduced by the amount of the scheduled amortization and any prepayments. The pass-through will bear a rate of interest 0.5 percent less than that on the mortgages. If the rate on the mortgages is 10 percent, that on the pass-through will be 9.5 percent. The difference is split between the originator (44 basis points) for servicing the loans and Ginnie Mae (6 basis points) for its guarantee of timely payments. Ginnie Mae uses these funds to make payments (on defaulted loans) to the pass-through investors in the event the originator cannot.

In 1983 Ginnie Mae loosened the provision that all mortgages in a pool had to have the same interest rate. Under the Ginnie Mae II program, loans can be mixed as long as the difference in rates among the mortgages is no greater than 1 percent. The program also allows seasoned or existing mortgages to be included in the pool.

Table 10–4 shows the recent activity of the GNMA. As of 1990 GNMA pass-throughs represented 42 percent of all pass-throughs and 14 percent of all mortgage-related securities.

Federal Home Loan Mortgage Corporation

In 1970 mortgage-backed securities backed by pools of FHA- and VA-insured loans were well established. A large percentage of mortgage loans was conventional, however. Sixty-five percent of all one- to four-family mortgages that were originated in that year were conventional. Furthermore, thrifts dominated the conventional loan market. Seventy percent of loans originated by thrifts were conventional. Mortgage bankers, on the other hand, dominated the FHA and VA market. Ninety-four percent of their loans were this type. Thus, up to 1970 the government support of the secondary mortgage market aided the FHA and VA sector and mortgage bankers. There was a perceived need of government support for conventional lenders and thrifts that were experiencing interest rate risk.

In 1970 Congress passed the Emergency Home Finance Act. Title III of this act chartered the Federal Home Loan Mortgage Corporation (FHLMC), or Freddie Mac. It authorized the corporation to purchase conventional and FHA and VA loans. It also authorized the purchase of conventional loans by Fannie Mae. To date, Freddie Mac has specialized in conventional mortgages and Fannie Mae in FHA and VA mortgages. The corporation's initial capital came from the sale of $100 million in nonvoting common stock that was sold to the (twelve) district Federal Home Loan Banks. It also issued 15 million shares of preferred stock at the end of 1984 to the Federal Home Loan Banks which in turn issued them to their members (thrifts). This issuance was part of the effort to help troubled thrifts survive in the mid-1980s. Freddie Mac stock is traded on the New York Stock Exchange.

Freddie Mac obtains its funds by issuing a wide variety of debt and mortgage-related securities as follows.

TABLE 10–4

Government National Mortgage Association Outstanding Guarantee of Mortgage Pools (millions of dollars)

	1- to 4-Family	*Multifamily*	*Total*
1986	256,920	5,777	262,697
1987	309,806	7,749	317,555
1988	331,257	9,270	340,527
1989	358,142	10,225	368,367
1990	391,505	12,108	403,613
1991	415,767	9,528	425,295
1992	410,625	8,841	419,516
1993	414,700	9,000[a]	423,000
1994	451,500	10,000[a]	461,500
1995	472,300	12,000[a]	484,300

[a]Estimate.

Discount Notes and Debentures.   Freddie Mac issues debentures in minimum denominations of $10,000 and increments of $5000. It also issues discount notes (maturity of 1 year or less) with a minimum denomination of $25,000 and increments of $1.

Mortgage Participation Certificates (PCs).   The Freddie Mac PC is the corporation's pass-through security. First sold in 1971, pools now consist of conventional fixed-rate, 30-year mortgages, 15-year mortgages, adjustable-rate mortgages, and multifamily mortgages. The corporation guarantees the timely payment of interest and principal.

Collateralized Mortgage Obligations.   First issued in 1983, Freddie Mac CMOs are available with several classes with varying stated maturities. Semiannual principal payments are allocated to each class of the CMO in the order of the stated maturity. No principal is paid to an investor in a class until earlier maturity classes are retired. Holders of each class of CMOs receive semiannual interest payments on the unpaid principal balance of their bonds at the coupon rate for the class. Interest on the accrual class is paid out only upon the full payment of all other classes of bonds. While they are the general obligation of Freddie Mac, each CMO is backed by its own pool of mortgages that is owned by, and held in, its own portfolio.

Guaranteed Mortgage Certificates (GMCs).   Issued early on, GMCs have not been sold directly by Freddie Mac since 1979. They represent an undivided interest in a pool of mortgages owned by Freddie Mac. The certificates pay a guaranteed minimum principal annually and interest semiannually.

Table 10–5 shows the recent activity of the Federal Home Loan Mortgage Corporation. The bulk of the mortgages that are purchased by Freddie Mac are pooled and "sold" (held in trust) as backing for (PCs), the agency's pass-through security. This constitutes its "sold" portfolio, and the values of the securities or the underlying mortgages do not appear on the balance sheet. Only the "retained" portfolio is shown there. Fee income for Freddie Mac's guarantee of timely payment is recorded on their income statement, however.

Federal Credit Agencies

There are several federal credit agencies that, in part, support the primary and secondary mortgage market.

Farm Credit System.   In 1987 Congress passed the Agricultural Credit Act. The purpose was to consolidate and coordinate the activities of three agriculturally related systems: the Federal Land Banks, the Federal Intermediate Credit Banks, and the Banks for Cooperatives. The first two were merged into a system of 37 farm credit banks and the latter renamed the Federal Credit Banks. The farm credit system is divided into 12 farm credit districts. The farm credit banks make direct loans for agricultural purposes, including the purchase of rural homes. The banks obtain their funds by issuing securities through the Credit Banks Funding Corporation located in New York. The securities are called Farm Credit Systemwide Obligations and consist of both discount notes and long-term bonds.

Farm Credit Assistance Financial Corporation.   This agency was approved pursuant to the Agricultural Credit Act in early 1988. Its purpose was to provide capital to farm credit banks that were experiencing financial difficulty. It was authorized to issue up to $2.8 billion of uncollateralized debt guaranteed by the U.S. Treasury. The guaranteed debt securities have maturities of 15 years and may be issued no later than September 1992.

Federal Agricultural Mortgage Corporation (Farmer Mac).   A third creation of the Agricultural Credit Act, this corporation was intended to act similarly to GNMA and FNMA, but for farm mortgages. This institution, housed in the Farm Credit System, examines pools of farm mortgages, places a guarantee on the timely payment of principal and interest, and permits underwriters to sell pass-throughs in the secondary market. Unlike the full guarantee of timely payments granted by GNMA, FAMC guarantees the timely payment of 90 percent of the principal and interest payments. Credit enhancement (funds to allow the guarantee of payments)

TABLE 10–5

Federal Home Loan Mortgage Corporation Financial Activity (in millions) Quarter Ended September 1997

Part A: Balance Sheet

Assets:*		Liabilities:	
Mortgages	156,972	Short-term Notes and Bonds	74,420
Cash and Investments	10,881	Long-Term Notes and Bonds	85,118
Reverse Repurchase	5,874		
Acct's Receivable	7,991	Total Debt	159,538
Other	1,783		
Total	184,275	Principal & Interest Due	
		to PC Investors	10,162
		Other Liabilities	2,713
		Equity	7,148
		Total	184,275

Part B: Components of Revenue

	Effective Interest Rate	
Income from Retained Portfolio	3,232	7.06%
Interest on Debt Liability	2,753	6.00%
Spread on Retained Portfolio	479	1.06%
Management and Guarantee Income	325	
Other	32	
Total Revenue	836	
Non-Interest Expense	262	
Total Income	574	

Part C: Mortgage Activity

Purchases of Mortgages

	30-year Fixed***	15-year Fixed	ARMS	Multifamily	Other**	Total
1985	34,757	6,496	823	1,902	33	44,012
1986	74,680	22,904	2,262	3,538	90	103,474
1987	54,880	15,097	4,779	2,016	69	76,840
1988	28,843	6,729	7,253	1,191	59	44,075
1989	49,116	8,613	17,835	1,824	1,207	78,591
1990	47,815	9,393	16,286	1,338	686	75,518
1991	93,540	18,190	7,793	236	206	99,965
1992	113,377	62,203	15,512	27	7	191,126
1993	139,407	68,470	21,172	191	466	229,706

Part D: Debt Outstanding

Mortgage-backed Securities Outstanding

	PCs	CMOs + Other	Totals
1985	99,908	5,047	104,955
1986	169,186	5,333	174,519
1987	212,634	3,652	216,286
1988	226,406	4,594	231,150
1989	272,870	5,292	278,162
1990	316,359	4,687	321,046
1991	359,163	4,019	363,182
1992	407,514	1,717	409,231
1993	439,029	1,056	440,085

*Not shown on Balance Sheet are mortgage participation certificates backed by same amount of mortgages: Freddie Mac refers to this as the "sold" portfolio.

**Due to timing differences of receipt and payment of interest on the sold portfolio.

***Includes 20-year fixed rate mortgages and balloon resets.

***Includes second mortgages and mobile home loans.

comes from three sources: (1) a $1.5 billion line of credit from the Treasury; (2) $20 million in equity raised by selling stock to banks, insurance companies, and farm system institutions; and (3) the fees the agency charges for the guarantee. FAMC charges 50 basis points plus an annual fee of 0.5 percent of the outstanding pool balance.

Farmer Mac was originally capitalized by a $20 million subscription sale of common stock which was sold primarily to financial institutions that deal with agricultural loans. To qualify as an agricultural loan, a loan must be secured by land or improvements used for the production of at least one agricultural commodity. This includes rural housing loans that finance single-family residential dwellings in rural areas with populations not greater than 2500 and with a maximum purchase price of $100,000.

Although established in 1987, the implementation of Farmer Mac's underwriting program was delayed to 1992. In that year Farmer Mac issued its first guaranty certificates worth $233 million. These securities were collateralized by agricultural loans originated by Travelers Insurance Company.

Rural Housing Service (RHS). The Rural Housing Service (formerly the Farmers Home Administration), housed in the Department of Agriculture, extends loans to rural areas for farms, houses, and community facilities. Until 1975 the agency raised some funds through the sale of Certificates of Beneficial Ownership (CBOs). Current sources of funds include a line of credit with the Treasury and the sale of its loans to the private sector or to trusts which in turn create pass-through securities. The direct loans made by RHS are restricted to areas with a population less than 10,000 and to low- and moderate-income families. Maximum income limits (adjusted family income) are set and vary by section of the country and size of the family. The loans made by the agency are typically below-market-rate loans. They are sold at a discount, with the agency bearing the loss. The term for a direct loan is typically 33 years, however, loans for up to 38 years may be made for applicants whose annual income does not exceed 60 percent of the median income for the area. Each county has a different maximum loan amount that may not exceed the market value of the property. The PITI cannot exceed 29 percent for very-low-income families or 33 percent for low-income families and the family must personally occupy the dwelling. Section 504 loans are for repair of existing properties. It is for families with very low income (less than 50 percent of the median income in the area), and who cannot obtain repair loans elsewhere. The loan cannot exceed $20,000 and the interest payment is 1 percent annually.

Financing Corporation (FICO).   The Financing Corporation was chartered by the Federal Home Loan Bank Board in 1987, pursuant to the Competitive Equality Banking Act of the same year. It was formed to help solve the deepening crisis of widespread insolvency among thrifts. The purpose of FICO was to recapitalize the FSLIC, which was in danger of insolvency itself as a result of the costly resolutions of many failed thrifts. FICO was authorized to issue $3 billion in nonvoting capital stock and up to $10.825 billion (no more than $3.75 billion in any 1 year) in debt securities. The proceeds are to be transferred to the FSLIC for use in resolving problems with failed thrifts. The bonds are not guaranteed by either the U.S. government or the FSLIC. Since 1989 the annual level of debt for this agency has been $8.17 billion.

Federal Financing Bank (FFB).   This bank was established by the Federal Financing Bank Act of 1973 to consolidate and reduce the government's cost of financing a variety of federal agencies and other borrowers whose obligations are guaranteed by the federal government. The bank issues debt to obtain funds with which to purchase the obligations of two dozen or so federal agencies. Most of the mortgage- and housing-related agency obligations are excluded. Examples of agencies whose obligations are purchased include the TVA, REA, NASA, SBA, postal service, and many others. Two housing-related obligations that the bank can purchase are those issued by HUD to support Section 108 guaranteed loans and low-rent public housing. In 1993 the bank had $127.3 billion in debt outstanding.

State and Local Credit Agencies

We saw in Chapter 7 how the various state Housing Finance Agencies (HFAs) issue mortgage revenue bonds that carry a low rate of interest because of their tax exemption. Another activity of the HFAs is their outreach to the secondary mortgage market. HFAs fund FHA-insured and

VA-guaranteed loans that are packaged into securities guaranteed by GNMA. They also participate in affordable housing initiatives offered by Freddie Mac and Fannie Mae. In 1989, HFAs originated approximately $9 billion in collateralized mortgage obligations through the secondary mortgage market.

Private Firms

Numerous private firms have entered the secondary mortgage market. Once the government agencies demonstrated the need for the market and Congress passed enabling legislation, many private firms saw a profit in securitizing mortgages. The private companies do everything that the government-related agencies do. They purchase mortgages for securitization and exercise swaps. Credit enhancement comes from pool insurance or overcollateralization or both. The mortgage-related securities that they issue are rated by the rating agencies. Many of the private firms specialize in loans that the government agencies either cannot or do not wish to securitize, such as nonconforming and jumbo loans. Some large thrifts or other financial institutions create subsidiaries to carry on the specialized function of mortgage securitization.

An example of a private effort was the short-lived Home Mortgage Acceptance Corporation (HOMAC), founded to aid builders finance houses that they sold. This firm was very successful in the early 1980s because it took advantage of tax savings afforded by the installment sales treatment for recognition of income. To understand its benefits, consider a homeowner (not a builder) who sells a property with a basis of $50,000 for $100,000. Under certain circumstances, the $50,000 gain may be taxable. If the owner takes back a second mortgage for, say, $40,000, then it is considered an installment sale; the seller has not received all of the gain in cash. The seller is allowed to recognize $40,000 of the gain over time as he or she receives it in payments from the buyer. For a long-term loan, little of the initial payments will be principal and therefore included in the income of the seller. In this fashion, the seller spreads out the gain over many years and pays taxes as received.

Home builders took advantage of the installment sales treatment to defer taxes on the profits on the houses they built. Assume a home builder builds many $100,000 houses, with the profit on each being $20,000. The builder can defer recognition of the profit to the extent the builder extends a loan to the buyer. If the builder extends a $95,000 loan, he will recognize an immediate $5000 profit, but defer the remainder and recognize it as the home buyer makes payments. Since many builders did not have the financial strength to make loans to every buyer of the properties they constructed, HOMAC was formed. As the builder extended loans to home buyers, HOMAC would securitize the loans and sell them in the secondary market. In this way, the builder was the lender of record, even though the funds came from investors in the mortgage-related securities. The installment sales treatment afforded by this technique was valuable, but unfortunately it was eliminated by the Tax Reform Act of 1986.

More recently, several large investment bankers, such as First Boston Corporation and Salomon Brothers, have been active in issuing CMOs and REMICs.

DEVELOPING A SECONDARY MORTGAGE MARKET: A YEAR-BY-YEAR SUMMARY

There have been more changes in the mortgage market in the last dozen or so years than in any other comparable period. We review some of the events during this period on a year-by-year basis. These events paint a picture of a revolution in mortgage financing. There appears to be no limit to the imagination of market participants in creating financial instruments designed to provide funds to the ultimate user, the mortgage borrower.

1981   Freddie Mac introduces Guarantor, the first swap program for conventional, fixed-rate mortgages. Disintermediation is a problem for thrifts, and they can use the Freddie Mac PCs as collateral for borrowing funds outside of Regulation Q limits. They also can sell the PCs to raise funds to meet deposit withdrawals without reporting a loss on their income statement. A sale of the original loans that were swapped would have generated losses, because they were predominantly low-rate loans.

1982   Conventional mortgage rate peaks at 16.5 percent. GNMA securitizes more than $12 billion in one- to four-family mortgages. Freddie Mac more than doubles its holdings of one- to four-family mortgages, from $19.5 billion in 1981 to $42.6 billion in 1982.

1983   In June, Freddie Mac issues the first CMO for $1 billion. The issue sells out in one week. By December, there are 12 issues of CMOs for nearly $4.7 billion. Life insurance companies and pension funds are the major investors in the long-term tranches of the CMOs.

Private firms such as First Boston and Salomon Brothers purchase Ginnie Mae pass-throughs and convert the cash flows to CMOs.

American Southwest Financial forms a consortium of 35 builders to securitize mortgages on the properties they sell.

1984   The Home Mortgage Acceptance Corporation (HOMAC) is started. This firm will aid the home building industry by securitizing FHA- and VA-insured mortgages made by builders on their properties. In February they sell $18 million in CMOs.

Freddie Mac begins buying 1-, 3-, and 5-year ARMs for the first time. Later in the year, they move to standardize ARMs by setting restrictions on the terms of ARMs that they will purchase. Lenders begin to adopt this standardization, since many desire the ability to sell their loans in the secondary market.

Cumulative CMOs reach $3 billion.

Citicorp Homeowners Mortgage Acceptance Corporation introduces the first CMO backed by mortgages without a federal (FHA or VA) guarantee.

The Secondary Mortgage Market Enhancement Act is passed. It provides secondary mortgage market issuers an exemption from state security registration laws and legal investment restrictions. To qualify under the act, the mortgage securities must be rated in one of the two top categories by at least one rating agency. This act effectively placed Freddie Mac and Fannie Mae obligations on a par with Treasury securities. The act also authorized these two agencies to purchase second mortgages and increase their activity in the securitization of multifamily mortgages.

1985   Freddie Mac issues PCs in book-entry form through the Federal Reserve Bank of New York book-entry system. Rapid expansion of the secondary mortgage market requires that action. Trading volume of mortgage-related securities jumps from $131 billion in 1981 to nearly $1 trillion in 1984. Later in the year, Fannie Mae also converts to the book-entry system.

The first CMO backed by commercial mortgages is issued by Penn Mutual Life Insurance Company. It is a $204.8 million AAA-rated issue.

Fannie Mae issues its first mortgage-related security denominated in yen.

In further "layering" of the secondary market, EPIC Acceptance Corporation issues a $100 million CMO backed by Freddie Mac PCs. It is overcollateralized by 30 percent.

HOMAC expands its activities to include conventional mortgages (including jumbo loans).

1986   The Tax Reform Act (TRA) is passed. The act authorizes the issuance of Real Estate Mortgage Investment Conduits (REMICs). They offer alternative tax treatment for multiclass pass-through securities. REMICs avoid the double-taxation problem for actively managed pass-throughs, yet allow the issue to be treated as a sale of assets for accounting purposes. The act also places limits on the total amount of mortgage revenue bonds that can be offered by state housing agencies. It eliminates the installment sales treatment of builder bonds, effectively closing down HOMAC.

Secondary mortgage market activity heats up:

Freddie Mac increases the maximum loan amount on single-family properties to $133,250.

Freddie Mac sells a record $2.6 billion in PCs in February and closes a single $3 billion swap deal in June. It begins selling multifamily PCs on a weekly basis.

Ginnie Mae issues a record $135 million in ARM securities and reaches the $300 billion milestone for total securities guaranteed.

Fannie Mae purchases a record $6.6 billion in mortgages in the second quarter. Fearing interest rate risk, it sells off $10 billion in fixed-rate loans.

1987   Freddie Mac raises the maximum loan limit on single-family residences to $153,100. It also swaps $1 billion in PCs for fixed-rate mortgages with Amerifirst Mortgage Company.

Fannie Mae issues its first REMIC, backed by $500 million of FHA and VA loans. It is a stripped security divided into two classes. One class receives 99 percent of the principal payments and 62 percent of the interest payments (resulting in a 5 percent coupon rate). The other class receives 1 percent of the principal and 38 percent of the interest (resulting in a 3.05 percent coupon rate). The agency also announces it will purchase 7- and 10-year balloon mortgages to create a market for this type of loan.

Ginnie Mae announces an increase in its guarantee fee from 6 to 10 basis points, and then later rescinds the increase after heavy criticism from lenders.

Private firms become more active and innovative. Mechanics and Farmers Saving Bank issues the first publicly offered security backed by biweekly mortgages. First Boston Corporation issues the first CMO with a securitized residual class. This means that the class shares some of the scheduled principal payments, making it more liquid and easy to understand. The first REMIC backed by commercial mortgages is a $200 million issue by Security Pacific Merchants Bank.

1988   To avoid problems with excessive teaser-rate discounts, Freddie Mac requires that borrowers qualify for the loan at the maximum rate for the second year (or it will not purchase the loan). The agency also announces a $1 billion multiclass PC to be issued through a REMIC, the largest ever.

Fannie Mae issues the first REMIC backed by ARMs; Glendale Federal Savings and Loan of California is the originator of the $200 billion in loans in the pool. The agency also issues its first "megapool," allowing investors to combine existing mortgage-backed securities into larger instruments.

HUD announces that it will consider having the FHA insure price-level adjusted mortgages.

Federal Home Loan Bank Board Chairman Danny Wall raises his estimate of the cost of resolving insolvent thrifts from $22 billion to $30 billion.

1989   Federal Home Loan Bank Board announces a new rule to take over troubled thrifts before they become insolvent. It also announces plans to sue large accounting firms that failed to detect financial problems in thrifts that they audited.

The Government Accounting Office suggests that the thrift industry should be overhauled, starting with a split of the Federal Home Loan Bank Board and the FSLIC.

The Chicago Board of Trade announces a new cash-settled, mortgage-backed futures and a futures/options contract. They are listed monthly, based on the current GNMA coupon, and traded four months in the future.

Freddie Mac announces a stripped Giant PC program. The interest-only and principal-only strips will be formed by using several fixed-rate PCs. The agency also issues the one-hundreth series of multiclass mortgage PC.

The Financial Institutions Reform, Recovery, and Enforcement Act is passed.

1990   Jack Kemp, Secretary of HUD, launches a nationwide search for certified public accountants to put his agency in fiscal order.

President Bush says the $164 billion financing enacted to solve the thrift problem may not be enough.

The Office of Thrift Supervision issues Bulletin 38, which places seven types of CMO/REMIC products in the 100 percent risk class for the purpose of determining thrift capital requirements.

Freddie Mac issues its first MBS backed by ARMs pegged to the London Interbank Offer Rate (LIBOR). It also announces five REMICs, backed by gold PCs.

1991   U.S. House of Representatives approves $78 billion in funding to keep the Resolution Trust Corporation running so it can solve the thrift problem.

The RTC swaps $70 million in loans with the Federal Home Loan Mortgage Corporation. The loans came from the failed Imperial Federal Savings and Loan Association. It also sells $833 million in mortgage-backed securities, the largest single MBS sale ever.

Congress considers passing legislation that would require government-sponsored enterprises (GSEs), such as Fannie Mae and Freddie Mac, to be adequately capitalized and supervised. Provisions of any legislation would require GSEs to obtain Triple-A ratings on their MRSs by the rating agencies.

By mid-year, 84 percent of all FHA/VA mortgages and 32 percent of conventional mortgages have become securitized.

1992   Congress passes the Housing and Community Development Act, an extensive housing law that consists primarily of modifications to existing programs. It includes the Federal Housing Enterprises Financial Safety and Soundness Act which rewrites the congressional charters for Fannie Mae and Freddie Mac to establish safe goals for financing affordable housing and housing in central cities and other underserved areas. The revised charters also set standards to protect against any savings-and-loan-type failure.

1993   Mortgage debt held by all mortgage pools and trusts reaches $1.5 trillion; 36 percent of all mortgage debt outstanding in the nation.

1994   At the end of March, 87 percent of all FHA/VA and 42 percent of conventional mortgages have been securitized.

1995   The fiscal 1995 HUD appropriations act revises the mortgage limits under the Federal Housing Administration Section 203(b) home mortgage program such that the maximum limit is 75 percent of the current Federal Home Loan Mortgage Corporation limit.

1996   Freddie Mac announces the purchase of $1.075 billion in mortgage revenue bonds from housing finance agencies.

THE FLOW OF FUNDS THROUGH THE PRIMARY AND SECONDARY MORTGAGE MARKETS

The Federal Home Loan Mortgage Corporation has assembled primary and secondary mortgage market data from various sources. The data show the importance of originators and secondary market agencies and firms. The data allow an analysis of the flow of funds and the relative importance of the various agencies and firms. Tables 10–6 and 10–7 show the mortgage data for 1985 through 1996. Mortgage-loan activity consists of originations, sales, and purchases of mortgages. Mortgage-security activity involves the creation of mortgage-related securities collateralized in various degrees by mortgages.

Part A of Table 10–6 shows direct originations of mortgage loans by seven different types of mortgage lenders. In 1995, $678,620,000 in residential mortgages were originated, most of that in conventional one- to four-family loans. For the most part, the data come from the HUD Survey of Mortgage Lending Activity that polls 1500 lending institutions and agencies in the seven groups. The groups represent about 95 percent of all residential mortgages originated. The Federal Credit Agencies listed in the table are not the secondary mortgage market agencies but rather the Farmers Home Administration, the Federal Land Banks, and other agencies issuing a small amount of direct loans in the primary market.

Primary market lenders sell many of the mortgages they originate in the secondary market. Part B of Table 10–6 shows the sales and purchases of mortgages by 10 different types of sellers and buyers. In 1995 originators sold $657,702,000,000 worth of loans, the bulk by thrifts and mortgage bankers. This represents 97 percent of the loans originated in that year. Several things should be noted about the data in this table. First, the secondary market agencies record no sales of mortgages. They purchase mortgages in order to securitize them. Second, although by definition total sales must equal total purchases, the table does not reflect this because of the absence of certain lender/investor categories in the HUD survey (for example, credit unions). The data also do not include the activities of dealers. If the omitted groups are large net sellers or purchasers in a given year, the discrepancy will emerge. Third, the purchases recorded for Ginnie Mae are not actually purchases, since the agency only guarantees the pass-throughs backed by the mortgages. The figure for Ginnie Mae purchases represents the value of the pass-throughs created by originators with the agency's guarantee. Fourth, the net acquisition for any group will equal originations plus purchases less sales.

Part A of Table 10–7 shows the originations of mortgage-related securities by various agencies and firms. There are three types of securities listed: pass-throughs, CMOs, and debt. Virtually all of the pass-throughs of Freddie Mac and Fannie Mae include those that result from swap transactions. The four issuers of CMOs include Freddie Mac, Fannie Mae, state and local agencies, and private firms. The debt issue of the agencies reflects the amount issued to finance new acquisitions of mortgages. Any debt issued to refinance existing debt is excluded. In Part B of Table 10–7,

TABLE 10–6

Mortgage Loan Activity (millions of dollars)

Part A: Originations of Residential Mortgage Loans

Conventional 1- to 4- Family	Thrifts	Commercial Banks	Mortgage Bankers	Life Insurance Companies	Pension Funds	State & Federal Credit Agencies	Local Credit Agencies	Total
1985	113,976	50,928	28,717	951	12	3,154	1,320	199,058
1986	201,839	100,922	52,502	3,196	104	2,676	887	362,126
1987	200,022	112,380	57,578	2,726	23	2,890	557	376,176
1988	182,717	95,815	52,282	2,995	50	2,858	1,041	337,759
1989	151,362	117,335	33,730	997	186	2,694	882	307,186
1990	131,722	137,412	103,018	411	64	3,056	1,051	376,734
1991	133,153	147,964	214,785	314	7	3,050	602	499,875
1992	211,122	225,267	377,864	436	355	3,362	442	818,848
1993	207,717	249,847	423,189	525	228	4,073	264	895,328
1994	141,510	191,665	285,879	450	505	4,827	809	625,645
1995	112,478	148,284	299,739	454	778	2,241	776	564,750

Conventional Multifamily

1985	16,254	4,497	2,387	2,772	69	1,647	824	28,450
1986	22,439	7,133	4,267	3,723	19	1,625	1,922	41,128
1987	22,318	8,291	1,046	3,547	27	1,120	1,912	38,261
1988	20,259	6,899	2,525	3,732	103	1,153	527	35,198
1989	13,299	7,654	4,294	2,786	35	1,194	935	30,197
1990	10,604	10,686	4,683	2,172	44	1,565	805	30,559
1991	7,215	12,088	1,894	1,575	0	918	895	24,584
1992	8,299	11,634	2,058	1,406	208	1,049	501	25,155
1993	7,207	18,797	1,134	1,486	150	933	334	30,043
1994	7,905	20,920	0	1,257	655	627	358	31,722
1995	5,639	23,109	5,535	1,611	790	733	488	37,905

FHA/VA 1- to 4-Family

1985	2,777	6,103	34,579	335	0	0	188	44,017
1986	5,342	7,691	74,116	618	0	0	151	87,919
1987	8,758	12,171	86,414	483	0	0	167	107,998
1988	6,154	6,048	49,470	336	0	0	245	67,550
1989	6,314	5,858	45,828	446	19	0	327	58,789
1990	7,268	15,873	58,135	195	12	0	221	81,704
1991	7,263	5,359	49,132	250	0	0	195	62,199
1992	7,670	6,798	59,740	261	187	0	162	74,818
1993	11,016	9,617	103,313	282	128	0	124	124,480
1994	10,871	8,331	122,262	212	489	675	263	143,103
1995	6,378	7,075	58,960	216	390	1,354	307	74,686

FHA Multifamily

1985	229	1	359	0	2	353	2,538	3,482
1986	330	43	2,905	0	0	114	5,348	8,740
1987	285	9	1,363	0	0	0	5,175	6,831
1988	292	21	2,001	0	13	2	631	2,960
1989	170	15	149	0	13	0	601	950
1990	150	280	853	0	2	0	719	2,004
1991	90	74	138	0	0	0	614	916
1992	102	108	0	0	8	0	358	571
1993	84	23	866	0	44	0	642	1,659
1994	76	4	0	0	92	0	791	693
1995	61	9	573	0	151	6	485	1,279

TABLE 10–6 *(continued)*

Total Residential Originations

Year								Total
1985	133,236	61,529	66,042	4,078	98	5,154	4,870	275,007
1986	229,950	115,789	183,158	7,537	123	4,415	8,308	549,279
1987	231,383	132,851	169,462	6,756	50	4,010	7,811	552,322
1988	209,422	108,783	152,530	7,063	166	4,013	2,444	489,421
1989	171,145	130,862	170,937	4,229	253	3,881	2,745	484,054
1990	149,744	164,251	166,689	2,778	122	4,587	2,796	490,967
1991	147,721	165,485	625,949	2,139	7	3,968	2,306	587,575
1992	227,193	243,807	439,662	2,103	758	4,411	1,478	919,412
1993	226,036	287,805	528,502	2,293	550	5,006	1,364	1,051,563
1994	160,362	220,920	408,141	1,919	1,741	6,120	2,221	801,433
1995	124,556	176,477	364,813	2,281	2,109	4,328	2,056	678,620

Part B: Trading of New and Existing Residential Mortgage Loans

Sales	Thrifts	Commercial Banks	Mortgage Bankers	Life Insurance Companies	Pension Funds	Freddie Mac	Fannie Mae	Ginnie Mae	Federal Credit Agencies	State & Local Credit Agencies	Total
1985	106,484	21,784	82,797	1,574	81	0	0	884	5,844	0	219,448
1986	173,037	39,135	177,741	1,573	295	0	0	1,008	15,425	1	463,783
1987	132,830	50,353	164,115	1,160	467	0	0	232	7,234	0	461,917
1988	112,661	39,555	122,505	3,675	386	0	0	258	6,728	21	370,956
1989	118,613	46,352	113,345	1,523	171	0	0	148	4,041	0	427,143
1990	122,038	69,765	218,226	500	74	0	0	0	32,214	45	443,662
1991	136,424	67,427	294,015	562	33	0	0	5	31,416	14	529,735
1992	186,789	101,878	519,776	774	56	0	0	6	28,762	0	838,041
1993	172,014	136,290	667,997	1,257	0	0	0	0	15,244	113	992,920
1994	103,985	85,850	579,872	772	0	0	0	13	8,933	96	779,521
1995	77,094	73,075	498,896	1,014	0	0	0	23	7,543	51	657,702

Purchases

Year	Thrifts	Commercial Banks	Mortgage Bankers	Life Insurance Companies	Pension Funds	Freddie Mac	Fannie Mae	Ginnie Mae	Federal Credit Agencies	State & Local Credit Agencies	Total
1985	53,665	6,708	31,813	319	645	44,012	43,840	112,178	31,707	6,005	330,892
1986	67,782	11,037	62,094	962	913	103,474	80,435	259,984	38,966	5,677	631,324
1987	62,929	21,407	87,476	1,602	1,376	76,840	77,609	230,675	25,136	4,235	589,285
1988	56,111	24,382	60,426	2,407	1,009	44,075	72,052	148,436	31,097	6,116	446,111
1989	40,812	27,109	105,442	2,299	1,636	78,589	84,835	196,497	30,867	6,374	574,460
1990	42,292	33,667	51,541	1,206	298	75,518	114,166	232,875	79,240	4,997	635,810
1991	55,375	26,738	39,230	488	973	99,965	136,927	276,370	83,409	4,363	723,838
1992	59,130	42,837	79,981	581	1,210	191,126	251,715	467,154	104,466	3,493	1,201,865
1993	65,891	59,870	139,134	910	698	229,242	294,160	564,240	121,126	3,189	1,478,460
1994	48,111	50,369	147,767	645	1,262	123,410	164,061	357,418	89,250	4,751	987,044
1995	43,257	85,040	130,807	983	1,501	91,536	132,602	269,290	95,877	6,111	857,004

Source: Federal Home Loan Mortgage Corporation

TABLE 10–7

Mortgage Securities Activity (millions of dollars)

Part A: Issues of Mortgage-related Securities

Pass-through Securities	Freddie Mac	Fannie Mae	Federal Ginnie Mae	State & Local Credit Agencies	Credit Agencies	Private Firms	Total
1985	38,829	23,649	45,980	0	0	6,916	115,374
1986	100,198	60,566	101,433	0	0	13,163	275,360
1987	75,018	63,229	94,929	0	0	18,576	251,752
1988	39,777	54,878	55,248	0	0	20,699	170,602
1989	73,518	69,764	57,190	0	0	12,010	212,482
1990	73,815	96,695	64,651	0	0	14,341	249,502
1991	92,340	112,903	62,630	0	0	NA	267,873
1992	179,207	194,037	81,917	0	0	NA	455,166
1993	207,948	221,444	137,989	0	0	NA	567,381
1994	117,111	130,622	111,185	0	0	NA	358,918
1995	85,877	110,457	72,826	0	0	NA	269,160
1996	119,702	149,869	101,207	0	0	NA	370,778

Mortgage-Collateralized Securities

1985	2,905	0	0	0	10,875	12,973	26,753
1986	1,573	0	0	0	13,984	46,494	62,051
1987	0	916	0	0	12,046	58,137	71,099
1988	14,985	10,782	0	0	8,539	50,984	85,290
1989	39,731	44,043	0	0	9,119	16,730	109,623
1990	40,479	60,917	0	0	7,748	21,064	130,208
1991	72,032	101,805	0	0	NA	NA	173,837
1992	131,284	154,781	0	0	NA	NA	286,065
1993	143,396	167,992	0	0	NA	NA	311,328

Debt

1985	2,278	20,191	(884)	31,017	0	0	52,602
1986	1,703	19,869	(1,152)	27,956	0	0	48,376
1987	1,822	15,317	(475)	21,912	0	0	38,576
1988	4,298	18,063	(402)	28,382	0	0	50,341
1989	5,071	19,482	0	30,714	0	0	55,267
1990	1,703	18,114	0	26,475	0	0	46,292
1991	7,487	30,037	0	37,238	0	0	74,762
1992	NA	NA	NA	NA	NA	NA	NA
1993	NA	NA	NA	NA	NA	NA	NA

Total New Issues of Mortgage-related Securities

1985	44,012	43,840	45,096	31,017	10,875	19,889	194,729
1986	103,474	80,435	100,281	27,956	13,984	59,657	385,787
1987	76,840	79,462	94,454	21,912	12,046	76,713	361,427
1988	59,060	83,723	54,846	28,382	8,539	71,683	306,233
1989	118,320	133,289	57,190	30,714	9,119	28,740	377,372
1990	115,997	175,726	64,395	26,475	7,748	35,405	425,746
1991	171,859	244,745	62,630	37,238	0	0	516,472
1992	310,491	348,818	81,922	0	0	0	741,231
1993	351,284	389,436	138,041	0	0	0	878,761

T A B L E 1 0 − 7 *(c o n t i n u e d)*

Part B: Agency Issues of Pass-Through Mortgage-backed Securities

Freddie Mac	Conventional 1- to 4-Family Fixed-Rate	Conventional ARMs	FHA/VA	Multifamily	Total
1986	93,708	1,619	1,471	3,400	100,198
1987	67,040	4,993	833	2,152	75,018
1988	31,354	7,287	849	287	39,777
1989	54,492	17,864	575	587	73,518
1990	55,398	16,194	406	1,817	73,815
1991	64,522	7,574	144	0	92,340
1992	163,960	15,181	61	5	179,207
1993	187,876	20,052	20	0	207,948
1994	100,297	16,591	14	209	117,111
1995	71,253	14,267	2	355	85,877
1996	112,443	6,446	53	770	119,702

Fannie Mae					
1986	43,102	6,197	10,718	549	60,566
1987	50,665	7,969	3,433	1,162	63,229
1988	32,144	18,407	569	3,758	54,878
1989	52,239	13,501	749	3,275	69,764
1990	84,171	11,703	132	689	96,695
1991	97,919	12,411	1,158	1,415	112,903
1992	180,776	12,108	303	850	194,037
1993	205,920	14,300	265	959	221,444
1994	112,879	15,305	201	2,237	130,622
1995	86,834	18,807	630	4,187	110,457
1996	128,393	15,273	535	5,668	149,869

Ginnie Mae					
1986	97,634	962	896	1,941	101,433
1987	89,802	2,067	824	2,197	94,890
1988	50,659	1,777	482	2,263	55,181
1989	54,529	520	543	1,482	57,074
1990	61,781	716	598	1,300	64,395
1991	57,477	3,516	653	984	62,630
1992	69,371	11,211	434	901	81,917
1993	115,299	20,208	454	2,028	137,989
1994	115,383	28,798	139	1,944	146,264
1995	47,888	22,712	86	2,140	72,826
1996	75,538	22,960	56	2,653	101,207

Source: Federal Home Loan Mortgage Corporation.

the originations of the three principal agencies are broken down by the type of mortgages that back the securities. For example, of the $119,702,000,000 in securities issued by Freddie Mac in 1996, $112,433,000,000 were backed by conventional one- to four-family mortgages.

The data in this table tell us several things about the major secondary mortgage market agencies. First, the three agencies originate about 75 to 90 percent of all mortgage-related securities issued by the secondary mortgage market. Second, they rely more heavily on pass-throughs than on CMOs or debt. Third, state and local agencies and private firms rely on CMOs to raise funds. Generally, the private firms originate MRSs backed by conventional one- to four-family mortgages, while Ginnie Mae supports much of the FHA/VA mortgages that are securitized. Finally, Table 10–8 shows the amount of all mortgage debt outstanding that has been securitized. Overall, 55 percent of all one- to-four-family mortgage debt has been securitized through the secondary market—49 percent of all conventional and 90 percent of all FHA/VA loans. In contrast, 33 percent of multifamily mortgages have been securitized. As recently as 1994 only 49 percent of single-family and 11 percent of multifamily mortgages were securitized.

TABLE 10–8

Securitized Mortgage Debt Outstanding (as of March 31, 1997)

	1-to 4-Family			Multifamily		
	Total	*Conventional*	*FHA/VA/RHS*	*Total*	*Conventional*	*FHA/RHS*
Percent of debt securitized	55	49	90	33	29	49
Amount securitized ($ billions)	2,187	1,655	532	102	72	30
Amount not securitized ($ billions)	1,780	1,718	61	211	180	31
Total mortgage debt	3,967	3,373	593	313	252	61

Source: Federal Home Loan Mortgage Corporation. RHS is the Rural Housing Service.

REGULATION OF GOVERNMENT SPONSORED ENTERPRISES

Government sponsored enterprises (GSEs) is a term used to describe FNMA and FHLMC. These agencies are not official departments or branches of the U.S. government. Yet, they were originated through federal legislation and in the eyes of the investing public appear to enjoy the backing of the federal government. In fact, while the federal government does not guarantee the obligations of these two GSEs, Congress has expressed the feeling that in the event of default, they may be required to expend federal dollars to pay off investors who may have purchased their obligations. Because of this perceived obligation, there has been a recent move in Congress to pass legislation requiring some sort of federal regulation of the GSEs. The regulation would address the risk that the agencies face and would focus on the amount of capital they have.

Notice that these two agencies operate similarly to (but not exactly as) thrifts. They issue debt to purchase long-term mortgages. Some of the debt is short-term. Thus, the agencies face interest rate risk. In addition, any uninsured mortgages held by the agencies would pose a threat of default risk. Finally, the GSEs also face management and operating risk if the management of the GSEs fails to operate them efficiently.

In 1992 Congress passed the Federal Housing Enterprise Financial Safety and Soundness Act. This act set capital guidelines for Fannie Mae and Freddie Mac and, to monitor those guidelines, established the Office of Secondary Market Examination and Oversight (OSMEO) within the Department of Housing and Urban Development. The act sets two levels of capital guidelines, minimum and critical. In addition, it authorizes the Director of OSMEO to establish a third, and more rigorous, risk-based guideline. Under this guideline the director will simulate a 10-year "stress" period (high default rates) that includes large movements in interest rates. The capital sufficient to meet the default risk during this stress period establishes this guideline.

While the director establishes the risk-based guideline, the act sets the minimum and critical guidelines. The minimum capital is equal to 2.5 percent of the aggregate on-balance sheet assets plus 0.45 percent of the unpaid principal balance of mortgage-backed securities plus 0.45 percent of the off-balance sheet obligations of the enterprise. The critical capital level is established at 1.25, 0.25, and 0.25 percent of the same items. An enterprise is deemed adequately capitalized if its capital exceeds the rigorous risk-based capital guideline. It is deemed undercapitalized if its capital is less than the risk-based but greater than the minimum. It is considered significantly undercapitalized if its capital is less than the minimum but above the critical guideline. Finally, an enterprise is considered critically undercapitalized if its capital is less than the critical guideline. In the latter case it must submit a capital restoration plan and can be placed into conservatorship. In addition, the director of OSMEO can limit the growth and activities of the enterprise.

SUMMARY

The secondary mortgage market is one in which existing mortgages are bought and sold. Purchased mortgages are "repackaged" and their cash flows converted into various types of mortgage-related securities, such as mortgage-backed bonds and collateralized mortgage obligations. These mortgage-related securities also are bought and sold in the secondary mortgage market. The secondary market exists to facilitate the flow of funds from areas or institutions with a surplus to areas or institutions with a deficit. The flow is facilitated by the creation of liquid, default-free, mortgage-related securities. The secondary market also allows originators of mortgages to shift interest rate risk to investors, who are in a better position to handle the risks. Players that facilitate transactions in the secondary market include government agencies, such as the Government National Mortgage Association and the Federal National Mortgage Association, as well as private firms, such as First Boston or Salomon Brothers. These agencies and firms specialize in rearranging the cash flows from pools of mortgages into debt instruments that appeal to investors.

The federal government has actively supported the secondary mortgage market by its guarantee of some bonds (GNMA), its line of credit from the Treasury (FNMA), and legislation that facilitates the formation of conduits (REMICs) that have favorable tax rules. The secondary mortgage market has been so successful in meeting the needs of its participants that, by 1990, 40 percent of all residential mortgage debt had been securitized.

Because two agencies, FNMA and FHLMC, were established by federal legislation and enjoy the perception of federal backing, legislation was recently passed aimed at regulating these government sponsored enterprises (GSEs) in terms of capital requirements reflecting their credit, interest rate, and management risks.

KEY TERMS

Collateralize	Market-to-market
Collateralized mortgage obligation (CMO)	Mortgage-backed bond (MBB)
Credit enhancement	Mortgage pay-through bond
Federal Agricultural Mortgage Corporation	Mortgage-related security
Federal credit agencies	(Farmer Mac) (FAMC)
Federal Financing Bank (FFB)	Participation certificate (PC)
Federal Home Loan Mortgage	Pass-through
Corporation (FHLMC)	Private mortgage insurance (PMI)
Federal National Mortgage Association (FNMA)	Pool insurance
Financial Accounting Standards Board (FASB)	Real Estate Mortgage Investment Conduit (REMIC)
Government National Mortgage	Secondary mortgage market
Association (GNMA)	Senior/subordinated pass-through
Government sponsored enterprises (GSEs)	Subordinated tranche
Grantor trust	Swap
Guaranteed mortgage certificate	Tranche

SUGGESTED READINGS

Anders, G. 1988. How a home mortgage got into a huge pool that lured investors. *Wall Street Journal* 17 Aug.

Dougherty, A. J. 1989. The (next-to-the) last word in financial innovation. *Secondary Mortgage Markets* Vol. 6, Spring.

Federal Home Loan Mortgage Corporation. 1988. *A Citizen's Guide to the Secondary Mortgage Market.* Publication No. 67.

Federal Home Loan Mortgage Corporation. 1994. *Secondary Mortgage Markets, Mortgage Market Review.* McLean, VA.

Gatti, J. F., and R. W. Spahr. Value of Federal Sponsorship: The Case of Freddie Mac. *Real Estate Economics* 25, 3 (1997): 453–485.

Lore, K. G. 1987. *Mortgage-Backed Securities.* New York: Clark Boardman.

McElhone, J. 1987. The bare facts about strips. *Secondary Mortgage Markets* Vol. 4, Summer.

U.S. Department of Housing and Urban Development. 1986. *GNMA: Ginnie Mae Investment Facts.* Publication HUD-1047-GNMA. Government National Mortgage Association.

REVIEW QUESTIONS

10–1   What are the benefits of a well-organized secondary mortgage market? List at least three.

10–2   What are two forms of a supply and demand mismatch solved by the secondary mortgage market?

10–3   What are mortgage-related securities?

10–4   What are desirable characteristics of mortgage-related securities?

10–5   List and give a brief description of the types of mortgage-related securities.

10–6   What are the advantages of a collateralized mortgage obligation over a straight pass-through security?

10–7   Explain what credit enhancement is, and list a few ways in which it is accomplished in the secondary mortgage in debt.

10–8   What is a stripped mortgage-backed security?

10–9   Define a swap and indicate why some lenders use them.

10–10   Explain what a REMIC is and why Congress passed legislation to provide for it.

10–11   List and briefly describe several secondary mortgage market agencies.

10–12   Compare and contrast the three federally sponsored agencies. Include in your comparison the types of mortgages they purchase and the types of securities they issue.

10–13   Describe current regulation of government sponsored agencies.

10–14   List the characteristics of mortgage-related securities that make them acceptable to investors.

ENDNOTE

1. In the early years of operation, GNMA had two programs: a straight pass-through, which provided for the payment of interest and principal only if paid by the mortgagors, and a partially modified pass-through, which provided for interest payment (but not principal) whether or not collected. Recent GNMA programs are all gully modified pass-throughs which pay interest and principal whether or not collected.

WEB SITES

www.ginniemae.gov   information on GNMA programs and securities

www.freddiemac.com   information on the Federal Home Loan Mortgage Corporation including articles from its journal, *Secondary Mortgage Markets*

www.grad.usda.gov   information on Rural Housing Service programs.

CHAPTER **11**

Valuation of Mortgage Securities

LEARNING OBJECTIVES

The topic of this chapter is the valuation of mortgage securities. After you have read this chapter, you should understand how the cash stream from a pool of mortgages flows through to investors in various types of mortgage securities. You should understand how the cash flows of mortgage securities differ from one another in terms of their amount and timing. You also should know how changes in interest rates affect the value of mortgage securities. You will see why the values of mortgage securities behave differently from one another in response to changes in interest rates. You will discover how some mortgage securities can be used to hedge against interest rate risk inherent in more traditional debt securities.

INTRODUCTION

In this chapter, we analyze the cash flows and valuation of several types of mortgage securities: pass-throughs, mortgage-backed bonds, collateralized mortgage obligations (including the interest-only and principal-only strips), and servicing rights. These securities are called mortgage-related and mortgage-derivative securities. A **mortgage-derivative security** is any security for which the cash flows derived from mortgages are rearranged in terms of amount and timing. They include all of the securities discussed so far except for pass-throughs. In valuation, particular attention is paid to how changes in the market rate of interest affect the cash flows and value of these securities.

It is well-known how changes in the rate of interest affect the value of traditional debt securities. For these securities, future expected cash flows are fixed in terms of amount and payment dates. For fixed-rate obligations such as Treasury bonds or (noncallable) corporate debt, an increase in the market rate of interest will lower their values. The amount and timing of the future cash flows are unchanged, while the discount rate is raised. The reverse is true for a decrease in the market rate. Furthermore, the longer the duration (similar to maturity) of the obligation, the greater will be the change in value as a result of a change in market rates. However, mortgage securities are very dissimilar to these traditional types of debt.

The most striking difference is that for mortgage securities, both the timing and the amount of future expected cash flows are dependent upon changes in the rate of interest. Not only does a change in the market rate of interest affect the rate used to discount the cash flows of a mortgage security, the change also affects the time pattern of the cash flows. Since the amount and timing of the cash flows are contingent on interest rates, they are referred to as **interest rate contingent securities.** All of this makes the valuation of mortgage-derivative securities somewhat of an intricate exercise. As a foundation, we begin with a review of the valuation of traditional debt securities and then move to mortgage-related securities.

VALUATION OF TRADITIONAL DEBT SECURITIES

By a traditional debt security, we mean an obligation for which the issuer has promised a fixed payment on certain dates. A noncallable corporate security, for example, pays a semiannual interest payment fixed in dollar amount and a return of the face principal amount at maturity. The size and timing of the payments are not contingent on future levels of interest rates. The value of the security depends on the discount rate employed to find the present value of the cash flows. Initially, if the coupon rate of interest equals the market discount rate for the security, it sells at face (par) value. This is usually the case when the bond is originally issued, because the corporation will attempt to set the coupon payment equal to the current market rate. As market rates change over the life of the bond, so will its value—in the typical inverse relationship. As an illustration, consider the value of the bond described in Table 11–1. The bond is a noncallable corporate bond with a remaining life of 19 years. It carries a 10 percent coupon and was issued and sold at par a year earlier. Three concepts are important: valuation, yield-to-maturity, and the sensitivity of the value to changes in interest rates.

Valuation.   Note that the bond in the example promises to pay $100 annually—$50 every six months. This promised payment is fixed. Its value can be found by discounting the expected cash flows by the current discount rate. Two elements comprise the remaining cash flows—the 38 semiannual payments of $50 and the face value of $1000, to be paid at the end of the 19th year. Again, higher discount rates create lower values, and vice versa. As an illustration, if the market rate of interest is 12 percent, then the value is found by

$$\$851.54 = \frac{50}{(1.06)^1} + \frac{50}{(1.06)^2} + \cdots + \frac{50}{(1.06)^{38}}$$

Yield-to-Maturity.   The function of the discount or premium on a bond is to cause its yield to equal the current discount rate. When the market rate of interest is 12 percent, investors require that the expected yield on the bond in our example also will be 12 percent. For a bond selling at a discount, the higher yield is obtained in two parts—coupon payments and capital gain. The latter is the difference between the amount paid for the bond and its face value at maturity

TABLE 11–1
Valuation of Traditional Debt Security

Bond description:
Annual coupon rate 10%; face value, $1000; semiannual coupon, $50; number of periods to maturity, 38 (19 years); duration, 9.9 years

Current Market Rate	Value
6%	$1,449.85
7	1,312.62
8	1,193.68
9	1,090.25
10	1,000.00
11	920.97
12	851.54
13	790.31
14	736.13
15	688.01

Valuation Formula: $PV = \dfrac{\$50}{1 + r/2} + \dfrac{\$50}{(1 + r/2)^2} + \cdots + \dfrac{\$1050}{(1 + r/2)^{38}}$

or

$$PV = PVIFAr_{\%,38} \times \$50 + PVIFr_{\%,38} \times \$1000$$

($1000 − 851.54). An approximation of the yield-to-maturity (YTM) can be found by utilizing the following formula:

$$\text{YTM} = \frac{C + [FV - P_0]/N}{(P_0 + FV)/2} \qquad \text{(Equation 11–1)}$$

where C is the annual cash coupon, N is the number of years to maturity, P_0 is the purchase price, and FV is the face value at maturity. The formula puts the yield on an annual basis and has two components—the cash coupon and the amount of appreciation in the value of the security. This latter component is represented by the total capital gain $(FV - P_0)$ divided by the number of years to maturity. Together, these two components of annual return are divided by the average investment in the security. You should note that this is an approximation only. It is used here to show how the yield is affected by the discount from the face value. For our example,

$$\text{YTM} = \frac{\$100 + [(\$1000 - \$851.54)/19]}{(\$851.54 + \$1000)/2} = \frac{107.81}{925.77} = 11.65\%$$

which is close to the precise yield of 12 percent.

Sensitivity of Prices to Changes in Interest Rates: Duration.   Note that although the bond's current maturity is 19 years, its duration is 9.9 years. It is the bond's duration that determines the change in its value as a result of changes in the rate of interest. This can be seen by reviewing the formula that relates the percentage change in the price of a debt security to its duration:

$$\Delta P/P = -D(\Delta r/(1 + r)) \qquad \text{(Equation 11–2)}$$

As an exercise, note the change in the price of the corporate bond in Table 11–1 when the market interest rate changes from 10 percent to 9 percent. The percentage change in the price of the security is given by

$$0.0925 = -9.9(-0.01/1.1)$$

If the duration of a security is unknown, one can avoid the tedious calculations necessary to determine it by using Equation 11–2. If one accepts the fact that securities trading in liquid markets are priced efficiently, then simply rewrite the equation as:

$$D = (-\Delta P/P \times ((1 + r)/\Delta r) \qquad \text{(Equation 11–3)}$$

and solve for its duration. This is a quick and easy way in which to approximate the duration of a security. In the above example, note that

$$9.9 = 0.090 \times (1.1/0.01)$$

Later, we will use this estimation method to determine the duration of mortgage-related securities.

The value profile of the corporate bond in Table 11–1 is shown in Figure 11–1. It relates the value of the bond as a function of the market (discount) rate of interest. It is downward sloping throughout and has a convex shape. One characteristic of securities is their convexity, which refers to the extent to which the value profile in Figure 11–1 is more or less convex. The value of the security increases as the discount rate approaches zero. This is because the bond is noncallable; the issuer must make the remaining coupon payments as promised even if the market rate falls. A callable bond would not increase in value below a certain low interest rate. Its value profile would appear as the dashed line in Figure 11–1. When the market rate of interest falls sufficiently below the coupon rate, the company will call it and pay an amount equal or close to its face value. It will raise the funds necessary to call the bond by issuing new bonds at the lower market rate.

The principles of valuation, yield-to-maturity, and the sensitivity of prices to changes in interest rates can be very different for mortgage-related securities, which we consider next.

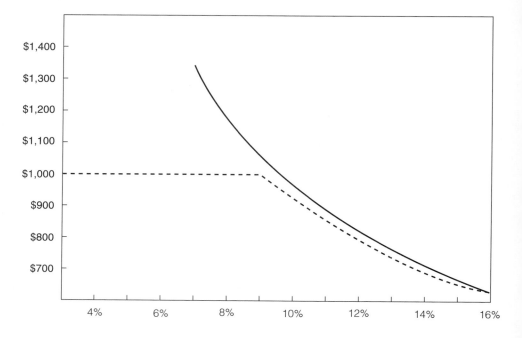

FIGURE 11–1

Value of Traditional Debt Security Coupon, 10%; Maturity, 19 Years

MORTGAGE-RELATED SECURITIES

The cash flows and valuation of mortgage-related securities differ from traditional debt securities of the type examined above. This is because the amount and timing of the cash flows depend upon changes in the level of interest rates. To see this, consider a pool of several hundred mortgages. In any one period (month), the cash flows from that pool will consist of three elements: (1) scheduled amortization of principal, (2) interest on the remaining principal, and (3) prepayments of a portion of the pool.

The first two elements are the standard principal and interest payments. For a standard fixed-rate, fixed-payment mortgage, the payment is constant, with a declining portion represented by interest and an accelerating portion as principal. The third element is any prepayment of one or more mortgages prior to the maturity. Most loans are prepaid prior to maturity. The average life of standard mortgages is from 9 to 15 years.

For a pool of mortgages (with no defaults), the following is true. First, the total amount of principal (both scheduled and prepayments) that will be paid from the pool will not depend upon changes in the interest rate. Changes in the interest rate may cause the principal payments to be delayed or accelerated, but the total amount paid will equal the initial principal in the pool. In other words, there is no question as to the amount to be received in the future, only to its timing. Second, the interest payments in any one month will depend on the amount of principal outstanding at the beginning of that month. Thus, if the principal payments are delayed, there will be more total interest payments coming from the pool. Conversely, if principal payments are accelerated by early prepayments, the total amount of interest payments will be reduced. For interest payments, there is uncertainty about both the amount and the timing of the payments.

Third, changes in the market rate of interest will affect the timing of prepayments. If interest rates remain unchanged, there is a "normal" rate of prepayment that results from homeowners selling their properties due to lifestyle changes. (Also, a default and foreclosure will result in a prepayment.) A change of occupation, a divorce, a decision by the homeowner to consume more or less housing than at present may lead to a prepayment of the existing loan. Beyond this normal rate, changes in interest rates will have an impact on prepayment rates. If interest rates rise, then more loans will have a coupon rate that is lower than the market rate. Prepayments of these low-rate loans will slow. Some homeowners will defer taking on a new job or a move to a new residence because they would face a higher house payment for the same amount of housing. Conversely, if rates fall, prepayments will accelerate. Even if the homeowner does not anticipate selling the residence, he will have an incentive to refinance his loan at a lower rate. By exercising his call option, his loan is prepaid. Thus, changes in the rate of interest will affect the amount and timing of the cash flows from a pool of mortgages and, in turn, the cash flows to the mortgage-related securities. We begin by reviewing the cash flows of a pass-through security.

Pass-throughs

As with all mortgage-related securities, the timing and amount of cash flows from a pool of mortgages backing a pass-through are crucial for valuation. The expected rate at which mortgages from a pool will prepay is critical to the valuation exercise. There are several models of expected prepayments that have been or are currently used to value pass-through securities.

Twelve-year Prepaid Life

At one time (1970s) the standard approach to valuing pass-throughs was to assume that the mortgages in the pool would all prepay at the end of 12 years, the so-called average life of mortgages. The 12-year average life was based on FHA data. It was soon discovered that this assumption led to misleading results. All pass-throughs do not prepay at the same rate. Changes in interest rates will cause some to prepay faster than others. Pools of mortgages with coupon rates above the market rate will prepay faster than those with coupons at the market rate. Pools with low-coupon mortgages will prepay more slowly. This method has been abandoned in favor of more sophisticated models.

Constant Prepayment Rate

One commonly used method is to assume that mortgages in a pool prepay at a constant rate. A pool's constant prepayment rate (CPR) for a given period is the percent of the mortgage principal in the pool at the beginning that prepays during the period. The beginning balance is computed net of scheduled amortization. For example, consider a pool with a monthly CPR of 1 percent (12 percent annually). If, at the beginning of the month, the principal in the pool is $1,000,000 and the scheduled amortization is $10,000, then the expected prepayment is $9900 ($1,000,000 − $10,000 × 0.01).

The effective annual CPR for this example is 11.36 percent. (Total prepayments for the year will be $113,600 (11.36% × $1,000,000), not 12 × $9.900 = $118,800.) The reason it is less than 12 percent is that the 1 percent prepayment rate is applied each month to a declining principal balance (sort of compounding in reverse). The assumed CPR for a given pool will depend on the coupon rate of the pool in relation to market rates.

FHA Experience

The FHA periodically publishes a schedule of the survivorship of FHA loans for each of the 30 years of their maturity. The schedule is based on the prepayment behavior of all FHA loans insured since 1957. An example is presented in Table 11–2. Note that 87.289 percent of all FHA loans originated since 1957 survived 5 years, and 82.38 percent survived 6 years. This tells us that 4.91 percent (87.289 − 82.38) of all FHA mortgages outstanding at the beginning of their sixth year were prepaid in that year. The prepayment rates can be used to estimate those on a pool of mortgages. Different models of prepayments may assume faster or slower attrition than the FHA experience. A rate-200 percent FHA indicates that a pool is expected to prepay twice as fast as the overall FHA experience, while a rate-50 percent FHA indicates a prepayment rate one-half that of the FHA experience.

The advantage of using the FHA experience is that it allows for a variation in the assumed prepayment rate by year. This reflects the fact that the probability of prepayment varies by year. The probability of prepayment is low in the initial years of a mortgage, rises and reaches a peak between 5 and 8 years, and falls thereafter. The disadvantage is that these rates are based on the

TABLE 11–2
FHA Mortality Table; Original Term, 30 Years

Year	Percent Existing at Beginning of Year	Period During Year	Year	Percent Existing at Beginning of Year	Prepaid During Year
1	1.00	0.00837	16	0.44062	0.03028
2	0.99163	0.03100	17	0.41034	0.03037
3	0.96063	0.04171	18	0.37997	0.03057
4	0.91892	0.04603	19	0.34940	0.03074
5	0.87289	0.04909	20	0.31866	0.03105
6	0.82380	0.04956	21	0.28761	0.02953
7	0.77424	0.04668	22	0.25808	0.02793
8	0.72756	0.04399	23	0.23015	0.02625
9	0.68357	0.04093	24	0.20390	0.02450
10	0.64264	0.03784	25	0.17940	0.02271
11	0.60480	0.03595	26	0.15669	0.02089
12	0.56885	0.03399	27	0.13580	0.01907
13	0.53486	0.03241	28	0.11673	0.01725
14	0.50245	0.03127	29	0.09948	0.02181
15	0.47118	0.03056	30	0.07767	0.07767

behavior of all FHA loans. If the FHA experiences were broken down by periods, radically different prepayment rates might be observed. Loans originated in a year of high interest rates (such as 1981) and followed by a drop in interest rates would prepay much faster in the early years. The reverse would be true for loans originated in a year of low rates (such as 1974) and followed by an increase.

Public Securities Association Model

The current industry standard is the **Public Securities Association Prepayment Rate (PSA)** model. It combines the information contained in the FHA experience tables with the simplicity of the CPR model. The PSA benchmark assumes that the annual CPR on a monthly basis is 0.2 percent in the first month and increases by 0.2 percent each month thereafter until month 30, at which time the CPR is 6 percent. The annual CPR remains at that level for the remaining 330 months. Multiples of the PSA benchmark are interpreted in terms of this base model. A 200 percent PSA assumes that the loans prepay at 0.4 percent in the first month, 0.8 percent the second month, and so forth, until they level off at 12 percent in month 30. Figure 11–2 shows the base PSA and two multiples.

Future cash flows are estimated by taking the scheduled principal and interest payments and adding the assumed PSA prepayment rate. Once the cash flows are so estimated, the value of the pass-through can be determined by use of the standard discounted cash flow model.

Econometric Prepayment Models

Many Wall Street firms as well as the secondary mortgage market agencies have developed econometric (statistical) models to predict prepayments of pools of mortgages for each month remaining for the pool. A number of variables that affect prepayments are included in the model: the age of the mortgages, the season of the year, current and projected interest rates relative to the coupon on the mortgages, geographical location of the properties that back the mortgages, and borrower characteristics such as age, income, and wealth. Such a model was developed by Merrill Lynch's Mortgage-Backed Securities Research Department and based on the prepayment rates on a portfolio of conventional loans held by Freddie Mac. The model explained 85 percent of the historical variation in prepayment rates. The level of interest rates is important, of course, because these determine the probability that mortgagors will exercise the prepayment option. Location also can be important because mortgages turn over more frequently in some parts of the country than in others. Also, seasonal patterns in home sales will translate into seasonal patterns of prepayment rates. Borrower characteristics may indicate the propensity to relocate.

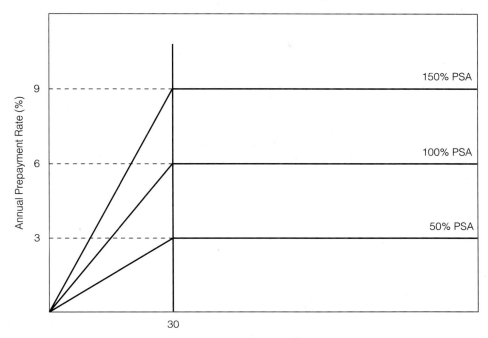

FIGURE 11-2

PSA and Multiples of PSA

Econometric models can be used to forecast the prepayment rate for each month in the future. The accuracy of any such models becomes diminished for more distant months. Also, the predicted prepayment rates may appear very unlike the PSA-model rates. But once the prepayment rates are determined, then the cash flows can be estimated and a value placed on the pool via standard discounted cash flow analysis. The results can be expressed in terms of a PSA prepayment rate by finding that PSA-type rate that yields the same value for the security.

Refinancing Models

Telerate Advanced Factor Service.   In May 1991 Telerate Mortgage Market Services introduced a market data base for the purpose of predicting prepayment activity. Their Advanced Factor Service (AFS) estimates prepayments based on data gathered from title search companies. When homeowners decide to prepay their existing mortgage, a title search is performed as part of the refinancing process. Thus, title search activity will precede the actual refinancing by one to several months. This information can be used, essentially, as an early warning of near future refinancings (prepayments).

Mortgage Bankers Association Weekly Mortgage Application Survey.   A similar data set is the weekly report issued by the Mortgage Bankers Association. The data are compiled from a survey of approximately 20 large national mortgage bankers. Data relating to the purpose of the loan are collected and of interest is the purchase or refinance decision. Changes in application volume are related to a baseline index date of March 16, 1990. Here, again, the data provide an early warning of near future refinancings.

Changes in Interest Rates and Prepayment Behavior

Many studies have demonstrated that one of the most important variables that affects the prepayment behavior of a mortgage pool is the relationship between current market rates and pool rates. Common sense would tell us that if the current rate is above the contract rate, borrowers will have little incentive to prepay. Moreover, regardless of the size of the positive differential, prepayments will occur at a uniformly slower pace, dictated by noneconomic factors such as job relocation, divorce, and so forth. When market rates fall below the contract rate, prepayments should accelerate until a sufficiently large negative differential is reached, at which point they should level off. Some have suggested that this behavior leads to a relationship characterized in Figure 11–3. Tests confirm that this is, in fact, the case. Navratil looked at the prepayment behavior of several hundred GNMA pools.[1] He found that the interest rate differential between the current market rate and that on a pool was the single most important determinant of prepayments and, furthermore, that the data fit the curve in Figure 11–3 very well.

As an example, for the average 12 percent pool in Navratil's study, the expected prepayment rate was 1.5 percent with no interest differential. It rose to 8.4 percent when the market rate fell 200 basis points below the pool, and to 30.9 percent for a 400-basis point differential. When the market rate was above the contract rate, there was little change in the prepayment rate. It fell to 1 percent for a 200-basis point differential. He also found that the elasticity of the change in the prepayment rate with respect to the interest rate differential was greatest for the 200 to 300 basis point negative differential. The duration of the mortgage pool was similarly affected. With no differential, the duration on the average 12 percent pool was 6.4 years. It fell dramatically to only 2.5 years for a 400-basis point negative differential but remained between 5 and 6 years for all positive differentials.

Green and Shoven analyzed the probability of a given mortgage prepaying as a function of changes in interest rates.[2] They looked at the prepayment behavior of nearly 4000 mortgages held by California savings and loans from 1975 through 1982. As market rates rose, the value (to the lender) of low-rate loans and the probability of their prepayment fell. Their average time to payoff was extended. They analyzed both loans with a due-on-sale feature and those without one. They found that a 10 percent reduction in value reduced the probability of prepayment by 35 percent for loans with a due-on-sale clause and by 63 percent for those that were assumable. The average time to payoff for a 10 percent mortgage was 5.83 years, if the market rate was also

FIGURE 11–3

Interest Rate Differential and Prepayment Rates

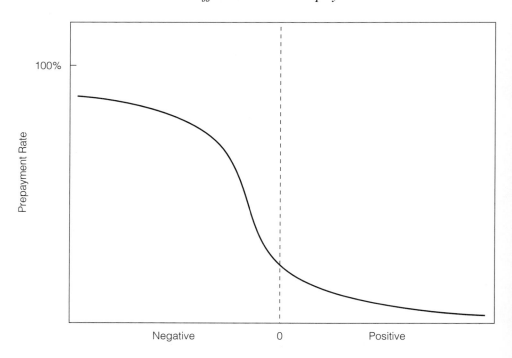

10 percent. It rose to 7.331 years if the market rate increased to 12 percent and the loan had a due-on-sale clause, and to 10.337 years if the mortgage was assumable. Milonas and Lacey found that both the interest rate differential and the shape of the term structure affected prepayment rates.[3] They found that the interest rate differential was the key to predicting prepayments, but they also discovered that expected future rates were important. Even if the current rate was above the contract rate (the prepayment option was out-of-the-money), they found there was a greater likelihood of increased prepayments if rates were expected to rise further. Instead of maximizing the value of the prepayment option, homeowners were maximizing their utility from relocating. They also found that prepayment behavior operated with a lag. As interest rates fell, prepayments rose—but with at least a three-month lag.

Next, we explore how the prepayment rate affects the cash flows, values, and yields on pass-through securities. Later, we analyze their effect on other mortgage-related securities.

Effect of Prepayments on the Cash Flows of Pass-throughs

The assumed rate of prepayments will have a significant impact on the timing of the cash flows from a pool of mortgages. In turn, it will affect the value of those cash flows. Consider the examples presented in Tables 11–3 and 11–4.

The pool of mortgages at issue consists of $106 million in fixed-rate, 30-year amortizing loans that carry a 10.25 percent coupon rate. It might be useful to consider the pool one big mortgage for the total amount of the pool. In Table 11–3, we assume that the prepayment rate is 0 percent PSA. This means that there are no prepayments at all. The table can be used as a comparison for models that assume a positive PSA prepayment rate. The annual payment necessary to amortize a $106 million fixed-rate mortgage is $11,479,564. As with this type of loan, the payment consists of interest and principal. The former portion falls and the latter rises through time.

If one were to discount the cash flows presented in Table 11–3 at the mortgage coupon rate (10.25 percent), the present value of all the payments would be, of course, $106 million. The present value of the interest portion would be $89,277,157, or 84 percent of the total present value of the cash flows. Since there are no prepayments at all, the total interest payments and their present value are larger than any model that includes positive prepayments.

The cash flows from this pool, assuming a 100 percent PSA, are shown in Table 11–4. In year one, scheduled principal and interest payments are the same as in the case of no prepayments. At the end of the first year, it is assumed that approximately 1.3 percent of the remaining

T A B L E   1 1 – 3
Cash Flows from Pool of Mortgages

Initial balance, $106,000,000; PSA 0%; coupon, 10.25%

Year	Balance End of Year	Principal	Interest	Prepayments	Total
0	$106,000,000	—	—	—	—
1	105,385,436	$ 614,564	$10,865,000	0	$11,479,564
2	104,707,878	677,557	10,802,007	0	11,479,564
3	103,960,871	747,007	10,732,558	0	11,479,564
4	103,137,296	823,575	10,655,989	0	11,479,564
5	102,229,304	907,992	10,571,573	0	11,479,564
.	.	.	.	.	.
.	.	.	.	.	.
.	.	.	.	.	.
.	.	.	.	.	.
.	.	.	.	.	.
29	10,412,303	9,444,266	2,035,298	0	11,479,564
30	0	10,412,303	1,067,261	0	11,479,564
Total		106,000,000	238,386,935	0	344,386,935
PV at 10.25%		16,722,843	89,277,157	0	106,000,000

TABLE 11-4

Cash Flows from Pool of Mortgages

Initial balance $106,000,000; PSA, 100%; coupon, 10.25%

Year	Balance End of Year	Principal	Interest	Prepayments	Total
0	$106,000,000	—	—	—	—
1	104,015,425	$ 614,564	$10,865,000	$1,370,011[a]	$12,849,575
2	99,523,055	668,749	10,661,581	3,823,620	15,153,950
3	93,135,241	710,017	10,201,113	5,677,797	16,588,928
4	86,860,047	737,815	9,546,362	5,537,378	15,821,555
5	80,935,662	764,691	8,903,155	5,159,695	14,827,541
.	.	.	.	.	.
.	.	.	.	.	.
.	.	.	.	.	.
.	.	.	.	.	.
.	.	.	.	.	.
29	1,870,495	1,804,751	388,935	119,245	2,312,931
30	0	1,870,493	191,725	0	2,062,218
Total		34,958,128	138,017,824	71,041,872	244,017,824
PV at 10.25%		8,399,418	66,083,742	31,516,840	106,000,000

[a](106,000,000 − 614,564) × 0.013

balance prepays. The beginning balance in year two is less than that in the case of no prepayments. As a result, the interest payments in year two will also be less. Total scheduled amortization and prepayments are $106 million ($34,958,128 + $71,041,872), but the timing of their receipt is accelerated. The present value of the cash flows remains $106 million but is now distributed differently between principal and interest. The present value of interest payments is only $66,083,742, or 62 percent of the total, mainly because the total amount of the interest payments is reduced. The present value of the principal payments is increased, not because that total is any different, but because principal payments are accelerated in timing. The earlier a cash flow is received, the greater will be its present value. Further increases in the PSA rate will lead to additional reductions in the present value of the interest payments relative to that of the principal payments. The relationship between the present values of the two components as a function of the PSA rate is shown in Figure 11–4.

Recall that the PSA model assumes that the prepayment rate on a pool of mortgages will rise through month 30 and then level off. This produces a "spike" in the third year of the cash flows. Cash flows under the PSA model will rise for 3 years and then decline. Larger PSA rates produce more pronounced "spikes" in the third year. The profiles of the cash flows of a pool of mortgages under various PSA assumptions are shown in Figure 11–5.

Discount and Premium Pass-throughs

The effect of the assumed prepayment rate is crucial to the valuation of pass-throughs that sell at a discount or premium. Debt obligations sell at a discount when the market rate is above the coupon rate, and at a premium when the rates are reversed. For pass-throughs, prepayments complicate their valuation. To see this, consider first traditional debt securities that sell at a discount. The appreciation in value from purchase to maturity is part (or all) of the yield. A debt obligation maturing in 2 years with a $1000 face value (and no coupon payments) will be priced at $826.44 to yield 10 percent. Over the 2-year period, the $173.56 appreciation represents the yield to the investor. But what would happen to the yield if, for some reason, the debt issuer were to prepay the face value 1 year after purchase? The $173.56 1-year gain on the investment would represent a yield of 21 percent. Conversely, a delay of the repayment of the principal would lower the yield. For discounted debt securities, accelerated prepayments increase the realized yield and delayed prepayments lower the yield. Investors that price pass-through securities on

FIGURE 11-4

Proportion of Total Present Value of Cash Flow of Principal and Interest

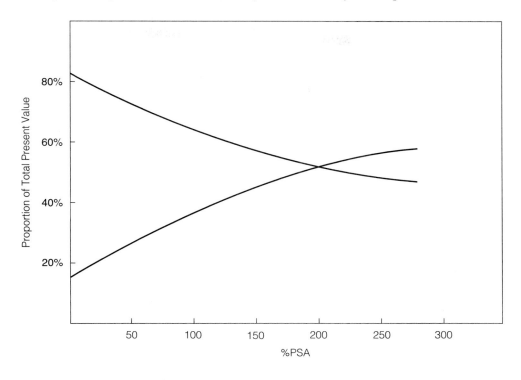

FIGURE 11-5

Cash Flows of GNMA 9 for Various PSA Rates ($100,000,000 pool)

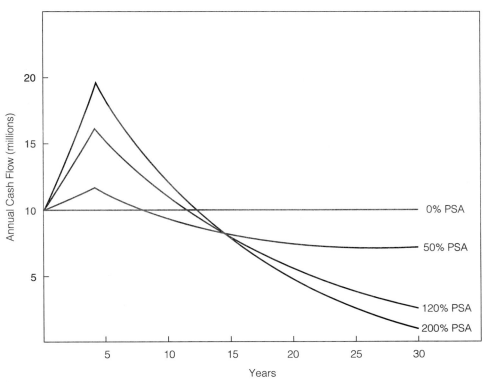

an expected rate of prepayment will realize yields that are different from expected if prepayments accelerate or slow. The reverse is true, of course, for premium pass-throughs. Here, the coupon on the mortgages is above the market yield, and investors benefit if the prepayments are delayed and suffer if they are accelerated.

Price and Yield Behavior of Pass-throughs

We can now analyze how the price and yield-to-maturity of pass-through securities behave in response to changes in interest rates. Their behavior is different from standard debt instruments because of their prepayment (call option) feature.

Pass-through Prices.   At any time, pass-throughs of several different coupons are trading in the market. A pass-through will have a coupon reflecting the level of mortgage rates when it was issued. Since interest rates have been cyclical over the last dozen years or so, presently available pass-throughs reflect a range of coupons. Figure 11–6 shows the prices on June 1, 1991, of seasoned GNMA and FNMA pass-throughs. On that date, the market rate on new mortgages was approximately 9 percent. Note that the price curves became flat above the 9 percent coupon level. This is called **price compression** and reflects the market perception of prepayment behavior for high coupon pass-throughs. The value of the high coupon is offset by the higher expected prepayments. Recall that accelerated prepayments reduce the yield on premium pass-throughs. The higher prepayments are expected on these pass-throughs because of the opportunity of mortgagors to call the loan and refinance it. Another way of viewing the price of premium pass-throughs is to realize that investors require a higher yield (lower price) to compensate for the fact that they are purchasing a callable debt instrument. Furthermore, the call option is "in the money" for premium pass-throughs.

For rates below 10 percent, the prices reflect the differences in coupons. This is so because there are no expectations of accelerated prepayments for the discounted pass-throughs.

FIGURE 11–6

Prices of GNMA and FNMA Pass-through; December 1990

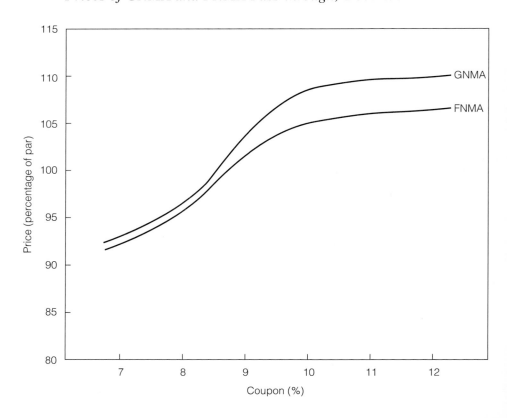

Changes in the market rate of interest will have two impacts on the value of pass-throughs. Both the discount rate and the assumed rate of prepayments will change. Figure 11–7 shows the projected price paths for a discounted and a premium GNMA pass-through (9 percent and 11 percent coupon, respectively, when the market rate is 10 percent). The shapes of the curves are different from one another and reflect the difference in the prepayment rates. The price of the GNMA 9 changes for either a decrease or increase in the market (discount) rate. It currently sells at a discount. If rates increase, prepayments are expected to slow. In this case, the discount rate rises and the prepayments slow. Both factors cause a decrease in price. If there is a moderate decline in rates, the price of the GNMA 9 will rise. The discount rate is lower and prepayments are expected to accelerate as rates drop. For large reductions in the interest rates, the value will continue to increase, but at a slower rate, because the large amount of the refinancing would have already occurred.

The shape of the price path of the GNMA 11 is somewhat different. It lies everywhere above that of the GNMA 9 because of the larger coupon. It is a premium security and its price will fall with an increase in rates for the same reasons as the GNMA 9. For a moderate decline in rates, the value will not change much, however. The increase in the value caused by the lower discount rate is offset by a reduction in value caused by the acceleration of prepayments. Recall that accelerated prepayments reduce the yield on a premium pass-through. Investors will require compensation in the form of a lower price. For a large reduction in the level of rates, the effect of the lower discount rate will dominate the prepayment behavior as, again, much of the prepayment activity would have occurred during a moderate decline in rates.

Pass-through Yields.   Figure 11–8 illustrates the effect of changes in the market rate of interest on the yield-to-maturities of the GNMA 9 and 11. First, consider an increase in rates. Prepayments for both pass-throughs will slow. A slower prepayment rate will reduce the yield on the discounted pass-through, as the principal is received later in the security's life. The slower prepayment rate raises the yield on the premium, however. The higher coupon rate is earned on a loan balance that does not contract as rapidly as ordinary. As interest rates fall, prepayment rates accelerate. This causes the yield on the GNMA 9 to rise and that on the GNMA 11 to drop.

FIGURE 11–7

Price Profile of GNMA 9 and 11

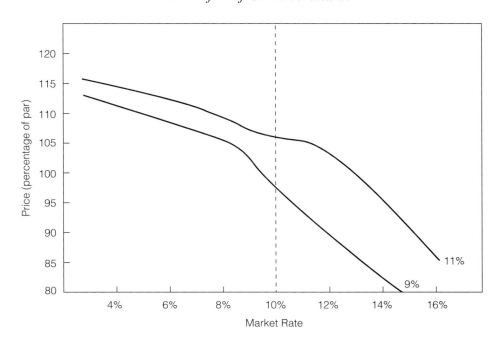

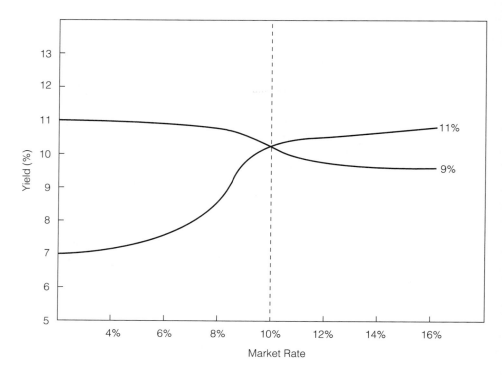

FIGURE 11–8

Projected Yield-to-Maturity, GNMA 9 and 11

TABLE 11–5

Calculation of Effective Duration of GNMA 11

	Interest Rate		
	9.75	*10.0*	*10.25*
Projected prepayment rate	230	200	180
Price at 200 PSA	105.25	104.25	103.16
Price at projected prepayment rate	104.80	104.25	103.46

The prepayment rate on the GNMA 11 will be faster than that of the GNMA 9 because the interest rate relative will be larger, making a refinancing more profitable for the mortgagor.

Because the yields of the two pass-throughs react differently for both increases and decreases in market rates, a good hedging strategy would be to purchase a balanced portfolio of both.

We saw above that, under some circumstances, there may not be a large change in the price of a pass-through as a result of a change in market rates. This was true, for example, for the premium GNMA 11 for moderate declines in interest rates. In that example, an increase in value due to the decline in the discount rate was offset by an acceleration in the prepayment rate. In effect, the duration of the security was shortened, thereby moderating the effect of the change in rates on price.

Effective Duration of Pass-throughs. The duration of pass-throughs is impossible to measure by calculating the amount and timing of future cash flows because they are affected by uncertain prepayments. Nonetheless, it is possible to determine the **effective** or **implied duration** by observing the price behavior of various pass-throughs in response to changes in interest rates. The example in Table 11–5 will clarify this. The market prices of a GNMA 11 are given for the base rate, 10 percent, and a change of the rate by 25 basis points in both directions. The price at the base rate ($104.25) is that necessary to produce an expected yield of 10 percent. If market rates rise by 25 basis points, the price of the pass-through will fall. The price will increase with a fall in rates. However, the expected prepayment rate also rises and falls with changes in the market interest rate. The change in the assumed prepayment rate has the effect of moderating the price changes as a result of changes in market rates.

The example shows two prices of the pass-through for a fall in market rates and two prices for an increase. In each case, one price is that required to produce the new yield, assuming the prepayment rate remains constant and does not change with the market rate. The other price is that necessary to produce the new yield, assuming the prepayment rate does change when the market rate changes, which is much more likely. Take, for example, an increase in the market rate by 25 basis points. This will produce a fall in the value of the security. If one assumes that the prepayment rate is not affected by the rise in the market rate, then the new price will be $103.16. But if it is assumed that the prepayment rate will slow, then the market price will fall but will still be higher, $103.46. The increase in value ($103.46 − $103.16) is the result of the slowing of the prepayment rate on a premium pass-through. Of course, the reverse argument can be used to demonstrate that when market rates fall, the increase in value will be moderated by the acceleration in prepayments.

The effective or implied duration of the security under each set of assumptions can be calculated with Equation 11–3. If this is done, it can be shown that the changes in the prepayment rates reduce the effective duration of pass-through securities. In other words, the change in the prices of pass-throughs as a result of changes in interest rates is not as dramatic as with conventional debt securities with the same duration. As an illustration, the duration calculated using the unadjusted price data is

$$D = \frac{104.25 - 103.16}{104.25} \times \frac{1.1025}{0.0025}$$

$$= \frac{1.09}{104.25} \times 441 = 4.61 \text{ years}$$

Using the adjusted price data the duration is

$$D = \frac{104.25 - 103.46}{104.25} \times \frac{1.1025}{0.0025}$$

$$= 0.007578 \times 441 = 3.34 \text{ years}$$

The uncertainty surrounding the prepayment rates on pools of mortgages complicates their valuation. The complication has led to the creation of other mortgage-related securities that are more easily priced by investors. Nonetheless, pass-throughs remain popular and provide returns from 100 to 200 basis points above those on other default-free securities such as Treasury obligations. As long as they exist, prepayment assumptions will play an intricate part of the pricing in the marketplace. The following three examples illustrate the importance of prepayment assumptions for one discounted and two premium pass-throughs.

■■ EXAMPLE ONE

In the late 1970s and early 1980s market interest rates were at high levels. Ginnie Mae pass-throughs originated a few years earlier were selling at substantial discounts. An investor's realized yield would depend, in part, upon the prepayment rate. Realized yields would be greater than expected if prepayment rates were faster than expected. As a result, there was a great deal of attention devoted to the identification of pools that were likely to have prepayment rates faster than the average. Some members of the Ginnie Mae Dealers Association claimed a specialization in identifying the "fast-pay" Ginnie Maes and promised superior returns to their clients who purchased them.[4] They were called "speed freaks" in the financial press. Their identification of the pools that would prepay at a fast rate was based primarily on the pools' prepayment histories to date, a rather naive model. Simply put, pools that had prepaid faster than the average were expected to continue that behavior. Interest in identifying the so-called "fast-pay" pools declined with the introduction of more sophisticated econometric models to estimate future prepayment rates. It was also soon realized that, historically, fast-pay pools had a tendency to slow their rate of prepayment. Needless to say, this led to undesirable investment results. ▮▮

EXAMPLE TWO

The second example concerns premium GNMAs. In March 1989, when mortgage rates were in the neighborhood of 10 percent, the FHA sent out several thousands of letters to homeowners who still had insured mortgages with a 15 percent coupon or higher. The FHA was concerned about the risk posed by the homeowners' possible inability to meet the payments on these high-rate mortgages. They offered a Streamline Refinance Plan (SRP), whereby homeowners could refinance their existing loan with lower-rate, FHA-insured loans with virtually no refinance costs. The moderate refinance costs could furthermore be included in the amount of the new loan. Basically, the homeowner could refinance the existing loan with no out-of-pocket funds and still reduce the monthly payment. The result, of course, would be a dramatic one-shot increase in the amount of prepayments of GNMA 15s and above. The marketplace realized this, and over the next several weeks the price of GNMA 15s fell, relative to other GNMAs, by about 200 basis points. Holders of GNMA 15s lost about $22 million in the value of their securities as a result of the unexpected acceleration in prepayments.[5] ▮▮

EXAMPLE THREE

Our third example continues with the SRP program. In mid-1990 the Office of the Inspector General of HUD announced that it was investigating certain scams associated with the SRP program. Apparently, several lenders were profiting from the program by offering to refinance high-rate loans, but only at a half-point or so below the contract rate and not at the market rate. These lenders would place newspaper ads that read "Lower Your FHA Mortgage with No Out-of-Pocket Costs and No Paper Work." With the market rate at about 10 percent, the lenders involved in the scam would offer the no-cost refinancing plan to those with, say, 13 percent loans. By offering the refinance at 12 percent, they could sell the new loans into Ginnie Mae pools that would sell for about 102 to 104 percent of par. The lenders would absorb the refinancing costs, which were less than the premium earned on the pool. Then a few months later, they would offer the same borrower an opportunity to refinance down again, but still at an above-market rate. The lender would insure a profit on the second and any subsequent refinancings that were above market. Losses were suffered by the pass-through security holders, who purchased their pass-throughs at a premium, only to have them prepaid shortly thereafter. On the first refinancing, the involved lenders would tell borrowers that only one refinancing rate was available at the time, but would give them a "Free Refinance Certificate" or a "Preferred Borrower Certificate" for the next refinancing. ▮▮

Senior/Subordinated Pass-throughs

In the previous chapter, we discussed the structure of a senior/subordinated pass-through. With this arrangement, a pool of mortgages is securitized into a senior pass-through with a principal balance somewhat less than the principal of the pool. The senior security has enhanced rights to the cash flows from the entire pool. The subordinated security, usually retained by the lender who sells the senior pass-through, bears all of the default risk. Since there is little or no default risk with the senior security, it will command a premium. The lender captures this premium as a reward for enhancing the credit of the senior by absorbing the entire default risk in the subordinated position. If the premium exceeds the present value of future default risks of the pool, the lender benefits. If, however, there is a severe incidence of default in the pool, the lender may receive a very low or negative return on the subordinated position.

    Figure 11–9 is an approximation that compares the yields on a whole mortgage pool with those on the subordinated position as a function of various foreclosure rates. For low foreclo-

FIGURE 11–9

*Yield Comparison of Whole Mortgage Pool and Subordinated Security;
Senior Security Sold to Yield 40 Basis Point Difference, GNMA 10*

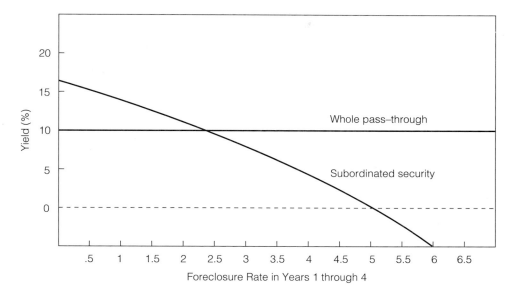

sure rates, the lender's return on the subordinated position is greater than that on the pool as a whole. This is so because the lender receives a premium on the sale of the senior position. This premium is considered a cash flow to the subordinated position. As long as the foreclosure rates in years two to four are less than 2 percent, the yield on the subordinated position will exceed that on the whole pool. Lenders who may be in a better position to judge the default risk of a portfolio of loans that they originate can obtain better yields by creating the senior/subordinated securities. This is, in effect, a form of leveraging. Superior expected yields are created on the subordinated position. The tradeoff is the increased risk of the subordinated position. With sufficient foreclosures, the yield on the subordinated position becomes less than that on the whole pool and can even become negative.

We next look at pricing considerations of mortgage-backed bonds.

Mortgage-backed Bonds

The cash flows of mortgage-backed bonds are designed to appear as traditional noncallable debt. They promise periodic coupon payments and a return of the face value at maturity. They are priced the same as traditional debt securities. The discount rate may reflect risk if the issue is not sufficiently overcollateralized, however. In addition, there is the issue of valuing the residual interest. Let's consider the simple example in Table 11–6. There, we see that $100 million in mortgage-backed bonds are collateralized by $110 million in conventional, fixed-rate, 30-year mortgages, each having a 10.5 percent coupon. The mortgage-backed bonds promise a 9.5 percent coupon payable semiannually for 20 years with repayment of face value at maturity. The cash flows are analyzed on an annual basis for simplicity. At first, we make the assumption that there are no prepayments, but that there is a default rate of 0.5 percent annually for 10 years, applied to the beginning pool balance less scheduled amortization. Cash inflows from the pool not delivered as interest to bond investors are placed in a sinking fund for the repayment of principal at maturity. The fund earns 8 percent. No payments are made to the residual (equity) position until after the bonds mature.

Two important observations can be made. First, the fund balance in year 20 in this example is $105,760,237, sufficient to make the maturity payment ($100 million). Second, the residual payments in the last column have a net present value of $224,138 when discounted at the

TABLE 11–6
Cash Flows of Mortgage-backed Bonds

Year	Pool Balance	Principal and Interest	Prepayment	Default	Cash Inflow	Payment to Bond Holders	Fund	Residual Payment
1	$110,000,000	$12,158,133	0	$546,959[a]	$12,158,133	$9,500,000	$ 2,658,133[b]	$ 0
2	108,844,908	12,097,342	0	540,881	12,097,342	9,500,000	5,468,126[c]	0
3	107,635,399	12,036,856	0	534,501	12,036,856	9,500,000	8,442,432	0
4	106,365,759	11,976,671	0	527,787	11,976,671	9,500,000	11,594,497	0
5	105,029,705	11,916,788	0	520,705	11,916,671	9,500,000	14,938,845	0
6	103,620,331	11,857,204	0	513,216	11,857,204	9,500,000	18,491,157	0
.	.	.	.	.	.	.	.	.
.	.	.	.	.	.	.	.	.
.	.	.	.	.	.	.	.	.
.	.	.	.	.	.	.	.	.
19	76,898,349	11,563,723	0	0	11,563,723	9,500,000	96,015,290	0
20	73,408,952	11,563,723	0	0	11,563,723	109,500,000	5,760,237	5,760,237
21	69,553,168	11,563,723	0	0	11,563,723	0	0	$11,563,723
.	.	.	.	.	.	.	.	.
30	10,464,908	11,563,723	0	0	11,653,723			11,563,723

Mortgage $110,000,000
Coupon 10.5%
Bonds $100,000,000
Coupon 9.5%
Maturity 20 years
Equity $10,000,000
%PSA 0
Default rate
First 10 years .005
NPV equity 224,138[d]
Fund balance
Year 20 105,760,237

[a]0.005 × ($110,000,000 − $608,133)
[b]12,158,133 − $9,500,000
[c]$2,658,133 × 1.08 + ($12,097,342 − $9,500,000)
[d]$10,224,138 − $10,000,000

rate of the pool, 10.5 percent. Taken together, this means that the securitization was successful. The overcollateralization was sufficient to make the promised payments to the bondholders, and the residual payments provided a return-on-equity to the agency issuing the bonds.

The firm issuing the bonds would like to keep the amount of equity (overcollateralization) as small as possible to maximize the return on investment. The bond buyers, on the other hand, would like to see the amount of equity as large as possible to guarantee payment of interest and principal. As noted above, one of the things that the rating agencies will examine closely in the rating process is the amount of overcollateralization. The rating agencies will determine the adequacy of the overcollateralization by considering the impact of several key variables on the balance in the sinking fund at maturity (year 20, in this example). Variables that affect the sinking fund balance include the prepayment rate on mortgages in the pool, the reinvestment rate on the sinking fund, the initial overcollateralization, and the default rate.

The effect of changes in these variables on the sinking fund balance at maturity is shown in Table 11–7. Each variable is changed in isolation from the others in order to show the effect on the fund balance. There are several interesting relationships.

First, a small increase in the initial amount of overcollateralization has a magnified impact on the terminal fund balance. An increase in initial equity of $2.5 million (from $110 million) raises the sinking fund balance in year 20 by $12,284,070. This is due to the reinvestment of a larger volume of cash flowing into the sinking fund. Second, even a slight increase in the default rate has a dramatic impact on the sinking fund balance. An increase to 0.007 percent for the first 10 years is sufficient to drop the fund balance below that necessary to redeem the bonds. Not only is the value of the defaulted mortgages lost, but so are the principal and interest payments and reinvested funds. Third, an increase in the yield on the sinking fund has a positive effect on the fund balance, but not as dramatically as one might think. Finally, the fund balance will rise with increases in the PSA prepayment rate, reach a maximum, and then fall. For small levels of the prepayment rate, more cash flows are available to be placed in the sinking fund prior to year 20. That is, some payments from the mortgage pool that would have been paid subsequent to the maturity date of the bonds are paid prior to that date. This increases the balance of the fund at maturity. But if the prepayment rate is too great in the early years of the pool's life, there will be a reverse effect. The prepayments are made into the pool that is earning a rate of return generally less than that on either the mortgages or the bonds. Thus, excessive prepayment rates adversely affect the sinking fund balance at maturity, because principal is taken from a mortgage pool earning 10.5 percent and placed in a fund earning 8 percent.

Some factors may interact in their effect on the sinking fund balance. If market interest rates fall, prepayments will accelerate. Furthermore, the excess payments are placed in a sinking fund for which the reinvestment rate also has fallen. In this example, if the interest rate earned on the fund balance drops to 7.5 percent and the prepayment rate rises to 10 percent in the first year, the fund balance in year 20 will be only $94,202,239.

These considerations point out the need for sufficient overcollateralization. Rating agencies will consider some worst-case scenarios when determining the minimum acceptable level for overcollateralization. If their overcollateralization is insufficient, the bonds will receive a low rating and not be available for investment by a wide class of regulated investors. To obtain a high

TABLE 11–7
Year 20 Fund Balance for MBB

Initial Mortgage Pool	Fund Balance	Default Rate	Fund Balance	Yield on Fund	Fund Balance	PSA Prepayment Rate Fund (year one)	Balance
$110,000,000	$105,760,237	0.005	$105,760,237	0.08	$105,760,237	0	$105,760,237
112,500,000	118,044,303	0.006	102,651,606	0.08125	107,295,582	0.05	126,269,237
115,000,000	130,328,368	0.007	99,565,138	0.0825	108,855,597	0.075	122,217,256
117,500,000	142,612,434	0.008	96,500,677	0.08375	110,440,682	0.10	117,341,525
120,000,000	154,896,000	0.009	93,458,067	0.085	112,051,241	0.125	113,015,338
125,000,000	179,464,632	0.01	90,437,154	0.08675	113,687,688	0.15	109,482,052

rating, the issuer will have to provide more collateralization or provide other forms of credit enhancement, such as pool insurance or insurance on the individual loans. The rating on the bonds (and the current level of market rates) will determine the discount rate for valuing the mortgage-backed bonds. If the rating is adequate and the discount rate equals the coupon rate, the bonds will sell at par when issued. A subsequent change in market rates or a change in their rating will affect the discount rate and the value of the bonds in the same manner as in Table 11–1.

Collateralized Mortgage Obligations

The cash flows from a pool of mortgages to the various tranches and residual class of a collateralized mortgage obligation (CMO) can be complicated. We continue with the example discussed in the previous chapter. For convenience, the structure of the CMO is repeated in Table 11–8. Before you analyze the cash flows, notice some relevant characteristics of this CMO. First, the coupon yield on the mortgages is 10.25 percent. This is greater than the coupon yield on the first two tranches, which make up the majority (60 percent) of the total CMO issue. Additionally, the CMO is overcollateralized by $6 million. Thus, assuming no default risk, the cash flows from the mortgage pool will be sufficient to meet the payments on the CMO. Recall that any prepayments from the mortgage pool are passed along to the bondholders; there is no sinking fund that will have the potential of earning less than the coupon rate on the bonds. In other words, the CMO issuer faces no interest rate or reinvestment risk. The longest maturity tranche does have a higher yield than the shorter maturity tranches and the yield on the mortgage pool. But it has a small outstanding principal.

With this in mind, let's look at the cash flows from the mortgage pool to the security holders and the residual class. One possible scenario is presented in Tables 11–9 through 11–12.

Column 6 of Table 11–9 shows the total cash flows from the pool for each year of its 30-year life. The total cash flows are the total of the scheduled principal and interest and the prepayments. Prepayments are based on the 100 percent PSA model, which implies a first-year rate of approximately 1.3 percent of the pool balance after scheduled amortization.[6] The last column in this table shows the remaining principal owed to the security holders. The amount for the first year is the original principal less scheduled amortization and prepayment from the pool ($100,000,000 − $614,564 − $1,370,011). All principal reductions from the pool are passed through to security holders.

Next, Table 11–10 shows the payments to the first two classes of securities. Bondholders for Tranche A receive all principal payments from the pool plus the deferred interest from the Z Tranche bondholders. Skipping down to Table 11–11, you will notice that in the first year the accrued interest for this class is $1,575,000. This amount is added to the principal prepayments ($1,370,011) and scheduled amortization ($614,564) from the pool, and the total ($3,559,575) is paid to the Tranche A bondholders as a reduction in their principal. These bondholders also receive their 9.25 percent coupon payments of $2,775,000, for a total of $6,334,575. The B and C Tranche bondholders only receive coupon payments ($2,850,000 and $2,500,000, respectively). Total cash flows to all bondholders equal $11,684,575. Since there is $12,849,575 available from the pool, the difference ($1,165,000) goes to the residual (equity) holders.

This process continues year-by-year until year five. In that year, the total cash available from the pool ($14,827,541) is more than sufficient to pay off the remaining principal and ac-

TABLE 11–8
Structure of CMO Example

Pool balance; $106,000,000; coupon rate, 10.25%; maturity; 30 years

CMO Tranches	Coupon	Maturity	Amount
Tranche A	9.25	5–9 years	$30,000,000
Tranche B	9.50	9–14 years	30,000,000
Tranche C	10.00	12–17 years	25,000,000
Tranche Z	10.50	26–30 years	15,000,000

crued interest for the A Tranche bonds. The excess principal payment from the pool in this year is next applied to the principal of the B Tranche. Coupon payments for the C Tranche bonds are made and deferral of the interest on the Z Tranche continues. By now, the total owed to the Z Tranche bondholders is $24,711,701. The B Tranche bondholders are paid off by year nine, and the C Tranche bondholders by year twelve. After year 12, the accrued interest is paid each year along with principal reductions from the pool. Because the pool's balance is still sizable in relationship to that of the Z Tranche ($47.5 million versus $41.5 million), there will be some payments left over for the residual tranche. After the Z Tranche is paid off in year 26, all remaining pool payments accrue to the residual class.

The final table, Table 11–12, shows the cash flows accruing to the residual class beginning with the $6 million investment. The internal rate-of-return and the net present value of the cash flows also are given.

Because CMOs are structured differently than pass-throughs, prepayment behavior affects their pricing and yield behavior in a different fashion. The price and yields on the shorter-term classes will not vary in response to prepayments as much as with pass-throughs. It is this characteristic which makes CMOs appealing to some investors. The importance of the prepayment

TABLE 11–9

Cash Flows from Mortgage Pool

Initial Balance, $106,000,000; Coupon Rate, 10.25%; Maturity, 30 Years; PSA, 100%

Year	(1) Pool Balance End of Year	2=(3)+(4) Scheduled Principal and Interest	(3) Amortization	(4) Interest	(5) Prepayments	6=(2)+(5) Total Available For Distribution	(7) Amount Owed To Security Holders
0	$106,000,000						$100,000,000
1	104,015,425	$11,479,564	$ 614,564	$10,865,000	$1,370,011[a]	$12,849,575[b]	98,015,425[c]
2	99,523,055	11,330,330	668,749	10,661,581	3,823,620	15,153,950	93,523,055[d]
3	93,135,241	10,911,131	710,017	10,201,113	5,677,797	16,588,928	87,135,241
4	86,860,048	10,284,177	737,815	9,546,362	5,537,378	15,821,555	80,860,048
5	80,935,662	9,667,846	764,691	8,903,155	5,159,695	14,827,541	74,935,662
6	75,340,138	9,088,452	792,547	8,295,905	4,802,977	13,891,429	69,340,138
7	70,052,814	8,543,781	821,417	7,722,364	4,465,907	13,009,688	64,052,814
8	65,054,231	8,031,753	851,339	7,180,413	4,147,244	12,178,997	59,054,231
9	60,326,059	7,550,410	882,351	6,668,059	3,845,821	11,396,230	54,326,059
10	55,851,031	7,097,914	914,492	6,183,421	3,560,535	10,658,449	49,851,031
11	51,612,876	6,672,536	947,805	5,724,731	3,290,350	9,962,886	45,612,876
12	47,596,257	6,272,651	982,331	5,290,320	3,034,289	9,306,939	41,596,257
13	43,786,714	5,896,731	1,018,114	4,878,616	2,791,428	8,688,159	37,786,714
14	40,170,614	5,543,340	1,055,201	4,488,138	2,560,900	8,104,239	34,170,614
15	36,735,091	5,211,127	1,093,639	4,117,488	2,341,883	7,553,010	30,735,091
16	33,468,009	4,898,824	1,133,477	3,765,347	2,133,605	7,032,429	27,468,009
17	30,357,908	4,605,238	1,174,767	3,430,471	1,935,334	6,540,572	24,357,908
18	27,393,967	4,329,246	1,217,560	3,111,686	1,746,381	6,075,627	21,393,967
19	24,565,960	4,069,794	1,261,913	2,807,882	1,566,094	5,635,888	18,565,960
20	21,864,223	3,825,891	1,307,880	2,518,011	1,393,857	5,219,748	15,864,223
21	19,279,614	3,596,606	1,355,523	2,241,083	1,229,086	4,825,692	13,279,614
22	16,803,481	3,381,061	1,404,901	1,976,160	1,071,232	4,452,293	10,803,481
23	14,427,634	3,178,434	1,456,077	1,722,357	919,770	4,098,204	8,427,634
24	12,144,309	2,987,951	1,509,118	1,478,833	774,207	3,762,157	6,144,309
25	9,946,146	2,808,883	1,564,091	1,244,792	634,072	3,442,955	3,946,146
26	7,826,158	2,640,546	1,621,066	1,019,480	498,922	3,139,468	1,826,158
27	5,777,708	2,482,298	1,680,117	802,181	368,332	2,850,631	0
28	3,794,488	2,333,534	1,741,319	592,215	241,901	2,575,435	0
29	1,870,493	2,193,686	1,804,751	388,935	119,245	2,312,931	0
30	0	2,062,218	1,870,493	191,725	0	2,062,218	0

[a]($106,000,000 − $614,564) × 0.013
[b]$11,479,564 + $1,370,011
[c]$100,000,000 − $614,564 − $1,370,011
[d]$98,015,425 − $668,749 − $3,823,620

TABLE 11–10
Payments to Tranche A and B Bond Holders

	Tranche A				Tranche B			
Year	(1) Principal Outstanding	(2) Reduction in Principal from Pool and Tranche Z	(3) Coupon	(4) Total 5 213	(5) Principal Outstanding	(6) Reduction in Principal from Pool and Tranche Z	(7) Coupon	(8) Total
0	$30,000,000				$30,000,000			
1	26,440,425[a]	$3,559,575[b]	$2,775,000[c]	$6,334,575	30,000,000	0	$2,850,000	$2,850,000
2	20,207,680	6,232,744	2,445,739	8,678,484	30,000,000	0	2,850,000	2,850,000
3	11,896,751	8,310,929	1,869,210	10,180,139	30,000,000	0	2,850,000	2,850,000
4	3,496,517	8,400,234	1,100,450	9,500,683	30,000,000	0	2,850,000	2,850,000
5	0	3,496,517	323,428	3,819,945	25,223,961	$4,776,039[d]	2,850,000	7,626,039
6					17,033,708	8,190,252	2,396,276	10,586,529
7					8,879,209	8,154,499	1,618,202	9,772,702
8					712,397	8,166,812	843,525	9,010,337
9					0	712,397	67,678	780,075

[a] $30,000,000 − $3,559,575
[b] 614,564 + 1,370,011 (Table 11–9) + 1,575,000 (Column 6, Table 11–11)
[c] 30,000,000 × .0925
[d] 764,691 + 5,159,695 (Table 11–9) + 2,348,171 (Column 6, Table 11–11) − 3,496,517 (Payoff of Tranche A)

TABLE 11-11
Payment to Tranche C and Z Bond Holder

| | Tranche C | | | | Tranche Z | | | | | |
| | (1) | (2) | (3) | (4) | (5) | (6) | (7) | | | |
Year	Principal Outstanding	Reduction in Principal from Pool and Tranche Z	Coupon	Total	Principal Outstanding	Accrued Interest	Accumulated Accrued Interest	Prepayment	Interest	Total
0	$25,000,000				$15,000,000	$1,575,000	$1,575,000			
1	25,000,000	0	$2,500,000	$2,500,000	16,575,000	1,740,375	3,315,375	0	0	0
2	25,000,000	0	2,500,000	2,500,000	18,315,375	1,923,114	5,238,489	0	0	0
3	25,000,000	0	2,500,000	2,500,000	20,238,489	2,125,041	7,363,531	0	0	0
4	25,000,000	0	2,500,000	2,500,000	22,363,531	2,348,171	9,711,701	0	0	0
5	25,000,000	0	2,500,000	2,500,000	24,711,701	2,594,729	12,306,430	0	0	0
6	25,000,000	0	2,500,000	2,500,000	27,306,430	2,867,175	15,173,605	0	0	0
7	25,000,000	0	2,500,000	2,500,000	30,173,605	3,168,229	18,341,834	0	0	0
8	25,000,000	0	2,500,000	2,500,000	33,341,834	3,500,893	21,842,726	0	0	0
9	17,483,333	$7,516,667	2,500,000	10,016,667	36,842,726	3,868,486	25,711,213	0	0	0
10	9,139,819	8,343,514	1,748,333	10,091,847	40,711,213	4,274,677	29,985,890	0	0	0
11	626,986	8,512,833	913,982	9,426,814	44,985,890	4,723,518	26,596,257	0	0	0
12	0	626,986	62,699	689,685	41,596,257	4,723,518	22,786,714	$3,389,633	$4,723,518	$8,113,152
13					37,786,714	4,367,607	19,170,614	3,809,542	4,367,607	8,177,149
14					34,170,614	3,967,605	15,735,091	3,616,101	3,967,605	7,583,706
15					30,735,091	3,587,914	12,468,009	3,435,522	3,587,914	7,023,437
16					27,468,009	3,227,185	9,357,908	3,267,082	3,227,185	6,494,267
17					24,357,908	2,884,141	6,393,967	3,110,101	2,884,141	5,994,242
18					21,393,967	2,557,580	3,565,960	2,963,941	2,557,580	5,521,522
19					18,565,960	2,246,367	864,223	2,828,007	2,246,367	5,074,373
20					15,864,223	1,949,426	(1,720,386)	2,701,737	1,949,426	4,651,163
21					13,279,614	1,665,743	(4,196,519)	2,584,609	1,665,743	4,250,353
22					10,803,481	1,394,359	(6,572,366)	2,476,132	1,394,359	3,870,492
23					8,427,634	1,134,366	(8,855,691)	2,375,847	1,134,366	3,510,213
24					6,144,309	884,902	(11,053,854)	2,283,325	884,902	3,168,226
25					3,946,146	645,152	(13,173,842)	2,198,163	645,152	2,843,316
26					1,826,158	414,345	(15,000,000)	2,119,988	414,345	2,534,334
27					0	191,747		1,826,158	191,747	2,017,904

TABLE 11–12

Residential Cash Flows to Equity

IRR, 13.89%; net present value at 13%, $325,940

Year	Cash Flow
0	$(6,000,000)
1	1,165,000[a]
2	1,125,467
3	1,058,788
4	970,871
5	881,556
6	804,900
7	736,987
8	668,660
9	599,488
10	566,602
11	536,072
12	504,103
13	511,009
14	520,533
15	529,573
16	538,162
17	546,330
18	554,105
19	561,515
20	568,585
21	575,339
22	581,801
23	587,991
24	593,931
25	599,639
26	605,135
27	832,727
28	2,575,435
29	2,312,931
30	2,062,218

[a]12,849,575 (Column 6, Table 11–9) − 6,334,575 (Column 4, Table 11–11) − 2,850,000 (Column 8, Table 11–10) − 2,500,000 (Column 4, Table 11–11)

behavior on the effect of yields on the various tranches is greater for bonds sold at a discount or premium. Recall, that for a discounted security, an acceleration in prepayments increases the yield and a delay reduces the yield. The opposite is true for securities sold at a premium.

Assume that the market initially employs a discount rate different from the coupon rate on the securities and prices them under a 100 percent PSA model. In this case, the market assumes that the cash flows displayed in Tables 11–10 and 11–11 will occur. Table 11–13 shows the effect of changes in the prepayment rate on yields.

For example, assume that investors initially employ a 10.25 discount rate to value the cash flows of Tranche A under the 100 percent PSA model. Since the coupon rate is 9.25 percent, the issue will sell at a discount. The present value for the cash flows of Tranche A shown in Table 11–13 is $29,257,585. Given this price for the security at issue, the actual yield will depend on the realized prepayment behavior of the pool. The yield will be as low as 9.87 percent for 0 percent PSA prepayments and as high as 10.92 for 500 percent PSA prepayment rates.

If the Tranche A cash flows are initially discounted at 8.25 percent, the issue will command a premium ($30,772,244). Slower realized prepayment rates will increase the actual yield, and accelerated prepayment rates will lower the yield. The changes in the yield for the discounted and premium cases are comparable for this tranche. The example for the Tranche A securities is repeated for the other tranches. Several things should be noted. First, for the shorter tranches, there is little change in the yield as prepayment behavior changes. The change in the yield for

TABLE 11–13
Prepayment Rates and Yield Behavior; CMO Tranches and Residual Class

Initial Discount Rate and Price		PSA Rate					
		0%	50%	100%	150%	200%	500%
Tranche A:							
Coupon, 9.25%;	0.1025						
Principal, $30,000,000	$29,257,585	0.0987	0.1009	0.1025	0.1038	0.1049	0.1092
	0.0825						
	$30,772,244	0.0863	0.0841	0.0825	0.0812	0.0801	0.0798
Tranche B:							
Coupon, 9.50%;	0.105						
Principal, $30,000,000	$28,611,057	0.1019	0.1034	0.105	0.1064	0.1077	0.1132
	0.085						
	$31,482,680	0.0881	0.085	0.0835	0.0823	0.0823	0.0768
Tranche C:							
Coupon, 10.00%;	0.11						
Principal, $25,000,000	$24,159,905	0.1081	0.1092	0.11	0.1110	0.1121	0.1179
	0.09						
	$26,610,312	0.092	0.091	0.09	0.0889	0.0878	0.0821
Tranche Z:							
Coupon, 10.50%;	0.115						
Principal, $15,000,000	$16,928,790	0.1069	0.1117	0.115	0.1166	0.1184	0.1291
	0.095						
	$17,373,272	0.0919	0.0944	0.095	0.0934	0.0916	0.081
Residual Class							
Investment, $6,000,000		0.158	0.142	0.1389	0.1348	0.1322	0.1302

the longer-maturity Tranche Z is more pronounced, however. This is expected, since changes in prepayments will have a greater effect on the actual maturity (duration) of this class. Second, since the price paid for the residual is the amount of the equity investment ($6 million), we report only the internal rate-of-return (yield-to-maturity) for this class as prepayment behavior is modified. The effect of prepayments is greatest for the residual. Figure 11–10 depicts the relationship between yields and prepayment behavior for a hypothetical CMO (other than the example used here). Here, you can see how prepayment behavior affects the yields on the various tranches of a CMO.

We also can demonstrate the effect on the price of the various tranches in the simple case where each tranche has the same coupon rate and it is below the market rate (so that the securities sell at a discount when initially issued). Figure 11–11 shows that the value of each later-maturity tranche is progressively lower, as would be expected. Also, all values increase with expectations of accelerated prepayments. For zero prepayments, the values converge. They also draw near in value for very fast prepayments because their values become close to the remaining balance.

Interest-only and Principal-only Strips

One interesting way in which the cash flows from a mortgage pool have been rearranged has been to **strip** off the rights to receive the principal payments and the interest payments from the mortgages. An investor who purchases the **principal-only (PO) strip** will have the right to receive all the principal payments whenever they are received. The same is true for the **interest-only (IO) strip.** The total amount of the principal payments will equal the initial pool balance. Because prepayments are unpredictable, the exact timing of the PO payments will not be known. If prepayments accelerate, more of the principal will be returned sooner than later. The total amount of interest payments will not be known. Interest payments are made each period on the basis of the principal outstanding in that period. Here, accelerated prepayments reduce the principal outstanding and, therefore, the interest payments for all remaining periods. Thus, accelerated payments may be advantageous for the PO investor and disadvantageous for the IO investor.

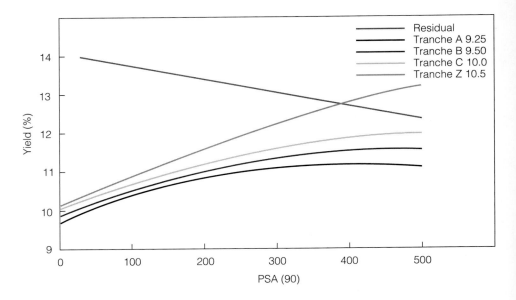

FIGURE 11–10

Yield-to-Maturity for CMO Tranches (discounted)

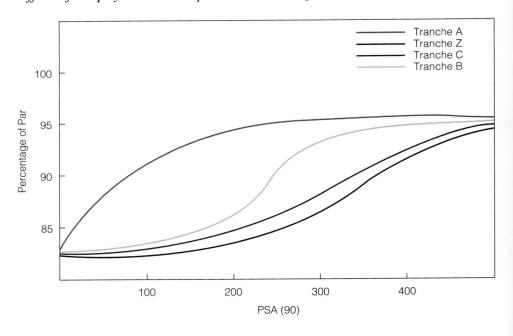

FIGURE 11–11

Effect of Prepayment Assumptions on Value of Discounted CMO Tranches

The role of market interest rates in the value of the POs and IOs is interesting. Changes in interest rates will have two impacts on each of these strips. First, a move in interest rates changes the discount rate used to value all securities. Second, a move in rates alters the prepayment behavior of mortgage pools and, therefore, the amount and timing of the cash flows of the POs and IOs. Thus, for the strips, we have

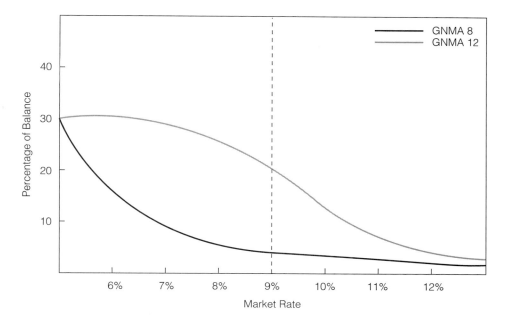

FIGURE 11–12

Annual Prepayment Assumptions as a Percent of Outstanding Balance, GNMA 8 and 12

PO:	interest rate ↑	discount rate ↑	value ↓
	interest rate ↑	prepayments ↓	value ↓
	net effect		value ↓
IO:	interest rate ↑	discount rate ↑	value ↓
	interest rate ↑	prepayments ↓	value ↑
	net effect		value ↑

To understand how changes in interest rates affect the cash flows and values of the strips, first refer back to Figure 11–3, which shows the prepayment rates on a mortgage pool as a function of the market rate of interest. The figure shows that prepayments change little as rates rise but accelerate sharply as they fall until they reach a sufficiently low market rate, at which point they level off again. We reproduce this curve in Figure 11–12 for two GNMAs, one with an 8 percent coupon and one with a 12 percent coupon, and assuming that the current market rate is 9 percent. Note the inflection points (the point at which the curves become flat) in the two curves. Those points occur approximately where the market rate would equal the coupon rate for each pool. At the base market rate of 9 percent, the prepayment rate on the 12 percent pool is significantly greater than that on the 8 percent pool, as would be expected. If rates rise, there is little change in the prepayment rate on the 8 percent pool because the prepayment option, which is already "out-of-the-money" for this pool, becomes even more so. Also, as rates rise, the call option on the 12 percent pool, which is "in-the-money," becomes less valuable and eventually becomes "out-of-the-money." Thus, prepayments for this pool drop dramatically as the market rate rises. The important thing to note is that the inflection point in each curve occurs where the market rate would equal the coupon rate. With this in mind, we can turn to a valuation of the IOs and POs.

Figure 11–13 shows the value of a GNMA 8 and its component IO and PO for various market interest rates. When the market rate equals the coupon rate, the pass-through is valued at or near par. The actual value will depend upon investors' expectation of future interest rates and the expected volatility of interest rates. If investors expect high volatility in interest rates, this will increase the value of the call option, raise the required yield, and result in a lower price. Here, we assume the rates are not expected to change and that there is low volatility.

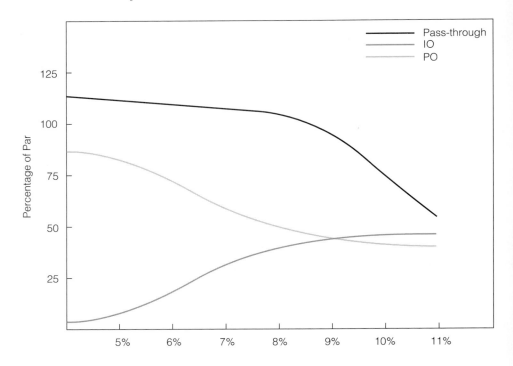

FIGURE 11–13

Value of GNMA 8, IO, and PO; Various Market Rates

The value of the pass-through is the sum of the component IO and PO. The shape of the value profiles can be explained as follows. If interest rates rise above the coupon rate, prepayments will slow. The effect of the increased rate and the slowing of the prepayments will combine to reduce the value of the PO. The increase in the market rate raises the discount rate used to value the PO cash flows. At the same time, the slowing of the prepayments will push the PO cash flows (unaltered in total amount) further back in time. The same is not true of the IO. Although there is an increase in the discount rate, the total amount of interest payments to be received is augmented. These two effects tend to cancel each other, and there is little change in the value of the IO for rising market rates. The sum of the components, the value of the pass-through, declines as the effect on the value of the PO outweighs that on the IO. When market rates decline, there is little change in the value of the pass-through.

For a sufficiently large drop in rates, prepayment of much of the pool becomes likely, so that it is valued at or near par. The values of the two strips nearly mirror each other. The decline in the market rate makes prepayments accelerate and substantially reduces the total cash flows expected on the IO. The cash flows on the PO are again unaltered but now accelerated. The combined effect of a reduction in the discount rate and the expectation that more of the cash flows will be received sooner rather than later raises the value of the PO. For very low rates, the prepayment rate is so high that the value of the PO approaches that of the pass-through and the value of the IO approaches zero.

The shapes of the value profiles for the IO and PO will not be the same for all pass-throughs. Figure 11–14 shows the profiles for a GNMA 12, a premium GNMA. For an increase in the market rate, the value of the IO increases dramatically, as the "in-the-money" call option approaches the "out-of-the-money" range (12 percent). The rise in the value of the IO is matched by a decline in the value of the PO, again for the same reason—the fall in the value of the call option. Since the base market rate is 3 percentage points below the coupon, prepayment behavior is not expected to change dramatically for further reduction in the market rate. This, in turn, leads to little change in either strip or the pass-through itself.

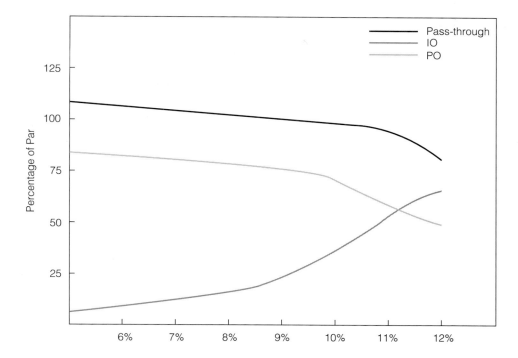

FIGURE 11–14

Value of GNMA 12, IO, and PO; Various Market Rates

As opposed to traditional debt securities, the value of the IO strip moves in the same direction as market interest rates. This means that an IO strip has **negative duration.** This does not mean that the weighted average life of the cash flows is negative. That does not appear to be sensible. What it means is that the value of the IO strip will not decline with a rise in rates, as a traditional debt security will. This makes the IO strip a useful security to hedge interest rate risk. For a lender or other institutional investor with traditional debt securities, the addition of IO strips will hedge the return on the portfolio. If rates rise, a decline in the market value of the traditional debt securities will be partially offset by a rise in the value of the IO strip. The curves in Figures 11–13 and 11–14 indicate that the value of the IO strip is most sensitive to changes in the market rate when this rate is between 100 and 300 basis points below the coupon on the pool. Thus, investors who desire to obtain the hedging benefits of the IO strip should purchase strips of pass-throughs 100 to 300 points above the market rate.

Floaters and Inverse Floaters

Some investors in mortgage-backed securities may have a need for bonds with a rate of interest that moves with the market rate. Financial institutions, for example, have short-term liabilities (savings deposits) with interest rates that move with the market. They thus have a need to invest in assets with rates that match those on their liabilities. **Floaters** are classes of a CMO that have a rate that moves with the market. They operate just like an adjustable-rate mortgage would. A floater can be created out of a particular tranche of a CMO while the remaining tranches have the more typical bond-like payments described above. The interest payment on the floater is usually pegged to a short-term interest rate such as the monthly London Interbank Offered Rate. This rate, called the **LIBOR,** is a short-term rate which European banks charge one another for short-term borrowing. It is similar to the federal Funds Rate in the United States. The rate on a floater will be set at a certain number of basis points over the LIBOR rate (similar to a margin on an ARM).

One of the problems with creating a floater from a CMO tranche lies in the possibility that market rates may rise significantly above the rate on the underlying mortgage pool. If the pool of mortgages is receiving an 8 percent coupon and the rate on the floater rises above this rate there will be a loss on this tranche. To solve this problem an inverse floater is created out of the same tranche. An **inverse floater** is a bond for which the interest rate moves in the opposite direction to market rates. The rate on the inverse floater will move opposite to the rate on the floater. The formula for determining the rate on the inverse floater will be such as to insure that the total interest payment from the tranche will be constant regardless of the movement of interest rates.

As an example, assume that a $100,000,000 tranche supported by 8 percent coupon mortgages is structured to create floaters and inverse floaters with a total interest payment of 7.5 percent. Next, assume that the floater portion of the tranche is backed by 75 percent of the tranche or $75,000,000 and the inverse floater is supported by the remainder. The rate on the floater is set at the one-month LIBOR plus 0.5%. If the one-month LIBOR is initially 3.75% then the rate on the floater will be 4.25 percent. The rate on the inverse floater, I, will be set at

$$I = C - 3 \times \text{LIBOR}$$

In this formula, C is a cap on rate for the inverse floater, the highest rate possible assuming that the LIBOR goes to zero. If, for example, the cap is set at 28.5 percent then the initial rate on the inverse floater, I, will be

$$I = 28.5\% - 3 \times 3.75\% = 17.25\%$$

The "value" of 3 in the formula reflects the fact that the floater portion of the tranche is three times as large as the inverse floater portion. In this case the weighted-average coupon rate of the entire tranche is

$$0.75 \times F + 0.25 \times I$$

$$= 0.75 \times (L + 0.5) + 0.25(C - 3 \times L)$$

$$= 0.75 \times L + 0.375 + 0.25 \times C - 0.75 \times L$$

$$= 0.375 + 0.25 \times C$$

If the weighted-average coupon is set at 7.5 percent then

$$7.5 = 0.375 + 0.25 \times C$$

and

$$7.125 = 0.25 \times C.$$

Thus, C is set at $7.125/0.25 = 28.5$ percent.

Although beyond the scope of this text, you should realize that many other securities can be created from a pool of mortgages. As an example floater/inverse IO floaters have been created from IO strips. The combinations of interest contingent securities (derivatives) that can be created are, quite literally, infinite.

Servicing Rights

Next we turn to the valuation of another derivative of mortgages, servicing rights. When lenders sell off loans that they originate, they often retain the servicing rights to those loans. Sometimes they may sell the servicing rights as a separate package. In either case, the proper valuation of the servicing rights is important. Servicing a pool of loans includes some or all of the following:

collecting monthly payments, maintaining escrow accounts for property taxes and hazard insurance, forwarding proper payments to purchasers of the loans, sending notices of delinquency and default, initiating foreclosure procedures on defaulted loans, and making claims to the mortgage insurer for losses on defaulted loans. The revenues associated with servicing loans include the servicing fee, float on the escrow accounts, and float between the receipt of the monthly payment and the payment of proceeds to the purchaser of the loans. Costs associated with servicing a pool include administrative costs and overhead. The cash flows available from servicing will equal the revenue less the costs.

The servicing fee is generally between 0.25 and 0.5 percent of the mortgage balance, usually three-eighths of a percent. The costs will vary with the balance of the mortgages but will include a fixed component, such as administrative and overhead costs. The value of the servicing rights is the present value of the net income from servicing. Those cash flows will behave similarly to an IO strip. This is because the major portion consists of the servicing fee, which is expressed as a percentage of the outstanding balance of the pool, just as interest payments are.

To make the analysis more concrete, we provide an example of the servicing cash flows from a pool of mortgages in Table 11–14. For simplicity, we assume there are no revenues associated with float on the escrow account or on the timing of payments from the pool to the investors. Servicing costs in the first year equal $30 per year plus 0.0002 percent of the ending pool balance. They grow at 4 percent annually thereafter. For the 100 percent PSA model, the value of the servicing rights is $1588 per $100,000 in mortgages.

The value of the servicing rights under the 200 percent model is only $1235, or 78 percent of the value under the zero percent model.

Changes in interest rates will affect the value of the servicing rights in much the same way as they do an IO strip. A rise in rates will cause the discount rate to rise and the rate of prepayments to accelerate. Prepayments eliminate all future revenue associated with the terminated loan, although fixed expenses for the pool may continue. All of these factors will combine to reduce the value of the servicing rights significantly.

TABLE 11–14
Valuation of Servicing Rights

Discount rate, 12%; pool balance, $100,000; coupon rate, 10%; initial P&I, 10,608

Year	Beginning Balance	Payment	Ending Balance	Prepayment	Servicing Income	Servicing Cost	Net
1	$100,000	$10,608	$99,392	$1,292	$375.00	$52.00	$323.00
2	98,100	10,470	97,440	3,605	367.87	53.67	314.21
3	93,835	10,083	93,136	5,352	351.88	54.86	297.02
4	87,784	9,503	87,059	5,217	329.19	55.63	273.56
5	81,842	8,934	81,092	4,860	306.19	56.41	250.49
6	76,232	8,398	75,457	4,522	285.87	57.25	228.62
7	70,935	7,895	70,133	4,203	266.01	58.15	207.86
8	65,930	7,422	65,102	3,902	247.24	59.10	188.14
9	61,200	6,977	60,343	3,616	229.50	60.12	169.38
10	56,727	6,559	55,840	3,347	212.72	61.20	151.52
11	52,494	6,166	51,577	3,091	196.85	62.35	134.51
12	48,486	5,796	47,538	2,849	181.82	63.56	118.27
13	44,689	5,449	43,709	2,620	167.59	64.83	102.75
.	.	.	.	.	.	.	.
.	.	.	.	.	.	.	.
.	.	.	.	.	.	.	.
25	11,305	2,596	9,839	590	42.39	86.00	(43.61)
26	9,250	2,440	7,735	464	34.69	88.30	(53.62)
27	7,271	2,294	5,704	342	27.27	90.69	(63.43)
28	5,363	2,156	3,742	224	20.11	93.18	(73.07)
29	3,518	2,027	1,843	110	13.19	95.75	(82.56)
30	1,732	1,906	(0)	(0)	6.50	98.43	(91.93)
						PV at 12%	$1,588

Often, mortgage originators will retain excess servicing rights. Excess servicing consists of servicing fees greater than the "normal" compensations for the services provided. This generally occurs when the mortgages are sold with a promised rate somewhat less than the coupon on the mortgage. For example, a mortgage originator may sell a pool of 9.5 percent mortgages with a promised 9 percent rate to the investor or secondary mortgage market agency. The originator retains the 50 basis points (if there is no guarantee fee) for servicing. This is greater than the normal 25 or so basis points. Sometimes the spread may be 100 or more basis points. The greater the spread, the larger the excess servicing retained by the originator.

There are several reasons why originators may retain excess servicing fees. First, mortgage-backed securities usually have coupons in one-half-point intervals; one-quarter-point interval securities trade at relatively unattractive prices. In the above example, the mortgage-backed security has a 9 rather than a 9.25 rate. Second, premium securities may sell at relatively unattractive prices because of investors' apprehension about paying a premium for a security that may repay at par at any time. If mortgages are originated at 10 percent and rates decline to 9.25 percent, the originator may prefer to sell a 9 percent security below par rather than a 9.5 percent security above par. The lower rate results in higher excess servicing fees. Third, originators often mix loans with different coupons in the same pool. As a result, some loans in the pool may have excess servicing, even when the pool on average has no excess servicing.

Financial Accounting Standards Board Statement Number 65 ("Accounting for Certain Mortgage Banking Activities," September 1982) requires that excess servicing, after adjustment for expected prepayments, be capitalized at the time of the mortgage sale. The resulting asset is designated "excess servicing rights" and is generally amortizable over the expected life of the servicing contract. Although originators followed these guidelines for accounting purposes, many used a different tax treatment. To see why, consider the notion that the lower the promised coupon on the mortgages sold, the lower the price obtained by the seller (originator). Thus, by retaining excess servicing, the loans were sold at a discount or a loss over their basis at origination. By retaining excess servicing, originators could show a loss on their mortgage sales for tax purposes. For example, a $100 million pool of mortgages may be sold for only $95 million, producing a $5 million loss.

In 1991 the IRS put a stop to this practice with Revenue Ruling 91-46. The ruling required that the fair market value of the excess servicing be allocated between the servicing rights and the mortgage pool. In the above example, if the value of excess servicing is determined to be $5 million, then the basis of the pool is considered to be $95 million. Since that is also the sales price in the example, there would be no loss for tax purposes. Internal Revenue Service Procedure 91-50 also indicates the acceptable amount of normal servicing for one- to four-family residential mortgages. Those normal servicing fees are 25 basis points for conventional, fixed-rate loans, 44 basis points for FHA and VA loans, 44 basis points for loans with an original balance less than $50,000, and 37.5 basis points for other loans, including adjustable rate loans.

Data on Mortgage Pools

The market value of mortgage-backed securities depends to a certain extent on individual characteristics of the mortgages in the pools that back them. Pool characteristics can affect the rate of delinquency, default, and prepayment. For this reason, MBS investors demand as much information as possible about pool characteristics. As an example, when GNMA pools were first formed and pass-throughs issued, the pools often were formed from mortgages from a defined geographic area. Thus, knowing which mortgage banker may have issued the pool gave investors knowledge about the geographic area the loans were originated in. This information was valuable because mortgages from some areas, such as Southern California, had higher prepayment rates than those from other areas. Some geographic areas also may be more vulnerable to high default rates. By the early 1980s, many lenders had expanded into the national market and GNMA mortgage pools were formed from mortgages originated over wide geographic (national) areas. As a result, such pool information was no longer valuable for these pass-throughs.

However, other pool characteristics, including those for nonstandard loans, remain available and are important to investors. As an example, a mortgage pool may consist of a variety of adjustable rate mortgages with many different terms. One pool may have a complexity of terms, including periodic rate cap, lifetime cap, index, margin, adjustment frequency, and convertibility. Secondary market agencies such as Freddie Mac will issue pool information on the amount of the principal balance having these various features. Other pools may consist of relocation mortgages. Relocation mortgages are mortgages given to key employees of firms as part of a relocation package. They may have different prepayment behavior than standard mortgages. Still other pools may be buydown mortgages. The ability of the borrower to meet the regular payments after the buydown period likewise may cause the prepayment behavior to vary from that of standard mortgages.

If a pool of mortgages consists of standard fixed-rate, fixed-payment mortgages with a variety of coupons and ages, there is valuable investor information that is pertinent. Since 1983 Freddie Mac has made available information on the original weighted-average coupon (WAC) and weighted-average remaining maturity (WARM) of each pool, so investors could judge the likely prepayment rate and age of the loans in those pools. Beginning in 1987, the WAC and WARM of each pool were updated annually and quartiles reported. Quartiles are the sequential interest rate and age ranges into which one-quarter of the loans in a pool fall. Since 1991, WACs and WARMs and quartiles have been updated monthly. Also since 1991, data are available monthly on a pool's weighted-average loan age (WALA), weighted-average original loan term (WAOLT), updated longest maturity date (ULMD), and average original loan size (AOLS). All of this pool information can be used, along with current market rates, to judge the future prepayment behavior of the pool. As an example, investors may have different prepayment projections if the loans in a pool average $50,000 as opposed to $200,000.

Each of the secondary market agencies has automated telephone services through which investors can obtain detailed information on pools. Ginnie Mae has a service through Chemical Bank, Freddie Mac has Freddie Answers, and Fannie Mae has PoolTalk. Often, the investors can download information on many pools into their personal computers. They then can analyze the pool information to make pricing decisions. Also, data on pools are available from private firms that specialize in such services. Examples include the Bond Buyer, Capital Market Decisions, Inc., Financial Publishing Co., Interactive Data Corporation, and Telerate Systems, Inc. Given the increase in the volume of data available on pools, the market for mortgage-backed securities is very efficient compared to markets for other assets.

VALUE CREATION IN MORTGAGE-RELATED SECURITIES

In each case of the creation of mortgage-related securities, the cash flows from a pool of mortgages is delivered, often rearranged in terms of amount and timing, to investors in the securities. No additional cash flows are added to the pool. Cash flows available to investors come from the pool only. In fact, some cash flows are absorbed by the owners of the additional resources used to create the mortgage-related securities. Such parties as underwriters, investment bankers, trustees that hold the mortgages, security brokers, and their staffs absorb cash flows from mortgage pools. The question that presents itself is, How can value be created through a system which does not add additional productive resources, but rather absorbs cash flows from the existing portfolio? The three most common answers follow.

First, securitization makes the mortgage market larger and more liquid. By eliminating liquidity risk, value is created.

Second, mortgage securitization often rearranges the cash flows of a pool into less and more risky components. Different investors may have a need and therefore value differently the partition of the cash flows. As an example, investors seeking a hedge against interest rate risk may value the IO strip for this reason. Certainly, the different risk preference of investors gives rise to value creation by rearranging the cash flows in this manner.

Third, value can be created for one party by the existence of asymmetric information. In the case of the senior/subordinated pass-through, the lender may have superior information concerning the credit risk of the pool. Since outsiders do not have this information, they will attach greater value to the senior security than would be the case if they had full information. The lender with the information captures the increased value by selling the senior at a premium and retaining the subordinated interest, which the lender knows not to have significant default risk.

The fact that such a great percentage of mortgages has been securitized in the secondary mortgage market indicates that the process creates value over and above the value of the resources required to accomplish the securitization.

SUMMARY

The valuation of mortgage-related securities, including the behavior of their yield-to-maturity and duration, is different from traditional debt securities. The cash flows depend, to various degrees, on the payment behavior of pools of mortgages. The cash flows from a pool of mortgages consist of the scheduled amortization, interest on the remaining balance, and any prepayments of loans. As such, the cash flows associated with mortgage-related securities are interest-contingent. This means that changes in the market interest rate have two effects on the value of the MRS. First, the discount rate changes. As with traditional debt securities, the change in the market rate will have an effect on the value of the MRS in the opposite direction. Second, the timing and/or amount of the cash flows will change. This effect can either reinforce or counteract that of the discount rate. If the change in the market rate causes the total payments to increase or to occur sooner, the value of the MRS will increase, and vice versa.

Pass-through securities represent an ownership interest in a pool of mortgages. The cash flows of pass-throughs behave precisely as those of the mortgages in the pool. Prepayment behavior will have an impact on the yield of discounted and premium pass-throughs. If the principal on a discounted pass-through is received sooner than expected, the yield-to-maturity will be greater than anticipated. Thus, a drop in interest rates will increase the yield-to-maturity on discounted pass-throughs as prepayments accelerate. The opposite is true for premium pass-throughs.

Several types of MRSs rearrange the cash flows from a pool of mortgages into various components, some of which are more and some of which are less interest-contingent. The extent of the repackaging can either reduce or enhance the interest-contingent character of their payments. Some tranches of a CMO, for example, are constructed so that interest only is received and the maturity of the obligation occurs within a narrow range of years, regardless of the prepayment behavior of the mortgage pool. They go the furthest in creating MRSs that mimic the cash flow payments of traditional debt securities. The creation of the tranches also produces a residual component, which may be more interest-contingent than the pool as a whole.

A CMO of particular interest is the interest-only and principal-only division of the cash flows. The holder of the IO receives only the interest payments from the pool of mortgages, while the PO holder receives only principal payments (both scheduled and prepayment). When market interest rates change, the value of these securities behave very differently from each other. When market rates rise, the value of the PO drops considerably as the discount rate increases and the fixed amount of principal payments are extended in time through the slowing of prepayments. When rates fall, the value of the PO drops considerably for the same reasons. When interest rates rise, the value of the IO actually may increase. Because prepayments from the pool are slowed, the increase in the total amount of cash received on the IO enhances its value. The IO is one security used by investors to hedge their portfolio of traditional debt securities against changes in value through the interest rate cycle.

The value of servicing rights behaves similarly to the IO. The servicer of a pool of loans receives compensation defined as a percent of the outstanding balance—thus the similarity to an IO. When prepayments accelerate, the total payments for the servicing decrease. The value of servicing rights on the marketplace will depend upon expectations of charges in interest rates and the effect on the prepayment behavior of the mortgage pool.

The interest-contingent nature of the cash flows of MRSs makes the estimation of future prepayments essential to proper valuation. Several models have been used, including the history of FHA loans, a constant CPR, and the repayment model of the Public Securities Association. In addition, econometric models have been used to estimate future prepayment behavior. These models identify the functional relationship between various variables (such as interest rates and the yield curve) and the prepayment behavior of a pool of mortgages. Finally, value is created through mortgage securitization if the resulting securities trade in a more liquid market or meet the risk preferences of different types of investors. Value also is created for one party when there is asymmetric information concerning the risk of a mortgage pool.

KEY TERMS

Constant prepayment rate (CPR)
Econometric prepayment models
Effective (implied) duration
FHA prepayment experience
Interest rate contingent security
Mortgage-derivative security
Negative duration

Price compression
Public Securities Association (PSA) prepayment rate
Strips (IO and PO)
Servicing rights
Streamline refinance plan (SRP)
Value creation

SUGGESTED READINGS

Andrukonis, D., and B. Preiss. 1984. Projecting mortgage cash flow. *Secondary Mortgage Markets* Vol. 1, May.

Biasucci, J., and M. Martell. 1990. Buying and selling mortgage servicing. *Secondary Mortgage Markets* Vol. 6, Winter.

Fabozzi, F. J., C. Ramsey, and F. R. Ramirez. 1994. Collateralized Mortgage Obligations, 2nd ed. Frank J. Fabozzi Associates, Buckingham, PA.

Hendershott, P., and S. Buser. 1984. Spotting prepayment premiums. *Secondary Mortgage Markets* Vol. 1, August.

Hess, A., and C. W. Smith, Jr. 1989. Mortgage Securitization: A low cost hedge against interest-rate risk. *Simon Research Review*. University of Rochester, Fall.

Hjerpe, E., 1987. Stripped mortgage-backed securities: An economic analysis and valuation simulation. Research Paper no. 130. Washington, DC: Federal Home Loan Bank Board.

Stanton, R. 1995. Rational Prepayment and the Valuation of Mortgage-backed Securities. *Review of Financial Studies* 8:3 677–708.

REVIEW QUESTIONS

11–1   a. What is meant by interest (rate) contingent securities?
        b. Give three examples of a claim on cash flows that is interest rate contingent. Explain.

11–2   Why are pass-through securities considered "callable" bonds?

11–3   List and explain three methods of predicting prepayments on a pool of mortgages.

11–4   Given a GNMA 10 pool of mortgages, would you expect prepayments to accelerate greatly if the market rate of interest fell from 15 percent to 14 percent? From 10 percent to 8 percent? Explain any difference in your answer.

11–5   Explain what "overcollateralized" means and why it exists. Give an example.

11–6   a. What is meant by the "effective" or "implied" duration of a mortgage pool?
        b. How does it differ from the duration of a traditional noncallable corporate bond?
        c. How can it be measured?

11–7   What are senior/subordinated pass-throughs? How do they provide for credit enhancement?

11–8   Compare and contrast the characteristics of mortgage-backed bonds with those of collateralized mortgage obligations.

11–9   a. Explain what interest-only and principal-only strips are.
        b. Explain why the value of an interest-only strip goes up when market rates of interest go up.
        c. Explain why interest-only strips are excellent investment vehicles to hedge against interest rate risk. In this regard, define negative duration.

11–10   a. What are servicing rights?
        b. Explain why the value of servicing rights declines as prepayments are expected to accelerate.

11–11   Explain how the securitization of mortgages can create value.

PROBLEMS

11–1   Given the following information about a pool of fixed-rate mortgages, perform the calculations indicated.

Amount	$110 million
Coupon rate	11%
% PSA	100%

year one, 1.3%; year two, 3.7%; year three, 5.75%; year four, 6%

For the first 4 years, show (a) the end-of-year pool balance; (b) scheduled principal and interest payments; and (c) total cash flows.

11–2   Perform the calculations in Problem 11–1 assuming a PSA of 50 percent.

11–3   a. Calculate the effective duration from the following yield and price data on a FNMA 11.

	Market Rate	
	10%	10.25%
Price	105.125	104.25

b. Would the duration calculated be greater or less if the price change did not reflect a change in the assumed PSA prepayment rate? Explain.

11–4   Given the following information on a mortgage-backed bond, perform the calculations indicated.

Pool Data	
Amount	$120 million
Coupon rate	11%
Maturity	30 years
% PSA	0%
Default rate	0.5% first 5 years

Bond Data	
Amount	$110 million
Coupon rate	10%
Maturity	20 years
Yield on fund	7%

For the first four years, show
a. End-of-year pool balance.
b. Default losses.
c. Cash inflow from pool.
d. Payment to bondholders.
e. End-of-year fund balance.

11–5   a. Perform the calculations in Problem 11–4 assuming no default rate at all.
b. When the default rate drops from 0.005 to zero, who benefits, the bondholders or the equity holders? Explain.

11–6   Given the following information, perform the calculations indicated.

Pool Data	
Amount	$106 million
Coupon rate	10.5%
Maturity	30 years
PSA	100%

year one, 1.3%; year two, 3.7%; year three, 5.75%; year four, 6%

Tranche Data	Coupon	Amount
Tranche A	9.5%	$ 30,000,000
Tranche B	9.75	30,000,000
Tranche C	10.25	25,000,000
Tranche Z	10.50	15,000,000
Equity		$ 6,000,000
Total		$106,000,000

    a. For the first four years, show the:
       1. End-of-year pool balance.
       2. Total funds available for distribution.
       3. End-of-year amount owed to security holders.
    b. For the first 4 years, show the principal outstanding and cash distributions to holders of the A, B, and C tranches.
    c. For the first 4 years, show the principal outstanding for Tranche Z.
    d. For the first 4 years, show the cash flows to the residual (equity) interest.

11–7   Assume that the rate on a floater is set at LIBOR + 2.5%, that the floater portion of a class is 80 percent and that the weighted average coupon of the floater plus inverse floater should be eight percent. Determine the cap on the formula for the inverse floater that will accomplish this.

ENDNOTES

1. Frank Navratil, "The Estimation of Mortgage Prepayment Rates," *Journal of Financial Research* (Summer 1985): 107–117.
2. Jerry Green and John Shoven, "The Effects of Interest Rates on Mortgage Prepayments," *Journal of Money, Credit, and Banking* (February 1986): 41–59.
3. Nikolaos Milonas and Nelson Lacey, "An Examination of GMNA Prepayments," Office of Policy and Economic Research, Federal Home Loan Bank Board (May 1988).
4. This association was subsequently merged into the Public Securities Association.
5. See Terrence M. Clauretie, Mel Jameson, and Ronald Rogers, "A Note on Refinancing Costs, Prepayment Assumptions, and the Value of Mortgage Backed Securities," *Journal of Real Estate Finance and Economics* (September 1990): 295–330.
6. Years two, three, and four will have prepayment rates of 3.7 percent, 5.75 percent, and 6 percent, respectively.

WEB SITES

www.psa.com   site for the Public Securities Association
www.ginniemae.gov   site for GNMA

CHAPTER 12

Controlling Default Risk Through Borrower Qualification, Loan Underwriting, and Contractual Relationships

LEARNING OBJECTIVES

This chapter discusses controlling default risk through borrower qualification, loan underwriting, and contractual relationships in the note and mortgage or deed-of-trust. After reading this chapter, you should be familiar with the important borrower and property characteristics which are the focus of borrower qualification. You also should understand the legal relationship between the lender and the borrower and how contractual provisions give each party rights and obligations. You should see how many of the contractual relationships protect the lender from default risk. In short, you should understand how the lender controls for default risk from the qualification of the borrower through the structuring of the legal contracts supporting the loan. (Please note that the exhibits referenced in this chapter can be accessed through Microsoft Word on the CD packaged with this textbook.)

INTRODUCTION

One of the major risks faced by mortgage lenders is **default risk,** the risk that the borrower will fail to make timely payments or repay the principal amount of the loan when it is due. The risk is greater when general property values fall, for the likelihood increases that the value of a particular property will fall below the balance of the loan used to purchase it. Lenders use several precautionary measures to mitigate default risk, including closely scrutinizing the financial position of the borrower, accurately estimating the value of the property that serves as collateral, and employing legal instruments (deeds of trust and mortgages) with provisions that protect the interest of the lender. Although the lender garners as much information as possible and uses legal instruments to guard against default risk, the legal system affords some rights to borrowers as well. These rights, along with such unforeseen events as localized recessions that dampen property values, ensure that some default risk will remain for the mortgage lender. In Chapter 14, we will discuss the business of default risk insurance.

BORROWER QUALIFICATION AND LOAN UNDERWRITING

Borrower qualification and loan underwriting refers to the process of determining and controlling the risk of loss on a residential loan. In general, mortgage credit analysis includes: (a) determining the maximum loan amount, (b) estimating settlement requirements and costs, (c) analyzing credit history, (d) calculating effective income, (e) estimating monthly housing expense, and (f) assessing ability to repay mortgage and other liabilities in a timely fashion. Specifically, lenders are concerned with default risk, the chance that the borrower may default on the loan obligations. Interest rate risk is not an underwriting concern. In Chapter 14 we explore the costs of borrower default and mortgage insurance in detail. Briefly, however, when a borrower defaults on his loan obligation, the lender must take legal action (foreclosure) to obtain title to the property. He then will liquidate the property and make a claim to the insurer. (Alternatively, he can make a claim and deliver a deed to the property to the insurer.) The process can be time-consuming and expensive, as the lender must pay legal fees, property taxes, maintenance expenses, hazard insurance, repairs, and so forth. A loss equal to 40 or 50 percent of the loan amount is not uncommon for foreclosure procedures that are lengthy and expensive. Proper borrower qualification can minimize this risk and is therefore the concern of both the lender and the mortgage insurer. Some reasons for rejection are: (a) borrower cannot support the payments, (b) borrower has a bad credit history (especially pertaining to mortgage repayment), and (c) borrower is currently delinquent.

Theories of Default

There are two theories of default risk: the **ability-to-pay theory** and the **equity theory.** Borrower qualification addresses both theories.

Ability-to-Pay Theory

This theory states that default and default risk occur when the borrower cannot make the monthly payments on the loan. Loss of employment, disputes that emerge from a divorce proceeding, and an unexpected addition to the family are typical reasons why borrowers may fail to make their loan payments. After several payments are missed, the expensive foreclosure procedure will begin. Borrower qualification involves an analysis of borrower characteristics, such as the number of dependents and the amount and stability of family earnings. Research conducted to explain or predict default and delinquency under this theory has focused on such borrower characteristics as family size and source of income.

Equity Theory (The "Put" Option)

The equity theory of default focuses on the amount of equity in the property. This theory states that no borrower with substantial positive equity would default, even if unable to make the monthly payment. The borrower instead would sell the property in the market and pay off the loan, capturing the equity for himself. On the other hand, if there is negative equity (the value of the property is less than the value of the loan), default may occur even if the borrower is able to make the monthly payment. This would be especially true when the borrower faces a move from the property because of an employment change or divorce. It would appear that the equity theory dominates the ability-to-pay theory.

The equity theory of default is also termed the "put" option theory of default. When the loan is made, the lender also gives the borrower a put option. Simply stated, whenever the value of the house is less than the value of the loan and the borrower contemplates a move, it is optimal for the borrower to give (put to) the lender the house rather than repay the loan. The borrower benefits if he puts a $90,000 house to the lender in satisfaction of a $100,000 mortgage debt. Although many borrowers in this situation may decide not to default because they may personally value the property more than the market, an event such as a divorce or unexpected unemployment may "force" the default.

Although the lender can seek a judgment in court for the difference (called a deficiency judgment), this may, in practice, be difficult. The cost of pursuing the judgment in court and the ability of defaulters to declare personal bankruptcy (thereby avoiding the consequences of the judgment) mitigates the power of the deficiency judgment. Also, a few states prohibit deficiency judgments by statute.

At the time the loan is originated, the lender will make certain that the appraised value of the house will be greater than the amount of the loan. Nonetheless, even then, the put option will have value since there is a chance that at some time over the life of the loan the value of the property may fall below the value of the loan. When this occurs, one might say that the put option is "in the money." The put option will have greater value where the loan-to-value ratio is large and the variance in property price changes is expected to be great. Research conducted to explain default under this theory has focused on the role of the original loan-to-value ratio.

Studies of Delinquency and Default

Studies of delinquency and default have included variables which are expected to be related to both the equity theory and the ability-to-pay theory. A survey of the mortgage default literature by Quercia and Stegman shows that, consistently, home equity or the related measure, loan-to-value ratio, are the main characteristics influencing the default decision.[1] Other factors found to be important are transactions costs and the difficulty of estimating the value of the default option. In an early study of defaults, von Furstenberg analyzed the default rates on FHA loans grouped by the policy year (the year the loans were originated and insured).[2] He considered the original maturity of the loans, the original loan-to-value ratio, and whether or not the loan was for a new or existing property. He found that shorter maturity loans (20-year versus 30-year) and loans on new houses were much less likely to default. Holding these two variables constant, he discovered the original loan-to-value ratio was the single most important factor governing defaults over the life of the loans. In a similar study of VA loans, von Furstenberg considered not only the original loan-to-value ratio but the age (time from origination to default) of defaulted loans.[3] He found that defaults peak between 3 and 5 years subsequent to origination, and the loan-to-value ratio is the predominant determining factor in explaining defaults. In another study (with Green) of the loan portfolio of a large Pittsburgh savings and loan association, von Furstenberg found that delinquencies behaved similarly to defaults; they were related primarily to the loan-to-value ratio, the age of the mortgage, and the type of property (new or existing).[4]

Variables related to the ability-to-pay theory, such as family size and source of income, also have been used to explain default. In an early study, Morton analyzed borrower characteristics in terms of their importance in causing delinquency or foreclosure.[5] He analyzed the loan performance of 24 Connecticut lenders and found that the number of dependents and the employment status of the borrower were very important in explaining defaults. Employment as a salesman was by far the most significant job classification related to defaults.

On a macro level, unemployment may be expected to affect defaults. In a study of mortgages insured nationally by the Mortgage Guaranty Insurance Corporation, Campbell and Dietrich found that the regional rate of unemployment contributed to an explanation of delinquency and default rates.[6]

Finally, in a test of the ability-to-pay and equity theories of default, Jackson and Kaserman concluded that the evidence supports the latter theory.[7] Using a large number of FHA loans that were originated in or close to the year 1969, they found the loan-to-value ratio a better predictor of default than the payment-to-income ratio of the borrower.

It should be pointed out that there is no inherent conflict between the two theories of default. Negative equity is likely a necessary condition for default, but it may not be sufficient in and of itself. A homeowner with negative equity in his residence may prefer to make the monthly payments. He may do so out of a sense of obligation, a fear of a bad credit rating, or because the house has more value to him than it would in the market (the owner personally installed the sauna). As stated above, an untimely event, such as involuntary unemployment or divorce, may lead to delinquency. At that time, the homeowner may "put" the house to the lender in satisfaction of the debt. The untimely event has moved the exercise date of the put option to the present, and it is exercised. Borrower qualification practices that scrutinize both the characteristics of the property and those of the borrower recognize the dual role of negative equity and ability to make payments in causing default.

Once default occurs, the natural progression is for the lender to initiate foreclosure proceedings. However, as Ambrose and Capone point out in a 1996 study,[8] foreclosure can be the most costly post-default outcome. As a result, lenders may attempt to recover the debt without going through the foreclosure process by offering the borrower some alternatives such as deed-in-lieu of foreclosure (voluntary title transfer), allowing the borrower to sell the property even at a loss, or arranging a work-out agreement to lower payments. Ambrose and Capone do a simulation where the results show that lenders can find profitable opportunities in extending foreclosure alternatives.

Lenders, however, face a "moral hazard" problem by offering alternatives to foreclosure. The willingness of lenders to negotiate a less costly solution to default may act as a signal to other borrowers that their cost of default has decreased and this, in itself, may lead to more defaults. In this regard, Clauretie and Jameson[9] conclude that loan renegotiation does not occur frequently enough to warrant its consideration in mortgage pricing models.

Characteristics of the Property

All lenders will require that an appraisal of the property be performed as part of the qualification procedure. The appraisal may be done by an independent person or by someone on the lender's staff, but it must be ordered by the lender. For all FHA, VA, and conventional loans regulated by a federal financial institution, the appraisal process and form are standardized, and federal law requires the appraiser be state-licensed or certified. A Freddie Mac/Fannie Mae uniform report is shown in Exhibit 13–1 (on the CD). The appraiser will note on the form the physical characteristics of the property, such as the square footage, number of bedrooms, structure (frame, masonry, concrete), description (split level, bi-level), and condition of the electrical, plumbing, and heating systems. The appraiser also will indicate the property's location, such as urban, rural, or in a floodplain. Next, the appraiser will determine the recent selling price of at least three nearby and comparable properties in forming an opinion of value. Finally, the value of the residence as a rental property will be considered. Even though the intended use is for owner occupancy, its value as reflected by the economic market rent it could command is considered as an appraisal method.

Conforming conventional loans have guidelines set by the major secondary market agencies that purchase them. Other conventional loans have no set guidelines. Loans in excess of 95 percent loan-to-value ratio are not common, and most lenders require private mortgage insurance on all loans with loan-to-value ratios in excess of 80 percent. The private mortgage insurers will impose their own borrower qualification guidelines.

Characteristics of the Borrower

Though different in detail, procedures for borrower qualification for conforming conventional, FHA, and VA loans are all similar. They involve a determination of the ability of the borrower to make mortgage payments out of the family income. The qualification procedures consider the type and stability of income, supplemental sources of income, nonmortgage debt obligations, and living expenses.

Borrower qualification for conforming conventional, FHA, and VA loans all compare maximum ratios of housing-related expenses to either gross or after-tax income. Table 12–1 compares these definitions and ratios. Ratios for nonconforming conventional loans will vary by lender but will approximate those in the table.

HUD/FHA Guidelines

The Department of Housing and Urban Development (HUD) requires that FHA-approved lenders use a percentage calculation to help determine an applicant's eligibility for a loan. Lenders follow a mortgage credit analysis worksheet in which two **payment-to-income ratios** are utilized: (1) the ratio of the monthly **total mortgage payment (TMP)** to **gross monthly effective income** and (2) the sum of TMP and other monthly expenses to monthly effective income. Effective income is the borrower's and co-borrower's regular plus supplemental gross income. Payment-to-income ratios that exceed 29 percent and 41 percent, respectively, generally will lead to a denial of the loan application. However, HUD will permit the qualifying ratios to be increased by two percentage points (to 31 and 43 percent, respectively) on newly constructed

TABLE 12-1

Comparison of Borrower Qualification Guidelines

	Conforming Conventional	FHA	VA	
			Residual Method	Income Ratios (as of March 1991)
(1) Monthly income	Gross income	Gross income	Net effective income (gross less federal taxes)	Gross income
(2) Monthly housing expense	Principal, interest, taxes, insurance. (PITI)	Principal, interest, taxes, insurance, association fees (TMP)	Principal, interest, taxes, insurance, utilities, maintenance	Principal, interest, taxes, insurance association fees
(3) Other monthly expense	State and local taxes, car payment	Installment debt, loan payments, child support	State and local taxes, social security taxes, installment debt, retirement contributions, life insurance premiums, loan payments	Installment debt, loan payments, child support
(4) Minimum residual			Food, clothing, transportation, medical care, personal items; by region and family size	
Maximum ratio 2/1	Generally 28% 25% [95% L/V]	29%		
Maximum ratio (2+3)/1	Generally 36% 33% [95% L/V]	41%		41%
Minimum excess residual ratio [(1)−(2)−(3)−(4)]/(4)			20%	

homes that are identified as being "energy efficient homes." In fact, the FHA has an "energy efficient mortgage" in which the borrower can buy or refinance and incorporate in the cost of energy efficient improvements.

Definition of Housing Expenses

Whereas borrower qualification for conventional loans may focus on only the principal, interest, insurance, and taxes (**PITI**), the FHA adds to PITI the **monthly mortgage insurance premium (MIP)** and any homeowner association or condominium fees.

The total fixed payment is determined by adding to the total mortgage payment installment debt, child support, and other debt payments (as on an automobile loan). Any installment payment that is scheduled to be paid off within six months can be excluded from this definition. The idea is to estimate the total monthly obligation for which the borrower will be committed over an extended period of time. This total should not exceed 41 percent of gross monthly effective income.

Definition of Income

Gross monthly effective income is determined by HUD as the gross income from all sources that can be expected to continue for the first 5 years of the mortgage. The dual qualifying ratios computed with respect to gross income can be exceeded if there are significant compensating factors such as:

1. The borrower has a conservative attitude toward the use of credit and has accumulated liquid assets (other than by gift).
2. The borrower has at least a 10 percent investment in the property.
3. The borrower's housing expenses are increased only slightly as a result of the purchase.
4. The borrower has other compensation not reflected in the effective income figure.
5. A considerable amount of the borrower's effective income is from nontaxable sources.

Self-employed borrowers can pose some difficult problems for estimating effective income. A borrower is considered self-employed if she has a 25 percent or greater ownership in a business. For such borrowers, the lender must verify at least 2 years of income. An average income figure must be used for the purpose of qualification. Furthermore, the self-employed borrower must have been self-employed for a minimum of 2 years. A person who has been self-employed between 1 and 2 years must have at least 2 years' previous employment in order to qualify. No person self-employed for less than a year can qualify for an FHA-insured loan.

HUD/FHA employs an accept/reject decision based on the following four factors of credit rating:

1. Credit characteristics
2. Stability of effective income
3. Adequacy of effective income
4. Adequacy of wealth or assets

A rejection in any category will lead to a denial of the loan.

VA Borrower Qualification

The main purpose of the VA mortgage loan program is to help veterans finance the purchase of homes with favorable loan terms and at competitive interest rates. VA mortgages are available to buy homes, townhomes, condominiums, and mobile homes, to repair or improve a home, and to refinance. Basic characteristics of VA loans are no down payment, limits on closing costs paid by the buyer, and no prepayment penalty. Typical requirements are: (a) eligibility with loan entitlement, (b) the home must be owner-occupied, (c) the borrower must meet income requirements, and (d) the borrower must have good credit. The VA makes direct loans only to Native Americans on trust land or in some cases of veteran disability. Otherwise, loans are made by local lenders and are guaranteed by the VA.

The VA offers loans with a maximum term of 30 years and 32 days and can be a fixed-rate loan, a graduated-payment loan, or a growing equity mortgage. The growing equity mortgage allows for gradual annual increases in payments with all extra applied to the mortgage principal. Increases may be fixed (3 percent per year, for example) or tied to some index. No down payment is required if the value of the property exceeds the purchase price or cost. A down payment is required on the graduated-payment mortgage because of negative amortization. The interest rate is negotiated and only reasonable closing costs can be charged. These might include VA appraisal, credit report, survey, title insurance, recording fees, origination fee, and discount points.

Wartime veterans are eligible for a VA loan if they have served 90 days of active duty during a "hot war." This would include: (1) World War II (1940–1947), (2) Korean Conflict (1950–1955), (3) Vietnam War (1964–1975), and (4) Persian Gulf War (1990–1991). Peacetime service requires a minimum of 181 days of continuous active duty. For reservists and national guardsmen, 6 years of service is required for eligibility.

The VA employs a two-step method using ratios similar to those employed in FHA qualification. The ratios are displayed in Table 12–1. The residual method has been used for many years; the income ratio method was added in October 1986.

Residual Method

This method is similar to that used by the FHA, except that an additional category of obligations is added to the analysis—monthly living costs such as food, clothing, and transportation. The

VA begins with the same definition of housing expenses as the FHA—PITI—and then adds utilities and maintenance costs. Additional monthly payments are added as well. Here, the VA includes state and local taxes, retirement contributions, social security taxes, and life insurance premiums. Finally, the VA adds cost-of-living expenses to this total. Estimates of these costs, called minimum residual income, are made by region and family size.

The total of all these costs is then subtracted from net effective income (gross income less federal income taxes) to arrive at excess residual income. Under VA guidelines, this excess residual income should be at least 20 percent of the minimum required residual if the borrower fails the income ratio method described next.

Income Ratio Method

This method, similar to the FHA's method, is used in conjunction with the residual method. The income concept is gross income as opposed to net effective income. Here, PITI is used as a definition of housing expense, and other monthly expenses include loan repayments, installment obligations, and child support. The sum of the housing plus other expenses should not exceed 41 percent of gross income. If the expenses exceed this ratio, then the residual method can be employed. Also, the previous credit history of the applicant as indicated by his wealth, borrowing decisions, and credit history is considered by the VA. The VA will look at the work history and stability of earnings of the borrower. The number and ages of dependents is also a factor, as is the size of the down payment on the property.

Conforming Conventional Loan Qualification

Unlike government-insured loans, there are no nationally uniform guidelines for conventional loan underwriting. The Federal National Mortgage Association (FNMA) and the Federal Home Loan Mortgage Corporation (FHLMC) purchase conventional loans from lender/originators. These agencies have established qualification guidelines to which the loan application must conform. Since nonconforming loans would not be purchased by these large secondary market agencies, most conventional loans are originated under their guidelines. If these guidelines are not met, the loan will not be available for purchase by the agencies and is therefore unlikely to be offered by lenders that do not hold their originations in their own portfolio. Due to the efficiencies of the secondary mortgage market, conforming loans often carry interest rates 10 to 50 basis points lower than nonconforming loans. Exhibit 13–8 (on the CD) shows a FNMA/FHLMC residential loan application form used for borrower qualification.

For 95 percent loan-to-value loans, FNMA requires that the mortgage payment not exceed 25 percent of gross income and that the total of the payment and other obligations not exceed 33 percent of gross income. The limits are 28 and 36 percent, respectively, for less than 95 percent loan-to-value loans.

Table 12–2 indicates that the federal agencies have other guidelines that pertain to loans other than the standard fixed-rate type. As an example, FNMA will not purchase adjustable-rate mortgages (ARMs) with negative amortization. The FHLMC will, but requires a 10 percent down payment. The same is true for graduated-payment ARMs.

Also, Freddie Mac and Fannie Mae determine a loan limit subject to an annual survey of home purchase prices conducted by the Federal Housing Finance Board. As of January 1, 1995, that limit has been set at $203,150. By law, since 1981 the Fannie Mae and Freddie Mac loan purchase limit is adjusted annually on the basis of the October-to-October percent change in the average home price reported in the FHFB's monthly survey of terms on conventional home mortgages.

Borrower Qualification Comparison

Table 12–3 shows the relevant values and ratios for the Smith family example. The family meets all of the ratio tests with the exception of a high loan-to-value conventional loan and a low residual income ratio. If the family were to fail the VA test using the income-ratio method, the VA would look next to the residual income. Here, the family appears to have difficulty, since the residual income is less than the 20 percent guideline.

TABLE 12–2
Federal Agency Guidelines for Purchased Conventional Mortgages

	Investor Loans Allowed?	Minimum Down Payment	Minimum Down Payment for Regular ARMS	Minimum Down Payment for Reg. Am. ARMS	Graduated Payment ARM	Builder Buydowns	Refinanced Loans	PMI Mortgage Insurance Required	Title Insurance Required
Fannie Mae	Yes, maximum 80% loan-to-value ratio	10% (with tougher income-standards if less)	10%	Not acceptable	Not acceptable	Fixed rate, less than 10% down limited to 3%; 10% down limited to 6%. ARM, no contributions	10%	Yes, if loan-to-value ratio more than 80%	Yes
Freddie Mac	Yes	5%	5%	10% Max 125% neg. amotization	10% down 5%, 7.5% adjustment for first five years	Value of buydown less than 10% of loan amount; annual increase in payment 7.5% or less	10%	Yes, if loan-to-value ratio more than 80%	Yes

261

TABLE 12–3

Borrower Qualification Ratios for Smith Family

	Conforming Conventional	FHA	VA Residual Method	VA Income Ratios Method
(1) Income	$3,600	$3,600	$3,200	$3,600
(2) Housing expense	800	800	950	800
(3) Other monthly expenses	600	600	850	600
(4) Minimum residual			1,193	
Ratio one (2/1)	22.22%	22.22%		
Ratio two (2+3)/1	38.99%	38.89%		38.89%
Minimum expense [(1)−(2)−(3)−(4)]/4			17.35%	

Computing the various ratios involved in borrower qualification can be time-consuming. Fortunately, there are software programs available that make the computations easy. As additional information is made known, the user can simply input the new data into the program to automatically calculate the new ratios. Spreadsheet programs are also ideal for this type of analysis.

Recently lenders have been assigning letter grades to loans based on the credit history of the applicant. Lenders commonly refer to loans as "A," "B," and "C" loans. Under the "A" rating the borrower can have no more than 38 percent of income allocated to pay debt, has no late mortgage payments in the last 2 years, no bankruptcy in 10 years, no more than one 30-day late installment payment or 60-day late credit card payment. For a "B" loan, no more than 50 percent of the borrowers income may be allocated to debt service, no more than three 30-day late mortgage payments in the last year (no 60-day late payments at all), no more than four 30-day late installment loan payments or two 30-day late credit card payments. Also, the borrower must have no declared bankruptcy in the last 2 to 4 years. A "C" loan limits debt payments to 55 percent of income, allows no more than four 30-day late installment loan payments or four 60-day late credit card payments. The borrower must not have declared bankruptcy in the last 2 years.

CONTRACTUAL RELATIONSHIPS IN RESIDENTIAL LOANS

In this section, we describe the generic characteristics of legal instruments that deal with residential finance. The actual characteristics of such instruments vary greatly from state to state and from region to region. Many provisions are subject to negotiation between the borrower and the lender, although this seldom occurs. Many of the provisions of the legal instruments discussed here may be modified or obviated by law in some states. In addition, there may be conflicts between provisions allowed or prohibited by the various states and those required by the federal government through such regulatory agencies as the Office of Thrift Supervision (previously the Federal Home Loan Bank Board).

Often, state legislatures pass laws (or state courts make decisions) that protect the borrower in a financial transaction. As an example, many state laws allow a prepayment of the mortgage without penalty, thus preserving the value of the prepayment option for the borrower. Or, state laws may attempt to override any due-on-sale provision in a mortgage. We saw in Chapter 5 how California sought to protect the value of an assumable loan by declaring the due-on-sale provision to be void in a mortgage held by the Wellenkamps. It did so on the basis that the new buyers of the property met the credit rating criteria of the lender. Recall that the lender was not so much concerned with the credit risk of the loan as with the interest rate risk.

Assumable mortgages have their greatest value and likelihood of being assumed by new buyers when market interest rates are high. This is precisely when financial institutions will be faced with paying higher rates on their deposits, and the maturity mismatch problem rears its ugly head. The federal regulatory agencies perceive their duty to be preserving of the solvency of the lending institutions, rather than enhancing the value of mortgages to borrowers. Accordingly, we observed that the Federal Home Loan Bank Board overrode the California legislation for all federally chartered savings and loans. Later, the override was extended to all members of the Federal Home Loan Bank Board, including state-chartered thrifts.

Remember, then, that many of the provisions discussed below may not be valid in some states or for some mortgages originated by federally regulated thrifts or purchased by federal secondary mortgage agencies.

Promissory Notes

In a residential finance arrangement, the borrower promises to repay the lender by signing a promissory note. The loan is usually secured by the residence through another instrument—either a mortgage or a deed-of-trust (also called a trust deed). Together, these instruments contain the contractual provisions that spell out the rights and obligations of the borrower and lender. The promissory note contains the important provisions of the loan. The mortgage or trust deed are instruments that collateralize the property for the lender in the event of borrower default. The mortgage or trust deed also have important provisions. Default generally is defined as any failure on the part of the borrower to meet the terms of the promissory note. That can include failure to make interest and principal payments, property tax payments, hazard insurance payments, and so forth.

The promissory note can be sold by the lender to another investor. When this is done, the mortgage or trust deed also is transferred. A sale or assignment of the latter without the sale of the note is meaningless. The security for the debt has no value apart from the debt itself.

Types of the Promissory Notes

A promissory note can be either a recourse note or a nonrecourse note. A **recourse note** is one in which the lender has the right to pursue other assets of the borrower in the event that, through a default and foreclosure, the liquidation value of the residence is insufficient to satisfy the debt. In this situation, there is a deficiency and the lender can obtain a court-ordered judgment for the amount of the deficiency. A **nonrecourse note** limits the lender's remedy to the value of the residence that serves as collateral. This is done through the exculpatory clause, which literally means "to hold blameless." Although the terms of a note may determine its status, there may be state legislation that prohibits certain loans from being recourse notes. Seller carryback loans and home improvement loans often are required to be nonrecourse. A seller carryback exists when the owner-seller of the residence agrees to grant a loan to the buyer instead of receiving cash. A handful of states (six, at the present time) require that first mortgages be nonrecourse through antideficiency judgment legislation. In these states, the lender is unable to pursue a judgment for the deficiency. His recourse is only to the residence securing the loan. Most states allow **deficiency judgments** on first mortgages so that the lender can proceed against the borrower's remaining assets. Of course, if the borrower has few remaining assets, his ability to declare personal bankruptcy may discourage the lender from incurring the legal expenses required to pursue a deficiency judgment. Deficiency judgments are discussed in detail in Chapter 14.

Provisions of Promissory Notes

Amount, Consideration, and Payer.   Since a note has value, the lender must give consideration to make it enforceable. Usually that consideration is the amount of the loan (cash). It also can be personal property, or in the case of seller carrybacks, real estate. The amount to be repaid must be contained in the note as well as the person or entity to be repaid. If the words "or order" appear after the identification of the lender as payee, the lender can sell the note or designate another to collect the payments. Because of the large secondary mortgage market, virtually all notes have this provision.

Interest and Payment. The note will indicate the annual rate of interest and the date from which interest begins to accrue. For adjustable-rate mortgages, the note will indicate the date that the interest rate may change (anniversary date), the basis upon which the new rate will be calculated (index), and any limitations (caps) on the interest change or the payment change. In the case where payments (but not the interest rate) are capped, the note also will explain the provisions for negative amortization. For the standard fixed-rate, amortizing loan, the amount of the installment payment (principal and interest) and due dates will be noted. Some notes may provide that the loan be amortized over a period longer than the final payment date. In this case, there will be some unamortized principal remaining on the final due date. The entire principal will come due and is referred to as a "balloon payment." Legislation in some states requires written notice by the note holder within a certain time frame (say, six months) that the balloon payment is coming due.

Interest can be charged using an "accrual" or an "add-on" method. The former is by far the most common method and exists when the installment payment covers both interest and principal reduction. Interest is charged only on the unpaid balance. The latter exists mainly in debt not related to real estate. Here, interest is computed for the entire amount of the loan and added on at the beginning.

Assignment Provision. Many notes provide that in the case of default, the borrower assigns the right to receive rents or other income from the property to the lender. This prevents the borrower from obtaining benefits from ownership while not paying the interest payments to the lender.

Lock-in Clause and Prepayments. Mortgage notes contain a phrase similar to "and the borrower promises to pay the installment amounts or more. . . " The "or more" portion of the clause allows the borrower to prepay any portion or all of the debt at any time prior to the term of the loan. Borrowers are more likely to prepay their loan when interest rates fall below the note rate. They refinance the existing note with a new note in order to take advantage of lower market rates. Since this prepayment (call) option has value, lenders may prefer to "lock in" the borrower by excluding this portion of the installment payment clause. Competition between lenders, state legislation, case law, and the regulations of federal agencies that insure loans (FHA, VA) have virtually eliminated the lock-in feature. As a result, the bulk of residential mortgages give the borrower the right to prepay at any time.

An alternative to the lock-in provision is a lender-imposed prepayment penalty fee. If the fee is large enough, the borrower will not prepay the loan when interest rates fall below the note rate. Here again, competitive forces, state legislation, and federal regulations have severely limited the use of prepayment penalties. Where they do exist, they are likely to be limited by legislation. The penalty may be limited in amount (say, the next six months' interest) or in time (within only the first 3 years of the loan). Prepayment penalties are not allowed in the case where the loan is accelerated because of a transfer of the property and the lender's exercise of the due-on-sale provision (below). Prepayment penalties are common on commercial real estate loans.

The general disuse of the lock-in clause or prepayment penalties on residential mortgages means that the majority of borrowers are free to exercise prepayments while it is advantageous to do so.

Default, Late Performance, and Acceleration. The note often will stipulate that if the borrower is late in paying the installment amount, a fee can be charged for the late performance. It also will indicate the number of days that the payment can be late before the loan is considered to be in default. In the event of default, the note will stipulate that the borrower is required to pay attorney's and other legal fees necessary to cure the default. These fees are added to the amount of the indebtedness that is secured by the residence. The acceleration clause indicates that in the event of default, the lender can require that the entire amount of the debt become due. There will be statutory limitations on the exercise of this lender option, however. The equitable right of redemption, available in all states, allows the borrower to cure the default up to several days before a trustee's sale of the property by bringing the debt (including any legal and other foreclosure fees) current. Additionally, most states require that a sale date be set at least three months subsequent to the Notice of Default (NOD). In the unusual event that the note is unsecured, the acceleration clause may be immediately enforceable.

Escrow (Impound) Accounts.   Since the residence is security for the note, lenders often require that payments for hazard insurance and property taxes be made as part of the regular installment payment and placed in an account for disbursement to the proper parties. It is in the interest of the lender to require such accounts. The lender needs to ensure that the hazard insurance is paid, because a loss of value due to a fire, for example, would reduce or eliminate the security for the note. Property tax payments also must be made, because any lien placed on the property for failure to pay taxes is superior to the lien of the lender. In some states, lenders can require an escrow account on some types of loans. Such accounts generally will be present on loans of greater than 90 percent loan-to-value ratio and on loans guaranteed by a government agency (FHA, VA). Lenders may not charge a fee for handling the account, and the borrower has the right to an end-of-year accounting and to have any excess accumulated funds returned.

Lenders can require a cushion of one-sixth of the total amounts paid out of the account (approximately two months worth). **RESPA** does not require escrows to be present. This is up to the lender. Also, HUD does not require interest to be paid on accounts. Some states do but many do not.

Guarantor.   Often an individual other than the borrower may guarantee the payment of the note. Lenders will require a personal guarantee when the borrower is a corporation or a limited partnership. This alleviates an agency problem. A major stockholder of a corporation could borrow money in the corporation's name and then waste the assets of the corporation (transfer them to another corporation, for example). In the event of default, the lender could foreclose on the note but would not have any security. For this reason, personal guarantees also are required. Additionally, the note may be secured by the corporation's property and not the stock of the corporation. In an unusual twist, the guarantor may end up with a greater liability than the borrower in states where antideficiency judgment legislation exists. Such legislation may not apply to guarantors. Thus, the borrower, even if a corporation, would be protected by the antideficiency legislation, but the guarantor would not. The lender would pursue the guarantor for any deficiency.

Due-on-Sale Clause.   We learned in Chapter 5 that assumable loans contain a valuable option. If market rates rise above the rate on the loan, it will have greater value if assumed than if prepaid when the property is sold. We saw in Chapter 7 that the value of the assumability option is capitalized to a certain extent into the value of the property. We also learned that the right to assumability was so valuable as to be the subject of expensive litigation. Since the Garn–St. Germain Act, virtually all due-on-sale clauses are enforceable. Recall that the regulatory authorities convinced Congress that enforcement was required to mitigate the interest rate risk faced by depository institutions and protect their solvency. Also under the act, a sale means any conveyance of any interest, including a lease, further encumbrance, or some types of transfers.

Rather than sell a property financed with a due-on-sale note, the owner may attempt to take advantage of the low rate on the note by leasing the property. A long-term lease would have a present value close to that of the property, yet the owner would make payments based on the note's low rate. Under the Garn Act, any leasehold interest greater than 3 years in length could represent a transfer of interest for the purpose of enforcing the due-on-sale clause. A lease with an option to purchase the property would also trigger the due-on-sale provision, even if less than 3 years.

Also, the creation of a junior lien on the property may trigger the due-on-sale clause for properties that contain more than one residential unit or are not owner-occupied (transfer of the right of occupancy). In addition, a foreclosure on the junior trust deed can activate the due-on-sale clause for all residential properties.

Residential properties often are transferred from one party to another upon death, divorce, or simply through a voluntary transfer (parents to children). In such situations, the transfer of the property will not activate the due-on-sale clause, unless the new owner does not occupy the residence or the property is not a single-family residence.

A transfer of the property to a trust likewise will not trigger the due-on-sale clause if the owner remains the beneficiary and there is no change in occupancy. The Office of Thrift Supervision regulations generally will not require an enforcement of the clause upon transfers involving single-family residences to be owner-occupied. Also, a lender that accepts payments on the original note from the new owners of the property may have waived his right to enforce the due-on-sale clause. OTS regulations are not intended to override state laws in regard to waivers.

Then there is involuntary conversion. If a fire completely destroys a residence, the lender has the right to require that the proceeds from insurance be applied to paying off the note rather than to rebuilding the property. The lender is more likely to require the repayment if market interest rates are substantially higher than that on the note. The borrower would be forced to rebuild the residence via a high-rate loan. In some states, however, the courts have sided with the property owner and required the lender to extend the terms of the original note. They cite the long-term expectations of each party to the contract and indicate that, as long as there is no threat to the security for the note, the borrower should be able to use insurance proceeds to rebuild the house.

Lenders may allow a loan to be assumed even if there is a due-on-sale clause. In such cases, the lender is allowed to, and may, charge an assumption fee. However, the fee cannot consist of "points" ordinarily associated with new loans. Case law in some states has made it clear that large assumption fees imposed by lenders during high-interest-rate periods constitute an unreasonable constraint on alienation (the right to convey property to another).

In order not to be unreasonable, the fee should reflect the expenses incurred by the lender in transferring the note to the new owner (credit evaluation, for example).

Sale, Transfer, or Assignment of the Note

The sale of notes and transfer of mortgages and trust deeds are two independent events. There are several means by which the sale (transfer) of the note can occur. One is by absolute assignment. Here, the seller retains no property rights or liabilities. The buyer of the note will not have recourse to the seller in the event of a default. To ensure no future liability, the seller may endorse the back of the note with the words "endorsed without recourse."

A second type of transfer is by endorsement. This leaves the seller personally liable to the buyer. In the case of future default on the note, the buyer can seek compensation from the seller for any loss incurred.

Finally, a transfer by guarantee occurs when a third party, not a party to the transaction, guarantees to the buyer that the note will be paid in full. The guarantee is really a separate transaction between the note buyer and the guarantor.

Deed-of-trust or Trust Deeds

The trust deed is an instrument that serves as security for the note. A third party to the lender-borrower relationship is added to hold the deed in trust. The trustee is usually a bank, attorney, title company, or other individual. There is generally no prohibition of the lender also serving as trustee, but this is unusual. The trust deed usually will say something to the effect that "the borrower grants and conveys to the trustee in trust, the following real property. . . ." In reality, the borrower retains the right to use the property as he sees fit—to possess, encumber, or sell it. Should the borrower default, the trustee, having a deed, is in position to quickly liquidate the property. A typical trust deed will identify the parties and have several provisions.

Parties to the Trust Deed

There are three parties to the trust deed: the borrower (trustor, who is also usually the owner of the property), the lender (beneficiary), and the trustee. The trustor can own and encumber a part-interest in real estate (for example, of two individuals owning real estate, one can encumber his part-interest). The beneficiary is the individual entitled to repayment of the note. Thus, if the note is sold, the buyer becomes the beneficiary under the new arrangement. Most of the provisions of a note are designed to protect the interest of the lender/beneficiary. Under most provisions, he can require that taxes and insurance be paid (placed in escrow), that the property be maintained, and most important, that he may liquidate the property if the borrower fails to make his payments. The borrower/trustor has the right to use the property within any limitations established by the covenants and restrictions (see below). He can also sell or lease the property. Many of the borrower's rights are given by state law rather than the trust deed. State law may require that interest be paid on the tax and insurance escrow account, or that the borrower has a right to an accounting of all amounts paid and owing if he has received a notice of default. Some state laws are potentially valuable to the borrower. They may give him the right to redeem the property even after foreclosure (for a specified period of time). We will discuss state laws in more detail in Chapter 14.

The only duties of the trustee are to act fairly without bias and to return the property title to the borrower when he receives documentation that the note has been paid.

Provisions of a Trust Deed

The provisions of the trust deed outline the rights and obligations of the lender/beneficiary and the borrower/trustor. In addition, the trust deed also may include many of the same provisions of the promissory note, such as those related to payments, escrow accounts, the due-on-sale clause, actions in the event of default, and so forth.

Assignment of Rents.   In the event of a default, this provision allows the lender to collect any rents from the property and apply them to the debt. In the unlikely event that the rents are substantial, they may be sufficient to cure the default. This provision prevents "equity skimming" by the borrower. Equity skimming occurs when an original or subsequent borrower (by assuming the loan) invests little equity in the property. He then collects rents from the property but makes no repairs or debt payments. The amount pocketed easily can exceed the initial equity after a few months. The borrower then defaults on the loan. If the lender has the right to intervene and collect the rents, this behavior is discouraged.

Waste.   The borrower agrees to keep the property in good condition so as not to lose value. In this way, the value of the collateral is not impaired.

Nonwaiver.   The lender's failure to exercise a right given in the trust deed is not to be construed to prohibit the exercise of the right in the future.

Security Protection.   The borrower must reimburse the lender for the costs of protecting the property from adversary interests in the event that the borrower fails to do so.

Successors and Assigns.   Any person or entity who receives an interest in the property must adhere to the same provisions as the borrower.

Substitution of Trustee.   This provision allows the lender to replace the trustee, assuming the proper papers are filed with the county recorder.

Reconveyance.   Upon payment of the indebtedness, this provision directs the lender to give the note and trust deed to the trustee, who in turn delivers the title to the borrower.

Release Clause.   This provision is typical for large residential real estate developments, where the land is used as collateral for a development loan. It allows the borrower to have some portion of the collateral (land) released from the provisions of the note and trust deed in return for a partial payment of the debt. This allows the borrower/developer to sell off parcels of the development without having to pay the entire debt. Usually, the lender will make sure that the value of the remaining collateral still exceeds the amount of the remaining debt.

Owner-occupancy.   By this provision, the owner promises to occupy the property. This prevents borrowers from purchasing the property as an investment. As we will see in Chapter 14, "investment properties" have a higher incidence of default than do owner-occupied properties. This also prevents equity skimming.

Award from Eminent Domain.   Should the property be expropriated by a governmental authority, the lender can claim the proceeds from the action to satisfy the debt. Otherwise, if the borrower received the proceeds, he could default on the debt and the lender would have no collateral.

Covenants and Restrictions.   These appear in the trust deed and can limit the use of the property by the borrowers in many ways. They may be as substantial as a prohibition of the use of the property as a business, or as minor as a limitation on the number of pets.

SUMMARY

In this chapter we saw how lenders manage default risk from the borrower qualification stage to the provisions in the mortgage and/or trust deed. At the borrower qualification stage, lenders are concerned that the value of the property that serves as collateral is greater than the amount of the loan. They also are concerned with the ability of the borrower to make the monthly payments. A great deal of stress is placed on the amount and stability of applicants' income, the size of the mortgage payments, and other nonmortgage debt obligations. Both government (FHA, VA) and private mortgage insurers have an interest in managing default risk. Many borrower qualification standards are set by them. Government agencies, such as the Federal National Mortgage Association and the Federal Home Loan Mortgage Corporation, purchase conventional mortgages and also are concerned with default risk. They establish their own qualification standards for "conforming" loans.

Most of the provisions in the mortgage and/or deed-of-trust protect the lender in case of default. The lender can step in and collect any rents or proceeds from insurance claims or eminent domain awards. The lender also can foreclose on and sell the property to recover the amount of the indebtedness. The lender can require the owner to maintain the property in good condition. Although the deed-of-trust may give the borrower some rights, most are given by state law. They include the right to cure a deficiency and reinstate the loan by making required payments. In some states, the right extends for a period beyond the foreclosure and liquidation of the property.

KEY TERMS

Ability-to-pay theory of default	Monthly effective income
Deed-of-trust	Mortgage
Default risk	Nonrecourse
Equity theory of default	Promissory note
Guarantor	Recourse
Income ratios	Residual method
Lock-in clause	Total mortgage payment

SUGGESTED READINGS

Ambrose, B., and C. Capone. 1996. Cost-Benefit Analysis of Single-Family Foreclosure Alternatives. *Journal of Real Estate Finance and Economics* Vol. 13, 105–120.

Clauretie, T. M., and M. Jameson. 1995. Residential Loan Renegotiation: Theory and Evidence. *Journal of Real Estate Research* Vol. 10, 153–161.

Dennis, M. W. 1989. *Residential Mortgage Lending.* Englewood Cliffs, NJ: Prentice-Hall, ch. 16.

Jackson, J. R., and D. L. Kaserman. 1980. Default risk on home mortgage loans: A test of competing hypotheses. *Journal of Risk and Insurance* Vol. 47, December.

Melicher, R. W., and M. Unger. 1989. *Real Estate Finance.* Cincinnati, OH: South-Western Publishing Co., ch. 1.

Sirmans, C. F. 1989. *Real Estate Finance*, 2nd ed. New York: McGraw-Hill, ch. 3.

Waller, N. 1988. Residential mortgage, default: A clarifying analysis. *Housing Finance Review* Vol. 7, Fall/Winter.

Wiedemer, J. P. 1990. *Real Estate Finance.* Englewood Cliffs, NJ: Prentice-Hall, ch. 5.

REVIEW QUESTIONS

12–1 a. State and explain the two theories of default.

b. Which theory makes more "intuitive" sense?

12–2 a. What is a deficiency judgment?

b. How useful are deficiency judgments in mitigating losses through borrower default?

12–3 Explain default as a "put option" held by the borrower.

12–4 Define borrower qualification.

12–5   Contrast borrower qualification under VA and FHA procedures. Describe the residual and income-ratio methods.

12–6   List four contractual relationships in a mortgage that are designed to protect the interest of the lender.

12–7   Indicate how state laws can require provisions in mortgages to protect the borrower.

12–8   What is the difference between a recourse and a nonrecourse promissory note?

12–9   List at least seven important provisions of promissory notes.

12–10   a. What is a trust deed?
        b. Who are the parties to a trust deed?
        c. What are the duties of the trustee?

12–11   List and explain at least five provisions of a typical trust deed.

PROBLEM

12–1   Assume the following monthly data for the Jones family:

Jones family	loan amount, $85,000
Gross income	$3,400
Federal taxes	425
PITI	795
Utilities and maintenance	160
Other debt payments	625
Social Security, retirement, life insurance, state and local taxes	235
Minimum residual	1,200

a. Compute the relevant qualifying ratios for (1) an FHA loan and (2) a VA loan.
b. Under which ratios, if any, would the Jones family qualify for a loan?

ENDNOTES

1. R. G. Quercia and M. A. Stegman, "Residential Mortgage Default: A Review of the Literature," *Journal of Housing Research,* 3(2) (1992): 341–379.

2. G. von Furstenberg, "Default Risk on FHA Insured Home Mortgages as a Function of the Terms of Financing: A Quantitative Analysis," *Journal of Finance* 24 (1969): 459–477.

3. G. von Furstenberg, "The Investment Quality of Home Mortgages," *Journal of Risk and Insurance* 37 (1970): 437–445.

4. G. von Furstenberg and J. R. Green, "Estimation of Delinquency Risk for Home Mortgage Portfolios," *AREUEA Journal* 2 (Summer 1974): 5–19.

5. T. G. Morton, "A Discriminant Function Analysis of Residential Mortgage Delinquency and Foreclosure," *AREUEA Journal* 3 (Fall 1975): 73–90.

6. T. Campbell and J. Kimble Dietrich, "The Determinants of Default on Insured Conventional Residential Mortgage Loans," *Journal of Finance* 38 (1983): 1596–1581.

7. J. R. Jackson and D. L. Kaserman, "Default Risk on Home Mortgage Loans: A Test of Competing Hypotheses," *Journal of Risk and Insurance* 47 (1980): 678–690.

8. B. Ambrose and C. Capone, "Cost-Benefit Analysis of Single-Family Foreclosure Alternatives," *Journal of Real Estate Finance and Economics* 13 (1996): 105–120.

9. T. Clauretie and M. Jameson, "Residential Loan Renegotiation: Theory and Evidence," *Journal of Real Estate Research* 10 (1995): 153–161.

WEB SITES

www.boston-financial.com   information on risk mitigation for lenders, investors, and REITs.

www.maxsol.com   provides a comprehensive guide for buying a home.

www.reinfonet.com   provides information for buyers and sellers of homes plus a nationwide referral network for finding real estate agents.

www.hsh.om/mort_calc.html   income qualification, housing affordibility calculator.

13

Loan Origination, Processing, and Closing

LEARNING OBJECTIVES

After reading this chapter, you should have an understanding of the steps involved in processing a loan application and closing a mortgage. You should know the data that must be collected and analyzed, the forms used throughout the process, and the regulations that must be observed. You also should understand the operation of mortgage bankers. Mortgage bankers originated, processed, and closed 51 percent of all residential loans in the United States in 1993. Savings and loan associations and commercial banks originated 22 percent and 27 percent, respectively. (Please note that all exhibits referred to in this chapter can be accessed through Microsoft Word on the CD packaged with the textbook.)

INTRODUCTION

In most cases, processing a residential loan transaction is a detailed step-by-step procedure. For government-insured loans, there is little leeway for variation, either in the process or in the documents used. The general process is the same for all types of residential loans, but for convenience our description will rely heavily on FHA loan transactions. The forms and procedures employed in loan processing are changing almost daily. As a result, should you ever be engaged in this type of activity, you will need to refer to the latest guidelines and practices.

LOAN PROCESSING

Loan processing involves several steps, including property appraisal, analysis of application (borrower information collection and verification), submission for credit approval, and closing the loan. At each step of the way, there are forms to organize the processing. Some of the forms are uniform and standardized by whatever government agency may be involved in the loan.

Property Appraisal

Property appraisal is one of the first steps in the loan process. The appraisal is generally made after the application for a loan. However, a developer who contemplates building and selling houses with FHA/VA financing will request an appraisal in conjunction with a master certificate of reasonable value (MCRV). The MCRV process allows for an appraisal of the property prior to the loan application and will establish both maximum values of the properties and maximum loan amounts if financed with FHA/VA loans.

There are three stages in the appraisal process: ordering the appraisal, monitoring the appraisal, and evaluating (reviewing) the appraisal.

Ordering the Appraisal.   The procedures for ordering conventional appraisals vary from lender to lender and from investor to investor. Most lenders are free to choose their own appraiser. Since January 1995, a **uniform residential appraisal report** has been used for nearly all loans, including those intended for sale to FNMA or Freddie Mac and those insured by the FHA or VA. They are available only to direct endorsement lenders. (See Exhibit 13–1 on CD.) Separate forms are used for condominiums (Exhibit 13–2) and for small (generally, up to four families) residential income properties. (Exhibit 13–3.) Since 1994, lenders have been able to choose the appraiser in FHA/VA loan applications whereas previously these agencies assigned appraisers to the property.

The regulatory environment of appraisers is shown in Figure 13–1. The Financial Institutions Reform, Recovery, and Enforcement Act of 1989 (FIRREA) mandated that state-certified or licensed appraisers must be used for the appraisal of properties involving federally related mortgage transactions after July 1, 1991.[1]

Under the act, each federal regulatory agency (Federal Reserve Board, FDIC, Office of the Comptroller of the Currency, Office of Thrift Supervision [formally the FHLBB], and the National Credit Union Administration) establishes appraisal guidelines for the appraising of federally related transactions. Virtually all mortgages are federally related, as they are insured by the FHA, guaranteed by the VA, originated by federally insured institutions, or originated for sale to federal secondary mortgage market agencies. FIRREA mandates that, at a minimum, all appraisal work must conform to the Uniform Standards of Professional Appraisal Practices (USPAP) as established by the Appraisal Standards Board of the Appraisal Foundation.[2]

The regulatory agencies can establish additional standards for the institutions they regulate. The act distinguishes between certified and licensed appraisers, the former meeting a stricter set of requirements. It delegated the certification and licensing to individual states. The state certification agencies must establish certification requirements in conformity with criteria established by the Appraiser Qualification Board of the Appraisal Foundation. The Appraiser Qualification Board assists the states by administering the Uniform State Certification Examination.

To see that the state certification agencies are doing their job in screening appraisers for certification and licensing, the act further establishes a government regulatory authority, the

FIGURE 13–1

Appraisal Regulation

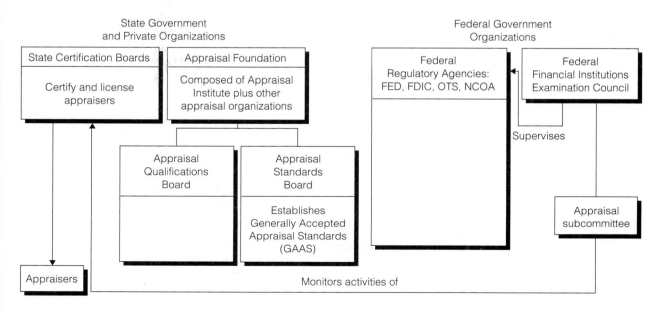

Appraisal Subcommittee of the Federal Financial Institutions Examination Council. This council oversees the various federal regulatory agencies.

Using a noncertified or nonlicensed appraiser in connection with a federally related mortgage transaction can result in a fine of $25,000 for the first violation and $50,000 for subsequent violations.

Monitoring the Appraisal.   At this stage, the loan processor makes sure that the appraisal is performed within the time specified by HUD (if an FHA loan) or by a private investor or secondary market agency. The processor makes certain that the appraiser gains access to the property and is paid upon receipt of the report.

Evaluating the Appraisal.   For government-insured loans, the lender will not receive a copy of the appraisal itself, only a conditional commitment (HUD-FHA) or certificate of reasonable value. The lender has somewhat less concern with the appraisal, since he is not at risk. If the appraised value appears to be low, the lender may request a reconsideration. To do so, the lender must provide detailed data on at least three comparable properties. The same appraiser makes the second appraisal, and if the lender is still dissatisfied, HUD will assign a staff appraiser to handle a second reconsideration.

For VA-guaranteed loans, the value established is an "as-is" value and requires that the veteran acknowledge the condition of the property prior to closing. HUD-FHA appraisals, on the other hand, may require that repairs be made if the health and safety of the occupants are endangered by a defect. Some appraisers become zealous at this point and require the property be almost "like new." This is not a strict requirement, however, and recently HUD has relaxed this rule. In some cases, the lender can request that HUD-FHA waive repairs if he feels that the defects do not materially affect the value of the property. If repairs are not waived, the seller must be informed so that he can make the necessary repairs and the loan can be processed.

The lender will receive a complete appraisal report for conventional loans. An **underwriter** or **review appraiser** will review the report for acceptability. The review may include visits to the property and a check on the transaction prices of any comparables used by the original appraiser. If the review is done only in the office of the review appraiser, it is called a **desk review.** The review appraiser will consider several important elements of the appraisal, including the physical characteristics of the subject property, the neighborhood, present and alternative land uses, predominant occupancy (owner-occupied versus rental units), price range of single-family properties, and range in age of properties. The appraisal report must indicate if the property is located in a HUD-identified flood hazard area. Flood zones are rated "A" if it is likely the property will be invaded by water, "B" if there is only a minimal chance of water invasion, and "C" if there is virtually no chance of flooding. Flood insurance is required for properties located in an "A" zone but is optional for "B" and "C".

It should be noted that under the *di minimus* rule lenders do not have to have an appraisal performed if the loan is for less than $200,000 and the lender will retain the loan in its own portfolio instead of selling it in the secondary market. However, since most lenders would like to reserve the option to sell the loan they will, as a general rule, have an appraisal done.

The valuation section of the appraisal will indicate how the appraiser arrived at the opinion of value. Generally Accepted Appraisal Standards require that the appraiser consider three approaches to the determination of value: cost, market, and income.

The **cost approach** is based on the premise that the buyer will not pay more for a property than for a comparable property with the same utility. Thus, the value of the property cannot be greater than the cost of replacing it. The steps in the cost approach are

1. Estimate the value of the land as vacant.
2. Estimate the cost of replacing the improvement.
3. Estimate depreciation for the improvement. This may be three types:
    a. physical deterioration (deferred maintenance, peeling paint, sagging shutters, etc.),
    b. functional obsolescence (bad floor plan, no air conditioning in south Florida, etc.), and/or
    c. economic obsolescence (changing neighborhood characteristics, busy street, etc.).

4. Subtract 3 from 2.
5. Add 1 plus 4 to arrive at total value.

In estimating depreciation, physical and functional obsolescence are generally internal to the property and may be **curable.** A problem is considered curable if the cost to remedy is not greater than the value added by making the repair. Economic obsolescence is external to the property and is generally **incurable.** Economic depreciation is generally caused by factors that are beyond the control of the individual homeowner. The amount of street traffic is an example. We should point out, however, that all external factors are not detrimental. A property that adjoins a golf course, for example, would have its value affected favorably.

The general limitation of the cost approach is that cost is not necessarily equal to value. For example, if you built an expensive home in an industrial district you would likely soon discover the difference between cost and value.

The **market approach** is based on the premise that transaction prices of similar properties (comparables) in the neighborhood are good indicators of value. The appraiser will generally utilize at least three comparables. The appraiser will make adjustments to the comparables for differences in physical characteristics of the properties relative to the subject property. For example, the appraiser may deduct $1300 from the value of the comparable because it had a fireplace and the subject property does not. Typically, there will be several adjustments. Besides physical characteristics, the review appraiser also will examine factors such as location, time on the market, and financing. The appraiser should make certain that the comparables do not involve creative or advantageous financing. We saw in Chapter 7 that transaction prices reflect the value of such financing. Failure to adjust for the effects of financing on the price of the creatively financed comparable could result in an overappraisal for the subject property.

The **income approach** says that the value of the property is a function of the income that accrues to it. Thus, this approach arrives at a value by capitalizing the potential rent on the property using either an income multiplier or overall capitalization rate. For example, if a property produces $1000 per month in gross rent and the appropriate gross rent multiplier (value divided by gross monthly rent) is 100, then the estimated value for the property is $100,000. The gross rent multiplier can be derived by dividing the transaction prices of recently sold comparable properties by the rent paid on those properties.

Alternatively, the appraiser may use the overall capitalization rate to determine value. The overall cap rate is the reciprocal calculation of income multiplier and is defined as net operating income (NOI as defined in chapter 15) divided by the value of the property. Again, comparable properties are generally used to determine the overall cap rate. Thus, if a property has NOI of $10,000 per year and the applicable capitalization rate is 10 percent, the indicated value of the property is $100,000.

The review appraiser will next determine the loan-to-value ratio. A loan guaranteed by the VA may not exceed the value of the property, and the FHA sets limits on the loan-to-value ratio. These limits vary from program to program but are generally above 90 percent. Conventional lenders will establish a maximum loan-to-value ratio for loans without private mortgage insurance. Generally, loans above 80 percent loan-to-value ratio will require insurance. The cost of the insurance will vary with the loan-to-value ratio. Loan-to-value ratios are computed by using the appraisal value or the contract price, whichever is less.

The estimates of value produced by the three approaches will generally not be identical. Thus, in the **reconciliation phase** of the appraisal, the appraiser will consider each estimated values and arrive at a final estimate. At this point, the appraisal becomes a "subjective art" rather than an "exact science" as the appraiser considers the reliability of each estimate based on such factors as quality and quantity of data.

Analysis of Application

This stage of loan processing involves a complete analysis of the financial position of the borrower and the disclosure of information required by RESPA, Regulation Z, and ECOA. RESPA requires that lenders provide, in advance, general information about the settlement costs (Exhibit 13–4) and, within three days after receiving the application, a statement of the estimated costs of settlement and monthly payments. (Exhibit 13–5.) Also within this three-day period, the lender must provide the borrower with a good-faith estimate (Exhibit 13–6) of the cost of the loan over its term, and it must include an estimate of the annual percentage rate (APR). The actual APR and total finance changes must be provided at or prior to settlement.

The FHA and VA use a joint application form for mortgages they insure. (Exhibit 13–7.) FNMA and FHLMC (Exhibit 13–8) have their preferred form for loans that will be sold to them. Some lenders prefer to take all loan applications on their own form and then transfer the data to the relevant application form. Some applications may be taken by an outside agent, such as a realtor or builder. HUD requires that FHA loans entail a face-to-face meeting between lender and borrower at some time during the application stage.

Some of the more important items collected on the application form include the type of loan applied for, terms of the loan applied for, purpose of the loan (construction loan, construction-permanent loan, existing property), names in which the title will be held, down payment and settlement charges, and borrower information. Important borrower information includes gross monthly income, other income, monthly housing expense, previous employment data, assets, liabilities, net worth, previous credit references, and a schedule of other real estate owned. These data are used for borrower qualification, which is part of the risk management outlined in Chapter 12.

In this phase of the loan process, the lender is concerned with two items: (1) the borrower's ability to make the down payment and monthly payments on the loan and (2) the accuracy of the financial data provided on the loan application. To address the first concern, the lender examines the borrower's liquid assets, the amount and stability of the borrower's income relative to housing expenses, and the past credit history of the borrower. On the second point, the lender must verify the accuracy of the financial data from independent, third-party sources. Financial data is verified as soon as possible, so that figures will not become outdated (verifications more than 90 days old are generally not acceptable for FHA loans). Requests for verification will be sent by the processor directly (not through the borrower) to the person from whom the verification is requested. If a lender asks the applicant to secure the verification, its status as an FHA/VA-approved lender may be revoked.

The FHA, VA, and Fannie Mae use a common form for the verification of deposit. (Exhibit 13–9.) The FHA and VA use one form for the verification of employment (Exhibit 13–10), while Fannie Mae uses a separate form. (Exhibit 13–11.) The verification forms must be signed by the applicant and sent directly to the depository institution and employer for their signatures. Often the lender will have to verify the existence and worth of other assets, such as stocks, bonds, retirement funds, equity in other real estate, and the cash surrender value of life insurance policies. Lenders have their own forms for these verifications. The lender also will require at least a 2-year history of income from all sources. The history is required to judge the amount and stability of income.

Finally, the lender will verify the credit standing of the applicant. The lender will request a credit report from a credit reporting agency (bureau) in the local area. If the applicant lived in another area within the last 2 years, then a credit report from that area will be required. The credit report will indicate any failure of the applicant to make timely payments to other creditors that report to the bureau. Some creditors of the applicant may not report information to the credit bureau. Typically, other mortgage lenders and credit unions do not provide credit histories to bureaus. In such a case, the lender will have to obtain a direct verification from them. The lender also will determine if there are any outstanding liens or judgments against the applicant in the public record.

Most verifications (credit reports) will be returned within two to seven (employment) days. The lender must monitor the process to see that all verifications are received in a timely manner.

Submission for Insurance

When the verification of borrower information has been made and it appears there are no major problems, the loan will be submitted for insurance. The FHA and VA have a common form for the submission. (Exhibit 13–12.) Most of the items on the form are self-explanatory, but a few comments are in order. If FHA credit approval is applied for, the lender will have to indicate which of the many FHA insurance programs is applicable. Each approved lender is assigned a ten-digit ID number which must be included in the application. Information on the borrower's race or national origin is sought for monitoring purposes. However, if the borrower prefers not to provide this information, it will not be included in the application for insurance.

Information on housing expenses, such as interest, hazard insurance, property taxes, utilities, and maintenance, must be included in the application. Information on the borrower's income assets and liabilities also is included. The FHA is particularly concerned with the financial position of the borrower and his or her ability to meet the monthly housing expenses.

The lender's certification portion of the application includes important information for the FHA or VA. By signing this portion, the lender certifies that all provisions and regulations of the FHA have been complied with. The lender also agrees to be responsible for any acts of its agents, such as the appraiser, employed to value the property.

The borrower's certification portion of the application also contains important information for both the borrower and the insuring agency. The FHA is particularly interested in knowing if the borrower has ever defaulted on a previous residential loan, has other FHA-guaranteed loans, or intends to rent the property covered by the insurance. All these factors affect the credit risk of the borrower. The FHA/VA also informs the borrower that, in the event the contract price exceeds the appraised value of the property, it is the borrower's responsibility to make up the difference through a cash down payment. The borrower also certifies that all information provided in the application is true and complete to the best of his or her knowledge.

Next, for FHA and VA insured loans, the lender prepares a loan analysis worksheet. (Exhibit 13–14.) The worksheet organizes the borrower qualification process that is a part of the risk management discussed in Chapter 12. If the worksheet is prepared properly by the lender, it will be given "priority" in processing by the local HUD office. The worksheet includes information on the borrower's (and co-borrower's) gross and net income, monthly payments for principal, interest, taxes, and insurance, other housing expenses, and other nonhousing monthly obligations. One purpose of the worksheet is to organize sufficient information to compute the ratios of net-effective-income to total housing expenses and total fixed payments. Another purpose is to determine if the borrower has sufficient liquid assets to meet the settlement requirements.

For FHA approval, the lender will submit a package consisting of the following documents:

1. Mortgage Credit Analysis Worksheet, (Exhibit 13–14)
2. Application for commitment of insurance, (Exhibit 13–12)
3. Copy of the sales contract,
4. All verifications of deposits, (Exhibit 13–9)
5. All verifications of employment, (Exhibit 13–10)
6. Credit reports,
7. Verifications of indebtedness, and
8. Other supporting documents, such as sales contract on former residence, schedule of payments on a GPM, any buydown escrow agreement, and evidence of security for secondary financing.

Many lenders participate in the FHA's **direct endorsement program.** Under this program, the lender essentially performs the underwriting process. To become a direct endorser, a lender will have to submit 15 or so test cases that the FHA will check. If there are no substantial differences between the underwriting process or decisions of the lender and the FHA for the test cases, approval will be granted for direct endorsement of subsequent loans. A lender that is a direct endorser is essentially an agent of the FHA. The lender may hire independent appraisers or use an FHA appraiser. By becoming a direct endorser, a lender will save several days in the total processing time.

If the application for insurance is accepted, the FHA will issue a mortgage insurance certificate. The certificate will indicate the maximum mortgage amount (which may include the financing of the mortgage insurance premium), the interest rate on the loan, and the monthly payment. The commitment will have an expiration date beyond which the loan cannot be closed. If the commitment is conditional on modifications of the loan arrangement, the expiration date is six months after issue for existing properties and 1 year for new properties. For firm commitments, the expiration date is the expiration date of the conditional commitment, or 90 days from the date of the firm commitment, whichever is later.

Loan Closing

The loan closing is composed of two distinct, but related, transactions. In one transaction, title to the property passes from the seller to the buyer. In the other, the buyer signs a promissory note. The closing involves preparing and assembling the legal documents necessary in the jurisdiction to carry out the closing transaction. In some areas of the country, the closing agent will prepare all of the documents. In other areas, the lender will prepare the documents and forward them to a closing agent to complete the process. In still other locations, the lender prepares the documents, carries out the closing, and records the documents. Regardless of the system used, there are certain documents that must be included in the closing transaction and recorded in the local courthouse.

The **note** represents the borrower's promise to repay the loan. It states the terms of the loan, including the loan amount, interest rate, payments, due date, and so forth.

For some jurisdictions, the **mortgage** or **deed-of-trust** are standard. FNMA and FHLMC use a joint form; the FHA and VA have similar but somewhat different forms, due to the nature of their programs. The mortgage or deed-of-trust will include much of the same basic information as the note and, in addition, will provide a legal description of the property.

The **deed** conveys title to the property from the seller to the buyer. It is important that the sellers identified in the deed as the grantors are the same as the owners-of-record and that the buyers indicated as the grantees are the same as the borrowers identified in the mortgage or deed-of-trust. The property identified on the deed also must be the same as that on the mortgage.

The **settlement statement** is a record of what went on at the closing. The record is kept on form HUD-1, a standardized settlement statement designed to comply with the Real Estate Settlement Procedures Act (RESPA). RESPA requires that the form be used for all "federally related" loans. There may be more than one copy of the HUD-1 form. The form given to the seller may or may not show the costs paid by the buyer, and vice versa.

The **commitment** should be part of the closing file. If an FHA commitment is involved, the borrower must sign certain certifications. (Exhibit 13–15.)

Truth-in-lending disclosure must be given to the borrower and must include the major financial terms of the loan (see Chapter 8).

Disbursement.   Disbursement is part of the closing process and can be handled in a couple of different ways. The lender may give the closing agent several checks payable to the ultimate recipients (title company, mortgage insurer, real estate agent, and so forth). Alternatively, the lender can give the closing agent one check for the full amount of the loan and payable to the agent. The agent then issues its own checks to the ultimate recipients.

Recording.   The deed and the mortgage are recorded, so as to give notice to the public that the buyer is the new owner of the property and the mortgagee has a lien on the property. Recording is not necessary to enforce any claims made in regards to the transfer of the property or the indebtedness. It is necessary, however, to protect the owner against others that may claim also to have a valid deed or to protect the lender against those that may claim to have a senior lien against the property.

Mortgage Insurance Payments.   We will limit our discussion of mortgage insurance to FHA insurance. The lender will instruct the closing agent to make a check payable to the Secretary of Housing and Urban Development for the full amount of the mortgage insurance premium (MIP). The amount must agree with that indicated on the HUD-1 settlement form. Late charges and interest are assessed by HUD if the check is delayed. The check will accompany a Mortgagee's One-Time MIP Transmittal Form. (Exhibit 13–16.) In return, HUD will send the lender a "Statement of Account" which summarizes the transaction. The lender then will file a submission for insurance, certifying that all FHA requirements have been met. The submission will include the statement of account, a mortgage insurance certificate, a copy of the note and mortgage, the original FHA firm commitment, the settlement statement, the federal truth-in-lending disclosure statement, a builder's warranty (if new construction), a mortgagee certification of repairs, and a mortgagee review certification.

The mortgagee's review certification is a signed document whereby the lender certifies that (1) the borrower has made at least the minimum cash investment, (2) the borrower has not paid any prohibited fees or charges, (3) all of the conditions imposed by the firm commitment have been met, (4) all repairs required by the firm commitment have been made, and (5) the terms of the mortgage conform to HUD requirements and the terms of the firm commitment.

MORTGAGE BANKING

Mortgage banking is the origination, servicing, and sale of mortgage loans by a firm or individual. Mortgage bankers specialize in the details of loan origination discussed in this chapter. Mortgage bankers are not bankers in the sense of institutions that take customer deposits; that is, they are not depository institutions. Nor do mortgage bankers hold the loans they originate; they are not "portfolio" lenders. They are simply originators that process, close, and sell the loans they make. They often retain servicing rights, however. Loan servicing consists of several duties. It involves collecting monthly payments from the borrower, making sure escrow payments (impounds) are made for insurance and taxes, handling delinquencies and defaults, forwarding payments to the investor, and even inspecting properties on occasion. Mortgage bankers collect a fee for servicing the loans they originate. They have an expertise in these functions and do not share in either the returns or the risk of investing in and holding mortgage loans.[3]

The position of mortgage bankers relative to other mortgage originators is indicated in Table 13–1. The numbers show that the share of mortgages written by mortgage bankers has steadily increased over time such that, in the 1990s, they have written more mortgages than commercial banks and savings and loan associations combined.

TABLE 13-1
Originations of Residential Mortgages (billions of $)

Year	Commercial Banks	Mutual Savings Banks	Savings and Loans	Mortgage Bankers	Other Lenders	Total
1970	7.8	2.1	14.8	8.9	1.9	35.6
1971	12.6	3.5	26.6	12.5	2.6	57.8
1972	17.7	5.1	36.7	13.3	3.0	75.9
1973	18.8	5.9	38.4	12.7	3.3	79.1
1974	16.1	3.9	30.9	13.0	3.5	67.5
1975	14.5	4.3	41.2	14.0	3.9	77.9
1976	24.5	6.4	61.9	15.7	4.2	112.8
1977	36.7	8.7	86.3	25.7	4.7	162.0
1978	43.9	9.4	90.0	34.4	7.3	185.0
1979	41.4	9.0	82.8	45.3	8.6	187.1
1980	28.8	5.4	61.1	29.4	9.0	133.8
1981	21.7	4.0	42.0	24.0	6.5	98.2
1982	25.2	4.0	34.8	28.0	5.0	97.0
1983	44.8	10.8	81.5	59.8	5.0	201.9
1984	41.9	12.7	96.2	47.6	5.3	203.7
1985	57.0	7.5	109.3	110.0	6.0	289.8
1986	108.6	31.1	176.1	176.0	7.6	499.4
1987	124.6	34.2	174.5	167.1	6.8	507.2
1988	101.9	28.4	160.4	148.0	7.5	446.2
1989	121.2	23.2	134.5	166.5	7.5	452.9
1990	153.3	18.0	121.0	161.2	5.0	458.4
1991	153.3	18.5	121.9	263.9	4.4	562.1
1992	232.1	34.2	184.5	437.6	5.2	893.7
1993	269.0	39.4	179.3	526.5	5.6	1,019.9
1994	200.0	29.3	123.1	408.1	8.2	768.7
1995	151.3	23.7	95.6	358.7	6.5	635.8

Sources of Funds

Mortgage bankers have two principal sources of funds. One is commercial paper. Commercial paper is a short-term (180 to 270 days) obligation that carries a rate about equal to the prime rate, but that can be somewhat higher or lower through the interest rate cycle. Only large mortgage bankers can issue commercial paper. A second source of funds for mortgage bankers is short-term loans from commercial banks; these are called **warehousing loans.** A mortgage banker will ask for a line-of-credit for, say, $2 million. The mortgage banker will agree to a compensating balance, usually 20 percent of the maximum line-of-credit. As mortgage loans are made from this line-of-credit, the mortgage banker will pledge those loans as collateral for the line-of-credit. That is, when the mortgage banker originates a mortgage for $100,000, he will simultaneously "take down" $100,000 of the $2 million line-of-credit and pledge the mortgage note for collateral. After the mortgage banker has originated $2 million in mortgages, he will sell them to an investor. The proceeds of the sale will pay off the line-of-credit at the commercial bank. Often, the mortgage banker will have received a commitment from an investor (FHLMC, for example) to purchase the loans for a set price. The warehousing cycle is complete and can be repeated. Each time, the mortgage banker usually retains the servicing of the loans.

Revenues

Revenues for mortgage bankers come from four main sources. Mortgage bankers charge origination fees, usually 1 percent of the amount of the mortgage. They also charge a servicing fee, from 0.25 to 0.5 percent of the outstanding balance annually. Mortgage bankers also make some income on the difference between the rate earned on the mortgage and the rate paid for the line-of-credit at the commercial bank while the mortgages are being held and prepared for sale. This revenue is called the **warehousing rate difference.** Mortgage bankers also may earn revenue from a **marketing rate difference.** This is the difference between the amount originated and the amount received from the sale. Origination and servicing fees represent the largest portion of mortgage bankers' revenues.

Some mortgage bankers grow through purchasing the servicing rights of other originators. There are definite economies of scale in mortgage banking. Because of fixed costs, as a mortgage banker grows in size, the average cost per serviced loan declines. Thus, profit per loan serviced increases with size. Mortgage bankers who may be limited in the amount of mortgages they can originate will grow by purchasing the service rights to mortgages from other originators. Servicing rights are a sort of mortgage-derivative security in their own right, and their value depends upon a host of assumptions regarding future interest rates and prepayments. Most rights sell for between 1.5 percent and 2.25 percent of the amount to be serviced. The valuation of servicing rights was discussed in Chapter 11.

Mortgage bankers are not regulated by any government agency as are thrifts and commercial banks. They are partnerships or corporations and, as such, are governed somewhat by state laws which address these forms of business. Other than that, there is no active regulation of mortgage bankers. Their activities are subject, however, to periodic audits if they are approved as lenders by the FHA or as lender/servicers by FNMA.

SUMMARY

The steps involved in loan origination, processing, and closing are designed to reassure the parties to the transaction that their interests are protected. The buyer will want a clear (unencumbered) title to the property. The lender will want security for the loan. He will want to be assured that the buyer will make the required payments and that the value of the collateral (property) will be preserved through an accurate appraisal and by payment of property taxes and hazard insurance.

The lender also will desire insurance against events that would cause a loss, such as would result from a borrower default (mortgage insurance) or a clouded title that would jeopardize the lender's interest (title insurance). The insurance agencies will take steps necessary to verify that sufficient information has been gathered to assess the risk of default and loss.

At each step throughout the process, verifications of relevant facts, data, or information by outside parties will be required. The entire process can be appreciated as one in which each party takes the necessary steps to protect against loss.

Mortgage bankers are specialists in the origination, processing, and closing of residential loans. They do not hold loans in their own portfolios. They obtain sources of funds for lending by borrowing short-term from commercial banks (warehousing). After selling the loans, the mortgage bankers will repay this loan.

Mortgage bankers obtain revenue primarily from servicing the loans they originate. Other sources of revenue include their warehousing rate difference and marketing rate difference.

KEY TERMS

Appraisal	Marketing rate difference
Cost approach	Mortgage banking
Income approach	Review appraiser
Market approach	Underwriter
Desk review	Warehousing loans
Direct endorsement program	Warehousing rate difference
Loan processing	

SUGGESTED READINGS

Stowe, A.M. 1997. Servicing FHA Single-Family Loans. *Mortgage Banking* 57:8, 91–97.

REVIEW QUESTIONS

13–1   List and explain the steps in loan processing.

13–2   What is the importance of an appraisal in loan processing?

13–3   List and briefly explain the three basic appraisal methods.

13–4   What information concerning a loan applicant must be verified, and how is it verified?

13–5   In the realm of FHA insurance, what is a "direct endorsement"?

13–6   What two transactions take place in the loan closing?

13–7   What is a settlement statement?

13–8   What documents must be recorded and why?

13–9   Define mortgage banking.

13–10   What are the sources of revenue of mortgage bankers?

13–11   What is meant by the term "warehousing" of loans?

ENDNOTES

1.   Because many states were late in passing legislation and establishing the rules and procedures for licensing and certification, the Federal Appraisal Subcommittee of the Federal Financial Institutions Examination Council extended the deadline to January 1, 1992. Then, in late 1991, Congress included a provision in some banking legislation that extended the deadline again, until January 1, 1993.

2.   The Appraisal Foundation is a private organization made up of representatives of several appraisal groups, the largest of which is the Appraisal Institute (resulting from a merger in 1991 of the former American Institute of Real Estate Appraisers and the Society of Real Estate Appraisers).

3.   An exception would occur if a secondary market agency required a mortgage banker to take back a nonperforming loan.

WEB SITES

www.mortgages.infopages.net   example of information required for loan processing

14

Mortgage Default Insurance, Foreclosure, and Title Insurance

LEARNING OBJECTIVES

After reading this chapter, you should understand how each of three different default insurance plans—VA, FHA, and private mortgage insurance (PMI)—operate. You should understand the basic differences between the three insurance plans and be able to distinguish between partial insurance, full insurance, and coinsurance. You should also understand how foreclosure laws of the various states differ and how those laws affect mortgage insurance claims under the different insurance plans. Finally, you should understand the risk that is insured by title insurance and appreciate the economics of the title insurance industry.

INTRODUCTION

In this chapter, we review the essentials of default insurance, foreclosure laws, and title insurance. We begin with a description and comparison of three default insurance plans: VA, FHA, and private mortgage insurance (PMI). These plans are different in terms of eligibility requirements, costs (premiums), loan limits, underwriting procedures, and coverage. Next, we will look at the foreclosure laws in various states. We will discuss the differences between judicial and power-of-sale procedures, equitable and statutory rights of redemption, and recourse and nonrecourse (antideficiency judgment) provisions. We will analyze the impact of the various foreclosure laws on default risk and on insurance claims under the coverage of the different insurance plans. We then will discuss title insurance—its purpose, nature, and cost.

MORTGAGE DEFAULT INSURANCE

There are four principal types of mortgage default insurance. All insure the lender against losses that result from borrower default and subsequent foreclosure. One type provides **partial coverage,** in which the insurer will cover losses up to a certain percentage of the original amount of the loan. If the coverage is 20 percent, then all claims up to $20,000 on a $100,000 loan would be covered. A second type provides for **full coverage.** Under full coverage, all lender losses are covered. A third type is **coinsurance.** With coinsurance all losses up to a certain portion of the loan are covered. Losses above this amount are shared between the lender and the insurer in the same ratio. Thus, if the coverage ratio is 20 percent and there is a $30,000 loss on a $100,000 loan, the lender will cover $22,000 of the loss ($20,000 + 20 percent of the remainder). Later, we will see that the type of insurance affects the extent to which lenders have an incentive to control losses. The fourth type of mortgage insurance is **self-insurance.** With this insurance, lenders absorb the default risk themselves.

With respect to mortgage insurance and lenders, however, a couple of points should be made. First, the cost of the insurance is typically borne by either the borrower (in the case of

FHA and PMI) or the federal government (VA). Second, the borrower may have no choice in carrying mortgage insurance since it may be a qualifying contingency. For example, the guarantee on a VA loan is provided at no cost except for a funding fee paid by the borrower at origination. This funding fee is not optional for the borrower. On FHA loans and loans covered by private mortgage insurance, there is an up-front fee and a yearly premium both paid by the borrower. Since FHA insurance covers the entire loan amount, historically the premium had to be paid by the borrower for the entire life of the loan (this has changed and will be discussed later) and payment of the premium is not optional but mandatory. The same is true in general for conventional mortgages that have loan-to-value ratios greater than 80 percent; private mortgage insurance is generally a requirement.

Government Insurance

There are two government insurance programs: the VA and FHA. The VA is a partial insurance program; it covers losses up to a certain proportion of the loan amount. The FHA is a full insurance program; it covers all losses. Most private mortgage insurance is coinsurance. Insurance firms cover losses up to a certain percent of the loan and additional losses are shared by the lender.

Veterans Administration (VA)

VA insurance was created by the Serviceman's Readjustment Act of 1944 with Section 501 of the GI Bill of Rights. The Veterans Administration (VA) was elevated to cabinet rank in 1989. The VA provides a guarantee program to assist eligible veterans and their immediate families (generally the spouse) in acquiring a home with little or no down payment. The veteran must occupy the home as his/her primary residence. Veterans on overseas active duty may purchase a home as a primary residence for his/her immediate family. The VA guarantees a portion of the loan to the lender depending on the amount of the veteran borrower's eligibility. The VA does not protect the veteran against losses of any kind.

To be eligible for a VA loan, veterans must serve a minimum time on active duty. As discussed in an earlier chapter, the time runs from 90 days for "hot" wars to 6 years for the reserves and National Guard. In general, service during peacetime requires 181 days of continuous active duty for eligibility. A veteran not on active duty must hold a discharge other than dishonorable. Unmarried surviving spouses of individuals who died while in service or as the result of a service connected disability are generally eligible for a VA loan.

A veteran's Certificate of Eligibility certifies his/her **entitlement.** As of October 1994, the maximum available entitlement is $50,750. In contrast, the maximum entitlement at the inception of the program in 1944 was $2000. As house prices have increased over the years, Congress has likewise increased the entitlement limit.

The VA guarantees the lender against losses up to 25 percent of the original loan, or $50,750, whichever is less. This establishes a maximum loan amount of $203,000. Most VA loans are sold to Ginnie Mae which requires at least 25 percent guaranty. Thus, Ginnie Mae will purchase VA loans with original principal balances up to this amount.

VA loans approved prior to March 1, 1988, are fully assumable, and those approved subsequently are assumable subject to credit qualification of the buyer. For the former loans, the veteran is liable for the default of the buyer unless the veteran obtains a release of liability. For the latter loans, the buyer must assume full liability to repay the loan, including the indemnity liability of the VA. In either case, the VA loan always must have an entitlement attached to it. Thus, when a property is sold to a nonveteran, the selling veteran's entitlement remains with the property. Entitlement can only be restored by replacing it with another entitlement or by repaying the mortgage. One should note that restoration of entitlement is different from release of liability. For example, a veteran may allow the mortgage to be assumed by a nonveteran who qualifies. In this case the nonveteran could assume liability for the loan giving the veteran a release of liability. However, the veteran's entitlement would continue to be encumbered by the loan. Veterans who previously have used their entitlement may have an unused portion which they may apply to the purchase of another residence, even though the initial loan has not been paid off.

The VA guarantee entails a funding fee which varies with the amount of down payment. For a 0 to less than 5 percent down payment, the funding fee is 2 percent of the loan amount. With at least 5 percent but less than 10 percent down payment, the fee is 1.5 percent and for a 10 percent or greater down payment the fee is 1.25 percent. The fee is higher for reservists and for mortgage refinancings. The fee is waived for veterans entitled to compensation for service-connected disabilities. The fee may be included in the loan amount, provided the total does not exceed the VA limit. Existing single-family, two- and four-unit dwellings are eligible for insurance as long as the veteran occupies the property after the closing. New units are not eligible unless the builder has received prior approval or provides the veteran with an approved 10-year warranty.

The VA also will guarantee qualifying graduated-payment loans. Because of the negative amortization feature, the veteran will be required to make a down payment and the rate on the loan may be slightly higher than on a standard loan. Starting in 1992, the VA has an adjustable-rate mortgage program. These are 1 year adjustables using the Treasury Bill yield index with annual and life-of-loan interest rate caps of 1 and 5 percent and a margin of 2.00.

Since 1992, market interest rates and discount points can be charged on VA loans. Any discount points paid by the borrower cannot be added to the loan amount. Previously, interest rates were set by the VA Director and no points except the funding fee could be paid by the borrower.

FHA Insurance

The Federal Housing Administration (FHA) was created by the National Housing Act in 1934 to encourage improvement in housing standards and conditions. The primary function for FHA is and has always been to provide a system of mutual mortgage insurance. FHA has been part of the Department of Housing and Urban Development since 1965. The mortgage insurance programs are designed to provide protection to private lenders against losses caused by defaults by borrowers. Like the VA, the FHA does not protect the borrower against losses of any kind, nor does it lend government funds directly. The FHA has more than 50 different programs providing loans for homes purchases, home improvement, nursing homes, mobile home parks, and multifamily projects, among others.

Along with typical mortgage financing, the FHA will make construction/permanent loans that can assist builders by allowing borrowers to be approved prior to construction. Also, the FHA will do reverse annuity mortgages allowing borrowers to convert equity into a monthly income and/or a line of credit. Borrower requirements for this type loan are: (1) at least 62 years of age, (2) own property, (3) occupy as principal residence, and (4) participate in a consumer information session. For this type loan there are no income qualifications and no repayment as long as the home is occupied as principal residence by the borrower. Closing costs may be financed and financing is available for one to four unit properties.

Coverage under FHA insurance is different from the VA guarantee. FHA insures the full amount of the loan in the event of default and foreclosure. To control risk, FHA places a limit on the amount of the loan it will insure and underwrites the loan taking into consideration the borrower's income, credit and work history, funds available for settlement, and monthly housing expense. FHA insurance is open to any qualified resident of the United States. Citizenship is not required but the property must be the borrower's principal residence and must be located in the United States.

The interest rate and amount of discount points are negotiable with the lender. Discount points can be paid by either the buyer or the seller. Prior to November 30, 1984, FHA had set a maximum rate the lender could charge and prohibited the buyer from paying the points (except one point origination fee). The purpose of these limits was to protect borrowers. The reality was, however, that when the market rate exceeded the pegged FHA rate, lenders charged points on FHA loans in order to equalize the rates. Since the borrower could not pay the points, they were charged to the seller who often raised the price of the house. This policy created such distortions in the credit market that FHA abandoned the practice in favor of the current policy.

Loan Limits.   The upper limit on the loan amount used to be uniform nationally. This caused a shortage of FHA insurance in areas where housing was particularly expensive, such as Hawaii, Alaska, and portions of California. Consequently loan limits are allowed to vary depending on the cost of housing for a given area. Currently the high cost limit is $160,950 for a single-family home, but in many high-cost areas the limit is set at 95 percent of the median house price in the SMA or county. Limits for Alaska, Guam, Hawaii, and the Virgin Islands may be adjusted up to 150 percent of loan limits. The limits are higher for multifamily properties. The FHA will finance up to four-unit properties as long as one unit is owner-occupied.

Loan Assumptions.   Prior to December 1, 1986, all FHA loans were simple assumptions. This meant that the buyer did not have to qualify to assume the mortgage. Furthermore, there was no release of liability for payments for the seller unless requested and if the purchasor agreed to assume such liability. This remains the status of those loans. For loans originated between December 1, 1986, and December 14, 1989, rules regulating assumptions changed. Assumptions made within 1 year of origination required a creditworthiness review of the persons seeking to assume the mortgage. The period was extended to 2 years if the assuming parties did not intend to occupy the residence. (Loans made to, or assumed by, nonowner occupants are called investor loans.) For loans originated subsequent to December 14, 1989, the rules governing assumptions were changed again. For the entire life of the loan, a creditworthiness review is required of all borrowers seeking to assume the loan. Furthermore, no nonowner occupants (investors) may assume any of these loans. That is, the assumptor must be an owner-occupant.

Refinancing.   FHA loans can be refinanced, and cash can be obtained on owner-occupied properties up to 85 percent of the acquisition cost (appraised value plus closing costs). A borrower can refinance out of an insured, graduated-payment loan, but not into one. In March 1989, FHA announced its Streamline Refinance Plan (SRP) for very-high-rate mortgages (15 percent and above). Under the plan, FHA offered refinancing with little paperwork and the refinancing costs included in the new loan. Alternatively, the borrower could refinance without any costs whatsoever by obtaining a new loan with a rate slightly above the market rate. Because mortgage rates at the time were approximately 10 to 11 percent, the plan offered borrowers tremendous savings on their payments.

Loan-to-value Ratios.   The FHA has several loan programs, the most popular being the Section 203b program. This program insures standard 30-year, fixed-rate mortgages on one- to four-family houses. FHA had set the maximum loan-to-value ratio at 97 percent of the first $25,000 and 95 percent of the remainder up to $125,000 (after which it goes to 90 percent), based on the lesser of the appraised value or selling price (including closing costs). The Omnibus Budget Reconciliation Act of 1990 (OBRA) modified the National Housing Act to set additional limits on the loan-to-value ratio under this program. For a property with an appraised value of $50,000 or less, the maximum loan-to-value ratio is 98.75 percent of the lesser of the appraised value or sales price (excluding closing costs). For properties with an appraised value of more than $50,000, the maximum loan-to-value ratio is 97.5 percent of the lesser of the above two values. Thus, two calculations must be made. If the FHA rules result in the lower amount, then the closing costs are considered to be financed. However, it is important to note that in 1991 HUD announced additional regulations that limited the percent of closing costs that could be financed to 57 percent. Examples of the calculations for properties over and under $50,000 in value are demonstrated in Table 14–1.

The Section 245a program is the FHA's graduated payment mortgage plan. The borrower can qualify with less monthly income, but the down payment requirement is larger than the standard 203b loan because of the negative amortization. Depending upon the plan selected, the payments will increase annually for 5 or 10 years and for various growth rates. Appendix A to this chapter compares the payments on three popular plans and the percent of the acquisition price that can be financed under the FHA GPM Plan III. As an example, for interest rates around 10 percent, the borrower must have a down payment of approximately 9 percent of the acquisition price.

Mortgage Insurance Premium.   Prior to 1984 the FHA charged an annual premium (paid monthly) over the life of the loan. The annual premium was 0.5 percent of the outstanding balance. This amount was divided by twelve and added to the monthly payment. If a loan was pre-

T A B L E   1 4 – 1

Calculation of Maximum Loan-to-value
Ratio for Section 203b Program

A. Examples for a property with a value exceeding $50,000:

Example No. 1; $2,000 closing costs

First Calculation (per FHA rules)

$90,000   Lesser of sales price or appraised value
+ 1,140   Add allowable closing costs (57% × $2,000)
$91,140
−25,000 × 97% = $24,250
$66,140 × 95% = $62,833
$87,083

Second Calculation (per OBRA amendments)

$ 90,000   Lesser of sales price or appraised value
×97.75%   Do not add closing costs
$ 87,975

In this example, the maximum mortgage would be $87,083, and $1140 of the closing costs are financed.

Example No. 2; $5,000 closing costs

First Calculation (per FHA rules)

$90,000   Lesser of sales price or appraised value
+ 2,850   Add allowable closing costs (57% × $5,000)
$92,850
−25,000 × 97% = $24,250
$67,850 × 95% = $64,458
$88,708

Second Calculation (per OBRA amendments)

$ 90,000   Lesser of sales price or appraised value
×97.75%   Do not add closing costs
$ 87,975

In this example, the maximum mortgage is $87,975, and no closing costs are financed.

B. Examples for a property with a value less than $50,000:

Example No. 1; $800 closing costs

First Calculation (per FHA rules)

$48,000   Lesser of sales price or appraised value
+   456   Add allowable closing costs ($800 × 57%)
$48,456
× 97%
$47,002

Second Calculation (per OBRA Amendments)

$ 48,000   Lesser of sales price or appraised value
×98.75%   Do not add closing costs
$ 47,400

In this example, the maximum mortgage is $47,002 because it is the lesser of the two calculations. Here, $456 in closing costs are financed.

Example No. 2; $2000 closing costs

First Calculation (per FHA rules)

$48,000   Lesser of sales price or appraised value
+ 1,140   Add allowable closing costs ($2,000 × 57%)
$49,140
× 97%
$47,666

Second Calculation (per OBRA amendments)

$ 48,000   Lesser of sales price or appraised value
×98.75%   Do not add closing costs
$ 47,400

In this example the maximum mortgage is $47,400, and no closing costs are financed.

paid, the borrower simply ceased to make premium payments but did not receive a refund of any sort. From 1984 to 1991, the annual premium was dropped and the FHA charged a one-time, up-front premium only (except for loans on condominiums, which continued to have a monthly premium charged. The one-time mortgage insurance premium was either paid in cash at closing or financed into the mortgage. If financed into the mortgage, the premium was 3.8 percent of the amount of the loan. If paid in cash at closing, the premium was 3.661 percent. The full premium structure is shown in Table 14–2.

In 1990 a new law established a phased-in reduction of the rate to a permanent 2.25 percent. This portion of the premium was renamed the up-front MIP. The permanent rate became effective in 1994. The up-front premium can be financed and is the same whether it is paid in cash or financed into the mortgage. The new law also reinstated the annual premium so that currently the FHA borrower pays both an up-front premium and an annual premium.

Since the up-front premium is a lump-sum payment that covers the life of the loan, it is subject to a partial refund when a loan is prepaid. The FHA calculates the refund using a scale based on the number of years the loan has been outstanding. There is no refund if the loan is assumed.

The amount of the reinstated annual premium is 0.5 percent of the outstanding balance. The length of time the premium has to be paid depends on the amount of down payment. With a loan-to-value ratio less than 90 percent, the annual premium is assessed for the first 11 years of the loan life. With a loan-to-value ratio from 90 percent through 95 percent, the premium must be paid for the full 30 years. If a mortgage has a loan-to-value ratio greater than 95 percent the premium charge jumps to 0.55 percent and must be paid for the full life of the loan. Table 14–3 shows the fee structure since 1991. This fee structure is also applicable to graduated payment loans. The fee structure gradually transfers the cost of insurance from an up-front to a "pay-as-you-go" basis. Many real estate professionals urged this change because it lowered the initial cost of purchasing a residence.

The Rural Housing Service

The Rural Housing Service (formerly the Farmers Home Administration) has a guaranteed housing loan program. The program is designed to provide mortgage financing for rural areas. The program provides financing for new home loans, for construction-to-permanent loans, and loans to purchase existing homes, including repairs/improvements. Typical advantages of this program are: (1) 100 percent loan-to-value ratio, (2) no mortgage insurance, (3) closing costs and the guarantee fee can be financed in many cases, (4) conventional appraisals are used, (5) not limited to first-time home buyers, and (6) 29 percent and 41 percent payment-to-income ratios.

TABLE 14–2
One-time MIP Factor Table
1984–1990

Portion of MIP Financed	Term of Loan in Years			
	Less Than 18	18–22	23–25	More Than 25
100%	0.024	0.030	0.036	0.038
0%	0.02344	0.02913	0.03475	0.03661

TABLE 14–3
FHA Mortgage Insurance Premiums

Fiscal Year	Up-front MIP	LTV	Term of Annual Premium	Annual Premium
1991 & 1992	3.80%	89.99 & under	0.50	5 years
	3.80	90.00–95.00	0.50	8 years
	3.80	95.01 & over	0.50	10 years
1993 & 1994	3.00	89.99 & under	0.50	7 years
	3.00	90.00–95.00	0.50	12 years
	3.00	95.01 & over	0.50	30 years
1995 & later	2.25	89.99 & under	0.50	11 years
	2.25	90.00–95.00	0.50	30 years
	2.25	95.01 & over	0.55	30 years

The program does impose some restrictions such as no swimming pools are allowed and financing does not cover manufactured homes. There is also a limit on the maximum loan amount.

Private Mortgage Insurance

Private mortgage insurance (PMI) is provided by private companies that insure the lender against losses caused by borrower default. The industry dates to the early 1900s, when title companies would acquire and resell mortgages—sort of a small secondary market. To make the market work, the loans were sold with a guarantee of payment as well as a guarantee of title. By the time of the Great Depression, there were hundreds of mortgage guaranty firms. Many of the firms were undercapitalized. Years of rising real estate values insulated them from default risk. The depression years created a tremendous number of defaults, and many mortgage insurance companies failed and were unable to honor their commitments.

The widespread failure of the mortgage insurance companies was one of the motivations for the creation of FHA insurance during the depression. Then, after World War II, the FHA insurance program was joined by the VA program. Both government programs were aimed at low-to-moderate income home buyers and placed limits on the amount of the loan. Bureaucratic rules also led to delays in processing on occasion. Because of the limitations of government insurance, conventional loans occupied a not insignificant part of the mortgage market.

Private mortgage insurance reemerged in the late 1950s in Wisconsin with the formation of the Mortgage Guaranty Insurance Corporation. Other firms followed, and by the 1970s, there were a dozen or so large and mostly well-capitalized firms offering mortgage insurance. The restructured industry was based on solid capital requirements. Although PMIs are regulated by individual state agencies, all states require that insurers hold large reserves for possible losses. In addition to reserves for normal losses, PMIs must maintain a reserve sufficient to weather a severe economic recession or catastrophic depression.

Coverage

In general, PMI covers the top portion of the loan where the down payment is less than 20 percent. The lower the down payment, the greater the amount of coverage required. Coverage under a typical PMI policy is as follows. Assume the lender desires coverage for the amount of the loan in excess of 75 percent of the value of the property. The minimum mortgage insurance coverage that will accomplish this is:

$$\text{Coverage Ratio} = \frac{\text{Mortgage Balance} - (0.75 \times \text{Value})}{\text{Mortgage Balance}} \qquad \text{(Equation 14-1)}$$

In the case of a \$90,000 mortgage on a \$100,000 house, the coverage would be

Coverage Ratio = (\$90,000 − \$75,000)/\$90,000 = 16.67% or 17%, rounded.

A typical claim with 17 percent coverage might appear as follows:

Principal balance due	\$88,915
Accumulated interest	7,900
Attorney fees	2,400[a]
Property taxes	1,040
Hazard insurance	650
Maintenance expense	360
Other foreclosure costs	200
Subtotal	101,465
Less rent received	1,300
Total claim	\$100,165

[a]In most policies, the attorney fees are limited to 3 percent of the principal balance, plus accumulated interest.

If the insurer believes that the property could be sold for more than $100,165 after additional holding and transaction costs, the insurer will pay the claim and take possession of the house. If house prices are depressed, which is likely the case when borrowers default, the insurer will elect to pay the amount of the insurance, $17,028 ($100,165 × 0.17). This means that the lender could sell the property for $83,137 ($100,165−$17,028) after transaction costs and not suffer a loss.

Table 14–4 shows the payoff (indemnity) to the lender for various values of the total claim and a given house value. The insurance payoff is equal to the amount of the loss or 17 percent of the amount of the claim, whichever is less. Thus, after the claim reaches $102,410 in our example, the lender shares a portion of the loss. When the loss jumps from $110,000 to $120,000, the loss absorbed by the lender increases by $8,300 ($14,600–$6,300), or 83 percent of the increase in the claim. The PMI company pays the remaining 17 percent. The indemnity (*I*) from a PMI can be expressed as

$$I = \text{Min}\,(E - H,\ \alpha E) \qquad \text{(Equation 14–2)}$$

where E equals the exposure, H is the value of the house, and α is the coverage ratio.

This coinsurance factor provides an incentive for lenders to try to mitigate losses as much as possible, since, after they reach the limit, they share the bulk of additional default losses. Each PMI company has what is called a master policy, which governs the terms and conditions of the individual insurance policies. These master policies contain additional provisions intended to control losses. The following are some typical provisions.

The lender shall pursue whatever foreclosure process is the quickest, unless the procedure precludes the possibility of pursuing a deficiency judgment (see below for state foreclosure laws).

Voluntary conveyance of title, or a deed-in-lieu-of-foreclosure is encouraged, so as to avoid the legal expense of a foreclosure. Also, in many states a foreclosure action entitles the borrower to a lengthy period during which the property can be redeemed, and during which the borrower may be entitled to occupy the property rent-free.

Attorney's fees are limited to 3 percent of the total claim (this prevents lenders from running up legal expenses for any attorney "friends"). Additional attorney's fees are allowed, if they are required to pursue a deficiency judgment against the borrower.

Since the insurance company may reserve a right of subrogation (if allowed by state law, the insurer can pursue the borrower under any rights the lender has but does not exercise), the lender is not to undertake any action that would diminish the company's legal ability to seek compensation (if it does, a claim can be denied).

The lender must make any repairs on the property to bring it to a condition that existed at the time the policy was taken out. This prevents the lender from neglecting the property to the detriment of the insurer. If the repairs are not made, a claim cannot be filed. Only normal maintenance expenses can be included in the claim; major repairs are disallowed. So if the lender has allowed the property to deteriorate, repairs must be made prior to a claim being filed, and the cost of repairs cannot be included in the claim.

TABLE 14–4

Private Mortgage Insurance Payoff (house value = $85,000)

Claim	Payoff	Loss (claim value)	Loss Incurred by Lender
90,000	5,000	5,000	0
100,000	15,000	15,000	0
102,410	17,410	17,410	0
110,000	18,700	25,000	6,300
120,000	20,400	35,000	14,600

Figure 14–1 shows the procedures for the filing and resolution of a claim to a mortgage insurer (MI). For example, a loan is considered in default after three or four monthly payments have been missed. At that time, the lender must file a notice of default with the insurance company. If the loan is not brought current by the borrower, then the lender will seek to take title to the property, either through foreclosure or voluntary conveyance. After title is obtained, the lender will either sell the property for more than the amount of debt (there is no loss), sell the property for less than the amount of debt and submit a claim to the MI, or not sell the property but submit a preliminary claim. In the latter case, the MI will have two options—to pay the lender the percentage of the liability established by the policy or to pay the claim in full and take title to and sell the property.

Fee Structure

The fee structure for private mortgage insurance is somewhat different from that of government insurance. With PMI there is a relatively small up-front fee and an annual charge. If, after some

FIGURE 14–1

Claims Cycle

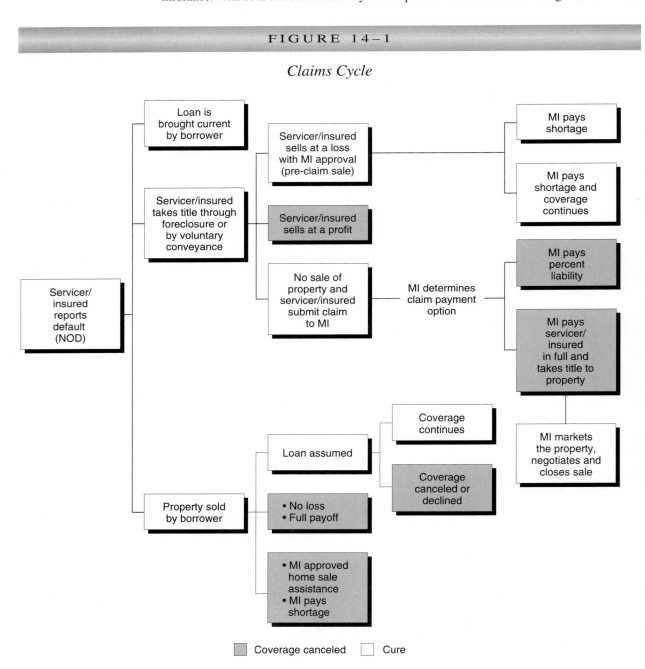

Coverage canceled   Cure

years, the lender decides not to renew the policy, the annual fees cease. This fee structure has caused problems for the PMI industry. First, there is an adverse selection problem. What this means is that lenders have a tendency to cancel mortgage insurance on loans that, after the fact, turn out not to be risky. Local property prices may have risen significantly, for example. If loans continue to be risky, lenders continue to keep the policy in force by making payments (insurance companies cannot cancel insurance). Thus, after a period of time, insurance companies lose business on the good loans, but keep it on the more risky ones. Second, since the insurance can be canceled at any time, lenders may switch insurance companies if they feel that the claims-paying ability of a company is threatened by heavy losses or insolvency. Despite the heavy capitalization in the industry, several PMI companies failed in the mid- to late-1980s as a result of recessions in portions of the country and the tendency for lenders to switch policies away from financially weak insurance companies.

Comparison of Government and Private Mortgage Insurance Programs

Table 14–5 provides a summary of the similarities and differences between the FHA, VA, and private mortgage insurance. The government programs have restrictions on the size of the loan that is insured, whereas PMIs do not. While PMIs dominate the high-priced end of the mortgage insurance market, they still compete with FHA and VA insurance in the moderate price range. The VA has a modified coinsurance feature to the extent that all losses above the insured amount are absorbed by the lender. PMI companies engage in locational underwriting and can charge different premiums according to the risk of the loan, particularly the loan-to-value ratio. While the FHA insurance program charges annual premiums based on the loan-to-value ratio, the VA has a one-time, uniform, up-front fee. Both make insurance available irrespective of the location of the property. As stated above, PMI firms charge an initial fee plus an annual charge. If the lender drops insurance, the PMI premium stops.

With both FHA insurance and PMI, the premium is canceled when the mortgage is paid in full. In the case of PMI, generally the coverage can be dropped once the equity has reached 20 percent of the value of the property, through loan amortization and/or property appreciation.

STATE FORECLOSURE LAWS

The following discussion of state foreclosure laws will provide a background to assess the riskiness of the different mortgage insurance programs.

Foreclosure

Foreclosure is a legal process by which the property that serves as collateral on a loan is sold. Foreclosure takes place when the borrower defaults on the contractual obligations of the loan,

TABLE 14–5
Mortgage Insurance Comparison

	FHA	VA	PMI
Limit on size of loan	Yes	Yes	No
Coinsurance feature	No	Modified	Yes
Uniform premium	Yes	N/A	No
Underwriting	No	No	Yes
Very low down payment loans	Yes	Yes	No
Fee structure	Partial up-front and annual	Up-front one-time	Partial up-front and annual
Available for new houses	Yes	Generally no	Yes

usually by failing to make the required payments. Through the foreclosure process, the lender exercises his power to compel the sale of the property so as to minimize any loss. In each state the process is governed by the terms of the loan contract and applicable state law. State laws differ in terms of the procedure that is permitted or mandated. There are three principle areas in which state laws differ: in procedure, in redemption rights, and in regard to deficiency judgments.

Procedure

There are two methods by which mortgaged property is sold in satisfaction of a defaulted obligation—foreclosure by **judicial procedure** and foreclosure by **power-of-sale.** In a limited number of states there is also a "strict foreclosure," which does not involve the sale of the property.

In a judicial procedure, the lender must proceed through the courts to get a judgment against the borrower and a court order authorizing the sale of the property by an officer of the court. All states allow a judicial procedure, but in about half of the states, it is the only process permitted. All requirements for advertising the sale and giving notice to the appropriate parties are established by the statutes of each state. After the sale, a confirmation report is made to the court that ordered the sale. Then an officer of the court records and delivers the deed to the new owner and gives the proceeds of the sale, less court costs, to the lender(s) in order of their priority. Second and successive lien holders are paid after each prior lien holder has been paid in full. Any excess is given to the former owner (borrower). The priority of payment—court costs, lien holders in order, and the former owner—is mandated by the Uniform Land Transaction Act, which most states adhere to. If the proceeds of the sale are insufficient to pay court costs plus the amount due the lender(s), then there is a deficiency. As long as a state does not prohibit it, a deficiency judgment (see below) will be entered against the borrower for the amount of the deficiency. Because the foreclosure proceeds through the court, it generally results in a title that is solidly marketable. However, the procedure is often complicated, costly, and time-consuming. Just getting the case heard may take considerable time. In the meantime, the expenses associated with maintaining the property fall on the lender.

An alternative procedure allowed in many states is the power-of-sale foreclosure. The sale of the property can take place without a court order if the terms of the mortgage confer upon the lender the right to sell the property in the event of a default. In such cases, there will most likely be a deed-of-trust held by a trustee. It is the duty of the trustee to make sure that the rights of both parties are protected and that there is no foreclosure sale without evidence of a default. The trustee is usually an attorney or bank. State laws protect the borrower by requiring that the sale be held at public auction and that ample notice of the sale be given. Proceeds of the sale go first to the cost of conducting the sale, including the reasonable costs of securing and holding the property, next to the amount of indebtedness, and finally, any excess goes to the borrower.

If the proceeds from the sale are insufficient to cover the amount of the debt, then the lender will have to initiate a court action to secure a deficiency judgment. Many states, however, require that a judicial procedure be used in order to obtain a deficiency judgment, denying it in the case of a power-of-sale foreclosure. The power-of-sale procedure is much quicker and less costly than the judicial procedure and is the preferred method in cases where it is permitted and there is a deed-of-trust.

Equitable and Statutory Rights of Redemption

In all states a mortgagor who defaults on the loan may prevent foreclosure by paying the full amount of the outstanding debt, including any back interest and expenses incurred by the lender. This is called the **equitable right of redemption.** The mortgagor can get a recordable release to clear the title. The equitable right of redemption is terminated by the foreclosure. The Uniform Land Transactions Act limits the borrower's right to cure a default to once every twelve months. A defaulted borrower may sell his equitable right of redemption. The purchaser will then cure the loan and assume its liability.

A **statutory right of redemption** is a right given to the borrower that enables him or her to regain the property lost in a foreclosure sale. The statutory right of redemption commences with foreclosure or the termination of the equitable right of redemption. This right is given by state law, and not all states provide for this right. Two dozen or so states do. State statute determines the length of redemption, which varies between one and eighteen months. The right is transferable. In a few states, the redemption period is available only if the foreclosure was by power-of-sale. The cost to redeem the property during this period is usually the amount paid at the sale plus interest and expenses (determined by the statute).

Some argue that the statutory right of redemption results in a weak title at foreclosure and discourages many from bidding at the sale of the property and thus increases the cost (loss) to the lender.

Deficiency Judgments

A **deficiency judgment** is a court-ordered judgment against the borrower for the difference between the value of the property (at foreclosure sale) and the amount of indebtedness (including delinquent interest and foreclosure costs).

Prompted by the large losses during the Great Depression, several states passed antideficiency legislation. Often, in a depressed real estate market, the only bidder at a sale of the property would be the lender. The lender would end up with the property and a judgment against the borrower. This appeared unfair to many. Antideficiency judgment legislation addressed this apparent inequity. Some states adopted modified antideficiency judgment legislation, whereby the amount of the deficiency was limited. In such cases, the amount was limited to the difference between the amount of the indebtedness and the fair market value of the property (not what the lender bid). The fair market value in such cases is determined by the court. Other states disallow a deficiency judgment if the lender bids at the sale of the property. Antideficiency legislation typically does not allow the borrower to waive this right in the mortgage contract.

Table 14–6 summarizes foreclosure procedures by state. There are additional subtle differences not indicated in the table. Some states may apply somewhat different rules to residences located on certain size parcels of land, for example.

Default Risk, Mortgage Insurance, and State Foreclosure Laws

Default risk on residential loans is often measured in terms of any negative equity in the property at the time of default. The presumed loss on a $100,000 loan when the property value is $90,000 is $10,000. The actual loss on a defaulted loan is much greater than the negative equity, however. When a lender forecloses on a property, there are significant costs. The cost of foreclosing and liquidating properties can be divided into three categories: transaction costs, property costs, and opportunity costs. Transaction costs include those involved with the foreclosure: attorney's fees, trustee's fees, sheriff's cost of sale, broker's commission, title charges, and so forth. Property costs include those fees incurred by the lender to carry the property until liquidated: property taxes, hazard insurance, utilities, and repairs and maintenance. Opportunity costs include interest foregone on the investment value of the property.

The longer and more costly the foreclosure procedure, the greater these costs will be. An early study done for the Federal Home Loan Bank Board found that the loss on a defaulted loan as a percent of the loan balance was as little as 6.4 percent in states with quick and inexpensive foreclosure procedures and as great as 53 percent in states with lengthy and expensive procedures.[1] Clauretie found that the average loss suffered by the FHA on foreclosed loans in Illinois from 1972 through 1988 was $25,316.[2] Illinois law requires a judicial procedure and provides a statutory right of redemption. The average loss in the neighboring state of Michigan, for the same period, was $15,847. Michigan allows a power-of-sale foreclosure. Thus, it appears that the risk of default comes not only from a decline in property prices that might produce negative equity, but also from the cost of the foreclosure and property liquidation process. Some state laws facilitate the process, while others create an economic burden on the lender.

A process that helps contain costs would allow a power-of-sale foreclosure and provide for no statutory right of redemption. By shortening the process, the power-of-sale provision reduces the carrying costs, foregone interest, and opportunity costs. Bidding should be more rigorous at the liquidation sale if there is no statutory right of redemption. Laws that provide for deficiency

TABLE 14-6

Comparison of Foreclosure Aspects by State

State	Predominant Method of Foreclosure	Months to Complete Initial Action	~~Equitable~~ Statutory Period of Redemption
ALASKA	Power of sale	3	None (A)
ARIZONA	Power of sale	4	None (B)
ARKANSAS	Power of sale	5	None (C)
CALIFORNIA	Power of sale	5	None (A)
COLORADO	Power of sale	2	2.5 mo. (D)
CONNECTICUT	Strict foreclosure	6	None (E)
DELAWARE	Judicial	9	None
DIST. OF COLUM	Power of sale	2	None
FLORIDA	Judicial	6	None
GEORGIA	Power of sale	1	None
HAWAII	Judicial (F)	6	None (F)
IDAHO	Judicial (G)	6	6 mo. (G)
ILLINOIS	Judicial	6	6 mo. (H,I)
INDIANA	Judicial	7	3 mo. (J,K)
IOWA	Judicial	6	6 mo. (L)
KANSAS	Judicial	4	12 mo. (M)
KENTUCKY	Judicial	9	None (N)
LOUISIANA	Judicial	4	None
MAINE	Entry & possession	1	12 mo.
MARYLAND	Power of sale	2	None
MASSACHUSETTS	Power of sale	9	None
MICHIGAN	Power of sale	4	6 mo. (O)
MINNESOTA	Power of sale	3	6 mo. (P)
MISSISSIPPI	Power of sale	1	None
MISSOURI	Power of sale	2	None (Q)
MONTANA	Power of sale(R)	1	None (R)
NEBRASKA	Judicial	7	None (J,S)
NEVADA	Power of sale	5	None (T)
NEW HAMPSHIRE	Power of sale	2	None
NEW JERSEY	Judicial	6	None (U)
NEW MEXICO	Judicial	6	1 mo. (V)
NEW YORK	Judicial	8	None
NORTH CAROLINA	Power of sale	1	None
NORTH DAKOTA	Judicial	3	6 mo. (L)
OHIO	Judicial	8	None
OKLAHOMA	Judicial	6	None (W)
OREGON	Power of sale	9	None (X)
PENNSYLVANIA	Judicial	6	None
RHODE ISLAND	Power of sale	1	None
SOUTH CAROLINA	Judicial	5	None (U)
SOUTH DAKOTA	Judicial	6	6 mo. (L,Y,Z)
TENNESSEE	Power of sale	1	None (C)
TEXAS	Power of sale	1	None
UTAH	Power of sale	5	3 mo. (J,A1)
VERMONT	Strict foreclosure	1	6 mo. (A2)
VIRGINIA	Power of sale	2	None
WASHINGTON	Power of sale	1(A3)	None
WEST VIRGINIA	Power of sale	2	None
WISCONSIN	Power of sale (A1)	3	12 mo. (A1)
WYOMING	Power of sale (A1)	3	3 mo. (A1)

Notes:

(A) Deed of trust. However, if there is a judicial foreclosure, there is a twelve-month redemption period.

(B) Judicial foreclosure under mortgage is also available. Time to complete would be four months followed by a six-month redemption. However, if property was abandoned, the redemption can be reduced to one month if so stated in the decree.

(C) Provided redemption rights have been expressly waived in the security instrument; if no waiver, redemption period is 12 months in Arkansas, 24 months in Tennessee.

T A B L E 1 4 – 6 (*Continued*)

(D) Redemption period is five months on security instruments executed before July 1, 1965.

(E) Redemption (law date) depends entirely on the equity in the property. If little or no equity exists, there is a 30-day law date prior to completion; otherwise, length is determined by the court.

(F) Foreclosure by power of sale on entry and possession also available under deed of trust.

(G) For properties of more than 20 acres, redemption is twelve months. Power of sale foreclosure also available under trust deed.

(H) Statute permits both strict foreclosure (where value of property does not exceed 90% of debt) and foreclosure with consent of the mortgagor; in either case, the foreclosure sale is eliminated, the mortgagee waives deficiency judgment, and the decree vests title directly in the mortgagee subject to a three-month redemption period.

(I) Redemption is six months for sale if the judgment date is after January 1, 1982 (previously was twelve months from date of service).

(J) The redemption period precedes sale in Indiana, Nebraska (court stays sale on mortgagor's request), Oklahoma (without court appraisement), Wisconsin (if judicial foreclosure is used), and Utah (if foreclosure is by power of sale). In Nebraska redemption can be only between day of sale and confirmation of sale.

(K) On security instruments executed before July 1, 1975, redemption period is six months before sale, time to complete is then ten months with a twelve-month transfer time.

(L) If security instruments specifically provide for six-month redemption, period is twelve months. For Iowa, if the property was abandoned, redemption can be reduced to two months.

(M) Provided no suit is instituted for deficiency, redemption period is reduced to six months in cases of abandoned property or on purchase money mortgages with less than a third down.

(N) If foreclosure sale brings less than two-thirds of appraised value (court appraiser), there is a twelve-month redemption period.

(O) Redemption period is twelve months on security instruments dated prior to January 1, 1965. Redemption may be reduced if the property was abandoned.

(P) If deed is executed after July 1, 1967, the redemption is six months provided the deficiency judgment was waived.

(Q) Within ten days after sale, mortgagor may give notice of intention to redeem, including security deposit for taxes, interest, etc.; the redemption period is then twelve months.

(R) For estates of more than 15 acres, a mortgage is used and foreclosed judicially, one year redemption.

(S) Foreclosure by power of sale is available under a deed of trust, effective 1965. Time of completion then would be three months; no redemption following sale.

(T) Judicial foreclosure is available under a mortgage with a twelve month redemption following the sale.

(U) Provided no suit is instituted for deficiency; otherwise, redemption is six months. In South Carolina, the redemption is one month if a deficiency judgment was obtained.

(V) Provided mortgage specifically calls for shorter redemption period; otherwise, redemption period is six months.

(W) Provided sale is with court appraisement; otherwise, there is a six-month redemption period preceding the sale.

(X) If security instrument was executed prior to May 26, 1959, judicial foreclosure is necessary with a twelve-month redemption period following sale.

(Y) Foreclosure by power of sale with service is also available for properties of less than 40 acres.

(Z) Redemption period can be extended to 24 months upon filing of affidavit to mortgagor, including provision of accruing taxes, interest, etc.

(A1) Judicial foreclosure is also available. If used, the six-month redemption period precedes the sale. In Utah the six-month redemption would follow the sale. In Wyoming a three-month redemption follows the sale plus 30 days for successive lien holders.

(A2) For mortgages executed after April 1, 1968, the redemption period is six months from date of judgment unless a shorter period is granted per the complaint. Redemption is twelve months for mortgages executed before April 1, 1968.

(A3) Loan must be in default at least 120 days before day fixed for sale.

Source: Mortgage Bankers Association, *A State Legislative Compilation.*

judgments also should reduce default losses. Lenders can pursue a judgment to reduce losses. Even if the borrower lacks funds to pay the full amount of the deficiency judgment, a threat of its use by the lender may suggest a settlement which, to some extent, reduces the loss.

In short, lenders can liquidate the property quickly, obtain a better price, and pursue the borrower for deficiencies in states with laws that are favorable to the lender.

Lender–Insurer Incentive Conflicts

Since most residential loans are insured by either the government agencies or by private companies, the risk of loss from default and foreclosure becomes a concern of the insurers as well. Moreover, the form of the insurance contract, in combination with various state laws, may affect the risk exposure of the insurer.

This risk results from any incentive provided by the insurance contract for the lender to control foreclosure costs. Consider, for example, that the FHA provides full coverage for losses, while PMI is a coinsurance relationship. Since all losses are covered under FHA insurance, lenders would have no incentive to either pursue the most expeditious foreclosure process or a deficiency judgment. Under PMI, however, lenders share a portion of the loss in excess of the coverage ratio. They will have an incentive to foreclose quickly, if they have a choice of procedure (judicial versus power-of-sale) and will pursue a deficiency judgment. There is some evidence that this is exactly what occurs. Clauretie and Herzog analyzed the risk faced by mortgage insurers in terms of dollar losses from claims per dollar insured.[3] The average loss rate for PMIs from 1980 through 1987 was 1.2 percent. The loss rate varied by state, from a low of 0 in Hawaii (1980) to a high of 9.75 in Wyoming (1987).

Some of the variation was due to local economic conditions, but much was due to differences in state foreclosure laws. The authors found that the PMI loss rates were 12 and 25 percent higher in states that required a judicial procedure and mandated a statutory right of redemption, respectively. Losses were reduced by 29 percent in states that allowed a deficiency judgment. For FHA loans, the judicial procedure and statutory right of redemption increased the loss rate by 60 and 65 percent, respectively. FHA losses were not affected by the presence of a deficiency judgment. This would be expected since lenders have no incentive to pursue these judgments under FHA insurance.

TITLE INSURANCE

Real estate property is exchanged through a transfer of the title to the property. Title conveys legal rights to the use of the property from the seller to the buyer. The buyer desires to have a bundle of legal rights to the property that is as unencumbered as possible. Government may always restrict or deny certain property rights through its police powers. Examples include the ability to restrict the use of the property through zoning ordinances, the right to take the property for public purposes (eminent domain or expropriation), the need to require that all or portions of the property be used for public services (easements for utilities, for example), and the right to place taxes on property for revenue generation. Beyond these government powers, however, the buyer desires an unencumbered and "clear" title, free from restrictions by private parties.

Title insurance is obtained at the point that property is transferred. It insures against the risk that clear title may not be transferred to the buyer. It does not insure against any loss that may result from government restriction of property rights, such as zoning legislation or eminent domain. Title insurance also involves **title search,** a process that reviews each transfer of title to the property throughout its history. The search reviews public records for occasions where clear title to property may not have been transferred. Most people think that clear title to property may be endangered by some ancient event in the history of the property. They envision the discovery of a document that shows there was a fraudulent transfer by an unscrupulous long-lost relative sometime in the 1800s, or that an ancient treaty with Native Americans was misinterpreted, or a land grant from an early Spanish king was never really made. They look upon title insurance as protection against such claims by Native Americans, Mexican Americans, or others. While title insurance may cover such events, that is not the primary purpose of a title search or title insurance. Most failures of a transfer of clear title occur as a result of much more recent events.

Another common misconception that some people have is that title insurance is generally not necessary. They reason that if the seller of the property had a title search and received clear title when he purchased the property, then the title must still be unencumbered. Nothing could be further from the truth. Most encumbrances or obstacles to a transfer of clear title are recent and subsequent to the last transfer. The most obvious is a mortgage (deed-of-trust) that exists because the present owner financed the purchase of the real estate. But other encumbrances also may exist. There may be a second mortgage, taken out subsequent to the last transfer of the property. There may be a lien on the property as a result of the failure of the present owner to pay local property taxes. The Internal Revenue Service may have placed a lien on the property if the owner has not paid his federal income taxes. There could be a mechanic's lien on the property if the owner had repairs or additions made and did not pay the contractor. There may even be a lien for failure to pay water or sewerage bills. Furthermore, these liens can appear quite quickly on the property. A title search is designed to discover these encumbrances. They will be listed on a preliminary title search and must be removed (generally by paying them off) when title is transferred.

When property is transferred, there will be a search of the title, and a title insurance policy will be issued. There is a standard policy called the **American Land Title Association (ALTA)** policy which is used nationally by the dozen or so national title insurance companies. That policy insures the lender and the new owner separately against certain losses.

Both parties are insured for losses if (a) title to the property is vested with the wrong party; (b) a lien or encumbrance remains after the transfer; (c) title is unmarketable; (d) the land physically abuts one or more streets, yet the owner fails to receive ordinary access rights; (e) the mortgage is unenforceable; (f) the lien of the mortgage is shown incorrectly as far as its order of priority; or (g) an assignment of the mortgage is invalid.

If a property is purchased without financing (all cash), then the new owner does not have to purchase title insurance. He can assume the risk. If he does purchase insurance, it will involve an "owner's policy." In this case, only items (a) through (d) will be covered. The amount of the coverage can vary up to the value of the property. Owner's policies will not cover any losses that result from liens on the property known to exist prior to the sale. In other words, if a lien on the property is discovered by the title search and it is not removed upon transfer of title, the title insurance will not insure against any loss that results from the lien. Liens discovered through the title search will be listed as "exceptions" on the insurance policy; that is, they are not covered. While this does not appear to be fair to the property buyer, note that he or she will have recourse to the conveyer (title transfer company or attorney) if clear title is not transferred. So, if the conveyer makes a search of the title, discovers a lien, transfers title, and does not cause the lien to be removed, the new owner will have recourse to the conveyer but not the title insurance company.

The lender, on the other hand, will require the new owner to purchase a "lender's policy" that will cover the additional factors (e) through (g) above. Also, the lender's policy will cover losses that result from known liens or other encumbrances discovered in the search process. Because of the additional coverage, the lender's policy is somewhat more expensive than the owner's policy. The amount of the coverage is usually equal to the amount of the loan, which can be less than the value of the property. Finally, if a new owner purchases a property with all cash, he may wish to pay a larger premium to obtain a lender's policy. This is permissible.

Title insurance is different from other types of insurance (property and casualty insurance, for example) in several respects. First, title insurance covers losses caused by events that occur prior to the payment of the premium. Property and casualty, life, and health insurance all cover losses that occur subsequent to the payment of the premium. Second, and as a result, the title insurance company or its agent will make every effort to ensure that losses do not occur as a result of past events in the chain of title. The largest element of cost for title insurers is that necessary to search the public records for encumbrances and evidence of errors in the transfer of title prior to the current transaction. The company must hire individuals trained in searching the records. In many areas of the country, insurers maintain their own records, which replicate the public records. This is termed a title plant. The daily updating of the information in the title plant can be costly. The costs of maintaining a title plant and searching the records is the largest single expense for title insurers. In short, the administrative expenses associated with title insurance are substantially greater than those for other types of insurance.

Losses from claims are much less, however. As a percent of revenues, claims may run 40 to 90 percent for property and casualty companies. During particularly bad years, claims losses may exceed 100 percent of premium revenues for certain of these companies. For title insurance companies, claim losses run between 4 and 7 percent of premium income. Thus, the bulk of the premium for property and casualty insurance covers the risk of loss from a claim, while that for title insurance covers the cost of maintaining the title plant and searching the records.

Finally, since a large proportion of the premium is used to pay administrative and operating expenses, there is less available to employ for investment income. Net investment income averages about 11 percent of premiums earned for property and casualty companies and only 4 percent for title companies.

The large fixed administrative costs associated with running a title plant makes title insurance companies vulnerable to the real estate cycle. Premium income is earned on real estate transactions, obviously, and when interest rates rise and there is a drop in, especially, commercial real estate activity, the premium income of title insurance companies drops substantially.

SUMMARY

Lenders that desire to insure their loans against the risk of loss have a choice of government or private insurance programs. In either case, the loans must meet the qualifications of the insurers. The FHA and VA set loan-to-value and size limits on loans they insure. For this reason, many large loans are insured by private mortgage insurers (PMIs). The VA provides partial coverage, while the FHA provides full coverage for all losses. PMI insurance covers up to an agreed-upon proportion of the loan. If the loss exceeds this proportion, the lender and insurer share the additional loss. This is a coinsurance relationship.

If there is a default on a loan, state laws regulate the foreclosure process. Some states require the process to be carried out in a judicial arena, while others permit a trustee to sell the property under a power-of-sale procedure. The latter is by far the least expensive of the two procedures. If the value of the property is insufficient to cover the amount of indebtedness, a deficiency results. Most states allow the lender to pursue a judgment on this deficiency, but a half-dozen or so prohibit deficiency judgments if a power-of-sale foreclosure procedure is implemented.

State laws regulating foreclosure can affect the total loss incurred on defaulted loans. Judicial procedures and statutory rights of redemption increase the cost of foreclosure (and the loss) as a result of a default. Antideficiency statutes also increase the loss by limiting the recourse of the lender.

Historical data on claims made to mortgage insurers, both private and government, indicate that required judicial procedures and statutory rights of redemption increase the risk of loss on default.

Title insurance insures the lender (and borrower) against a loss due to a defect in the title. Borrowers' policies do not insure against liens or defects on the property known to exist before its sale. Lenders' policies insure against loss from any lien or defect that exists prior to the sale, known or unknown.

KEY TERMS

American Land Title Association
California Land Title Association
Coinsurance
Coverage ratio
Deficiency judgment
Equitable right of redemption
Foreclosure
Judicial foreclosure
Lien
Mortgage default insurance
   Partial
   Full

Coinsurance
Self-insurance
Mortgage insurance premium
Power-of-sale foreclosure
Private mortgage insurance (PMI)
Statutory right of redemption
Title insurance redemption
Title plant
Title search

SUGGESTED READINGS

Clauretie, T. M., and T. Herzog. 1990. The effect of state foreclosure laws on loan losses: Evidence from the mortgage insurance industry. *Journal of Money, Credit and Banking* 22(2): 221–233.

Epperson, J. F., et al. 1985. Pricing default risk in mortgages. *Journal of the American Real Estate and Urban Economics Association* Vol. 13, Fall.

Foster, C., and R. Van Order. 1984. An option based model of default. *Housing Finance Review* Vol. 3, October.

Meader, M., 1982. The effect of mortgage laws on home mortgage rates. *Journal of Economics and Business.*

Plotkin, I. H. 1978. On the theory and practice of rate review and profit measurement in title insurance. Cambridge, MA: Arthur D. Little, Inc.

Touche, Ross & Co. 1975. *The cost of mortgage foreclosure: Case studies of six savings and loan associations.* Washington, DC: Touche, Ross & Co.

Wiedemer, J. P. 1995. *Real Estate Finance,* 7th ed. Englewood Cliffs, NJ: Prentice-Hall.

REVIEW QUESTIONS

14–1   Define and explain the different types of mortgage insurance coverage. Give an example of each.

14–2   Compare and contrast the FHA and VA insurance programs.

14–3   How does the FHA determine its premium on its standard (203b) program?

14–4   Compare private mortgage insurance programs to the government programs.

14–5   Compare and contrast the two predominant methods of foreclosure as determined by state law.

14–6   Differentiate between an equitable right of redemption and a statutory right of redemption.

14–7   Explain how state foreclosure laws can affect the loss on a loan and the claim made to the mortgage insurer.

14–8   Define title insurance and indicate what losses it is intended to cover.

14–9   Differentiate between an owner's (borrower's) and a lender's title policy in terms of coverage.

14–10   Compare and contrast title insurance with property and casualty insurance.

PROBLEMS

14–1   Given the following information, determine (A) the maximum mortgage amount for which the applicant will qualify; and (B) the percentage of the allowable closing costs that can be financed with FHA insurance.

Value of Property	
Sales price	$80,000
Appraised value	79,500
Allowable closing costs	2,400

14–2   What would be your answer to parts (A) and (B) in Problem 14–1 if the sales price and appraised value were both $46,000 and the allowable closing costs were $1,200?

14–3   Assume the following information on a residential loan default:

Value of house at foreclosure sale	$100,000
Balance of loan at time of last payment	120,000
Original loan amount	125,000
Delinquent interest payments	4,000
Foreclosure costs	
Attorney fees	5,000
Court expense	300
REO expenses	
Maintenance	800
Hazard insurance	400
Property taxes	550
Repairs	700

Determine the amount of the loss for which the lender will receive reimbursement if the loan was insured or guaranteed by (a) the FHA, (b) the VA, or (c) a typical PMI with a 15 percent coverage ratio.

In each case indicate the proportion of the loss that would not be covered and, thus, must be borne by the lender.

14–4   For Problem 14–3, what would the value of the house have to be, other things unchanged, for the lender to bear no portion of the loss under a private mortgage policy?

14–5   Alternatively for Problem 14–3, if the value of the house remains at $100,000, what would the private mortgage insurance coverage ratio have to be in order for the lender to bear no portion of the loss?

ENDNOTES

1. Touche, Ross & Co. "The Costs of Mortgage Loan Foreclosures: Case Studies of Six Savings and Loan Associations," Washington, DC. (April 1975).
2. T. Clauretie, "Foreclosed Laws and FHA Losses: Illinois and Neighboring States" (Office of Real Estate Research Paper No. 79, University of Illinois at Champaign-Urbana, May 1990).
3. T. Clauretie and T. Herzog, "The Effect of State Foreclosure Laws on Loan Losses: Evidence from the Mortgage Insurance Industry," *Journal of Money, Credit, and Banking* 22 (2) (May 1990): 221–233.

WEB SITES

www.FannieMae.com   for information about the Federal National Mortgage Association and the housing finance system.

www.FreddieMac.com   for information about the Federal Home Loan Mortgage Corporation.

www.hud.gov   for housing information (FHA included) and consumer alerts from the Department of Housing and Urban Development.

www.va.gov   for information on VA mortgages.

www.financenet.gov/exsales/auto/hud/agents/startup-agent/35000a73.html   FHA maximum mortgage limits by high cost areas.

APPENDIX A

FHA GPM Program

FHA GPM Program (245a); Comparing Monthly Payments

Loan Amount, $90,400; Interest, 10%; Term, 30-Years

Graduation Rate:	245a Plan 1 2.50%	245a Plan 2 5.00%	245a Plan 3 7.50%	203b FHA Standard Mortgage at 10%
Year 1	723.72	660.45	603.00	793.50
Year 2	741.80	693.48	648.22	793.50
Year 3	760.35	728.14	696.84	793.50
Year 4	779.37	764.56	749.11	793.50
Year 5	798.85	802.79	805.29	793.50
Year 6	818.82	842.93	865.69	793.50

Maximum Loan Factors; FHA GPM Plan III (245a)

Interest Rate	Principal Balance Factor	Year 1 P&I Factor	Interest Rate	Principal Balance Factor	Year 1 P&I Factor
8.00	94.087	5.5101	12.50	89.452	8.2358
8.25	93.793	5.6500	12.75	89.225	8.3982
8.50	93.505	5.7915			
8.75	93.225	5.9344	13.00	89.004	8.5618
13.25	88.787	8.7263			
9.00	92.951	6.0788	13.50	88.575	8.8917
9.25	92.684	6.2246	13.75	88.367	9.0580
9.50	92.423	6.3719			
9.75	92.169	6.5204	14.00	88.164	9.2252
14.25	87.966	9.3933			
10.00	91.920	6.6704	14.50	87.771	9.5621
10.25	91.677	6.8216	14.75	87.581	9.7318
10.50	91.440	6.9740			
10.75	91.200	7.1277	15.00	87.394	9.9023
15.25	87.212	10.0736			
11.00	90.932	7.2826	15.50	87.033	10.2456
11.25	91.970	7.4387	15.75	86.857	10.4183
11.50	90.415	7.5960			
11.75	90.166	7.7543	16.00	86.685	10.5918
16.25	86.519	10.7660			
12.00	89.922	7.9138	16.50	86.350	10.9408
12.25	89.685	8.0743	16.75	86.188	11.1168

MIP Monthly Payment Factors

Condominium, 30-Year Mortgage

Rate	Factor	Rate	Factor	Rate	Factor	Rate	Factor
7.00%	.4148	8.00%	.4151	9.00%	.4153	10.00%	.4156
7.25	.4149	8.25	.4152	9.25	.4154	10.25	.4157
7.50	.4149	8.50	.4153	9.50	.4155	10.50	.4158
7.75	.4150	8.75	.4153	9.75	.4156	10.75	.4158
11.00	.4158	12.00	.4160	13.00	.4161	14.00	.4163
11.25	.4158	12.25	.4160	13.25	.4162	14.25	.4163
11.50	.4159	12.50	.4161	13.50	.4162	14.50	.4163
11.75	.4159	12.75	.4161	13.75	.4162	14.75	.4163
15.00	.4163	16.00	.4164	17.00	.4164		
15.25	.4163	16.25	.4164	17.25	.4164		
15.50	.4163	16.50	.4164	17.50	.4164		
15.75	.4164	16.75	.4164				

PART

3

Commercial Real Estate Finance

In this section, we cover topics related to financing commercial real estate properties. Commercial real estate includes all nonresidential properties and multifamily residential properties. Commercial real estate is varied, including office facilities, warehouses, industrial complexes, shopping centers, hospitals, hotels, motels, and many other types of properties. In this section, we will focus on attributes of financing that are unique to commercial real estate projects. We also will cover issues related to taxation and different forms of ownership structure, such as partnerships, corporations, and real estate investment trusts.

CHAPTER 15

Value, Leverage, and Capital Structure

LEARNING OBJECTIVES

This chapter deals with issues surrounding the use of debt to finance commercial or income-producing real estate properties. After reading this chapter, you should understand that the value of an equity investment in real estate is dependent upon the level and risk of the after-tax cash flows available to the equity investor. You also should understand how the use of debt can alter these cash flows. When the use of debt alters the amount and/or risk of the cash flows to equity investors, the value of the equity position likewise will change. In this regard, there may be an optimal amount of debt to use. Too much or too little debt may not maximize the value of the equity. You should understand the concept of an optimal balance of debt and equity financing. There are arguments on both sides of the issue of whether or not the use of an optimal amount of debt can change the value of a real estate equity investment. You also should understand how more practical institutional matters, such as the peculiarities of the tax laws and the risk of individual property types, affect the debt structure of real estate investments.

INTRODUCTION

Regarding commercial real estate properties, we are concerned with three fundamental principles in this chapter: value, financial leverage, and optimal capital structure. They are all interrelated. In this chapter, we will be concerned with the central issue of the value of using debt financing in real estate investments. Even without considering such institutional factors as tax laws and the legal aspects of debt contracts, there is one set of arguments that suggests that financial leverage, or the use of debt to finance the purchase of real estate, can affect the value of the equity position in a positive way. That is to say, leverage has value in and of itself. Within this set of arguments, there is also the suggestion that the use of too much debt can be risky and not desirable. Although the use of debt can be fruitful, there are also reasons why real estate properties cannot or should not be financed totally with debt. This suggests the use of an optimal amount of debt or an optimal capital structure. The idea of an optimal capital structure follows from the suggestion that the use of some debt can be "good," but the use of too much debt can be "bad." Beyond this consideration, we also will see that an optimal capital structure may be enforced by lenders, who will see it in their interest to restrict the amount of debt used to finance real estate investments. This, and other institutional factors, will affect the amount of debt financing.

On the other side of the issue is a proposition that the use of debt does not or cannot, per se, enhance the value of a real estate investment. This side of the argument implies that, ignoring institutional factors, there is no benefit from the use of debt and, therefore, no optimal capital structure. Leverage by itself has no value, according to this argument. Whichever series of arguments appears to be most reasonable, we are left with explaining the widespread use of debt financing in real estate. So we conclude this chapter with possible explanations for the persistence of this form of real estate investment financing, as well as a discussion of some institutional factors that affect the amount of debt used to finance real estate investments. We first begin with some broad concepts.

VALUATION OF REAL ESTATE INVESTMENTS

General Principles

The valuation of real estate is conceptually no different from the valuation of any asset. Simply put, the (present) value of any asset is the expected future cash flows discounted by the appropriate interest rate. The **discounted cash flow (DCF) model**

$$\text{Value} = \sum_{i=1}^{n} \frac{\text{CF}_i}{(1 + r)^i} \qquad \text{(Equation 15–1)}$$

can be applied to any asset. For some assets, such as Treasury obligations, the valuation exercise is simple because the cash flows of the security are easily and accurately ascertained. For other investments, the determination of the cash flows and the proper discount rate may be a more formidable and less certain task. In Chapter 11, for example, we discussed the problems associated with predicting the prepayment rate on mortgage-related securities. Furthermore, the more difficult it is to accurately predict the cash flows of an asset, the more likely mistakes in valuation will be made.

Commercial real estate investment is one of the most difficult areas in which to apply the valuation mode. For many real estate investments, both the expected cash flows and the proper discount rate are difficult to determine. Consider the following nonexhaustive list of commercial real estate investments: hotels, motels, urban office buildings, suburban office buildings, shopping malls, strip centers, warehouses, mini-warehouses, theme parks, restaurants, fast-food facilities, nursing and convalescence centers, hospitals, apartment complexes, casinos, and (private) schools.

The value of an enterprise that occupies each of the above types of real estate is a function of the amount and risk of its cash flows. But those cash flows will derive from two different sources: the nature of the real estate and the nature of nonreal estate sources of value, such as the talent of the management team that directs the business enterprise. This is an important distinction because it is often difficult to separate the two sources of value, and failure to value the business enterprise component may lead to mistakes in valuing the real estate. For example, a potential investor in an existing fast-food facility may value it by discounting the expected cash flows. The expected cash flows, in turn, may be based on the present cash flows, which would be a function of two separate considerations. One consideration would be the value of the real estate: its location, state of repair, attractiveness of the facility, and so forth. Another consideration would be the managerial talent of the present owners, the franchise name, and other assets unrelated to real estate. If the investor buys the facility at the full value of the cash flows generated by the two sources and then cannot replicate the managerial talent or other non-real-estate sources of cash flow, he may have paid too much. Whether because of a lack of managerial talent or because of a well-known franchise name, the cash flows subsequent to purchase may fall short of those expected. Although the value of the whole enterprise would be less than expected (and paid for), the value of the real estate may not have changed at all.

The identification of the cash flows that derive from the real estate is less of a problem for those facilities that are essentially rental in nature. Examples include office buildings, warehouses, and apartment complexes. But even in these cases, the property management function can be very important. An investor can purchase such a property, finance it with debt, fail to manage it properly, and be forced to default on the loan. Because, for some real estate investments, so much of the cash flows depend upon non-real-estate sources, mistakes in valuation are common. Many improperly managed real estate investments have failed, but in other cases properties have been purchased, managerial talent applied, and fortunes made. What may appear to be a failure to value real estate properly may have been a failure to measure the non-real-estate sources of cash flows. Bear in mind as we discuss the valuation of real estate that a portion of the cash flows may be derived from the non-real-estate assets that occupy the realty.

The more uncertainty there is in the amount and timing of the cash flows of an asset, the more difficult it is to apply the valuation formula with precision. However, the use of debt financing for a real estate investment acquisition will have the effect of partitioning the cash flows from the investment into two parts: the return to debt and the return to equity. Of the two, the payments to the debt holders will be the more stable and predictable. In fact, if the debt is noncallable[1] and sufficiently collateralized by the real estate (so that the probability of default is minimal), then the amount and timing of the payments will be nearly certain. The rate of interest on such debt may approach that on Treasury obligations. As we will see next, the partitioning of the cash flows in this manner will make the uncertainty (riskiness) of the return to equity greater. We begin by defining leverage.

Financial Leverage

Financial leverage (henceforth referred to simply as leverage)[2] is the use of debt to finance a portion of a real estate investment. Although not all debt is structured alike, it is generally characterized by an obligation fixed in amount. Interest payments on the fixed obligation also can be fixed or vary with the market rate of interest. When debt is fixed in amount and interest, the debt service or payments are stable and predictable. Equity is the difference between the value of the asset and the amount of debt and is therefore a residual. Equity holders have a claim on the cash flows of the asset after all obligations, including interest on the debt, have been met. For this reason, it is said that equity holders have a claim on the residual cash flows of the asset.

The use of debt is prevalent in the acquisition of real estate investments. In 1997 mortgage debt on commercial properties totaled more than $698 billion, and debt on multifamily residential properties topped $243 billion. Several arguments support the use of debt in financing real estate investments. Before we look at a complex real estate investment, it will help to present the arguments in favor of leverage by using the very simple example that follows.

Assume an asset "valued" at $100 produces an expected annual cash flow of $10 in perpetuity (forever). Although the expected cash flow is $10 each year, also assume there is a 50-50 chance that the cash flow will either be $8 or $12 (you should verify that, with these probabilities, the expected cash flow is $10). With this example in mind, let's look at leverage and value.

Leverage, the Return to Equity, and Value

There are several general arguments that the use of debt enhances the value of an equity interest in real estate. One argument for the use of leverage claims that debt financing increases the return on equity and its value. The trick that accomplishes this task is the use of debt at a cost less than the expected return on the asset. Consider an investor whose total wealth is $100 in cash. If he purchases our simple asset with his cash (he does not borrow), the expected return on the investment will be 10 percent ($10/$100). Now, if the investor can borrow up to 80 percent of the value of the asset at, for example, 8 percent, he can purchase the investment with only $20 of his own equity. From the $10 expected annual cash flow, he pays $6.40 ($80 × 0.08) in interest. The residual $3.60 represents an 18 percent ($3.60/$20) return on his investment. If there are four other like assets available, the investor could purchase them with his remaining $80 in cash. Total expected cash flow after paying interest would be $18 (5 × $3.60), or 18 percent on his $100 investment. Had he purchased only one asset with all equity, his return would be only 10 percent. The advantage of leverage comes from the opportunity to borrow (use outside sources of funds) at a cost (rate) less than the return from the asset acquired with the borrowed funds.

Another way of looking at the effects of leverage in this simple example is to analyze the investor's wealth position. If he purchases one asset with all equity, his wealth position is $100. If he uses leverage and purchases five assets, his wealth position is the value of the five equity interests. The annual cash flows from those five equity interests total $18. The value of the equity cash flows depends on the investor's discount rate. Even using a 10 percent discount rate, the value of his wealth position is $180 ($18/0.10). It is clear that those with a limited access to equity would desire to use as much debt as possible. This allows those with limited equity to control as much in the way of real estate assets as possible and thereby increase their wealth.

There is a caveat here, however. Since the annual cash flow from the asset is uncertain and may vary from an expected value of $10, the risk is magnified by the leverage and transferred to the equity position. Recall that there is a 50-50 chance that the cash flows from the asset can either be $8 or $12. In the first case, the cash flow to the residual is $1.60 after payment of the $6.40 in interest, and in the second case it is $5.60. The return on equity is either 8 percent or 28 percent. Below, we will consider an argument that the increase in risk eliminates the value enhancement. For example, if the augmentation in risk causes the investor's discount rate to increase to 18 percent, then the value of the equity position in the five assets would be $100 ($18/0.18), the same as the 100-percent-equity investment in one asset. Nonetheless, the ability for an investor to acquire more real estate assets with a given amount of equity leads to a second consideration for the use of debt financing—portfolio effects.

Portfolio Considerations

Beyond these theoretical arguments the case can be made that leverage allows for an increase in the diversification of a portfolio of assets. In the above example, the use of leverage has allowed the investor with limited equity funds to invest in five assets as opposed to one. In the context of real estate, diversification has potential benefits. It has been shown that the returns on different property types or on properties in different regions of the country are not perfectly correlated. As you will see in a later chapter, the lack of perfect correlation allows portfolio construction to reduce the risks associated with investment in one or a few properties. Thus, debt financing is particularly attractive to those desiring to construct a portfolio but with limited access to equity funds. As you will see next, debt also may have value in terms of risk allocation to investors with different risk preferences.

Division of the Cash Flows

Leverage divides the uncertain cash flows of the asset into two components—one of less risk and one of more risk—than that of the asset. In the above example, as long as the annual cash flow from the asset does not drop below $6.40, the interest payment on the debt will be made. Ignoring default risk (which can be managed), the debt lender has the right to a $6.40 annual payment. The amount is known and will not vary. The equity investor has the right to the residual. But given the possible cash flows in the example above, the return on equity will be either 8 or 28 percent.

Value can be created through this division of the cash flows of the asset, if the debt holder and the equity holder have different risk-return preferences. Simply put, more risk-averse "investors" will become debt lenders, and less risk-averse investors will become equity holders. The equity investors take on more risk for the increased return. But their risk preference is such that it is a desirable tradeoff. The debt holders take on less risk for less return (8 percent on debt versus 10 percent on the asset). Their risk-return preference makes the tradeoff for them desirable as well. The situation is graphically displayed in Figure 15–1.

The utility indifference curves for the more and less risk-averse investors are shown in the left and right panels, respectively. A utility curve shows the tradeoff of risk and return for which an investor is indifferent. One can begin by assuming they are equal equity partners in a real estate investment. The cash flows of the investment have risk equal to $2 \times \sigma_1$, so each share the risk, σ_1. The total expected return is $R1$, so they each share that as well. It may be possible to rearrange the risk and return of the cash flows and move each "partner" to a higher indifference curve. The strongly risk-averse investor has a steeply sloped utility curve. This means he is willing to give up substantial expected return for a reduction in risk. The mildly risk-averse investor has a gradually sloped utility curve, indicating it takes relatively little added return to take on additional risk. The risk-averse investor can agree to a debt position with little risk, σ', in exchange for a reduction in return to R' and still move to a higher indifference curve. This transfers more risk σ and return R to the less risk-averse equity investor, who also moves to a higher utility curve.

The actual ending positions will be determined by the relationship of the tradeoff of risk and return. That relationship will depend on the nature of the risk and return of the cash flows of the investment. Offhand, one cannot determine any "formula" for the tradeoff. However, given the slopes of the curves in Figure 15–1, it certainly appears reasonable that both investors can move to higher utility curves by rearranging the cash flows into debt and equity (residual). Since both types of security holders move to higher levels of utility, value is created by the division of the cash flows in the manner indicated.

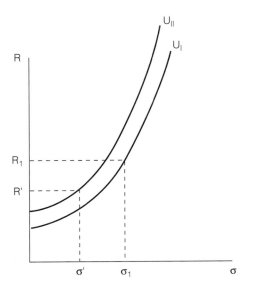
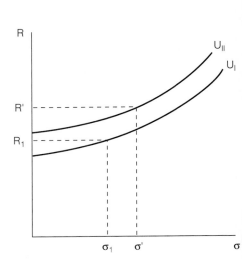

FIGURE 15–1

Risk-Return Preferences

Tax Deduction of Interest Payments

Now consider that interest payments are deductible as an expense for tax purposes. For each dollar in interest paid, net income is reduced by one dollar. This means that the government "rebates" a portion of the interest expense in the form of tax relief. If the tax rate of the holder of the real estate is 28 percent, then for every dollar in interest expense the after-tax cost is only 72 cents. This has the effect of lowering the after-tax cost of the investment and makes debt financing advantageous. Another way of visualizing the benefit of debt financing is to consider that a property generates only so many dollars of net operating income. If fewer dollars are given to the U.S. Treasury because of the tax laws, more can be divided between the debt and equity security holders, raising their values. An example of tax savings is illustrated in the next section.

Finally, it should be noted that the above example illustrates what can be termed **positive leverage.** That is, the use of debt at a cost less than the return on the asset increases the return on equity. (Whether it also increases the required return, or discount rate on equity has been mentioned and is another consideration.) Leverage also can be negative or neutral. **Negative leverage** occurs when the cost of debt is greater than the expected return on the asset. In this case, the return on the asset must be used to compensate the lender at a higher rate, reducing the expected return to the equity position. In our simple example, if the cost of debt is 12 percent, then the interest charge on an $80 loan would be $9.60, leaving only $0.40 for the equity holder, or a 2 percent rate of return.

As you might guess, **neutral leverage** occurs when the cost of debt equals the expected return on the asset.[3] In this case the return on equity is not affected by the use of debt.

In summary, leverage may create value if the return on assets exceeds the cost of debt, there is a portfolio effect, and interest is tax deductible.

DEBT AND RETURNS TO EQUITY: A REAL ESTATE EXAMPLE

To understand the effect of leverage on the value of a real estate investment, one must first understand the cash flow structure of a real estate project. The total cash flows are comprised of two components: (1) operating cash flows (rental revenues, etc.) and (2) cash flow from the resale of the property. Tables 15–1 and 15–2 show the calculation of the after-tax cash flows from

TABLE 15–1
After-tax Cash Flow from Operations

```
    Gross rent (GR)
 −  Vacancy (VAC)
 +  Other income (OI)
 =  Effective gross income (EGI)
 −  Operating expenses (OE)
 =  Net operating income (NOI)
 −  Mortgage payment (MP)
 =  Before-tax cash flow (BTCF)
 −  Taxes (savings) from operations (TXS)
 =  After-tax cash flow (ATCF)
```

Taxes from Operations

```
    Effective gross income (EGI)
 −  Operating expenses (OE)
 =  Net operating income (NOI)
 −  Interest (INT)
 −  Depreciation (DEP)
 =  Taxable income from operations (TI)
 ×  Marginal tax rate (t)
 =  Taxes (savings) from operations(TXS)
```

TABLE 15–2
After-tax Cash Flow from Resale of Property

```
    Estimated resale price (ESP)
 −  Selling expenses (SE)
 =  Net sales price (NSP)
 −  Unpaid mortgage balance (UMB)
 =  Before-tax equity reversion (BTER)
 −  Total tax on resale (TXR)
 =  After-tax Equity Reversion (ATER)
```

Taxes from Resale of Property

Taxable Income From Resale

```
    Estimated resale price (ESP)
 −  Selling expenses (SE)
 =  Amount realized on sale (AR)
 −  Adjusted basis (AB)
 =  Total gain from sale (TG)
 −  Depreciation Recapture (DR)
 =  Capital gain from resale (CG)
```

Taxes Due on Resale

```
    Depreciation recapture (DR)
 ×  Tax rate on depreciation recapture ($t_d$) (Maximum of 25%)
 =  Tax on depreciation recapture (DRT)

    Capital gain
 ×  Capital gain tax rate ($t_g$) (Maximum of 20%)
 =  Capital gains tax (CGT)

    Tax on depreciation recapture (DRT)
 +  Capital gains tax (CGT)
 =  Total tax on resale (TXR)
```

operations and resale of the property. Table 15–1 shows that, beginning with gross rent (GR), one subtracts vacancy (VAC) and adds other income (OI) (sources such as paid parking, vending machines, and late fees on rents) to achieve effective gross income (EGI). Subtracting operating expenses (OE) from effective gross income yields net operating income (NOI). To account for debt service, the mortgage payment (MP) is then subtracted from NOI to calculate the before-tax cash flow from operations (BTCF). The remaining item to account for is the tax liability (or tax savings) which is calculated in the bottom portion of Table 15–1. This calculation is shown separately since taxes are based on taxable income and not cash flow.

As a general rule, a cash flow calculation will contain every item that is an actual cash inflow or outflow regardless of whether it is tax deductible. On the other hand, a taxable income calculation would contain all items that are tax deductible whether or not they are actual cash outflows. The upper part of Table 15–1 is consistent with the lower part down to NOI since operating expenses are tax deductible. From this point, however, only the tax deductible portion (interest) of the mortgage payment is considered. Also, items that are tax deductible but not actual cash outlays (depreciation) are included.

Depreciation is a tax deductible expense but not an actual cash outlay. Improvements on real property are considered physical structures that will deteriorate over time to a value of zero. (In actuality, properly maintained properties generally will increase in value over time.) Based on this, Congress has included in the tax laws a schedule by which real properties (along with other items) can be depreciated. The specifics of this schedule are discussed in Chapter 16. For now it is sufficient to say that the basis for depreciation is the sum of the value of the capital improvements and acquisition costs. Acquisition costs are costs related to acquiring the property, such as an appraisal or a survey. The current schedule is straight-line depreciation with mid-month convention. Residential income properties are depreciated 27.5 years straight-line while nonresidential income properties are depreciated over 39 years straight-line.

Once taxable income is known, the appropriate marginal tax rate is applied to calculate the tax liability or tax savings. Negative taxable income would produce an operating loss which in turn would produce a tax savings. Thus, it may be possible to have a zero or negative before-tax cash flow but a positive after-tax cash flow.

Table 15–2 shows the after-tax cash flow from the resale of the property and the accompanying tax liability (savings) from the total gain. As seen, the sales price is derived net of selling expenses. Then the mortgage payoff is considered by subtracting the outstanding balance of the debt. Finally, the amount of tax (savings) is deducted (added) to produce the after-tax equity reversion.

The lower portion of Table 15–2 shows that the total tax due at resale is determined by the amount of total gain. The total gain has two components: the capital gain and the depreciation portion of the total gain. The total gain is the amount realized on sale minus the adjusted basis. Adjusted basis is the original purchase price plus any subsequent capital improvements plus acquisition costs minus accumulated depreciation. The depreciation portion of total gain is taxed at a maximum rate of 25 percent whereas the capital gain (assuming long-term) is taxed at a maximum rate of 20 percent. Thus the total tax is the sum of the tax on the depreciation portion and the tax on the capital gain.

Once Tables 15–1 and 15–2 are in place, all the after-tax cash flows that accrue to the property are known except the initial outlay, that is, the initial equity investment. Mortgage lenders generally require the investor to make some equity investment in the project. This is reflected in the down payment. In addition, any acquisition costs and financing costs (costs related to acquiring the mortgage) are paid at the outset. These are typically paid from equity funds. Thus, the total equity outlay required at the outset will usually be the down payment plus acquisition costs plus financing costs. In general, the initial equity investment would include any outlay paid by the equity investor.

We are now ready to construct investor cash flows and to illustrate the effect of leverage. Table 15–3 provides an example of multifamily investment property.

Basic Assumptions

Table 15–4 calculates the after-tax cash flows assuming no financial leverage, that is, no debt. We begin with this assumption so we can demonstrate the effects of leverage on the cash flows and value of the equity. Gross rent in year one is $522,100, the vacancy rate is 6 percent each year,

T A B L E   1 5 – 3

Property Data for Multifamily Investment Property

Project cost	
Land	$300,000
Building	$2,500,000
Total cost	$2,800,000
Equity investment	
Down payment	$2,800,000 less loan amount
Debt financing	
Loan amount	Varies
Interest rate	Varies
Loan term	30 years
Operating data	
Initial rent	$522,100
Growth in rent	8% per year
Vacancy rate	6% of gross rent
Other Income	1% of gross rent
Operating expenses	16% of first year gross rent (83,536)
Growth in expenses	7% per year
Growth in resale price	6%
Selling expenses	5% of resale price
Depreciation	Straight-line 27.5 years, mid-month convention, put into service at beginning of year
Holding period	5 years
Marginal tax rate	28%
Capital gains tax rate	20%
Depreciation recapture tax rate	25%

and other income is 1 percent of gross rent. Gross rent is expected to grow at 8 percent annually. The operating expense in the first year is 16 percent of the gross rent and grows at 7 percent annually thereafter. The property increases in value by 6 percent annually and is sold at the end of year five.[4] There is a 5 percent selling commission. It should be noted that operating expenses may alternatively be stated as a percentage of EGI. The choice may be determined by local custom or maybe by the client. Consistency with available benchmarks would be the objective.

Annual Operating Cash Flows

To begin, let's analyze the first and fifth year's cash flows in Table 15–4. In year one the gross rent is $522,100. A 6 percent vacancy factor and 1 percent other income results in EGI of $495,995. A deduction of the operating expenses (16 percent of the gross rent) results in a net operating income (NOI) of $412,459. At this point in the income statement, we have only discussed cash flows. That is, the NOI is a net cash inflow—cash income less cash expenses. Since there is no mortgage payment in this initial example, the NOI is also the before-tax cash flow. To compute the after-tax cash flow, it is only necessary to compute the tax due. Expenses for tax purposes include depreciation and interest on debt. Depreciation is rounded to $87,000, assuming that the property was purchased on January 1 and sold on December 31, using the mid-month convention.[5] Since there is no debt, there are no interest expenses. The tax due is 28 percent of the taxable income ($325,459), or $91,129. For the first year, the after-tax cash flow is, therefore, $321,330 ($412,459−$91,129). The after-tax cash flow can be computed similarly for each year.

For year five the after-tax cash flow is larger because revenues have grown faster than expenses.

Sale of Property

In this example, the property is sold at the end of the fifth year. The bottom portion of Table 15–4 shows the computation of the after-tax cash flow from the sale. By year five the value of the property has reflected the 6 percent annual growth in value, and the property is sold for $3,747,032. The sales commission (5 percent) is $187,352, so that the net sales price is

TABLE 15–4

Cash Flows from Operations

Year	1	2	3	4	5
Before-tax Cash Flows					
Gross rent(GR)	$522,100	$563,868	$608,977	$657,696	$710,311
− Vacancy (VAC)	31,326	33,832	36,539	39,462	42,619
+ Other Income	5,221	5,639	6,090	6,577	7,103
= Effective gross income (EGI)	495,995	535,675	578,529	624,811	674,796
− Operating expenses(OE)	83,536	89,384	95,640	102,335	109,499
= Net operating income (NOI)	412,459	446,291	482,888	522,476	565,297
− Mortgage payment (MP)	0	0	0	0	0
= Before tax cash flow (BTCF)	412,459	446,291	482,888	522,476	565,297
Income Tax Liability (Savings)					
NOI	$412,459	$446,291	$482,888	$522,476	$565,297
− Depreciation (DEP)	87,000	91,000	91,000	91,000	87,000
− Interest (INT)	0	0	0	0	0
= Taxable income (TI)	325,459	355,291	391,888	431,476	478,297
× Marginal tax rate (t)	× .28	× .28	× .28	× .28	× .28
= Taxes (savings)	91,129	99,482	109,729	120,813	133,923
After-tax Cash Flows					
Before-tax cash flow (BTCF)	$412,459	$446,291	$482,888	$522,476	$565,297
− Taxes (savings)	91,129	99,482	109,729	120,813	133,923
= After-tax cash flow (ATCF)	321,330	346,810	373,160	401,662	431,374

After-tax Cash Flow From Resale of Property

Before-tax Cash Flow from Sale

Estimated sale price (ESP	$3,747,032
− Selling expenses (SE)	187,352
= Net sales price (NSP)	3,559,680
− Unpaid mortgage balance (UMB)	0
= Before-tax equity reversion (BTER)	3,559,680

Tax (Savings) on resale

Estimated sale price (ESP)	$3,747,032
− Selling expenses (SE)	187,352
= Amount realized on sale (AR)	3,559,680
− Adjusted basis (AB)	2,353,999
= Total gain (loss) on sale (TG)	1,206,680
Depreciation recapture (DR)	447,000
× t_d	x 0.25
= Tax on depreciation recapture (DRT)	111,750
Capital gain (CG)	759,680
× t_g	0.20
= Capital gains tax (CGT)	151,936
Tax on depreciation recapture (DRT)	111,750
+ Capital gains tax (CGT)	151,936
= Total tax on resale (TXR)	263,686

After-tax Cash Flow from Sale

Before-tax equity reversion (BTER)	$3,559,680
− Total tax on resale (TXR)	263,686
= After-tax equity reversion (ATER)	3,295,994

$3,559,680. The basis of the property has been reduced by accumulated depreciation and is $2,353,000. The resulting gain on the sale is $1,206,680. Of this amount, depreciation recapture (accumulated depreciation) is $447,000 which is taxed at 25 percent producing a tax of $111,750. The remaining $759,680 is capital gain which is taxed at 20 percent yielding a tax of $151,936. Thus the total tax on resale is $263,686. The after-tax cash flow from the sale of the property is equal to the net sales price less the repayment of debt (none in this case) less the payment of taxes.

Value of the Cash Flows

Table 15–5 summarizes the annual cash flows from this property. If the after-tax discount rate for equity is 15 percent, then the value of the cash flows accruing to the owner is $2,832,944, or very close to the proposed purchase price of $2,800,000. Using Equation 15–1 one calculates the net present value (NPV_e) of the equity position to be $32,944. The net present value is the present value of the cash inflows minus the present value of the cash outflows using the investor's risk-adjusted required rate of return as the discount rate. The net present value measures the increase or decrease in the investor's wealth by making this investment. This leads to the decision rule that projects with positive NPVs would be accepted and negative NPVs would be rejected. Zero NPVs would lead to indifference. If the investor faces capital rationing or is choosing between mutually exclusive investments, in general, that project or combination of projects with the highest NPV would be preferred. The equation for net present value is

$$NPV = \sum_{t=1}^{n} \frac{CF_t}{(1 + r)^t} - II \qquad \text{(Equation 15–2)}$$

where CF are the cash flows, r is the discount rate, t is the number of time periods, and II is the initial (cash) investment. For our example the NPV would be:

$$NPV = \frac{\$321,330}{(1.15)^1} + \frac{\$346,810}{(1.15)^2} + \frac{\$373,160}{(1.15)^3} + \frac{\$401,662}{(1.15)^4}$$
$$+ \frac{(\$431,374 + 3,295,994)}{(1.15)^5} - \$2,800,000$$

Also by using Equation 15–2 to solve for r, one can derive the after-tax internal rate of return (IRR_e) for the equity. In this case, the after-tax IRR is slightly greater than the discount rate, 15.70 percent. This makes sense because the present value of the cash flows using a 15 percent discount rate is only slightly greater than the cost of the property. We know that the internal rate of return is that rate at which the present value of the cash inflows equals the present value of the cash outflows, that is, the discount rate at which the net present value is zero.

To make accept/reject decisions with IRR, the investor's risk-adjusted required rate of return is used as a benchmark. Projects with IRRs greater than the required return would be accepted whereas those with IRRs less than the required return would be rejected. The investor is indifferent at the point where the two rates are equal. With our example, the project is acceptable since the IRR is greater than the required return.

TABLE 15–5
Summary of After–tax Cash Flows; Multifamily Investment Property (debt,0)

Year	0	1	2	3	4	5
After-tax cash flows	($2,800,000)	$321,330	$346,810	$373,160	$401,662	$431,374 +3,295,994
NPV at 15%,	$69,827					
After-tax IRR,	15.70%					

Comparing NPV and IRR. In our above example we were making a simple accept/reject decision on an independent project (investing in this project has no effect on our investing in other projects). In a simple accept/reject decision framework, the NPV and IRR techniques must agree on acceptance or rejection. By nature of the calculations, there can be no conflicting recommendations. In more complex decision-making, however, there is a possibility that the two techniques may present conflicting recommendations. For example, given two mutually exclusive projects, A and B, NPV may say choose project A whereas IRR says choose project B. This conflict is generally resolved in favor of NPV because it is a direct measure of the investor's change in wealth.

Another problem sometimes encountered with IRR is multiple rates of return; that is, it may be possible to calculate more than one internal rate of return for a given set of cash flows. A general rule of thumb is that there is the possibility of having as many internal rates of return for a given set of cash flows as there are the number of sign changes in the cash flows. For example, a set of cash flows with three sign changes may have three IRRs, two IRRs, or only one IRR. It is also possible to have a set of cash flows for which the IRR cannot be calculated.

Inherent in the discounting process used for deriving NPV and IRR is the assumption that the cash flows are reinvested at the rate of return used in the analysis. NPV assumes that cash flows are reinvested at the required rate of return. IRR assumes reinvestment at the internal rate of return. Some would argue that NPV is more appropriate since it may be impossible to reinvest funds at the internal rate of return and it is more logical to assume that the investor will reinvest at least at the required rate of return.

Leverage and Value

We are now in a position to analyze the effect of debt on the value of the equity position. Tables 15–6 and 15–7 show the cash flows for the property, assuming that the owner can borrow $1 million at 9 percent for 30 years with annual payments. The first year's debt service payment, $97,336, will have to be paid from the cash flows of the property. In essence, the owner is dividing up the cash flows into two components—a less risky debt payment and a (more risky) residual allocated to the equity interest. Table 15–7 shows that the value of the equity is $2,151,506, assuming that the owner applies the same 15 percent after-tax discount rate. He may not, but we will pursue this argument below. Since the owner's contribution is $1,800,000, the

TABLE 15–6
Operating Cash Flows; Years One through Five (debt, $1,000,000)

Year	1	2	3	4	5
Before-tax Cash Flows					
NOI	$412,459	$446,291	$482,888	$522,476	$565,297
− Mortgage payment	97,336	97,336	97,336	97,336	97,336
= Before tax cash flow	315,123	348,955	385,552	425,129	467,961
After-tax Cash Flows					
− Depreciation	$87,000	$91,000	$91,000	$91,000	$87,000
− Interest	90,000	89,340	88,620	87,836	86,980
= Taxable income	235,459	265,951	303,268	343,640	391,317
− Tax	65,929	74,466	84,915	96,219	109,569
= After-tax cash flow	249,194	274,488	300,637	328,920	358,392
After-tax Cash Flow from Sale (Year Five)					
Resale price	$3,747,032				
− Selling expenses	187,352				
− Mortgage balance	956,094				
− Tax on resale	263,686				
= After-tax cash flow	2,339,900				

net present value is $351,506, and the internal rate of return is 20.26 percent. Because the net present value of the equity is greater, it appears that the use of leverage has created value.

One driving mechanism that has created the value in this example is the use of debt with an after-tax rate that is less than the after-tax rate of return on the (all equity) property. The after-tax cost of debt is 6.3 percent (9% × [1 − 0.28]) and the after-tax internal rate of return on the all-equity property is 15.33 percent. In essence, the investor is using outside funds with an after-tax cost of 6.3 percent to finance a property with an after-tax return of 15.33 percent. The "profit" on the portion financed by debt accrues to the investor.

Another factor creating value in this example is the reduction in taxes paid to the government. Whatever the cash flows generated by the intrinsic economic worth of the property, they will have greater value if a larger portion can be retained by the claimants (debt holders and equity holders) to those cash flows. In other words, if the use of debt causes the amount of taxes paid to fall, there will be a greater amount of cash flows to distribute to the lender (debt) and to the investor (equity). It stands to reason that they will reach an agreement (insofar as the interest rate on debt) that divides these tax-generated cash flows between them. In short, if the total available cash flows are greater, their value will be greater.

Optimal Capital Structure

Optimal capital structure refers to that proportion of debt and equity which maximizes the value of the property (or the value of both the debt and equity components). If value can be created, as indicated in the above fashion, then how much debt should be secured by the property? At first, one would be tempted to finance as much as possible, say, 99.9 percent. However, some practical considerations dictate against the use of so much debt. The risk of default increases with the use of debt. The cash flows available from the real estate investment are expected, not certain. If the cash flows of the property turn out to be substantially below expectations, both the value of the property and the ability of the owner to meet debt payments will fall. The property's value may fall below the amount of debt. If the debt is nonrecourse, the owner of the property will have a put option. He can put the (diminished) value of the property to the lender in satisfaction of the nominal amount of debt. To reduce the value of the put option, the lender will limit the amount of debt that the property can carry. Alternatively, the lender will require a higher interest charge for the greater use of debt. Since the greater use of debt increases the probability of default and the loss to the lender, it is reasonable to expect the lender to demand higher interest. If the interest charge becomes too great, the benefit of leverage will disappear. When the after-tax cost of debt exceeds the after-tax rate of return on the (all-equity) property, then reverse leverage will occur. In this case, more debt will cause the value of the equity to fall.

This analysis suggests that the use of debt creates value. Next we shall review some counter-arguments to this claim. However, keep in mind that the widespread use of debt to finance real estate properties implies that its use is valuable to owners and developers of real estate properties. It is likely some institutional factors also play a part in driving the use of debt to finance real estate.

Arguments Against an Optimal Capital Structure

If we ignore the increase in the cash flows that occur because of deductibility of interest for tax purposes, there are some sound arguments to suggest that the use of debt financing cannot create value. The best way to proceed, then, is to assume that there are no taxes applicable to

T A B L E 1 5 – 7
Summary of After-tax Cash Flows; Multifamily
Investment Property (debt, $1,000,000)

Year	0	1	2	3	4	5
After-tax cash flows	($1,800,000)	$249,194	$274,488	$300,637	$328,920	$358,392 +2,339,900
NPV at 15%	$351,506					
After-tax IRR,	20.26%					

investment in real estate or the investor's tax bracket is zero. The first cogent argument that the use of debt cannot create value was first put forth by Modigliani and Miller in the context of corporate finance and stock values.[6] They argued that the use of debt by a corporation could not affect the value of the equity of the corporation. The basis of the argument was that the value of the corporation was determined by the amount and risk of the cash flows generated by the assets of the corporation and that dividing those cash flows into two components could not increase their value. More precisely, they argued that the division of the cash flows by the corporation could not create value because that division could occur outside the corporation through the use of "homemade" leverage. Investors will not value activities of the corporation that they can perform themselves. The authors proved their proposition through the use of an arbitrage argument. An arbitrage argument basically says that if riskless profits are available through the simultaneous buying and selling of securities (in their example, corporate stock), then such buying and selling will cause the prices of securities to change to eliminate the excess profits. We will illustrate this argument in the context of our real estate example.

Modigliani–Miller Proposition in a Real Estate Context.   To understand this argument against value creation by the use of debt, assume the following:

1. There are two (or two sets of) real estate properties identical in all respects, including the physical characteristics and the expected amount and the risk of the annual cash flows.
2. One property (set) has no debt; it is an all-equity property. The other has $2 million in debt.
3. There are no taxes (interest is not tax deductible).
4. Investors can borrow personally at the same rate as they can get for a mortgage on the property.
5. There are no transaction costs involved in buying and selling real estate properties.

Table 15–8 shows the expected cash flows for year one and the values of the properties obtained from discounting the cash flows to equity at 15 percent. In this version, the values are somewhat higher than those shown elsewhere because we have eliminated taxes. (We want to show the Modigliani–Miller hypothesis in a no-tax situation.) As expected, the value of the debt-financed

TABLE 15–8
Cash Flow and Values

	All Equity vs. Debt Finance Properties Year One Cash Flows	
	Property A *All Equity*	*Property B* *$2 Million Debt (10.75%)*
Gross revenue	$522,100	$522,100
Net revenue	495,995	495,995
Operating expenses	83,536	83,536
NOI	412,459	412,459
Interest	0	215,000
After tax cash flow	412,459	197,459
Value of property	3,363,197	3,648,130
Value of equity	3,363,197	1,648,130

	Arbitrage	
	Sell B for	$3,648,130
	Pay off mortgage	2,000,000
	Difference	1,648,130
	Borrow $2.0 million	2,000,000
		3,648,130
	Buy A for	3,363,197
	Difference	284,933

property is higher than the all-equity property. The increase in value is due purely to the ability to borrow at a rate less than the return on the assets (equity).

The Modigliani–Miller (MM) argument would proceed as follows. If the property values indicated in Table 15–8 existed, then the owner of Property B could engage in arbitrage. He would sell the property for $3,648,130 and pay off the mortgage ($2,000,000). He would take the remaining $1,648,130 and borrow (personally) $2,000,000 at 10.75 percent. He now has $3,648,130. He uses $3,363,197 to purchase Property A and puts the remaining $284,933 "in the bank," so to speak. The first year, after-tax cash flow from Property A will appear as in Table 15–8—$412,459, from which he must make a $215,000 payment on the (personal) $2,000,000 loan, leaving $197,459.

This amount is the same as the cash flow from Property B. The investor thus has the same expected cash flow and the same risk, but now has an extra $284,933 "in the bank." He is clearly better off and therefore has an incentive to arbitrage in this fashion. But what does the arbitrage do to the property prices? If there is a sufficient amount of properties of the types described, and if there is pressure to sell property of Type B and buy property of Type A, their prices will change. Property A prices will rise, and Property B prices will fall. In fact, the process will continue until their prices are identical. At that point, one cannot say that the values of properties with debt financing are greater than all-equity properties.

It is important to note the heart of the MM argument. It says that as long as investors can borrow at the same rate offered by lenders on mortgaged properties, the creation of debt adds no value to the property. This is so because the debt can be created at the personal level (MM call this homemade leverage). Any value created by the use of debt can occur outside of the property level and, therefore, will not attach to the property. Also, if two properties, one with debt and the other with all-equity financing, must sell for the same value, then the total value of the debt and equity for each property must be the same. But, we know that the use of debt financing at a rate less than the return on the property increases the expected return to the property. The implication, according to the MM model, is that the required rate of return on equity must rise with the use of debt. Referring back to Table 15–8, this means that the value of the equity would fall by the precise amount of the increase in debt. This would occur with a rise in the required return on equity. If, for example, the required return on equity rose to 29.53 percent when $2,000,000 in debt is used, then the value of the equity cash flows would be $832,944, and the total value of debt and equity would be $2,832,944, the same as the all-equity value.

What would cause the required return on equity to rise with the use of debt? The answer is an increase in the risk (variance) of the cash flows accruing to the equity holder. Recall from Chapter 3 and our simple example in this chapter that the variance in the cash flows to the equity holders increased with leverage. Although the expected return increases, so does the risk. Furthermore, for any given risk (of the cash flows from the property), as more debt is used, the variance in the cash flows to equity increases at accelerating rates. For sufficiently high levels of debt, the variance becomes so great that very high discount rates may be appropriate for valuing the equity position. The MM model argues that the equivalence of property prices implies that the discount rate must rise by precisely the amount necessary to equate the reduction in the value of the equity to the increase in the amount of debt.

Given the assumptions of the MM model, the conclusions are unarguable. But how do we reconcile this with the overwhelming use of debt to finance real estate properties? In the next section, we consider the effect of agency costs and the legal structure of debt financing for real estate.[7] Then we look at some other institutional and practical reasons for the use of debt financing.

Resolution of the Modigliani–Miller Proposition with the Use of Debt Financing for Real Estate Properties

There are a couple of ways in which we can reconcile the inescapable conclusions of the MM argument with the widespread use of debt financing.

One, of course, is the introduction of taxes. If the property is held in a nonpersonal form, as by a corporation, then the use of debt increases the amount of after-tax cash flows available to the owners. This was demonstrated above.[8] A second important reason is agency costs.

There may be agency problems associated with the use of personal debt. In the case where the investor borrows personally and purchases a property with all equity, he has access to the same cash flows to pay the interest on the personal debt. The lender appears to be in no more of a risk position than if the loan were collateralized by the property, the cash flows being identical. However, if there is a default, our legal system provides first priority of loan payment to lenders who have a lien (mortgage) on the property. This means that there is added safety for the lender if the loan is secured by the property and not personally. Another way of looking at the situation is as follows. Suppose that the investor who borrows personally to purchase Property A in the above arbitrage example seeks another loan from another lender and pledges the property against that second loan. (He can add the $2 million loan to the amount he has in the bank if he desires.) In the event of default, the second lender will have priority in a claim to the property in satisfaction of the debt. The first lender will have to pursue the investor personally. However, the first lender is likely to anticipate the added risk this situation poses. The upshot is that the first lender will either require a much higher interest rate (eliminating the value of the debt financing) or insist on a first lien on the property. In the end, the value-creating debt financing is applied at the property level.

This situation does not run counter to the MM argument. What it does say is that if debt creates value, it is the legal system, whereby properties can serve as collateral for loans, that creates a situation where the leverage occurs at the property level and not personally. Also, it should be noted that many investors do not use debt to acquire real estate investments. Some large institutional investors, such as life insurance companies and pension funds, purchase properties with all equity. The National Council of Real Estate Investment Fiduciaries (NCREIF) is an organization of more than 50 such institutional investors and real estate managers of equity properties. They own or manage more than 1000 all-equity properties totaling more than $15 billion. Many such institutional investors do not have to pay taxes on income as received, however. This removes an incentive for them to use debt with its associated deductibility of interest payments.

Finally, let's consider some other institutional and practical considerations that affect the amount of debt used to finance real estate.

Some Practical Considerations in the Use of Debt to Finance Real Estate Properties

The above theoretical discussion on optimal capital structure can be used to explore the effect of some practical considerations on the use of debt in financing real estate properties. There are several considerations that will dictate the relative amounts of debt and equity that will be used by real estate investors. They include the form of ownership, access to equity capital markets, the risk of the property type, the cost of bankruptcy, special tax regulations, and the interest rate or cost of debt. Let's consider each in turn.

Form of Ownership.   If real estate is owned by a corporate entity, the returns will be subject to double taxation. The value of the debt and equity of the real estate investment can be increased through the use of debt. Given the alternative legal structures under which real estate may be held (such as limited partnerships or nontaxable real estate investment trusts), it makes little sense to hold real estate in corporate structure and incur the double taxation. If real estate is held in the corporate form, one would expect a liberal use of debt so as to reduce the taxable income of the corporation.

Access to Equity Capital Markets.   The equity market for real estate is very limited. While there is a limited market for interests in real estate investment trusts, there is not a market for other forms of equity interests. Pension funds and life insurance companies do own substantial amounts of equity real estate (though not in proportion to their total asset portfolios), but these equity interests are not traded on a market. They are held for long-term investments by those institutions. Thus, most investors will have to make whatever equity resources they have go as far as possible in acquiring real estate investments. That is, relatively small, noninstitutional investors with limited equity will have to rely on debt financing to acquire real estate, since it is difficult to raise additional equity funds in any organized and liquid market. One would expect that small, noninstitutional investors would use a larger proportion of debt to acquire larger and more expensive properties.

Risk of the Property.   Lenders that provide debt financing for the acquisition of real estate properties are risk averse. For this reason, they will require larger equity contributions for the purchase of real estate properties that they perceive to be risky. Certain property types are likely to be inherently more risky than others. Historically, the variance in the cash flows of urban office buildings has been greater than that for apartment complexes. In some regions of the country, the risk of a particular property type may be more or less than in other areas of the country. Knowledgeable local lenders will likely require higher equity contributions (lower debt ratios) to finance the purchase of real estate properties they perceive to be risky.

The Cost of Bankruptcy.   This consideration is closely related to the risk of the property type. A note secured by the property can either be recourse or nonrecourse. A nonrecourse note means that the lender may look only to the property to satisfy the debt. From the lender's point of view, such a note is obviously more risky. A recourse note, on the other hand, is more risky for the investor. If the operating cash flows from the property fail to cover the debt service, the result may be default and foreclosure. If this should occur, then the investor may be personally liable for any deficiency between the amount of the debt obligation and the market value of the property. Taken together, this implies that lenders will prefer to advance greater amounts of debt only on less risky properties and only if the note is a recourse note. Investors will prefer nonrecourse notes on all properties but especially on risky properties. Other things being equal, one would expect to see investors maximize the use of debt when it is nonrecourse.

Special Tax Regulations.   Here there are two issues to consider: the extent to which operating losses from the real estate investment can be used to offset other income and the tax rate. You will see in the next chapter that present tax laws severely limit the extent to which an investor can use an operating loss on a real estate property to offset other positive (taxable) income and thereby reduce tax liability. There are also limitations on the extent to which interest deductions can be used to reduce taxes. It was not always this way. These changes have reduced the value of the interest deduction and, therefore, the value of debt financing. If the depreciation deductions on a property are sufficient to minimize the operating net income, this will further reduce the value of the interest deduction. Thus, one would expect to see less debt used to finance properties with large depreciation components. These are basically newer properties where the value of the improvements are large relative to the value of the (undepreciable) land. Of course, the lower the tax rate, the less the value of the interest deductions.

Interest Rate.   One would expect that the lower the market rate of interest, the more debt would be utilized to purchase real estate properties. This is especially true if the factors that lower the market rate of interest have no effect on the cost of equity. In this case, debt becomes relatively cheaper than equity. Given the limited amount of equity available for real estate investment, this would imply that the market rate of interest is an important determinant of market values and activity. In fact, we know that over the cycle, lower interest rates bring about an increase in real estate transactions and real estate prices.

In summary, debt will represent a greater portion of the capital structure of real estate investments when (1) the corporate structure is used to acquire the investments, (2) the value of the investment is large (access to equity is limited), (3) the risk of the property as measured by the variance in the operating cash flows is small, (4) the cost of bankruptcy to the investor is low (the note is nonrecourse), (5) operating losses are available to offset other income and thereby reduce current taxes, (6) the depreciation component is small, (7) the tax rate is high, and (8) the market interest rate is low.[9]

Several of these factors may interact. If a property has a large depreciable base but tax laws allow operating losses to offset other positive income, debt financing still will be valuable. If, however, there are restrictions on such a use of operating losses, there will be less of a need for the use of debt.

The considerations discussed in this chapter have favored the use of debt to finance real estate investments. Historically, the tax laws have been favorable, access to equity markets limited, and the after-tax cost of debt relative to equity low. Regardless of the theoretical arguments on the existence of an optimal capital structure, more practical considerations such as limited equity markets, tax rules, property risk, and the legal enforcement of debt covenants have driven the use of debt in real estate finance.

REAL ESTATE INVESTING IN THE REAL WORLD

The cash flow examples presented in this chapter are designed to provide a good basis for making real estate investment decisions. The tables give a basis for structuring cash flows from different types of real estate investments. In reality, some projects may have additional factors that must be considered. These are discussed below.

Financing costs may be a consideration. In the process of purchasing property the buyer may encounter various costs, referred to as closing costs. A buyer may incur costs such as an appraisal, mortgage origination fees, and document recording fees. These costs are typically paid by the buyer at the time the property is acquired. These costs, however, are not fully tax deductible in the year they are paid. To start, the buyer has to distinguish between **acquisition costs** and **financing costs.** Acquisition costs are costs related to acquiring the property. These are prorated relative to the value of the land versus the value of the improvement in relation to the total value of the project. The portion prorated to the improvement is included in depreciation and written off over the depreciable life of the asset. Financing costs, on the other hand, are costs related to acquiring the mortgage. These would include such costs as mortgage origination fees and discount points. Financing costs are written off on a straight-line basis over the life of the mortgage. Thus, for example, if a buyer incurred $15,000 in financing costs on a 30-year mortgage, the annual deduction would be $500. This amount would be reflected in both cash flow and taxable income. If the property is sold before financing costs are fully amortized, the remaining balance of financing costs can be deducted in the year of sale.

Another financing consideration is a mortgage **prepayment penalty.** Some mortgages assess the borrower a penalty if the mortgage is prepaid, that is, repaid before maturity. These penalties may be stated as a percentage of the outstanding balance at the time of prepayment. A prepayment penalty can be treated as interest and is fully tax deductible in the year it is paid. The amount of the prepayment penalty would be included in both the cash flow and taxable income calculations.

A final factor that may have to be considered is a **replacement reserve.** In some investment projects the owner may be required to maintain a reserve to replace items which are prone to wear out. This would include such things as heating and cooling systems, appliances, carpet, etc. If a reserve is required, it is likely to be included in operating expenses. However, a set-aside of funds is not a tax deductible expense. If reserves are included in operating expenses (and therefore deducted from EGI to derive NOI), they must be added back to taxable income.

SUMMARY

The division of risky cash flows of a real estate investment can be beneficial if lenders and equity holders have different risk/return preferences. Lenders may be willing to accept a relatively low rate of return on debt as a tradeoff for less risk. In turn, the equity holder is exposed to more risk, including that of losing the entire investment. The use of debt at a rate less than the expected return on an all-equity property will magnify the return (and the risk) to the equity position. For the less risk-averse equity investor, the tradeoff is again beneficial. Some will argue that the arrangement creates value, and this explains the widespread use of debt to finance real estate properties.

Others would argue along the lines of the Modigliani–Miller hypothesis that, in a world without taxes, the use of leverage cannot increase the value of real estate properties. The value of the property will be based only on the amount and risk of the cash flows it generates and not on how they are divided among different classes of claimants (debt and equity). An arbitrage example can be used to demonstrate this point. The arbitrage argument is based on the assumption that the property owner can use homemade leverage to produce the same cash flows as would result from debt financing on the property.

However, two major institutional factors drive the use of debt financing for the acquisition of real estate properties. First, our legal system allows lenders to receive priority of payment from the liquidation of a property in the event of default. This is one reason why debt may be applied at the property level and not the personal level. Second, in a world of taxation, the deductibility of interest payments for tax purposes may increase the total cash flows accruing to the claimants. This factor alone would provide an incentive for debt financing. If the total cash flows to the claimants are greater by virtue of debt financing, they can arrange financing terms that make them both better off at the expense of the Treasury. Institutional investors that have no need for the tax deduction are more inclined to purchase properties with all equity. Other factors also affect the optimal capital structures, including the risk of the property, the risk of bankruptcy, the availability of nonrecourse financing, the amount of the depreciation tax shield, the tax rate, and, of course, the level of market interest rates. In the next chapter, you will see how tax laws affect the financing of real estate properties.

KEY TERMS

Bankruptcy costs	Optimal capital structure
Debt	Positive leverage
Discounted cash flow model (DCF)	Prepayment penalty
Equity	Property risk
Financing costs	Recourse
Financial leverage	Replacement reserve
Modigliani–Miller hypothesis	Return on equity
Negative leverage	Risk
Neutral	Value
Nonrecourse	

SUGGESTED READINGS

Jaffe, A. 1982. On the theory of finance, equity models and optimal financing decision of real property. In *Real Estate Research* Vol. 1. Greenwich, CT: JAI Press.

Jaffe, A., and K. Lusht. 1982. On the relevance and irrelevance of finance and the market value of real property. Paper presented at the annual meeting of the American Real Estate and Urban Economics Association, Washington, DC.

Lusht, K. M. 1977. A note on the favorability of leverage. *Real Estate Appraiser and Analyst* Vol. 43, May–June.

Lusht, K. M. 1986. Finance theory and real estate valuation. In W. Kennard, ed., *Real Estate Valuation Colloquium.* Cambridge, MA: Lincoln Land Institute.

Mao, J. C. T. 1979. Wealth maximizing criterion for profitable leverage in real estate investments. *Real Estate Appraiser and Analyst* Vol. 45, May–June.

REVIEW QUESTIONS

15–1 Define the terms *debt* and *equity.* What are the major characteristics that distinguish *debt* and *equity?*

15–2 Define *leverage.*

15–3 Under what condition will the use of debt financing raise the return on equity?

15–4 How does the use of debt affect the cash flows of a real estate property in terms of a division of risk and return?

15–5 What is meant by optimal capital structure?

15–6 Why is 100 percent debt financing rare for real estate investments?

15–7 Present the arguments for and against the view that the use of debt can add value to the equity position in a real estate investment. Assume a no-tax situation.

15–8 Explain why the deductibility of interest payments for tax purposes has a positive effect on the use of debt.

15–9 How does our legal system influence the use of debt to finance real estate investments?

15–10 List several institutional factors that will affect the use of debt to finance real estate. Explain how each affects the use of debt.

PROBLEMS

15–1 Consider the following information on a real estate property with a value (cost) of $1 million:

Annual Cash Flow	Probability
$150,000	0.5
90,000	0.5

a. What is the expected return on this property?

b. If an investor can borrow 80 percent of the value of the property at 10 percent interest, what will be the expected return on equity?

c. Will the investor be in danger of insolvency by borrowing 80 percent of the value of the property (i.e., will the annual cash flow be sufficient to meet debt obligation)?

d. Should the investor borrow to finance the acquisition of the property or purchase the property with 100 percent equity? Explain.

For Problems 15–2 through 15–5, assume the following basic data about a residential development.

Land cost	$300,000
Building cost*	$2,500,000
Total cost	$2,800,000
Holding period	5 years
Gross rent, year one	$500,000
Vacancy rate	4%
Operating expense, year one	15% of gross rent
Growth rates	
Gross rent	7%
Operating expense	7%
Resale price	7%
Resale expense rate	5%
Investor's tax bracket	28% on ordinary income
	25% on recapture of depreciation
	20% on excess gain over cost
Depreciation, residential	27.5 years
Property purchased	January 1
Financing:**	

Debt (in millions)	Cost of Debt	After-tax Cost of Debt	Discount Rate on Equity
$0	N/A	N/A	0.15
1.4	0.09	0.0648	0.15
2.4	0.18	0.1296	0.15

*Depreciation year one = $87,121; years 2 through 5, $90,909
**All debt amortized over 30 years

15–2 a. Calculate the after-tax cash flows for the project, assuming no debt. (Check figures: after-tax cash flow from operations in year five, $439,936; tax on sale of property in year five, $112,689 on recapture, $186,158 on excess.

b. Calculate the present value of the equity position. (Note: not the net present value.)

15–3 a. Calculate the after-tax cash flows for the project, assuming $1.4 million in debt. (Check figures: after-tax cash flow from operations in year five, $305,508; tax on sale of property in year five, same as in 15.2)

b. Calculate the present value of the equity position.

15–4   a. Calculate the after-tax cash flows for the project, assuming $2.4 million in debt. (Check figures: after-tax cash flow for operations in year five, $95,838; sale price in year five, $3,927,145.)

b. Calculate the present value of the equity position.

15–5   Show the total value of the property (value of debt and equity) for each of the debt levels in the above three problems. What is the optimal capital structure?

ENDNOTES

1. Unlike owner-occupied residential financing, the use of prepayment penalties in commercial real estate financing is widespread.

2. This term should not be confused with operating leverage, which relates to the relationship between fixed costs and variable costs in business operations.

3. These relationships can be demonstrated algebraically. If the return on assets (ROA) is defined as net operating income (NOI) divided by assets (A), and the return on equity (ROE) defined as NOI minus interest expense (rD, where r is the interest rate and D is debt) divided by equity, then

$$ROA = NOI/A$$

and

$$ROE = (NOI - rD)/Equity$$

Positive leverage implies that the return on equity is greater than the return on assets if the cost of debt r is less than ROA. That equation,

$$(NOI - rD)/(A - D) > NOI/A$$

can be reduced to

$$r < NOI/A$$

4. One could argue that with revenue increasing by 8 percent and expenses increasing by 9 percent the property's value should increase by more than 6 percent. All other things being equal, this may be true. However, for purposes of illustration, here we assume other market factors do not allow the property to grow at an amount in excess of 6 percent.

5. The current tax code requires that depreciation for multifamily housing be based on a straight-line write-off over 27.5 years. The property is assumed to be placed in service and also sold in the middle of the month. A full year's depreciation would be $2,500,000/27.5 = $90,909. Prorated over 11.5 months, the precise depreciation for the first year and the last year would be $87,121. The remaining year's depreciation is rounded to $91,000 from $90,909.

6. Franco Modigliani and Merton Miller, "The Cost of Capital, Corporation Finance, and the Theory of Investment," *American Economic Review* 48 (June 1958): 261–297.

7. Recall that agency costs refer to costs incurred by a principal to insure that an agent operates in a manner that protects the interests of the principal. In the example that follows, the principal will be the lender, and the agent will be the investor-borrower. As you know, borrowers often may have an incentive to act in their own interest and not that of the lender.

8. In a later paper, Modigliani and Miller recognize this tax issue and conclude that corporations should use as much debt as possible. Franco Modigliani and Merton Miller, "Corporation Income Taxes and the Cost of Capital," *American Economic Review* 53 (June 1963): 433–443.

9. George Gau and Ko Wang looked at the debt (loan-to-value) ratios on 759 properties that were sold in Vancouver, Canada, between 1971 and 1985. They did not have sufficient data to test the effect of the tax environment, but they did find that many of the above considerations affected the debt ratio. Apartment complexes (considered to be low-risk) had higher debt ratios than other property types. Older properties (with smaller depreciation bases) also had higher debt ratios, as did properties held by corporations. Higher valued properties (where access to the equity market would be a concern) also had higher debt ratios. In short, they found that the theoretical and practical considerations discussed here played an important part in determining the capital structure of real estate investments. George Gau and Ko Wang, "Capital Structure Decisions in Real Estate Investment," *Journal of the American Real Estate and Urban Economics Association* 18 (Winter 1990): 501–521.

16

Federal Taxation and Real Estate Finance

LEARNING OBJECTIVES

After reading this chapter, you should understand how the rules and regulations of federal income taxation affect both the value of real estate investments and financing decisions for real estate investments. You will understand how changes in the tax rules have altered the return on real estate investment over the last 20 or so years. Despite the complexity of the tax regulations and despite the fact that some rules appear to be without logic, you will understand the motivation behind them.

INTRODUCTION

Federal income tax rules and regulations affect both the value and return on real estate investments in many different ways. An outline of the effect of current and recent tax rules on real estate investments and real estate finance is given in Figure 16–1, which also orders the discussion in this chapter.

Figure 16–1 shows that federal tax rules affect real estate investments through two primary channels: how income is defined for tax purposes and, given the definition of income, how tax payments are determined.

The definition of income is affected by two considerations: allowance of items not involving cash outlays to be treated as expenses (namely, depreciation) and allowance of interest payments on debt to be treated as expenses. Limitations on these expenses, such as the rate at which real estate can be depreciated and the application of both original issue discount (OID) and investment interest rules to interest expenses, will affect the attractiveness of real estate investments.

As to the second major way in which tax rules affect real estate investments—determining the actual amount of taxes to be paid—there are several considerations to keep in mind. First, there is the differential treatment of capital gains (especially long-term gains) versus ordinary income. A lower rate on the former will provide an incentive for taxpayers to hold long-term investments and to convert ordinary income to capital gains when possible. To the extent that real estate can be used as a vehicle to do this, a differential rate will favor real estate as an investment. Currently the maximum tax rate on long-term capital gains (held at least 18 months) is 20 percent. The amount of capital gain that had been allowable as depreciation is taxed at a maximum rate of 25 percent. Second, allowing losses on real estate investments to offset income from other sources will reduce the investor's overall tax bill and increase the investment value of real estate. However, under current rules, the extent to which losses from real estate may be used to offset income from other sources will be restricted by rules that (1) limit the amount of capital loss that can offset income from other sources, (2) allocate income into increasingly more narrow categories and prevent cross category offsets, and (3) limit the

FIGURE 16–1

Tax Regulations and Their Effects on the Value of Real Estate Investment

---

After-tax cash flows are affected in two primary ways:

First

The definition of income for tax purposes differs from before-tax cash flows because:

1. Non-cash expenses such as depreciation (which often creates "paper losses") are allowed

2. Interest payments on debt can be expensed, subject to
   a. original issue discount (OID) rules
   b. investment interest rules
   c. amortization of discount points

Second

Given income for tax purposes, the actual amount of taxes paid are affected by:

1. Differential tax rates on ordinary income and capital gains

2. Offset of losses against other sources of income; such losses are restricted by
   a. capital loss limitation rules
   b. defining narrow income classes and prohibiting cross-class offsets of losses
   c. establishing "at risk" rules

3. Providing for alternative minimum tax

4. Establishing favorable classes of real estate investment, such as
   a. low-income housing
   b. historical structures

---

amount of losses that may be recognized to the amount the taxpayer has "at risk" in the property. Third, other rules limit the total amount of tax advantages that a taxpayer can exploit. Currently called alternative minimum taxes (AMTs), they may limit the use of some of the tax advantages present in real estate investments. Finally, the establishment of favored classes of real estate will encourage investment in real property. Special rules such as tax credits for developing low-income housing or rehabilitating historic buildings will encourage investment in those real estate projects.

Table 16–1 summarizes the effect of tax rules on the value of real estate as an investment and indicates the rules' current status (in boldface). You will note quickly that most of the current rules do not favor real estate investment as they did in previous years. Prior to 1987 (the effective year of the Tax Reform Act of 1986), many of the tax rules would have favored real estate as an investment. Now, real estate is placed on a more equal plane with other investments.

In general, there are four changes in the tax laws which can affect real estate: (1) changes in marginal tax rates, (2) changes in methods of depreciation, (3) changes in the treatment of capital gains, and (4) changes in the ability to write off losses. The discussion in this chapter will help you understand how these factors affect investors' real estate investment decisions.

In this chapter, we introduce the concept of a tax shelter and use a real estate example to show how value is affected by tax laws. Then, we will follow the outline presented in Figure 16–1, using this example where possible. We will conclude by looking at the effect of recent tax legislation on the financing of an investment in real estate.

Tax Rules and Real Estate Investment

Tax Rule	Tax Rule Favors Real Estate as Investment	Tax Rule Does Not Favor Real Estate as Investment	Impact on Real Estate Investment
Depreciation			Substantial
A. Accelerated over short period	X		
B. Straight-line over extended period		**X**[a,b]	
Capital gains treatment			Substantial
A. Rate less than ordinary income	**X**		
B. Rate same as ordinary income		X	
Interest payments on debt			
A. Deductible as an expense	**X**		Substantial
B. Lender and borrower on different basis	X		Moderate
C. Lender and borrower on same basis		**X**	
D. Not imputed	X		Moderate
E. Imputed		**X**	
F. Investment interest limitation		**X**	Minor
Definition of income			
A. Broad categories	X		Substantial
B. Narrow categories		**X**	
Alternative minimum tax			Minor
A. Not Enforced	X		
B. Enforced		**X**	
Favored types of investment			Moderate
A. Allowed	**X**		
B. Not allowed		X	

[a]boldface = Current tax rules.
[b]Real estate may still have an advantage over other assets that may not be depreciated.

CLASSIFICATION OF REAL PROPERTY

For income tax purposes, real estate is classified into four categories depending on the purpose for which the property is used:

1. Property held as principal residence
2. Property held for investment
3. Property held for resale to others
4. Property held for use in trade or business

Our focus in this chapter is on income-producing real estate and not *property held as principal residence.* The tax treatment of this type property (commonly called owner-occupied) has some major differences from the other categories. Briefly, these are: (1) individuals can deduct mortgage interest up to $1,000,000 of acquisition indebtedness plus $100,000 of additional indebtedness for any purpose, (2) losses from the sale and most operating expenses are not tax deductible (only mortgage interest and property taxes are deductible), and (3) depreciation is not allowed. Effective for transactions after May 6, 1997, individuals who sell or exchange a principal residence that they owned and occupied for at least 2 of the 5 years preceding the sale or exchange can elect a $250,000 ($500,000 for joint filers) exclusion from income of gain from the sale or the exchange. This applies to only one sale or exchange every 2 years. This new exclusion replaces the rollover provision and the age 55 exclusion.

   Contrary to what you might think initially, most real estate investments do not fall into the category *property held for investment.* This category applies when the real estate is held strictly for income or investment and the owner has no participation in the operations of the investment. This will generally include unimproved land and net leases. Recall that a net lease is one in which the tenant pays operating expenses (such as maintenance, property taxes, and insurance);

thus, the property is held strictly for income and is not used in trade or business. Investments in this category are subject to limitations not placed on other classifications. First, the owner may face limitations on interest deductibility. Second, investments sold at a loss are subject to the limitations imposed by the capital loss provisions of the law.

When *property is held for resale to others,* it is viewed as inventory and profits from its sale are taxed as ordinary income (as opposed to capital gains). Individuals who hold real estate as inventory in the ordinary course of business are treated as dealers and not investors. Examples are developers developing lots and home builders building houses for immediate resale. Real estate held in this fashion cannot be depreciated; however, losses on the sale of this inventory can be treated as operating losses and are tax deductible.

Property held for use in trade or business, referred to as a Section 1231 asset, is the most prevalent (and in general the most favorable) classification for income-producing real property. In fact, most income-producing real estate investments fall into this category. The key words establishing this category are *real estate owned* and *operated for the purpose of deriving rental income.* All operating expenses, mortgage interest, and depreciation are fully deductible from rental income. In addition, losses from the sale of the property are fully deductible.

TAX SHELTERS

A **tax shelter** is an investment structured so that tax rules and regulations are utilized to enhance its value. The value of the investment is increased because a significant portion of the investor's return is derived from tax savings on other income or tax-favored income on the investment itself. In other words, the total value of the asset would be the sum of its fundamental economic value and the tax shelter value. The tax laws are used to alter the amount and timing of the cash flows, as well as the discount rate used to value the cash flows. Real estate is one investment that has the potential to be used as a tax shelter. The organizational form of ownership of the real estate combined with tax laws causes the cash flows from the real estate investment to be larger, occur sooner, or both, than they otherwise would. Organizational forms for holding real estate investments include corporations (both subchapter S and C corporations), limited and general partnerships, real estate investment trusts, and sole ownership. Since tax rules are applied differently according to the organizational structure of the investment, both the rules and the structure combine to create a shelter.

In many cases, favorable tax rules will enhance the value of real estate investments that would, nonetheless, have value in their absence. More importantly, tax rules may create value for real estate investments that otherwise would not have value or be economically feasible. It is this latter case that most aptly fits the definition of a tax shelter. Given sufficiently favorable rules, a real estate investment that otherwise would generate negative cash flows may provide the investor with positive cash flows. Although any investment that utilizes tax rules to enhance the value of its cash flows can be considered a tax shelter, the term is generally applied to situations where positive cash flows result strictly from the application of tax regulations. In the absence of the tax regulations, the cash flows would be negative.

Taxes, Cash Flows, and Discount Rates: Some Examples

First, let's distinguish between the before- and the after-tax discount rate used to value cash flows. Investors are concerned with the cash flow they receive after paying income taxes. If an investor in a 40 percent tax bracket owns a 5-year corporate (taxable) bond that pays $100 annually (a 10 percent coupon bond), her after-tax cash flow will be $60. If the (before-tax) market discount rate for this bond is 10 percent, we know it should be valued at par, $1000. That is,

$$\$1000 = \$100/(1.1)^1 + \$100/(1.1)^2 + \ldots + \$1000/(1.1)^5$$

The investor employing a 10 percent discount rate values the asset at $1,000, even though it pays only $60 annually after taxes. That is, one way to value the asset is to apply a before-tax rate to the before-tax cash flows.

How would this same investor value an equally risky municipal bond of the same maturity that promised to pay $60 annually on which there would be no taxes? The apparent answer is that she would place the same value on the municipal as on the corporate bond. And this is the case. If the two equally risky assets promise the same cash flows after taxes, they should be valued identically. But this would require that the after-tax cash flows be valued not by a before-tax market discount rate but rather by the investor's after-tax discount rate. For each asset, the after-tax cash flow is the same, $60. If they have the same value, they should be valued with the same discount rate. In this case, the discount rate is the after-tax rate of $r(1 - T)$, where r is the before-tax market rate and T is the investor's tax rate. For each asset, we have

$$\$1000 = \$60/(1.06)^1 + \$60/(1.06)^2 + \ldots + \$1000/(1.06)^5$$

where $60 is the after-tax annual cash flow and 0.06 is the after-tax discount rate, $0.1 \times (1 - 0.4)$.

Confusing cash flows and the discount rates would lead to incorrect valuations. If, for example, the investor valued the municipal bond with a 10 percent discount rate, the resulting value would be

$$\$848.26 = \$60/(1.1)^1 + \$60/(1.1)^2 + \ldots + \$1000/(1.1)^5$$

Or, if the investor discounted the before-tax cash flows of the corporate bond with an after-tax discount rate, the erroneous value would be

$$\$1168.50 = \$100/(1.06)^1 + \$100/(1.06)^2 + \ldots + \$1000/(1.06)^5$$

In short, the proper method of valuation applies an after-tax discount rate to after-tax cash flows.

With this in mind, let's look at another example. Tables 16–2 and 16–3 show the operating data and assumptions for a multifamily investment under the current tax laws (after the *Tax*

TABLE 16–2
Property Data for Multifamily Investment Property

Project cost:	
Land	$165,000
Building	$660,000
Acquisition costs	$ 14,000
Additional capital improvements	none
Total	$839,000
Financing data:	
Loan amount	$660,000
Interest rate (monthly pmt)*	10%
Term	20 years
Financing costs	4% of loan amount
Prepayment penalty	5% of outstanding balance
Equity investment	$205,400
Operating data:	
Gross rent year one	$141,000
Vacancy rate	6% of gross rent
Other income	3% of gross rent
Operating expense	40% of gross rent
Replacement Reserve	20% of operating expenses
Growth rates:	
Gross rent	5% per year
Property value	5% per year
Other:	
Selling Expenses at reversion	8% of selling price
Depreciation	residential straight-line
Marginal tax rate	28%
Capital gains tax rate	20%
Holding period	5 years
Required equity yield	10%

*The monthly payment is converted to an annual debt service by multiplying the monthly payment by 12.

TABLE 16-3

After-Tax Cash Flow from Operations for 5-Year Holding Period

Year	1	2	3	4	5
Gross Revenue	141,000	148,050	155,452	163,225	171,386
− Vacancy	−8,460	−8,883	−9,327	−9,794	−10,283
+ Other Income	+4,230	+4,442	+4,664	+4,897	+5,142
Effective Gross Income	136,770	143,609	150,789	158,328	166,245
− Operating Expenses	−56,400	−59,220	−62,181	−65,290	−68,554
Net Operating Income	80,370	84,389	88,608	93,038	97,691
− Mortgage Payment	−76,430	−76,430	−76,430	−76,430	−106,065
Before-Tax Cash Flow	3,940	7,959	12,178	16,608	−8,374
− Taxes	−401	−1,719	−3,420	−5,226	+6,414
After-Tax Cash Flow	3,539	6,240	8,758	11,382	−1,960

Taxes from Operations

Year	1	2	3	4	5
Effective Gross Income	136,770	143,609	150,789	158,328	166,245
− Operating Expenses	−56,400	−59,220	−62,181	−65,290	−68,554
Net Operating Income	80,370	84,389	88,608	93,038	97,691
− Interest	−65,508	−64,365	−63,101	−61,706	−89,799
− Amortized Financing Cost	−1,320	−1,320	−1,320	−1,320	−21,120
− Depreciation	−23,390	−24,407	−24,407	−24,407	−23,390
+ Replacement Reserve	+11,280	+11,844	+12,436	+13,058	−13,711
Taxable Income	1,432	6,141	12,216	18,663	−22,907
× t	×0.28	×0.28	×0.28	×0.28	×0.28
Taxes	401	1,719	3,420	5,226	−6,414

After-Tax Cash Flow from Resale of Property

Estimated Selling Price	1,052,932
− Selling Expense	−84,235
Net Sales Price	968,697
− Unpaid Mortgage Balance	−592,696
Before Tax Equity Reversion	376,001
− TXR	−55,940
After Tax Equity Reversion	320,061

Taxes from Resale of Property
Taxable Income from Resale

Estimated Selling Price	1,052,932
− Selling Expense	−84,235
Amount Realized	968,697
− Adjusted Basis	−718,999
Capital Gain	249,698

Taxes from Resale

Depreciation Recovery	120,000
× t_d	×0.25
Depreciation Recovery Tax	30,000
Capital Gain	129,698
× t_g	×0.20
Capital Gain Tax	25,940
Depreciation Recovery Tax	30,000
+ Capital Gain Tax	+25,940
TXR	55,940

Summary of After-Tax Cash Flows

Year	0	1	2	3	4	5
After-Tax Cash Flow	−205,400	3,539	6,240	8,758	11,382	−1,960
After Tax Equity Reserve						320,061
NPV at 10%	$14,844					
IRR	11.62%					

Reform Act of 1986). Recall that the 1986 law (and the subsequent *Tax Act of 1993*) ushered in widespread changes in the tax law which resulted in a reduction in the attractiveness of real estate as a tax shelter. Later, we will show the cash flows under the lenient tax rules of the early 1980s. This will allow us to demonstrate the effect of changes in the tax regulations on the value of real estate investments. The details of the tax laws before and after the 1986 act and the 1993 Tax Act are discussed in detail below, but the following is a summary.

The Tax Reform Act of 1981 established depreciation based on the **accelerated cost recovery system (ACRS).** The first-year depreciation was approximately three times greater under this system than under current rules. The investor had the choice of the accelerated depreciation rate or a straight-line depreciation schedule over 15, 35, or 45 years. For a residential property using ACRS, the excess depreciation over straight-line was subject to **depreciation recapture.** For nonresidential properties, the entire amount of depreciation deductions had to be recaptured. Recaptured depreciation was taxed as ordinary income and was not subject to the 60 percent capital gains exclusion. There were also different maximum tax rates applied to ordinary income and capital gains—50 and 20 percent, respectively. It was this differential that induced investors to seek ways to transform ordinary income into capital gains income.

Table 16–3 shows the cash flows from operations for a 5-year holding period. To calculate the after-tax cash flows, it is necessary to determine the tax liability. Depreciation and interest expenses are deductions for tax purposes. Negative taxable income is generated for year five. This loss produces a tax savings which is reflected in the after-tax cash flow for that year. This loss can be written off against other income in the year the property is sold. For the other years, we have taxable income; however, the after-tax cash flows are still positive. Likewise, the after-tax reversion from the sale of the property is a positive $320,061. With an initial equity investment of $205,400 (down payment plus financing costs plus acquisition costs), this project is acceptable at the required return of 10 percent. The NPV is $14,844 and the IRR is 11.62 percent.

By contrast, Table 16–4 shows a very different picture for the same project under the tax treatment of the 1981 Tax Act. The generous depreciation allowances produce negative taxable income. These losses could be written off against income from other sources to produce tax savings and generate even larger after-tax cash flows. Even more interesting, the project now generates a much higher rate of return and has a greater NPV. This clearly shows that tax rules can affect the investment value of real property.

Because the initial equity investment for the project is an after-tax cost, the proper discount rate is the after-tax discount rate. Recall that acquisition costs must be included in depreciation and written off over the depreciable life of the asset and that financing costs must be written off over the life of the mortgage. Thus, since the down payment is not tax deductible, these equity expenditures are after-tax costs.

Two tax considerations drive the increase from pre-tax to post-tax value in this example. The first is the deduction of a noncash item, depreciation, to compute taxable income. The favorable depreciation allowance creates large and early tax rebates. The second is the conversion of ordinary income to capital gains and its favorable treatment. Each dollar of depreciation reduces ordinary income by one dollar and taxes by 50 cents in the year in which it occurs. It also reduces the book value of the property and, given the ultimate sale price, increases the capital gain in the year of sale. The capital gain in the year of sale is taxed at the 20 percent rate, however. Thus, the tax rules allow the investor to postpone 50 cents in taxes in the early years in exchange for a payment of 20 cents later when the property is sold—a good deal.

The example just discussed is a good illustration of how a property without economic merit or worth can be made into an attractive investment through the application of the favorable tax laws that existed prior to 1986. There is some suggestion that the lenient tax laws of the early 1980s encouraged the development of real estate projects that were not economically feasible but were, rather, pure tax shelters. The overbuilding of rental properties, such as office buildings and apartments, led to declining real estate values in many areas of the country as owners granted ever attractive rent concessions to lure tenants. Lenders sometimes advanced funds on the basis of appraisals that failed to reflect the consequences of overbuilding. Investors in commercial properties that fell in value exercised their put option and forfeited the properties to

T A B L E   1 6 – 4

Comparison of Pre- and Post-1986 Tax Reform Act After-Tax Cash Flows

Year	Post-1986 Tax Treatment After-Tax Cash Flow	Pre-1986 Tax Treatment After-Tax Cash Flow
0	−205,400	−205,400
1	3,539	34,621
2	6,240	29,206
3	8,758	27,180
4	11,382	25,186
5	−1,960 + 320,061	26,719 + 262,805
NPV at 10%	$14,844	$67,606
IRR	12.34%	18.15%

lenders. The losses suffered by lenders during the mid-1980s in this fashion were one of the motivating factors leading to the change in the tax laws. One purpose of the 1986 act was to remove incentives to develop real estate properties that had no economic feasibility.

REAL ESTATE TAX REGULATIONS

Figure 16–1 presents a useful outline to discuss tax regulations and their impact on real estate. Some of the regulations will have a major impact on the value of real estate projects, while others will have only a minor impact. Also, the value of real estate will be affected by the interaction of several of the tax rules. We begin with a discussion of the manner in which tax regulations affect the definition of income.

Definition of Income

The definition of taxable income will differ from the before-tax cash flows for two reasons. One is the treatment of noncash expenses such as depreciation, and the other is the treatment of interest as an expense.

Noncash Expenses, Notably Depreciation

Since depreciation is a noncash expense, each dollar of depreciation results in a proportional tax savings equal to the marginal tax rate of the taxpayer. This is true whether the depreciation reduces reported profits, whereby tax dollars are saved, or whether it creates a loss that can be offset against other income, creating a tax "rebate." Three factors affect the value of the tax savings that result from depreciation—the amount of depreciation, the speed of write-off, and the marginal tax rate. The tax shelter provided by depreciation will be greater if the tax laws allow a greater amount of depreciation to be recorded early in the life of the investment and tax rates are high. The general formula for the present value (PV) of the depreciation tax shield is

$$PV = \sum_{t=1}^{n} \frac{D_t \times T}{(1 + r)^t}$$

(Equation 16–1)

where D_t is the dollar amount of depreciation in period t, n is the period over which depreciation occurs (not necessarily the period over which the investment is held), T is the marginal tax bracket of the investor, and r is the discount interest rate. To repeat, tax rules can affect the amount of depreciation D, the time t in which it occurs, and the tax rate T.

There are different views on the issue of the discount rate used to value the depreciation tax shield. One view holds that a risk-free rate should be used because the tax savings are certain. Given the tax rules, there will be known tax savings generated by the depreciation, regardless of the operating cash flows of the real estate investment. This argument divides the present value of the real estate investment into two components: the operating cash flows computed without regard to the tax shield and the tax shield itself. Under this view, the present value (PV) of the equity position in the real estate is given by

$$PV = \sum_{t=1}^{n} \frac{CF_T}{(1 + r^*)^t} + \sum_{t=1}^{n} \frac{D_t \times T}{(1 + r_f)^t} \qquad \text{(Equation 16–2)}$$

where CF_t is the cash flow only from operations in period t, and r^* is a discount rate that reflects the risk of those cash flows. The second term in Equation 16–2 is the depreciation tax shield from above, employing a risk-free discount rate r_f.

Another argument suggests that the real estate investment should be valued as a whole, using the proper risk-adjusted discount rate.

$$PV = \sum_{t=1}^{n} \frac{CF_t}{(1 + r^{**})^t} \qquad \text{(Equation 16–3)}$$

where r^{**} reflects the risk of the cash flows CF_t determined by including depreciation.

There is no irreconcilable conflict in the two views. One can choose two discount rates, r^* and r^{**}, that produce the same present value in Equations 16–2 and 16–3. If this is done, r^{**} would be less than r^*. The cash flows in the latter equation are less risky than those of operations alone because they combine the risky cash flows of operations with the riskless cash flows of depreciation. Viewing the depreciation of the tax shield as riskless has its merits. Tax rules that allow large and accelerated depreciation and impose high tax brackets increase the proportion of real estate that is represented by tax shield. This reduces the risk of real estate investments and, other things being equal, encourages (overbuilding) real estate projects. The previous example shows this. A real estate project which could not be economically justified without depreciation becomes profitable with favorable tax rules.

Over the last two decades or so, there have been five distinct periods marked by different tax treatment of depreciation. In the several years prior to 1981, real estate was depreciated over relatively long periods. This disadvantage was offset by the ability of investors to select one of a few accelerated methods of depreciation. A high top marginal tax bracket, 70 percent, added to the value of the depreciation tax shield during this time. From 1981 through 1986, the tax shield held its value. Although the top marginal tax bracket was reduced to 50 percent, the depreciation allowance was accelerated. After 1986, however, the value of the tax shield was reduced by lengthening the period of depreciation, eliminating accelerated methods, and reducing the top tax bracket to 28 percent. The Tax Act of 1993 raised marginal tax rates on ordinary income to a maximum of 39.6 percent and extended the term of depreciation for nonresidential property. Finally, in 1997 capital gains treatment was reintroduced. Let's review these five periods.

Pre-1981.   Prior to the Economic Recovery Act of 1981, tax regulations placed commercial real estate into classes with rather long lives for the purpose of depreciation. Residential real estate (multifamily housing) was depreciated over 40 years. The rules allowed for several methods of accelerated depreciation, including the double-declining balance and sum-of-the-year's digits methods. It also allowed a taxpayer to shift from one method to another during the depreciation period if the switch resulted in a greater depreciation over the remaining period. The taxpayer also could choose a straight-line depreciation. During this time, the top marginal tax bracket was 70 percent.

Depreciation in year t, (D_t) under the **straight-line method** is given by

$$D_t = C/n \qquad \text{(Equation 16–4)}$$

where C is the cost basis of the depreciable portion of the real estate and n is the term over which it is depreciated. Under the straight-line method, the property is considered to deteriorate at a constant rate over its depreciable life.

Under the **double-declining method,** the depreciation in the first year is double that under straight-line. For the second year, depreciation is double the amount that would be calculated if the remaining balance were depreciated under a straight-line method. This method provides for relatively large depreciation in the initial years and little in the later years.

Annual depreciation under the **sum-of-the-year's digits method** is given by a ratio for which the numerator n is the number of years remaining, the denominator (SYD) is the sum of the years in the depreciable life taken individually, and C is the cost basis of the depreciable portion of the real estate.

1981–1986. The most notable feature affecting real estate in the Tax Reform Act of 1981 was the establishment of a new method of depreciation, the accelerated cost recovery system (ACRS). Real estate was placed in a category of 15 years. This increased to 18 years for 1984 and 1985 then to 19 years for 1986 (see Part A of Table 16–5). The percentages of depreciation for the 15-year ACRS are shown in Part B of Table 16–5. Note that the depreciation is accelerated such that 46 percent of the total depreciation can be taken in the first 5 years of life. The alternative straight-line depreciation for real estate in the 15-year class would be 6.67 percent in each year (1/15). Using ACRS, the actual allowance in the first year is nearly double that, or 12 percent. From 1981 to 1986, the top tax bracket was 50 percent. This system allowed for somewhat greater depreciation in the early years but also reduced

TABLE 16–5
Rules for Real Estate Depreciation

Part A

Depreciation Rules Since 1981

1981–1983*	15 year ACRS based on 175% of straight-line depreciation
1984–1985*	18 year ACRS based on 175% of straight-line depreciation
1986*	19 year ACRS based on 175% of straight-line depreciation
1987–1993	27.5 years straight-line for residential properties (mid-month convention)
	31.5 years straight-line for nonresidential properties (mid-month convention)
1994–	27.5 years straight-line for residential properties (mid-month convention)
	39 years straight-line for nonresidential properties (mid-month convention)

Part B

ACRS Depreciation Percentages for Real Estate (15 year depreciable life)**

Recovery Year	Month Placed in Service											
	1	2	3	4	5	6	7	8	9	10	11	12
1	12	11	10	9	8	7	6	5	4	3	2	1
2	10	10	11	11	11	11	11	11	11	11	11	12
3	9	9	9	9	10	10	10	10	10	10	10	10
4	8	8	8	8	8	8	9	9	9	9	9	9
5	7	7	7	7	7	7	8	8	8	8	8	8
6	6	6	6	6	7	7	7	7	7	7	7	7
7	6	6	6	6	6	6	6	6	6	6	6	6
8	6	6	6	6	6	6	6	6	6	6	6	6
9	6	6	6	6	5	6	5	5	5	6	6	6
10	5	6	5	6	5	5	5	5	5	5	6	5
11	5	5	5	5	5	5	5	5	5	5	5	5
12	5	5	5	5	5	5	5	5	5	5	5	5
13	5	5	5	5	5	5	5	5	5	5	5	5
14	5	5	5	5	5	5	5	5	5	5	5	5
15	5	5	5	5	5	5	5	5	5	5	5	5
16		1	1	2	2	3	3	4	4	4	4	5

*Residential properties required recapture of excess depreciation; nonresidential properties required recapture of all depreciation.
**Not applicable for taxable years less than 12 months.

the value of the depreciation shield by lowering the top tax rate (from 70 percent in previous years). Recall that the value of depreciation will increase as the investor's marginal tax rate increases.

1986–1993. The Tax Reform Act of 1986 (TRA 1986) created the **modified accelerated cost recovery system (MACRS).** This system eliminated accelerated depreciation and placed commercial real estate investments in two separate classes. Residential properties such as apartment houses were to be depreciated over 27.5 years, and other commercial properties (office buildings, shopping centers, warehouses, and so on) over 31.5 years, both on a straight-line basis. Thus for real estate, this change eliminated accelerated depreciation and lengthened the depreciation period. At the same time, the top tax bracket was reduced to 28 percent.[1] These changes of lengthening the depreciation schedule, switching to straight-line depreciation, and lowering the marginal tax rates for personal income led to a significant reduction in the value of the depreciation tax shield.

The MACRS requires the mid-month convention which assumes that the asset is placed into service in the middle of the month acquired. It also assumes that the asset is sold in the middle of the month. Thus, even if the asset is purchased on January 1, the maximum depreciation for the first year is 11.5 months. Likewise, if the asset is sold on December 31 of a later year, the maximum depreciation allowed for that year is 11.5 months.

1993–1997. The Tax Act of 1993 provided some further changes in the personal income tax structure: (1) the top marginal tax rate increased from 31 percent for 1992 to 39.6 percent for 1993; (2) the long-term capital gains tax remained at a maximum of 28 percent;(3) starting in 1994, losses and credits from certain real estate activities were no longer disallowed by the passive rules; and (4) the depreciation write-off for nonresidential real estate increases from 31.5 years to 39 years straight-line for properties put in service after May 12, 1993.

Thus, marginal tax rates have been increased gradually since the initial compression of the maximum tax rate to 28 percent by TRA 1986. For 1997, the marginal tax rates for married filing jointly are:

Income if taxable income is		Tax Liability regular income tax liability before credit is			
more than	but not more than				
$ 0	$ 41,200	$ 0.00	+	15%	$ 0
41,200	99,600	6,180.00	+	28%	41,200
99,600	151,750	22,532.00	+	31	99,600
151,750	271,050	38,698.50	+	36	151,750
271,050		81,646.50	+	39.6	271,050

Post–1997. The *Taxpayer Relief Act of 1997* increased the holding period for long-term capital gains to 18 months. For sales and exchanges after July 28, 1997, the long-term capital gains rate will only apply if the taxpayer holds the asset for more than 18 months. For sales with long-term gains after May 6, 1997, the maximum capital gains rate is 20 percent (10 percent in a 15 percent marginal bracket). Mid-term capital assets (capital assets held for more than 1 year and less than 18 months) sold after July 28, 1997, are subject to tax at a rate no higher than 28 percent. Capital gain property acquired after December 31, 2000, and held for more than 5 years will be taxed at the reduced rate of 18 percent. This provision does not benefit anyone until the year 2006. For individuals in the 15-percent bracket, the 10 percent rate for capital gains is reduced to 8 percent for assets meeting the 5-year holding period, regardless of the acquisition date. This reduction is only for capital gains after December 31, 2000.

The maximum tax rate on gain attributable to the depreciation of section 1250 property is reduced to 25 percent. It is important to note that the section 1250 recapture applies to all depreciation of real estate assets and not to just excess depreciation. The remaining portion of the total gain from the sale is treated as capital gain and is taxed at a rate up to 20 percent.

The depreciation methods for the 1981–1986 and post-1986 tax periods are summarized in Table 16–6. The table shows the annual depreciation for a multifamily residential property with a depreciable base of $100,000. The 1981–1986 tax environment afforded much larger depreciation in the initial years of the investment than the post-1986 environment. The best measure of the value of a depreciation method is the present value of the tax savings that results from the method. For each method, the table shows both the present value (using an arbitrary, but reasonable, discount rate of 10 percent) of the depreciation amount and the present value of the tax savings. The latter value is the former multiplied by the relevant top tax rate. For the ACRS, the present value of the tax savings is $28,395 with a top tax rate of 50 percent. For the post-1986 period, the present value of the tax savings is $8,396 with a top tax rate of 25 percent.

Thus, the tax shelter component of the asset's value has declined significantly as a result of the shift to straight-line, a lengthening of the depreciation period, and a reduction in marginal tax rates.[2] Figure 16–2 shows the value of depreciation under the previous allowable methods.

At first glance, one might be tempted to ask how a tax law (such as TRA 1986) that significantly lowers the tax rate can have an adverse effect on the value of real estate as an investment. After all, if the investor pays less taxes, should that not increase the value of any capital investment? The answer is yes. One recalls that the 1986 tax law not only lowered tax rates but also

TABLE 16–6

Annual Depreciation: ACRS and Post-1986 Methods, Multifamily Residential Property

	Depreciable Base, $100,000; Placed in Service, January 1	
Year	1981–1986 Accelerated Cost Recovery System (ACRS)[a]	Post–1986 Tax Reform Act of 1986 (TRA 1986)
1	$12,000	$ 3,485[b]
2	10,000	3,636
3	9,000	3,636
4	8,000	3,636
5	7,000	3,636
6	6,000	3,636
7	6,000	3,636
8	6,000	3,636
9	6,000	3,636
10	5,000	3,636
11	5,000	3,636
12	5,000	3,636
13	5,000	3,636
14	5,000	3,636
15	5,000	3,636
16	—	3,636
17	—	3,636
18	—	3,636
19	—	3,636
20	—	3,636
21	—	3,636
22	—	3,636
23	—	3,636
24	—	3,636
25	—	3,636
26	—	3,636
27	—	3,636
28	—	1,979
Present value at 10%	$56,790	$33,586
Present value × the marginal tax rate[c]	$28,395	$ 8,396

[a]Fifteen-year depreciable term
[b]Reflects the mid-month convention
[c]Assumed to be 50 percent and 25 percent, respectively

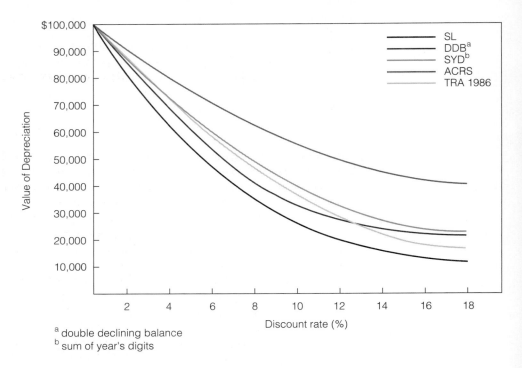

FIGURE 16–2

*Present Value of Depreciation; Various Methods
(depreciable base: $100,000)*

ª double declining balance
ᵇ sum of year's digits

reduced the value of depreciation and eliminated the advantage of capital gains. These changes would have the greatest effect on those real estate projects that are not economically feasible. High tax brackets favor real estate projects that produce paper losses, because a greater portion of the loss results in a tax savings on other income. Paper losses are enhanced by generous depreciation allowances. Low tax rates favor real estate investments that will show a profit, because fewer taxes are paid on such investments. To this extent, the change in the depreciation method accomplished one intended goal—to reduce investment in real estate projects that are not economically justifiable.

Taxes and Interest Payments

Income for tax purposes also is affected by the treatment of interest payments on debt. Generally, interest payments are considered an expense. Thus, for every dollar of interest paid, the tax due to the government is reduced by one dollar times the tax rate. We saw in the previous chapter on leverage and capital structure how the equity yield is enhanced by the use of debt. This would encourage the use of debt financing. Were it not for default risk, it might be optimal to finance real estate projects with 99.9 percent debt.

In the past, real estate developers and investors have used—some would say abused—this rule to reduce or avoid taxes in much the same fashion as the depreciation tax shield. When it became obvious that the terms of financing were often arranged solely to reduce or avoid taxes, the tax laws were changed to restrict abuses. Two examples of changes in the tax laws are the original issue discount (OID) rules and the investment interest limitation rules.

Original Issue Discount Rules

By way of background, the term original issue discount (OID) refers to debt that is issued at a discount from the face value. Such debt may have no coupon or interest payments during its life but simply promises a face amount at maturity. Zero coupon bonds issued by corporations are a good example. The present value (at 10 percent) of a $1000 bond that pays no coupon interest and matures in 10 years is $385.54. The investor who purchases the bond receives a 10 percent return through appreciation in its value over the term of the bond. During this time, the investor receives no cash interest payments. Assuming interest rates do not change, the value of the bond will increase each year as it approaches maturity. At one time investors did not have to pay tax on the accretion in value, since they were receiving no interest payments. Later, the IRS ruled that investors had to pay tax on the annual accretion in value. Prior to 1984, the set of regulations covering these requirements were referred to as original issue discount rules, and they were applied only to corporate debt securities. The Tax Reform Act of 1984 extended the OID rules to real estate lending such as mortgages. The rules are applied to the financing of real estate whenever the periodic interest payment is different from market rates. There were several abusive practices that led to the OID rules being applied to real estate.

One practice concerned the conversion of ordinary income to capital gains during times when there is a differential tax rate. Even though the differential has been eliminated, the OID rules still apply, so it is necessary to understand the background in this regard. A simple example will illustrate. A property owner may desire to sell a parcel valued at $1 million that originally was purchased for $800,000. The seller, in a high tax bracket, has no immediate need for cash, only future income. The seller is willing to finance the purchase price at 12 percent over 30 years. The annual payment would be $124,144, of which $120,000 would be interest in the first year. The seller must pay taxes on interest at the ordinary tax rate. What would happen if, instead, the seller raised his asking price to $1.4 million and charged 8 percent interest on a loan for $1.4 million over the same term? The annual payment would remain relatively the same at $124,358 of which interest in the first year would be $112,000. The seller would receive the same payment and be able to trade off less ordinary income in the future for more capital gains in the present (the capital gain increases to $600,000 from $200,000). Even on a time unadjusted basis, the seller pays less total tax and has greater after-tax income.

Another abusive practice that led to the OID rules was the use of large amounts of nonrecourse debt to sell properties at inflated prices. Without getting too technical, nonrecourse debt is a loan for which the borrower is not personally liable. Generally, the lender can only look to the property as collateral and for payment of the debt. Recourse debt means that the lender can look to the personal assets of the borrower in the event of default. In seller-financed transactions, the seller of the property becomes the lender, and the buyer becomes the borrower. As an example of abusive practices, assume that an owner of a property valued at $1 million sells it for $1.8 million and finances the major portion of the loan at a very low rate—for example, 4 percent. The payments on the loan may be no greater than a market interest loan for a smaller amount and a sale at the true value. But the higher transaction price allows the borrower to write off much larger amounts of depreciation. Taxpayers in high tax brackets can then use the loss to offset other income, a typical tax shelter. Meanwhile, the seller of the property reports the sale on an installment basis, avoiding immediate capital gains tax. If the value of the property rises sufficiently, the buyer will continue to make payments on the loan and eventually pay off the debt. If the property does not rise in value, the buyer may default on the loan, giving the property back to the original owner. The total tax savings to the buyer because of the depreciation may well exceed the down payment, so there is no loss on the default. The parties also benefit if the loan called for the accrual of interest. If the buyer was on an accrual and the seller on a cash basis, the former could take a deduction for the interest accrued but not paid, while the latter would not have to report interest income.

As a result of these practices, the OID rules were enacted. At-risk limitations also were introduced as a result of the use of nonrecourse debt. (The at-risk limitation rule is discussed later in the chapter.) First applied to real estate under the Tax Reform Act of 1984, the OID rules remain intact under the more recent TRA of 1986. These rules require two things: that a market rate be imputed to seller-financing if it carries a below-market rate and interest charge, and that income be reported annually. There are two tests to determine if the OID rules apply.

The adequacy of interest test says that if the stated interest rate is less than 110 percent of the applicable federal rate, an interest rate will be imputed at 120 percent of the applicable federal rate. The applicable federal rate is determined with reference to the rate on Treasury obligations with a maturity equal to that on the loan. There are three categories established: loans of maturity less than 3 years, loans of maturity from 3 to 9 years, and loans of maturity after 9 years.

■ EXAMPLE

Assume that the applicable federal rate is 10 percent. The rate on a loan is 9 percent. Since the rate is less than 11 percent (110 percent of 10 percent), the imputed rate on the loan will be set at 12 percent (120 percent of 10 percent). ■ ■

The time-value-of-money test is applied only in cases where the stated interest meets the adequacy of interest test, but payments are not paid at least annually or an interest rate must be imputed. In either case, the test requires that the effective interest rate on the loan is determined and the amount of interest treated as income to the lender and expense to the borrower. In short, the OID rules require that interest be imputed and reported as revenue (expense) annually.

There are some exceptions to the OID rules. They fall into two categories: those exempted under the 1984 act and those subsequently exempted under an amendment passed in October 1985. Exemptions under the original act include sales of farms by individuals for not more than $1 million, sales of personal residences under $250,000, and transactions between related parties under $500,000. For these transactions the imputed interest rule applies, but the rate is set at 10 percent for loans that carry a rate less than 9 percent. Also, the time-value-of-money rule is not applied. This means that a cash-basis seller need not report interest income until actually received, while the accrual-basis buyer can deduct the interest expense as incurred.

The amendments in 1985 liberalized the OID rules further. For transactions where the amount of the seller-financing does not exceed $2.8 million, the interest rate for tax purposes will be the lower of 9 percent or 100 percent of the applicable federal rate. Also, the $2.8 million figure has been indexed for inflation since 1990. This reduces the minimum interest rate from either the 110 percent or 120 percent of the applicable federal rate requirement. For sales involving a sale/leaseback with any amount of seller financing, the OID rules apply. The OID rules also apply to any seller financing greater than $2.8 million. The amendments provide for the use of the cash-basis method of accounting for interest provided the financing is $2 million or less and both the lender and the borrower agree to elect the cash-basis method.

Investment Interest Payments

Another example of the use of tax laws to minimize after-tax income involved holding property for investment purposes. Again, at a time when there was a tax-rate differential or ordinary and capital gains income, it was possible to transfer ordinary income into capital gains using interest expense as the tax shield. Assume an investor purchases an asset that is not likely to produce an operating income, only capital gains. An example would be the purchase of raw land to be held for appreciation in value. The investor takes out a loan to purchase the property with only a small down payment. On an annual operating basis, the investor will show no income, only an interest expense. The resulting loss can be used to offset other income. Here, interest expense and not depreciation creates the tax shelter. Later, when the property is sold, the gain is taxed at a lower capital gain rate.

To curtail such arrangements, a limitation was placed on the deduction of interest payments by the Tax Reform Act of 1969. It was aimed at those instances where an investment was made in an asset that provided no annual operating income. Most such assets include stocks and bonds. Examples in real estate singled out by the 1969 act included raw land and net leased investments. With a net leased investment, the owner holds property for which all operating expenses, including property taxes, repairs, and other expenses, are paid by the tenant. The investment replicates the holding of an investment for which the investor makes no managerial decisions or incurs no operating expenses. TRA 1986 removed net leased investments from the limitation because such properties under the act were placed under passive loss limitations (discussed below). The purpose of the rule as it now stands is to limit the amount of an individual's annual interest deduction to the amount of the net investment income received. If there is insufficient net income generated, interest expense may not be deductible on loans used to carry raw land investments.

■ EXAMPLE

An investor borrows $1 million at 10 percent to purchase land valued at $1.2 million in the hopes that it will appreciate in value. In the first year, she allows some development of minerals and receives royalties of $110,000. Investment expenses in the first year consist solely of property taxes of $35,000. The interest expense will be $100,000 (0.1 × $1,000,000). The investor may make the following deductions:

Royalty income	$110,000
Less property tax expense	35,000
Equals net investment income	75,000
Interest allowed	75,000
Interest deferred	25,000

Determination of Taxes

The above rules specify how income and expenses are defined for the purpose of determining taxable income. Given taxable income, other rules determine the amount of the tax liability. The tax liability will be determined by

1. Differential tax rates on ordinary income and capital gains,
2. Offsetting losses from one income source against other sources (passive loss limitations),
3. Applicability of alternative minimum taxes, and
4. Establishment of favored classes of investment.

Differential Tax Rates

Prior to TRA 1986 and subsequent to 1997, ordinary income and capital gains income were taxed at different rates. The lower rate on capital gains encouraged the conversion of ordinary income into capital gains whenever possible. The 1986 act retained the distinction between the two types of income but required capital gains to be treated as ordinary income up to a maximum rate of 28 percent. Recall that the maximum tax rate for individuals for 1997 is 39.6 percent. Tax regulations continue to require that income be distinguished because differential rates seem to come and go, and there continues to be restrictions on capital losses (discussed below). However, the closer to equalization the rates, the less the incentive to design tax schemes and shelters that convert ordinary income into capital gains.

Limitation of Losses

There are three ways in which tax regulations limit the use of losses from one source to offset income from another source. They are the capital loss limitation, passive loss limitation, and "at-risk" rules.

Capital Loss Limitation.   The **capital loss limitation** rule allows the taxpayer to offset capital losses only against capital gains. This is so even if tax rates are the same for ordinary income and for capital gains. Capital losses in excess of capital gains can be used to offset other sources of income only up to $3000 annually. The remainder must be carried forward and used in subsequent years to offset capital gains or another $3000 in other income. This rule really does not prevent the use of real estate as a tax shelter. The value of real estate as a tax shelter derives mainly from operating losses that could, if allowed by the tax rules, be used to offset other sources of income. Present rules, such as the passive loss limitation, severely restrict such an offset, however.

Passive Loss Limitation.   Real estate tax shelters existed because losses created through a depreciation write-off could be offset against other (non-real-estate) income. The tax savings were a bonus to the positive cash flow of the investment. The government's answer to this "problem" was to create narrow categories of income. Losses in one class cannot be used to offset positive income in other classes. There are two general types of income, which we will refer to as business income and outside income. The latter generally includes salaries and wages from an occupation. TRA 1986 created the passive activities loss limitation (PALL) rule and established three classes within the category of business income: active, portfolio, and passive income. **Active income** consists primarily of earnings received from actively working in a business.

Income from an active trade or business is further subdivided into income from real estate or business. **Portfolio income** is income received from investments, such as interest on bonds, dividends on stock, and capital gains from these investments. **Passive income,** the focus here, is income received primarily from real estate activities. Figure 16–3 summarizes the categories of income and indicates the extent to which loss can be offset by outside income.

A loss generated by an active trade or business can be used to offset outside income, just as under prior law. The taxpayer must participate "materially" in the active trade or business. To participate materially means to be involved on a regular, continuous, and substantial basis. Real estate is not generally considered to be an active business. Losses from real estate activities cannot be used to offset outside income (except for a $25,000 special exemption discussed below).

FIGURE 16–3

Tax Reform Act of 1986 and Income Classification

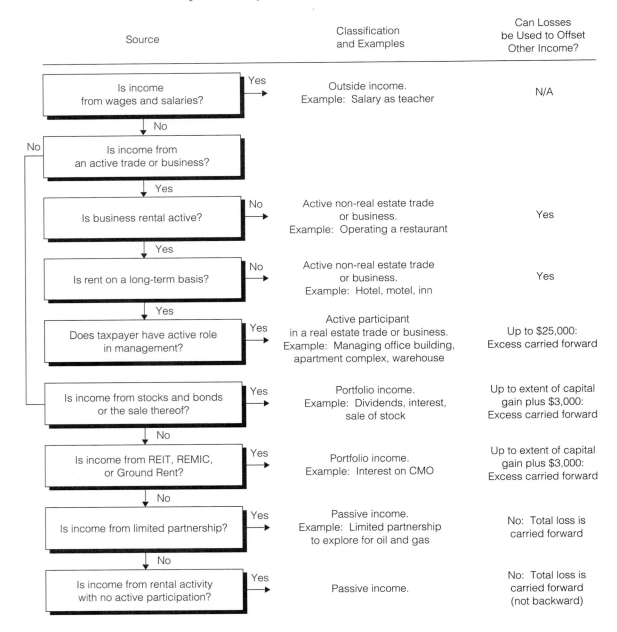

In essence, no real estate business, regardless of the taxpayer's participation, can be considered an active trade or business. A real estate business is usually characterized by rental activity. Rental activity is activity that produces revenue for the use of tangible real property. One exception here is the lodging industry, which rents living space on a short-term basis. Thus, hotels and motels are one example of real estate in an active business class.

Portfolio losses (losses in this class occur almost exclusively through a capital loss—a loss on the sale of the capital asset) can be offset against portfolio gains and up to $3000 in ordinary income annually. Dividends from a real estate investment trust (REIT) or income from a real estate mortgage investment conduit (REMIC) are considered portfolio income. These instruments, although real-estate-related, are actually stocks and bonds. Income from REITs and REMICs cannot be used to offset passive losses.

Passive income consists of income not in the above classifications. It includes all nonactive real estate activity and all income from limited partnerships. Income from limited partnerships is passive income by definition. Thus, whether or not a limited partnership is engaged in a non-real-estate trade or business or a real estate trade or business, the income is still classified as passive. Income received for personal services performed for a limited partnership is not passive income, however. If a limited partner receives a salary for preparing the accounts of the partnership, such income is considered outside income.

Given these classes, losses from one are not available to offset income from the others. The one exception is the active participant in a real estate investment. Up to $25,000 in losses from this class can be used to offset income from other classes (active non-real-estate, portfolio, or outside income). The loss must be from actively participating in real estate. This means that the taxpayer must be actively involved in the real estate rental activity. To be actively involved is not the same as to be materially involved (the requirement for the non-real-estate trade or business). Active involvement only requires that the taxpayer participate in a significant sense, such as managing the property, making repairs, or arranging for repairs to be made. Taxpayers with an adjusted gross income (AGI) of less than $100,000 can use the entire $25,000 exemption. The exemption is reduced by 50 percent of the taxpayer's AGI above $100,000. It is eliminated for an AGI of $150,000 or above.

Use of Passive Losses.   Unless the taxpayer is actively involved in a rental property, his or her gain or loss is categorized as passive income and losses. For each tax year, the taxpayer must net those losses and income. Each rental property is considered as a separate "activity." For each activity, positive net passive income is taxable and net passive losses must be carried forward to a future date. Passive losses cannot be carried back. The deferred (also called suspended) passive losses can be used to offset any positive passive income in future years, including any gain in the year the taxpayer disposes of the real estate activity. Any suspended passive losses that remain after the disposition of the entire activity can be used to offset outside income. Passive losses from an activity are suspended, but they are not lost.

The Tax Act of 1993 provides some easing of the passive loss rules for real estate brokers, salespersons, and other real estate professionals. The major benefit is that eligible taxpayers can deduct unlimited real estate activity losses from active income and portfolio income. Under the new law, individuals must meet these requirements: (1) more than half of all personal services they perform during the year are for real property trades or business in which they materially participate and (2) they perform more than 750 hours of service per year in those real estate activities. Thus, material participation requirements are met if the taxpayer is involved in real estate operations on a regular, continuous, and substantial basis. Real estate trades and businesses include real estate brokerage, management, rental, operation, leasing, development, construction, reconstruction, acquisition, or conversion.

Separate records should be kept for each passive activity of a taxpayer. The unused passive loss from an activity may be used to offset outside income in the year of disposition, even if there is positive passive income from other activities. An abandonment is considered a disposition of the property and will trigger the recognition of suspended losses. However, if the taxpayer transfers property to a related individual, the transfer will not be considered a disposition. Unused passive losses remain with the seller, who may use them to offset positive passive income until the property is fully disposed of. The government must have anticipated that a taxpayer would sell a property to a relative, use the suspended losses, and then repurchase the property.

Form of Organization.   The passive loss limitation rules are modified, depending on the form of organization of the owner. Real estate property can be held by an individual, personal service corporation, limited partnership, a closely held C corporation, a regular C corporation, or an S corporation. A closely held C corporation (closed corporation) is one that is owned by a few stockholders or is a family business. It is not the same as an S corporation, which is also owned by a few stockholders but is taxed as a partnership. That is, it avoids the double taxation of a C corporation.

A closed corporation may use passive losses to offset active business income but not portfolio income. A regular C corporation can use passive losses to offset both active business income and portfolio income. Table 16–7 summarizes the use of passive losses to offset income according to the form of ownership.

▮▮ EXAMPLE

A closely held C corporation has $200,000 in passive losses from an apartment complex (which it does not actively manage), $350,000 in positive income from a restaurant, and $50,000 in interest from bonds. The $200,000 can be used to reduce the income from the restaurant to $150,000 but cannot be used to reduce the portfolio income. Had the loss from the apartment complex been $400,000, it would reduce the income from the restaurant to zero and the remaining $50,000 loss would be carried forward. ▮ ▮

The limitation of passive losses was clearly designed to curtail the use of real estate as a pure tax shelter. Under the new rules, passive activity is synonymous with real estate activity. These limitations, involving some rather complex rules, may have been overkill, however. TRA 1986, which defined the passive loss limitation, also extended the period of depreciation and lowered the top tax bracket. The treatment of depreciation alone probably would have been sufficient to eliminate most real estate tax shelters. A good example is the one used in the beginning of this chapter where the change in the depreciation rules destroyed the tax shelter character of the real estate investment. Certainly, the combination of the change in the treatment of depreciation and the limitation of passive losses has caused investors to concentrate on the true economic feasibility of real estate developments.

Capital Loss Limitation and Passive Loss Rule.   Unused passive losses can be used to offset other sources of income upon the disposition of the property. But what if there is a capital loss on the sale of the property? Is this loss a passive loss that can now be used to offset other income, or is a capital loss subject to the capital loss limitation? The answer is the latter. A capital loss is not exempt from the capital loss limitation rule simply because it is from a passive activity.

▮▮ EXAMPLE

Assume a taxpayer sells an apartment complex with a book value of $1 million for $950,000, incurring a $50,000 loss. The taxpayer also has $10,000 of suspended passive losses from previous years. The $10,000 can be used in full to offset other income. The $50,000 capital loss can be used only to offset capital gains plus $3000 of ordinary income in the year of sale. ▮ ▮

TABLE 16–7
Passive Loss Limitations

Form of Ownership	Can Passive Losses Offset	
	Active Business?	*Portfolio?*
Individual	No	No
Limited partnership	No	No
Personal service company	No	No
S corporation	No	No
Closely held C corporation	Yes	No
C corporation	Yes	Yes

At-risk Limitation

At-risk limitations were introduced by the Tax Reform Act of 1976 and originally aimed at non-real-estate shelters, such as oil and gas exploration ventures. Prior to the act, investors could purchase an "asset" at inflated prices with little of their own money and finance the remainder with nonrecourse debt. The heavy write-off of expenses would shelter other income from taxes. The cash flows from the tax shield were likely to be greater than the meager investment. If the venture failed, the investor would simply default on the nonrecourse debt. The 1976 act introduced the **at-risk** concept. Essentially, this rule limits cumulative losses on an investment to the amount that the investor actually has at risk.

The Tax Reform Act of 1986 applied the at-risk rules to real estate investments held by individuals, partnerships, and corporations, including closely held corporations. The crucial determination in applying the rule is the amount considered to be at risk. For a real estate investment, that amount is generally and initially the investor's cash contribution to the investment; the tax basis of any property that the investor contributes; amounts borrowed for use in the investment for which the investor is personally liable or has pledged other property; and/or amounts borrowed for use in the investment for which the investor is not personally liable but which are made by a qualified lender who is engaged in the business of making loans, such as a commercial bank, a savings and loan association, an insurance company, or a pension fund.

The qualified lender cannot be a promoter or a seller of the investment property. A lender becomes a promoter when a fee is received for a loan that is contingent on the amount of the investor's contribution. A qualified lender can have an equity participation in the investment property as long as the terms of the loan are common to those in the trade. If a lender who has an equity position in the investment makes a loan with an interest rate substantially below the market, with a term in excess of the life of the property, or with severe restrictions on the ability to foreclose, then the lender may be determined to be unqualified and the loan not considered an amount at risk.

Subsequent to the initial investment, the at-risk amount is increased by any additional contributions of the investor and reduced by any payments made to the investor.

The at-risk test is applied before consideration of passive losses. If there is any loss denied because of the at-risk test, that loss is not eligible to be a suspended passive loss and will therefore never be allowed to offset other income.

Alternative Minimum Tax Rules

Alternative minimum tax (AMT) rules were established in 1978 because some taxpayers with high incomes had so much of their income sheltered by tax preference items. A number of the tax preference items relate to real estate. Essentially, the AMT rule establishes a minimal amount of income upon which a tax is based and then sets a minimum tax rate. It does this by adding back some preference items to the adjusted income. Applied to both individuals and corporations, TRA 1986 broadened the definition of income subject to the AMT and raised the rate to 21 percent. The rate was increased to 24 percent starting in 1991. The Tax Act of 1993 replaces the single rate with a two-tier rate structure starting in 1993 that is 25 percent ($0 to $175,000) and 28 percent (above $175,000). Also starting in 1993, contributions of appreciated real, personal, and intangible property no longer create a tax preference item for the alternative minimum tax. Tax preference items that must be added back are listed in Appendix A to this chapter.

The procedure for computing the alternative minimum tax is as follows. The taxpayer begins with his regular taxable income and adds items known as tax preference items. He then makes deductions that are determined under the AMT rule and substitutes them for the regular deductions. The result is alternative minimum taxable income (AMTI). From AMTI an exemption of $40,000 ($30,000 for single taxpayers) is deducted. The $40,000 exemption is reduced by 25 percent of the amount by which AMTI exceeds $150,000 ($112,500 for single returns). Finally, the appropriate AMT rate is applied. The taxpayer pays the higher of the regular tax or the AMT. Any AMT in excess of regular tax is carried forward to be available as a credit against regular tax in future years.

Table 16–8 shows an example of the alternative minimum tax calculation.

TABLE 16–8

Example of Alternative Minimum Tax Calculation

	Regular Tax	Amount
Salary	$200,000	$200,000
Portfolio income	25,000	25,000
Tax shelter losses	(75,000)[a]	0
Deductions		
Mortgage interest	22,000	22,000
Taxable income	128,000	203,000
Amount exemption		26,750[b]
AMTI		176,250
Tax at 28%	38,840	
Tax at 24%		42,300
AMT	42,300	

[a]This amount is from the tax preference items shown in Appendix A.
[b]$40,000 − [0.25 × (203,000 − 150,000)].

Favored Classes of Real Estate Investment

A favorite tool by which the government encourages activity that has social and economic value is tax incentives, specifically the tax credit. A tax credit is different from a tax deduction. With a one-dollar tax deduction, the taxpayer saves an amount equal to one dollar times the tax rate. With a one-dollar tax credit, the taxpayer saves one dollar. Tax credits can be a powerful motivating tool.

There are two types of real estate investment that the federal government desires to encourage by extending tax credits. One is the rehabilitation of historic structures, and the other is low-income housing.

Rehabilitation of Historic Structures. The Revenue Act of 1978 established tax credits for the rehabilitation of historic structures. The credit was equal to 10 percent of the expenses required to rehabilitate qualified structures. In 1981, the credit was liberalized. The credit was raised to 15 percent on nonresidential structures 30 to 39 years of age, 20 percent on nonresidential structures 40 or more years of age, and 25 percent on certified historic structures (CHS), either residential or nonresidential. TRA 1986 changed the credits again. It authorized a 10 percent credit for nonresidential structure built prior to 1936 and a 20 percent credit for any certified historic structure, regardless of the year in which it was built. CHS's are structures that are on the National Register of Historic Places or are within registered historic districts. The rehabilitation must be certified by the Secretary of the Interior.

The tax credit can be used to offset taxes only on passive income, but it is treated as if it comes from a rental activity with active participation (management) by the taxpayer. Thus, the taxpayer is entitled to the $25,000 exemption for passive activities. This is so even if the rehabilitation is carried out by a limited partnership. In other words, regardless of the nature of the facility or the organization form of ownership, the credit is available only for passive income but with the $25,000 exemption. The taxpayer actually claims the credit equivalent of the $25,000 exemption against outside income. The credit is phased out by 50 cents on the dollar for AGI over $200,000. A tax deduction of $25,000 will save $7000 in taxes for a taxpayer in the 28 percent bracket. Therefore, the taxpayer may use up to $7000 of the credit to offset outside income.

EXAMPLE

A taxpayer rehabilitates a non-CHS (nonresidential) structure built in 1924. It is eligible for the 10 percent credit. The taxpayer spends $120,000 to rehabilitate the structure, creating a $12,000 credit. He can use $7000 of the credit to offset taxes on outside income. The remaining $5000 may be used to offset taxes on passive income. If there is insufficient passive income, the unused tax credit is carried forward for use in future years.

Finally, if the taxpayer uses the tax credit, the depreciable basis of the property must be reduced by the amount of the credit and depreciated with a straight-line method. This reduces the value of the credit somewhat.

Low-income Housing Credits.   Investors are eligible for tax credits on their investment in qualified low-income housing. There are two types of eligible property. The first type includes new structures for which there are no other federal subsidies. The credit will equal 9 percent of the "qualified basis" for each of the first 10 years. The qualified basis is that portion of the property used for low-income housing. The second type of credit includes those properties for which there is some other form of federal subsidy, such as below-market interest loans or loans arranged through tax-exempt issues such as mortgage revenue bonds (see Chapter 7). In this case, the credit is limited to 4 percent of the qualified basis over the first 10 years. If the project fails to meet the requirements for a credit in any 1 year, then the previous tax credits can be recaptured. The credits are subject to the $25,000 exemption on passive losses. This means that the investor may use the credit to offset tax on up to $25,000 on nonpassive income annually. Again, for taxpayers in the 28 percent bracket, this results in a tax savings of $7000. Any excess credit can be used to offset passive income or carried forward. The 1993 tax act makes the credit available for units occupied by full-time students and also eases various operating requirements for low-income housing.

EFFECT OF TAX REFORM ACT OF 1986 ON REAL ESTATE INVESTMENT

The Tax Reform Act of 1986 had a more dramatic impact on real estate than on any other investment activity. Rule changes were aimed specifically at reducing the value of real estate as a tax shelter. In this regard, there were three major changes: (1) a lengthening of the period of depreciation, (2) a limitation on the use of losses from real estate investment to offset other income, and (3) a lowering of the top tax rate. Real estate investment did retain some benefits, however. Interest on debt is deductible for tax purposes, and there are credits for investing in certain types of properties.

With the limitation of the pass-through of losses to partners, the advantage may have shifted to the corporate form of ownership. If the corporation has other sources of income, it can realize substantial tax savings. Furthermore, if these savings are reinvested in other assets (rather than declared as dividends), they will continue to generate cash flows free from taxation at the individual level. Nonetheless, the continued double taxation of corporation income will mean that some real estate will be developed through the partnership entity. Lentz and Fisher studied the impact of TRA 1986 on the form of ownership.[3] They concluded that while there were no conditions under which the corporate form of ownership would dominate prior to the act, that form of ownership may now be the value-maximizing organizational form. The corporate form of ownership, they claim, may be desirable for highly levered (interest tax deduction) depreciable property where a substantial amount of cash flows are retained by the corporation. The motivating factor is the ability of the corporation to utilize more of the losses to offset income. Also, cash flows are reinvested without being taxed. The authors also state that it is relatively more costly to set up a partnership and distribute the partnership interests than it is to establish the corporation. They suggest that real estate may be held less in the form of partnerships as a result of the 1986 act.

There is some evidence that this may be the case. In 1989 Nelson and Petska did a study of the number of real estate limited partnerships and their profit and losses for years before and after TRA 1986.[4] Using tax returns, they found that the number of limited partnerships in real estate fell as a result of the act. They also found that substantial losses were suspended and unavailable for tax relief. Table 16–9 shows the number of partnerships by type of partnership and gain or loss status from 1981 through 1987. It shows that the number of limited partnerships with losses grew dramatically for several years prior to the 1986 act. In 1987 that number dropped dramatically.[5] Table 16–10 shows the gain or loss in ordinary income by type of partnership and gain or loss status. For all partnerships, losses rose steadily through 1986 and then declined by $12 billion (−$17.4 to −$5.4 billion) in 1987. Of the $12 billion improvement in income, $6.2 billion came from partnerships engaged in finance, insurance, and real estate.

TABLE 16-9

Number of Partnerships by Type of Partnership and Gain or Loss Status, Income Years 1981–1987 (in thousands)

Income Year	All Partnership	General Partnership		Limited Partnership	
		With Gain (1)	*With Loss* (2)	*With Gain* (3)	*With Loss* (4)
1981	1,461	677	576	75	133
1982	1,514	707	581	87	139
1983	1,542	707	601	82	152
1984	1,644	750	636	101	157
1985	1,714	774	660	107	173
1986	1,703	766	663	92	181
1987	1,648	769	617	96	166

Source: *SOI Bulletin*, Winter, 1989–1990, p. 33.

TABLE 16-10

Partnerships Gain or Loss in Ordinary Income by Type of Partnership and Gain or Loss Status, Income Years 1981–1987 (in billions of dollars)

Income Year	Total Gain Less Loss	General Partnership		Limited Partnership	
		With Gain (1)	*With Loss* (2)	*With Gain* (3)	*With Loss* (4)
1981	− 2.7	42.8	−29.8	7.8	−23.5
1982	− 7.3	44.4	−34.2	9.2	−26.7
1983	− 2.6	48.6	−32.5	11.7	−30.4
1984	− 3.5	55.7	−36.6	14.0	−36.6
1985	− 8.9	60.5	−42.4	16.6	−43.5
1986	−17.4	63.5	−45.3	16.8	−52.3
1987	− 5.4	66.2	−43.4	21.5	−49.6

Source: *SOI Bulletin*, Winter, 1989–1990, p. 33.

TABLE 16-11

Partnerships Ordinary Income and Losses Reported on Individual Income Tax Returns, 1980–1987 (in billions of dollars)

Income Year	Net Loss* (1)	Total Income (2)	Total Loss (3)
1980	9.6	29.8	20.2
1981	−0.1	31.1	31.2
1982	−0.7	33.0	33.8
1983	−2.3	36.2	38.5
1984	−8.2	38.6	46.8
1985	−8.5	45.5	54.0
1986	−13.0	48.2	61.2
1987	8.2	52.0	43.8

Source: *SOI Bulletin*, Winter, 1989–1990, p. 35.

Next, Table 16–11 shows the partnership ordinary income reported on the individual tax returns of the partners. Again, total losses increased steadily through 1986 and then declined dramatically in 1987. Contrary to the previous years, the reported net income for all partners was positive in 1987. By looking closely at the partners' returns, the authors concluded that only 23.4 percent of all losses were "active" and therefore eligible to offset other income. Another 25.6 percent of the losses were passive, but offset passive income. The remaining losses, about half of all losses, were subject to passive loss limitation rules. The authors concluded that the tax changes of 1986 provided an incentive for high income taxpayers to move out of real estate tax shelters.

TAX-DEFERRED EXCHANGES OF REAL ESTATE PROPERTIES

There is one tax rule that does not affect the after-tax cash flows of operations from real estate or the ownership structure for holding real estate. Nonetheless, the rule has important implications for real estate investors. The rule is the Section 1031, or so-called tax-deferred exchange rule. It applies to all types of properties, but we will focus on the rule insofar as real estate is concerned.

Many real estate owners hold properties which, for various reasons, they would like to sell. Perhaps they do not envision the property as the type that would appreciate greatly in the future. Or perhaps there are too many management responsibilities with the property. The owner would like to remain a real estate investor, however. A sale (and purchase of another property) would accomplish the desired goal but may result in large tax payments if the basis in the property is low relative to the sales price. If a property worth $10 million (with a basis of zero dollars) is sold, the owner in a 30 percent tax bracket would have only $7 million after taxes to reinvest. One way around the problem is the use of the Section 1031 provisions. If the rules are followed, the investor may exchange one (or more) property for another. The new properties need only be "like-kind" properties. Virtually all real estate properties are considered like-kind. Owners may exchange farm land for apartment complexes, or office buildings for warehouses. There are several basic requirements that have to be met for the exchange to qualify as tax-deferred.

It is possible under Section 1031 to permanently defer the gain on investment real estate properties. As long as the investor keeps exchanging properties instead of selling, the equity buildup is not taxed. At the investor's death, the basis of the properties will automatically adjust to market value, eliminating all capital gains.

Basic Requirements

There are four requirements under Section 1031 rules. First, both the relinquished and the acquired property must be held for productive use in a trade or business or for investment. Thus, owner-occupied residences would not be eligible for a like-kind exchange. Second, both the property exchanged and the one received must be of like-kind. For real estate, this involves most any type as mentioned above. Third, the exchange must occur. The owner cannot sell one property for cash and immediately use the cash proceeds to purchase another property. There can be no intervening sale of the relinquished property, no matter how quickly the new acquired property is purchased. Finally, the basis in the acquired property will be equal to the basis in the relinquished property. The calculation of the basis must be adjusted if there is any non-real-estate property (boot) involved. This is discussed shortly.

Three-party Exchanges

You may wonder what transactions are available if an owner identifies a new property to be acquired, but the owner of the identified property does not wish to exchange it for the property in question. This is likely to be the case. One way around this impasse is the three-party exchange. Assume that the owner has a property A and desires to exchange it for property B. The owner of property B has no interest in owning property A, however. Under a three-party exchange, a third party interested in property A is found. Instead of buying A, the third party buys property B and then exchanges it for property A. All parties end up with the property they want: The third party gets A, the original owner gets B, and the owner of B gets cash.

Delayed Exchanges

What would happen if a third-party buyer for property A were available who wanted to own property A immediately, before the owner of A could identify another desirable property. In this case, there can be a delayed exchange. The owner of property A would transfer title (not sell) to the third party who, in turn, would agree to transfer a property identified by the owner of A at some time in the future. In such a case, the third-party buyer usually would deposit a sufficient sum of money in escrow to purchase the identified property at a later date. In this type of exchange, the owner of property A simply transfers title to the third party and says, "Some time in the future, I will identify other properties that you can purchase and deliver title to me."

Boot

Boot is a general term for property that is not like-kind. In a like-kind exchange, it is difficult to believe that real estate properties exchanged will have precisely identical values. If property A is worth $10 million, the owner may exchange it for another property worth $8 million and $2 million in cash. The cash is boot. In this case, the boot is a taxable portion of the exchange. If the investor is in the 30 percent tax bracket, then the tax due will be $600,000 (0.3 × $2,000,000). This is still better than a tax bill for $3 million if the property were sold outright. The basis of the acquired property will still be the basis of the relinquished property. In this example, it is zero.

Boot is not limited to cash. It can be any non-like-kind property, including the relief of a mortgage obligation. Assume in this example that there is a $1 million mortgage on the property to be relinquished. If the owner of the property to be exchanged (worth $8 million) exchanges that property and pays off the mortgage on the relinquished property plus $1 million, then the boot will consist of $1 million in cash and $1 million in mortgage relief.

Technical Requirements

There are numerous technical requirements that must be met if a like-kind exchange is to avoid taxation. Those who contemplate such an exchange are wise to seek the counsel of a tax specialist or a specialist in such exchanges. Most large urban areas have several such specialists who belong to a society or group of real estate exchangers. Here, we will mention a few of the most important technical requirements.

Time Limitation on Delayed (Deferred) Exchanges

The regulations contain three requirements that, if met, will satisfy a tax-deferred exchange. First, the replacement property must be identified by the owner of the relinquished property within an identification period. Second, the exchange must be completed within an exchange period. Third, the owner of the relinquished property must not be in constructive receipt of the proceeds from the transfer of the property.

The identification period begins on the date the relinquished property is transferred and ends 45 days thereafter. If there is more than one property involved in the exchange, the period begins with the first transfer of a property. The exchange period begins on the date of the transfer of the relinquished property and ends 180 days later or on the due date of the tax return for the taxable year, whichever occurs sooner.

Multiple Property Tests

In a delayed transaction it may be difficult, if not impossible, to identify the property to be acquired within 45 days. The IRS rules permit the owner to identify several prospective properties within this time period, provided the three-property test, the 200 percent test, and the 95 percent test are met.

The three-property test permits property owners to identify any three other properties to be exchanged without regard to their fair market values. The 200 percent test limits the identified properties to 200 percent of the fair market value of the properties relinquished. The 95 percent rule kicks in if the first two criteria are not met. Under this rule, the identification requirement is still met if at least 95 percent of the identified property is actually received by the termination of the 180-day exchange period.

Other Considerations

You should be aware of some other minor points concerning tax-deferred real estate exchanges. Incidental property may be involved in the exchange. This type of property is usually considered personal property (such as furniture and fixtures) but can be included in the real estate package as long as its value does not exceed 15 percent of the aggregate value of the replacement property. If the property to be acquired does not exist but is to be constructed, then the regulations require that as much detail as possible about the property be described within the identification period. Variations due to typical production changes are allowed. However, any additional construction after the property is received is not considered like-kind property, but rather will be considered boot. For the 200 percent test, the fair market value of the property to be produced is its value at the time it is to be received.

Recall that the owner of the property to be relinquished cannot receive any money from the transaction. Yet there is always the possibility that in a delayed transaction the other party may not deliver title to the property as required under the exchange agreement. In this case, the property owner may require that the other party deposit a sum of money in an escrow account so as to guarantee delivery of the property to be acquired. Tax rules allow this arrangement as long as the property owner has not received any cash upon the delivery of the property to be relinquished.

Tax-deferred exchanges have obvious benefits for the property owner who desires to change the type of real estate investment without having to pay taxes and thereby reduce the size of the investment portfolio. Like so many other tax regulations, the rules involved in the tax-deferred exchange can be complicated. Property owners who anticipate an exchange are advised to seek professional help in structuring the transaction so as to comply with the applicable regulations.

TAX-DEFERRED EXCHANGE EXAMPLE

Suppose that Investor A owns a triplex that was bought 5 years ago and is currently worth $150,000. The property has an adjusted basis of $75,000 and Investor A owes $67,500 on the mortgage. She is seeking to buy a larger property and has found a quadraplex for sale by Investor B. This property is valued at $300,000 and is subject to a $217,500 mortgage. Table 16–12 shows the process of Investor A and Investor B doing a tax-deferred exchange.

In doing the exchange, the equities must balance. This may be done by giving cash (boot) or maybe refinancing one of the mortgages.

The recognized gain of $0 for Investor A shows that the $66,000 realized gain is completely deferred. The effect on the tax basis of the new property now owned by Investor A is shown on the last line ($234,000). The $66,000 gain on the old property has been subtracted from the new property's $300,000 value. While this lowers the property's depreciable basis, Investor A has more cash. Plus she has achieved her goals of disposing of the old property while deferring the tax on the gain and acquiring a property worth more than the old one. ▮▮

INSTALLMENT SALE FINANCING

When a property is sold, it is treated as an **outright sale** if the seller pays income tax on the full capital gain in the year of sale. An alternative method of sale is the installment sale which occurs when the seller takes back a promissory loan from the buyer. Ordinarily the IRS would consider the receipt of a promissory note as taxable income, the same as cash. This would require payment of taxes in the year of sale. However, there is a section in the tax code that allows different treatment for a qualified installment sale.

To qualify as an installment sale, the seller must receive at least one payment after the year of sale. The typical scenario would have the seller receiving a down payment in the year of sale followed by a series of payments over the installment period. The installment method can be used only when a gain results from the sale. Losses incurred on the sale of business assets must be deducted in the year of sale, and losses from property held for personal use are not tax deductible. Installment sales are used most frequently on income properties in order to postpone taxes. The financing provided by the seller may take a first, second, etc. mortgage position.

TABLE 16–12

Tax-Deferred Exchange Calculations

	Investor A	Investor B
A. Equities Must Balance		
Market Value of		
Property Given	$150,000	$300,000
− Mortgage Balance	67,500	217,500
= Equity Given	82,500	82,500
+ Boot (Unlike Property)	0	0
= Total	82,500	82,500
B. Realized Gain		
Market Value of		
Property Given	150,000	300,000
− Selling Expenses	9,000	18,000
− Adjusted Basis	75,000	270,000
= Realized Gain	66,000	12,000
C. Recognized Gain		
Net Mortgage Relief	0	150,000
− Boot Given	0	0
− Selling Expenses	9,000	18,000
+ Boot Received	0	0
= Net Boot Received	0	132,000
Recognized Gain	0	12,000
(Lesser of Realized		
Gain or Net Boot		
Received)		
D. Tax Basis of Property Received		
Adjusted Basis	75,000	270,000
− Boot Received	0	0
− Old Mortgage	67,500	217,500
+ Boot Given	0	0
+ Selling Expenses	9,000	18,000
+ Mortgage on New Property	217,500	67,500
+ Recognized Gain	0	12,000
= Tax Basis of New Property	234,000	150,000

Since this results in a series of payments, the seller is taxed only on the portion of capital gain received with each payment. The major task in an installment sale is distinguishing with each payment the portions of taxable profit and the return of original investment. The capital gains percentage is called the gross profit percentage. It is calculated as a percentage of the contract price. Once the gross profit percentage is determined, it stays constant and is applied to each payment as received to determine the taxable portion of the payment.

Previously, if payments were to be received by the seller the installment method had to be elected if desired. Currently, however, under these circumstances the installment method is required and the seller must elect out if she wants the sale to be treated as an outright sale. Interestingly, a sale can be treated as an outright sale where taxes are paid on the full capital gain in the year of sale even though the seller receives the proceeds from the sale over future periods. Other tax rules include the related-persons rule which says if an installment sale is made to a related person (defined as spouse, children, parents, and grandparents; brothers and sisters do not qualify) who, in turn, sells the property within a two-year period, the original seller must recognize the balance of her gain at the time the related person makes the sale. Exceptions to this rule include involuntary conversion by the related person.

TABLE 16–13
After-tax Cash Flows from Installment Sale Agreement

A. ATCF in Year of Sale				
Down payment	$60,000			
− Selling expenses	− 5,000			
− Taxes	− 6,110			
= ATCF	$48,890			

D. ATCF from Installments		Yr. 1	Yr. 2
Debt service payment		$51,857	$51,857
+ Balloon payment		+ 0	+ 0
− Tax on installment		− 6,884	− 6,120
= ATCF		$44,973	$45,737

B. Tax in Year of Sale	
Down payment	$60,000
+ Excess of mortgage over Adj. basis and selling expenses	+ 0
= Total payment in year of sale	$60,000
× Profit percentage	× .4333
= Taxable portion of gain	$25,998
× Tax rate on gain	× .235*
= Taxes in year of sale	$6,110

C. Profit Percentage	
Sale price	$150,000
− Selling expenses	− 5,000
− Adjusted basis	− 80,000
= Total capital gain	$ 65,000
Sale price	$150,000
− Mortgage balance assumed	− 0
+ Excess of mortgage over Adj. basis and selling expenses	+ 0
= Contract price	$150,000

Total gain/contract price = profit percentage 65,000/150,000 = .4333

E. Taxes on Installments	Yr. 1	Yr. 2
Repayment of principal	$42,857	$47,143
+ Balloon payment	+ 0	+ 0
= Principal portion	42,857	47,143
× Profit percentage	× .4333	× .4333
= Taxable principal	18,570	20,427
× Tax rate on principal	0.235*	× 0.235*
= Tax on principal	4,364	4,800
+ Interest earned	9,000	4,714
× Marginal tax rate	× 0.28	× 0.28
= Tax on interest	2,520	1,320
Tax on principal	4,364	4,800
+ Tax on interest	2,520	1,320
Tax on installment	$6,884	$6,120

*Tax rate on gain = (0.70) (0.25) + (0.30) (0.20) = 0.235. The depreciation recapture is 70% of the total gain and is prorated equally across the installment period.

Installment sales are also subject to the imputed interest rate rules. A seller might have an incentive to set an interest rate below the market rate and raise the contract price to capture the lost interest. This transforms income from interest to capital gains, which may have more favorable tax treatment. To avoid this the IRS instituted the imputed interest rule. This rule is addressed in the system of applicable federal rates which was established by Congress in 1985. This is not designed to be a form of credit control or the setting of interest rates.

▌▌ INSTALLMENT SALE EXAMPLE

Suppose that Smith sells property to Jones for $150,000 in a 2-year installment agreement with 40 percent down and the balance financed at 10 percent. The adjusted basis of the property is $80,000 with accumulated depreciation of $45,500. Smith has selling expenses of $5000 and is in a 28 percent marginal tax bracket. The property has been depreciated on a straight-line basis and the buyer will make annual debt service payments. What are the seller's ATCF in the year of sale and ATCFs from the installment receipts?

These cash flows are calculated in Table 16–13. The calculation in the upper left corner shows the ATCF in the year of sale. It is the down payment minus selling expenses and taxes. The tax liability in the year of sale is shown in the middle left side. The entry excess of mortgage over adjusted basis and selling expenses is applicable if the transaction includes the assumption of a loan by Jones from Smith. If there is no loan assumption, this entry is zero. If there is an assumption, the sum of adjusted basis plus selling expenses is subtracted from the balance of the assumed mortgage. A positive difference is entered in the table. If this difference is negative or zero, then the entry is zero. Calculating the tax also requires the profit percentage, which is shown in the table in the bottom left side. The profit percentage is the total gain (selling price minus selling expenses minus adjusted basis) divided by the contract price.

The tables on the right side show the ATCFs for the installment receipts and the corresponding tax liabilities. The principal portion of the payment must be distinguished from the interest portion in order to determine the portion of the principal which is taxable in a given year. ▮ ▮

Other Considerations in an Installment Sale

Note in the above example the debt is fully amortized over the installment period of 2 years. In some cases, however, the note may be amortized over a longer period than the installment agreement. This results in a balloon payment in the last year of installment receipts. This is usually done to make the debt service payments more affordable. This would have the effect of rearranging the cash flows from the installment receipts. Also, if a sale is greater than $150,000 and the seller has a large amount of other debt, the seller may have to recognize additional gain through the allowable installment indebtedness rule.

SUMMARY

Historically, tax rules and regulations have favored real estate as an investment. Prior to 1986 the rules allowed real estate to be depreciated over a relatively short period. These noncash expenses reduced taxes and, given their ability to offset paper losses against other income, actually increased the after-tax cash flows over the before-tax cash flows. The lower tax rate on capital gains income allowed real estate investors to transfer ordinary income to capital gains through the depreciation write-off. Also, interest payments on debt were tax deductible. Depreciation and interest expenses combined to produce losses that could be used to offset other income. The high tax rates at the time meant that the rebate substantially increased the amount of after-tax cash flows.

Certain limitations were placed on losses to avoid abusive practices, however. Such limitations included those on the amount of interest that could be deducted for nonoperating real estate investments (land) and those on the rate of interest that could be charged on loans, especially seller-supplied, nonrecourse loans. Reported losses also were limited to the amount the investor had at risk. Finally, investors who used too many tax preferences were subject to an alternative minimum tax. Despite these limitations, the preponderance of favorable rules caused real estate to become the tax shelter of choice.

This situation changed with the Tax Reform Act of 1986. Four major changes reduced the value of real estate as a tax shelter. First, the depreciation period was extended, substantially reducing the amount of depreciation in the early life of the investment. Second, the preferable tax rate on capital gains was eliminated, removing the incentive to use real estate to transform ordinary income into capital gains income. Third, with minor exceptions, losses on real estate activity could not be used to offset income from non-real-estate activities. Fourth, the top tax rate was reduced. This diminished the value of tax losses. The investment income, original issue discount, and at-risk limitation rules were retained. The combined effect of these changes was to remove real estate as a favored tax shelter and cause investment in real estate projects to be based more on their economic feasibility and less on their ability to generate tax losses. About the only remaining tax shelters involve investment in historic structures or low-income housing. Even here, though, the tax credits are limited to the $25,000 exemption amount. The Tax Act of 1993 raised marginal tax rates and extended depreciation to 39 years straight line for nonresidential income properties. It did ease to some extent the passive loss limitation rules for real estate professionals. The 1997 Tax Act reintroduced capital gains.

Tax-deferred exchanges of real estate property represent an excellent way in which property owners can alter their real estate investment portfolio without having its value reduced by tax payments. The owner of the relinquished property must receive another property in exchange within 180 days of relinquishing the property. The basis of the acquired property is generally that of the relinquished property. The installment sales agreement is an alternative to the outright sale and allows the seller to defer payment of taxes on capital gains by electing to receive a series of installment payments.

KEY TERMS

Accelerated cost recovery system (ACRS)

Active income

Adequacy of interest test

After-tax cash flows

After-tax discount rate

Alternative minimum tax (AMT)

At-risk limitation

Before-tax cash discount rate

Before-tax cash flows

Boot

Capital gains tax

Capital loss limitation

Certified historic structure

Contract price

Depreciation

Depreciation tax shield

Double-declining balance

Historic rehabilitation credit

Imputed interest rule

Installment sale

Investment interest limitation

Limited partnership

Low-income housing credit

Modified accelerated cost recovery system (MACRS)

Nonrecourse debt

Net leased investment

Ordinary income tax

Original issue discount

Passive loss

Passive loss limitation

Portfolio income

Profit percentage

Recourse debt

Related persons rule

Straight-line depreciation

Sum-of-the-year's digits

Suspended losses

Tax Reform Act of 1986

Tax shelter

Time-value-of-money test

SUGGESTED READINGS

Brode, G. 1986. Structuring real estate entities in view of the new limitation on loss rules. *Journal of Taxation* Vol. 65, November.

Follain, J. R., and J. K. Brueckner. 1986. Federal income taxation and real estate: A survey of tax distortions and their impacts. Office of Real Estate Research Paper No. 26. Champaign-Urbana, IL: University of Illinois.

Howard, R. 1989. Selected tax issues of real estate ownership and use. *Real Estate Accounting and Taxation* Vol. 4, Summer.

Lentz, G., and J. Fisher. 1989. Tax reform and organizational forms for holding investment in real estate: Corporations vs. partnerships. *Journal of the American Real Estate and Urban Economics Association* Vol. 17, Fall.

Sanger, G., C. F. Sirmans, and G. K. Turnbull. 1990. The effects of tax reform on real estate: Some empirical results. *Land Economics* Vol. 66, November.

Wechter, T., and D. Kraus. 1991. The ABC's of low-income housing credit. *Real Estate Accounting and Taxation* Vol. 6, Spring.

REVIEW QUESTIONS

16–1   Explain what a tax shelter is, and indicate at least three different tax rules that favor an investment as a tax shelter.

16–2   Explain, in general, the following tax "limitations" in the present tax code:

   a. Investment interest limitation

   b. Capital loss limitation

   c. Passive loss limitation

16–3   Explain why the tax code "imputes" interest rates on loans under the original issue discount (OID) rules.

16–4   Discuss, in general terms, the recent three tax regimes, insofar as the treatment of depreciation expense is concerned: pre-1981, 1981 to 1986, and post-1986. Which was the most and which the least favorable for real estate investment and why?

16–5   Explain the use of tax credits to encourage investment in certain types of real estate properties.

16–6   Explain how the $25,000 exemption under the passive loss limitation rules works.

16–7   How are passive losses treated when real estate is held under the corporate form versus the limited partnership form?

16–8   Explain the at-risk limitation rule and why it was introduced.

16–9   Why is a nonrecourse loan provided by the seller of a property not considered to be at risk?

16–10   Indicate the way in which you believe the Tax Reform Act of 1986 has affected investment in real estate. Indicate specific facets of the act.

16–11   What is the purpose of allowing like-kind exchanges of real estate properties?

16–12   Indicate two main criteria that must be met so that a like-kind exchange of real estate property will satisfy the rules of a tax-deferred exchange.

16–13   List the major differences between the four tax categories of real estate.

16–14   What is the profit percentage in an installment sale, and why is it important?

16–15   Explain the treatment of an assumed mortgage in an installment sale.

PROBLEMS

For Problems 16–1 and 16–2, assume a real estate investor is considering the purchase of an office building and knows the following information:

The purchase price is $800,000 with acquisition costs of $25,000.

The project is two 2-story office buildings containing a total of 42,000 leasable square feet.

The rents are expected to be $6.00 per square foot per year and are expected to increase 5 percent per year.

The vacancy rate is expected to be 8 percent each year.

The project has concession vendors that generate other income in the amount of 8 percent of gross revenue.

Operating expenses are estimated at 45 percent of the gross revenue each year.

Eighty percent of the purchase price can be borrowed with a 20 year, annual payment mortgage at an interest rate of 12 percent plus 2 percent financing costs. The loan has a prepayment penalty of 4 percent of the outstanding balance.

Of the total cost, 85 percent is depreciable.

The value of the investment is expected to increase 5 percent per year. Selling expenses are expected to be 8 percent of the selling price.

The investor plans to hold the project for 5 years, is in a 28 percent marginal tax bracket, and requires a 14 percent equity return.

16–1   Compute the after-tax cash flows from operations and the after-tax equity reversion for the investor's holding period.

16–2   Calculate the net present value (NPV) and the internal rate of return (IRR) for the investment.

16–3   Assume the following data related to the purchase of raw land and calculate the amount of the interest charge that must be deferred under the investment interest limitation rules.

Purchase price	$1,500,000
Loan amount	$1,100,000
Interest rate	12%
First year income royalties	$150,000
First year expenses property tax	$ 55,000

16–4   Determine the amount an investor is at risk at the end of year one for the following investment:

Asset	Limited partnership interest
Initial cost	$100,000
Financed as follows:	
	$ 5,000 cash down payment
	$25,000 promissory recourse note
	$40,000 seller-financed, nonrecourse note
	$30,000 land (tax basis)
Year one payments from partnership to investor	$10,000

16–5   Given a $500,000 building (land valued separately), determine the present value of the tax shield, assuming a 12 percent discount rate for the tax rules in effect from 1981 through 1986 and for the tax rules in effect after 1986. What accounts for the difference?

16–6   Under OID rules, what rate of interest will the IRS apply to determine the interest expense on a loan under the following conditions:

Stated Rate	Applicable Federal Rate	Imputed or Allowable Rate
10%	10%	_____
12	10	_____
11	10	_____

16–7   Determine the tax due for the following investors. Assume the investment is real estate for which passive loss limitations apply.

	Investor A	Investor B	Investor C
Participates in management	Yes	Yes	No
Other taxable income	$90,000	$120,000	$200,000
Marginal and average tax rate	28%	28%	28%
Income for real estate	($100,000)	($100,000)	($100,000)
Taxable income	_____	_____	_____
Tax due	_____	_____	_____

16–8   Mr. Lunt sells property to Mr. Deen for $250,000 on a 3-year installment basis. Mr. Deen will pay 30 percent down and the balance will be financed over a 5-year period at 8 percent interest, annual payments. Mr. Lunt's original purchase price was $160,000 with acquisition costs of $10,000. He has made no capital improvements, and his accumulated depreciation is $37,000 on a straight-line basis. Mr. Lunt also has selling expenses of $8000 and is in a 28 percent tax bracket. Calculate Mr. Lunt's ATCF in the year of sale and the ATCFs from the installment receipts.

ENDNOTES

1.   For incomes between $71,901 and $180,850, the marginal rate was actually 33 percent. Beyond that the marginal rate is 28 percent. We will use the convention of referring to 28 percent (and not the 33 percent "bubble rate") as the highest rate, since it applies to the highest income categories.

2.   Note that the value of depreciation has increased since 1986 as marginal tax rates have gradually increased even though the depreciation schedule has not changed. For example, with the maximum tax rate of 39.6 percent in 1994, the value of depreciation goes to $13,300 from $9405.

3.   George Lentz and Jeffrey Fisher, "Tax Reform and Organizational Forms for Holding Investment Real Estate: Corporation vs. Partnership," *AREUEA Journal* 17 (3) (Fall 1989): 314–337.

4.   Susan Nelson and Tom Petska, "Partnerships, Passive Losses, and Tax Reform," *Statistics of Income Bulletin,* Internal Revenue Service 9 (3) (Winter 1989–1990): 31–39.

5.   Partnerships report income on their own form even though they do not pay taxes. Individual partners pay taxes on the gain or loss passed through to them.

WEB SITES

www.uni.edu/schmidt/bookmark.html   tax, accounting, and law site
www.best.com//~ftmexpat/html/taxsites.html   income tax laws and related news

APPENDIX A

Tax Preference Items for Alternative Minimum Tax

Certain deductions are allowed when determining regular income. The following items must be added back to regular income in the process of determining the alternative minimum tax:

- For taxpayers using a 27.5- or 31.5-year life under the Tax Reform Act of 1986, the difference between the depreciation under those lives and that of straight-line for a 40-year life.
- Losses of passive (no material participation) farming activity. (Losses from one passive farming activity cannot be used to offset income from another passive farming activity.)
- The amount of capital gains on an appreciated real estate property that has been donated to a qualified charity.
- The additional income realized by the taxpayer by using the percentage of completion method for accounting for real estate developments.
- Tax-exempt interest for certain private activity bonds.
- Intangible drilling costs to the extent they exceed 65 percent of net income from oil and gas properties.
- Excess of depreciation of pollution control facilities (amortized over 60 months as opposed to regular life).
- The excess of percentage depletion over the property's adjusted basis.
- The excess of the expending of research and development expenditures over that which would result from a 10-year amortization.
- Income deferred by installment sales.

CHAPTER **17**

Sources of Funds for Commercial Real Estate Properties

LEARNING OBJECTIVES

Chapter 17 describes debt financing and equity financing—the major sources of investment funds for real estate. The chapter is short and descriptive. After reading it, you should be familiar with these sources of funds that support the development and purchase of real estate. You also should understand the difference between debt and equity sources of funds and understand how different institutions specialize in either debt or equity financing or in financing various types of real estate. You should know how government regulations affect the real estate investment decisions of financial institutions.

INTRODUCTION

The current estimated value of America's real estate is approximately \$5.0 to \$6.1 trillion.[1] The ownership of this property is financed by both debt and equity. While much of the property is financed with mortgage debt, significant amounts are predominantly or entirely financed with equity. At the beginning of 1997, \$4.7 trillion of all real estate was financed by mortgage debt. Some institutions supply debt financing only, others equity financing only, and others a combination of the two. Some institutional lenders that preferred one type of financing in the past have redirected their priorities and now prefer another type of financing. Also, the type of financing that a particular institution prefers is determined by its liquidity needs—its short-term and long-term cash flow requirements.

DEBT FINANCING OF REAL ESTATE PROPERTIES

Estimates of the Stock of Debt

The U.S. Department of Housing and Urban Development estimated there was \$4.7 trillion in mortgage debt outstanding in America at the beginning of 1997. Eleven types of institutional lenders held that debt. Table 17–1 shows the mortgage debt of the eleven institutional lenders according to type of property: land, residential, and commercial (nonresidential). Multifamily housing is included in residential properties. Also shown in the table is debt related to construction activity. In 1997 construction loans stood at \$107 billion. The data in Table 17–1 indicate that the bulk of commercial construction activity has been financed by commercial banks. Commercial properties are primarily hotels, office buildings, shopping malls, warehouses, and so forth. The data in Table 17–1 reveal the following about the various institutional lenders.

TABLE 17–1

End of Quarter Holdings of Land, Construction, and Long-term Mortgage Loans by Eleven Major Lender Groups for the End of the First Quarter, 1997

(millions of dollars)

Property Type	Commercial Banks	Mutual Savings Banks	Savings & Loan Assns	Life Insurance Companies	Noninsurance Pension Funds	Mortgage Companies	Private MBS Conduits	ST&L Ret Funds	Federal Credit Agencies	Mortgage Pools	ST&L Credit Agencies	Totals Groups Shown
Loans for Construction												
1–4 family homes	22,341	2,737	7,671	0	0	2,366	0	0	52	0	4	35,171
Multifamily	7,706	406	1,116	129	52	515	0	0	64	0	814	11,001
All nonresidential	48,263	1,079	1,560	650	0	8,051	0	0	64	0	1,100	60,767
Total construction	78,310	4,222	10,347	779	57	10,932	0	0	374	0	1,918	106,939
Long-term Mortgage Loans												
1–4 family homes												
FHA insured	1,101	147	5,031	1,009	1,985	19,957	0	468	12,501	344,124	13,088	389,411
VA guaranteed	1,821	497	2,680	508	0	2,120	0	40	4,454	165,205	1,392	178,717
Conventional	653,907	109,624	319,985	4,233	2,071	51,543	329,339	6,190	409,322	1,131,315	45,582	3,063,111
Subtotal	656,829	110,268	327,696	5,750	4,056	73,620	329,330	6,698	426,277	1,630,644	60,062	3,631,239
Multifamily												
FHA insured	729	356	416	518	0	705	0	1,855	11,683	8,422	27,950	52,634
Conventional	37,660	10,265	33,465	22,060	922	3,175	13,848	2,202	29,608	21,592	16,799	191,232
Subtotal	38,389	10,621	33,881	22,587	922	3,880	13,484	4,057	41,291	30,014	44,749	243,866
Nonresidential	314,401	16,875	27,954	154,548	13,460	1,954	63,377	13,587	3,557	6,692	9,581	625,986
Farm properties	25,313	131	0	10,068	0	0	0	0	27,842	8,378	20	71,752
Total long-term mortgage loans	1,034,932	137,895	389,531	192,944	18,438	79,454	406,200	24,342	498,967	1,675,728	114,412	4,572,843
Land loans	13,696	575	3,252	752	0	195	0	0	167	0	55	18,692
Total mortgage loan credits	1,126,938	142,692	403,130	194,475	18,495	90,581	406,200	24,342	499,508	1,675,782	116,385	4,698,474

Source: U.S. Department of Housing and Urban Development.
Note: Sum of components may not equal totals due to rounding.

Commercial banks are by far the largest single source of commercial real estate debt. They hold 50.2 percent of all nonresidential, long-term commercial real estate debt, which represents 28 percent of their total real estate debt lending. They also funded 15.7 percent of all multifamily mortgages outstanding in 1997.

Life insurance companies have by far the largest concentration of commercial loans in their portfolio. In 1997, these loans represented 79.5 percent of all their mortgage debt holdings. In fact, life insurance companies held 24.6 percent of all commercial mortgage loans outstanding in that year. They are also big lenders for multifamily residential properties, holding 9.26 percent of all multifamily residential debt in 1997. The large amount of commercial real estate loans (as a percent of total mortgage debt) held by life insurance companies in 1997 was actually down somewhat from 1990, when the share was 83.3 percent. This drop may have been due to the risk-based capital (RBC) requirements imposed on life insurance companies by the National Association of Insurance Commissioners (NAIC) in December 1993. These RBC guidelines require life insurance companies to maintain minimum levels of capital based on the riskiness of their operations and their investments. Under these standards a commercial mortgage in foreclosure has been assigned a 20 percent capital requirement while a delinquent commercial loan only requires a 3 percent ratio. As a result, life insurance companies have an incentive to sell off nonperforming properties rather than take possession through a foreclosure action. Taking back such nonperforming properties would not only lead to continued operating losses but erode capital and increase the likelihood of a downgrade in their investment rating by the rating agencies. As long as RBC guidelines are in place, we may see more reluctance on the part of life insurance companies to acquire commercial mortgages. However, they remain an important source of real estate debt.

Thrifts continue to specialize in residential properties, especially single-family properties. Still, because of deregulation in the early 1980s, thrift holdings of nonresidential commercial mortgages have increased steadily. In 1997, their holdings represented 7.2 percent of all nonresidential commercial property debt and 8.2 percent of thrift debt holdings. These first four institutional lenders shown in Table 17–1 together held 82.1 percent of all commercial real estate debt in 1997. Commercial banks held 50.2 percent of the total, and life insurance companies held an additional 25 percent.

Pension funds held $18.5 billion in mortgage-related investments in the beginning of 1997, which represented about 4.2 percent of their total assets. Pension funds held $4.3 billion (11 percent of the total mortgage-related securities) in private collateralized mortgage obligations. The vast bulk of the private CMOs are backed by commercial, not single-family residential, properties.

In summary, commercial banks represent the largest single type of lender for commercial real estate loans. Thrifts continue to specialize in residential loans, but they have recently increased their lending for commercial properties. Life insurance companies specialize in debt on commercial properties. Pension funds hold little debt at all, but of the amount they hold, they specialize in commercial properties. Private mortgage-backed security conduits hold only residential mortgages. State and local retirement funds invest more heavily in residential mortgages than they do in commercial mortgages, which is also true for the mortgage pools. State and local credit agencies were created to support residential housing, so it is not surprising that more than 90 percent of their debt holdings are in residential mortgages.

Flow of Debt Funds

Institutions invest in real estate debt securities by either lending funds directly or by purchasing debt obligations from another originator. The holder of the securities, either by origination or by purchase, is the ultimate source of funds. Nonetheless, originators who may sell off much of their debt are important players in directing the funds from their source to their use. The data in Table 17–2 show the gross flows of long-term mortgage loans for eleven institutional lenders and investors during the first quarter of 1997. For a particular institution, the net change in its end-of-year holding of debt securities will equal its originations plus its purchases less sales and less repayment of the debt outstanding at the end of the previous year.

TABLE 17-2

Quarterly Gross Flows of Long-term Mortgage Loans
by Eleven Lending Groups for the First Quarter, 1997
(millions of dollars)

	Total Loan Originations	Loan Purchases	Gross Acquisi- tions	Loan Sales	Net Acquisi- tions	Repay- ments	Net Change
Commercial banks							
1–4 family homes	48,116	18,737	66,853	20,704	46,149	37,207	8,942
Multifamily	5,659	188	5,847	25	5,822	5,105	717
Nonresidential	35,738	3,872	39,610	879	38,731	35,776	2,955
Farm properties	2,648	8	2,656	76	2,580	2,228	352
Totals	92,161	22,805	114,966	21,684	93,282	80,316	12,966
Mutual savings banks							
1–4 family homes	5,651	369	6,020	2,240	3,780	4,793	−1,013
Multifamily	441	14	455	0	455	494	−39
Nonresidential	883	18	901	4	897	1,373	−476
Farm properties	8	0	8	0	8	0	8
Totals	6,983	401	7,384	2,244	5,140	6,460	−1,520
Savings & loan associations							
1–4 family homes	24,953	10,173	35,126	17,015	18,111	20,695	−2,584
Multifamily	1,144	125	1,269	249	1,020	2,080	−1,060
Nonresidential	1,206	134	1,340	202	1,138	1,974	−836
Farm properties	0	0	0	0	0	0	0
Totals	27,303	10,432	37,735	17,466	20,269	24,749	−4,480
Life insurance companies							
1–4 family homes	79	165	244	126	118	186	−68
Multifamily	341	26	367	55	312	191	121
Nonresidential	4,407	81	4,488	142	4,346	14,995	−10,649
Farm properties	183	6	189	8	181	123	58
Totals	5,010	278	5,288	331	4,957	15,495	−10,538
Priv. noninsured pension funds							
1–4 family homes	210	417	627	0	627	531	96
Multifamily	200	0	200	0	200	179	21
Nonresidential	1,310	0	1310	0	1310	993	317
Farm properties	0	0	0	0	0	0	0
Totals	1,720	417	2,137	0	2,137	1,703	434
Mortgage companies							
1–4 family homes	0	14,736	14,736	0	14,736	6,786	7,950
Multifamily	0	0	0	0	0	287	−287
Nonresidential	0	5,222	5,222	0	5,222	1,250	3,972
Farm properties	0	0	0	0	0	0	0
Totals	0	19,958	19,958	0	19,958	8,323	11,635
Priv. mortgage-backed conduits							
1–4 family homes	0	13,665	13,665	0	13,665	6,784	6,881
Multifamily	0	2,254	2,254	0	2,254	302	1,952
Nonresidential	0	5,222	5,222	0	5,222	1.250	3,972
Farm properties	0	0	0	0	0	0	0
Totals	0	21,141	21,141	0	21,141	8,336	12,805
State & local retirement funds							
1–4 family homes	93	171	264	0	264	113	151
Multifamily	105	52	157	0	157	95	62
Nonresidential	100	202	302	0	302	303	−1
Farm properties	0	0	0	0	0	0	0
Totals	298	425	723	0	723	511	212
Federal credit agencies							
1–4 family homes	640	19,601	20,241	545	19,696	8,935	10,761
Multifamily	153	643	796	46	750	1,681	−931
Nonresidential	207	3	210	53	157	181	−24
Farm properties	1,743	0	1,743	0	1,743	1,696	47
Totals	2,743	20,247	22,990	644	22,346	12,493	9,853
Mortgage pools							
1–4 family homes	0	74,371	74,371	0	74,371	55,265	19,106
Multifamily	0	1,420	1,420	0	1,420	842	578
Nonresidential	0	0	0	0	0	0	0
Farm properties	0	0	0	0	0	0	0
Totals	0	75,791	75,791	0	75,791	56,303	19,488

TABLE 17 – 2 (*Continued*)

	Total Loan Originations	Loan Purchases	Gross Acquisitions	Loan Sales	Net Acquisitions	Repayments	Net Change
State & local credit agencies							
1–4 family homes	166	1,086	1,252	0	1,252	679	573
Multifamily	494	68	562	0	562	606	−44
Nonresidential	172	2	174	0	174	42	136
Farm properties	0	0	0	0	0	0	0
Totals	832	1,156	1,988	0	1,988	1,327	661
Totals for eleven groups							
1–4 family homes	176,877	164,584	341,461	164,367	177,094	135,190	41,904
Multifamily	10,197	2,536	12,733	2,065	10,668	11,560	−892
Nonresidential	44,023	9,534	53,557	1,280	52,277	57,083	−4,806
Farm properties	4,582	14	4,596	84	4,512	4,047	465
Totals	235,679	176,668	412,347	167,796	244,551	207,880	36,671

Source: U.S. Department of Housing and Urban Development, Office of Financial Management

The origination plus purchases less sales is referred to as net acquisitions. These relationships may be presented as:

$$\text{Originations} + \text{Purchases} = \text{Gross Acquisitions} - \text{Sales}$$

$$= \text{Net Acquisitions} - \text{Repayments}$$

$$= \text{Net Change in Holdings}$$

Several important features of the flow of funds in Table 17–2 stand out. First, commercial banks and thrifts sell off much of the debt they originate, especially residential mortgages. In 1997, sales of residential mortgages represented 44.9 percent of net acquisitions for commercial banks. For thrifts, sales represented nearly 90 percent of their net acquisitions. Thrifts sell off proportionately many more mortgages than commercial banks. They sell these mortgages primarily to federal credit agencies and mortgage pools. Second, life insurance companies purchased very few debt securities—either residential or nonresidential commercial loans. They originated more than 99 percent of their gross acquisition of commercial real estate debt and sold off very few of the loans. Third, as expected, mortgage bankers sold off all of their originations of residential mortgages, while the mortgage pools purchased virtually all of their acquisitions. Finally, the purchase and sale of debt securities was restricted almost entirely to residential properties. Sales of mortgages on one- to four-family houses represented 92.8 percent of total net acquisitions for all institutions. In contrast, the sale of mortgages on nonresidential, commercial properties represented 2.4 percent of net acquisitions.

Some institutions provide sources of funds by purchasing mortgage-related securities. Two institutions that have increased their share of this market are private pension funds and life insurance companies. The 1989 holdings of mortgage-related securities by these institutions are shown in Table 17–3. For comparison, we include for each institutional investor the amount of direct mortgage holdings as well as their holdings of the mortgage-related securities of federal agencies and pools. Mortgage-related securities holdings represented 11.5 percent of the holdings of union-sponsored pension funds, as compared to only 3.1 percent of corporate-sponsored funds. Also, note that life insurance companies held a much greater proportion of their mortgage debt in direct debt than did the pension funds. Many CMOs held by pension funds and insurance companies were commercial—securities backed by commercial mortgages. Compared to their residential counterparts, commercial CMOs are relatively new. However, we expect that the success in the residential area will spill over to the commercial area, and the commercial CMO will become an increasingly popular source of funds. For this reason we will take a closer look at commercial CMOs.

TABLE 17–3

Mortgage-related Investments of Private Pension Funds
and Life Insurance Companies
March 1989 (billions of dollars)

	Private Pension	Funds	
	Corporate Sponsors	*Union Sponsors*	*Life Insurance Companies*
FNMA notes and debentures	4.4	1.5	5.6
FHLBB notes and debentures	2.2	1.2	3.4
FHLMC notes and debentures	0.5	0.2	0.7
FHLMC CMOs	0.6	0.1	0.7
FHA debentures	0.9	0.2	1.1
GNMA pass-throughs	7.3	5.0	12.3
FHLMC REMICS and certificates	3.4	1.9	5.3
FNMA pass-throughs and REMICS	1.8	0.9	2.7
Mortgage-backed bonds	0.5	0.4	0.9
CMOs	3.9	0.4	4.3
Total mortgage related securities	26.2	11.5	37.7
Direct mortgage holdings	2.1	3.8	5.9
Total mortgage related investments	28.3	15.1	43.6
Total assets	904.0	131.0	103.5
Percent of assets	3.1%	11.5%	4.2%

Source: U.S. Department of Housing and Urban Development.

A Closer Look at Commercial Collateralized Mortgage Obligations (CMOs)

CMOs are becoming an important source of debt financing for commercial properties. Like their counterpart in residential financing, these are securities backed by commercial mortgages. The first commercial CMOs were securities backed by a mortgage on a single, large property, such as an office building in a large metropolitan area. Later, mortgages on different and smaller property types were packaged and collateralized. Presently, many commercial CMOs are backed by a mix of mortgages on different property types in different geographical locations. Commercial CMOs were introduced for the same reason as residential CMOs—to provide liquidity through a secondary market mechanism. Unlike residential CMOs, commercial CMOs may be more risky for several reasons. First, they may lack the mortgage insurance that is nearly always present in residential mortgages (such as FHA and VA insurance). Second, the mix of mortgages on various properties may prevent a thorough analysis of the risk of the underlying properties. Third, even for CMOs backed by a single mortgage, the risk of the underlying property may be difficult to ascertain for the average investor.

For these reasons, most commercial CMOs, unlike their residential counterparts (except for residuals), are rated by rating agencies such as Moody's and Standard and Poor's. The rating provides investors with a snapshot, as it were, of the risk of the CMO. For example, the Structured Finance Division of Moody's Investors Service considers many variables and factors when rating a particular commercial CMO. First, they assign a quality rating (QR) of A, B, C, D, or E to the CMO by considering financial factors of the mortgage and property, such as the loan-to-value ratio, debt-to-service coverage, and current loan balance per square foot. They also consider qualitative factors, such as the state of repair of the property, the trend in the economic stability of the neighborhood, and the financial strengths of the tenant of the property. Table 17–4 summarizes the mortgage characteristics used by Moody's in their quality rating of CMOs.

After Moody's assigns a quality rating, it makes a final rating based on the regional market strength of the state and city in which the property is situated. In the late 1980s, for example, California was rated as a strong regional economy, Michigan an average regional economy, and Texas a weak regional economy. Table 17–5 shows how the strength of the regional economy is used with the quality rating to assist rating agencies in arriving at a final rating assignment. The

TABLE 17-4
Summary of Mortgage Characteristics Used in the QR System

Quality Ratings:	A	B	C	D	E
Loan-to-value ratio	<65%	<70%	<75%	<80%	>85%
Debt-service coverage	>1.35x	>1.25x	>1.15x	>1.05x	<1.05x
Number of 30-day delinquencies/months	0/36	0/24	1/24;0/12	1/12;0/6	1/6
Mortgage seasoning (months)	>36	>24	>24	<12	—
Balloon risk	Minor	Minor	Average	Substantial	Substantial
Occupancy level	>95%	>90%	>90%	>85%	<85%
Property age (years)	<10	<15	<20	<25	>25
Deferred maintenance	None	Minor	Average	Excessive	Substantial
Construction quality	Excellent	Good	Average	Fair	Poor
Neighborhood					
Trends	Stable/impr	Stable/impr	Stable	Stable/decl	Declining
Current status	Excellent	Good	Average	Below average	Poor
Property size					
Multifamily (units)	>200	>150	>75	>10	<10
Office, industrial & retail (sq.ft.)	>100,000	>75,000	>50,000	>25,000	<25,000
Multitenancy	Yes	Yes	—	—	—
Retail	Credit anchor	Credit anchor	Credit anchor	Anchor	No anchor
Owner/tenant credit	Excellent	Good	Average	Fair	Poor

Source: Moody's Structured Finance.

TABLE 17-5
Benchmark Credit Support Levels[a]

Regional Market Strength														
Strong					Average					Weak				
QR:	Aaa	Aa	A	Baa	QR:	Aaa	Aa	A	Baa	QR:	Aaa	Aa	A	Baa
A	8	4	2	1	A	12	8	6	5	A	18	14	12	11
B	9	5	3	2	B	13	9	7	6	B	19	15	13	12
C	11	7	5	4	C	15	11	9	8	C	21	17	15	14
D	14	10	8	7	D	18	15	12	11	D	24	20	18	17
E[b]	—	—	—	—	E[b]	—	—	—	—	E[b]	—	—	—	—

[a]The above benchmarks are offered as a guideline only. The actual level of credit enhancement will reflect the specifics of each rated transaction and therefore may diverge significantly.
[b]Credit enhancement of mortgages with a QR of E must be determined on a case-by-case basis because of the large variance in credit risk for these mortgages.
Source: Moody's *Structured Finance*.

benchmark figures show the relative change in credit enhancement or support that must occur to obtain a given rating.

Exhibit 17–1 (at the end of this chapter) shows that the market classification for Boston was relatively low-risk in 1987. We chose this example to demonstrate how risk can change. Even though Moody's rated Boston a low-risk region in 1987, property values subsequently suffered, and defaults and foreclosures rose for awhile. Since 1992, however, the Boston real estate market has revived. Thus, the Boston experience demonstrates that investors in commercial CMOs must be aware of the cyclical nature of regional economies. Since real estate investments typically have a long investment horizon, current market conditions must be tempered with the reality that regional economies can change quickly.

Since the early 1990s there has been an acceleration in the securitization of commercial loans. In 1993 commercial mortgage securitization was at $17 billion, up $3 billion over 1992's level of $14.4 billion. This increase occurred despite a drop in RTC (Resolution Trust

Corporation) activity to $3 billion from $9 billion in 1992. By 1997 the annual volume of new CMOs approached $40 billion. As of March, 1997 the total market size of all CMOs was $118.8 billion according to *The Roulac Group*. One must remember, however, that even this total amount is small relative to the total debt and equity of all commercial real estate. The 1997 size of this total market is estimated at $1.5 trillion.

A key to the future growth of this source of real estate financing is the standardization of the assets backing the commercial CMOs. To obtain the best ratings from rating agencies, CMOs at a minimum will have to

1. Standardize loan documents,
2. Extend amortization beyond the popular "bullet" loans of 5 to 7 years,
3. Establish minimum debt service and loan-to-value ratios, and
4. Establish a prohibition against any prepayments for some standard initial number of years.

Given the diversity of terms and conditions in commercial loans, it will be difficult to achieve full standardization of these loans.

Recent Trends in Debt Financing

Several trends in debt financing are worth noting. First, regional economies behave differently from the national economy. While some areas are depressed, others are growing. Commercial banks not only provide a large amount of commercial real estate debt, but have intimate knowledge of their respective local economies. It is not surprising, then, that a bank's commercial lending trends parallel local economic trends. As an example, back in 1990, the Federal Deposit Insurance Corporation performed a survey of commercial real estate bank lending in 40 large cities. The survey revealed that construction loan originations increased by more than 20 percent in 10 of 40 local markets, even though there was a slowdown in the national economy. Table 17–6 shows the percentage of change in construction loan originations in the top ten and bottom ten markets at that time. Construction loan activity increased by between 32 percent and 54 percent in the top five cities (all in California), whereas loan originations declined substantially in depressed markets in Texas and other cities. The data reflect the local role that commercial banks play in financing commercial real estate construction.

Second, acquisition, development, and construction (ADC) loans for large residential real estate developers are not as plentiful as in the 1970s and 1980s. FIRREA made changes that limit the number of loans thrifts can make to a single borrower, thereby forcing many developers to

TABLE 17–6
Bank Construction Loan Origination by Metropolitan Area:
Annual Percentage Change, 1989 to 1990

Top Ten				Bottom Ten			
Rank	Metro Area	State	Loan Origination Growth	Rank	Metro Area	State	Loan Origination Decline
1	San Jose	CA	53.7%	1	Austin	TX	258.0%
2	Anaheim	CA	47.0	2	San Antonio	TX	241.8
3	Riverside	CA	40.3	3	Phoenix	AZ	233.8
4	Los Angeles	CA	37.4	4	Houston	TX	233.5
5	San Diego	CA	32.3	5	Dallas/Ft. Worth	TX	230.2
6	Cleveland	OH	31.0	6	Honolulu	HI	215.4
7	Seattle	WA	24.1	7	Oklahoma City	OK	214.4
8	Detroit	MI	23.9	8	Boston	MA	213.2
9	Sacramento	CA	22.6	9	Denver	CO	28.5
10	Orlando	FL	20.5	10	New Orleans	LA	27.0

Sources: Roulac Group & Touche; Federal Deposit Insurance Corporation.

either cut back on their development or seek out several, often unfamiliar, lenders. In 1990, the National Association of Home Builders surveyed developers to determine the availability of ADC loans. About 50 percent of the developers had been using thrifts as a source of financing. Fifty-eight percent of all developers and 60 percent of large-scale developers reported difficulty in obtaining adequate ADC financing. They also reported that they were paying higher interest rates to obtain ADC financing because they had to work with unfamiliar lenders. Many developers responded to the problem in several ways: reducing the number of their developments, building smaller-scale office/commercial projects, building only for those who could afford their own construction financing, and putting more of their equity into the projects. One result of FIRREA limits of loans to one borrower will be that more developments will be financed with equity sources, such as limited partnerships and real estate investment trusts, which are discussed in the next section. Although there has been some discussion about relaxing this rule, as of 1997, no such action has been taken.

EQUITY FINANCING OF REAL ESTATE PROPERTIES

Investors can hold equity positions in commercial real estate either through direct investment or through securities. With direct investment, institutional and individual investors hold the equity real estate by purchasing the property. With indirect investment, investors purchase securities that represent an equity interest. There are two popular types of securities that allow for indirect investment: shares of interest in limited partnerships that own real estate and shares of stock in companies that purchase and hold real estate (real estate investment trusts). Real estate limited partnerships (RELPs) and real estate investment trusts (REITs) represent the bulk of equity real estate investment through securities. The structures of limited partnerships and real estate investment trusts are discussed in Chapter 20. Here, we only discuss the relative importance of each investment vehicle in providing equity financing for commercial real estate.

Equity Financing Through Securities

Data on funds raised through RELPs and REITs are available from several sources. Table 17–7 shows the amount of funds raised through RELPs and REITs through November 1992, as estimated by the Stephen Roulac Group. Real estate limited partnerships are of three types: public real estate partnerships, identified private real estate partnerships, and master limited partnerships. Public real estate partnerships are those offered to the investing public, whereas private offerings are designed for sale to particular institutional investors. The Securities and Exchange Commission (SEC) requirements are less strict for private placements. Master limited partnerships are a vehicle for purchasing and consolidating existing limited partnerships. They have decreased in popularity since the Tax Reform Act of 1986, because the act removed many of the benefits of investing in partnerships. Fund raising through REITs has increased substantially to fill the gap (not shown in Table 17–7 are sales of $18.3 billion in 1993).

TABLE 17–7

Real Estate Securities Sales
(millions of dollars)

	1987–89	*1991*	*1992*
Real estate partnerships	31,770	781.4[a]	782.4[a]
Real estate investment trusts	9,831	2,288.6	6,515.1
Total	41,601	3,070.0	7,297.5

[a]Through November 30.

Source: *Roulac's Strategic Real Estate,* published by the Roulac Real Estate Consulting Group of Deloitte Haskins & Sells.

Institutional Investors

The two primary institutional investors in equity real estate are life insurance companies and pension funds.

Life Insurance Companies

Mortgages by far represent the majority of real estate asset holdings of life insurance companies, with equity representing a smaller proportion. Table 17–8 shows the equity real estate holdings of all life insurance companies from 1970 through 1992 and demonstrates that life insurance companies invest only moderately in equity real estate. The proportion of their total equity real estate assets has held steady at approximately 3 percent for the last two decades. In contrast, they held $246,702 million in mortgages in 1992, about 20 percent of their total assets over this period. Life insurance companies have held about one-third of their equity real estate in separate accounts. A separate account is a fund established by a life insurance company and held separately from other assets. State laws provide that assets in separate accounts may be invested without regard to restrictions that are normally placed on other investments. The separate account may be comprised of only stocks, only mortgages, or only equity real estate. In 1992, for example, they held $10,733 million of equity real estate in separate accounts, which represented 4.5 percent of all assets held in separate accounts. The role of life insurance companies in financing equity real estate has been limited because of concern about the liquidity of equity real estate. Their primary role remains in providing debt financing.

Pension Funds

The growth of pension funds has been phenomenal. In 1970 they held only $135 billion in assets. In 1991 their assets had skyrocketed to $2.5 trillion. Their interest in real estate as an investment has been recent. In 1980 pension funds held a negligible amount of equity real estate, but their interest in real estate grew throughout the decade. By the late 1980s dozens of investment advisors managed real estate investments for pension funds and by 1990, their holdings of real estate had grown modestly to represent about 5 percent of their assets. Table 17–9 shows the top advisors for both commingled and direct accounts in 1994. Commingled funds are investments that are made on behalf of several firms or groups. A manager may invest in a real estate property with funds allocated from the pension funds of several firms. Direct investment refers to a situation where the investment property is held by one, and only one, pension plan.

Pension plans may be categorized into two classes: **defined-contribution plans** and **defined-benefit plans.** In short, the former specifies a certain contribution made during the working years of the employee. Retirement benefits are based on the accumulation of the fund at the

TABLE 17–8

Equity Real Estate Holdings of Life Insurance Companies: 1970–1992
(millions of dollars)

Year	Amount	Percentage of Assets	Year	Amount	Percentage of Assets
1970	6,320	3.0	1983	22,234	3.4
1971	6,905	3.1	1984	24,767	3.6
1972	7,295	3.0	1985	28,822	3.5
1973	7,693	3.0	1986	31,615	3.4
1974	8,331	3.2	1987	34,172	3.3
1975	9,621	3.3	1988	37,371	3.2
1976	10,476	3.2	1989	39,908	3.1
1977	11,060	3.0	1990	43,367	3.2
1978	11,764	3.0	1991	46,711	3.2
1979	13,007	3.0	1992	50,595	3.3
1980	15,033	3.1			
1981	18,278	3.5			
1982	20,624	3.5			

Source: American Council of Life Insurance, *1993 Life Insurance Fact Book.*

time of retirement. Defined-benefit plans specify a certain pension payment. Employees contribute sufficient funds to guarantee the defined payment when they retire. The amount they contribute may vary with the investment performance of the fund.

Defined-contribution plans are by far the largest of the pension plans, both in the amount and in number. Their administrators have been reluctant, until recently, to invest in equity real estate. As late as 1988, the largest defined-contribution plan held only 0.7 percent of its assets in real estate. The largest 200 funds held only 4.3 percent of their assets in real estate.[2] The equity real estate investment of the top 200 funds is shown in Table 17–10. Participants in defined-contribution plans usually have a say in how the funds are invested. They may prefer not to invest in real estate for several reasons. They may not understand that adding real estate to a portfolio of assets significantly affects portfolio diversification. Second, they may have been unimpressed with the generally weak returns generated by real estate securities in the 1970s and early 1980s. Even today, real estate returns are weak in certain areas of the United States. Finally, participants may value liquidity and the option to quickly sell and buy assets for the fund.

A survey by Elebash and Yost revealed that most pension fund managers believe that diversification is the most attractive feature of equity real estate investment. On the other hand, 64 percent of managers of corporate pension funds and 47 percent of managers of public pension funds cited lack of liquidity as an unattractive feature of real estate as an investment.[3] Indeed, lack of liquidity can be a significant problem for defined-contribution pension funds because many of the funds allow their participants to switch from one investment option to another. Essentially, the liquidity problem would require that real estate be packaged similarly to mutual funds or in REITs. While there has been some limited attempt to create mutual fund types of programs for real estate, the success of these programs has been limited. Some observers believe that pension funds will accelerate their investment in REITs in the last half of the 1990s.

Restrictions on Pension Fund Investments.   Pension fund investments can be affected in at least three ways—by rules and regulations established under the Employee Retirement

TABLE 17–9

Twenty-five Largest Equity Real Estate Managers, 1994

Firm	Millions of Dollars
Equitable real estate	12,192
JMB Institutional Realty	7,082
Copley Real Estate	6,036
RREEF Funds	4,382
Prudential Real Estate	4,014
Heitman Advisory	3,033
Yarmouth Capital	2,944
TCW	2,914
GE Investments	2,547
TCW Realty Advisors	2,301
Aeltus Investment	2,193
LaSalle Advisors	2,100
O'Connor Group	1,900
CIGNA Investments	1,878
Mellon/McMahan Real Estate	1,843
Corporate Property Investors	1,610
J. P. Morgan	1,600
Aetna Life Guaranteed	1,280
Sentinel Real Estate	1,247
Kennedy Associates	1,139
Aldrich, Eastman & Waltch	1,060
L&B Real Estate	948
Citicorp Realty	881
Metropolitan Life	873
Balcor	846
Total	68,870

Source: Pensions and Investments, May 1994

T A B L E   1 7 – 1 0
Top 200 Funds with Assets in Real Estate Equity, 1994

Defined Benefit

Fund	Assets $ Millions	Fund	Assets $ Millions	Fund	Assets $ Millions
California Public Employees	5,019	Exxon	219	S. Baptist Convention	48
AT&T	3,603	Mass. Teachers/Employees	213	Johnson & Johnson	45
General Electric	2,272	Alabama Retirement	204	Travelers	35
IBM	1,736	Los Angeles Fire & Police	201	American Airlines	30
Ohio State Teachers	1,621	World Bank	195	K Mart	30
Illinois Teachers	1,605	North Carolina	192	Bank of America	27
California State Teachers	1,505	Monsanto	191	Chemical Bank	22
State of Michigan	1,416	Xerox	182	American Electric Power	20
Virginia Retirement	1,160	Ohio Police & Fireman	182	New York Life	17
New York State & Local	1,154	Caterpillar	180	Hewlett-Packard	13
Ameritech	1,100	Textron	169	District of Columbia	11
Connecticut Trust Funds	1,069	Owens-Illinois	168	Federal Express	8
Ohio Public Employees	1,000	Boilermakers-Blacksmiths	168	General Dynamics	4
New York State Teachers	961	Idaho Public Employees	167	TOTAL	47,109
NYNEX	912	Atlantic Richfield	163		
Wisconsin State Board	885	Honeywell	157		
Pennsylvania Employees	849	Minnesota Mining & Mfg.	155	**Defined Contribution**	
Ford Motor	800	Los Angeles City Employees	136		
Florida State Board	755	Chrysler	135		Assets $ Millions
Oregon Public Employees	650	Citicorp	125	Fund	
Washington State Board	645	Operating Engineers	120		
Teamsters, Western	642	Alaska Retirement	114	TIAA-CREF	6,984
Colorado Public Employees	574	ITT	109	United Methodists	102
Los Angeles County	537	Du Pont	107	Bechtel Power	12
Pacific Telesis	501	Rhode Island Employees	100	American Stores	57
Texas Teachers	480	Grumman	100	Xerox	26
Illinois Municipal	440	United Airlines	100	Halliburton	19
Prudential Insurance	417	S. California UFCW	97	Evangelical Lutheran	16
U S WEST	415	RJR Nabisco	90	Metropolitan Life	13
Minnesota State Board	396	Southern Cos.	86	Texton	5
Southwestern Bell	381	BP America	85	Shell Oil	1
Iowa Public Employees	381	Sears, Roebuck	84	TOTAL	7,295
Westinghouse Electric	380	S. New England Telephone	81		
Unisys	360	GTE	81		
Nevada Public Employees	360	CIGNA	80	**Defined Contribution**	
Illinois State Universities	354	Philip Morris	73		
Shell Oil	342	Bakery & Confectionery	73		Assets $ Millions
San Francisco City/County	336	Chicago Municipal	72	Fund	
Kansas Public Employees	326	Aluminum Co. of America	70		
Utah State	300	J.C. Penney	69	TIAA-CREF	4,600
Illinois State Board	300	Aetna	68	Trans World Airlines	93
Kentucky Retirement	300	FPL Group	66	Bechtel Power	83
Maryland State	291	Deere	65	American Stores	77
USX	260	Goodyear Tire & Rubber	62	United Methodist Church	61
UMWA	252	Kentucky Teachers	62	United Parcel Service	35
Ohio School Employees	250	Missouri State Employees	54	Halliburton	24
Massachusetts PRIM	233	TRW	53	Xerox	24
United Technologies	231	Hanson Industries	52	Evangelical Lutheran	7
Pacific Gas & Electric	220	Union Carbide	48	Equitable Life	4
				TOTAL	5,908

Source: Pensions and Investments, January 1994.

Income Security Act, by tax regulations concerning unrelated business income, and by Generally Accepted Accounting Principles.

In 1974, Congress passed the **Employee Retirement Income Security Act (ERISA).** It was designed to protect the integrity of pension funds and, thus, the retirement benefits of workers covered by retirement plans. ERISA regulations can affect the real estate investments of pension funds in several ways. First, the stipulations of a retirement plan must be adhered to only to the extent that they do not conflict with ERISA rules. Second, pension funds must invest as "a prudent man" would invest his own funds. Third, pension funds must undertake to diversify their respective portfolios.

ERISA does not restrict the types of real estate properties that pension funds can purchase. However, it discourages a pension fund from purchasing the property of the company that funds the plan, because the company may be tempted to sell property of low value to the fund at an inflated price. Apart from this minor restriction, ERISA places no constraints on real estate investment by pension funds. However, tax rules may affect the types of real estate pension funds may invest in.

Pension funds are exempt from paying federal taxes. This does not mean that pension funds can take advantage of the tax exemption to compete unfairly for debt financing as a source of investment funds. For this reason, tax regulations prohibit pension funds from engaging in any business that is not related to their primary purpose. If a pension fund does earn unrelated business income by engaging in a business unrelated to its purpose, it is subject to a tax on that income. The tax is referred to as **unrelated business income tax (UBIT).**

Until 1981 a pension fund that purchased real estate that was in part financed by a mortgage had to treat a portion of the income (rents, for example) as unrelated business income and pay taxes on it. This discouraged pension fund investment in real estate, except for an occasional all-equity investment. In 1980 the tax law was changed to allow investment in debt-financed properties without the burden of UBIT. Even here, there are some restrictions. The purchase price of the property must be fixed in amount and not be contingent on future revenues or profits from the property. The property cannot be leased to the seller (sale-leaseback), and the financing must be standard (no nonrecourse purchase money mortgage or below-market-rate financing). In addition, pension funds must comply with the **fractions rule** in leveraged real estate through a partnership in which at least one of the other partners is not an organization that qualifies for tax exempt status (qualifying organization, QO). The fractions rule was established to prevent such a partnership from allocating a disproportionate amount of annual expenses to the taxable partner in the early years of the partnership and a similar disproportionate amount of revenues to the tax exempt pension fund in the later years of the partnership (remember the time value of money). The rule states that revenue and expenses allocated to a QO partner for any taxable year cannot exceed the partner's fraction rule percentage. That percentage, in turn, is its percentage share of overall partnership loss for the taxable year for which that partner's percentage loss share will be the smallest. This rule prevents a pension fund or other QO from "lending" its tax exempt status to a taxable partner. Pension funds must be very careful not to violate the fractions rule since any violation is incurably fatal. Once a partnership flunks the fractions rule, it does so for all remaining taxable years of the partnership. Also, a violation of the fractions rule can be highly contagious. Compliance with the rule is tested at the partnership level and not at the partner level. Thus, where there are numerous partners that are QOs, a bad allocation to one of them taints all of the QOs in the partnership, including those in compliance with the fractions rule. Although the fractions rule can be complicated and difficult to adhere to, the Department of Treasury established regulations in May 1994 that clarify exactly what can and cannot be done under the rules. The permitted and excluded activities are beyond the scope of this text, but in general they allow "preferred returns" to a QO to compensate for cash equity investments, distribution of the proceeds of subsequently obtained nonrecourse debt to the partners, and a *di minimus* rule that allows QOs with very small interests in a partnership to avoid the fractions rule entirely.

As you can see from this very casual discussion, the rules governing UBIT, as they relate to real estate securities, are extremely complex and beyond the scope of this discussion. In brief, income from or the gain on the sale of RELPs is generally considered UBIT for pension funds. Because of potential tax problems, many pension funds do not invest in limited partnerships. Partnerships with other taxable entities require careful compliance with the fractions rule. Income from real estate investment trusts, however, generally is not considered UBIT. Thus, many pension funds that invest in real estate securities avoid RELPs and invest in REITs.

The Future of Pension Fund Investment in Real Estate.   Although lack of liquidity is a problem for defined-contribution plans, the outlook for increased pension fund investment in real estate is bright, because plan managers better understand portfolio theory and the need to diversify investments and because Financial Accounting Standards Board (FASB) statement Number 87 made changes, effective in 1990, for the reporting of pension liabilities. These changes will encourage pension funds to invest in equity real estate, because FASB-87 limits the range in the discount rate that companies can use to determine their pension liability and requires unfunded portions of the liability to be recorded on the company's balance sheet. Here's how it works.

Under FASB-87, companies report as a liability on their respective balance sheets the present value of future retirement benefits that they are expected to incur, based on the number, ages, salaries, and so forth, of their employees. The annual pension expense that is reported in the income statement is the change in the liability (present value) reported on the balance sheet from year to year. Prior to FASB-87, companies had a wide latitude in the selection of the discount rate. If their profits for any one year were low, they could increase the discount rate. This would reduce the amount of the pension liability at year end and, therefore, the change in the pension liability, which was reported as an expense. It was this abuse that led FASB-87 to restrict a company's choice of discount rates.

A financially distressed company would fear a fall in interest rates. A large drop in rates, given the lack of choice of discount rate, would require a company to record a large increase in its pension liability. This would appear on the income statement as a large pension expense, which would reduce the company's net profit. It also would cause pension liability to exceed the value of the assets placed in the pension fund, unless the assets also rose with the drop in interest rates.

FASB-87, therefore, has caused many firms to invest in noncallable bonds that rise with a fall in rates. Many professional pension plan managers offer such "immunization" from changes in rates, but as some companies have learned, investing a large proportion of a pension plan's assets in bonds provides lower yields and little protection from inflation. Investment in real estate, on the other hand, may solve some of the problems for pension funding. Real estate values tend to rise when interest rates drop, which would give funds some immunization against a large drop in rates. Real estate investments are also less volatile than bonds or stocks and appear to offer better protection from unanticipated inflation than does a bond portfolio.

Public/Private Partnerships

Public funds are also a source for real estate investment and development. In a public/private partnership, the local government provides land, money, or both, and the developer provides the skill. In such partnerships, the land or funds provided by the government can make some projects feasible that otherwise would not be undertaken on a purely economic basis. The most common government subsidies include contributions of land (or the sale of land at below-market prices), cash, grants, subsidies, or outright investments in the real estate, with the expectation of below-market rates-of-return, low-interest loans (often from funds obtained through the issue of tax-free bonds), and credit enhancement.

In addition to government financial support, the real estate developer may benefit from community support and from visibility arising from the public/private partnership. Such partnerships also mean that the developer can move more quickly through the otherwise lengthy approval process. However, the accelerated approval process may be offset by a more lengthy planning process. Divided votes within the local governing body could stall the project, and the developer also may face restrictions from local ordinances that must be dealt with. Examples include conflict of interest laws, public hearing requirements, minority employment and affirmative action requirements, environmental regulations, wage requirements, and land use limitations.

The local government may benefit from projects that serve a community need. Often the development will improve the appearance of blighted locations, reduce crime, and improve nearby property values (and, therefore, property taxes). Some developments may involve more risk than the local government is willing or legally able to assume. Although most states have prohibitions of some sort against local governments selling land at reduced values or lending funds to private enterprises, the courts in many of these states have allowed public/private partnerships where a public benefit from the project is clearly demonstrated, even though there may be an incidental private benefit.

Public/private partnership developments are restricted by federal tax regulations if they are financed by the sale of tax-free municipal bonds. Under current federal laws, the interest on such bonds will not be tax-exempt if more than 10 percent of the project financed with the proceeds of the bonds is used by a private business and more than 10 percent of the interest payments on the bonds are paid from private business sources. Limited exceptions to the rules allow specifically for the development of airports, public water facilities, sewage facilities, solid-waste-disposal facilities, structures for charitable organizations, mass transportation facilities, and docks and wharves.

Finding Sources of Financing

Most large real estate developers are well connected with sources of funding. They work well with these sources and develop and cultivate strong ties. Some large developers and most smaller and emerging developers may not have strong ties to large lenders or investors, however. They will more likely work through brokers or mortgage bankers that specialize in funding small- and medium-size projects, either with their own equity or with large amounts of funds provided to them by institutional investors.

For real estate developers who have no permanent source of funding, there are income property financing source books that list lenders and investors interested in real estate developments. The information in the source books indicates the terms of the loans that the source is willing to consider, such as the size of the loan, its purpose, geographical location, maximum loan-to-value ratio, participation terms, and so forth. An example of a description sheet from one popular source book, *Fleets Guide,* is given in Exhibit 17–2. Cross-section referencing allows the developer to seek those lenders or investors interested in certain size loans, certain property types, or in certain geographical locations.

SUMMARY

Sources of commercial real estate financing can be divided into debt sources and equity sources. The bulk of debt financing for commercial real estate is provided by three institutional lenders: commercial banks, thrifts, and life insurance companies. These three lenders hold approximately 85 percent of all commercial real estate debt. Commercial banks are generally very close to, and knowledgeable about, local economic conditions. For this reason, they advance the most debt for construction and purchase of real estate developments. Their lending follows the local economic cycle closely.

Commercial banks and thrifts are active in the purchase and sale of mortgages backing multifamily residential properties. Life insurance companies, on the other hand, originate more than 97 percent of their total acquisition of real estate debt.

Recently, there has been a trend to collateralize commercial property debt or mortgages. Some private financial institutions have created commercial CMOs that are the counterpart to residential CMOs. Since the risks of investing in commercial CMOs are different from those of residential CMOs, the former are likely to be rated by the rating agencies. The rating agencies will take into account characteristics of the property and loan, such as the loan-to-value ratio, debt-to-service ratio, and current loan balance per square foot, as well as the local economy in which the property is located. Some complex CMOs are created by packaging mortgages for different types of properties in different locations.

Investors can provide equity financing by direct purchase of commercial properties or by purchasing securities that represent an equity interest. Two examples of the latter form of investment are real estate limited partnerships and real estate investment trusts. Limited partnerships are declining in importance as a result of the Tax Reform Act of 1986, which limited the pass-through of passive losses to partners. In the late 1980s and early 1990s, real estate investment trusts gained in market share to fill the gap left by the decline in real estate limited partnerships. Life insurance companies and pension funds also invest directly in commercial real estate. Pension funds, in particular, have increased their investment in recent years. The desire to diversify their portfolios and accounting regulations make real estate more attractive for pension funds now than in the past. The major problem faced by pension funds to date has been the lack of liquidity. This is particularly true for defined-contribution plans, where the participants have a say and an inclination to determine the investment vehicles for their contributions.

KEY TERMS

Collateralized mortgage obligations (CMO)
Defined-benefit plan
Defined-contribution plan
Employee Retirement Income
   Security Act (ERISA)
Fractions rule

Gross acquisitions
Net acquisitions
Originations
Pension funds
Quality rating
Unrelated business income tax (UBIT)

SUGGESTED READINGS

Berra, J., and S. M. Breitstone. 1994. Pension funds and realty: The rigorous tax guidelines for institutional investors, 3 Oct.

Books, R. 1988. Commercial real estate as a capital market. *Real Estate Finance* Vol. 5, Fall.

Healy, J. J., P. Healy, and E. Lindner. 1994. Emerging trends in commercial mortgage securitization. *Real Estate Issues,* August, 44–47.

Her, M. 1990. Attracting Asian investment: East meets southwest. *Real Estate Finance* Vol. 6, Winter.

Levitan, D. R. 1990. Alternative financing sources for the 1990s. *Real Estate Finance Journal* Vol. 6, Fall.

McCoy, B. 1988. The new financial markets and securitized commercial real estate financing. *Real Estate Issues* Vol. 20, Spring/Summer.

Roulac, S., and N. Dimick. 1991. Real estate capital markets undergo fundamental changes. *Real Estate Finance Journal* Vol. 6, Winter, 7–17.

Roulac Real Estate Consulting Group. A quarterly survey of trends in commercial financing. *Real Estate Finance* Various Issues.

Sprayregen, R. 1990. REITs may make a comeback as a development financing vehicle. *Real Estate Finance Journal* Vol. 6, Fall, 35–41.

REVIEW QUESTIONS

17–1   What are the three major financial institutions that provide debt financing of commercial properties?

17–2   Discuss the role that life insurance companies play in financing commercial real estate.

17–3   Which institutions specialize in originating and selling commercial mortgage debt?

17–4   Which institutions purchase much of the commercial mortgage debt they hold?

17–5   How do commercial CMOs differ from residential CMOs?

17–6   What factors do the rating agencies consider when rating a commercial CMO?

17–7   How did FIRREA affect the sources of acquisition, development, and construction loans?

17–8   Why have pension funds become interested in acquiring equity real estate? What is the major drawback of real estate investment for pension funds?

17–9   What is unrelated business income, and how does it affect pension fund investments in real estate?

17–10   Give a general explanation of the fractions rule for pension fund investment in real estate partnerships.

17–11   Explain how accounting rules may affect the assets that pension funds acquire.

17–12   How do risk-based capital requirements affect the real estate investment decisions of life insurance companies?

ENDNOTES

1.   M. Miles, "What Is the Value of All U.S. Real Estate?" *Real Estate Review* 20 (Summer 1990): 69–75. Values updated to current estimates by 20 percent to reflect the known addition to mortgage debt since 1990.

2.   "Real Estate Assets up 26%," *Pensions and Investment Age* (January 23, 1989): 69–71.

3.   C. Elebash and G. Yost, "Real Estate Attitudes Differ Greatly," *Pension and Investment Age* (August 7, 1989): 35.

WEB SITES

www.aptfunding.com   information on apartment loans

EXHIBIT 17–1

Moody's Market Classification

MARKET ANALYSIS   March 1987

Boston   Market Classification: I

Compound Employment Growth[1] (1981 – 1985) :	2.9%	Vacancy Rate [2] :	8%
Export base size[1]:	24%	New Construction Rental Range[2] : $19.00–26.00 per sq. ft.	
Key Industries[1] : Health Services, Educational Services, Insurance, Business Services, Banking.		New Construction [2] 1987: 2.7 1988: 2.0	
		Years of Supply [2] 1987: 3.0 1988: 3.8	

Source: 1 Wharton Econometric Forecasting Associates. 2 Cushman & Wakefield, New Construction in mil. sq. ft.

Summary Opinion

Boston's office market falls within the lowest risk classification because of its low vulnerability to a decrease in demand for office space and strong controls on commercial development. Office space demand in Boston should be relatively less vulnerable to a downturn because of above-average industrial diversity, improving trends in employment growth, and high representation of less volatile industries. On the supply side, Boston's development process is highly controlled as a result of both a lack of readily developable sites and a strict approval process. In addition, commercial development in the areas surrounding the central business district tends to be complementary rather than competitive in nature.

Market Fundamentals

Employment Growth: The city of Boston has benefited in recent years from strong economic growth in the surrounding region. More specifically, the finance, insurance, and service sectors that the city specializes in have expanded significantly. The metropolitan area has recently experienced excellent growth in "high tech" and other manufacturing industries. This growth, combined with subsequent increased growth in nonmanufacturing sectors, has given the region a growth rate equal to or higher than the nation's since 1976. Boston itself has also participated in this upsurge in growth, moving from substantial declines in the pre-1976 period to substantial positive growth since the late 1970s, at about 1 percentage point below national rates.

Employment Volatility: The mix of industries in Boston heavily favors the less volatile nonmanufacturing sectors, with a notable de-emphasis on the more volatile durable manufacturing, construction, and mining sectors. Some of the industries which dominate in Boston (such as insurance, educational services, and health services) are among the least volatile sectors.

Industry Diversification: The industries in which Boston is relatively specialized form a diverse economic base for trade outside the local economy. The "extra" employment in these industries is distributed in significant amounts across enough different industries to indicate a high amount of economic diversity in the export base. This export base is also large relative to the rest of the local economy, with total "extra" employment in export-base industries accounting for about 24 percent of employment in the city. This indicates good connections to the rest of the world and less dependence on purely local factors.

Commercial Development Controls: The Boston Redevelopment Authority (BRA) strictly controls commercial development through one of the most comprehensive planning processes in the United States. These controls should continue to limit Boston's vulnerability to overbuilding in the furure as the BRA gains additional community support. Boston's progressive linkage program, which requires the developer to pay certain fees to the community in order to gain the right to build, also adds significantly to the cost of development and therefore slows the pace of new construction. Additionally, the lack of readily available quality locations for new development will further restrict the rate of future commercial building.

CBD/Suburban Dynamics: Boston's central business district has only limited vulnerability to out-migration of tenants to the suburbs. This is because the service firms located there have exhibited a strong preference for a dowtown location. In fact, the strong performance of the metropolitan area's economy has supported the service firms located in the central business district. In addition, Boston's downtown tenants tend to maintain contiguous space for all levels of employees, in contrast with long-standing trends in other major cities.

Moody's Structured Transactions Group Newsletter

Source: *Moody's Market Report*, 1991.

EXHIBIT 17–2

Lender Profile

SAMPLE LIFE INSURANCE COMPANY

Life Company   Info Date - June 19,1991

PARENT: Sample Holding Company   **HQ COUNTRY**: USA

U.S. INCOME PROPERTY FINANCINGS (Debt and/or Equity as Principal or Discretionary Manager):

    1990 Vol.: $350MM   **# Of Deals:** 150   **Exp. 1991 Vol.:** $400MM

PROPERTY TYPES CONSIDERED (Current *Preferences* Noted by ▸):

Multitenant Office	Single-Tenant Office	▸ Owner-Occupied Office	Medical Office
Strip Retail W/ Anchor(s)	▸ Warehouse/Distribution	R&D/Flex Space	Mini-Storage
▸ Garden Apartments	Student Apartments	Limited/No Care Elderly	

PROPERTY LOCATIONS CONSIDERED: Nationwide (except New York State)

LOAN OR INVESTMENT SIZE: Minimum: $750K   **Maximum:** $5.0MM   **Preferred:** $3.5MM – $5.0MM

FINANCING TYPES:

First Mortgages   Second Mortgages   Participating Mortgages

Fixed Rates: 3 Yr., 5Yr., X Yr. + Rewrite (5 + 5)

TYPICAL RATE STRUCTURE(S) FOR TODAY'S BUSINESS: Corresponding Treasury Yield + 150 – 200 Basis Points

    Pricing varies based on specific deal and prevailing market. Check source for current pricing.

DEPOSITS & FEES: Refundable Good Faith Deposit: 2% – 3%. Site Inspection Fee: $400

RATE LOCKED AT: Commitment

PREPAYMENT PENALTY: Yield Maintenance Basis

MAXMIMUM LOAN-TO-VALUE (Typical Deal): 75%

MINIMUM DEBT SERVICE COVERAGE (Typical Deal): 1.20X

PARTIAL OR FULL RECOURSE REQUIRED: Usually

TYPE OF APPRAISAL REQUIRED: Will accept correspondent's appraisal

ENVIRONMENTAL REVIEW REQUIREMENT: Clean Phase 1 prior to closing

CHANNELS (Accepted Deal Sources): Exclusive correspondent's **ONLY**

SERVICING: Available to correspondents

WILL PARTICIPATE DEALS WITH OTHER LENDERS/INVESTORS?: Yes occasionally, as lead

WILL PURCHASE EXISTING LOANS?: No

COMMENTS: Limited/no care elderly must be within two miles of hospital. Call for nearest correspondent.

MAIN CONTACT(S):   Mr. Buck Lender   919-444-0000   (FAX: 919-444-0005)
                                         Senior Vice President
                                         Sample Life Insurance Company
                                         8800 Security Boulevard
                                         Suite 500
                                         Raleigh, NC   22222

REGIONAL CONTACTS:

Southeast	West	Central/Southwest	East Coast
Daniel Ambrose	Kathy Bressler	Ann Caroline	Michael Thomas
919-444-0001	919-444-0002	919-444-0003	919-444-0004

READER'S NOTES:

Source: *Fleet's Guide: Income Property Financing Sourcebook*, July–December 1991 Edition.

CHAPTER **18**

Acquisition, Development, and Construction Financing

LEARNING OBJECTIVES

In this chapter, you will read about financing commercial developments from the land acquisition stage through the construction stage. While most of the chapter is descriptive, one concept permeates the relationship of the lender, the developer, and the contractor—that of the agency cost problem. You should understand that a large proportion of the covenants and restrictions contained in loans to finance the acquisition and development of commercial properties are directed at agency problems. Several parties may be involved in one project: the developer, the contractor, and two or more different lenders. They each have an incentive to act in their own interest. Agency costs are those costs necessary to prevent parties from acting in their own interest to the detriment of others. You should view many of the loan covenants and restrictions as methods to avoid agency costs.

On the factual side, you should understand those loan provisions that are common to commercial developments and how they may differ from residential loans. You also should understand the basic mechanics involved in determining the loan amount and periodic disbursements.

█████ **INTRODUCTION**

Commercial real estate financing is covered in this and the following chapter. The subject matter is divided between the two chapters according to the time sequence involved in the financing of commercial properties. In this chapter, we discuss the financing associated with the purchase of raw land, the development of the raw land to ready it for construction, and the construction of the facility. In the following chapter, we discuss the forms that the permanent, long-run financing of commercial properties takes. Permanent financing takes over once the real estate project is completed and ready to generate operating income.

We divide the nonpermanent financing discussed in this chapter into three stages: acquisition, development, and construction. In the trade, this type of financing is referred to as ADC financing. We will proceed as if the financing of the acquisition of the property, development for construction, and construction is done in stages and involves different sources from different lenders. While this is often the case in practice, there is no reason why the total financing of acquisition through construction cannot be done at one time, through one source, and with one set of loan package documentation. In fact, it can be accomplished in both ways.

When the ADC process is financed in stages, the separate lenders often require that a detailed set of provisions be met by the other lenders. For example, a lender that finances the development of a property may require that a commitment from another to finance the construction of the facility be in place at the time of the development loan. The development loan lender often will stipulate the terms of the construction loan. Likewise, the construction lender often will require that there be a permanent lender, sometimes referred to as a "takeout" lender, ready to commit to a permanent loan when the facility is completed and ready for operation. It would appear that lenders involved in the various stages of the acquisition, development, construction, and permanent lending process could simplify matters and avoid agency problems (not to mention litigation expenses) by financing the project from the initial land acquisition stage through the operation of the completed facility.

Although such full-scale financing has occurred, the more popular method involves different lenders financing distinctly different stages of the development process. The most likely reason for the persistence of this practice is the specialization developed by various types of lenders. Some lenders have developed an expertise in, for example, construction financing. They can monitor the construction process and make sure that loan proceeds are disbursed only according to the development of the project. They also make sure that the project is developed at or under the original cost projections. They may have little expertise in determining the economic viability of the completed project, however. Other lenders, on the other hand, may have an expertise in determining the economic worth of the completed project but cannot monitor the disbursement of the proceeds (perhaps because they are not located in the community where the project is constructed). In this case, the construction lender will require that a permanent takeout lender be secured before it will agree to finance construction of the project. The permanent lender will have judged the economic viability of the project and determined that, if completed as designed, the project could support the payments on the permanent loan. Such specialization appears to be the only rational reason for the separation of the financing by the stages of acquisition and development.

In this chapter, we will review the stages of acquisition and development and indicate how these stages are financed. We also will indicate where agency problems arise between the various lenders in the acquisition and development process and how those agency problems are handled. Finally, we will review the mechanics of how the total amount of the loan and its disbursements are determined.

ACQUISITION

The Land Loan

The first stage of the process involves the acquisition of the raw land to be developed. Raw land is acquired by two types of investors, the speculator and the developer. The **speculator** has no particular development plans for the land. The speculator sees an opportunity for price appreciation because of growth constraints, new transportation facilities, zoning changes, and other economic or institutional changes that will cause the value of the property to appreciate over the near term. The **developer,** on the other hand, has definite plans for the property. The developer is likely to be a specialist in a particular type of development, such as housing, shopping centers, or industrial facilities. Developers may specialize even further within these categories, so that some developers may only develop low-income housing or upscale housing. Some shopping center developers may specialize in malls, others in strip shopping centers. Whatever the specialization, the developer has immediate plans for the land and likely will proceed as quickly as possible to complete the project.

Warehousing

Large developers, especially those that specialize in large residential developments, may desire to warehouse substantial amounts of property. **Warehousing** refers to the holding of large parcels of properties in advance of the development process. As one residential development is completed, the next has housing units under construction, the next has housing construction started, and the next has the land being prepared for development (roads, utilities, and so on being installed). In this way, the developer creates residential developments in a continual process. As part of the process, the developer is continually looking for additional parcels to purchase to begin a new development process, even as he is completing the latest development. Here, financing becomes very important because the developer desires to tie up as little equity as possible in large parcels of land. That is, since assets must be financed, the developer that holds large quantities of land will seek out the lowest cost financing possible. There are several sources of such financing.

Institutional Lenders

One source of land acquisition financing is the traditional financial institution. We saw in the previous chapter that commercial banks and thrifts were the dominant sources of land financing. These local lenders are in the best position to judge the risks (underwrite) involved in a land loan. Land loans are risky for several reasons. First, raw land usually does not provide any operating income, so that the proceeds of the loan must be repaid either from appreciation in the value of the land or from subsequent loans made for the purpose of development and construction. Also, there are few tax benefits from holding raw land. Land cannot be depreciated, and there are limitations on the deductibility of interest costs. If the land falls in value and is not developed, the owner may default on the loan, putting the property to the lender. Second, the raw land may not be physically suited for its ultimate highest and best use, and the cost of preparing land for that use is uncertain. The cost of preparing land for development may be unexpectedly high, or development may even be impossible if certain geological formations are discovered that preclude development as planned. Also, there may be no guarantees that the legal factors, such as zoning changes, necessary for development will be forthcoming. Many developments have been approved by local planning commissions only to have further legal objections raised by local citizens opposed to the project. In short, unforeseen physical and legal problems may raise the cost of development of the land to prohibitively high amounts. In such cases, the lender would be stuck with a lien on a nearly valueless piece of land. Because of these risks, land loans will seldom exceed 50 or 60 percent of the appraised value of the land.

A financial institution that makes a loan on raw land will have a lien on the property as collateral for the loan. If the land is to be used for a residential development, provisions will have to be made for a release of a portion of the land from the lien, the so-called release provision. For example, assume that a residential developer purchases 1000 acres of land on which he desires to develop and sell 2000 residences. It is unlikely the developer will be able to build and sell the houses over a very short period of time. The "absorption" (sales) rate for the development may take several years in some cases. The developer will want to sell the first houses in the development long before the final houses are even constructed. However, the land lender will have a lien on the entire acreage of the development. The potential home buyers of the initial houses will demand unencumbered, or free, title to their property, subject only to their own mortgage. To accommodate the sale of the initial phase of the development, the land loan will contain a provision for the **partial release** of the lien on those portions of the development that are sold. As the properties are sold, the developer will use the sales proceeds to pay off a portion of the land loan in exchange for a release of the lien on that portion of the development that is sold.

The provisions detailing the partial release will be included in the original loan documents and must be carefully thought out. Specifically, the lender must make sure that after a significant portion of the development has been sold, the value of the remaining land (upon which the lender still has a lien) is greater than the remaining amount of indebtedness. The indebtedness can exceed the value of the land if the developer was not required to reduce the debt sufficiently as each parcel was sold. This would be the case if the partial release provision required the developer to only pay off 10 percent of the debt when 10 percent of the land was sold. Here, the developer may sell off the more valuable parcels first, leaving less valuable parcels to secure the remainder of the debt. In this regard, the release provision may establish a "release pattern" that describes the order in which various parcels will be developed and sold. This ensures that the developer will not develop and sell the more desirable parcels without adequately reimbursing the lender.

The mechanics of the partial release are handled in escrow. When the developer sells the property, a new lien (buyer's mortgagee) will be substituted for the developer's lien.

Seller Accommodation

Another source of land acquisition financing is the seller of the property. Often the seller of the property will be asked to accommodate the developer in financing the sale. This can be done in several ways, including option financing, seller financing, and subdivision trusts.

Options

Rather than purchasing land outright, many developers will prefer to purchase an **option** to purchase the land at a future time. The terms of a **land purchase option** will include the purchase price, the expiration date of the option, and the premium or cost of the option. In this way, the developer can secure the land that he wishes to develop without securing immediate financing or tying up equity in land. If, at a later time, the development of the property is not economically feasible, the developer can let his option lapse. His loss will be the option premium, which may very well be less than the loss of the equity investment in the land.

The cost of the option will depend on several factors. The longer the term of the option, the higher the premium. This is especially so where the purchase price of the land is set in the option contract. The longer the period of exercise, the greater the chance that the market value of the land will rise substantially above the contract price in the option agreement. In essence, the seller has agreed to hold the land for the developer until the last day of the option period. The seller incurs the carrying costs of the property (such as property taxes), while the developer receives the benefits from appreciation in the value of the property over the exercise period. Thus, the longer the exercise period, the higher the premium demanded by the seller. Second, the option price will depend on the volatility of land prices. If land prices have been or are expected to be very stable, then the premium price for the option will be low. Stable prices reduce the probability that at the time of exercise the value of the land will be substantially above the contract price. Third, the option premium will be smaller if the contract price of the land is allowed to float with some sort of index. This reduces the chance that the market value of the land will be substantially above the contract sales price when the option is exercised.

In some cases, the seller of the land will inflate the cost of the land but then give a credit for the option premium. In other cases, the seller will give a declining portion of the option premium as a credit as time elapses. This provision will encourage an earlier exercise of the option than otherwise.

Rolling Options

Some developers will contract for rolling options. **Rolling options** give the developer additional options on more land as the existing options are exercised. Residential developers, especially, use rolling options. As they purchase land and develop it with housing, they want to be in a position of having options on other parcels. They often will have a rolling option agreement to purchase land that is contiguous with the land already purchased.

Seller Financing

In some cases, the seller of the land will agree to finance the purchase by taking back a note from the buyer. In this way, the seller becomes a lender as well. The sales price of the land under such arrangements is higher than otherwise. The reason is that the seller almost always will provide nonrecourse financing. Since the seller is granting the developer a put option should the project fail, the seller will be compensated with a higher selling price for the property. Seller financing can complicate the development process, because the seller will have a lien on the property. Lenders will advance funds for development and construction only if they can have a priority lien, however. In cases of seller financing, there is nearly always a provision in the loan documents that allows the seller's lien to become **subordinated** to a subsequent construction loan. The seller's note is subject to an increase in risk through the subordination process. This is another reason the sales price of the property will be higher than if the seller financing were not used.

Where a subordination clause exists, it is likely to be quite detailed. There is a severe agency problem here. Once the seller's note is subordinated to a construction lender, there is no one to look after the interests of the seller. The developer has an incentive to maintain as much flexibility as possible in the development process. The construction lender will stand ahead of the land seller through the subordination process, concerned only that the value of the property exceed the amount of the construction loan and not the entire amount of indebtedness (construction loan plus seller's note). Thus, after the seller's note is subordinated, the remaining parties will act on their own behalf and not in the seller's interest.

Because of these agency costs, the seller will insist on as many restrictive covenants as possible. The seller must act like a construction lender in this case. The subordination provision often will spell out the terms of the construction loan, such as the amount of the loan, its maturity, the interest rate (as in 2 percent over prime at the time of the loan, and so on), and loan-to-value ratio. The subordination agreement also will give the seller the right to make payments on the construction loan and supervise the disbursement of the loan as construction takes place, should the developer default. In short, the terms of the subordination agreement will, as much as possible, insure that the total value of the property as it is developed always exceeds the total amount of indebtedness as the construction loan is paid out. The total amount of indebtedness, of course, will include the seller's note.

When a construction loan is made and the subordination of the seller's note takes place, the construction lender will have the senior position in case of default. Although the construction lender will have no interest in the land seller's now junior lien, the construction lender will have to be sure not to recklessly jeopardize the position of the junior lien holder. If the construction lender inappropriately endangers the collateral of the junior lien holder, it may be held legally responsible and have its position moved behind that of the land seller. There are certain procedures the construction lender can follow to ensure that it does not open itself to litigation and damages from a junior lien holder.

First, it should ascertain that there is a specific subordination agreement with the original sale documents. A general statement that the land seller "agrees to at some point in the future consider a subordination of the security" is too vague to be enforceable. The subordination agreement should be as specific as possible. Second, the construction lender must make sure that the disbursement of the proceeds of the construction loan are used as intended and not misappropriated by the developer. If the funds are not used as intended, the value of the property may not rise in step with the indebtedness, placing the junior lien holder in an increasingly disadvantageous position. Third, in regards to the disbursement of the construction funds, the construction lender should clarify the difference between those disbursements that are optional and those that are obligatory. Fourth, the construction lender should acquire from the junior lien holder a specific waiver for disbursing any funds that are not in strict accordance with the construction loan and/or subordination agreement. Finally, the construction lender should avoid any oral commitments to the junior lien holder, such as an agreement to continue to advance more funds to the developer.

Subdivision Trusts

Under a **subdivision trust,** the developer puts up only a portion of the sales price and agrees to pay the balance when the property is developed and sold. The seller of the land transfers title to a trust and is designated the first beneficiary of the trust. As the developer, designated the second beneficiary, sells off parcels of the developed property, he is entitled to have portions of the lien released by the trustee. Under the typical subdivision trust, the developer will have the right to develop the property as he sees fit. This arrangement avoids the vesting of the title to the property in the hands of the developer, and this provides certain safeguards in the event of developer default and bankruptcy.

DEVELOPMENT

Once the land is acquired, the next stage of the development process involves making the site ready for construction. This involves several steps, including:

1. *Zoning.* If necessary, the proper application and legal procedures must be taken to assure that the area is zoned in accordance with the intended development.
2. *Engineering and surveying.* Engineers and other experts must work out the details of grading, drainage, removal of natural obstacles, and preparing accurate maps of the area. This must all be done before any physical work can be done on the project.
3. *Subdividing.* If applicable, a subdivision of the land into smaller sections may be necessary. This is particularly so for residential developments.
4. *Physical work.* The final stage of preparation will involve the physical work of grading the land and putting in streets, utilities, landscaping, and so forth.

All of these elements of site preparation are costly. In fact, it is not unusual for the expenses associated with the first three steps to be greater than those of the actual physical work. Even though no physical changes in the land occur in the first three steps, value is added through the expenditures made in these efforts. The land development lender, just as the construction loan lender discussed below, will want to make sure that value is added to the project as loan proceeds are disbursed. The loan documents generally will state that in the event of default, the lender will have the right to the work materials produced by the various experts and technicians involved in the site preparation process. Such work materials will include maps, surveys, engineers reports, and so forth. In the event of default, the lender may wish to proceed with the development as planned. These work papers will be invaluable in that case. Also, the engineers, surveyors, planners, and architects will have a lien on the property for any work performed but not paid for.

Lenders of funds for land development are specialized in that they can judge how the development of the land will increase its value and if the loan proceeds plus the developer's equity will be less than or equal to the value of the land when it is ready for construction. They are also aware of local land use regulations and required governmental approvals for developing the land. The lender will make sure that the loan documentation provides for deadlines for obtaining the necessary government approvals.

Some of the more important government approvals concern subdivision control ordinances and impact fees. Subdivision control ordinances usually relate to residential developments and require the developer to construct a minimum infrastructure. The ordinances exist in every state and nearly every locality and are designed to protect the consumer from the unkept promises of developers. Before such ordinances were introduced, it was not unusual for a developer to sell residential lots with a promise to install the necessary roadways, utilities, drainage, and such after a sufficient number of lots had been sold and ready for construction. Then, after many of the lots were sold, the developer would refuse to make the promised improvements, leaving the consumers with buildable lots but no utilities or roads.

Subdivision control ordinances take two forms. Under one form, the developer is required to construct the infrastructure prior to building residences or selling lots. The infrastructure must be built to minimum specifications. Under another method, the builder must post a performance bond, place cash in escrow, or obtain a letter of credit. This is where the land development lender comes into play. The developer often will ask this lender to lend the funds to be placed in escrow or issue a letter of credit to secure the bond.

Impact fees are fees placed on developers by municipalities to cover the added costs of the burden to the infrastructure that results from the new development. Municipalities argue that new developments increase the local population and therefore require additional highways, schools, libraries, firehouses, wastewater and sewer treatment facilities, and so forth.

There are two popular types of impact fees: dollar-based fees and non-dollar-based fees. **Dollar-based fees** are payments made to municipalities or other local governments. An example is a fee imposed on the developer for new construction (usually based on a formula) which may or may not be paid over a period of years. Another dollar-based fee is the **cost recovery fee,** paid by the developer to help recover the cost of the infrastructure built by the local government. Non-dollar-based fees are contributions in lieu of cash payments. An example is an **exaction,** whereby a developer agrees to construct and donate a public facility such as a park, school, or firehouse. Sometimes developers will be allowed to construct more houses per acre than usually provided by zoning regulations if the exaction is valuable. This is called a **density bonus.** Another example of a non-dollar-based fee is **inclusionary zoning,** whereby the developer agrees to build low-income housing, either on-site or off-site, in return for a right to develop the property or for a density bonus. Finally, there is **tax increment financing.** Here, improvements in the infrastructure are financed by additional property taxes applied to properties in the geographical area of the development.

As was discussed above, the lender must consider partial release clauses. The land developer may desire to sell off some of the developed lots rather than proceed with construction. The usual approach is to set the release price at a fraction of the sales proceeds so that the developer can pay the expenses associated with the sale (such as a broker's commission) and make a reasonable profit for his efforts. The partial release clause also will likely set a minimum sales price to ensure that sufficient funds are given to the lender in exchange for the partial release of the lien.

CONSTRUCTION

The **construction loan** is the final type of financing for a project prior to the permanent or "take-out" loan, when the project is completed and set for operation. Most construction loans have the following characteristics.

1. They are short-term and cover the length or period of construction only.
2. The interest rate is variable and usually set at a given number of percentage points over the prime rate of the lender.
3. Since the project provides no operating revenues during the construction stage, interest payments are deferred and "financed" by the lender.
4. Loan-to-value ratios are generally in the 70 to 80 percent range for commercial projects built for sale and 60 to 70 percent for speculative projects.

Underwriting Construction Loans

As in the case with land development lenders, construction lenders tend to be very knowledgeable, both about local policies and about the risks involved in construction lending. They are specialists in assessing and controlling the risks that result from the construction process itself and from local conditions. The risks involved in construction lending include the following.

1. The collateral for the loan includes unfinished or partially completed projects.
2. There are unknown construction risks, such as unexpected increases in material costs, strikes, poor weather, and financial difficulties of subcontractors.
3. There are intervening rights of third parties, such as mechanic's liens or claims for personal injury by construction workers.
4. There may be loss of permanent financing should the permanent lender fail to honor a commitment.
5. Failure to meet with building codes may result in a denial of certificate of occupancy.

For these reasons, the construction lender usually will be a specialist in assessing and controlling the risks of the construction phase of the project. In assessing and controlling the risk, the construction lender will do all of the following.

1. The lender will request an appraisal of the finished project based on generally accepted appraisal methods. The lender should make sure that the appraiser is independent of the developer. Federally related lenders must ensure that key federally mandated requirements of the appraisal are met. The appraisal should be based on a financial analysis of the finished project. If a financial analysis is missing or inadequate, then the lender should have its own analysis performed.
2. The lender will have its staff review all construction plans, engineer's reports, applications for government permits, applications for zoning changes, and so forth, so as to determine if the project can be built for the amount estimated and in the time frame indicated. The lender will make sure the loan documents indicate which parties are responsible for cost overruns or failure to meet the deadlines set for completion.
3. The lender will make sure that the proceeds of the loan are disbursed only for approved expenditures and made to the parties responsible for the construction. This has a twofold impact. First, it insures that the work has been done so that the collateral for the loan increases step-by-step with the increase in the loan balance outstanding. Second, it insures that no mechanic's liens will be placed by parties who performed work on the project but were not paid. By law, mechanic's liens can be given priority over the lender's lien.
4. The lender will monitor "holdbacks." A holdback is a reserve of funds held back from payment to subcontractors until the work of the subcontractor has been inspected and accepted by the general contractor.
5. The lender will make sure there is a takeout commitment from the permanent lender and will analyze that commitment. The financial stability and reputation of the takeout lender are important in this analysis.

The Construction Loan Commitment

As part of the planning process for a real estate project, the developer at some point will desire to have a lender commit to make a construction loan. A **construction loan commitment** is a separate agreement whereby a lender makes a commitment to make a loan in exchange for a fee. Even though the construction loan commitment is a separate agreement, it will provide extremely detailed information about the construction loan itself. In fact, to be enforceable (in court), the commitment will have to be as specific as possible and contain no vague language. The following are among the more important terms of the construction loan itself that should be covered in a commitment: (1) the loan amount, and when the proceeds of the loan are to be disbursed; (2) the interest rate, which can be fixed or floating and may include a floor and ceiling for the protection of both parties; (3) a description of the collateral; (4) a commitment for a permanent loan and the details of the permanent loan; (5) the amount of equity that the developer is required to contribute to the construction phase; (6) a statement indicating that the project will comply with legal restrictions, such as environmental laws and zoning regulations; (7) a requirement that rental agreements with major tenants of the project have been completed; (8) statements of personal liability in the event of default; and (9) a statement to the effect that the commitment is not assignable to another party.

The commitment fee paid by the developer is intended to assure the availability of the construction loan. When the construction loan calls for a fixed interest rate at the time the commitment is made, the developer may have an option. The developer can exercise the option and take the construction loan if the market rate is at or above the commitment rate. If the market rate is below the commitment rate, the developer will have an incentive to seek alternative financing. In many cases, the commitment is two-sided, however. That is, even if market rates fall below the commitment rate, the developer may be obligated under the commitment to finance the project at the higher commitment rate. Thus, commitment fees tend to be higher if the developer has the option to seek alternative financing. Stated differently, the commitment fee will be lower if the developer is obligated to take the construction loan at the rate indicated in the loan commitment, regardless of the market rate at the time of the funding. If the market rate does drop and the developer is obligated to the higher rate stated in the commitment, this may lead to some interesting legal procedures.

First, if the developer fails to initiate construction, he generally will have no right to a return of the commitment fee. The fee would be refundable only if the developer fails to initiate the project for any reason specifically allowed in the loan commitment documents, or because he is prevented by some legal restriction from developing the project.

Second, in the event that the lender fails to make the construction loan as committed (perhaps because interest rates have risen above that in the commitment), the developer may be able to recover the costs of development that were expended prior to the loan commitment date. The developer also can recover for any alternative financing costs that are greater than those indicated in the loan commitment. Recovery for future profits on the project are more speculative and are generally not available.

Construction Loan Provisions

An example of a building loan agreement is shown in Exhibit 18–1 at the end of this chapter. The agreement sets out the rights and obligations of the lender and the developer. There are several general things that the agreement accomplishes. First, the agreement refers to the promissory note (the collateral which serves as security to the note) and the deed of trust (the instrument that actually secures the collateral). The note and deed are separate documents from the loan agreement. They are, however, executed simultaneously with the agreement. Second, the agreement spells out the details of how the construction is to proceed and how the loan proceeds are to be disbursed. By these details, the lender attempts to cover every contingency that may impair the security of the loan. Essentially, the details are designed to ensure that the facility is constructed as expeditiously as possible, within the designed budget, and without additional liens intervening in priority to that of the lender. It is not our intent here to describe each of the details in all of the items included in the agreement. However, we will explore certain important provisions that stand out and should be given attention.

First, the essential terms of the note and reference to the security for the note are included in Item 3 of the exhibit. Items 4 and 5 describe the security for the loan. These items make certain that, in addition to the land and building, equipment, furnishings, and the like also serve as collateral for the loan. Also, the lender may require written statements from subcontractors and vendors that they have no cause for a lien on the property. Item 6 requires the borrower to obtain a title insurance policy on the property. This is designed to protect the collateral for the lender. The title company must meet with the approval of the lender (that is, it has to be a financially strong title company). Also, the lender must approve any exceptions in the policy. (Exceptions are liens and claims against the property by others that the title company specifically mentions in the title policy as not being covered under the policy.) Items 7 through 10 relate to the disbursement of the loan funds. These provisions insure that the proceeds are used as intended and lead to an increase in the value of the property in step with the disbursement of the loan. Item 7 indicates that the lender may use an agent (often referred to as a voucher control agent) to monitor the disbursement of the loan proceeds. Item 8 assures the lender that the actual cost of each of the stages of development will not exceed the cost established in the loan agreement. Item 10 is a detailed description of the mechanics of disbursement to the contractor and subcontractors. It also names an architect to ensure that the facility is being constructed as indicated in the preapproved plans. Item 13 provides the details of how the physical work on the construction of the facility will be carried out. Here, the lender wants to make sure that the work is carried out expeditiously, in conformity with local construction codes, and in accordance with the authorized architectural plans.

Item 15 indicates that before the lender will make the final disbursement, the designated architect will verify that the facility has been constructed as planned and that all contractors have been paid and given releases from any mechanics' liens. Sometimes this item will include a reference to a verification by an engineer that the construction meets the required specifications. Items 17 and 18 indicate that it is the responsibility of the borrower to make sure there are no mechanics' or tax liens on the property that may have priority over the lender's security interest. Item 21 identifies those actions that constitute a default by the borrower. They include the failure to pay interest or a deposit of principal as called for in the loan amortization schedule, bankruptcy or insolvency of the borrower, delay in the construction of the project, and allowing items of security to be transferred to another party. Item 22 indicates the lender's remedies in the event the borrower breaches the agreement. One of the more important of the remedies is the right to accelerate (demand immediate payment of the entire balance) the loan. The next important item is Item 27, which states that the loan agreement is part of the deed of trust (security) and that if there appears to be any conflict between terms in the deed and terms in the loan agreement, then the latter will control. The reason for this provision is that the loan agreement is usually much more detailed and explicit in many of the terms and conditions of the construction loan.

What happens if the state takes the property under an eminent domain action before the project is completed? Who is entitled to the proceeds from the state, the property owner (borrower) or the lender? Item 29 protects the interest of the lender by stating that the proceeds will be applied to the loan balance at the time. This prevents the developer from taking the proceeds for himself and defaulting on the loan, leaving the lender with no collateral. Items 32 and 33 together prevent the developer from assigning (selling) his rights under the loan agreement to another party, but allow the lender to assign (sell) the loan to another lender.

Item 37 is very important in light of recent court cases on the liability of lenders for the costs of cleaning up hazardous waste found on properties which serve as loan collateral. If there is a loan default and the lender forecloses on the property, the lender will own the property. Under certain interpretations of the Comprehensive Environmental Response, Compensation, and Liability Act of 1980 (CERCLA), the courts have held lenders (as owners) liable for the cost of cleaning up any hazardous waste on the sites that they own through a foreclosure. To escape liability, the lender must prove that it was unaware of the presence of hazardous waste and that it took all necessary steps to ensure that there was no hazardous process undertaken. This provision is one step the lender takes in this regard. Other steps will include what is called an **environmental audit.** The lender may require that the borrower hire a specialist to explore the property, including its history of use and its current physical condition. A loan will be made only if there is a clean audit. Issues of lender liability under CERCLA are explored more fully in Chapter 22. Item 37 is an attempt by the lender to insulate itself from liability under CERCLA.

Item 38 requires that the borrower waive the right to a jury trial in the event of a dispute over the terms of the loan agreement. Basically, lenders feel that juries can come up with some pretty weird decisions. They would rather trust the knowledge of a judge if there is a dispute. This makes sense, given the detailed and exhaustive nature of the terms of the loan agreement.

Finally, Item 41 allows the borrower to prepay the loan at any time without a prepayment penalty. Since construction loans have short maturities, the lender does not worry about the risk of prepayment in a falling interest rate environment. Long-term, permanent, commercial (take-out) loans generally have prepayment penalties to protect the lender in the event that interest rates fall subsequent to loan origination.

Construction Loan Administration

After a construction loan has been made, the lender must monitor the construction process and oversee the disbursements of the loan to the contractors. The administration of the loan will include:

1. Making sure that construction proceeds as scheduled. A delay in the construction process means that the amount of the outstanding debt, which includes accrued interest, is becoming larger and larger. The lender does not want the amount of the indebtedness to exceed the value of the completed project.
2. Making sure that the construction work conforms to all specifications. The lender does not want a finished project that will require additional expenditures to cure defects in workmanship.
3. Making sure that the cost of the project does not exceed the original estimates. This ensures that at all times the remaining portion of the loan exceeds the cost to complete the project.
4. Making sure that no other liens intervene ahead of the lender's. The best way to accomplish this is to make sure that the contractors are paid for the work as done, so that there will be no mechanics' liens placed on the property.
5. Making sure that none of the conditions of the permanent lenders are violated. The construction lender does not want to give the permanent lender any excuse for not financing the finished project.

Usually, a loan administrator is placed in charge of the administration of the loan. The loan administrator will make sure that all the requirements of the loan agreement are met as the project is constructed. The developer will make periodic applications for payment to the contractors and subcontractors involved in the construction of the facility. The loan administrator will make sure that the request for the disbursement includes an indication of the value (or percentage) of the work done and that which remains to be done. The loan administrator will request that an architect verify that the work is being done according to the approved specifications.

Also, many lenders use the services of voucher control agents. A **voucher control agent** is an independent third party that specializes in monitoring the disbursement of the loan to the proper contractors. These agents also regularly inspect the job site to ensure that construction is proceeding as indicated and that materials paid for have been delivered. They also collect material and labor releases (to guard against mechanics' liens) when the funds are paid.

Determination of Loan Amount and Disbursements

In this section we outline the "mechanics" of the determination of the loan amount, payments (disbursements), and repayment. The determination of these amounts will hinge on the cost and the timing of the construction of the project. In this regard, there are several general considerations.

First, the lender will require that the developer put some equity into the project. When the project is completed, the loan-to-value ratio of the ADC loan should reflect the lender's perception of the risk of the project. An 80 percent loan-to-value ratio for a typical commercial project is not uncommon. Second, the developer will want to borrow the funds only as needed to complete the project. By borrowing funds only to finance the construction, the developer will minimize the interest cost of the loan. Third, since the project will generate no cash flows until completed, the developer will not be in a position to make interest payments on the loan until permanent financing is secured. In other words, each advance by the lender will continue to accrue interest until the project is completed. At the time of completion, a permanent loan will be used to repay the construction loan.

Fourth, as with many types of real estate financing, the lender will charge a contract rate of interest and also assess loan fees or points. In the case of an ADC loan, the points may be determined at the time the loan is paid off when the actual balance is known. Fifth, even though the actual balance of the loan will not be known until the project is complete and the loan is to be repaid, a reliable estimate of the amount must be made. For one thing, the lender must be assured that the final loan amount will not be so large as to exceed a desirable loan-to-value ratio. Finally, there are several risks associated with ADC loans, for both the lender and the borrower. We will address these risks following a review of an example ADC loan.

ADC Loan Example

Table 18–1 shows the basic cost data for a multifamily project similar to the example used throughout the text. The ultimate investment in the project will be approximately $2.8 million. The amount that is invested, or "put into," the project will not determine its final value, however. A value based on anticipated cash flows will be used to justify the expenditures for development of the project. Thus, for simplicity, we assume that the value of the project upon completion is approximately the amount invested in it, in terms of the cost of developing it, including interest costs associated with the ADC loan. The cost of the land is $300,000 (five acres at $60,000 each). The project is estimated to take 18 months to complete, once funding is approved

TABLE 18–1
Project Data

Basic data	
Site area 5 acres	$60,000/acre
Units	35
Square footage	42,000 rentable
	52,500 total
Development period	18 months
Cost Information	
Site acquisition	
(including settlement costs)	$300,000
Site preparation	
Sewer and water	$60,000
Paving and curbs	100,000
Landscaping	35,000
Total	$195,000
Construction costs	
Hard costs	
Structure	$1,025,000
Heating and air conditioning	100,000
Electrical	85,000
Plumbing	70,000
Finish work	660,000
Total	$1,940,000
Soft costs	
Architect fees	$40,000
Legal fees	15,000
Loan costs	$55,000
Interest	$199,143
Fees	47,783
Contingency	60,000

by the lender. Site preparation expenses total $195,000, hard costs total $1,940,000, and soft costs, $55,000. Total costs, excluding acquisition of the land, are $2,190,000. For now, we will assume that the developer purchases the land with cash as a portion of his equity interest in the property and the lender funds the remaining development costs.

Table 18–2 shows the construction schedule as agreed upon by the developer and the lender. It shows the disbursement of the $2,190,000 in development expenses over the 18-month period. In this example, the lender charges a 12 percent (annual, 1 percent monthly) contract rate, with two percentage points at the termination of the loan. Table 18–3 shows the "mechanics" of the loan disbursement and repayment.

Disbursements are assumed to be made at the beginning of each month. At the beginning of the first month, the lender advances the developer $105,000 as indicated by the construction cost schedule. At the end of the month, the balance due reflects this first disbursement and the 1 percent monthly interest rate on the loan. At this time, the lender advances the second month's disbursement, $95,000. The balance due at this point is $106,050 + $95,000, or $201,050. This sum, likewise, accrues interest at the 1 percent monthly rate, so that the balance due at the end of the second month is $201,050 × 1.01, or $203,061. This process continues, so that if the construction proceeds as planned, the balance of the loan at the end of the 18 months will be $2,389,143.

Another way to arrive at this figure is to compute, for each disbursement, its future value at the end of the 18 months (Column 5) and sum those values. For example, the future sum of $105,000 compounded at a 1 percent monthly rate for 18 months is $125,595 ($105,000 × $[1.01]^{18}$ = $125,595). The future value of the second month's disbursement is $95,000 × 1.01^{17}, or $112,509. The sum of the future values in Column 5 of Table 18–3 is $2,389,143 (neglecting the $47,783 charge for points). The lender will add 2 percent of this amount ($47,783) to arrive at the balance due, $2,436,926.

Recall, that in order to simplify this example, we have assumed that the developer contributes the value of the land and the lender funds the construction of the project. Also, we assume that the developer is responsible for any contingencies or overruns (which we have assumed will equal $60,000). In the end, the capitalized value of the property will be $2,436,926 + $300,000, or $2,736,926, if there are no contingencies or overruns. If the overrun occurs as estimated ($60,000), then the total cost of the project will be near the $2.8 million assumed value used throughout the text. In this case, the loan-to-value ratio at the end of the 18 months will be $2,436,926/$2,800,000, or 87 percent, a rather high amount. Most likely, the lender would not fund the full amount of the development costs as portrayed in this simplified example. To reduce risk, the lender would require the developer to add equity to the project by funding a portion of the development costs.

Yield Calculation

The lender's yield can be determined by finding that rate which equates the present value of the disbursements to the present value of the loan repayment. The lender's yield in this example is *r,* such that:

$$\$105,000 + \$95,000/(1 + r)^1 + \$45,000/(1 + r)^2 + \ldots + \$85,000/(1 + r)^{17}$$

$$= \$2,436,926/(1 + r)^{18}$$

The rate which solves the equation is 1.23 percent monthly, or 14.71 percent annually.

Risks of ADC Loans

There are several risks associated with ADC loans for both developers and lenders. From the lender's perspective, the major risk involves a failure of the value of the property (collateral) to increase in proportion to the expenditures for construction. Some development expenditures may not increase the value of the property. Costs to obtain the proper government permits, legal expenses, and other soft costs may not improve the value of the property at all. For this reason, the lender may require the developer to incur the soft costs as an equity contribution. Also, as

TABLE 18–2
Construction Cost Schedule

Month	Sewer and Water	Paving and Curbs	Land-scaping	Structure	Heating and Air Conditioning	Electrical Expenses	Plumbing Expenses	Finishing Expenses	Architect	Legal Expenses	Total(%)
1	$30,000	$ 25,000							$40,000	$10,000	$105,000 (4.8)
2	30,000	50,000	$15,000								95,000 (4.3)
3		25,000	20,000								45,000 (2.1)
4				$ 20,000							20,000 (1.9)
5				50,000							50,000 (2.3)
6				100,000							100,000 (4.6)
7				100,000							100,000 (4.6)
8				125,000							125,000 (5.7)
9				125,000							125,000 (5.7)
10				300,000							300,000(13.7)
11				125,000	$ 20,000		$30,000				175,000 (8.0)
12				80,000	40,000	$40,000	20,000	$ 80,000			260,000(11.9)
13					20,000	30,000	15,000	100,000			165,000 (7.5)
14					20,000	10,000	5,000	100,000			135,000 (6.2)
15						5,000		100,000			105,000 (4.8)
16								100,000			100,000 (4.6)
17								100,000			100,000 (4.6)
18								80,000		5,000	85,000 (3.9)
TOTAL	$60,000	$100,000	$35,000	$1,025,000	$100,000	$85,000	$70,000	$660,000	$40,000	$15,000	$2,190,000

TABLE 18-3
Construction Loan Disbursement

Month	Loan Amount	Contract Rate = 12% of Total	Balance Due	Future Value
1	$ 105,000	4.79%	$ 106,050	$ 125,595
2	95,000	4.34	203,061	112,509
3	45,000	2.05	250,541	52,766
4	20,000	0.91	273,247	23,219
5	50,000	2.28	326,479	57,474
6	100,000	4.57	430,744	113,809
7	100,000	4.57	536,051	112,683
8	125,000	5.71	667,662	139,459
9	125,000	5.71	800,588	138,078
10	300,000	13.70	1,111,594	328,106
11	175,000	7.99	1,299,460	189,500
12	260,000	11.87	1,575,055	278,755
13	165,000	7.53	1,757,455	175,151
14	135,000	6.16	1,911,380	141,886
15	105,000	4.79	2,036,544	109,263
16	100,000	4.57	2,157,909	103,030
17	100,000	4.57	2,280,488	102,010
18	85,000	3.88	2,389,143	85,850
Loan fees				47,783
Total	$2,190,000			$2,436,926

Yield: 1.23% monthly, 14.71% annually
P.V. Disbursements $1,957,035 at 0.0123
P.V. Repayment $1,957,035 at 0.0123

indicated earlier, the lender will monitor all aspects of the development to make certain that the loan disbursements are used to develop the property in conformity with architectural and engineering plans.

The lender also will be concerned that the project be completed on time. Delays in construction will result in a larger balance due on the ADC loan at completion. If the project is delayed too long, the amount due on the ADC loan may begin to approach or exceed the value of the property. In this regard, the risk of bad weather, worker strikes, or material shortages affects the riskiness of the loan. Many ADC lenders will require the developer to incur some of the development costs if the project is delayed beyond the agreed-upon schedule.

The lender also will require that permanent financing be approved prior to formalizing the ADC loan. The amount of the permanent financing must be sufficient to cover the expected balance of the ADC loan when the project is terminated.

The developer also faces risks. A delay in construction can cause losses for the developer. The developer will incur greater interest charges as a result of a delay and may have to put more equity into the project. An increase in materials costs also will expose the developer to risk. For short-term projects, this risk can be reduced by contracting for a fixed price on materials at the commencement of the project.

Also, some ADC loans carry a floating interest rate. The lender may change a monthly interest rate equal to the prime rate plus a margin. A rise in the rate of interest during construction will increase the developer's interest costs. (Very-short-term ADC loans may be made at a fixed rate, the floating rate occurring more frequently on lengthy ADC loans.) Small developers likely will not have the incentive or the resources to hedge this interest rate risk with sophisticated financial instruments.

SUMMARY

There are three stages in the construction of a real estate project: acquisition of the land, development or preparation of the land, and construction of the facility. Loans for these stages are referred to collectively as acquisition, development, and construction (ADC) loans. There is no reason why one lender could not finance all stages of the construction process, and some in fact do. In many cases, however, lenders specialize in financing one or two stages. There is definite specialization between ADC lenders and lenders that finance the completed project—the so-called *takeout* or *permanent lenders.* The reason that various stages of the development process are financed by different lenders lies in specialization. Local lenders, especially, know the legal and institutional parameters of the construction process in their area. They are in a better position to underwrite (analyze) the risks involved in the development and construction process.

Two types of buyers acquire raw land: speculators and developers. Speculators rely on an increase in the value of the land to make a return-on-investment. Developers intend to create a commercial real estate project on the land. Residential developers have a need to warehouse large amounts of land to assure that the development and sale of residential properties flows at an even pace and in step with the demand (absorption) of the houses. Institutional lenders, such as commercial banks and thrifts, are by far the largest of the land acquisition lenders. For residential developments, it is necessary for the developer and the lender to work out a well-designed, partial release program that allows a release of the lender's lien on those portions of the land that the developer desires to sell when construction is completed.

Landowners often will finance the sale by taking back a note on the property. The seller will almost always have to agree to a subordination of his lien to a construction lender at some time in the future. The risk of default by the developer and the eventual subordination of the seller's lien increase the risk for the seller. For these reasons, the price of the property with seller financing is generally greater than a third-party-financed sale.

When land is prepared for construction, the developer often will have to meet the provisions of subdivision control ordinances. These ordinances require that the developer put in place an adequate infrastructure before he can sell off any of the property. Alternatively, the developer can post a bond or letter of credit guaranteeing that the infrastructure will be put in place prior to sale of the finished development. The lender that finances the developer often will be called on to provide the financing to meet the provisions of the subdivision control ordinances.

Construction lenders are specialists in analyzing and managing risks of the construction process. The major risk factor is that loan disbursements are made as the construction takes place and value is added to the site. The loan administrator must make sure that the proper payments (collateral) increase step by step with the loan balance. The loan administrator also must make sure that there are no additional items of indebtedness that intervene and jeopardize the security of the construction lender. This means that the administrator must verify that the payments have been made to the proper parties, so as to avoid mechanics' liens and the like. Some construction lenders use the services of voucher control agents to handle all of the verification necessary to protect the collateral of the lender.

KEY TERMS

Construction loan	Land purchase option
Construction loan administration	Loan administration
Construction loan commitment	Partial release provision
Cost recovery fee	Release provisions
Density bonus	Rolling option
Developer	Senior financing
Dollar-based fees	Speculator
Environmental audit	Subdivision control ordinances
Exaction	Subdivision trust
Impact fees	Subordination
Inclusionary zoning	Tax increment financing
Junior financing	Voucher control agent
Land acquisition loan	Warehousing
Land development loan	

SUGGESTED READINGS

Brueggeman, W., J. Fisher, and L. Stone. 1989. *Real Estate Finance.* Homewood, IL: Irwin Publishing Co., chs. 17 and 18.

Sirmans, C. F. 1989. *Real Estate Finance,* 2d ed. New York: McGraw-Hill, ch. 12.

Wiedemer, J. P. 1995. *Real Estate Finance,* 7th ed. Englewood Cliffs, NJ: Prentice Hall, ch. 11.

REVIEW QUESTIONS

18–1   Discuss the differences in the motives of the land speculator and the land developer.

18–2   Discuss the advantages of the arrangement whereby each of the stages of acquisition, development, and construction are financed separately by different lenders.

18–3   What is the purpose of partial release provisions? What are the dangers of an improperly designed partial release provision for the lender?

18–4   Explain why a developer would purchase an option to buy land rather than purchase the land outright and immediately.

18–5   Indicate two reasons the sales price of a parcel of land will be higher if the seller provides some of the financing.

18–6   Explain what a subordination agreement is and why it is necessary in the presence of seller financing.

18–7   Indicate the steps involved in land development—that is, the development of the land in preparation for construction.

18–8   What are subdivision control ordinances, and why have they been enacted?

18–9   Indicate at least four areas of risk that construction lenders must analyze and control when designing a loan package.

18–10 Indicate at least four control measures that a construction lender will implement to monitor and manage the risk involved in construction lending.

18–11 What are the benefits to both the developer and the lender of a construction loan commitment?

18–12 Indicate at least four procedures involved in construction loan administration.

18–13 What is a voucher control agent, and what are the agent's duties?

PROBLEMS

Use the following project cost schedule data to answer Problems 18–1 and 18–2.

Month	Utilities and Landscaping	Structure	Heating and Air Conditioning	Electrical and Plumbing	Finishing	Soft Costs
1	$75,000	0	0	0	0	$40,000
2	125,000	0	0	0	0	8,000
3	52,000	$14,000	0	0	0	0
4	0	126,000	0	0	0	0
5	0	452,000	0	0	0	0
6	0	318,000	0	0	0	0
7	0	200,000	0	0	0	0
8	0	125,000	0	0	0	0
9	0	52,000	$ 40,000	0	0	0
10	0	4,000	72,000	$ 48,000	0	0
11	0	0	115,000	152,000	0	0
12	0	0	0	26,000	$122,000	0
13	0	0	0	0	216,000	0
14	0	0	0	0	146,000	22,000
Total	$252,000	$1,291,000	$227,000	$226,000	$484,000	$70,000

Land value (cost) $750,000

18–1   Assume a lender agrees to finance all costs (except for the acquisition of the land) at 14 percent interest and 2 points.
a. What will be the final payment due the lender at the end of month 14?
b. What will be the yield on the loan to the lender?
c. What will be the loan-to-value ratio at the end of month 14?

18–2   Assume the lender reviews the above loan and decides to reduce the risk by requiring the developer to pay all costs associated with installing utilities and landscaping.
a. What will be the final payment due at the end of month 14?
b. What will be the loan-to-value ratio?

WEB SITES

www.boma.org   information on Building Owners and Managers Association, a trade group that collects data on revenues and expenses of operating commercial real estate.

EXHIBIT 18–1

Building Loan Agreement

BUILDING LOAN AGREEMENT

THIS AGREEMENT is made and entered into at

County,   , on the
day of   , 19   by and between

a   (**"BORROWER"**),
qualified to do business in the County of   ,
State of   , and
(**"LENDER"**).

R E C I T A L S:

WHEREAS, **BORROWER** is the owner and holder of fee simple title estate in that property (**"SECURITY"**) situated in
, described
in legal description attached hereto as Exhibit A and made a part hereof; and

WHEREAS, **BORROWER** has applied to **LENDER** for a construction loan in the total aggregate principal amount of
DOLLARS
($ U.S.) (**"LOAN"**) for a loan term
ending no later than   ,   at an interest
rate on the daily outstanding balance as hereinafter provided and

WHEREAS, the **LOAN** shall be advanced as hereinafter provided, said advances being evidenced by a Promissory Note (**"NOTE"**)
payable to the order of **LENDER** for the principal sum as above stated; and

WHEREAS, the **NOTE** shall be secured by a first lien on the **SECURITY** evidenced by Deed of Trust (**"DEED"**); and

WHEREAS, **BORROWER** has represented to **LENDER** that the **SECURITY** is to be improved (the **"IMPROVEMENT"**) in the
manner set forth in plans and specifications and/or other documents heretofore made available to **LENDER** by **BORROWER,** a description or copy of which plans and specifications and/or documents are attached hereto; and

WHEREAS, **BORROWER** has represented to **LENDER** that the **LOAN** funds are to be used solely for the purposes set forth herein
and for no other purpose;

NOW, **THEREFORE,** in consideration of the sum of One Dollar ($1.00) and other good and valuable consideration, the receipt and
sufficiency of which is hereby acknowledged, it is stipulated and agreed as follows:

1. **RECITALS:** The foregoing recitals are true and correct.

2. **DEFINITIONS:** Wherever used herein, the following words shall be considered in the context of these definitions:

    (a) **DEED:** The Deed of Trust, Assignment of Rents and Security Agreement, used to establish the first priority lien of **LENDER**
against the **SECURITY;**

    (b) **NOTE:** The Promissory Note or Notes or other evidence of the indebtedness created by the **LOAN;**

    (c) **LOAN:** The **LOAN** which is the subject matter of this Agreement and the other documents to which this Agreement refers;

    (d) **LENDER:** The named party to this Agreement, and any subsequent owner and holder of the rights and obligations established
under this Agreement, the **NOTE** and **DEED;**

    (e) **BORROWER:** The named **BORROWER** in this Agreement and any successor in interest to **BORROWER** whose
designation as such shall be previously consented to in writing by **LENDER;**

    (f) **SECURITY:** The real property described in legal description and the improvements thereon upon which the lien of the
DEED attaches, including all fixtures and other personal property identified in Paragraph 4 hereinbelow;

    (g) **IMPROVEMENT:** The improvements, or any portion therof, contemplated by this Agreement to be constructed on
the **SECURITY;**

    (h) **AGENT:** Any person or entity, other than a **LENDER,** acting as disburser of the **LOAN** funds, or any portion thereof,
under the terms of this Agreement; and

3. **NOTE: LENDER** shall make to **BORROWER** and **BORROWER** shall accept from **LENDER** a **LOAN** in the aggregate
principal sum of **DOLLARS**
($ U.S.) for a term ending   which
LOAN shall be evidenced by **BORROWER'S NOTE** and **DEED.** The **NOTE** and **DEED** are to be simultaneously executed
with this Agreement. The interest rate payable under the **NOTE** may be increased or decreased   by
LENDER based on the increase or decrease in

referred to in **NOTE** as "Index", plus a margin of   percentage points as defined in the **NOTE.**

Although the **NOTE** evidencing the indebtedness of **BORROWER** to **LENDER** may provide that it shall bear interest
from a specific date therein, the parties herein agree that the **NOTE** shall bear interest, which shall be payable monthly, from
the date of each advance and on the sum outstanding from time to time under this Agreement. Said interest shall be computed
on a per diem basis on a   -day year.

It is the intention of the parties that under no circumstances shall **BORROWER** be charged more than the highest lawful
rate of interest under the applicable law, and notwithstanding anything contained herein to the contrary, the amount of interest
payable under the terms of the **NOTE** shall in no event exceed the maximum amount of interest permitted to be charged by
law at the date hereof. Interest shall be computed and accrued on the daily outstanding principal balance after each advance-
ment or disbursement under the **LOAN** from the date thereof until the **LOAN** is fully paid. In the event that **BORROWER**
fails to make any interest payments when due, then all such outstanding amounts may be deducted by **LENDER** from any
subsequent advance or disbursement without notice to **BORROWER.** All interest as well as principal due under the **NOTE**
shall be secured by the lien created by the **DEED.**

ML23 (4/88)

Building Loan Agreement

4.   SECURITY: The **LOAN** shall be secured by a first lien in the form of a **DEED** encumbering the **SECURITY** set forth and described in legal description. Such lien shall be subject only to those encumbrances, limitations, restrictions, or easements which are listed in the Preliminary Title Report or are approved by Counsel designated by **LENDER** as more fully provided hereinbelow in Paragraph 6.

5.   ADDITIONAL SECURITY: **BORROWER** shall contemporaneously with the execution and delivery of this Agreement, execute in favor of **LENDER** any Security or Collateral Agreement creating a security interest in personal property or any assignment or pledge of other property, all as may be required hereunder by **LENDER,** which additional security shall include, but not be limited to, the following:

(a)   the Note to evidence the Loan;

(b)   the Deed of Trust encumbering the Real Property and the Project;

(c)   a Security Agreement granting **LENDER** a Security Interest in all building materials, equipment, fittings, furniture, furnishings, fixtures and all other articles of personal property of every kind or character now owned, or hereafter acquired by **BORROWER** in connection with or for use in constructing, equipping, furnishing, operating or maintaining the Project;

(d)   a Security Agreement granting a Security Interest in and an assignment of all Leases ("**LEASES**") between **BORROWER** and Lessees of space in the Project, whether now, or hereafter, in existence, together with the rents, issues, proceeds and profits therefrom; and

(e)   a Title Policy insuring **LENDER'S** lien under the Mortgage as a first lien upon the Real Property.

6.   TITLE INSURANCE: **BORROWER** shall provide, at its own expense, title insurance in form satisfactory to **LENDER** and issued by a title insurance company acceptable to **LENDER.** The title policy is to be issued without exceptions, except for those exceptions which are acceptable to Counsel for **LENDER,** insuring the **DEED** required hereunder as a first, valid, and paramount lien against the **SECURITY** and insuring against loss or change in priority as a result of the filing of any lien or special assessment for any materials and/or work either under construction or completed.

Designation by **BORROWER** of the title insurer shall be subject to **LENDER'S** approval of the financial ability of said insurer to pay the face amount of the new policy and all of its other policies insuring **LENDER** in the event of loss.

The designated title insurer shall also provide at **BORROWER'S** expense, on **LENDER'S** demand and at an appropriate time, an endorsement that the foundations and/or pad of the premises do not violate setback requirements of the appropriate municipal agencies and copies of all easements and restrictions of record, as shown on the report of binder. If for any reason the title insurer does not or cannot provide this endorsement as to any of the aforesaid information, then **BORROWER** shall provide **LENDER** with such other certifications or documentation as may be required by **LENDER** at **LENDER'S** discretion.

Prior to making any disbursement under the **LOAN**, **LENDER** shall receive evidence satisfactory to it that the title insurance company is prepared to issue its title insurance endorsement insuring the amount being disbursed and that the **MORTGAGE,** as of said date, remains a first, valid and permanent lien on the **SECURITY,** free and clear of any and all Mechanics', Materialmen's and/or Laborer's Liens and subject only to such exceptions as **LENDER** may approve, as more specifically set forth in Paragraph 11 below.

7.   DISBURSING AGENT: **LENDER** may, at its election and at **BORROWER'S** cost, disburse the **LOAN** proceeds to **BORROWER** through a title insurance company, mortgage company, or other third party ("**AGENT**") selected by **LENDER** or directly to the sub-contractors, materialmen and laborers. Such election, however, except as required by agreements with the title insurance company insuring the **LOAN,** does not prevent **LENDER** from making subsequent disbursements in a different manner and through a different party.

The account of any selected **AGENT** for **LENDER,** maintained with **LENDER** for **BORROWER,** as may be referred to herein, shall be deemed a direct account of **BORROWER** with **LENDER** and shall be maintained at **BORROWER'S** expense. Any disbursements to be paid by **AGENT** to **BORROWER** shall be payable in accordance with the provisions of this Agreement.

In no event shall **AGENT** be construed as the **AGENT** of **BORROWER,** nor shall said **AGENT** be construed as assuming **BORROWER'S** responsibility for proper payments. Said **AGENT** shall at all times be entitled, and is hereby authorized by **BORROWER,** to rely upon representations of **BORROWER.** This latter provision shall in no way alter **AGENT'S** liability to **LENDER** as its disbursing **AGENT** pursuant to the terms hereof.

8.   CONDITIONS PRECEDENT TO DISBURSEMENT: **LENDER** shall incur no obligations hereunder, nor shall it deposit any monies in AGENT'S account for **BORROWER** or to the account of **BORROWER** maintained with **LENDER,** until all of the following are completed:

(a)   **BORROWER** has, if required by **LENDER,** either deposited with **AGENT** or to BORROWER'S account with **LENDER,** as the case may be, an amount equal to the difference, if any, between the **LOAN** and the estimated cost of construction, or has expended **BORROWER'S** own funds in an amount equal to said difference. The deposit to be made by **BORROWER** under the provisions of this subsection, together with the proceeds of the **LOAN,** shall constitute the total fund to be disbursed hereunder. If such a deposit is not required by **LENDER,** then **BORROWER** shall provide **LENDER** or **AGENT,** whichever may be applicable, with paid bills and waivers of lien to the extent of the difference between the amount of the **LOAN** and the estimated cost of construction of the **IMPROVEMENT** before the disbursement of any of the proceeds of the **LOAN;**

(b)   **BORROWER** has recorded the **DEED** in the office of the Recorder of the County in which the **SECURITY** is located; and

(c)   **BORROWER'S** condition title, as certified by the title insurer, by issuance of a form of title insurance as acceptable to the **LENDER.**

(d)   After the initial recording draw for purposes other than construction and upon **LENDER'S** request, **BORROWER** shall supply to **LENDER** executed subcontracts with assignments to the **LENDER.**

LENDER may, at its election, require that **BORROWER** furnish, in addition to the foregoing, executed construction contracts between **BORROWER** and all contractors, executed copies of all subcontracts between the general contractor or contractors and all of their subcontractors and suppliers, including contracts, subcontracts, and purchase orders for all fixtures and equipment required to be installed for the operation of the premises. **LENDER** may require executed copies of firm bids or estimates of costs from any or all of the contractors and subcontractors.

The amounts called for under any of the aforesaid contracts shall not be in excess of the total amount allocated for the purpose in the schedule entitled "Use of Funds" set forth below.

LENDER, at its election, may verify the correctness of the amount of any contract, subcontract, estimate or bid furnished pursuant to the terms hereof.

USE OF FUNDS

Subject to the provisions herein set forth, **LOAN** funds contemplated in this Agreement have been allocated as follows and shall only be disbursed in accordance therewith:

A.	Land Acquisition consisting of	$
B.	Acquisition and Development consisting of	$
C.	Acquisition of Developed Lots consisting of	$
D.	Construction consisting of	$

ML23 (4/88)

(continued)

E X H I B I T   1 8 – 1   *(Continued)*

Building Loan Agreement

9.   **ADDITIONAL DEPOSIT BY BORROWER:** If, at any time pending or during the disbursement of the **LOAN** proceeds or any portion thereof, it appears that the amount remaining undisbursed will be insufficient to complete the construction of the **IMPROVEMENT** in accordance with the plans and specifications and/or to pay for any of the necessary labor, material, and costs, **BORROWER** shall, within ten (10) banking days of **LENDER'S** demand, deposit with the **LENDER** or assign or hypothecate to **LENDER** in a form acceptable to **LENDER** additional monies which shall, when added to the undisbursed proceeds of the **LOAN**, be sufficient to pay for the cost of completion of the **IMPROVEMENT** and the costs and expenses in connection therewith. The amount so deposited shall be disbursed to pay for the cost of completion of the **IMPROVEMENT** before any additional **LOAN** proceeds will be disbursed.

10.   **DISBURSEMENT OF LOAN FUNDS:** Upon recordation of the **DEED** and delivery to **LENDER** of all items required and specified hereunder or herein by **LENDER, LENDER** shall periodically disburse the **LOAN** funds to **BORROWER** in accordance with the Cost Breakdown, and in the following manner:

(a)   Each request for disbursement shall be made on a Construction Loan Requisition form (**"VOUCHER"**) furnished to **BORROWER** by **LENDER** or **AGENT**, which shall, if applicable, be accompanied by a contractor's cost breakdown and request for partial payment form, which shall be executed by **BORROWER** and Contractor, the contents of which must meet the approval of **LENDER** or **AGENT**. At no time shall **LENDER** or **AGENT** disburse any monies from the proceeds of the **LOAN** when the total of such disbursement would be in excess of twenty percent (20%) of the value of the **SECURITY** and the **IMPROVEMENT** at the time of the request. No funds shall be disbursed prior to an inspection by such persons designated by the **LENDER** (**"Inspector"**). Said Inspector's function is solely for the purpose of verifying the voucher and not for the inspection of the quality of the work or compliance with any applicable building codes.

(b)   Upon the application for the first disbursement and each subsequent disbursement thereafter, **BORROWER** shall furnish **LENDER** or **AGENT** with waivers of lien, receipted bills and such other items as may be required by them or either one of them pursuant to subsection (d) below, evidencing the payment of all sub-portions of construction paid out of the last preceding disbursement. It is the intention and agreement of the parties that no disbursement shall be applied for or made at any time when the waivers of lien and receipted bills, when added to the balance of undisbursed portion of the **LOAN**, equal an amount in excess of the amount shown in the Contractor's Cost Breakdown spread sheet as necessary for completion of the construction of the **IMPROVEMENT**. However, in any event, **BORROWER** shall only be entitled to payment in the specific amount approved by **LENDER** as to each requisition or application for disbursements under this Agreement;

(c)   If required by **LENDER**, an architect (**"ARCHITECT"**) shall be designated to verify with each requisition of **LOAN** proceeds that all construction to the date requisition has been completed to the extent indicated in the Contractor's requisition form and in accordance with the final plans and specifications previously submitted to **LENDER**. **ARCHITECT** shall be subject to **LENDER'S** approval. Any fees incurred in connection with this subsection shall be paid by **BORROWER**;

(d)   **LENDER** or **AGENT** shall make disbursements for contract items to **BORROWER'S** Contractor or to **BORROWER**, if **BORROWER** is the Contractor, in accordance with the Contractor's Cost Breakdown spread sheet, and shall impose such additional conditions to this approval of requisitions and to disbursements of advances by way of sworn statements, waivers, partial waivers or releases of lien, proof of paid bills, inspection of payroll vouchers and submission of **ARCHITECT'S** certificates and progress surveys as it may deem necessary to protect the priority of the **DEED** and comply with the provisions of this Agreement;

(e)   Ten percent (10%) of all disbursements shall be withheld until **BORROWER** has complied with the provisions of Paragraph 15 below;

(f)   **BORROWER** (or **AGENT**) shall utilize all portions of the Mechanics' Lien Law which will shorten the time in which such liens can be filed, and shall comply with all applicable laws, as a prerequisite to any requested disbursements;

(g)   **LENDER** shall not be obligated to make disbursements hereunder until **BORROWER** has delivered to it all requisitions and other proofs as may be required. Tendered requisitions and other proofs shall be deemed acceptable to **LENDER** unless, within ten (10) days after delivery, **LENDER** notifies **BORROWER** of the deficiencies;

(h)   Each request shall be submitted in sufficient time prior to **BORROWER'S** requested date for an advance hereunder to enable **LENDER** or **AGENT** to process such request. Funds shall be characterized as disbursed to **BORROWER** when disbursed by **LENDER**, irrespective of instruction by **BORROWER** to disburse to another entity. **LENDER** shall disburse within ten (10) days of receipt of all necessary documentation for a draw request; and

(i)   **LENDER** may deduct from any disbursements, where necessary and in addition to the amount withheld pursuant to subsection (e) of this Paragraph, the amount of any retainage, fees, expenses, reserves, advances or deposits specified in the Cost Breakdown. **BORROWER** shall advance in cash any sums not provided in said Exhibit to pay premiums on casualty and title insurance, taxes, assessments, recording expenses, filing fees, or such other sums as **LENDER** may deem necessary for the protection and preservation of the **SECURITY**, and payment of the premiums for insurance required by **LENDER** during the life of this **LOAN**. In the event **BORROWER** does not make timely payment of any of the aforesaid sums, **LENDER** is hereby authorized, if **LENDER** so elects, to advance out of **LOAN** proceeds and at **BORROWER'S** expense, after thirty (30) days' notice or such lesser time as allotted by an insurer, etc., any sums necessary to make such payments.

11.   **ENDORSEMENTS TO TITLE INSURANCE POLICIES:** Periodically, at the **LENDER'S** discretion, the **LENDER** may request the title insurance company to issue a title certificate to **LENDER** which shall certify that there are no changes in the condition of title of the **SECURITY** from the condition thereof as set forth in the original title policy. In the event said title certificate indicates an objection, defect in, or cloud upon the title to the **SECURITY** which arose subsequent to the issuance of the original title policy, **BORROWER** shall pay such monies, take such action or do whatever else may be necessary in the opinion of **LENDER** to cure any such objection, defect or cloud, and **LENDER** shall not be required to disburse any monies until the title insurance company is able to certify to **LENDER** that such objection, defect or cloud has been cured.

Any surveys delivered to **LENDER** to support advances shall be accompanied by a certificate from the title company listing the legal description of the **SECURITY** and certifying that such survey has been inspected by the title company and no condition has been found to exist thereon which will in any way affect the original title policy.

12.   **MISREPRESENTATION BY BORROWER:** Unless otherwise specified herein, if any representation contained in this Agreement, or in any agreement, report, or statement given to **LENDER** regarding any transaction hereunder or submitted in support thereto, is untrue and incorrect in any material respect, or in the event of any breach on the part of **BORROWER** of any of the terms contained in this Agreement, or in the **NOTE** or other instrument given by **BORROWER** to **LENDER**, then, in any such event, **LENDER** shall have all of the rights and remedies provided in this Agreement as well as those provided for by applicable law and, in addition to such rights and remedies, all obligations hereunder of **BORROWER** to **LENDER** shall become immediately due and payable without demand or notice and shall forthwith be paid and discharged by **BORROWER** notwithstanding any time or credit otherwise allowed. Upon the failure of **BORROWER** to pay or discharge all such liabilities and obligations forthwith, or upon the failure of **BORROWER** to pay the **NOTE** or other obligation to **LENDER** on demand, or at the expressed or declared maturity thereof, **LENDER** may proceed to exercise all of its rights and remedies as provided herein. Every term contained in the **NOTE** or other obligation shall be deemed

Building Loan Agreement

incorporated into this Agreement. All rights, remedies, and powers granted to **LENDER** herein, or in the **NOTE** or other instruments, or implied in law, shall be cumulative and may be exercised separately or concurrently with such other rights as **LENDER** may have and shall include, among other rights, the right to apply to a court of equity for an injunction to restrain a breach or threatened breach by **BORROWER** of this Agreement. **LENDER** may exercise such rights from time to time as to all or part of the **SECURITY** as **LENDER**, in its sole discretion, may determine.

13.   **WORK:**

(a)   **Development Work Criteria:** The development of the subject property shall be in accordance with the proposed plans and specifications submitted as the basis for this **LOAN** and in compliance with all restrictions, conditions, ordinances, codes, regulations and laws of governmental departments and agencies having direction or jurisdiction over, or an interest in, said premises and improvements. No extra work nor change in plans and specifications shall be authorized by **BORROWER** without the prior express written consent of **LENDER**. **LENDER** shall respond to all such requests within five (5) Banking days of receipt. If **LENDER** shall consent to any such extra work or change in plans and specifications, **BORROWER** shall immediately deposit the amount of the cost thereof with **LENDER** (or **AGENT**), such deposit to be held in an interest bearing account and disbursed by **LENDER** or **AGENT** in accordance with normal disbursement procedures;

(b)   **Commencement and Continuity of Work:** Development of the property shall commence within one (1) month of recording the Deed of Trust and shall be carried on diligently, continuously and with dispatch until completed. **BORROWER** agrees to devote its full effort and energy to the immediate development, construction and completion of the **IMPROVEMENT** without any abandonment thereof;

(c)   **Construction Costs:** No development work may commence or continue under this **LOAN** until (i) engineering cost estimates have been provided to **LENDER** and such cost estimates have been reviewed and found acceptable by **LENDER**, and (ii) firm construction contracts have been provided to and approved by **LENDER;**

(d)   Not withstanding the above, the improvements shall be completed on or before twelve (12) months from the date of the **DEED'S** being recorded; and

(e)   **Use of First Class Materials: BORROWER** shall use first class materials in construction of the project. Such material shall be owned by the **BORROWER** and not subject to any liens or liabilities.

14.   **REPRESENTATIONS AND WARRANTIES OF BORROWER: BORROWER,** based upon its best knowledge and belief, makes the following warranties and representations:

(a)   **Correctness of Documents:** The documents furnished in support of the **LOAN** and those documents listed in the Opinion of Counsel are true and correct and accurately set out the facts contained therein.

(b)   **Absence of Proceedings and Actions:** There are no actions, suits, or proceedings pending or, to the knowledge of **BORROWER**, threatened against or affecting **BORROWER** except as set forth in the Credit Report which is attached hereto.

(c)   **BORROWER'S Powers, Status of Authority and Compensation of Employees:** There is a true, complete, and correct statement with respect to **BORROWER'S** powers, and status of authority contained in the Credit Report attached hereto.

(d)   **Absence of Judgments and/or Awards and/or Orders:** There are no outstanding and unpaid judgments or arbitration awards against **BORROWER** except as are set forth in the Credit Report. **BORROWER** is not in default or violation with respect to any valid regulation, order, writ, judgment or decree or any court or other governmental or municipal department, commission, board, bureau, agency or instrumentality.

(e)   **Non-Default of BORROWER Contractually: BORROWER** is not in default under and has not breached in any material respect any agreement or instrument to which it is a party or by which it may be bound. The execution and delivery of this Agreement, the **NOTE** and **DEED**, and the consummation of the other transactions contemplated by this Agreement do not and will not conflict with or result in violation of any valid regulations, order, writ, judgment, injunction or decree of any court or governmental or municipal instrumentality or in the breach of or default under any indenture, contract, agreement, or other instrument to which **BORROWER** is a party or by which it is bound, except where the amount of all such liability is, in the aggregate less than $ and no one item exceeds $ provided all such items are bonded. Neither the execution and delivery of this Agreement, nor the **DEED**, nor the issuance of the **NOTE** will result in the creation or imposition of, or be any cause for imposing, any lien, charge or encumbrance of any nature whatsoever upon any of the **SECURITY** or assets of **BORROWER** other than those created, imposed or required by this Agreement or the **DEED**.

(f)   **Marketable Title in BORROWER Without Liens:** Except as stated in the Preliminary Title Report, **BORROWER** has, and at all times until payment of this **LOAN** in full will have, good and marketable title in fee simple to the **SECURITY**. The **SECURITY** is subject to no liens, charges or encumbrances except as shown on the Preliminary Title Report or as may be acceptable to counsel designated by **LENDER**.

(g)   **Use of Proceeds:** The proceeds of this **LOAN** will be used solely for the purposes specified herein and in supporting documents.

(h)   **Licenses: BORROWER** has, or has applied for, all necessary licenses to effect the use of the **SECURITY**, but not limited to, business licenses.

15.   **FINAL DISBURSEMENT:** The obligation of **LENDER** hereunder to make the final disbursement to **BORROWER** shall be conditioned upon the following in a form and substance acceptable to **LENDER:**

(a)   Receipt of evidence of approval by all applicable authorities for permanent occupancy of the **IMPROVEMENT** in its entirety by issuance of a certificate of occupancy;

(b)   Written notice from an **ARCHITECT** approved by **LENDER** to the effect that the **IMPROVEMENT** has been completed in accordance with plans and specifications;

(c)   A final survey showing the completed **IMPROVEMENT;**

(d)   The Contractor's final affidavit pursuant to the   Statutes, final waivers and releases of liens from all subcontractors and suppliers as well as any parties that have served a notice to owner's affidavit in accordance with the   Statutes; and

(e)   Final signoff by the title insurer.

16.   **INSURANCE POLICIES AND CERTIFICATES: BORROWER** at its expense shall maintain with insurers acceptable to **LENDER** and furnish **LENDER** certificates from the insurance carrier evidencing the following: (i) insurance against loss from fire, windstorm, theft, vandalism and other perils generally included in "extended coverage" policies, and for such other hazards as may be reasonably required by **LENDER**; (ii) public liability and property damage insurance; (iii) Workmen's Compensation Insurance; and, (iv) such other insurance coverage as **LENDER** may reasonably require and which is usually obtained for ownership and use of property similar to the use contemplated of the **SECURITY**. As to the insurance described in (i) of the preceding sentence, said policy shall contain a Mortgagee's "Loss Payable" clause (Form CF-1219 or its equivalent) providing for payment to **LENDER** and its successors and/or

(continued)

EXHIBIT 18 – 1 *(Continued)*

Building Loan Agreement

assigns to the extent of its interest in the event of loss. Said policy may, during construction, be in "Builder's Risk" form so far as the same relates to the **IMPROVEMENT**. In the event said policy is cancelled, **BORROWER** shall notify **LENDER** in writing within five (5) days of receipt of notice of such cancellation, and shall advise insurer to forward any and all refunds resulting from such cancellation to **LENDER** for the account of **BORROWER**. All such insurance shall be in amounts acceptable to **LENDER**, and in such form and amounts as will comply with applicable law; and said insurance shall, where necessary or permissible, name **LENDER** as an additional insured as its interest may appear. The aforesaid public liability insurance shall be carried during the full course of construction work on the premises, naming **LENDER** and its successor and/or assigns as an additional insured, and with minimum limits of coverage for death of or injury to persons of not less than $300,000.00/$500,000.00 and for damage to property of not less than $_____ unless otherwise agreed to in writing by **LENDER**. Copies of such policies shall be delivered to **LENDER** at, or before, disbursement of the **LOAN** proceeds with proof of premium payment. At the election of **LENDER** any proceeds of such insurance in excess of _____ **DOLLARS** ($_____ U.S.) shall be paid to **LENDER** and its successors and/or assigns and shall be applied first to payment of accrued interest and then to reduction of principal or, at **LENDER'S** option, said excess proceeds may be made available under usual disbursing procedures to rebuild the project. In the event **LENDER** must place coverage in order to protect **LENDER'S** security interest, the premium for such coverage shall be disbursed from the loan proceeds and will accrue interest at the **NOTE** rate.

   17.   REMOVAL OF MECHANICS' LIENS: **BORROWER** specifically agrees to have any and all Mechanic's and/or Materialmen's Liens which may be filed against the **SECURITY** released or bonded within twenty (20) calendar days of the date **BORROWER** receives notice of the same, time being of the essence. **BORROWER** need not secure the release of a Mechanic's Lien against the **SECURITY** within such period, if, and so long as, the priority of **LENDER'S** lien as against such Mechanic's Lien is affirmatively insured by the title insurance policy. **BORROWER'S** failure to promptly insure **LENDER'S** priority or promptly remove such liens shall constitute an act of Default.

   18.   PAYMENT OF TAXES: BORROWER agrees to promptly pay and discharge any taxes, assessments, charges, levies or indebtedness upon the **SECURITY**, which may become due or payable during the existence of this **LOAN**. At least ten (10) days before delinquency, **BORROWER** shall furnish to **LENDER** evidence satisfactory to **LENDER** that taxes and assessments have been paid. **LENDER** may pay such sums as may become due out of undisbursed **LOAN** proceeds in the event **BORROWER** fails to promptly pay as aforesaid.

   19.   ACCESS TO BORROWER'S BOOKS AND RECORDS: LENDER, or its agents, shall at all reasonable times have unrestricted access to the records, accounting books, contracts, subcontracts, bills and statements of **BORROWER**, including any supporting or related vouchers or other instruments as relate in any manner to the **IMPROVEMENT** contemplated to be constructed by the funds disbursed under this Agreement, and shall have the right to make copies of the same. If **LENDER** so requires, the records, books, vouchers, or other instruments shall be made available to an accountant of **LENDER'S** choice for audit, examination, inspection, and photocopying or other type of duplication; such audit to be done at **BORROWER'S** office.

   20.   FINANCIAL STATEMENTS: BORROWER shall furnish to LENDER signed monthly Profit and Loss statements, including current leasing data, quarterly un-audited statements of financial condition; and, **BORROWER** shall also furnish **LENDER** with a signed and audited or un-audited annual statement acceptable to **LENDER**. The quarterly statements shall be delivered by **BORROWER** to **LENDER** within thirty (30) days of the end of each quarter and the annual audited statement within ninety (90) days after close of the fiscal year. Upon the event of any default, **LENDER** may choose to request any reasonable financial data.

   21.   EVENTS OF DEFAULT: The happening of any one, or more, of the following events shall constitute a default under this Agreement, the NOTE, and DEED:

   (a)   **Nonpayment of Interest:** BORROWER failing to make the required interest payments on any due date;

   (b)   **Non-Deposit of Principal:** BORROWER failing to make any required deposit of principal, or any portion thereof, on any due date;

   (c)   **Breach of Condition:** BORROWER violating any material term, condition or representation contained in this Agreement, the **NOTE**, or **DEED**, or the determination by **LENDER** of the existence of a material misrepresentation of fact as set forth in Paragraph 15 not cured after thirty (30) days' notice;

   (d)   **Bankruptcy or Insolvency:** BORROWER being insolvent by being unable to pay its debts when they become due or by having the amount of its liabilities exceed the amount of its assets; or **BORROWER** committing an act of bankruptcy, making a general assignment for the benefit of creditors; or if there is filed by or against **BORROWER** a voluntary or involuntary Petition in Bankruptcy or for the appointment of a receiver; or if **BORROWER** admits in writing to a creditor that he is financially unable to pay such creditor any indebtedness due him; or if there commences under any law relating to bankruptcy, insolvency, reorganization or relief of debtors proceedings for **BORROWER'S** relief or for the composition, extension, arrangement or adjustment of any of **BORROWER'S** obligation's or affecting the **SECURITY**, which is not withdrawn or dismissed within thirty (30) days after the filing of, or the entry into, the same; or if **BORROWER'S** business is discontinued as a going concern; or if there is a suspension of **BORROWER'S** business or if **BORROWER** defaults on any other obligation it may have to **LENDER**; or if a Writ of Attachment, execution, or any similar process is issued or levied against any significant part of **BORROWER'S** property which is not released, stayed, bonded or vacated within a reasonable time after its issue or levy;

   (e)   **Liens or Foreclosures:** The institution of foreclosure action against the **SECURITY** or the filing of a valid lien against the **SECURITY**, which is not removed of record, bonded, vacated, released or dismissed within thirty (30) days after **BORROWER** receives notice of such filing, except as provided above in Paragraph 18;

   (f)   **Substantial Discontinuance of Construction or Development:** The substantial discontinuance of construction or development work for a period of ten (10) days which discontinuance is, in the sole determination of **LENDER**, without cause;

   (g)   **Transfer of Security:** The sale, assignment, pledge, transfer hypothecation or other disposition of the **SECURITY** by **BORROWER** to some other person or entity without the prior express written consent of **LENDER** as proscribed in the **DEED** unless as provided under the release agreement, Section 14 hereof and Opinion of Counsel;

   (h)   **Ability of BORROWER to Perform:** The sale, assignment, pledge, transfer, hypothecation, or other disposition of any proprietary or beneficial interest in **BORROWER** or its property by the owner thereof, or, any change in the executive management or operating control of **BORROWER** unless, in **LENDER'S** sole judgment, such sale, assignment, pledge, transfer, hypothecation, other disposition or change does not materially and adversely affect the ability of **BORROWER** to perform in accordance with the terms of this Agreement;

   (i)   **Impairment of Security:** Any condition or situation which, in the sole determination of **LENDER**, constitutes a danger to, or impairment of, the **SECURITY** or repayment of the **LOAN**, where such condition or situation is not remedied within thirty (30) days after written notice to **BORROWER** to remedy such condition or situation, or, where it is not possible to fully remedy such condition or situation within thirty (30) days and no action has yet been commenced to remedy such condition or situation. **LENDER** agrees that it will not exercise this right in an unreasonable manner.

Building Loan Agreement

(j) **Failure to Pay Taxes:** Should **BORROWER** fail to pay taxes as they become due or fail to make such payment within ten (10) days after written notice that such payments are due.

(k) **Cross Default:** Any default on this Agreement or the **NOTE** is a default on any other **NOTES** to the **LENDER** executed by the **BORROWER**, successors or assigns in any capacity. Conversely, any default on any other Agreement or **NOTE** to the **LENDER** executed by the **BORROWER**, successors or assigns in any capacity, is a default on this Agreement or **NOTE**. Further, in the event of any default on this Agreement or **NOTE**, or any other Agreements or **NOTES** to the **LENDER** executed by the **BOR-ROWER**, successors or assigns in any capacity, the **LENDER** may, at its option, declare the remainder of any and all said debts due and payable and any failure to exercise that option shall not constitute a waiver or a right to exercise the same at any other time, nor shall such failure to exercise the option be construed as any form of acceptance of said default. Notice of the exercise of said option is hereby waived. Upon exercise of said option, interest shall accrue at the then prevailing rate of the **NOTE**.

22. **LENDER'S REMEDIES:** Upon the occurrence of any event of default hereunder, **LENDER** shall have the absolute right to refuse to disburse any funds provided in the Cost Breakdown hereof. If said default is not remedied by **BORROWER** within the time periods as may be elsewhere herein provided, if any, **LENDER**, at its option and election and in its sole discretion, shall have the absolute right to do any of the following, singly or in combination:

(a) **Cancellation:** Cancel this Agreement by written notice to **BORROWER**;

(b) **Specific Performance:** Institute appropriate proceedings to specifically enforce performance of the terms and conditions of this Agreement;

(c) **Withhold Advances:** Withhold further advances hereunder;

(d) **Taking of Possession:** Take immediate possession of the **SECURITY** encumbered by the **DEED**, as well as all other **SECURITY** given hereunder, as is necessary to fully complete all on-site and off-site **IMPROVEMENTS** contemplated to be developed and/or constructed under this Agreement;

(e) **Receivership:** Appoint a Receiver, as a matter of strict right without regard to the solvency of **BORROWER**, for the purpose of preserving the **SECURITY**, preventing waste and protecting all rights accruing to **LENDER** by virtue of this Agreement and of the **DEED** executed in connection with this Agreement, and expressly to make any and all further improvements, whether on-site or off-site, as may be determined solely by **LENDER** to be necessary to complete the development and construction in accordance with this Agreement. All expenses, including attorney's fees, incurred in connection with the appointment of said Receiver, or in protecting, preserving, or improving the **SECURITY**, shall be chargeable against **BORROWER** and shall be enforced as a lien against the **SECURITY**, any statutes or judicial decisions to the contrary notwithstanding;

(f) **Acceleration:** Accelerate maturity of said **DEED** and **NOTE** and demand payment of the principal sums due thereunder, with interest, advances, costs and attorneys' fees, and in default of said payment or any part thereof, to enforce collection of such payment by foreclosure of the said **DEED** and/or other appropriate action in any court of competent jurisdiction;

(g) **Other:** Exercise any other right, privilege, or remedy available to **LENDER** as may be provided by applicable law and/or any other document executed in connection herewith.

In addition to the rights hereinabove granted, in the event of default by **BORROWER**, **LENDER** may, at its option, enter into and upon the **SECURITY** and the **IMPROVEMENT** and complete the construction thereof, **BORROWER** hereby giving to **LENDER** full power and authority to make such entry and to enter into such contracts or arrangements as may be necessary to complete the construction of the **IMPROVEMENT**. If **LENDER** does not enter upon the **SECURITY** and undertakes the completion of construction of the **IMPROVEMENT**, **LENDER** shall be entitled to have any funds then on deposit with the **AGENT** or in the account of **BORROWER** maintained with **LENDER** disbursed to it or, under its direction, disbursed in the payment of bills theretofore or thereafter contracted in connection with the construction of the **IMPROVEMENT**. In addition, **LENDER** may, at its option, expend money in completing the construction of the **IMPROVEMENT** which shall be over and above the amount of the **NOTE**; and, any such monies, when so expended, shall be added to the principal of the **LOAN** and the same, together with interest thereon at the rate specified in the **NOTE**, shall be secured by the lien of the **DEED**.

The said remedies and rights of **LENDER** shall be cumulative and not mutually exclusive. **LENDER** shall have the absolute right to resort to any one, or more, or all, of said remedies, neither to the limited exclusion of the other.

Further, in the event of any such default or breach of this Agreement, the **NOTE** or **DEED** by **BORROWER**, **LENDER** shall have the absolute right to refuse to disburse the balance of the **LOAN** funds, as aforesaid, and no other party, whether contractor, materialmen, laborer, subcontractor, or supplier, shall have any interest in **LOAN** funds so applied and, further, shall not have any right to garnish, require, or compel payment thereof to be applied toward discharge or satisfaction of any claim or lien which they or any of them have, or may have, for work performed or materials supplied for the development and/or construction work. Any additional funds advanced by **LENDER** to complete development and/or construction shall be secured by the lien of said **DEED** and considered a part of the **LOAN** as though initially included therein.

23. **ASSIGNMENT OF PLANS AND SPECIFICATIONS:** In the event **BORROWER** fails to construct and complete the **IMPROVEMENT** in accordance with the terms and provisions of this Agreement, **BORROWER** hereby assigns to **LENDER** the right to possess and use the architectural plans and specifications and engineering drawings for the purpose of completing the **IMPROVEMENT**.

ARCHITECT and **ENGINEER** shall agree to continue his or their services on behalf of **LENDER** in such an event and if so requested, and shall further agree that **LENDER** shall, without cost, be entitled to use all plans, specifications, and drawings with all modifications thereof, prepared for use in the construction of the **IMPROVEMENT** and the Contractor shall agree to continue its services for **LENDER**, pursuant to its agreement with **BORROWER**.

24. **UNLIMITED ACCESS TO PROPERTY:** Until the **LOAN** has been repaid in full, **LENDER**, **ARCHITECT** and/or **AGENT** and their agents shall, at all reasonable times, have the right of entry and free access to the **SECURITY** and the right to inspect all work done, labor performed, and material furnished on, or about, the **SECURITY**.

25. **WAIVER OF DEFAULTS:** The waiver by **LENDER** of any breach or default by **BORROWER** under any of the terms of the **NOTE**, **DEED** or this Agreement, shall not be deemed, nor shall the same constitute, a waiver of any subsequent breach or default on the part of **BORROWER**.

26. **LENDER'S RIGHT TO APPEAR IN LITIGATION:** **LENDER** shall have the right to commence, to appear in, or to defend any action or preceding purporting to affect the rights or duties of the parties hereunder and, in connection therewith, to pay out of the **LOAN** all necessary expenses and reasonable attorney's fees. **BORROWER** hereby agrees to repay all of the foregoing to **LENDER** upon demand, and all **SECURITY** given hereunder shall secure any such sums.

27. **THIS AGREEMENT PART OF DEED:** The **DEED** and other Security Agreements provided for herein shall specifically incorporate this Agreement by reference and, in the event that the same and the **NOTE** are duly assigned, this Agreement shall be considered assigned in like manner. In the event of a conflict between any of the provisions of the **NOTE**, **DEED**, or this Agreement, then the provisions of this Agreement shall control. A breach or default by **BORROWER** of any term or condition of this Agreement shall constitute a default under the **NOTE** and **DEED**.

ML23 (4/88)

—6—

(continued)

EXHIBIT 18-1 *(Continued)*

Building Loan Agreement

28. **EXCLUSIVE OF AGREEMENT:** This Agreement, and the **NOTE** and **DEED** are made for the sole protection of **BORROWER**, **LENDER**, and **LENDER'S** successors and assigns, and no other person or entity shall have any right of action pursuant to, or because of, any of the terms hereof.

29. **CONDEMNATION:** All of the right, title, and interest which **BORROWER** and its successors or assigns have, or shall have, to any award or awards as a result of the taking of, or damage to, the **SECURITY** or any part thereof, including any award or awards for any change or changes of grade or route of streets affecting said **SECURITY**, by reason of condemnation proceedings under the power of eminent domain, is hereby assigned to **LENDER** to be applied to the indebtedness secured by the **DEED**. **LENDER** is hereby authorized, directed, and empowered, at its option, to collect and receive the proceeds of all awards from the authorities making same and to give proper receipts and acquittances therefore and to apply the same toward the payment of the amount owing on account of the **NOTE** and **DEED**, notwithstanding the fact that such amount may not then be due and payable. **BORROWER** agrees to make, execute and deliver any and all assignments and other instruments sufficient for the purpose of assigning the aforesaid awards to the holder of the **NOTE** and **DEED** free, clear and discharged of any and all encumbrances of any kind or nature whatsoever. Any sums received by **LENDER** pursuant to the terms of this Paragraph in excess of the sum of the outstanding amount owed by **BORROWER** to **LENDER**, and the additional interests, if any, shall be remitted to **BORROWER**.

30. **NOTICE TO PARTIES:** All notices provided for herein shall be mailed by Certified or Registered Mail—Return Receipt Request—addressed to the appropriate party as follows:

BORROWER:

LENDER:

or such other address as the party who is to receive such notice may designate in writing. Notice shall be completed by depositing the same in a letter box or other means provided by the United States Post Office for the posting of mail and shall have the proper amount of postage affixed thereto. Actual receipt of notice shall not be required to affect notice hereunder.

31. **LOAN FUND:** **LENDER** shall not be required to segregate the **LOAN** funds or to earmark such funds in any manner. The sole obligation of **LENDER** shall be to disburse the funds as set forth herein, provided there exists no default under this Agreement, the **NOTE** or **DEED** at the time of any request for disbursement.

32. **NON-ASSIGNABLE BY BORROWER:** **BORROWER** shall not assign this Agreement or any part of any advance to be made hereunder, nor convey, nor encumber the **SECURITY** by mortgage or other lien, without the prior written consent of **LENDER**. Any Assignment, conveyance or encumbrance made without such consent of **LENDER** shall constitute an immediate default under this Agreement, the **NOTE** and **MORTGAGE**. Consent of **LENDER** hereunder shall not be unreasonably withheld.

33. **LENDER'S RIGHT TO ASSIGN:** The rights of **LENDER** under this Agreement are assignable, wholly or in part, and any assignee of **LENDER** shall succeed to and be possessed of the rights of **LENDER** hereunder to the extent of any such assignment, including the right to make advances to **BORROWER** or any approved assignee of **BORROWER** in accordance with this Agreement.

34. **BROKER'S COMMISSIONS:** **LENDER** shall be furnished with a statement in writing signed by **BORROWER**, fully disclosing all fees and commissions paid or to be paid to any licensed mortgage broker or other in connection with the obtaining of the **LOAN**, including an affirmative statement indemnifying and holding **LENDER** harmless from any and all claims for any such fees and commissions.

35. **CLOSING COSTS:** All expenses incurred in connection with the making, closing, servicing and/or modification of the **LOAN** shall be paid by **BORROWER**, including, but not limited to, charges for title examination and title insurance, recording and filing fees, mortgage and documentary taxes, all other applicable excise and intangible property taxes and fees of all appraisers, architects, attorneys, engineers, escrow agents and surveyors incurred in connection with the **LOAN**. Where there are funds provided in the **LOAN** for the payment of any of the foregoing costs, fees, expenses or other charges, **LENDER** is hereby authorized to disburse those funds directly in payment thereof.

Any fees and expenses of **LENDER** paid at the time of closing by **BORROWER** are for services rendered and expenses incurred to date of closing only.

36. **NO AGENCY RELATIONSHIP:** **BORROWER** understands and agrees that **LENDER** is not the agent or representative of **BORROWER**, and this Agreement shall not be construed to make **LENDER** liable to materialmen, contractors, craftsmen, laborers, or others for goods delivered to or services performed by them upon the **SECURITY**, or for debts or claims accruing to said parties against **BORROWER**, and it is further understood and agreed that there is not a contractual relationship, either expressed or implied, between **LENDER** and any materialmen, subcontractors, craftsmen, laborers or any other person supplying any work, labor, or materials for the **IMPROVEMENT** of the **SECURITY**.

37. **HAZARDOUS WASTE:** Neither the **BORROWER** nor, to the best knowledge of the **BORROWER**, any other person has ever caused or permitted any Hazardous Material to be placed, held, located or disposed of on, under or at the Premises or the Land or any part thereof or into the atmosphere or any watercourse, body of water or wetlands or any other real property legally or beneficially owned (or any interest or estate in which is owned) by the **BORROWER** (including, without limitation, any property owned by a land trust the beneficial interest in which is owned, in whole or in part, by the **BORROWER**), and neither the Premises, the Land, any part of either thereof, nor any other real property legally or beneficially owned (or any interest or estate in which is owned) by the **BORROWER** (including, without limitation, any property owned by a land trust the beneficial interest in which is owned, in whole or in part, by the **BORROWER**) has ever been used (whether by the **BORROWER** or, to the best knowledge of the **BORROWER**, by any other person) as a treatment, storage or disposal (whether permanent or temporary) site for any Hazardous Material. For purposes of this Agreement, ''Hazardous Material'' means and includes any hazardous substance or any pollutant or contaminant defined as such in (or for purposes of) the Comprehensive Environmental Response, Compensation, and Liability Act, any so-called ''Superfund'' or ''Superlien'' law, the Toxic Substances Control Act, or any other Federal, state or local statute, law, ordinance, code, rule, regulation, order or decree regulating, relating to, or imposing liability or standards of conduct concerning, any hazardous, toxic or dangerous waste, substance or material, as now or at any time hereafter in effect, asbestos or any substance or compound containing asbestos, or any other hazardous, toxic or dangerous, waste, substance or material.

BORROWER hereby indemnifies the **LENDER** and agrees to hold the **LENDER** harmless from and against any and all losses, liabilities, damages, injuries, costs, expenses and claims of any and every kind whatsoever, including reasonable attorney's fees, paid, incurred or suffered by, or asserted against, the **LENDER** for, with respect to, or as a direct or indirect result of, the presence on or under, or the escape, seepage, leakage, spillage, discharge, emission, discharging or release from, the Premises or into or upon the land, the atmosphere, or any watercourse, body of water or wetland or any Hazardous Material (including, without limitation, any losses, liabilities,

Building Loan Agreement

damages, injuries, costs, expenses or claims asserted or arising under the Comprehensive Environmental Response, Compensation and Liability Act, any so-called ''Superfund'' or ''Superlien'' law, or any other Federal, state or local statute, law, ordinance, code, rule, regulation, order or decree regulating, relating to or imposing liability or standards of conduct concerning any Hazardous Material.

38.   WAIVER OF JURY TRIAL: BORROWER hereby expressly waives any right to trial by jury in any action or proceeding to enforce any right under this Agreement, the Promissory Notes or Deeds of Trust, or under any amendment, instrument, document, or other Note(s) delivered (or which may in the future be delivered) in connection herewith or arising from any banking relationship existing in connection with this Agreement. BORROWER agrees that any such action or proceedings shall not be tried before a jury. To the extent permitted by law, any dispute by and between the parties shall be resolved by arbitration. Any arbitration for which provision is made herein shall be conducted in accordance with the Uniform Arbitration Act, as provided in the Nevada Revised Statutes, 38.015 et seq, as it may be amended from time to time. The fees and expenses of the arbitrator(s) shall be divided equally between the parties. LENDER and BORROWER shall each bear their own expenses (including, but not necessarily limited to, attorney's fees and expenses of witnesses) in any arbitration proceedings. The arbitration proceedings shall be held in the County of   , State of   . Judgment upon the award rendered by the arbitrator(s) may be entered in any court having jurisdiction thereof.

_____ (initials)   _____ (initials)

39.   MISCELLANEOUS PROVISIONS: All inspections and other services rendered by, or on behalf of, **LENDER**, whether or not paid for by **BORROWER** or its successors in title, shall be rendered solely for the protection and the benefit of **LENDER**. **BORROWER** or its successors in interest, shall not be entitled to claim any loss or damage against **LENDER**, or against its agents or employees for failure to properly discharge their duties to **LENDER**.

This Agreement, the **NOTE** and **DEED**, are executed and delivered in the State of   The laws of the State of Nevada shall govern in the interpretation, enforcement and all other aspects of the obligations and duties created under this **LOAN**.

BORROWER and **LENDER** agree that, by mutual consent evidenced by a written instrument, this Agreement, **NOTE** and **DEED**, from time to time, may be extended or renewed in whole or in part or the rate of interest thereon may be changed or fees in consideration of **LOAN** extensions imposed. Any related right to security therefore waived, exchanged, surrendered or otherwise dealt with any of the acts mentioned in the **NOTE** may be done, all without affecting, limiting, or negating the liability of the **BORROWER** and all other obligors, endorsers, and guarantors under this Agreement, the **NOTE** and **DEED**.

The release of any party liable upon the **NOTE** shall not release any other such party who may be liable. **BORROWER** hereby waives presentment, demand of payment, protest and notice of non-payment and protest, and any and all other notices and demands whatsoever except as may be elsewhere provided herein.

Nothing contained in this Agreement, the **NOTE** and **DEED** shall impose upon **LENDER** any obligation to see to the proper application of any disbursements and advances of funds made pursuant to this **LOAN**.

No provisions of this Agreement shall be amended, waived, or modified except by an instrument in writing signed by the parties hereto.

All covenants, agreements, representations and warranties made herein and in documents delivered in support of the **LOAN** request shall be deemed to have been material and relied on by **LENDER** and shall survive the execution and delivery to **LENDER** of the **NOTE** and **DEED** hereunder and the disbursements and advances of funds made pursuant to this **LOAN**. Title Instructions, attached hereto, identify, but are not an exclusive list of, such documents.

All sections and descriptive headings of paragraphs in this Agreement are inserted for convenience only and shall not affect the construction or interpretation hereof.

This Agreement may be executed in any number of counterparts, each of which, when executed and delivered, shall be an original; but such counterparts shall, together, constitute one and the same instrument.

If any provision of this Agreement, **NOTE** or **DEED** is deemed unenforceable or illegal by a court competent to so rule, then the offending words will be stricken and all remaining provisions shall remain in full force and effect.

40.   LOAN PROCEEDS LIMITATION: **BORROWER** shall, under no circumstances, use any of the **LOAN** proceeds disbursed by **LENDER** hereunder for the payment of any item, purchase, or obligation not directly connected with the **IMPROVEMENT** being financed under this **LOAN** program or shown on the Cost Breakdown. All **LOAN** proceeds are to be utilized solely in connection with the **IMPROVEMENT** and for no other purpose as shown on the Cost Breakdown and the letter of commitment.

41.   PREPAYMENT: **BORROWER** shall have the right to prepay without penalty the monies provided for under the terms and conditions of this Agreement and the **NOTE** and **DEED**.

42.   The use of the masculine form shall be inclusive of the feminine form and the singular inclusive of the plural.

43.   ATTORNEY'S FEES: **LENDER** shall be entitled to recover attorney's fees, cost and expenses should lawsuit be instituted to enforce this Agreement.

BORROWER

By_____

CO-BORROWER   **LENDER**

By_____   By_____

STATE OF   **STATE OF**

                              ss: ss:
COUNTY OF   **COUNTY OF**
  On   , 19   ,   On   , 19   ,
before me, the undersigned Notary Public in and for said County   before me, the undersigned Notary Public in and for said County
and State, personally appeared   and State, personally appeared

                                          ,   ,
proven to me on the basis of satisfactory evidence to be the person   proven to me on the basis of satisfactory evidence to be the person
                          who executed the within   who executed the within
instrument on behalf of the   instrument on behalf of the
therein named, and acknowledged to me that such   therein named, and acknowledged to me that such

executed the within instrument pursuant to its   executed the within instrument pursuant to its

_____   _____
          NOTARY PUBLIC   **NOTARY PUBLIC**

CHAPTER **19**

Permanent Financing of Commercial Real Estate Properties

LEARNING OBJECTIVES

By now you have solid information about the principles of real estate finance. Many of the concepts that you have learned can be applied to standard long-term commercial real estate finance. Therefore, after reading this chapter, you should be able to show how such concepts as agency problems, interest rate risk, and leverage apply to permanent commercial property financing. In addition, you should be able to indicate the differences between permanent commercial property finance covered in this chapter and residential or acquisition, development, and construction finance covered in earlier chapters. Specifically, you should know the terms and conditions that are standard to and characteristic of long-term, fixed-rate financing of commercial properties.

After reading this chapter, you also should understand how equity participation loans are structured and what the benefits of such loans are to property investors and lenders. You should understand the arguments on each side of the issue of the lease-versus-own decision. In this regard, you should understand what factors influence an owner of commercial real estate to sell the property and lease it back from the new owner. Finally, you should know the mechanics of a sale-leaseback and the accounting rules that govern the reporting of such transactions on the seller's financial statements.

INTRODUCTION

In this chapter, we discuss the permanent financing of commercial real estate properties. By permanent financing, we mean long-term financing of existing operating properties. Financing commercial real estate ownership refers simply to the alternative of all-equity ownership. First, we consider a standard, long-term, fixed-rate loan. This type of loan is very similar to a standard, fixed-rate, residential loan. Some differences would include a provision for a prepayment penalty and more vigorous underwriting for a given loan-to-value ratio. Next, we look at two variations in long-term financing. One variation is referred to as the equity participating loan, so called because, by its terms, the lender shares in the income or cash flows from the property. Then we look at leasing as an alternative to ownership and as a means of financing. In particular, we investigate the economics of and accounting for sale-leaseback transactions.

LONG-TERM, FIXED-RATE LOANS

A long-term, fixed-rate loan is a common instrument with which to finance a commercial real estate property. Most of these loans are originated by financial institutions such as commercial banks and life insurance companies. Pension funds also purchase some of these loans, and there exists some collateralization in the secondary mortgage market. These loans are very similar to long-term, fixed-rate loans on residential properties, with several exceptions.

First, long-term commercial loans involve a more intricate underwriting process. With a residential loan, the value of the property is determined primarily with reference to sales of comparable properties. While this method also is used to appraise commercial properties, underwriting here relies more heavily on the income capitalization approach. For commercial properties, the lender is very concerned with the value of the collateral, as determined by its income-earning capacity. Lenders realize that changes in the marketplace, including competition from newly added properties, can quickly alter the earnings picture of existing properties. For this reason, lenders are cautious with these types of loans, in the sense that they generally lend a smaller portion of the value. While residential properties may have loan-to-value ratios of 90 to 95 percent, commercial properties may carry loan-to-value ratios in the neighborhood of 60 to 70 percent. Despite the generally lower loan-to-value ratios on commercial properties, changing market conditions can cause great swings in property values. Many lenders suffered losses on their commercial property loans when regional economies suffered in the 1980s. Also in this regard, there is less reliance on mortgage insurance in the commercial loan market than in the residential loan arena.

A second major difference between long-term commercial and residential loans is the exposure to interest rate risk. You saw earlier that residential mortgages involve substantial interest rate risk because of the option granted to the borrower to prepay the loan in the event that interest rates drop subsequent to origination. This option is associated with residential mortgages because of the lack of **prepayment penalties.** This is not the case for commercial loans. Most long-term loans on commercial properties have prepayment penalties. Furthermore, prepayment penalties are usually set at an amount related to the spread between the market rate and the contract rate. The larger the spread between the market rate and the contract rate, the larger the prepayment penalty on a commercial loan. A properly constructed prepayment penalty will eliminate the value of the refinancing option, regardless of the spread between the rates. It is called a **yield maintenance prepayment penalty.**

A third difference between residential and commercial loans relates to the nature of the collateral. Since the lender has a security interest in a commercial property, there will likely be an **assignment of rents clause** in the note. This clause allows the lender to step in and collect lease payments directly from the tenants in the event the borrower defaults (becomes delinquent) on the loan.

ALTERNATIVES TO STANDARD LONG-TERM, FIXED-RATE LOANS

There are two popular alternatives to the standard, fixed-rate commercial loans discussed above: equity-participation loans and sale-leaseback agreements.

Equity-participation Loans

Equity-participation, or equity "kicker," loans have become a popular method for financing commercial properties. Often they are referred to simply as participation loans. However, you should be aware that the term *participation loan* may have another meaning. The term may refer to a situation where more than one financial institution agrees to participate in a loan by each advancing a portion of the total loan amount. The loan may be a regular, long-term, fixed-rate loan, for example. Here, however, a participation loan refers to the participation in the income of the property by a sole lender—thus, the term equity participation. With an equity-participation loan, the lender offers a lower interest rate on the loan in return for a share of the income from the property and/or a share of the appreciation of the property. In most cases, the share of the income is a portion that exceeds a specified minimum amount. Essentially, a portion of the loan can be viewed as an equity interest in the property, because of the nature of equity as a claim on residual income. With an equity-participation loan, the lender has a claim to a portion of the income if it exceeds a certain amount—that is, a residual amount.

Basic Principles

Before we present an example of an equity-participation loan, it will be useful to consider some basic principles of such an arrangement. First, the arrangement represents a tradeoff between the owner/borrower and the lender. The lender gives up some interest for a right to share in a residual. The owner gives up some of the rights to income for a reduction in the interest rate. In one respect, it is difficult to see how the arrangement can create new value. One would expect that in an efficient market, with full knowledge of the expected cash flows by each party, the tradeoff would be priced appropriately. That is, under the "no free lunch" theory, neither party could gain or lose at the expense of the other. Or, the value of the property would be determined by its expected cash flows, and the riskiness of those cash flows, and not how those cash flows would be divided between the investor and the lender.

Second, there appears to be no value creation from a tax savings. If the loan arrangement is structured properly, the share of income paid to the lender qualifies as an interest deduction for the borrower. In other words, the borrower obtains a lower interest payment on the loan in return for a portion of the income, both of which are deductible for tax purposes.

Third, given that the parties to the tradeoff will attempt to determine the terms of the loan, there are certain considerations that they will use to do so. In a participating loan, the lender is exposed to an increase in risk (over a standard loan) of the payment stream. The lender gives up a portion of the interest payments associated with a conventional loan for a residual interest in the income from the property. Essentially, the lender advances funds (for the purchase of the property) that are part debt and part equity. For a conventional loan, the lender would discount the interest payments by the contractual interest rate to arrive at the present value of the payment stream. Once the payment stream includes a participation in the income of the property, the risk is increased. So, the discount rate necessary to value the payment stream will be greater than that on an interest-only loan. Even though the lender's risk is increased by the share in the equity position, the standard arrangement calls for the lender to share in the positive cash flows. While risk is increased, it is nonetheless limited.

Likewise, the risk to the owner is reduced by the participation agreement. In return for a portion of the income, the borrower receives a lower interest obligation. For a loan of a given size, the debt-coverage ratio will increase and the probability of insolvency and default will be reduced. Therefore, the discount rate used to value the cash flows to equity will be lower by virtue of the participation agreement. In short, an equity-participation agreement increases the total equity component and reduces the debt component of financing. But, the larger equity component is shared by the owner and the lender. The result increases the risk position of the lender and decreases the risk position of the property owner. Commensurate changes in their respective discount rates used to value their expected cash flows are justified.

These considerations taken together imply that the tradeoff in the terms of participation should be priced efficiently and that the discount rates used by the lender and owner should reflect the value of the tradeoff. In an efficient market, it is difficult to imagine how the agreement can increase value to both parties.

The Popular View of Equity-participation Loans

You should understand that some suggestions presented in the popular finance literature point out the advantages of equity-participation agreements for the borrower. None of them address the question of the efficient pricing of the terms of the loans, however. Nonetheless, they bear repeating here. One argument indicates that borrowers benefit because they give up a portion of the equity without giving up ownership of the property. This gives the borrower control over the property and the right to the depreciation write-off (although the depreciation write-off may be less valuable in light of the passive loss limitations on real estate investments). Also, the agreement will lower the debt service costs and reduce the break-even point. The cost of reducing the break-even point is the share of the profits and property appreciation that is traded to the lender. Another advantage mentioned is the increase in leverage. Since the owner shares a portion of the equity, the equity base is lower than would occur otherwise, leading to the increase in leverage.

None of these so-called advantages addresses the question of any increase in value for the borrower. Logically, knowledgeable lenders should extract the value of the lower interest payment in terms of the share of profits and property appreciation such that, when efficiently priced, the borrower would be neither better nor worse off under the participation agreement. After we present an example of an equity-participation loan, we suggest one reason why these loans exist and how value can be created by the agreement.

Equity-participation Loan Example

Next, we explore the nature of the tradeoff of terms of an equity-participation loan through an example of a familiar, standard loan discussed earlier in the text. Consider a long-term (30 years), fixed-rate (12 percent) loan for approximately 70 percent of the value of the property. Data on the operating revenues and expenses, as well as the growth rates in key variables of this example, are shown in Table 19–1. Table 19–2 shows the before- and after-tax cash flows for a 5-year holding period. The property has positive income each year, so there are no passive losses to be suspended. The debt ratio (NOI/payment) rises from 1.66 in year one to 2.28 in year five. Table 19–3 shows the cash flows from reversion (sale) of the property at the end of the fifth year. Finally, Table 19–4 pulls the example together and summarizes the cash flows and net present value of the equity position of the investor. Assuming a discount rate of 15 percent, the net present value of the equity position is $492,675. The cash flows to the lender are not shown. Be aware, though, that assuming the lender charges a rate reflective of the risk of the loan, then the net present value would, of course, be zero, and the internal rate-of-return would be the loan contract rate, 12 percent.

Now, let's consider an equity-participation loan. Note that we have constructed the following participation loan to demonstrate a point. We purposely have chosen the terms of the tradeoff and the discount rates to show no increase in value to either the investor (borrower) or the lender. Table 19–5 shows the terms of the participating mortgage. Several items should be noted. First, the interest rate on the loan is 10 percent, less than the 12 percent rate on the standard loan. The loan amount remains the same in this example. Next, note the terms of the participation. In this example, the lender receives the right to 15 percent of any net operating income over $280,000, and 10 percent of the appreciation in the value of the property. The appreciation in the value of the property will be measured as the difference between the gross selling price in year five and the current value ($2.8 million). Both participation amounts are deductible for tax purposes.

TABLE 19–1
Analysis of Commercial Real Estate Project

Project Cost:		
Land	$300,000	
Building	$2,500,000	
Total	$2,800,000	
Project Financing:		
Loan amount	$2,000,000	
Interest rate	12%	
Amortization period	30 years	
Initial-equity investment	$800,000	
Gross Rent:		
[Year one]	$522,100	
Vacancy Rate	5%	
Operating Expense:		
Year one	$83,536	(16% of gross revenue)
Growth Rates:		
Gross rent	8%	
Operating expense	7%	
Resale price	6%	
Resale Expense Rate	5%	
Investor's Marginal Tax Rate	28%	

TABLE 19-2

Cash Flows from Operations

Before-tax Cash Flows					
	Year 1	*Year 2*	*Year 3*	*Year 4*	*Year 5*
Gross Rent	$522,100	$563,868	$608,977	$657,696	$710,311
Vacancy	26,105	28,193	30,449	32,885	35,516
Effective gross income	495,995	535,675	578,529	624,811	674,796
Operating expense	83,536	89,384	95,640	102,335	109,499
NOI	412,459	446,291	482,888	522,476	565,297
Mortgage payment	248,287	248,287	248,287	248,287	248,287
Before-tax cash flow	164,172	198,004	234,601	274,188	317,010
Debt coverage ratio	1.66	1.80	1.94	2.10	2.28

After-tax Cash Flows					
	Year 1	*Year 2*	*Year 3*	*Year 4*	*Year 5*
NOI	$412,459	$446,291	$482,888	$522,476	$565,297
Depreciation	87,000	91,000	91,000	91,000	87,000
Interest	240,000	239,006	287,892	236,644	235,247
Taxable income	85,459	116,286	153,996	194,831	243,050
Loss carry forward	0	0	0	0	0
Net carry forward	0	0	0	0	0
Net taxable income	85,459	116,286	153,996	194,831	243,050
Tax due	23,929	32,560	43,119	54,523	68,054
Before-tax cash flow	164,172	198,004	234,601	274,188	317,010
After-tax cash flow	140,243	165,444	191,482	219,636	248,956

TABLE 19-3

Cash Flows from Sale of Property, Year 5

Sale price	$3,747,032
Less sales expense	187,352
Less mortgage balance	1,947,352
Less tax	263,660[a]
	$1,348,668

[a]Tax rate = 0.2185 = (0.37)(0.25) + (0.63)(0.20). Total gain = 1,206,680 of which 447,000 (37%) is depreciation recapture. Adjusted basis = 2,353,000.

TABLE 19-4

Present Value and Yield Calculations

	Year 1	Year 2	Year 3	Year 4	Year 5
Cash flows	$140,243	$165,444	$191,482	$219,636	1,597,624
Discount rate: 15%					
Net present value: $492,675					
IRR, 30%					

There is an infinite combination and variety of participation terms that can be arranged. In addition to alternative percentages, the participation terms can specify a proportion of either cash flows or net income. Also, the terms of the equity participation loan may indicate that the participation in income begins only after a given period of time. In short, there is no limit to the design of the terms of the tradeoff in a participating loan. All will have a common theme, however. The lender will receive a right to some sort of residual in return for reducing the rate on the loan. While the investor and the lender will bargain for the best terms possible, the investor will not wish to give up participating cash flows that are significantly greater than the reduction of

TABLE 19–5

Analysis of Commercial Real Estate
Project With Lender Participation

Project cost:	
Land	$ 300,000
Building	$2,500,000
Total	$2,800,000
Project financing	
Loan amount	$2,000,000
Interest rate	10%
Amortization	30 Years
Participation terms	
Share of NOI	
Over $280,000	15%
Share of appreciation	10%
Initial equity investment	$800,000
Gross rent: Year 1	$522,100
Vacancy rate	5%
Operating expense: Year 1	$83,536
Growth rates	
Gross rent	8%
Operating expense	7%
Resale price	6%
Resale expense rate	5%
Investor's marginal tax rate	28%

interest payments. Obviously, the greater the discount in the rate on the loan, the greater the share of the cash flows that the investor will be willing to give up.

To repeat, risk as well as cash flows are shifted between the parties of the participation agreement. The investor is in a lower risk position, while the lender is in a higher risk position. This means that the investor's discount rate should fall, while that of the lender will rise.

Table 19–6 shows the before- and after-tax cash flows of the equity-participation loan. Table 19–7 shows the calculation of the after-tax cash flow from the sale of the property, including the revisionary participation. The data in Tables 19–6 and 19–7 can be used to determine the returns to the investor and the lender. Table 19–8 summarizes the present value and yield calculations for the investor and the lender. The cash flows that accrue to the investor are not significantly different from those in Table 19–4. This is so because the lender has given up a portion of the net operating income in return for a reduction in the interest expense. If one assumes that there has been a slight decrease in the investor's discount rate because of the reduction in risk (for example, from 15 percent to 14.75 percent), then the net present value of the investment is virtually the same as with a standard, fixed-rate loan.

The annual cash flows that accrue to the lender include the mortgage and participation payments. Because of the slight increase in risk, the lender's discount rate is raised (for example, from 12 percent to 12.25 percent). The result is a net present value of the loan of zero, the same as in the case of the standard loan. Thus, neither the investor nor the lender obtains an increase in value under the terms and assumptions of this participation loan. If one accepts the changes in the discount rates as reflective of the changes (sharing) of the risk of the equity to each party, then it appears as though the terms of the participation loan have been priced efficiently. In other words, given the changes in the discount rates, the tradeoff of the lower interest payments for a portion of the returns to equity leaves neither party better off.

Of course, if the changes in the discount rates do not reflect the sharing of the risk, then these results are not valid. If, for example, the lender's discount rate does not rise as much as indicated in the example, then the lender would be better off with the participating loan. If this is the case, one would expect that the lender may be in a position to offer the investor an even better participation agreement (other things being equal, a lower interest rate). Accordingly, creation of value would seem to result simply by a rearrangement of the terms of the participation loan.

TABLE 19–6

Equity Participation Loan

| | Before-tax Cash Flows | | | | |
	Year 1	Year 2	Year 3	Year 4	Year 5
Gross rent	$522,100	$563,868	$608,977	$657,696	$710,311
Vacancy	26,105	28,193	30,449	32,885	35,516
Effective gross income	495,995	535,675	578,529	624,811	674,796
Operating expense	83,536	89,384	95,640	102,335	109,499
NOI	412,459	446,291	482,888	522,476	565,297
Mortgage payment	212,158	212,158	212,158	212,158	212,158
Cash flow before participation	200,301	234,133	270,730	310,317	353,139
Participation	19,869[a]	24,944	30,433	36,371	42,795
Before-tax cash flow	180,432	209,189	240,296	273,946	310,344
Debt coverage ratio	1.94	2.10	2.28	2.46	2.66

| | After-tax Cash Flows | | | | |
	Year 1	Year 2	Year 3	Year 4	Year 5
NOI	$412,459	$446,291	$482,888	$522,476	$565,297
Depreciation	87,000	91,000	91,000	91,000	87,000
Interest	200,000	198,784	197,447	195,976	194,357
Participation	19,869	24,944	30,433	36,371	42,795
Taxable income	105,590	131,563	164,008	199,129	241,145
Loss carried forward	0	0	0	0	0
Net carry forward	0	0	0	0	0
Net taxable income	105,590	131,563	164,008	199,129	241,145
Tax due	29,569	36,838	45,922	55,756	67,521
Before-tax cash flow	180,432	209,189	240,296	273,946	310,344
After-tax cash flow	150,866	172,351	194,374	218,190	242,823

[a][$412,459 − $280,000] × 0.15

TABLE 19–7

Sale of Property: Year 5

Sale price	$3,747,032
Less sales expense	187,352
Less mortgage balance	1,925,771
Less participation	94,703[a]
Less tax	244,635[b]
	$1,294,571

[a]10% × ($3,747,032 − $2,800,000)
[b]22% × ($3,747,032 − $187,352 − $94,703 − $2,353,000).
Depreciation recapture is 40 percent of total gain.

We suggest that this may be the case for lenders that do not experience a significant increase in the required discount rate as a result of the equity-participation agreement. A couple of reasons may account for this result. First, the lender may not perceive the participation loan as more risky than a standard loan because of its hedging qualities. If the lender has a particular need to hedge against inflation risk and views real estate as a particularly useful investment for this purpose, then the equity-participation loan may appear to offer no additional risk. Indeed, it may offer risk-reduction benefits because of the inflation-hedging qualities of this type of loan. Second, some lenders may not view a participation loan as more risky because they may, at the time, have negative net worth. This concept was discussed earlier in the text as it relates to thrifts. A thrift with a negative net worth (yet operating with the

T A B L E   1 9 – 8

Present Values and Yield Calculations

	Year 1	Year 2	Year 3	Year 4	Year 5
Owner					
Cash flows	$150,866	$172,351	$194,374	$218,190	$1,537,394
Discount rate, 14.75%					
Net present value	$489,566				
IRR, 29.87%					
	Year 1	Year 2	Year 3	Year 4	Year 5
Lender					
Cash flows	$232,027[a]	$237,102	$242,592	$248,530	$2,275,427[b]
Discount rate, 12.25%					
Net present value, $0					
IRR, 12.25%					

[a]$212,158 + $19,869
[b]$212,158 + 1,925,771 + 94,703 + 42,795

grace of the regulators) has an incentive to take on risky investments. If the investments fail, the thrift is in no worse position, and if the investments succeed, the thrift may extricate itself from insolvency.

During the mid- to late 1980s many thrifts entered into participation loan arrangements. In those sections of the country that experienced falling real estate values in the late 1980s and early 1990s, the gamble by thrifts was unsuccessful, and their losses were much greater than they would have been had they not sought out the equity-participation loans.

The key is that there may be reasons why a participating loan for a lender does not warrant a significant (or any) increase in the discount rate used to value the loan. If this is the case, then the risk-sharing created by an equity-participation loan can be beneficial to both parties.

While we have considered only one example of an equity-participation loan, you should realize that there is a virtually limitless number of combinations of terms that can characterize this type of loan. For each combination, the investor and the lender must estimate the value of the arrangement and agree to a tradeoff that makes at least one party better off and no party worse off than with a traditional, fixed-rate loan.

Lease Versus Own Analysis

An alternative to owning for the real estate investor who needs to occupy space is to lease the property. If the property is purchased, the investor would most likely incur debt to pay the purchase price and would have to make the down payment. In this case, the interest paid on the debt would be tax deductible. Additionally, the investor could depreciate the property and would receive any price appreciation. On the other hand, by leasing the property, the investor avoids having to make a down payment, avoids the expense of incurring debt, and can fully tax deduct the lease payments. However, the investor does not enjoy any price appreciation which may accrue to the property. The preferable option depends on the after-tax return and risk of each alternative. There are certain cautions to consider. For example, if the lease payments are not reasonable and an option to purchase is allowed, the IRS may consider the lease to actually be a financing arrangement.

EXAMPLE

Suppose that Mr. Max A. Million, a small businessman, needs to occupy office space for 5 years. He is considering buying an office building but that would also entail buying equipment and furniture, incurring acquisition costs to make the purchase, and paying financing costs to acquire the mortgage. His thoughts turn to leasing.

Mr. Million has found a building for sale that suits his needs. The purchase price is $225,000 of which $180,000 is the building value and $45,000 is the value of the land. He can purchase the building with a $175,000 interest-only mortgage at a rate of 10 percent. The loan would be due and payable at the end of year five. Mr. Million expects to sell the property at the end of year five for $280,000. He is in a 28 percent marginal tax bracket and requires a 12 percent equity return.

Alternatively, Mr. Million can lease this same building for 5 years at $20,000 per year. In either case, there will be no cash inflow (since it is owner-occupied) and Mr. Million will pay property taxes, insurance, and maintenance. Thus, interest and depreciation are the only factors if he buys the property and the lease payment is the only factor to be considered if he leases.

Table 19–9 shows the after-tax cash flows from owning the property. This produces a net present value of −$40,718. Alternatively, Table 19–10 gives the after-tax cash flows from leasing the same property and the net present value is −$51,909. In this case, the least cost alternative is to own the property. At a lease payment of $15,688, Mr. Million would be indifferent between the two options. In this case, the two alternatives would have the same net present value. At any lease payment less than $15,688, he would prefer to lease the property. ▪ ▪

Leases and Sale-leaseback Agreements

Consider an all-equity owner (individual or corporation) of a commercial property that is fully depreciated. The owner wants to finance the property because she has an immediate need for cash. There are two alternatives, outlined in Table 19–11, that may accomplish this task. As you can see, the two alternatives are essentially identical. One alternative is to take out a loan on the property. The other, **a sale-leaseback,** is to sell the property and lease it from the new owner with an option to repurchase. In either case, the current owner will retain use of the facility.

In our example, the value of the property is $10 million. If the owner obtains a loan for 80 percent of its value ($8 million) at 10 percent for 20 years, the annual (interest-only) payments will be $800,000. With an interest-only loan, the balance at the end of 20 years will be $8 million. On the other hand, the owner can sell the property for $8 million and enter into a 20-year lease with annual payments of $800,000. The sale-leaseback arrangement also will provide that

T A B L E 1 9 – 9
After-tax Cash Flow from Owning the Property

	Year					
	0	*1*	*2*	*3*	*4*	*5*
Net operating income	–	0	0	0	0	0
− Mortgage payment	–	− 17500	− 17500	− 17500	− 17500	− 17500
= Before-tax cash flow	–	− 17500	− 17500	− 17500	− 17500	− 17500
− Taxes	–	+ 6138	+ 6192	+ 6192	+ 6192	+ 6138
= After-tax cash flow	− $50,000	− 11362	− 11308	− 11308	− 11308	− 11308
After-tax equity reversion						88335

NPV at 12% − $40,718
ATER = Sales price   280,000
          − Mortgage balance   − 175,000
          − Tax   − 16,665
          = After-tax equity reversion   = 88,335
TX   = Sales price   280,000
          − Adjusted basis   − 202,309
          = Gain   = 77,691
          × Tax rate   × 0.2145
          = Tax   = 16,665
NPV at 12% = −$40,678

Tax rate = (0.29)(0.25) + (0.71)(0.20) = 0.2145
(Depreciation recovery is 29 percent of total gain).

the seller has the right (option) to repurchase the property at the end of the lease term for $8 million. For each alternative, the cash flows are the same and the current owner is guaranteed use of the property. Interest payments and lease payments are both deductible for tax purposes. Therefore, from the standpoint of the cash flows, there is essentially no difference between the two alternatives. For this reason, leasing property can be viewed as a method of financing.

One could argue that the lease alternative is superior, since it involves the same cash flows and grants the current owner the option to purchase the property at the end of the lease term. If property values fall, the current owner will not exercise that option and is in a better position than if the property was owned. However, many sale-leaseback agreements provide that the seller guarantee a certain value of the property at the end of the lease and agree to indemnify the buyer in the event property prices fall and the option to repurchase is not exercised. To the extent such an agreement is included in the sale-leaseback, both of the alternatives are identical.

The Economics of Lease Versus Ownership of Assets

Before we look at an example of a real estate sale-leaseback agreement, it would be useful to discuss the economics of leasing versus ownership of assets in general. This will help us to focus on the issue of the advantages and disadvantages of sale-leasebacks of real estate. An argument can be made that a firm should never lease an asset that it anticipates using for a long period of time. The reason is that leasing an asset requires that a separate structure be created to own the asset. This separate ownership structure requires the expenditure of resources (management, secretarial personnel, and so on), but does not affect the productivity of the asset. That is, the productivity of the asset is in no way influenced by the entity that has legal title to it. The cash flows generated by the asset are not affected by who owns it. Yet, if a separate entity is established to own the asset and lease it to the firm that uses it, some of the cash flows produced by the asset must be diverted to the resources necessary to establish that entity. If one also considers that the selling firm may have to pay tax on any appreciation in the asset, then it becomes even more uneconomical to enter into a sale-leaseback arrangement.

One may be quick to point out that one advantage of leasing rather than owning an asset is the probability that the asset may become obsolete before the end of its physical life. However, if one assumes that knowledge of the probability of obsolescence is available to all market participants, then there is still no advantage to leasing. While the risk and cost of obsolescence is shifted to the

TABLE 19–10
After-Tax Cash Flow from Leasing

	Year					
	0	1	2	3	4	5
Net operating income	–	0	0	0	0	0
– Lease	–	– 20000	– 20000	– 20000	– 20000	– 20000
– Taxes	–	+ 5600	+ 5600	+ 5600	+ 5600	+ 5600
= After-tax cash flow	0	– 14400	– 14400	– 14400	– 14400	– 14400
NPV at 12% – $51,909						

After-tax cost of lease = 20,000 $(1 - t)$ = 20,000 (0.72) = $14,400

TABLE 19–11
Comparison of Financing Methods[a]

Debt			Sale-leaseback		
Borrow	$8,000,000	Cash Inflow	Sale	$8,000,000	Cash Inflow
Interest payments	800,000	Cash Outflow	Lease payments	800,000	Cash Outflow
Repayment of loan	8,000,000	Cash Outflow	Repurchase	8,000,000	Cash Outflow

[a]Value of Property: $10,000,000

lessor, the lessor will charge for the risk in terms of the size of the lease payments. Thus, the firm that uses the asset cannot shift the risk of obsolescence to another firm without paying for it.

There are some reasonable arguments why leasing may have its advantages, however. First, leasing is advantageous if the firm expects to use only a portion of the asset (which is indivisible), or if the firm expects to use the asset for only a relatively short period of time. Ownership, by purchase and later by sale, involves transaction costs. It does not make sense to incur transaction costs in the purchase and sale of an asset if the firm intends to use the asset for a short period of time. The firm is better off leasing, even at relatively high lease payments, if it anticipates using the asset only briefly. Since firms often require use of only a portion of a real estate property, or use for only a short period of time, leasing of real estate is common. However, this argument cannot be used to justify the sale-leaseback of a property that will be used for a lengthy period of time.

Second, there is the tax argument. A firm may benefit more from leasing than from owning if the lessor can use the tax benefits from depreciation more than the property user. Thus, an owner of a real estate property that cannot use the depreciation benefits (because of no other income with which to offset passive losses) may be better off selling it to a firm that can use the depreciation writeoff and then leasing the facility from the new owner. Since the new owner of the property can use the tax benefits, the lease terms may be more favorable than the terms (interest) on a loan on the property.

Also in this regard, a property may have been fully or nearly fully depreciated on the books of the owner. A sale of the property is the only way to obtain a **"stepped-up" basis** to its current market value. Once the new book value of the property is stepped up to its market value, a larger amount of depreciation can be taken. If that depreciation is taken by the new owner, that new owner in turn can provide favorable lease terms to the seller. In this way, both parties to the sale-leaseback transaction will benefit at the expense of the Treasury.

Third, there is the **window-dressing** argument for the firm's financial statements. Consider a firm that sells a property and leases it for lease payments that are similar to interest payments it would make if it incurred debt. In such a case, the total assets on the firm's balance sheet are less, so that the return on assets will be greater. There is also less debt (mortgage) on the balance sheet. So the firm's rate-of-return on assets increases, and its debt-to-equity ratio declines if it sells and then leases back the property. In an efficient market, the window-dressing ploy may have no value. After all, financial analysts would recognize the present value of the future lease obligations as an implicit debt for the firm. Regardless of these arguments, current accounting rules prohibit these window-dressing techniques.

In short, sale-leaseback transactions that are structured to reduce taxes or improve the financial statements of the property owner may not be entirely successful in accomplishing these goals. Tax regulations state that any transaction that is designed for the express purpose of avoiding taxes can be voided by the Internal Revenue Service. And, accounting rules require that the firm's financial statements reflect the substance of a transaction and not the form.

Substance Versus Form: An Example

A perspective on the advantages and disadvantages of a sale-leaseback transaction can be gained by considering the following example. Table 19–12 shows the data on a commercial real estate property owned by a noncorporate investor. It is clear that the investor has owned the property for some time, because the book value (undepreciated) of the property is very low. The remaining annual depreciation amounts are also very low. Likewise, the amount of debt on the property is low. The low depreciation and debt levels mean that there are only small deductions from the annual net operating income for depreciation and interest expenses. For simplicity, we will assume that there is no expected growth in the revenue, expenses, net operating income, or value of the property for the next 10 years. If the investor retains the property for 10 years, then the annual cash flows will appear as in Table 19–13.

The before-tax cash flow calculations begin with the net operating income (NOI). From NOI, the mortgage payment is deducted to arrive at the before-tax cash flow. The after-tax cash flows are determined by calculating the tax charge for each year. From NOI, interest and depreciation are deducted to determine taxable income. Note that the tax charge each year is substantial, due to the low interest and depreciation expense. We will return to an analysis of the

TABLE 19–12

Property Characteristics

Original cost	$2,000,000
Book value	$60,000
Market value	$2,000,000
Debt balance	$100,000
Rate	12%
Remaining term	10 years
Payment	17,698
Investor's tax rate	28%
Annual depreciation	$6,000
Growth rates	0%

TABLE 19–13

Retention of Property

Before-tax Cash Flows						
	Year 1	Year 2	Year 3	Year 4	. . .	Year 10
Net operating income	$338,900	$338,900	$338,900	$338,900		$338,900
Mortgage payment	17,698	17,698	17,698	17,698		17,698
Cash flow	321,202	321,202	321,202	321,202		321,202

After-tax Cash Flows						
Net operating income	$338,900	$338,900	$338,900	$338,900		$338,900
Interest	12,000	11,316	10,550	9,693		1,896
Depreciation	6,000	6,000	6,000	6,000		6,000
Taxable income	320,900	321,584	322,350	323,207		331,004
Tax	89,852	90,043	90,258	90,498		92,681
Cash flow	231,350	231,158	230,944	230,703		228,521

cash flows in this table shortly. For now, let's analyze the cash flows that would result from a sale-leaseback of the property.

Terms of Sale-leaseback

For ease of comparison, assume that the investor enters into a sale with a leaseback of 10 years. The sale price is $2 million. The investor agrees to repurchase the property at the end of 10 years for the same amount. The annual lease payments are set at $275,000. You should note three things. First, after the 10-year period, the investor owns the property just as he would have had he not agreed to the sale-leaseback. Second, we assume for simplicity that there are no taxes due on the sale of the property. The annual lease payment is close to what the payment would be on a loan for $2 million for 10 years. Taken together, you can see how the sale-leaseback agreement has all of the characteristics of a loan on the property. With either a loan or the sale-leaseback, the investor owns the property after the 10-year period. With the sale-leaseback, the buyer advances $2 million to the investor, receives lease payments that behave as loan payments, and gets a return of the $2 million at the end of the 10-year period (repurchase of the property). It is for this reason that accounting rules have been developed that force property owners to treat sale-leaseback agreements on their financial statements just as if they were loan arrangements; that is, taxpayers must carry the property on the books as an asset, record the lease obligation as a liability, and treat lease payments as interest expense. Such accounting rules are discussed further below.

    Table 19–14 shows the cash flows to the investor from the sale-leaseback agreement. The seller receives $2 million from the buyer at the outset. The cash flow in year ten reflects the $2 million repurchase price. Table 19–15 compares the cash flows associated with owning the property for the next 10 years (from Table 19–13) and from a 10-year sale-leaseback agreement

(Table 19–14). In both cases, a 15 percent discount rate is used to value the cash flows. (The risks associated with ownership are not transferred with the sale-leaseback, since the seller agrees to repurchase the property at an agreed-upon price. Typically in sale-leasebacks, the owner agrees to insulate the buyer from a decline in the market value of the property.) Note that the present value of the cash flows from the sale-leaseback agreement is greater than that of the continued ownership.

The first thought is that the increase in value for the owner has come at the expense of the buyer. However, we can show that this is not the case. Table 19–16 shows the cash flows accruing to the new owner (lessor). The first year's cash flow includes the cash outflow of the purchase price, while the last year's cash flow reflects the cash inflow from the repurchase. We also have assumed that the new owner can take a larger amount of depreciation because of the higher sales price of the property. In this example, the discount rate for the new owner is lower than the rate for the original investor. Recall that the original investor has retained all of the risks of ownership, including the possibility of a decline in the property's market value. The new owner is really in the position of a lender. The present value of the cash flows discounted at (a lender's) discount rate is zero, which is to say that the lease payments replace the 12 percent loan payments of a lender. One of the factors that makes the sale-leaseback arrangement work is the larger depreciation deductions resulting from the stepped-up basis of the property.

There are a few considerations that may mitigate the value of a sale-leaseback, however. First, we have not considered the impact of any taxes due on the gain on the sale of the property. Consideration of capital gains taxes will reduce the value of the sale-leaseback. Second, the original owner may have been able to accomplish much the same result by borrowing against the property. Although it is likely the investor could not borrow as much as the sales price, any additional debt (at a 12 percent rate) may have the same impact as the sales-leaseback, since interest payments would replace lease payments and both are tax deductible. In

TABLE 19–14
Sale-leaseback Cash Flows[a]

	Year 0	Year 1	Year 2	Year 3	Year 4	Year 10
Net operating income		$ 338,900	$338,900	$338,900	$338,900	$ 338,900
Lease expense		275,000	275,000	275,000	275,000	275,000
Taxable income		63,900	63,900	63,900	63,900	63,900
Tax		17,892	17,892	17,892	17,892	17,892
Cash flow	2,000,000	46,008	46,008	46,008	46,008	(1,953,992)

[a]Sale price, $2,000,000; lease payment; $275,000

TABLE 19–15
Net Present Value: Own vs. Lease[a]

	Own				
	Year 1	Year 2	Year 3	Year 4	Year 10
Net present value = $1,156,744	$231,350	$231,158	$230,944	$230,703	$228,521

	Lease					
	Year 0	Year 1	Year 2	Year 3	Year 4	Year 10
Present value = $1,736,534	$2,000,000	$46,008	$46,008	$46,008	$46,008	$(1,953,992)

[a]Cash flow discount rate 15%

other words, the leveraging effect can occur by incurring new debt at 12 percent or by a sale-leaseback with a new owner with a similar discount rate. Next, if there is no significant increase in the amount of depreciation, one of the main elements driving this type of transaction would be missing. Our example allows for significantly more depreciation than would be allowed for under current tax regulations. In fact, the volume of sale-leasebacks has fallen since the Tax Reform Act of 1986, which lowered the depreciation allowance on commercial real estate.

Finally, if accounting rules require that sale-leasebacks be treated as debt financing on the financial statements of the original owner, the impact of window-dressing will be lost. It is instructive to look briefly at the accounting rules for sale-leasebacks and see how they often view such arrangements as alternatives to debt financing.

Leases and Accounting Regulations

The accounting treatment for leases in general, and real estate sale-leasebacks in particular, are very detailed and complicated. In establishing accounting rules, the Financial Accounting Standards Board (FASB) has attempted to cover virtually every type of sale-leaseback arrangement imaginable. It is not our purpose here to give you thorough training in the rules of real estate sale-leaseback accounting. Instead, we will provide an overview and an example or two to show the nature and intent of the accounting regulations. If you are interested in an exhaustive analysis of accounting for real estate sale-leasebacks, you may consult authoritative accounting sources for that material.[1]

Accounting for Leases in General.   Accounting standards attempt to distinguish between a normal business lease and a lease that is a substitute for debt financing. The former types of leases are termed **operating leases,** and the latter are called **capital leases.** In general, if it appears that a lease is a substitute or alternative for debt financing, the accounting rules will require that the leased property and the present value of the future lease payments be carried on the balance sheet as an asset and liability, respectively. Lease payments are accordingly treated as interest expense. A lease will be considered a capital lease if the risks and rewards of ownership are basically retained by the firm that uses the asset. Specifically, a lease is a capital lease if it meets any one of the following criteria:

1. The lease terms provide for the transfer of the ownership (title) of the property to the lessee at the end of the lease term.
2. The lease contains an option to purchase the asset at a bargain price.
3. The lease term is equal to or greater than 75 percent of the estimated economic life of the asset.
4. The present value of the minimum lease payments is equal to or greater than 90 percent of the current fair market value of the asset (less any investment tax credit retained by the lessor).

As you can see, each of these criteria establishes some sort of ownership position for the lessee.

TABLE 19–16
Cash Flows for Buyer-lessor

	Year 0	Year 1	Year 2	Year 3	Year 4 . . .	Year 10
Lease income	0	$ 275,000	$275,000	$275,000	$275,000	$ 275,000
Depreciation	0	150,000	150,000	150,000	150,000	150,000
Tax	0	35,000	35,000	35,000	35,000	35,000
Cash flow	(2,000,000)	240,000	240,000	240,000	240,000	2,240,000

Discount rate = 12%
Net present value = $0

Accounting for Real Estate Sale-leasebacks.   The primary accounting rules that govern the sale-leaseback transaction are set out in the following Statement of Financial Accounting Standards (SFAS):

1. **SFAS No. 13** Accounting for leases
2. **SFAS No. 28** Accounting for sales with leasebacks
3. **SFAS No. 66** Accounting for sale of real estate
4. **SFAS No. 98** Accounting for leases: Sale-leaseback transactions involving real estate, sales-type loans of real estate, definition of lease term, initial direct costs of direct financing leases.

The last statement, issued in May 1988, encapsulates the rules of the earlier statements for all sale-leaseback transactions involving real estate. SFAS 98 amends Paragraph 40 of SFAS 66, which previously directed the accountant to SFAS 13 for guidance in recognizing gain in sale-leaseback transactions. SFAS 13 had less stringent requirements for sale recognition than did SFAS 66. In particular, Paragraph 28 of SFAS 66 prohibits a seller from recognizing a sale in a sale-leaseback transaction, since lease payments were interpreted as a guarantee of return to the buyer. Some accountants, therefore, relied on Paragraph 40, which directed them to the more liberal rules of SFAS 13. Now, SFAS 98 clears any confusion and establishes rather strict rules before a sales-leaseback transaction can be treated as a sale.

Under SFAS 98 rules, not all sale-leaseback arrangements will be considered capital leases, however. An owner of a commercial real estate property can sell it and lease it back, yet treat the transaction as a sale. That is, the property will be removed from the balance sheet, and lease expenses will not be treated as interest expense. If this is done, then the accounting rules indicate the sale can be treated as a sale-leaseback. However, if certain very strict criteria are met, then the owner may not treat the sale-leaseback as such, but must treat the arrangement as a capital lease and retain the asset on the balance sheet, along with a liability for the lease payments. In general, to be treated as a sale-leaseback (and not as a capital lease), the arrangement must transfer the risks and rewards of ownership to the new owner. There are two very widely used features of sale-leasebacks which do not transfer risk and returns and which will prohibit accounting for the transfer as a sale. First, the seller-lessee either has an obligation or an option to repurchase the property. Often it is an obligation to repurchase the property at a given price, so as to insulate the buyer from the risk of depreciation. A right of first refusal on an offer from a third party ordinarily is not considered as an option or an obligation to repurchase the property. Second, the seller-lessee guarantees the buyer-lessor's return on the investment for either a limited or extended period of time.

Either one of these two provisions indicate that the **risks and returns of ownership** are not transferred to the buyer-lessor and, therefore, treating the transaction as a sale would not be warranted. There are several additional commonly used terms of sale-leaseback agreements that indicate that the risk and rewards of ownership are not transferred, or that, subsequent to sale, the seller-lessee has some continued involvement with the property in an ownership capacity. A third term is that the seller-lessee is required to compensate the buyer-lessor for a decline in the fair market value of the property at the end of the lease term (except for a decline resulting from normal wear and tear). Fourth, the seller-lessee provides nonrecourse financing for all or a portion of the sales price. Fifth, the seller-lessee is not relieved of any existing debt on the property that may be assumed by the buyer-lessor. Sixth, the seller-lessee lease payment is contingent on the economic performance of the property. Seventh, the buyer-lessor is obligated to share with the seller-lessee a portion of the appreciation in the value of the property over the term of the lease.

If any of these (or other criteria outlined in FASB 98) are met, the seller-lessee cannot account for the transaction as a sale of the property. The seller-lessee will have to carry the asset on the balance sheet, will report sales proceeds as a liability (called a finance obligation), will report all or a portion of the lease payments as interest expense, and will defer the recognition of any gain or loss on the sale until such a time that the transaction can be considered a sale. Sometimes the terms of a sale-leaseback will indicate that, for example, the seller-lessee has an option to repurchase the property within 5 years of a 10-year lease. After the fifth year, if the option is not exercised, then the transaction may qualify for sales treatment. At that time, the accounting statements will be adjusted to reflect the sale, including the recognition of any gain or loss on the property.

Examples of Sale-leaseback Accounting.   It will be instructive at this point to provide a couple of examples of accounting for sale-leaseback transactions. The examples show how certain arrangements must be treated as though the property is retained by the seller and financed with debt.

EXAMPLE 1

Investor B (the seller-lessee) sells a building to a buyer-lessor for $1 million and enters into an agreement to lease the building for 5 years at $120,000 annually. The lease agreement includes an option to repurchase the property, and the seller guarantees that the residual value of the property will be at least $1 million at the end of the lease term. The historical cost of the property is $1.3 million and the accumulated depreciation is $450,000. Annual depreciation is $75,000. After the initial lease term is up, the seller-lessee decides not to exercise the option to repurchase the property but instead purchases another, unrelated property. The fair market value of the property at the time is $965,000, so the seller-lessee pays the buyer-lessor $35,000 to honor the guarantee of residual value.

At the time of the sale-leaseback, the transaction cannot be accounted for as a sale because of the option to repurchase and the guarantee of the residual value. At the end of the 5-year lease term, the seller-lessee has no further involvement with the property. It qualifies for treatment as a sale at that time.

Table 19–17 shows the calculation of the gain on the sale of the property. Recall that the gain will be recognized only in year five after the purchase option has expired. The gain is calculated with reference to the accumulated depreciation at the end of the lease term. Table 19–18 shows the journal entries associated with the sale-leaseback transaction. The sale of the property in year one establishes a liability called **finance obligation.** Annual entries for the lease payments are recorded as interest expense. After the lease term expires and the repurchase option expires, the property and finance obligation are removed from the books of the seller-lessee. Also at this time, the gain on the sale of the property is recognized. ■ ■

This first example illustrates a relatively simple transaction. The following example illustrates a somewhat more complicated arrangement.

EXAMPLE 2

In this example, we assume the same set of circumstances as in the first example, with the following changes: (1) there is no guarantee of the residual value of the property at the end of the lease term, and (2) the seller-lessee finances a portion of the sales price by making a nonrecourse note for $950,000.

No other changes are made. The option to purchase expires unexercised at the end of the 5-year lease term. There are two consequences of the nonrecourse seller financing. First, the transaction cannot be accounted for as a sale, but must be treated as a financed lease. Second, the note complicates the accounting for the finance obligation. Recall that the finance obligation is set up as a liability on the balance sheet of the seller-lessee. This is part of the arrangement establishing the transaction as a financing and not a sale. Lease payments to the new owner are treated just as payments on a debt would be—part interest expense and part reduction in the "debt" li-

TABLE 19–17

Calculation of Gain on Sale of Property Example 1

Sales price	$1,000,000
Basis	475,000[a]
Gain to be recognized	525,000

[a]$1,300,000 − $450,000 − [5 × $75,000]

TABLE 19–18

Journal Entries for Example 1

	Debit	Credit
Year 1		
Cash	$1,000,000	
Finance obligation		$1,000,000
Annual Journal Entries: Years 1 through 5		
Depreciation expense	$ 75,000	
Accumulated depreciation		$ 75,000
Interest expense	120,000	
Cash		120,000
Year 5		
Recognition of gain on sale:		
Accumulation depreciation	$ 825,000	
Finance lease obligation	1,000,000	
Property		$1,300,000
Cash		35,000
Gain on sale		490,000[a]

[a]$525,000 gain less $35,000 payment or guarantee.

TABLE 19–19

Calculation of Gain on Sale of Property Example 2

Sale price	1,000,000	
Basis	475,000	
	525,000	
Adjustments		
Lease expense charged to finance obligation; Years 1–5		$(600,000)
Interest expense charged to income; Years 1–5		76,178
Interest income credited to finance obligation; Years 1–5		452,748
Gain to be recognized		453,926

ability (finance obligation). However, in this case, the transaction involves annual payments by the buyer on the seller's note. A portion of these expenses will be considered interest income, and a portion will be considered an increase in the finance obligation (not a reduction in an asset, called a note receivable, as no such asset is recorded). Thus, there are two things going on with the finance obligation. Lease payments by the seller-lessee reduce this liability item, and note payments by the buyer-lessor increase it.

Also, at the time that the transaction can be recognized as a sale, the effects of the interest expense and income over the 5-year term of the lease must be adjusted (reversed). The adjustment is made to the retained earnings of Investor B but through the recognition of the gain on the sale. The calculation of the gain is shown in Table 19–19. The adjustments reflect the reversal of the interest charges and credits on the lease and note payments, respectively. The supporting schedules for the items in Table 19–19 are included in Appendix A to this chapter. Table 19–20 shows the journal entries for this transaction. The interest expense portion of the lease payment is established assuming a 10 percent rate. The actual rate used must be computed using the so-called interest method, a discussion of which is beyond the scope here. For simplicity, we assume a 10 percent rate. Because the sale is recognized at the end of the lease term, the finance obligation is removed as a liability and the balance of the note receivable is established as an asset. Also, the property, along with its accumulated depreciation, is removed from the balance sheet, and the gain is recognized. ▮ ▮

The essence of the accounting rules is to treat the sale-leaseback transaction as a financing until the criteria used to determine sales status are met. This generally occurs when all of the

TABLE 19–20
Journal Entries for Example 2

Description	Debit	Credit
Year 1		
Cash	$ 50,000	
Finance obligation		$1,050,000
Annual Journal Entries; Years 1–5		
Cash	161,311	
Finance obligation		161,311
(Collection of Payment on $900,000 Note)		
Depreciation expense	75,000	
Accumulation depreciation		75,000
Nonrecurring Journal Entries; Years 1–5		
Year 1		
Finance obligation	$115,000	
Interest expense	5,000	
Cash		$1,120,000
Year 2		
Finance obligation	$110,369	
Interest expense	9,631	
Cash		$1,120,000
Year 3		
Finance obligation	$105,275	
Interest expense	14,725	
Cash		$1,120,000
Year 4		
Finance obligation	$ 99,671	
Interest expense	20,329	
Cash		$1,120,000
Year 5		
Finance obligation	$ 93,507	
Interest expense	26,493	
Cash		$1,120,000
Year 5		
Finance obligation	$332,733[a]	
Note receivable	596,193[a]	
Accumulation depreciation	875,000	
Property		$1,300,000
Gain on sale		453,926

[a]From Appendix A.

risks and rewards have been transferred to the buyer and the lender has no involvement with the property from the perspective of ownership.

There is a virtually limitless number of variations of sale-leaseback agreements that can be constructed. Each will involve variations as to the magnitude and timing of the transfer of the risks and rewards to the buyer. You should be aware that the accounting rules on the more complex transactions can be very complicated. The accounting rules and regulations are designed to cause the financial statements of the seller-lessee to reflect the substance of the sale-leaseback transaction and not the form.

GROUND LEASE MORTGAGES

Sometimes lenders will write a loan against a ground lease.[2] A ground lease loan is unusual because the borrower does not own the land. The land is leased from the owner/developer for construction of improvements. These arrangements are most common in densely populated areas.

Usually the terms of the lease call for ownership of the improvement to pass to the land owner at expiration of the lease. Sometimes the lease will give the tenant an option to purchase.

The treatment of ground lease loans can vary. In some states loans made to the owner/developer secured by the lease are viewed as real property and treated the same as a mortgage loan. In other states the lease is viewed legally as personalty and is secured under the Uniform Commercial Code Financing Statement. In either case, the lender can foreclose on the lease if the borrower defaults.

The Bankruptcy Reform Act enacted in 1994 provided some clarification of lenders' rights to collateralize leases. It also provided some protection for lenders in the event of landowner bankruptcy.

CREDIT-BASED FINANCING

Credit-based financing uses the tenant's good credit rather than the real estate asset itself as the basis for financing. This type of financing may be useful when the tenant has stronger credit than the landlord. There are two available formats for credit-based financing.[3] Both require a direct financing agreement with the tenant. In either case, credit-based financing falls outside the traditional real estate financing areas of mortgage and general obligation bond financing.

In the first format, **multisite securitization,** a pool of facilities are net leased to the tenant. A third-party entity is established to build the facilities and repay debt backed by the properties and the rental receivables. Securitized debt in this fashion may be more desirable by the tenant than having the developer finance each site separately if the funds are less costly. Also, securitization would allow the tenant to pool a number of small and/or scattered facilities. Various types of lease arrangements may allow the tenant to repay the debt and purchase the facilities.

The second format is **tenant improvements financing.** In this case tenant improvements are financed in a personal property lease. The tenant improvements—but not the real estate—is conveyed to the third-party financier. The accounting treatment of this arrangement is acceptable to the tenant since it is the same as if the tenant improvements were included in rents paid to the landlord.

Both tenants and landlords may have incentives to use credit-based financing. For a tenant these may be financing an expensive new facility or financing a group of facilities. Other advantages for the tenant are off-balance-sheet accounting, 100 percent financing, and the flexibility to take real estate as is (thereby obtaining a better economic deal). For landlords the incentives may be the ability to deliver substantial allowances, thereby attracting more and/or new tenants and enhancing their property values.

SUMMARY

In this chapter, we discussed the different ways of financing existing income-producing properties. One common method is by a standard, long-term loan not much different from a loan on a residential property. These permanent loans do not reflect the nature of the collateral, however. Generally, the underwriting criteria are more strict than with residential loans. The riskiness of the cash flows of commercial properties requires a careful analysis of the property and generally leads to lower loan-to-value ratios than on residential properties. The risk of commercial loans also is reduced by an assignment of rent provision in the note. Prepayment penalties are also common with these loans. The prepayment penalties, which may be determined with reference to market interest rates, reduce the interest rate risk exposure for the lender.

Alternative loan arrangements include equity-participation loans and sale-leaseback transactions. Equity-participation loans grant a share of the income of the property or a share of the property's appreciation to the lender in return for a lower interest rate. Essentially, this type of loan increases the amount of equity in the deal and gives a portion of the equity to the lender. The risk for the lender is increased, and the risk for the investor is decreased. In an efficient market, one would expect that the investor could not gain from the tradeoff, since its terms should be priced to reflect the transfer of risk. There are no tax benefits to either party for equity-participation loans; both the interest and the participation payments are tax deductible to the investor and are also taxable income to the lender.

There may be some benefit to the arrangement for both parties if the discount rate used to value the cash flows does not change commensurate with the transfer of risk. Briefly, the lender may not view the increase in risk as warranting an increase in the discount rate. This may be true for lenders seeking an inflation hedge or for lenders with negative net worth seeking more risky investments to extricate themselves from their insolvency.

Sale-leaseback transactions can be viewed as an alternative to debt financing. It can be shown that the cash flows from such a transaction are identical to those of a debt financing. There appears to be little advantage to a sale-leaseback transaction compared to more traditional debt financing of the property. At one time, such a transaction might have led to fewer taxes because of the greater depreciation allowed by a stepped-up basis. With the new tax laws in place, there may be little tax relief from a larger basis generated by a sale. Window-dressing advantages (where the financial statements reflect a greater return on assets and a smaller debt-to-equity ratio) have been frustrated by accounting regulations that require the transaction be recorded on the financial statements as a debt financing. FASB 98 requires that, if certain criteria are met, the property be carried on the books as an asset and a liability be established for the debt. This is so even if title to the property has been transferred to the buyer. The criteria that require this type of financial reporting hinge on whether or not the risks and returns of property ownership have been transferred to the buyer. If not, then the transaction cannot be reported as a sale but must be reported as a financing.

KEY TERMS

Assignment of rents	Prepayment penalty
Capital lease	Risk and return of ownership
Credit-based financing	Sale-leaseback
Equity-participation loan	Sale-leaseback accounting
FASB 98	Stepped-up basis
Finance obligation	Tenant improvements financing
Ground lease mortgage	Window-dressing
Multisite securitization	Yield maintenance prepayment penalty
Operating lease	

SUGGESTED READINGS

Arcudy, A. T., R. K. Herdman, and M. T. Strianese. 1989. Real estate sale-leasebacks under FASB 98. *Journal of Accountancy,* June.

Lieberman, M. J., and E. Kosoffsky. 1989. Sale-leaseback accounting: The rules have changed. *Real Estate Accounting and Taxation* Vol. 4, Spring.

McGrath, W. T. 1989. Sale-leasebacks of corporate property: A response to new financial reporting requirements. *Real Estate Review* Vol. 19, Fall.

McNiff, J. 1988. Share the risks: Share the profits. *Mortgage Banking,* January.

Smith, C., and E. McDonough. 1989. A sale and leaseback case study. *Real Estate Finance* Vol. 6, Spring.

Urdang, S. 1986. Participating mortgages, determining true returns. *Mortgage Banking,* April.

REVIEW QUESTIONS

19–1   Compare long-term commercial property loans with their residential counterparts. Explain the reasons for any differences.

19–2   a. Define an equity-participation loan.

   b. Give an example of the terms of an equity-participation loan.

19–3   Concerning an equity-participation loan:

   a. What are the advantages for a property investor?

   b. What are the advantages for a lender?

   c. How can both parties benefit from this type of loan?

19–4   Compare a sale-leaseback transaction to the alternative of standard debt financing by noting the similarities and differences between the two.

19–5 Indicate the factors that would have made sale-leaseback transactions attractive in earlier times. Indicate the recent tax and accounting changes that have reduced the attractiveness of sale-leasebacks.

19–6 Distinguish, by definition, between operating and capital leases in general. Indicate the criteria that establish a lease as a capital lease.

19–7 List 5 terms of a sale-leaseback transaction that would require accounting as a financing rather than as a sale.

19–8 If a sale-leaseback must be treated as a financing, generally describe how the financial statements reflect the transaction.

PROBLEMS

19–1 An investor can purchase a property for which the net present value of the expected cash flows to equity (15 percent discount rate) is $400,000 for a 5-year holding period. The purchase can be made with a standard, long-term, fixed-rate loan. Now, consider the following alternative equity-participation loan.

Basic Terms

Project cost	
Land	$300,000
Building	$2,500,000*
Total	$2,800,000
Project financing	
Loan amount	$2,000,000
Interest rate	9%
Amortization	30 years
Participation terms	
Share of NOI	20% over $250,000
Share of appreciation	15%
Discount rates	
Investor	14.75%
Lender	12.25%
Holding period	5 years
Operating data	
Gross rent, year one	$522,100
Vacancy rate	5%
Operating expense, year one	$83,536 (16% of gross rent)
Growth rates	
Gross rent	8%
Operating expense	7%
Resale value	6%
Resale expense rate	5%
Investor's marginal tax rate	28%

*Depreciation years one and five 5 $87,000; other years 5 $91,000

a. Determine the after-tax cash flows from operations for the 5-year holding period. (Check figure: year three value is $193,113.)

b. Determine the after-tax cash flow from the sale of the property in year five. (Check figure: share of participation to the lender upon sale is $142,055.)

c. Determine the net present value of expected after-tax cash flows to the investor.

19–2 For the loan in Problem 19–1:

a. Determine the cash flows to the lender for the 5-year holding period. (Check figure: year two value is $233,931.)

b. Determine the total cash flow to the lender in the year of the sale of the property. (Check figure: share of NOI in year five is $63,059.)

c. Determine the net present value of the expected cash flows to the lender.

19–3   Compare the net present values of the equity-participation loan in the above problems to a standard loan. Should the investor agree to the loan? Should the lender agree to the loan?

19–4   You are trying to decide whether to lease or buy warehouse space for the next 5 years. Since you will pay property taxes, insurance, and maintenance in either case (a triple net lease), the major factors to consider are the debt service and depreciation versus the cost of the lease. The property that suits your needs has the following characteristics:

Purchase price	$300,000
Building value	$240,000
Land value	$ 60,000
Selling price EOY5	$400,000
Interest-only mortgage	$225,000 at 9%, balance paid end of year 5
Marginal tax rate	28%
Required equity yield	14%
Lease payment if leased	$22,000 per year

a. Which alternative is preferable?

b. What is the break-even point at which you would be indifferent between the two options?

19–5   Assume the following information about a commercial warehouse facility.

Original cost	$1,500,000
Book value	0
Market value	$1,800,000
Value of building	$1,500,000
Value of land	$300,000
Annual depreciation	0
Debt	$100,000
Rate	12%
Term	10 years
Payment	$17,698
Investor's tax rate	28%
Year one NOI	$338,900
Growth in NOI	0%

a. Calculate the after-tax cash flows from operations for the next 10 years. (Check figure: year three value is $229,264.)

b. Assuming the investor has a 15 percent required rate-of-return (discount rate), calculate the present value of the after-tax cash flows from operations for the 10-year period.

c. Calculate the after-tax cash flows from a sale-leaseback assuming: (1) annual lease expense of $275,000; (2) the property is sold and repurchased for $1,800,000; and (3) repurchased in year ten.

d. Calculate the cash flows to the buyer/lessor. (Assume the buyer/lessor is in the 28 percent tax bracket.)

e. Assuming the buyer/lessor has a discount rate of 12 percent, calculate the present value of the cash flows.

f. Assuming no objections to the arrangement from the IRS, should the sale-leaseback be undertaken? Why or why not?

ENDNOTES

1. A good source is Financial Accounting Standards Board, *Current Text: Accounting Standards, General Standards* (Homewood, IL: Irwin Publishing Co., 1991).

2. See T. Cornwell, "Ground Lease Mortgages Easier Now," *National Mortgage News* 19 (December 5, 1994): 2.

3. A good discussion of credit-based financing is found in Miller Blew, "Credit-Based Financing: New Tools for Tenants and Landlords" in *Corporate Real Estate Executive* (Boston: Greyfield Finance, Oct. 1993).

APPENDIX A

Supporting Schedules for Example 2

Calculation of Finance Obligation Account; Years 1–5

	Year 1	Year 2	Year 3	Year 4	Year 5
Beginning balance	$50,000[a]	$96,311	$147,253	$203,289	$264,929
Plus note payment	161,311	161,311	161,311	161,311	161,311
Less lease payment	(115,000)	(110,369)	(105,275)	(99,671)	(93,507)
Ending balance	$96,311	$147,253	$203,289	$264,929	$332,733

Amortization of Note; Years 1–5

	Year 1	Year 2	Year 3	Year 4	Year 5
Beginning balance	$950,000	$893,189	$830,129	$760,132	$682,436
Plus note payment	104,500	98,251	91,314	83,615	75,068
Less lease payment	(161,311)	(161,311)	(161,311)	(161,311)	(161,311)
Ending balance	$893,189	$830,129	$760,132	$682,436	$596,193
Sum of interest portion =	$452,748				

[a]Initial deposit.

CHAPTER **20**

Ownership Structures for Financing and Holding Real Estate

LEARNING OBJECTIVES

$\mathbf{R}$eal estate properties can be held in several forms of ownership, including individual, corporate, partnership, and trust ownership. After reading this chapter, you should understand that the ownership form is defined by legal considerations, but that the choice of ownership form is driven by institutional and economic considerations. You should know the three main determinants of the form in which real estate is held: the federal tax environment, issues of personal liability, and access to equity capital markets. In addition, investors will be concerned with issues related to control and transfer of the property, as well as the continuity of the ownership structure. Unless there are overriding considerations, real estate will be held by that structure which tends to pass on to the owners the most after-tax dollars. You also will understand that investors are averse to incurring liability beyond the amount of their investment. You will see that the illiquid nature of individual real estate properties affects the choice of ownership form. Next, you should understand the basic tax regulations and legal considerations that govern each type of ownership form. Finally, you should be able to compare the risks and returns of various ownership forms.

INTRODUCTION

There are several ownership structures that can be used to hold real estate properties. Properties can be held by an individual, a corporation (both chapter C and chapter S), a partnership (private or publicly traded), or a trust. The choice of ownership is driven by tax regulations and institutional constraints on the access to large equity markets. The federal government has played an active role in determining the ownership form of real estate by passing legislation affecting how the various ownership forms are taxed. One can say that the federal government uses the tax code intentionally and actively to push the ownership form of real estate in certain directions. Investors will choose that ownership form which provides them with the most after-tax cash flows. The intrinsic value of a real estate property is determined by its expected cash flows and the risk of those cash flows. Beyond that, the ownership form is determined primarily by tax regulations. Investors desire to obtain as many of those cash flow dollars without a diversion to the Treasury. You will see that the corporate form of organization is not well suited in this regard, while the partnership form is.

Of course, other considerations come into play. Legal factors, such as personal liability, will affect the ownership form. Investors desire to be insulated from personal liability should the real estate investment fail. In other words, in the event of bankruptcy, investors want to be liable only for the amount they have invested. As you may expect, in an efficient market, insulation from liability has a price. There are ownership forms that shift liability from some investors to others. The tradeoff is priced in terms of return on the various interests: those accepting more personal liability obtain a greater return. Both the corporate form and the real estate limited partnership (RELP) form insulate investors from personal liability beyond the amount invested.

Also, economic factors such as access to capital markets affect the ownership form. Access to large, efficient capital markets lowers liquidity risk. Real estate properties are not liquid. Liquidity can be enhanced by virtue of the form of ownership, however. Although a corporation can purchase real estate, and the shares of a sufficiently large corporation can be exchanged in the large, efficient equity market, the double taxation associated with the corporate form of organization presents a major deterrent to the use of this structure. Fortunately, tax rules allow a certain specially designed form of corporation to avoid the double taxation. This form, called a real estate investment trust (REIT),[1] provides liquidity by access to large capital markets without the burdensome double taxation. It is not surprising that increasing amounts of real estate have been securitized, or held in the form of REITs. Tax regulations have, in fact, pushed this structure to the forefront.

In summary, access to large, efficient capital markets lowers the financing cost through the reduction in liquidity risk. Also, flotation costs of securities, relative to the size of the investment, are lower when they are issued in large capital markets. Other ownership forms remain because of the special advantages they may provide investors.

In the next section, we present the various ownership forms that can be used to hold real estate and give a brief description of each. Then we will make a more detailed examination of two forms of ownership structure: the real estate limited partnership and the real estate investment trust.

FORMS OF REAL ESTATE OWNERSHIP

Table 20–1 outlines the various forms by which real estate properties can be owned. Each of these forms is discussed briefly here.

Sole Ownership

This form of ownership is exactly as the term implies. Real estate can be owned at the individual investor level. Usually, sole owners will have modest portfolios of properties. They may hold several residential properties, occasionally a small apartment complex or small strip shopping center. Such investors will have to rely heavily on debt to secure any sizable portfolios because of their limited equity. Individual owners do not have access to the large equity markets. In such cases, the property will secure the debt, which is likely to take the form of a recourse note. If the note is recourse, the investor is personally liable for any loss. Thus, if the value of the property falls below the amount of the indebtedness and the investor defaults on the loan, the lender can seek a judgment for the deficiency. Antideficiency statutes in some states usually do not apply to investor-owned (commercial) properties. There is no double taxation as with the corporate form of ownership. Losses sustained by the individual owner can be used to offset other positive income, but only if the owner actively participates in the management of

TABLE 20–1
Ownership Forms for Real Estate

Form	Major Characteristics
Sole Ownership	Low liquidity, control over property
Corporations:	
C corporation	Double taxation
S corporation	No double taxation, limited number of shareholders
Partnerships:	
General	Unlimited liability, control over property
Limited	Limited liability, centralized management
Publicly traded partnership	Limited liability, access to capital markets
Real estate investment trusts	No double taxation, access to capital markets high liquidity

the properties. Annual operating losses that can be used in this manner are limited to the $25,000 exemption.

For all these reasons there is little investor-owned (as opposed to owner-occupied housing) real estate at the personal level.

Characteristics of Sole Ownership	
Tax environment	Fair to moderate
Personal liability	Significant
Access to capital markets	Poor
Overall	Poor to moderate

Corporate Form of Ownership

Legally, corporations have identities separate from that of their stockholders. There are two types of corporate structure: the regular **C corporation** and the **S corporation**. They are named after different chapters in the tax code that set forth how each is treated from the tax standpoint. Since a regular C corporation is recognized as having a legal identity separate from its stockholders, it earns income and incurs liabilities; the stockholders do not. Taxes must be paid on the corporate income. The corporation also distributes dividends to the stockholders from any excess after-tax earnings. Because the corporation pays a tax on its income and then the stockholders pay a tax on their dividends, the term double taxation applies to this form of ownership. The impact of double taxation can be onerous.

Consider a small real estate investment. Assume that a strip shopping center produces $100,000 annually after operating expenses and after interest payments on debt. If the shopping center is owned by an individual, the owner will pay federal income taxes based on his tax rate—for example, 28 percent. The cash flow after tax is $72,000 for this investor. On the other hand, if the shopping center is owned by a corporation, the sole shareholder of which is the same hypothetical investor, then the after-tax cash flows will be somewhat less. If the corporate tax rate is 35 percent, then the corporation will have a $65,000 after-tax cash flow to distribute to the stockholder in the form of a dividend. The stockholder must then pay personal taxes, equal to $18,000 ($65,000 × 28%), on this amount. The after-tax cash flow to the stockholder is now only $46,800, much less than the $72,000 he would have as a sole owner.

Regular C corporations exist and endure the double taxation because they provide limited liability to the stockholders, allow access to large equity markets, and often invest in unique assets. There are better vehicles for holding real estate, however—vehicles that provide limited liability but avoid double taxation. For these reasons, C corporations are not a desirable ownership structure for investments that are purely or mostly real estate.

Characteristics of Corporate Ownership (C Corporations)	
Tax environment	Poor
Personal liability	None
Access to capital markets	Good
Overall	Poor to moderate

An S corporation provides for the same limited liability as the C corporation, but it does not have the double taxation problem. Tax regulations allow the income (and losses) to be passed through to each stockholder and reported on their individual income tax returns. The major drawback of the S corporation as a real estate ownership form is the limitation on the number of shareholders; an S corporation is limited to 35 shareholders. This restriction severely limits the ability of an S corporation to raise substantial amounts of equity, which may be needed for many large real estate investments. Prior to 1983, S corporations were not allowed to receive more than 20 percent of their gross revenue from what is now referred to as passive investment income (for example, rents from commercial real estate properties). However, the Subchapter S

Revision Act of 1982 eliminated this restriction, so that S corporations can now invest in real estate properties.

Characteristics of Corporate Ownership (S Corporations)

Tax environment	Good
Personal liability	None
Access to capital markets	Poor
Overall	Moderate

Partnerships

A **partnership** is an association made up of individuals who pool their resources to carry out an enterprise. There are two types of partnerships defined by law: **general** and **limited**. Neither type is taxed at the partnership level, so double taxation is avoided for each. The partners of a general partnership may be held personally liable for the debts of the partnership, however. For those seeking limited liability, the general partnership is not a recommended ownership vehicle. For this reason, general partnerships, where they exist, tend to have only a few partners. The affairs of the enterprise can be attended to by those who may incur potential liabilities. Also, because investors do not wish to expose themselves to unlimited liability, few would even consider becoming a partner in a general partnership. For this reason, general partnerships have little, if any, access to the capital markets. General partnerships usually carry out endeavors for which human rather than money capital is required: law firms, accounting firms, and the like.

A limited partnership allows for some of the "investing" partners to avoid liability beyond the amount of their investment. A limited partnership must have at least one general partner with unlimited liability. Because of the limited liability, investors are more likely to purchase "interests" in a limited partnership than in a general partnership. There is, likewise, no double taxation. Profits and losses are passed through to the limited partners. Prior to the Tax Reform Act of 1986, when partners' losses could be used to offset other positive income, limited partnerships were one of the dominant ownership forms of real estate. Limited partnerships can be small, private placement partnerships or large publicly traded partnerships (PTPs). We will look more closely at real estate limited partnerships in the next section.

Characteristics of Partnership Ownership

Tax environment	Good
Personal liability	None
Access to capital markets	Good (for PTPs)
Overall	Good

Real Estate Investment Trusts

Real Estate Investment Trusts (REITs) can either be a trust or a corporation. Prior to 1960 some real estate was held in trust form to avoid the double taxation associated with the corporate structure. Beneficial interests in the trusts were then sold in the capital markets. In 1960 Congress passed the Real Estate Investment Trust Act. The act authorizes the corporate form of real estate ownership, but with no double taxation as long as certain restrictive conditions are met. The restrictions, described below, relate primarily to the form of assets that a REIT can invest in and the type of income it can generate. There are also restrictive conditions relating to the distribution of income to shareholders. Now, virtually all REITs have a corporate form of ownership. Their limited liability, favorable tax status, and access to capital markets make them a favored vehicle for ownership of large portfolios of properties.

Characteristics of REITs

Tax environment	Good
Personal liability	None
Access to capital markets	Good
Overall	Excellent

Because tax regulations, liability issues, and access to capital markets are important in the determination of the ownership structure of real estate, we will take a closer look at two forms of ownership that successfully meet investment criteria in these areas. Both real estate limited partnerships (RELPs) and real estate investment trusts (REITs) are important investment vehicles and sources of financing for real estate properties. In 1990, together they accounted for nearly $3 billion of equity funds raised for investment in real estate.

A CLOSER LOOK AT REAL ESTATE LIMITED PARTNERSHIPS AND REAL ESTATE INVESTMENT TRUSTS

Real Estate Limited Partnerships

Real estate limited partnerships are associations of individuals that form a "partnership" for the purpose of investing in real estate properties. There must be at least one general partner liable for the debts of the partnership. The remaining limited partners have no liability beyond their actual or promised contribution to the partnership. The structure and financial arrangements of limited partnerships are governed by the **Uniform Limited Partnership Act (ULPA),** promulgated in 1916, and the **Revised Uniform Limited Partnership Act**, published in 1976 (more about this revision shortly). The acts establish rules for the determination of when a partnership exists and the relationship among the partners, and between the partners and outside creditors of the partnership. Under ULPA a limited partnership is one formed by two or more limited partners. The general partners administer the affairs of the partnership and are personally liable for the partnership's debts. As such, the general partners must have sufficient personal financial resources to meet any expected liabilities. As previously stated, the limited partners have no liability beyond their investment and are prohibited from managing the affairs of the partnership or even having their name appear in the partnership name.

All limited partners stand on an equal footing regarding the right to distribution of the partnership assets. Although they are not liable for partnership debts beyond their contribution, they may be required to give the partnership a sum equal to a promised but unpaid contribution or, in some cases, a return of any amounts given to them in the past that may have rightfully belonged to a creator of the partnership.

The 1976 revision (adopted by about 70 percent of the states) made it easier for limited partnerships to raise needed capital. Prior to the revision, certain restrictions of the original ULPA had hindered the ability of partnerships to attract investors. For one, the original act prohibited a limited partner from obtaining a security interest on any partnership property in exchange for a loan. Thus, limited partners were not willing to loan the partnership additional capital, since they could not get a security interest. Such rules certainly would discourage large financial institutions from issuing a mortgage on a partnership property and simultaneously being a limited partner. The revision allows any partner to lend money or transact business with the partnership on the same basis as any other person who may not be a partner.

The original act also prevented limited partners from taking part in the control of the partnership without risking their limited-liability status. Many potential investors did not like this provision, since they wanted to have some say in the management of the partnership's assets. Under the revision limited partners may consult with and advise the general partner; approve or disapprove amendments to the partnership agreement; vote on the dissolution of the partnership; vote on the sale, exchange, mortgage, or transfer of substantially all of the assets of the partnership (other than in the ordinary course of business); and vote on the removal of a general partner. Also prior to the revision, ULPA allowed disgruntled partners to sue for the dissolution of the partnership in order to obtain a return of their contribution. The revision now protects the integrity of the partnership by requiring a disgruntled partner to sue for his contribution just as any general creditor must. In short, the 1976 revision liberalizes the participation of limited partners in the partnership, gives the partnership greater access to additional funds (loans from partners), and protects its integrity from injurious dissolution by dissenting partners.

Limited partnerships experienced their greatest popularity from 1983 through 1989. Limited partnerships were attractive to investors because they could offer benefits of direct ownership without the burden of management responsibility and personal liability. The limited partnerships of the early 1980s were tax driven mainly due to the accelerated depreciation provided in the Economic Tax Recovery Act of 1981. By the end of the 1980s, however, tax law changes and increased scrutiny had caused limited partnerships to lose favor with investors. The Tax Reform Act of 1986, which instituted the passive loss limitation and extended the "at-risk" limitations to real estate tax shelters, was the biggest factor.

For a time in the mid-1980s master limited partnerships (MLPs) were formed to deal with the Tax Reform Act of 1986. These were designed to produce income so that passive losses could be used to offset the passive income. Favorable income tax rates gave MLPs an advantage over corporations. However, the Revenue Act of 1987 eliminated the tax advantages of MLPs. The consequences in the 1990s for investors already holding limited partnerships were not good due to tax reform and falling real estate prices. The choices have been to continue to own or to sell in the secondary market at deep discounts. Limited partnerships have clearly lost their luster.

Distinguishing a Partnership from a Corporation

A partnership offers significant advantages over the corporate form of ownership, notably the absence of double taxation. However, the Internal Revenue Service requires that certain tests be made to determine if a partnership is indeed a partnership and not a corporation. Actually the tests were designed at a previous time, when many professional partnerships (such as medical firms established by a small number of physicians) wanted to be considered corporations for liability purposes. There are four tests that a partnership must consider. In order not to be considered a corporation, the partnership must meet no more than two of the following tests.

Continuity of Life. Because corporations are considered to have a perpetual life, an indication that the partnership will have a termination date points to a partnership and not a corporation. This test is easy to meet. If the partnership has a termination date, even 50 years in the future, it has not passed the first test. Also, if the partnership indicates that the retirement, death, or insanity of the general partner constitute grounds for the termination and dissolution of the partnership, then it is considered to have a finite life.

Centralized Management. Corporations have a centralized management, as do limited partners. The general partners make the major decisions for the limited partners, with the exceptions discussed above. This test would indicate that a limited partnership was a corporation.

Limited Liability. This, of course, is a hallmark of corporations. Limited partnerships must make at least one (general) partner liable for the debts of the partnership. The general partner also must have sufficient assets to meet any contingent liabilities.

Free Transferability of Interest. Stocks of corporations are freely transferable from one owner to another. If there is any doubt about failing to meet two of the first three tests, the limited partnership agreement should specify that interests in the partnership are not transferable without the consent of the general partner. A condition that allowed a transfer of the rights to share in the profits of the partnership but not the management would probably be considered a restriction of the free transferability of the interest. Of course, restrictions on the transferability of interests will lead to a reduction in access to capital markets. Thus, most limited partnerships which contain restrictions on the transferability of interest tend to be small, often intrastate, offerings designed for a small real estate investment. Limited partnerships that desire access to the capital markets will be large, **publicly traded partnerships (PTPs),** sometimes referred to as master limited partnerships.

Master Limited Partnerships

Master limited partnerships (MLPs) or publicly traded partnerships (PTPs) had their origin in the need to make the interests in small limited partnerships more liquid. Essentially, one who creates an MLP issues partnership interests in the new, larger partnership in exchange for those in the smaller, less liquid partnerships. Thus, an investor that previously had an interest in a small partnership equal to, for example, 5 percent of the partnership may end up having an interest in the new MLP equal to a much smaller percentage. This MLP "roll-up," as it is called, creates one large partnership out of many smaller ones.[2] The newly formed MLP will have greater liquidity. In fact, interests in MLPs trade on the New York, American, and NASDAQ markets. They were first listed on the New York Stock Exchange in March 1987.

MLPs got their start in February 1981 in the petroleum industry when Apache Petroleum rolled up the interests of many small oil and gas partnerships into a single large one. In all, 33 separate limited partnerships were rolled into one large limited partnership. If the partnership is structured to fail to meet the test for corporate designation, then interests can be traded freely. Notice the use of the term "interest." What is really transferred is not the ownership in the partnership but rather an assignment of the beneficial interest (units), beneficial assignment certificates (BACs), or depository unit receipts (DURs). These terms indicate that rather than the ownership in the partnership being traded, what is traded is the right to share in the profits and cash distribution of the partnership.

Although MLPs got their start in the petroleum industry, virtually all MLPs today are real-estate-related. The Omnibus Budget Reconciliation Act of 1987 provided that all MLPs would be treated as corporations for the purpose of taxation. However, certain MLPs were exempted from this rule—namely, those that derived at least 90 percent of gross income from qualifying income. Qualifying income includes interest, dividends, real property rents, gain on sale of real property, and other items of less interest here. As you can see, the exemptions allow an MLP to be treated as a partnership if it invests heavily in real estate properties. The 1987 act went further, however. It reclassified income from an MLP from passive to portfolio income and indicated that losses could not be offset until the MLP had sufficient positive income in subsequent years. A loss from an MLP cannot be used to offset any other income from another MLP or any other passive income. Neither can MLP partners use their $25,000 exemption for passive activities. About the only tax relief MLP partners receive is an allowance for low-income housing and rehabilitation tax credits.

Given this reclassification of income and the restriction on losses, it became apparent that real estate property could be held more effectively by the REIT structure. The number of MLP offerings has declined since 1987. In 1990 virtually no MLPs came on the market. This is in contrast to $2.7 billion in REIT offerings.

Real Estate Investment Trusts

A **real estate investment trust (REIT)** is a corporate form of organization structured under the rules of the Real Estate Investment Trust Act of 1960 and designed as an investment in real estate properties, the income from which is not taxed at the corporate level. In order to qualify as a REIT, the organization must meet certain requirements.

The Internal Revenue Code lists a number of criteria for a REIT to qualify as a tax-free intermediary. (1) It must distribute at least 95 percent its net annual income (net cash flow) to its shareholders. (2) At least 75 percent of its assets must be real estate loans secured by real estate, mortgages, shares of other REITs, cash, or government securities. (3) It must derive at least 75 percent of gross income from its real-estate-related investments. (4) It must be managed by one or more trustees or directors who may be individuals or corporations. (5) It must engage independent advisory and management firms to manage its real estate properties. (6) It must issue transferable shares. (7) It may not be a financial institution or insurance company.

The Taxpayer Relief Act of 1997 included the following provisions affecting REITs. A REIT may earn up to 1 percent of its gross income on a property by property basis from nominal services to customers. An example would be occasionally helping a tenant move in or out. Also, the 30 percent gross income test was repealed allowing greater sales of properties held for less than 4 years. In addition, hedging rules were relaxed so that income from all types of derivatives are considered qualifying income for purposes of the 95 percent gross income test.

These rules were established to ensure that REITs operate basically as mutual funds for the purpose of holding real-estate-related assets. The first three rules ensure that the REIT invests in and engages in real estate activities. Shareholders in the REIT may be individuals, corporations, partnerships, trusts, and estates. Depending upon whether the REIT is a trust or corporation, it is run by either a board of trustees or a board of directors. Next, the board must employ an outside advisor to manage the assets of the REIT. The advisor can be a bank, real estate advisory company, life insurance company, or even an individual. The advisor is paid an annual management fee, usually equal to a percentage of the assets managed or the income and gains realized during the year. The advisory fees are not subject to any federal limits, but may be subject to restrictions set by the North American Securities Administration Association (NASAA) in conjunction with state securities regulators. The advisors often can use the REIT as a source of financing. Thus, if the advisor is a mortgage banker, it can use the REIT as a short-term source of financing (warehousing) to originate loans. An advisor who is in real estate development may use the REIT to provide short-term acquisitions, development, and construction (ADC) loans.

Finally, there is a provision that prevents the REIT from engaging in short-term speculative real estate transactions. A REIT cannot hold real estate property primarily for sale (in the ordinary course of business). It can sell a property only under certain conditions: (1) It must have held the property for at least 4 years. (2) During the 4-year period prior to sale, it must not have incurred capital expenditures on the property in excess of 20 percent of its sales price. (3) It must not have sold more than five properties during the same year. (4) It must not have acquired the property through a foreclosure.

As you can see, REITs must meet a highly restrictive set of conditions to retain favorable tax treatment. The avoidance of double taxation and access to capital markets are sufficient incentives for REITs to meet these conditions. Since the Tax Reform Act of 1986 placed limits on the pass-through of losses to real estate partnerships, REITs have gained a dominant share of the real estate securities market. The equity REIT industry reached a total market capitalization of about $45 billion as of August 1994. Despite the surge in REIT offerings, however, the percentage of real estate securitized—both equity and debt—as of 1994 remained relatively small, with an estimated 1.5 percent of the $3 trillion domestic real estate market securitized.

Because of their nature, measuring the operating performance of REITs has historically been a problem. In 1991 the National Association of REITs (NAREITs) developed a definition of **funds from operations (FFO)** to provide a more accurate measure of operating performance of REITs. Industry analysts have generally felt that basing performance on historical cost accounting approaches could be misleading. In addition, REIT analysts agree that company prices of REIT stocks in terms of conventional price/earnings (P/E) ratios are not meaningful.

FFO is net income, excluding gains or losses from debt-restructuring and sales of property, plus depreciation and amortization, and after adjustments for unconsolidated partnerships and joint ventures. FFO is not a deviation from generally accepted accounting principles (GAAP). However, it was designed to not have some of the drawbacks associated with net income under GAAP. Since its introduction in 1991, this supplemental measurement to net income has significantly benefited the REIT industry by providing an "industry standard" measurement of operating performance.

Types of REITs

There are several types of REITs. **Equity REITs** invest in and operate properties. As you will see below, equity REITs can be subclassified if they specialize in the acquisition and operation of certain types of properties. **Mortgage REITs** acquire mortgages, primarily commercial. Here again, some mortgage REITs may specialize in certain types of mortgages just as equity REITs may specialize in certain types of properties. A third type of REIT is a **hybrid REIT**. These REITs invest in both mortgages and properties. Regardless of the type of REIT, equity or mortgage, a given REIT can have its own preferred capital structure. For example, a REIT can issue stock and debt and use the proceeds to purchase only equity properties. It would be an equity REIT, even though it had debt in its capital structure.

A fourth type of REIT is a **finite-life,** or **self-liquidating**, REIT. This type is established to purchase and operate properties for a limited and defined period of time. At the expiration of the time frame for the finite-life REIT, the board of directors will sell off the properties, pay off any liabilities, and distribute the remainder to the stockholders. Equity REITs generally liquidate their assets in 5 to 10 years, whereas mortgage REITs may establish a 12-year horizon. As the liquidation date approaches, the market value of the shares will approximate the market value of the properties held by the REIT. For this reason, market values of self-liquidating REITs track the values of the underlying assets much better than is the case for perpetual REITs. The self-liquidating REIT was established, in part, to compete with limited partnerships that almost universally establish liquidation dates. They have several advantages over partnerships, however. The minimum purchase price is generally lower, and the shares can be traded on a liquid market. Shareholders may have more control over the management decisions of the REIT, because the managers must be independent and elected by the stockholders.

REITs can be either open- or closed-ended. An **open-end** fund continually offers new stock for sale to investors and uses the proceeds to purchase additional real estate assets. When new stock is issued, the existing assets must be valued so that a price can be set on it. Continuous valuation may prove difficult, especially for REITs that invest in equity properties. For this reason, most REITs are not open-end funds. Rather, they are **closed-end** funds. This means that after the initial stock is issued and assets purchased, no further stock is issued. The value of the existing stock will depend upon the performance of the assets in the REIT's portfolio. A closed-end REIT can purchase additional properties from the small amount of earnings (5 percent) it is allowed to retain or from the cash flow afforded by depreciation of existing properties.

REIT Specialization

Many REITs specialize in the types of real estate assets that they acquire, some being formed for a special purpose. Some REITs will invest in hotel/motel properties only, while others may be formed to purchase distressed real estate in recession-hit portions of the country. As of October 31, 1997, the approximate composition of the equity REIT market was retail (24 percent), residential (18 percent), health care (6 percent), office (10 percent), industrial (5 percent), self storage (3 percent), hotel (7 percent), manufactured homes (2 percent), diversified (13 percent), mortgage-backed securities (7 percent), and other (5 percent). REITs often specialize because of the expertise of their advisor group. New Plan Realty Trust and Federal Realty Trust are examples of REITs that purchase only shopping centers. Specialization can be carried even further. New Plan invests only in smaller shopping centers in rural areas of the mid-Atlantic states. New Plan managers are good at finding somewhat distressed properties, restoring the facility, and finding anchor tenants.

Many REITs focus on properties only in particular geographic regions. There is no reason why REITs should consider diversification as essential. We know that potential shareholders of REITs can diversify their portfolio by purchasing shares in numerous REITs. If investors can diversify at the personal level, there will be no reward to the individual REIT for diversifying. In fact, because of particular expertise in certain areas of real estate, it may be worthwhile for a REIT to specialize.

Some REITs specialize in residential mortgages. They may purchase FHA- and VA-insured loans and hold them for investments. In this way, they really replicate some of the secondary mortgage market agencies. It is not unusual to find REITs specializing in derivative mortgage securities, such as (residential) CMO residuals. Investors may buy the shares of such REITs as an interest-hedging device. Recall from Chapter 11 that the returns on CMO residuals rise when interest rates increase. Thus, if an investor, such as a bank, has a heavy portion of its portfolio in traditional bonds, it may wish to invest in derivative securities that increase in value when rates rise. One way to accomplish this is to invest in REITs that hold the residuals.

REIT Advisors

REIT legislation requires that the assets of the REIT be managed by an independent advisor. Most advisors are financial institutions or firms that specialize in real estate advisory services. Some, such as mortgage bankers and developers, may use the REIT as a short-term source of financing for their non-REIT business. The performance (rate-of-return) of a REIT will be a function of the quality of its investments, the managerial ability of the advisor, and the fees that the advisor charges. Theoretically, there should not be any difference of REIT performance based on the type of advisor. However, at least one study showed that there was such a difference. In a study of 105 REITs, Howe and Shilling found that the rates-of-return on REITs advised by mortgage bankers were significantly less than those on others.[3] The return on REITs advised by life insurance companies and real estate advisor firms performed the best. Thus, there appears to be some evidence that the selection of advisors for a REIT is important.

Development of REITs

A perspective on the performance of REITs can be gained by looking at Table 20–2. The table shows the total annual return on all, equity, mortgage, and hybrid REITs over the period 1972–1996. As seen, returns on REITs have been somewhat volatile. For example, in 1974 REITS overall earned a negative 42 percent while the return was 36 percent and 49 percent for the two years following, respectively. In general, returns were lower for REITs in the 1980s. Recently, REITs earned 18 percent in 1995 and 36 percent in 1996.

Subsequent to moderate initial growth in the early 1970s, the growth of REITs declined in the mid-1970s. You will see shortly that the per-share value of REITs also fell significantly during the mid- to late-1970s. After the decline in the importance of REITs in the mid-1970s, REITs made a comeback in the 1980s, the major growth occurring in the late 1980s after the 1986 Tax Reform Act. On the asset side, REITs have significantly reduced their holdings of acquisition, develop-

T A B L E   2 0 – 2
Annual Total Return for REITs

Year	All	Equity	Mortgage	Hybrid
1972	11.19%	8.01%	12.17%	8.01%
1973	−27.22	−15.52	−36.26	−15.52
1974	−42.23	−21.40	−45.32	−21.40
1975	36.34	19.30	40.79	19.30
1976	48.97	47.59	51.71	47.59
1977	19.08	22.42	17.82	22.42
1978	−1.64	10.34	−9.97	10.34
1979	30.53	35.86	16.56	35.86
1980	28.02	24.47	16.80	24.37
1981	8.58	6.00	7.07	6.00
1982	31.64	21.60	48.64	21.60
1983	25.47	30.64	16.90	30.64
1984	14.82	20.93	7.26	20.93
1985	5.92	19.10	−5.20	19.10
1986	19.18	19.16	19.21	16.41
1987	−10.67	−3.64	−15.67	−4.48
1988	11.36	13.49	7.30	15.75
1989	−1.81	8.84	−15.90	4.64
1990	−17.35	−15.35	−18.37	−23.62
1991	35.68	35.70	31.83	29.42
1992	12.18	14.59	1.92	20.66
1993	18.55	19.65	14.55	18.70
1994	0.81	3.17	−24.30	2.99
1995	18.31	15.27	63.42	14.21
1996	35.75	35.27	50.86	36.40

Source: NAREIT Web Page—www.NAREIT.com

ment, and construction loans. In 1992 these loans represented less than 1 percent of total assets, as opposed to 53.3 percent in 1972. On the liability side, REITs have reduced their short-term borrowing. Short-term borrowing was only 13.6 percent of assets in 1992 versus 43.8 percent in 1972. The reasons for the shift in asset and liability position is the widespread failure and losses attributed to REITs in the mid-1970s. REIT values fell precipitously in the early and mid-1970s. Share value did not reach its 1972 value until 1983. The decline in share values depressed the access of REITs to the capital markets. Investors, aware of the sharp drop, were wary of investing in REITs. Table 20–3 shows the volume of public offerings from 1970 through 1997. It is clear from this table that the decline in REIT values depressed the market for new offerings of REITs.

The widespread failure of REITs in the 1970s gave a black eye to this type of ownership form, and REITs did not recover until the late 1980s. There were two primary reasons for the decline in the number, assets, and value of REITs. One was the maturity mismatch problem that occurred about the same time for thrifts and was discussed earlier in the text. Essentially, the structure of some of the REITs was almost exactly that of a thrift. In 1974, for example, 34 percent of the assets of all REITs consisted of long-term (other) loans, while nearly half of their sources of funds was in short-term loans (bank borrowings and commercial paper). As you might expect, as interest rates ratcheted upward in the 1970s, REITs had to refinance their borrowing at increasingly higher rates while the return on their assets remained stable. As the market value of REIT assets fell relative to their liability, their equity was eroded.

A second reason that many REITs failed was related to an agency problem. In 1974, 47 percent of REIT assets were in land, construction, and development loans. These types of loans can be risky, since they are made to develop a property rather than purchase an existing property. As

TABLE 20–3
Public Offerings of Securities by REITs
(millions of dollars)

Year	All Offerings		Initial Offerings		Secondary Offerings	
	Number	*Total*	*Number*	*Total*	*Number*	*Total*
1970	72	1,687.4	41	1,358.4	31	329.0
1971	78	1,987.3	32	1,183.4	46	803.9
1972	67	1,223.3	29	563.2	38	660.1
1973	68	852.1	18	156.8	50	695.3
1974	17	23.7	5	1.5	12	22.2
1975	5	0.4	1	0.0	4	0.4
1976	8	19.7	0	0.0	8	19.7
1977	8	91.9	0	0.0	8	91.9
1978	12	91.5	3	8.4	9	83.1
1979	18	110.5	4	0.0	14	110.5
1980	20	264.0	4	30.0	16	234.0
1981	22	244.7	5	100.0	17	144.7
1982	12	453.6	3	315.0	9	138.6
1983	23	741.3	4	159.0	19	582.3
1984	34	2,729.9	9	378.8	25	2,351.1
1985	59	4,270.6	29	2,791.9	30	1,478.7
1986	63	4,668.9	20	1,204.4	43	3,464.5
1987	50	2,929.2	12	634.4	38	2,294.8
1988	37	3,068.7	13	1,374.2	23	1,694.6
1989	34	2,440.8	11	1,074.5	23	1,366.3
1990	24	1,765.2	10	882.0	14	883.2
1991	35	2,288.6	8	808.4	27	1,480.2
1992	57	6,515.1	8	919.2	49	5,595.5
1993	141	18,326.6	50	9,335.4	91	8,991.2
1994	145	14,721.0	45	7,175.8	100	7,545.2
1995	195	12,493.4	8	939.3	187	1,554.1
1996	225	17,455.8	6	1,107.8	219	16,348.0
1997	350	35,180.8	18	4,844.4	332	30,336.4

Source: REIT Web Page—www.NAREIT.com.

was pointed out earlier in the text, loans for a purchase are less risky because the property will have some sort of a track record to gauge its value. With a development loan, all of the cash flows are speculative. The interest rate on development loans is higher than for loans for purchase because of the added risk.

The agency problem that arose in the 1970s had to do with originators of development loans selling them off to REITs at their face value, when in fact they may have declined in value. Thus, a commercial bank that may be an advisor to a REIT might cause the REIT to purchase development loans that it has originated and subsequently determined to be very speculative. If a bank (also the REIT advisor) sells the loan to the REIT at face value, it captures a wealth premium at the expense of the stockholders in the REIT. This sort of activity, where REIT advisors sold real estate assets to REITs, caused investors to take a cautious view of REITs. The data in Table 20–3 indicate the public offerings of REITs fell to a trickle in the mid- to late 1970s. Today, land development and construction loans only represent a small percentage of the assets of all REITs.

REITs: A Laboratory for Analyzing Capital Structure Decisions

Regardless of the form of assets held by REITs (equity, mortgage, or hybrid), they may choose to finance a portion of their acquisitions by issuing debt. Those REITs that choose to issue debt are leveraged REITs. They may represent an interesting case. As you know, REITs are not taxed at the entity level. They do not benefit from the tax deductibility of interest payments as do regular corporations. Thus, the tax reasons for leverage are absent in the case of REITs. In this sense, they present an opportunity to view the effect of leverage in a "no-tax world."

Arguments can be presented on either side of the issue of whether or not the use of leverage should increase the value of a REIT. That is, should a REIT use debt to finance its asset acquisitions? Here are some arguments.

First, there is the personal tax issue. Even though the REIT entity is not taxed, the bondholders and stockholders of the REIT are. If the personal tax rate on equity is lower than that on interest, then more equity should be used. Fewer dollars will go to the Treasury. The tax shelter nature of real estate (cash flows greater than income per books) suggests that the tax rate on equity is less than on debt and the use of leverage would negatively impact the value of REITs. Second, if the use of debt increases the probability of bankruptcy and default, there should be a negative impact from the use of debt. Third, REITs that borrow funds must compete with taxable firms, for which a portion of their interest payments represent a tax savings. This implies they are at a disadvantage in the marketplace in bidding for debt. The rate they pay will be too high. All these arguments weigh against the use of debt for REITs.

On the other hand, real estate assets are immovable and readily identifiable. From this standpoint, they generally represent excellent collateral for debt. There is also the argument that firm managers may have better information about the value of the firm than does the marketplace. If management believes that the equity of the REIT is undervalued, they will prefer to issue debt to finance asset acquisitions. (Why issue equity if the firm is not going to receive the full value for the new shares?) This may be a signal to the marketplace that the value of the REIT is greater than that set by the marketplace. We also know that some REIT investors are institutional investors such as pension funds. Pension funds are prohibited from borrowing money to invest in assets. They cannot leverage themselves. Even if they purchase mortgage properties, they may run the risk of incurring the unrelated business income tax (UBIT) discussed earlier in the text. However, REIT investments are specifically exempt from the UBIT provisions. Thus, purchasing leveraged REITs may be a way for such institutional investors to obtain leverage they cannot obtain for themselves. As you can see, the theoretical arguments for the use of debt by REITs are mixed.

The evidence on the effectiveness of REIT leverage is also mixed. Maris and Elayan looked at the cost of capital for 61 REITs in the 1980s.[4] They found there was a slight increase in the cost of capital as a result of the use of leverage. This would imply that the value of the REITs should fall if debt is used. Additional debt raises the average cost of acquiring funds.

On the other hand, Howe and Shilling found that the value of a large sample of REITs increased concurrently with the announcement of a debt offering.[5] Conversely, the value of REITs that announced new equity issues fell.

In neither study were the changes substantial, however. This indicates that the use of leverage by REITs likely has offsetting impacts.

A CLOSER LOOK AT CORPORATE VERSUS PARTNERSHIP FORM OF OWNERSHIP

We conclude this chapter with another, more in-depth comparison between the corporate and partnership forms of ownership of real estate. These two ownership forms are alternatives when the REIT form is not a candidate for holding real estate. For example, when the scale of the investment is moderate, there is the need or desire to retain earnings for reinvestment, or there is no need for access to large capital markets. Depending upon the characteristics of the real estate investment, one or the other form will yield superior returns. Here, we will assume that limited liability is not an issue, since limited partnerships can be used to hold real estate in the partnership form.

The form of ownership that dominates is the one that provides the highest present value of after-tax cash flows to the investor. Several items are important. First, it is the present value of the cash flows that matter, not the total over time. Second, it is after-tax dollars that are measured, not before-tax returns. Thus, tax laws have an important impact on the most advantageous form by which to hold real estate. Finally, it is the return to the investor that matters, not the holding entity. If real estate is held by a corporation, then the proper measure of value is the returns to the shareholder, not the returns at the corporate level.

Prior to the Tax Reform Act of 1986, it was almost always advantageous to hold real estate in the partnership form because of the double taxation of corporations and the pass-through of losses for partnership. If income and cash flows were positive, they would be subject to double taxation under the corporate form of ownership, but only at the investor level if under partnership ownership. If income was negative (regardless of the cash flows), the losses could not be passed through with corporate ownership as they could be with partnership ownership. Thus, prior to 1986, the partnership form dominated. The 1986 Tax Reform Act removed this dominance. Recall that the main provisions of the 1986 Act are the restrictions on the availability of passive losses to offset other income. While investors in a partnership cannot use passive losses (except to offset passive income), the corporation can use such losses to offset other income. This reduces the sting of the double taxation and gives some advantage to the corporate form. The major disadvantage of the corporate form, however, remains the double taxation of income.

Given the tax environment, there are several factors that will determine the best ownership form of real estate.

Amount of Depreciation.   Depreciation is a noncash expense which is deductible for tax purposes. Given sufficient depreciation, the net operating income (NOI) of the real estate investment may be near zero (but with positive cash flows). If the NOI of the real estate investment is near zero for a significant portion of the holding period, the double taxation problem nearly disappears. Thus, high levels of depreciation expense will favor the corporate form of ownership. Lower levels of depreciation will result in positive levels of (taxable) NOI, which will favor the partnership form of ownership.

Holding Period.   If an investor anticipates a long holding period, this will favor the corporate form of ownership. Any cash flows that are retained by the corporation will not be taxed until distributed. With a long holding period, the cash flows can be reinvested and the longer reinvested cash flows escape the double taxation. The taxes are eventually paid but at a future date, reducing their present value (cost).

A shorter holding period favors the partnership form, especially if there are suspended passive losses in the early years of the investment. The suspended losses are available to offset other income only when the property is sold. Thus, a short holding period will result in the use of the suspended loss and the associated tax benefits at an earlier date.

Amount of Retained Earnings.   If the investor desires to reinvest a large portion of the cash flows back into the real estate investment, then the corporate form of ownership will be beneficial. Again, the reason is the double taxation. If a large portion of the cash flows is to be retained, the corporation can do so and avoid taxes at the individual investor level. With a partnership, any income flows through to the partner (investor) and is taxed at that level.

Tax Credits. If there are low-income or rehabilitation tax credits available for the property, the partnership form may be the best of the two alternatives. With the corporate form, the tax credit accrues at the corporate level. The corporation pays less taxes than otherwise, but this means that the investor will eventually receive more cash flows (by virtue of the tax saving at the corporate level) on which taxes must be paid at the personal level. Under a partnership, the tax credits are passed through directly to the investor.

Use of Debt Financing. In the case where the property is well suited as collateral for debt and equity sources of funding are scarce, the use of a large amount of debt to finance the property may be desirable. This will favor the corporate form of ownership because of the tax shield nature of the interest payments. This argument is the same as the one used above for large depreciation expenses. Thus, for properties where there is both large depreciation and interest expenses, the corporate form of ownership may be the most advantageous.

Passive Loss Limitations. An investor may have positive passive income with which to offset passive losses. In such a case, the passive loss limitation is going to be less binding and the partnership form of ownership will be preferred. If the investor has no passive income to offset, this would favor the corporate form since only the corporation can use the passive losses to offset nonpassive income.

Table 20–4 presents a summary of the characteristics of real estate investments that affect the choice of type of ownership—corporate or the partnership form. In general, the double taxation of corporate income places this form of ownership at a distinct disadvantage, relative to the partnership form. It may take several factors to cause the corporate form of ownership to dominate the partnership form, even with the limitation of passive losses. Yet, for properties that (1) have large amounts of depreciation, (2) are expected to be held for a long period of time, (3) have a need for reinvested cash flows, (4) are not eligible for tax credits, and (5) are debt financed, the corporate form may dominate for the reasons stated above.

The final determination of the best form of ownership can be made by finding the present value of the after-tax cash flows that accrue at the investor (not holding entity) level. The after-tax cash flows will take into effect the lack or presence of double taxation, the deductibility of depreciation and interest expenses, reinvestment of cash flows, and the use of passive losses to offset other income. The present value will take into account the timing of the after-tax cash flows.

The preceding discussion is summarized in Table 20–5. There is no perfect ownership vehicle for real estate. Even a sole ownership may be warranted for investors interested in small acquisitions which they can manage by themselves. However, if one considers the effect of tax legislation, access to capital marketing (liquidity), and the large scale of many real estate investments, then a form of ownership such as a RELP or REIT is likely to be the overall best ownership form.

TABLE 20–4

Factors Affecting Optimal Holding Form for Real Estate

Favors Corporate Ownership	*Favors Partnership Ownership*
1. Large depreciable base	1. Small depreciable base
2. Long holding period	2. Short holding period
3. Need to retain cash flows	3. Need to distribute cash flows
4. No tax credits available	4. Tax credit available
5. Financed by debts	5. Financed by equity
6. No passive income available	6. Passive income available to be offset by passive losses

T A B L E 20–5

Summary of Real Estate Ownership Forms

Attribute	Sole Ownership	C Corporation	S Corporation	Private Limited Partnership	Publicly Traded Partnership	Real Estate Investment Trust
Personal Liability	Unlimited	Limited	Limited	Limited	Unlimited	Limited
Tax treatment:						
Double taxation	No	Yes	No	None	None	None
Pass-through of losses	up to $25,000	Offset active business and portfolio	Offset active business loss only	None	None	None
Liquidity	Low	Low	Low	Low	Good	Excellent
Access to equity capital markets	None	Moderate	None	Limited	Good	Excellent
Minimum investment requirement	Burdensome	Moderate	Moderate	Moderate	Moderate	Minimum
Scale of asset acquisition	Small	Medium	Medium	Medium	Medium to large	Large
Government restrictions of financial decisions	None	None	None	None	None	Substantial
Participation in management decisions	Great	Moderate	Great	Moderate	None	None
Overall	Poor to moderate	Poor to moderate	Great	Moderate	Moderate to good	Good to excellent
Comments	Good for small investors seeking small properties, ability to diversify limited.	Good for real estate investments with no income but positive cash flow to reinvest.	Mimics a partnership but with limits on number of shareholders.	Useful for small scale investments. Relatively large cost of raising funds.	Similar to REITs since passive losses cannot be used, REITs may be better vehicle.	Tax regulation makes this a good choice for large investments.

SUMMARY

There are three major factors that influence the ownership form for real estate investments: tax regulations, personal (investor) liability, and access to capital markets. Tax regulations affect the investor's after-tax cash flow from the real estate acquisition. Other things being equal, those ownership forms that allow greater (and sooner) after-tax cash flows will be the preferred ownership vehicle. The double taxation of the corporation puts this form at an immediate disadvantage. But the restriction on the pass through or losses (1986 Tax Reform Act) also has diminished the value of the partnership form.

Investors also value limited liability. Leveraged real estate can be especially risky. Should the value of the property fall below that of the indebtedness, the lender will seek judgments to recover the difference. Investors do not desire to become liable for any such amounts beyond their initial investment. Sole ownership will expose investors to this risk. Most other forms of ownership, including corporate, limited partnership, and REIT structures afford limited liability.

For large real estate investments, access to capital markets may be important. Here, the ownership form will have to involve shares or interests that trade on large, efficient, capital markets. Large MLPs and REITs offer much better access to capital markets than do the private limited partnership, S corporation, or sole ownership forms.

Real estate limited partnerships were very popular prior to the Tax Reform Act of 1986. Losses could be passed through to the limited partners at that time. In many cases, investors in highly leveraged limited partnerships would often receive tax deductions over the first few years at least equal to their initial investment. The restrictions on the use of passive losses introduced by the act have diminished the value of this form of ownership. Unless the partnership has access to large capital markets (MLPs), this form may not be the one of preference.

The REIT structure was created by Congress in 1960. The act that created REITs eliminated the double taxation that is usually present for the corporate form of ownership. REITs did poorly in the 1970s, however, because of maturity mismatch and investment in risky and speculative acquisition, construction, and development loans. Rising market interest rates in the 1970s increased the cost of short-term funds for REITs at the same time that the yield on their mortgage portfolio remained low. While their equity was being eroded by the squeeze play from interest rates, many of their speculative ADC loans were going bad. The combination led to widespread failure of REITs, a loss of confidence in this form of real estate ownership, and a drought in new public offerings. REITs made a comeback in the mid- to late 1980s. The maturity of the assets and liabilities was structured better, and the Tax Reform Act of 1986 diminished the value of the partnership form of investment.

The best forms of ownership for large-scale investments remains the large, publicly traded partnership and the REIT. For smaller-scale investments, the corporate form may offer some benefits despite the double taxation. The corporate form of investment may prove prudent if the real estate property is intended to be held for a long period of time, if it is financed with debt, if it has a significant depreciable base, and if the corporation has other income with which to offset losses from the property. Otherwise, for moderate-size investments, the private limited partnership may dominate simply because of the absence of double taxation.

All ownership forms of real estate exist because of the wide variety of investors' needs and desires. Even the sole ownership form may be preferred by small investors who desire to have maximum control over the management of the property and can use the $25,000 exemption of pass-through losses allowed to active manager-investors.

KEY TERMS

C corporation	Limited partnership
Closed-end REIT	Master limited partnership (MLP)
Continuity of life	Mortgage REIT
Double taxation	Open-end REIT
Equity REIT	Publicly traded partnership (PTP)
Finite-life REIT	Real estate investment trust (REIT)
Free transferability of interest	Revised Uniform Limited Partnership Act
General partnership	S corporation
Hybrid REIT	Self-liquidating REIT
Limited liability	Uniform Limited Partnership Act (ULPA)

SUGGESTED READINGS

Corgel, J. B., W. McIntosh, and S. Ott. 1995. Real Estate Investment Trusts: A Review of the Financial Economics Literature. *Journal of Real Estate Literature* Vol. 3, No. 1, 13–46.

Erickson, J. R., and A. Friedman. 1987. Estimating the cost of capital for a REIT: A case study. *The Real Estate Appraiser and Analyst,* Fall/Winter.

Glascock, J. L., and W. T. Hughes. 1995. NAREIT Indentified Exchange Listed REITs and Their Performance Characteristics: 1972–1991. *Journal of Real Estate Literature* Vol. 3, 63–83.

Gould, A., and A. Van Dyke. 1990. Property ownership: Key considerations in choice of entity. *Real Estate Accounting and Taxation* Vol. 15, Summer, 43–51.

Healey, T., R. Papert, and S. Shepherd. 1990. Real estate finance alternatives in corporate restructurings. *Real Estate Finance Journal* Vol. 5, Spring, 9–16.

Investment Partnership Association. 1990. Partnership in America: An analysis of limited partnerships. *Real Estate Accounting and Taxation* Vol. 4, Winter.

Kapplin, S. D., and A. L. Schwartz, Jr. 1988. Public real estate limited partnership returns: A preliminary comparison with other investments. *Journal of the American Real Estate and Urban Economics Association* Vol. 16, Spring, 63–68.

Lentz, G., and J. Fisher. 1989. Tax reform and organizational forms for holding investment real estate: Corporation vs. partnership. *Journal of the American Real Estate and Urban Economics Association* Vol. 17, Fall.

Maris, B., and F. Elayan. 1990. Capital structure and the cost of capital for untaxed firms: The case of REITs. *Journal of the American Real Estate and Urban Economics Association* Vol. 18, Spring, 22–39.

McIntosh, W., C. Rogers, C. F. Sirmans, and Y. Liang. 1994. Stock Price and Management Changes: The Case of REITs. *AREUEA Journal* Vol. 22, 515–526.

Wang, K., J. Erickson, and G. W. Gau. 1993. Dividend Policies and Dividend Announcement Effects for REITs. *AREUEA Journal* Vol. 21, 185–201.

Webb, J. R. 1984. Real estate investment acquisition rules of life insurance companies and pension funds: A survey. *Journal of the American Real Estate and Urban Economics Association* Vol. 12, Winter, 495–500.

Webb, J. R., and W. McIntosh. 1986. Real estate investment acquisition rules for REITs: A survey. *Journal of Real Estate Research* Vol. 1, Fall, 465–495.

REVIEW QUESTIONS

20–1   There are three general factors that affect the form in which investors choose to hold real estate. List each and explain how they affect the ownership form.

20–2   List each ownership form by which investors can hold real estate. List at least one advantage and one disadvantage of each form.

20–3   Explain what is meant by double taxation of corporation income.

20–4   Why would a limited partnership be a better ownership form for real estate than an S corporation?

20–5   How is a limited partnership different from a general partnership?

20–6   List the four IRS tests that distinguish a partnership from a corporation. Indicate which of the four differentiate a partnership from a corporation.

20–7   What is a master limited partnership, and how does it differ from a regular limited partnership?

20–8   List at least six requirements for an association of investors to qualify as a real estate investment trust.

20–9   List and define four types of REITs.

20–10   Explain why large numbers of REITs failed in the 1970s.

20–11   What characteristics of a real estate property investment would favor the corporate form of ownership over the partnership form? What characteristics would favor the partnership form? Explain each answer.

ENDNOTES

1.   Originally, in order to avoid taxation, real estate investment trusts were established whereby the real estate was held in trust form, and beneficial interests in the trust were sold in the capital markets. Later, in 1960, the Treasury allowed real estate to be held in the corporate form and still avoid the

double taxation as long as certain restrictive conditions were met. Today, what is still referred to as a real estate investment trust is most probably a corporate form of organization that holds real estate assets.

2.   There are other ways of creating MLPs that are beyond the scope of this text.

3.   J. Howe and J. Shilling, "REIT Advisor Perfomance," *AREUEA Journal* 18 (4) (Winter 1990): 479–500.

4.   B. Maris and F. Elayan, "Capital Structure and the Cost of Capital for Untaxed Firms: The Case of REITs," *AREUEA Journal* 18 (1) (Spring 1990): 22–39.

5.   J. Howe and J. Shilling, "Capital Structure Theory and REIT Security Offerings," *Journal of Finance* 43 (4) (September 1988): 983–993.

WEB SITES

www.NAREIT.com   Web page for the National Association of Real Estate Investment Trusts.

PART

4

Special Topics in Real Estate Finance

The two chapters in this section deal
with topics tangential to financing real
estate properties. Here, we look at portfolio construction and the role of diversification in reducing the risk of investment in real estate. We also look at
issues of lenders' legal liabilities and
fraud and ethics in real estate lending.

CHAPTER 21

Real Estate in a Portfolio Context

In this chapter, we discuss the relevance of real estate investments in constructing portfolios of assets. A **portfolio** is a set or combination of assets. Although a portfolio can consist of only one asset, it is generally viewed as a mixture of different types of assets. After you have read this chapter, you should understand how the risk and return of a portfolio of assets can differ from that of the individual assets that make up the portfolio. You should understand how diversification, the process of forming portfolios consisting of different types of assets, affects the risk of a portfolio. You also will understand what characteristics of assets are important insofar as constructing "efficient" portfolios. Efficient portfolios are those that maximize expected return for a given level of risk, or minimize risk for a given level of expected return. You will see what characteristics of real estate investments contribute to the construction of efficient portfolios. Finally, you will see that diversification of real estate assets can be achieved in several ways, including by property type and by location.

INTRODUCTION

In this chapter, we will explore the role of real estate investment in the context of a portfolio of assets. We begin with a discussion of the nature of diversification and the effect of diversification on the risk and return of a portfolio of assets. You will see the difference between the risk of an asset held in isolation and the risk of a portfolio of assets. We will then move to a discussion of some asset-pricing theories that incorporate the concept of portfolio risk. Here you will view the risk of an asset only in terms of its relationship to a portfolio of other assets.

In the following section of this chapter, we will consider the role of real estate in a **mixed-asset portfolio**—that is, one that includes different types of assets. Finally, we will analyze the diversification of a portfolio that consists only of real estate assets. Here, diversification means different property types in different geographical locations.

THE NATURE OF DIVERSIFICATION

Investors are concerned with both the expected return and the risk of an asset. Return and risk cannot be considered in isolation. A basic premise of finance theory states that investors must be rewarded with higher expected returns for taking on added risk. This is the reason that more risky investments, say junk bonds, have initially higher yields than riskless investments, such as Treasury obligations. Fortunately, investors need not invest in assets in isolation: they can form portfolios that are mixtures of different assets with different expected returns and risks. The main thrust of portfolio diversification is the disproportionate reduction of risk compared to return. We will see shortly that it is possible to employ diversification to reduce risk while having a negligible or no impact on return. In essence, investors are able to eliminate some (but not all) risk simply by combining assets into a portfolio.

Risk can be defined as the possibility (and probability) that the actual return on an investment will be different from the expected return. It can be measured as the volatility of an asset's returns. There are two implicit elements in this definition of risk. First, there is the notion of the absolute difference that can occur between the actual return and the expected return. Second, there is the consideration that the probability of the actual return will be different from the expected return. Consider the following simple example. Table 21–1 shows the expected and possible returns on two assets for the coming year. The possible returns for Asset A differ from the expected returns by a substantial amount, while those for Asset B are close to the expected return. At first glance, one is tempted to view Asset A as the more risky of the two. However, note the probabilities that have been assigned to the possible and expected returns in each case. There are very low probabilities associated with the possible returns of Asset A (other than the expected). It is possible to assign such small probabilities to the alternative returns as to make Asset A virtually riskless. The probabilities associated with the different returns for Asset B indicate it may be more risky. Shortly, we will review the formulas for determining the risk of an asset held in isolation. If that formula is applied to the data in Table 21–1, it would indicate that the risk of Asset B is indeed greater than that of Asset A.

To understand the risk reduction that is possible through diversification, consider the following simple example. Table 21–2 shows the expected and possible returns on two assets, X and Y. The expected return $E(R)$ for an asset is calculated by considering the possible returns and their probabilities ($P_1R_1, P_2R_2 \ldots P_nR_n$) with the following formula:

$$E(R) = P_1R_1 + P_2R_2 + \cdots + P_nR_n = \sum_{i=1}^{n} P_iR_i \qquad \text{(Equation 21–1)}$$

where i represents each asset.

For both assets X and Y the expected return is

$$E(R) = (0.06 \times 0.2) + (0.07 \times 0.2) + (0.08 \times 0.2) + (0.09 \times 0.2) + (0.10 \times 0.2) = 0.08$$

T A B L E 2 1 – 1
Distribution of Returns for Upcoming Year

	Asset A		Asset B	
	Possible Return	*Probability*	*Possible Return*	*Probability*
	2%	0.02	7%	0.30
	9	0.96	9	0.40
	16	0.02	11	0.30
Expected return	9%		9%	

T A B L E 2 1 – 2
Distribution of Returns for Upcoming Year

	Asset X		Asset Y	
	Possible Return	*Probability*	*Possible Return*	*Probability*
	6%	0.2	6%	0.2
	7	0.2	7	0.2
	8	0.2	8	0.2
	9	0.2	9	0.2
	10	0.2	10	0.2
Expected return	8%		8%	
Variance	0.00020		0.00020	
Standard deviation	0.01414		0.01414	

Likewise, the formula for risk takes into account not only the difference between the expected return and the possible returns but also their probabilities. That is, the (squared) differential between each possible return and the expected return $[R_1 - E(R)]_2$ is multiplied by the probability P of the possible return as follows:

$$\sigma^2 = [R_1 - E(R)]^2 \times P_1 + [R_2 - E(R)]^2 \times P_2 + \cdots + [R_n - E(R)]^2 \times P_n$$

$$= \sum_{i=1}^{n} [R_i - E(R)]^2 P_i \qquad \text{(Equation 21–2)}$$

In this equation, σ is the standard deviation or risk and n is the number of assets. Thus, for the example in Table 21–2, the risk of each asset can be computed as

$$\sigma^2 = (0.06 - 0.08)^2 \times 0.2 + (0.07 - 0.08)^2 \times 0.2 + (0.08 - 0.08)^2$$

$$\times 0.2 + (0.09 - 0.08)^2 \times 0.2 + (0.10 - 0.08)^2 \times 0.2$$

The statistical measure of risk derived in Equation 21–2 is called the **variance.** Its square root σ is called the standard deviation.

The expected return and the risk of each asset in Table 21–2 have been made identical for the purpose of illustration. It is obvious that the two assets are identical insofar as their risk/return structure is concerned. Each has the same expected return, 8 percent, and the same risk, $\sigma = 0.01414$. The probability distribution of returns for either asset is shown in Figure 21–1.

A rational investor should be indifferent between the two assets if he is to hold either one in isolation, because both provide the same expected return and the same risk. But what if the investor chooses to invest half his wealth in each asset. What would be the expected return and risk of a portfolio so divided? One may be tempted to conclude that the risk and the return of a portfolio of two identical assets would be the same as that of the assets held in isolation. However, this is likely not to be the case.

To see why, assume that the returns on assets X and Y are completely independent of one another. (In statistical terms, the correlation between the returns of the two assets is zero.) This means that the return on one asset will have no influence on the return on the other asset. A more precise way of stating the relationship of independence of returns is to say that knowledge of the actual return on one asset will be useless in predicting the return on the other. In other words, if someone were to tell you that the actual return on Asset X for the past year was 7 percent, that information would be useless for you to predict the return on Asset Y. If the returns on the two

FIGURE 21–1

Distribution of Returns for an Individual Asset

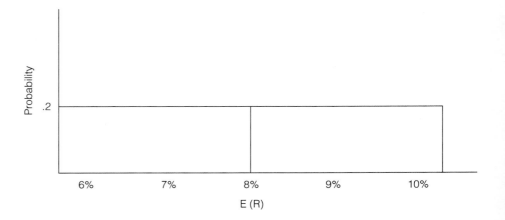

assets are completely independent, then the expected return and the risk of a portfolio consisting of an equal share of X and Y will be as indicated in Table 21–3.

The values in Table 21–3 are derived as follows. Note that the first listed possible return on the portfolio is 6 percent. For this to occur, however, both assets would have to have a return of 6 percent. From probability theory, we know that the probability of two independent events occurring simultaneously is equal to the product of their separate probabilities. Thus, the probability that both assets (and, therefore, the portfolio) will return 6 percent is $0.2 \times 0.2 = 0.04$. The next listed possible return is 6.5 percent. This portfolio return can occur two ways: if Asset X has a return of 6 percent and Asset Y a return of 7 percent, or the reverse. Since each of these two possibilities has a probability of 0.04, their combined probability is 0.08.

The same thinking applies to the other listed probabilities. For example, a portfolio return of 8 percent can occur in five different ways (X and Y returns of 6 and 10 percent, 7 and 9 percent, 8 and 8 percent, 9 and 7 percent, and 10 and 6 percent, respectively), so that the probability here is 20 percent (5×0.04). The entire probability distribution is shown in Figure 21–2, where you should notice two things. First, the probabilities of the extreme rates of return, 6 and 10 percent, have been reduced significantly—from 20 to 4 percent.

TABLE 21–3
Distribution of Returns for Upcoming Years

Portfolio of Assets X and Y	
Possible Return	*Probability*
6.0%	0.04
6.5	0.08
7.0	0.12
7.5	0.16
8.0	0.20
8.5	0.16
9.0	0.12
9.5	0.08
10.0	0.04
Sum	1.00
Expected	8%
Variance	0.0001
Standard deviation	0.01

FIGURE 21–2

Distribution of Returns for a Portfolio

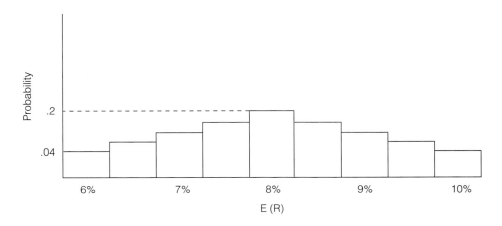

Second, the expected value (and its probability) has remained the same. Taken together, this indicates that the risk of the portfolio is less than that of either asset held in isolation. However, the expected return is not less. The standard deviation for this simple two-asset portfolio is 0.01, less than that of either asset held in isolation. In fact, if 100 assets identical to X or Y could be combined into a portfolio, the expected return would remain 8 percent but the risk, as indicated by the standard deviation, would be negligible. It would be extremely unlikely that the return on such a portfolio would be much less than 7.9 or more than 8.1 percent. Given a sufficient number of assets all identical to X or Y, it would be possible to construct a portfolio for which an 8 percent return would be virtually assured.

It should be clear that the amount of risk reduction that takes place through diversification is determined by the extent to which the returns of the assets are correlated. For example, if the returns of X and Y are perfectly correlated, then there would be no benefit from diversification. If the return on Asset X is 6 percent and the return on Y is also 6 percent, there is no benefit from diversification. The portfolio will behave precisely as either asset held alone. On the other hand, if the returns of the two assets are perfectly negatively correlated, diversification may reduce the risk of the portfolio to zero with just two assets. If the return on Asset X is 6 percent and that on Y is 10 percent, the portfolio return will be 8 percent. Conversely, if the return on X is 10 percent and that on Y is 6 percent, the portfolio return will again be 8 percent.

The (historic) correlation in the returns of two assets can be determined from a statistical sample of past returns and is indicated by the **correlation coefficient r_{xy}**:

$$r_{xy} = \frac{\sum_{t=1}^{n}(R_{x,t} - \overline{R}_x)(R_{y,t} - \overline{R}_y)/N}{\sigma_x \sigma_y}$$

(Equation 21–3)

where N is the number of time periods in the sample, $\overline{R}_x$ and $\overline{R}_y$ are the average returns on assets X and Y, $R_{x,t}$ and $R_{y,t}$ are the actual returns on assets X and Y in each time period t, and σ_x and σ_y are the standard deviations of the returns of assets X and Y.

Note that whenever R_x and R_y are both above their respective average return, the numerator in Equation 21–3 is positive. When both are below their respective average, then the numerator is also positive. Thus, if the returns vary together in a positive manner (rising together and falling together), the correlation coefficient is positive. It is negative if the return on one rises as the other falls. Of course, if there is no relationship at all between the returns, the correlation coefficient is near zero.

From these relationships, you can see that the risk of a portfolio of two (or more) assets will depend, in part, on the correlation coefficient(s) between their returns. For a two-asset (x, y) portfolio, the standard deviation in the return on the portfolio σ_p can be given by

$$\sigma_p = \sqrt{(\alpha \cdot \sigma_x)^2 + [(1 - \alpha) \cdot \sigma_y]^2 + 2\alpha \cdot \sigma_x[(1 - \alpha) \cdot \sigma_y r_{xy}]}$$

(Equation 21–4)

where α is the weight of the portfolio represented by Asset x.

This formula was developed in the late 1950s by Harry Markowitz and is referred to as the Markowitz diversification.[1] Note that the smaller r_{xy} is, the smaller will be the risk of the portfolio. In fact, if r_{xy} is sufficiently negative, the standard deviation in the returns of the portfolio can be zero.

The returns in Table 21–3 were constructed under the premise that the correlation in the returns of assets X and Y was zero. Employing Equation 21–4 and the standard deviation from Table 21–2, one can confirm that the standard deviation is 0.01.

$$0.01 = \sqrt{(0.5 \times 0.01414)^2 + (0.5 \times 0.01414)^2 + 0}$$

While the risk of a portfolio may be reduced by diversification, this is not necessarily so for its return. The return on a portfolio of assets will be equal to an average of the individual returns weighted by the relative proportion that each asset represents in the portfolio. Thus, the return on a portfolio can be expressed as:

$$R = \alpha R_x + (1 - \alpha)R_y$$

(Equation 21–5)

FIGURE 21–3

Risk Return Tradeoff for Two Assets

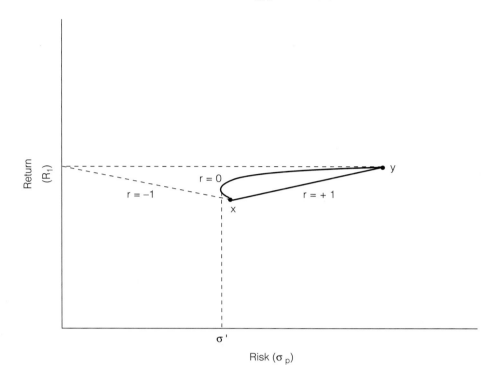

Benefits of Diversification

Diversification derives its value from the reduction in risk that occurs when assets are combined into portfolios. Even where the returns on assets are independent (not correlated), portfolio construction reduces risk associated with holding assets in isolation. Furthermore, the reduction in risk comes at no cost to the investor. Aside from slightly higher (and in some cases no higher) transaction costs, the diversification achieves a costless reduction in risk. Yet, diversification does not reduce the return. Equation 21–5 indicates that the return on a portfolio is the weighted average of the return on the individual assets. These relationships are shown in Figure 21–3. There we consider the expected risks and returns of two assets in isolation and in a portfolio. Points X and Y represent the expected risk and return of two separate assets. Asset Y is more risky and has a higher expected return than Asset X. A rational investor may be indifferent between the two, since the asset with the higher risk also has the larger expected return. But what if the two assets are combined into a portfolio? Equation 21–4 indicates that the risk (standard deviation) of the portfolio will depend on the risk of the individual assets, the correlation of their returns, and their weights in the portfolio. Equation 21–5 indicates that the expected return on the portfolio will depend upon the expected returns of the individual assets and their relative weights in the portfolio.

Here we consider three cases, each with a different correlation coefficient: perfect positive correlation ($+1$), no correlation (0), and perfect negative correlation (-1). In Figure 21–3 the straight-line segment between points X and Y corresponds to the assumption that the returns are perfectly positively correlated. There are no benefits from diversification. Portfolios constructed with more of Asset Y will have a larger return but also a larger risk, giving no benefits to the investor beyond investing in a single asset. The curved-line segment shows the risk/return tradeoff when the correlation coefficient is assumed to be zero. Risk can be reduced (to a theoretical minimum of σ'). Including some of the Y asset in a portfolio that begins with a concentration of the X asset has two benefits: return is increased and risk is reduced. No rational investor would

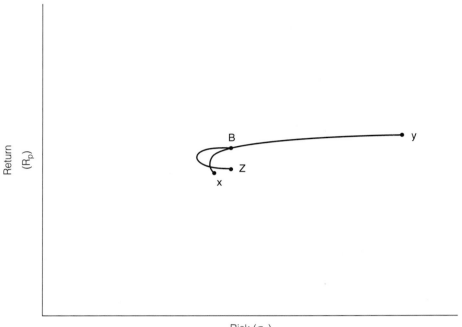

FIGURE 21–4

Risk Return Tradeoff for Multiple Assets

ever invest totally in Asset A, since he can increase his return and reduce his risk through diversification. The kinked-line segment associated with a correlation coefficient of -1 shows that the proper proportion of X and Y can yield a zero risk. That proper proportion will depend upon the risk of the individual assets.

From here we will assume that most assets have a zero correlation coefficient, so that the risk/return tradeoff can be characterized by curved-line segments such as that in Figure 21–3. A rational investor will choose a portfolio with a risk/return tradeoff in the upper portion of the curve, say at Point B.

Next, we can consider the results from introducing a third, fourth, and other assets into the portfolio. Figure 21–4 shows how other assets can be considered. If we introduce a third asset, Z, we can think of a portfolio that can be formed by adding Asset Z to a portfolio already consisting of X and Y at Point B. Thus, the new risk/return tradeoff will appear as the line segment designated by the points Z, B, and Y. Adding more assets in such a fashion will introduce new curves, and eventually the risk/return tradeoff of an almost infinite number of possible portfolios will appear as in Figure 21–5.

The dark, heavy line represents all those portfolios that have the greatest expected return for a given amount of risk or have the lowest risk for a given expected return. This portion of the curve is called the efficiency frontier, and all rational investors will choose a portfolio with a risk/return tradeoff on this curve. Portfolios located on the efficiency frontier are often referred to as mean-variance efficient, since they have the greatest return for the risk or the lowest risk for the return. Investors will choose their portfolio from among those on the frontier according to their risk preferences. More risk-averse investors will locate to the left portion of the curve, while less risk-averse investors will seek the higher returns on the rightward, more risky portion of the curve.

The important thing to remember from this discussion is that assets that have little, no, or negatively correlated returns with each other can be combined to create efficient portfolios. The efficient portfolios reduce risk without reducing return at nearly no cost. The key to portfolio construction is the search for assets with negatively correlated returns.

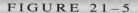

FIGURE 21–5

Efficiency Frontier

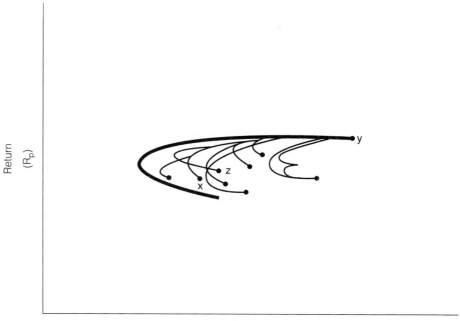

Theories of Asset Pricing

A formula such as Equation 21–4 is useful to determine the risk of a portfolio of a few or several assets. The formula can be used to determine the impact of an additional asset on the risk of a portfolio. The relevant risk of an asset then becomes that associated with its contribution to the risk of the portfolio. Assets with returns that are negatively correlated to assets in the existing portfolio are excellent candidates for inclusion in the portfolio. One can use the formula to judge how much risk is reduced by adding another asset. Unfortunately, the formula has some drawbacks.

The major shortcoming of using such a formula to determine the contribution to the risk of a portfolio from including an asset is the large number of terms and calculations that must be made. Even with modern computers the data collection, data entry, and calculations can be a monumental task for portfolios with more than a few assets. The formula for portfolio risk must consider not only the risk (standard deviation) of each asset but also the correlation coefficient between each asset and every other asset in the portfolio. As the number of assets included in the portfolio increases, the number of terms required to determine the new portfolio risk (and thus the contribution of the added assets to portfolio risk) explodes geometrically until the task is unmanageable. For this reason, the Markowitz formula was of limited use to practitioners who desired to create efficiently diversified portfolios.

Capital Asset Pricing Model

An alternative to the Markowitz methodology was offered about a decade later by William Sharpe,[2] who noted that it was not necessary to relate the correlation of returns of each asset to each other but only to an overall index (or portfolio). The mathematical demonstration of this model is shown in Appendix A to this chapter. Here, however, we opt for an intuitive explanation of Sharpe's model by considering the following example in the context of the stock market.

Assume that the only market for assets of interest is the stock market, and that the portfolio managers of larger institutional investors seek to eliminate as much risk as possible. Since diversification is costless, they begin by diversifying their portfolios as much as possible. A naive diversification process occurs at first, with portfolio managers simply adding stock without regard to the stock's individual risk or its contribution to the risk of the portfolio. Now, every stock that exists will be held by someone. After all, if no one desired a stock to be held in a portfolio, the demand would fall and so too would the price until it was attractive for someone to hold. The result of this naive process is that all portfolio managers would end up with a portfolio of all stocks. Their portfolios would be small representations of the large overall stock market. By definition, they would have eliminated all the risk that can possibly be eliminated through the diversification process. They would have eliminated all **diversifiable risk**. Does this mean that none of the portfolios would contain any risk? Not at all. They would each represent a portfolio of the stock market and therefore, each would have a risk associated with the market. Investing in the stock market is not riskless. The return on the market fluctuates from year to year.

Now imagine that each of the portfolio managers attempts to reduce the risk of his portfolio further. How can this be done? There is no more diversifiable risk left to eliminate, only the **nondiversifiable risk** of the market as a whole. Assume that each manager identifies stocks that appear to move with the market but by more than the market. When the market returns increase, the returns on these stocks increase more, and conversely when the returns decrease. In other words, the return on a portfolio is the average of the returns on the assets in the portfolio. If the return on the market portfolio increases, it must be because the return on some stocks increase more than the average, while the return on other stocks increase less than the average. The same can be said about decreases in the return on the market.

The optimal strategy of the managers would appear to be to sell off those stocks whose returns fluctuate more than the market. In this way, they not only get rid of all the diversifiable risk, they eliminate some of the nondiversifiable market risk. Thus, the Sharpe method concentrates on the relationship between the return of a stock (or other asset) and the return on a portfolio (market index). To continue the example, imagine that each portfolio manager has identified the stocks that fluctuate more than the market. This is not a difficult task, given the quantity of price data that is available. Each will attempt to sell those stocks and purchase stocks that fluctuate less than the market. But in the process of doing so, the price of the former type stock will fall and the price of the latter will rise. Falling prices imply, other things being equal, a higher expected return. Rising prices imply a lower expected return. In this simple way, stocks that fluctuate more than the market and represent added risk to a portfolio must have a higher expected return to be candidates for investment. The relationship expressed mathematically by Sharpe is called the **capital asset pricing model (CAPM)** or:

$$R_J = R_f + \beta(R_m - R_f) \qquad \text{(Equation 21–6)}$$

where R_J is the return on stock J, R_f is the risk-free rate, and R_m is the return on the market. In the CAPM, β (beta) represents the relationship between the return on a stock and the return on the market portfolio. Assets with a beta greater than 1 will command an expected return greater than the return on the market and vice versa. Note that the CAPM formula implies assets with a beta of 1 will have an expected return equal to the return on the market, which is reasonable since the returns on the asset behave like those on the market.

The same result can be obtained by noting that investors also will hold risk-free assets, notably Treasury obligations. When risk-free assets are added to a portfolio, the efficiency frontier changes shape. If we consider adding a risk-free investment to a portfolio represented by Point B in Figure 21–6, then the new efficiency frontier appears as the line segment R_fBC, a straight line. The new frontier, also called the capital market line, is straight because adding a risk-free asset affects the return on the new portfolio but does not affect the risk from a diversification standpoint (risk-free assets have no variance in return). Note that the new frontier as drawn will contain a set of portfolios that dominate all others in terms of higher returns and less risk. Thus, Point B represents the optimal mix of assets with some risk. Investors will, according to their risk preference, locate their portfolios along this capital market line. Some may invest only in risk-free securities (Point R_f), others only in portfolios of assets with some degree of risk (Point B), and others in a combination of the two.

FIGURE 21–6

Portfolio Construction with a Risk-free Asset

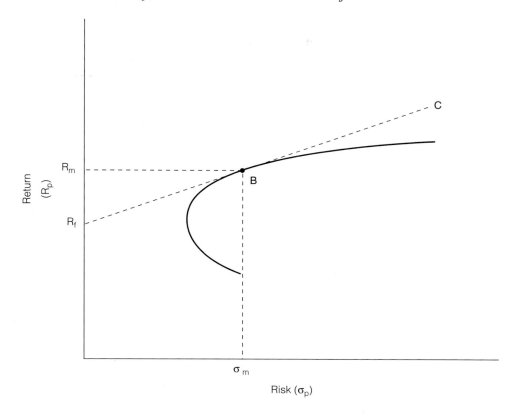

It is easy to develop an equation for the capital market line. Linear equations take the form:

$$Y = A + BX \qquad \text{(Equation 21–7)}$$

where A is the intercept on the vertical axis and B is the slope of the line. The slope of the line is equal to the rise over the run. If in Figure 21–6 the market portfolio is Point B, its expected return and its risk will be those of the market: $E(R_m)$ and δ_m, respectively. Beginning at point R_f the slope (rise over run) of the capital market line is

$$\frac{R_m - R_f}{\sigma_m - 0} = \frac{R_m - R_f}{\sigma_m} \qquad \text{(Equation 21–8)}$$

The equation for the capital market line can be expressed as

$$R_p = R_f + \frac{R_m - R_f}{\sigma_m}\sigma_p = R_f + (R_m - R_f)\frac{\sigma_p}{\sigma_m} \qquad \text{(Equation 21–9)}$$

which is similar to the capital asset pricing model for individual securities.

Subsequent to the development of the CAPM, many empirical studies were conducted to determine its validity as a pricing model. Most of these studies were confined to the returns on stocks alone. The form of the tests was simple. Historical data up to a cutoff point were employed to determine the beta of a stock. Then, using the beta and the risk-free rate, predictions were made for the return on the stock subsequent to the cutoff date. Predicted returns were then compared to actual returns. The predictability of the model met with limited success. Most studies confirmed the basic relationship but with less than ideal accuracy. In general, the tests showed:

1. A positive and linear relationship exists between a stock's beta and its return in excess of the market.
2. The slope of the capital market line was generally less than predicted.
3. The overall predictive results were disappointing.

The two main reasons given for the disappointing empirical results were the use of historical beta to predict future returns and the choice of assets to test the model. Most tests of the model utilized stock returns when, in fact, a proper portfolio should consist of every possible asset that can be held, including bonds, real estate, and human capital.

Arbitrage Pricing Theory

Following a critique of the CAPM by Roll[3] in the late 1970s, Roll and Ross[4] proposed the **arbitrage pricing theory (APT).** The central theme of this model was that the return on an asset is likely to be a function of more than one index (return on the market). The CAPM is a special case of the APT in the sense that the former only includes one factor, the return on the market. The APT model does not rely on a mean-variance efficient portfolio, but rather on asset pricing such that no arbitrage profits exist. Tests of the APT suggest that several factors affect assets' returns, including the return on the market, inflation, industrial production, and the return on the industry within which a company is located. Tests of the APT have been generally restricted to the stock market, however.

Both the CAPM and the APT indicate that diversification can reduce some risk with no sacrifice of expected return. The sole condition necessary for this result is that the mix of assets have returns that are not perfectly correlated with each other. Furthermore, the smaller the correlation, the greater the risk reduction that can be accomplished through diversification.

In the next portion of this chapter, we look at the role of real estate in a mixed-asset portfolio. That is, does the addition of real estate to a portfolio consisting of non-real-estate assets have diversification benefits?

REAL ESTATE IN A MIXED-ASSET PORTFOLIO

Here we discuss the advantages of adding real estate investments to a portfolio of mixed assets. A 1992 study by Louargand found that real estate represents about 4 percent of total investing by pension funds.[5] This produces a total equity investment of about $100 billion; however, their total real estate investment is closer to $400 billion when mortgages and mortgage-backed securities are considered. This total amounts to about 15 percent of the total pension asset portfolio.

The crucial test is the extent to which the returns on real estate investments are correlated with a wide variety of other assets such as stocks, bonds, human capital, and collectibles. One of the difficult tasks in this determination has been an accurate measurement of the returns on real estate properties. Stocks and bonds are traded frequently in large, efficient markets. Their market prices and, therefore, their returns over time can be determined with ease and accuracy. Real estate investments, on the other hand, are traded infrequently, and their prices are not reported to some centralized market as is the case for stocks and bonds.[6] The prices of real estate properties that are traded relatively frequently, such as single-family homes, also are not reported to a centralized market. An additional problem concerns capital improvements to real estate properties. Even where traded prices for a particular property on two different dates may be available, lack of information on any capital improvements made in the interim will lead to a miscalculation of the return.

The Problem with Appraised Values

Much of the data that are available on real estate property values are based on periodic appraisal and not on actual sales. This is so because many properties are held by one owner for long periods of time. Many properties held for investment by institutions such as pension funds and insurance companies must be appraised regularly so that the institutions can file financial statements with their regulators. Often, the institutions may make an "inside" appraisal on a quarterly basis but will have an outside independent appraisal made at least annually. The appraisal data can be used to estimate the value of the properties at various dates, but the estimates of value will not be transaction prices. Measures of return based on appraised values rather than transaction prices will show less variation through time. In other words, the return series based on appraised values is "smoothed" and does not exhibit the fluctuations that would result from returns based on transaction prices.

A primary reason for this smoothing process lies in the method of appraising properties—the income method. This method, combined with what Geltner calls the "lack of confidence" factor, causes the smoothing.[7] Lack of confidence refers to the subjective nature of the appraisal process and the tendency for appraisers to rely too much on the most recent past appraisals of the property in forming a new opinion of value. Often, new appraisals may be simply past appraisals adjusted upward for inflation. Inside appraisals may be made much in this fashion—an adjustment of the latest outside appraisal for whatever inflation has occurred.

A 1993 study by Myer and Webb seems to substantiate this problem with smoothing.[8] They found that the return on properties of securitized real estate (REITs) appears to be much more like the returns on common stocks and closed-end funds than like the returns on unsecuritized commercial real estate. They attribute this to the fact that REITs, commons stocks, and closed-end funds are all traded in the same markets and the returns on unsecuritized real estate are appraisal/accounting based rather than market/transaction based.

Follain and Calhoun, in a 1997 study, provide some insight into the multifamily housing market by examining price movements during the 1980s and early 1990s.[9] By developing price indices, they draw several conclusions about the national multifamily housing market. First, various methods of creating indexes yield similar patterns of price movement. Second, regional variation in price movements seems to be great. Third, the impact of the Tax Reform Act of 1986 does not appear to have been as dramatic as some have suggested given that price declines do not appear in either the 1986 or 1987 indices.

Before we further explore the relationship between the return on real estate and other assets, we will look briefly at some typical sources of data that can be used to estimate real estate returns.

Sources of Real Estate Data

When one speaks of the returns to real estate and their role in a mixed-asset portfolio, one is generally concerned with the return to the equity portion of real estate and not debt or mortgage returns. The ideal source of data of such a return series would be the transaction prices of all equity properties adjusted for any capital improvements. Such clean data is difficult, if not impossible, to obtain. There are, however, some sources that allow estimates of returns to equity real estate to be made. These sources have been used in various studies of real estate portfolios.

The Russell–NCREIF.   The Russell–NCREIF Property Index measures the historical performance of all-equity, income-producing properties owned by commingled funds on behalf of qualified pension and profit-sharing trusts, or owned directly by these trusts and managed on a separate account basis. The index gets its name from the Frank Russell Company, which computes the index on the basis of the value of properties held by members of the National Council of Real Estate Investment Fiduciaries. The index began in 1977 and calculations are based on quarterly returns of individual investment-grade properties. In 1987, Russell–NCREIF began tracking a separate index for apartments. It is the most widely quoted index of property values. The net income of the properties and their values are used to construct a quarterly return series divided into two components: income and appreciation. The Russell–NCREIF Property Index contains performance data on five different property types: apartments, office buildings, retail properties (including regional community and neighborhood shopping centers), research and development facilities, and warehouses.

National Association of Real Estate Investment Trusts.   Real estate investment trusts (REITs) are trusts that invest in real estate properties and issue shares of stock. The REITs invest in mortgages on real estate, real estate equity, or a combination of the two (hybrid REITs).

The advantage of return data based on REIT performance derives from the fact that prices of REIT stock are market transaction prices and not appraisals. The disadvantage is that, except for a few very large REITs, most are not traded in large, efficient markets. The return on nontraded REITs will reflect a lack of liquidity. Studies that have employed data on REIT prices have taken the information from the major stock exchanges or have obtained data from the National Association of Real Estate Investment Trusts (NAREIT), a trade organization that collects and maintains data on REIT transactions. From the transaction data, this organization publishes the **NAREIT Equity Index,** based on the return to equity REITs.

Commingled Real Estate Funds.   Commingled real estate funds (CREFs) are managed by large financial institutions for investors such as pension funds. The funds are called commingled because they take and combine funds from several investors and purchase real estate properties. Some of these funds track their return record. An example is the Prudential Property Investment Separate Account (PRISA), managed by Prudential Realty Group.

National Association of Realtors.   This trade organization for the nation's real estate salespeople and brokers surveys its members periodically to determine selling prices of residential properties. The data are released on a quarterly basis and indicate the median selling prices in four geographical areas of the country. A limitation is that data are not adjusted for any changes in the quality of the houses sold. Other sources of data on residential properties include *Finnegan's Financial Green Sheet Rates of Return* and the U.S. Department of Commerce series on prices for constant quality houses. The main problem with all such data on residential properties is the lack of transaction data on identified properties—that is, so-called repeat sales. The transaction data in the time series are, for the most part, on different properties.

U. S. Department of Agriculture.   The U.S. Department of Agriculture publishes a series called *Farm Real Estate Market Developments: Outlook and Situation,* based on recent transactions. The data suffer from the same problem as the data for residential sales—lack of data on repeat transactions. It is one of the more widely used sources for data on farmland values.

R. G. Ibbotson Associates.   Under the direction of Roger Ibbotson, this company annually publishes rates of return on various investments including real estate. The real estate component is a combination of residential, commercial, and farm properties. It is a good source for comparing rates of return and risk (variance in rates of return) on various investments.

The Diversification Benefits of Real Estate

Using these and other sources of data on real estate returns, many researchers have attempted to judge the diversification value of real estate. The results overwhelmingly support the notion that real estate offers substantial diversification benefits while at the same time offering protection against unanticipated inflation. An early 1980s study by Ibbotson and Siegel indicated that the average annual return on real estate from 1947 to 1982 was 8.27 percent.[10] This compared to 3.98 percent on U.S. government securities and 3.56 percent on corporate debt. Only corporate stock had a higher annual rate of return—11 percent. The standard deviation in the annual returns was very low for real estate, 3.71 percent. It was moderately higher for U.S. government securities, 4.92 percent, and corporate debt, 6.47 percent, and substantially higher for corporate stock, 17.52 percent. Over this period, the risk/return tradeoff for real estate indicated that it was a superior investment to any other asset. The diversification benefits of real estate were also substantial. Table 21–4 shows the correlation coefficients between real estate and other assets from 1947 to 1982. The returns on real estate are a composite of those on residential, farm, and commercial real estate. The return series was based on appraised values, so it suffered from the smoothing problem discussed above. The conclusion reached by Ibbotson and Siegel was that real estate offered superior returns if held as an asset in isolation, and excellent diversification benefits if held in a mixed-asset portfolio.

TABLE 21–4

Selected Cross Correlations of Asset Returns
1947–1982
Ibbotson & Siegel

	Real Estate	S&P Common Stock	Small Company Stock	Long-Term Corporate Bonds	Long-Term Government Bonds	U.S. Treasury Bills
Real estate	1.0					
S & P common stock	−0.06	1.0				
Small company stock	0.04	0.79	1.0			
Long-term corp. bonds	−0.06	0.14	0.05	1.0		
Long-term gov't bonds	−0.08	0.01	−0.06	0.95	10	
U.S. treasury bills	0.44	−0.25	0	0.15	0.21	1.0

Source: Ibbotson and Siegel, "Real Estate Returns: A Comparison With Other Investments," *AREUEA Journal* Vol. 12, No. 3, 1984, Table 3, p. 231.

Norman, Sirmans, and Benjamin provide a review of the literature on real estate returns and risk.[11] They find, when adjusting for risk, that real estate has a higher return per unit of risk than bonds or common stocks.

Bajtelsmit and Worzala examined the decision-making process used by pension plans in either their mixed portfolio allocations or within asset class.[12] The most interesting result was that most are making the between-class allocations before and independently of within-class allocations. The primary diversification techniques used by pension managers were not surprising. The mixed-asset portfolio was diversified by risk and return and by asset class, whereas the individual asset classes were most often diversified by asset type. They also found that pension funds' portfolio allocations to real estate were substantially less than the theoretically derived allocations suggested by research.

Zietz, Worzala, and Sirmans examined investment decisions and allocation patterns for large insurance companies and found evidence that larger companies are more likely to have direct real estate, mortgage, and mortgage-backed security investments.[13]

New Equilibrium Theory. The superior returns to real estate outlined in the Ibbotson and Siegel paper led them to introduce the **new equilibrium theory.** Returns to real estate appeared to be greater than that predicted by either the capital asset pricing model or the arbitrage pricing theory. The new equilibrium theory suggests that the apparent excess returns to real estate are a reward for some of the unique risk characteristics of that asset. While there appears to be a small stock beta for real estate (the correlation between real estate returns and stock market returns), the major risk elements are residual risk, marketability costs, and information costs. **Residual risk** refers to the difficulty for other than very large investors to diversify real estate holdings. Most real estate assets are very large relative to the portfolio of the typical investor. In other words, for the typical investor, it is not possible to own only a small portion of a particular real estate asset, making diversification difficult. **Marketability risk** refers to the liquidity of real estate. Again, because real estate is not divisible and does not trade frequently in large, efficient markets as does corporate stock, liquidity risk can be a problem for the average investor. **Information risk** refers to the cost of obtaining all the information sufficient to make an informed and rational investment in real estate. Information such as proposed zoning changes, changes in the infrastructure, and changes in the local economy is costly to obtain. Yet, these factors will play an important role in the returns of a real estate asset. In short, these risks, unique to real estate, are the source of the apparent excess returns to real estate relative to its risk.

Webb and Rubens also investigated the role of real estate in a mixed-asset portfolio.[14] They constructed a "restricted" portfolio and included two types of real estate: farm and residential properties. A **restricted portfolio** includes only those assets that are eligible by law for investment by large institutional investors such as pension plans. Some of the correlation coefficients from their study are presented in Table 21–5. The farm and residential real estate returns data were taken from *Finnegan's Financial Green Sheet Rates of Return*. Once again, the negative correlations attest to the diversification benefits of real estate. When optimal portfolios were

TABLE 21–5
Selected Cross Correlations of Asset Returns
1967–1986
Webb and Rubens

	Farm	Residential	Common Stock	Small Stock	Corporate Bonds	Government Bonds
Farm	1.0					
Residential	−0.37	1.0				
Common stock	−0.36	−0.37	1.0			
Small stock	0.01	−0.23	0.73	1.0		
Corporate bonds	−0.57	−0.47	0.32	−0.07	1.0	
Government bonds	−0.55	−0.55	0.42	0.04	0.96	1.0

Source: James Webb and Jack Rubens, "The Effect of Alternative Return Measures on Restricted Mixed Asset Portfolios," *AREUEA Journal* Vol. 16, No. 2, 1988, Exhibit 5, p. 132.

constructed based on the return and risk data, they were dominated by real estate. Webb and Rubens found that the optimal portfolios would consist of nearly 75 percent real estate, approximately 15 percent small corporate stock, and only 5 percent common stock. Government bonds represented a negligible part of the optimal portfolio. The dominance of real estate in the optimal portfolio persisted, even when the returns on real estate were held to their historic levels but the risk (standard deviation in returns) was arbitrarily increased fivefold.

Geltner used return data from the Russell—NCREIF, PRISA, and NAREIT indexes to judge the value of real estate in mixed-asset portfolios.[15] Geltner used a statistical technique to "de-smooth," so to speak, the return series. That is, he estimated return series after adjusting for the smoothing effects of appraised values in the series. The adjusted series naturally exhibited more risk (variance) than that based strictly on appraised values. As a result, real estate taken in isolation did not exhibit excess returns for the risk involved. However, it did present solid diversification benefits. Geltner computed the correlation coefficient between the various real estate indexes and the stock market over a period of time from the early 1970s to the late 1980s. He found no coefficients that were significantly different from zero.

Pagliari, Webb, and Del Casino also used the Russell–NCREIF data to compare ex ante and ex post portfolios.[16] Their goal was to point out the problems of using ex post (after the fact) historical to build ex ante (before the fact) portfolios. In fact, their results showed that using data from previous periods may yield suboptimal ex ante allocations when examined historically since, for none of the subperiods examined, did the ex ante strategies generate portfolios which were on the ex post efficient frontier.

In summary, most of the studies of real estate in a mixed-asset portfolio find that the returns of real estate are high relative to the risk and offer substantial risk-reduction through diversification. Most studies imply that real estate should occupy a larger role in the portfolios of large institutional investors. They indicate that lack of liquidity is one of the primary reasons why large institutional investors have not increased their investment in real estate to portions that would appear to be optimal.

Next, we look at the advantages of diversifying within real estate—that is, taking a portfolio of real estate assets only and diversifying by such characteristics as property type and geographical location.

WITHIN-REAL-ESTATE DIVERSIFICATION

For various reasons, some portfolios may be constructed entirely or mostly out of real estate properties or real-estate-related investments. This may be the case, for example, for institutions that because of regulation or by choice invest in real estate or real estate securities (such as mortgages). Other funds, such as CREFs, have been established for the primary purpose of investing in real estate. Here, we discuss the advantages of diversification within a real estate portfolio.

There are several ways in which within-real-estate diversification can take place. One is by property type, in which the portfolio is constructed with investments in various property types such as hotels, warehouses, office buildings, and apartment complexes. The idea here is, of course, that even within one local area, all property types may not prosper or fail together. Often, office buildings may do well at a time when apartment complexes are doing poorly. However, there certainly are cases where all property types may do well or poorly together, depending on the state of the local economy. Another method of diversification is by geography. This involves constructing a portfolio from properties in various parts of the country or the world. This strategy can involve a single property type or a mix of properties. The strategy can be accomplished in a naive way, selecting properties in the East, West, South, and Northeast, for example, or in a more sophisticated way by looking closely at the economies of the various regions. These more sophisticated types of diversification can be accomplished by analyzing the correlation of the economies of the various regions or by looking at the extent to which the local economies are themselves economically diversified.

Diversification by Property Type

It should not be surprising to see that diversification by property type is beneficial in terms of risk reduction. In a 1982 study, Miles and McCue tested diversification strategies that consisted of dividing the country into four geographic regions versus a strategy that diversified the portfolio by property type.[17] They found that diversification by property type showed better risk/return characteristics than a four-region geographic strategy. They looked at the returns of REITs that specialized in investment of property types from 1972 through 1978 and found the correlation in returns between REITs that held office facilities and those that held retail properties was 0.48. The correlation coefficient between REITs involved in the acquisition of residential properties and those with office properties was -0.49. The retail to residential coefficient was only 0.0806. The negative coefficient between residential and office properties indicates that the addition of residential properties to an existing real estate portfolio would provide risk-reduction benefits. This corresponds to the heavy emphasis on residential properties in the efficient portfolios analyzed by Webb and Rubens. More recently, Firstenberg, Ross, and Zisler analyzed the quarterly performance of nearly 600 individual properties from 1974 through 1987.[18] The authors divided the properties into four types: office, retail, industrial, and apartments. The returns were used to create mean-variance efficient portfolios (those that would lie on the efficiency frontier) that would return at least 10.5 to 11.5 percent annually. Their results indicated that the efficient tradeoff between risk and return depended crucially on the property types included in the portfolio. As an example, the authors demonstrated the beneficial impact of adding a fourth property type to one with the other three. Table 21–6 shows decline in risk (for selected levels of return) accomplished by adding apartments to a portfolio of office, industrial, and retail properties.

TABLE 21–6
Impact of Adding Apartments on Portfolio Risk/Return Relationship

Expected Return	Standard Deviation of 3 Property Portfolio	Standard Deviation of Portfolios with Apartments	Basis Point Decline in Risk (%)
10.8	3.41	3.29	0.12
10.9	3.59	3.33	0.19
11.0	3.88	3.45	0.43
11.1	4.24	3.63	0.61
11.2	4.67	3.87	0.80

Source: Managing Portfolio and Reward, Paul Firstenberg and Charles Wurtzebach, *Real Estate Review,* Vol. 19, No. 2, Summer 1989, Exhibit 2, p. 64.

Geographic Diversification

There is strong evidence that diversification of real estate investments by geographic area can have substantial risk-reduction benefits. Miles and McCue calculated a reward-to-variability ratio (excess return divided by the standard deviation in returns) for the REITs in their study.[19] With the calculated value as the dependent variable, they regressed it against the number of types of properties held by each REIT and the number of states the properties were located in. Both variables had a positive impact on the reward-to-variability ratio, indicating that in addition to property diversification, geographic diversification had positive benefits. However, the statistical significance of the geographic diversification variable was much weaker than that of the property diversification variable. In another paper, Hartzell, Hekman, and Miles analyzed the returns to commingled real estate funds from 1973 to 1983 and concluded that geographic diversification was not nearly as important as diversification by property type.[20] However, their geographic diversification was based on placing properties into one of four broad regional classifications: East, West, South, and Midwest. It is suggested that if investors construct portfolios on the basis of such naive geographic diversification, there will be little benefit from the effort.

Thus diversification of real estate portfolios historically has been accomplished by using either a geographic or property-type strategy. A new direction was taken in a 1987 paper by Hartzell, Shulman, and Wurtzebach.[21] They divided the United States into eight sections based on a commonality of their regional economies. State borders were ignored in the partitioning. As an example, southern California was joined with southern Nevada but both were separate from northern California. As much as possible, the regions were based on local economies. Montana and Wyoming were considered to be mineral-extraction states and placed in the same section as Texas and Louisiana. Some Midwestern states were split, as that area was partitioned into two segments: an industrial sector and a farming sector. The authors used the same database as did Hartzell, Hekman, and Miles but expanded the data to include returns through mid-1987.

A more recent 1993 study by Mueller reexamined the efficiency of the existing geographic and geographic/economic strategies against an economically based diversification strategy using government groupings.[22] His study found that the addition of the economic aspect to a geographically constrained model creates a higher risk and return efficient frontier than the purely geographical diversification model. Table 21–7 shows the correlation coefficients for the four

T A B L E   2 1 – 7

Correlation Coefficients Based on Geographic Diversification

Four Region 1973 IV–1990 IV				
	East	*Midwest*	*West*	*South*
East	1.0			
Midwest	0.308	1.0		
West	0.282	0.459	1.0	
South	−0.038	0.076	0.199	1.0

Eight Region Diversification 1973 IV–1990 IV								
	New England	*Mid-Atlantic*	*Old South*	*Industrial*	*Farm Belt*	*Mineral*	*So. Calif.*	*No. Calif.*
New England	1.0							
Mid-Atlantic	−0.212	1.0						
Old South	−0.170	−0.077	1.0					
Industrial	−0.042	0.306	0.025	1.0				
Farm Belt	−0.013	0.125	0.167	0.323	1.0			
Mineral	−0.238	0.070	0.136	0.177	0.205	1.0		
So. Calif.	−0.045	0.378	0.085	0.473	0.361	0.102	1.0	
No. Calif.	−0.007	0.095	0.139	0.207	0.139	0.145	0.371	1.0

Source: Glenn Mueller, "Refining Economic Diversification Strategies for Real Estate Portfolios" *Journal of Real Estate Research,* Vol. 8 (Winter, 1993), pp. 55–68.

major and the eight geographic regions. As you can see, the correlation coefficients based on the more sophisticated diversification are smaller than those based on a naive four-section identification of property location. This is evidence that geographic diversification can yield substantial risk-reduction benefits, if it is done with respect to the regional economies and not strictly physical location. The importance of this study is that geographic diversification has been resurrected and given more importance than indicated by earlier studies.

Other Methods of Diversification

There are other ways in which investment managers can diversify their real estate portfolios. Corgel and Gay studied the correlations of employment between large U.S. cities in the context of investing in mortgages.[23] Their thinking was that employment reflects the economies of the cities, and investment managers should construct real estate mortgage portfolios based on such correlations, investing in mortgages in cities with low or negative employment correlations. Of course, their implications can be extended to investment in real estate equity as well. They used monthly rates of change in employment levels for the 30 largest metropolitan areas from 1969 through 1984, and demonstrated that there was no large systematic component. That is, sufficient independence of employment rates existed to allow portfolio managers to exploit geographic diversification. Furthermore, the geographic diversification based on correlation in employment rates is superior to naive geographic diversification (North, South, and so on).

Clauretie suggested that substantial diversification benefits can be achieved by managers of small portfolios by investing in properties in locations that are themselves economically diversified.[24] He considered several measures of economic diversification. He showed that foreclosure rates on residential mortgages were related to the economic diversification of the region. Localities with greater economic diversification had fewer foreclosure rates than areas that were economically specialized. The conclusion here is that managers of small portfolios that cannot achieve substantial diversification by investing in properties in many diverse locations can achieve some of the benefits of diversification by investing in a few properties that are in locations where the economy is itself economically diversified.

Ziobrowski and Curcio addressed the issue of international diversification by combining the notions that international diversification enhances portfolio performance and that adding real estate to financial asset portfolios improves yield.[25] They hypothesized that the greatest gains should be available from international mixed-asset portfolios. They investigated this hypothesis as an explanation for investment in U.S. real estate by foreign investors. Their results showed that U.S. real estate does not improve foreign portfolio performance. The evidence suggests that volatile exchange rates induce a level of risk that offsets potential diversification benefits.

SUMMARY

The diversification of a portfolio into several or many assets can have a significant effect on reducing the risk of the portfolio while maintaining or even increasing the expected yield. Furthermore, the cost of the diversification is negligible. For this reason, rational investors take advantage of the opportunity to diversify. The size of the risk reduction due to the diversification depends on the correlation in the returns of the added assets with the existing portfolio. The correlation of the returns of the assets to be included in a portfolio with that of the portfolio is the relevant risk that must be priced and is the basis of the capital asset pricing model.

The returns on equity real estate investments indicate that those investments should be included in all portfolios of any size. The historic returns to real estate have been far in excess of their risk, and they appear to have no or negative correlation with other assets. This is particularly true of residential properties. The apparent excess returns to real estate has been the basis of the new equilibrium theory, which states that those returns must be due to the peculiar risk characteristics of real estate, such as liquidity, residual, and information cost risks. Nonetheless, many large institutional investors have responded by increasing their real estate holdings.

Within-real-estate diversification also appears to have risk-reduction benefits. At one time, it was thought that only diversification by property type produced benefits. Recent evidence suggests that if regions are defined in terms of their economies and not by state boundaries, then geographic diversification also can produce risk-reduction benefits. Investors with small- to medium-size portfolios also can take advantage of other methods of diversification. They can invest in properties in metropolitan areas that exhibit negative employment correlations, or they can invest in localities where the regional economy is itself diversified.

KEY TERMS

Arbitrage pricing theory (APT)

Capital asset pricing model (CAPM)

Correlation

Correlation coefficient

Diversifiable risk

Diversification

Geographic diversification

Information risk

Marketability risk

Mixed-asset portfolio

NAREIT Equity Index

New equilibrium theory

Nondiversifiable risk

Portfolio

Property diversification

Residual risk

Restricted portfolio

Risk

Russell–NCREIF property index

Variance

SUGGESTED READINGS

Corgel, J. B., and G. Gay. 1987. Local economic base, geographic diversification, and risk management of mortgage portfolios. *Journal of the American Real Estate and Urban Economics Association* Vol. 5, Fall.

Firstenberg, P. B., and C. H. Wurtzebach. 1989. Managing portfolio risk and reward. *Real Estate Review* Vol. 19, Summer.

Follain, J. R., and C. A. Calhoun. 1997. Constructing Indices of the Price of Multifamily Properties Using the 1991 Residential Finance Survey. *Journal of Real Estate Finance and Economics* Vol. 14, 235–255.

Goetzmann, W. N., and M. Spiegel. 1997. A Spatial Model of Housing Returns and Neighborhood Substitutability. *Journal of Real Estate Finance and Economics* Vol. 14, 11–31.

Hartzell, D. J., D. G. Shulman, and C. H. Wurtzebach. 1987. Refining the analysis of regional diversification for income producing properties. *Journal of Real Estate Research* Vol. 2, Winter.

Miles, M., and T. McCue. 1982. Historic returns and institutional real estate portfolios. *Journal of the American Real Estate and Urban Economics Association* Vol. 10, Summer.

Norman, E., G. S. Sirmans, and J. D. Benjamin. 1995. The Historical Environment of Real Estate Returns. *Journal of Real Estate Portfolio Management* Vol. 1, No. 1, 1–24.

Sirmans, G. S., and C. F. Sirmans. 1987. The historical perspective of real estate returns. *Journal of Portfolio Management* Vol. 14, Spring.

Webb, J. R., and J. H. Rubens. 1988. The effect of alternative return measures on restricted mixed-asset portfolios. *Journal of the American Real Estate and Urban Economics Association* Vol. 16, Summer.

Webb, J. R., R. J. Curcio, and J. H. Rubens. 1988. Diversification gains from including real estate in mixed-asset portfolios. *Decision Sciences*.

REVIEW QUESTIONS

21–1   Explain how diversification can reduce the risk of a portfolio of assets.

21–2   Provide a definition of an efficiency frontier.

21–3   Define beta and explain why it is the only risk of an asset that is relevant to investors.

21–4   Why is it difficult to measure historical returns on real estate investments?

21–5   Explain the new equilibrium theory in regards to the historical returns to real estate.

21–6   Do the historical returns on real estate suggest it should be included in a mixed-asset portfolio? Explain.

21–7   Describe several methods to accomplish within-real-estate diversification.

21–8   Describe a successful geographic diversification program for a real estate portfolio.

ENDNOTES

1.   H. Markowitz, *Portfolio Selection: Efficient Diversification of Investments* (New York: John Wiley, 1959).

2.   W. Sharpe, *Portfolio Theory and Capital Markets* (New York: McGraw-Hill, 1970).

3. R. Roll, "A Critique of the Asset Pricing Theory's Tests," *Journal of Financial Economics* 5 (May 1977): 129–176.

4. R. Roll and S. Ross, "An Empirical Investigation of the Arbitrage Pricing Theory," *Journal of Finance* 35 (December 1980): 1073–1103.

5. Louargand's study finds two interesting results: (1) methodological sophistication has increased over time (as measured by the increase of discounted cash flow models) and (2) a subset of 20 percent of pension investors make no explicit adjustment for risk in their real estate investment decision-making. See M. A. Louargand, "A Survey of Pension Fund Real Estate Portfolio Risk Management Practices," *Journal of Real Estate Research* 7 (Fall 1992): 361–373.

6. For a review of the literature showing returns and risk on real estate relative to other assets see E. J. Norman, G. Stacy Sirmans, and J. D. Benjamin, "The Historical Environment of Real Estate Returns," *Journal of Real Estate Portfolio Management* (1995).

7. D. Geltner, "Estimating Real Estate's Systematic Risk from Aggregate Level Appraisal-Based Returns," *AREUEA Journal* 17 (Winter 1989): 463–481. See also D. Geltner, "Smoothing in Appraisal-Based Returns," *Journal of Real Estate Finance and Economics* 4 (September 1991): 327–345.

8. F. C. Neil Myer and J. R. Webb, "Return Properties of Equity REITs, Common Stocks, and Commercial Real Estate: A Comparison," *Journal of Real Estate Research* 8 (Winter 1993): 87–106.

9. J. R. Follain and C. A. Calhoun, "Constructing Indices of the Price of Multifamily Properties Using the 1991 Residential Finance Survey," *Journal of Real Estate Finance and Economics* 14 (1997): 235–255.

10. R. Ibbotson and L. Siegel, "Real Estate Returns: Comparison with Other Investments," *AREUEA Journal* 12 (Fall 1984): 219–242.

11. E. Norman, G. Stacy Sirmans, and J. D. Benjamin, "The Historical Environment of Real Estate Returns," *Journal of Real Estate Portfolio Management* 1 (1995): 1–24.

12. V. L. Bajtelsmit and E. M. Worzala, "Portfolio Decision-Making by Pension Fund Managers: A Survey of Corporate, Public, and Union Plans" (Paper presented at the American Real Estate and Urban Economics Association meeting, 6 January 1995).

13. E. Norman Zietz, E. Worzala, and G. Stacy Sirmans, "Insurer Portfolio Allocations: An Exploration of Investment Decision-Making Techniques" (Paper presented at the American Real Estate Society Meeting, March, 1996).

14. J. R. Webb and J. Rubens, "The Effect of Alternative Return Measures on Restricted Mixed-Asset Portfolios," *AREUEA Journal* 16 (Summer 1988): 123–137.

15. D. Geltner, "Estimating Real Estate's Systematic Risk from Aggregate Level Appraisal-Based Returns," *AREUEA Journal* 17 (Winter 1989): 463–481.

16. J. L. Pagliarti, Jr., J. R. Webb, and J. J. Del Casino, "Applying MPT to Institutional Real Estate Portfolios: The Good, the Bad and the Uncertain," *Journal of Real Estate Management,* 1995.

17. M. Miles and T. McCue, "Historic Returns and Institutional Real Estate Portfolios," *AREUEA Journal* 10 (1982): 184–197.

18. P. Firstenberg, S. A. Ross, and R. C. Zisler, "Managing Real Estate Portfolios," Goldman Sachs & Co. (November 1987).

19. Miles and McCue, "Historic Returns and Institutional Real Estate Portfolios."

20. D. Hartzell, J. Hekman, and M. Miles, "Diversification Categories in Investment Real Estate," *AREUEA Journal* 14 (Summer 1986): 230–259.

21. D. Hartzell, D. Shulman, and C. Wurtzebach, "Refining the Analysis of Regional Diversification of Income-Producing Real Estate," *Journal of Real Estate Research* 2 (Winter 1987): 85–95.

22. G. Mueller, "Refining Economic Diversification Strategies for Real Estate Portfolios," *Journal of Real Estate Research* 8 (Winter 1993): 55–68.

23. J. B. Corgel and G. Gay, "Local Economic Base, Geographic Diversification, and Risk Management of Mortgage Portfolios," *AREUEA Journal* 15 (Fall 1987): 256–267.

24. T. M. Clauretie, "Regional Economic Diversification and the Residential Default Rate," *Journal of Real Estate Research* 3 (Spring 1988): 87–97.

25. A. J. Ziobrowski and R. J. Curcio, "Diversification Benefits of U.S. Real Estate to Foreign Investors," *Journal of Real Estate Research* 6 (Summer 1991): 119–142.

■■■■■   **APPENDIX A**   ■■■■■

The Capital Asset Pricing Model Derived from Combining an Asset with the Existing Market Portfolio

If an asset X is added to the market portfolio, the expected return and risk on the new portfolio can be given as

$$E(R_p) = \alpha E(R_y) + 1 - \alpha\ E(R_m) \qquad \text{(Equation A21-1)}$$

and

$$\sigma_p = \sqrt{\alpha^2\sigma_x2 + (1 - \alpha)^2\sigma_m2 + 2\alpha(1 - \alpha)\sigma_x\sigma_m r_{xm}} \qquad \text{(Equation A21–2)}$$

But, if X already exists in the portfolio in its optimal ratio, the excess demand for X must be 0, or

$$\left.\frac{\partial E(R_p)}{\partial \alpha}\right| = E(R_x) - E(R_m) \qquad \text{(Equation A21–3)}$$

$$\left.\frac{\partial \sigma_p}{\partial \sigma}\right| = r_{ym}\sigma_x - \sigma_m \qquad \text{(Equation A21–4)}$$

$$\frac{E(R_m) - R_f}{\sigma_m} = \frac{E(R_m) - E(R_x)}{\sigma_m - r_{xm}\sigma_x}$$

rearranging,

$$E(R_x) = R_f + \frac{r_{xm}\sigma_x\sigma_m}{\sigma_m^2}(E(R_m) - R_f)$$

or

$$E(R_y) = R_f + \text{ß}[E(R_m) - R_f]$$

where

$$\text{ß} = \frac{r_{xm}\sigma_x\sigma_m}{\sigma_m^2}$$

CHAPTER 22

Liability, Agency Problems, Fraud, and Ethics in Real Estate Finance

LEARNING OBJECTIVES

In this chapter, we review several topics related to the legal environment of real estate finance. After reading this chapter, you should understand how parties to real estate finance transactions can be held liable for their actions, including fraud, misrepresentation, negligence, and, in some cases, violation of state and federal laws. You should also understand the structure of agency relationships within real estate finance and how those relationships can create incentives for parties to behave in their own interest and against the interest of others. Such behavior may include fraud or unethical practices. You also should see that there are costs—agency costs—associated with preventing parties from acting solely in their own interest and against the interests of others. You will see how insufficient agency monitoring costs lead to agency problems. The failure of many federally insured savings and loans is an example where some parties used fraud and unethical practices to enrich themselves at the expense of others, mainly the general taxpayers. You should understand how insufficient agency costs allowed this wealth transfer.

INTRODUCTION

The central topic of this chapter is the legal environment that surrounds those involved in real estate finance. We also are concerned here with agency relationships, agency costs, fraud, and ethics—both within and outside of the legal system.

In terms of the legal environment, one focus is on the contractual relationships among the parties to real estate finance transactions, the duties which such contractual relationships impose upon the parties, and the liabilities faced by the parties for failure to fulfill those duties. Another focus concerns liabilities that arise from violations of state and federal laws. Whether by failure to abide by contractual obligations or by violation of state and federal law, the liabilities faced by lenders, borrowers, and property owners can be substantial. Here, we concentrate on the liabilities faced by lenders, although other parties such as real estate developers and brokers also may incur liabilities. Lenders face liability which may arise from many areas, including enforcement of laws related to the disposal of hazardous waste, laws related to drug enforcement, misrepresentation or fraud in a contract to loan funds, abrupt termination of loan arrangements, or the exercise of undue influence in managing the affairs of a delinquent borrower.

In the remainder of the chapter, we will discuss agency relationships between the parties to real estate finance transactions and the role that fraud and ethics plays in those relationships.

LENDERS' LEGAL LIABILITY

In this section, we discuss the legal liability of lenders and other parties involved in financing real estate transactions. The greatest focus over the last several years has been on the liability for a variety of acts or omissions, and the awards have been substantial. Lenders who are not vigilant to the legal environment may find themselves in the role of the debtor. Others, such as real estate developers, brokers, and property owners, must also be aware of the legal environment of real estate finance.

To repeat, there are two broad areas in which lenders may be subject to liability. The first occurs when lenders are found liable under state or federal laws regulating certain activities. An example is the liability that results from the improper disposal of hazardous waste on a property for which the lender has a secured interest. The second occurs when lenders have been found to violate contractual obligations involving loan arrangements. Recently, lenders have been held increasingly liable under actions in both arenas.

Hazardous Waste Disposal

As a result of the growing problem associated with the improper disposal of hazardous and toxic waste, the federal government passed the Comprehensive Environmental Response, Compensation, and Liability Act of 1980 (**CERCLA**) and its companion legislation, the Superfund Amendments and Reauthorization Act of 1986 (**SARA**). A central purpose of the acts was to pass the cost of cleaning up contaminated sites to those parties that had benefited from the generation and disposal of the waste materials. In 1986 the Environmental Protection Agency (EPA) estimated that American industry generated about 266 million metric tons of hazardous waste annually, of which 68 percent came from the chemical industry.[1] The EPA currently estimates that there are approximately 27,000 sites in need of cleanup at a cost of more than $300 billion. The cost of cleaning up the most contaminated sites can be overwhelming. In 1986 Union Carbide Corporation agreed to pay at least $40 million to clean up a hazardous waste site in Colorado.[2]

CERCLA and SARA attempt to make the parties responsible for the problem bear these large cleanup costs. Lenders may be involved in the process because of the language of the acts and because of recent court decisions that have interpreted that language.

Liability under CERCLA is *strict, retroactive,* and *joint and several. Strict liability* means that a charged party may not offer as a defense a claim that its actions were not in violation of any law prior to CERCLA. Parties can act in good faith, adhere to a standard of care of a reasonable manufacturer in a similar situation, and still be liable. If they discharged hazardous waste and contaminated a site, they are liable for the cost of cleanup even though they may not have violated previous laws. *Retroactive* means that parties may be held responsible for previous discharges even though they may no longer own the contaminated property. *Joint and several liability* means that each potentially liable party can be made to bear the entire cost of cleanup even though several parties may have been responsible for the contamination. Also, one or more liable parties may force contribution from other potentially liable parties. Section 113(f) of the act provides that any person may seek contribution from any other person who is liable. Congress wrote the act in this way so as to include as many potentially liable parties as possible, making cleanup more expeditious and less costly to the taxpayer. This feature of the legislation is particularly dangerous for lenders, since the government and other parties to the contamination may look for so-called deep pockets in the cleanup effort.

If a facility is found to be contaminated by hazardous waste, the act defines *potentially responsible parties (PRPs)* as

1. Current owner(s) and operator(s) of the facility
2. Owner(s) or operator(s) at the time of discharge
3. Generator(s) of the hazardous substance or the party or parties who arranged for its disposal and treatment
4. Transporter(s) of the hazardous substance

By facility the law means "any site or area where a hazardous substance has been deposited, stored, disposed of, or otherwise come to be located."[3] This definition includes a parcel of raw land. Hazardous waste disposal includes any inadvertent leaking and spilling. Under CERCLA, PRPs can be held for damages defined as the cost to remove or mitigate the effect of the hazardous waste as well as injury to any natural resources, and the costs of any studies necessary to determine the effect of the contamination of public health. In writing the law, Congress did not intend to extend liability to lenders in their capacity as lenders. The law excludes from the category of an owner or operator "a person, who, without participating in the management of a vessel or facility, holds an indicia of ownership primarily to protect his security interest in the vessel or facility."[4] This is termed the *secured-lender exemption* and means that a PRP owner or operator does not include a lender that holds a mortgage or deed-of-trust on a property as security for a note.

Lenders may lose this exemption, however, if they foreclose on the contaminated property (and through a foreclosure sale become an owner) or if, in an effort to avoid foreclosure, they become involved in the operations of a contaminated facility. When a company is losing money and cannot make its loan payments, a lender frequently becomes involved in the firm's operations. The lender would like to restore profitability so that the company can resume loan payments and costly foreclosure can be avoided. It is likely Congress did not foresee issues related to liability under the act when lenders foreclose or influence the operations of contaminated facilities. The lack of congressional guidance in the act for such circumstances left a void to be filled by the judiciary. As you will see shortly, interpretive court decisions have not been kind to lenders.

Lender Defenses

There are several defenses available to a lender who may be a PRP, through either a foreclosure or a loan workout whereby the lender influences the business operations of the borrower. Under the first defense, the lender simply claims not to be a PRP. Under a second defense, the lender claims the contamination resulted solely from an act of God, an act of war, or the act or omission of a third party being neither an employee or agent nor having a contractual relationship with the lender. This is the "Hey, how did that happen?" defense. For this defense to hold, the actual contaminator cannot have any contractual relationship with the lender. CERCLA broadly defines a contractual relationship as "including but . . . not limited to land contracts, deeds, or other instruments transferring title or possession."[5]

A third defense is the *innocent landowner defense.* Here, the lender claims to have had no knowledge of the contamination when it foreclosed and obtained title to the property. Under this defense, there is no liability if the lender can demonstrate that it acquired the property after the disposal or placement of the hazardous waste and did not know or have any reason to know that there was hazardous waste on the property. There is a "catch 22" to this defense, however. Courts have ruled that in order not to have any reason to know of the contamination, the lender would have had to make an appropriate inquiry into the previous ownership and use of the property. Furthermore, the discovery of hazardous waste at a site is sufficient evidence that the lender failed to make the necessary inquiry to discover its existence. In any event, it is likely that lenders for commercial real estate will be held to a higher standard of inquiry than lenders for residential real estate, since hazardous waste is much more likely to occur on commercial and industrial sites. An owner that discovers the hazardous waste and then sells the property also loses this defense. Finally, a fourth defense is the secured-lender exemption discussed above.

Initial Judicial Decisions

Several early court cases have addressed each of the above defenses. We review the important cases.

United States v. Mirable.[6]   This 1985 case involved three lenders that had a secured interest in a property. Anna and Thomas Mirable obtained title to the property from American Bank and Trust (ABT) after the latter had foreclosed on its loan to Turco Coatings Inc., the former owner. Of the three lenders, ABT was the high bidder at the foreclosure sale. ABT did not immediately accept the deed to the property from the sheriff, but instead secured the property against vandalism, showed the property to prospective buyers, and made some inquiries about disposing of some drums containing hazardous waste. It was about four months after the foreclosure sale that ABT assigned its right to the deed to the Mirables. Then, about a year later, the Environmental Protection Agency discovered the drums, ordered a cleanup, and sued the Mirables for recovery of the cleanup costs, $249,702.52. The Mirables then joined the three lenders as defendants.

The federal district court found that ABT was not liable, since it had simply foreclosed on the property and taken steps to secure it against further depreciation. A second lender, the Small Business Administration (SBA), also was held not liable under CERCLA. Although SBA regulations called for extensive management assistance when borrowers faced default, no such assistance was ever provided by the SBA. Their failure to follow their own administrative procedures may have saved the SBA from liability.

A third lender was not so fortunate. One of the loan officers attended advisory meetings with the borrower. The purpose of the meetings was to improve the management of the financial and marketing affairs of the company. A second loan officer was even more involved with the running of the company's business affairs. Testimony indicated that he was always at the plant site and was in "control" of the day-to-day operations of the facility. He reassigned personnel, determined which orders were to be filled, and made changes in the manufacturing process. As a result, the court held that the third lender exercised sufficient control over the operations of the business and facility as to make it a responsible party.

United States v. Maryland Bank and Trust Company.[7] This 1986 case involved a secured lender that foreclosed on a property and took title through a sheriff's sale. The lender, Maryland Bank and Trust (MBT), still had title to the property 4 years later when the EPA inspected the site and discovered that hazardous waste had been improperly disposed on the site in the 1970s. After MBT refused to clean up the site, the EPA had the job done and then sued MBT to recover the costs. MBT pleaded the secured-lender exemption defense. The court rejected this defense, however. It stated that the law grants the exemption if the PRP "holds" (present tense emphasized) an indicia of ownership. The foreclosure, the court noted, changed the indicia of ownership to actual ownership at the time of the cleanup. Because of the foreclosure, the security interest did not exist at the time of the cleanup; rather, actual ownership existed. Furthermore, it interpreted the phrase "owner and operator" in the CERCLA legislation in the disjunctive—that is, a PRP need not be both an owner and an operator but only one or the other. The court also was concerned that granting MBT a secured-lender exemption would allow it to benefit from the government's cleanup of the wastes. If the bank were held to be unaccountable, it could purchase the contaminated property cheaply at a foreclosure sale, wait for the government to clean it up, and sell the property at a profit. This would simply "convert CERCLA into an insurance scheme for financial institutions by protecting them against possible losses due to the security of loans with polluted properties."[8] We will return to this issue when we discuss the next case.

The MBT ruling seems a little harsh and for reasons discussed below would likely lead lenders to think twice before foreclosing on delinquent loans. It could even have more extended effects. As a result of the ruling, lenders may be reluctant to loan funds where the security is any property on which there is even the remote possibility that hazardous waste could have been disposed in the past or even subsequent to the loan. Funding for industrial and commercial developments may be severely reduced. Fortunately, the court gave hope that not all foreclosures on contaminated properties would result in lender liability for cleanup costs. In the MBT decision, the court added that the lender had owned the property for nearly 4 years before the EPA cleanup. The court emphasized that it was not considering the issue of the exemption when applied to a lender who quickly resells the property after a foreclosure, although the court gave no indication why the length of time that a lender holds ownership is important in determining liability for cleanup costs.

Guidice v. BFG Electroplating Co.[9] This 1989 case is interesting for the court's recognition of option values related to the CERCLA legislation first hinted at in the Maryland Bank case. To set the scene, imagine a parcel of real estate with great market value, except for the presence of hazardous waste. Its value with waste present will be its value with no waste less the cost of cleanup. It could have negative value if the cost of cleanup is substantial. Now, consider what may occur if secured lenders could never be held responsible for the cost of cleaning up hazardous waste. They would have a call option on contaminated properties. The strike price would be the value of the property with the waste present, and the market value would be the value with no waste. To see how this works, assume the value of a property is $1 million without waste present and $100,000 with waste present (the cost of cleanup is therefore $900,000). The owner of the property is unable to sell it in the marketplace for more than $100,000. If the amount of the loan securing the property is more than $100,000, the owner may default and give the property to the lender by default (exercise the put option). The lender need only bid $100,000 at the sheriff's sale to acquire the property. If the lender cannot be held responsible for the cleanup, the lender can sell the property for its higher market value, $1 million. There is a wealth redistribution from the party that pays for the cleanup (taxpayers, in this example) to the lender.

In *Guidice* v. *BFG Electroplating Co.* the court recognized this problem. In this case, the owner of a metal polishing company defaulted on his loan from National Bank. The lender did not immediately foreclose but preferred to work toward solving the borrower's financial problems. For about a year, representatives of the lender met with company officials to discuss management affairs such as work shifts, customer accounts, and so forth. The lender also attempted to find buyers for the business. Despite these efforts, the company failed and defaulted on its loan. The borrower owned the property for nine months subsequent to a foreclosure sale, before selling it to members of the family of the former owner. During this time, the lender arranged for the removal of drums of hazardous materials inherited at the foreclosure sale. Two years after resale of the property, nearby residents claimed damage from toxic waste and sued several parties. National Bank was named as a potentially responsible party because it was an owner and operator for nine months. National Bank claimed a secured-lender exemption.

The court found no excessive involvement in the management of the business by the lender prior to foreclosure and certainly no involvement in the disposal of waste materials. However, citing the Maryland Bank and Trust case, the court held that once National Bank foreclosed and held title to the property, it lost its secured-lender exemption. There was no reference to the period of time that National held the property, however. Recall that the length of time of ownership appeared to be a crucial element in the Maryland Bank and Trust case. In this case, the court noted that there was leaking and dripping of hazardous waste during the nine months that National Bank owned the property. This was sufficient to find the lender liable as an owner or operator that allowed contamination during its tenure as owner. Additionally, the court noted another concern. It stated that all prospective buyers at a foreclosure sale would have to factor in the cost of cleaning up hazardous waste in their bids. Moreover, they would not have secured-lender exemptions. This would give the secured lender a comparative advantage and allow it to obtain the property for a very low amount. The court added that the lender could then hold the property while the government cleaned it up. The lender then could sell the property at a substantial profit, putting the cleanup cost to the taxpayers.

The court was clearly influenced by this option value in making its decision. (It should be noted, however, that in this case, the lender sold the property before any cleanup was attempted. The court appears to have been concerned with a general situation of enhancement rather than any enrichment in this particular case.) As a result of the *Maryland Bank* and *Guidice* decisions, the optimal policy for lenders may be to avoid foreclosing on contaminated properties. Foreclosure may be optimal only after the EPA has cleaned up the property. Although the EPA can obtain a lien for the cost of cleaning up the property, it is a judgment lien and would not have priority over the lender's secured lien, since the secured lien was recorded first. In this way, the lender never becomes an owner and would not become a PRP, providing that the lender also avoided controlling the facility. As we see in the following case, the exercise of control over a facility can cause a lender to become a PRP.

Fleet Factors Corporation.[10]   Lender liability may have been extended even further by this 1990 case. Here, the focus returned to lender involvement with management decisions in a case where the lender did not foreclose on the real estate. Fleet Factors Corporation advanced funds to Swainsboro Print Works and secured the loan principally with Swainsboro's accounts receivable, but also with equipment and real estate. After the business encountered some difficulties, it filed for bankruptcy and continued operations under the supervision of the bankruptcy court. Things did not get better, and Swainsboro eventually ceased operations and began selling off its inventory and collecting accounts receivable. Before any inventory was sold, Fleet Factors checked the credit of the buyer before authorizing shipment. Any factor would do this, since the inventory and accounts receivable are collateral for the loan.

Several months after Swainsboro ceased operations, Fleet Factors foreclosed on its loans, taking title to the equipment but not the real estate. Fleet Factors then auctioned off a portion of the equipment and removed the remainder and washed its hands of the affair. Two months later the EPA discovered 700 leaking drums of hazardous waste and damaged asbestos on the premises. The defunct Swainsboro still owned the real estate. However, it was revealed that the auctioneers that sold the equipment for Fleet Factors had moved the leaking drums, and the contractor that removed the unsold equipment damaged the asbestos, making it hazardous. Both the auctioneer and the contractor would have had a contractual relationship with the lender, Fleet Factors. The EPA sued Fleet Factors as a potentially responsible party.

The federal district court found that financial advice and actions as a factor did not involve or influence the day-to-day operations of the facility and, thus, Fleet Factors was not liable on this account. On the question of whether Fleet Factors should be held liable for the actions of the auctioneer and the contractor, the district court noted that there was a dispute about the facts. It suggested that the parties allow the appellate court to rule on this issue. Fleet Factors took the district court's invitation and appealed the case (even though it was not liable under the management of the business issue). The appellate court took another look at all the issues and facts. The result was remarkable. First, the court rejected the distinction between influencing the financial decisions of a firm and influencing or controlling its day-to-day operations. It concluded that influencing a firm's financial decisions can affect the day-to-day operations. The court noted that "a secured creditor may incur CERCLA liability, without being an operator, by participating in the financial management of the facility to a degree indicating a capacity to influence the (borrower's) treatment of hazardous wastes."[11] Thus, under this interpretation, a secured lender can incur liability if its involvement with the financial management of the business is sufficiently broad to conclude that it may affect how the firm disposes of its hazardous waste. It should be added that Fleet Factors had somewhat more control of the company than indicated by the testimony at the district court trial. The appellate court pointed out that Fleet Factors required Swainsboro to obtain permission before shipping products, established prices on excess inventory, determined when employees should be laid off, processed the firm's employment and tax forms, and even controlled access to the facility. This was sufficient involvement in the management of the firm to warrant liability under CERCLA. The court was also quick to point out that nothing in its decision gutted the secured-lender exemption. Lenders simply must be careful to restrict their involvement in the debtor's business to only the purely financial aspects.

Although the holding of Fleet Factors to be liable for the cleanup costs appears to be harsh, there are several considerations of this decision that blunt its impact on lenders. The nature of the liability established by this decision is that any participation by the lender must have the capacity to influence the manner in which hazardous wastes are treated. The simple fact that a lender may have influence with a borrower by virtue of the loan arrangement does not expose the lender to CERCLA liability. Even agreements in the loan document that give the lender the right to control the business in the event of delinquency or default may not establish liability. Only lender actions that influence or have the capacity to influence disposal of hazardous waste will create a potential CERCLA liability. Also, because the case was on appeal for a summary judgment, the facts as indicated by the EPA were accepted as true. The case was remanded back to the district court for a hearing on the merits of the case. Finally, in this case, two principals of Fleet Factors were also principals of Swainsboro Paint Works. The appellate court may have been influenced by the close relationship of the parties. That is, the court may have considered Fleet Factors and Swainsboro Paint Works to be the same entity.

Bergsoe Metal Corporation.[12]   This is another 1990 case that addressed the issue of lender control of business activities. This decision backed away somewhat from the broad sweep of the Fleet Factors decision. The case involved a municipal corporation in Oregon, the Port of St. Helens, that had issued industrial revenue bonds and advanced the proceeds to various industrial firms to locate in the port. After Bergsoe purchased the property in question, it entered into a sale-leaseback agreement with Port of St. Helens Authority. Thus, legal title vested with the authority. As owner of the property and as lender, the authority gave some financial advice to Bergsoe. When the plant site was found to be contaminated, the authority was declared to be the owner for the purpose of CERCLA liability. It claimed secured-lender exemption.

The court ruled in the authority's favor in this case. The court recognized that the focus was on the extent of lender control over management. The court stated that under any reasonable standard there must be "some actual management of the facility" before CERCLA liability can be established. This opinion appeared to retreat somewhat from the Fleet Factors decision in terms of establishing liability in cases where lenders may exercise some control over the strictly financial decisions of the borrower.

APRIL 1992 EPA REGULATION

As a result of the uncertainty surrounding the liability of lenders caused by these various court cases, many lenders lobbied the EPA to clarify the rules under which they could foreclose on a property and escape liability under CERCLA. In April 1992 the EPA responded by promulgating such rules. The new rules gave guidance by categorically providing examples of management activity that a lender can participate in and not incur a liability for cleanup costs. Specifically, the rules are:

1. Any and all actions that occur prior to the creation of the security interest,
2. Periodic monitoring and/or inspection of the property,
3. Ongoing involvement that results from an inspection of the property,
4. Requiring the borrower to clean up any contamination,
5. Requiring the borrower to comply with any laws,
6. Restructuring the loan arrangement,
7. Requiring the payment of more rent or interest,
8. Exercising the right the lender may have under the law or under any warranties, covenants, conditions, or promises of the borrower, and
9. Providing specific or general financial or administrative advice, suggestions, or even control.

Recent Court Decision

If lenders thought that the new EPA regulation would clarify the risk faced under foreclosure proceedings, they were wrong. In 1994 an appeals court invalidated the 1992 EPA regulation. In *Chemical Manufacturers Association* v. *Environmental Protection Agency,*[13] a federal appeals court ruled that the EPA regulation exceeded its authority. In its decision the court said that "it cannot be argued that Congress intended EPA, one of many potential plaintiffs, to have authority to, by regulation, define liability for a class of potential defendants." Thus, it appears that any relief of the sort intended by the 1992 EPA regulation will have to occur in Congress. Currently, there is a pending Clinton administration proposal that would give the EPA the authority that the court says it now lacks.

As a result of case law, it is clear that lenders face increased exposure to liability for the cleanup costs of improperly disposed hazardous waste. The exposure becomes greater when lenders foreclose on or participate in the management of the firm that owns the contaminated facility. This increased exposure to liability may have an effect on real estate finance that was hinted at by the court in the Fleet Factors decision. If lenders become increasingly liable for the risk posed by hazardous wastes (beyond the risk of a decline in the market value of property which serves as collateral), they will, in an efficient market, incorporate the higher expected risk into loan terms, say, the interest rate. Firms that are likely to produce hazardous waste will find financing more expensive. Such firms will either be unable to obtain financing (eliminating the hazardous waste at the source) or will behave in a fashion that reduces the risk of contamination. For example, a firm may incur added costs of safety measures to avoid contamination. These added costs may be more than offset by lower interest costs imposed by lenders. In this way, contamination risks are reduced through terms in the real estate finance market.

Risk Management for Lender Liability

There are several ways in which lenders can mitigate their exposure to liability for the cleanup costs of hazardous wastes. First, they can avoid taking a security interest in any industrial facility that is likely to be used in such a fashion as to produce hazardous waste as a byproduct. Second, they can make sure that any site is absolutely free of contamination before making a loan. Third, the lender should avoid any loan covenants that may negatively impact the borrower's ability to properly dispose of wastes. Subsequent to a loan, a borrower may need to obtain additional financing to install equipment to eliminate wastes. Covenants in the original note that prevent such additional financing may be considered an action that affects the borrower's ability to treat waste. The same may be true if the lender finances the borrower with a continuing line of credit and then refuses to advance funds for a waste prevention or cleanup program. Recall that under the appeal in Fleet Factors, the standard for the court was the lender's capacity to influence the borrower's treatment of toxic wastes.

Fourth, lenders may seek a separate indemnity agreement from the borrower. A typical indemnity agreement would provide for the borrower to reimburse the lender for any liability that the lender incurs as a result of an improper disposal of hazardous materials. Such indemnities are not disallowed under CERCLA. Recall that Section 113(f) of CERCLA provides that "any person may seek contribution from any other person who is liable or potentially liable under Section 107(a) (and) . . . such claims . . . shall be governed by Federal law." Despite this wording, there is some question as to whether an indemnity agreement may be enforceable after a foreclosure where state laws preclude deficiency judgments. That is, although federal law allows for actions that seek contribution, the act does not provide any guidance as to where state laws may affect the indemnity agreements. Some lenders in California, the largest antideficiency judgment state, have executed separate nonsecured indemnity agreements to cover environmental claims. They are nonsecured so as to place them outside of the antideficiency judgment statutes.

Even if a state court were to deny a judgment on an indemnity contract because it violated antideficiency statutes designed to prevent double recovery, the lender may proceed on other grounds. The lender could seek recovery, for example, for bad faith waste of the property. That is, most deeds of trust that secure a property contain provisions that preclude the borrower from taking actions that destroy the market value of the collateral. Improperly disposing of hazardous waste on the property would certainly qualify as bad faith waste. Also, if the borrower did not divulge the true nature of the anticipated use of the facility on the loan application, the lender may recover by alleging fraud.

The area of lender liability for hazardous waste costs is a developing area of the law. Certainly, lenders are exposed to greater risks as a result of CERCLA, SARA, and recent court cases. Secured-lender exemption and innocent-owner defenses are not as solid as one may think. In an effort to solve the huge hazardous waste cleanup problem, the judicial arena in which many of these issues are played out is disposed toward finding as many responsible parties with adequate resources (deep pockets) as possible.

Lenders may find themselves on the losing end of real estate transactions for other reasons. Another area fraught with dangers for lenders is the war on drugs.

Lenders and the Drug War

As a result of a growing drug problem in this country, Congress passed the Comprehensive Drug Abuse Prevention and Control Act in 1970. This act authorizes the federal government to confiscate property used to manufacture, transport, store, and dispense illicit drugs. The original focus of the act was on personal property, such as cars and boats. Real estate could be confiscated only if purchased with the proceeds of drug sales. In 1984 the act was amended to include real estate. Now, all rights and interests in real estate property are subject to forfeiture if the real estate is used in any way to facilitate the drug trade. This means that real estate may be confiscated from an owner, even if the owner rented the property to someone who used it to carry out drug transactions. It also means that a lender who forecloses on a property may lose it under the same circumstances. The 1984 amendment did include an innocent-property-owner defense which said, "that no property shall be forfeited under this paragraph, to the extent of an interest of an owner by reason of any act or omission established by that owner to have been committed or omitted without the knowledge or consent of the owner." Lenders run the risk of losing property held as collateral for the loan because of several features of this federal legislation.

First, the seizure of the property is a civil, not a criminal, proceeding. The property, not the owner, is charged with the offense. This means that the owner need not be convicted or even charged with a drug-related offense. Second, the federal government claims a right to the property interests at the moment the property is used for illegal drug transactions. This means that if a lender obtains title to a property previously used for drug sales (for example, by way of a foreclosure), the lender may lose it even though it is no longer used for such purposes. Third, all of the owner's real estate may be confiscated, even though only a portion has been used for illegal purposes. Fourth, property of great value may be seized, even if the illegal activity involved minor amounts of drugs. The amount of drugs involved need only be sufficient to be punishable by at least 1 year in jail. (In *Calero-Toledo* v. *Pearson Yacht Leasing Co.,*[14] the U.S. Supreme court upheld the seizure of a $19,800 yacht after authorities discovered two marijuana cigarettes on board.) Fifth, the owner or mortgagee of the property may be completely innocent. Someone who leases the property and conducts an illegal drug trade will expose the property to forfeiture. Finally, the owner or mortgagee does not have any rights to the income from the property after it has been seized. In *U.S.* v. *Property Known as 708–710 West 9th St., Erie, Pa.,*[15] the owner-mortgagor defaulted on a loan after he was arrested for selling drugs. The government seized the rental property and began collecting rents but paid nothing to the mortgagee. The court held that the mortgagee was not entitled to any income from the property, despite an assignment-of-rents provision in the deed of trust. The court did allow the mortgagee to collect the balance of the mortgage when the government disposed of the property, however.

The danger for the lender is greatest when it forecloses on property that has previously been used to support illegal drug transactions. The lender may lose the property to the government if it fails in an innocent owner defense. To establish this defense, the owner (lender) must prove more than simple ignorance that the property was used for drug sales. The owner must demonstrate that all reasonable measures to investigate the use of the property were taken. This is called a "due diligence" defense and may be an enormously difficult task for some lenders, especially those that advance many loans on properties in diverse geographical locations. Furthermore, the lender may run into trouble if it attempts to avoid this risk by denying loans in areas of known drug activity. It runs the risk of violating the Home Mortgage Disclosure Act (1975) and the Community Reinvestment Act (1978). In Chapter 7 we saw that these anti-redlining acts impose penalties on lenders who identify neighborhoods within which they will not make loans.

Liability from Lender/Borrower Relationship

Lenders and borrowers enter into contractual relationships. These relationships are governed by both statutory law and the interpretation of that law by the courts. Since real estate loans are considered commercial transactions, the applicable law governing the lender/borrower relationship is the **Uniform Commercial Code (UCC).** The code specifies the rights and obligations of contracting parties. The courts interpret the meaning and intent of the code, assess or absolve liability, and fix judgments (monetary damages or awards). Often the decision of the trial court may be reversed by an appeals court. Judicial law is determined ultimately at the appeals level.

There are two primary and several minor areas of lender behavior that can give rise to liability. The two primary areas involve nonperformance of oral commitments and failure to extend credit beyond a certain date. In the latter case, a common cause of legal action is the calling of a demand note by the lender without notification. We will discuss these two problem areas first and then consider other sources of lender liability.

Oral Commitments for Extension of Credit

First, consider how most real estate projects are developed. A developer will have a plan to construct a commercial real estate project. The plans may call for the acquisition of the land, the development of the property (roads, utilities, and so on), and the construction of the facility. In most cases, the developer will sell the property when completed. The developer's financing need is limited to the acquisition, development, and construction (ADC) phase of the investment. Since few developers have the means or the desire to finance the ADC stage from their own equity, they seek out lenders for this purpose. The typical ADC loan will be for only the period through completion of the project, at which time the loan will be repaid from the proceeds of the sale of the facility by the developer.

To see how a lawsuit may result, consider the following scenario. A real estate developer desires to purchase a piece of raw land for $1 million and build a $7 million office building on the site. The seller of the land requires an earnest money deposit of $50,000 before signing a sales contract. Before the developer gives the seller of the land the $50,000, he requests a loan from a loan officer, who is also his friend, at a local bank. He has done business with this loan officer for many years. The loan officer assures the developer that, based on his past credit history, there will be no problem in obtaining a loan for the acquisition and development of the property. Based on this oral commitment the developer, unwisely, gives the seller of the land a $50,000 deposit and signs a contract to purchase the land one month hence. Two weeks later, when the developer arranges for the loan to purchase the property, the bank, concerned with a recent reversal in the local real estate market, refuses to make the loan. The developer loses not only the $50,000 deposit but any profits that he would have made on the deal. He may attempt to seek compensation through the court system on the basis that an oral commitment to make a loan was breached.

Consider a second example. Assume that the developer had been successful in arranging the ADC loan. Also, assume that the bank was concerned with some cost overruns in previous projects developed by the borrower. If the bank lends the developer several million dollars to construct a project, it does not wish to see those funds exhausted when the facility is only half-completed. It would have only a half-completed facility as collateral for the loan. Thus, the bank puts in a demand feature to the line-of-credit. The developer can "take down" as needed as the project is developed, but if the bank's construction auditors (experts in the field of construction costs) determine that there are insufficient safeguards to prevent cost overruns, the bank can freeze the remaining line-of-credit and call the amount due on the note immediately. Demand notes (payable upon the demand of the lender at any time) are common in commercial transactions. By their terms, they do not require prior notification before payment is demanded.

In this example, if the bank were to determine that its collateral was in danger when the project was half-completed and called the note, the developer would be unable to make the payment on short notice. The developer can neither quickly sell a half-completed real estate project nor arrange for a substitute loan. If the bank forecloses on the note and sells the property at a foreclosure sale, the developer not only loses the original deposit but also the profits on the development. Again, the developer may attempt to seek relief from the court system.

In the one case above, there is a failure to make a loan based on an oral commitment. In the other case, there is a failure to make a loan extension (extend an existing loan) beyond the demand date. In both cases, it would appear that the developer has little hope of success in court. As explained below in the text, contracts for real estate financing must be in writing to be enforced. Also, the Uniform Commercial Code allows parties to contract for loans that are payable on demand without notice. But, suppose you were a member of a jury in a case brought by the developer and were made aware of the following facts: That the developer had always received oral commitments in the past and had come to rely on this method of doing business; that in the case where the demand note was called, the bank had no reason to believe that the collateral was in jeopardy; that the loan was called because a new loan officer was hired who simply "didn't like" the developer. In whose favor would you decide? In many such cases jurors have sided with the developer. But, before we review some actual lender liability cases, consider the following arguments that suggest the lender in our example might, or should, prevail.

Oral Commitments by Lenders

Lenders may orally commit to make a loan. At first, one might think that there would be little room for liability in cases of oral commitments, since contracts to borrow funds to finance real estate are always in writing and usually quite detailed. In fact, the statute of frauds requires such contracts to be in writing. Specifically, the statute of frauds says that the following contracts must be in writing in order to be enforced:

- Agreements that cannot be performed within 1 year,
- Promises to answer for the debts of another (surety contracts),
- Promises made in consideration of marriage,
- Agreements relating to real property,
- Contracts exceeding $500 for the sale of goods, and
- Contracts by executors

If the agreement is not in writing, then the provisions of the agreement will not be binding on either party (unless some exception, not discussed here, may apply). It is obvious that nearly every real estate loan will fall under the provisions of the statute of frauds. Yet, there have been several successful suits brought by borrowers against lenders for oral statements or commitments related to a real estate loan. Lenders have been increasingly subject to suits concerning items in the contractual relationship of a real estate loan that have not been part of some written agreement. In their suits borrowers generally do not claim that the lender violated any technical terms of a written loan agreement, only that it reneged on oral commitments or violated long-standing practices.

As a result of the moderate success that borrowers have had in such suits in the past, lenders in many states have sought legislation implementing one of two types of modification—**statute of fraud** amendments or **credit agreement statutes.** Statute of fraud amendments would invalidate any oral commitment for granting or extending credit. These relate primarily to loans made by financial institutions for other than personal, family, or household extension of an existing line of credit and typically consist of three main sections. The first section defines certain terms such as creditor, debtor, credit agreement, and financial institution. The second section requires extensions of credit to be in writing and signed by both parties. The third section generally contains what are known as safe harbors for lenders. Safe harbors are actions that the lender can take that cannot be interpreted as implying an extension of credit. Examples include giving financial advice to the borrower, agreeing with the borrower not to take certain actions under the existing loan contract such as accelerating the loan, and so forth.

Statute of fraud amendments and credit extension agreements are similar in that they both give added support to lenders by explicitly requiring modification of loan contracts to be in writing before either party can enforce them.

Termination of Demand Notes Without Notification

As you can imagine, a call of a demand note without notification can be financially distressing to a cash-short real estate developer or other business that depends on the line-of-credit for its day-to-day operations. Many lawsuits have resulted from a short notice call of a demand note. The damages often may include the value of a business that has failed because of the call of the demand note by the lender. The plaintiff (borrower) will assert that the lender failed to act in "good faith" as required by law. Although the requirement to act in good faith is a well-accepted legal concept, it is not clear if it should apply to situations where the terms of contracts are spelled out, such as with demand notes and other types of real estate financing.

Section 1-203 of the Uniform Commercial Code provides that "every contract or duty within this chapter imposes an obligation of good faith in its performance or enforcement," while Section 1-201 defines **good faith** as "honesty in fact in the conduct or transaction concerned."[16] Most of the concern in the code about good faith centered on commercial sales (and not loans) where one or more of the terms of a contract may have been left open-ended. This is to say that the framers of the code were concerned that one party to an open-ended sales contract might be disadvantaged if the other were not required to bargain in good faith. As an example, assume that a buyer of a product signs a contract to purchase an item for a given price plus an unstipulated charge for shipping and handling. When the item is delivered, the bill reflects an outrageously high shipping and handling charge. The courts would probably not require the buyer to pay for the charges.

Yet, the code does address good faith in loan contracts as well. In Section 1-208 it states that when the terms of a note allow the lender to "accelerate payment or performance . . . 'at will' or 'when he deems himself insecure' . . . he shall have the power to do so only if he in good faith believes that the prospect of payment or performance is impaired."[17] This remark is aimed more at term notes (those with a specific maturity date) that can be accelerated than at demand notes. The Official Commentary to Section 1-208 states that the section has no application to demand notes because their nature permits call at any time with or without good reason. The difference between calling a term note "at will" and a demand note is confusing, to say the least. Some court decisions have required good faith practices for demand notes, even though it is clear from the Official Commentary that good faith should be applicable only to term notes that have acceleration clauses. Other court decisions, on the other hand, have held the opposite view and have refused to consider whether the lender has acted in good faith in calling a demand note.

Oral Commitments and Credit Termination: Court Cases

Lenders generally have been successful in defending themselves against liability on these issues, but the success has occurred primarily at the appeals level. In *Kruse* v. *Bank of America*[18] an apple grower in California claimed damage as a result of the lender's failure to make a loan after making an oral commitment. Although the jury at the trial level awarded the apple grower almost $47 million, the appeals court overturned the decision based on the fact that the commitment was not in writing. The results in this case are typical of many suits brought against lenders for failure to advance funds for which there is no written agreement. The results of suits are more mixed when an existing loan is accelerated (terminated), either before its maturity date or, if a demand note, without any notification.

In *Centerre Bank of Kansas City* v. *Distributors, Inc.,*[19] the lender extended a line-of-credit to the sole shareholder of Distributors, Inc., in return for a $900,000 demand note, a security interest in the firm's inventory and accounts receivable, and the personal guarantee of the owner. In the early 1980s the owner had sold 20 percent of the stock to the firm's general manager, who desired to purchase the remainder. The general manager was concerned that the lender might not continue the financing arrangement under new management. The loan officer at Centerre assured the general manager that the financing arrangement would continue as long as the original owner continued to provide a personal guarantee. After the general manager purchased the firm, the loan officer informed him that his personal guarantee also would be required, in addition to that of the former owner. These additional guarantees would assure the continued financing, according to the loan officer. Three days after the guarantees were delivered, the bank gave 60 days notice that it was calling the demand note. During this time, the bank extended funds and received payments on the line-of-credit. To no avail, it also helped the new owners seek alternative financing. Ultimately, the new owners were forced to turn over the assets of the business and cease operations. Evidence at the trial suggested that the bank knew that the call of the demand note would put Distributors out of business, but the president of the bank did not think that the new owner could manage the business and, in fact, did not like the new owner personally.

Although the jury found for the plaintiff in this case (undoubtedly as a result of the behavior of the lender), the appellate court held that a good-faith obligation does not apply to the decision of a lender to call a demand note.[20] Citing the appellate court in another case,[21] it stated that the application of Section 1-203 of the UCC would add another term to the loan arrangement that was not intended by either party.

The lender in similar case did not fare as well. In *K.M.C. Co., Inc.* v. *Irving Trust Co.*[22] the lender called a demand note on a line-of-credit without any notification. The jury found for the debtor, K.M.C., and the appeals court affirmed, undoubtedly because of the apparently callous nature of the lender's actions. The evidence indicated that the lender called the demand note without prior notice despite the fact that the bank had a policy of notification in such events. Also in the past, the bank had covered previous K.M.C. overdrafts via a line-of-credit. The evidence demonstrated that the bank knew that calling the note would lead to financial ruin for the firm. Finally, the call of the demand note was motivated by a personality conflict between a bank officer and the president of K.M.C.

Given this scenario, one can see why the case focused on the "good-faith" concept. In its decision the trial court stated that the lender had a good-faith obligation to notify K.M.C. prior to discontinuing the line-of-credit arrangement, this despite the express written provisions of the line-of-credit agreement that did not call for notification. The demand provision, it said, is like a general insecurity or default clause and is therefore subject to the good-faith standard outlined in Section 1-208 of the UCC. Although that section allows acceleration upon default, it requires that the lender feel that the security is jeopardized. That, according to the K.M.C. court, was not the motivation in the call of the line-of-credit. This decision was made in spite of the Official Commentary on this section that stated that such good-faith standards did not apply to demand notes whose very nature permitted a call at any time and for any reason. It is clear that the K.M.C. court was confused between the acceleration clause of a loan with a maturity date and the acceleration of a demand note or line-of-credit. The court justified its decision by way of analogy to another section of the UCC that addresses contracts for sales of goods (Sec. 2-309(3)), stating that "the application of principles of good faith and sound commercial practice normally call for such notification of the termination of a going contract relationship as will give the other party reasonable time to seek a substitute arrangement."

The court in this case likely failed to understand the nature of a demand note. Demand notes have the provision of call at the will of the lender precisely because notification may give the debtor an opportunity to waste more of the secured assets or take other actions that may be injurious to the lender. If lenders have the ability to call a demand note or line-of-credit at will, they will have greater protection and less risk. For the reduced risk, lenders will require a lower initial interest rate. Both the lender and the borrower profit from the arrangement. This is stating the obvious, since demand notes or lines-of-credit are very popular loan instruments sought out by borrowers because of these favorable terms. The very fact that borrowers and lenders freely enter into such loan arrangements indicates that the terms are advantageous to both parties.

The decision in K.M.C. is likely to be an anomaly. In cases where a line-of-credit is called by a lender, most courts have held that the demand note is callable by definition at the will of the lender and is outside the scope of good-faith requirements. The requirements that contracts for loans be in writing and that the call of demand notes be exempt from good-faith restrictions both provide relief for lenders from liability in these areas. However, there are other areas where lenders may be held liable; these include loans with fixed termination dates, such as many real estate loans.

Other Theories of Lender Liability

There are several other legal theories of actions that may give rise to lender liability. They are not addressed as frequently as breach of oral commitments or a lack of good faith, but they do arise and should be mentioned.

Prima Facie Tort

A **tort** is a breach of a duty created by law, whereby the injured party seeks compensation from the wrongdoer. **Prima facie tort** is described in Section 870 of Restatement (Second) of Torts thus: "One who intentionally causes injury to another is subject to liability to the other for that injury, if his conduct is generally culpable and not justifiable under the circumstances. This liability may be imposed even though the actor's conduct does not come within the traditional category of tort liability." Although an act may be lawful, it becomes a tort if it is done with the intent to cause injury, it results in an injury, and there is no justification for the act. The wrongdoer's state of mind and intention transform a lawful act into one that is unlawful. It may be insufficient that the person performing the act knew that the consequence would be injurious. What may be required is that the actor desired to bring about the outcome. Since the thrust of a prima facie tort goes to the intention of the wrongdoer, it is particularly difficult to establish liability without the wrongdoer admitting to his frame of mind.

Promissory Fraud

Fraud is an intentional misrepresentation intended to deceive, whether by misstating or concealing the truth. It can also be a statement made with reckless disregard for whether it is true or not. Promissory fraud involves the making of a promise with no intention of fulfilling it. **Promissory fraud** may be difficult to prove, because proof of the fraud requires that the wrong-doer intended not to perform at the time when the promise was made. The failure to perform is not sufficient proof to demonstrate promissory fraud.

Promissory fraud was one of the principal foundations in a $19 million verdict in the *State National Bank of El Paso* v. *Farah Manufacturing Co.*[23] In this case, the lender did not approve of the new management proposed by the firm. The provisions of its loan to the company allowed it to declare default at its option if there was a change of management. The lender induced the company not to install Mr. Farah as president and chief executive officer by stating it would not declare a default if someone else were selected. The evidence showed that the lender, in fact, had not determined what its action would have been if Mr. Farah had been installed as CEO. The company failed under the alternative management, which was shown to be inexperienced and to have divided loyalty. The failure of the company was the damage claimed in this case.

Contrary to a claim for a breach of contract, a claim for fraud can include punitive damages. For this reason, if there is any hint that promissory fraud may be involved, the plaintiff will include it as part of the claim.

Nondisclosure Fraud and Breach of Fiduciary Duty

Fiduciary means "characterized by trust." **Nondisclosure fraud** involves not only a misrepresentation but also the duty of one party to make a disclosure to another based on a fiduciary duty. Many relationships involve a fiduciary duty. The managers of a company have a fiduciary duty to act in the interests of the stockholders. The rules of agency require that agents have a fiduciary duty to act in the interests of the principal. There are numerous other examples of the relationship. In terms of lender liability, the issue centers on whether or not a lender has a fiduciary duty with the borrower.

Consider the following example. Assume that a real estate developer approaches a lender to obtain a loan to purchase a property. The purchase price is above its true value because of facts known to the lender but not to the buyer. To thicken the plot, also assume that the lender has a secured interest in the property, having made a nonrecourse loan to the present owner. In the event of default, the lender may look only to the property as collateral. The lender also knows that the current owner is delinquent. The lender would like to make a loan to the prospective buyer for the amount of the purchase price for the following reason: the amount of the new loan will be equal to that of the existing delinquent loan, and the lender can require that the buyer assume personal liability for the loan. The sale and loan would benefit the lender because of the additional security interest. It would disadvantage the buyer because the true value is much less than the purchase price. If the lender makes the loan and the buyer eventually defaults and makes up any deficiency out of personal funds, is the lender liable for nondisclosure fraud? That is, does the lender have a duty to disclose to the buyer the facts that make the true value of the property less than the purchase price?

Generally, to be liable under this theory, the lender should have a duty to disclose information only if there exists an inequality of position, a fiduciary relationship, or knowledge by one of the parties of facts that are not within the reasonable reach of the other. It is not clear how the courts would rule in the above example. In *Hill* v. *Securities Investment Co. of St. Louis*[24] the court ruled that a lender did not have an obligation to tell a borrower who desired a loan to invest in a company that the lender had refused financing for the company. Also, in *Denison State Bank* v. *Maderia,*[25] the court held that the bank did not have to disclose to a potential borrower that a company in which the borrower had plans to invest had overdrafts at the bank. In many such cases the courts generally have found that there is no fiduciary relationship between the lender—for example, a bank—and customers and depositors.

Breach of Contract

Plaintiffs may attempt to establish liability under the assertion that a lender failed to extend the existing financing after an oral agreement to do so. Generally, this attempt will run head on against the **parole evidence rule** that states that the terms of a written contract cannot be contradicted by any prior or contemporaneous oral agreement. The reasons for the parole evidence rule are:

1. There can be no contract without a meeting of the minds of the parties, and
2. There can be no meeting of the minds unless the terms of the contract are certain and ascertainable—in other words, definite.

Generally, oral agreements to extend credit are not sufficiently definite to create a contract. One needs to state the interest rate, date of maturity, default provisions, and many other terms to be definite. As an example, the court in *Labor Discount Center, Inc.* v. *State Bank and Trust Co. of Wellston*[26] held that an oral agreement to continue interim financing is insufficiently definite to be enforceable. Many other cases have confirmed that lenders do not incur liability for breaching alleged oral commitments to extend credit.

Duress and Lender Control

It is difficult for many start-up firms and emerging real estate development companies to obtain pure equity financing. Even if they could, the owners frequently do not wish to give up control of the firm through large stock issues. These firms will seek out debt financing but with an equity complexion. They will attract funds from lenders interested in financing the operations of new and emerging start-up real estate firms because of the potential for excess returns. The loan arrangements will, in many respects, have the complexion of equity. The lender will insist on an exclusive lending arrangement, cutting off competition from other lenders. The lender also will be rewarded in some fashion according to the success of the firm. Equity-participation loans whose terms are tied to the performance of the firm are not uncommon. Examples include arrangements for participating in the annual operating profits of the firm or sharing in the appreciation of the value of the property.

Many of these loan agreements stipulate that, in the case of financial difficulties, the lender has the right to take over certain operations of the borrowing company. Such control arrangements are designed to reduce the risk of the lender. If the management of the borrowing company does a poor job, then the lender has the opportunity to substitute management. In this case it is difficult to deny that the lender is, in reality, an equity holder. It has a "loan" with equity characteristics and can take over management of the firm in the event it perceives financial mismanagement.

If a lender exercises a right of control under such an agreement, it will run the risk of incurring some liability. If the business ultimately fails despite the control of the lender, several parties may wish to seek compensation from the lender. Those parties would include, in addition to the stockholders of the corporation, such third parties as creditors of the corporation, including suppliers, and the government, if taxes are unpaid. The magnitude of the liability will be a function of the extent and character of the actual control. There are several legal areas where lenders may be liable for control. For third parties, two areas are bankruptcy and agency law. Lenders may be liable to the debtor (owner of the firm) under tort or fiduciary law.

Liabilty to Third Parties: Bankruptcy and Agency Law

The legal rules that are followed in bankruptcy can be complex. Of interest here are the so-called voidable preference rules. Generally, if a debtor transfers assets to a preferred creditor within 90 days of filing for bankruptcy, the trustee in bankruptcy may require that those assets be returned to the debtor for the satisfaction of the general creditors. The voidable preference period of 90 days can be extended to 1 year if the creditor to which the assets are transferred is an insider. An insider is one who owns a certain amount of stock in the company or controls the operations of the company. You can see where problems may arise in this area. If a lender takes over control of a company, it will have an incentive to make payments on its own debt to the detriment of other creditors. Thus, a lender could be held liable by the trustee in bankruptcy for all payments made to itself within 1 year of filing for bankruptcy, if it takes over control. If the lender does not take over control but simply forecloses on its loan, then only payments made within the 90-day period may be considered a preference item.

A second area of the law where lenders may become liable to third parties is agency law. Restatement (Second) of Agency states that "**Agency** is the fiduciary relationship which results from the manifestation of consent by one person to another such that the other shall act on his behalf and subject to his control, and consent by the other so to act."[27] Three essential elements are necessary for an agency relationship to exist. First, both parties must consent to the relationship. Second, the agent must act in the interest of the principal. Third, the agent must be subject to the direction and control of the principal.

Agency law comes into play with lender control in this way: If the lender undertakes sufficient control of the operations of the creditor's business, then the debtor becomes an agent of the lender. Suppose, for example, that a lender takes control of the development of a real estate project in the belief that the developer is mismanaging the project. The lender may be within its rights to do so by the terms of the loan agreement. But now, the lender may have assumed the role of a **principal.** The lender takes over control and directs the operations of the business. Assume, further, that in the role of managing the business, the lender has the business order some construction material. If the developer (business) fails prior to paying for the material and declares bankruptcy, who is responsible for paying for the material? Under the laws of agency, the lender may be. The material supplier likely will claim that the business was acting as an agent on behalf of a principal, not the (failed) business. Section 140 of the Restatement (Second) of Agency states that "A creditor who assumes control of his debtor's business for the mutual benefit of himself and his debtor may become a principal, with liability for the acts and transactions of the debtor in connection with the business."[28] The extent of liability in such cases depends upon the amount of control. If, in the above example, the lender did not control an aspect of ordering materials, it would not likely be found to be a principal in this regard and therefore would not be liable for payment.

Finally, a lender may be liable for the unpaid payroll taxes of a debtor. This would be the case where lender control extended to hiring, firing, and other payroll decisions or the lender made a loan for the purpose of paying the payroll taxes and was aware that the debtor firm did not use the funds to pay the taxes.

The greatest exposure to liability is undoubtedly harm done to debtors when a lender exercises control over the business operations. As indicated above, many loan agreements call for the lender to take various actions in the case that a loan becomes troubled. The actions may range from giving management advice to suggesting a new management consulting team to actually controlling the affairs of the business. When a lender takes some control over the day-to-day affairs of the debtor's business, the lender may have a fiduciary duty to act in the interest of the firm's owners. A breach of that duty may expose the lender to liability. The greater the degree of control that a lender exercises, the larger the potential liability may be if the business ultimately fails. Not all cases of lender control will lead to liability, however. The fiduciary duty of the lender does not require that the lender abandon its self-interest. The controlling factor would be the extent to which the lender operates outside of a contract and its fiduciary duty to act in the interest of the borrower.

In summary, lenders can be liable for damages anytime they exercise some control over a borrower. The liability will be minimized if the control that is exercised is within the scope of the loan agreement and if the lender does not operate capriciously and in bad faith against the interest of the debtor. In many cases where juries have found lenders to be liable, the verdict has been reversed at the appellate level. Liability will result generally in cases of extreme lender misbehavior.

In cases where lenders have intervened in real estate developments, the lender likely will avoid liability if the developer has acted in violation of the loan agreement. Examples of the latter scenario include the use of project funds or materials for other developments or projects, appropriation of funds from an operating account for personal uses, and failure to exercise proper project supervision and cost controls.

BANKRUPTCY AND AGENCY COSTS

Lenders must be aware that the bankruptcy laws can be used by creditors to serve their own interest against that of the lender. Although bankruptcy laws have been formulated and designed primarily for ongoing business enterprises, they can and have been used in the context of the development of real estate projects. The usual scenario involves a real estate developer that borrows funds, contributes a small amount of equity, and develops a real estate project that is not economically feasible. In this situation the value of the completed development is often less than the amount of debt secured by that property. Faced with the loss of the property through a foreclosure, the developer/debtor may attempt to use the bankruptcy laws to salvage an interest in the property. If successful, the developer may be able to reduce the amount of debt that is owed the lender.

Bankruptcy Law and the "Cramdown" Process

Potentially bankrupt debtors have access to what is referred to as a Chapter 11 bankruptcy. The purpose of this type of bankruptcy is to allow the troubled "firm" to continue operations in the hope that eventually economic success will allow it to pay its debts and continue operation. From a social policy standpoint, the government views this as preferable to an immediate liquidation of the firm and its assets. Since a real estate development can be considered a firm with business operations, developers have employed the provisions of Chapter 11 bankruptcy to fight off an immediate foreclosure by a lender and, in some cases, to reduce the amount owed by the developer to the lender. The term cramdown refers to the ability, under the law, to force a restructuring of the debt owed by the developer. The types of restructuring that occur include extending the maturity date of the loan, reducing the interest rate on the loan, or even reducing the principal balance of the loan.

A simple example will demonstrate the value of the cramdown to the developer and the danger to the lender. If a property with a market value of $4 million is secured by a $6 million loan, the loss of the property through foreclosure will leave the developer with no equity and, most likely, a deficiency judgment of $2 million. If the developer can use bankruptcy laws to cramdown the loan principal to $4 million, there is an immediate capture of $2 million in wealth. Should the market value of the property increase subsequent to the cramdown—to $5 million, for example—then the developer gains $1 million in positive equity in the property that would not have existed without the cramdown. Obviously, lenders would prefer to foreclose if there is the possibility of obtaining a valuable deficiency judgment against the developer's other assets.

To be successful in a cramdown, the developer must obtain a confirmation of a bankruptcy plan in federal court. In such a reorganization plan, the developer/debtor must segregate the claims of all creditors into various classes, each of which receives a special treatment under the plan. For a real estate developer, other creditors might include subcontractors, tenants of the facility, and others. All the claims in a class must be similar in nature, but not all similar claims need to be placed in the same class. Thus, the developer/debtor may form two classes of creditors, all with similar characteristics. A class of creditors is considered "impaired" if the plan alters equitable or contractual rights of the creditors in a class, fails to cure prebankruptcy arrearages and damages, or does not pay the claims of the debtors in cash for the full amount of the debt owed. Obviously, a lender with a secured interest in the real estate property will be impaired under a plan that attempts to reduce the principal amount of the debt. For any impaired class of creditors, if two-thirds by amount or one-half by number agree to the bankruptcy plan, it is considered approved by the class. The lender has a choice of how to be classified. Using the above example, the lender may elect to be placed in two classes: a secured class with a debt of $4 million (the value of the real estate collateral) and an unsecured class for the remaining $2 million (a deficiency claim). Alternatively, the lender may elect to be placed only in one class, a secured class, where the entire claim is treated as secured. This selection is important because of the cramdown rules. Those rules address the treatment of the claims in each class and the approval of the plan by all classes.

Insofar as the treatment of the creditors in each class, the cramdown rules require that a secured creditor must receive deferred cash payments which both total and have a present value at a minimum equal to the value of the security and some treatment of the unsecured deficiency. In effect, this rule states that since through foreclosure the lender is likely to recover only the value of the collateral, he is in no worse position after the reorganization than before. Thus, in our example, the lender would have to be assured of future payments with a total and a present value of $4 million and some payment of the $2 million residual. In most situations, the creditor will offer a very small fraction of the dollar claim of the residual.

If all classes of debtors approve of the reorganization plan, then it will be binding on all creditors, even those minority debtors in classes that did not approve of the plan. If one impaired class does not approve the plan, it will not be binding unless the court feels that the plan is equitable and fair to all parties, in which case the plan is "crammed down" on that dissenting impaired class.

The developer/debtor who wishes to salvage value from the uneconomic real estate investment will attempt to establish several classes of debtors. Some will consist of a small number of unsecured creditors with small claims, and the remaining class will be made up of the secured lender. The developer hopes that the acceptance of the plan by the classes of the unsecured creditors will be sufficient to cramdown a reduction in the principal amount of the loan of the secured creditor. Here is where the lender must choose into which class(es) to place the claim. If the lender places all of the claim into the secured class, then he will be entitled to future payments with a total equal to the amount of the loan and a present value equal to the value of the collateral. In our example, the lender would be entitled to deferred payments that total at least $6 million and have a present value of $4 million. The lender is in a better position financially under this election. But if this choice is made, then the lender is represented in only one class and may be forced to have its claim crammed down by the other classes which may approve the plan. Strategy is the key in this regard.

Practical Considerations

From the above discussion, you can see that there are agency relationships with which the real estate lender must be concerned. If the value of a completed real estate project fails to meet projections, the lender may not feel secure in the foreclosure process which gives him the property and a deficiency judgment. The developer/debtor may be able to use the bankruptcy laws to reduce the amount of the debt to the value of the property. If successful, any subsequent increase in value will accrue to the developer and not the lender. For this reason, lenders will have to pursue the strategy that has the greatest probability of defeating the plan.

Although it is in the interest of the creditor to put forth a successful plan that will result in a reduction of the principal due the lender, it may not be an easy task. First, the plan must show that it is likely that the future cash flows from the project will be sufficient to meet the new debt payments under the plan. Second, all classes of creditors must approve the plan. Third, the courts are not likely to approve a plan designed solely to reduce the amount of debt owed the lender.

In the case where a loan is secured by a single real estate asset, the above criteria may be difficult to meet. A severely distressed property may not show sufficient cash flows to meet even the reduced amount of debt. Second, creating several classes of creditors to cramdown the plan on the lender may be difficult if there are very few other creditors. Even if such classes can be "manufactured," it is likely the court will view the plan as being unfair to the lender.

An excellent example of such a situation is the case of *In Re Meadow Glen, Ltd.*[29] where the debtor created four classes of unsecured creditors, including the tenants (total, $2000), unsecured creditors with claims less than $100 (total, $500), unsecured creditors with claims more than $100 (total, $23,000), and the deficiency claim of the lender ($5.5 million). The bankruptcy plan proposed to pay the claims as follows: tenants, 90 percent of allowed claims; unsecured claims less than $100, also 90 percent; unsecured claims more than $100, 75 percent of claims; and the deficiency claim, 10 percent equity interest in the property. The court reasoned that the plan was unfair to the lender. It stated there was no justification for distinguishing between the unsecured creditors. Also, it noted the high payoff to the small classes, and that the payment to the lender of a 10 percent equity interest was a dubious value at best. The court found that since the amount of the nondeficiency claims was so small, the impairment of these classes produced no material benefit for the secured lender. It ruled that the creation of the classes was done solely to produce impaired classes for the purpose of the cramdown in the debt owed the secured lender.

In short, the lender needs to be aware of the possibility that bankruptcy laws may be used to reduce the amount of principal owed, but that plans created for this sole purpose are unlikely to be approved by the courts. It should prove very difficult for developer/debtors of single properties to effectively reduce indebtedness and retain the property through bankruptcy proceedings. It may be more likely that developers of many properties under one firm name may succeed in such a strategy, however, because it may be easier to create multiple impaired classes for the purpose of effectuating the cramdown.

ETHICS, FRAUD, AND AGENCY COSTS

In many circumstances ethics, fraud, and agency costs are all related. **Ethics** deals with the moral duties and obligations that individuals have to deal justly with each other. In a real estate finance text, we prefer to leave it to the philosophers to discuss the meanings of such terms as just, fair, and moral. Here, it is sufficient to say that there is no scientific manner in which to determine if a particular action is moral or not. No standard can be applied to measure how moral or how ethical an action may be. We will state simply here that it is to the benefit of society if individuals deal with each other in a fair and just way.

One should not confuse ethical actions with legal actions. Some actions can be legal but not ethical, and vice versa. However, many laws are passed with ethical standards in mind. That is, many laws reflect the desire to have people treat others fairly and justly. We saw a good example of this earlier in the chapter. The Uniform Commercial Code specifically requires that parties to a contract deal in good faith with one another. Other examples of such laws are those that make it illegal for individuals to trade in securities based on inside information. Laws also restrict the dealings of public officials who may have inside information or whose actions can affect their private well-being through legislation.

Finally, agency relationships have legal and ethical implications. As explained earlier, an agency relationship exists when an agent is held to act on behalf of, or for the interests of, another. Often, but not always, the agent is compensated by the principal, so that the agent has a legal and ethical obligation to act on behalf of the principal only. There are numerous situations where the nature of the relationship provides an incentive for the agent to act on his own (or another's) behalf, rather than for the benefit of the principal. In these cases, the principal must expend resources to make sure that the agent acts only in the principal's interest. These resource expenditures are referred to as agency costs. An example will clarify these comments.

When a real estate developer requests a loan to finance a new project, the lender will require an appraisal of the property (in its completed form). The appraised value of the property will serve as a guide to the amount of financing the lender is willing to advance. To avoid default risk the lender may agree to finance only 80 percent of the appraised value. To obtain an appraisal of value, the lender will hire an appraiser. The appraiser is, therefore, an agent of, and is required to act on behalf of, the lender. But the appraiser may wish to obtain other appraisal assignments from the developer. If there are many appraisers competing for assignments, the appraiser may have an incentive to make sure the loan is approved. In this way, he gains the favor of a real estate developer, who may be able to give him additional assignments.

Let's assume that the value of the completed project is $1 million but that the developer does not desire to risk an equity position of $200,000. He may ask the appraiser to value the property at $1.3 million so that the lender will feel comfortable in advancing $1 million or so. Many areas of an appraisal report call for a judgment to be made. The appraiser may have to make a judgment as to the value of a proposed new highway intersection near the property. Also, it is possible for the appraiser to make out-and-out false statements. The appraiser has a conflict of interest between providing a fair report for the lender or an exaggerated or falsified one for the borrower. Ethically, the appraiser must be unbiased where any judgment is called for in the appraisal report. Legally, the appraiser is liable if he makes a false statement in the appraisal report. If the appraiser makes a biased judgment in favor of the developer, but it does not involve a false statement, the issue becomes clouded. While ethically wrong, the appraiser may escape legal liability, because it would be difficult to prove that the appraiser acted in his own interest against that of the lender.

Where do agency costs come in? Most large commercial real estate lenders employ a staff of review appraisers. It is their function to review the appraisal reports done by outside appraisers for inaccuracies and mistakes. Review appraisers are retained because lenders recognize that appraisers may act against the interests of the lender. The cost of maintaining a review appraiser staff can be considered an agency cost.

The following examples illustrate agency relationships in real estate finance. Two examples involve mortgage insurance, and one discusses the failure of many thrifts in the late 1980s and early 1990s.

Agency Relationships and Mortgage Insurance

Government (FHA, VA) and private mortgage insurance protects the lender against losses on defaulted loans. The major element in the loss on many defaulted loans is the carrying costs of the property during and after the foreclosure process. The lender pays these costs and is then reimbursed by the insurer (FHA pays the full costs, while private mortgage insurers pay only a portion over a minimum amount). These costs include property taxes, hazard insurance, maintenance costs, and foregone interest on the loan. Foregone interest is reimbursed at a rate equal to the contract rate on the loan. Although the premium is paid by the borrower, the agency relationship is between the lender and the insurer. In the event of a default, the lender will have two basic options: forebear and seek an arrangement to restructure the loan with the borrower or foreclose on the loan and file a claim with the insurer for any loss. If the lender chooses the second option, it faces several other decisions. One would be the method of foreclosure in a state where a choice is allowed between a judicial and power-of-sale procedure. As indicated in Chapter 14, the judicial procedure is the more time-consuming and expensive method. Another decision would be whether or not to monitor the property and make repairs. From these decisions, two different agency relationships arise.

Consider first the agency relationship between the lender and the FHA. Here, foregone interest is reimbursed at the contract rate on the loan. How would the current level of interest rates affect the decision of the lender in its choice of foreclosure method? If the current market rate is above the rate on the loan, the lender will have an incentive to foreclose as quickly as possible, so as to obtain the insurance funds and lend them at the higher rate. If, on the other hand, the current market rate is below that on the loan, the lender will have an incentive to slow the foreclosure process. This is so because the lender is being reimbursed for foregone interest during the foreclosure process at the higher (loan) rate. In this second case, the lender's incentive is contrary to that of the FHA. A drawn-out foreclosure process causes the carrying costs, borne entirely by the FHA, to increase. There is evidence to suggest that some lenders do, in fact, behave in this fashion.[30]

It should be noted that the FHA is an agent of U.S. taxpayers and should act on their behalf to reduce claim costs. The agency relationship among government departments, government employees, and taxpayers is beyond the scope of this example, however.

A second example of an incentive conflict between lenders and insurers involves maintenance costs of foreclosed properties. Lenders generally have no incentive to make repairs on a property, since such repairs would require managerial resources and any loss on the value of the property is covered by insurance.[31] Here, the private mortgage insurer may have to expend resources (agency costs) to make sure the lender makes the repairs on the property. The insurer may require that the lender make repairs to bring the property up to the condition at the time the policy was taken out before a claim can be filed. The lender would have to inspect the property to see that the repairs had in fact been made. All these efforts are costly procedures required to control the incentive conflicts between agents (lenders) and principals (mortgage insurers).

Agency Relationships and Recent Thrift Failures

A final example of the relationship of the law, ethics, and fraud involves the recent failure of many thrifts. To set the stage, consider the environment of thrifts after the deregulation legislation in the early 1980s. Also assume that you are an enterprising person bent on exploiting the agency relationships that exist in such an environment, and that you have no regard for ethics. You only want to create as much wealth for yourself as possible. Here is how you might proceed.

First you would identify a target savings and loan to purchase. You would look for a small- to medium-size thrift that had financial difficulties: perhaps its assets had declined in value because of rising interest rates. The value of the thrift's stock might be very low or even near zero. You can purchase the stock in the thrift for next to nothing. After you purchase the thrift, you place an ad in all the leading national newspapers offering extremely high rates of interest on large ($100,000) deposits. The rate you offer on the deposits is irrelevant because you have no intention that the thrift will ever make a profit. Let's say that $100 million arrives shortly from around the country. Since the deposits are guaranteed by the government, there is no concern on the part of the depositors that the thrift is near insolvency. Next, with all the deposit funds arriving, you seek out some real estate developers who have perhaps been turned down for loans by other lenders. You do not care if their developments are risky. You lend $10 million to one developer for a project worth only $8 million. The developer is so happy, he agrees to pay a loan commitment fee (not points) of $1 million. If you make several such loans, your thrift will earn millions in commitment fees. The earnings of the thrift look impressive. But the assets are all bad loans, loans for values greater than the property. At the end of the year, you report that the thrift made record earnings under the new ownership. In fact, you as the major stockholder take a $5 million bonus in your salary. You continue to do this year after year. If depositors want their money back, you issue new deposits in a continuing "Ponzi" scheme. After several years, the loans eventually default, the thrift is insolvent, and you hand the operation over to the FSLIC. All of your bonuses are personal pay, and you get to keep that.

Dozens of similar actual stories played themselves out in the late 1980s and early 1990s as a result of a regulatory situation that permitted such activities. Although different in detail, many such stories have been reported in the press. One story involved a sleepy little Texas thrift that was purchased in 1982, moved to Dallas, and opened up dozens of branches.[32] The thrift then sold millions of dollars in "jumbo" certificates of deposits ($100,000) in a "boiler room" type operation. At times, $20 to 25 million a day was pouring into the thrift through this operation. The thrift then made dozens of bad loans on which it charged a 6 percent loan fee. The fees, in turn, went to the bottom line of its income statement. Often the borrower was not even required to submit any supporting paperwork for the loan. Less than 4 percent of the thrift's loans in the first 2 years were to homeowners. The same article reported that the new owner of the thrift took more than $3 million in dividends over a 2-year period. The ultimate cost to the FSLIC (taxpayers) was more than $1 billion.

The thrift actions described in this particular article may or may not be within the letter of the law. The loosened regulation of the early 1980s created the environment that allowed these agency problems to evolve. Nonetheless, the Financial Institutions Reform, Recovery, and Enforcement Act (FIRREA) of 1990 authorized $75 million annually from 1990 through 1992 for U.S. Department of Justice investigations and prosecutions involving fraud at financial institutions. Additionally, the Dallas Bank Fraud Task Force was established in 1987 to investigate and prosecute fraud connected with thrift failures in Texas. At least one thrift CEO has been sentenced to 30 years imprisonment as a result of the efforts of the task force.

A final note: Some actions involve out-and-out and blatant fraud that victims must be on the outlook for. A common example is the sale of bogus mortgages—notes that have been fabricated. It is not too difficult for a seller of mortgages to make up fictitious home buyers and place their names and other information on bogus mortgage notes. The seller may intend to pay only the first several installment payments on the mortgage before defaulting, just so as to stay in business. Or the seller may plan to disappear with the sale proceeds. In 1991 the former president of the American Mortgage Company, a Milwaukee mortgage banking firm, pleaded guilty to selling 92 fictitious mortgages worth $10.7 million to a secondary mortgage market agency. In the same year, the president of a Detroit mortgage company forged 99 mortgage loan notes worth approximately $10 million and promptly left the country. In another scam, a Washington, D.C. mortgage broker set up a bogus loan operation and siphoned off an estimated $3 million in fraudulent loan proceeds. He was arrested in 1996 and in 1997 sentenced to 51 months in prison. (In 1990 the Federal Sentencing Guidelines were changed by a Congressional mandate to require a 51-month minimum sentence for fraud convictions where the perpetrator stole more than $1 million or jeopardized the financial soundness of a federally insured financial institution. Estimates place the number of bogus mortgages at about 1 percent of those held by the secondary mortgage market agencies.

Often, the fraud involves loan application information by potential borrowers. Table 22-1 shows the percentage of fraudulent information by type that appeared on mortgages sampled in 1993 and 1994. Incorrect income and employment data head the list of false information pro-

TABLE 22−1

Fraudulent Information Appearing on Mortgage
Applications: 1993–1994

Information	Percent
Incorrect Income	56
Incorrect Employment	36
Correct Occupancy Status	24
Incorrect Debt Structure	13
Fictitious Application	6
Straw Buyer	6
Forged Signature	6

Source: Mortgage Asset Research Institute

TABLE 22−2

Financial Institution Fraud by Type:
1996 Dollar Loss in Millions

Type	Number	Dollar Loss
Check fraud	19,876 (44.5%)	442 (13.4%)
Credit card/ATM	1,965 (4.4%)	1.6 (.5%)
Check kiting	2,992 (6.7%)	696 (21.1%)
Mortgage loan	1,429 (3.2%)	426 (12.9%)
Other	18,403 (41.2%)	1,719 (52.1%)
Total	44,665	3,300

Source: Federal Bureau of Investigation

vided on loan applications. Table 22-2 shows the financial institution fraud cases reported to the Federal Bureau of Investigation in 1996. Although mortgage loan frauds represented only 3.2 percent of all fraud cases they represented 12.9 percent of the loss.

SUMMARY

It is clear that there is more to real estate finance than the simple notion of lenders advancing loans to developers and investors and then collecting interest and principal. Legal issues and agency relationships complicate what otherwise might be such a simple relationship. Lenders may face liability from a variety of circumstances. The court's interpretation of potentially responsible parties under CERCLA may make lenders liable for hazardous waste cleanup costs, despite the secured-lender exemption, when lenders obtain ownership or exercise some control over the day-to-day operations of the debtor. Lenders also risk the loss of their security if the property has been used in any aspect of the illegal drug trade.

Lenders may be liable for their actions in their contractual relationship with borrowers. Secured loans come under the provisions of the Uniform Commercial Code. One provision of the code requires parties to contract to act and bargain in good faith. Several lenders have been found liable for failure to act in good faith, although in many cases the decisions have been reversed on appeal. Even if lenders do act in good faith, they may be liable for other reasons. Typical causes of action by borrowers include a breach of an oral agreement, promissory fraud, misrepresentation, and undue control over the business affairs of the debtor. The likelihood of liability from a breach of an oral agreement is mitigated by the Statute of Fraud and Credit Agreement Statutes. Liability from promissory fraud and undue control is greater, however.

Agency problems and costs permeate the real estate finance market. Parties to real estate finance arrangements that are also agents have an incentive to act in their own behalf and against the interests of the principal. Lenders may act in their own interest and against that of the government mortgage insurer or the government deposit insurer. The problem is compounded when one considers that the government programs are also agents of the general taxpayers. Government bureaucrats may prefer to act in their own interest and not that of the taxpayers. This "layering" of agency relationships has resulted in large losses sustained by the agencies and/or the taxpayers. Many of the self-serving activities of lenders, developers, and appraisers may have been technically legal, but certainly not ethical. Other activities may have involved fraud and were therefore illegal.

KEY TERMS

Agency costs

Agent

Breach of contract

CERCLA

Credit agreement statute

Due diligence defense

Ethics

Fiduciary

Fraud

Good faith

Joint and several liability

Lender control

Nondisclosure fraud

Oral commitment

Parole evidence rule

Potentially responsible party (PRP)

Prima facie tort

Principal

Promissory fraud

SARA

Secured-lender exemption

Statute of frauds

Strict liability

Tort

Uniform commercial code (UCC)

SUGGESTED READINGS

Cross, F. B. 1995. Establishing environmental innocence. *Real Estate Law Journal* Vol. 23, Spring.

Finegan, J. 1989. "Bankers' Suits." *Inc.* November.

Freddie Mac Reports. 1991. Fighting fraud and winning. Washington, DC: Federal Home Loan Mortgage Corporation, pp. 1–2.

Kellman, M., and R. F. Triana. 1989. CERCLA and nonjudicial foreclosure: The effect of California's antideficiency statutes on unsecured indemnities. *Real Estate Finance* Vol. 6, Summer.

Mack, W. F. 1989. No letup seen in lender liability cases. *Bottomline,* July.

Messer, J. S. 1990. New superfund risks. *Mortgage Banking,* August.

Ryan, D. F. 1989. A Lender's View of Hazardous Substances . . . and Appraiser Responsibility. *The Real Estate Appraiser and Analyst* Vol. 55, Fall.

Pivar, W., and D. Harlan. 1995. Real Estate Ethics, 3rd ed. Chicago, IL: Dearborn Financial Publishing. Chicago, IL.

Schulman, P. L. 1988. Shut the door on fraud. *Mortgage Banking,* January.

Ullman, L. S. 1991. Decision in Fleet Factors case expands lender liability. *Real Estate Finance Journal* Vol. 6, Winter.

Vickory, F. A. 1990. Regulating real estate appraisers: The role of fraudulent and incompetent real estate appraisals in the S & L crisis and the FIRREA solution. *Real Estate Law Journal* Vol. 19, Summer.

REVIEW QUESTIONS

22–1   Explain how a lender is likely to become liable as a potentially responsible party for hazardous waste cleanup costs.

22–2   How can lenders avoid liability for cleanup costs under CERCLA?

22–3   Explain the reasoning by the court in the Mirables case for assigning liability to the lender for hazardous waste cleanup costs.

22–4   What is meant by joint and several liability under CERCLA?

22–5   How does the statutory law protect lenders from liability for breach of oral commitments?

22–6   List a lender's four defenses from liability under CERCLA.

22–7   Explain the major risk that lenders face from enforcement of laws against trading in illicit drugs.

22–8   Explain the term "good faith" and the requirement of parties to a contract to deal in good faith.

22–9 Are demand loans covered by the good-faith requirement to provide notification of the demand feature?

22–10 Define each of the following and give an example of how a lender might be liable under each action.

a. Prima facie tort

b. Promissory fraud

c. Nondisclosure fraud

d. Breach of fiduciary duty

e. Lender control

22–11 Give an example whereby a lender might become liable as a principal under agency law.

22–12 Give an original real estate finance example (not one from the text) of an agency relationship that invokes a conflict of interest and involves agency costs.

22–13 Distinguish between illegal and unethical acts.

ENDNOTES

1. *The Wall Street Journal,* October 31, 1986, p. 48.
2. *The Wall Street Journal,* November 3, 1986, p. 47.
3. 42 U.S.C. 9601(9).
4. 42 U.S.C. 9607(a)(1).
5. 42 U.S.C. 1906 (35)(A).
6. 15 Envtl. L. Reg. 20, 992 (E.D. Pa. Sept. 4, 1985).
7. *United States* v. *Maryland Bank and Trust Co.,* 632 F. Supp. 573 (D. Md. 1986).
8. *Id.* at 580.
9. *Guidice* v. *BFG Electroplating Co.,* 732 F. Supp. 556 (W.D. Pa. 1989).
10. *Fleet Factors Corp.,* 724 F. Supp. at 955. (S.D. Ga. 1988).
11. *Fleet Factors,* 901 F. 2nd at 1557. (11th Cir. 1990).
12. *In Re Bergsoe Metal Corporation,* 1990 U.S. App. Lexis 13541 (9th Cir., Aug. 9, 1990).
13. 15 F. 3d 1100 (D.C. Cir. 1994).
14. *Calero-Toledo* v. *Pearson Yacht Leasing Co.,* 416 U.S. 663.
15. *U.S.* v. *Property Known as 708–710 West 9th St., Erie, Pa.,* (715 F. Supp. 1323).
16. U.C.C. 1-203, 1-201(19).
17. U.C.C. Sec 1-208.
18. *Kruse* v. *Bank of America* 202 Ca 3rd 38 (1st Dist, 1988).
19. *Centerre Bank of Kansas City* v. *Distributors, Inc.,* 705 S.W. 2d42 (Mo. Ct. App. 1985).
20. As a technical note, the court did not cite the official commentary to the U.C.C. that states that a demand note is callable by its nature but, rather, said that a call of a demand note was not related to the "performance or enforcement" of a contract mentioned in Sec. 1-203.
21. *Fulton National Bank* v. *Willis Denny Ford, Inc.,* 154 Ga. App. 8416, 269 S.E. 2nd 916 (1980).
22. *K.M.C. Co., Inc.* v. *Irving Trust Co.,* 757 F2d 752 (6th Cir 1985).
23. *State National Bank of El Paso* v. *Farah Manufacturing Co.,* 678 S.W. 2d 661 (Tex. Ct. App. 1984).
24. *Hill* v. *Securities Investment Co. of St Louis.* 423 S.W. 2d 836, 842 (Mo. 1968).
25. *Denison State Bank* v. *Madeira,* 230 Kan. 684, 640 P2d. 1235 (1982).
26. *Labor Discount Center, Inc.* v. *State Bank and Trust Co. of Wellston,* 526 S.W. 2d 407, 425 (Mo. App. 1975).
27. Restatement (Second) of Agency 1(1958).
28. Restatement (Second) of Agency 140 (1958).
29. *In Re Meadow Glen, Ltd.,* 87 Banker, 421, 424–425 (Banker, W.C. Tex. 1988).
30. T. M. Clauretie and M. Jameson, "Interest Rates and the Foreclosure Process: An Agency Problem in FHA Mortgage Insurance," *Journal of Risk and Insurance* Vol. 47 (December 1990): 701–711.
31. J. H. Mulherin and W. J. Muller, "Resolution of Incentive Conflicts in the Mortgage Industry," *Journal of Real Estate Finance and Economics* Vol. 2 (February 1989): 35–46.
32. "How Texas S&L Grew Into a Lending Giant and Lost $1.4 Billion." *The Wall Street Journal,* April 27, 1989. p. 1.

WEB SITES

www.webcom.com/~staber   environmental law information

APPENDIX 1

A REFRESHER ON THE TIME VALUE OF MONEY AND RELATED CONCEPTS

The material presented in this appendix is intended to be a refresher on the important concepts involved with what is known as the time value of money. Here, we reacquaint you with the mechanics of the time value of money, including the process of discounting and compounding. We strongly recommend that you understand the concepts in this appendix before you attempt to read the main body of the text. For those of you who have had several courses in finance, this material will be repetitive and you may skip this section. For those of you who may not come to this course with a strong background in finance, we recommend that you learn this material.

Discounting and Compounding (Coming and Going)

Compounding; Finding a Future Value of an Investment

To set the stage for what follows, consider this situation. Assume that someone offers you an "investment": If you will give him $10,000 now, he will return to you a sum of $16,000 at the end of 5 years. To make the example simple, assume that there is no default risk whatsoever. That is, you are certain to receive the $16,000 at the end of 5 years. Also, assume that interest rates are not expected to change in the next 5 years and that you are content to tie up your investment for the entire period. These assumptions are made so that we can concentrate on the value of this investment in terms of its rate-of-return without consideration of risk.

In this example you are in the position of being the lender, and the seller of the investment is the borrower. You are lending money to the borrower in return for the promise to return a greater sum in the future. The "interest" that you will earn over the 5-year period is the difference between the amount you lend today and the amount returned at the end of the term. What we want to do at this point is determine if this is a "good" investment for you. One way to determine the worth of this investment is to consider what other alternatives are out there in the "market." If there are investments with the same risk characteristics that offer superior returns, you will not want to take this deal. What we do at this point is to consider an alternative market investment—for example, putting your money in the bank.

Assume that your local banker is willing to give you 10 percent interest at the end of each and any year on the amount of funds you have in an account at the beginning of that year. This is termed annual compounding. Furthermore, assume that the banker is willing to guarantee this 10 percent rate for the next 5 years. You are now in a position to judge the value of the above investment by comparing the results to the alternative of placing your funds in the local bank. If you put the $10,000 in the bank, we can ask several questions. For example, how much will the account be worth at the end of the first year? The end of the second year? The third year? And, most important, the end of the fifth year?

The answer to the first question is easy. At the end of the first year, the amount in the account will equal the initial fund plus 10 percent, or

$$\text{Year one balance } = \$10{,}000 + (0.1 \times \$10{,}000) \qquad \text{(Equation A–1)}$$
$$= \$10{,}000 \times (1 + 0.1)$$
$$= \$11{,}000$$

Since the year-end balance for year one is the beginning balance for the second year, the year-end balance for year two will be

$$\text{Year two balance } = \$11{,}000 \times (1 + 0.1) \qquad \text{(Equation A–2)}$$
$$= \$10{,}000 \times (1 + 0.1) \times (1 + 0.1)$$
$$= \$10{,}000 \times (1 + 0.1)^2$$
$$= \$12{,}100$$

Similarly the year-end balance for year three will be

$$\text{Year three balance } = \$12{,}100 \times (1 + 0.1) \qquad \text{(Equation A–3)}$$
$$= \$10{,}000 \times (1 + 0.1) \times (1 + 0.1) \times (1 + 0.1)$$
$$= \$10{,}000 \times (1 + 0.1)^3$$

As you might guess, continuing this process will produce an end-of-year balance for year five equal to

$$\text{Year five balance } = \$10{,}000 \times (1 + 0.1)^5 \qquad \text{(Equation A–4)}$$

To generalize for any present value amount compounded at a given interest rate over a given time period, the equation can be written as

$$FV_n = PV (1 + i)^n$$

where

$$FV_n = \text{the future (compounded value at time } n\text{),}$$
$$PV = \text{present value amount (initial investment),}$$
$$i = \text{periodic interest rate, and}$$
$$n = \text{the number of compounding periods.}$$

The $(1 + i)^n$ portion of the equation is called the future value interest factor (FVIF).

There are two easy ways to compute this value. One way is to use a table which provides a factor for the future amount of each one dollar invested in the present. An example of such a table is Table A–1. This table includes the future value interest factors (FVIF) of one dollar for a large number of combinations of years and interest rates. The value in Table A–1 for a 10 percent interest for 5 years is 1.611. This means that each dollar invested now at 10 percent annual compounding will return $1.611 at the end of 5 years. So, $10,000 invested now will return $16,110 at the end of 5 years. Can you confirm from Table A–1 that $10,000 invested today will result in a future value of $19,740 if invested for 6 years and compounded annually at 12 percent?

A second way to find the terminal or future value is to use a financial calculator. An equation such as A–4 involves four elements: the present amount of the investment ($10,000), the interest rate (10 percent), the term of the investment (5 years), and the amount to be returned at the end of the term (the future value). Given any three of the four terms, the fourth can be determined with the use of a financial calculator. Most financial calculators will have (at least) four buttons representing the terms of an equation such as A–4. Generally, the buttons will be marked as:

Beginning amount (present value)	PV
Interest Rate	% or I/YR
Term	N
Future Value	FV
Payment (or Cash Flow)	PMT

By entering values for any of three elements in an equation, the fourth can be determined. For a Hewlett-Packard 10-B, the keystroke entries would appear as follows:

10000	+/− PV
10	I/YR
5	N

then press the FV key. The calculator will display $16,105.10 which is different, but more accurate, than the answer from the table because the factor in the table is rounded off. Other types of financial calculators may have somewhat different notation or keystroke entries. However, they will come with an operator's manual that will include many typical examples. Note that the HP 10-B should be set to one payment per year to account for annual compounding.

Since you can accumulate a larger end-of-year-five endowment by placing your funds in the bank than by purchasing this investment, it makes sense that you would do the former and not purchase the investment. Recall that the investments are identical in all respects except the future value. You should select the one with the largest future value.

Discounting: Finding the Present Value of a Future Sum

Now that you have rejected the investment, the seller of this investment may turn to you and say, "Well, if you will not give me $10,000 for the promise to return $16,000 at the end of 5 years, how much will you give me for it?" You know that the investment is not worth $10,000, but it must be worth something. How can you find out what it is worth? Since the investment is similar to placing your funds in the bank, you simply ask, "How much would I have to put in the bank to have $16,000 at the end of 5 years?" This question in equation form is

$$X(1 + 0.1)^5 = \$16,000 \qquad \text{(Equation A–5)}$$

What is the value of X? Rearranging Equation A–5 we find the value of X to be

$$X = \$16,000/(1 + 0.1)^5 \qquad \text{(Equation A–6)}$$
$$= \$9,934.74$$

That is, if you were to put $9,934.74 in the bank and it earned 10 percent annually, it would grow to an amount equal to $16,000 at the end of the fifth year. This is the present value of the investment opportunity. Again, there are two ways in which the value may be determined.

First, you can utilize a table of factors that show the present value of one dollar for a large set of interest rates and terms. Table A–3 shows that the present value interest factor of one dollar to be received in 5 years and discounted at 10 percent is 0.621. Or, 0.621 × $16,000 = $9936 (the difference is due, again, to rounding). Can you show that the present value of the $16,000 payment to be received at the end of the fifth year is worth only $9072 if the discount rate is 12 percent? Can you explain why it is less?

Alternatively, the financial calculator can be used. The following entries would accomplish the purpose.

$16,000	FV
10	I/YR
5	N

then press the PV key. The answer should be $9934.74.

The general equation for the present value of a future lump sum is

$$PV = FV_n \left[1/(1 + i)^n\right]$$

where the terms are as described above. The portion of the equation in brackets is the present value interest factor (PVIF).

Discounting and Compounding Annuities

The same principles noted here can be applied to a series of payments rather than just one. A series of payments, all of which are identical, is called an annuity. When the payments are identical, it becomes easy to calculate factors and place them in tables just as in the above examples.

Discounting

First, let's work backward. Assume that someone offers you the following investment opportunity. In return for you giving him $10,000 now, he would return to you $2,500 at the end of each of the next 5 years. The cash flows look like this:

End of Year	Year 1	Year 2	Year 3	Year 4	Year 5
Cash Flow	$2500	$2500	$2500	$2500	$2500

To find out if this is a good deal, proceed as follows. Envision putting a sum of money in the bank (again at 10 percent annual interest) that would provide you with these exact cash flows. What sum would accomplish this goal? To make the calculation simple, consider opening 5 different accounts in the bank. The entire contents of account #1 will be removed at the end of the first year. The entire contents of account #2 will be removed at the end of the second year. The entire contents of account #3 will be removed at the end of the third year, and so forth.

The amount that must be deposited in account #1 is simply

$$\$2500/(1 + 0.1) = \$2272.73 \qquad \text{(Equation A–7)}$$

The amount to be deposited in account #2 is

$$\$2500/(1 + 0.1)^2 = \$2066.11 \qquad \text{(Equation A–8)}$$

This amount also can be determined by applying the present value interest factor for 10 percent for year two from Table A–2, 0.826. That is, $0.826 \times \$2500 = \$2065$. Continuing, the amount needed to be deposited in the remaining accounts would be

$$\$2500/(1 + 0.1)^3 = \$1878.28$$
$$\$2500/(1 + 0.1)^4 = \$1707.53$$

and

$$\$2500/(1 + 0.1)^5 = \$1552.30$$

Thus, the total to be deposited will be

$$\$2272.73 + \$2066.11 + \$1878.28 + \$1707.53 + \$1552.30 = \$9476.97$$

Depositing $9476.97 at the outset will allow you to withdraw $2500 at the end of each of the next 5 years and have no money remaining in the bank. This is equivalent to

$$\$9476.97 = \$2500/(1 + 0.1) + \$2500/(1 + 0.1)^2 + \$2500/(1 + 0.1)^3 \cdots$$
$$\$2500/(1 + 0.1)^5 \qquad \text{(Equation A–9)}$$

This formula can be rewritten as

$$\$9476.67 = \$2500 \times [1/(1 + 0.1) + 1/(1 + 0.1)^2 + 1/(1 + 0.1)^3 \cdots + 1/(1 + 0.1)^5]$$

This can be generalized to

$$PV_a = PMT\left[\frac{(1 + i)^n - 1}{i(1 + i)^n}\right]$$

where:

$$PV_a = \text{present value of an annuity}$$

and

$$PMT = \text{the annuity payment}$$

The term in brackets is called the present value interest factor of an annuity (PVIFA). Again, a table can be constructed that will show the factors for a large array of discount rates and time periods. Table A–4 is an example. Note the entry under the 10 percent column and row five: 3.791. If one multiplies this factor times the amount of the annuity payment, the result will be the present value of the annuity. That is,

$$3.791 \times \$2500 = \$9477 \qquad \text{(Equation A–10)}$$

Can you demonstrate that the present value of an annuity of $4400 for 6 years at 9 percent is $19,738.40?

Another way to determine the present value of an annuity is by using the financial calculator. For our example the entries would appear as follows:

2500	PMT
5	N
10	I/YR

Then press PV. The display should show $9476.97.

You should pay no more than $9476.97 for this investment since you can replicate its cash flows by placing this sum in the bank. Of course, you need not set up five different accounts; one will do. We only set the problem up in this fashion to draw a clear picture of the cash flows.

One can always verify the answer by setting up an amortization schedule of the funds placed in, and withdrawn from, the bank as follows:

Year	Beginning Balance	+	Interest Earned	−	End of Year Withdrawal	=	Ending Balance
1	$9476.97		$947.70		$2500		$7924.67
2	7924.67		792.47		2500		6217.13
3	6217.13		621.71		2500		4338.85
4	4338.85		433.88		2500		2272.73
5	2272.73		227.27		2500		0

Compounding Annuities

One also can ask, "If I place $2500 in a bank account at the end of each of 5 years, beginning with a deposit 1 year from today, how much will I have in the account at the end of the fifth year?" The answer, called the future value of an annuity, can be determined by considering the amount to which each of the deposits will accumulate. That is, one can "decompose" the annuity into a series of deposits and solve the problem by considering the future value of each of the payments. For example, the first cash flow will be deposited 1 year from the present and will, thus, accumulate interest for 4 years by the time of the end of the fifth year. The future value will be

$$\$2500 \times (1 + 0.1)^4 = \$3660.25 \qquad \text{(Equation A–11)}$$

(The future value interest factor from Table A–1 for 10 percent and 4 years is 1.464 and 1.464 × $2500 = $3660.)

Likewise, the future value of the second payment at the end of the fifth year will be

$$\$2500 \times (1 + 0.1)^3 = \$3327.27 \qquad \text{(Equation A–12)}$$

Continuing the future values of the remaining three payments will be

$$\$2500 \times (1 + 0.1)^2 = \$3024.79$$

$$\$2500 \times (1 + 0.1)^1 = \$2749.81$$

$$\$2500 \times 1 = \$2500.00$$

The sum of these five values is $15,262.12. This sum is equivalent to

$$\$2500 \times [\,(1.1)^4 + (1.1)^3 + (1.1)^2 + (1.1)^1 + 1\,] \qquad \text{(Equation A–13)}$$

$$FV_a = PMT\left[\frac{(1 + i)^n - 1}{i}\right]$$

The term in brackets is called the future value interest factor of an annuity (FVIFA). As you might expect by now, the future value interest factor of an annuity can be determined for a large combination of interest rates and number of payments. The value for this case is included in Table A–2 under the 10 percent column and the fifth row, 6.105. So, 6.105 × $2500 is equal to $15,262.

Can you confirm that the future value of a $1000 annuity deposited at the end of each of the next 11 years will be worth $17,560 if the funds earn 9 percent interest?

The financial calculator can be used to solve these types of problems as well. For our example the entries would appear as follows:

$2500	PMT
5	N
10	I/YR

Then press FV, the display should show $15,262.75.

Discounting and Compounding at Intervals Other than 1 Year

In the examples used thus far, we assumed that the relevant interval for compounding and discounting was 1 year. It is a simple step to consider intervals of other lengths. For example, how do the calculations change if one assumes that the relevant interval is 6 months? That is, assume that the bank in the above examples credits the account with interest at the end of 6 months based on the amount in the account at the beginning of the period. Consider the initial deposit of $10,000. At the end of the first 6 months, the bank will credit the account with 6 months worth of interest at the 10 percent annual rate, or 5 percent of the beginning balance. The amount in the account at the end of the first 6 months will be

$$\$10,000 \times (1 + 0.05) = \$10,500 \qquad \text{(Equation A–14)}$$

This is the beginning balance for the next 6-month period. Thus at the end of the second 6-month period, the amount in the account will be

$$\$10,500 \times (1 + 0.05) = \qquad \text{(Equation A–15)}$$
$$\$10,000 \times (1 + 0.05)^2 = \$11,025$$

Note that when the bank credited the account with interest only at the end of the year, the amount (from the first example) in the account at the end of the first year was $11,000. The extra $25 in this example results from interest being paid in the second 6 months on the interest earned in the first six months. That is,

$$0.05 \times \$500 = \$25$$

The amount in the account at the end of 5 years will be

$$\$10{,}000 \times (1 + 0.05)^{10} = \$16{,}288.94 \qquad \text{(Equation A–16)}$$

which is greater than the amount when the compounding was done annually. When interest is compounded semiannually rather than annually, the formula is changed by halving the interest rate and doubling the number of time periods. To find the future value interest factor in Table A–1 simply find the factor in the column for 5 percent and the row for ten periods. There you will see that the factor is 1.629. Alternatively, the financial calculator can be used as follows:

Enter	then	Press
10,000		PV
5		%
10		N

Then press FV. If using an HP 10-B, the calculator should be set to one payment per year.

More frequent compounding leads to a larger future value in this case. If the compounding is accomplished monthly, the future value will be

$$\$10{,}000 \times (1 + 0.1/12)^{60} = \$16{,}453.09 \qquad \text{(Equation A–17)}$$

More frequent compounding will lead to yet higher future values. The future value at the end of 5 years will not increase without limit, however. If the compounding is accomplished every day, minute, or second, the future value will reach a limit. Indeed, if the compounding is accomplished over an infinitesimal interval, called continuous compounding, the future value will be given by the following:

$$\$10{,}000 \times e^{rt} = \$16{,}487.21 \qquad \text{(Equation A–18)}$$

Here e is the base of the natural logarithm and is equal to 2.7182818, r is the rate of interest, and t is the term of the investment.

When we reverse the process and find the present value of a future cash flow, more frequent compounding leads to a smaller present value. Thus, the present value of $10,000 to be received at the end of the second year when discounted at 10 percent annually is

$$\$10{,}000/(1.1)^2 = \$8264.46$$

When discounted semiannually, the present value is

$$\$10{,}000/(1.05)^4 = \$8227.03$$

When discounted continuously, the present value is

$$\$10{,}000/e^{rt} = \$8187.31 \qquad \text{(Equation A–19)}$$

Annuity Due

An annuity sometimes is received at times other than the end of each period. When an annuity payment falls at the beginning of a time period, it is known as an **annuity due.** To account for this situation, the PVIFA and the FVIFA can be revised in the following manner:

$$\text{PVIFA}_{ad} = \left[\frac{(1 - i)^N - 1}{i(1 + i)^N} \right](1 + i)$$

$$\text{FVIFA}_{ad} = \left[\frac{(1 + i)^N - 1}{i} \right](1 + i)$$

In each case the ordinary annuity factor is multiplied by the payment to determine the annuity due. For our earlier example, the present value of an annuity due is $10,245, and the future value of an annuity due is $16,789.

Concluding Remarks

The equations that show the present value of a future (stream of) cash flows(s) can be referred to as a basic valuation equation. Such an equation essentially capitalizes future cash flows into a present value. These equations all have one thing in common. They consist of four elements: the present value, the amount of the cash flows(s), the interest or discount rate, and the term over which the cash flows are to be received. Given any three of the elements in the equation, the fourth can be determined. Furthermore, different situations in real estate finance will call for the determination of the various elements in the equation. This concept is developed further in the Appendix to Chapter 4. You are encouraged to read this appendix.

TABLE A-1

Future Value Interest Factors for One Dollar Compounded at k Percent for n Periods: $\text{FVIF}_{kn} = (1 + k)^n$

Period	1%	2%	3%	4%	5%	6%	7%	8%	9%	10%
1	1.010	1.020	1.030	1.040	1.050	1.060	1.070	1.080	1.090	1.100
2	1.020	1.040	1.061	1.082	1.102	1.124	1.145	1.166	1.188	1.210
3	1.030	1.061	1.093	1.125	1.158	1.191	1.225	1.260	1.295	1.331
4	1.041	1.082	1.126	1.170	1.216	1.262	1.311	1.360	1.412	1.464
5	1.051	1.104	1.159	1.217	1.276	1.338	1.403	1.469	1.539	1.611
6	1.062	1.126	1.194	1.265	1.340	1.419	1.501	1.587	1.677	1.772
7	1.072	1.149	1.230	1.316	1.407	1.504	1.606	1.714	1.828	1.949
8	1.083	1.172	1.267	1.369	1.477	1.594	1.718	1.851	1.993	2.144
9	1.094	1.195	1.305	1.423	1.551	1.689	1.838	1.999	2.172	2.358
10	1.105	1.219	1.344	1.480	1.629	1.791	1.967	2.159	2.367	2.594
11	1.116	1.243	1.384	1.539	1.710	1.898	2.105	2.332	2.580	2.853
12	1.127	1.268	1.426	1.601	1.796	2.012	2.252	2.518	2.813	3.138
13	1.138	1.294	1.469	1.665	1.886	2.133	2.410	2.720	3.066	3.452
14	1.149	1.319	1.513	1.732	1.980	2.261	2.579	2.937	3.342	3.797
15	1.161	1.346	1.558	1.801	2.079	2.397	2.759	3.172	3.642	4.177
16	1.173	1.373	1.605	1.873	2.183	2.540	2.952	3.426	3.970	4.595
17	1.184	1.400	1.653	1.948	2.292	2.693	3.159	3.700	4.328	5.054
18	1.196	1.428	1.702	2.026	2.407	2.854	3.380	3.996	4.717	5.560
19	1.208	1.457	1.753	2.107	2.527	3.026	3.616	4.316	5.142	6.116
20	1.220	1.486	1.806	2.191	2.653	3.207	3.870	4.661	5.604	6.727
21	1.232	1.516	1.860	2.279	2.786	3.399	4.140	5.034	6.109	7.400
22	1.245	1.546	1.916	2.370	2.925	3.603	4.430	5.436	6.658	8.140
23	1.257	1.577	1.974	2.465	3.071	3.820	4.740	5.871	7.258	8.954
24	1.270	1.608	2.033	2.563	3.225	4.049	5.072	6.341	7.911	9.850
25	1.282	1.641	2.094	2.666	3.386	4.292	5.427	6.848	8.623	10.834
30	1.348	1.811	2.427	3.243	4.322	5.743	7.612	10.062	13.267	17.449
35	1.417	2.000	2.814	3.946	5.516	7.686	10.676	14.785	20.413	28.102
40	1.489	2.208	3.262	4.801	7.040	10.285	14.974	21.724	31.408	45.258
45	1.565	2.438	3.781	5.841	8.985	13.764	21.002	31.920	48.325	72.888
50	1.645	2.691	4.384	7.106	11.467	18.419	29.456	46.900	74.354	117.386

TABLE A – 1 (Continued)

Period	11%	12%	13%	14%	15%	16%	17%	18%	19%	20%
1	1.110	1.120	1.130	1.140	1.150	1.160	1.170	1.180	1.190	1.200
2	1.232	1.254	1.277	1.300	1.322	1.346	1.369	1.392	1.416	1.440
3	1.368	1.405	1.443	1.482	1.521	1.561	1.802	1.643	1.685	1.728
4	1.518	1.574	1.630	1.689	1.749	1.811	1.874	1.939	2.005	2.074
5	1.685	1.762	1.842	1.925	2.011	2.100	2.192	2.288	2.386	2.488
6	1.870	1.974	2.082	2.195	2.313	2.436	2.565	2.700	2.840	2.986
7	2.076	2.211	2.353	2.502	2.660	2.826	3.001	3.185	3.379	3.583
8	2.305	2.476	2.658	2.853	3.059	3.278	3.511	3.759	4.021	4.300
9	2.558	2.773	3.004	3.252	3.518	3.803	4.108	4.435	4.785	5.160
10	2.839	3.106	3.395	3.707	4.046	4.411	4.807	5.234	5.695	6.192
11	3.152	3.479	3.836	4.226	4.652	5.117	5.624	6.176	6.777	7.430
12	3.498	3.896	4.334	4.818	5.350	5.936	6.580	7.288	8.064	8.916
13	3.883	4.363	4.898	5.492	6.153	6.886	7.699	8.599	9.596	10.699
14	4.310	4.887	5.535	6.261	7.076	7.987	9.007	10.147	11.420	12.839
15	4.785	5.474	6.254	7.138	8.137	9.265	10.539	11.974	13.589	15.407
16	5.311	6.130	7.067	8.137	9.358	10.748	12.330	14.129	16.171	18.488
17	5.895	6.866	7.986	9.276	10.761	12.468	14.426	16.672	19.244	22.186
18	6.543	7.690	9.024	10.575	12.375	14.462	16.879	19.673	22.900	26.623
19	7.263	8.613	10.197	12.055	14.232	16.776	19.748	23.214	27.251	31.948
20	8.062	9.646	11.523	13.743	16.366	19.461	23.105	27.393	32.429	38.337
21	8.949	10.804	13.021	15.667	18.821	22.574	27.033	32.323	38.591	46.005
22	9.933	12.100	14.713	17.861	21.644	26.186	31.629	38.141	45.923	55.205
23	11.026	13.552	16.626	20.361	24.891	30.376	37.005	45.007	54.648	66.247
24	12.239	15.178	18.788	23.212	28.625	35.236	43.296	53.108	65.031	79.496
25	13.585	17.000	21.230	26.461	32.918	40.874	50.656	62.667	77.387	95.395
30	22.892	29.960	39.115	50.949	66.210	85.849	111.061	143.367	184.672	237.373
35	38.574	52.799	72.066	98.097	133.172	180.311	243.495	327.988	440.691	590.657
40	64.999	93.049	132.776	188.876	267.856	378.715	533.846	750.353	1051.642	1469.740
45	109.527	163.985	244.629	363.662	538.752	795.429	1170.425	1716.619	2509.583	3657.176
50	184.559	288.996	450.711	700.197	1083.619	1670.669	2566.080	3927.189	5988.730	9100.191

(<i>continued</i>)

TABLE A−1 (*Continued*)

Period	21%	22%	23%	24%	25%	26%	27%	28%	29%	30%
1	1.210	1.220	1.230	1.240	1.250	1.260	1.270	1.280	1.290	1.300
2	1.464	1.488	1.513	1.538	1.562	1.588	1.613	1.638	1.664	1.690
3	1.772	1.816	1.861	1.907	1.953	2.000	2.048	2.097	2.147	2.197
4	2.144	2.215	2.289	2.364	2.441	2.520	2.601	2.684	2.769	2.856
5	2.594	2.703	2.815	2.932	3.052	3.176	3.304	3.436	3.572	3.713
6	3.138	3.297	3.463	3.635	3.815	4.001	4.196	4.398	4.608	4.827
7	3.797	4.023	4.259	4.508	4.768	5.042	5.329	5.629	5.945	6.275
8	4.595	4.908	5.239	5.589	5.960	6.353	6.767	7.206	7.669	8.157
9	5.560	5.987	6.444	6.931	7.451	8.004	8.595	9.223	9.893	10.604
10	6.727	7.305	7.926	8.594	9.313	10.086	10.915	11.806	12.761	13.786
11	8.140	8.912	9.749	10.657	11.642	12.708	13.862	15.112	16.462	17.921
12	9.850	10.872	11.991	13.215	14.552	16.012	17.605	19.343	21.236	23.298
13	11.918	13.264	14.749	16.386	18.190	20.175	22.359	24.759	27.395	30.287
14	14.421	16.182	18.141	20.319	22.737	25.420	28.395	31.691	35.339	39.373
15	17.449	19.742	22.314	25.195	28.422	32.030	36.062	40.565	45.587	51.185
16	21.113	24.085	27.446	31.242	35.527	40.357	45.799	51.923	58.808	66.541
17	25.547	29.384	33.758	38.740	44.409	50.850	58.165	66.461	75.862	86.503
18	30.912	35.848	41.523	48.038	55.511	64.071	73.869	85.070	97.862	112.454
19	37.404	43.735	51.073	59.567	69.389	80.730	93.813	108.890	126.242	146.190
20	45.258	53.357	62.820	73.863	86.736	101.720	119.143	139.379	162.852	190.047
21	54.762	65.095	77.268	91.591	108.420	128.167	151.312	178.405	210.079	247.061
22	66.262	79.416	95.040	113.572	135.525	161.490	192.165	228.358	271.002	321.178
23	80.178	96.887	116.899	140.829	169.407	203.477	244.050	292.298	349.592	417.531
24	97.015	118.203	143.786	174.628	211.758	256.381	309.943	374.141	450.974	542.791
25	117.388	144.207	176.857	216.539	264.698	323.040	393.628	478.901	581.756	705.627
30	304.471	389.748	497.904	634.810	807.793	1025.904	1300.477	1645.488	2078.208	2619.936
35	789.716	1053.370	1401.749	1861.020	2465.189	3258.053	4296.547	5653.840	7423.988	9727.598
40	2048.309	2846.941	3946.340	5455.797	7523.156	10346.879	14195.051	19426.418	26520.723	36117.754
45	5312.758	7694.418	11110.121	15994.316	22958.844	32859.457	46897.973	66748.500	94739.937	134102.187
50	13779.844	20795.680	31278.301	46889.207	70064.812	104354.562	154942.687	229345.875	338440.000	497910.125

TABLE A-2

Future Value Interest Factors for a One-Dollar Annuity Compounded
at k Percent for n Periods: $FVIFA_{kn} = \sum_{t=1}^{n} (1 + k)^{t-1}$

Period	1%	2%	3%	4%	5%	6%	7%	8%	9%	10%
1	1.000	1.000	1.000	1.000	1.000	1.000	1.000	1.000	1.000	1.000
2	2.010	2.020	2.030	2.040	2.050	2.060	2.070	2.080	2.090	2.100
3	3.030	3.060	3.091	3.122	3.052	3.184	3.215	3.246	3.278	3.310
4	4.060	4.122	4.184	4.246	4.310	4.375	4.440	4.506	4.573	4.641
5	5.101	5.204	5.309	5.416	5.526	5.637	5.751	5.867	5.985	6.105
6	6.152	6.308	6.468	6.633	6.802	6.975	7.153	7.336	7.523	7.716
7	7.214	7.434	7.662	7.898	8.142	8.394	8.654	8.923	9.200	9.487
8	8.286	8.583	8.892	9.214	9.549	9.897	10.260	10.637	11.028	11.436
9	9.368	9.755	10.159	10.583	11.027	11.491	11.978	12.488	13.021	13.579
10	10.462	10.950	11.464	12.006	12.578	13.181	13.816	14.487	15.193	15.937
11	11.567	12.169	12.808	13.486	14.207	14.972	15.784	16.645	17.560	18.531
12	12.682	13.412	14.192	15.026	15.917	16.870	17.888	18.977	20.141	21.384
13	13.809	14.680	15.618	16.627	17.713	18.882	20.141	21.495	22.953	24.523
14	14.947	15.974	17.086	18.292	19.598	21.015	22.550	24.215	26.019	27.975
15	16.097	17.293	18.599	20.023	21.578	23.276	25.129	27.152	29.361	31.772
16	17.258	18.639	20.157	21.824	23.657	25.672	27.888	30.324	33.003	35.949
17	18.430	20.012	21.761	23.697	25.840	28.213	30.840	33.750	36.973	40.544
18	19.614	21.412	23.414	25.645	28.132	30.905	33.999	37.450	41.301	45.599
19	20.811	22.840	25.117	27.671	30.539	33.760	37.379	41.446	46.018	51.158
20	22.019	24.297	26.870	29.778	33.066	36.785	40.995	45.762	51.159	57.274
21	23.239	25.783	28.676	31.969	35.719	39.992	44.865	50.422	56.764	64.002
22	24.471	27.299	30.536	34.248	38.505	43.392	49.005	55.456	62.872	71.402
23	25.716	28.845	32.452	36.618	41.430	46.995	53.435	60.893	69.531	79.542
24	26.973	30.421	34.426	39.082	44.504	50.815	58.176	66.764	76.789	88.496
25	28.243	32.030	36.459	41.645	47.726	54.864	63.248	73.105	84.699	98.346
30	36.784	40.567	47.575	56.084	66.438	79.057	94.459	113.282	136.305	164.491
35	41.659	49.994	60.461	73.651	90.318	111.432	138.234	172.314	215.705	271.018
40	48.885	60.401	75.400	95.024	120.797	154.758	199.630	259.052	337.872	442.580
45	56.479	71.891	92.718	121.027	159.695	212.737	285.741	386.497	525.840	718.881
50	64.461	84.577	112.794	152.664	209.341	290.325	406.516	573.756	815.051	1163.865

(continued)

TABLE A−2 (*Continued*)

Period	11%	12%	13%	14%	15%	16%	17%	18%	19%	20%
1	1.000	1.000	1.000	1.000	1.000	1.000	1.000	1.000	1.000	1.000
2	2.110	2.120	2.130	2.140	2.150	2.160	2.170	2.180	2.190	2.200
3	3.342	3.374	3.407	3.440	3.472	3.506	3.539	3.572	3.606	3.640
4	4.710	4.779	4.850	4.921	4.993	5.066	5.141	5.215	5.291	5.368
5	6.228	6.353	6.480	6.610	6.742	6.877	7.014	7.154	7.297	7.442
6	7.913	8.115	8.323	8.535	8.754	8.977	9.207	9.442	9.683	9.930
7	9.783	10.089	10.405	10.730	11.067	11.414	11.772	12.141	12.523	12.916
8	11.859	12.300	12.757	13.233	13.727	14.240	14.773	15.327	15.902	16.499
9	14.164	14.776	15.416	16.085	16.786	17.518	18.285	19.086	19.923	20.799
10	16.722	17.549	18.420	19.337	20.304	21.321	22.393	23.521	24.709	25.959
11	19.561	20.655	21.814	23.044	24.349	25.733	27.200	28.755	30.403	32.150
12	22.713	24.133	25.650	27.271	29.001	30.850	32.824	34.931	37.180	39.580
13	26.211	28.029	29.984	32.088	34.352	36.786	39.404	42.218	45.244	48.496
14	30.095	32.392	34.882	37.581	40.504	43.672	47.102	50.818	54.871	59.196
15	34.405	37.280	40.417	43.842	47.580	51.659	56.109	60.965	66.260	72.035
16	39.190	42.753	46.671	50.980	55.717	60.925	66.648	72.938	79.850	87.442
17	44.500	48.883	53.738	59.117	65.075	71.673	78.978	87.067	96.021	105.930
18	50.396	55.749	61.724	68.393	75.836	84.140	93.404	103.739	115.265	128.116
19	56.939	63.439	70.748	78.968	88.211	98.603	110.283	123.412	138.165	154.739
20	64.202	72.052	80.946	91.024	102.443	115.379	130.031	146.626	165.417	186.687
21	72.264	81.698	92.468	104.767	118.809	134.840	153.136	174.019	197.846	225.024
22	81.213	92.502	105.489	120.434	137.630	157.414	180.169	206.342	236.436	271.028
23	91.147	104.602	120.203	138.295	159.274	183.600	211.798	244.483	282.359	326.234
24	102.173	118.154	136.829	158.656	184.166	213.976	248.803	289.490	337.007	392.480
25	114.412	133.333	155.616	181.867	212.790	249.212	292.099	342.598	402.038	471.976
30	199.018	241.330	293.192	356.778	434.738	530.306	647.423	790.932	966.698	1181.865
35	341.583	431.658	546.663	693.552	881.152	1120.699	1426.448	1816.607	2314.173	2948.294
40	581.812	767.080	1013.667	1341.979	1779.048	2360.724	3134.412	4163.094	5529.711	7343.715
45	986.613	1358.208	1874.086	2590.464	3585.031	4965.191	6879.008	9531.258	13203.105	18280.914
50	1668.723	2399.975	3459.344	4994.301	7217.488	10435.449	15088.8705	21812.273	31514.492	45496.094

T A B L E   A – 2 (*Continued*)

Period	21%	22%	23%	24%	25%	26%	27%	28%	29%	30%
1	1.000	1.000	1.000	1.000	1.000	1.000	1.000	1.000	1.000	1.000
2	2.210	2.220	2.230	2.240	2.250	2.260	2.270	2.280	2.290	2.300
3	3.674	3.708	3.743	3.778	3.813	3.848	3.883	3.918	3.954	3.990
4	5.446	5.524	5.604	5.684	5.766	5.848	5.931	6.016	6.101	6.187
5	7.589	7.740	7.893	8.048	8.207	8.368	8.533	8.700	8.870	9.043
6	10.183	10.442	10.708	10.980	11.259	11.544	11.837	12.136	12.442	12.756
7	13.321	13.740	14.171	14.615	15.073	15.546	16.032	16.534	17.051	17.583
8	17.119	17.762	18.430	19.123	19.842	20.588	21.361	22.163	22.995	23.858
9	21.714	22.670	23.669	24.712	25.802	26.940	28.129	29.369	30.664	32.015
10	27.274	28.657	30.113	31.643	33.253	34.945	36.723	38.592	40.556	42.619
11	34.001	35.962	38.039	40.238	42.566	45.030	47.639	50.398	53.318	56.405
12	42.141	44.873	47.787	50.895	54.208	57.738	61.501	65.510	69.780	74.326
13	51.991	55.745	59.778	64.109	68.760	73.750	79.106	84.853	91.016	97.624
14	63.909	69.009	74.528	80.496	86.949	93.925	101.465	109.611	118.411	127.912
15	78.330	85.191	92.669	100.815	109.687	119.346	129.860	141.302	153.750	167.285
16	95.779	104.933	114.983	126.010	138.109	151.375	165.922	181.867	199.337	218.470
17	116.892	129.019	142.428	157.252	173.636	191.733	211.721	233.790	258.145	285.011
18	142.439	158.403	176.187	195.993	218.045	242.583	269.885	300.250	334.006	371.514
19	173.351	194.251	217.710	244.031	273.556	306.654	343.754	385.321	431.868	483.968
20	210.755	237.986	268.783	303.598	342.945	387.384	437.568	494.210	558.110	630.157
21	256.013	291.343	331.603	377.461	429.681	489.104	556.710	633.589	720.962	820.204
22	310.775	356.438	408.871	469.052	538.101	617.270	708.022	811.993	931.040	1067.265
23	377.038	435.854	503.911	582.624	673.626	778.760	990.187	1040.351	1202.042	1388.443
24	457.215	532.741	620.810	723.453	843.032	982.237	1144.237	1332.649	1551.634	1805.975
25	554.230	650.944	765.596	898.082	1054.791	1238.617	1454.180	1706.790	2002.608	2348.765
30	1445.111	1767.044	2160.459	2640.881	3227.172	3941.953	4812.891	5873.172	7162.785	8729.805
35	3755.814	4783.520	6090.227	7750.094	9856.746	12527.160	15909.480	20188.742	25596.512	32422.090
40	9749.141	12936.141	17153.691	22728.367	30088.621	39791.957	52570.707	69376.562	91447.375	120389.375
45	25294.223	34970.230	48300.660	66638.937	91831.312	126378.937	173692.875	238384.312	326686.375	447005.062
50	65617.200	94525.280	135992.150	195372.640	280255.690	401374.470	573877.870	819103.070	1167041.000	1659760.000

Present Value Interest Factors for One Dollar Discounted at k Percent for n Periods: $PVIF_{kn} := 1/(1 + k)^n$

Period	1%	2%	3%	4%	5%	6%	7%	8%	9%	10%
1	0.990	0.980	0.971	0.962	0.952	0.943	0.935	0.926	0.917	0.909
2	0.980	0.961	0.943	0.925	0.907	0.890	0.873	0.857	0.842	0.826
3	0.971	0.942	0.915	0.889	0.864	0.840	0.816	0.794	0.772	0.751
4	0.961	0.924	0.888	0.855	0.823	0.792	0.763	0.735	0.708	0.683
5	0.951	0.906	0.863	0.822	0.784	0.747	0.713	0.681	0.650	0.621
6	0.942	0.888	0.837	0.790	0.746	0.705	0.666	0.630	0.596	0.564
7	0.933	0.871	0.813	0.760	0.711	0.665	0.623	0.583	0.547	0.513
8	0.923	0.853	0.789	0.731	0.677	0.627	0.582	0.540	0.502	0.467
9	0.914	0.837	0.766	0.703	0.645	0.592	0.544	0.500	0.460	0.424
10	0.905	0.820	0.744	0.676	0.614	0.558	0.508	0.463	0.422	0.386
11	0.896	0.804	0.722	0.650	0.585	0.527	0.475	0.429	0.388	0.350
12	0.887	0.789	0.701	0.625	0.557	0.497	0.444	0.397	0.356	0.319
13	0.879	0.773	0.681	0.601	0.530	0.469	0.415	0.368	0.326	0.290
14	0.870	0.758	0.661	0.577	0.505	0.442	0.388	0.340	0.299	0.263
15	0.861	0.743	0.642	0.555	0.481	0.417	0.362	0.315	0.275	0.239
16	0.853	0.728	0.623	0.534	0.458	0.394	0.339	0.292	0.252	0.218
17	0.844	0.714	0.605	0.513	0.436	0.371	0.317	0.270	0.231	0.198
18	0.836	0.700	0.587	0.494	0.416	0.350	0.296	0.250	0.212	0.180
19	0.828	0.686	0.570	0.475	0.396	0.331	0.277	0.232	0.194	0.164
20	0.820	0.673	0.554	0.456	0.377	0.312	0.258	0.215	0.178	0.149
21	0.811	0.660	0.538	0.439	0.359	0.294	0.242	0.199	0.164	0.135
22	0.803	0.647	0.522	0.422	0.342	0.278	0.226	0.184	0.150	0.123
23	0.795	0.634	0.507	0.406	0.326	0.262	0.211	0.170	0.138	0.112
24	0.788	0.622	0.492	0.390	0.310	0.247	0.197	0.158	0.126	0.102
25	0.780	0.610	0.478	0.375	0.295	0.233	0.184	0.146	0.116	0.092
30	0.742	0.552	0.412	0.308	0.231	0.174	0.131	0.099	0.075	0.057
35	0.706	0.500	0.355	0.253	0.181	0.130	0.094	0.068	0.049	0.036
40	0.672	0.453	0.307	0.208	0.142	0.097	0.067	0.046	0.032	0.022
45	0.639	0.410	0.264	0.171	0.111	0.073	0.048	0.031	0.021	0.014
50	0.608	0.372	0.228	0.141	0.087	0.054	0.034	0.021	0.013	0.009

T A B L E   A − 3 (*Continued*)

Period	11%	12%	13%	14%	15%	16%	17%	18%	19%	20%
1	0.901	0.893	0.885	0.877	0.870	0.862	0.855	0.847	0.840	0.833
2	0.812	0.797	0.783	0.769	0.756	0.743	0.731	0.718	0.706	0.694
3	0.731	0.712	0.693	0.675	0.658	0.641	0.624	0.609	0.593	0.579
4	0.659	0.636	0.613	0.592	0.572	0.552	0.534	0.516	0.499	0.482
5	0.593	0.567	0.543	0.519	0.497	0.476	0.456	0.437	0.419	0.402
6	0.535	0.507	0.480	0.456	0.432	0.410	0.390	0.370	0.352	0.335
7	0.482	0.452	0.425	0.400	0.376	0.354	0.333	0.314	0.296	0.279
8	0.434	0.404	0.376	0.351	0.327	0.305	0.285	0.266	0.249	0.233
9	0.391	0.361	0.333	0.308	0.284	0.263	0.243	0.225	0.209	0.194
10	0.352	0.322	0.295	0.270	0.247	0.227	0.208	0.191	0.176	0.162
11	0.317	0.287	0.261	0.237	0.215	0.195	0.178	0.162	0.148	0.135
12	0.286	0.257	0.231	0.208	0.187	0.168	0.152	0.137	0.124	0.112
13	0.258	0.229	0.204	0.182	0.163	0.145	0.130	0.116	0.104	0.093
14	0.232	0.205	0.181	0.160	0.141	0.125	0.111	0.099	0.088	0.078
15	0.209	0.183	0.160	0.140	0.123	0.108	0.095	0.084	0.074	0.065
16	0.188	0.163	0.141	0.123	0.107	0.093	0.081	0.071	0.062	0.054
17	0.170	0.146	0.125	0.108	0.093	0.080	0.069	0.060	0.052	0.045
18	0.153	0.130	0.111	0.095	0.081	0.069	0.059	0.051	0.044	0.038
19	0.138	0.116	0.098	0.083	0.070	0.060	0.051	0.043	0.037	0.031
20	0.124	0.104	0.087	0.073	0.061	0.051	0.043	0.037	0.031	0.026
21	0.112	0.093	0.077	0.064	0.053	0.044	0.037	0.031	0.026	0.022
22	0.101	0.083	0.068	0.056	0.046	0.038	0.032	0.026	0.022	0.018
23	0.091	0.074	0.060	0.049	0.040	0.033	0.027	0.022	0.018	0.015
24	0.082	0.066	0.053	0.043	0.035	0.028	0.023	0.019	0.015	0.013
25	0.074	0.059	0.047	0.038	0.030	0.024	0.020	0.016	0.013	0.010
30	0.044	0.033	0.026	0.020	0.015	0.012	0.009	0.007	0.005	0.004
35	0.026	0.019	0.014	0.010	0.008	0.006	0.004	0.003	0.002	0.002
40	0.015	0.011	0.008	0.005	0.004	0.003	0.002	0.001	0.001	0.001
45	0.009	0.006	0.004	0.003	0.002	0.001	0.001	0.001	*	*
50	0.005	0.003	0.002	0.001	0.001	0.001	*	*	*	*

*PVIF is zero to three decimal places.

(*continued*)

TABLE A – 3 (*Continued*)

Period	21%	22%	23%	24%	25%	26%	27%	28%	29%	30%
1	0.826	0.820	0.813	0.806	0.800	0.794	0.787	0.781	0.775	0.769
2	0.683	0.672	0.661	0.650	0.640	0.630	0.620	0.610	0.601	0.592
3	0.564	0.551	0.537	0.524	0.512	0.500	0.488	0.477	0.466	0.455
4	0.467	0.451	0.437	0.423	0.410	0.397	0.384	0.373	0.361	0.350
5	0.386	0.370	0.355	0.341	0.328	0.315	0.303	0.291	0.280	0.269
6	0.319	0.303	0.289	0.275	0.262	0.250	0.238	0.227	0.217	0.207
7	0.263	0.249	0.235	0.222	0.210	0.198	0.188	0.178	0.168	0.159
8	0.218	0.204	0.191	0.179	0.168	0.157	0.148	0.139	0.130	0.123
9	0.180	0.167	0.155	0.144	0.134	0.125	0.116	0.108	0.101	0.094
10	0.149	0.137	0.126	0.116	0.107	0.099	0.092	0.085	0.078	0.073
11	0.123	0.112	0.103	0.094	0.086	0.079	0.072	0.066	0.061	0.056
12	0.102	0.092	0.083	0.076	0.069	0.062	0.057	0.052	0.047	0.043
13	0.084	0.075	0.068	0.061	0.055	0.050	0.045	0.040	0.037	0.033
14	0.069	0.062	0.055	0.049	0.044	0.039	0.035	0.032	0.028	0.025
15	0.057	0.051	0.045	0.040	0.035	0.031	0.028	0.025	0.022	0.020
16	0.047	0.042	0.036	0.032	0.028	0.025	0.022	0.019	0.017	0.015
17	0.039	0.034	0.030	0.026	0.023	0.020	0.017	0.015	0.013	0.012
18	0.032	0.028	0.024	0.021	0.018	0.016	0.014	0.012	0.010	0.009
19	0.027	0.023	0.020	0.017	0.014	0.012	0.011	0.009	0.008	0.007
20	0.022	0.019	0.016	0.014	0.012	0.010	0.008	0.007	0.006	0.005
21	0.018	0.015	0.013	0.011	0.009	0.008	0.007	0.006	0.005	0.004
22	0.015	0.013	0.011	0.009	0.007	0.006	0.005	0.004	0.004	0.003
23	0.012	0.010	0.009	0.007	0.006	0.005	0.004	0.003	0.003	0.002
24	0.010	0.008	0.007	0.006	0.005	0.004	0.003	0.003	0.002	0.002
25	0.009	0.007	0.006	0.005	0.004	0.003	0.003	0.002	0.002	0.001
30	0.003	0.003	0.002	0.002	0.001	0.001	0.001	0.001	*	*
35	0.001	0.001	0.001	0.001	*	*	*	*	*	*
40	*	*	*	*	*	*	*	*	*	*
45	*	*	*	*	*	*	*	*	*	*
50	*	*	*	*	*	*	*	*	*	*

*PVIF is zero to three decimal places.

TABLE A-4

Present Value Interest Factors for a One Dollar Annuity
Discounted at k Percent for n Periods: $PVIFA_{kn} = \sum_{t=1}^{n} 1/(1 + k)^t$

Period	1%	2%	3%	4%	5%	6%	7%	8%	9%	10%
1	0.990	0.980	0.971	0.962	0.952	0.943	0.935	0.926	0.917	0.909
2	1.970	1.942	1.913	1.886	1.859	1.833	1.808	1.783	1.759	1.736
3	2.941	2.884	2.829	2.775	2.723	2.673	2.624	2.577	2.531	2.487
4	3.902	3.808	3.717	3.630	3.546	3.465	3.387	3.312	3.240	3.170
5	4.853	4.713	4.580	4.452	4.329	4.212	4.100	3.993	3.890	3.791
6	5.795	5.601	5.417	5.242	5.076	4.917	4.767	4.623	4.486	4.355
7	6.728	6.472	6.230	6.002	5.786	5.582	5.389	5.206	5.033	4.868
8	7.652	7.326	7.020	6.733	6.463	6.210	5.971	5.747	5.535	5.335
9	8.566	8.162	7.786	7.435	7.108	6.802	6.515	6.247	5.995	5.759
10	9.471	8.983	8.530	8.111	7.722	7.360	7.024	6.710	6.418	6.145
11	10.368	9.787	9.253	8.760	8.306	7.887	7.499	7.139	6.805	6.495
12	11.255	10.575	9.954	9.385	8.863	8.384	7.943	7.536	7.161	6.814
13	12.134	11.348	10.635	9.986	9.394	8.853	8.358	7.904	7.487	7.013
14	13.004	12.106	11.296	10.563	9.899	9.295	8.745	8.244	7.786	7.367
15	13.865	12.849	11.938	11.118	10.380	9.712	9.108	8.560	8.061	7.606
16	14.718	13.578	12.561	11.652	10.838	10.106	9.447	8.851	8.313	7.824
17	15.562	14.292	13.166	12.166	11.274	10.477	9.763	9.122	8.544	8.022
18	16.398	14.992	13.754	12.659	11.690	10.828	10.059	9.372	8.756	8.201
19	17.226	15.679	14.324	13.134	12.085	11.158	10.336	9.604	8.950	8.365
20	18.046	16.352	14.878	13.590	12.462	11.470	10.594	9.818	9.129	8.514
21	18.857	17.011	15.415	14.029	12.821	11.764	10.836	10.017	9.292	8.649
22	19.661	17.658	15.937	14.451	13.163	12.042	11.061	10.201	9.442	8.772
23	20.456	18.292	16.444	14.857	13.489	12.303	11.272	10.371	9.580	8.883
24	21.244	18.914	16.936	15.247	13.799	12.550	11.469	10.529	9.707	8.985
25	22.023	19.524	17.413	15.622	14.094	12.783	11.654	10.675	9.823	9.077
30	25.808	22.396	19.601	17.292	15.373	13.765	12.409	11.258	10.274	9.427
35	29.409	24.999	21.487	18.665	16.374	14.498	12.948	11.655	10.567	9.644
40	32.835	27.356	23.155	19.793	17.159	15.046	13.332	11.925	10.757	9.779
45	36.095	29.490	24.519	20.720	17.774	15.456	13.606	12.108	10.881	9.863
50	39.196	31.424	25.730	21.482	18.256	15.762	13.801	12.233	10.962	9.915

(*continued*)

TABLE A − 4 (*Continued*)

Period	11%	12%	13%	14%	15%	16%	17%	18%	19%	20%
1	0.901	0.893	0.885	0.877	0.870	0.862	0.855	0.847	0.840	0.833
2	1.713	1.690	1.668	1.647	1.626	1.605	1.585	1.566	1.547	1.528
3	2.444	2.402	2.361	2.322	2.283	2.246	2.210	2.174	2.140	2.106
4	3.102	3.037	2.974	2.914	2.855	2.798	2.743	2.690	2.639	2.589
5	3.696	3.605	3.517	3.433	3.352	3.274	3.199	3.127	3.058	2.991
6	4.231	4.111	3.998	3.889	3.784	3.685	3.589	3.498	3.410	3.326
7	4.712	4.564	4.423	4.288	4.160	4.039	3.922	3.812	3.706	3.605
8	5.146	4.968	4.799	4.639	4.487	4.344	4.207	4.078	3.954	3.837
9	5.537	5.328	5.132	4.946	4.772	4.607	4.451	4.303	4.163	4.031
10	5.889	5.650	5.426	5.216	5.019	4.833	4.659	4.494	4.339	4.192
11	6.207	5.938	5.687	5.453	5.234	5.029	4.836	4.656	4.486	4.327
12	6.492	6.194	5.918	5.660	5.421	5.197	4.988	4.793	4.611	4.439
13	6.750	6.424	6.122	5.842	5.583	5.342	5.118	4.910	4.715	4.533
14	6.982	6.628	6.302	6.002	5.724	5.468	5.229	5.008	4.802	4.611
15	7.191	6.811	6.462	6.142	5.847	5.575	5.324	5.092	4.876	4.675
16	7.379	6.974	6.604	6.265	5.954	5.668	5.405	5.162	4.938	4.730
17	7.549	7.120	6.729	6.373	6.047	5.749	5.475	5.222	4.990	4.775
18	7.702	7.250	6.840	6.467	6.128	5.818	5.534	5.273	5.033	4.812
19	7.839	7.366	6.938	6.550	6.198	5.877	5.584	5.316	5.070	4.843
20	7.963	7.469	7.025	6.623	6.259	5.929	5.628	5.353	5.101	4.870
21	8.075	7.562	7.102	6.687	6.312	5.973	5.665	5.384	5.127	4.891
22	8.176	7.645	7.170	6.743	6.359	6.001	5.696	5.410	5.149	4.909
23	8.266	7.718	7.230	6.792	6.399	6.044	5.723	5.432	5.167	4.925
24	8.348	7.784	7.283	6.835	6.434	6.073	5.746	5.451	5.182	4.937
25	8.422	7.843	7.330	6.873	6.464	6.097	5.766	5.467	5.195	4.948
30	8.694	8.055	7.496	7.003	6.566	6.177	5.829	5.517	5.235	4.979
35	8.885	8.176	7.586	7.070	6.617	6.215	5.858	5.539	5.251	4.992
40	8.951	8.244	7.634	7.105	6.642	6.233	5.871	5.548	5.258	4.997
45	9.008	8.283	7.661	7.123	6.654	6.242	5.877	5.552	5.261	4.999
50	9.042	8.304	7.675	7.133	6.661	6.246	5.880	5.554	5.262	4.999

TABLE A − 4 (*Continued*)

Period	21%	22%	23%	24%	25%	26%	27%	28%	29%	30%
1	0.826	0.820	0.813	0.806	0.800	0.794	0.787	0.781	0.775	0.769
2	1.509	1.492	1.474	1.457	1.440	1.424	1.407	1.392	1.376	1.361
3	2.074	2.042	2.011	1.981	1.952	1.923	1.896	1.868	1.842	1.816
4	2.540	2.494	2.448	2.404	2.362	2.320	2.280	2.241	2.203	2.166
5	2.926	2.864	2.803	2.745	2.689	2.635	2.583	2.532	2.483	2.436
6	3.245	3.167	3.092	3.020	2.951	2.885	2.821	2.759	2.700	2.643
7	3.508	3.416	3.327	3.242	3.161	3.083	3.009	2.937	2.868	2.802
8	3.726	3.619	3.518	3.421	3.329	3.241	3.156	3.076	2.999	2.925
9	3.905	3.786	3.673	3.566	3.463	3.366	3.273	3.184	3.100	3.019
10	4.054	3.923	3.799	3.682	3.570	3.465	3.364	3.269	3.178	3.092
11	4.177	4.035	3.902	3.776	3.656	3.544	3.437	3.335	3.239	3.147
12	4.278	4.127	3.985	3.851	3.725	3.606	3.493	3.387	3.286	3.190
13	4.362	4.203	4.053	3.912	3.780	3.656	3.538	3.427	3.322	3.223
14	4.432	4.265	4.108	3.962	3.824	3.695	3.573	3.459	3.351	3.249
15	4.489	4.315	4.153	4.001	3.859	3.726	3.601	3.483	3.373	3.268
16	4.536	4.357	4.189	4.033	3.887	3.751	3.623	3.503	3.390	3.283
17	4.576	4.391	4.219	4.059	3.910	3.771	3.640	3.518	3.403	3.295
18	4.608	4.419	4.243	4.080	3.928	3.786	3.654	3.529	3.413	3.304
19	4.635	4.442	4.263	4.097	3.942	3.799	3.664	3.539	3.421	3.311
20	4.657	4.460	4.279	4.110	3.954	3.808	3.673	3.546	3.427	3.316
21	4.675	4.476	4.292	4.121	3.963	3.816	3.679	3.551	3.432	3.320
22	4.690	4.488	4.302	4.130	3.970	3.822	3.684	3.556	3.436	3.323
23	4.703	4.499	4.311	4.137	3.976	3.827	3.689	3.559	3.438	3.325
24	4.713	4.507	4.318	4.143	3.981	3.831	3.692	3.562	3.441	3.327
25	4.721	4.514	4.323	4.147	3.985	3.834	3.694	3.564	3.442	3.329
30	4.746	4.534	4.339	4.160	3.995	3.842	3.701	3.569	3.447	3.332
35	4.756	4.541	4.345	4.164	3.998	3.845	3.703	3.571	3.448	3.333
40	4.760	4.544	4.347	4.166	3.999	3.846	3.703	3.571	3.448	3.333
45	4.761	4.545	4.347	4.166	4.000	3.846	3.704	3.571	3.448	3.333
50	4.762	4.545	4.348	4.167	4.000	3.846	3.704	3.571	3.448	3.333

TABLE A–5

Monthly Mortgage Constants (payment = constant × loan amount)

Year	Annual Contract Interest Rate							
	9.00	9.25	9.50	9.75	10.00	10.25	10.50	10.75
1	0.08745	0.08757	0.08768	0.08780	0.08792	0.08803	0.08815	0.08827
2	0.04568	0.04580	0.04591	0.04603	0.04614	0.04626	0.04638	0.04649
3	0.03180	0.03192	0.03203	0.03215	0.03227	0.03238	0.03250	0.03262
4	0.02489	0.02500	0.02512	0.02524	0.02536	0.02548	0.02560	0.02572
5	0.02076	0.02088	0.02100	0.02112	0.02125	0.02137	0.02149	0.02162
6	0.01803	0.01815	0.01827	0.01840	0.01853	0.01865	0.01878	0.01891
7	0.01609	0.01622	0.01634	0.01647	0.01660	0.01673	0.01686	0.01699
8	0.01465	0.01478	0.01491	0.01504	0.01517	0.01531	0.01544	0.01557
9	0.01354	0.01368	0.01381	0.01394	0.01408	0.01421	0.01435	0.01449
10	0.01267	0.01280	0.01294	0.01308	0.01322	0.01335	0.01349	0.01363
11	0.01196	0.01210	0.01224	0.01238	0.01252	0.01266	0.01280	0.01295
12	0.01138	0.01152	0.01166	0.01181	0.01195	0.01210	0.01224	0.01239
13	0.01090	0.01104	0.01119	0.01133	0.01148	0.01163	0.01178	0.01192
14	0.01049	0.01064	0.04078	0.01093	0.01108	0.01123	0.01138	0.01154
15	0.01014	0.01029	0.01044	0.01059	0.01075	0.01090	0.01105	0.01121
16	0.00985	0.01000	0.01015	0.01030	0.01046	0.01062	0.01077	0.01093
17	0.00959	0.00974	0.00990	0.01005	0.01021	0.01037	0.01053	0.01069
18	0.00936	0.00952	0.00968	0.00984	0.01000	0.01016	0.01032	0.01049
19	0.00917	0.00933	0.00949	0.00965	0.00981	0.00998	0.01014	0.01031
20	0.00900	0.00916	0.00932	0.00949	0.00965	0.00982	0.00998	0.01015
21	0.00885	0.00901	0.00917	0.00934	0.00951	0.00968	0.00985	0.01002
22	0.00871	0.00888	0.00904	0.00921	0.00938	0.00955	0.00973	0.00990
23	0.00859	0.00876	0.00893	0.00910	0.00927	0.00944	0.00962	0.00979
24	0.00849	0.00866	0.00883	0.00900	0.00917	0.00935	0.00952	0.00970
25	0.00839	0.00856	0.00874	0.00891	0.00909	0.00926	0.00944	0.00962
26	0.00831	0.00848	0.00866	0.00883	0.00901	0.00919	0.00937	0.00955
27	0.00823	0.00841	0.00858	0.00876	0.00894	0.00912	0.00930	0.00949
28	0.00816	0.00834	0.00852	0.00870	0.00888	0.00906	0.00925	0.00943
29	0.00810	0.00828	0.00846	0.00864	0.00882	0.00901	0.00919	0.00938
30	0.00805	0.00823	0.00841	0.00859	0.00878	0.00896	0.00915	0.00933
31	0.00800	0.00818	0.00836	0.00855	0.00873	0.00892	0.00911	0.00930
32	0.00795	0.00813	0.00832	0.00851	0.00869	0.00888	0.00907	0.00926
33	0.00791	0.00810	0.00828	0.00847	0.00866	0.00885	0.00904	0.00923
34	0.00787	0.00806	0.00825	0.00844	0.00863	0.00882	0.00901	0.00920
35	0.00784	0.00803	0.00822	0.00841	0.00860	0.00879	0.00898	0.00918

TABLE A−5 (*Continued*)

	Annual Contract Interest Rate							
Year	*11.00*	*11.25*	*11.50*	*11.75*	*12.00*	*12.25*	*12.50*	*12.75*
1	0.08838	0.08850	0.08862	0.08873	0.08885	0.08897	0.08908	0.08920
2	0.04661	0.04672	0.04684	0.04696	0.04707	0.04719	0.04731	0.04742
3	0.03274	0.03286	0.03298	0.03310	0.03321	0.03333	0.03345	0.03357
4	0.02585	0.02597	0.02609	0.02621	0.02633	0.02646	0.02658	0.02670
5	0.02174	0.02187	0.02199	0.02212	0.02224	0.02237	0.02250	0.02263
6	0.01903	0.01916	0.01929	0.01942	0.01955	0.01968	0.01981	0.01994
7	0.01712	0.01725	0.01739	0.01752	0.01765	0.01779	0.01792	0.01806
8	0.01571	0.01584	0.01598	0.01612	0.01625	0.01639	0.01653	0.01667
9	0.01463	0.01476	0.01490	0.01504	0.01518	0.01533	0.01547	0.01561
10	0.01378	0.01392	0.01406	0.01420	0.01435	0.01449	0.01464	0.01478
11	0.01309	0.01324	0.01338	0.01353	0.01368	0.01383	0.01398	0.01413
12	0.01254	0.01268	0.01283	0.01298	0.01313	0.01329	0.01344	0.01359
13	0.01208	0.01223	0.01238	0.01253	0.01269	0.01284	0.01300	0.01315
14	0.01169	0.01185	0.01200	0.01216	0.01231	0.01247	0.01263	0.01279
15	0.01137	0.01152	0.01168	0.01184	0.01200	0.01216	0.01233	0.01249
16	0.01109	0.01125	0.01141	0.01157	0.01174	0.01190	0.01207	0.01223
17	0.01085	0.01102	0.01118	0.01135	0.01151	0.01168	0.01185	0.01202
18	0.01065	0.01082	0.01098	0.01115	0.01132	0.01149	0.01166	0.01183
19	0.01047	0.01064	0.01081	0.01098	0.01115	0.01133	0.01150	0.01167
20	0.01032	0.01049	0.01066	0.01084	0.01101	0.01119	0.01136	0.01154
21	0.01019	0.01036	0.01054	0.01071	0.01089	0.01106	0.01124	0.01142
22	0.01007	0.01025	0.01042	0.01060	0.01078	0.01096	0.01114	0.01132
23	0.00997	0.01015	0.01033	0.01051	0.01069	0.01087	0.01105	0.01123
24	0.00988	0.01006	0.01024	0.01042	0.01060	0.01079	0.01097	0.01116
25	0.00980	0.00998	0.01016	0.01035	0.01053	0.01072	0.01090	0.01109
26	0.00973	0.00991	0.01010	0.01028	0.01047	0.01066	0.01084	0.01103
27	0.00967	0.00985	0.01004	0.01023	0.01041	0.01060	0.01079	0.01098
28	0.00961	0.00980	0.00999	0.01018	0.01037	0.01056	0.01075	0.01094
29	0.00957	0.00975	0.00994	0.01013	0.01032	0.01052	0.01071	0.01090
30	0.00952	0.00971	0.00990	0.01009	0.01029	0.01048	0.01067	0.01087
31	0.00948	0.00968	0.00987	0.01006	0.01025	0.01045	0.01064	0.01084
32	0.00945	0.00964	0.00984	0.01003	0.01022	0.01042	0.01062	0.01081
33	0.00942	0.00961	0.00981	0.01000	0.01020	0.01039	0.01059	0.01079
34	0.00939	0.00959	0.00978	0.00998	0.01018	0.01037	0.01057	0.01077
35	0.00937	0.00956	0.00976	0.00996	0.01016	0.01035	0.01055	0.01075

(*continued*)

TABLE A−5 *(Continued)*

	Annual Contract Interest Rate							
Year	*13.00*	*13.25*	*13.50*	*13.75*	*14.00*	*14.25*	*14.50*	*14.75*
1	0.08932	0.08943	0.08955	0.08967	0.08979	0.08990	00.9002	0.09014
2	0.04754	0.04766	0.04778	0.04789	0.04801	0.04813	0.04825	0.04837
3	0.03369	0.03381	0.03394	0.03406	0.02418	0.03430	0.03442	0.03454
4	0.02683	0.02695	0.02708	0.02720	0.02733	0.02745	0.02758	0.02770
5	0.02275	0.02288	0.02301	0.02314	0.02327	0.02340	0.02353	0.02366
6	0.02007	0.02021	0.02034	0.02047	0.02061	0.02074	0.02087	0.02101
7	0.01819	0.01833	0.01846	0.01860	0.01874	0.01888	0.01902	0.01916
8	0.01681	0.01695	0.01709	0.01723	0.01737	0.01751	0.01766	0.01780
9	0.01575	0.01590	0.01604	0.01619	0.01633	0.01648	0.01663	0.01678
10	0.01493	0.01508	0.01523	0.01538	0.01553	0.01568	0.01583	0.01598
11	0.01428	0.01443	0.01458	0.01473	0.01489	0.01504	0.01520	0.01535
12	0.01375	0.01390	0.01406	0.01421	0.01437	0.01453	0.01469	0.01485
13	0.01331	0.01347	0.01363	0.01379	0.01395	0.01411	0.01428	0.01444
14	0.01295	0.01300	0.01328	0.01344	0.01360	0.01377	0.01394	0.01410
15	0.01265	0.01282	0.01298	0.01315	0.01332	0.01349	0.01366	0.01383
16	0.01240	0.01257	0.01274	0.01291	0.01308	0.01325	0.01342	0.01359
17	0.01219	0.01236	0.01253	0.01270	0.01287	0.01305	0.01322	0.01340
18	0.01200	0.01218	0.01235	0.01253	0.01270	0.01288	0.01306	0.01324
19	0.01185	0.01203	0.01220	0.01238	0.01256	0.01274	0.01292	0.01310
20	0.01172	0.01189	0.01207	0.01225	0.01244	0.01262	0.01280	0.01298
21	0.01160	0.01178	0.01196	0.01215	0.01233	0.01251	0.01270	0.01288
22	0.01150	0.01169	0.01187	0.01205	0.01224	0.01243	0.01261	0.01280
23	0.01142	0.01160	0.01179	0.01197	0.01216	0.01235	0.01254	0.01273
24	0.01134	0.01153	0.01172	0.01191	0.01210	0.01229	0.01248	0.01267
25	0.01128	0.01147	0.01166	0.01185	0.01204	0.01223	0.01242	0.01261
26	0.01122	0.01141	0.01160	0.01180	0.01199	0.01218	0.01238	0.01257
27	0.01117	0.01137	0.01156	0.01175	0.01195	0.01214	0.01234	0.01253
28	0.01113	0.01132	0.01152	0.01171	0.01191	0.01210	0.01230	0.01250
29	0.01109	0.01129	0.01148	0.01168	0.01188	0.01207	0.01227	0.01247
30	0.01106	0.01126	0.01145	0.01165	0.01185	0.01205	0.01225	0.01244
31	0.01103	0.01123	0.01143	0.01163	0.01182	0.01202	0.01222	0.01242
32	0.01101	0.01121	0.01141	0.01160	0.01180	0.01200	0.01220	0.01241
33	0.01099	0.01119	0.01139	0.01159	0.01179	0.01199	0.01219	0.01239
34	0.01097	0.01117	0.01137	0.01157	0.01177	0.01197	0.01217	0.01238
35	0.01095	0.01115	0.01135	0.01155	0.01176	0.01196	0.01216	0.01236

TABLE A−5 (*Continued*)

	Annual Contract Interest Rate							
Year	*15.00*	*15.25*	*15.50*	*15.75*	*16.00*	*16.25*	*16.50*	*16.75*
1	0.09026	0.09038	0.09049	0.09061	0.09073	0.09085	0.09097	0.09109
2	0.04849	0.04861	0.04872	0.04884	0.04896	0.04908	0.04920	0.04932
3	0.03467	0.03479	0.03491	0.03503	0.03516	0.03528	0.03540	0.03553
4	0.02783	0.02796	0.02808	0.02821	0.02834	0.02847	0.02860	0.02873
5	0.02379	0.02392	0.02405	0.02419	0.02432	0.02445	0.02458	0.02472
6	0.02115	0.02128	0.02142	0.02155	0.02169	0.02183	0.02197	0.02211
7	0.01930	0.01944	0.01958	0.01972	0.01986	0.02000	0.02015	0.02029
8	0.01795	0.01809	0.01824	0.01838	0.01853	0.01868	0.01882	0.01897
9	0.01692	0.01707	0.01722	0.01737	0.01753	0.01768	0.01783	0.01798
10	0.01613	0.01629	0.01644	0.01660	0.01675	0.01691	0.01706	0.01722
11	0.01551	0.01567	0.01582	0.01598	0.01614	0.01630	0.01646	0.01663
12	0.01501	0.01517	0.01533	0.01549	0.01566	0.01582	0.01599	0.01615
13	0.01460	0.01477	0.01493	0.01510	0.01527	0.01543	0.01560	0.01577
14	0.01427	0.01444	0.01461	0.01478	0.01495	0.01512	0.01529	0.01546
15	0.01400	0.01417	0.01434	0.01451	0.01469	0.01486	0.01504	0.01521
16	0.01377	0.01394	0.01412	0.01429	0.01447	0.01465	0.01483	0.01501
17	0.01358	0.01375	0.01393	0.01411	0.01429	0.01447	0.01465	0.01484
18	0.01342	0.01360	0.01378	0.01396	0.01414	0.01433	0.01451	0.01469
19	0.01328	0.01346	0.01365	0.01383	0.01402	0.01420	0.01439	0.01458
20	0.01317	0.01335	0.01354	0.01373	0.01391	0.01410	0.01429	0.01448
21	0.01307	0.01326	0.01345	0.01364	0.01382	0.01401	0.01420	0.01440
22	0.01299	0.01318	0.01337	0.01356	0.01375	0.01394	0.01413	0.01433
23	0.01292	0.01311	0.01330	0.01349	0.01369	0.01388	0.01407	0.01427
24	0.01286	0.01305	0.01325	0.01344	0.01363	0.01383	0.01402	0.01422
25	0.01281	0.01300	0.01320	0.01339	0.01359	0.01379	0.01398	0.01418
26	0.01276	0.01296	0.01316	0.01335	0.01355	0.01375	0.01395	0.01415
27	0.01273	0.01292	0.01312	0.01332	0.01352	0.01372	0.01392	0.01412
28	0.01270	0.01289	0.01309	0.01329	0.01349	0.01369	0.01389	0.01409
29	0.01267	0.01287	0.01307	0.01327	0.01347	0.01367	0.01387	0.01407
30	0.01264	0.01284	0.01305	0.01325	0.01345	0.01365	0.01385	0.01405
31	0.01262	0.01283	0.01303	0.01323	0.01343	0.01363	0.01384	0.01404
32	0.01261	0.01281	0.01301	0.01321	0.01342	0.01362	0.01382	0.01403
33	0.01259	0.01279	0.01300	0.01320	0.01340	0.01361	0.01381	0.01402
34	0.01258	0.01278	0.01299	0.01319	0.01339	0.01360	0.01380	0.01401
35	0.01257	0.01277	0.01298	0.01318	0.01338	0.01359	0.01379	0.01400

(*continued*)

TABLE A–6

Remaining Mortgage Balance Percentage for 9.00 Percent
(factor × original loan amount)

	Original Loan Term							
Age of Loan	*5*	*10*	*15*	*20*	*25*	*30*	*35*	*40*
1	0.83417	0.93537	0.96695	0.98127	0.98884	0.99317	0.99575	0.99733
2	0.65278	0.86467	0.93079	0.96079	0.97664	0.98570	0.99110	0.99441
3	0.45438	0.78734	0.89125	0.93838	0.96329	0.97752	0.98601	0.99121
4	0.23737	0.70276	0.84799	0.91388	0.94869	0.96858	0.98045	0.98771
5		0.61024	0.80068	0.88707	0.93272	0.95880	0.97436	0.98389
6		0.50904	0.74893	0.85775	0.91526	0.94810	0.96770	0.97971
7		0.39835	0.69232	0.82568	0.89615	0.93640	0.96042	0.97513
8		0.27728	0.63041	0.79060	0.87525	0.92361	0.95246	0.97012
9		0.14485	0.56268	0.75223	0.85239	0.90961	0.94375	0.96465
10			0.48861	0.71026	0.82739	0.89430	0.93422	0.95866
11			0.40758	0.66435	0.80004	0.87755	0.92380	0.95211
12			0.31895	0.61414	0.77013	0.85923	0.91240	0.94495
13			0.22201	0.55922	0.73741	0.83919	0.89993	0.93711
14			0.11598	0.49914	0.70162	0.81728	0.88629	0.92854
15				0.43343	0.66248	0.79330	0.87137	0.91917
16				0.36155	0.61966	0.76708	0.85505	0.90891
17				0.28294	0.57282	0.73840	0.83720	0.89770
18				0.19694	0.52159	0.70703	0.81768	0.88543
19				0.10288	0.46556	0.67272	0.79632	0.87201
20					0.40427	0.63518	0.77297	0.85733
21					0.33723	0.59413	0.74742	0.84127
22					0.26390	0.54922	0.71947	0.82371
23					0.18369	0.50010	0.68890	0.80450
24					0.09596	0.44638	0.65547	0.78349
25						0.38761	0.61890	0.76051
26						0.32334	0.57890	0.73537
27						0.25303	0.53514	0.70788
28						0.17613	0.48728	0.67780
29						0.09201	0.43493	0.64491
30							0.37768	0.60893
31							0.31505	0.56957
32							0.24654	0.52652
33							0.17161	0.47943
34							0.08965	0.42793
35								0.37159
36								0.30997
37								0.24257
38								0.16884
39								0.08820
40								

TABLE A−6 (*Continued*)

Percentage for 9.25 Percent

	Original Loan Term							
Age of Loan	*5*	*10*	*15*	*20*	*25*	*30*	*35*	*40*
1	0.83506	0.93620	0.96765	0.98184	0.98929	0.99351	0.99600	0.99752
2	0.65421	0.86624	0.93217	0.96192	0.97754	0.98639	0.99162	0.99479
3	0.45590	0.78953	0.89327	0.94009	0.96466	0.97858	0.98682	0.99181
4	0.23844	0.70542	0.85062	0.91614	0.95054	0.97003	0.98155	0.98854
5		0.61319	0.80385	0.88989	0.93505	0.96064	0.97577	0.98495
6		0.51205	0.75257	0.86110	0.91807	0.95035	0.96944	0.98101
7		0.40115	0.69633	0.82953	0.89945	0.93907	0.96249	0.97670
8		0.27955	0.63467	0.79492	0.87903	0.92669	0.95488	0.97196
9		0.14621	0.56705	0.75696	0.85664	0.91313	0.94652	0.96677
10			0.49291	0.71534	0.83209	0.89825	0.93737	0.96108
11			0.41161	0.66970	0.80517	0.88193	0.92733	0.95485
12			0.32247	0.61966	0.77565	0.86405	0.91632	0.94800
13			0.22472	0.56478	0.74329	0.84443	0.90424	0.94050
14			0.11753	0.50461	0.70779	0.82292	0.89100	0.93228
15				0.43864	0.66888	0.79934	0.87649	0.92326
16				0.36629	0.62620	0.77348	0.86057	0.91337
17				0.28696	0.57941	0.74512	0.84311	0.90252
18				0.19997	0.52810	0.71403	0.82397	0.89063
19				0.10459	0.47184	0.67994	0.80299	0.87759
20					0.41015	0.64255	0.77998	0.86329
21					0.34250	0.60156	0.75474	0.84761
22					0.26832	0.55661	0.72707	0.83042
23					0.18698	0.50732	0.69673	0.81157
24					0.09780	0.45327	0.66346	0.79090
25						0.39400	0.62698	0.76823
26						0.32902	0.58698	0.74338
27						0.25776	0.54312	0.71613
28						0.17963	0.49502	0.68624
29						0.09395	0.44229	0.65348
30							0.38446	0.61755
31							0.32105	0.57815
32							0.25152	0.53495
33							0.17527	0.48757
34							0.09167	0.43563
35								0.37867
36								0.31621
37								0.24773
38								0.17264
39								0.09029
40								

(*continued*)

T A B L E A − 6 (*Continued*)

Percentage for 9.50 Percent

Age of Loan	Original Loan Term							
	5	10	15	20	25	30	35	40
1	0.83596	0.93703	0.96834	0.98239	0.98972	0.99383	0.99625	0.99769
2	0.65563	0.86781	0.93353	0.96303	0.97841	0.98706	0.99212	0.99516
3	0.45741	0.79171	0.89527	0.94176	0.96599	0.97960	0.98758	0.99237
4	0.23952	0.70807	0.85322	0.91837	0.95233	0.97141	0.98260	0.98931
5		0.61612	0.80699	0.89265	0.93731	0.96241	0.97712	0.98594
6		0.51505	0.75617	0.86439	0.92081	0.95251	0.97109	0.98224
7		0.40395	0.70031	0.83332	0.90266	0.94163	0.96447	0.94817
8		0.28182	0.63890	0.79917	0.88272	0.92967	0.95719	0.97370
9		0.14757	0.57140	0.76163	0.86079	0.91653	0.94918	0.96878
10			0.49721	0.72036	0.83669	0.90208	0.94039	0.96338
11			0.41564	0.67500	0.81020	0.88619	0.93071	0.95744
12			0.32598	0.62513	0.78108	0.86873	0.92008	0.95091
13			0.22743	0.57032	0.74907	0.84954	0.90840	0.94373
14			0.11909	0.51007	0.71388	0.82844	0.89555	0.93584
15				0.44383	0.67520	0.80524	0.88143	0.92717
16				0.37103	0.63268	0.77975	0.86591	0.91763
17				0.29099	0.58595	0.75172	0.84885	0.90715
18				0.20301	0.53457	0.72091	0.83009	0.89563
19				0.10631	0.47809	0.68705	0.80948	0.88296
20					0.41601	0.64982	0.78681	0.86904
21					0.34777	0.60890	0.76190	0.85374
22					0.27275	0.56392	0.73452	0.83692
23					0.19029	0.51447	0.70442	0.81843
24					0.09964	0.46012	0.67133	0.79810
25						0.40037	0.63495	0.77575
26						0.33469	0.59497	0.75119
27						0.26250	0.55101	0.72419
28						0.18313	0.50270	0.69451
29						0.09590	0.44959	0.66189
30							0.39121	0.62603
31							0.32703	0.58660
32							0.25649	0.54327
33							0.17894	0.49563
34							0.09370	0.44327
35								0.38571
36								0.32244
37								0.25288
38								0.17643
39								0.09238
40								

TABLE A－6 (*Continued*)

Percentage for 9.75 Percent

Age of Loan	Original Loan Term							
	5	10	15	20	25	30	35	40
1	0.83685	0.93785	0.96902	0.98293	0.99013	0.99414	0.99647	0.99786
2	0.65705	0.86936	0.93487	0.96412	0.97925	0.98769	0.99259	0.99550
3	0.45893	0.79388	0.89725	0.94339	0.96727	0.98058	0.98831	0.99290
4	0.24060	0.71071	0.85579	0.92054	0.95406	0.97274	0.98359	0.99003
5		0.61905	0.81009	0.89537	0.93951	0.96411	0.97839	0.98688
6		0.51805	0.75974	0.86762	0.92347	0.95459	0.97266	0.98340
7		0.40675	0.70426	0.83705	0.90579	0.94411	0.96635	0.97956
8		0.28410	0.64312	0.80336	0.88632	0.93255	0.95939	0.97534
9		0.14894	0.57574	0.76624	0.86485	0.91982	0.95173	0.97068
10			0.50149	0.72533	0.84120	0.90579	0.94328	0.96555
11			0.41967	0.68025	0.81514	0.89032	0.93397	0.95990
12			0.32951	0.63057	0.78642	0.87328	0.92371	0.95367
13			0.23015	0.57583	0.75477	0.85451	0.91240	0.94680
14			0.12066	0.51550	0.71989	0.83381	0.89994	0.93924
15				0.44902	0.68145	0.81101	0.88621	0.93090
16				0.37576	0.63910	0.78588	0.87109	0.92171
17				0.29503	0.59242	0.75819	0.85441	0.91159
18				0.20607	0.54099	0.72768	0.83604	0.90043
19				0.10803	0.48431	0.69405	0.81580	0.88813
20					0.42186	0.65700	0.79349	0.87458
21					0.35303	0.61616	0.76890	0.85965
22					0.27718	0.57116	0.74181	0.84320
23					0.19360	0.52158	0.71195	0.82507
24					0.10150	0.46693	0.67905	0.80509
25						0.40671	0.64280	0.78307
26						0.34036	0.60285	0.75881
27						0.26723	0.55882	0.73207
28						0.18665	0.51030	0.70261
29						0.09785	0.45684	0.67014
30							0.39793	0.63436
31							0.33300	0.59494
32							0.26146	0.55149
33							0.18262	0.50361
34							0.09574	0.45085
35								0.39270
36								0.32863
37								0.25803
38								0.18022
39								0.09448
40								

(*continued*)

TABLE A−6 (*Continued*)
Percentage for 10.00 Percent

Age of Loan	Original Loan Term							
	5	10	15	20	25	30	35	40
1	0.83773	0.93866	0.96968	0.98345	0.99053	0.99444	0.99669	0.99801
2	0.65847	0.87089	0.93619	0.96517	0.98007	0.98830	0.99303	0.99582
3	0.46044	0.79603	0.89919	0.94498	0.96851	0.98152	0.98900	0.99339
4	0.24167	0.71333	0.85832	0.92267	0.95574	0.97402	0.98453	0.99071
5		0.62197	0.81317	0.89802	0.94164	0.96574	0.97960	0.98776
6		0.52105	0.76329	0.87080	0.92606	0.95660	0.97416	0.98449
7		0.40955	0.70818	0.84072	0.90884	0.94649	0.96814	0.98087
8		0.28638	0.64731	0.80750	0.88983	0.83533	0.96150	0.97689
9		0.15031	0.58006	0.77079	0.86882	0.92300	0.95416	0.97248
10			0.50577	0.73024	0.84561	0.90938	0.94605	0.96761
11			0.42370	0.68545	0.81998	0.89433	0.93709	0.96223
12			0.33303	0.63596	0.79166	0.87771	0.92719	0.95629
13			0.23288	0.58130	0.76037	0.85934	0.91625	0.94972
14			0.12223	0.52091	0.72581	0.83906	0.90418	0.94247
15				0.45419	0.68762	0.81665	0.89093	0.93446
16				0.38049	0.64544	0.79189	0.87609	0.92561
17				0.29907	0.59885	0.76454	0.85981	0.91584
18				0.20913	0.54737	0.73432	0.84182	0.90504
19				0.10977	0.49050	0.70094	0.82194	0.89310
20					0.42768	0.66407	0.79999	0.87992
21					0.35828	0.62333	0.77574	0.86536
22					0.28162	0.57833	0.74894	0.84928
23					0.19692	0.52862	0.71934	0.83151
24					0.10336	0.47370	0.68665	0.81188
25						0.41303	0.65052	0.79019
26						0.34601	0.61062	0.76624
27						0.27197	0.56654	0.73977
28						0.19018	0.51784	0.71054
29						0.09982	0.46404	0.67824
30							0.40461	0.64256
31							0.33895	0.60314
32							0.26642	0.55960
33							0.18630	0.51150
34							0.09778	0.45836
35								0.39965
36								0.33480
37								0.26316
38								0.18402
39								0.09659
40								

T A B L E A – 6 (*Continued*)

Percentage for 10.25 Percent

Age of Loan	Original Loan Term							
	5	10	15	20	25	30	35	40
1	0.83861	0.93946	0.97034	0.98396	0.99092	0.99472	0.99689	0.99816
2	0.65989	0.87242	0.93749	0.96620	0.98085	0.98888	0.99345	0.99612
3	0.46196	0.79817	0.90111	0.94653	0.96971	0.98241	0.98965	0.99385
4	0.24276	0.71594	0.86082	0.92475	0.95737	0.97525	0.98543	0.99135
5		0.62488	0.81620	0.90063	0.94371	0.96731	0.98075	0.98858
6		0.52404	0.76679	0.87392	0.92857	0.95852	0.97558	0.98551
7		0.41235	0.71207	0.84433	0.91181	0.94879	0.96985	0.98211
8		0.28867	0.65147	0.81157	0.89325	0.93801	0.96351	0.97834
9		0.15169	0.58436	0.77528	0.87270	0.92608	0.95648	0.97417
10			0.51003	0.73510	0.84993	0.91286	0.94870	0.96955
11			0.42772	0.69060	0.82472	0.89822	0.94008	0.96444
12			0.33656	0.64131	0.79680	0.88201	0.93053	0.95877
13			0.23561	0.58673	0.76588	0.86405	0.91996	0.95250
14			0.12381	0.52629	0.73164	0.84417	0.90825	0.94555
15				0.45935	0.69372	0.82215	0.89529	0.93786
16				0.38522	0.65172	0.79776	0.88093	0.92934
17				0.30312	0.60521	0.77075	0.86503	0.91990
18				0.21220	0.55370	0.74085	0.84742	0.90945
19				0.11151	0.49666	0.70722	0.82792	0.89788
20					0.43349	0.67104	0.80633	0.88506
21					0.36353	0.63042	0.78241	0.87087
22					0.28606	0.58543	0.75592	0.85515
23					0.20025	0.53560	0.72659	0.83774
24					0.10523	0.48043	0.69410	0.81847
25						0.41932	0.65813	0.79712
26						0.35165	0.61828	0.77347
27						0.27671	0.57416	0.74729
28						0.19371	0.52530	0.71829
29						0.10179	0.47118	0.68618
30							0.41125	0.65061
31							0.34488	0.61122
32							0.27138	0.56760
33							0.18998	0.51930
34							0.09983	0.46580
35								0.40655
36								0.34094
37								0.26828
38								0.18781
39								0.09869
40								

(*continued*)

TABLE A − 6 (*Continued*)

Percentage for 10.50 Percent

Age of Loan	Original Loan Term							
	5	10	15	20	25	30	35	40
1	0.83949	0.94026	0.97098	0.98446	0.99129	0.99499	0.99709	0.99829
2	0.66130	0.87393	0.93877	0.96721	0.98161	0.98944	0.99385	0.99639
3	0.46347	0.80029	0.90300	0.94806	0.97087	0.98327	0.99026	0.99429
4	0.24384	0.71854	0.86329	0.92679	0.95895	0.97642	0.98627	0.99195
5		0.62778	0.81921	0.90319	0.94571	0.96882	0.98185	0.98935
6		0.52702	0.77027	0.87698	0.93102	0.96038	0.97693	0.98647
7		0.41515	0.71593	0.84788	0.91470	0.95100	0.97148	0.98327
8		0.29096	0.65561	0.81558	0.89659	0.94060	0.96542	0.97972
9		0.15308	0.58864	0.77971	0.87648	0.92905	0.95870	0.97577
10			0.51428	0.73990	0.85415	0.91622	0.95123	0.97139
11			0.43174	0.69569	0.82937	0.90199	0.94294	0.96653
12			0.34010	0.64662	0.80185	0.88618	0.93374	0.96113
13			0.23836	0.59214	0.77130	0.86863	0.92352	0.95514
14			0.12540	0.53165	0.73739	0.84915	0.91218	0.94849
15				0.46449	0.69973	0.82752	0.89959	0.94110
16				0.38994	0.65793	0.80351	0.88561	0.93290
17				0.30717	0.61152	0.77685	0.87009	0.92380
18				0.21528	0.55999	0.74725	0.85286	0.91369
19				0.11326	0.50279	0.71439	0.83373	0.90247
20					0.43928	0.67791	0.81250	0.89001
21					0.36877	0.63741	0.78892	0.87618
22					0.29050	0.59245	0.76245	0.86083
23					0.20359	0.54253	0.73369	0.84378
24					0.10711	0.48711	0.70142	0.82486
25						0.42558	0.66560	0.80385
26						0.35727	0.62584	0.78052
27						0.28144	0.58169	0.75462
28						0.19724	0.53268	0.72587
29						0.10377	0.47827	0.69395
30							0.41786	0.65852
31							0.35079	0.61918
32							0.27633	0.57550
33							0.19366	0.52701
34							0.10189	0.47317
35								0.41341
36								0.34705
37								0.27339
38								0.19160
39								0.10080
40								

TABLE A−6 (*Continued*)

Percentage for 10.75 Percent

	Original Loan Term							
Age of Loan	5	10	15	20	25	30	35	40
1	0.84037	0.94104	0.97161	0.98495	0.99165	0.99525	0.99727	0.99842
2	0.66271	0.87543	0.94002	0.96819	0.98235	0.98997	0.99423	0.99665
3	0.46498	0.80240	0.90486	0.94954	0.97200	0.98409	0.99084	0.99469
4	0.24492	0.72113	0.86573	0.92879	0.96048	0.97754	0.98708	0.99251
5		0.63067	0.82218	0.90569	0.94766	0.97026	0.98288	0.99008
6		0.53000	0.77371	0.87998	0.93339	0.96215	0.97822	0.98737
7		0.41795	0.71976	0.85137	0.91752	0.95313	0.97302	0.98436
8		0.29325	0.65972	0.81952	0.89984	0.94309	0.96724	0.98101
9		0.15447	0.59290	0.78408	0.88017	0.93192	0.96081	0.97728
10			0.51853	0.74464	0.85828	0.91948	0.95365	0.97313
11			0.43575	0.70074	0.83392	0.90564	0.94569	0.96851
12			0.34363	0.65188	0.80681	0.89023	0.93682	0.96337
13			0.24111	0.59750	0.77663	0.87308	0.92695	0.95765
14			0.12700	0.53698	0.74304	0.85400	0.91596	0.95128
15				0.46962	0.70566	0.83276	0.90374	0.94419
16				0.39466	0.66406	0.80912	0.89013	0.93630
17				0.31122	0.61776	0.78281	0.87499	0.92752
18				0.21837	0.56623	0.75353	0.85814	0.91775
19				0.11502	0.50887	0.72095	0.83938	0.90687
20					0.44504	0.68468	0.81851	0.89477
21					0.37400	0.64431	0.79527	0.88130
22					0.29494	0.59939	0.76941	0.86631
23					0.20695	0.54939	0.74064	0.84962
24					0.10900	0.49374	0.70861	0.83105
25						0.43181	0.67296	0.81038
26						0.36288	0.63328	0.78738
27						0.28816	0.58913	0.76178
28						0.20078	0.53998	0.73329
29						0.10576	0.48529	0.70157
30							0.42442	0.66628
31							0.35667	0.62700
32							0.28127	0.58328
33							0.19735	0.53463
34							0.10395	0.48047
35								0.42021
36								0.35313
37								0.27847
38								0.19539
39								0.10292
40								

(*continued*)

TABLE A – 6 (*Continued*)

Percentage for 11.00 Percent

Age of Loan	Original Loan Term							
	5	10	15	20	25	30	35	40
1	0.84125	0.94182	0.97224	0.98542	0.99199	0.99550	0.99744	0.99853
2	0.66412	0.87692	0.94126	0.96915	0.98305	0.99048	0.99458	0.99689
3	0.46650	0.80450	0.90670	0.95099	0.97308	0.98487	0.99139	0.99507
4	0.24601	0.72370	0.86814	0.93074	0.96196	0.97862	0.98783	0.99303
5		0.63355	0.82512	0.90814	0.94955	0.97165	0.98386	0.99075
6		0.53297	0.77711	0.88293	0.93570	0.96386	0.97944	0.98822
7		0.42076	0.72356	0.85480	0.92025	0.95518	0.97450	0.98538
8		0.29555	0.66381	0.82341	0.90301	0.94549	0.96898	0.98223
9		0.15586	0.59714	0.78839	0.88378	0.93468	0.96283	0.97870
10			0.52276	0.74932	0.86232	0.92263	0.95597	0.97477
11			0.43977	0.70573	0.83838	0.90917	0.94831	0.97038
12			0.34717	0.65709	0.81167	0.89416	0.93977	0.96548
13			0.24386	0.60283	0.78187	0.87741	0.93024	0.96002
14			0.12860	0.54228	0.74862	0.85872	0.91960	0.95393
15				0.47473	0.71152	0.83787	0.90774	0.94713
16				0.39937	0.67012	0.81461	0.89450	0.93954
17				0.31528	0.62394	0.78866	0.87973	0.93108
18				0.22146	0.57241	0.75970	0.86325	0.92164
19				0.11679	0.51493	0.72739	0.84487	0.91110
20					0.45078	0.69134	0.82435	0.89935
21					0.37922	0.65112	0.80147	0.88623
22					0.29937	0.60625	0.77593	0.87160
23					0.21029	0.55618	0.74744	0.85527
24					0.11090	0.50033	0.71565	0.83706
25						0.43800	0.68019	0.81673
26						0.36847	0.64062	0.79406
27						0.29089	0.59647	0.76876
28						0.20433	0.54721	0.74053
29						0.10775	0.49225	0.70904
30							0.43094	0.67390
31							0.36252	0.63469
32							0.28619	0.59095
33							0.20103	0.54215
34							0.10601	0.48770
35								0.42695
36								0.35917
37								0.28355
38								0.19917
39								0.10503
40								

TABLE A – 6 (*Continued*)

Percentage for 11.25 Percent

Age of Loan	Original Loan Term							
	5	10	15	20	25	30	35	40
1	0.84212	0.94260	0.97285	0.98588	0.99232	0.99573	0.99760	0.99864
2	0.66552	0.87839	0.94248	0.94008	0.98374	0.99096	0.99491	0.99712
3	0.46801	0.80658	0.90851	0.95241	0.97413	0.98562	0.99191	0.99542
4	0.24709	0.72626	0.87051	0.93265	0.96339	0.97965	0.98855	0.99352
5		0.63642	0.82802	0.91054	0.95138	0.97297	0.98480	0.99139
6		0.53594	0.78079	0.88582	0.93794	0.96551	0.98059	0.98901
7		0.42356	0.72733	0.85816	0.92291	0.95715	0.97589	0.98635
8		0.29785	0.66786	0.82723	0.90610	0.94781	0.97064	0.98337
9		0.15726	0.60136	0.79264	0.88730	0.93736	0.96476	0.98004
10			0.52697	0.75394	0.86627	0.92567	0.95818	0.97632
11			0.44377	0.71067	0.84275	0.91259	0.95083	0.97215
12			0.35071	0.66226	0.81644	0.89797	0.94260	0.96749
13			0.24663	0.60812	0.78701	0.88161	0.93340	0.96228
14			0.13021	0.54756	0.75410	0.86332	0.92310	0.95645
15				0.47983	0.71729	0.84286	0.91159	0.94993
16				0.40407	0.67611	0.81997	0.89872	0.94264
17				0.31934	0.63006	0.79437	0.88432	0.93448
18				0.22456	0.57855	0.76574	0.86821	0.92536
19				0.11856	0.52094	0.73372	0.85019	0.91516
20					0.45650	0.69790	0.83004	0.90374
21					0.38442	0.65784	0.80750	0.89098
22					0.30381	0.61303	0.78229	0.87670
23					0.21365	0.56291	0.75410	0.86073
24					0.11280	0.50686	0.72256	0.84287
25						0.44416	0.68729	0.82289
26						0.37404	0.64784	0.80055
27						0.29560	0.60371	0.77556
28						0.20787	0.55436	0.74761
29						0.10975	0.49915	0.71634
30							0.43741	0.68137
31							0.36835	0.64226
32							0.29111	0.59851
33							0.20471	0.54958
34							0.10808	0.49485
35								0.43364
36								0.36518
37								0.28860
38								0.20295
39								0.10715
40								

(*continued*)

TABLE A – 6 (*Continued*)

Percentage for 11.50 Percent

Age of Loan	Original Loan Term							
	5	*10*	*15*	*20*	*25*	*30*	*35*	*40*
1	0.84298	0.94336	0.97345	0.98632	0.99264	0.99596	0.99775	0.99874
2	0.66693	0.87986	0.94367	0.97099	0.98440	0.99142	0.99523	0.99733
3	0.46952	0.80865	0.91029	0.95379	0.97515	0.98634	0.99240	0.99575
4	0.24818	0.72881	0.87286	0.93451	0.96478	0.98064	0.98923	0.99397
5		0.63929	0.83089	0.91289	0.95315	0.97425	0.98568	0.99198
6		0.53891	0.78383	0.88865	0.94011	0.96708	0.98169	0.98975
7		0.42636	0.73106	0.86147	0.92250	0.95904	0.97722	0.98725
8		0.30016	0.67190	0.83099	0.90911	0.95003	0.97221	0.98445
9		0.15866	0.60556	0.79682	0.89073	0.93993	0.96659	0.98130
10			0.53117	0.75851	0.87012	0.92860	0.96029	0.97777
11			0.44777	0.71555	0.84702	0.91590	0.95323	0.97382
12			0.35425	0.66738	0.82111	0.90166	0.94531	0.96939
13			0.24940	0.61337	0.79206	0.88569	0.93643	0.96442
14			0.13183	0.55281	0.75949	0.86779	0.92647	0.95884
15				0.48490	0.72297	0.84771	0.91530	0.95259
16				0.40877	0.68203	0.82520	0.90278	0.94559
17				0.32340	0.63611	0.79997	0.88875	0.93773
18				0.22767	0.58463	0.77167	0.87301	0.92892
19				0.12034	0.52691	0.73993	0.85536	0.91904
20					0.46219	0.70436	0.83557	0.90797
21					0.38962	0.66446	0.81339	0.89555
22					0.30825	0.61973	0.78851	0.88162
23					0.21701	0.56958	0.76061	0.86601
24					0.11471	0.51334	0.72934	0.84850
25						0.45028	0.69427	0.82887
26						0.37958	0.65494	0.80686
27						0.30031	0.61085	0.78219
28						0.21142	0.56142	0.75452
29						0.11175	0.50599	0.72349
30							0.44383	0.68870
31							0.37415	0.64969
32							0.29601	0.60596
33							0.20839	0.55692
34							0.11015	0.50193
35								0.44028
36								0.37115
37								0.29363
38								0.20672
39								0.10927
40								

TABLE A – 6 (*Continued*)

Percentage for 11.75 Percent

Age of Loan	Original Loan Term							
	5	10	15	20	25	30	35	40
1	0.84385	0.94412	0.97404	0.98676	0.99295	0.99617	0.99789	0.99883
2	0.66833	0.88131	0.94485	0.97187	0.98503	0.99186	0.99553	0.99753
3	0.47104	0.81070	0.91205	0.95514	0.97613	0.98702	0.99286	0.99605
4	0.24927	0.73134	0.87517	0.93633	0.96612	0.98158	0.98987	0.99440
5		0.64213	0.83372	0.91519	0.95487	0.97547	0.98651	0.99254
6		0.54186	0.78713	0.89143	0.94222	0.96859	0.98273	0.99045
7		0.42916	0.73476	0.86472	0.92801	0.96086	0.97848	0.98810
8		0.30247	0.67590	0.83470	0.91203	0.95218	0.97371	0.98546
9		0.16007	0.60973	0.80095	0.89407	0.94242	0.96834	0.98249
10			0.53536	0.76302	0.87389	0.93144	0.96231	0.97915
11			0.45176	0.72038	0.85120	0.91911	0.95553	0.97540
12			0.35780	0.67245	0.82569	0.90524	0.94790	0.97118
13			0.25217	0.61858	0.79703	0.88966	0.93933	0.96644
14			0.13345	0.55802	0.76480	0.87214	0.92970	0.96112
15				0.48996	0.72858	0.85245	0.91888	0.95513
16				0.41345	0.68787	0.83031	0.90671	0.94840
17				0.32745	0.64210	0.80544	0.89303	0.94083
18				0.23079	0.59066	0.77747	0.87766	0.93233
19				0.12213	0.53284	0.74604	0.86037	0.92277
20					0.46785	0.71070	0.84095	0.91202
21					0.39479	0.67099	0.81911	0.89994
22					0.31267	0.62635	0.79457	0.88637
23					0.22037	0.57617	0.76698	0.87111
24					0.11662	0.51977	0.73597	0.85395
25						0.45637	0.70112	0.83467
26						0.38511	0.66194	0.81300
27						0.30500	0.61790	0.78864
28						0.21497	0.56840	0.76126
29						0.11376	0.51276	0.73048
30							0.45021	0.69589
31							0.37991	0.65700
32							0.30089	0.61329
33							0.21207	0.56416
34							0.11223	0.50893
35								0.44685
36								0.37708
37								0.29864
38								0.21048
39								0.11139
40								

(*continued*)

TABLE A-6 (*Continued*)

Percentage for 12.00 Percent

	Original Loan Term							
Age of Loan	5	10	15	20	25	30	35	40
1	0.84471	0.94487	0.97461	0.98718	0.99325	0.99637	0.99803	0.99892
2	0.66972	0.88274	0.94601	0.97273	0.98564	0.99228	0.99581	0.99771
3	0.47255	0.81274	0.91377	0.95646	0.97707	0.98767	0.99330	0.99634
4	0.25036	0.73386	0.87745	0.93811	0.96741	0.98248	0.99048	0.99480
5		0.64497	0.83652	0.91744	0.95653	0.97663	0.98730	0.99306
6		0.54482	0.79040	0.89415	0.94427	0.97004	0.98372	0.99110
7		0.43196	0.73844	0.86791	0.93045	0.96261	0.97968	0.98889
8		0.30478	0.67988	0.83834	0.91488	0.95424	0.97513	0.98641
9		0.16148	0.61389	0.80501	0.89733	0.94481	0.97001	0.98360
10			0.53954	0.76746	0.87756	0.93418	0.96423	0.98045
11			0.45575	0.72515	0.85529	0.92220	0.95772	0.97689
12			0.36134	0.67747	0.83018	0.90871	0.95039	0.97288
13			0.25496	0.62375	0.80189	0.89350	0.94212	0.96836
14			0.13508	0.56321	0.77002	0.87637	0.93281	0.96327
15				0.49499	0.73410	0.85706	0.92232	0.95754
16				0.41813	0.69363	0.83530	0.91049	0.95107
17				0.33151	0.64802	0.81078	0.89717	0.94379
18				0.23391	0.59664	0.78316	0.88215	0.93558
19				0.12393	0.53873	0.75203	0.86524	0.92633
20					0.47348	0.71695	0.84617	0.91591
21					0.39995	0.67742	0.82469	0.90417
22					0.31710	0.63288	0.80049	0.89094
23					0.22374	0.58269	0.77321	0.87603
24					0.11854	0.52614	0.74248	0.85923
25						0.46241	0.70784	0.84030
26						0.39060	0.66882	0.81897
27						0.30969	0.62484	0.79493
28						0.21851	0.57529	0.76784
29						0.11577	0.51946	0.73732
30							0.45654	0.70293
31							0.38564	0.66418
32							0.30576	0.62051
33							0.21574	0.57130
34							0.11430	0.51585
35								0.45337
36								0.38297
37								0.30363
38								0.21424
39								0.11351
40								

TABLE A – 6 *(Continued)*

Percentage for 12.25 Percent

	Original Loan Term							
Age of Loan	*5*	*10*	*15*	*20*	*25*	*30*	*35*	*40*
1	0.84559	0.94561	0.97518	0.98759	0.99354	0.99656	0.99815	0.99900
2	0.67112	0.88417	0.94715	0.97357	0.98623	0.99268	0.99607	0.99788
3	0.47406	0.81477	0.91548	0.95774	0.97799	0.98830	0.99371	0.99660
4	0.25146	0.73636	0.87970	0.93985	0.96867	0.98334	0.99105	0.99517
5		0.64780	0.83929	0.91965	0.95814	0.97775	0.98805	0.99354
6		0.54776	0.79364	0.89682	0.94625	0.97143	0.98465	0.99171
7		0.43475	0.74207	0.87104	0.93282	0.96429	0.98082	0.98964
8		0.30710	0.68382	0.84191	0.91765	0.95622	0.97648	0.98730
9		0.16289	0.61802	0.80901	0.90051	0.94711	0.97159	0.98465
10			0.54369	0.77185	0.88115	0.93682	0.96606	0.98167
11			0.45973	0.72987	0.85928	0.92520	0.95982	0.97829
12			0.36488	0.68245	0.83458	0.91207	0.95276	0.97448
13			0.25774	0.62888	0.80667	0.89723	0.94479	0.97018
14			0.13672	0.56836	0.77515	0.88047	0.93579	0.96532
15				0.50001	0.73954	0.86155	0.92562	0.95982
16				0.42279	0.69932	0.84016	0.91414	0.95362
17				0.33556	0.65388	0.81601	0.90116	0.94661
18				0.23703	0.60255	0.78872	0.88651	0.93869
19				0.12573	0.54457	0.75790	0.86995	0.92975
20					0.47908	0.72309	0.85125	0.91965
21					0.40509	0.68376	0.83012	0.90824
22					0.32152	0.63933	0.80626	0.89535
23					0.22711	0.58915	0.77930	0.88078
24					0.12047	0.53246	0.74884	0.86433
25						0.46842	0.71444	0.84575
26						0.39608	0.6755ε	0.82476
27						0.31436	0.63169	0.80105
28						0.22206	0.58210	0.77427
29						0.11779	0.52609	0.74401
30							0.46282	0.70983
31							0.39134	0.67122
32							0.31061	0.62761
33							0.21940	0.57835
34							0.11638	0.52269
35								0.45983
36								0.38882
37								0.30860
38								0.21799
39								0.11563
40								

(continued)

TABLE A−6 (*Continued*)

Percentage for 12.50 Percent

	Original Loan Term							
Age of Loan	5	10	15	20	25	30	35	40
1	0.84642	0.94634	0.97574	0.98799	0.99381	0.99675	0.99827	0.99908
2	0.67251	0.88558	0.94826	0.97439	0.98680	0.99306	0.99632	0.99803
3	0.47557	0.81677	0.91715	0.95899	0.97887	0.98889	0.99410	0.99685
4	0.25255	0.73886	0.88192	0.94155	0.96988	0.98417	0.99159	0.99551
5		0.65062	0.84202	0.92180	0.95970	0.97882	0.98875	0.99400
6		0.55070	0.79684	0.89944	0.94817	0.97276	0.98554	0.99228
7		0.43755	0.74568	0.87411	0.93512	0.96590	0.98189	0.99034
8		0.30942	0.68774	0.84543	0.92034	0.95813	0.97777	0.98813
9		0.16431	0.62213	0.81296	0.90361	0.94933	0.97310	0.98564
10			0.54784	0.77618	0.88465	0.93937	0.96781	0.98282
11			0.46370	0.73453	0.86319	0.92809	0.96182	0.97962
12			0.36843	0.68737	0.83888	0.91531	0.95504	0.97600
13			0.26054	0.63396	0.81136	0.90085	0.84735	0.97190
14			0.13836	0.57348	0.78019	0.88447	0.93866	0.96726
15				0.50500	0.74490	0.86591	0.92881	0.96200
16				0.42744	0.70493	0.84491	0.91765	0.95604
17				0.33962	0.65967	0.82112	0.90502	0.94930
18				0.24016	0.60841	0.79417	0.89072	0.94167
19				0.12754	0.55037	0.76367	0.87452	0.93302
20					0.48465	0.72912	0.85617	0.92323
21					0.41022	0.69000	0.83540	0.91214
22					0.32593	0.64570	0.81188	0.89959
23					0.23048	0.59553	0.78524	0.88537
24					0.12240	0.53871	0.75508	0.86927
25						0.47438	0.72092	0.85103
26						0.40153	0.68224	0.83039
27						0.31903	0.63843	0.80701
28						0.22560	0.58883	0.78053
29						0.11981	0.53266	0.75055
30							0.46904	0.71659
31							0.39701	0.67814
32							0.31544	0.63460
33							0.22306	0.58529
34							0.11846	0.52946
35								0.46623
36								0.39463
37								0.31354
38								0.22172
39								0.11775
40								

TABLE A–6 (*Continued*)

Percentage for 12.75 Percent

| | Original Loan Term | | | | | | | |
Age of Loan	5	10	15	20	25	30	35	40
1	0.84728	0.94707	0.97629	0.98838	0.99408	0.99692	0.99838	0.99915
2	0.67390	0.88698	0.94936	0.97519	0.98735	0.99343	0.99655	0.99818
3	0.47708	0.81877	0.91880	0.96021	0.97971	0.98946	0.99447	0.99708
4	0.25365	0.74133	0.88411	0.94321	0.97105	0.98495	0.99210	0.99584
5		0.65343	0.84472	0.92391	0.96121	0.97984	0.98942	0.99442
6		0.55363	0.80001	0.90200	0.95004	0.97403	0.98637	0.99281
7		0.44034	0.74925	0.87713	0.93736	0.96744	0.98292	0.99099
8		0.31174	0.69163	0.84889	0.92296	0.95996	0.97899	0.98892
9		0.16574	0.62622	0.81684	0.90662	0.95147	0.97453	0.98657
10			0.55196	0.78045	0.88807	0.94183	0.96947	0.98390
11			0.46767	0.73914	0.86701	0.93088	0.96373	0.98087
12			0.37197	0.69224	0.84310	0.91846	0.95721	0.97743
13			0.26333	0.63901	0.81596	0.90435	0.94981	0.97353
14			0.14000	0.57857	0.78515	0.88834	0.94140	0.96909
15				0.50997	0.75017	0.87016	0.93186	0.96406
16				0.43208	0.71046	0.84953	0.92104	0.95835
17				0.34367	0.66539	0.82610	0.90874	0.95187
18				0.24329	0.61422	0.79951	0.89479	0.94451
19				0.12935	0.55613	0.76932	0.87894	0.93615
20					0.49018	0.73505	0.86096	0.92666
21					0.14532	0.69614	0.84054	0.91590
22					0.33033	0.65197	0.81736	0.90367
23					0.23386	0.60184	0.79105	0.88979
24					0.12433	0.54492	0.76118	0.87404
25						0.48030	0.72727	0.85615
26						0.40695	0.68878	0.83585
27						0.32367	0.64508	0.81280
28						0.22914	0.59547	0.78664
29						0.12183	0.53915	0.75693
30							0.47522	0.72321
31							0.40264	0.68493
32							0.32025	0.64148
33							0.22672	0.59215
34							0.12054	0.53614
35								0.47257
36								0.40039
37								0.31846
38								0.22545
39								0.11987
40								

(*continued*)

TABLE A–6 (*Continued*)

Percentage for 13.00 Percent

	Original Loan Term							
Age of Loan	*5*	*10*	*15*	*20*	*25*	*30*	*35*	*40*
1	0.84813	0.94779	0.97682	0.98876	0.99433	0.99708	0.99849	0.99921
2	0.67529	0.88837	0.95045	0.97596	0.98788	0.99377	0.99677	0.99832
3	0.47859	0.82075	0.92043	0.96140	0.98053	0.99000	0.99481	0.99730
4	0.25474	0.74380	0.88627	0.94483	0.97218	0.98570	0.99258	0.99614
5		0.65622	0.84739	0.92597	0.96267	0.98082	0.99005	0.99481
6		0.55656	0.80315	0.90451	0.95184	0.97526	0.98717	0.99331
7		0.44314	0.75280	0.88008	0.93952	0.96893	0.98388	0.99160
8		0.31406	0.69550	0.85229	0.92551	0.96172	0.98015	0.98965
9		0.16717	0.63029	0.82065	0.90955	0.96353	0.97590	0.98744
10			0.55608	0.78466	0.89140	0.94420	0.97106	0.98492
11			0.47162	0.74369	0.87074	0.93358	0.96555	0.98205
12			0.37551	0.69707	0.84723	0.92150	0.95929	0.97878
13			0.26613	0.64401	0.82047	0.90775	0.95215	0.97506
14			0.14166	0.58363	0.79002	0.89211	0.94404	0.97084
15				0.51491	0.75536	0.87430	0.93480	0.96602
16				0.43671	0.71592	0.85403	0.92429	0.96054
17				0.34771	0.67104	0.83097	0.91233	0.95431
18				0.24643	0.61996	0.80473	0.89872	0.94722
19				0.13117	0.56184	0.77486	0.88323	0.93914
20					0.49568	0.74087	0.86560	0.92996
21					0.42040	0.70219	0.84554	0.91950
22					0.33473	0.65817	0.82270	0.90760
23					0.23723	0.60807	0.79672	0.89406
24					0.12627	0.55106	0.76715	0.87865
25						0.48618	0.73350	0.86111
26						0.41234	0.69520	0.84115
27						0.32831	0.65162	0.81844
28						0.23268	0.60202	0.79259
29						0.12385	0.54558	0.76317
30							0.48134	0.72970
31							0.40824	0.69160
32							0.32504	0.64824
33							0.23036	0.59890
34							0.12262	0.54275
35								0.47884
36								0.40612
37								0.32336
38								0.22917
39								0.12198
40								

TABLE A-7
Annual Percentage Rate (APR)
(term of loan: 20 years)

Contract Rate	Percentage Points Charged							
	0.50	*1.00*	*1.50*	*2.00*	*2.50*	*3.00*	*3.50*	*4.00*
7.00	7.0648	7.1301	7.1960	7.2623	7.3291	7.3965	7.4644	7.5329
7.25	7.3155	7.3814	7.4479	7.5149	7.5824	7.6505	7.7191	7.7882
7.50	7.5661	7.6328	7.6999	7.7676	7.8358	7.9045	7.9738	8.0437
7.75	7.8168	7.8841	7.9519	8.0203	8.0892	8.1586	8.2286	8.2992
8.00	8.0675	8.1354	8.2040	8.2730	8.3426	8.4128	8.4835	8.5548
8.25	8.3181	8.3868	8.4560	8.5258	8.5961	8.6669	8.7384	8.8104
8.50	8.5688	8.6382	8.7081	8.7786	8.8496	8.9212	8.9934	9.0661
8.75	8.8195	8.8896	8.9602	9.0314	9.1031	9.1755	9.2484	9.3219
9.00	9.0702	9.1410	9.2123	9.2842	9.3567	9.4298	9.5035	9.5778
9.25	9.3209	9.3924	9.4645	9.5371	9.6104	9.6842	9.7586	9.8337
9.50	9.5717	9.6439	9.7167	9.7901	9.8641	9.9386	10.0138	10.0897
9.75	9.8224	9.8953	9.9689	10.0430	10.1178	10.1931	10.2691	10.3457
10.00	10.0731	10.1468	10.2211	10.2960	10.3715	10.4477	10.5244	10.6019
10.25	10.3239	10.3983	10.4734	10.5491	10.6253	10.7023	10.7798	10.8580
10.50	10.5746	10.6498	10.7257	10.8021	10.8792	10.9569	11.0353	11.1143
10.75	10.8254	10.9014	10.9780	11.0552	11.1331	11.2116	11.2908	11.3706
11.00	11.0761	11.1529	11.2303	11.3083	11.3870	11.4663	11.5464	11.6270
11.25	11.3269	11.4045	11.4827	11.5615	11.6410	11.7211	11.8020	11.8835
11.50	11.5777	11.6560	11.7350	11.8147	11.8950	11.9760	12.0577	12.1400
11.75	11.8285	11.9076	11.9874	12.0679	12.1490	12.2309	12.3134	12.3966
12.00	12.0793	12.1592	12.2399	12.3212	12.4031	12.4858	12.5692	12.6533
12.25	12.3301	12.4109	12.4923	12.5744	12.6573	12.7408	12.8250	12.9100
12.50	12.5809	12.6625	12.7448	12.8278	12.9114	12.9958	13.0810	13.1668
12.75	12.8317	12.9142	12.9973	13.0811	13.1657	13.2509	13.3369	13.4237
13.00	13.0826	13.1658	13.2498	13.3345	13.4199	13.5061	13.5929	13.6806
13.25	13.3334	13.4175	13.5024	13.5879	13.6742	13.7612	13.8470	13.9376
13.50	13.5843	13.6692	13.7549	13.8413	13.9285	14.0165	14.1052	14.1946
13.75	13.8351	13.9209	14.0075	14.0948	14.1829	14.2717	14.3613	14.4518
14.00	14.0860	14.1727	14.2601	14.3483	14.4373	14.5270	14.6176	14.7089
14.25	14.3368	14.4244	14.5128	14.6019	14.6917	14.7824	14.8739	14.9662
14.50	14.5877	14.6762	14.7654	14.8554	14.9462	15.0378	15.1302	15.2235
14.75	14.8386	14.9280	15.0181	15.1090	15.2007	15.2933	15.3866	15.4808
15.00	15.0895	15.1798	15.2708	15.3626	15.4553	15.5488	15.6431	15.7383
15.25	15.3404	15.4316	15.5235	15.6163	15.7099	15.8043	15.8996	15.9957
15.50	15.5913	15.6834	15.7763	15.8700	15.9645	16.0599	16.1562	16.2533
15.75	15.8422	15.9352	16.0290	16.1237	16.2192	16.3156	16.4128	16.5109
16.00	16.0931	16.1871	16.2818	16.3774	16.4739	16.5712	16.6694	16.7685
16.25	16.3441	16.4389	16.5346	16.6312	16.7286	16.8269	16.9261	17.0263
16.50	16.5950	16.6908	16.7875	16.8850	16.9834	17.0827	17.1829	17.2840
16.75	16.8459	16.9427	17.0403	17.1388	17.2382	17.3385	17.4397	17.5419

(continued)

TABLE A-7 (*Continued*)

(term of loan: 20 years)

Contract Rate	Percentage Points Charged							
	4.50	*5.00*	*5.50*	*6.00*	*6.50*	*7.00*	*7.50*	*8.00*
7.00	7.6018	7.6714	7.7415	7.8121	7.8834	7.9552	8.0276	8.1007
7.25	7.8579	7.9282	7.9990	8.0704	8.1424	8.2149	8.2881	8.3619
7.50	8.1141	8.1850	8.2566	8.3287	8.4015	8.4748	8.5488	8.6233
7.75	8.3703	8.4420	8.5143	8.5872	8.6607	8.7348	8.8095	8.8849
8.00	8.6266	8.6991	8.7721	8.8458	8.9200	8.9949	9.0704	9.1466
8.25	8.8830	8.9562	9.0300	9.1044	9.1795	9.2551	9.3314	9.4084
8.50	9.1395	9.2134	9.2880	9.3632	9.4390	9.5155	9.5926	9.6704
8.75	9.3960	9.4707	9.5461	9.6221	9.6987	9.7760	9.8539	9.9325
9.00	9.6526	9.7281	9.8043	9.8811	9.9858	10.0366	10.1154	10.1948
9.25	9.9093	9.9856	10.0626	10.1402	10.2184	10.2973	10.3769	10.4572
9.50	10.1661	10.2432	10.3210	10.3994	10.4784	10.5582	10.6386	10.7198
9.75	10.4230	10.5009	10.5794	10.6587	10.7386	10.8192	10.9005	10.9825
10.00	10.6799	10.7586	10.8380	10.9181	10.9988	11.0803	11.1624	11.2453
10.25	10.9369	11.0165	11.0967	11.1776	11.2592	11.3415	11.4246	11.5083
10.50	11.1940	11.2744	11.3554	11.4372	11.5197	11.6029	11.6868	11.7715
10.75	11.4512	11.5324	11.6143	11.6969	11.7803	11.8644	11.9492	12.0347
11.00	11.7084	11.7905	11.8733	11.9568	12.0410	12.1260	12.2117	12.2982
11.25	11.9657	12.0487	12.1323	12.2167	12.3018	12.3877	12.4743	12.5617
11.50	12.2231	12.3069	12.3914	12.4767	12.5627	12.6495	12.7371	12.8254
11.75	12.4806	12.5653	12.6507	12.7369	12.8238	12.9115	13.0000	13.0893
12.00	12.7381	12.8237	12.9100	12.9971	13.0849	13.1736	13.2630	13.3533
12.25	12.9957	13.0822	13.1694	13.2574	13.3462	13.4358	13.5262	13.6174
12.50	13.2534	13.3408	13.4289	13.5179	13.6076	13.6981	13.7895	13.8817
12.75	13.5112	13.5995	13.6885	13.7784	13.8691	13.9606	14.0529	14.1461
13.00	13.7690	13.8582	13.9482	14.0390	14.1307	14.2231	14.3164	14.4106
13.25	14.0269	14.1171	14.2080	14.2998	14.3924	14.4858	14.5801	14.6783
13.50	14.2849	14.3760	14.1679	14.5606	14.6542	14.7486	14.8439	14.9401
13.75	14.5430	14.6350	14.7278	14.8215	14.9161	15.0115	15.1078	15.2050
14.00	14.8011	14.8941	14.9879	15.0826	15.1781	15.2745	15.3719	15.4701
14.25	15.0593	15.1532	15.2480	15.3437	15.4402	15.5377	15.6360	15.7353
14.50	15.3175	15.4125	15.5082	15.6049	15.7025	15.8009	15.9003	16.0006
14.75	15.5759	15.6718	15.7686	15.8662	15.9648	16.0643	16.1647	16.2661
15.00	15.8343	15.9312	16.0289	16.1276	16.2272	16.3278	16.4292	16.5317
15.25	16.0927	16.1906	16.2894	16.3891	16.4898	16.5913	16.6939	16.7974
15.50	16.3513	16.4502	16.5500	16.6507	16.7524	16.8550	16.9586	17.0632
15.75	16.6099	16.7098	16.8106	16.9124	17.0151	17.1188	17.2235	17.3292
16.00	16.8685	16.9695	17.0713	17.1742	17.2779	17.2827	17.4885	17.5953
16.25	17.1273	17.2292	17.3321	17.4360	17.5409	17.6467	17.7536	17.8615
16.50	17.3861	17.4891	17.5930	17.6980	17.8039	17.9108	18.0188	18.1278
16.75	17.6449	17.7490	17.8540	17.9600	18.0670	18.1750	18.2841	18.3942

TABLE A – 7 (*Continued*)
(term of loan: 20 years)

Contract Rate	Percentage Points Charged							
	8.50	*9.00*	*9.50*	*10.00*	*10.50*	*11.00*	*11.50*	*12.00*
7.00	8.1743	8.2486	8.3235	8.3990	8.4752	8.5521	8.6296	8.7078
7.25	8.4363	8.5114	8.5871	8.6634	8.7405	8.8181	8.8965	8.9756
7.50	8.6985	8.7744	8.8509	8.9280	9.0059	9.0844	9.1636	9.2435
7.75	8.9609	9.0375	9.1148	9.1928	9.2715	9.3509	9.4309	9.5117
8.00	9.2234	9.3008	9.3790	9.4578	9.5373	9.6175	9.6985	9.7801
8.25	9.4860	9.5643	9.6433	9.7230	9.8033	9.8844	9.9662	10.0488
8.50	9.7488	9.8280	9.9078	9.9883	10.0696	10.1515	10.2342	10.3177
8.75	10.0118	10.0918	10.1725	10.2539	10.3360	10.4188	10.5024	10.5868
9.00	10.2749	10.3558	10.4373	10.5195	10.6026	10.6863	10.7709	10.8561
9.25	10.5382	10.6199	10.7023	10.7855	10.8694	10.9541	11.0395	11.1257
9.50	10.8016	10.8842	10.9675	11.0516	11.1364	11.2220	11.3084	11.3955
9.75	11.0652	11.1487	11.2329	11.3179	11.4036	11.4901	11.5774	11.6656
10.00	11.3290	11.4133	11.4984	11.5843	11.6710	11.7585	11.8467	11.9358
10.25	11.5928	11.6781	11.7642	11.8510	11.9386	12.0270	12.1163	12.2063
10.50	11.8569	11.9431	12.0301	12.1178	12.2064	12.2958	12.3860	12.4770
10.75	12.1211	12.2082	12.2961	12.3848	12.4774	12.5647	12.6559	12.7480
11.00	12.3854	12.4735	12.5624	12.6520	12.7425	12.8339	12.9261	13.0192
11.25	12.6499	12.7390	12.8288	12.9194	13.0109	13.1033	13.1965	13.2906
11.50	12.9146	13.0046	13.0954	13.1870	13.2795	13.3728	13.4671	13.5622
11.75	13.1794	13.2703	13.3621	13.4547	13.5482	13.6426	13.7379	13.8340
12.00	13.4444	13.5363	13.6290	13.7227	13.8172	13.9126	14.0089	14.1061
12.25	13.7095	13.8024	13.8961	13.9908	14.0863	14.1827	14.2801	14.3784
12.50	13.9747	14.0686	14.1634	14.2590	14.3556	14.4531	14.5515	14.6509
12.75	14.2401	14.3350	14.4308	14.5275	14.6251	14.7237	14.8232	17.9236
13.00	14.5056	14.6016	14.6984	14.7961	14.8948	14.9944	15.0950	15.1966
13.25	14.7713	14.8683	14.9661	15.0649	15.1647	15.2654	15.3670	15.4697
13.50	15.0371	15.1351	15.2341	15.3339	15.4347	15.5365	15.6393	15.7431
13.75	15.3031	15.4022	15.5021	15.6031	15.7050	15.8079	15.9117	16.0167
14.00	15.5692	15.6693	15.7704	15.8724	15.9754	16.0794	16.1844	16.2905
14.25	15.8355	15.9366	16.0388	16.1419	16.2460	16.3511	16.4572	16.5644
14.50	16.1019	16.2041	16.3073	16.4115	16.5167	16.6230	16.7303	16.8386
14.75	16.3684	16.4717	16.5760	16.6813	16.7877	16.8951	17.0035	17.1131
15.00	16.6351	16.7395	16.8449	16.9513	17.0588	17.1673	17.2769	17.3877
15.25	16.9019	17.0074	17.1139	17.2215	17.3301	17.4398	17.5506	17.6625
15.50	17.1688	17.2754	17.3831	17.4918	17.6015	17.7124	17.8244	17.9375
15.75	17.4359	17.5436	17.6524	17.7622	17.8732	17.9852	18.0984	18.2127
16.00	17.7031	17.8119	17.9218	18.0328	18.1450	18.2582	18.3725	18.4881
16.25	17.9704	18.0804	18.1915	18.3036	18.4169	18.5313	18.6469	18.7636
16.50	18.2378	18.3490	18.4612	18.5746	18.6890	18.8046	18.9214	19.0394
16.75	18.5054	18.6177	18.7311	18.8456	18.9613	19.0781	19.1961	19.3154

(*continued*)

TABLE A–7 (*Continued*)

(term of loan: 25 years)

Contract Rate	Percentage Points Charged							
	0.50	*1.00*	*1.50*	*2.00*	*2.50*	*3.00*	*3.50*	*4.00*
7.00	7.0556	7.1117	7.1682	7.2251	7.2825	7.3404	7.3987	7.4575
7.25	7.3063	7.3631	7.4203	7.4780	7.5361	7.5947	7.6538	7.7133
7.50	7.5570	7.6145	7.6725	7.7309	7.7897	7.8491	7.9089	7.9693
7.75	7.8078	7.8660	7.9246	7.9838	8.0434	8.1036	8.1642	8.2253
8.00	8.0585	8.1174	8.1769	8.2368	8.2972	8.3581	8.4195	8.4814
8.25	8.3092	8.3689	8.4291	8.4898	8.5510	8.6127	8.6749	8.7376
8.50	8.5600	8.6205	8.6814	8.7429	8.8049	8.8673	8.9304	8.9939
8.75	8.8107	8.8720	8.9337	8.9960	9.0588	9.1221	9.1859	9.2503
9.00	9.0615	9.1236	9.1861	9.2491	9.3127	9.3768	9.4415	9.5067
9.25	9.3123	9.3751	9.4385	9.5023	9.5667	9.6317	9.6972	9.7632
9.50	9.5631	9.6267	9.6909	9.7556	9.8208	9.8866	9.9529	10.0199
9.75	9.8139	9.8783	9.9433	10.0088	10.0749	10.1416	10.2088	10.2766
10.00	10.0647	10.1300	10.1958	10.2622	10.3291	10.3966	10.4647	10.5333
10.25	10.3155	10.3816	10.4483	10.5155	10.5833	10.6517	10.7206	10.7902
10.50	10.5664	10.6333	10.7008	10.7689	10.8376	10.9068	10.9767	11.0471
10.75	10.8172	10.8850	10.9534	11.0223	11.0919	11.1620	11.2328	11.3042
11.00	11.0681	11.1367	11.2060	11.2758	11.3462	11.4173	11.4890	11.5613
11.25	11.3189	11.3885	11.4586	11.5293	11.6006	11.6726	11.7452	11.8184
11.50	11.5698	11.6402	11.7112	11.7828	11.8551	11.9280	12.0015	12.0757
11.75	11.8207	11.8920	11.9639	12.0364	12.1096	12.1834	12.2579	12.3330
12.00	12.0716	12.1438	12.2166	12.2900	12.3641	12.4389	12.5143	12.5904
12.25	12.3225	12.3956	12.4693	12.5437	12.6187	12.6945	12.7708	12.8479
12.50	12.5734	12.6474	12.7221	12.7974	12.8734	12.9501	13.0274	13.1055
12.75	12.8243	12.8992	12.9748	13.0511	13.1281	13.2057	13.2841	13.3631
13.00	13.0752	13.1511	13.2276	13.3049	13.3828	13.4614	13.5408	13.6208
13.25	13.3262	13.4030	13.4805	13.5587	13.6376	13.7172	13.7975	13.8786
13.50	13.5771	13.6549	13.7333	13.8125	13.8924	13.9730	14.0544	14.1365
13.75	13.8280	13.9068	13.9862	14.0664	14.1473	14.2289	14.3112	14.3944
14.00	14.0790	14.1587	14.2391	14.3203	14.4022	14.4848	14.5682	14.6524
14.25	14.3300	14.4106	14.4921	14.5742	14.6571	14.7408	14.8252	14.9104
14.50	14.5809	14.6626	14.7450	14.8282	14.9121	14.9968	15.0822	15.1658
14.75	14.8319	14.9146	14.9980	15.0822	15.1671	15.2528	15.3394	15.4267
15.00	15.0829	15.1666	15.2510	15.3362	15.4222	15.5090	15.5965	15.6849
15.25	15.3339	15.4186	15.5040	15.5902	15.6773	15.7651	15.8538	15.9433
15.50	15.5849	15.6706	15.7571	15.8443	15.9324	16.0213	16.1110	16.2016
15.75	15.8359	15.9226	16.0101	16.0985	16.1876	16.2776	16.3684	16.4601
16.00	16.0869	16.1747	16.2632	16.3526	16.4428	16.5339	16.6258	16.7185
16.25	16.3380	16.4267	16.5163	16.6068	16.6980	16.7902	16.8832	16.9771
16.50	16.5890	16.6788	16.7695	16.8610	16.9533	17.0466	17.1407	17.2357
16.75	16.8400	16.9309	17.0226	17.1152	17.2086	17.3030	17.3982	17.4944

TABLE A-7 (*Continued*)
(term of loan: 25 years)

Contract Rate	Percentage Points Charged							
	4.50	*5.00*	*5.50*	*6.00*	*6.50*	*7.00*	*7.50*	*8.00*
7.00	7.5168	7.5766	7.6368	7.6976	7.7589	7.8207	7.8831	7.9459
7.25	7.7734	7.8340	7.8950	7.9566	8.0187	8.0813	8.1445	8.2082
7.50	8.0301	8.0915	8.1533	8.2157	8.2786	8.3421	8.4061	8.4707
7.75	8.2869	8.3491	8.4118	8.4750	8.5387	8.6030	8.6679	8.7333
8.00	8.5439	8.6068	8.6703	8.7344	8.7989	8.8641	8.9298	8.9961
8.25	8.8009	8.8647	8.9290	8.9939	9.0593	9.1253	9.1919	9.2591
8.50	9.0580	9.1226	9.1878	9.2535	9.3198	9.3867	9.4542	9.5223
8.75	9.3152	9.3806	9.4467	9.5133	9.5805	9.6483	9.7167	9.7856
9.00	9.5725	9.6388	9.7057	9.7732	9.8413	9.9100	9.9793	10.0492
9.25	9.8299	9.8971	9.9649	10.0332	10.1022	10.1718	10.2420	10.3129
9.50	10.0873	10.1554	10.2241	10.2934	10.3633	10.4338	10.5050	10.5768
9.75	10.3449	10.4139	10.4835	10.5537	10.6245	10.6960	10.7681	10.8408
10.00	10.6026	10.6725	10.7430	10.8141	10.8859	10.9583	11.0313	11.1051
10.25	10.8604	10.9312	11.0026	11.0746	11.1474	11.2207	11.2948	11.3695
10.50	11.1182	11.1899	11.2623	11.3353	11.4090	11.4833	11.5583	11.6340
10.75	11.3762	11.4488	11.5221	11.5961	11.6707	11.7461	11.8221	11.8988
11.00	11.6342	11.7078	11.7821	11.8570	11.9326	12.0089	12.0860	12.1637
11.25	11.8923	11.9669	12.0421	12.1180	12.1947	12.2720	12.3500	12.4288
11.50	12.1505	12.2261	12.3023	12.3792	12.4568	12.5351	12.6142	12.6940
11.75	12.4088	12.4854	12.5626	12.6405	12.7191	12.7985	12.8786	12.9594
12.00	12.6672	12.7447	12.8229	12.9019	12.9815	13.0619	13.1431	13.2250
12.25	12.9257	13.0042	13.0834	13.1634	13.2440	13.3255	13.4077	13.4907
12.50	13.1843	13.2638	13.3440	13.4250	13.5067	13.5892	13.6725	13.7566
12.75	13.4429	13.5234	13.6047	13.6867	13.7695	13.8531	13.9374	14.0226
13.00	13.7016	13.7832	13.8655	13.9485	14.0324	14.1171	14.2025	14.2888
13.25	13.9604	14.0430	14.1264	14.2105	14.2954	14.3812	14.4677	14.5551
13.50	14.2193	14.3029	14.3873	14.4726	14.5586	14.6454	14.7331	14.8216
13.75	14.4783	14.5629	14.6484	14.7347	14.8218	14.9098	14.9986	15.0882
14.00	14.7373	14.8230	14.9096	14.9970	15.0852	15.1743	15.2642	15.3550
14.25	14.9964	15.0832	15.1709	15.2594	15.3487	15.4389	15.5300	15.6219
14.50	15.2556	15.3435	15.4322	15.5218	15.6123	15.7036	15.7958	15.8890
14.75	15.5149	15.6039	15.6937	15.7844	15.8760	15.9685	16.0618	16.1561
15.00	15.7742	15.8643	15.9552	16.0471	16.1398	16.2334	16.3280	16.4235
15.25	16.0336	16.1248	16.2169	16.3098	16.4037	16.4985	16.5942	16.6909
15.50	16.2931	16.3854	16.4786	16.5727	16.6677	16.7437	16.8606	16.9585
15.75	16.5526	16.6461	16.7404	16.8357	16.9319	17.0290	17.1271	17.2262
16.00	16.8122	16.9068	17.0023	17.0987	17.1961	17.2944	17.3937	17.4940
16.25	17.0719	17.1676	17.2642	17.3618	17.4604	17.5599	17.6604	17.7620
16.50	17.3316	17.4285	17.5263	17.6251	17.7248	17.8255	17.9273	18.0300
16.75	17.5914	17.6894	17.7884	17.8884	17.9893	18.0912	18.1942	18.2982

(*continued*)

TABLE A−7 (*Continued*)
(term of loan: 25 years)

Contract Rate	Percentage Points Charged							
	8.50	*9.00*	*9.50*	*10.00*	*10.50*	*11.00*	*11.50*	*12.00*
7.00	8.0094	8.0733	8.1379	8.2030	8.2687	8.3349	8.4018	8.4693
7.25	8.2725	8.3373	8.4027	8.4687	8.5353	8.6024	8.6702	8.7386
7.50	8.5358	8.6015	8.6678	8.7347	8.8021	8.8702	8.9389	9.0083
7.75	8.7993	8.8659	8.9331	9.0008	9.0692	9.1383	9.2079	9.2782
8.00	9.0630	9.1305	9.1986	9.2673	9.3366	9.4065	9.4771	9.5484
8.25	9.3269	9.3953	9.4643	9.5339	9.6042	9.6751	9.7467	9.8189
8.50	9.5910	9.6603	9.7302	9.8008	9.8720	9.9439	10.0165	10.0897
8.75	9.8553	9.9255	9.9964	10.0679	10.1401	10.2130	10.2865	10.3608
9.00	10.1197	10.1909	10.2628	10.3353	10.4084	10.4823	10.5568	10.6321
9.25	10.3844	10.4565	10.5293	10.6028	10.6770	10.7519	10.8274	10.9037
9.50	10.6492	10.7223	10.7961	10.8706	10.9458	11.0217	11.0983	11.1756
9.75	10.9143	10.9884	11.0632	11.1386	11.2148	11.2918	11.3694	11.4478
10.00	11.1795	11.2546	11.3304	11.4069	11.4841	11.5621	11.6408	11.7203
10.25	11.4449	11.5210	11.5978	11.6753	11.7536	11.8327	11.9125	11.9930
10.50	11.7105	11.7876	11.8654	11.9440	12.0234	12.1035	12.1844	12.2660
10.75	11.9762	12.0544	12.1333	12.2129	12.2933	12.3745	12.4565	12.5393
11.00	12.2422	12.3214	12.4013	12.4820	12.5635	12.6458	12.7289	12.8128
11.25	12.5083	12.5885	12.6696	12.7514	12.8340	12.9174	13.0016	13.0866
11.50	12.7746	12.8559	12.9380	13.0209	13.1046	13.1891	13.2745	13.3607
11.75	13.0410	13.1235	13.2066	13.2907	13.3755	13.4611	13.5476	13.6350
12.00	13.3077	13.3912	13.4755	13.5606	13.6466	13.7334	13.8210	13.9096
12.25	13.5745	13.6591	13.7445	13.8308	13.9179	14.0058	14.0947	14.1844
12.50	13.8415	13.9272	14.0137	14.1011	14.1894	14.2785	14.3685	14.4595
12.75	14.1086	14.1954	14.2831	14.3717	14.4611	14.5514	14.6426	14.7348
13.00	14.3759	14.4639	14.5527	14.6424	14.7330	14.8245	17.9169	15.0103
13.25	14.6434	14.7325	14.8225	17.9134	15.0051	15.0979	15.1915	15.2861
13.50	14.9110	15.0013	15.0924	15.1845	15.2775	15.3714	15.4663	15.5621
13.75	15.1788	15.2702	15.3625	15.4558	15.5500	15.6451	15.7413	15.8384
14.00	15.4467	15.5393	15.6328	15.7273	15.8227	15.9191	16.0165	16.1148
14.25	15.7148	15.8086	15.9033	15.9990	16.0956	16.1933	16.2919	16.3915
14.50	15.9830	16.0780	16.1739	16.2708	16.3687	16.4676	16.5675	16.6685
14.75	16.2514	16.3476	16.4447	16.5429	16.6420	16.7421	16.8433	16.9456
15.00	16.5199	16.6173	16.7157	16.8151	16.9155	17.0169	17.1194	17.2229
15.25	16.7886	16.8872	16.9868	17.0874	17.1891	17.2918	17.3956	17.5005
15.50	17.0573	17.1572	17.2581	17.3600	17.4629	17.5669	17.6720	17.7782
15.75	17.3263	17.4274	17.5295	17.6327	17.7369	17.8422	17.9486	18.0561
16.00	17.5953	17.6977	17.8011	17.9055	18.0110	18.1177	18.2254	18.3343
16.25	17.8645	17.9681	18.0728	18.1785	18.2853	18.3933	18.5024	18.6126
16.50	18.1338	18.2387	18.3446	18.4517	18.5598	18.6691	18.7795	18.8911
16.75	18.4033	18.5094	18.6166	18.7250	18.8344	18.9450	19.0568	19.1698

T A B L E   A − 7 (*Continued*)

(term of loan: 30 years)

Contract Rate	Percentage Points Charged							
	0.50	*1.00*	*1.50*	*2.00*	*2.50*	*3.00*	*3.50*	*4.00*
7.00	7.0497	7.0999	7.1504	7.2014	7.2527	7.3045	7.3568	7.4094
7.25	7.3005	7.3514	7.4027	7.4545	7.5066	7.5592	7.6123	7.6658
7.50	7.5513	7.6029	7.6551	7.7076	7.7606	7.8140	7.8679	7.9222
7.75	7.8020	7.8545	7.9074	7.9608	8.0146	8.0688	8.1236	8.1787
8.00	8.0528	8.1061	8.1599	8.2140	8.2687	8.3238	8.3793	8.4354
8.25	8.3037	8.3578	8.4123	8.4673	8.5228	8.5788	8.6352	8.6921
8.50	8.5545	8.6094	8.6648	8.7207	8.7770	8.8338	8.8911	8.9489
8.75	8.8053	8.8611	8.9173	8.9740	9.0313	9.0890	9.1472	9.2059
9.00	9.0561	9.1128	9.1699	9.2275	9.2856	9.3442	9.4033	9.4629
9.25	9.3070	9.3645	9.4225	9.4810	9.5399	9.5994	9.6595	9.7200
9.50	9.5579	9.6162	9.6751	9.7345	9.7944	9.8548	9.9157	9.9772
9.75	9.8087	9.8680	9.9278	9.9880	10.0489	10.1102	10.1721	10.2345
10.00	10.0596	10.1198	10.1805	10.2417	10.3034	10.3657	10.4285	10.4919
10.25	10.3105	10.3716	10.4332	10.4953	10.5580	10.6212	10.6850	10.7494
10.50	10.5614	10.6234	10.6859	10.7490	10.8127	10.8769	10.9416	11.0070
10.75	10.8124	10.8753	10.9387	11.0028	11.0674	11.1325	11.1983	11.2647
11.00	11.0633	11.1271	11.1916	11.2565	11.3221	11.3883	11.4551	11.5224
11.25	11.3142	11.3790	11.4444	11.5104	11.5769	11.6441	11.7119	11.7803
11.50	11.5652	11.6309	11.6973	11.7642	11.8318	11.9000	11.9688	12.0382
11.75	11.8161	11.8829	11.9502	12.0182	12.0867	12.1559	12.2257	12.2962
12.00	12.0671	12.1348	12.2032	12.2721	12.3417	12.4119	12.4828	12.5543
12.25	12.3181	12.3868	12.4561	12.5261	12.5967	12.6679	12.7399	12.8124
12.50	12.5691	12.6388	12.7091	12.7801	12.8517	12.9240	12.9970	13.0707
12.75	12.8201	12.8908	12.9622	13.0342	13.1068	13.1802	13.2543	13.3290
13.00	13.0711	13.1428	13.2152	13.2883	13.3620	13.4364	13.5115	13.5874
13.25	13.3221	13.3949	13.4683	13.5424	13.6172	13.6927	13.7689	13.8458
13.50	13.5731	13.6469	13.7214	13.7966	13.8724	13.9490	14.0263	14.1044
13.75	13.8242	13.8990	13.9745	14.0508	14.1277	14.2054	14.2838	14.3630
14.00	14.0752	14.1511	14.2277	14.3050	14.3830	14.4618	14.5413	14.6216
14.25	14.3262	14.4032	14.4809	14.5593	14.6384	14.7183	14.7989	14.8804
14.50	14.5773	14.6553	14.7341	14.8135	14.8938	14.9748	15.0566	15.1392
14.75	14.8284	14.9075	14.9873	15.0679	15.1492	15.2314	15.3143	15.3980
15.00	15.0794	15.1596	15.2405	15.3222	15.4047	15.4880	15.5720	15.6569
15.25	15.3305	15.4118	15.4938	15.5766	15.6602	15.7446	15.8298	15.9159
15.50	15.5816	15.6639	15.7471	15.8310	15.9158	16.0013	16.0877	16.1749
15.75	15.8327	15.9161	16.0004	16.0855	16.1713	16.2580	16.3456	16.4340
16.00	16.0838	16.1683	16.2537	16.3399	16.4269	16.5148	16.6036	16.6932
16.25	16.3349	16.4206	16.5071	16.5944	16.6826	16.7716	16.8615	16.9523
16.50	16.5860	16.6728	16.7604	16.8489	16.9383	17.0285	17.1196	17.2116
16.75	16.8371	16.9250	17.0138	17.1035	17.1940	17.2854	17.3777	17.4709

(*continued*)

TABLE A – 7 (*Continued*)

(term of loan: 30 years)

Contract Rate	Percentage Points Charged							
	4.50	*5.00*	*5.50*	*6.00*	*6.50*	*7.00*	*7.50*	*8.00*
7.00	7.4625	7.5161	7.5701	7.6246	7.6796	7.7350	7.7910	7.8474
7.25	7.7197	7.7741	7.8290	7.8844	7.9402	7.9965	8.0534	8.1107
7.50	7.9770	8.0323	8.0880	8.1442	8.2010	8.2582	8.3159	8.3742
7.75	8.2344	8.2905	8.3472	8.4043	8.4619	8.5201	8.5787	8.6379
8.00	8.4919	8.5489	8.6065	8.6645	8.7230	8.7821	8.8417	8.9018
8.25	8.7495	8.8074	8.8659	8.9248	8.9843	9.0443	9.1049	9.1660
8.50	9.0073	9.0661	9.1254	9.1853	9.2457	9.3067	9.3682	9.4303
8.75	9.2651	9.3249	9.3851	9.4460	9.5074	9.5693	9.6318	9.6949
9.00	9.5231	9.5837	9.6450	9.7068	9.7691	9.8320	9.8955	9.9596
9.25	9.7811	9.8428	9.9050	9.9677	10.0310	10.0950	10.1595	10.2246
9.50	10.0393	10.1019	10.1651	10.2288	10.2931	10.3581	10.4236	10.4897
9.75	10.2976	10.3611	10.4253	10.4900	10.5554	10.6213	10.6879	10.7551
10.00	10.5559	10.6205	10.6856	10.7514	10.8178	10.8848	10.9524	11.0206
10.25	10.8144	10.8800	10.9461	11.0129	11.0803	11.1483	11.2170	11.2864
10.50	11.0730	11.1396	11.2067	11.2746	11.3430	11.4121	11.4819	11.5523
10.75	11.3317	11.3993	11.4675	11.5363	11.6059	11.6760	11.7469	11.8184
11.00	11.5904	11.6591	11.7283	11.7983	11.8688	11.9401	12.0120	12.0847
11.25	11.8493	11.9190	11.9893	12.0603	12.1320	12.2043	12.2774	12.3511
11.50	12.1083	12.1790	12.2504	12.3225	12.3952	12.4687	12.5429	12.6178
11.75	12.3673	12.4391	12.5116	12.5848	12.6586	12.7332	12.8085	12.8846
12.00	12.6265	12.6994	12.7729	12.8472	12.9222	12.9979	13.0743	13.1515
12.25	12.8857	12.9597	13.0344	13.1097	13.1859	13.2627	13.3403	13.4187
12.50	13.1450	13.2201	13.2959	13.3724	13.4497	13.5277	13.6064	13.6860
12.75	13.4044	13.4806	13.5575	13.6352	13.7136	13.7928	13.8727	13.9535
13.00	13.6639	13.7412	13.8193	13.8981	13.9776	14.0580	14.1391	14.2211
13.25	13.9235	14.0019	14.0811	14.1611	14.2418	14.3233	14.4057	14.4888
13.50	14.1832	14.2627	14.3431	14.4242	14.5061	14.5888	14.6724	14.7567
13.75	14.4429	14.5236	14.6051	14.6874	14.7705	14.8544	14.9392	15.0248
14.00	14.7027	14.7846	14.8672	14.9507	15.0350	15.1201	15.2061	15.2930
14.25	14.9626	15.0456	15.1294	15.2141	15.2996	15.3860	15.4732	15.5613
14.50	15.2225	15.3067	15.3917	15.4776	15.5643	15.6519	15.7404	15.8298
14.75	15.4826	15.5679	15.6541	15.7412	15.8292	15.9180	16.0077	16.0984
15.00	15.7426	15.8292	15.9166	16.0049	16.0941	16.1842	16.2752	16.3671
15.25	16.0028	16.0906	16.1792	16.2687	16.3591	16.4504	16.5427	16.6359
15.50	16.2630	16.3520	16.4418	16.5326	16.6242	16.7168	16.8104	16.9049
15.75	16.5233	16.6135	16.7045	16.7965	16.8894	16.9833	17.0781	17.1739
16.00	16.7836	16.8750	16.9673	17.0606	17.1547	17.2499	17.3460	17.4431
16.25	17.0440	17.1366	17.2302	17.3247	17.4201	17.5165	17.6139	17.7124
16.50	17.3045	17.3983	17.4931	17.5889	17.6856	17.7833	17.8820	17.9817
16.75	17.5650	17.6601	17.7561	17.8531	17.9511	18.0501	18.1502	18.2512

TABLE A – 7 (*Continued*)

(term of loan: 30 years)

Contract Rate	Percentage Points Charged							
	8.50	9.00	9.50	10.00	10.50	11.00	11.50	12.00
7.00	7.9043	7.9618	8.0197	8.0782	8.1372	8.1968	8.2569	8.3176
7.25	8.1685	8.2269	8.2858	8.3453	8.4052	8.4658	8.5269	8.5886
7.50	8.4330	8.4923	8.5522	8.6126	8.6735	8.7351	8.7972	8.8599
7.75	8.6976	8.7579	8.8188	8.8801	8.9421	9.0047	9.0678	9.1315
8.00	8.9625	9.0238	9.0856	9.1480	9.2110	9.2745	9.3387	9.4035
8.25	9.2277	9.2899	9.3527	9.4161	9.4801	9.5447	9.6100	9.6758
8.50	9.4930	9.5562	9.6201	9.6845	9.7495	9.8152	9.8815	9.9485
8.75	9.7585	9.8228	9.8877	9.9532	10.0193	10.0860	10.1534	10.2214
9.00	10.0243	10.0896	10.1555	10.2221	10.2892	10.3571	10.4256	10.4947
9.25	10.2903	10.3566	10.4236	10.4912	10.5595	10.6284	10.6980	10.7683
9.50	10.5565	10.6239	10.6920	10.7607	10.8300	10.9001	10.9708	11.0422
9.75	10.8229	10.8914	10.9605	11.0303	11.1008	11.1720	11.2439	11.3165
10.00	11.0895	11.1591	11.2293	11.3003	11.3719	11.4442	11.5172	11.5910
10.25	11.3563	11.4270	11.4984	11.5704	11.6432	11.7167	11.7909	11.8658
10.50	11.6234	11.6952	11.7676	11.8408	11.9147	11.9894	12.0648	12.1410
10.75	11.8906	11.9635	12.0371	12.1115	12.1866	12.2624	12.3390	12.4164
11.00	12.1580	12.2320	12.3068	12.3824	12.4586	12.5357	12.6135	12.6921
11.25	12.4256	12.5008	12.5768	12.6535	12.7309	12.8092	12.8882	12.9681
11.50	12.6934	12.7698	12.8469	12.9248	13.0035	13.0830	13.1632	13.2444
11.75	12.9614	13.0389	13.1172	13.1963	13.2762	13.3570	13.4385	13.5209
12.00	13.2295	13.3082	13.3878	13.4681	13.5492	13.6312	13.7140	13.7977
12.25	13.4978	13.5778	13.6585	13.7401	13.8225	13.9057	13.9898	14.0748
12.50	13.7663	13.8475	13.9295	14.0123	14.0959	14.1804	14.2658	14.3521
12.75	14.0350	14.1174	14.2006	14.2846	14.3696	14.4554	14.5420	14.6296
13.00	14.3038	14.3874	14.4719	14.5572	14.6434	14.7305	14.8185	14.9074
13.25	14.5728	14.6577	14.7434	14.8300	14.9175	15.0059	15.0952	15.1855
13.50	14.8420	14.9281	15.0151	15.1029	15.1917	15.2815	15.3721	15.4637
13.75	15.1113	15.1986	15.2869	15.3761	15.4662	15.5572	15.6492	15.7422
14.00	15.3807	15.4694	15.5589	15.6494	15.7408	15.8332	15.9266	16.0209
14.25	15.6503	15.7402	15.8311	15.9229	16.0156	16.1094	16.2041	16.2999
14.50	15.9201	16.0113	16.1034	16.1966	16.2906	16.3857	16.4818	16.5790
14.75	16.1899	16.2824	16.3759	16.4704	16.5658	16.6623	16.7598	16.8583
15.00	16.4599	16.5538	16.6486	16.7444	16.8412	16.9390	17.0379	17.1378
15.25	16.7301	16.8252	16.9213	17.0185	17.1167	17.2159	17.3162	17.4175
15.50	17.0003	17.0968	17.1943	17.2928	17.3923	17.4929	17.5946	17.6974
15.75	17.2707	17.3685	17.4673	17.5672	17.6681	17.7701	17.8732	17.9775
16.00	17.5412	17.6403	17.7405	17.8418	17.9441	18.0475	18.1520	18.2577
16.25	17.8118	17.9123	18.0138	18.1165	18.2202	18.3250	18.4310	18.5381
16.50	18.0825	18.1844	18.2873	18.3913	18.4964	18.6027	18.7101	18.8187
16.75	18.3534	18.4566	18.5608	18.6663	18.7728	18.8805	18.9893	19.0994

TABLE A–8

Mortgage Pricing as a Percent of Loan Amount
(30-year term and 12-year prepayment)

Required Percentage Yield	Net Percentage Contract Rate							
	9.00	9.25	9.50	9.75	10.00	10.25	10.50	10.75
7.00	1.15426	1.17390	1.19360	1.21337	1.23319	1.25307	1.27300	1.29298
7.25	1.13329	1.15264	1.17206	1.19154	1.21108	1.23067	1.25031	1.27001
7.50	1.11283	1.13190	1.15104	1.17024	1.18949	1.20881	1.22817	1.24758
7.75	1.09286	1.11166	1.13052	1.14944	1.16843	1.18747	1.20656	1.22569
8.00	1.07338	1.09190	1.11050	1.12915	1.14787	1.16664	1.18546	1.20433
8.25	1.05436	1.07262	1.09095	1.10934	1.12780	1.14630	1.16486	1.18347
8.50	1.03580	1.05381	1.07188	1.09001	1.10820	1.12645	1.14475	1.16310
8.75	1.01768	1.03544	1.05325	1.07114	1.08908	1.10707	1.12512	1.14322
9.00	1.00000	1.01751	1.03508	1.05271	1.07040	1.08815	1.10595	1.12380
9.25	0.98274	1.00000	1.01733	1.03472	1.05217	1.06967	1.08723	1.10484
9.50	0.96588	0.98291	1.00000	1.01715	1.03436	1.05163	1.06895	1.08632
9.75	0.94943	0.96622	0.98308	1.00000	1.01698	1.03401	1.05110	1.06824
10.00	0.93337	0.94993	0.96656	0.98325	1.00000	1.01681	1.03366	1.05057
10.25	0.91768	0.93402	0.95042	0.96689	0.98342	1.00000	1.01663	1.03332
10.50	0.90236	0.91848	0.93467	0.95091	0.96722	0.98358	1.00000	1.01647
10.75	0.88740	0.90331	0.91928	0.93531	0.95140	0.96755	0.98375	1.00000
11.00	0.87279	0.88848	0.90424	0.92007	0.93595	0.95188	0.96787	0.98391
11.25	0.85852	0.87401	0.88956	0.90518	0.92085	0.93658	0.95236	0.96820
11.50	0.84458	0.85986	0.87521	0.89063	0.90610	0.92163	0.93721	0.95284
11.75	0.83096	0.84605	0.86120	0.87641	0.89169	0.90702	0.92240	0.93783
12.00	0.81765	0.83255	0.84751	0.86253	0.87760	0.89274	0.90792	0.92316
12.25	0.80466	0.81936	0.83413	0.84896	0.86384	0.87878	0.89378	0.90882
12.50	0.79195	0.80647	0.82105	0.83569	0.85039	0.86515	0.87996	0.89481
12.75	0.77954	0.79388	0.80827	0.82273	0.83725	0.85182	0.86644	0.88112
13.00	0.76742	0.78157	0.79579	0.81006	0.82440	0.83879	0.85323	0.86773
13.25	0.75556	0.76954	0.78358	0.79768	0.81184	0.82605	0.84032	0.85464
13.50	0.74398	0.75778	0.77165	0.78558	0.79956	0.81360	0.82770	0.84184
13.75	0.73266	0.74629	0.75999	0.77374	0.78756	0.80143	0.81535	0.82932
14.00	0.72159	0.73505	0.74858	0.76218	0.77582	0.78953	0.80328	0.81708
14.25	0.71076	0.72407	0.73744	0.75086	0.76435	0.77789	0.79148	0.80512
14.50	0.70018	0.71333	0.72654	0.73980	0.75313	0.76650	0.77993	0.79341
14.75	0.68984	0.70283	0.71588	0.72899	0.74215	0.75537	0.76864	0.78196
15.00	0.67973	0.69256	0.70545	0.71841	0.73142	0.74448	0.75760	0.77076
15.25	0.66983	0.68252	0.69526	0.70806	0.72092	0.73383	0.74679	0.75981
15.50	0.66016	0.67269	0.68529	0.69794	0.71065	0.72341	0.73623	0.74909
15.75	0.65070	0.66308	0.67553	0.68804	0.70060	0.71322	0.72589	0.73860
16.00	0.64144	0.65369	0.66599	0.67836	0.69077	0.70325	0.71577	0.72834
16.25	0.63239	0.64449	0.65666	0.66888	0.68116	0.69349	0.70587	0.71830
16.50	0.62353	0.63550	0.64752	0.65961	0.67175	0.68394	0.69618	0.70847
16.75	0.61487	0.62670	0.63859	0.65054	0.66254	0.67459	0.68670	0.69885

TABLE A – 8 (*Continued*)

Required Percentage Yield	Net Percentage Contract Rate							
	11.00	*11.25*	*11.50*	*11.75*	*12.00*	*12.25*	*12.50*	*12.75*
7.00	1.31300	1.33307	1.35317	1.37331	1.39348	1.41369	1.43392	1.45418
7.25	1.28974	1.30952	0.32934	1.34920	1.36909	1.38901	1.40896	1.42893
7.50	1.26704	1.28654	0.30608	1.32566	1.34527	1.36491	1.38458	1.40429
7.75	1.24488	1.26410	1.28337	1.30268	1.32201	1.34139	1.36079	1.38022
8.00	1.22324	1.24220	1.26120	1.28024	1.29931	1.31841	1.33755	1.35671
8.25	1.20212	1.22082	1.23955	1.25833	1.27714	1.29598	1.31485	1.33376
8.50	1.18150	1.19994	1.21842	1.23693	1.25549	1.27407	1.29269	1.31134
8.75	1.16136	1.17955	1.19777	1.21604	1.23434	1.25268	1.27105	1.28944
9.00	1.14170	1.15964	1.17762	1.19564	1.21369	1.23178	1.24990	1.26805
9.25	1.12249	1.14019	1.15793	1.17571	1.19352	1.21137	1.22925	1.24716
9.50	1.10374	1.12120	1.13870	1.15624	1.17382	1.19143	1.20907	1.22675
9.75	1.08542	1.10265	1.11992	1.13723	1.15457	1.17195	1.18936	1.20681
10.00	1.06753	1.08453	1.10157	1.11865	1.13577	1.15292	1.17011	1.18732
10.25	1.05005	1.06683	1.08365	1.10050	1.11740	1.13433	1.15129	1.16828
10.50	1.03298	1.04954	1.06613	1.08277	1.09945	1.11616	1.13290	1.14968
10.75	1.01630	1.03264	1.04902	1.06545	1.08191	1.09840	1.11493	1.13149
11.00	1.00000	1.01613	1.03230	1.04852	1.06477	1.08105	1.09737	1.11372
11.25	0.98408	1.00000	1.01597	1.03197	1.04802	1.06410	1.08021	1.09635
11.50	0.96851	0.98424	1.00000	1.01580	1.03165	1.04752	1.06343	1.07937
11.75	0.95331	0.96883	0.98439	1.00000	1.01564	1.03132	1.04703	1.06277
12.00	0.93844	0.95377	0.96914	0.98455	1.00000	1.01548	1.03100	1.04655
12.25	0.92392	0.93905	0.95423	0.96945	0.98471	1.00000	1.01533	1.03068
12.50	0.90972	0.92467	0.93966	0.95469	0.96976	0.98486	1.00000	1.01517
12.75	0.89584	0.91060	0.92541	0.94026	0.95514	0.97006	0.98501	1.00000
13.00	0.88227	0.89685	0.91148	0.92614	0.94085	0.95559	0.97036	0.98517
13.25	0.86900	0.88340	0.89785	0.91234	0.92687	0.94143	0.95603	0.97066
13.50	0.85603	0.87026	0.88453	0.89885	0.91320	0.92759	0.94201	0.95647
13.75	0.84334	0.85740	0.87151	0.88565	0.89983	0.91405	0.92830	0.94259
14.00	0.83093	0.84483	0.85877	0.87274	0.88676	0.90081	0.91489	0.92901
14.25	0.81880	0.83253	0.84630	0.86012	0.87397	0.88785	0.90177	0.91572
14.50	0.80694	0.82050	0.83411	0.84777	0.86145	0.87518	0.88894	0.90272
14.75	0.79533	0.80874	0.82219	0.83568	0.84921	0.86278	0.87638	0.89001
15.00	0.78397	0.79723	0.81052	0.82386	0.83723	0.85064	0.86409	0.87756
15.25	0.77286	0.78597	0.79911	0.81229	0.82552	0.83877	0.85206	0.86538
15.50	0.76200	0.77495	0.78794	0.80098	0.81405	0.82715	0.84029	0.85346
15.75	0.75136	0.76417	0.77701	0.78990	0.80282	0.81578	0.82877	0.84180
16.00	0.74096	0.75362	0.76632	0.77906	0.79184	0.80465	0.81750	0.83038
16.25	0.73077	0.74329	0.75585	0.76845	0.78109	0.79376	0.80646	0.81920
16.50	0.72081	0.73318	0.74560	0.75806	0.77056	0.78309	0.79566	0.80825
16.75	0.71105	0.72329	0.73558	0.74790	0.76026	0.77265	0.78508	0.79754

(*continued*)

TABLE A – 8 (*Continued*)

Required Percentage Yield	Net Percentage Contract Rate							
	13.00	13.25	13.50	13.75	14.00	14.25	14.50	14.75
7.00	1.47446	1.49477	1.51510	1.53544	1.55581	1.57619	1.59658	1.61698
7.25	1.44894	1.46896	1.48901	1.50907	1.52916	1.54925	1.56937	1.58949
7.50	1.42401	1.44376	1.46353	1.48332	1.50313	1.52295	1.54276	1.56264
7.75	1.39967	1.41915	1.43865	1.45817	1.47771	1.49726	1.51683	1.53641
8.00	1.37590	1.39511	1.41435	1.43360	1.45288	1.47217	1.49147	1.51080
8.25	1.35269	1.37164	1.39061	1.40961	1.42862	1.44766	1.46670	1.48577
8.50	1.33001	1.34871	1.36743	1.38617	1.40493	1.42371	1.44251	1.46132
8.75	1.30786	1.32631	1.34478	1.36328	1.38179	1.40032	1.41886	1.43743
9.00	1.28623	1.30443	1.32266	1.34091	1.35918	1.37746	1.39577	1.41408
9.25	1.26510	1.28306	1.30105	1.31905	1.33708	0.35513	1.37319	1.39127
9.50	1.24445	1.26218	1.27993	1.29770	1.31549	1.33331	1.35114	1.36898
9.75	1.22428	1.24177	1.25929	1.27683	1.29440	1.31198	1.32958	1.34720
10.00	1.20456	1.22183	1.23913	1.25644	1.27378	1.29114	1.30851	1.32590
10.25	1.18530	1.20235	1.21942	1.23651	1.25363	1.27077	1.28792	1.30509
10.50	1.16648	1.18331	1.20016	1.21704	1.23394	1.25085	1.26779	1.28475
10.75	1.14808	1.16470	1.18134	1.19800	1.21468	1.23139	1.24811	1.26486
11.00	1.13010	1.14651	1.16294	1.17939	1.19587	1.21236	1.22888	1.24541
11.25	1.11252	1.12872	1.14495	1.16120	1.17747	1.19376	1.21007	1.22640
11.50	1.09534	1.11134	1.12736	1.14341	1.15948	1.17557	1.19168	1.20781
11.75	1.07855	1.09435	1.11017	1.12602	1.14189	1.15778	1.17370	1.18963
12.00	1.06213	1.07773	1.09336	1.10902	1.12469	1.14039	1.15611	1.17185
12.25	1.04607	1.06148	1.07692	1.09239	1.10788	1.12338	1.13891	1.15446
12.50	1.03037	1.04560	1.06085	1.07613	1.09143	1.10675	1.12209	1.13745
12.75	1.01502	1.03006	1.04513	1.06022	1.07534	1.09048	1.10564	1.12081
13.00	1.00000	1.01486	1.02975	1.04467	1.05960	1.07456	1.08954	1.10454
13.25	0.98531	1.00000	1.01471	1.02945	1.04421	1.05899	1.07379	1.08861
13.50	0.97095	0.98546	1.00000	1.01456	1.02915	1.04376	1.05839	1.07303
13.75	0.95690	0.97124	0.98561	1.00000	1.01442	1.02885	1.04331	1.05779
14.00	0.94315	0.95733	0.97153	0.98575	1.00000	1.01427	1.02856	1.04287
14.25	0.92970	0.94371	0.95775	0.97181	0.98589	1.00000	1.01413	1.02827
14.50	0.91654	0.93039	0.94427	0.95817	0.97209	0.98603	1.00000	1.01399
14.75	0.90367	0.91736	0.93107	0.94481	0.95858	0.97237	0.98617	1.00000
15.00	0.89107	0.90460	0.91816	0.93175	0.94536	0.95899	0.97264	0.98631
15.25	0.87874	0.89212	0.90552	0.91896	0.93241	0.94589	0.95939	0.97291
15.50	0.86667	0.87990	0.89315	0.90644	0.91974	0.93307	0.94642	0.95979
15.75	0.85485	0.86793	0.88104	0.89418	0.90734	0.92052	0.93372	0.94694
16.00	0.84329	0.85623	0.86919	0.88218	0.89519	0.90823	0.92128	0.93436
16.25	0.83197	0.84476	0.85758	0.87043	0.88330	0.89619	0.90911	0.92204
16.50	0.82088	0.83354	0.84622	0.85893	0.87166	0.88441	0.89718	0.90998
16.75	0.81003	0.82255	0.83509	0.84766	0.86025	0.87287	0.88550	0.89816

TABLE A – 8 (*Continued*)

Required Percentage Yield	Net Percentage Contract Rate							
	15.00	15.25	15.50	15.75	16.00	16.25	16.50	16.75
7.00	1.63740	1.65782	1.67826	1.69870	1.71915	1.73960	1.76006	1.78052
7.25	1.60963	1.62978	1.64993	1.67010	1.69027	1.71044	1.73063	1.75081
7.50	1.58250	1.60238	1.62226	1.64216	1.66205	1.68196	1.70187	1.72179
7.75	1.55601	1.57562	1.59523	1.61486	1.63449	1.65413	1.67378	1.69343
8.00	1.53013	1.54947	1.56883	1.58819	1.60757	1.62694	1.64633	1.66572
8.25	1.50484	1.52393	1.54303	1.56214	1.58125	1.60038	1.61951	1.63865
8.50	1.48014	1.49898	1.51782	1.53668	1.55554	1.57442	1.59330	1.61218
8.75	1.45600	1.47459	1.49319	1.51180	1.53042	1.54905	1.56768	1.58632
9.00	1.43242	1.45076	0.46912	1.48749	1.50587	1.52425	1.54265	1.56105
9.25	1.40937	1.42748	1.44560	1.46373	1.48187	1.50002	1.51818	1.53634
9.50	1.38684	1.40472	1.42261	1.44050	1.45841	1.47633	1.49425	1.51219
9.75	1.36483	1.38247	1.40013	1.41780	1.43548	1.45317	1.47087	1.48858
10.00	1.34331	1.36073	1.37817	1.39561	1.41307	1.43053	1.44801	1.46549
10.25	1.32228	1.33948	1.35669	1.37392	1.39116	1.40840	1.42566	1.44292
10.50	1.30172	1.31870	1.33570	1.35271	1.36973	1.38676	1.40380	1.42085
10.75	1.28161	1.29839	1.31517	1.33197	1.34878	1.36560	1.38243	1.39927
11.00	1.26196	1.27852	1.29510	1.31169	1.32830	1.34491	1.36153	1.37816
11.25	1.24274	1.25910	1.27548	1.29186	1.30826	1.32467	1.34109	1.35752
11.50	1.22395	1.24011	1.25628	1.27247	1.28867	1.30488	1.32110	1.33733
11.75	1.20557	1.22154	1.23751	1.25350	1.26951	1.28552	1.30155	1.31758
12.00	1.18760	1.20337	1.21916	1.23495	1.25076	1.26658	1.28242	1.29826
12.25	1.17002	1.18560	1.20120	1.21681	1.23243	1.24806	1.26370	1.27936
12.50	1.15283	1.16822	1.18363	1.19905	1.21449	1.22994	1.24539	1.26086
12.75	1.13601	1.15122	1.16644	1.18168	1.19694	1.21220	1.22748	1.24277
13.00	1.11955	1.13458	1.14963	1.16469	1.17977	1.19485	1.20995	1.22506
13.25	1.10345	1.11831	1.13318	1.14806	1.16296	1.17787	1.19280	1.20773
13.50	1.08770	1.10238	1.11708	1.13179	1.14652	1.16126	1.17601	1.19077
13.75	1.07229	1.08680	1.10133	1.11587	1.13043	1.14499	1.15957	1.17417
14.00	1.05720	1.07155	1.08591	1.10028	1.11467	1.12908	1.14349	1.15792
14.25	1.04244	1.05662	1.07082	1.08503	1.09926	1.11349	1.12775	1.14201
14.50	1.02799	1.04201	1.05605	1.07010	1.08416	1.09824	1.11233	1.12643
14.75	1.01385	1.02771	1.04159	1.05548	1.06939	1.08331	1.09724	1.11118
15.00	1.00000	1.01371	1.02743	1.04117	1.05492	1.06869	1.08246	1.09625
15.25	0.98645	1.00000	1.01357	1.02716	1.04076	1.05437	1.06800	1.08163
15.50	0.97317	0.98658	1.00000	1.01344	1.02689	1.04035	1.05383	1.06731
15.75	0.96018	0.97344	0.98671	1.00000	1.01330	1.02662	1.03995	1.05329
16.00	0.94746	0.96057	0.97370	0.98684	1.00000	1.01317	1.02636	1.03955
16.25	0.93499	0.94797	0.96095	0.97395	0.98697	1.00000	1.01304	1.02610
16.50	0.92279	0.93562	0.94847	0.96133	0.97421	0.98710	1.00000	1.01291
16.75	0.91084	0.92353	0.93624	0.94896	0.96170	0.97446	0.98722	1.00000

TABLE A–9

Real Property Depreciation System
(straight-line method for mid-month conventions)

27.5-Year Recovery Period

If the Recovery Year Is:	And the Month in the First Recovery Year the Property Is Placed in Service Is:											
	1	2	3	4	5	6	7	8	9	10	11	12
	The Depreciation Rate Is:											
1	3.485	3.182	2.879	2.576	2.273	1.970	1.667	1.364	1.061	0.758	0.455	0.152
2	3.636	3.636	3.636	3.636	3.636	3.636	3.636	3.636	3.636	3.636	3.636	3.636
3	3.636	3.636	3.636	3.636	3.636	3.636	3.636	3.636	3.636	3.636	3.636	3.636
4	3.636	3.636	3.636	3.636	3.636	3.636	3.636	3.636	3.636	3.636	3.636	3.636
5	3.636	3.636	3.636	3.636	3.636	3.636	3.636	3.636	3.636	3.636	3.636	3.636
6	3.636	3.636	3.636	3.636	3.636	3.636	3.636	3.636	3.636	3.636	3.636	3.636
7	3.636	3.636	3.636	3.636	3.636	3.636	3.636	3.636	3.636	3.636	3.636	3.636
8	3.636	3.636	3.636	3.636	3.636	3.636	3.636	3.636	3.636	3.636	3.636	3.636
9	3.636	3.636	3.636	3.636	3.636	3.636	3.636	3.636	3.636	3.636	3.636	3.636
10	3.637	3.637	3.637	3.637	3.637	3.637	3.636	3.636	3.636	3.636	3.636	3.636
11	3.636	3.636	3.636	3.636	3.636	3.636	3.637	3.637	3.637	3.637	3.637	3.637
12	3.637	3.637	3.637	3.637	3.637	3.637	3.636	3.636	3.636	3.636	3.636	3.636
13	3.636	3.636	3.636	3.636	3.636	3.636	3.637	3.637	3.637	3.637	3.637	3.637
14	3.637	3.637	3.637	3.637	3.637	3.637	3.636	3.636	3.636	3.636	3.636	3.636
15	3.636	3.636	3.636	3.636	3.636	3.636	3.637	3.637	3.637	3.637	3.637	3.637
16	3.637	3.637	3.637	3.637	3.637	3.637	3.636	3.636	3.636	3.636	3.636	3.636
17	3.636	3.636	3.636	3.636	3.636	3.636	3.637	3.637	3.637	3.637	3.637	3.637
18	3.637	3.637	3.637	3.637	3.637	3.637	3.636	3.636	3.636	3.636	3.636	3.636
19	3.636	3.636	3.636	3.636	3.636	3.636	3.637	3.637	3.637	3.637	3.637	3.637
20	3.637	3.637	3.637	3.637	3.637	3.637	3.636	3.636	3.636	3.636	3.636	3.636
21	3.636	3.636	3.636	3.637	3.636	3.637	3.637	3.637	3.637	3.637	3.637	3.637
22	3.637	3.637	3.637	3.636	3.637	3.636	3.636	3.636	3.636	3.636	3.636	3.636
23	3.636	3.636	3.636	3.637	3.636	3.637	3.637	3.637	3.637	3.637	3.637	3.637
24	3.637	3.637	3.637	3.636	3.637	3.636	3.636	3.636	3.636	3.636	3.636	3.636
25	3.636	3.636	3.636	3.637	3.636	3.637	3.637	3.637	3.637	3.637	3.637	3.637
26	3.637	3.637	3.637	3.636	3.637	3.636	3.636	3.636	3.636	3.636	3.636	3.636
27	3.636	3.636	3.636	3.636	3.636	3.636	3.637	3.637	3.637	3.637	3.637	3.637
28	1.970	2.273	2.576	2.879	3.182	3.485	3.636	3.636	3.636	3.636	3.636	3.636
29	0.000	0.000	0.000	0.000	0.000	0.000	0.152	0.455	0.758	1.061	1.364	1.667

TABLE A–10
Real Property Depreciation System
(straight-line method for mid-month conventions)

31.5-Year Recovery Period

If the Recovery Year Is:	And the Month in the First Recovery Year the Property Is Placed in Service Is:											
	The Depreciation Rate Is:											
	1	2	3	4	5	6	7	8	9	10	11	12
1	3.042	2.778	2.513	2.249	1.984	1.720	1.455	1.190	0.926	0.651	0.397	0.132
2	3.175	3.175	3.175	3.175	3.175	3.175	3.175	3.175	3.175	3.175	3.175	3.175
3	3.175	3.175	3.175	3.175	3.175	3.175	3.175	3.175	3.175	3.175	3.175	3.175
4	3.175	3.175	3.175	3.175	3.175	3.175	3.175	3.175	3.175	3.175	3.175	3.175
5	3.175	3.175	3.175	3.175	3.175	3.175	3.175	3.175	3.175	3.175	3.175	3.175
6	3.175	3.175	3.175	3.175	3.175	3.175	3.175	3.175	3.175	3.175	3.175	3.175
7	3.175	3.175	3.175	3.175	3.175	3.175	3.175	3.175	3.175	3.175	3.175	3.175
8	3.175	3.174	3.175	3.174	3.175	3.174	3.174	3.175	3.174	3.174	3.174	3.175
9	3.174	3.175	3.174	3.175	3.174	3.175	3.175	3.174	3.175	3.175	3.175	3.174
10	3.175	3.174	3.175	3.174	3.175	3.174	3.174	3.175	3.174	3.174	3.174	3.175
11	3.174	3.175	3.174	3.175	3.174	3.175	3.175	3.174	3.175	3.175	3.175	3.174
12	3.175	3.174	3.175	3.174	3.175	3.174	3.174	3.175	3.174	3.174	3.174	3.175
13	3.174	3.175	3.174	3.175	3.174	3.175	3.175	3.174	3.175	3.175	3.175	3.174
14	3.175	3.174	3.175	3.174	3.175	3.174	3.174	3.175	3.174	3.174	3.174	3.175
15	3.174	3.175	3.174	3.175	3.174	3.175	3.175	3.174	3.175	3.175	3.175	3.174
16	3.175	3.174	3.175	3.174	3.175	3.174	3.174	3.175	3.174	3.174	3.174	3.175
17	3.174	3.175	3.174	3.175	3.174	3.175	3.175	3.174	3.175	3.175	3.175	3.174
18	3.175	3.174	3.175	3.174	3.175	3.174	3.174	3.175	3.174	3.174	3.174	3.175
19	3.174	3.175	3.174	3.175	3.174	3.175	3.175	3.174	3.175	3.175	3.175	3.174
20	3.175	3.174	3.175	3.174	3.175	3.174	3.174	3.175	3.174	3.174	3.174	3.175
21	3.174	3.175	3.174	3.175	3.174	3.175	3.175	3.174	3.175	3.175	3.175	3.174
22	3.175	3.174	3.175	3.174	3.175	3.174	3.174	3.175	3.174	3.174	3.174	3.175
23	3.174	3.175	3.174	3.175	3.174	3.175	3.175	3.174	3.175	3.175	3.175	3.174
24	3.175	3.174	3.175	3.174	3.175	3.174	3.174	3.175	3.174	3.174	3.174	3.175
25	3.174	3.175	3.174	3.175	3.174	3.175	3.175	3.174	3.175	3.175	3.175	3.174
26	3.175	3.174	3.175	3.174	3.175	3.174	3.174	3.175	3.174	3.174	3.174	3.175
27	3.174	3.175	3.174	3.175	3.174	3.175	3.175	3.174	3.175	3.175	3.175	3.174
28	3.175	3.174	3.175	3.174	3.175	3.174	3.174	3.175	3.174	3.174	3.174	3.175
29	3.174	3.175	3.174	3.175	3.174	3.175	3.175	3.174	3.175	3.175	3.175	3.174
30	3.175	3.174	3.175	3.174	3.175	3.174	3.174	3.175	3.174	3.174	3.174	3.175
31	3.174	3.175	3.174	3.175	3.174	3.175	3.175	3.174	3.175	3.175	3.175	3.174
32	1.720	1.984	2.249	2.513	2.778	3.042	3.175	3.174	3.175	3.174	3.175	3.174
33	0.000	0.000	0.000	0.000	0.000	0.000	0.132	0.397	0.661	0.926	1.190	1.455

TABLE A–11
General Depreciation System
Applicable Depreciation Method
(straight-line applicable recovery period: 39 years)

If the Recovery Year Is:	And the Month in the First Recovery Year the Property Is Placed in Service Is:											
	1	2	3	4	5	6	7	8	9	10	11	12
	The Depreciation Rate Is:											
1	2.461	2.247	2.033	1.819	1.605	1.391	1.177	0.963	0.749	0.535	0.321	0.107
2–39	2.564	2.564	2.564	2.564	2.564	2.564	2.564	2.564	2.564	2.564	2.564	2.564
40	0.107	0.321	0.535	0.749	0.963	1.177	1.391	1.605	1.819	2.033	2.247	2.461

Source: IRS publication no. 534 (depreciation)

APPENDIX 2

ACRONYM LIST

ACRS–Accelerated cost recovery system

ADC loan–Acquisition, development, and construction loan

ALTA–American Land Title Association

AMT–Alternative minimum tax

APR–Annual percentage rate

ARC–Accelerated remittance cycle

ARM–Adjustable rate mortgage loan

BSPRA–Builder/sponsor profit and risk allowance

CERCLA–Comprehensive Environmental Response, Compensation, and Liability Act

CLO–Computerized loan origination systems

CMB–Certified mortgage banker

CMO–Collateralized mortgage obligation

COFI–Cost of funds index

CPM–Certified property manager

CPR–Constant prepayment rate

CRV–Certificate of reasonable value

ECOA–Equal Credit Opportunity Act

EPA–Equity-participation agreement

ERISA–Employee Retirement Income Security Act

FASB–Financial Accounting Standards Board

FDIC–Federal Deposit Insurance Corporation

FHA–Federal Housing Administration

FHLMC–Federal Home Loan Mortgage Corporation

FIDA–Financial Institutions Deregulation Act

FIRREA–Financial Institutions, Reform, Recovery, and Enforcement Act

FIRSTS–Floating interest-rate short-tranche securities

FmHA–Farmers Home Administration

FNMA–Federal National Mortgage Association

FRM–Fixed rate mortgage

GAAP–Generally Accepted Accounting Principles

GEM–Growing equity mortgage

GMC–Guaranteed mortgage certificate

GNMA–Government National Mortgage Association

GPAM–Graduated payment adjustable mortgage

GPM–Graduated payment mortgage

GSE–Government-sponsored enterprise

HMDA–Home Mortgage Disclosure Act

HOLC–Home Owners Loan Corporation

HTG yield–"Honest to God" yield

HUD–Department of Housing and Urban Development

ILSFDA–Interstate Land Sales Full Disclosure Act

IOs–Interest-only bonds

IRB–Industrial revenue bond

IRS–Internal Revenue Service

LIBOR–London inter-bank offer rate

MACRS–Modified accelerated cost recovery system

MAI–Member, Appraisal Institute

MBS–Mortgage-backed securities

MCA–Financial Institutions Deregulation and Monetary Control Act

MCF–Mortgage cash flow obligation

MIP–Mortgage insurance premium

MLP–Master limited partnership

NOD–Notice of default

NOO–Nonowner-occupied

OCC–Office of the Comptroller of Currency

OID–Original issue discount

OILSR–Office of Interstate Land Sales Registration
OTS–Office of Thrift Supervision
PAC Bond–Planned amortization class bond
PAM–Pledged account mortgage
PC–Participating certificate
PITI–Principal, interest, taxes, and insurance
PLAM–Price level adjusted mortgage
PMI–Private mortgage insurance
POs–Principal-only bonds
PSA–Public Securities Association
PUD–Planned unit development
PV–Present value
QMI–Qualified monthly income
RAM–Reverse annuity mortgage
RAP–Regulatory accounting principles
REIT–Real estate investment trust
REMIC–Real estate mortgage investment conduit
REO–Real estate owned
RESPA–Real Estate Settlement Procedures Act

RFC–Residential Funding Corporation
RTC–Resolution Trust Corporation
SAM–Shared appreciation mortgage
SARA–Superfund Amendments and Reauthorization Act
SEC–Securities and Exchange Commission
SF–Single family
SMM–Single monthly mortality
SMM–Secondary mortgage market
SMMEA–Secondary Mortgage Market Enhancement Act
SREA–Senior real estate analyst
TRA–Tax Reform Act
UCC–Uniform Commercial Code
VA–Veterans Administration
VRM–Variable rate mortgage
WAC–Weighted average coupon
WAL–Weighted average life
WAM–Weighted average maturity

APPENDIX 3

SOFTWARE TO ACCOMPANY REAL ESTATE FINANCE

Software is included with this text to allow you to analyze several types of real estate finance situations. The software can be used to solve complicated homework problems, to manipulate variables to determine their effect on key financial ratios, or to gain an understanding of how variables interact in different models. There are many situations where input variables are both numerous and interactive. Analyzing such situations with a financial calculator would be extremely time consuming or nearly impossible. So, in order to save precious time, we have included this software with the text. The software is a menu driven spreadsheet analysis. It uses a Windows-based Excel spreadsheet in a menu driven format.

FINANCIAL MODELS

There are ten different financial models in ten different sheets as follows:

ADC EXAMPLE   is an example of an ADC loan.

ARM EXAMPLE   is an example of a simple 1-year adjustable rate mortgage.

CMO   is an example of the cash flows from collateralized mortgage obligations with four tranches and a residual class.

EQUITY PARTICIPATION   is an example of financing an income property with equity participation loan.

FINSALE   is an example of financing an income property through a sale-leaseback.

INCOME PROPERTY   is an analysis of the cash flows from operations of an income producing property.

MBB   is an example of the cash flows of a mortgage backed bond.

PRE 1986   is an example of the cash flows from operating an income property under tax rules prior to the Tax Reform Act of 1986.

REFINANCE   is an example of refinancing a residential loan when interest rates drop below that on the mortgage.

SERVICE RIGHTS   is an example of the cash flows associated with retention of servicing rights on a pool of residential mortgages.

ABOUT THE MENUS

All the sheets operate off the same menu driven format. When a sheet is selected, a menu will appear as follows:

GO BACK TO MAIN MENU
INPUT VALUES
VIEW CHART
PRINT

> **INPUT VALUES**   allows you to input information to be analyzed by the spreadsheet. Examples include the cost of a commercial project for INCOME PROPERTY, the PSA prepayment rate for a CMO, or the rate caps on ARM EXAMPLE.
>
> **VIEW CHART**   allows you to view a graph of some of the output data on most of the sheets.
>
> **PRINT**   allows you to print the results of a spreadsheet operation.

USING THE SOFTWARE

To use this software first insert the CD diskette in the proper drive (usually "d" or "e" drive). Next, activate your Windows program by typing WIN (enter). From the main menu of Windows select the latest version of EXCEL. Select the drive in which you inserted the CD and click on "ALLFILES."

ADC Example

Purpose

This sheet allows you to determine the effective rate of interest on an ADC loan. Although there is usually a contract rate on the loan, lenders will often add loan fees to the balance due at the termination of the loan. These fees result in an increase in the effective rate on the loan above the stated contract rate. Recall from Chapter 18 that the effective rate can be found by solving the following equation for *r:*

$$cf_1 + cf_2/(1 + r)^1 + cf_3/(1 + r)^2 + \cdots + cf_n/(1 + r)^{n-1} = \text{bal}/(1 + r)^n$$

where the *cf* are the monthly cash flows provided by the lender to the developer, bal is the amount due to the lender at the termination of the loan including the loan fees, and *r* is the effective interest rate.

Using the Sheet

The first screen in the sheet appears as follows:

> GO BACK TO MAIN MENU
> INPUT VALUES
> VIEW CHART
> PRINT

Selecting **INPUT** allows you access to the input data. The sheet opens on the contract rate of interest for the loan (cell E23). Next, monthly loan disbursements are entered in the appropriate cells in column C. Cell C44 allows the user to enter the amount of the loan fees in percent. This percent is multiplied by the amount due in the terminal month of the loan. The fees are then added to the amount due to arrive at an adjusted balance. Finally, the user inputs a guess as to the monthly rate of interest in Cell C50. Cell D52 uses this guess to calculate the present value of column D (the left side of the above equation) while Cell D53 uses the same guess to calculate the present value of the balance due in Cell I46 (the right hand side of the above equation). The user can try alternative guesses until the amounts in cells D52 and C50 are nearly equal (as indicated by a near zero amount in Cell D54). The guess in cell C50 is multiplied by 12 to convert to an annual effective yield, and displayed in Cell C46. Clicking the **FINISHED INPUT KEY** will return you to the main menu. Selecting the **PRINT** option will print out the results of this sheet.

ARM Example

Purpose

This sheet allows you to analyze a very simple adjustable rate mortgage. The ARM in this example is restricted to a 1-year adjustable. Also, even though there is a cap in the interest rate change, this cap does not set a floor. That is, a 1 percent cap on the rate change limits an increase in the rate to one percentage point per year but establishes no limit on the decrease in the rate from one year to the next.

Using the Sheet

The first screen appears as that in the above ADC EXAMPLE. Input data include the amount of the loan (D26), the initial (first year) interest rate on the loan (D27), the rate cap (D28), the margin over the index (D29), the life-of-loan cap (D30), maturity of the loan in months (D31), and the present index (index at the beginning of the loan), D32. The user will also input data on the expected index for each of the next 30 years in the appropriate cells.

Output is displayed in columns E through G. For each year the output displays the monthly payment during the year, the ending balance of the loan, and the contract rate of interest (which may have been limited by an interest cap). To go back to the original position click on **FINISHED INPUT.** The **PRINT** option can be used to print the results.

CMO

Purpose

This sheet allows you to analyze the cash flows from a pool of mortgages to the various bond holders and the equity position in a CMO. With a CMO there are various tranches with maturities of various lengths. There also is a residual class which is that of the equity position. As the earlier tranches are paid off more cash flows are diverted to the longer tranches and the residual. The prepayment rate on the pool of mortgages will have a large impact on the cash flows to the equity or residual position.

Using the Sheet

As with the other sheets the first screen allows one to input values and print the results. If the **INPUT VALUES** option is selected you will be able to provide information on the pool of mortgages such as the amount of the pool, the contract rate of interest, maturity, and the assumed PSA prepayment rate. Recall the 100 percent rate is 0.013 for the first year. You also will provide information on the bonds including their face amounts and coupon rates. The difference between the pool balance and the amounts of the bonds is the equity position or the residual class. If you select the **PRINT** option you will print the input data, cash flows generated by the mortgage pool, cash flows to each tranche, and the cash flows to the residual class.

Income Property

Purpose

This sheet allows you to analyze the cash flows from a commercial real estate property (income property). You may analyze the cash flows for any time period up to 5 years. The output shows the cash flows from both operations and sale of the property (reversion), net present value, and internal rate of return.

Using the Sheet

As with the other sheets the first screen will contain the familiar options of **MAIN MENU, INPUT VALUES, VIEW CHART,** and **PRINT.** Input data include cost of land, cost of building, amount of the loan, interest rate on the loan, gross rent, operating expenses, vacancy rates, and growth rates in expenses, rent, and value of the property as well as the ordinary and capital gains tax rate of the property owner. Selecting the **PRINT** option will print the input data, before-tax cash flows and after-tax cash flows for each of the 5 years holding period. For each of the 5 years the cash flows from sale are calculated as if the sale occurred in that year. In this way one can determine the net present value and internal rate of return as if the property were sold in any of the 5 years of the holding period.

Pre-1986

Purpose

The purpose of this sheet is to allow you to analyze the cash flows, net present value, and internal rate of return for an income property under tax rules that existed prior to the Tax Reform Act of 1986. The only difference between this sheet and the INCOME PROPERTY sheet is that there is no provision for passive loss limitations. In the case of negative taxable income, the income tax is negative and treated as cash inflow.

Equity Participation

Purpose

The purpose of this sheet is to analyze the cash flows from a property financed by a participation loan. This sheet operates very much as the INCOME PROPERTY sheet except that added input and output includes the participation terms for the lender. Participation terms include both a share of the net operating income and a share of the appreciation of the property.

Using the Sheet

Again, the first screen will appear as usual with the input and print options. In this sheet **SHARE OF NOI** is the share (percentage) of net operating income shared by the lender. **OVER** is the threshold amount of the NOI that triggers a share for the lender. **APPRECIATION SHARE** refers to the share (percentage) of the appreciation in the property that goes to the lender at the time of sale. The final two screens request information on the discount rate applied by the property owner (investor), and that required by the lender.

FINSALE

Purpose

This sheet allows you to analyze the benefits of financing through a sale-leaseback arrangement. The sheet analyzes the cash flows of both the seller/lessee and the buyer/lessor.

Using the Sheet

The first screen will show the familiar options of all sheets. The **INPUT VALUES** option allows you access to cell locations D24 through D38 where you may enter data on the book value of the property, current depreciation, lease costs if the sale-leaseback is executed, new depreciation on the stepped up basis, discount rates for the two parties, and other self-explanatory data. You may **PRINT** the results of the calculations to see the cash flows, net present value, and internal rate of return to the owner/lessee and buyer/lessor.

MBB

Purpose

This sheet allows you to analyze the workings of a typical mortgage backed bond. A mortgage backed bond is one that is backed by a pool of mortgages and is often overcollateralized. This sheet assumes that there is only one bond that is backed by the pool of mortgages with a single contract rate. You will be asked to provide basic information about the pool (contract rate, default rate, prepayment rate, etc.) and about the bond (contract rate, maturity, etc.). The program computes the payments from the pool of mortgages and payments to the bondholders and the residual class.

Using the Sheet

The standard options are available with this sheet. If you choose the **INPUT VALUES** option then you can enter the basic data in cells C24 through C32. Data here include, for the pool, the pool balance, contract rate on the mortgages, the year-one PSA prepayment rate, and the default rate. For the bonds it includes the maturity of the bonds (MBBs), interest rate on the bonds, and the principal amount.

The **PRINT** option will produce, year-by-year, the following: beginning pool balance, total payment, scheduled amortization, interest payment, default rate (for the first 10 years only), prepayment rate, payments to the bondholders, the residual that is to be placed in a sinking fund, the balance on the sinking fund, and finally, the cash flows to the equity position. Once you have chosen a discount rate for the equity position, the program uses this rate and the cash flows to the equity position to determine the present value of the cash flows.

Refinance

Purpose

This sheet allows you to analyze, in terms of net present value, the refinancing decision on a mortgage. A loan should be refinanced if the present value of the future payment savings exceeds the cost of obtaining the new loan. Costs include prepayment penalties on the existing loan as well as origination costs on the new loan.

Using the Sheet

The **INPUT VALUES** option allows you to input data in cells F42 through F50. The data include the original balance on the existing loan, the current contract rate, original maturity, age of the existing loan, prepayment penalties, new loan fees and new loan costs, in addition to the new loan contract interest rate. Finally, you will provide the opportunity cost or discount rate for the determination of the net present value.

The **PRINT** option for the program includes the payment on the existing loan, payment on the new loan, payment savings, costs of obtaining a new loan, present value of the payment savings and the net present value.

Service Rights

Purpose

This sheet allows you to analyze the cash flows from servicing rights. Servicing rights collectively refers to the fees received for servicing a portfolio of mortgages. The servicers usually will have sold the portfolio but will, for fees referred to as servicing rights, collect the payments from the mortgagors and forward them to the new mortgage owner.

Using the Sheet

The **INPUT VALUES** option includes data on the pool or portfolio of mortgages being served, including the interest rate, pool balance, servicing rate (usually a quarter to a half of a percent), the percent PSA prepayment, fixed costs, variable costs percent, and the assumed growth rate in costs to service. Finally, you will input the discount rate used to solve for the present value of the cash flows. **PRINT** output includes the payments received to service the pool of mortgages as well as the present value of the cash flows.

Comments about this software and suggestions for improvement should be sent to

Real Estate Finance Editor
Prentice Hall
1 Lake Street Drive
Upper Saddle River, NJ 07458
or e-mail Terrence Clauretie at MikeC@ccmail.nevada.edu

GLOSSARY OF REAL ESTATE FINANCE TERMS

Ability-to-pay theory of default The theory that mortgage defaults occur because the mortgagor is unable to meet the monthly payment (see **equity theory of default**).

Abstract of title A condensed written history of the title transactions and recorded instruments or condition bearing on the title to designated real estate. An abstract of title covers the period from the original source of title to the present and is prepaid by an abstractor who may be an attorney, public official, or employee of a title company.

Accelerated cost recovery system (ACRS) A system of depreciation in existence from 1981 through 1986 in which assets were placed into several classes with various expected useful lives and depreciated under an accelerated rate (see **modified accelerated cost recovery system**).

Accelerated remittance cycle (ARC) An option available to Freddie Mac sellers and servicers that allows the seller to decrease the management and guarantee fee in return for remitting principal and interest payments early.

Acceleration clause A common provision of a mortgage, trust deed, or note providing that the entire principal shall become immediately due and payable in the event of default (see **default**).

Accrued interest Unpaid interest that already has been earned.

Acknowledgment A formal declaration to a public official by a person who has signed (executed) an instrument which states the signing was a voluntary act.

Acquisition cost The FHA-appraised value or purchase price (whichever is less) plus closing costs, such as origination fees, appraisal fees, and attorney fees.

Acre A measure of land, 43,560 square feet or 4,840 square yards.

Action to quiet title A court action taken to remove any interest or claim on the title to real property.

Active income A category of income established by TRA 1986. Refers to income from working in a trade, profession or business.

Ad valorem A Latin prefix meaning "according to the value." Local and state governments levy taxes on real property based on the assessed value of the property.

Adequacy of Interest Test An IRS rule inputs the rate of interest on a loan if the contract rate is less than 110% of the applicable federal rate.

Adjustable rate mortgage loan (ARM) A type of mortgage in which the interest rate adjusts periodically according to a preselected index, such as Treasury Bill rates, and a margin. This adjustment results in the mortgage payment either increasing or decreasing. Limits can be set on the amount by which interest rates or payments can change.

Administrator A person appointed by a probate court to administer and settle the estate of a person who died intestate (without a will).

Advance The word has two common meanings in real estate finance: (1) to pay or advance money before it is due, and (2) to disburse working capital to a builder-developer through a construction loan.

Advantageous financing Generally a loan with a contract rate of interest below the current market rate.

Adverse possession or Title by Prescription A method of acquiring title to real property by possession. The occupant's possession must be actual (open and visible), continuous and uninterrupted, hostile and notorious for a statutory period of time.

Affidavit Latin meaning "has pledged his faith." A written statement of facts made voluntarily and sworn to under oath to a public official (see **acknowledgement**).

Affordability index An index of housing cost which uses the cost of housing, interest rates, and familiar income to track the affordability of housing over time.

After-acquired title Legal ownership in real property acquired by someone who had previously transferred his or her legal interest in the property.

After-tax cash flow The cash flow from an investment after all applicable taxes have been paid.

Agency by estoppel Results when a principal causes a third person to believe that another person is acting as an agent, and the third person acts to his or her detriment in reasonable reliance on that belief.

Agency costs Costs incurred by a principal to insure that his or her agent operates in the interest of the principal. They include bonding, monitoring, and structuring costs.

Agency coupled with an interest A relationship that results in the agent holding an interest in the property he or she is representing.

Agent One who legally represents another, called a principal, from whom authority has been granted.

Agreement for sale A written document in which the purchaser agrees to buy certain real estate (or personal property), and the seller agrees to sell under stated terms and conditions. Also called sales contract, binder, or earnest money contract.

Air rights The ownership of the right to use, control, or occupy the air space above a particular parcel of real estate.

Alienation clause Provision in mortgage or deed of trust that legally permits the mortgagee to demand payment of the outstanding principal in the event the property is sold (see **due-on-sale clause**).

Alienation of title A voluntary transfer of an interest in real property from one person to another.

All-inclusive trust deed See **wraparound.**

Alternative minimum tax (AMT) The minimum federal tax that a taxpayer must pay if there are substantial tax preference items that would otherwise result in low or no taxes due.

Alternative mortgage instrument Any one of the various mortgage loans differing from a traditional, fixed-rate, 30-year amortizing mortgage because the monthly payment, interest rate, term, or other provisions are changed.

Amenity An feature of a property that enhances its value to its owner. Examples are off-street reserved parking within a condominium community, the nearness of public transportation, tennis courts, a scenic view, or proximity to shopping.

American Land Title Association (ALTA) A national association, founded in 1907, representing 2,100 title abstractors, title insurance companies, title insurance agents, and associate members. It is the role and responsibility of the title industry and its ALTA members to guarantee the safe, efficient transfer of real property and to provide protection for consumers and lenders alike. The association speaks for the title industry and establishes standard procedures and title policy forms.

Amortization Periodic repayment of a debt in installments of principal and interest (as opposed to interest-only payments).

Amortization rate The percentage of a periodic payment that represents reduction in principal.

Anniversary date Date when the new payment on an ARM is calculated.

Annual percentage rate (APR) The actual annual cost of credit which represents the relationship of the total finance charge (interest, loan fees, points) to the amount of the loan.

Annuity A series of fixed sum payments for a specified number of payments. A standard fixed-rate mortgage with equal monthly payments is an example.

Appraisal An estimate or opinion of value supported by factual data by a qualified person. Also, the process by which this estimate is obtained.

Appraised value An estimate of value based on the appraiser's analysis of data within the context of the appraisal problem that the appraiser was employed to solve.

Appraiser An individual who has the experience, training, and legal qualifications to appraise the value of real or personal property.

Appreciation An increase in an assets market value over its value at some previous point.

Appurtenance Anything attached to the land which thus passes with the property, such as a barn, garage, garden, or an easement.

Arbitrage The simultaneous purchase and sale of a commodity or security in different markets with the purpose of obtaining a sure profit from the differential between the buying and selling price.

Assessed valuation The worth or value of a piece of property as determined by the taxing authority for the purpose of levying an ad valorem (property) tax.

Assessment A determination of value on property for the purpose of taxation. May also refer to a levy against property for a special purpose, such as a sewer assessment.

Assessment appeal board Local governmental body which hears and rules on property owner complaints of overassessment.

Assessment roll A list of all property showing the assessed value of each parcel. Such information is public and is normally available in the tax assessor's office or in the local land records.

Assignee The person or entity to whom a claim, benefit, or right in property is made.

Assignment of mortgage A document that evidences a sale of a mortgage from one party to another.

Assignment of rents clause An agreement between a property owner and lender which gives the lender rights to the rents of the property if the owner defaults.

Assignor The person transferring a claim, benefit, or right in property to another.

Assumption Taking title to property which has an existing mortgage and agreeing to be personally liable for the payment of the existing mortgage.

Assumption fee The fee paid to a lender resulting from the assumption of an existing mortgage.

At the money An option with a strike price that is equal to the current market price of the underlying security.

At risk limitation An IRS rule that limits the losses on an investment to the amount the taxpayer has at risk in the investment.

Attachment The act of taking a person's property into the legal custody of a court for the purpose of serving as security for satisfaction of a judgment which has been filed.

Attestation clause The act of witnessing a person's signing of a written instrument.

Balance sheet A financial statement showing assets, liabilities, and the net worth of an entity as of a specific date.

Balloon mortgage A mortgage in which periodic payments do not fully amortize at the end of the loan; thus, the last principal payment is substantially higher than those made during the life of the mortgage. Generally, the mortgage payments are determined with reference to a period longer than the term of the loan.

Balloon payment The final payment of principal under a balloon mortgage, possibly representing a substantial portion of the original amount borrowed.

Band of investment One of the common techniques used by appraisers and investors to derive an appropriate capitalization rate for a particular income-producing property. The band of investment method is related to the typical capital structure of a particular project and how much income would be necessary to compensate each provider of funds. A weighted average is developed to determine the composite capitalization rate.

Bargain and sale deed A deed conveying all of the grantor's interest in real property to the grantee by reciting a valuable consideration. Such deeds may be with or without covenants.

Base lines Imaginary lines running east-west (latitude) which intersect with lines running north-south (longitude and referred to as meridians) to form the starting points in the rectangular survey or U.S. government survey system of land descriptions.

Basic rent In government subsidized housing, the amount of rent charged assuming the tenant qualifies for the maximum rent subsidy.

Basis points A basis point is 1-100 of 1 percent interest; thus, 50 basis points equal 0.5 percent or $\frac{1}{2}$ of 1 percent. The term is used to explain the absolute change in the marketplace of debt instruments, such as mortgages and bonds.

Basket loan A type of loan made by insurance companies, savings and loan associations, and mutual savings banks not otherwise permitted by regulatory authorities. A small percentage of assets can be placed in such loans.

Before-tax cash flow The cash flow from an investment before applicable taxes are considered.

Beneficiary The person who benefits from the act or acts of another.

Bequeath To transfer personal property by will.

Bill of sale A written instrument used to transfer ownership of personal property in contrast to real property which is transferred by a deed.

Binder Receipt for the earnest money deposit paid by the purchaser to secure his or her right to buy property at the specific price and terms agreed to by both buyer and seller.

Biweekly mortgage A mortgage with payments due every two weeks, totalling 26 payments per year.

Blanket mortgage A mortgage in which two or more pieces of property are used to cover a single debt. It is frequently incurred by subdividers or developers who have purchased a single tract of land for the purpose of dividing it into smaller parcels for sale or development over a period of time.

Blockbusting The illegal practice of inducing panic selling in a neighborhood for financial gain.

Blue Sky laws State laws to regulate and supervise the sale of securities to avoid investments in fraudulent companies or high-risk investments. Prevents the unscrupulous from selling the "Blue Sky" to unsophisticated buyers.

Bona fide In good faith, sincere, honest.

Breach Violation of a legal obligation. Failure to perform as promised on part or all of the terms and conditions of a contract.

Break-even point In residential or commercial property, the point at which income is equal to operating expenses and debt service (interest and principal).

Bridge loan (swing loan, interim financing) A loan or loan offer that is taken on a property and applied to the purchase of another property prior to the sale of the first property. It can be used to offset the sale of a residence by having the seller named as beneficiary of the buyer's junior mortgage or trust deed. If the buyer's house is sold prior to or concurrent with the seller's house, the bridge loan can be cashed out before being consummated.

Broker A middleman who, for a commission or fee, brings parties together and assists in negotiating contracts between them.

Builder-seller sponsor The sponsor of a project that is specifically organized to be built (or rehabilitated) and sold, immediately upon completion, to a private nonprofit organization at the certified cost of the project. The nonprofit sponsor buys a total package.

Builder/sponsor profit & risk allowance (BSPRA) The fee that may be collected by developers of government-assisted low-income housing (e.g., FHA Section 236 housing; the amount of fee is regulated by the government). The amount allowed is based on total estimated costs of on-site utilities, landscape work, structures, general overhead structures, general overhead expense, architects' fees, carrying charges, financing, and legal and organizational expense.

Building code Local ordinances and regulations that set standards for design, construction, maintenance, and materials used in both new and existing buildings.

Building residual technique The process of estimating the contribution of improvements to the present worth or value of the entire property over and above the value of the site, in which the following occur: (1) return attributable to the land, valued independently of the building, is deducted from net operating income; and (2) the residual income, representing return to the building (including recapture), is capitalized to indicate the building's value.

Bundle of rights A legal concept of real estate which gives the owner of real estate an aggregate of rights, powers, and privileges which are guaranteed and protected by the government.

Buy-down mortgage A mortgage made by a lender with a below-market interest rate for a certain period of time in return for money received from a builder or seller.

Buy-sell agreement An agreement that an interim lender will assign a mortgage to a permanent lender when a building has been completed. Often the mortgagor is a party to this agreement on the theory that the mortgagor should have a contractual right to insist that the permanent lender buy the mortgage. This is termed a tripartite agreement.

Call protection A feature of mortgage-backed securities designed to minimize the risk of prepayment. Examples would include prepayment penalties and lock-out periods in mortgages that back securities or structuring an issue so that if loans are prepaid, the funds are not passed through immediately to the investor. Investors desire call protection because it provides a more consistent cash flow and keeps them from having to reinvest prepayments.

Call provision A clause in the mortgage or deed of trust giving the lender or beneficiary the right to accelerate payment of the mortgage debt in full on a certain date or on the happening of specified conditions. An example is a due-on-sale clause.

Callability risk The risk that a debt instrument, including a mortgage, will be paid off prior to maturity if the market rate of interest falls.

Capital lease A lease of an asset that is treated as ownership on the balance sheet with an entry for the present value of the lease payments as a liability (see **property lease**).

Capital loss limitation An IRS rule that limits the tax deductibility of a loss on a capital investment to the amount of gains on other capital investments plus $3,000 of ordinary income.

Capital market security A financial instrument, including both debt and equity securities with maturities greater than one year. Those instruments with maturities of less than a year are money market securities.

Capital structure The proportion of debt and equity used to finance the acquisition of assets.

Capitalization The process of determining the present value of a series of future payments or cash flows by discounting them into a present worth using an appropriate discount rate (or rate of return).

Capitalization rate The rate used to convert future payments to present value.

Caps Limits on the interest rate increase of either the periodic or lifetime rate or both, or a limit on any payment change for adjustable rate mortgages.

Carrying charges Costs incurred by a developer, principally interest on construction loans, insurance, and property taxes, to carry non-income-producing land or land currently under development or construction.

Cash equivalent value The value of a property when purchased either with all cash or with financing at market rate of interest.

Cash flow Cash inflows less cash outflows. Usually found by taking after-tax net income and adding back noncash expenses such as depreciation.

Cash-on-cash return The rate of return on an investment measured by the cash returned to the investor based on the investor's cash investment without regard to income tax savings or the use of borrowed funds. The before-tax cash flow divided by the equity interest.

Cash to loan A method of acquiring property wherein the buyer assumes the seller's mortgage and pays the seller cash for the remaining balance.

Certificate of limited partnership A summary of the major provisions of a limited partnership agreement. It is to be filed in the county recorder's office of the county in which the particular partnership is doing business.

Certificate of occupancy Written authorization given by a local government that allows a newly completed or substantially completed structure to be inhabited.

Certificate of reasonable value (CRV) A document issued by the Veterans Administration (VA) establishing maximum value and loan amount for a VA-guaranteed mortgage.

Certificate of title A written statement issued by a title attorney or title examiner stating his or her opinion of the quality of the title to a particular parcel of real estate.

Certificate rate The rate of interest which Freddie Mac pays to investors as specified on the participation certificate.

Certified historic structure A designation given by the Department of Interior to structures that meet certain age and-or site conditions. Designation may be important for a taxpayer to claim a credit for restoring such a structure.

Certified property manager (CPM) A member of the Institute of Real Property Management of the National Association of Realtors.

Cession deed A deed that conveys street rights to a county or municipality.

Chain of title The history of all the documents transferring title to a parcel of real property, starting with the earliest existing document and ending with the most recent.

Chattel mortgage A pledge of personal property to secure a mortgage.

Closed-end mortgage A mortgage which prohibits the mortgagor (borrower) from pledging the mortgaged property as security for additional loans.

Closed period The portion of the term of a mortgage during which the loan cannot be repaid.

Closing The consummation of a transaction. In mortgage lending this means the delivery of a deed, signing of notes, mortgages, and other loan documents, and disbursement of the loan proceeds.

Closing costs Expenses incidental to a sale of real estate, such as loan origination fees, title fees, appraisal fees, mortgage insurance premiums, termite inspection fees, attorney fees, and so forth.

Closing statement A financial disclosure accounting for all funds received and expected at the closing, including the escrow deposits for taxes, hazard insurance, and mortgage insurance for the escrow account.

Cloud on title Any conditions revealed by a title search that adversely affect the clear title to real estate. A cloud on title is usually removed through an action to quiet title.

Certified mortgage banker (CMB) A professional designation of the mortgage banking industry provided by the mortgage banker's association.

Co-insurance A sharing of insurance risk between insurer and owner depending on the relation of the amount of the policy and a specified percentage of the actual value of the property insured at the time of loss.

Collateral Property pledged as security for the satisfaction of a loan or debt.

Collateralized mortgage obligation (CMO) A multiple-class, pay-through bond, first issued by the FHLMC in June 1983. They are secured by a pool of mortgages or a portfolio of pass-through securities. The CMO provides a type of call protection and pays principal and interest semiannually rather than monthly, as a pass-through security does.

Color of title In the conveyance of property, an instrument that appears to convey title to the property, but in fact conveys no title at all.

Co-maker A second party who signs a note with the borrower in order to increase the security of the loan. The co-maker becomes jointly liable for repayment of the loan.

Commercial bank A financial institution that specializes in commercial, industrial, and agricultural loans.

Commercial loan A mortgage loan on property that produces income.

Commercial paper Short-term unsecured promissory notes of large firms sold to meet short-term capital needs.

Commission An agent's fee for negotiating a real estate or loan transaction.

Commitment A written promise to make or insure a loan for a specified amount, on specified terms, on a certain date.

Commitment fee Any fee paid by a borrower to a lender for the lender's promise to lend money at a specified date in the future and at specified terms.

Common law A body of legal principles and rules of action derived from accepted practices and procedures in England and used to an extent in the United States.

Community property In some states a form of ownership under which property acquired during a marriage is presumed to be owned jointly unless otherwise exempted.

Community Retirement Act An act passed by Congress in 1978 that requires federally insured thrifts to adopt a community reinvestment statement that defines the community in which the institution makes loans and maintains a file of loans for public inspection.

Comparables Properties used for comparative purposes in the appraisal process. They will have much the same characteristics as the subject property and a known value.

Compound interest Interest upon interest; that is, interest that is paid on interest in addition to being paid on the original principal.

Comprehensive Environmental Response, Compensation, and Liability Act (CERCLA) A federal act passed in 1980 that requires owners of properties to bear the cost of cleaning up toxic or hazardous waste found on the properties.

Computerized loan origination systems (CLO) Computerized networks that offer information or process loans of various lenders that participate in the network.

Condemnation The court proceedings for taking private property for public use with just compensation to the owner under the right of eminent domain.

Condominium A form of ownership of residential real property. The owner receives title to an identified unit and a prorated interest in common areas such as a swimming pool.

Conduit An entity issuing mortgage-backed securities backed by mortgages which were originated by traditional mortgage originators.

Consolidated obligations The bonds issued by the Federal Home Loan Bank System.

Consolidated-rate mortgage A refinancing mortgage, typically offered by a lending institution wherein a new loan is created

carrying an interest rate that reflects a compromised average rate between the old loan and a new market-rate loan. The borrower would like to sell his house and have the buyer assume the existing low-rate mortgage, while the lender would like to enforce the due-on-sale clause, but does not want the seller to refuse to sell and keep the low-rate loan.

Constant The percentage of the original loan represented by the monthly payment of interest and principal. It varies by interest rate and loan maturity.

Constant prepayment rate (CPR) The rate at which the principal balance on a pool of mortgages is being paid, stated on an annualized basis.

Construction contract An agreement between a general contractor and an owner-developer stating the specific duties the general contractor will perform according to blueprints and specifications at a stipulated price and terms of payment.

Construction loan A short-term loan for financing the cost of construction. The lender makes payments to the builder at periodic intervals after he is assured that work on the project is progressing on schedule.

Construction loan agreement A written agreement between a lender and a builder or borrower in which the specific terms and conditions of a construction loan, including the schedule of payments, are spelled out.

Construction loan draw or takedown The partial disbursement of the construction loan, based on the schedule of payments in the loan agreement.

Constructive notice Notice given through public records and by visible possession, and the legal presumption that all persons are thereby notified.

Contingent interest Interest that may be added to a loan is fixed interest rate. Commitment calls for an additional fixed interest rate, which is a percentage of the annual gross or net project income exceeding an agreed base amount to be paid to the lender.

Conventional loan A mortgage loan in which real estate serves as the security without any government agency either insuring (FHA) or guaranteeing (VA) the loan.

Convertible adjustable rate mortgage An adjustable rate mortgage whereby the mortgagor can convert the mortgage to a fixed-rate mortgage during a predetermined time period for a small conversion fee.

Conveyance The transfer of title to land from one person to another by use of a written instrument, such as a deed, assignment of lease, or mortgage.

Contract for deed A method of selling and financing property whereby the buyer obtains possession but the seller retains the title.

Cooperative A form of multiple ownership of real estate in which a corporation or business trust entity holds title to property and grants occupancy rights to apartments or units to shareholders by means of proprietary leases or similar arrangements.

Correspondent A mortgage banker who services mortgage loans he has originated as an agent for the owner of the mortgage (investor). Also applies to the mortgage banker's role as originator of mortgage loans for an investor.

Cosigner A person who signs a legal instrument and therefore becomes individually and jointly liable for repayment or performance of an obligation.

Cost approach An appraisal technique used to establish value by first estimating the cost to reproduce the facility, then deducting for depreciation and finally adding the value of the land.

Cost-of-development method A method of valuing undeveloped acreage by estimating the maximum amount an investor-developer would be warranted in paying for land, given the cost of development, the probable proceeds from the sale of the developed sites, and appropriate discounting techniques. This is also called the subdivision method or subdivision analysis method.

Cost of Funds Index (COFI) Index for an adjustable rate mortgage based on the average of interest rates paid by thrifts to their depositors (their cost of funds).

Cost of uncompleted contracts in excess of related billing An asset

item that may arise under the completed-contract and percentage-of-completion methods of recognizing income. It represents the costs (and earned fees under the percentage-of-completion method) incurred that have not been billed.

Coupon rate The annual interest rate on a bond or the contract interest rate on a mortgage note.

Covenant Promise or restriction in a mortgage. For example, the borrower may covenant to keep the property in good repair, adequately insured against fire and other casualties, and pay property taxes. The breach of a covenant in a mortgage usually creates a default.

Covenant of seizin A covenant which gives assurance that the grantor has the exact estate in the quantity and quality which in fact is being conveyed.

Coverage ratio For private mortgage insurance, that portion of the exposure (potential loss) that is covered by the insurance and for which the lender will be indemnified.

Creative financing Any method of financing the purchase of (usually) a residence with a loan that is other than offered by traditional mortgage lenders. These include loans with rates below the current market rate, such as assumable loans, owner financed loans, and interest rate buy-downs.

Credit enhancement The process whereby the issuer of a mortgage-related security adds support to the underlying assets by contributing capital or overcollateralizing the assets.

Credit report A detailed financial history of a person or company used by a lender in determining whether to extend credit.

Cross-defaulting clause A clause in a junior mortgage that specifies that a default on a senior mortgage triggers a default on the junior mortgage.

Curtesy By common law, the legal rights a husband acquires in his wife's property at the time of her death.

Custodian Usually a commercial bank which holds for safekeeping mortgages and related documents backing an MBS. Custodian may be required to examine and certify documents.

Debt coverage ratio The ratio of effective annual net operating income to annual debt service of a mortgage loan.

Debt service The periodic payment of both principal and interest paid on mortgage loans.

Deed A written legal document which purports to transfer ownership of land from one party to another.

Deed-in-lieu-of foreclosure A deed given by a borrower to a lender to satisfy the debt and avoid foreclosure.

Deed of reconveyance The transfer of legal title from the trustee to the trustor (borrower) after the trust deed debt is paid in full.

Deed of trust A type of security instrument conveying title (in trust) to a third party (trustee). It is used to secure the payment of a note. A conveyance of the title land to a trustee as collateral security for the payment of a debt with the condition that the trustee shall reconvey the title to the borrower (trustor) upon the payment of the debt. The trustee has the power to sell the real estate and pay the debt in the event of a default on the part of the debtor.

Deed restriction A limitation placed in a deed limiting or restricting the use of real property.

Default Breach or nonperformance of a clause in either a note or mortgage which, if not cured, could lead to foreclosure.

Default risk The risk of incurring a loss on a loan as a result of a default.

Defeasance clause The clause in a mortgage that gives the mortgagor the right to redeem property upon payment to the lender of the obligation due. This "defeats" the passage of title to the lender.

Deficiency judgment A judgment levied against the borrower personally (personal assets) for the difference between the mortgage debt (including payments in arrears) and the liquidation value of the property.

Delinquent A loan with payments past due.

Demand note A note that is due whenever the holder demands payment.

Deminimis PUD A planned unit development in which the common property has little effect upon the value of the property securing the PUD unit mortgage.

Density bonus A waiver of regular limits on the density of housing in a development in return for the developer paying the local government in-kind or dollar-based impact fees.

Deposit Money offered by a prospective purchaser to indicate his or her good faith in entering into a sales contract. Also known as earnest money.

Depository Institutions Deregulation and Monetary Control Act of 1980 (DIDMCA, also DIDA) A bill that authorized deregulation of all depository financial institutions and the phaseout of most deposit interest rate ceilings by 1986.

Depreciation A loss of value, particularly in real estate property, brought about by age, physical deterioration, and-or functional or economic obsolescence.

Depreciation allowance An accounting charge (expense) made to allow for the fact that an asset may be becoming economically or physically obsolete. The purpose is to write off the original cost by distributing it over the estimated useful life of the asset.

Development loan A loan made for the purpose of preparing raw land for the construction of one or more buildings.

Direct endorsement program An FHA program whereby qualified lenders are authorized to approve borrowers prior to all information being provided to the FHA.

Disbursements The payment of monies on a previously agreed-to basis. Used to describe construction loan draws.

Discount For a mortgage, discount refers to an amount withheld from loan proceeds by a lender. In secondary market sales, a discount is the amount by which the face value of a note exceeds its selling price. In both instances, the purpose of a discount is to adjust the yield upward, over the coupon rate of interest. The amount of the discount depends on money market conditions, the credit of the borrower, and the rate and terms of the note.

Discount point A fee charged by a lender at closing or settlement that

results in increasing the lender's effective yield on the money borrowed. An amount equal to 1 percent of a loan's principal.

Discounted cash flow The present value of future cash flows, determined by applying an appropriate discount rate that reflects the maturity and risk of the cash flows.

Disintermediation The flow of funds out of savings institutions into short-term investments in which interest rates are higher. It occurred primarily when short-term money market rates rose above institutional deposit rates.

Diversifiable risk Risk that can be reduced by combining several assets into one portfolio (see **nondiversifiable risk**).

Diversification The process of constructing a portfolio of different assets where returns are not expected to be perfectly correlated with each other. A method of risk reduction.

Documentary tax A fee or tax on deeds and other documents payable at the time of recording.

Dollar-based fees Fees charged to developers by local governments that are denominated in dollars.

Double declining balance A depreciation method allowed prior to 1981 where the depreciation of an asset in the early years was double the straight-line amount on whatever the nondepreciable difference was.

Down payment Cash portion of purchase price paid by a buyer from his or her own funds, as opposed to that portion which is financed.

Due-on-sale clause A type of acceleration clause included in many mortgages permitting the lender to require the borrower to repay the outstanding balance when the property is sold.

Duration A measure of the extent to which the cash flows of a security are "pushed back" in time. It is found by taking a weighted average of the present values of the cash flows. Similar to maturity of a security.

Easement A right to the limited use or enjoyment by one or more persons in the land of another. The specific limited use may include laying a sewer, putting up electric power lines, or crossing the property.

Easement appurtenant An easement which belongs to and passes with a particular tract of land.

Effective gross income (personal) For loan qualification purposes, annual income including overtime that is regular or guaranteed. It may be from more than one source.

Effective duration The duration of an interest contingent security found by observing the percentage price change in the market as a result of a change in interest rates.

Effective gross income (property) Gross actual cash receipts (net of vacancy and collection losses) from an income-producing property.

Effective yield The actual rate of return to the investor. It may vary from the coupon rate due to sale at a discount or premium.

Efficient market (theory) The theory that asset markets are efficient in that assets prices reflect all known and available information. No excess returns can be gained by trading on information known to market participants.

Eminent domain The right of a government to take private property for public use upon payment of its fair value (see **condemnation**).

Employee Retirement Income Security Act (ERISA) A federal law that regulates the investments that pension and profit-sharing plans can make, and the conduct of their fiduciaries.

Encroachment An improvement that intrudes illegally upon another's property.

Encumbrance Any interest in or claim on the land of another that in some manner burdens or diminishes the value of that property.

Equal Credit Opportunity Act (ECOA) A federal law that requires lenders to make credit equally available without discrimination based on race, color, religion, national origin, age, sex, marital status, or receipt of income from public assistance programs. Also known as Regulation B.

Equitable (right of) redemption The common law right to redeem property during the foreclosure period by paying past due amounts. In some states the mortgagor has a statutory right to redeem property after a foreclosure sale. This is limited to several months or a year.

Equity   In real estate, equity is the difference between the fair market value of the property and the amount of debt.

Equity kicker   A term usually applied to the income participation given to a lender as part of the consideration for making the loan.

Equity participation   An interest in income property, given by the owner to the lender as part of the consideration for making the loan. The loan is usually made at a below-market rate of interest.

Equity-participation agreement (EPA) A mortgage financing arrangement involving a third-party investor who joins with the borrower to finance a property. The investor-participant's involvement can have the impact of reducing the home buyer's borrowing needs or lowering the effective interest rate.

Equity REIT   A real estate investment trust that invests in the equity of real estate (see **mortgage REIT**).

Equity theory of default   A theory that states that mortgage defaults only occur if there is negative equity in the property (see **ability-to-pay theory of default**).

Escalator clause   A clause permitting an increase or decrease in rent payments to cover specified contingencies, such as the provision in a lease to provide for increases in property tax and operating expenses or inflation.

Escheat   The reversion of property to the state if the owner dies intestate and without descendants or heirs.

Escrow   A relationship whereby a third party, acting as the agent for a buyer and a seller of real estate, carries out instructions of both and assumes the responsibilities of handling all the paperwork and disbursement of funds.

Escrow analysis   The periodic review of an escrow account to determine if current monthly deposits will provide sufficient funds to pay taxes, insurance, and other bills when due.

Escrow payment   That portion of a mortgagor's monthly payment held by the lender to pay for taxes, hazard insurance, and mortgage insurance as they become due. Also called impounds in some states (such as California).

Estoppel letter   A statement that in itself prevents its issuer from later asserting different facts.

Eviction   The lawful expulsion of an occupant from real property.

Exclusive listing   A written contract giving a licensed real estate agent the exclusive right to sell a property for a specified time, but reserving the owner's right to sell the property alone without the payment of a commission.

Exclusive right to sell   The same as exclusive listing, but the owner agrees to pay a full commission to the broker even though the owner may sell the property.

Exculpatory clause   A clause inserted in a contract, such as a mortgage or lease, which frees a party from liability. For example, a debt agreement may contain an exculpatory clause that limits the recourse of the lender in the event of default solely to the assets pledged as collateral for the debt agreement.

Executor   A male named in a will to administer an estate. Executrix is the feminine equivalent.

Expectations theory   A theory that says the structure of the yield curve incorporates the market's expectations of future interest rates.

Face value   The value of notes, mortgages, etc., as stated on the face of the instrument itself.

Fair Housing Law   Title VII of the Civil Rights Act, prohibiting discrimination in residential housing on the basis of race, religion, color, sex, or national origin. Does not apply to commercial or industrial properties.

Fair market value   An economic concept denoting the price, in terms of money, at which a willing seller and buyer will agree when both parties are acting prudently, knowledgeably, and under no compulsion.

Falling market   A market in which interest rates are moving in an overall downward direction.

Fannie Mae   See **Federal National Mortgage Association.**

Federal credit agencies   Federally sponsored and-or supported agencies that support various activities such as housing or agriculture through credit availability.

Farmers Home Administration (FmHA)   An agency within the Department of Agriculture which operates principally under the Consolidated Farm and Rural Development Act of 1921 and Title V of the Housing Act of 1949. This agency provides residential property financing to farmers and other qualified borrowers who are unable to obtain loans elsewhere.

Federal Deposit Insurance Corporation (FDIC)   An organization originally established by the Banking Act of 1933 to insure the deposits of banks.

Federal Home Loan Mortgage Corporation (FHLMC)   A private corporation authorized by Congress with an independent board of directors to provide secondary mortgage market support for conventional mortgages. It also sells participation certificates secured by pools of conventional mortgage loans. Popularly known as Freddie Mac, it is under the oversight of HUD.

Federal Housing Administration (FHA)   Its main activity is the insuring of residential mortgage loans made by private lenders. FHA is a division of HUD which sets standards for construction and underwriting and charges a fee, generally 3.8 percent of loan amount.

Federal National Mortgage Association (FNMA)   A privately owned corporation created by Congress to support the secondary mortgage market. It purchases and sells residential mortgages insured by FHA or guaranteed by VA, as well as conventional home mortgages. Popularly known as Fannie Mae, it is under the oversight of HUD.

Federal Reserve Board   A government institution that controls and regulates the operation of all nationally chartered or FDIC-insured commercial banks.

Fee simple   An estate under which the owner is entitled to unrestricted powers to dispose of the property and which can be left by will or inherited; commonly, the greatest interest a person can have in real estate.

FHAing   The practice by lenders of only making FHA loans in certain risky or transition neighborhoods. Lenders suffer no loss with FHA insurance as they may with private mortgage insurance.

FHA prepayment rate A model of mortgage prepayments based on the historical record of prepayments of all FHA loans.

Fiduciary A person in a position of trust and confidence for another.

Financial Accounting Standards Board (FASB) An independent, private entity that establishes standards for financial accounting and reporting and derives its authority from the SEC.

Financial Institutions Deregulation Act and Monetary Control Act (MCA) A law enacted in March 1980, authorizing the deregulation of several aspects of the banking and financing industry, in particular the deregulation of interest and earnings limits and the approval for savings and loans to have trust powers and make more consumer loans. One effect of MCA is a lessening of the distinction between banks and savings and loan associations.

Financial Institutions Reform, Recovery, and Enforcement Act (FIRREA) An act passed in 1989 to help bail out the failing savings and loan industries. It established the Resolution Trust Corporation (RTC) and changed the regulatory structure of financial institutions.

Financial intermediary An institution that accepts funds from surplus income units and lends them to deficit income units.

Financing package The total of all financial interest in a project. It may include mortgages, partnerships, joint venture capital interests, stock ownership, or any financial arrangement used to carry a project to completion.

Firm commitment A lender's agreement to make a loan to a specific borrower for a specified property. An FHA or PMI agreement with a designated borrower to insure a loan on a specific property.

First mortgage A lien on property in which the lender's claims are superior to the rights of subsequent lenders.

Fixture Personal property that becomes real property when attached in a permanent manner to real estate.

Floating Interest-Rate Short-Tranche Securities (FIRSTS) A type of

floating-rate CMO, issued by Shearson Lehman Brothers, that pays LIBOR (London Inter-Bank Offer Rate) plus a prespecified spread, subject to caps.

Floating rate tranche A class of bonds in a CMO or REMIC where the interest rate to investors varies according to a specified market index.

Floor loan A portion or portions of a mortgage loan commitment that is less than the full amount of that commitment. It may be funded upon conditions less stringent than those required for funding the full amount. For example, the floor loan, equal to 80 percent of the full amount, may be funded upon completion of construction without occupancy requirements, but substantial occupancy of the building may be required for funding the full amount of the loan.

Flow-of-funds accounts A system that shows how funds flow through the financial system from the saving sector to the borrowing sector.

FNMA See **Federal National Mortgage Association.**

Forbearance The act of refraining from taking legal action despite the fact that a mortgage is in arrears. It is usually granted only when a mortgagor makes a satisfactory arrangement by which the arrears will be paid at a future date.

Foreclosure A legal procedure taken by a mortgagee or lender under the terms of a mortgage or deed of trust for the purpose of having the property sold and the proceeds applied to the payment of a defaulted debt.

Forward commitment An agreement by a lender or investor to either make or purchase a loan within a certain period or time.

Forward delivery The delivery of mortgages or mortgage-backed securities to satisfy cash or future market transactions of an earlier date.

Front-end money Funds required to start a development and generally advanced by the developer or equity owner as a capital contribution to the project.

Fully indexed rate The rate of interest on an adjustable rate mortgage when no discount or "teaser" rate applies.

Gap financing A loan given to fulfill the temporary need of a borrower

until the permanent loan is funded. For example, a permanent lender may require a minimum occupancy level in a new office building before he will fund the total permanent loan. To fill the "gap" between reduced and permanent loans, the developer needs gap financing. Gap financing also generally is required during the construction period to finance the difference in the lower permanent loan commitment.

Garn–St. Germain Act An act passed in 1982 to place savings and loans on a more equal footing with commercial banks.

Garnishment A legal process whereby the property or money of a debtor that is under control of a third party (garnishee) can be legally applied toward those debts.

Generally Accepted Accounting Principles (GAAP) Accounting principles established by the accounting profession which are intended to produce a uniform and consistent set of accounting rules and practices.

Geographic diversification In real estate investment, the process of adding properties to a portfolio from different areas of the country. An area may be defined in terms of a commonality of its economy.

Gibson paradox An apparent paradox that recognizes that interest rates move in the same (not opposite) direction from changes in the money supply.

GNMA-backed bond A "mortgage-backed bond" using GNMA Certificates as the collateral rather than the individual mortgages.

GNMA futures market A regulated central market organized by the Chicago Board of Trade in which standardized contracts for the future delivery of GNMA securities are traded.

GNMA mortgage-backed securities Securities, guaranteed by GNMA, that are issued by mortgage bankers, commercial banks, savings and loan associations, savings banks, and other institutions. The GNMA security holder is protected by the "full faith and credit of the United States." GNMA securities are backed by FHA, VA, or FmHA mortgages. All mortgages in original pools have the same contract rate.

GNMA II Similar to GNMA certificates, except that the mortgages within the pool may have interest rates that vary within 100 basis points.

Government National Mortgage Association (GNMA) Nicknamed Ginnie Mae, this HUD agency operates as a participant in the secondary mortgage market. It is involved with special government financing programs for urban renewal projects, elderly housing, and other high-risk mortgages. GNMA also carries out the liquidation and special assistance functions performed by the Federal National Mortgage Association prior to its reorganization in 1968. The association is involved with the mortgage securities pool and the tandem plan.

Government-sponsored enterprise (GSE) Examples are Freddie Mac, Fannie Mae, and Ginnie Mae.

Graduated payment adjustable mortgage (GPAM) A new financing alternative which is essentially an adjustable mortgage loan version of the GPM. It provides a graduated payment schedule for the principal and interest, with a variable interest factor built into the payment schedule and-or term and-or principal balance owed (see **graduated payment mortgage**).

Graduated payment mortgage (GPM) A residential mortgage designed to overcome the "tilt" effect. The monthly mortgage payments that start at a level below that on a FRM and increase at a predetermined rate with later payments above that on a FRM. They may level off at some predetermined point.

Grantee The person who receives an interest in real property.

Grantor The person conveying an interest in real property.

Gross rent multiplier A figure used to compare rental properties to determine value. The multiplier is derived by dividing the sales price of comparable properties by their gross annual or monthly rents. Synonyms are gross multiplier and gross income multiplier.

Ground rent or lease A long-term lease for a parcel of unimproved land. If it is developed, the first lienholder often takes a junior position to another lienholder through a subordination clause.

Growing equity mortgage (GEM) A type of loan in which annual increases in monthly payments are used to reduce outstanding principal and shorten the term of the loan.

Guarantee of principal and interest payment A promise of a mortgage security issuer that principal and interest due investors will be paid by issuer if not paid by borrower.

Guaranteed mortgage certificate (GMC) A bond-like instrument issued by Freddie Mac that represents ownership in a large pool of residential mortgages. Principal is returned annually and interest is paid semiannually.

Guarantor A person or entity that guarantees the performance of a loan taken out by another party.

Hard money mortgage A mortgage given in return for cash, rather than to secure a portion of the purchase price, as with a purchase money mortgage.

Hazard insurance An insurance policy designed to protect the owner's property from physical damage.

Hedging In mortgage lending, the purchase or sale of mortgage futures contracts to protect cash market transactions to be made at a future date.

Highest and best use The legal use of a parcel of land which, when capitalized, will generate the greatest net present property value of income.

Historic rehabilitation credit A credit for federal taxes computed as a percent of the amount of funds used to restore historic properties.

Holdback That portion of a loan commitment not funded until some additional requirement such as rental or completion is attained (see **floor loan**). Quite often the amount withheld is equal to the contractor's profit.

Home Mortgage Disclosure Act (HMDA) A federal act passed in 1975 that requires disclosure of an institution's loans by census tract or by zip code.

Home Owners Loan Corporation (HOLC) An agency formed in 1933 to help stabilize the economy. HOLC issued government-guaranteed bonds to lenders for delinquent mortgages and then refinanced homeowner indebtedness.

Homeowners policy A multiple-peril policy commonly called a "package policy." In addition to hazard insurance, it covers the property owners for loss due to burglary, injury to other, and damages caused by the owner to another's property.

Homestead estate In some states the home and property occupied by an owner are protected by law up to a certain amount from attachment and sale for the claims of creditors.

"Honest-to-God" (HTG) yield A phrase coined in 1977 by The First Boston Corporation, an estimate of a pass-through's cash flow yield.

HUD The Department of Housing and Urban Development, established by the Housing and Urban Development Act of 1965 to supersede the Housing and Home Finance Agency. It is responsible for the implementation and administration of government housing and urban development programs. The broad range of programs includes community planning and development, housing production and mortgage credit (FHA), equal opportunity in housing, and research and technology.

Hypothecate The process of pledging something as security but retaining possession of it. The borrower who gives a mortgage to a lender but keeps possession of the mortgaged property has hypothecated the property.

Impact fee A fee charged a developer by a local government to cover the added government expenditures (fire, police protection, etc.) necessitated by the development.

Impound See **Escrow**.

Income approach to value One of three traditional means of appraising property, based on the assumption that value is equal to the present value of future rights to income. Others are comparable sales and cost of construction.

Income property Real estate developed or improved to produce income. Also called commercial property and distinguished from owner-occupied residence.

Income ratios Ratios of monthly payments on debt to total income used to qualify borrowers for mortgage loans.

Index A rate of interest, such as a T-bill rate, used to measure periodic interest rate adjustments for an adjustable rate mortgage.

Industrial park A large parcel of real estate specifically zoned to be used as a manufacturing facility or other light industrial uses. Normally, facilities needed by industrial plants, such as roads, water, rail service, and automobile parking, are made available by the developer of the park.

Industrial revenue bond (IRB) A form of financing whereby a municipality or development corporation issues bonds to finance revenue-producing projects. Project revenues are used to pay the debt service on the bonds and to retire the bonds at maturity.

Installment One payment of principal and interest, required as a periodic payment on a mortgage loan.

Installment contract A method of selling and financing property whereby the seller retains title but the buyer takes possession while he makes payments.

Installment sale The selling of an appreciated property on terms rather than for cash so as to postpone the payment of capital gains taxes on the profits.

Institutional lender A financial institution that originates mortgages that it carries in its own portfolio. Mutual savings banks, life insurance companies, commercial banks, pension and trust funds, and savings and loan associations are examples.

Insured loan A loan insured by FHA, VA, or a private mortgage insurance company.

Interest The sum paid for the use of money. Also, the degree of rights in the ownership of property.

Interest only (IOs) A mortgage-related security that gives the holder the right to receive all interest payments (only) from a pool of mortgages.

Interest rate Rate of return on a principal amount. The rate is normally expressed as an annual percentage.

Interest rate contingent security A security (usually a mortgage-related security) for which the amount and timing of the cash flows is dependent upon (changes in) market rates.

Interest rate risk The risk that, subsequent to the purchase of a debt security, interest rates will change, thereby affecting the value of the security.

Interest reduction programs HUD programs (e.g., Sections 235 and 236) that subsidize the market interest rate on mortgage loans for low- and moderate-income housing, thus lowering the borrower's cost.

Interim financing Financing provided from project commencement to closing of a permanent loan, usually in the form of a construction loan or development loan.

Interstate Land Sales Full Disclosure Act (ILSFDA) A federal act passed in 1968 that requires a developer to provide complete disclosure of all relevant facts concerning the interstate sale of undeveloped land.

Intestate To die leaving no valid will.

Investment interest limitation An IRS rule that limits the amount of interest on debt used to finance the acquisition of an asset (usually raw land) that a taxpayer can deduct to determine taxable income.

Investor One who acquires investment property. Any person or institution investing in mortgages.

Involuntary lien A lien imposed against property without consent of an owner. Examples include taxes, special assessments, federal income tax liens, mechanic's liens, and materials liens. A mortgage is a voluntary lien.

Joint and several liability A situation in which a creditor may sue one or more of the parties separately, or all of them together. For example, partners are jointly and separately liable for all debts and obligations incurred by the partnership.

Joint tenancy A concurrent ownership by two or more persons with the right of survivorship.

Joint venture An agreement by two or more individuals or entities to engage in a single project or undertaking. A joint venture is used in real estate development as a means of raising capital and spreading risk. It is formed for a specific purpose and duration and is dissolved when the purpose of the venture is accomplished.

Judgment The final legal determination of rights between disputants, such as a mortgagor and a mortgagee, by a court of competent jurisdiction.

Judgment lien A lien upon the property of a debtor resulting from the decree of a court.

Judicial foreclosure A means of selling property through a court procedure to satisfy a lien (see **foreclosure**).

Junior mortgage A mortgage that has a lower priority or lien position than a first (senior) mortgage.

Kicker The right of a mortgage lender or other investor to share in income, in addition to principal and interest receipts.

Land contract A contract ordinarily used in connection with the sale of property in cases where the seller does not convey title until all or a substantial portion of the purchase price is paid by the buyer. Often used to avoid a due-on-sale clause.

Land-use control A broad term that describes any legal restriction which controls the use of a parcel of land.

Late charge A financial charge made to a borrower for failure to pay a loan installment when due.

Lease An agreement by which a landlord (lessor) gives the right to a tenant (lessee) to use and have exclusive possession but not ownership of realty for a period of time in consideration for the payment of rent.

Leasehold An interest in real property held by virtue of a lease. A leasehold and a leased fee are valuable property rights which may under certain circumstances be sold, assigned, or mortgaged.

Leasehold mortgage A loan to a lessee secured by a leasehold interest in a property.

Legal description A description of a parcel of real estate complete and specific enough so that a competent civil engineer or surveyor could locate the exact boundaries of the property.

Legal lists A term describing investments as different types of bonds or securities that life insurance companies, mutual savings banks, or other regulated investors may make under a state charter or court order.

Lessee (tenant) The person(s) holding rights of possession and use of property under terms of a lease.

Lessor (landlord) The one leasing property.

Level payment mortgage A method of loan repayment in which the dollar amount of each payment is the same. Part of each payment is credited to interest with the balance of the payment used to reduce the principal.

Leverage The use of borrowed money to increase the return on a cash investment. For leverage to be profitable, the rate of return on the investment must be higher than the cost of borrowed funds.

Lien A legally recognized hold or claim of one person on the property of another as security for a debt, duty, or obligation.

Lien theory The legal position that a mortgage creates a charge against property rather than conveying it to the lender.

Life-of-loan cap The maximum rate of interest allowed under the terms of an adjustable rate mortgage.

Limited partner A partner in a business venture whose liability to creditors is restricted to the money which he or she has invested in the partnership.

Limited partnership A partnership that consists of one or more general partners who are fully liable and one or more limited partners who are liable only for the amount of their investment. A substitute for a corporation in terms of liability but without being taxed as a corporate entity.

Line of credit The maximum amount of money that a customer of a bank may borrow without further need for approval. The borrower will "take down" the line of credit as it is needed.

Liquidity The cash position of an individual or business as it relates to the ability to pay obligations due. The ease with which an asset may be converted to cash.

Liquidity effect A short-term effect on interest rates resulting from a change in the growth rate of the money supply. Generally, when the money supply is increased, there is a short-term drop in interest rates.

Liquidity risk The risk that an asset may not be easily and rapidly sold for cash at its current value.

Lis pendens A notice filed in the public records for the purpose of serving as notice that title or some matter involving a particular parcel of real property is in litigation.

Loan (mortgage) constant The ratio of a payment (principal and interest) on a loan to its original loan balance. If a $100,000 loan requires $9,000 in annual interest and principal payment, the constant is 0.09.

Loan submission A package of papers and documents usually including pro forma income statements regarding a specific property. It is delivered to a lender for review and consideration for the purpose of making a mortgage loan.

Loan-to-value ratio The relationship between the amount of money borrowed and the appraised value of the property.

Lock-out (lock-in) period The portion of the term of a mortgage loan or line of credit during which the loan cannot be prepaid.

London Inter-Bank Offer Rate (LIBOR) An average of daily lending rates from several major London banks, used as a common international interest rate index.

Loss payable clause A clause in a fire insurance policy which lists the priority of claims in the event of destruction of the insured property. Generally, a mortgagee, or beneficiary under a deed of trust, is the party appearing in the clause to be paid prior to the owner.

Low-income housing credit A credit against federal taxes for investing in low-income housing.

MAI (Member, Appraisal Institute) A professional designation awarded by the American Institute of Real Estate Appraisers to persons who have met minimum education, experience, and demonstration requirements in the areas of valuation and appraisal.

Mandatory delivery A type of loan purchase program in which delivery of loans by a seller-servicer is mandatory.

Margin The number of basis points a lender adds to an index to determine the interest rate of an adjustable rate mortgage.

Market approach to value Also called comparable sales method. A method of appraisal valuation that estimates value based on the recent sale of properties with comparable characteristics.

Market rent The rental income that a property is likely to command in the current market. Market rent may be either higher or lower than what the property is actually renting for under the terms of the lease.

Market-to-market A procedure where an asset (or liability, but usually an asset) is revalued periodically (can be as frequently as daily) on the books of the holder.

Market value The price in terms of cash or its equivalent upon which a willing buyer and a willing seller will agree, where neither is under undue pressure and both are typically motivated, have adequate knowledge, and are acting in their own best interests.

Marketable title A title to property which is free from reasonable doubts or objections and which the courts would compel a purchaser to accept under the terms of the sale.

Marketing rate difference The difference between the amount a mortgage banker sells a loan for and the amount originated. A source of revenue for mortgage bankers.

Master limited partnership (MLP) A large limited partnership usually holding multiple projections either directly or through ownership of subsidiary partnerships. It is publicly traded on a secondary security market and can have several hundred investors.

Master servicer For MBS, the master servicer is responsible for servicing and administering mortgage loans in a mortgage pool. This function may be contracted to the originator of each mortgage loan under the supervision of the master servicer.

Maturity The date when a note or negotiable instrument is due and payable.

Maturity mismatch A difference in the maturity of the assets and liabilities of a financial institution. Usually refers to assets with a longer maturity than liabilities.

Maturity risk The increase in risk due to the increase in the maturity of a debt obligation due to possible changes in interest rates or inflation rates.

Metes and bonds A method of land description in which the dimensions of the property are measured by distance and direction.

Modified accelerated cost recovery system (MACRS) A system of depreciation in effect since 1986 whereby the expected lives of assets under the previous ACRS system were lengthened.

Modified pass-through A variation of the "pass-through security" which guarantees and pays the investor the scheduled monthly principal and interest payment, regardless of amounts collected from the pool of mortgages.

Money market The market where short-term (less than one year) debt obligations are exchanged.

Moratorium A period during which a borrower is granted the right to delay fulfillment of an obligation. Sometimes imposed by state law during periods of economic depression. In regard to the development of land, a temporary suspension or delay in the granting or approval of building permits, sewer and water hookups, or rezoning requests.

Mortgage A conveyance of an interest in real property given as security for the payment of a debt.

Mortgage-backed bonds A "bond" or debt instrument which is backed by a pool (large group) of mortgages and for which the cash flow of the mortgages serves as the source of repayment.

Mortgage-backed securities (MBS) Securities purchased by investors that are secured by mortgages. Such securities are also known as pass-through securities since the debt service paid by the borrower is passed through to the purchaser of the security.

Mortgage banker or mortgage company A firm or individual active in the field of mortgage banking (see next entry). Mortgage bankers, as local representatives of regional or national institutional lenders, act as correspondents between lenders and borrowers.

Mortgage banking The packaging of mortgage loans to be sold to a permanent investor or to be packaged into mortgage-backed securities with servicing retained for the life of the loan for a fee. Mortgage banking includes the origination, sale, and servicing of mortgage loans by a firm or individual. The investor-correspondent system is the foundation of the mortgage banking industry.

Mortgage broker A firm or individual who brings the borrower and lender together and receives a commission. A mortgage broker does not retain the servicing of the instrument.

Mortgage cash flow obligation (MCF) The unsecured general obligations of Freddie Mac which resemble a corporation's CMOs, except that the underlying mortgages are not pledged in trust as collateral.

Mortgage derivative securities A debt obligation for which the cash flows derive from those of the underlying assets which are mortgages.

Mortgage discount The difference between the principal amount of a mortgage and the amount for which it actually sells. Sometimes called points, loan brokerage fee, or new loan fee.

Mortgage insurance The function of mortgage insurance (whether government or private) is to insure a mortgage lender against loss caused by a mortgagor's default. This insurance will cover a percentage of or virtually all of the mortgage loan depending on the type of mortgage insurance. It also will cover all or a portion of REO expenses such as hazard insurance and property taxes that are paid by the lender after the property is taken over.

Mortgage insurance premium (MIP) The charge paid by a mortgagor for mortgage insurance either to FHA or a private mortgage insurance (PMI) company. On an FHA loan, the payment is 3.8 percent of the loan balance.

Mortgage life insurance A decreasing-term life insurance policy purchased by a borrower which will pay off the outstanding balance in the event of the death of the borrower (mortgagor). The premium is paid as part of the monthly mortgage payment.

Mortgage note A written promise to pay a sum of money at a stated interest rate during a specified term. The note is secured by real property.

Mortgage portfolio The total of all mortgages held by an investor or serviced by a mortgage lender.

Mortgage REIT A real estate investment trust that invests in mortgages on real estate properties (see **Equity REIT**).

Mortgage revenue bond A bond issued by a public entity payable from revenues derived from repayments of principal and interest on mortgage loans that were financed from the proceeds of the bonds.

Mortgagee A lender who receives a pledge of property to secure a debt.

Mortgagee in possession A mortgagee who, by virtue of a default under the terms of a mortgage, has obtained possession but not ownership of the property.

Mortgagor A borrower who pledges property through a mortgage to secure a loan.

Mutual mortgage insurance fund One of four FHA insurance funds into which all mortgage insurance premiums and other specified revenue of the FHA are paid and from which the losses are met.

Naked title Title that lacks the rights and privileges usually associated with ownership.

National Credit Union Association Board The federal supervisory agency for the nation's credit unions.

Negative amortization A loan payment schedule in which the outstanding principal balance goes up, rather than down, because the payments do not cover the full amount of interest due. The unpaid interest is added to the principal.

Negative duration Refers to a security whose value varies positively with a change in interest rates. An example is an interest-only strip of a mortgage pool.

Net income In accounting and taxation, income remaining after all expenses or deductions. The term may be qualified as net income before depreciation and debt service (interest).

Net lease A lease calling for the lessee to pay all fixed and variable expenses associated with the property, such as utilities, property taxes and maintenance expenses.

Net present value The excess of the present value of an asset's future cash flows over its current cost. A positive net present value indicates an asset should be acquired.

Net worth An amount equal to the value of total assets, including cash, less total liabilities; also known as equity.

Net yield interest rate The rate of interest remitted to an investor after the servicing fee has been deducted from the gross rate.

Nonconforming loan A loan that does not meet the purchase requirements of Fannie Mae and Freddie Mac (including "jumbo" loans).

Nondisturbance agreement An agreement that permits a tenant under a lease to remain in possession despite any foreclosure.

Nondiversifiable risk Risk that remains in a well-diversified portfolio of assets and thus cannot be reduced through further diversification (see **diversifiable risk**).

Nonowner-occupied (NOO) A term used to describe single-family investment property.

Nonrecourse loan A type of loan in which the borrower (mortgagor) is not personally liable for payment of the debt if the value of the property securing the loan is less than the amount necessary to repay the loan.

Notice of default (NOD) A notice recorded after default under a deed of trust or mortgage, or a notice required by an interested third party insuring or guaranteeing a loan.

Obsolescence The loss of value due to a decrease in the usefulness of property caused by decay, changes in technology, people's behavior patterns and tastes, or environmental changes.

Office of Interstate Land Sales Registration (OILSR) An agency within the Department of Housing and Urban Development (HUD) responsible for the registration of retail land programs being offered for sale to interstate customers.

Office of the Comptroller of Currency (OCC) The federal entity that regulates nationally chartered banks; the parallel organization to the Federal Home Loan Bank Board.

Open-end mortgage A mortgage written without a prepayment clause and which thus can be repaid in part or in full at any time during the term of the loan without the borrower having to pay a prepayment penalty.

Operating lease A lease for which the asset is not carried on the balance sheet of the user. Lease payments are treated as an operating expense (see **capital lease**).

Optimal capital structure That ratio of debt and equity which maximizes the value of the two components. Refers primarily to corporate finance but can be used in reference to financing real estate properties.

Option A right, given for consideration to a party (optionee) by a property owner (optionor), to purchase or lease within a specific time at a specific price and terms.

Optional delivery A type of loan purchase program in which the seller-servicer pays a fee for the option of delivering loans.

Original issue discount (OID) A tax concept that requires investors to pay taxes on the effective yield of an investment rather than on the coupon rate of the cash flows when debt is issued at a below-market coupon.

Origination The process of making a mortgage loan.

Origination fee A fee or charge for the work involved in the evaluation, preparation, and submission of a proposed mortgage loan.

Originator A person who solicits builders, brokers, and others to obtain applications for mortgage loans.

Out of the money A put option with a strike price that is below the current market price of the underlying security.

Overcollateralization Sufficient mortgages placed into a collateral pool so that their market value is sufficient to cover the bond they back plus a reserve. Overcollateralization is usually defined as a percentage of the bond, such as 110 percent.

Package mortgage A real estate loan which, in addition to real property, covers certain personal property items and equipment, such as appliances, carpeting, and draperies.

Par The principal or face amount of a mortgage with no premium or discount.

Partially modified pass-through A variation of the "pass-through security" which guarantees, to a certain extent, that monthly principal and interest payments will be made to the investor, even if not collected from the mortgage pool. A regular pass-through only promises principal and interest payments as collected.

Participating certificate (PC) Mortgage-backed security issued by FHLMC which is backed by mortgages purchased from eligible sellers. Called PC because seller retains some interest (5 or 10 percent) in the mortgages sold to FHLMC.

Participation loan A mortgage made by one lender, known as the lead lender, in which one or more other lenders, known as participants, own a mortgage or a part interest in a mortgage originated by two or more lenders. It is usually a large loan.

Passive income One of three classifications of income under TRA 1986. Most real estate and all limited partnerships are placed in this class of income.

Pass-through security A security issued by the Government National Mortgage Association which provides for the interest and principal to pass through to the holder of the security.

Pay-through security A form of "mortgage-backed bond" which is secured by a mortgage pool and for which the payment features closely resemble those of a "modified pass-through security." The bond is fully amortizing with scheduled principal and interest payments which closely track the scheduled collections on the collateral mortgage pool.

Payment cap A limit on the size of the payment (for a particular adjustment period) for an adjustable rate mortgage.

Percentage lease A lease in which a percentage of the tenant's gross sales or net profits constitutes all or a part of the rental payment. Although a straight percentage lease is occasionally encountered, most percentage leases contain a provision for a minimum rent amount. Common for shopping malls.

Percentage of completion A method of recording income from construction contracts based on the percentage of construction completed. Performance is often measured on a cost incurred basis.

Performance bond A bond given by someone such as a contractor to guarantee the completion of a construction project within a specified period of time.

Personal property Any property that is not real property.

PITI (principal, interest, taxes, and insurance) A measure of housing expense which is commonly used in borrower qualification as a measure of monthly obligation. In residential finance it is common for the lender to require payment of all four each month.

Planned amortization class bond (PAC bond) A tranche of a CMO or REMIC that is retired according to a predetermined amortization schedule independent of the prepayment rate on the underlying collateral. The amortization of the other tranches may have to be slowed down or accelerated so that the PAC schedule may be met.

Planned unit development (PUD) A one- to four-family individually owned unit situated upon a parcel of land which also contains common property for the benefit and use of individual PUD owners. The common property is maintained and owned by a homeowners' association, corporation or trust, which requires automatic membership of each individual unit owner, with mandatory assessments.

Plat A plan, map, or chart of a city, town, section, or subdivision indicating the location, boundaries, and ownership of individual parcels of real estate.

Plat book A record showing the location, size, and ownership of each plot of land in a stated area.

Pledged account mortgage (PAM) A graduated payment mortgage in which part of the buyer's down payment is deposited in a savings account. Funds are drawn from the account to supplement the buyer's monthly payments during the early years of the loan.

Point An amount equal to 1 percent of the principal amount of an investment or note. Loan discount points are a one-time charge assessed at closing by the lender to increase the yield on the mortgage loan.

Police power That right by which the state or other government authority may take, condemn, destroy, limit the use of, or otherwise invade property rights. It must be shown affirmatively that the property was taken for the public interest in a reasonable and equitable manner.

Portfolio A combination of distinct assets into one group, often for the purpose of diversification.

Portfolio income One of three classes of income under TRA 1986. Income from stocks and bonds is the primary type of income in this class.

Portfolio theory The theory that the risk of individual assets can be reduced by combining them into a portfolio and that there need be no reduction in expected return.

Potentially responsible party Under CERCLA, a party that will be considered legally responsible for the cost of cleaning up hazardous or toxic waste found on a property.

Power of sale A clause normally included in a mortgage or deed of trust giving the lender the legal right, upon default of the borrower, to sell the property at public auction.

Premium The amount, often stated as a percentage, paid in addition to the face value of a note or bond. A premium also may be defined as the dollar payment made by the insured to the insurance company for an insurance policy.

Prepayment (recovery of principal) Payment in full on a mortgage before the loan has been fully amortized due either to a sale of the property or to foreclosure.

Prepayment assumption A calculated guess of how a portfolio of single-family loans will prepay over time. Often the assumption is expressed as a percentage of long-term FHA experience of prepayments.

Prepayment fee The dollar amount levied against a borrower by a lender for paying off a loan before its maturity date. Also known as a prepayment penalty.

Prepayment penalty See **prepayment fee.**

Prepayment privilege The right given by a lender to a borrower to pay all or part of a debt prior to its maturity.

Present value (PV) Stated in terms of one dollar, PV represents today's value of an amount of money that is not to be received until some time in the future. Present value may be understood as the current value of money less the compounded interest that would have been earned over a given time period.

Price anticipation effect A change in the market rate of interest in the same direction as recent inflation. Market investors incorporate expectations of future inflation in their required yield.

Price level adjusted mortgage (PLAM) An alternative mortgage instrument that provides the lender with a real rate of interest in the form of a contract rate and inflation premium through an adjustment of the mortgage balance by the most recent amount of inflation.

Primary market The market where financial securities are first originated.

Principal The face value of a note or mortgage. In a real estate transaction, the principal is the person who hires a real estate broker to sell his or her property.

Principal balance The outstanding balance of a mortgage, exclusive of interest and other charges.

Principal only (POs) A mortgage-related security that gives the holder the right to all principal payments (only) from a pool of mortgages.

Priority Having legal precedence over others, such as a first mortgage in contrast to a second mortgage. In such a case, the priority determines which creditor receives first payment in case of foreclosure.

Private mortgage insurance (PMI) Insurance written by a private (nongovernmental) company protecting the mortgage lender against loss caused by a mortgage default or foreclosure.

Private pass-through securities Securities that carry no agency guarantee. Bank of America issued the first private pass-through in 1977.

Pro forma statement A financial statement used to project anticipated revenues and expenses for a real estate project. The information is based upon assumptions and estimates regarding the operation of the property.

Public Securities Association (PSA) An organization representing the major dealers in mortgage-related and government-sponsored securities that provides nonenforceable guidelines to the industry. "PSA experience" refers to the model used for prepayment assumptions.

Public Securities Association prepayment rate A widely used model of mortgage prepayment rates established by the PSA.

Publicly traded partnership A large partnership, the interests of which are traded on the major security exchanges.

Purchase contract The contract between a seller and Freddie Mac covering a commitment to purchase, in whole or in part, a specific dollar amount of mortgages.

Purchase money mortgage A mortgage given by the purchaser of real property to the seller as part of the sales price.

Purchase procedures The procedure under which a secondary market corporation reviews a loan package and decides to purchase or reject it.

Put option An agreement giving the holder the right to deliver specified securities at a fixed price during a particular period of time.

Qualification In real estate finance, the process of obtaining a sufficient amount of information from a buyer and seller to determine the seller's financial objectives and the buyer's purchasing capacity.

Qualified monthly income (QMI) The amount of a borrower's monthly income necessary to qualify for a loan of a given amount at a given interest rate for a given term. Used as a lender's standard to determine how much a borrower can afford to borrow without creating undue risk or hardship. In most cases a QMI must be three to four times the monthly principal and interest payments on the loan.

Qualified thrift investments Investments which thrifts are allowed to acquire under the 1989 FIRREA act.

Quitclaim deed A deed that transfers (with no warranty) only what present interest, title, or right a grantor may have at the time the conveyance is executed.

Rate cap A limit on the contract rate of interest (for a particular adjustment period) on an adjustable rate mortgage.

Real estate investment trust (REIT) An organized association whereby individual investors pool their funds for the purpose of investing in real estate. A REIT is created in the form of a business trust. If the tax requirements are met, it provides for a pass-through of income without double taxation.

Real estate mortgage investment conduit (REMIC) A type of mortgage-backed security that allows for income to be taxed only to the holders of the bond and not to the entity holding the mortgages.

Real estate owned (REO) A term used by lending institutions referring to its ownership of real property usually acquired as a result of foreclosure.

Real Estate Settlement Procedures Act (RESPA) A federal law that deals with procedures to be followed in certain types of real estate closings. RESPA requires lenders to provide loan applicants with pertinent information so that the borrower can make an informed decision as to which lender to use in financing the purchase.

Real property The aggregate of rights, powers, and privileges inherent in the ownership of land and appurtenances, including anything of a permanent nature.

Real rate of interest The nominal rate of interest adjusted for inflation.

REALTOR A real estate broker or an associate holding active membership in the National Association of Realtors. Realtor is a registered trademark of the NAR.

Reciprocal easement agreement The basic agreement relating to the development, construction, and operation of a shopping center entered into between the developer and the major department stores' anchor tenants around which the center is planned and developed.

Recision The cancellation or annulment of a transaction or contract by operation of law or mutual consent.

Reconveyance The transfer of the title of real estate from one person to the immediately preceding owner. It is used when the performance of debt is satisfied under the terms of a deed of trust.

Record date The date which determines holder of record entitled to receive payment of principal, interest, and any prepayment from the loan servicer.

Recorder The public official in a political subdivision who keeps records of transactions affecting real property in the area. Sometimes known as a registrar of deeds or county clerk.

Recording The noting in the registrar's office of the details of a properly executed legal document, such as a deed, mortgage, a satisfaction of mortgage, or an extension of mortgage, thereby making it a part of the public record. A recording often is required to establish priority of claim.

Recourse The right of the holder of a note secured by a mortgage or deed of trust to look personally to the borrower or endorser for payment, not just to the property.

Redlining The practice by lenders of refusing to make loans in certain risky or transitional neighborhoods.

Redemption period The statutory period of time within which a borrower may make good on a defaulted loan and thus regain his or her property by paying the principal amount accumulated, interest, and legal costs.

Redemption, right of The legal right of a borrower to make good on a defaulted loan within a statutory period of time and thus regain his property.

Refinance To repay one or more existing mortgage loans by simultaneously borrowing funds through another mortgage loan.

Regulation Z A regulation issued by the Federal Reserve System to implement the Truth-in-Lending Act.

Regulatory accounting principles (RAP) The accounting principles required by regulation that allow savings institutions to elect annually to defer gains or losses on the sale of assets and amortize these deferrals over the average life of each loan group or the stated life of each security sold.

Release of lien An instrument discharging secured property from a lien.

Release provision A provision in a land development loan that allows parcels to be released from the lien of the lender so that they may be sold.

Rent Payments made by a tenant to a landlord for the use of real estate owned by the landlord.

Reproduction cost The current cost of constructing an exact duplicate of the property being appraised. One of three methods of appraising the property's value.

Residential Funding Corporation (RFC) A private company that engages in secondary market activities. It specializes in buying loans which do not conform to Freddie Mac and Fannie Mae requirements.

Residual method One of two income ratio tests applied by the VA for loan qualifications. The method concentrates on the residual income after housing payments sufficient to meet other living expenses, such as food and clothing.

Resolution Trust Corporation (RTC) A government organization set up by the 1989 FIRREA act to dispose of property acquired by the federal government when it acquired the assets of failed savings and loans.

RESPA Real Estate Settlement Procedures Act.

Restrictive covenant A clause in a deed which puts a private limitation on the use of real estate.

Return on equity The ratio of cash flow after debt service to the difference between the value of property and total financing (see **cash-on-cash return**).

Reverse annuity mortgage (RAM) A financing arrangement whereby a lender pays the borrower a fixed annuity or periodic payment based on a percentage of the property's value.

Reverse leverage The financial condition experienced when expenses incurred to repay an interest-bearing debt exceed the financial benefits of the assets that were acquired with the borrowed money (see **negative cash flow**).

Reverse repurchase agreement An agreement to purchase mortgage-backed securities from a party with a simultaneous agreement to resell them at a specified future date and price.

Reversion A right to future possession retained by an owner at the time of a transfer of the owner's interest in real property.

Reversionary clause A clause providing that any violations of restrictions will cause title to the property to revert to the party who imposed the restriction.

Right of rescission The right to rescind (undo) a contract if certain legal requirements are not fulfilled.

Right of survivorship In joint tenancy and tenancy by the entirety, the right of survivors to acquire the interest of a deceased joint tenant.

Right of way The legal right of one person to cross over the land belonging to someone else. Such a right may be either private or public and can be created either by contractual agreement or through continued use.

Risk The possibility combined with the probability that the actual future outcome will differ from the expected outcome.

Risk-based capital guidelines Rules established by Office of Thrift Supervision (OTS) which determine the amount of capital a thrift must have as a function of the riskiness of its assets.

Rolling option An option to purchase more land to be developed as the existing development is completed.

Sale-leaseback A technique in which a seller deeds property to a buyer for a consideration and the buyer simultaneously leases the property back to the seller, usually on a long-term basis.

Sandwich lease A lease in which the "sandwiched party" is simultaneously lessee and lessor paying rent on a leasehold interest to one party and collecting rent from another party.

Satisfaction of mortgage A written release issued by a mortgagee (lender) stating that a mortgage has been paid in full. Sometimes known as a release deed.

Savings and loan association (S&L) A mutual or stock association chartered and regulated by either the federal or a state government. S&Ls accept time deposits and lend funds primarily on residential real estate.

Second mortgage A mortgage that is second in priority because of the timing of recording the mortgage or of the subordination of the mortgage.

Secondary financing Financing real estate with a loan, or loans, subordinate to a first mortgage or first trust deed.

Secondary market The market where existing securities are exchanged.

Secondary mortgage market A market where existing mortgages are bought and sold. It contrasts with the primary mortgage market, where mortgages are originated.

Secondary Mortgage Market Enhancement Act of 1984 (SMMEA) A federal law that enhanced development of the private mortgage securities markets, amended federal securities laws, and preempted certain state laws.

Secured lender exemption Under CERCLA, an exemption from responsibility for cleanup costs given to lenders with a security interest in a property (collateral) on which toxic or hazardous waste is found.

Secured party The party holding a security interest or lien.

Securities and Exchange Commission (SEC) The federal agency which regulates securities and the securities industry. It is involved in real estate and mortgage lending when MBS, certain limited partnerships, and REITs are issued.

Securitization The process of creating new securities backed by (collateralized) a package of other securities or assets.

Security The collateral given, deposited, or pledged to secure the fulfillment of an obligation or payment of a debt.

Security instrument The mortgage or trust deed evidencing the pledge of real estate security as distinguished by the note.

Security interest A general term designating the interest of the creditor in the property of the debtor in all types of credit transactions.

Seller carryback An idiom commonly used in real estate for whenever the seller, acting as a lender, holds or "carries back" a first or second mortgage note from the buyer. An example would be a purchase-money mortgage.

Seller-servicer FNMA term for an approved financial institution or mortgage banker that sells and services mortgages for FNMA.

Seller's points Loan discount points paid by a seller so that a buyer can obtain a loan.

Senior mortgage The mortgage against a property that holds first priority in the event of foreclosure.

Senior/subordinated securities A mortgage pass-through security issued in two classes. The subordinated class absorbs payment risk for both classes.

Servicing The duties of the mortgage lender as a loan correspondent as specified in the servicing agreement for which a fee is received. The periodic, normally monthly, collection of mortgage interest and principal repayment and other mortgage related expenses, such as property taxes and property insurance.

Servicing agreement A written agreement between an investor and mortgage servicer stipulating the rights and obligations of each party.

Servicing income The income derived from servicing a portfolio of mortgages.

Set-back ordinance An ordinance prohibiting the erection of an improvement or structure between the curb and the set-back line.

Settlement The closing of a real estate transaction at which time prorations and adjustments are made between buyer and seller for the purpose of concluding the transactions.

Settlement services Services provided by the participants in a loan settlement: attorneys, lenders, title companies, escrow companies, and others.

Shared appreciation mortgage (SAM) A mortgage in which a borrower receives a below-market interest rate in return for which the lender receives a portion of the future appreciation in the value of the property.

Single family (SF) Any residential one- to four-family zoned property.

Single-family (SF) loan Any loan secured by a one- to four-family property.

Single monthly mortality (SMM) A prepayment measurement that reflects monthly average prepayment rates.

Sinking fund Periodic deposits of money into an account that, with its interest earnings, will be used to replace assets or retire loans. Provides investors assurance that the principal portion of an investment will be repaid within a specified maturity.

Soft costs Architectural, engineering, and legal fees as distinguished from land and construction costs.

Special limited obligation debt Bonds issued by a housing agency which are secured only by the revenues and funds pledged in the specific indenture. Funds held by the agency for other programs or in general funds are not pledged for debt service. Opposite of a general obligation debt.

Special warranty deed A deed in which the seller (grantor) warrants only against defects of title that have occurred after the grantor acquired title.

Specific performance A remedy in a court of equity compelling the defendant to carry out the terms of an agreement or contract.

SREA The appraisal designation denoting Senior Real Estate Analyst (SREA), awarded by the Society of Real Estate Appraisers. The designations are: senior residential appraiser (SRA), senior real property appraiser (SRPA), and senior real estate analyst (SREA).

Standby commitment An agreement between a real estate lender and a builder whereby the lender stands ready to make a certain loan amount available to the builder for a specified period of time. Such commitments are used typically to enable the borrower to obtain construction financing at a lower cost on the assumption that permanent financing of the project will be available on more favorable terms when the improvements are completed and the project is generating income.

Standby fee A fee charged by an investor for a standby commitment. The fee is earned upon issuance and acceptance of the commitment.

Statute of frauds A state law requiring that certain contracts be in writing and contain certain essential elements to be enforceable. A contract for the sale of real estate must be in writing to be enforceable.

Statute of limitations The period of time limited by statute within which certain court actions may be brought by one party against another. The period of time varies from state to state as well as between the various types of action.

Statutory (right of) redemption The right of a borrower after a foreclosure sale to reclaim his property by repaying his defaulted loan.

Step-down lease A lease calling for reductions in the initial rent over a stated period of time.

Step-up lease A lease calling for increases in the initial rent over a stated period of time.

Stepped-up basis An increase in the depreciable basis of an asset usually brought about by its sale.

Straight-line depreciation Depreciation based on dividing the depreciable basis of an asset by the number of years of its remaining useful life.

Strips A mortgage pass-through security created by separating and reassembling the principal and interest payments on a pool of long-term mortgages.

Subdivision control ordinances Local government ordinances that require developers to put in place the necessary infrastructure before development may take place. Alternatively, the developer may place funds in a trust for this purpose.

Subject to mortgage A real estate transaction in which the grantee (purchaser) takes over the existing mortgage payments from the grantor (seller) but assumes no personal liability on the mortgage. When a mortgage is taken subject to, the purchaser can walk away from the mortgage and lose nothing but the equity already invested.

Sublease A lease transferred by a lessee to a third person for a term no longer than the remaining portion of the original lease.

Subordinate Not in a position of priority, junior to.

Subordination A clause which may be included in a written recorded instrument in which the mortgagee (lender) agrees to permit a later-acquired debt to have priority. Subordination may apply not only to mortgages, but to leases, real estate rights, and any other types of debt instruments.

Subrogation The substitution of one person into another person's legal position in reference to a debt, claim, or right.

Superfund Amendments and Reauthorization Act (SARA) A federal law, passed by Congress in 1986, stipulating that any party entering into a contractual relationship (e.g., a mortgage) with the owner of a toxic waste site also may be liable for cleanup.

Suspended losses Passive losses that cannot be used in the year they occur to offset other types of income. They are cumulated until they can be used or the property is sold.

Swap The selling of mortgages in exchange for PCs representing interests in those same mortgages under the Guarantor program.

Takeout commitment A promise to make a loan at a specified future time. It is commonly used to designate a higher cost, shorter term, backup commitment as support for construction financing until a suitable permanent loan can be secured.

Tandem plan A mortgage assistance program in which a federal agency agrees to purchase below-market interest rate mortgages at near par prices. The mortgages purchased are accumulated and periodically sold at auction as either mortgage-backed securities or whole mortgages. As the subsidy cost of the program, the agency absorbs the difference between the price it paid for the loan and the market price paid by the investor.

Tax deed A deed on property purchased at public sale to satisfy delinquent taxes.

Tax increment financing Exists where the infrastructure for a new development is paid for by property taxes on properties within the development.

Tax lien A claim against property for the amount of unpaid taxes.

Teaser rate A below market rate of interest for an initial period of time only on an adjustable rate mortgage.

Tenancy A tenant's legal interest in real property. A tenancy may be created either by title or by lease.

Tenancy at will The possession of real estate belonging to another with their permission for an indefinite period of time which can be terminated by the lessor (owner) or lessee (tenant).

Tenancy by entirety A special form of joint tenancy, limited to husband and wife, where both are viewed as one person under common law. This form also provides for the right of survivorship.

Tenancy in common In law, the type of tenancy or estate created when real or personal property is granted, devised, or bequeathed to two or more persons, in the absence of expressed words creating a joint tenancy. There is no right of survivorship (see **joint tenancy**).

Tenant One who holds or has the legal right to occupy the property belonging to someone else. The tenant is entitled to exclusive possession, use, and enjoyment of the property, usually for a rent specified in a lease.

Terminal wealth The amount in a fund at a future time where the fund accumulates periodic deposits and earns market rates of return. A tool to compare investment performance of a series of cash flows of a security to other securities.

Testate To leave a will at death.

Tilt effect The effect of a rise in interest rates whereby the real payments on a standard fixed rate mortgage (FRM) are much greater at the beginning of the loan than at the end.

Title The legally recognized evidence of a person's right to possess property. In the case of real estate, the documentary evidence of ownership is the title deed which specifies in whom the legal right is vested and the history of ownership.

Title insurance policy An insurance policy that protects the named insured against loss or damage due to defects in the property's title.

Title plant A duplicate set of public records maintained by a title company.

Title search A search of the public records to discover any liens or other impediments to a transfer of an unencumbered title.

Tranche A class of securities in a multiclass securities offering.

Trust deed The instrument given by a borrower (trustor) to a trustee vesting title to a property in the trustee as security for the borrower's fulfillment of an obligation (see **deed of trust**).

Trustee A person who holds title and control over property for another person known as a beneficiary.

Truth-in-Lending Law Enacted in 1969 under the National Consumer Credit Protection Act; implemented by Regulation Z of the Federal Reserve Board. The law ensures disclosure of credit costs by lenders, including disclosure of all fees and charges associated with a loan but separate from its quoted interest rate.

Underwriting The process of analyzing risk and determining an appropriate charge for taking on the risk. It involves a review of borrower's credit, value of security, and certain legal documents.

Unencumbered property Property that is free and clear of any legal claims or liens.

Unrelated business income tax (UBIT) A tax law that requires otherwise tax exempt organizations (such as pension funds) to pay tax on income earned from any business endeavor not related to its main purpose.

Uniform Commercial Code (UCC) A comprehensive law regulating commercial transactions. It has been adopted, with modification, by all states.

Uniform Settlement Statement A standard form required by HUD that stipulates the fees and charges to be paid by the buyer and seller at a loan closing.

Usury Charging a higher interest rate than allowed by law.

Vacancy factor A percentage rate expressing the loss from gross rental income due to vacancy and collection losses.

Variable rate mortgage (VRM) A mortgage agreement that allows for adjustment of the interest rate according to the market rate. Also called an adjustable rate mortgage.

Velocity of circulation The average number of times the money supply "turns over" in one year. Measured by dividing the gross national product by the supply of money.

Vendee The party to whom personal or real property is sold.

Veterans Administration (VA) Established in 1930, the Servicemen's Readjustment Act of

1944 authorized this agency to administer a variety of benefit programs designed to facilitate the adjustment of returning veterans to civilian life. The VA home loan guaranty program is designed to encourage lenders to offer long-term, low-down-payment mortgages to eligible veterans by guaranteeing the lender against loss.

Voucher control agent   An independent company that verifies that all monies advanced by a lender on an ADC loan have been used to construct the facility and that there are no mechanic's or other liens on the property being developed.

Warehousing   The holding of a mortgage on a short-term basis pending either a sale to an investor or other long-term financing. These mortgages may be used as a collateral security with a bank to borrow additional funds. A builder "warehouses" mortgages when he takes back a mortgage from a home buyer and holds the mortgage for a time period. A mortgage banker "warehouses" mortgages until a sufficient number is accumulated to package into a mortgage-backed security.

Warehousing rate difference   The difference between the interest rate on a mortgage (revenue) and the rate on a warehouse loan (cost) for a mortgage banker. A source of funds for a mortgage banker.

Warranty deed   A deed in which the grantor or seller warrants or guarantees that good title is being conveyed, as opposed to a quitclaim deed that contains no representation or warranty as to the quality of title.

Waste   The destructive use of property by someone in possession who holds less than full and clear title such as a tenant or mortgagor.

Weighted average coupon (WAC)   The weighted average coupon (or contract rate) on the mortgages underlying a mortgage-backed security.

Weighted average life (WAL)   The average time required to receive full repayment of principal, weighted by the principal payments.

Weighted average maturity (WAM)   The average term of the mortgages underlying a mortgage-backed security, weighted for the dollar amounts of the mortgages.

Wellenkamp case   A famous court case in California that established the right of a borrower to assume a mortgage even though it had a due-on-sale clause.

Whole loan   The entire mortgage loan package representing 100 percent ownership, and not prorated ownership as in a mortgage pool.

Wraparound   A mortgage which secures a debt that includes the balance due on an existing senior mortgage and an additional amount advanced by the wraparound mortgagee. The wraparound mortgagee thereafter makes the amortizing payments on the senior mortgage. For example, when a landowner has a mortgage securing a debt with an outstanding balance of $4 million, a lender can then advance the same mortgagor another $2 million and makes the remaining payments on the $4 million debt by taking a $6 million wraparound junior mortgage on the real estate to secure the total indebtedness. The mortgage will involve an all-inclusive deed of trust.

Yield to maturity   The annual return on an investment equal to the annual interest rate plus or minus the discounted gain or loss realized at time of maturity.

Zoning   The act of city or county authorities specifying the type of use to which property may be put in specific areas.

NAME INDEX

A

Agarwal, Vinod B., 133
Ahlbrandt, Roger, 180
Altman, E. I., 177
Ambrose, B., 256–257
Aquinas, Thomas, 45
Asabere, Paul K., 128
Avery, R. B., 52, 176

B

Bajtelsmit, Vickie L., 453
Becker, Gary S., 174–175
Beeson, P. E., 52
Benjamin, John, 137, 450, 453
Berkovec, J., 180
Blew, Miller, 416
Boczar, G. E., 175
Boehm, Thomas P., 114
Boyes, W. J., 176
Brimelow, Peter, 178
Browne, Lynne, 178
Brueggeman, William, 127
Bush, George, 82, 208

C

Calem, P., 180
Calhoun, C. A., 451
Campbell, Tim, 256
Cannaday, Roger, 131
Canner, G., 180
Capone, C., 256–257
Carr, James, 178
Chandler, G. G., 176, 177
Clauretie, Terrence M., 131, 137, 232, 257, 291, 294, 457, 480
Colwell, Peter F., 127, 131
Corgel, John B., 39, 457
Cornwell, Ted, 415
Curcio, Richard J., 457

D

Dale-Johnson, David, 131
Del Casino, Joseph J., 454
Dickinson, Amy, 117
Dietrich, J. Kimble, 256
Do, A. Quang, 109
Dougherty, Ann, 112
Downs, David H., 4
Dunsky, Robert M., 150
Durning, Dan, 137

E

Edgren, John A., 135
Ehrhardt, Michael C., 114
Elayan, Fayez, 432
Elebash, Clarence, 365
Elledge, B., 105
Ewert, D. C., 176, 177

F

Ferreira, Eurico J., 131
Findlay, M. Chapman, 131
Firstenberg, Paul, 455
Fisher, Irving, 17
Fisher, Jeffrey, 343
Fletcher, S., 105
Follain, J. R., 150, 451
Forgey, Fred, 84
Friedman, Jack, 131
Friedman, Milton, 17

G

Gabriel, S., 180
Gau, George, 317
Gay, Gerald, 457
Geltner, David, 451, 454
Gibson, A. H., 19

Goebel, Paul, 84, 181
Green, Jeffrey R., 256
Green, Jerry, 224
Guntermann, Karl L., 127

H

Hannon, T., 180
Hanz, J. Andrew, 128
Hartzell, David, 4, 456
Hayworth, Steven, 135
Hekman, J., 456
Hendershott, Patric, 73, 151–152
Herzog, Thomas, 294
Heuson, Andrea, 117
Hoffman, D., 176
Houston, Arthur L., 109
Houston, Joel F., 101
Howe, John, 430, 432
Huffman, Forrest E., 128
Hutchinson, P., 179

I

Ibbotson, Roger, 452, 453

J

Jackson, J. R., 256
Jameson, Mel, 232, 256, 480

K

Kane, Ed, 82
Kapplin, Stephen D., 131
Kaserman, D. L., 256
Kemp, Jack, 208
Keynes, John Maynard, 19
Klein, Linda, 114

L

Lacey, Nelson, 225
Larson, J. E., 39
Lentz, George, 343
Linneman, Peter, 154
Louargand, Marc A., 450
Low, S., 176
Lusht, Kenneth M., 128

M

Manchester, Joyce, 111
Marans, Robert W., 181
Maris, Brian, 117, 432
Markowitz, Harry, 444
Marshall, J., 177
Mayer, Christopher J., 113

McCue, Tom, 455, 456
McCulloch, J. Huston, 111, 146
McEneaney, James, 178
Megbolugbe, Isaac F., 178
Mehdian, Seyed, 128
Merkle, Paul, 137
Miceli, Thomas J., 114
Miles, Mike, 355, 456
Miller, Merton, 33, 314
Milonas, Nikolaos, 225
Modigliani, Franco, 33, 314
Morton, T. Gregory, 256
Mueller, Glenn, 456
Mulherin, J. Harold, 480
Muller, Walter J., 480
Munnell, Alicia, 178
Myer, F. C. Neil, 451

N

Navratil, Frank, 224
Nelson, Susan, 343
Norman, Emily J., 450, 453
Norris, G., 105

O

Ostas, J., 179
Ozanne, Larry, 73

P

Pagliari, Joseph L., Jr., 454
Pesando, James, 111
Peterson, C. M., 183
Peterson, R. L., 183
Petska, Tom, 343
Phillips, Richard A., 133
Pittman, Robert H., 4
Plotkin, Irving, 159

Q

Quercia, Roberto G., 256
Quigley, John, 137

R

Reed, D., 179
Rogers, Ronald, 232
Roll, Richard, 450
Rosen, Kenneth T., 130
Rosenberg, Sidney, 39, 181
Ross, Stephen, 450, 455
Rubens, Jack, 453, 455
Rutherford, Ronald C., 84

S

Sa-Aadu, J., 101, 105, 137
Sartoris, W. L., 175
Saulnier, R. J., 47
Schultz, William R., 73
Schwartz, A. L., 130, 131
Scott, William, 109
Sexton, D. E., 177
Sharpe, William, 447
Shay, R. P., 175, 177
Shilling, James, 101, 105, 430, 432
Shinkel, B. A., 177
Shoven, John, 224
Shulman, David, 456
Siegel, Laurence, 452, 453
Simons, Katerina, 113
Simonson, John, 159
Sirmans, C. F., 114, 127, 130, 137
Sirmans, G. Stacy, 130, 131, 450, 453
Smith, Stanley D., 130
Sniderman, M. S., 52
Spencer, Leslie, 178
Stegman, Michael A., 256
Sunderman, Mark A., 131

T

Tootell, Geoffrey, 178
Turnbull, Stuart, 111

V

Vanderhart, Peter, 113
Van Order, Robert, 112, 151–152
Villani, Kevin, 112, 159
Voith, Richard, 154
von Furstenberg, George, 256

W

Wall, Danny, 208
Wang, Ko, 317
Webb, James, 451, 453–455
Worzala, Elaine, 453
Wurtzebach, Charles, 456

Y

Yang, T. L. Tyler, 117
Yost, Gregory, 365

Z

Zerbst, Robert, 127
Zietz, E. Norman, 453
Ziobrowski, Alan, 457
Zisler, R. C., 455
Zorn, T. S., 39

SUBJECT INDEX

A

Ability-to-pay theory, 255
Abusive practices, regulation of, 157–158
Accelerated cost recovery system (ACRS), 328, 331
    modified (MACRS), 332
Acceleration clause, promissory notes, 264
Accounting issues of mortgage-related
        securities (MRSs), 196–197
Accounting regulations for leases, 411–415
Acquisition, 374–377
    institutional lenders, 375
    land loan, 374, 375
    seller accommodation, 375–377
Acquisition costs, 318
Acquisition, development, and construction
        (ADC) loans, 6, 362–363, 373–386,
        428, 470
    example of, 383–384
    risks of, 384, 386
    and yield calculation, 384, 386
ACRS, *See* Accelerated cost recovery
        system (ACRS)
Active income, 337
**Adaptations model of inflationary
        expectations, 17**
ADC loans, *See* Acquisition, development, and
        construction (ADC) loans
Adequacy of interest test, 335
Adjustable caps and periods, 101
Adjustable-rate mortgages (ARMs), 37, 69,
        93–106, 118–119, 260, 264
    adjustable caps and periods for, 101
    characteristics of, 118
    COFI indices, 94–95
    convertible, 95
    description of, 94–95
    example of, 95–98
    frequency of rate change, 94
    FRMs and, 93–94, 105–106
    fully indexed rate, 95
    index, 94

initial-period discount for, 95, 101–102
interest rate and, 168–169
interest rate caps, 95
interest rate risk and, 93–94
interest rate volatility and trend,
        103–105
life-of-loan caps for, 95, 102
margin for, 94–95, 103
monthly payment changes, 169
negative amortization, 95
payment caps, 95
performance comparison of, 98–100
pricing of, 100–105
and Regulation Z, 155
teaser rate for, 95, 101–102
value of, 103, 104
Adjustment rate caps, 95
Administration of construction loans, 382
Advantageous financing, 125, *See* Creative
        financing
Advertising in print media, 156
Affordability:
    of FRMs and ARMs, 106
    housing, *See* Housing affordability
    tilt effect and, 108
Affordability index, 67
Affordability problem, 108
After-tax cash flows, 29, 306–311, 313,
        325–329, 349, 350
    and asset valuation, 29
After-tax discount rate, 325–326, 328
Agency, 476
Agency costs, 39–40
    bankruptcy and, 476–479
    ethics and, 479–482
Agency law, bankruptcy and, 475–476
Agency problems, definition of, 39
Agency ratings, 20
Agency relationships:
    and mortgage insurance, 480
    and thrift failures, 480–482
Agency theory, 39–40
Agent, 39

voucher control, 382
Agricultural Credit Act (1987), 202
ALTA, *See* American Land Title
    Association (ALTA)
Alternative minimum taxes (AMTs),
    323, 341
    calculation example of, 342
    tax preference items for, 354
Alternative mortgage instruments
    (AMIs), 68, 69, 93–119
    adjustable rate mortgages (ARMs),
        37, 69, 93–106, 118, 155,
        168–169, 260, 264
    fixed-rate mortgages (FRMs),
        48–53, 93–94, 105–106, 118
    graduated payment mortgages
        (GPM), 69, 106–109, 116,
        118, 155
    introduction of, 68–70
    pledged-account mortgage,
        114–115, 118
    price level adjusted mortgage
        (PLAM), 69, 109–112, 116, 118
    and Regulation Z, 154–156
    reverse annuity mortgage (RAM),
        113–114
    shared appreciation mortgages
        (SAMs), 69, 112–113, 116,
        118, 155
    tax treatment of, 116
**American Land Title Association
    (ALTA), 295**
American residential finance, history
    of, 46–48
American Southwest Financial, 206
Amerifirst Mortgage Company,
    207, 481
AMIs, *See* Alternative mortgage
    instruments
Amortization, 49–50
    negative, 69, 95, 106–108, 111, 116
Amortization schedule, 50, 107
Amount, promissory notes, 263
AMTs, *See* Alternative minimum taxes
    (AMTs)
Annual percentage rate (APR), 51,
    153–154
    calculation of, 51
    with no points/fees, 51
    with two discount points, 51
Appraisal Standard Board of the
    Appraisal Foundation, 271
Appraisals:
    and ethics, 479
    problems with, 450–451
    property, 270–273
    smoothing process and, 451
    uniform residential appraisal
        report, 271
Appraiser Qualification Board, 271

APR, *See* Annual percentage rate
    (APR)
APT, *See* Arbitrage pricing theory
    (APT)
Arbitrage pricing theory (APT), 450
ARMs, *See* Adjustable-rate mortgages
    (ARMs)
Asset pricing, theories of, 447–450
    arbitrage pricing theory, 450
    capital asset pricing model
        (CAPM), 32, 447–450, 460
Asset valuation, 28–32
    after-tax cash flows, amount of, 29
    cash flows:
        risk of, 29–32
        timing of, 29
    role of risk in, 32
Assignment of rents, trust deeds, 267
Assignment of rents clause, 399
Assignment provisions, promissory
    notes, 264
Assumability, federal regulators and,
    72–73
Assumability option, 70–73
Assumable loans, 75, 125, 128–132
    cash-equivalent value, 128–129
    efficient markets/value of
        assumption financing, 129–130
    and house price capitalization,
        130–132
    See also Assumability option
At-risk limitations, 335, 341, 426
Audit, environmental, 381
Award of eminent domain provision,
    trust deeds, 267

B

Bank capital requirements, thrift vs.,
    86, 87
Banking, mortgage, 277–278
Bankruptcy:
    and agency costs, 476–479
    and agency law, 475–476
    Chapter 11, 477
    cost of, 317
Bankruptcy Reform Act (1994), 416
Banks:
    capital requirements of, 86, 87
    commercial, 6, 357
Banks for Cooperatives, 202
Before-tax cash flows, 308, 310,
    325–326, 350
Before-tax discount rate, 325–326
Benchmark credit support levels, 361
Beneficial assignment certificates
    (BACs), 427
Bergsoe Metal Corporation, 466–467
Blockbusting, 173
Bonding costs, 39

Bonds:
    mortgage-backed, 193–194,
        233–236
    mortgage pay-through, 194
    mortgage revenue, 135–141
    noncallable, 21, 35
    price of, and market-required yield,
        15–16
    supply and demand for, 16
    Treasury, 8
    zero coupon, 108, 334
Boot (non-real estate property), **346**
Borrower qualification:
    comparison, 260, 262
    for conventional loans, 260
    and loan underwriting, 254–262
    VA, 259–260
Borrowers, characteristics of, 257
Breach of contract, 474–475
Breach of fiduciary duty, 474
Brokers, 6
Building and loan associations, 46
Building loan agreement, 390–397
Buydown mortgages, 76–77, **125,**
    132–133
    and Regulation Z, 155

C

*Calero-Toledo v. Pearson Yacht Leasing
    Co.,* 469
Call options, 33, 35
Callability risk, 21–22
Capital, risk-based guidelines for,
    85–89
Capital asset pricing model (CAPM),
    32, 447–450, 460
Capital gains, 322, 328, 332, 334–338,
    345, 347–350
Capitalization:
    categories of, 86, 88
    house price, 130–132
Capitalized payment savings, 129
Capital leases, 411
    criteria for, 411
Capital loss limitation, 337
    and passive loss rule, 340
Capital market line, 448
Capital markets, 8
    equity, 316–317
Capital structure, 33
    optimal, 32, 313–315
CAPM, *See* Capital asset pricing model
    (CAPM)
Caps on ARMS, 95, 101, 102
Carryback financing, 125
Cash-equivalent value, 128–129
Cash flows, 28, 304–305, 325–329
    after-tax, 29, 306–311, 313,
        325–329, 349, 350

before-tax, 308, 310, 325–326, 350
of collateralized mortgage
    obligations (CMOs), 196, 236,
    237
discounted, 28, 57–58, 303
division of, 305
of mortgage-backed bonds (MBBs),
    193, 233, 234
operating, 309, 310
and pass-through securities, effect
    of prepayments on, 225–226
for REMICs, 197
risk of, 29–32
tailoring, 191
timing of, 29
value of, 311–312
C corporations, 325, 340, 423
ownership characteristics of, 423
and passive loss limitation rules,
    340
*Centerre Bank of Kansas City v.
    Distributors, Inc.,* 472
CERCLA, *See* Comprehensive
    Environmental Response,
    Compensation, and Liability
    Act of 1990 (CERCLA)
Certificates of Beneficial Ownership
    (CBOs), 204
Certified historic structures (CHSs), 342
Chancery Court, 45
CHAP, *See* Comprehensive homeless
    assistance plan (CHAP)
Chapter 11 bankruptcy, 477
*Chemical Manufacturers Association v.
    Environmental Protection
    Agency,* 467
*Cherry v. Home Savings and Loan
    Association,* 72
Chicago Board of Trade, 208
Citicorp Homeowners Mortgage
    Acceptance Corporation, 206
Citicorp Mortgage Power Program, 161
Civil and criminal remedies, 158
Closed-ended REITs, 429
Closing, loan, 276–277
CMOs, *See* Collateralized mortgage
    obligations (CMOs)
CMO tranches, 195, 241, 242,
    245–246
Coast Bank v. Minderhout, 71
COFI, *See* Cost of Fund Index (COFI)
Coinsurance, 280
**Collateralized mortgage obligations
    (CMOs), 31,** 194–197, 202,
    236–241, 429
cash flows of, 196, 236, 237
commercial, 359–362
and risk of cash flow, 31
Collateralized securities, 188
Commercial banks, 6, 357

Commercial real estate investments:
    debt and returns to equity, 306–318
    options on, 36
    risk of cash flows, 30
    source of funds, 278
    valuation of, 303–306
Commingled real estate funds
    (CREFs), 364, 452
Commitment, 276
    in construction loans, 380
Commitment fees, 81
**Community Development Block
    Grants, 147**–148
Community Reinvestment Act (CRA),
    113, 177–180, 469
Comprehensive Drug Abuse
    Prevention and Control Act
    (1970), 468
Comprehensive Environmental
    Response, Compensation, and
    Liability Act of 1990
    (CERCLA), 380–381, 462–468
Comprehensive homeless assistance
    plan (CHAP), 148
**Computer loan origination systems
    (CLOs), 160**–161
Consideration, promissory notes, **263**
Constant prepayment rate (CPR), 221
Construction loan commitment, 380
Construction loans, 379–386
    administration of, 382
    commitment in, 380
    loan amount and disbursements,
        determination of, 382–386
    provisions of, 380
    underwriting, 379
Consumer Credit Protection Act
    (1968), 152–156
    annual percentage rate (APR),
        153–154
    total finance charge, 153
Continuity of life, 426
Contract, breach of, 474–475
Contract price, 349
Contractual relationships in residential
    loans, 262–267
Conventional loans, 257, 260
Convertible ARMs, 95
Corporate form of ownership, 423–424
    characteristics of, 423–424
    partnerships vs., 433–435
Corporations and real estate
    investments, 325
Correlation coefficient, 444
Cost approach, 272–273
Cost of Fund Index (CFI), 94, 95
Cost recovery fee, 378
Costs:
    acquisition, 318
    agency, 39–40, 476–479

of bankruptcy, 317
bonding, 39
effective, 50–51
financing, 318
monitoring, 39
structuring, 39
Covenants/restrictions provision, trust
    deeds, 267
Coverage ratio, 287
CRA, *See* Community Reinvestment
    Act (CRA)
Cramdown, 477–478
Cranston–Gonzalez National
    Affordability Act (1990), 147,
    149
Creative financing, 73–77, **125**–135
    and appraisal practices/market
        studies, 135
    assumable loans, 75, 125, 128–132
    buydown financing, 76–77, 125,
        132–133
    FHA/VA discount points,
        126–128
    government-underwritten loans,
        73–75
    house price capitalization, empirical
        tests of, 130–132
    land contracts, 125, 134–135
    owner financing, 77
    wraparound loans, 75–76, 133–134
Credit:
    evaluation of, 37
    oral commitments for extension of,
        469–470
Credit agreement statutes, 471
Credit-based financing, 416
Credit enhancement, 190, 205
Credit evaluation, 37
Credit risk, 146
    and group membership, 176
Credit termination and oral
    commitments, 472–473
CREFs, *See* Commingled real estate
    funds (CREFs)
Curable obsolescence, 273
Curves, *See* Yield curves

D

Dallas Bank Fraud Task Force, 481
DCF, *See* Discounted cash flow (DCF)
Debentures, 202
Debt:
    estimates of stock of, 355–357
    and interest rates, 317–318
    nonrecourse and recourse, 335
    for real estate financing, 316–318
    and returns to equity, 306–318
Debt financing, 355–363
    considerations in, 316–318

Modigliani–Miller Proposition and, 315–316
and ownership form, 434
trends in, 362–363
Debt funds, flow of, 357–360
Debt securities, valuation of, 218–219
Deed, 276
recording of, 276
Deed-of-trust, 266–267, 276
parties to, 266–267
provisions of, 267
Default:
promissory notes, 264
studies of, 256–257
theories of, 255–256
ability-to-pay theory, 255
equity theory, 255–256
Default insurance, mortgage, 280–289
Default risk, 20–21, 108, 115, **254**–268, 291, 293
and interest rates, 20–21
on residential loans, 291
Deficiency judgments, 263, 291
Deficit Reduction Act (1984), 136
Defined-benefit plans, 364–365
Defined-contribution plans, 364–365
Delayed exchanges, 345–346
time limitation on, 346
See also Tax-deferred exchange rule
Demand notes, termination of, without notification, 471–472
Denison State Bank v. Maderia, 474
Density bonus, 378
Deposit insurance, 86, 146
Depository institutions, regulators of, 11–14
Depository Institutions Deregulation and Monetary Control Act (1980), 78, 151
Depository Institutions Deregulation Committee, 78
Depository unit receipts (DURs), 427
Depreciation, 308, 328, 350, 433
annual, 333
double-declining balance method of, 331
as noncash expense, 329–334
and ownership form, 433
present value of, 333, 334
rules of, for real estate, 331
straight-line method of, 308, 328, 330
sum-of-the-year's digits method of, 331
Depreciation recapture, 328
Depreciation tax shield, 329–330, 332
Depression, *See* Great Depression
Deregulation, 151–152
Desk review, 272
Developer, 374
Development, 377–378

Differential tax rates, 337
Di minimus rule, 272, 367
Direct endorsement program, 275
Direct financing, 6, 7
Direct grants, 147–148
Disbursement, 276
Disclosure requirements, RESPA, 157
Discount, initial-period, 95, 101–102
Discounted cash flow (DCF), 28, 303
Discounted cash flow (DCF) model, 57–58, **303**
Discount notes, 202
Discount pass-throughs, 226, 228
Discount points, 51, 52
FHA/VA, 126–128
Discrimination:
economic theory of, 174–176
effects method and, 174
empirical evidence of, 176–177
existence of, 176–177
intent approach to, 174
in lending behavior, identifying, 174
practices approach to, 174
Disintermediation, 64
Diversifiable risk, 448
Diversification:
benefits of, 445–446, 452–454
geographic, 456–457
nature of, 440–450
by property type, 455
within-real-estate, 454–457
Dollar-based fees, 378
Double-declining balance method of depreciation, **331**
Double taxation, 191, 422, 426, 433
C corporations, 423
mortgage-related securities (MBS), 191
Drug war and lenders, 468–469
Due diligence defense, 469
Due-on-sale clause, 265–266
Duration, 59, 108, 219
effective, 230–231
implied, 230–231
negative, 245
of pass-through securities, 230–231
Duress and leader control, 475

E

ECOA, *See* Equal Credit Opportunity Act (ECOA)
Econometric prepayment models, 222–223
Economic Recovery Act (1981), 330, 426
Economics of information, 175–176
Economic theory of discrimination, 174–176
economics of information, 175–176
"taste" for discrimination, 174–175

Effective cost of mortgage, 50–51
Effective duration, 230–231
Effects method, discriminatory lending, **174**
Efficient markets, 38, 150–151
and value of assumption financing, 129–130
Efficient market theory, 38–39
Eisenberg v. Comfed Mortgage, 161
Elizabeth I (queen of England), 45
Emergency Home Finance Act (1970), 151, 201
Emergency Shelter Grants Program, 148
Employee Retirement Income Security Act (ERISA), 365, **367**
England, real estate law developments and, 45
Entitlement, 281
Environmental audit, 381
Environmental Protection Agency (EPA), 462
April 1992 regulation, 467
See also Hazardous waste disposal
EPIC Acceptance Corporation, 206
Equal Credit Opportunity Act (ECOA), 173–177
discriminatory lending behavior, identifying, 174
economic theory of discrimination, 174–176
effects of, 177
empirical evidence of discrimination, 176–177
Equation of Exchange, 17
Equitable right of redemption, 45, 290
Equity capital markets, 316–317
Equity financing, 363–369
institutional investors, 364–368
public/private partnerships, 368–369
through securities, 363
sources of, finding, 369
top 200 funds, 365
Equity in housing, 172–182
Community Reinvestment Act, 177–180
Equal Credit Opportunity Act (ECOA), 173–177
Fair Housing Act (FHA), 172–173
Fair Housing Amendments Act (FHAA), 181–182
Home Mortgage Disclosure Act (HMDA), 177–180
redlining, 178–180
Equity managers, twenty-five largest, 365
Equity-participation loans, 399–405
basic principles of, 400

example of, 401–405
popular view of, 400–401
Equity REITs, 30, **428**
Equity theory, 255–256
ERISA, *See* Employee Retirement
Income Security
Act (ERISA)
Escrow accounts, promissory notes, 265
Ethics, 479–482
Exaction, 378
Excess returns, 38
Exchanges, tax-deferred, 345–347
Expectations theory, 24–25
Explicit options, 36
Extended term wrap, 134

F

FADA, *See* Federal Asset Disposition
Association (FADA)
Fair Housing Act (FHA), 172–173
Fair Housing Amendments Act
(FHAA), 181–182
Fannie Mae, *See* Federal National
Mortgage Association
Farm Credit Assistance Financial
Corporation, 202
Farm Credit System, 202
Farm Credit Systemwide
Obligations, 202
Farmer Mac, *See* Federal Agricultural
Mortgage Corporation
(Farmer Mac)
Farmer's Home Administration
(FmHA), 209, 285
*Farm Real Estate Market
Developments: Outlook and
Situation,* 452
FASB 87, 368
FASB 98, 412, 417
Favored classes of real estate
investment, 342–343
FDIC, *See* Federal Deposit Insurance
Corporation (FDIC)
Federal Agricultural Mortgage
Corporation (Farmer Mac),
202, 204
Federal Asset Disposition Association
(FADA), 84
Federal credit agencies, 202, 204, 209
Federal Deposit Insurance Corporation
(FDIC), 6, 47–48, 79, 84,
145, 362
Federal Deposit Insurance Corporation
Improvement Act, 86, 89
Federal Financial Institutions
Examination Council,
268, 272
Federal Financing Bank (FFB), 204
Federal Home Loan Bank (FHLB),
145, 178, 201

Federal Home Loan Bank Act (1932),
47, 144–145
Federal Home Loan Bank Board
(FHLBB), 6, 72, 78, 82, 84,
144, 208, 263, 291
and "appraised equity capital," 80
**Federal Home Loan Bank System
(FHLBS), 47**
Federal Home Loan Mortgage
Corporation (FHLMC), 7, 66,
85, 151, 198, 205–209, 213,
249, 260, 274
and MRS, 201–205
**Federal Housing Administration
(FHA), 48,** 73–75, **146**–147,
198–201, 232, 257–259,
272–276, 296, 480
direct endorsement program, 275
FHA experience, 221–222
FHAing a neighborhood, 179
FHA/VA discount points, 126–128
loans, 125
mortgage insurance, 282–285
Federal Housing Enterprise Financial
Safety and Soundness Act
(1992), 208, 214
Federal Housing Finance Board,
84, 178
Federal housing policies, 144–162
efficiency/stability, 150–152
equity in housing, 172–182
housing affordability, 144–150
real estate finance market
competition, 152–162
Real Estate Settlement Procedures
Act (RESPA), 156–162
See also Housing affordability
Federal Intermediate Credit Banks, 202
Federal Land Banks, 202, 209
**Federal National Mortgage
Association (FNMA),** 7, **48,**
66, 151, 198, 199, 206–207,
209, 260, 268, 274
and MRS, 198
Federal regulators:
assumability and, 72–73
depository institutions and, 11–14
financial institutions and, 11–14
Federal Reserve System, 6, 46, 64, 89,
152, 156, 178, 180
**Federal Savings and Loan Insurance
Corporation (FSLIC), 6, 47,**
77, 79–82, 84, 145
forbearance of, 80
Federal taxation, *See* Taxes
Federal Truth-in-Lending Disclosure
Statement, *See* Regulation Z
FFB, *See* Federal Financing
Bank (FFB)
FHA, *See* Federal Housing
Administration (FHA)

FHAA, *See* Fair Housing Amendments
Act (FHAA)
FHA experience, 221–222
FHAing, 179
FHA insurance, 282–285, 289
loan assumptions, 283
loan limits, 282–283
loan-to-value ratios, 283
mortgage insurance premiums
(MIPs), 283–285
refinancing, 283
FHA prepayment experience,
221–222
FHLB, *See* Federal Home Loan Bank
(FHLB)
FHLBB, *See* Federal Home Loan Bank
Board (FHLBB)
FHLBS, *See* Federal Home Loan Bank
System (FHLBS)
FHLMC, *See* Federal Home Loan
Mortgage Corporation
(FHLMC)
FICO, *See* Financing Corporation
(FICO)
*Fidelity Federal Savings and Loan
Association v. de le Cuesta,* 72
Fiducia, 44
Fiduciary, 474
Finance, 2–3
residential, *See* Residential finance
subdisciplines of, 3–4
See also Real estate finance
Finance obligation, 413
Finance theory:
agency theory, 39–40
capital structure, 33
efficient market theory, 38–39
financial intermediation, 36–37
financial leverage, 32–33
options, 33–36
portfolio theory, 37–38
Financial Accounting Standards Board
(FASB), 196, 368, 411, 412
Financial institutions:
deregulation of, 151–152
economic support of, 144–146
regulatory environment of, 11–14
Financial Institutions Deregulation and
Monetary Control Act
(1980), 70
Financial Institutions Reform,
Recovery, and Enforcement
Act, *See* FIRREA
Financial intermediaries, 6–8
capital markets, 8
commercial banks, 6
direct financing, 7
insurance companies, 7
investment companies, 7
money markets, 8
pension funds, 7

primary vs. secondary markets, 7–8
secondary mortgage market, 7
thrift institutions, 6–7
Financial intermediation, 36–37, 64
Financial leverage, 32–33, **304**–306
division of cash flow, 305
negative, 32, 306
neutral, 306
portfolio considerations, 305
positive, 32, 306
tax deduction of interest payments, 306
and value, 304–305, 312–313
Financial marketplace, 5–8
Financing:
advantageous, 125, *See* Creative financing
buydown, 76–77, 125, 132–133, 155
carryback, 125
creative, 73–77, 125–135
credit-based, 416
debt, *See* Debt financing
direct, 6, 7
equity, 363–369
installment sale, 347–350
owner, 77
owner-second, 125
tax increment, 378
tenant improvements, 416
Financing Corporation (FICO), 204
Financing costs, 318
Finite-life REITS, 429
Finnegan's Financial Green Sheet Rates of Return, 452, 453
FIRREA, 70, 208, 271, 481
and the Bush initiative, 82–84
limits of loans to one borrower, 362, 363
mandated changes in mortgage market regulation, 85
mandated changes in thrift institutions, 83
regulatory structure from, 84–86
First Boston Corporation, 205, 206
First-in-first-out (FIFO), 29
Fisher Equation, 17–19
Fixed-rate mortgages (FRMs), 48–53, 93–94, 105–106
amortization of, 49–50
characteristics of, 118
demand problems, 66–68
and early payment, 51–52
effect of inflation of real payment of, 67
effective cost of, 50–51
in inflationary environment, problem of, 66–70
and interest rate risk, 53

mortgage payment, 48–49
outstanding balance of, 50
and prepayment penalties, 52–53
supply problems, 68
Fleet Factors Corporation, 465–467
Fleets Guide, 369, 372
Flexible loan insurance program (FLIP), 114–115, 118
characteristics of, 118
FLIP mortgage, *See* Pledged-account mortgage (FLIP mortgage)
Floaters, 245–246
Flow of funds, 5
through primary and secondary mortgage market, 209–214
in savings-investment cycle, 5
FmHA, *See* Farmers Home Administration (FmHA)
FNMA, *See* Federal National Mortgage Association (FNMA)
Forbearance, FSLIC, 80
Foreclosure, 256–257, **289**–294, 296
deficiency judgments, 291
equitable right of redemption, 290
procedure, 290
state foreclosure laws, 289–294, 296
statutory right of redemption, 45, 290–291, 296
Fractions rule, 367
Fraud, 473
ethics and, 479–482
nondisclosure, 474
promissory, 473–474
Freddie Mac, *See* Federal Home Loan Mortgage Corporation (FHLMC)
Free transferability of interest, 426
Frequency of rate change, 94
FRM–ARM rate spread, 105–106
FRMs, *See* Fixed-rate mortgages (FRMs)
FSLIC, *See* Federal Savings and Loan Insurance Corporation (FSLIC)
Full coverage, 280
Fully amortized loans, 47
Fully indexed rate, 95
Funds:
flow of, 5, 209–214
mortgage banking, 278
pension, 7, 357, 364–368
Funds from operations (FFO), 428

G

GAAP, *See* Generally Accepted Accounting Principles (GAAP)
Gage, 45
Garn-St. Germain Act, 72, 79, 145, 265

Generally Accepted Accounting Principles (GAAP), 80, 367, 428
RAP compared to, 80–82
Generally Accepted Appraisal Standards, 272–273
General partnerships, 424
Geographic diversification, 456–457
German customs and real estate law, 45
Gibson paradox, 19
Ginnie Mae, *See* Government National Mortgage Association (GNMA)
Ginnie Mae Dealers Association, 200, 231
Glendale Federal Savings and Loan, 207
GMCs, *See* Guaranteed mortgage certificates (GMCs)
GNMA, *See* Government National Mortgage Association (GNMA)
Good faith, 471–472
Good faith estimate of settlement costs, 157
Government:
loans underwritten by, 73–75
See also Federal housing policies
Government Accounting Office, 208
Government insurance, 281–285, 289
See also Federal Housing Administration (FHA); Veterans Administration (VA)
Government National Mortgage Association (GNMA), 7, 21–22, 66, 151–152, 191, 207, 209, 213, 231, 232
and MRS, 198–201
Government sponsored enterprises (GSEs), regulation of, 208, 214
Government-underwritten loans, 73–75
Graduated payment mortgages (GPM), 69, 106–109, 116
characteristics of, 118
computation of initial payment on, 123–124
example of, 106–109
and Regulation Z, 155
and tilt effect, 106–108
Grantor trusts, 196
Grants, direct, 147–148
Great Depression, 47, 286, 291
Gross acquisitions, 359
Gross monthly effective income, 257
Gross profit percentage, 348
Ground lease mortgages, 415–416
GSEs, *See* Government sponsored enterprises (GSEs)
Guaranteed mortgage certificates (GMCs), 202

Guarantor, promissory notes, 205, 265
Guidice v. BFG Electroplating Co.,
        464–465

H

Hazardous waste disposal, 462–467
HELCPA, *See* Home Equity Loan
        Consumer Protection Act
        (HELCPA)
HELs, *See* Home equity loans (HELs)
Hill v. Securities Investment Co. of St.
        Louis, 474
Historical replication, 100
Historic structures, rehabilitation
        of, 342
HMDA, *See* Home Mortgage
        Disclosure Act (HMDA)
HOLC, *See* Home Owners Loan
        Corporation (HOLC)
Holding period and ownership form, 433
HOMAC, *See* Home Mortgage
        Acceptance Corporation
        (HOMAC)
Home Equity Loan Consumer
        Protection Act (HELCPA), 156
Home equity loans (HELs) and
        Regulation Z, 155–156
Home Mortgage Acceptance Corporation
        (HOMAC), 205, 206
Home Mortgage Disclosure Act
        (HMDA), 177–180, 469
Home Owners Loan Act (1933), 47
Home Owners Loan Corporation
        (HOLC), 47
HOME program, 149
HOPE (Homeownership and
        Opportunity for People
        Everywhere) program, 149
House price capitalization, 130–132
Housing Act (1968), 136
Housing affordability, 144–150
        direct grants, 147–148
        financial institutions, economic
                support of, 144–146
        HOME/HOPE programs, 149
        income tax provisions, 149–150
        mortgage insurance, 147
        subsidies, 148
Housing and Community Development
        Act, 172, 208
Housing expenses, definition of, 258
Housing Finance Agency (HFA),
        135–136, 204–205
Housing and Urban Development,
        Department of (HUD),
        146–149, 214, 257–259, 274,
        276, 355
        borrower qualification, 257–259
        fair housing and, 173

and ILSFDA, 152
programs, legislation/executive
        orders authorizing, 164–168
VAMAs, 173
Housing and Urban Development
        Act, 66, **151,** 198, 272
Hybrid REITs, 30, **428**
Hypotheca, 45

I

ICC, *See* Income Capital Certificate
        (ICC)
ILSFDA, *See* Interstate Land Sales Full
        Disclosure Act (ILSFDA)
Impact fees, 378
Imperial Federal Savings and Loan
        Association, 208
Implied duration, 230–231
Impound accounts, promissory
        notes, 265
Imputed interest rule, 336, 349
Incentive conflicts, 294
Inclusionary zoning, 378
Income:
        active, 337
        classification of, 338
        definition of, 258–259
        passive, 338, 339
        portfolio, 338
        and taxes, 329–337
Income approach, 273
Income Capital Certificate (ICC),
        79–81
Income classification and Tax Reform
        Act (1986), 337
Income effect, 19
Income ratio method of borrower
        qualification, 260
Incurable obsolescence, 273
Index, 94
        affordability, 67
        and ARM, 94
        Cost of Fund Index (COFI), 94–95
        NAREIT Equity Index, 452
        Russell–NCREIF Property Index,
                451, 454
Information:
        economics of, 175–176
        and efficient market theory, 38–39
        about financing sources, 451–452
Information risk, 453
Initial-period discount, 95, 101–102
In Re Meadow Glen, Ltd., 478
Installment sale:
        after-tax cash flows from, 349
        definition of, 347
        example of, 349–350
        qualifications for, 347
Installment sale financing, 347–350

Institutional investors and equity
        financing, 364–368
Institutional lenders, 364–368
        and acquisition, 375
Institutional risk, sources of, 146
Insurance:
        deposit, 86, 146
        mortgage, *See* Mortgage insurance
        mortgage default, 280–289
        mortgage insurance premium (MIP),
                276, 283–285
        pool, 192
        private mortgage, 179, 257,
                286–289, 296
        submission of loan for, 274–276
        title, 294–296
Insurance companies, 7
Intent approach to discrimination, **174**
Interest:
        free transferability of, 426
        money-inflation-interest rate
                mechanism, 17
        promissory notes, 264
Interest-only (IO) securities, 195
        and risk of cash flows, 31
Interest-only (IO) strips, 241–245
Interest payments:
        investment, 336–337
        tax deduction of, 306, 350
        and taxes, 334–336
Interest Rate Adjustment Act (1966), 64
Interest rate caps, 95
Interest rate contingent securities, 217
Interest rate risk, 37, 58–60
        and adjustable-rate mortgages
                (ARMs), 93–94
        assumptions and, 70–71
        definition of, 22
        determination of, 168–169
        and fixed-rate mortgages (FRMs), 53
        and graduated-rate mortgages
                (GRMs), 108
        and maturity mismatch, 79
        and reverse annuity mortgage
                (RAM), 113–114
        and risk-based guidelines, 89
Interest rates:
        and callability risk, 21–22
        changes in, 223–225, 229
        and credit market instruments,
                20–22
        and debt, 317–318
        and default risk, 20–21
        general level of, 15–16
        and liquidity risk, 22
        and marketability risk, 22
        and maturity risk, 22
        price sensitivity to, 219
        real rate of interest, 16
        and yield curve, 22–25

Interest rate volatility:
    and loan value, 104
    and trend, 103–105
Interest volatility risk, 146
Intermediaries, financial, 6–8
Intermediation, financial, 36–37, 64
Internal fraud risk, 146
Internal rate of returns, 311, 312
Interstate Land Sales Full Disclosure
    Act (ILSFDA), 152
Initial-period discount, 95
Inverse floater, 246
Investment companies, 7
Investment interest payments, 336–337
IO securities, *See* Interest-only (IO)
    securities
IO strips, *See* Interest-only (IO) strips

J

Joint and several liability, 462
Judicial foreclosure, 290
Junior financing, 377

K

Kickbacks, 157–159
K.M.C. Co., Inc. v. Irving Trust Co., 472
Kruse v. Bank of America, 472

L

Labor Discount Center, Inc. v. State
    Bank and Trust Co. of
    Wellston, 475
"Lack of confidence" factor, 451
Land acquisition loan, 374
    risk of, 375
    warehousing, 374
Land contracts, 125, 134–135
Land development loan, 377–386
Land purchase option, 376
LaSala v. American Savings and Loan
    Association, 72
Last-in-first-out (LIFO), 29
Late performance, promissory notes, 264
Leases, 405–415
    and accounting regulations, 411–415
    capital, 411
    economics of ownership of assets
        vs., 407–408
    operating, 411
Legislation:
    affecting real estate, 184–187
    authorizing HUD programs,
        164–168
Lender-insurer incentive conflicts, 294
Lender liability, 461–475
    breach of contract, 474–475
    breach of fiduciary duty, 474

duress and lender control, 475
and hazardous waste disposal,
    462–467
initial judicial decisions, 463–467
from lender/borrower
    relationship, 469
lender defenses, 463
nondisclosure fraud, 474
prima facie tort and, 473
promissory fraud, 473–474
risk management for, 468
Lenders:
    and drug war, 468–469
    institutional, 364–368
    oral commitments by, 470–471
    profile of, 372
Leverage, 32–33, **304**–306
    division of cash flow, 305
    negative, 32, 306
    neutral, 306
    portfolio considerations, 305
    positive, 32, 306
    tax deduction of interest
        payments, 306
    and value, 304–305, 312–313
Liability:
    lender, 461–475
    limited, 423–426
    to third parties, 475–476
LIBOR, *See* London Interbank Offer
    Rate (LIBOR)
Liens, 290, 295
    subordinated, 376
Life insurance companies:
    and debt financing, 357
    and equity financing, 364
Life-of-loan rate caps, 95
    for ARMs, 102
    and loan value, 102
Limitation of losses, 337–340, 350
    at-risk limitations, 341
    capital loss limitation, 337, 340
    form of organization, 340
    passive loss limitation, 337–340
    passive loss rule, 340
    use of passive losses, 339, 340
Limited liability, 423–426
Limited partnerships, 30, 343, **424**
    and risk of cash flow, 30
Liquidity effect, 19
Liquidity premium theory, 24
Liquidity risk, 8, 37, 146
    and interest rates, 22
Loan closing, 276–277
Loan processing, 270–277
    application analysis, 273–274
    insurance, submission for,
        274–275
    loan closing, 276–277
    property appraisal, 270–273
Loans:

acquisition, development, and
    construction (ADC), 6,
    362–363, 373–386, 428, 470
assumable, 75, 125, 128–132
building loan agreement, 390–397
construction, 379–386
conventional, 257, 260
discount points, 51, 52, 126–128
equity-participation, 399–405
fully amortized, 47
government-underwritten, 73–75
home equity, 155–156
long-term, fixed rate, 398–399
    alternatives to, 399–415
nonamortizing, 46
underwriting, 73–75, 254–262, 379
warehousing, 278
wraparound, 75–76, 133–134
Loan-to-value ratios, 283–285, 379
Lock-in clause, promissory
    notes, 264
London Interbank Offer Rate
    (LIBOR), 208, **245**–246
Long-term, fixed rate loans,
    398–399
    alternatives to, 399–415
Low-income housing credits, 343

M

Margin, 94
    for ARMs, 94–95, 103
    and loan value, 103
Marketability risk, 8, **22, 453**
Market approach, 273
Marketing rate difference, 278
Marketplace, financial, 5–8
Market segmentation theory, 24
Mark-to-market, 194
Master certificate of reasonable value
    (MCRV), 270
Master limited partnerships (MLPs),
    363, 426–427
Maturity mismatch, 62–64
    and interest rate risk, 79
Maturity risk, 22
MBBs, *See* Mortgage-backed
    bonds (MBBs)
MBSs, *See* Mortgage-backed securities
    (MBSs)
MCRV, *See* Master certificate of
    reasonable value (MCRV)
Mechanics and Farmers Savings
    Bank, 207
Merrill Lynch, 222
Minorities, HOME and HOPE
    programs, 149
MIPs, *See* Mortgage insurance
    premiums (MIPs)
Miscellaneous risk, 146
Mixed-asset portfolio, 440, 450–454

Modified accelerated tax recovery system (MACRS), 332
Modigliani–Miller Proposition, 314–315
  and debt financing in real estate properties, 315–316
Monetary Control Act (1980), 78
Monetary theory of inflation, definition of, 17
Money and capital markets, 8
Money-inflation-interest rate mechanism, 17–18
Money markets, 8
Monitoring costs, 39
Monthly mortgage insurance premium (MIP), 258
Moody's Investor Service, 20, 190, 192, 194
  market classification, 371
  Structured Finance Division of, 360
Mortgage, 276
  adjustable-rate, *See* Adjustable-rate mortgages (ARMs)
  buydown, 76–77, 125, 132–133, 155
  fixed-rate, *See* Fixed-rate mortgages (FRMs)
  graduated payment, 69, 106–109, 116, 118–119, 155
  ground lease, 415–416
  home equity loans (HELs), 155–156
  maturity, duration, and interest rate risk of, 22
  pledged-account, 114–115, 118
  prepayment-protection, 53
  price level adjusted, 69, 109–112, 116, 118
  recording of, 276
  residential, 30, 35–36
  reverse annuity, 113–114
  securitization, 151
  servicing rights, 30–31, 246–248
  shared appreciation, 69, 112–113, 116, 118, 155
Mortgage-backed bonds (MBBs), 193–194, 233–236
  cash flows of, 193, 233, 234
Mortgage-backed securities (MBSs):
  and risk of cash flows, 30–31
  stripped, 195
Mortgage Bankers Association Weekly Mortgage Application Survey, 223
Mortgage banking, 277–278
  revenues, 278
  source of funds, 278
Mortgage constant, 48–49
Mortgage default insurance, 280–289
  comparison of types of, 289
  government insurance, 281–285
  private mortgage insurance, 286–289
Mortgage-derivative security, 217

Mortgagee's One-Time MIP Transmittal Form, 376
Mortgage Guaranty Insurance Corporation, 256, 286
Mortgage insurance, 147, 157, 276–277
  and agency relationships, 480
  private, *See* Private mortgage insurance (PIP)
  and VA, 281–282, 289
Mortgage insurance premium, 276, 283–285
Mortgage loans, *See* Debt financing
Mortgage market:
  post-FIRREA regulatory structure of, 84–86
  secondary, *See* Secondary mortgage market
Mortgage Participation Certificates (PCs), 151, 202, 205–208
Mortgage pass-through securities, 191–193
  See also Pass-through securities
Mortgage payment, 48–49
Mortgage pay-through bonds (MPTBs), 194
Mortgage pools, 192–196, 220
  cash flows from, 225–249
  data on, 248–249
  GNMA, 224
  See also Pass-through securities
Mortgage refinancing, 116–117
Mortgage REITs, 30, 428
Mortgage-related securities (MRSs), 7, 188, 190–197, 220–251
  agencies/firms issuing, 197–205
  cash flows, tailoring of, 191
  collateralized mortgage obligations (CMOs), 31, 194–197, 236–241, 429
  credit enhancement, 190
  double taxation, 191
  mortgage-backed bonds (MBBs), 193–194, 233–236
  mortgage pass-through securities, 191–193, 221–233
  mortgage pay-through bonds, 194
  pass-throughs, *See* Pass-through securities
  swaps, 195–196
  tax/accounting issues of, 196–197
  types of, 191–195
  value creation in, 249–250
Mortgage revenue bonds (MRBs), 135–141
  and house prices/wealth distribution, 137
  and state HFA, 135–137
Mortgage Subsidy Bond Tax Act (1980), 136
MPTBs, *See* Mortgage pay-through bonds (MPTBs)

MRBs, *See* Mortgage revenue bonds (MRBs)
MRSs, *See* Mortgage-related securities (MRSs)
Multisite securitization, 416

N

NAIC, *See* National Association of Insurance Commissioners (NAIC)
NAREIT, *See* National Association of Real Estate Investment Trusts (NAREIT)
NAREIT Equity Index, 452
National Association of Home Builders, 363
National Association of Insurance Commissioners (NAIC), 357
National Association of Real Estate Investment Trusts (NAREITs), 428, 451–452
National Association of Realtors, 67, 452
National Banking System, 46
National Commission on Consumer Finance (NCCF), 173
National Council of Real Estate Investment Fiduciaries (NCREIF), 316, 451
National Council of State Housing Agencies, 136
National Credit Union Association Board (NCUAB), 6–7
National Credit Union Share Insurance Fund, 7
National Housing Act (1934), 145–146, 282, 283
National Mortgage Association of Washington (1938), 48, 151
National Register of Historic Places, 342
NCREIF, *See* National Council of Real Estate Investment Fiduciaries (NCREIF)
NCUAB, *See* National Credit Union Association Board (NCUAB)
Negative amortization, 69, 95
  GPM, 106–108, 116
  PLAMs, 111, 116
Negative duration, 245
Negative equity, 255
Negative leverage, 32, 306
Net acquisitions, 359
Net leased investment, 336
Net operating income (NOI), 29, 309, 433
Net present value (NPV), 311, 312
Net Worth Certificate, 79–81
Neutral leverage, 306
New equilibrium theory, 453
New York Bond Exchange (NYBE), 7

New York Stock Exchange (NYSE), 7,
    201, 427
NOI, *See* Net operating income (NOI)
Nonamortizing loan, 46
Noncallable bonds, 21, 35
Noncash expenses, depreciation as,
    329–334
Nondisclosure fraud, 474
Nondiversifiable risk, 448
Nonrecourse debt, 335
Nonrecourse note, 263, 317
Nonwaiver provision, trust
    deeds, 267
Notes, 276
    promissory, 263–266

O

OBRA, *See* Omnibus Budget
    Reconciliation Act (1987)
Office of Interstate Land Sales
    Registration (OILSR), 152
Office of Secondary Market
    Examination and Overnight
    (OSMEO), 214
Office of Thrift Supervision (OTS), 6,
    72, 82, 84, 86, 88, 208, 262
    thrift bulletins, 86
OID, *See* Original issue discount
    (OID) rules
Omnibus Budget Reconciliation Act
    (1987), 283, 427
One-to-Four-Family Home Mortgage
    Insurance Program 147
Open-ended REITs, 429
Operating leases, 411
Optimal capital structure, 32, 313
    arguments against, 313–315
Options, 33–34, 376
    on commercial properties, 36
    examples of, 34–36
    explicit, 36
    land purchase, 376
    and real estate finance, 33–36
    residential mortgage, 35–36
    rolling, 376
Oral commitments:
    and credit termination, 472–473
    for extension of credit, 469–470
    by lenders, 470–471
Ordinary income, 328, 335–337, 344
Original issue discount (OID) rules,
    322, 334–336
    exceptions to, 336
Origination fee, 50–51
Originations; 357, 359
OTS, *See* Office of Thrift
    Supervision (OTS)
Outright sale, 347
Outstanding balance, 50
Owner financing, 77

Owner-occupancy provision, trust
    deeds, 267
Owner-occupied property, 150
    refinancing of, 117–118
    tax treatment of, 324
Owner-second financing, 125
Ownership:
    real estate, forms of, 316, 422–42
    corporate vs. partnership form
        of, 423–424, 433–435
    risks and returns of, 412
Oxford Provident Building
    Association, 46

P

Parole evidence rule, 475
Partial coverage, 280
Partial release, 375
Participation Certificates (PCs), 151,
    202, 205–208
Partnerships, 343–344, 424
    corporate form of ownership vs.,
        433–435
    and equity financing, 363
    general, 424
    limited, 30, 343, 424
    master limited (MLPs), 363,
        426–427
    ownership characteristics of, 424
    publicly traded partnerships (PTPs),
        368–369, 424, 426–427
    See also Real estate limited
        partnerships (RELPs)
Passive activities loss limitation
    (PALL), 337
Passive income, 338, 339
Passive losses, use of, 339, 340
Passive loss limitation rule, 340
Passive loss limitations, 337–340, 426
    and ownership form, 434
Pass-through securities, 191–193,
    221–233
    cash flow, effect of prepayments on,
        225–226
    constant prepayment rate (CPR), 221
    discount, 226, 228
    duration of, 230–231
    econometric prepayment models,
        222–223
    FHA experience, 221–222
    interest rates, changes in, 223–225
    premium, 228
    prepayment behavior, changes in,
        223–225
    prices of, 228–229
    Public Securities Association
        Prepayment Rate (PSA), 222
    refinancing models, 223
    senior/subordinated, 192–193,
        232–233

    twelve-year prepaid life, 221
    yield behavior of, 229–230
Payer, promissory notes, 263
Payment, promissory notes, 264
Payment caps, 95
Payment-to-income ratios, 257
PCs, *See* Mortgage Participation
    Certificates (PCs)
Penn Mutual Life Insurance
    Company, 206
Pension funds, 7
    and debt financing, 357
    Employee Retirement Income
        Security Act (ERISA), 367
    and equity financing, 364–368
    future of real estate investments, 368
    restrictions on investments, 365, 367
    taxes on, 367
Performance, promissory notes, 264
Pigus, 44
PLADs, *See* Price level adjusted
    deposits (PLADs)
PLAMs, *See* Price level adjusted
    mortgages
Pledged-account mortgage (FLIP
    mortgage), 114–115, 118
    characteristics of, 118
PMI, *See* Private mortgage
    insurance (PMI)
Pool insurance, 192
Portfolio, 305, 440
    diversification, 440–450
    mixed-asset, 440, 450–454
    restricted, 453
Portfolio income, 338
Portfolio losses, 339
Portfolio theory, 37–38
PO securities, *See* Principal-only (PO)
    securities
Positive leverage, 32, 306
PO strips, *See* Principal-only (PO) strips
Potentially responsible parties (PRPs),
    462–463
Power-of-sale foreclosure, 290, 296
Practices approach to
    discrimination, **174**
Preference for discrimination, 174
Premium pass-throughs, 228
Prepayment, 220–232
    promissory notes, 264
Prepayment option, *See* Call option
Prepayment penalties, 40, 318, 399
**Prepayment-protection mortgage
    (PPM), 53**
Price-anticipation effect, 19
Price compression, 228
Price level adjusted deposits (PLADs),
    111–112
**Price level adjusted mortgages
    (PLAMs), 69, 109–**112, 116
    characteristics of, 118

drawbacks of, 111–112
example of, 109–112
negative amortization, 111, 116
Prices, sensitivity of, to changes in
interest rates, 219
Pricing:
of ARMs, 100–105
asset, theories of, 32,
447–450, 460
Prima facie tort, 473
Primary market, 7–8
Principal, 476
Principal, interest, insurance, and taxes
(PITI), 258
Principal-only (PO) securities, 195
and risk of cash flows, 31
**Principal-only (PO) strips,
241**–245
Private credit firms, 205
Private mortgage insurance (PMI), 179,
257, 286–289, 296
claims cycle, 288
coverage, 286–288
fee structure, 288–289
master policy, 287
Private partnerships and equity
financing, 368–369
Profit percentage, gross, 348
Promissory fraud, 473–474
Promissory notes, 263–266
provisions of, 263–266
sale/transfer/assignment of, 266
types of, 263
Property:
appraisal of, *See* Property appraisals
characteristics of, 257
classifications of, 324–325
diversification by type of, 455
owner-occupied, 117–118,
150, 324
risk of, 317
sale of, 309–311
Property appraisals, 270–273
evaluating, 272–273
Generally Accepted Appraisal
Standards, 272–273
monitoring, 272
ordering, 271–272
uniform residential appraisal
report, 271
Provisions of construction loans, 380
Prudential Property Investment Separate
Account (PRISA), 452
PTPs, *See* Publicly traded partnerships
(PTPs)
Public Housing Agency (PHA), 148
Publicly traded partnerships (PTPs),
424, **426**–427
and equity financing, 368–369
Public Securities Association (PSA), 200
model of, 222

**Public Securities Association
Prepayment Rate (PSA), 222**
Purchase money mortgages, 62
Purchasing power risk, 22
Put option, 33, 36, 255–256, 313

Q

QTIs, *See* Qualified Thrift Investments
(QTIs)
Qualifications of buyer, 254–262
**Qualified Thrift Investments
(QTIs), 83**
Quality rating, 360, 361

R

RAM, *See* Reverse annuity mortgage
(RAM)
RAP, *See* Regulatory Accounting
Practices (RAP)
Rating agencies, 20, 360
Real estate:
classification of, 324–325
data sources, 451–452
major federal legislation affecting,
184–187
ownership forms of, 422–425
securities sales, 363
Real estate finance, 3–4
environment of, 4–6
and federal taxation, 322–350
nature of, 2–6
and options, 33–36
study areas included in, 3–4
Real estate investments:
and corporations, 325
favored classes of, 342–343
and Tax Reform Act (1986),
343–345
and tax rules, 324
Real Estate Investment Trust Act,
424, 427
**Real estate investment trusts
(REITs), 7, 30,** 339, 363, 365,
422, 424–425, 427–433,
451–452, 455, 456
advisors, 430
and capital structure decisions,
432–433
cash flows for, 197
characteristics of, 424–425
definition of, 427
development of, 430–432
fund raising through, 363
and Internal Revenue Code, 427
and risk of cash flows, 30
specialization, 429
types of, 428–429
Real estate limited partnerships (RELPs),
363, 367, 421, 425–427

and risk of cash flows, 30
tests for, 426
Real Estate Mortgage Investment
Conduits (REMICs), 197,
207, 339
Real estate ownership:
corporate form of, 423–424,
433–435
partnership form of, 424, 433–435
real estate investment trusts
(REITs), 424–425
sole, 422–423
**Real Estate Settlement Procedures
Act (RESPA),** 156–162,
265, 276
abusive practices, regulation of,
157–158
disclosure requirements, 157
effect of:
on real estate sales, 160–162
on settlement services, 158–159
remedies under, 158
Real property, classification of,
324–325
Real rate of interest, 16
Reconciliation phase, 273
**Reconstruction Finance Corporation
(RFC), 47,** 198
Reconveyance, trust deeds, 267
Recording of deed and mortgage, 276
Recourse debt, 335
Recourse note, 263, 317
Redlining, 178
empirical evidence on, 179–180
Refinancing, 283
mortgage, 116–117
of owner-occupied property,
117–118
Refinancing models, 223
Regulation:
of abusive practices, 157–158
of appraisers, 271–272
and assumability, 72–73
of financial institutions, 11–14
FIRREA mandated changes in, 85
and savings and loan failures, 77–84
and thrift failures, 480–482
See also specific acts
Regulation Q, 64–66, 151, 196
Regulation Z, 152–156
and advertising in print media, 156
and alternative mortgage
instruments, 154–156
annual percentage rate (APR),
153–154
and civil remedies/criminal
penalties, 156
total finance charges, 153
Regulatory Accounting Practices
(RAP), 80
GAAP compared to, 80–82

REITs, *See* Real estate investment trusts (REITs)
Related-persons rule, 348
Release clause, trust deeds, 267
Release provisions, 375
RELPs, *See* Real estate limited partnerships (RELPs)
REMICs, *See* Real Estate Mortgage Investment Conduits (REMICs)
Rental Rehabilitation grants, **148**
Replacement reserve, 318
Rescission model form (general), 170–171
Residential finance:
    American history of, 46–48
    early history of, 44–54
    English developments in, 45
    fixed-rate mortgage (FRM), 48–53
    German influence on, 45
    in the 1950s, 62–64
    in the 1960s, 64–66
    in the 1970s, 66–70
    in the 1980s, 70–88
    in the 1990s, 88–89
    and Roman law, 44–45
Residential loans, contractual relationships in, 262–267
Residential mortgages:
    and options, 35–36
    and risk of cash flow, 30
Residual method of borrower qualification, 259–260
Residual risk, 453
Resolution Trust Corporation (RTC), 82, 84, 208, 361–362
RESPA, *See* Real Estate Settlement Procedures Act (RESPA)
Restricted portfolio, 453
Retained earnings and ownership form, 433–434
Retroactive liability, 462
Returns to equity, 315
    and debt, 306–318
    and leverage, 304–305
Revenue Act of 1978, 342, 426
Reverse annuity mortgage (RAM), 113–114
Review appraiser, 272
Revised Uniform Limited Partnership Act, 425
RFC, *See* Reconstruction Finance Corporation (RFC)
R. G. Ibbotson Associates, data from, 452
Right of rescission, 156, 170–171
Risk, 3, 441–444
    callability, 21–22
    of cash flows, 29–32
    collateralized mortgage obligations(CMOs), 31
    commercial projects, 30

interest-only/principal-only securities(IOs and POs), 31
    limited partnerships, 30
    mortgage-backed securities (MBSs), 30–31
    real estate investment trusts (REITs), 30
    residential mortgage, 30
    servicing rights, 31–32
    of construction loans, 384
    credit, 146, 176
    default, 20–21, 108, 115, 254–268, 291, 293
    diversifiable, 448
    information, 453
    institutional sources of, 146
    interest rate, 22, 37, 53, 58–60, 70–71, 79, 89, 93–94
    interest volatility, 146
    internal fraud, 146
    liquidity, 8, 22, 37, 146
    marketability, 8, 22, 453
    maturity, 22
    miscellaneous, 146
    nondiversifiable, 448
    of property, 317
    residual, 453
Risk-based capital guidelines, 85–88, 357
    and interest rate risk, 89
Rolling options, 376
Rural Housing Service, 199, 200, 204, 285–286
Russell–NCREIF Property Index, 451, 454

S

Sale-leaseback agreements, 406–415
    accounting for, 412–415
    example of, 408–409
    terms of, 409–411
Sales, RESPA and, 160–162
Sales-price-to-asking-price ratio (SP/AP), 127
Salomon Brothers, 205, 206
SAMs, *See* Shared appreciation mortgages (SAMs)
SARA, *See* Superfund Amendments and Reauthorization Act of 1986 (SARA)
Savings and loan associations, failures of, 77–84
Savings-investment cycle, 4
    flow of funds in, 5
S corporations, 325, 340, 423–424
    ownership characteristics of, 424
    and passive loss limitation rules, 340
Secondary market, 7–8, 65–66
    continued growth of, 70

Secondary mortgage market, 7, 188–215
    agencies/firms, 197–205
    development of, 205–209
    dominance of, 88–89
    flow of funds through, 209–214
    government sponsored enterprises (GSEs), regulation of, 214
    mortgage-related securities (MRS), 7, 188, 190–197
    nature of, 188–190
    purpose of, 189–190
Secondary Mortgage Market Enhancement Act (SMMEA), 190, 206
Section 8 Program, 148
Secured lender exemption, 463
Securities and Exchange Commission (SEC), 363
Securitization, 151
    multisite, 416
Security Pacific Merchants Bank, 207
Security protection, trust deeds, 267
Self-insurance, 280
Self-liquidating REITs, 429
Seller accommodation, 375–377
    options, 376
    roller options, 376
    seller financing, 376–377
    subdivision trusts, 377
Seller financing, 376–377
Semi-strong market efficiency, 38
Senior financing, 377
Senior/subordinated pass-throughs, 192–193, 232–233
Servicing rights, 31, 246–248
    and risk of cash flows, 31–32
Settlement charges, 157
Settlement services, RESPA, 158–159
Settlement statement, 276
SFAS, *See* Standard of Financial Accounting Standards (SFAS)
Shared appreciation mortgages (SAMs), 69, 112–113, 116
    characteristics of, 118
    and Regulation Z, 155
Shorter term wrap, 134
Simulation model, 101
Simultaneous term, fully amortized wrap loan, 134
Simultaneous term, partially amortized wrap loan, 134
SMMEA, *See* Secondary Mortgage Market Enhancement Act (SMMEA)
Sole ownership, 422–423
    characteristics of, 423
Speculator, 374
SRP, *See* Streamline Refinance Plan (SRP)

Standard and Poor's, 20, 190, 192, 194, 360
Standard fixed-rate mortgage, characteristics of, 118
Standard of Financial Accounting Standards (SFAS), 412
Standard variation, 442
State credit agencies, 204–205
State foreclosure laws, 289–294
State National Bank of El Paso v. Farah Manufacturing Co., 474
Statute of fraud, 471
Statutory right of redemption, 45, 290–291, 296
Stepped-up basis, 408
Stewart B. McKinney Homeless Assistance Act (1987), 148
Straight-line method of depreciation, 308, 328, **330**
Streamline Refinance Plan (SRP), 232, 283
Strict liability, 462
Strip, 241
Stripped mortgage-backed securities, 195
Strong market efficiency, 38
Structuring costs, 39
Subdivision control ordinance, 378
Subdivision trusts, 377
Subordinated lien, 376
Subordination, 376–377
Subsidies, 148
Substitution of trustee, trust deeds, 267
Successors/assigns provisions, trust deeds, 267
Sum-of-the-year's digits method of depreciation, **331**
Superfund Amendments and Reauthorization Act of 1986 (SARA), 462
Suspended losses, 339
Swaps, 195–196

T

Tailoring cash flows, 191
Tandem Plan, 199
Taste for discrimination, 174–175
Tax Act (1993), 330, 332, 339, 341, 350
Tax credits and ownership form, 434
Tax-deferred exchange rule, 345–347
   basic requirements of, 345
   boot, 346
   delayed exchanges, 345–346
   multiple property tests, 347
   technical requirements, 346–347
   three-party exchange, 345
Taxes, 322–350
   alternative minimum tax (AMT) rules, 341
   at-risk limitation, 341

capital gains, 322, 328, 332, 334–338, 345, 347–350
   definition of income, 329–337
   determination of, 337–343
   differential tax rates, 337
   favored classes of real estate investment, 342–343
   and interest payments, 334–336
   limitation of losses, 337–340
   on pension funds, 367
   on real estate investments, effect on value of, 322–323
   real property, classification of, 324–325
   tax-deferred exchanges of property, 345–347
   tax shelters, 325–329
Tax increment financing, 378
Tax Reform Act (1969), 336
Tax Reform Act (1976), 341
Tax Reform Act (1981), 328, 331
Tax Reform Act (1984), 335
Tax Reform Act (1986), 196, 205, 207, 323, 332, 335–337, 341, 350, 363, 411, 424, 426, 428, 433, 451
   effect of, on real estate investment, 343–345
   and income classification, 337
Tax Relief Act (1997), 150, 332, 427
Tax shelters, 325–329
Teaser rates, 95
   and ARMs, 101–102
   and loan value, 102
Technical and Miscellaneous Revenue Act (1988), 136
Telerate Advanced Factor Service, 223
Tenant improvements financing, 416
Terminal cash flow, 30
Terminal wealth, 99–100
Third parties, liability to, 475–476
Thrift institutions, 6–7, 357, 359
   bank capital requirements vs., 86, 87
   capitalization of, 86, 88
   deregulation of, 7
   failures of, and agency relationships, 480–482
   FIRREA-mandated changes in, 83
   negative net worth (insolvency) of, 79–80
   and residential properties, 357
   "zombie" theory of failures of, 82
Tier-one risk-based capital, 88
Tilt effect, 67, 106–108
Time-value-of-money test, 336
Title insurance, 294–296
Title plant, 295
Title search, 294
Tort, 473
Total finance charges, 153
Total mortgage payment (TMP), 257

Traditional debt securities, valuation of, 218–219
Tranches, 195, 236, 238–242, 245–246
Travelers Insurance Company, 204
Treasury bills, 8
Treasury bonds, 8
Trust deeds, 266–267
   parties to, 266–267
   provisions of, 267
Trusts:
   grantor, 196
   subdivision, 377
Truth-in-lending disclosure, 276
Truth-in-Lending Law, *See* Consumer Credit Protection Act (1968)
Tucker v. Lassen Savings and Loan Association, 72

U

UBIT, *See* Unrelated business income tax (UBIT)
ULPA, *See* Uniform Limited Partnership Act (ULPA)
Uncertainty, 29
Underwriter, 272
Underwriting:
   and borrower qualification, 254–262
   construction loans, 379
   government-underwritten loans, 73–75
Uniform Commercial Code (UCC), 469–473, 479
Uniform Commercial Code Financing Statement, 416
Uniform Land Transaction Act, 290
Uniform Limited Partnership Act (ULPA), 425
Uniform residential appraisal report, 271
Uniform Settlement Statement, 157
United States v. Graham Mortgage Corp., 161
United States v. Maryland Bank and Trust Company, 464
United States v. Mirable, 463–464
Unrelated business income tax (UBIT), 367, 432
Urban Homesteading Program, 148
U.S. Department of Agriculture, data from, 452
U.S. Department of Commerce, 452
U.S. Savings and Loan League, 6
Usury, 45
U.S. v. Property Known as 708–710 West 9th St., Erie, Pa., 469

V

VA, *See* Veterans Administration (VA)
VA borrower qualification, 259–260

income ratio method, 260
residual method, 259–260
Valuation, 217–251
of commercial real estate
investments, 303–306
of debt securities, 218–219
general principles of, 303–304
role of risk in, 32
See also Asset valuation
Value:
appraised, problem with, 450–451
of cash flows, 311–312
and leverage, 304–305, 312–313
Variance, 442
Velocity of circulation, 17
Veterans Administration (VA), 54,
73–75, 126–128, 198–201,
275, 296
borrower qualification, 259–260

FHA/VA discount points, 126–128
mortgage insurance, 281–282, 289
Voluntary affirmative marketing
agreements (VAMAs), 173
Voucher control agent, 382

W

Warehousing, 200, 374
Warehousing loans, 278
Warehousing rate difference, 278
Waste, trust deeds, 267
Weak-form market efficiency, 38
Wellenkamp v. Bank of America, 71–72
Window-dressing argument, 408, 411
Wraparound loans, 75–76, 133–134

Y

Yield calculation, 384
Yield curves, 23
expectations theory, 24–25
and future interest rates, 22–25
liquidity premium theory, 24
market segmentation theory, 24
Yield-to-maturity (YTM), 218–219

Z

Zero coupon bonds, 108, 334
"Zombie" theory, 82
Zoning, 377
inclusionary, 378